The Broadview Anthology of

RESTORATION & EARLY EIGHTEENTH-CENTURY DRAMA

CONCISE EDITION

"THE DUKE'S THEATRE IN DORSET GARDENS"

(*reproduced by permission of the Folger Shakespeare Library*)

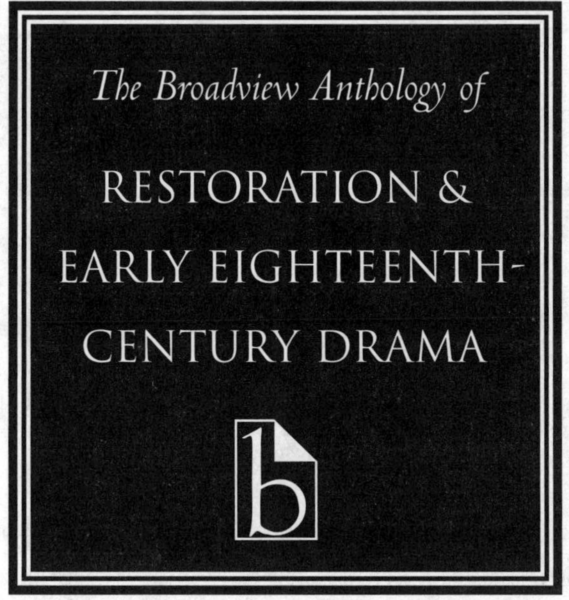

The Broadview Anthology of Restoration & Early Eighteenth-Century Drama

CONCISE EDITION

J. DOUGLAS CANFIELD

GENERAL EDITOR

MAJA-LISA VON SNEIDERN, ASSISTANT EDITOR

BROADVIEW ANTHOLOGIES OF ENGLISH LITERATURE

broadview press

National Library of Canada Cataloguing in Publication

The Broadview anthology of Restoration & eighteenth-century drama / general editor: J. Douglas Canfield ; assistant editor: Maja-Lisa von Sneidern. — Concise ed.

(Broadview anthologies of English literature)
ISBN 1-55111-581-6

1. English drama — Restoration, 1660-1700. 2. English drama — 18th century. I. Canfield, J. Douglas (John Douglas), 1941- II. von Sneidern, Maja-Lisa III. Series.

PR1265.B76 2003 822´.408 C2003-900886-X

Broadview Press Ltd. is an independent, international publishing house, incorporated in 1985. Broadview believes in shared ownership, both with its employees and with the general public; since the year 2000 Broadview shares have traded publicly on the Toronto Venture Exchange under the symbol BDP.

We welcome comments and suggestions regarding any aspect of our publications—please feel free to contact us at the addresses below or at broadview@broadviewpress.com
www.broadviewpress.com

North America:

PO Box 1243, Peterborough, Ontario, Canada K9J 7H5

3576 California Road, Orchard Park, NY, USA 14127

Tel: (705) 743-8990;
Fax: (705) 743-8353
E-mail: customerservice@broadviewpress.com

UK, Ireland, and continental Europe:

NBN Plymbridge
Estover Road
Plymouth PL6 7PY UK

Tel: 44 (0) 1752 202301;
Fax: 44 (0) 1752 202331
Fax Order Line: 44 (0) 1752 202333
Customer Service:
cservs@nbnplymbridge.com
Orders: orders@nbnplymbridge.com

Australia and New Zealand:

UNIREPS,
University of New South Wales
Sydney, NSW, 2052

Tel: 61 2 9664 0999;
Fax: 61 2 9664 5420
E-mail: info.press@unsw.edu.au

Broadview Press gratefully acknowledges the financial support of the Government of Canada through the Book Publishing Industry Development Program for our publishing activities.

PRINTED IN CANADA

For

James

Thompson

The editors gratefully acknowledge the conscientious work of our contributing editors—and that of Broadview Press in general and Eileen Eckert and Dawn Huck in particular. Thanks also to Danika Brown and Elise Marubbio for research assistance. Special thanks to Derek Hughes.

Contents

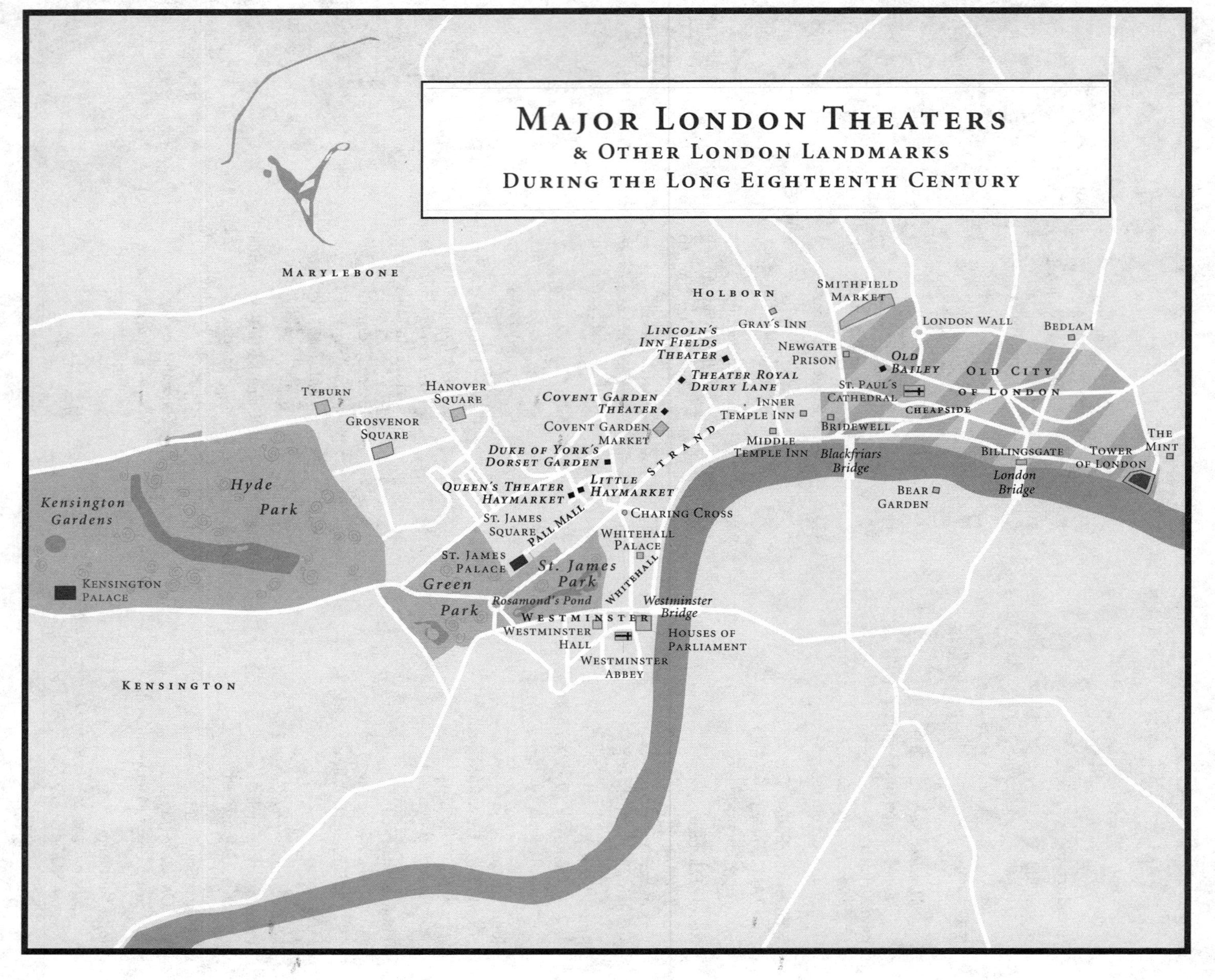
Major London Theaters
& Other London Landmarks
During the Long Eighteenth Century
Marylebone
Tyburn
Hanover Square
Grosvenor Square
Holborn
Gray's Inn
Smithfield Market
London Wall
Bedlam
Lincoln's Inn Fields Theater
Newgate Prison
Old Bailey
Old City of London
Theater Royal Drury Lane
St. Paul's Cathedral
Cheapside
Covent Garden Theater
Inner Temple Inn
Bridewell
Covent Garden Market
Middle Temple Inn
Blackfriars Bridge
Billingsgate
Tower of London
The Mint
Duke of York's Dorset Garden
Strand
London Bridge
Bear Garden
Queen's Theater Haymarket
Little Haymarket
Charing Cross
Hyde Park
Kensington Gardens
St. James Square
Pall Mall
Whitehall Palace
St. James Palace
St. James Park
Whitehall
Kensington Palace
Green Park
Rosamond's Pond
Westminster Bridge
Westminster
Westminster Hall
Houses of Parliament
Westminster Abbey
Kensington

Introduction

This anthology of English drama covers the years 1660 to 1737, with a glance at the resurrection of its kind of comedy toward the end of the eighteenth century. The years 1660 and 1737 mark major political events that affected the theater in England: the restoration of the monarchy in 1660 after the commonwealth of the mid-seventeenth century (an event that also restored public theaters to London) and the Licensing Act of 1737 (an event that marked the stifling of creativity through government censorship). Just as the closing of the public theaters in 1642 was a political act (the emerging powers buttressed their right to rule with a claim of moral superiority above the Court and its decadent entertainments), so their restoration was a political act: the triumphant Court gave patents to political supporters to run two theaters, aptly named the King's and the Duke's for the restored King Charles II and his brother, James, the duke of York. Thus the theaters were reopened rather explicitly as ideological state apparatuses, for the plays, subject to state censorship through the offices of Master of the Revels and the Lord Chamberlain (though exercised rather mildly except in times of political crisis), were expected to inculcate into their audiences the ideology that attempted to naturalize the right of the monarchists to rule.

Thanks to the "Puritans," who had torn most of them down, the new companies had no adequate theaters and had to make shift with tennis courts. They also had no new plays to hand and so had to make shift with the repertory of plays from before the Civil Wars. It is no accident that this repertory was dominated by the Elizabethan/Jacobean playwrights, William Shakespeare and John Fletcher, both of whose plays generally affirmed aristocratic, monarchist ideology. The new plays of the 1660s were often adaptations of earlier Cavalier drama, particularly its tragicomic romances about lost, dispossessed heirs to thrones and estates. One of the more original genres, the rhymed heroic play, with roots in Cavalier drama and in French drama witnessed by the Court in exile, was also, in the main, a form of romance with political ramifications. Both heroic and tragicomic romance usually restored the dispossessed to positions of power they merited by birth. Comedies too were political, uniting aristocratic couples whose inborn wit and energy entitle them to inherit and make new heirs for the estates that were the backbone of the political economy of the English aristocracy. The comedies also regularly disciplined Puritans and Cits, opponents of the Court who, because of religious or economic ties to new sources of power especially in the City of London, had demanded participation in their own government but were now caricatured as vain, hypocritical, vulgar, and eminently unworthy to rule. Paradoxically, these 1660s comedies were leavened by a folk energy that disrupted the very status hierarchy being reaffirmed, as enterprising soldiers and commoners and thieves and whores often stole the show and sometimes even estates themselves. And occasional tragedies allowed villains with enormous energy to get away with murder and to indict the ruling aristocracy with ideological hypocrisy.

The Restoration political compromise between the competing oligarchies of the civil war period began to unravel almost as soon as it was made. Just as Charles I had courted alliance with Catholic France and tried to run the country without Parliament, so did Charles II, especially in the infamous secret Treaty of Dover (1670), which in return for financial aid from Louis XIV promised to return England to the Catholic fold. James was already a Catholic, and Charles promised to declare his own conversion when it would not be too politically disruptive. Parliament was prorogued during the second half of the '70s, and Charles ran the country with subsidies from France. The country became suspicious, and the time was ripe for the Popish Plot of 1678.

After Henry VIII broke England away from the Roman Catholic Church in the middle of the sixteenth century, the Pope had, in effect, declared war: England was to be returned to the fold no matter how. Hence "Bloody" Mary I and her purges of Protestants; hence the attempted invasion of England by Mary's husband, King Philip II of Spain, which ended with the defeat of the Spanish Armada in 1588; hence Guy Fawkes and the Jesuit Gunpowder Plot to blow up Parliament in 1605; hence the Vatican's offer to finance a Catholic invasion of England to keep Charles I on the throne during the Civil Wars. Paranoid Protestants blamed Catholics for the Great Fire of London in 1666. So the rumor in 1678 of a Catholic plot to assassinate the king, murder Protestants, and invade England through Ireland was not so far-fetched. Titus Oates, who claimed to be a doctor of divinity, was the star witness, denouncing putative conspirators right and left. Indeed, several English Catholics were executed. The scare led powerful groups to agitate for the exclusion of the Catholic James from succession to the throne, to which he was heir-presumptive because Charles had no legitimate children, though he had several bastards. Hence the Exclusion Crisis of 1679-81, when opponents of the Court attempted not only to exclude James but have one of Charles's bastards, James Scott, duke of Monmouth, declared heir-apparent. Charles had repeatedly to prorogue or dissolve Parliament. By the dismissal of his last Parliament at Oxford in 1681, Charles won a Pyrrhic victory. He had to rely increasingly on France until his death in 1685, when James himself won a Pyrrhic victory over Monmouth, who was defeated and executed. The days of the monarchists were numbered. Immediately after the birth of a son to James II and his second (Catholic) wife, Maria of Modena, he was forced to abandon the throne to his Protestant daughter Mary and her Protestant Dutch husband, William of Orange. They became the co-sovereigns William III and Mary II in what their winning side dubbed the Glorious Revolution of 1688.

These major political events of course affected the drama. Already in the early 1670s comedies began to portray anti-bourgeois sentiments more aggressively. Puritan and Cit wives and daughters were seduced by Cavaliers whose *droit du seigneur* bestowed upon their actions not just impunity but the patina of a kind of benevolence: they were not only giving the women what they wanted but they were ennobling their backward City breed. Cit-cuckolding plays increased as the '70s careened on through the Popish Plot to the Exclusion Crisis. Heroic romances and tragedies portrayed political crises of succession, especially in adaptations of Shakespeare's history plays. As in Shakespeare's Roman tragedies (several of which were also adapted at this time), some Restoration neoclassical tragedies portrayed societies in crisis precisely because they did not have clear traditions to resolve the problem of succession; others presented protagonists great but flawed and unable to bequeath to their states political stability; still others (a rare few) portrayed a republican alternative to monarchism. A few comedies and dramatic satires enacted intra-class strife and exposed the fissures beneath the ostensibly smooth surface of the old ideology.

The Act of Settlement of the Revolution, with its accompanying Bill of Rights, did not mark a middle-class revolution, as was formerly assumed by historians. There was no Reign of Terror; the aristocracy persisted; land remained the symbol of wealth and power. Wealth of estates increased through enclosing lands and putting them into production and through improving yield. Much of this growth depended on infusions of money from trade, and power itself shifted from one oligarchy to another more responsive to the increasing wealth of the rising merchant class. Government monopolies were broken, resulting in virtual free trade. A national bank and the National Debt were instituted (1694), providing low-interest loans and venture capital for both government and industry. Paper money and checks increased the fluidity of the economic system. Wars were fought on the Continent that had serious ramifications for colonial trade. Victories under John Churchill, later duke of Marlborough, in the War of the Spanish Succession brought England much of New France and the *asiento*, the right to the exclusive slave trade with Spanish America. By the end of the Revolution period (1714), the wealth was increasingly invested in stocks and the moneyed interest came to dominate the landed interest. England, united formally with Scotland in 1707, was on the verge of becoming the empire of Great Britain.

The new ruling oligarchy required an ideology that embodied a new ethos (character) and ethics (morality). Revolution drama helped constitute it. Worth was increasingly portrayed as based no longer on birth but on merit. Heroic romances and political tragedies generally replace passionate, self-indulgent protagonists with stoic, self-controlled protagonists. Protagonists of personal tragedies are more often the victims of economic circumstance. And comic protagonists are not rewarded for their wit and sexual energy but for their good nature and generosity, a term that shifts from referring to nobility to referring to moral action: benevolence. A theory that maintains the essential goodness of human nature, benevolence emerged from the writings of the Latitudinarian divines (who would emphasize the broad latitudes of Christianity) and was codified by the third earl of Shaftesbury in the early eighteenth century. It formed the basis of this new comedy, a comedy based on an ethic of sentiment, of feelings. In such comedy, the Restoration comic libertine is bifurcated into an effete beau, who is easily defeated, and a downright villain, who is—not so easily—defeated, who stands for the rapacity of Lockean unlimited acquisition. From between these two husks emerges a good husband who is also a good husbandman—of his estate for the good of the new Nation. Comedy also becomes less about the socializing of the centrifugal sexual energy of the male rake than the socializing of the centrifugal sexual energy of the female coquette.

This movement in comedy was part of a general reform movement, summoned forth by the new King William himself: "We most earnestly Desire, and shall Endeavour a General Reformation of the Lives and Manners of all Our Subjects, as being that which must Establish Our Throne, and Secure to Our People their Religion, Happiness and Peace, all which seem to be in great Danger at this time, by reason of that overflowing of Vice, which is too Notorious in this as well as other Neighbouring Nations." The king's call was met by the establishment of societies for the reformation of manners. As today, such societies focused not on real corruption but on surface and style: in the drama, on satiric portrayals of the ruling establishment and its supporting clerics and on sexual "immorality." One of the most notorious attacks was the Reverend Jeremy Collier's *Short View of the Immorality, and Profaneness of the English Stage* (1698), the importance of which was less causal than symptomatic.

Dramatic theory accompanied this shift from aristocratic to bourgeois ethos. Following the Aristotelian tradition that had come to them from Italian and French "neoclassicism," Restoration dramatic theory legitimated a tragedy that portrayed "great people," because they were the only people whose fall might concern the audience, and that instilled in the audience not only Aristotle's pity and fear but also admiration for the great heroics as well as great passions of such protagonists. Restoration comedy was theorized in the manner of Molière: *corriger les hommes en les divertissant.* But the entertaining correction of vices and folly seems a theory more honored in the breach than in the observance and more designed to placate Puritan hostility than to accurately legitimate the practice of Restoration comedy. Theorists like Dryden actually spent more time celebrating Restoration drama in relation to previous English and current French practice. Its superiority was said to reside in its wit and elegant dialogue and its eschewing of vulgarities. At the same time, the theorists celebrated the "mixed way" of the English: their blurring of generic boundaries in the very popular mode of tragicomedy. Farce they explained as a sop to unsophisticated audience taste.

There lurks in this aristocratic theory an acceptance of a surplus exuberance that allows explicitly for genre—and implicitly for class—mixing: tragicomedies and comedies are invaded by successful, applauded disrupters from below. In a sense, it is bourgeois theory that demands purity, as if the taste Dryden pointed to is the cultural status symbol par excellence for the nouveaux riches. Thus neoclassical theory, as it develops toward the end of the Restoration and is adapted from a new wave of French theory, demands a purer adherence to Aristotle in terms of the dramatic unities of time, place, and action, for instance, and in terms of decorum of character and genre. That decorum will cleanse the stage of improprieties and vulgarities. Just as Joseph Addison and Richard Steele would attempt to mold the taste of the new ruling class through a series of essays in their periodicals, *The Tatler* and *The Spectator*, so dramatic theorists would attempt to justify a drama that invokes not so much admiration for heroic action and passion nor contempt for vice and folly but sympathy for models of exemplary behavior under stress, the register of which would gradually open to include merchants and even apprentices and servants.

This new decorum blurred generic distinctions between tragedy and comedy. And with regard to tragedy, Revolution theory introduced a strict interpretation of an old doctrine: poetical justice. Aristotle himself had argued that the fall of a totally good man would scandalize us because it could challenge the justice of the gods. The tragic protagonist, therefore, must not be perfect; his fall must be justified by at least a *hamartia*, an error in judgment. English Renaissance and Restoration dramatic practice portrayed a version of retributive justice: the evil are punished or disciplined (either onstage or in prophecy); the good may suffer in this life, but be rewarded in the next. The Revolution theorists insisted that such justice must be distributive: the evil must be punished and the good rewarded onstage. Again, a rule more honored in the breach, but as early as 1680 the ending of *King Lear* was altered so that Lear lives and Cordelia is happily married to Edgar—all so as not to violate our sense of decorum, here the decorum of God's justice.

* * *

Revolution comedies occasionally subvert the new order. Comic protagonists sometimes succeed because they parasitically feed off the new political economy, whose meritocratic rhetoric occludes those left out, who must resort to crime and trickery. Sometimes they make a mockery of bourgeois systems of order, from residual status hierarchy, to gender distinctions that deny equality and agency, to the military, with its impressment of a displaced surplus labor pool. Especially interesting are comedies and satires (both comical and tragical) that attack the institution of marriage, retained in the bourgeois ideology because power and property are still, in the main (despite the ideology of meritocracy and egalitarianism) transmitted through patrilineal genealogy. Women remain the sacred transmitters and must therefore be chaste—and monogamous. Some comedies indulge the fantasy of no-fault divorce. Some satires close with women standing alone in bas relief, their marital problems unresolved and unresolvable. Tragical satires attack the republican system as no more efficacious than the monarchal. One menippean, absurdist satire portrays usurpers as not accountable in a world where God himself is sheer Will-to-Power.

These trends continue after 1714-15, when occurred these three crucial events: the death of Mary II's younger sister, Anne, the last of the Stuart monarchs; the succession of the Hanoverian dynasty, distantly related to the Stuarts through marriage; and the failure of The Fifteen, a revolution that attempted, once again with Catholic backing, to restore James II's son, now called James III by his supporters, termed

Jacobites. Both this failure and this successful succession mark the full triumph of the Revolutionary Settlement; Parliament, backed by the army, clearly had the power to make or break a king. And they mark the dawn of the era of the strong chief minister, as this office took shape under the hands of Sir Robert Walpole, who consolidated the new constitutional monarchy at home and the new empire abroad. The new wealth called for new laws protecting property. Named for blackfaced Robin Hoods in the countryside, the infamous Black Act was passed in 1724, making most crimes against property, even the pettiest, capital, and giving rise to England's "Hanging Judge" and "Albion's Fatal Tree"—the gallows. The new oligarchy cut the slack built into the previous system for the poor and let it out to themselves. Although the act was repealed a short time later, it and other oppressive acts by the Walpole government, including the most successful intelligence agency until the twentieth century, gave rise to an opposition press and opposition literature, championed by the Scriblerists (named for their fictional blockhead creation, Martinus Scriblerus), who included Jonathan Swift, Alexander Pope, and John Gay.

Early Georgian drama (named after the Georges of the House of Hanover, who became England's monarchs for the rest of the eighteenth century) solidified bourgeois ideology, by extending tragedy and tragicomic romance, for example, to include as spokesmen for the new ethos (and for its discrimination from the aristocratic ethos) positive merchant characters with such telling names as Mr. Sealand and Mr. Thorowgood. Industry and prudence become key words. Wealth from the colonies (first the Indies, later India itself) is laundered, as it were, by crossing the seas to the metropolis. The appropriation of resources from them is justified in the name of superior culture, civilization, not to mention technology. Effete beaux of the decadent aristocracy continue to be defeated, while good husbands, in both senses of the word, continue to win wives, sometimes by bold strokes.

Even the Georgian heroic romance *Lucius*, however, continues to reveal the ineluctable Oedipal crisis of the patrilineal monarchy to which England stubbornly clings: the only way to the throne is over the dead body of the father. This repressed truth lurks at the heart of English heroic romance and tragedy. It surfaces with a vengeance around the time of the Exclusion Crisis. And it rears its beheaded ghost again around the time of The Fifteen.

One of the great delights of early Georgian theater is the invention of the ballad opera, precursor to the modern musical. In the hands of its greatest practitioners, John Gay and Henry Fielding, it strips bare the hypocrisy of the new bourgeois ethos, embodied in Walpole and his agents and placemen, revealing the inherent rapacity of mercantilism (as well as its frightful instability, as witnessed in the stock-market crash of 1720 known as the "South Sea Bubble") and escaping into the fantasies of art. Gay's *Polly*, unstaged but immensely popular in print, like Thomas Southerne's *Oroonoko* before it, reveals the ugly truth behind bourgeois cultural imperialism: that its ideology is bankrupt and untrue. The only nobles on the planet may well be the supposed savages, and they are headed toward the hinterlands to escape civilization.

Walpole could not stand such severe criticism, so at the very moment of his own demise (he lost power steadily after the death of his chief supporter at Court, George II's Queen Caroline, in 1737) he engineered the passage of the Licensing Act, which enforced zero tolerance for criticism of the ministry and effectively disciplined playwrights into conformity. In the atmosphere of crisis brought on by the American Revolution and the Gordon (anti-Catholic) Riots in the late 1770s and early 1780s, a few playwrights tried to resuscitate the theater by departing from sentimental comedy and returning to the greatest contribution of Restoration and Revolution drama, what Oliver Goldsmith called "laughing"—that is, satirical—comedy (though neither the departure nor the return was radical).

* * *

The Restoration theater itself, as it moved from the tennis courts to new buildings, implemented new designs and innovations. The typical theater comprised stage and backstage, pit, boxes, and galleries. Backstage contained the tiring rooms where actors and actresses dressed and made up, and they were the site of visitations by VIPs. This interaction between company and members of the audience continued on the stage itself, where some of the bolder young aristocrats might actually bring benches and sit and where the long apron allowed an immediacy and intimacy between actor and audience. Proscenium arches came to frame the action. Extending out from the arch into the architecture of the boxes were structures containing doors and balconies with windows. Moveable scenery became possible by sliding multiple pairs of screens or flats, representing different scenes, along grooves in the stage floor. These flats could be opened or "drawn" to reveal another scene upstage up to a final set scene, with cutouts to imply three-dimensional depth. As the theaters became more elaborate, they were capable of raising and lowering all kinds of "machines" with various "engines" operating on a pulley system. Such by the early 1670s were the Duke's Company's new theater in Dorset Garden and the King's Company's new Theater Royal in Drury Lane, designed by the great architect, Christopher Wren. These two theaters were the model for the theaters of the eighteenth century. Indeed, Drury Lane remained active as the most famous of London theaters. In the early eighteenth century another great architect, John Vanbrugh, designed the elegant Haymarket theater, which proved to be too grand for drama and housed mainly operas, which were becoming the new fad. Dorset Garden, in the meantime, fell into desuetude. When Betterton and Barry led their rebellion against the patent theaters, they were forced to return to—and renovate—the old Lincoln's Inn Fields tennis court.

The majority of the audience of Restoration drama sat either in the pit immediately in front of the stage or in galleries that tiered up and back. In the pit and middle gallery vendors, including prostitutes, plied their wares. In the upper gallery servants could sit at reduced prices. The boxes along the sides and across the back of the pit under the galleries were reserved for the upper crust, including members of the royal family, who often attended—and whose patronage was both indispensable and conveniently protective from residual antitheatrical prejudice. This Restoration audience was not limited to Court and the fashionable Town (and their servants), however: it contained increasing numbers of the middling sort, from wealthy merchants down to apprentices. During the eighteenth century, the royal family was less in evidence, the middling sorts more.

One of the more interesting aspects of theater history of the period is the gradual resistance to control, culminating in the repression of the Licensing Act of 1737. After finances and politics conspired to collapse the two patent companies into the United Company in 1682, the management of that company eventually devolved into the hands of Christopher Rich, a professional manager with no experience in the theater. When leading actors Thomas Betterton and Elizabeth Barry and their followers broke away in 1695, they established a tradition of actor managers. Rich was ousted as manager of Drury Lane in 1707 and replaced by another group of actor managers. Meanwhile, smaller non-patent theaters began to proliferate, the most interesting being the Little Haymarket, where Henry Fielding staged plays attacking the Walpole administration. By 1737 Walpole had had enough; the Licensing Act restricted London theater once again to two patented houses (Drury Lane, run by Colley Cibber and his fellow actors, and the new Covent Garden Theater, run by Rich's son John), though entrepreneurs like Samuel Foote developed elaborate ways to get around the laws in lesser venues around town. Out of such venues came the most successful actor-manager of the mid-eighteenth century, David Garrick.

But the enforcer of the theatrical ideological state apparatus became virtually directly the far more powerful Lord Chamberlain, who eventually quashed the upstarts.

It is essential to remember that the London stage was a profit-seeking enterprise, financed by wealthy investors, who were the major shareholders. Some of the leading actors and even playwrights held shares as well, but the majority of the workers in the theater were hirelings. In general during the period 1660–1737, theater was a profitable enterprise for the shareholders. Ticket prices early were four shillings for the boxes, two for the pit, one and a half for the middle gallery, and one for the upper. As audiences began demanding and theaters providing more elaborate productions, including operas and even entre acte and afterpiece pantomimes and entertainments, prices began to rise (though interesting subversions persisted, like not having to pay for attending only one act or getting a partial refund by leaving before the afterpiece). Playwrights were not usually shareholders or on salary, and they made a mere pittance from book sales, so their major income came from either wealthy patrons—a capricious lot—or benefit performances: if a play succeeded well enough to be extended to a third night, the profit went to the playwright. If he or she was really lucky, the play might extend to a sixth or a ninth night. Gay's *Beggar's Opera* had such a spectacular run that it is said to have made Gay rich and Rich gay.

* * *

One of the most important innovations of the Restoration stage was the presence of actresses. Previously in public theater in England the roles of women were played by boys. Like today's film stars, beautiful actresses were a great attraction. With their low-cut dresses they could show off their bosoms, and when they played "breeches" roles, they could show off their legs. They were not just objectified by the gaze of the audience, however; in their reciting of prologues and epilogues, in their asides, and merely in their making eye contact with the audience, they conveyed their personalities and enacted their own gaze of agency. And they enacted roles of significant agency, from queens to more private women of powerful passion and intelligence.

Great actresses earned important places in the repertory companies: the Marshall sisters, Rebecca and Anne, who dominated heroic roles in the early decades; Nell Gwynn, Charles II's mistress, who immortalized the witty heroine of the gay, lively couple that became a staple of comedy; Katherine Corey, the premier comedienne; Elizabeth Barry, the prima donna in the best sense, who became a manager of the breakaway company after the Revolution; her stage antagonist Anne Bracegirdle and her stage descendent Anne Oldfield; Letitia Fenton, who made a career acting Gay's Polly Peachum; the irrepressible Charlotte Charke, whose outrageous energy could not be contained within legitimate theater. The leading ladies were paired with brilliant leading men (and were sometimes married to them, as in the case of Susanna and William Mountfort): Charles Hart, the other half of the early gay couple; Thomas Betterton, the Olivier of his time; wild Jack Verbruggen and handsome Robert Wilks, who played the dashing young men of Revolution comedy and tragedy; Barton Booth, whose specialty was Shakespeare. Not to be left unmentioned are the great comic actors John Lacy, Edward Angel, Thomas Jevon, Cave Underhill, Jo Haines, and especially, James Nokes and Anthony Leigh. These comedians energized the ubiquitous farce of this comedy in ways we can now only imagine by analogy with W. C. Fields, Laurel and Hardy, Abbott and Costello, Guinness and Sellers, Belushi and Aykroyd and Murray, Chapman and Gilliam and Cleese and Idle.

* * *

The full *Broadview Anthology of Restoration and Early Eighteenth Century Drama* includes representatives of nine dramatic sub-genres: Heroic Romance, Political Tragedy, Personal Tragedy, Tragicomic Romance, Social Comedy, Subversive Comedy, Corrective Satire, Menippean Satire, and Laughing Comedy. Of these sub-genres, seven are represented in this concise edition.

Heroic romance pits heroes, representing hegemonic cultural values, against forces portrayed by that culture as threatening. Often those forces are figured as monstrous, foreign, other, but they are what Freud called *unheimlich*: seemingly strange but really at home in us. English baroque drama (late 16th to early 18th century) specialized in the character type of the Machiavel, the unscrupulous statesman or even prince (modeled after Florentine philosopher Niccolò Machiavelli's infamous treatise of that name, which preached that the end justifies the means). Juxtaposed to such unscrupulousness is the heroic code of virtue, honor, loyalty—supposedly underwritten by God. In the Restoration and early eighteenth century, a crucial issue in such plays, as one would expect given the political background, is who has the right to rule and why. Post-Revolution heroic romance begins to give us rulers who rule by merit and not by birth, who may even be outsiders. But the spectre of parricide remains, for the way to the throne lies over the dead body of the king, and playwrights still had to negotiate the Oedipal crisis. The three examples of this sub-genre included in the full *Broadview Anthology of Restoration and Early Eighteenth Century Drama* are Roger Boyle's *The History of Henry the Fifth*, Nicholas Rowe's *Tamerlane*, and Delarivier Manley's *Lucius, The First Christian King of Britain*.

Political tragedy focuses on conflicts that involve political systems. English baroque drama portrays monarchy and its discontents, which in Shakespeare's time are primarily dynastic, but as the period wears on, those discontents become revolutionary, threatening monarchism with republicanism. The figure of the grand, passionate aristocratic leader yields to that of the neostoic *primus inter pares* (first among equals), even as England moves to a constitutional, parliamentary monarchy. But peeping from behind the arras is the *iron law of oligarchy*, that despite proto-democratic rhetoric, power remains in the hands of the wealthy few and is put to the service of military, economic, and cultural imperialism, from Ireland to the Indies. The three examples of this sub-genre included in the full version of this anthology are John Banks' *The Unhappy Favorite*, Nathaniel Lee's *Lucius Junius Brutus*, and Joseph Addison's *Cato*.

Personal tragedy focuses on conflicts within individuals that have consequences for those around them. Classical, Aristotelean tragedy portrays aristocratic heroes flawed at least by errors of judgment. To paraphrase *King Lear*, when they run downhill, they drag the world along. Restoration neoclassical personal tragedy retains such protagonists, whose warring passions destroy them, leaving their states unstable. But as the revolutionary period develops, protagonists become more domestic, more bourgeois; their motivation more banal, less Herculean; and the consequences of their mistakes less cosmic, less communal. What is lost shifts from the world to a happy marriage, a career, peace of mind. The three representatives of this sub-genre that are included in the full version of the anthology also appear in these pages: John Dryden's *All for Love*, Nicholas Rowe's *The Fair Penitent*, and George Lillo's *The London Merchant*.

Tragicomic romance features lost heirs, lost lovers, lost rulers found again at last. It features protagonists gone on quests, often into dark and foreign lands, to retrieve some treasure, some beloved, some cultural talisman. Protagonists have brushes with death, but only villains die. The forces of evil are some dark version of the self, one's culture's greatest fear: incest, fratricide, parricide. This is the world of Shakespeare's and John Fletcher's early English baroque tragicomedies. The Restoration's great achievement in the genre is the split-plot play, juxtaposing heroic with comic plots, the conclusion of which is to compound idealistic with pragmatic rationales for societal order. The Revolution's achievement was twofold: injecting real tragedy into the genre to produce, so to speak, comitragic romance, where one of the plots ends tragically, with the death or exile of one or more of the good guys; injecting tragicomedy into the world of comedy, making it more somber, more serious, and producing novelistic melodrama, a genre which exalts the importance of the bourgeois self—and preoccupies us with that self rather than the world and its discontents. All three of the tragicomic romances that appear in the full version of the anthology are also included here: John Dryden's *Marriage à la Mode*, Thomas Southerne's *Oroonoko*, and Richard Steele's *The Conscious Lovers.*

Social comedy socializes threats against hegemonic culture either by disciplining upstarts (cits and commonwealthsmen, Puritans and parvenus, rich country boobies and scientific experimenters) or by marrying rebellious youth, within their own class, for the perpetuation of the estate economy. English baroque comedy still owes a great deal to the Roman comedies of Plautus and Terence for precisely these preoccupations. In the Restoration, sometimes that estate economy is enriched by union with wealthy cits and the ideology stretched to accommodate them. More often, cits are severely disciplined by the seduction of their wives and daughters by the "naturally" superior Cavaliers. A great contribution of this comedy is the development of the "gay couple" foreshadowed in, for example, Shakespeare's Beatrice and Benedick. Post-Revolution comedy continues to put the right couple to bed, but the male has been deprived of much of his libertine sting, and it is the female coquette who must be socialized into marriage. Good nature and generosity replace wit and energy as the supreme values, as comedy becomes more a matter of feelings, more sentimental—even as bourgeois morality becomes an ethic of sentiment, of benevolence, providing the rationale for patronizing the less fortunate, less civilized. Five social comedies appear here: George Etherege's *The Man of Mode*, Aphra Behn's *The Rover*, William Congreve's *The Way of the World*, Catherine Trotter's *Love at a Loss*, and Susannah Centlivre's *A Bold Stroke for a Wife*. Four additional social comedies appear in the full anthology: Sir Robert Howard's *The Committee*, John Crowne's *City Politics*, Colly Cibber's *Love's Last Shift*, and Mary Pix's *The Beau Defeated.*

Subversive comedy reveals fissures under the smooth surface of official ideology, even as the plays end in ritual celebration of society's centripetal power—usually a marriage. These fissures sometimes include sympathetic glimpses of the oppressed or cracks in ruling-class solidarity or threats to the genealogical system for the transmission of power and property. Jacobean city comedy is full of such fissures. In the Restoration, folk energy disrupts officialdom; aristocratic friends turn on one another, often seducing each other's wife; witty women get away with sexual promiscuity. Post-Revolution subversive comedy features women who even more thoroughly threaten: not just the order controlling sex through monogamy but that controlling gender difference and class difference. And it presents the new tricksters on the horizon as not sexual but economic. The omnivorous predation of capitalism gapes so widely in a few plays that the endings barely paper over its abyss as the audience takes refuge in the fantasy of art. Five subversive comedies appear in these pages: John Lacy's *The Old Troop*, William Wycherley's *The Country Wife*, Thomas Shadwell's *A True Widow*, George Farquhar's *The Beaux' Stratagem*, and John Gay's *The Beggar's Opera*. A further three subversive comedies appear in the full anthology: Edward Ravenscroft's *The Careless Lovers*, Thomas Otway's *Friendship in Fashion*, and Thomas Southerne's *Sir Anthony Love.*

Corrective satire condemns aberrant behavior by exposing it to ridicule and lashing it with a rod clearly representing the violated standard of behavior. Most comedies contain satire. What makes a comical satire is the ending. Comedies end in centripetal celebration, even if some aspect behaves centrifugally (as in subversive comedies), even if the ending represents wish-fulfillment. Satires either end with nothing really resolved, the aberrant behavior to continue ad infinitum, or they end with draconian poetical justice. Corrective comical satires judge behavior as morally reprehensible. Aristophanes was the classic master; Ben Jonson the Jacobean. Restoration corrective comical satire attacks the libertinism of its hegemonic class of aristocrats, as well as the selfishness, ineptitude, and pusillanimity of its competing class of bourgeois cits. Post-Revolution satire attacks the failure of the Revolution to extend its principles to other classes and genders, to provide real relief to the oppressed, especially women trapped in bad marriages. At its best, it reveals the total bankruptcy of England's—and Europe's—supposed moral superiority. John Vanbrugh's *The Relapse* is included here as a representative of corrective satire. Three other examples of the sub-genre appear in the pages of the full anthology: Nathaniel Lee's *The Princess of Clèves*, Aphra Behn's *The Lucky Chance*, and John Gay's *Polly*.

Menippean satire presents a jumble of competing voices, with no clear standard by which to judge behavior aberrant. Lucian and Petronius Arbiter are the classic exemplars. Shakespeare's *Antony and Cleopatra* pulls the rug out from under any set of values. Restoration menippean satire does the same, presenting us with endings that not only make no sense but make nonsense of previous positioning. Post-Revolution menippean satire forces us to confront a world grown secular and materialist, where God himself may be nothing but another tyrannical force of sheer will-to-power. The ludic is all that is left. Thomas Otway's *Venice Preserved* is included in these pages as an example of Menippean satire. Four other representatives of the sub-genre are included in the full anthology: John Tatham's *The Rump*, Thomas Durfey's *A Fond Husband*, John Dryden's *Amphitryon*, and Henry Fielding's *The Author's Farce*.

Laughing comedy is a later Georgian attempt to eschew sentimental comedy and melodrama, which portray, as Goldsmith put it, the "distresses" of the middle and lower classes—about which we do not care, as Aristotle insisted—and to return to earlier satirical comedy, which portrays the vices and follies of the members of those classes, leaving the upper classes to tragedy. But the values remain Revolutionary, bourgeois: good nature and generosity. And the satire within the comedies has not the bite of earlier comedy, much less that of earlier comical satire. Benevolence still reigns, and the sentimental still prevails. England as imperial metropolis basks in its newfound wealth and patronizingly disciplines its wayward sons and daughters—at home if not abroad. The three laughing comedies included in the full version of the anthology are all also included in these pages: Oliver Goldsmith's *She Stoops to Conquer*, Richard Brinsley Sheridan's *The School for Scandal*, and Hannah Cowley's *The Belle's Stratagem*.

Procedures

This concise anthology attempts to provide as many plays as might feasibly be taught in a semester, especially from the aesthetically richest genre of comedy, with a modicum of apparatus (general introduction, individual play headnotes, explanatory and textual notes). Accordingly, we have included as many different authors as feasible, doubling up only in the case of Dryden. We have organized the concise anthology chronologically.

Keeping in mind the primary audience for this text, students, we have tried to provide competently edited texts, modernized for their convenience. We have generally employed first editions, unless another edition demanded precedence, checking them against other early editions that might be presumed to have authority and against modern editions (whose scholarship has been enormously beneficial). We have kept textual annotation to a minimum, noting only substantive variants adopted or substantive variants of interest in other editions unadopted. We have simplified and often silently corrected and repositioned stage directions, though we have set major additions in brackets. We have also so marked additions to dramatis personae, to act and scene divisions, and to settings.

In order to maximize space for plays, we have omitted dedications and prefaces, referring to salient features occasionally in our headnotes. We have also eschewed the reproduction of the lists of all actors and actresses, mentioning only noteworthy names in headnotes. Those who wish to know more may consult such standard references as *The London Stage* and *A Biographical Dictionary of Actors, Actresses, Musicians, Dancers, Managers & etc.* More reluctantly, we have, in the main, omitted prologues and epilogues, since, witty and entertaining as they are, they rarely contribute to the thematics of the plays to which they are attached but rather most often carry on a banter with the audience over the state of the theater, the plight of actors, and so forth. Occasionally we have printed some on the grounds that they importantly relate to the thematics of the plays, to important political contexts, or to significant aesthetic developments. And we have retained (and translated) epigraphs.

We have omitted theoretical and practical texts about the theater; instead we refer students to the Garland series, *The English Stage: Attack and Defense, 1577–1730.* And we have eschewed a bibliography, although we have already mentioned here some of the standard reference works. Criticism is always both ephemeral and incremental; thus, bibliographies are always outdated—and hence increasingly misleading—during the life of an anthology. Students should have recourse to the various bibliographies on the drama and the dramatists—some reference books themselves, others carried in journals, from general bibliographies, like the *MLA International Bibliography*, to specialized, like *The Scriblerian* and *Restoration: Studies in English Literary Culture, 1660–1700.*

We have not glossed words that are in *Webster's Tenth Collegiate Dictionary*, readily available online. We have glossed words and facts not readily available to students, and we have provided a glossary of words not in the dictionary that appear in more than one play, and words that, although in the dictionary, have secondary meanings not readily apparent to students, and we have marked them in the text with asterisks; for example, *want** as *lack*, *parts** as *talents*, *glass** as *mirror*. We have not so marked repeated instances of such words when they follow hard upon one we have just marked. When Town and City refer to Westminster and London, we have capitalized them (and have also glossed their first use in each play) because they are specific, proper names for important geographical locations in these plays. Other important locations are also in our glossary: for example, the New Exchange, the Tower, St. James's Park.

We have modernized and regularized spelling and punctuation, although occasionally an old spelling will be retained for its dialectal flavor or its sound (especially in verse). We have retained dashes mostly to indicate pregnant pauses or (when preceded by another mark of punctuation) to indicate a change of subject or object of address. We have generally not emended grammar, but we have corrected foreign words and phrases, unless the mistakes are thematic, characteristic. We have occasionally emended a line for metrics' sake (preferably with warrant), but never by introducing elisions not in the original: students of foreign as well as English poetry quickly learn to perform such elisions themselves if only *sotto voce.*

We have regularized certain distinctions: for example, "Hah" is an exclamation, "ha" part of a laugh; "aye" is an affirmation, "ay" a sigh. Others we have collapsed as trivial: for example, we have changed all instances of "O" to "Oh." We have retained (or sometimes introduced) capitals in personifications: for example, "Heaven," "Love," "Fortune," "Nature," "Death" (but when the devil is part of a cliché, we have left him lower case).

Our principle throughout these procedures has been readability. We are not insensitive to original aspects of texts that might have facilitated performance, for example, punctuation that might have indicated phrasing. But we also know that published texts are not based, in the main, upon prompters' copies: those heavily marked with pointings and marginal stage directions—and excisions—all perhaps extraneous to the original script. Printed texts bear no absolute connection to plays as they were performed, any more than film scripts do today. Plays are always collaborative enterprises, refined through production, even from one night to another. If these texts are readable and therefore intelligible, they can provide the basis for performances in which the director—or the student—will decide how the lines should be read, how the play should be blocked and staged, how the sets would look, if only in his or her head.

One last word of justification for our enterprise here: We have tried, as have the best of our predecessors, to provide soundly edited and annotated texts. Others have provided texts, sometimes with a claim to inclusivity, with not so careful attention to the copytext chosen or to subsequent substantive emendations. For example, one series's reprint of *The Way of the World* is based upon a pirated Dublin edition. We do not claim that our texts are definitive. Students should have recourse to such editions, if they exist. But we do claim that ours are solid and, in some instances, are the only modern scholarly editions.

In short, we hope we have been of service to teachers, to students, to lovers (amateurs) of English drama.

The Old Troop; or, Monsieur Raggou[a]

by John Lacy (?-1681)

edited by Maja-Lisa von Sneidern

John Lacy was apprenticed to John Ogilby, a dancing master and theater owner (later made notorious by Dryden in "MacFlecknoe" and Pope in the *Dunciad*), in 1631. During the Civil War, Lacy served as a lieutenant and quartermaster for the royalist cause. After 1660, Lacy acted and wrote for the King's Company, and his performances were much admired by diarists John Evelyn and Samuel Pepys. Lacy's reputation as a comedian was well established by such roles as Scruple in *The Cheats*, Teague in *The Committee*, Bayes in *The Rehearsal*, and Raggou in his own play *The Old Troop*.

The play was first performed in 1664, some eight years prior to the publication of the first quarto, and was revived frequently over the next half century. Its debut was after Cromwell's body was exhumed, hanged and mutilated, after the frequent and barbarous executions of the regicides, and after the purge of Commonwealth's men (supporters of "The Good Old Cause" or "Saints" as the experiment in republicanism and its adherents were sarcastically called), but before the sobering events—the plague and fire of London—of 1665–66.

The Old Troop is particularly interesting because it worries less over Roundhead hypocrisy than Cavalier excess. It stages and then manages the most egregious accusations against the royalists. Rumor, as reported in lampoons, had it that some of Charles I's officials were overly fond of eating children. Act III proposes that, while originating in necessity, the threatened cannibalism was mere "mirth" that no reasonable person could take seriously; however, enemies of the king would "noise" the rumor as fact.

The problems of provisioning and quartering armies most central to the play are not so facilely resolved. The third amendment to the U. S. Constitution guarantees only that property owners must consent to quartering soldiers "in time of peace." As in Lacy's play, at war we can only trust that the "timbers" of state "would rather have" our "hearts than money."

The Old Troop is a farce, and students need to interpolate the slapstick and accept the crudity of the humor as they might a contemporary comedian-actor—the frequently bigoted, potty-mouthed, coarse buffoon, without apparent taste or values. In *The Old Troop*, the "serious" business, including the restoration of the King and the romantic interest, is thin at best. Raggou and most of "the old troop" wallow in their ill-gotten gains "like de dog dat tumbla in de carrion." But it is worthwhile to remember that the theater audience both reviled and admired the Reformation of the church, French savoir faire and cuisine, Dutch economic and political successes, and the events that restored Charles II to his throne. Lacy toys with stereotypes and these ambivalent attitudes to entertain his audience by making them feel more secure in their faith, their taste, their economy, their monarchy, and their King.

[I]

DRAMATIS PERSONAE

Captain [Honor], Lieutenant, Cornet } of the Troop.
Tom Tell-troth.
Raggou.[1]
Flea-flint, Plunder-master General.
Captain Ferret-farm.
Quartermaster Burndorp.
Biddy, the Cornet's Boy.
Dol Troop.
Troopers.
Constables.
[Watch.]
[Marshal.]
Painter.
Carpenter.
Servants.
Women and Children in abundance.
Roundheads:
Governor of a Garrison.
Captain Holdforth.
Captain Tubtext, and his two holy sisters.

The[b] *Old Troop; or, Monsieur Raggou*

Act I. [The camp of the Cavalier troop.]

Tell-troth and Dol Troop.

DOL.
I have heard your story and much pity you, but in truth, I am a wicked, very wicked woman, for I never did one good deed in all my life, and I doubt* you're unlucky that your fate directs you to me.

TELL-TROTH.
I find you have opportunity to do good and will to serve me. And for reward, if that—

DOL.
Nay, y'are liberal enough, you understand the world, for money creates good and evil. And I, that never thought of doing good, will now heartily endeavor it. Go to my quarters, for I have a great deal of roguery to act for myself, besides the good I am to do for you.

TELL-TROTH.
Inquire all you can into the last thing you spoke of, for I confess that troubles me. If she proves but honest,* I'll forgive her wildness.

DOL.
I'll do it with all the craft I can.

Exeunt.

Enter Lieutenant, Flea-flint, Ferret-farm, and Burndorp.

FLEA-FLINT.
Good morrow, good morrow, Lieutenant.

LIEUTENANT.
Precious rogues! What brave honors and titles you have arrived at in the wars, rascals! Plunder-master General Flea-flint! What Prince can give thee so great a title? a great credit for my colonel, rogue. Then here's Captain Ferret-farm, an honorable gentleman: for always when we are fighting, you are ferreting the farms and searching the women for letters of intelligence, you damned rogue. Then, here's the quartermaster Burndorp, a rogue that, when we have brave* large quarters assigned, you sell half of 'em, and then truss us up nine or ten in one house together. A pox on you, rascal!

BURNDORP.
But why are you thus cruel, Lieutenant?

LIEUTENANT.
Hang you, dogs. Did not I know you at first to be three tattered musketeers, and by plundering a malt-mill of three blind horses, you then turned dragooners, and so, quartering in a farm where a good team was, you changed your blind horses for better, and then you commenced troopers at Oxford, and when you had plundered yourselves into good clothes, you impudently called yourselves Major and Captain and Quartermaster, and then you ran away from your own troop, and I entertained* you for reformado-officers?[2] You

---

[1] Raggou] or ragout, from the French for a highly seasoned stew

[2] Musketeers … reformado officers] musketeer: foot soldier; dragoon: infantryman on horseback; trooper: cavalryman; reformado officer: officer removed from command, but retaining rank and sometimes pay. Oxford, about midway between London and Bristol, was traditionally a royalist stronghold.

know I know this, and yet, you dull, ungrateful rascals, you will not know why I am angry.

FERRET-FARM.

Why are you angry?

FLEA-FLINT.

Why? I'll tell thee why. He wants* twenty pounds and a good gelding, coxcomb. He must have it, too; I know him well enough.

BURNDORP.

Is that it? He shall have it, and thank him, too. Pray, accept of this twenty pound, Lieutenant.

FERRET-FARM.

And we have a good gelding for you, Lieutenant, as ever you laid leg over.

LIEUTENANT.

Why so? Why will you put me to't to give you ill language? Cannot you understand me without scurvy usage?

FERRET-FARM.

I did not understand you, by my troth, Lieutenant.

LIEUTENANT.

Pray, understand me hereafter. Now are you three as honest, harmless fellows! How dost thou do? Who dares say that thou wilt flea a flint?[3] or he search for letters in a wench's placket? or the quartermaster burn a town? I'll set 'em by the heels that say it. Honest Robin, Tom, and Dick, when shall we drink a tub of ale together?

BURNDORP.

When you please, worthy Lieutenant.

LIEUTENANT.

Get a tub at one of your quarters, and I'll come to you. And pray, understand me thoroughly hereafter. I believe I shall be very angry within this week again; therefore, pray, take care to prevent it. (*Exit.*)

FLEA-FLINT.

It were a good deed ne'er to plunder more.

BURNDORP.

Why, prithee?

FLEA-FLINT.

No thriving on't for these damned officers. To put excise and custom upon plundering! to put toll upon fleaing a flint! I hold my own quarters to be my lawful inheritance as much as any man's land or office that is held by old custom and time out of mind.

FERRET-FARM.

Nay, I hold my quarters to be so much my own, that the wife, the daughter and maidservants ought to be in my occupation.

BURNDORP.

I deny that, for the man of the house ought to have his wife himself, in case he have a daughter to furnish you. Nay, the strictness of the statute of plundering says, that in case he has but barely a maidservant, you ought not to meddle with his wife, or indeed his daughter.

FLEA-FLINT.

I am of the opinion of the gentleman that spoke last, for I am (in my own quarter) lord of the manor, and all wefts[4] and strays are mine.

BURNDORP.

I'll say that for thee, a maid cannot go a-milking but thou mak'st a weft or stray of her.

Enter Cornet.

CORNET.

Here's the faithful fraternity, a league of knaves that's never to be broke. It is a joyful thing when brethren plunder together in unity. How d'ye, Plunder-master General?

FLEA-FLINT.

We have all arrived at excellent nicknames, to say truth, according to our several degrees and ways of plundering. But you, Cornet, have a name that's proper for all cornets to be called by, for they are all beardless boys in our army.[5] For the most part of our horse were raised thus: The honest country gentleman raises the troop at his own charge, then he gets a low-country lieutenant[6] to fight his troop

[3] flea a flint] flay or skin a flint, to obtain money in any cruel or hardhearted way, as in modern "skinflint"

[4] weft] waif

[5] cornet] (1) lowest ranking cavalry officer, (2) immature grain, without a "beard."

[6] low-country lieutenant] The sense is a professional soldier, but there is a possible allusion to Prince Rupert from Germany, who led Royalist troops for his uncle Charles I.

safely, then sends for his son from school to be his cornet, and he puts off his child's coat to put on a buff coat; and this is the constitution of our army. So I salute you, Cornet Beardless.—Thou art called Ferret-farm because thou are so terrible valiant amongst the country bumpkins, and Aspen because thou shakest and tremblest in a day of battle.

FERRET-FARM.

Whoo, pox, this is absolute malice.

CORNET.

There thou art out, for this is neither malice nor anger, but downright truth.

FLEA-FLINT.

You abuse him, i'faith. I have seen him up to the chin in blood.

CORNET.

'Twas in a saw-pit,[7] then. Yet, when the armies meet (I'll say that for him) he will draw up as confidently as if he would take a general by the beard. And he will as confidently ride out of the army before the battle joins, and if any man ask him whither he goes, he says he is sent for orders. So you hear of him no more, and the next day you find him as sure in a saw-pit.

FERRET-FARM.

Pray let the saw-pit alone and provoke me not. Good men have done the like; therefore, be not too bold with your betters.

FLEA-FLINT.

Provoke him not, for he's a devil at a sword though he tremble at a gun.

FERRET-FARM.

A gun, I confess, is as terrible to me as thunder and lightning; they're out of my element. Well, but leave this discourse, and, so you do not laugh at me, I'll tell you a story.

FLEA-FLINT.

What is't?

FERRET-FARM.

Why, faith, our Dol's with child and lays it to me.

[7] saw-pit] a pit over which timber is sawed by two men, one above and one below, hence a safe hole for hiding

BURNDORP.

Pox on her, she was with me this morning, and I compounded with her for five pound.

FERRET-FARM.

The whore had seven of me, by this light.

CORNET.

An excellent cunning quean! She knows the family of the Flea-flints are ever the moneyed men of the troop. I'll make use of my time too; give me ten pound to keep counsel, or I'll make you the laughingstock o'th'army.

FLEA-FLINT.

Thou wilt not turn treacherous rogue now, sure?

CORNET.

'Tis no treachery. Show me a soldier that will not take advantage.

FLEA-FLINT.

Aye, of the enemy.

CORNET.

For ten pound any man's my enemy or friend. There's another principle for you, and very fit for the Flea-flints to make use of.

BURNDORP.

We scorn to compound, but we will lend you so much money if you will mortgage[8] the next fresh quarters.

CORNET.

I'll do't.

BURNDORP.

Then there's your ten pound.

CORNET.

Now are you men of inheritance. Now you have a good title to every man's goods and chattels, and for ten pound more I'll help you to a lawyer shall plead it and make it good to you and your heirs forever.[9]

Enter Tell-troth.

TELL-TROTH.

God give you good morn, sirs. I pray you, which of you is the Captain Commander?

[8] mortgage] promise

[9] men of inheritance … forever] The cornet implies that the cash loan can be converted into "real" property; until 1867 only male landowners deriving income from real estate could vote.

FLEA-FLINT.

Why, friend, we have ne'er a captain here. He lies leiger[10] at Oxford to give the King intelligence when his troop beats or is beaten.

CORNET.

There y'are a scandalous rascal. Some captains, I confess, have that trick, but our captain always fights his troop himself. But we have a good lieutenant here, if that will serve your turn.

BURNDORP.

Aye, he's too good for us; I would the devil had him.

CORNET.

What's thy business?

TELL-TROTH.

I'd be a trooper.

FERRET-FARM.

And canst thou fight?

TELL-TROTH.

Wilt thou try?

FERRET-FARM.

No, faith friend, I believe thee. Wast ever a soldier?

TELL-TROTH.

Aye, a Parliament one.

FLEA-FLINT.

What, and didst thou run away?

TELL-TROTH.

No, I walked this pace; I scorn to run.

BURNDORP.

I believe this fellow's a spy.

TELL-TROTH.

You lie;* I am very honest. Now, dare you fight?

BURNDORP.

No, by my troth, not with thee.

TELL-TROTH.

Then remember, if anybody want the lie, you had it last.

FLEA-FLINT. [*Aside.*]

This is such a fellow as I never met with.—Yet why didst thou leave the Parliament?

TELL-TROTH.

For the same cause that I believe I shall leave you.

10 leiger] permanently

FLEA-FLINT.

What's that?

TELL-TROTH.

Because I liked 'em not.

FERRET-FARM.

Who was thy captain?

TELL-TROTH.

One Captain Verily Rett.

FERRET-FARM.

Of what profession was he?

TELL-TROTH.

Of everyone's profession, I think.

FERRET-FARM.

What's that?

TELL-TROTH.

An hypocrite.

BURNDORP.

And dost thou come out of love to the King?

TELL-TROTH.

No. I come to see fashions.

BURNDORP.

But why didst thou leave thy captain?

TELL-TROTH.

Because he is a hypocrite, a yea-and-nay knave. He cannot endure to plunder, but (in a godly manner) he will take all he can lay his hands on.

CORNET.

But wilt thou fight for the King out of stark love and kindness?

TELL-TROTH.

No; I'll fight for him as all men fight for kings, partly for love, partly for my own ends. I'll fight bravely for a battle or two, then beg an old house to make a garrison of, grow rich, consequently a coward, and then let the dog bite the bear, or the bear the dog,[11] I'll make my own peace, I warrant you. And, in short, this is my business hither.

Enter Lieutenant.

LIEUTENANT.

Where are you, sirs? The captain has brought orders to march, but whither I know not. And, better news than that, he has brought pay, boys.

11 dog bite … the dog] The outcome is irrelevant; a reference to bear-baiting, a popular entertainment.

FLEA-FLINT.
I hope you are not angry, Lieutenant?

LIEUTENANT.
I am not yet, but I shall be very suddenly; therefore, provide against it. The next fresh quarter you will have advantage enough. I hope we understand of all hands?

FLEA-FLINT.
'Tis sufficient, Lieutenant.

CORNET.
But here's the strangest fellow come to be a trooper.

LIEUTENANT.
He's welcome.—Hast thou a good horse, friend?

TELL-TROTH.
No, but I've a bridle, and if you'll entertain* me, I shall quickly have a horse. Are you the captain?

LIEUTENANT.
I am but lieutenant, friend.

TELL-TROTH.
Ho, I thought you had all been captains. I'm sure you are all called so.

Enter Captain.

LIEUTENANT.
But here comes one that is so; this is a very* captain.

TELL-TROTH.
I tell thee that's very much. What's his name?

LIEUTENANT.
Captain Honor.

TELL-TROTH.
Aye? Have you such a thing as honor amongst you?

CAPTAIN.
Lieutenant, get your corporals together and give 'em orders to make ready for a march, and be sure you charge 'em to see every horse in their squadron's shod; otherwise, we shall have 'em lie behind drinking and plundering and then pretend they stay to shoe their horses. Let me hear no more on't.

TELL-TROTH.
'Tis possible a very captain may be honest.

LIEUTENANT.
But, sir, before you do anything, talk with this fellow; he would fain be a trooper.

CAPTAIN.
Now, friend, wouldst thou be a soldier?

TELL-TROTH.
Yes, if I could light of a good side: a right cause and good men to manage it.

CAPTAIN.
On my word, that's shrewdly put. Well, I'll promise thee a good cause and some good men; in multitudes all are not virtuous, nor valiant.

TELL-TROTH.
That's well said; I think I shall begin to take a liking to you. But, Captain, I hear a man may learn to flea a flint amongst you, to drink and plunder.

CAPTAIN.
D'ye hear that, rascals?—But where didst thou hear this report of us?

TELL-TROTH.
In a London pulpit. But another sort of people told me; they preached interest more than Gospel, so that a man knows not which side to take.

CAPTAIN.
Nay, upon my word, thou art come to the right side.

TELL-TROTH.
I guess as much, for you talk worse than you do, and they do worse than they talk.

CAPTAIN.
This is an odd kind of fellow, and I believe a dangerous.—Friend, withdraw while I read my orders to my officers.

TELL-TROTH.
A word in your ear first: Are you wonderful honest?

CAPTAIN.
Thou art a strange, blunt fellow. Yes, I am honest.

TELL-TROTH.
But are you wise too? For else the want* of wit to manage your honesty may make you a knave. I know 'tis some men's cases.

CAPTAIN.
Thou dost surprise me. Sure thou hast more business than to be a trooper?

TELL-TROTH.
I have so, but I must ask you another question ere you know it. Are you staunch enough to keep a secret? Be not angry. Many of your party cannot hold, for tell you news and you fly like lightning

to the next man to disgorge it, and so it goes round till it comes to the enemy, and thus you betray your business and intend it not neither.

CAPTAIN.

I have not heard so dangerous a man.—Pray, friend, think me worthy to know your business.

TELL-TROTH.

You shall. And to show you that I have business, I know what your orders are.

CAPTAIN.

Why, 'tis impossible.

TELL-TROTH.

Nothing impossible, you are to remove your troop to Cilstow, there quarter till further orders, but not to go to bed, for you are within three miles of a little house called Thievesden Garrison, and you are to expect a company of foot to quarter with you. Is that your orders?

CAPTAIN.

You amaze me! How came you by this intelligence?

TELL-TROTH.

It came to Thievesden house this morning and so to me. I am their confidant and would fain be yours.

CAPTAIN.

Do you not know who sent it?

TELL-TROTH.

No, nor they neither. There's the subtle carriage of the thing.

CAPTAIN.

But pray, sir, let me ask you who you are?

TELL-TROTH.

I am a plain, honest-meaning man, a neighbor to that garrison of Thievesden, and one that has dived into the bottom of both your parties and find that you have faults, but the other great wickedness.

FLEA-FLINT.

I do not like this fellow; he had a fling against drink.

FERRET-FARM.

And plundering, but twenty to one he hath paid for't.

FLEA-FLINT.

He had a plaguy jerk* at flaying of flints too.

CAPTAIN.

What if you went to Oxford with me?

TELL-TROTH.

So I may be hanged when I come home again? for they will know it as sure. Pray let me eat and refresh myself, and then conclude of something.

Exeunt.

Enter Dol, and calls Lieutenant back.

DOL.

Lieutenant, I'd speak with you.

LIEUTENANT.

Dol, I'll come to thee presently. (*Exit.*)

DOL.

I cannot say I am with child, but with children, for here has been all nations and all languages to boot. If the several tongues should work upwards now, and I speak all languages? Why, I am not the first learned woman, but I believe the first that ever came by her learning that way. If I should have for every man that has been dealing here a child, and if the children should be born with every one a back and breast[12] on, as they were got? Bless me, what hard labor should I have! But, for all this, I hope I do not go with above a squadron of children. But to my business. I mean to lay this great belly to every man that has but touched my apron strings. I thank the law, 'tis very favorable in this point, for when I have played the whore, the law gives me leave to play the rogue, and lay it to whom I will.[13]

Enter Lieutenant.

LIEUTENANT.

Why, how now, Dol? How go matters with you, good Dol?

DOL.

I desire you stand my friend, sir. You see my condition.

---

12 back and breast] backplate and breastplate, armor parts

13 law … will] Prior to 1754 an unmarried pregnant woman would be brought before a Justice of the Peace by parish officials to name the father, who would then be arrested and offered the choice of on the spot marriage or prison.

LIEUTENANT.
Thou wilt not lay thy child to my charge, I hope?
DOL.
No, sir, I have more wit; my drift is to lay it to more than one man or one squadron. Sir, I understand there's a month's pay in your hands, and I am resolved to lay this great belly to every man round the troop. Some I have struck already, and they have very fairly compounded with me; some, I suppose, may bustle and stand out, but if you will countenance me, then they must compound at our rates.
LIEUTENANT.
But, Dol, what benefit is this to me? For I profess no friendship but follow the general principle of mankind, Dol, which is to pick the money out of thy pocket to put it into mine. So, Dol, in plain terms, what will you give me?
DOL.
Why, Lieutenant, you shall go snips.[14]
LIEUTENANT.
Why, Dol, we are agreed. But after we have struck the troop round, who dost thou pitch upon to father it?
DOL.
Why, faith, I did design to marry Monsieur Raggou, the French cook that rides in your troop.
LIEUTENANT.
Thou wilt never endure to live with him, 'tis such a nasty slovenly rogue.
DOL.
'Tis no matter for living with him, I want* a husband.
LIEUTENANT.
He stinks above ground. He has not had a shirt on's back time out of mind.
DOL.
That makes it a fit match, for by my troth, I do not deserve a man that's worth a shirt.
LIEUTENANT.
Well, Dol, upon the aforesaid terms you're sure of me; play your game with all confidence.
DOL.
Well, I'll to work amongst 'em presently,* or if I might gain you to advance my greater desires, which is my cornet's boy that waits on him. I am foolish, for I love him strangely, desperately. A hundred pounds, in plain terms, make him mine.
LIEUTENANT.
But, Dol, where is this hundred pound?
DOL.
I have sharked these four years and made a shift to scrape four hundred pounds together.
LIEUTENANT.
Still, I say, you're sure of me with ready money.

Enter Monsieur Raggou and his landlady.

Well, Dol, away; here comes Monsieur Raggou. Step aside.
DOL.
Oh, let him have his money. If our cornet's boy fail, I'll have him, or he shall certainly keep* the child. (*Exit.*)
RAGGOU.
Landlady, come, take-a my pistol and lock in your trunk very safe.
LANDLADY.
Yes, sir.
RAGGOU.
Take heed, for begar* you will be hang if my pistol run away.
LANDLADY.
Oh Lord, I'll take no charge on't!
RAGGOU.
You roundhead whore, lock it up, or me will kill you, begar.
LANDLADY.
I'll take all care I can on't, sir. (*Exit.*)
RAGGOU.
So, me will steal my pistol from her trunk, and say she carry it to de enemy, and den me will so plundra de dam whore.

Enter bumpkin.

Stand; who are you for, Bumpkin?
BUMPKIN.
Oh Lord, sir, I am for nobody.
RAGGOU.
You dog, be you for de King or de Parliamenta?

[14] go snips] have a share

BUMPKIN.

Why, I am for—pray, sir, who are you for?

RAGGOU.

Tank you for dat. Begar, you be very full wid cunning. You will be of my-a side if me name myself first. Speak, you dam dog. Who be you for?

BUMPKIN.

In truth it is not good manners to say who I am for; your worship ought to speak first.

RAGGOU.

Pox take you, me be for de Parliament, you dog.

BUMPKIN.

Oh, the Lord bless your worship, I am for the good Parliament, too.

RAGGOU.

Jernie,* I am for de King, you roundhead dog. Begar, me will plundra you, soul and body.

BUMPKIN.

Oh, good sir, spare me; I am for the King.

RAGGOU.

Diable, me will plundra you for being Jack[15] of both sides. [*Aside.*] Diantie,[16] he have but one silling about his soul and bodee.—Get you gone, you dog.

Exit bumpkin.

Begar, me have no luck. Zoun, me plundra every day dis tre years, and begar me never get but one silling or one sixpenne, begar. Hah! Monsieur Lieutenant, me hear very brave* ting of you.

LIEUTENANT.

What's that?

RAGGOU.

Me hear you have some largion[17] for Monsieur la Soldier. Pray, how much will come to Monsieur Moy?

LIEUTENANT.

Faith, monsieur, some three pounds.

RAGGOU.

How, tre pone? Whar be de tre pone? How much be tre pone?

LIEUTENANT.

Why, here 'tis, Monsieur, so much as you see.

RAGGOU.

Begar, sure you mock-a de moy; begar, me never see so much money togeder in my life. Me will lie down and tumble in my money like de dog dat tumbla in de carrion, it is so sweet. Oh brave Capitain, oh brave Lieutenant, Gad-a bless de King of England, and de King of France, too, when he give me tre pone. Lieutenant, be to be mad a dangerous ting?

LIEUTENANT.

Oh, very dangerous.

RAGGOU.

Begar, dere be your tre pone again. It will make-a me tark-a mad; me no know vat me sall do with all dis money. Begar, me admire tre pone of all ting in dis varle; it vill make de great Turk de Christian, or de Christian de Turk, better den all de argument in the varle. Pray, Lieutenant, keep dis money for me, one, two, tre year, till me take counsel of all my friend in France vat me sall do wid dat.

LIEUTENANT.

Go to Oxford and buy some necessaries with it; you are so nasty, nobody is able to come near you. Buy some shirts, to keep you sweet and clean.

RAGGOU.

Buy some shart? Me love you very vell, Lieutenant, but you no understand. For vat sall me have some shart?

LIEUTENANT.

To keep yourself sweet and from being lousy.*

RAGGOU.

Who can see my shart? Here be my doublet come close, my coat come over all dat, den who de devil see my shart? For vat sall me have a shart, when nobody see my shart?

LIEUTENANT.

But then you want* stockings and twenty necessaries.

RAGGOU.

Me pull up my boot, who see me have a stockin? You vill have a little English tricka and never understand. For vat vill you have more ting about you den vat vill make a show in de varle and

15 Jack] a knave, a nickname usually indicating a youthful or impish miscreant, not a dangerous felon

16 Diantie] probably a corruption of *Diantre*, a mild French oath perhaps best translated as "the dickens"

17 largion] *l'argent*, money

everybody can see? Pray, let me lay out my money to please my own fancee.

LIEUTENANT.

With all my heart.

RAGGOU.

Den me will lay it out for my honor, and for de honor of de King and my Lieutenant. So adieu. Buy shart? Who see my shart? (*Exit.*)

Enter Dol.

DOL.

Faith, Lieutenant, I'll at him and some of the rest presently;* therefore, leave me to work. I am ashamed; I am such a fool to dote on a boy, but no remedy. Remember, therefore, and about it.

LIEUTENANT.

Do you remember the hundred pound; I'll work him, fear not.

Exeunt severally.

Act II, scene i. [The troop's camp.]

Enter Dol Troop.

DOL.

Now to my business. My Flintflayer compounded with me very civilly, that I did fear would have outwitted me. I am afraid of nothing but an impudent rogue that has no shame in him, that will father the child rather than part with his money, and so spoil my compounding with the rest of the troop. I'll be as wise as I can, so have among 'em.

Enter a trooper.

TROOPER.

What a pox makes she here?

DOL.

How d'ye, Mr. William? I'm come to tell you I am gone half my time, that you may provide, for I am quick.*

TROOPER.

Art thou? Faith, I'll be as quick as thou art, for I'll be in Holland (if the wind serve) tomorrow. (*Exit.*)

DOL.

'Slife, if they should all boggle thus, I should make a thin troop on't.

Enter Raggou.

RAGGOU.

Oh, Madam Dol! Ow dee? Ow dee?

DOL.

You see how I do. I am near my time; I desire you to provide. You swore a thousand oaths to me you would keep* the child.

RAGGOU.

But me did but swear in French, Madam Dol, and dat vill no stand good in English law, Madam Dol.

DOL.

Come, sir, come, I'll make you father my child, or I'll make you do worse. Will you compound?

RAGGOU.

Me scorn to compone and scorn to fader your shild. You be a dam whore, Madam Dol.

DOL.

You are a rascal, Mr. Monsieur, and I'll make you father the child in spite of your French teeth.*

RAGGOU.

Begar, Madam Dol, you be de great whore de Babylon.* Begar, me vill make appear noting can get you wid shild but de maypole in de Strana,[18] and den me can make appear by good vitteness dat me have no maypole abouta me. So adieu, Madam Babylon. Pox take you, me fader your dam son of a whore shild! (*Exit.*)

DOL.

You fickle Frenchman, I shall be revenged on thee. I'll marry thee, but I'll be revenged on thee.

Enter Cornet, Lieutenant, and Biddy.

But here comes my cornet and his boy, and the lieutenant. I see he is mindful of my business. (*Exit.*)

LIEUTENANT.

Cornet, I have an earnest and (by my troth) a most pleasant suit to you.

CORNET.

You cannot miss the grant of it. What is't?

LIEUTENANT.

But first, do you love money?

CORNET.

By my troth, I know not, for I never had a sum worth loving in my life yet.

[18] de Strana] the Strand*

LIEUTENANT.

Will fifty pound do any hurt?

CORNET.

But what must I do for it? betray the troop to the enemy, or some garrison? For under that I cannot deserve fifty pound.

LIEUTENANT.

Towns are not so cheap yet. Though treason be plentiful, 'tis not grown a drug. But to my suit, you are to know that our Dol is desperately in love and with whom.

CORNET.

Not with me? I find I must earn this fifty pound.

LIEUTENANT.

No such matter; you have too great a conceit of your good face.

BIDDY. (*Aside.*)

Indeed you lie, Lieutenant, for he can never think too well of that face.

CORNET.

Who is it she is in love with?

LIEUTENANT.

By my troth, with thy boy here, desperately in love with thy boy.

BIDDY. (*Aside.*)

The devil take her for her pains. But why do I curse her, that am so desperately in love myself?

CORNET.

Why, this story is very pleasant, if you knew all.

BIDDY.

Oh Lord, you will not tell him what I am, I hope?

CORNET.

Lieutenant, I must deny your suit, for it must not be a match, for the boy is, in plain terms, a girl.

BIDDY.

The devil take you for telling him.

CORNET.

Why so? My lieutenant's very faithful.

LIEUTENANT.

A girl? Let me see your face.

BIDDY.

Oh, you unworthy man!—Good sir, forgive me, for I am even ready to scold.

LIEUTENANT.

This is the pretty young daughter that belonged to your winter quarters, and so came away for love?

BIDDY.

Yes, sir, but if your cornet had been true, I had been past love by this time. I had been married.

LIEUTENANT.

Why, are all married people past love?

BIDDY.

Yes, sir, of the men's side especially, but sir, I am naturally very merry, and shall be, if you will but do me the favor to think me very honest.*

LIEUTENANT.

I shall do you a great favor if I do, for I never thought anybody so yet. But if it please you, I'll try your honesty, and then I'll give you my opinion.

BIDDY.

Be not rude when you try me. If you be, you were better venture on a maiden cat at midnight, for I shall scratch worse and so mark you, not for my humble servant, but my humble caterwauler.

LIEUTENANT.

I could meet such a creature o'th'housetop at any hour, and scratch and squeak, and tumble down together, and get the prettiest kitlings as we fall.

BIDDY.

I am glad to see you merry, sir, for merry people are likely honest.

LIEUTENANT.

Well, we'll try, but if you love mirth, consent to marry with this Dol. There's money for us all. (*Exit.*)

BIDDY.

Content, i'faith. 'Twill be excellent sport to marry her, for I love roguery well enough, but the devil's in't; she'll know me to be a girl.

Enter Dol aloof.[19]

CORNET.

No, no. She shall not come near you, nor touch you, till she's brought to bed. Then two to one but the troop marches away and leaves her behind. Then I'm sure the country bumpkins will knock her o'th'head.[20]

---

19 aloof] at a distance, i.e., unseen by Biddy and the Cornet.

20 knock her o'th'head] bludgeon her to death

DOL. [*Aside.*]
There's a cornet in grain, i'faith.
BIDDY.
Troth, you are very charitable. Well, since my hand's in at wearing breeches, I'll do all the offices of a man. I would I had wherewithal to perform, for by my troth, I am weary of our own sex.
DOL. [*Aside.*]
She cries, i'faith; I like that well.
CORNET.
You little fool, you do not cry, I hope?
BIDDY.
No, faith, that was but a tear by chance. You made me leave my friends, you know, when you talked of marriage to me, but not one word on't now you have made me your be-de-boy.[21]
DOL. [*Aside.*]
I know not what to say to that.
CORNET.
We'll talk of those things when we are settled.
BIDDY.
By my troth, you have put me in such a gog* of marriage that it will not out of my head, and yet I scorn to ask you to marry me, and I scorn to crack a commandment with you. Was not that basely done of you to tempt me? But I shall scold, which is a thing I hate. Oh base fellow! You would be going o'th'score[22] with me for my virginity? Faith sir, I'd have you know 'tis worth ready money at any time, and, faith, I'll swear it shall ne'er go under matrimony.
DOL. [*Aside.*]
She is honest,* i'faith. I love a virtuous woman, though I am none myself, like him that loved the sound of Greek though he understood it not. She is right honest, i'faith.
BIDDY.
Marry me, and then halloo, dog, for thy silver collar, but till then I'll gnaw my under-sheet to the bedcord before you shall have your will of me. I am sometimes mad when I think how I left my friends. Sometimes I could scold, and sometimes I could cry, and the devil take that good face of yours, I can do neither for it.
CORNET.
Come, come, you trust your person with me, and why not your virginity? How long do you think you can hold out at this staunch rate?
BIDDY.
Faith sir, I can hold out till it's fit for nobody, till I'm past the use of man, before thou shalt have it, shameless wretch.
DOL. [*Aside.*]
She is certainly honest, and that's half our work done.
CORNET.
Come, prithee let's think of our mock-marriage with Dol, and after we'll be serious.
BIDDY.
Why, I'm for that too. But yet I cannot choose but cry to see how false you are, and how they talk at home of me, "She's run away with a soldier, and that rascal will not marry her." Oh, the devil take you; I shall never recover that credit again!
CORNET.
Come, we'll cozen 'em all at last.
BIDDY.
Nay, I believe thou'lt cozen more than me, for what woman can forbear running away with thee, that sees those leering eyes, thou bewitching devil, thou!
CORNET.
Oh, remember you hate scolding, Biddy.
BIDDY.
I had forgot that, indeed.
CORNET.
Nay, prithee, no more of this story.
BIDDY.
Well, I will not, but truly I grow weary of your unkindness, and I am served well enough for scorning a man that doted on me.
DOL. [*Aside.*]
Aha! Aye, marry,* that's somewhat, indeed.
BIDDY.
But I see, a cornet with his flying colors and his word, "Have at all," goes a great way with a virgin. Who can resist it?

Exeunt.

---

21 be-de-boy] bidding boy, an ad hoc servant who attends to light, ephemeral tasks; the character name, "Biddy," emphasizing the function

22 o'th'score] cross the line

[Scene ii. The troop's headquarters.]

Enter Captain, Lieutenant, and Tell-troth.

CAPTAIN.
Lieutenant, stay and receive orders. But, sir, how many companies are there in Thievesden Garrison?

TELL-TROTH.
Ne'er a company, for not one of 'em will be called captain of a company, but captain of a congregation. One is called Captain Holdforth; another Captain Tubtext, rogues marked at the font[23] for rebellion.

CAPTAIN.
Rebellion is the first point of Reformation always.

TELL-TROTH.
They are formed to a new stamp of villainy, the last impression——that which put the Devil into a cold sweat.[24] Take the wickedest and worst reputed men you have and turn 'em loose to plunder, and I defy 'em to make the tithe o'th'spoil these hypocrites have done!

CAPTAIN.
You are very bitter.

TELL-TROTH.
Malice cannot lay 'em open. They lecture[25] it thrice a week, and summon the country to come in. They that refuse, they take their goods and leave 'em ne'er a groat. And then they say they took but their own, for the good creature is the inheritance of the people of God.

CAPTAIN.
It seems every captain is a teacher, and his own company is his congregation, so that they hang and draw religion among themselves. No doubt most blasphemous villains.

TELL-TROTH.
Well sir, I'll home tonight. March your troop to Lavel tomorrow; stay till I come to you. So fare you well, and I wish a blessing upon your good meaning. (*Exit.*)

CAPTAIN.
Lieutenant, be careful how you march tomorrow, and take heed I hear no complaint. I'll to Oxford in the morning to give an account of this fellow.

LIEUTENANT.
I hope you'll allow us our old harmless drolleries.

CAPTAIN.
Aye, most freely. (*Exit.*)

Enter Cornet.

CORNET.
Lieutenant, half the troop will be gone. Dol has laid her child to 'em all, and they're for horse and away.

LIEUTENANT.
What shall we do?

CORNET.
Endeavor to prevent it, that is all that's to be said.

Exeunt.

Enter a trooper with his arms, and Monsieur Raggou meets him.

RAGGOU.
Ow dee, ow dee, Monsieur Lancashire?[26] Vat make you have your arms so late at night? Is dere alarm? Be de enemy in de quarteer?

FIRST TROOPER.
Worse than the enemy, the Devil's in the quarter. Our Dol is with child and would lay it to me, but I'll lay down my arms and go home.

RAGGOU.
Begar, me vil lay down my arms and go home too. Hah! Begar, now I tink, me have no home. (*Exit.*)

FIRST TROOPER.
Captain! Captain!

[VOICE.] (*Within.*)
Who's there? What's the matter?

FIRST TROOPER.
Thomas, 'tis I, the old mutineer. Tell the Captain I must speak with him.

---

23 at the font] at baptism, since birth

24 last impression … cold sweat] the image stamped would be of Armageddon prophesied in Revelation; hence the defeat of the Devil.

25 lecture] preach. After the Restoration, dissenters often privately hired lecturers or speakers to address congregations and supplement or counteract the teachings of the official Anglican church.

26 Lancashire] at the time a very rural northwestern county in England

[VOICE.] (*Within.*)
He is but just laid down on the bed to sleep a little. Come i'th'morning!

FIRST TROOPER.
Flesh and blood, I will speak with him.

[Enter] Captain above.

CAPTAIN.
What's the matter? an alarm?

FIRST TROOPER.
Aye, marry is there, Captain; there will be a whole squadron upon you presently.

CAPTAIN.
'Sdeath,* my horse presently.*

FIRST TROOPER.
The enemy, Dol, is fallen into our Lancashire quarters and has laid her child to our squadron. So here is your back and your breast, Captain, and I'll go home.

Enter four troopers and Raggou.

SECOND TROOPER.
Flesh! We'll father no child, not we.

RAGGOU.
Begar, me vil fader no shild too.—Hey, Monsieur Captain, here be your one pistol.

THIRD TROOPER.
Captain, we have brought you some Lancashire arms; here is some ten or eleven sowze kidgiors[27] for you.

CAPTAIN. (*Above.*)
What the devil ails the fellows?

RAGGOU.
Begar, Capitain, me vil keep* no shild; your dam madam Dol have get us all with a shild.

CAPTAIN.
Run for the quean to come to me. I shall have all my troop forsake me. Stay, sirs, I'll come to you.—I must as well humor 'em as be severe, or else no soldiers. (*Exit from above.*)

RAGGOU.
Vell, me do know very well how it sall be my shild or no.

FOURTH TROOPER.
Well monsieur, and I have a mark to know whether it be mine or no as well as you.

SECOND TROOPER.
And so we have all.

Enter Captain and Cornet.

CAPTAIN.
My masters, you might have had so much manners to have held your complaints till morning. But, however, I have sent for Dol, and I'll do you justice before I stir now. How now, Raggou? What are thy sleeves stuffed withal so?

RAGGOU.
Begar, dis sleeve be my stabla: dere be good oata for mine arse. And dis sleeve be my kitchin: dere be meat for myself. Vill you eat dis morning, Capitain?

CAPTAIN.
Faugh! Your sleeves stink abominably.

RAGGOU.
Zoun, do you call dat a stinka? 'Tis true, it have a little hogoe.* Begar, dis sleeve keep your troop alive; dis sleeve is de physician to all de troop. When any man be sick, me set on some hot vatera, dere let my sleeve boil one hour in it, and dat make de comfortable pottage in de varle. Have not me cure you all?

FOURTH TROOPER.
Yes, indeed, Captain, he has cured us twenty times.

RAGGOU.
Begar, Capitain, me have cure that dam whore Madam Dol, and yet for all dat she lay her shild a top upon me.

Enter Dol.

CAPTAIN.
Oh, here she is. Now, you audacious quean, what makes you alarm these people thus? Who got you with child? Speak, and speak truth, I charge you.

DOL.
Why, then, I will speak truth an't* please you. Good Captain, do not fright me.

CAPTAIN.
Well, then, is it his child? Did he get it?

DOL.
I cannot say absolutely 'tis his, Captain.

[27] sowse kidgiors] probably pig prods, useful for plundering

CAPTAIN.
Why, is it this fellow's?

DOL.
I cannot say directly 'tis his neither.

CAPTAIN.
Is it Monsieur Raggou's?

DOL.
I cannot say, to speak truth, 'tis his in particular.

CAPTAIN.
Death, you abominable quean, say whose 'tis, or I'll slit your nose.[28]

DOL.
Why, truly, I cannot lay it to any one man, but, Gad is my judge, 'tis the troop's child, Captain.

CAPTAIN.
Was ever such a slut heard of!

DOL.
I desire your worship to believe me in one thing. Truly, Captain, and, as Gad's my comfort, I have been as true and faithful a woman to the troop as ever wife was to a husband, Captain.

RAGGOU.
Oh ho! Are you so? Me tink now, Madam Dol, you are de whore de Babylon, for one whole troop may make a maypole.

CAPTAIN.
Why, this is some honesty yet, that she is true to the troop.

RAGGOU.
Ould, Capitain! For oughta me see, dis shild be your shild.

CAPTAIN.
How prove you that, sir?

RAGGOU.
Begar, she say de shild belong to de troop, and you say de troop belong to you; derefore, de shild is your shild, begar.

CAPTAIN.
But I'll make some of you father it. There is none of you but have some private mark to know it to be your own by.

FOURTH TROOPER.
Faith, Captain, if it be born with a gauntlet and a headpiece[29] on, I'll own it.

SECOND TROOPER.
Troth, Captain, if it be born with a bridle in its hand and boots and spurs on, I'll own it.

FIRST TROOPER.
Troth, Captain, I ne'er touched her. I was about it once, but the jade laid herself so like a constable tied neck and heels together, that I went to plunder her, and she up and beat me like a dog.

THIRD TROOPER.
And by my troth, if it be born leading a horse into the world, 'tis my child, Captain.

RAGGOU.
Ould, you every one have a mark to know your shild. Madam Dol, before my Capitain, if your shild be born wid never a shart, den it be my shild, for me have had no shart dis forty week.

Enter Ferret-farm.

FERRET-FARM.
By your leave, Captain.

CAPTAIN.
What want you, Aspen?

FERRET-FARM.
I come to free all these men and to own the child, Captain.

DOL.
How, own my child? The rogue never touched me in his life, Captain.

FERRET-FARM.
Hah, Dol! Confess, confess! Will you have the truth, Captain?

CAPTAIN.
Aye, prithee, with all my heart.

FERRET-FARM.
Why, then, I must confess she goes with two children; one I got on the great trunk's end and the other on a staircase, by my life, Captain.

CAPTAIN.
I never heard of staircase children before.

---

[28] slit your nose] Mutilating (branding) petty criminals to identify them as such was part of the official criminal code, particularly in the military, until the mid-19th century. Nose-slitting, cutting the nostril up as far as the bridge, appears to be a practice of hooliganism or vigilantism.

[29] headpiece] helmet

RAGGOU.
But vat if de shild be born wid no shart? You sall be hang before you fader my shild.
DOL.
Captain, if I were to die tomorrow, the rogue never touched me.
FERRET-FARM.
I'll cudgel the rogue to death, Captain.
CAPTAIN.
Hold! Hold!
RAGGOU.
Let him come, Captain! Me vill kill him, begar! (*Draws and throws off his coat.*)
CAPTAIN.
Hold, Dol.—I charge you to put up, monsieur.
RAGGOU.
Me vill put up, den.
CAPTAIN.
Not one word more, I charge you, but all to your quarters. Be gone!—Cornet, 'tis time to sound to horse, and take heed I hear of no complaints.
RAGGOU.
Begar, me never see all dat before. Diable, me be Monsieur Raggou indeed. Me vill put on my coat presan,* for, begar, if Monsieur Dunghill-raker see me, begar he vill put me in his sack.

Exeunt.

[Scene iii. The troop's camp.]

Enter twelve troopers at six doors, two at a door.

FIRST TROOPER.
Pox of this French fool. What, does he mean to give us all ribbons? We do but laugh at him.
THIRD TROOPER.
His business is to be admired. I admire he has bought him ne'er a shirt.
SECOND TROOPER.
He is like the hypocrites that will not sing psalms because they've ne'er a room to the street, they cannot be heard.
FOURTH TROOPER.
And so he'll have ne'er a shirt because it cannot be seen.

Enter Lieutenant, Flea-flint, Ferret-farm, and Burndorp.

LIEUTENANT.
Come, to horse, to horse.
FLEA-FLINT.
Lieutenant, pray let Monsieur Raggou ride before and make the quarters tonight.
FERRET-FARM.
Pray do, sir, for every fresh quarter we know you expect, and therefore you must wink.
LIEUTENANT.
But, sirs, I dare not own you, for my captain is so severe that I protest he'll hang any man that plunders, especially you flint-flayers that he has forgiven so often.
BURNDORP.
Why, sir, we'll venture that, for we have a way to come off.
LIEUTENANT.
Pray, how? For if the country complain (and they discover you) the world cannot save you.
FLEA-FLINT.
Why, sir, you know Monsieur Raggou has a remarkable coat with one sleeve always full of meat for himself and the other full of oats for his horse.
LIEUTENANT.
Well, what then?
FLEA-FLINT.
Why, I have such a coat, and I will stuff up the sleeves and rob like him. I can spatter French and have everything so like him that yourself cannot distinguish.
LIEUTENANT.
Well, and how rob the rest?
FERRET-FARM.
To satisfy you, in such disguises as the devil cannot find us out in.
LIEUTENANT.
You'll do well to keep in those disguises still,* for, i'faith, he'll find you at the long run else. Well, if you will venture, do; I'll aid you in what I can.
BURNDORP.
If the country complain, they come directly to you, Lieutenant.
FERRET-FARM.
Then you bid 'em describe the men, and without peradventure they fall upon the Frenchman with his remarkable sleeves.

LIEUTENANT.
But suppose he stand it out and make it out where he was in the time of plundering?
FLEA-FLINT.
That's shrewd, I confess.
LIEUTENANT.
Come, I'll help you. If the countrymen come in and describe him, I'll go directly to him and tell him I have orders to seize him, for my captain is resolved to hang him. So, out of my kindness to him, I'll let him make his escape, and I'll warrant he'll away as if the devil drove him.
FERRET-FARM.
But suppose he will not go at that neither? For he's impudent enough.
LIEUTENANT.
Hah! If he will not (let me see) I'll write a letter and have it ready in my hand, and we'll pretend to search him for letters of intelligence, and so clap the letter into his pocket and pull it out again, which shall be as if it came from the enemy, and that, according to his promise, they hope he will betray the troop.
FERRET-FARM.
Aye, marry, this is something. Needs must he go that the devil drives.
FLEA-FLINT.
Then much more must he go that the Lieutenant drives. I warrant he goes to some purpose.
FERRET-FARM.
Good, and when he is gone and fled for't—
LIEUTENANT.
The case is plain, he's guilty. None but he could do it.
BURNDORP.
Why, this is plot and intrigue, Lieutenant, bravely* laid, i'faith.
FLEA-FLINT.
Why then, *Esperanza*,[30] Flea-flint.
FERRET-FARM.
What work we'll make!

Enter Raggou and his landlady.

LIEUTENANT.
Here comes the poor rogue and his landlady. He little thinks of our tragical design against him. I'll step aside and see what work he'll make.

Exeunt.

RAGGOU.
Come, Landlady, bring me my pistol, me must march.
LANDLADY.
Aye, sir, I'll fetch it you; 'tis safe enough. (*Exit.*)
RAGGOU.
Begar, me have steal my pistol. Me vill make her believe she vill be hang, and den she vill endure plundering de betra. But, pox take her, me have search, and she have noting to plundra.

Enter Landlady.

LANDLADY.
Oh Lord! What shall I do, Monsieur? Your pistol's gone.
RAGGOU.
Hah!
LANDLADY.
It is gone; it is stolen.
RAGGOU.
Hah! You have carry my pistol to de enemy, you dam whore. Begar, you sall hang tre pair of stair higher den Haman.
LANDLADY.
Truly, I know not what's become on't. I hope you have it yourself.
RAGGOU.
Oh, you dam whore, me vill plundra your house for slander a moy.
LANDLADY.
Good sir, I have nothing worth plundering but a great cheese.
RAGGOU.
Give me your sheese, you devil you.
LANDLADY.
Here it is, sir, and all I have in the world.
RAGGOU.
Pox take you, give me one silling for my sheese.
LANDLADY.
With all my heart. Truly it's all the money I have.

30 *Esperanza*] Hope

RAGGOU.
Now give me my sheese agen, you dam whore.—Vat sall me do wid dis sheese? It vill not go into my kitchin sleeve.—Begar, for one shilling more you sall have the sheese indeed.
LANDLADY.
You'll plunder it again?
RAGGOU.
Begar, it go agen my conscience to take your sheese, because it vill no go in my kitchin sleeve.
LANDLADY.
I have not a penny to save my life.
RAGGOU.
Begar, me sell it to your neighbor.

Enter Neighbor.

Vat vill you give me for my sheese?
LANDLADY.
It's my cheese.
RAGGOU.
Begar, she lie. Me plunder it very fair from her.
NEIGHBOR.
Then I hope I may buy plundered goods as well as other people. What's your price?
RAGGOU.
Begar, dog-sheap: one silling.
NEIGHBOR.
There's your money.
LANDLADY.
Will you offer to buy my cheese?
NEIGHBOR.
'Tis my cheese.
LANDLADY.
I'll try that.

Fight and exeunt [neighbor and landlady].

RAGGOU.
Begar, fight till de devil part you.

Enter Lieutenant and all the troopers.

Oh, Monsieur Lieutenant!
LIEUTENANT.
What dost with that cheese?
RAGGOU.
My landlady love me vera dear, and she give me dis sheese as a token to wear for her sake.
LIEUTENANT.
Raggou, you must needs go make the quarters for the troop.
RAGGOU.
Wid all min heart! But, Lieutenant, dere be a favor* for you. (*Gives him a knot of ribbon.*)
LIEUTENANT.
But what is the meaning of this?
RAGGOU.
Begar, it be for my honer; me have lay out all my tre pone in ribbon and give all de troop my favor to wear in de hat.
LIEUTENANT.
What, and is all thy three pound gone in ribbon, and bought never a shirt? 'Tis very fine.
RAGGOU.
Begar, and so it be very fine. As me tell you before, who de devil see my shart? All de varle see Monsieur Raggou in de hat; every man vill admire, and ask, "Who gave all that favor to de troop?" Den dey cry, "Monsieur Raggou, de French cook." Begar, dat sall be more honer for me den ever you sall get by your shart.
LIEUTENANT.
Thou art a right Frenchman.—My horse there, groom. Let's march away.

Exeunt.

Act III, scene i.
[Various locations near the troop's camp.]

Enter Flea-flint, Ferret-farm, and Burndorp.

FLEA-FLINT.
Is not this like him as can be?
BURNDORP.
'Tis like enough to delude the people with.
FLEA-FLINT.
I'll rant and tear the ground, boys. I will so plundra all de dam bumpkin dog.
FERRET-FARM.
That will pass; that's his word; 'tis like him.
FLEA-FLINT.
Be you pretty modest, sirs, and let me play the devil among 'em. I will so terrify 'em with French gibberish that you shall appear nobody amongst 'em.

BURNDORP.

Good, for the more active and terrible thou art, they will the more remember thee when they come to complain, and so we shall be sure to 'scape.

FLEA-FLINT.

Come away, sirs; we must be quick and ride hard for't.

Exeunt.

Enter Raggou, like Flea-flint.

RAGGOU.

Begar, me have maka myself like Flea-flint, and me vill burn one, two town as me go to make-a de quarter, and me vill speak English, and me vill call myself Flea-flint. Let me see.—Come, where is this constable? Where are all these damn'd, dery[31] damned, rogues and whores? I'll flay your very souls, you beastly bawds.—Begar, all dat be very good English, and it be very much like Monsieur Flea-flint, and begar, me hope he vill be taken and hang for dat, for begar me vill plundra de devel if me catch him. (*Exit.*)

Enter Cornet and Biddy.

CORNET.

Come, let me see, Biddy, how finely you'll court your mistress, now.

BIDDY.

I can court her as all men court women. You shall lend me two or three hundred oaths, your dissembling tongue, and your false heart, and then I cannot miss the right way of wooing her.

CORNET.

This comes very near scolding, Biddy. (*Takes her by the chin.*)

BIDDY.

You make me forget myself. Look you now, would any honest man take a maid so kindly by the chin and yet not mean to marry her?

CORNET.

Thou little fool, at that rate every man i'th'kingdom would have ten thousand wives. If you'll part with your maidenhead, have at you, Biddy. Come, come, you loving worm, I know I shall have it at last.

BIDDY.

Nay, o'my conscience, I believe thee, yet I have held fast hitherto.

CORNET.

I am glad to hear that, i'faith.

BIDDY.

But I find I must look no more on those eyes; if I do, i'faith, I shall flutter so long about the candle that I shall singe my virgin wings at last. I will therefore now conclude I am a man and must go court my mistress.

Enter Lieutenant and Dol.

CORNET.

Here's the lieutenant and Dol; now behave yourself like a man.

BIDDY.

Could you show me how to behave myself like an honest man? That's out of your way, I doubt.*

DOL. [*Aside.*]

Still better and better! This confirms me.

BIDDY.

Well, give me thy hand. I'm resolved to be very virtuous and very merry and never think more of thee.

CORNET.

Well, Mrs.* Dol, here's one has consented in part to marry you.

DOL.

Pretty creature!

BIDDY. (*Aside.*)

Ugly toad.

DOL.

Well, and will you be content to ride before me lovingly a days?

LIEUTENANT.

Aye, and behind thee, too; ride thee all points o'th'compass, wench, fear not.

BIDDY.

Oh Lord! But is there so many ways of riding, Lieutenant?

LIEUTENANT.

Hast thou lived to these years and not known that yet?

---

[31] dery] direly

CORNET.
Well, but when will you marry?
BIDDY.
Nay, by my faith, let us woo first and then marry, because I believe there is more pleasure in wooing than in the effects of it.
CORNET.
Why do not you begin and court her then?
BIDDY.
Nay, by my faith, let her begin first.
LIEUTENANT.
That's not the mode for the woman to woo the man.
BIDDY.
That is, if the man love the woman, but that's not my case, for 'tis she loves me, not I her.
LIEUTENANT.
Oh, but in complaisance you must begin. It is not civil to put a woman to't.
BIDDY.
Not I, faith. Pray, forsooth, do you begin.
DOL.
Indeed it shall be yours.
BIDDY.
I protest it shall be yours; therefore, begin or I vow I'll break off the match.
DOL.
Nay, rather than so, I'll begin. Sweet sir, I am much and greatly ashamed.
BIDDY.
Were you ever so before, mistress?
DOL.
Yes, truly, I have been ashamed, but it is so long since—
BIDDY.
That you have forgot it, I suppose. But I disturb you, forsooth.
DOL.
No disturbance, sweet sir; I want* fine words to express my love in. I am sorry that the cart-wheel of Fortune should drive me into the coach-box[32] of your affection.
BIDDY.
Fortune will take it scurvily to call her wheel a cartwheel. Besides, coach-box and cartwheel did never agree in this world yet.
DOL.
I am not able to express my love as it deserves, but I have four hundred pound in gold, if that will do it.
BIDDY.
By my faith, you express yourself very well, and I will woo you heartily for it. Madam, you have struck me with such a desperate dart from those fair somewhat or other that you have about you.—Are you sure you have the gold you spoke of?
DOL.
Yes, my dear heart, very sure.
BIDDY.
Then if I do not love you above all womankind, perish me, and sink me, refuse me, rot me, and renounce me.
CORNET.
Hold, hold, hold! Do you call this wooing?
BIDDY.
Yes, faith, I had a sister cast away with the very same speech; therefore, do not interrupt me, for I know all mankind woos thus.—And as I was swearing, madam, the devil take—
LIEUTENANT.
Enough, enough, enough, enough!
BIDDY.
But, madam, are you satisfied?
DOL.
I am, to the full, and do believe you.
BIDDY.
But if you please, madam, now my hand is in, to accept of a hundred or two of oaths more.
DOL.
No, no, no, by no means. I believe you without 'em, and I am yours.
BIDDY.
I have not sworn out half my alphabet yet.
DOL.
You have done sufficiently, indeed.
BIDDY.
Well, give me your hand, then. You are the first woman, certainly, that was ever gained with so little swearing.
CORNET.
Thou hast wooed her and won her most bravely.*

[32] coach-box] tool box carried along to repair the coach

BIDDY.

Have I? Why, then, I'm thine. But hark you, Lieutenant and Cornet, we will be married privately and in the dark, because her face shall not turn my stomach.—Madam, I have one ill-humor: I cannot abide a woman with a bare face. Therefore, if I could buy you a mask that would stick to your face and never come off, I believe I should love you very well.

DOL.

I have a mask, or what you please, my dear.—
Next bout, I hope, will be my turn to jeer.

LIEUTENANT.

Come, let's in, and visit our new quarters.

Exeunt.

[Scene ii. In a nearby village.]

Enter Raggou making quarters, constables and neighbors.

FIRST NEIGHBOR.

I beseech your worship do not quarter so many upon me; I'm but a poor man.

SECOND NEIGHBOR.

Alas, poor man! You have overcharged him. Rogue, he has more money than half the town.

RAGGOU.

You be a dam dog to betray your neighbor. Who would tink to find de devel in a country bumpkin! Begar, me vill make use of your develry.

FIRST NEIGHBOR.

I pray your worship, take four horse from me.

RAGGOU.

You be a dam rich dog; begar, you sall have a squadron upon you if you no understand me.

FIRST NEIGHBOR.

How should I understand you?

RAGGOU.

You be a dam dog; begar, me vill put twenty horse upon your back till you understand a moy. Vat vill you give me if I take all de horse from you?

FIRST NEIGHBOR.

Indeed, I'll pray for your worship.

RAGGOU.

Oh ho! Be dat all? Do you understand noting but prayer? Divel, you fool, vat be prayer to de quarteermaster? But can you pray in French?

FIRST NEIGHBOR.

Alas! Not I, an't* please you.

RAGGOU.

Den, begar, your English prayer will no save a Frenchman; you sall have ten arse more fo dat.

SECOND NEIGHBOR.

An't please you, monsieur, I understand you. [*Puts money in his pocket.*]

RAGGOU.

You sall have no arse upon you.

THIRD NEIGHBOR.

And I understand you very well, sir. [*Puts money in his pocket.*]

RAGGOU.

Begar, you have very mush, a great deal of understanding.

THIRD NEIGHBOR.

Here are more of our neighbors that understand you, sir.

RAGGOU.

Begar, den me understand too. Get all your money togedra, and put in my pocket yourself, den me can swear, begar, me never take no penny of you, aha!

THIRD NEIGHBOR.

We will do it gladly, sir, and pray for you too.

RAGGOU.

Begar, me no care for dat.—But you dam dog that no understan a moy sall quarteer all de troop, and den look to your wife, for, begar, Flea-flint vill so get your shild for you.

Exeunt.

Enter Flea-flint, Ferret-farm, Burndorp, Lieutenant, Cornet, Raggou, and Dol.

BURNDORP.

Lieutenant, we have done the work.

FERRET-FARM.

We have burnt seven towns.

FLEA-FLINT.

We have raised fourscore pound.

LIEUTENANT. (*Aside.*)

Y'are dexterous at your trade. You have made quick dispatch; but peace, we'll share anon.—Now you're welcome. Come, where's the boors o'th'house? We'll see what my quarters can afford. Where are you all? What house here, ho?

Enter woman and maid.

WOMAN.
What want you, sir?

LIEUTENANT.
Art thou the woman o'th'house?

WOMAN.
Yes, sir, a poor woman.

LIEUTENANT.
Art thou poor? What a pox do I in such a quarter? Why, Quartermaster Raggou, is this the best house in the village?

RAGGOU.
Zoun, hang 'em, they're very rich dog, but you sall have no meat for yourself, no oat for your arses, but her dam husband vill feast you all wid pray for you.

LIEUTENANT.
Diable, you Rotterdam[33] whore, I'll make you bring out your things. Where's your cows, your calves, and your sheep?

WOMAN.
Alas! We have none, sir.

CORNET.
Hast thou any drink, good woman?

WOMAN.
No, truly, we have none.

FLEA-FLINT.
Nor hast thou no wine nor strong water, good woman?

WOMAN.
No, indeed, we have none.

RAGGOU.
Why, den, a pox take you, good woman.

LIEUTENANT.
No hens, nor turkeys, nor swine, nor nothing?

RAGGOU.
Hang her, begar, she hide everyting when dey hear me come to make-a de quarteer.

FERRET-FARM.
Send to the market town and buy provision, and be hanged, or I'll set fire o'your house, you damned, dery damned, whore.

RAGGOU. [*Aside.*]
Zoun, dis dam coward, how he domineer over de bumpkin woman.

WOMAN.
Alas, we have no money, sir, not we.

FERRET-FARM.
What dost thou tremble and shake so for? What a pox ails thee?

CORNET. [*To the Troop.*]
What shall we do? Threatening will not serve the turn.

LIEUTENANT. [*To the Troop.*]
Do but second me, and I'll make 'em bring out all they have, I warrant you. Do but talk as if we used to eat children.

FERRET-FARM. [*To the Troop.*]
'Tis enough!

LIEUTENANT.
Why, look you, good woman, we do believe you are poor, so we'll make a shift with our old diet. You have children i'th'town?

WOMAN.
Why do you ask, sir?

LIEUTENANT.
Only to[c] have two or three to supper.—Flea-flint, you have the best way of cooking children.

FLEA-FLINT.
I can powder 'em[34] to make you taste your liquor. I'm never without a dried child's tongue or ham.

WOMAN.
Oh, bless me!

FLEA-FLINT.
Mine's but the ordinary way, but Ferret-farm is the man; he makes you the savoriest pie of a child's chaldron[35] that ever was eat!

LIEUTENANT.
A pox, all the world cannot cook a child like Monsieur Raggou.

---

33 Rotterdam] rich Dutch seaport. The Dutch republic was anathema to royalists.

34 powder 'em] reducing human parts for medicinal purposes

35 chaldron] entrails

RAGGOU.

Begar, me tink so. For vat was me bred in de King of Mogul's kitchin for? Tere ve kill twenty shild of a day. Take you one shild by both his two heels and put his head between your two leg, den take your great knife and slice off all de buttack, so fashion; begar, dat make a de best Scots'[36] collop in de varle.

LIEUTENANT.

Ah! He makes the best pottage of a child's head and purtenance! But you must boil it with bacon. Woman, you must get bacon.

FERRET-FARM.

And then it must be very young.

LIEUTENANT.

Yes, yes. Good woman, it must be a fine squab child of half a year old: a man-child. Dost hear?

WOMAN.

Oh Lord! Yes, sir.

RAGGOU.

Do you hear? Get me one she-shild, a little whore-shild, and save me all de lamb-stone[37] and sweetbread, and all de pig-petty-toe of de shild. Do you hear, you Roundhead whore?

WOMAN.

Aye, sir, aye.—Oh, that ever I should live to see such men! (*Exit.*)

LIEUTENANT.

I warrant you it works. If there be provision in the country, we shall have it.

FLEA-FLINT.

How the whore trembled for fear!

CORNET.

We shall have all the women in the village about our ears, hide-bound whores! It's a question whether they'll part with their meat or their children first.

LIEUTENANT.

This foolery will be noised about the country, and then the odium will never be taken off.[38]

CORNET.

Why, what can they make on't? All understanding people will know it to be mirth.

LIEUTENANT.

I know they will, but the envious priests will make fine talk on't, and make a great advantage on't too. Though they know it to be nothing but mirth, they'll preach their parishioners into a real belief of it,[39] on purpose to make us odious. They'll preach against anything. I heard a scandalous sermon of two hours long against Prince Rupert's dog.[40]

CORNET.

Come, 'tis no matter what hypocrites preach. Let us see what the event will be.

Exeunt.

[Scene iii. A neighborhood in the village.]

Enter women in a fright, alarmed by their neighbor.

WOMAN.

Look to your children! If ever you mean to see your children alive, hide your children; they'll eat your children.

FIRST NEIGHBOR.

Woe is me! What's the matter, neighbor?

WOMAN.

I say, hide your children.

SECOND NEIGHBOR.

Ah! Good neighbor, what's the matter?

WOMAN.

Why, run away with your children.

THIRD NEIGHBOR.

Why, that ever we were born! What's the matter?

WOMAN.

They will eat your children.

---

36 Scots'] proverbially, Scots were cannibals.

37 lamb-stone] testicles, here a non-sequitur

38 odium … off] According to Sir Walter Scott, Sir Thomas Lunsford was rumored to have a taste for broiled child steaks, and when he fell at the Siege of Bristol in 1643 that he "had child's hand in his pocket."

39 They'll preach … of it] probably a reference to John Lilburne, a vocal enemy of Thomas Lunsford during the Civil War

40 Prince Rupert's dog] Nephew of Charles I, Prince Rupert was a staunch and effective Royalist commander during the English Civil War and, after the restoration of Charles II, against the Dutch. Republican factions tarred him with flamboyancy and affectation so permanent that even the 1970 film, *Cromwell*, depicts him cuddling his lapdog on the field of battle.

FOURTH NEIGHBOR.
Oh, these bloody Cavaliers! How, eat our children?

WOMAN.
They talk of boiling your children.

ALL.
Oh, mercy on us!

WOMAN.
And roasting your children.

ALL.
Oh, bloody villains!

WOMAN.
And baking your children.

FIRST NEIGHBOR.
Oh, hellish cavaliering devils!

WOMAN.
There's nothing to be thought of but hiding your children.

FIRST NEIGHBOR.
I would mine were in my belly again.

WOMAN.
That's not safe. They'll search there in the first place, to be sure.

SECOND NEIGHBOR.
I'll hide mine in the straw.

WOMAN.
And so we shall have one of 'em lay you down atop of it and smother one child whilst he is getting another. I say, run away with your children.

THIRD NEIGHBOR.
Oh, bloody wretches! I have heard much of their getting children, but never of their eating children before.

FOURTH NEIGHBOR.
Neighbor, their getting of children might be borne with, but eating 'em was never heard of.

WOMAN.
They have got a cook from the Great Mogul on purpose to kill children, and they talk of roasting their haunches, and baking the chaldron and broiling the chine.

MAID.
And making pottage of the child's head and purtenance.

ALL.
Oh, deliver our poor children.

WOMAN.
Do you stand whining and crying? Fetch out your sheep, and your calves, your hens, your pigs, and your geese, and your bacon, for there's no other way to save your children.

ALL.
Aye, with all our hearts.

FIRST NEIGHBOR.
I'll bring two fat sheep.

SECOND NEIGHBOR.
I'll bring turkeys and hens.

THIRD NEIGHBOR.
I have a brave* fat calf, worth eleven nobles; by my troth, I had as leave part with one of my children.

WOMAN.
Oh, you uncharitable beast! Go fetch your calf. Run, everybody, and bring your things to my house as fast as you can drive.

Exeunt.

[Scene iv. With the troop.]

Enter Lieutenant, Cornet, Flea-flint, Ferret-farm, Burndorp, and Raggou.

LIEUTENANT.
Meat or children to supper, for a wager, gentlemen?

CORNET.
Meat, for a wager, if they have it.

LIEUTENANT.
Aye, without doubt, for never was women and children so alarmed in this world.

FLEA-FLINT.
When they were got together and told their children would be eaten, they set up their throats and made a more horrid noise than a Welsh hubbub or an Irish dirge.

Enter nurse with two children.

FERRET-FARM.
How now! What think you if we be put to eat children indeed? By this light, here's a woman with two children.

LIEUTENANT.
We shall be crossbit* with these country whores. What shall we do?

RAGGOU.

Begar, me vill help you off; you sall eat no shildren.

NURSE.

By your leaves, your good worships, I make bold to bring you in some provisions.

FERRET-FARM.

Provisions! Where, where is thy provisions?

NURSE.

Here, an't* please you. I have brought you a couple of fine fleshy children.

CORNET.

Was ever such a horrid whore! What shall we do?

NURSE.

Truly, gentlemen, they're as fine squab children—shall I turn 'em up? They have the bravest brawny buttocks!

LIEUTENANT.

No, no. But, woman, art thou not troubled to part with thy children?

NURSE.

Alas, they are none of mine, sir. They are but nurse-children.[41]

RAGGOU.

Dere be a dam whore for you.

LIEUTENANT.

What a beast is this! Whose children are they?

NURSE.

A Londoner's, that owes me for a year's nursing. I hope they'll prove excellent meat. They're twins, too.

RAGGOU.

Aha! But, begar, we never eat no twin-shild; de law[42] forbid dat. But, hark you, have any woman with shild in de town?

NURSE.

Yes, half a dozen.

RAGGOU.

Lieutenant, it be de best meat in de varle. Begar, a woman with shild is better meat den one hen with egg at Shrovetide.

Enter Landlady and women with provision.

LIEUTENANT.

How now, what news, Landlady?

WOMAN.

Here is a great many poor women that have brought in provisions in hope you'll spare their children.

FIRST NEIGHBOR.

We beseech your worships, spare our poor children, and you shall want for nothing our country can afford.

LIEUTENANT.

Good woman, we are content to spare your children, but you must get us some strong drink.

SECOND NEIGHBOR.

Aye, aye, we'll get you everything you want.

LIEUTENANT.

Why, then, go all home and be contented, for we promise you, if we eat any children, it shall be the two nurse-children.

ALL.

Ah—preserve you all, gentlemen.

RAGGOU.

Take some comfort, for if we should eat your shildren you sall no be a loser by dat. For look you, good woman, how many shildren we eat in a parish so many shild we are bound to get before we leave it. Dat is very fair.

Exeunt women.

LIEUTENANT.

Why, is not this better than fasting?

FLEA-FLINT.

Well, and what harm is there in all this?

CORNET.

None i'th'world. Come, let's in and dress our supper.

RAGGOU.

Me will go eat at my own quarteer. It be a brave* ting to be in office. Begar, de clowns* worship me as if me were dere great god Bumpkin.

Exeunt.

Act IV, scene i. [Outside Raggou's quarters.]

Lieutenant, Flea-flint, Ferret-farm, and Burndorp.

FLEA-FLINT.

Lieutenant, here's all our country crew that we plundred yesterday.

---

41 nurse-children] babies turned over to wet-nurses until weaned

42 de law] a parody of biblical dietary restrictions

FERRET-FARM.
But our comfort is they know us not, but cry out of a Frenchman, with two coat sleeves stuffed like two country bag-puddings.

LIEUTENANT.
This cunning rogue has crossbit* you all. He has been plundering as he went to make his quarters, and in a buff coat, too, for here is a dozen fellows at my quarter, and they all describe a rogue so like thee that I protest thou wilt suffer for it. Nay, the rogue called himself Flea-flint, too.

FLEA-FLINT.
Ouns!* What shall we do, sir?

LIEUTENANT.
Upon my word, this is no jesting business.

FERRET-FARM.
'Sheart,* overreached thus!

LIEUTENANT.
You must e'en think of overreaching him again. You must first think of stopping the clamor of the bumpkins; that's your first point of security.

FLEA-FLINT.
But, Lieutenant, how should we do't? Faith, you must try your wits and stick to us.

LIEUTENANT.
I knew you would venture so far 'twould come to my turn to fetch you off at last, rogues.

FLEA-FLINT.
Why, sir, my man and his both shall swear Raggou borrowed a buff coat of them.

LIEUTENANT.
Let him be gone first, and then you may swear anything. One of you go, tell the bumpkins I am searching for the rogue; the rest go with me to Raggou.

Exit Ferret-farm.

BURNDORP.
This is his quarter.

LIEUTENANT.
This? Knock. It seems to be the best house i'th'town. (*Knocks.*)

MAID. (*Within.*)
Who would you speak with?

LIEUTENANT.
With Monsieur Raggou.

MAID. [*Opening the door.*]
Sir, he gave us strict charge to let nobody speak with him.

LIEUTENANT.
But I must and will speak with him.

MAID.
Indeed, sir, he charged us, upon pain of his displeasure, not to disturb him.

LIEUTENANT.
Pain of his displeasure? What an impudent rogue's this! Show us, show us.

[The scene draws.] Raggou is discovered in a taffeta bed, with a back, breast, and headpiece on.*

How now!—what, in taffeta curtains? The impudent rogue makes me laugh. You rascal, Raggou. Look, in his headpiece, too!

RAGGOU.
Who de devel disturb me? You dam whore, you know vat me do to you last night?

LIEUTENANT.
Why, what was that you did to her last night?

RAGGOU.
Begar, me lie with her at three motion, as de musketeer shoot off his gun—make ready, present, and give fire.

LIEUTENANT.
O'my word, that's good discipline.

RAGGOU.
Begar, she sall make ready for you, if you will present and give fire.

LIEUTENANT.
But how came it that I had not this good quarter?

RAGGOU.
Because me knew me should make-a de quarter but one night, and so, begar, me make-a de best use of my time, as all the whole varle do too.

LIEUTENANT.
But what a rogue art thou. Why dost thou lie in such a bed in thy arms?

RAGGOU.
For two gran reason, sir. First, because my French louse sall go great way about before he come to de clean sheet, next, because-a de dam English flea shall not bite-a my sweet French body.

LIEUTENANT.
Well, maid, go down; I must speak with him.

Exit maid.

RAGGOU.

Vat you have wid me, Lieutenant?

LIEUTENANT.

Faith, out of my love, I would save thee from hanging.

RAGGOU.

Hang! For vat? Begar, hang me if me deserve, so you hang all dat deserve-a de hang. Begar, dat is de whole troop—Lieutenant and all.

LIEUTENANT.

Here you plunder in one shape, and there in another—sometimes, like Flea-flint, in buff; sometimes like yourself—that here is all the country come in with such horrid complaints. Nay, they say you ravish women too.

RAGGOU.

Lieutenant, begar, me never ravish but one old woman, and she give me five shilling for my pain.

LIEUTENANT.

Nay, here is worse than all that. My captain has intelligence you're a dangerous man and hold correspondence with the enemy.

RAGGOU.

Me sall be hang, Lieutenant, if you tink so.

LIEUTENANT.

Nay, 'tis so; I have orders to search you. (*Aside.*) Put that in his pocket and pull it out again.

RAGGOU.

Ah, begar, me have no long life before me be hang.

BURNDORP.

Oh, sir! Are you good at that?—He was going to convey letters out on's pocket.

RAGGOU.

Begar, he lie, Lieutenant; me have no lettra. Begar, hang-a me if me can write an read. De hornbook be de Hebrew to me, begar.

LIEUTENANT.

Search him, search him.

*Search, and pulls a letter out and an engine.**

BURNDORP.

Here's a letter, Lieutenant, and an engine, I think.

FLEA-FLINT.

What's this?

LIEUTENANT.

Oh, you need not write and read if you have this. I'll be hanged if this be not the key of his character he writes to the enemy with.

RAGGOU.

Dat make-a de French pie, and make-a de garniture for de dish; dat be all.

LIEUTENANT.

Let's see. The case is plain; he sent his intelligence in characters of paste. This very thing will hang him. But let's read the letter.

RAGGOU.

Begar, me have no lettra. De devil send it in my pocket.

LIEUTENANT. (*Reads.*)

"Monsieur Raggou, in hope that under this poor disguise of a French cook you will show a rich faith"—

RAGGOU.

Vat he mean by fait? Begar, me have no fait.

LIEUTENANT. (*Reads.*)

"And when you have delivered up your troop to us, the Parliament will own you as yourself, and give you the respects due to your great and honorable family."

RAGGOU.

Devel, me have no honorable, nor family neider, begar.

FLEA-FLINT.

The case is plain; you are of some great family.

RAGGOU.

Lieutenant, me confess me come of de King of France kitchin, of de honorable family of de Turnspit. Begar, me tell you true, dere be all my family, and my honorable too.

BURNDORP.

Oh, sir, 'tis a very cunning fellow. My captain sends word he used to be conversant with the Roundheads and pray with them.

RAGGOU.

The devel take-a me, me never pray in my life. Me swear altogedra in de King of France kitchin!

LIEUTENANT.

I love you so well that I'd be loath to hang you, monsieur; therefore, I'm content to let you 'scape. But be sure you be not taken.

RAGGOU.

Begar, den hang a moy, for my arse vill no go very far.

LIEUTENANT.
Well, pray be gone and say you found a friend.

RAGGOU.
Gad-a bless you, Lieutenant. Ven me come in France, zoun, me vill so pray for you.

FLEA-FLINT.
And yet you say you never prayed in your life.

RAGGOU.
Begar, me tank Gad me never have occasion to pray till just now. Adieu, adieu-a.—Who send me dat dam lettra in my pocket? (*Exit.*)

LIEUTENANT.
Well, now we must keep the bumpkins here till he is gone and give 'em orders to search the countries for him.

BURNDORP.
And that will whidle[43] them as well as if you had given them their money again.

Exeunt.

[Scene ii. Thievesden Garrison.]

Enter Governor, Captain Holdforth, Mr. Tell-troth, and Captain Tubtext.

HOLDFORTH.
In truth, drinking is a harmless recreation, so we proceed not to drunkenness.

TUBTEXT.
Pray, how far forth may we proceed in drink? For I would take no more than is fit to be taken with a safe conscience.

TELL-TROTH.
Why, Captain Tubtext, if thy belly were as large as thy conscience, by that computation the great tun at Heidelberg[44] would be just thy morning's draught.

TUBTEXT.
Here is old Tom Tell-troth. Ha, ha, ha!

HOLDFORTH.
In truth, if he were not very faithful, we should never away with his boldness.

TUBTEXT.
Well said, Captain Holdforth, but to the question. How far may we proceed in drink?

GOVERNOR.
As far as the innocent recreation of knocking one another down with cushions come to. It is the exercise of our superior officers.

HOLDFORTH.
I have observed, indeed, they do three things together: they drink, then practice pulpit faces—

TELL-TROTH.
To cheat the people with.

TUBTEXT.
Ha, ha, ha! In truth, you hit so home.

HOLDFORTH.
And the third is throwing of cushions. The practicing and dissembling of holy looks is of great use and design.

TUBTEXT.
And drinking and throwing cushions, a great refreshing to the body.

GOVERNOR.
As, for example. (*Throws a cushion.*)

HOLDFORTH.
Ha, ha, ha! I have seen our grandee throw a cushion at the man with the great thumb, and say, "Colonel, wilt thou be a cobbler again?" (*Throws a cushion.*)

ALL.
Ha, ha, ha!

TUBTEXT.
Come, here's to you, Governor,—You, Colonel Goldsmith, with a conscience as dirty as a blacksmith, will you sell thimbles again? (*Throws a cushion.*)

ALL.
Ha, ha, ha!

HOLDFORTH.
Noble Colonel, wilt thou brew ale again? (*Throws a cushion, etc.*) What an everlasting cheat is Reformation and false doctrine! It has raised us from cobblers to commanders.[45]

---

43 whidle] quiet

44 great tun at Heidelberg] a cask of legendary capacity in Germany

45 cobblers to commanders] from tradesmen to politically influential people, a recurring Cavalier grouse about a changing social order. The former cobbler is probably

TUBTEXT.

There is no other way to raise rebellion but by religion.

ALL.

Ha, ha, ha!

GOVERNOR.

I never knew the use of religion before.

TUBTEXT.

The women tickle like trouts* at it. Ha, ha, ha!

All laugh.

TELL-TROTH.

I believe the country will find it so, for I hear of twenty wenches with child.

GOVERNOR.

In truth, I wonder at the witchcraft of it, for, notwithstanding the people have been bit through the chine-bone with it, yet, for all that, before the old wound is healed, they are ready to run after the lanthorn of new lights again. Ha, ha, ha!

TELL-TROTH.

Well, sirs, since you are in such an ingenious way of confessing, tell me one thing: Do not you wish your garrison afire, so you were at home with all the wealth you've got?

TUBTEXT.

Thought's free.[46] But talk no more of that; these are both treacherous rogues; I dare not trust 'em.

TELL-TROTH.

Well, you are merry, sirs. But faith, be plain, sirs, what says my seeming Saint* that drinks by the conscience? Dost not wish thyself at home wallowing in thy plunder?

HOLDFORTH.

You might find a better name for it. Hark in your ear:—We are all such treacherous rogues, we dare not trust one another, but we'll talk in private.

GOVERNOR.

But our contribution women will come in anon.

HOLDFORTH.

Ha, ha, ha! In truth, they edify as one would have 'em.

TELL-TROTH.

Well, now you ought to be serious and consider the enemy's[d] approaching.

TUBTEXT.

In truth, a good occasion to fetch in all the goods and chattels of the country upon pretence of securing them, and so make conditions with the enemy to march away with them. I see we shall be rascals to the last gasp.

HOLDFORTH.

And so we shall have provisions for a long siege.

GOVERNOR. [*Aside.*]

I'll make your siege short enough.

Exit Governor and one captain.

TUBTEXT.

You are faithful; they are rogues. Read that, and tell me whether you will undertake or no. (*Gives Tell-troth a letter, and exit.*)

TELL-TROTH.

How! Very good. Is't possible? This is a greater rogue in his own nature than the devil's invention can make him. He would not only betray his trust, but deliver up all the rest of the garrison to mercy, conditionally that he may have all their wealth and safe convoy to his own house. I need lay no plot; 'tis done to my hand. I love the King well, yet my own ends are mingled because I have a mistress among 'em and cannot have her but by serving the King. And I believe most men have their reasons for their loyalty as well as I, so that, good King, wheresoe'er you see me, trust to yourself. Yet I will do something. What if I betrayed this rogue and his letter to the governor to secure myself? But then, if they have a mind to deliver up the garrison, 'twill make 'em shy of me. I find I have a hard task on't.

Enter Governor.

GOVERNOR.

Oh, Tell-troth, I came to ask thee a question, and what thinkst thou?

George Fox (1624-91), founder of the Quakers, targets for ridicule in many English plays during the period. John Lilburne, a member of the gentry but apprenticed to a London cloth merchant, was a spokesman for the Levellers, a group with radically democratic notions.

46 Thought's free] here probably an allusion to "free thinking" or heretical, dissident religious notions

TELL-TROTH.
Troth, I know not.

GOVERNOR.
To know whether thou lov'st me truly or no.

TELL-TROTH.
If you be serious, I could be angry with you for raising such a doubt. To show you that I love you (I do not say your cause, but you) read there. Look you, one of your captain rogues gave me that letter, and the other gave me a whisper to the same purpose, too.

GOVERNOR.
Is't possible? What's to be done with these villains?

TELL-TROTH.
Something must be done; they'll betray you else.

GOVERNOR.
I thank thy honesty; I find it so.

TELL-TROTH.
Shall I speak boldly? Serve 'em in their own kind.

GOVERNOR.
In troth, I had it in my head before to betray 'em, for the rogues are rich.

TELL-TROTH.
Come, let not you and I be shy of one another. Do it yet.

GOVERNOR.
Art thou in earnest?

TELL-TROTH.
By my life, and I will put you in a way, too.

GOVERNOR.
Let's in, and consider how. Had we best secure 'em?

TELL-TROTH.
No. First command their two companies out, then draw 'em into several parties, and then with your own company disarm 'em, and so clap them up and their officers; then show 'em the reason, this letter. When that's done, send the letter to the Parliament and write how you have secured 'em, which will so ingratiate you with them that you'll never be suspected for betraying on't yourself.

GOVERNOR.
My worthy friend, shall I fall on my knees and worship thee?

TELL-TROTH.
Let's be wise and about our business.

Exeunt.

[Scene iii. The troop's camp.]

Enter Cornet and two troopers.

CORNET.
Where have you been, sirs?

FIRST TROOPER.
Why, we have been to take Flea-flint. My captain is resolved to hang him.

CORNET.
For what?

SECOND TROOPER.
For plundering, and so forth. But the rogue has intelligence of it and is gone, but he is in as bad a case as Raggou, for we must send hue and cry after him.

Exeunt.

[Scene iv. At some distance from the camp.]

Enter Raggou.

RAGGOU.
Ah, *jan povera de moy.* May arse can no carry me from de danger of de hang-a de moy, and yet me have spur two such great hole in his rib dat you may creep quite trow him. Me must go change mine coat and mine hat; begar, me sall be known by dat. Vat come here now?

Enter Frenchman with a show.[47]

What come?

FRENCHMAN.
Come, who see my fine shite,[48] my rare shite? Who see my fine shite, my rare shite?

RAGGOU.
Monsieur, where you go wid your shite?

[47] show] a pushcart that opened up to reveal a puppet theater. Puppeteers enacted a range of stories, from the biblical to the pornographic.

[48] shite] since the puppet master of ceremonies is later called "Monsieur Puppey," perhaps a corruption of *chiot*, French for puppy; if so, Lacy wants the English pun; *puppy*, however, is derivative from Middle French *poupée*, doll or toy.

FRENCHMAN.
To de Bristol Fair,[49] monsieur.

RAGGOU.
Dis Frenchman look as if he will be hang. Begar, me vill put a de sheat of de hang upon him! Monsieur, begar, me have de very fine shite too, and it vill come de Bristol Fair too. It be de great vonder of de varle; it be de great fat dromedary.[50] You hear of dat?

FRENCHMAN.
Wee, wee; all de varle know de fat dromedary.

RAGGOU.
Begar, you and me vill join partiner in de fair, because you be my countryman.

FRENCHMAN.
Aye, monsieur, and tank you too.

RAGGOU.
We vill give out in de bill of de two famous Frenchman; one inventra de show of all trade, and de oder make-a de invent of de fat dromedary.

FRENCHMAN.
Monsieur, wid all my heart!

RAGGOU.
Vera good. You sall go take-a de best house in de town. Dere be two piece, two jacoby[51] for you; get some vera good dinner. You shall take-a my coat and de hat, and leave your show wid me, for my waggon will come wid my dromedary presan.

FRENCHMAN. (*Aside.*)
I had good luck to light o'this Frenchman.

RAGGOU. [*Aside.*]
Begar, me have betra luck to light o'dis Frenchman.—So, help me wid your waistcoat. Vera good. So, now make all de haste in de varle. Adieu, adieu!

Exit Frenchman.

So now, begar, me be very safe. But how de devil sall me show mine shite? Begar, me forget to ask vat language all de puppet in de show speak. *Parla françois, Monsieur Puppey?* Owieda.* Aha! very good.

Enter constables.

FIRST CONSTABLE.
Sure we shall catch this fellow at last, for we hear of him everywhere.

SECOND CONSTABLE.
Aye, his two sleeves stuffed and his French hat edged with ribbons will discover* him.

RAGGOU.
Diable, dere be de constable and Mr. Hue-Cry come to catch-a me.—Who see my shite, my rare shite, my fine shite?—Begar, me sall shite myself indeed.

FIRST CONSTABLE.
What a pox does he mean?

SECOND CONSTABLE.
He would have you see his show.

FIRST CONSTABLE.
Come, faith, let us. You, fellow, come, let's see your show.

RAGGOU. [Aside.]
How sall me do now? Begar, me must show it as well as me can.

SECOND CONSTABLE.
Sirrah, did not you see a Frenchman pass by?

RAGGOU.
Frenchman? Vat have he upon him?

FIRST CONSTABLE.
Why, he has a greasy coat with the sleeves stuffed out.

RAGGOU.
A pox take him! Begar, he rob me just now of two piece, all me have in de varle. Dat make-a me cry.

SECOND CONSTABLE.
Oh rogue, rascal! Alas today! Give him a crown, churchwarden; we are at the parish charge.[52]

FIRST CONSTABLE.
Come, do not cry, poor fellow. Let's see thy shite. There's a crown for thee.

[49] Bristol] the major seaport in western England some sixty miles from Oxford, important for trans-Atlantic trade and a Royalist stronghold during the Civil War. The Bristol Fair would have been a major event in the region.

[50] fat dromedary] exotic animals were major news and attractions throughout England

[51] jacoby] jacobus, gold coin valued a little over a pound.

[52] parish charge] public expense

RAGGOU.

A Gad bless you. Here be de brave* shite of de varle. Here be de King of Spain play on de bagpipe to his Privy Council. Dat's a very good jest. Den dere be de King of Solomon; he give judgment upon de vise child. Dere is de first act. Now, put on your hat and look upon all de lady.

Plays and sings.

"Jam more cum povera bla cum povera,
Jam, jam, jam, jam tomba nette,
Jam, jang tombe nette equbla."[53]

Now, here be de Queen of Swiveland.[54] She sit in great majesty; her leg hang over de chair, vera full of temptation—make your chops watra. Vera good jest. Den dere be de whore of Babylon; she make great love to de Maypole in de Stran. Second act. "Jam more cum povera," etc. (*Plays and sings.*) Dere be de King of Denmarks and Norvay learning to juggle of de Bishop of Munsera.[55] Dat's a very good jest. Dere be de silent ministra; he make-a de long preach in de playhouse.[56] Dere is tre act; dat is all.

SECOND CONSTABLE.

I thought your plays had always had five acts.

RAGGOU.

Dey be de great puppet have five act; de little puppet have but tre. Vill you go catch dis dam dog for me and get-a my money for me agen, my two jacoby? Begar, me be undone if you no catch dis dam dog for me!

FIRST CONSTABLE.

We'll away. We'll have him, I warrant thee.

Exeunt.

RAGGOU.

Begar, me be very fine sheat, if it vill hold out. But hold-a—vat if dey catch my coat? Begar, den dey vill hang-a my coat. But dam dog vill confess me have his show, den. Begar, me sall be hang wid mine coat. Begar, me vill put away mine show.

Enter Flea-flint, with hue and cry after him.

Who de devil is dat?

FLEA-FLINT. [*Aside.*]

A pox on 't, I must be robbing alone, and without my lieutenant's advice. I must be careful or suffer for it. The rogues follow me with hue and cry; I am not able to go further; I must change my clothes. How now? What fellow's this? 'Sheart, would I could persuade him out of his show and take my cloak for it.

RAGGOU. [*Aside.*]

Begar, would me could persuade him to take my show and give me de cloak for dat!

FLEA-FLINT.

Come hither, honest fellow.

RAGGOU. [*Aside.*]

Devil, it is Flea-flint. Hah, me be povera de moy; begar, me be half hang already. Me vill no speak French, begar, den he vill know me; me vill belch Dutch at him.—*Yaw, min heer.*

FLEA-FLINT.

Come hither, honest man. What's that? A show?

RAGGOU.

Yaw, min heer.—Begar, me vill slit my mouth from one ear to de odra to speak good Dutch; and den when me speak French, begar, me vill sew it up again.[57] Dere's a vera good trick to save-a my life.

FLEA-FLINT.

Fellow, wilt thou sell thy show?

---

53 Jam … equbla] This fractured French means roughly "I am in love with a poor woman, a poor woman; I love to fall flat; I go down for everyone."

54 Swiveland] the land of sexual intercourse; perhaps an allusion to Queen Christine of Sweden, philosophical libertine who had abdicated in 1654

55 King … Munsera] a fractured version of seventeenth-century religious warfare probably alluding to the king of Denmark and Norway, Christian IV, negotiating for peace with both Sweden and France, perhaps (anachronistically) learning to "juggle" or play both sides from the famous warlike Bishop of Münster, Bernhard von Galen, erstwhile unreliable ally of England against the Dutch.

56 silent ministra … playhouse] perhaps an allusion to William Prynne, famous Puritan who attacked the English stage and who had his ears cropped for sedition

57 slit my mouth] The English actor's parody of Dutch or German emphasizes open and guttural sounds, of French closed and labial; thus, "sew it up again".

RAGGOU.

Yaw, min heer.—Begar, dis Dutch make me vera sick. Look! Begar, every time me cry *Yaw, min heer,* dere come up a pickle herring with it. *Yaw*—look, dere it go.

FLEA-FLINT.

Art thou a Dutchman?

RAGGOU.

Yaw, verathticke.

FLEA-FLINT.

Where hab you de neder lands go weston?

RAGGOU. [*Aside.*]

Diable, vat sall me say? Begar, me have no more Dutch!

FLEA-FLINT.

Hab you de neder lands go west, lanceman?

RAGGOU.

Ick haben de hoigh Dutch lander goe weston, lanceman.

FLEA-FLINT. [*Aside.*]

Nay, it may be what Dutch it will, for I can speak no more.

RAGGOU.

Ick maken weel vander slapan can helder hought.

FLEA-FLINT.

But wilt thou sell thy show?

RAGGOU.

Yaw, yaw, ick vill van hundred gilder haben.[58]

FLEA-FLINT.

That's ten pound; that's too much.—I would I had it at any rate.

RAGGOU. [*Aside.*]

Begar, never fear, you sall have it.

FLEA-FLINT.

Wilt thou take five pound?

RAGGOU.

Neave ick; ick maken de show myself, and ick maken dat better as dis, and dat's better as dat, and dat's better as all, begott.

FLEA-FLINT. [*Aside.*]

I hear 'em coming.—Here's ten pound for thee, and I'll give thee my cloak to boot, and hat.

RAGGOU.

Dere be my show and my cap. Me tank you, lanceman.—So, dis dam rogue never do no good in all his life before; and me hope, begar, he vill be hang for dat. (*Exit.*)

FLEA-FLINT.

Now, what shall I do with this show? for I cannot show it. Why, if anybody would see it, I must say it's locked up, the key is gone before to Bristol Fair; that's all I have for't.

Enter constables looking for Flea-flint.

FOURTH CONSTABLE.

Come sirs, we shall have him at last.

THIRD CONSTABLE.

Stay sirs. What fellow's this? Who are you, sir?

FLEA-FLINT.

A poor man, master, going with my show to the fair to get a penny, and a rogue has robbed me of all I have, almost ten pound.

FOURTH CONSTABLE.

Oh damned rogue! Had he not a gray cloak and hat?

FLEA-FLINT.

Aye (wicked villain!) the same, master.

THIRD CONSTABLE.

It's the same rogue we are looking for; we shall have him i'th'fair, I warrant you. Let's away.

Exeunt constables.

FLEA-FLINT.

This rogue thinks himself so safe now, and he'll be hanged sure enough if they catch him.

Enter the first constables with him that had Raggou's clothes.

FIRST CONSTABLE.

Look you, there's the notorious rogue with the show. Take him.

FLEA-FLINT.

What would you have with me, gentlemen?

FRENCHMAN.

Begar, me vill have my show from you.

FLEA-FLINT.

Pox take you and your show! A damned rogue that had it has robbed me of ten pound and my hat and cloak.

58 *Yaw … haben*] nonsense Dutch, though some words are recognizable, the most important of which is *gilder,* Dutch coins

FIRST CONSTABLE.
Come, these are both rogues; bring 'em away.

FIRST WATCH.
Hold, it will do us no good to have them hanged. What if we plunder them as they use to do us?

CONSTABLE.
'Tis a very good notion.—Do you hear? We are to ask you a question. Will you be hanged or be plundered?

FLEA-FLINT.
I'll be hanged before I part with my money.

SECOND WATCH.
Then let's hang him; we can take his money when he is dead.

CONSTABLE.
Then do you hang him.

Enter bumpkin, passing over the stage.

FIRST WATCH.
Not I; I know not how to hang him.

SECOND WATCH.
Troth, hang him yourself, if you'll have him hanged.

CONSTABLE. (*Calls to the bumpkin.*)
Dost hear, brother bumpkin? I'll give thee an angel,* and hang this fellow.

BUMPKIN.
It is not worthwhile for one, but I'll take angels apiece to hang you all.

CONSTABLE.
Hang you, rascal.—Come there, fall on boys and plunder him.

Plunder Flea-flint.

FLEA-FLINT.
Pray you, gentlemen, give me some money again to bear my charges home.

CONSTABLE.
There's a crown for thee, and farewell.

Exeunt all but bumpkin.

BUMPKIN.
Hey day! This will prove a very wonder,
That Bumpkin should a soldier plunder.

Act V, scene i. [Pre-dawn in a village street.]

Enter a joiner, servant, and a painter at one door, and Raggou at another.

SERVANT.
Joiner, make haste, and set your t'other post up, and painter, fetch your colors, your pots, and pipkins, and paint this post in the meantime. It must be dispatched before the people are stirring.

PAINTER.
My things are all ready, sir, at the next house. We can scarce see to work yet.

SERVANT.
And be hanged, then. Go, get some ale to clear your eyesight; I'll warrant you'll see the bottom of the pot well enough without daylight.

JOINER.
Make what haste you can. I'll bring my post as soon as you'll be ready to paint it. (*Exit.*)

PAINTER.
I'd laugh at that, i'faith. But friend, what noise was this all night? I think the watch was searching for somebody.

SERVANT.
Aye, aye, hark, you may hear 'em searching still. Why, it seems 'tis a kind of outlandish Frenchman that they look for; he has a gray hat and a gray cloak. But come, let us mind our business and make haste.

Exeunt.

RAGGOU.
Dat be me. Dey slandra a moy; me be no outlandish Frenchman. Begar, me be a French Frenchman. Hark, dey come. Vat sall me do? Begar, me vill stand for de odra post till de dam bumpkin be gone. A pox take 'em! De devel could not hue and cry me so close. How sall me do to be like a dat post? Hark, dey come now. (*Raggou gets upon the post and sits in the posture of the other post.*)

Enter constable and watch.

CONSTABLE.
Pox o' this outlandish French fellow for me. I'm as dry as a dog.

FIRST WATCH.

So we are all; let's go and knock 'em up at an alehouse and eat and drink a little.

SECOND WATCH.

With all our hearts.

Enter painter.

Honest painter, canst tell where we may have a little ale?

PAINTER.

Aye, sure; two or three doors off you'll find 'em up and a good fire, where you may toast your noses, boys.

CONSTABLE.

Thou didst not see an outlandish Frenchman this way?

PAINTER.

No, I saw no Frenchman.

Exeunt constables and watch.

Why, what a devil. This joiner has been here and set up his post before I came. How time slips away at an alehouse!

RAGGOU. [*Aside.*]

Begar, would a good rope would slip away you too.

PAINTER.

Now to work. (*Whistles and paints him.*)

RAGGOU. [*Aside.*]

He vill paint-a me; vat sall me do?

As he stoops, Raggou throws a stone at him.

PAINTER.

A pox o'these roguing prentices! Sirrah, I'll have you by the ears. A company of rogues, a man cannot work for you! If you serve me such another trick, I'll break all your windows.

RAGGOU. [*Aside.*]

De pox break all your neck. (*Throws the pipkin at him as he stoops.*)

PAINTER.

Why, you damned rogue, you have broke my head. 'Sheart,* I'll complain to your master. Spoiled all my colors, too! I'll not endure it; I'll be revenged, whatsoe'er it cost me. (*Exit.*)

RAGGOU.

A pox dis rogue, he murder mine face wid his dam paint. Now de coast be clear, me vill take-a de coat of Monsieur Jack Painter and go, for begar, dere be no stay in dis town for moy.

Enter joiner with his post.

Hark! Dere be someting; me must be de post agen. A pox on dat! (*He stands up for a post again.*)

JOINER.

Why, how now? What a devil, another post, and none of my work? 'Sheart, do you employ two men at once? I'll not be used thus; I'll be paid for my work, and then let the devil set up your posts. (*Exit.*)

RAGGOU.

So, now, begar, me vill take de coat of de Jack Paintra, and de post of de Jack Joiner, den no man will suspect a moy. (*Offers to lift a post.*) Diable, it is too much heavy for moy; begar, me betra be hang den have all dis dam joiner sit upon me. Diable, and vould me vere in bed wid all de king of France army, begar, me vould fain see vat dam English bumpkin, Mr. Hue-Cry, come fetch me from dem. (*Exit.*)

Enter servant, painter, and joiner.

SERVANT.

Why, what a foolish fellow art thou to be so angry. I employed no joiner but thyself.

JOINER.

'Sheart, there was two carved posts up, and I'm sure I brought the third.

SERVANT.

Thou art mad, and so is this fool, too, to complain of throwing stones at thee, when we have ne'er a prentice, nor none within six doors of us.

PAINTER.

I'm sure my pipkin's broke, and my head too; pray, look here.

SERVANT.

Why, what's here? Here's a broken pipkin indeed, but where's the three carved posts?

JOINER.

There was two stood up when I came to the house, and I set the third down here. Ouns,* my post and my tools and all's gone.

SERVANT.

I believe you are both drunk.

PAINTER.
Heart, man, I painted the post that stood there.

JOINER.
Well, and heart, man, I brought the t'other, an* you call it heart, man, and all's gone, you see.

SERVANT.
My masters, go look after your things and make an end of your work.

PAINTER.
Let's go search for this fellow that stole our goods here.

Exeunt.

[Scene ii. At the camp.]

Enter Tell-troth and Dol.

TELL-TROTH.
Oh, Dol, d'ye hear? Put her off till your friend come as before you pretended and say you'll marry when the garrison is delivered up.

DOL.
The lieutenant and cornet are very eager to have it dispatched, that they may have the money I promised, and then they are resolved to laugh me to death.

TELL-TROTH.
Well, but you know it will be our turn to laugh at them, if all be right you have told me.

DOL.
Upon my life, I have been faithful in all points, and I find I shall take pride in doing good since I have prospered so well in serving you.

TELL-TROTH.
Your reward shall answer your service. I must to the captain and give him an account of all I undertook, which will meet his expectation.

DOL.
Let me alone to manage my undertakings.

Enter Captain and Lieutenant.

TELL-TROTH.
Here's the captain. Be you gone, therefore; I would not be seen with you till I make him acquainted with everything.

Exeunt [Tell-troth and Dol].

LIEUTENANT.
But pray, sir, why are you thus severe now to banish the flint-flayers?

CAPTAIN.
The King's honor and interest is so abused with these scandalous fellows that I'm resolved to cashier 'em.

Enter Tell-troth.

Oh, friend Tell-troth! Look you, Lieutenant, my opinion seldom fails me.

TELL-TROTH.
So, you had some dispute, then, concerning me? Look you, sir, it's now in my power to do more than e'er I hoped for. You have a foot company?

CAPTAIN.
Yes; they are now marching into th'quarter.—Lieutenant, see they march fair and do no wrong.

Exit Lieutenant.

TELL-TROTH.
Read that. Upon my life there is but three companies and two of 'em are disarmed and prisoners, officers and all. I laid no plot to do it. I found 'em all ready to betray one another to get the wealth; the manner how, hereafter. The governor has commissioned me to make his conditions, which must be a convoy with all his wealth to his own home. The country bring in their plate and goods to secure 'em from your party, and he'll make conditions with you to march away with 'em and so cheat the people (precious rogues!), besides what they preach the women out of.

CAPTAIN.
That must not be, for the King has intelligence that they have great treasure there.

TELL-TROTH.
Does he know how they came by it?

CAPTAIN.
Yes, very well, with the cheat of preaching. (I mean tub-preaching[59] and lectures.) The lectures your wives read you never awed you so.

59 tub-preaching] ad hoc pulpit, dissenters' sermons

TELL-TROTH.

But faith, sir, give him his conditions.

CAPTAIN.

I'll storm it first.

TELL-TROTH.

I intend not to have you keep conditions when you have made 'em.

CAPTAIN.

That's base. I scorn that; my honor is at stake.

TELL-TROTH.

What, for breaking articles with a rebel? Had it been a fair enemy, I grant you. Suppose you storm it, and be beaten off? The King would give you little thanks for the punctilio of your own private honor. Let your lieutenant do it; the captain may with his honor break the conditions that his lieutenant makes.

CAPTAIN.

I may approve of that; I would not have my own hand appear against me. But I am glad to see you thus earnest for the King. Sure you have some design?

TELL-TROTH.

By my troth, I have, but so small a one it is not worth this labor; you shall know it, for you must assist me.

CAPTAIN.

With all faithfulness.

TELL-TROTH.

Come, then, let's sign articles. So, march and take possession.

Exeunt.

Enter Raggou like an old woman.

RAGGOU.

Me vill make-a me nose of wax like de old woman and vill go to Madame Dol and tell her me come from Monsieur Raggou. Vera good. And if she vill beg his pardon of de capitain, he vill come and marry her, although her shild be born wid a shart, and back and breast too; for begar, me find in mine conscience me had betra marry a dam whore dan be hang. (*Exit.*)

Enter Tell-troth, Captain, Lieutenant, Cornet, etc., with the Governor prisoner.

TELL-TROTH.

Now sir, are you satisfied in my faith?

CAPTAIN.

I am so, and I have found you a worthy person. Command me to anything.

TELL-TROTH.

Then I'll make you merry till I go about my design. Captain Tubtext, that got the two sisters with child, is now in bed with them eating a sack* posset, and that we may both shame and fright 'em, there are bears i'th'town and other shows that are going to Bristol Fair. Now, I'll speak to the bearward to muzzle a bear and turn him loose into the room, and I'll bring you where you shall see the sight.

CAPTAIN.

Content, for I am a great lover of sports.[60] Let not the shows go away, for I mean to celebrate Dol's wedding.

LIEUTENANT.

That's kindly done. You'll need no other sport than to see Dol rant and tear when she finds she has married a girl.

CAPTAIN.

But the sport will be when you and the cornet receive your fifty pound apiece you told me of.

LIEUTENANT.

Yes, faith, we shall have it sure enough.

CAPTAIN.

Yes, for 'tis deposited in my hands.

CORNET.

Never was jade so deeply in love! But the jest is, the girl has made conditions with Dol to put on a mask when she is marrying, for her face is so bad she cannot away with it.

CAPTAIN.

Give all the troop favors;* let 'em dispatch, and bring them in to the baiting of the sack posset, and let the country be summoned in.

Exeunt.

60 sports] games, and gaming occasions like bear-baiting, often played on Sundays and suppressed during the interregnum

[Scene iii.] Tubtext and his Sisters are discovered* in bed eating a sack posset.

Enter Captain, Lieutenant, Cornet, and Ferret-farm above.

TUBTEXT.
Here is this spoonful in remembrance of our sweet sister's precious fruit she goes with. (*He puts a spoonful in each of their mouths.*)

FIRST SISTER.
My tender and most shame-faced thanks be returned to you.

TUBTEXT.
Now, here is to the maiden-fruits of this our weeping sister. Wipe your tears. If they were cavaliering burthens you went with, your case were mournful, but as they are my offspring, repent not, for your infants, be assured, will be babes of grace.[61]

CAPTAIN.
What a damned rogue is this!

FIRST SISTER.
Why, then, it seems we religious lambs may play with one another without sinning?

CAPTAIN.
Was ever such blasphemous rogues and whores! I tremble to hear 'em! Let in the bear upon 'em.

FIRST SISTER.
Here is to this our sweet comforting man.

SECOND SISTER.
I am overjoyed to hear that religious lambs may play and yet not sin. (*Put their spoons in his mouth.*)

Enter bear.

TUBTEXT.
What's here, a bear? Mercy upon us!

ALL.
Help, help, help, help!

TUBTEXT.
Shift for yourselves, sweet sisters.

CAPTAIN.
Now bear! Now Saint*!

LIEUTENANT.
Halloo, Saint! Halloo, bear! I'll hold a—

CORNET.
Hundred pound of the bear, thou boy bear.

LIEUTENANT.
A hundred pound of the Saint. So now, take off[62] your bear.

FERRET-FARM.
By my faith, we must stave and tail[63] him off for aught I see, Captain. I have been at many a bear-baiting, but never at a Saint-bear-baiting before.

Exit bear, etc.

CAPTAIN.
Now, sir, is your name Tubtext?

TUBTEXT.
Yea.

CAPTAIN.
And do you think your two whores are with child with two babes of grace?

TUBTEXT.
Yea, foul mouth.

CAPTAIN.
What an audacious rogue is this!—And dost thou really believe thyself in such a degree of perfection that thou canst not sin, and so need no repentance?

TUBTEXT.
Yea, sure, we are past repentance.

CAPTAIN.
Thou damned villain, I believe thee. Blasphemous rogue! How many poor souls hast thou deluded? Sirrah, it were just to make thee marry these two women, and then hang thee for having two wives.[64]

Enter Ferret-farm.

FERRET-FARM.
Sir, our wedding folks are coming and are so merry and so pleased that, if their joy continue, the example will make us all marry.

---

61 babes of grace] a parody of the Calvinist notion of the elect. Some sects, notably the Ranters, held that they answered only to God and were not subject to civil, criminal, or ecclesiastical laws.

62 take off] close the wager, (your bet is covered)

63 stave and tail] in bear-baiting, to check the bear with a staff and hold back the dog by the tail

64 hang … two wives] Bigamy was a felony, and technically all felonies were capital crimes.

Enter Biddy as bridegroom, Tell-troth in her hand dressed in Dol's clothes, and Dol in other clothes, and Raggou dressed like an old woman with a muffler.

Look you, here they are, pleased as you see.

DOL.
Now stand you here till I beg your pardon of my captain.

BIDDY.
By your leave, Captain, I have made bold to espouse your old handmaid, Dol. And give us leave to laugh, for faith, my lieutenant and cornet has cheated her, Captain, for they have matched her to a girl. I am a very* girl, and yet I have not wronged you, for I told you before I could not get your children.

TELL-TROTH.
And we laugh to think how we have cheated you. For though you cannot get my children, if I can get yours we shall do well enough.

BIDDY.
Oh Lord, what's that? That is not Dol's voice.

DOL.
Y'are i'th'right; it is not Dol's voice, nor Dol that has married you,—Keep the money, Captain.—But your old love Tell-troth. Pray have your money, Lieutenant, before you laugh me to death.

BIDDY.
What? My old lover, Tell-troth!

TELL-TROTH.
Now the laugh is on our side, gentlemen.—Come, be not troubled, for I am the same honest lover that e'er I was.

BIDDY.
Nay, I'll swear thou deservest me; thou art a desperate lover to venture on a wench that has trooped so long under such a handsome cornet. But he's a fool too, for if he had followed his blow close at one time, he had had all that I could have given him.

TELL-TROTH.
I had spies upon you and am well assured of your honesty.* Ask Dol.

DOL.
Yes, faith, I watched your water* at every turn. Do you remember he would have gone o'th'score for your maidenhead? But you cried 'twas worth ready money at any time; but marry me, and then halloo dog for thy silver collar. You remember this?

BIDDY.
Aye, to my shame I do.

TELL-TROTH.
What, are you ashamed that you are honest?

BIDDY.
No, but I'm ashamed that I lost so much time, for I'm sure thou wouldst ha' had me honest or not honest.

TELL-TROTH.
Come, be not troubled; I pass by all.

BIDDY.
I love thee for thy confidence; give me thy hand. By my life, I'm very honest, but I have had as much ado to keep myself so as ever poor wench i'th'world had.

CORNET.
But I hope, Biddy, you and I shall not lose our acquaintance?

BIDDY.
If my husband will have it so, I cannot help it. But I hope he has more wit than ever to let me see you again.—If you have not, husband, in good faith, at your own peril.

TELL-TROTH.
I'll have wit enough; fear not.

Enter Ferret-farm.

FERRET-FARM.
Sir, here's the country gentlemen come.

CAPTAIN.
Pray, let 'em come in.

Enter country gentlemen.

Gentlemen, 'tis not unknown how publicly you have appeared against your Prince and how secure you thought yourselves under the protection of these hypocrites. But, to show you what rogues they are, all the wealth that you brought hither to be secured from us, they would have made conditions to have marched away with and so cheated the whole country. Look you, there's their articles. There's Reformation for you.

FIRST GENTLEMAN.
We are deceived indeed in them. To have used us thus!

CAPTAIN.
You must own, gentlemen, that all the wealth that's here is justly forfeited to the King.

SECOND GENTLEMAN.
We grant it, worthy Captain, and our lives to boot.

CAPTAIN.
Although the wealth that's here be great and the King's wants require it, yet, to show that he had rather have his subjects' hearts than money, he has commissioned me to return every man his own again.

FIRST GENTLEMAN.
Sir, this gracious act of the King, and your readiness to perform it, shall turn us all faithful subjects to the extent of our lives and fortunes.

CAPTAIN.
Now, you deserve his mercy.

DOL.
Sir, will you grant me a request? Poor Raggou has sent me word, if I can beg his pardon of you, he'll marry me.

CAPTAIN.
Dol, you have been instrumental to our friend Telltroth; I must grant you anything.

DOL.
Then pray, sir, let's make a little sport with him. Who do you think that old woman is?

CAPTAIN.
I know not.

DOL.
'Tis Raggou himself. Pray, fright him a little before you seal his pardon.

CAPTAIN.
What a devil has he done to his face?

DOL.
I know not. I believe he has clapped wax upon't.

CAPTAIN.
Now, good woman, what wouldst thou have?

RAGGOU.
Me come in de crowd, in hope to see a soldier hang. It would be great satisfaction to de country, truly.

CAPTAIN.
Well, good woman, where dost thou dwell?

RAGGOU. [*Aside.*]
Begar, me have no dwell; vat sall me say to him?—I live at Bristol town's end, an't* please your worship.

CAPTAIN.
But woman, if thou wouldst tell me where to find a plundering Frenchman called Raggou, the country should hang him with all my heart, for that's a notorious rogue, and he shall be hanged if he live above ground.

RAGGOU. (*Aside.*)
Begar, he serve-a me vera well to hang me. Vat a devil make-a me come here? Dis be my vit. A pox on mine French wit.

CAPTAIN.
Woman, find out that rascal for me. Here is ten shillings in earnest, and when thou takest him, I'll make it ten pound.

RAGGOU.
But will your worship secure me that I shall have no harm if I find him?

CAPTAIN.
Aye, upon my honor, before all this company, thou shalt have no harm.

RAGGOU.
Bear witness, gentlemen. Now give me ten pound, for begar, me be de man; me be Monsieur Raggou.

ALL.
How! Monsieur Raggou!

RAGGOU.
Wie, mafoy,[65] ha, ha! Me have sheat-a my capitain of ten pound, and save-a my life too. Dere be de French vit! Begar, me honor my vit very much for dat.

CAPTAIN.
Call the marshal. Take him, and hang him upon the next tree.

RAGGOU.
Hang a moy! Did not you before vitness engage your honor dat me sall have no harm? Begar, you vill do me great deal wrong if you hang me now.

CAPTAIN.
I promised, indeed, that the old woman should have no harm, but Raggou shall certainly be hanged.

RAGGOU.
Aha! Dere be a dam English trick vill hang a Frenchman. But hold, hold. If you hang Raggou, how can you save de old woman? Dere be law case for you! Let me have fair play for my life.

---

65 mafoy] my faith

CAPTAIN.
Take the old woman's garments and lay them up safe, and then they have no harm, then my honor is clear, and here is Raggou fairly to be hanged.

MARSHAL.
Come, come away. 'Tis a plain case; you must hang for't.

DOL.
Why were you such a fool as to come hither?

RAGGOU.
For the love of you, you dam whore, you.

DOL.
Why would you betray yourself for ten pound?

RAGGOU.
Dat be my cunning. De hangman sall have de ten pound because he sall no hurt[66] a me when he hang me. But, Capitain, begar you can no hang me in justice, for de old woman is Raggou, and Raggou is de old woman, and de devil can no part us. So, if you hang Raggou, you hang de old woman, and you hang your own honor too, begar.

CAPTAIN.
Well sir, you have pleaded so well for yourself that, conditionally you will marry Dol, I'll pardon you.

RAGGOU.
If you tink it better to marry den to be hang, Capitain, me leave all to your judgment.

CAPTAIN.
Why, then marry her.

RAGGOU.
But who sall keep* de shild?

CAPTAIN.
The troop shall keep it.

RAGGOU.
Why may not de troop as vell marry her, and me vill make one? Dat's very fair, me tinks.

CAPTAIN.
Nay, you may be hanged yet if you will.

[Raggou] takes the woman in one hand, and the halter in the other.

RAGGOU.
Let-a me see. Here be whore, and here be halter—vera fine shoice, begar! Me can no tell which to shuse; but me vill e'en stan to mine fortune, and cross and pile[67] for it.

CAPTAIN.
By my troth, it shall be so! And take your choice—cross or pile?

LIEUTENANT.
Why, cross he shall be hanged, and pile he shall be married.

RAGGOU.
No, begar. It sall be cross if me be married, and pile if me be hang.

LIEUTENANT.
Now, it's an even lay whether this farce be a comedy or a tragedy.

CORNET.
Come, gentlemen, whore or halter for a wager?

LIEUTENANT.
Whore, for a wager.

CORNET.
Halter, for a wager.

RAGGOU.
Hold, hold, vat if it be nedra cross nor pile?

CAPTAIN.
If it be neither cross nor pile, thou shalt neither be married nor hanged, upon my honor. Come, here is your fortune for you. [*Flips coin.*] I'faith, 'tis cross. Thou art to be married.

RAGGOU.
Den dere be your halter again, and me tank you.

CAPTAIN.
Come, take your beloved wife and strike a match.

RAGGOU.
Den let her take me and de devil in hell give her good of me.

CAPTAIN.
Then you have my pardon and all is well.

Enter Ferret-farm.

FERRET-FARM.
Sir, here are two of Queen Elizabeth's tilters, going to Bristol Fair, desire to dance before you.

---

66 no hurt] tipping the executioner was proverbial practice

67 cross and pile] flip a coin; cross (heads) generally had a human figure with a cross, pile (tails) generally a building.

CAPTAIN.
With all my heart, call 'em in.

A dance of two hobbyhorses in armor, and a jig.

You have done well. Where's my man? Give 'em half a piece. You have done prettily indeed. Lieutenant, cashier the flint-flayers. As for these hypocrites, I'll keep them prisoners till the King dispose of 'em, which will be but too mercifully, I'm sure.

CORNET.
I suppose, Governor, the Parliament will reward you with some Bishops' lands for being so honorably pulled by the ears out of your garrison?

CAPTAIN.
Come, upbraid 'em not; I hate that. Tomorrow, sirs, summon in the country and every man shall have his right.

ALL.
God bless the King and all his good soldiers!

CAPTAIN.
You see, Lieutenant, how with good usage the people return to their loyalty. I know you are a brave fellow, but you have been to blame in the country, and that disserves your Prince more than your courage can recompense.

LIEUTENANT.
Sir, you shall never have occasion to say this again.

CAPTAIN.
I believe you, and I wish that the great timber, the pieces of state, that lie betwixt the King and subjects—
I wish that they would take a hint from hence,
To keep the people's hearts close to their Prince.

Exeunt omnes.

FINIS.

Textual Notes

[a] The copytext is the 1672 first quarto (Q1), which exists in both uncorrected and corrected states. Also consulted are the 1698 second quarto (Q2) and an 1885 edition of the works (Maidmont and Logan—ML).

[b] *The*] *An* Q1, ML

[c] to] *om.* Q1, Q2, ML

[d] enemy's] ML; enemies Q1, Q2

Marriage à la Mode[a]

by John Dryden (1631-1700)
edited by Brian Corman

Marriage à la Mode is the quintessential Restoration split-plot tragicomedy. The form gained popularity in England in Shakespeare's time; *Much Ado About Nothing* is the best known example. The Restoration version of the form, perfected by Dryden, juxtaposes a comic plot of courtship and/or adultery with a heroic romance plot of love and/or courtship. The comic plot is one of private life, the heroic of the public world of politics and statecraft.

In this case, the Sicilian setting, conventionally associated with the idealized pastoral world of characters like Leonidas and Palmyra, was especially useful for distancing a play dealing with the always touchy subject of usurpation from the world of late Stuart England. That distancing is carefully balanced by the comic plot with its frequent allusions to post-Restoration London and to the English social hierarchy from the Court to its adjacent fashionable Town to the unfashionable, financial City, to the equally if not even more unfashionable Country. The relationship between two apparently dissonant plots marks the special feature of split-plot tragicomedy. No other aspect of the play has so caught the attention of critics since the initial production. Split-plot tragicomedy remains a self-consciously artificial form, and Dryden exploits its artificiality throughout with his scrupulous attention to such devices as symmetries, formal correspondences and linguistic echoes. Careful attention to detail characterizes the construction of the play throughout, leading to a whole that differs from and is greater than the sum of its parts.

Marriage à la Mode was first published in 1673, well after its initial performance. The precise date of that first performance remains uncertain, but the evidence points to late November, 1671. Like most of Dryden's plays, it was written for the King's Company, of which he was both principal playwright and shareholder. Some of the strongest actors in the company were cast in the comic plot, Charles Hart and Michael Mohun as Palamede and Rhodophil, Rebecca Marshall and Elizabeth Boutell as Doralice and Melantha (though the equally strong Edward Kynaston played Leonidas, the hero of the heroic plot). This highlighting of the comic plot no doubt reflected Dryden's own sense of where his play was strongest. *Marriage à la Mode* was a success, and it was performed and reprinted throughout Dryden's lifetime. By century's end, however, it met the fate of aristocratic tragicomic romance: neglect. The form went out of fashion, never to be revived. *Marriage à la Mode* had something of a performance afterlife in Colley Cibber's *The Comical Lovers; or, Marriage A-la-Mode* (1707), an amalgam of the comic plots of *Marriage à la Mode* and *Secret Love*, another of Dryden's tragicomedies. Cibber's play was a tribute to the staying power of Dryden's comic plot—and the absence of a similar staying power in his heroic plot.

DRAMATIS PERSONAE

MEN

Polydamas, Usurper of Sicily.
Leonidas, the rightful prince, unknown.
Argaleon, favorite to Polydamas.
Hermogenes, foster father to Leonidas.
Eubulus, his friend and companion.
Rhodophil, Captain of the Guards.
Palamede, a courtier.
[Straton, servant to Palamede.]

WOMEN

Palmyra, daughter to the usurper.
Amalthea, sister to Argaleon.
Doralice, wife to Rhodophil.
Melantha, an affected lady.
Philotis, woman* to Melantha.
Beliza, woman* to Doralice.
Artemis, a court lady.

SCENE: SICILY.

Marriage à la Mode.

Quicquid sum ego, quamvis
Infra Lucilli censum ingeniumque, tamen me
Cum magnis vixisse, invita fatebitur usque
Invidia, etc. fragili quaerens illidere dentem
Offendet solido. Horat. *Serm.*[1]

Act I, scene i. Walks near the court.

Enter Doralice and Beliza.

DORALICE.
Beliza, bring the lute into this arbor, the walks are empty: I would try the song the Princess Amalthea bade me learn.

They go in, and sing.

1.

Why should a foolish marriage vow,
Which long ago was made,
Oblige us to each other now
When passion is decayed?
We loved and we loved as long as we could,
Till our love was loved out in us both.
But our marriage is dead, when the pleasure is fled;
'Twas pleasure first made it an oath.

2.

If I have pleasures for a friend
And farther love in store,
What wrong has he whose joys did end
And who could give no more?

'Tis a madness that he
Should be jealous of me
Or that I should bar him of another.
For all we can gain
Is to give ourselves pain
When neither can hinder the other.

Enter Palamede, in riding habit, and hears the song. Re-enter Doralice and Beliza.

BELIZA.
Madam, a stranger.

DORALICE.
I did not think to have had witnesses of my bad singing.

PALAMEDE.
If I have erred, madam, I hope you'll pardon the curiosity of a stranger, for I may well call myself so after five years' absence from the court. But you have freed me from one error.

DORALICE.
What's that, I beseech you?

PALAMEDE.
I thought good voices and ill faces had been inseparable and that to be fair and sing well had been only the privilege of angels.

DORALICE.
And how many more of these fine things can you say to me?

PALAMEDE.
Very few, madam, for if I should continue to see you some hours longer, you look so killingly that I should be mute with wonder.

DORALICE.
This will not give you the reputation of a wit with

1 *Quicquid* ... Serm.] Horace, *Satires* 2.1.74-79: "Such as I am, however far beneath Lucillius in rank and native gifts, yet Envy, in spite of herself, will ever admit that I have lived with the great, and, while trying to strike her tooth on something soft, will dash upon what is solid" (Loeb).

me. You traveling monsieurs live upon the stock you have got abroad for the first day or two; to repeat with a good memory and apply with a good grace is all your wit. And commonly your gullets are sewed up like cormorants:[2] when you have regorged what you have taken in, you are the leanest things in nature.

PALAMEDE.

Then madam, I think you had best make that use of me. Let me wait on you for two or three days together, and you shall hear all I have learnt of extraordinary in other countries. And one thing which I never saw till I came home, that is, a lady of a better voice, better face, and better wit, than any I have seen abroad. And after this, if I should not declare myself most passionately in love with you, I should have less wit than yet you think I have.

DORALICE.

A very plain and pithy declaration. I see, sir, you have been traveling in Spain or Italy or some of the hot countries where men come to the point immediately. But are you sure these are not words of course? For I would not give my poor heart an occasion of complaint against me that I engaged it too rashly and then could not bring it off.

PALAMEDE.

Your heart may trust itself with me safely: I shall use it very civilly while it stays and never turn it away without fair warning to provide for itself.

DORALICE.

First then, I do receive your passion with as little consideration on my part as ever you gave it me on yours. And now see what a miserable wretch you have made yourself.

PALAMEDE.

Who, I miserable? Thank you for that. Give me love enough and life enough, and I defy Fortune.

DORALICE.

Know then, thou man of vain imagination, know to thy utter confusion, that I am virtuous.

PALAMEDE.

Such another word and I give up the ghost.

DORALICE.

Then, to strike you quite dead, know that I am married, too.

PALAMEDE.

Art thou married? Oh thou damnable virtuous woman!

DORALICE.

Yes, married to a gentleman, young, handsome, rich, valiant, and with all the good qualities that will make you despair and hang yourself.

PALAMEDE.

Well, in spite of all that, I'll love you. Fortune has cut us out for one another, for I am to be married within these three days. Married past redemption to a young, fair, rich, and virtuous lady. And it shall go hard, but I will love my wife as little as I perceive you do your husband.

DORALICE.

Remember, I invade no propriety.[3] My servant* you are only till you are married.

PALAMEDE.

In the meantime, you are to forget you have a husband.

DORALICE.

And you, that you are to have a wife.

BELIZA. (*Aside to her lady.*)

Oh madam, my lord's just at the end of the walks and, if you make not haste, will discover you.

DORALICE.

Some other time, new servant, we'll talk further of the premises; in the meanwhile, break not my first commandment, that is, not to follow me.

PALAMEDE.

But where, then, shall I find you again?

DORALICE.

At court. Yours for two days, sir.

PALAMEDE.

And nights, I beseech you, madam.

Exeunt Doralice and Beliza.

PALAMEDE.

Well, I'll say that for thee, thou art a very dexterous executioner; thou hast done my business at one stroke. Yet I must marry another—and yet I must

2 cormorants] When used for fishing, cormorants' lower necks were tied to prevent them from swallowing.

3 propriety] property

love this. And if it lead me into some little inconveniencies, as jealousies and duels and death and so forth, yet while sweet love is in the case, Fortune do thy worst, and avaunt, mortality.

Enter Rhodophil, who seems speaking to one within.

RHODOPHIL.
Leave 'em with my lieutenant while I fetch new orders from the King. (*Sees Palamede.*) How? Palamede!

PALAMEDE.
Rhodophil!

RHODOPHIL.
Who thought to have seen you in Sicily?

PALAMEDE.
Who thought to have found the court so far from Syracuse?

RHODOPHIL.
The King best knows the reason of the progress. But answer me, I beseech you, what brought you home from travel?

PALAMEDE.
The commands of an old, rich father.

RHODOPHIL.
And the hopes of burying him?

PALAMEDE.
Both together, as you see, have prevailed on my good nature. In few words, my old man has already married me, for he has agreed with another old man, as rich and as covetous as himself: the articles are drawn, and I have given my consent for fear of being disinherited and yet know not what kind of woman I am to marry.

RHODOPHIL.
Sure your father intends you some very ugly wife and has a mind to keep you in ignorance till you have shot the gulf.

PALAMEDE.
I know not that, but obey I will and must.

RHODOPHIL.
Then I cannot choose but grieve for all the good girls[4] and courtesans of France and Italy. They have lost the most kind-hearted, doting, prodigal, humble servant* in Europe.

PALAMEDE.
All I could do in these three years I stayed behind you was to comfort the poor creatures for the loss of you. But what's the reason that in all this time a friend could never hear from you?

RHODOPHIL.
Alas dear Palamede, I have had no joy to write nor indeed to do anything in the world to please me. The greatest misfortune imaginable is fallen upon me.

PALAMEDE.
Prithee, what's the matter?

RHODOPHIL.
In one word, I am married, wretchedly married, and have been above these two years. Yes faith, the Devil has had power over me in spite of my vows and resolutions to the contrary.

PALAMEDE.
I find you have sold yourself for filthy lucre: she's old or ill-conditioned.

RHODOPHIL.
No, none of these. I'm sure she's young, and for her humor,* she laughs, sings, and dances eternally. And which is more, we never quarrel about it, for I do the same.

PALAMEDE.
You're very unfortunate indeed. Then the case is plain: she is not handsome.

RHODOPHIL.
A great beauty, too, as people say.

PALAMEDE.
As people say? Why, you should know that best yourself.

RHODOPHIL.
Ask those who have smelled to a strong perfume two years together what's the scent.

PALAMEDE.
But here are good qualities enough for one woman.

RHODOPHIL.
Aye, too many, Palamede. If I could put 'em into three or four women, I should be content.

PALAMEDE.
Oh, now I have found it: you dislike her for no other reason but because she's your wife.

RHODOPHIL.
And is not that enough? All that I know of her

---

[4] good girls] wanton wenches (Partridge)

perfections now is only by memory; I remember, indeed, that about two years ago I loved her passionately. But those golden days are gone, Palamede. Yet I loved her a whole half year, double the natural term of any mistress, and think in my conscience I could have held out another quarter. But then the world began to laugh at me, and a certain shame of being out of fashion seized me. At last, we arrived at that point that there was nothing left in us to make us new to one another. Yet still I set a good face upon the matter and am infinite fond of her before company. But when we are alone, we walk like lions in a room, she one way and I another. And we lie with our backs to each other so far distant as if the fashion of great beds[5] was only invented to keep husband and wife sufficiently asunder.

PALAMEDE.

The truth is, your disease is very desperate, but though you cannot be cured, you may be patched up a little. You must get you a mistress, Rhodophil. That, indeed, is living upon cordials, but as fast as one fails, you must supply it with another. You're like a gamester who has lost his estate, yet in doing that you have learned the advantages of play and can arrive to live upon't.

RHODOPHIL.

Truth is, I have been thinking on't and have just resolved to take your counsel. And faith, considering the damned disadvantages of a married man, I have provided well enough for a poor humble sinner that is not ambitious of great matters.

PALAMEDE.

What is she, for a woman?

RHODOPHIL.

One of the stars of Syracuse, I assure you: young enough, fair enough, and, but for one quality, just such a woman as I would wish.

PALAMEDE.

Oh friend, this is not an age to be critical in beauty. When we had good store of handsome women and but few chapmen,[6] you might have been more curious* in your choice. But now the price is enhanced upon us, and all mankind set up for mistresses, so that poor little creatures, without beauty, birth, or breeding but only impudence, go off at unreasonable rates. And a man in these hard times snaps at 'em as he does at broad-gold,[7] never examines the weight, but takes light or heavy[8] as he can get it.

RHODOPHIL.

But my mistress has one fault that's almost unpardonable: for, being a town lady,[9] without any relation to the court, yet she thinks herself undone if she be not seen there three or four times a day with the Princess Amalthea. And for the King, she haunts and watches him so narrowly in a morning that she prevents* even the chemists* who beset his chamber to turn their mercury[10] into his gold.

PALAMEDE.

Yet hitherto, methinks, you are no very unhappy man.

RHODOPHIL.

With all this, she's the greatest gossip in nature, for besides the court, she's the most eternal visitor of the town and yet manages her time so well that she seems ubiquitary.[11] For my part, I can compare her to nothing but the sun, for like him, she takes no rest nor ever sets in one place but to rise in another.

PALAMEDE.

I confess she had need be handsome with these qualities.

RHODOPHIL.

No lady can be so curious of a new fashion as she is of a new French word. She's the very mint of the nation and, as fast as any bullion comes out of France, coins it immediately into our language.

PALAMEDE.

And her name is—?

---

5 great beds] double beds came into fashion after the Restoration

6 chapmen] traders, with a secondary meaning of consumers

7 broad-gold] or broad-piece (twenty shillings), so called to distinguish it from the guinea (introduced 1663), which was worth one shilling more

8 light or heavy] Broad-pieces, having smooth edges (as opposed to the milled edges of the guineas) could be clipped or mutilated.

9 town lady] a member of fashionable society

10 mercury] common treatment for syphilis

11 ubiquitary] ubiquitous

RHODOPHIL.
No naming, that's not like a cavalier. Find her if you can by my description, and I am not so ill a painter that I need write the name beneath the picture.

PALAMEDE.
Well then, how far have you proceeded in your love?

RHODOPHIL.
'Tis yet in the bud, and what fruit it may bear I cannot tell. For this insufferable humor* of haunting the court is so predominant that she has hitherto broken all her assignations with me for fear of missing her visits there.

PALAMEDE.
That's the hardest part of your adventure. But for aught I see, Fortune has used us both alike: I have a strange kind of mistress too in court, besides her I am to marry.

RHODOPHIL.
You have made haste to be in love then, for if I am not mistaken, you are but this day arrived.

PALAMEDE.
That's all one, I have seen the lady already who has charmed me, seen her in these walks, courted her, and received for the first time an answer that does not put me into despair.

To them, Argaleon, Amalthea, Artemis.

I'll tell you at more leisure my adventures. The walks fill apace, I see. Stay, is not that the young Lord Argaleon, the King's favorite?

RHODOPHIL.
Yes, and as proud as ever, as ambitious, and as revengeful.

PALAMEDE.
How keeps he the King's favor with these qualities?

RHODOPHIL.
Argaleon's father helped him to the crown. Besides, he gilds over all his vices to the King and, standing in the dark to him, sees all his inclinations, interests, and humors, which he so times and soothes that, in effect, he reigns.

PALAMEDE.
His sister Amalthea, who, I guess, stands by him, seems not to be of his temper.

RHODOPHIL.
Oh, she's all goodness and generosity.

ARGALEON.
Rhodophil, the King expects you earnestly.

RHODOPHIL.
'Tis done, my lord, what he commanded. I only waited his return from hunting. Shall I attend your lordship to him?

ARGALEON.
No, I go first another way. (*Exit hastily.*)

PALAMEDE.
He seems in haste and discomposed.

AMALTHEA. (*To Rhodophil after a short whisper.*)
Your friend? Then he must needs be of much merit.

RHODOPHIL.
When he has kissed the King's hand, I know he'll beg the honor to kiss yours. Come, Palamede.

Exeunt Rhodophil and Palamede bowing to Amalthea.

ARTEMIS.
Madam, you tell me most surprising news.

AMALTHEA.
The fear of it, you see,
Has discomposed my brother, but to me
All that can bring my country good is welcome.

ARTEMIS.
It seems incredible that this old King,
Whom all the world thought childless,
Should come to search the farthest parts of Sicily
In hope to find an heir.

AMALTHEA.
To lessen your astonishment I will
Unfold some private passages of state
Of which you yet are ignorant. Know first,
That this Polydamas, who reigns, unjustly
Gained the crown.

ARTEMIS.
Somewhat of this I have confus'dly heard.

AMALTHEA.
I'll tell you all in brief: Theagenes,
Our last great King,
Had by his queen one only son, an infant
Of three years old, called, after him, Theagenes.
The general, this Polydamas, then married,
The public feasts for which were scarcely past
When a rebellion in the heart of Sicily
Called out the King to arms.

ARTEMIS.

Polydamas

Had then a just excuse to stay behind.

AMALTHEA.

His temper was too warlike to accept it.
He left his bride and the new joys of marriage
And followed to the field. In short, they fought,
The rebels were o'ercome, but in the fight
The too bold King received a mortal wound.
When he perceived his end approaching near,
He called the general, to whose care he left
His widow queen and orphan son, then died.

ARTEMIS.

Then false Polydamas betrayed his trust?

AMALTHEA.

He did. And with my father's help, for which
Heav'n pardon him, so gained the soldiers' hearts
That in few days he was saluted King.
And when his crimes had impudence enough
To bear the eye of day,
He marched his army back to Syracuse.
But see how Heav'n can punish wicked men
In granting their desires: the news was brought him
That day he was to enter it that Eubulus,
Whom his dead master had left governor,
Was fled and with him bore away the Queen
And royal orphan. But what more amazed him,
His wife, now big with child and much detesting
Her husband's practices, had willingly
Accompanied their flight.

ARTEMIS.

How I admire her virtue!

AMALTHEA.

What became
Of her and them since that was never known.
Only some few days since, a famous robber
Was taken with some jewels of vast price,
Which, when they were delivered to the King,
He knew had been his wife's; with these, a letter,
Much torn and sullied, but which yet he knew
To be her writing.

ARTEMIS.

Sure from hence he learned
He had a son.

AMALTHEA.

It was not left so plain.
The paper only said she died in childbed.
But when it should have mentioned son or daughter,
Just there it was torn off.

ARTEMIS.

Madam, the King.

To them, Polydamas, Argaleon, guard, and attendants.

ARGALEON.

The robber, though thrice racked, confessed no more
But that he took those jewels near this place.

POLYDAMAS.

But yet the circumstances strongly argue
That those for whom I search are not far off.

ARGALEON.

I cannot easily believe it.

ARTEMIS. (*Aside.*)

No,
You would not have it so.

POLYDAMAS.

Those I employed have in the neighboring hamlet
Amongst the fishers' cabins made discovery
Of some young persons whose uncommon beauty
And graceful carriage make it seem suspicious
They are not what they seem. I therefore sent
The captain of my guards this morning early
With orders to secure and bring 'em to me.

Enter Rhodophil and Palamede.

Oh here he is.—Have you performed my will?

RHODOPHIL.

Sir, those whom you commanded me to bring
Are waiting in the walks.

POLYDAMAS.

Conduct 'em hither.

RHODOPHIL.

First, give me leave
To beg your notice of this gentleman.

POLYDAMAS.

He seems to merit it. His name and quality?*

RHODOPHIL.

Palamede, son to Lord Cleodemus of Palermo,
And new returned from travel.

Palamede approaches, and kneels to kiss the King's hand.

POLYDAMAS.

You're welcome.

I knew your father well. He was both brave
And honest; we two once were fellow soldiers
In the last civil wars.

PALAMEDE.
I bring the same unquestioned honesty
And zeal to serve your Majesty; the courage
You were pleased to praise in him
Your royal prudence and your people's love
Will never give me leave to try like him
In civil wars. I hope it may in foreign.

POLYDAMAS.
Attend the court, and it shall be my care
To find out some employment worthy you.
Go, Rhodophil, and bring in those without.

Exeunt. Rhodophil and Palamede. Rhodophil returns again immediately, and with him enter Hermogenes, Leonidas, and Palmyra.

(*Looking earnestly on Leonidas and Palmyra.*)
Behold two miracles!
Of different sexes but of equal form.
So matchless both that my divided soul
Can scarcely ask the gods a son or daughter
For fear of losing one. If from your hands,
You Powers, I shall this day receive a daughter,
Argaleon, she is yours. But if a son,
Then Amalthea's love shall make him happy.

ARGALEON.
Grant, Heav'n, this admirable nymph may prove
That issue which he seeks.

AMALTHEA.
Venus Urania,[12] if thou art a goddess,
Grant that sweet youth may prove the Prince of Sicily.

POLYDAMAS. (*To Hermogenes.*)
Tell me, old man, and tell me true, from whence
Had you that youth and maid?

HERMOGENES.
From whence you had
Your scepter, sir: I had 'em from the gods.

POLYDAMAS.
The gods then have not such another gift.
Say who their parents were.

HERMOGENES.
My wife and I.

ARGALEON.
It is not likely a virgin of so excellent a beauty
Should come from such a stock.

AMALTHEA.
Much less, that such a youth, so sweet, so graceful,
Should be produced from peasants.

HERMOGENES.
Why, Nature is the same in villages
And much more fit to form a noble issue
Where it is least corrupted.

POLYDAMAS.
He talks too like a man that knew the world
To have been long a peasant. But the rack
Will teach him other language. Hence with him.

As the guard are carrying him away, his peruke falls off.

Sure I have seen that face before. Hermogenes!
'Tis he, 'tis he who fled away with Eubulus,
And with my dear Eudoxia.

HERMOGENES.
Yes sir, I am Hermogenes.
And if to have been loyal be a crime,
I stand prepared to suffer.

POLYDAMAS.
If thou wouldst live, speak quickly.
What is become of my Eudoxia?
Where is the queen and young Theagenes?
Where Eubulus? And which of these is mine?
(*Pointing to Leonidas and Palmyra*).

HERMOGENES.
Eudoxia is dead, so is the queen,
The infant King her son, and Eubulus.

POLYDAMAS.
Traitor, 'tis false: produce 'em, or—

HERMOGENES.
Once more
I tell you, they are dead. But leave to threaten,
For you shall know no further.

POLYDAMAS.
Then prove indulgent to my hopes and be
My friend forever. Tell me, good Hermogenes,
Whose son is that brave* youth?

HERMOGENES.
Sir, he is yours.

[12] Venus Urania] heavenly Venus, i.e. epithet for Venus as goddess of the heavens

POLYDAMAS.
Fool that I am, thou see'st that so I wish it,
And so thou flatter'st me.
HERMOGENES.
By all that's holy.
POLYDAMAS.
Again. Thou canst not swear too deeply.
Yet hold, I will believe thee—yet I doubt.
HERMOGENES.
You need not, sir.
ARGALEON.
Believe him not: he sees you credulous
And would impose his own base issue on you
And fix it to your crown.
AMALTHEA.
Behold his goodly shape and feature, sir.
Methinks he much resembles you.
ARGALEON.
I say, if you have any issue here,
It must be that fair creature;
By all my hopes I think so.
AMALTHEA.
Yes brother, I believe you by your hopes,
For they are all for her.
POLYDAMAS.
Call the youth nearer.
HERMOGENES.
Leonidas, the King would speak with you.
POLYDAMAS.
Come near and be not dazzled with the splendor
And greatness of a court.
LEONIDAS.
I need not this encouragement.
I can fear nothing but the gods.
And for this glory, after I have seen
The canopy of state spread wide above
In the abyss of heaven, the court of stars,
The blushing morning, and the rising sun,
What greater can I see?
POLYDAMAS. (*Embracing him.*)
This speaks thee born a prince: thou art thyself
That rising sun and shalt not see on earth
A brighter than thyself.—All of you witness
That for my son I here receive this youth,
This brave,* this—but I must not praise him further
Because he now is mine.
LEONIDAS. (*Kneeling.*)
I wonnot, sir, believe
That I am made your sport,
For I find nothing in myself but what
Is much above a scorn. I dare give credit
To whatsoe'er a king, like you, can tell me.
Either I am or will deserve to be your son.
ARGALEON.
I yet maintain it is impossible
This young man should be yours, for if he were,
Why should Hermogenes so long conceal him
When he might gain so much by his discovery?*
HERMOGENES. (*To the King.*)
I stayed a while to make him worthy, sir, of you.
But in that time I found
Somewhat within him which so moved my love
I never could resolve to part with him.
LEONIDAS. (*To Argaleon.*)
You ask too many questions and are
Too saucy for a subject.
ARGALEON.
You rather overact your part and are
Too soon a prince.
LEONIDAS.
Too soon you'll find me one.
POLYDAMAS.
Enough, Argaleon,
I have declared him mine. And you, Leonidas,
Live well with him I love.
ARGALEON.
Sir, if he be your son, I may have leave
To think your queen had twins. Look on this virgin.
Hermogenes would enviously deprive you
Of half your treasure.
HERMOGENES.
Sir, she is my daughter.
I could, perhaps, thus aided by this lord,
Prefer her to be yours, but truth forbid
I should procure her greatness by a lie.
POLYDAMAS.
Come hither, beauteous maid. Are you not sorry
Your father will not let you pass for mine?
PALMYRA.
I am content to be what Heav'n has made me.
POLYDAMAS.
Could you not wish yourself a princess then?

PALMYRA.
Not to be sister to Leonidas.
POLYDAMAS.
Why, my sweet maid?
PALMYRA.
Indeed I cannot tell,
But I could be content to be his handmaid.
ARGALEON. (*Aside.*)
I wish I had not seen her.
PALMYRA. (*To Leonidas.*)
I must weep for your good fortune.
Pray pardon me, indeed I cannot help it.
Leonidas (alas, I had forgot,
Now I must call you Prince), but must I leave you?
LEONIDAS. (*Aside.*)
I dare not speak to her, for if I should,
I must weep too.
POLYDAMAS.
No, you shall live at court, sweet innocence,
And see him there.—Hermogenes,
Though you intended not to make me happy,
Yet you shall be rewarded for th'event.
—Come my Leonidas, let's thank the gods:
Thou for a father, I for such a son.

Exeunt all but Leonidas and Palmyra.

LEONIDAS.
My dear Palmyra, many eyes observe me,
And I have thoughts so tender that I cannot
In public speak 'em to you. Some hours hence
I shall shake off these crowds of fawning courtiers,
And then— (*Exit.*)
PALMYRA.
Fly swift, you hours. You measure time for me in vain
Till you bring back Leonidas again.
Be shorter now, and to redeem that wrong,
When he and I are met, be twice as long.

Exit.

Act II, scene i.

Melantha and Philotis.

PHILOTIS.
Count Rhodophil's a fine gentleman indeed, madam, and I think deserves your affection.

MELANTHA.
Let me die but he's a fine man: he sings and dances *en français*[13] and writes the *billets-doux* to a miracle.

PHILOTIS.
And those are no small talents to a lady that understands and values the French air, as your ladyship does.

MELANTHA.
How charming is the French air! and what an *étourdi bête*[14] is one of our untraveled islanders! When he would make his court to me, let me die, but he is just Aesop's ass,[15] that would imitate the courtly French in his addresses but, instead of those, comes pawing upon me and doing all things so *mal a droitly.*

PHILOTIS.
'Tis great pity Rhodophil's a married man, that you may not have an honorable intrigue with him.

MELANTHA.
Intrigue, Philotis! that's an old phrase. I have laid that word by: *amour* sounds better. But thou art heir to all my cast* words, as thou art to my old wardrobe. Oh Count Rhodophil! Ah *mon cher*! I could live and die with him.

Enter Palamede and a servant.

SERVANT.
Sir, this is my lady.

PALAMEDE.
Then this is she that is to be divine and nymph and goddess and with whom I am to be desperately in love.
(*Bows to her, delivering a letter.*) This letter, madam, which I present you from your father, has given me both the happy opportunity and the boldness to kiss the fairest hands in Sicily.

---

13 *en français*] Melantha obviously laces her discourse with French phrases (and Frenchified English)—here, as in the original, italicized (although there are other words that obviously should be spoken with a French accent, as suggested by the spelling or by Palamede's responses to her); those whose meaning seems obvious are unglossed.

14 *étourdi bête*] thoughtless beast

15 Aesop's ass] the ass who imitated the fawning of his master's lapdog

MELANTHA.

Came you lately from Palermo, sir?

PALAMEDE.

But yesterday, madam.

MELANTHA. (*Reading the letter.*)

"Daughter, receive the bearer of this letter as a gentleman whom I have chosen to make you happy." (Oh Venus, a new servant* sent me! And let me die but he has the air of a gallant *homme*). "His father is the rich Lord Cleodemus, our neighbor. I suppose you'll find nothing disagree-able in his person or his converse, both which he has improved by travel. The treaty is already concluded, and I shall be in town within these three days, so that you have nothing to do but to obey your careful father." (*To Palamede.*) Sir, my father, for whom I have a blind obedience, has commanded me to receive your passionate addresses. But you must also give me leave to avow that I cannot merit 'em from so accomplished a cavalier.

PALAMEDE.

I want* many things, madam, to render me accomplished, and the first and greatest of 'em is your favor.

MELANTHA. [*Aside to Philotis.*]

Let me die, Philotis, but this is extremely French. But yet, Count Rhodophil.—A gentleman, sir, that understands the *grand monde* so well, who has haunted the best conversations, and who (in short) has voyaged, may pretend to the good graces of any lady.

PALAMEDE. (*Aside.*)

Hey day! *Grand monde*! *conversation*! *voyaged*! and *good graces*! I find my mistress is one of those that run mad in new French words.

MELANTHA.

I suppose, sir, you have made the *tour* of *France* and, having seen all that's fine there, will make a considerable reformation in the rudeness of our court. For let me die, but an unfashioned, untraveled, mere Sicilian is a *bête* and has nothing in the world of an *honnête homme*.[16]

PALAMEDE.

I must confess, madam, that—

MELANTHA.

And what new *menuets* have you brought over with you? Their *menuets* are to a miracle! And our Sicilian jigs are so dull and fade to 'em!

PALAMEDE.

For *menuets*, madam—

MELANTHA.

And what new plays are there in vogue? And who danced best in the last grand ballet? Come, sweet servant, you shall tell me all.

PALAMEDE. (*Aside.*)

Tell her all? Why, she asks all and will hear nothing.—To answer in order, madam, to your demands—

MELANTHA.

I am thinking what a happy couple we shall be! For you shall keep up your correspondence abroad, and everything that's new writ in *France* and fine, I mean all that's delicate and *bien tourné*,[17] we will have first.

PALAMEDE.

But madam, our fortune—

MELANTHA.

I understand you, sir; you'll leave that to me. For the ménage of a family,* I know it better than any lady in Sicily.

PALAMEDE.

Alas madam, we—

MELANTHA.

Then, we will never make visits together nor see a play but always apart; you shall be every day at the King's *levee*, and I at the Queen's,[18] and we will never meet but in the Drawing Room.*

PHILOTIS.

Madam, the new prince is just passed by the end of the walk.

MELANTHA.

The new prince, say'st thou? Adieu, dear servant; I have not made my court to him these two long hours. Oh, 'tis the sweetest prince! So obligeant, charmant, ravissant, that—well, I'll make haste to kiss his hands and then make half a score visits more and be with you again in a twinkling.

Exit, running, with Philotis.

16 *honnête homme*] gentleman

17 *bien tourné*] neatly turned; well expressed

18 Queen's] Polydamas is a widower.

PALAMEDE.

Now Heaven, of thy mercy, bless me from this tongue; it may keep the field against a whole army of lawyers, and that in their own language, French gibberish.[19] 'Tis true, in the daytime 'tis tolerable, when a man has field-room to run from it. But to be shut up in a bed with her, like two cocks in a pit—humanity cannot support it. I must kiss all night, in my own defense, and hold her down like a boy at cuffs, nay, and give her the rising blow[20] every time she begins to speak.

Enter Rhodophil.

But here comes Rhodophil. 'Tis pretty odd that my mistress should so much resemble his: the same newsmonger, the same passionate lover of a court, the same— But *basta*,[21] since I must marry her, I'll say nothing, because he shall not laugh at my misfortune.

RHODOPHIL.

Well Palamede, how go the affairs of love? You've seen your mistress?

PALAMEDE.

I have so.

RHODOPHIL.

And how, and how? has the old Cupid, your father, chosen well for you? Is he a good woodman?[22]

PALAMEDE.

She's much handsomer than I could have imagined. In short, I love her and will marry her.

RHODOPHIL.

Then you are quite off from your other mistress?

PALAMEDE.

You are mistaken. I intend to love 'em both, as a reasonable man ought to do. For, since all women have their faults and imperfections, 'tis fit that one of 'em should help out t'other.

RHODOPHIL.

This were a blessed doctrine, indeed, if our wives would hear it, but they're their own enemies. If they would suffer us but now and then to make excursions, the benefit of our variety would be theirs. Instead of one, continued, lazy, tired love, they would in their turns have twenty vigorous, fresh, and active loves.

PALAMEDE.

And I would ask any of 'em whether a poor narrow brook, half dry the best part of the year and running ever one way, be compared to a lusty stream that has ebbs and flows?

RHODOPHIL.

Aye, or is half so profitable for navigation?

Enter Doralice walking by and reading.

PALAMEDE.

'Od's* my life, Rhodophil, will you keep my counsel?

RHODOPHIL.

Yes. Where's the secret.

PALAMEDE. (*Showing Doralice.*)

There 'tis. I may tell you as my friend, *sub sigillo*,[23] etcetera, this is that very numerical[24] lady with whom I am in love.

RHODOPHIL. (*Aside.*)

By all that's virtuous, my wife!

PALAMEDE.

You look strangely. How do you like her? Is she not very handsome?

RHODOPHIL. (*Aside.*)

Sure he abuses me.—Why the devil do you ask my judgment?

PALAMEDE.

You are so dogged now, you think no man's mistress handsome but your own. Come, you shall hear her talk too; she has wit, I assure you.

RHODOPHIL. (*Going back.*)

This is too much, Palamede.

PALAMEDE. (*Pulling him forward.*)

Prithee do not hang back so. Of an old, tried lover, thou art the most bashful fellow!

DORALICE. (*Looking up.*)

Were you so near and would not speak, dear husband?

---

19 French gibberish] legal French, a mixture of French, Latin, and English used in English law until the eighteenth century

20 rising blow] literally, an upper cut in a fight (cuffs)

21 *basta*] enough (It. and Sp.)

22 woodman] hunter

23 *sub sigillo*] under seal; in confidence (Lat.)

24 numerical] identical

PALAMEDE. (*Aside.*)
Husband, quotha! I have cut out a fine piece of work for myself.

RHODOPHIL.
Pray Spouse, how long have you been acquainted with this gentleman?

DORALICE.
Who, I acquainted with this stranger? To my best knowledge, I never saw him before.

Enter Melantha at the other end.

PALAMEDE. (*Aside.*)
Thanks, Fortune, thou hast helped me.

RHODOPHIL.
Palamede, this must not pass so. I must know your mistress a little better.

PALAMEDE.
It shall be your own fault else. Come, I'll introduce you.

RHODOPHIL.
Introduce me! Where?

PALAMEDE. (*Pointing to Melantha, who swiftly passes over the stage.*)
There. To my mistress.

RHODOPHIL.
Who? Melantha! Oh heavens, I did not see her.

PALAMEDE.
But I did. I am an eagle where I love; I have seen her this half hour.

DORALICE. (*Aside.*)
I find he has wit, he has got off so readily. But it would anger me if he should love Melantha.

RHODOPHIL. (*Aside.*)
Now I could e'en wish it were my wife he loved; I find he's to be married to my mistress.

PALAMEDE.
Shall I run after and fetch her back again to present you to her?

RHODOPHIL.
No, you need not, I have the honor to have some small acquaintance with her.

PALAMEDE. (*Aside.*)
Oh Jupiter! What a blockhead was I not to find it out! My wife that must be is his mistress. I did a little suspect it before. Well, I must marry her, because she's handsome and because I hate to be disinherited for a younger brother, which I am sure I shall be if I disobey. And yet I must keep in with Rhodophil, because I love his wife. (*To Rhodophil.*) I must desire you to make my excuse to your lady, if I have been so unfortunate to cause any mistake, and withal, to beg the honor of being known to her.

RHODOPHIL.
Oh, that's but reason. Hark you, Spouse, pray look upon this gentleman as my friend, whom, to my knowledge, you have never seen before this hour.

DORALICE.
I'm so obedient a wife, sir, that my husband's commands shall ever be a law to me.

Enter Melantha again, hastily, and runs to embrace Doralice.

MELANTHA.
Oh my dear, I was just going to pay my devoirs to you; I had not time this morning, for making my court to the King and our new Prince. Well never nation was so happy, and all that, in a young prince, and he's the kindest person in the world to me, let me die if he is not.

DORALICE.
He has been bred up far from court, and therefore—

MELANTHA.
That imports not. Though he has not seen the *grand monde*, and all that, let me die but he has the air of the court, most absolutely.

PALAMEDE.
But yet, madam, he—

MELANTHA.
Oh servant, you can testify that I am in his good graces. Well, I cannot stay long with you, because I have promised him this afternoon to— But hark you, my dear, I'll tell you a secret. (*Whispers to Doralice.*)

RHODOPHIL. (*Aside.*)
The Devil's in me, that I must love this woman.

PALAMEDE. (*Aside.*)
The Devil's in me, that I must marry this woman.

MELANTHA. (*Raising her Voice.*)
So the Prince and I— But you must make a secret of this, my dear, for I would not for the world your husband should hear it, or my tyrant there that must be.

PALAMEDE. (*Aside.*)
Well, fair impertinent, your whisper is not lost, we hear you.
DORALICE.
I understand then, that—
MELANTHA.
I'll tell you, my dear, the Prince took me by the hand and pressed it *à la dérobé*,[25] because the King was near, made the *doux yeux* to me,[26] and *ensuite*,[27] said a thousand gallantries, or let me die, my dear.
DORALICE.
Then I am sure you—
MELANTHA.
You are mistaken, my dear.
DORALICE.
What, before I speak?
MELANTHA.
But I know your meaning; you think, my dear, that I assumed something of *fierté*[28] into my countenance to *rebute*[29] him, but quite contrary, I regarded him, I know not how to express it in our dull Sicilian language, *d'un air enjoué*,[30] and said nothing but *à d'autre, à d'autre*,[31] and that it was all *grimace*[32] and would not pass upon me.

Enter Artemis: Melantha sees her and runs away from Doralice.

(*To Artemis.*)
My dear, I must beg your pardon. I was just making a loose from Doralice to pay my respects to you. Let me die if I ever pass time so agreeably as in your company and if I would leave it for any lady's in Sicily.
ARTEMIS.
The Princess Amalthea is coming this way.

Enter Amalthea: Melantha runs to her.

MELANTHA.
Oh dear madam! I have been at your lodgings in my new *calèche* so often to tell you of a new *amour* betwixt two persons whom you would little suspect for it, that, let me die if one of my coach horses be not dead and another quite tired and sunk under the *fatigue*.
AMALTHEA.
Oh Melantha, I can tell you news. The Prince is coming this way.
MELANTHA.
The Prince! Oh sweet Prince! He and I are to—and I forgot it. Your pardon, sweet madam, for my abruptness. Adieu, my dears. Servant, Rhodophil; servant, servant, servant all. (*Exit running.*)
AMALTHEA.
Rhodophil, a word with you. (*Whispers.*)
DORALICE. (*To Palamede.*)
Why do you not follow your mistress, sir?
PALAMEDE.
Follow her? Why, at this rate she'll be at the Indies within this half hour.
DORALICE.
However, if you can't follow her all day, you'll meet her at night, I hope?
PALAMEDE.
But can you in charity suffer me to be so mortified without affording me some relief? If it be but to punish that sign of a husband there, that lazy matrimony, that dull insipid taste, who leaves such delicious fare at home to dine abroad on worse meat and to pay dear for't into the bargain.
DORALICE.
All this is in vain. Assure yourself, I will never admit of any visit from you in private.
PALAMEDE.
That is to tell me, in other words, my condition is desperate.
DORALICE.
I think you in so ill a condition that I am resolved to pray for you this very evening in the close walk behind the terrace, for that's a private place, and there I am sure nobody will disturb my devotions. And so, goodnight, sir. (*Exit.*)
PALAMEDE.
This is the newest way of making an appointment

25 *à la dérobé*] secretly; on the sly
26 made the *doux yeux* to me] made eyes at me
27 *ensuite*] then
28 *fierté*] pride, haughtiness
29 *rebute*] discourage
30 *d'un air enjoué*] in a sprightly manner
31 *à d'autre, à d'autre*] Tell it to someone else.
32 *grimace*] affectation

I ever heard of. Let women alone to contrive the means; I find we are but dunces to 'em. Well, I will not be so profane a wretch as to interrupt her devotions, but to make 'em more effectual, I'll down upon my knees and endeavor to join my own with 'em. (*Exit.*)

AMALTHEA. (*To Rhodophil.*)

I know already they do not love each other and that my brother acts but a forced obedience to the King's commands, so that if a quarrel* should arise betwixt the Prince and him, I were most miserable on both sides.

RHODOPHIL.

There shall be nothing wanting* in me, madam, to prevent so sad a consequence.

Enter the King, Leonidas; the King whispers to Amalthea.

(*To himself.*)

I begin to hate this Palamede, because he is to marry my mistress, yet break with him I dare not for fear of being quite excluded from her company. 'Tis a hard case when a man must go by his rival to his mistress, but 'tis at worst but using him like a pair of heavy boots in a dirty journey. After I have fouled him all day, I'll throw him off at night. (*Exit.*)

AMALTHEA. (*To the King.*)

This honor is too great for me to hope.

POLYDAMAS.

You shall this hour have the assurance of it.
Leonidas, come hither: you have heard,
I doubt not, that the father of this Princess
Was my most faithful friend while I was yet
A private man, and when I did assume
This crown, he served me in that high attempt.
You see, then, to what gratitude obliges me:
Make your addresses to her.

LEONIDAS.

Sir, I am yet too young to be a courtier;
I should too much betray my ignorance
And want* of breeding to so fair a lady.

AMALTHEA.

Your language speaks you not bred up in deserts
But in the softness of some Asian court,
Where luxury and ease invent kind words
To cozen tender virgins of their hearts.

POLYDAMAS.

You need not doubt
But in what words soe'er a prince can offer
His crown and person, they will be received.
You know my pleasure, and you know your duty.

LEONIDAS.

Yes sir, I shall obey in what I can.

POLYDAMAS.

In what you can, Leonidas? Consider,
He's both your king and father who commands you.
Besides, what is there hard in my injunction?

LEONIDAS.

'Tis hard to have my inclination forced.
I would not marry, sir, and when I do,
I hope you'll give me freedom in my choice.

POLYDAMAS.

View well this lady,
Whose mind as much transcends her beauteous face
As that excels all others.

AMALTHEA.

My beauty, as it ne'er could merit love,
So neither can it beg. And sir, you may
Believe that what the King has offered you,
I should refuse, did I not value more
Your person then your crown.

LEONIDAS.

Think it not pride
Or my new fortunes swell me to contemn you;
Think less that I want* eyes to see your beauty;
And least of all think duty wanting* in me
T'obey a father's will. But—

POLYDAMAS.

But what, Leonidas?
For I must know your reason. And be sure
It be convincing too.

LEONIDAS.

Sir, ask the stars,
Which have imposed love on us like a fate,
Why minds are bent to one and fly another?
Ask why all beauties cannot move all hearts?
For though there may
Be made a rule for color or for feature,
There can be none for liking.

POLYDAMAS.

Leonidas, you owe me more
Than to oppose your liking to my pleasure.

LEONIDAS.
I owe you all things, sir, but something too
I owe myself.
POLYDAMAS.
You shall dispute no more: I am a king,
And I will be obeyed.
LEONIDAS.
You are a king, sir, but you are no god,
Or if you were, you could not force my will.
POLYDAMAS. (*Aside.*)
But you are just, you gods, oh you are just
In punishing the crimes of my rebellion
With a rebellious son!
Yet I can punish him, as you do me.
—Leonidas, there's no jesting with
My will. I ne'er had done so much to gain
A crown, but to be absolute in all things.
AMALTHEA.
Oh sir, be not so much a king as to
Forget you are a father. Soft indulgence
Becomes that name. Though Nature gives you pow'r
To bind his duty, 'tis with silken bonds.
Command him, then, as you command yourself.
He is as much a part of you as are
Your appetite and will, and those you force not
But gently bend and make 'em pliant to your reason.
POLYDAMAS.
It may be I have used too rough a way.
Forgive me, my Leonidas. I know
I lie as open to the gusts of passion
As the bare shore to every beating surge.
I will not force thee now. But I entreat thee,
Absolve[33] a father's vow to this fair virgin,
A vow which hopes of having such a son
First caused.
LEONIDAS.
Show not my disobedience by your prayers,
For I must still deny you, though I now
Appear more guilty to myself than you.
I have some reasons, which I cannot utter,
That force my disobedience, yet I mourn
To death that the first thing you e'er enjoined me
Should be that only one command in nature
Which I could not obey.

[33] absolve] discharge

POLYDAMAS. [*Aside.*]
I did descend too much below myself
When I entreated him.—Hence, to thy desert.
Thou'rt not my son or art not fit to be.
AMALTHEA. (*Kneeling.*)
Great sir, I humbly beg you, make not me
The cause of your displeasure. I absolve
Your vow. Far, far from me be such designs,
So wretched a desire of being great
By making him unhappy. You may see
Something so noble in the Prince his* nature
As grieves him more not to obey than you
That are not obeyed.
POLYDAMAS.
Then, for your sake,
I'll give him one day longer, to consider,[b]
Not to deny, for my resolves are firm
As Fate, that cannot change.

Exeunt King and Amalthea.

LEONIDAS.
And so are mine.
This beauteous Princess, charming as she is,
Could never make me happy. I must first
Be false to my Palmyra, and then wretched.
But then, a father's anger!
Suppose he should recede from his own vow.
He never would permit me to keep mine.

Enter Palmyra; Argaleon following her, a little after.

See, she appears!
I'll think no more of anything but her.
Yet I have one hour good ere I am wretched.
But oh! Argaleon follows her! So night
Treads on the footsteps of a winter's sun
And stalks all black behind him.
PALMYRA.
Oh Leonidas
(For I must call you still by that dear name),
Free me from this bad man.
LEONIDAS.
I hope he dares not be injurious to you.
ARGALEON.
I rather was injurious to myself,
Than her.
LEONIDAS.
That must be judged when I hear what you said.

ARGALEON.
I think you need not give yourself that trouble.
It concerned us alone.
LEONIDAS.
You answer saucily and indirectly.
What interest can you pretend in her?
ARGALEON.
It may be, sir, I made her some expressions
Which I would not repeat, because they were
Below my rank, to one of hers.
LEONIDAS.
What did he say, Palmyra?
PALMYRA.
I'll tell you all. First, he began to look,
And then he sighed, and then he looked again;
At last, he said my eyes wounded his heart.
And after that, he talked of flames and fires
And such strange words that I believed he conjured.
LEONIDAS.
Oh my heart! Leave me, Argaleon.
ARGALEON.
Come, sweet Palmyra,
I will instruct you better in my meaning.
You see he would be private.
LEONIDAS.
Go yourself,
And leave her here.
ARGALEON.
Alas, she's ignorant
And is not fit to entertain a prince.
LEONIDAS.
First learn what's fit for you: that's to obey.
ARGALEON.
I know my duty is to wait on you.
A great king's son, like you, ought to forget
Such mean converse.
LEONIDAS.
What? A disputing subject?
Hence, or my sword shall do me justice on thee.
ARGALEON.
Yet I may find a time. (*Going.*)
LEONIDAS. (*Going after him.*)
What's that you mutter,
To find a time?
ARGALEON.
To wait on you again.
(*Softly.*)
In the meanwhile I'll watch you. (*Exit, and watches during the scene.*)
LEONIDAS.
How precious are the hours of love in courts!
In cottages, where love has all the day
Full and at ease, he throws it half away.
Time gives himself and is not valued there
But sells at mighty rates each minute here.
There, he is lazy, unemployed, and slow;
Here, he's more swift and yet has more to do:
So many of his hours in public move,
That few are left for privacy and love.
PALMYRA.
The sun, methinks, shines faint and dimly here;
Light is not half so long nor half so clear.
But oh! when every day was yours and mine,
How early up! What haste he made to shine!
LEONIDAS.
Such golden days no prince must hope to see,
Whose ev'ry subject is more blessed than he.
PALMYRA.
Do you remember, when their tasks were done,
How all the youth did to our cottage run?
While winter winds were whistling loud without,
Our cheerful hearth was circled round about.
With strokes in ashes maids their lovers drew,[34]
And still* you fell to me, and I to you.
LEONIDAS.
When love did of my heart possession take,
I was so young my soul was scarce awake.
I cannot tell when first I thought you fair,
But sucked in love insensibly as air.
PALMYRA.
I know too well when first my love began,
When at our wake[35] you for the chaplet ran.
Then I was made the lady of the May[36]
And with the garland at the goal did stay.
Still,* as you ran, I kept you full in view.
I hoped and wished and ran, methought, for you.
As you came near, I hastily did rise

34 drew] represented

35 wake] an annual English parish festival held in honor of the church's patron saint

36 lady of the May] queen of the games on May Day

And stretched my arm outright that held the prize.
The custom was to kiss whom I should crown.
You kneeled and, in my lap, your head laid down.
I blushed and blushed and did the kiss delay.
At last my subjects forced me to obey.
But when I gave the crown and then the kiss,
I scarce had breath to say, take that—and this.

LEONIDAS.
I felt the while a pleasing kind of smart;
The kiss went tingling to my very heart.
When it was gone, the sense of it did stay;
The sweetness clinged upon my lips all day
Like drops of honey loath to fall away.

PALMYRA.
Life, like a prodigal, gave all his store
To my first youth and now can give no more.
You are a prince and in that high degree
No longer must converse with humble me.

LEONIDAS.
'Twas to my loss the gods that title gave;
A tyrant's son is doubly born a slave.
He gives a crown but, to prevent my life
From being happy, loads it with a wife.

PALMYRA.
Speak quickly: What have you resolved to do?

LEONIDAS.
To keep my faith inviolate to you.
He threatens me with exile and with shame,
To lose my birthright and a prince his* name.
But there's a blessing which he did not mean,
To send me back to love and you again.

PALMYRA.
Why was not I a princess for your sake?
But Heav'n no more such miracles can make,
And since that cannot, this must never be:
You shall not lose a crown for love of me.
Live happy and a nobler choice pursue;
I shall complain of Fate but not of you.

LEONIDAS.
Can you so easily without me live?
Or could you take the counsel which you give?
Were you a princess, would you not be true?

PALMYRA.
I would but cannot merit it from you.

LEONIDAS.
Did you not merit, as you do, my heart?
Love gives esteem and then it gives desert.
But if I basely could forget my vow,
Poor helpless innocence, what would you do?

PALMYRA.
In woods and plains where first my love began,
There would I live retired from faithless man:
I'd sit all day within some lonely shade
Or that close arbor which your hands have made;
I'd search the groves and ev'ry tree to find
Where you had carved our names upon the rind.
Your hook, your scrip, all that was yours, I'd keep
And lay 'em by me when I went to sleep.
Thus would I live, and maidens, when I die,
Upon my hearse white true love knots should tie.
And thus my tomb should be inscribed above,
"Here the forsaken virgin rests from love."

LEONIDAS.
Think not that time or fate shall e'er divide
Those hearts, which love and mutual vows have tied.[37]
But we must part: farewell, my love.

PALMYRA.
Till when?

LEONIDAS.
Till the next age of hours we meet again.
Meantime—we may,
When near each other we in public stand,
Contrive to catch a look or steal a hand.
Fancy will every touch and glance improve
And draw the most spirituous parts of love.
Our souls sit close and silently within
And their own web from their own entrails spin.
And when eyes meet far off, our sense is such
That, spider-like, we feel the tender'st touch.

Exeunt.

Act III, scene i.

Enter Rhodophil, meeting Doralice and Artemis. Rhodophil and Doralice embrace.

RHODOPHIL.
My own dear heart!

---

37 mutual vows have tied] Mutual vows, even unwitnessed, were as legally binding as public marriage ceremonies in Restoration England.

DORALICE.

My own true love! (*She starts back.*) I had forgot myself to be so kind;* indeed, I am very angry with you, dear: you are come home an hour after you appointed. If you had stayed a minute longer, I was just considering whether I should stab, hang, or drown myself. (*Embracing him.*)

RHODOPHIL.

Nothing but the King's business could have hindered me, and I was so vexed that I was just laying down my commission rather than have failed my dear. (*Kissing her hand.*)

ARTEMIS.

Why, this is love as it should be betwixt man and wife. Such another couple would bring marriage into fashion again. But is it always thus betwixt you?

RHODOPHIL.

Always thus! This is nothing. I tell you there is not such a pair of turtles* in all Sicily. There is such an eternal cooing and kissing betwixt us that indeed it is scandalous before civil company.

DORALICE.

Well, if I had imagined I should have been this fond fool, I would never have married the man I loved. I married to be happy and have made myself miserable by over-loving. Nay, and now my case is desperate, for I have been married above these two years and find myself every day worse and worse in love. Nothing but madness can be the end on't.

ARTEMIS.

Dote on to the extremity, and you are happy.

DORALICE.

He deserves so infinitely much that, the truth is, there can be no doting in the matter. But to love well, I confess, is a work that pays itself: 'tis telling gold and, after, taking it for one's pains.

RHODOPHIL.

By that I should be a very covetous person, for I am ever pulling out my money and putting it into my pocket again.

Embracing each other.

DORALICE.

Oh dear Rhodophil!

RHODOPHIL.

Oh sweet Doralice!

ARTEMIS. (*Aside.*)

Nay, I am resolved I'll never interrupt lovers. I'll leave 'em as happy as I found 'em. (*Steals away.*)

RHODOPHIL. (*Looking up.*)

What, is she gone?

DORALICE.

Yes, and without taking leave.

RHODOPHIL. (*Parting from her.*)

Then there's enough for this time.

DORALICE.

Yes, sure the scene's done, I take it.

They walk contrary ways on the stage: he with his hands in his pocket, whistling; she singing a dull melancholy tune.

RHODOPHIL.

Pox o'your dull tune, a man can't think for you.

DORALICE.

Pox o'your damned whistling: you can neither be company to me yourself nor leave me to the freedom of my own fancy.

RHODOPHIL.

Well, thou art the most provoking wife!

DORALICE.

Well, thou art the dullest husband. Thou art never to be provoked.

RHODOPHIL.

I was never thought dull till I married thee. And now thou hast made an old knife of me. Thou hast whetted me so long, till I have no edge left.

DORALICE.

I see you are in the husband's fashion: you reserve all your good humors for your mistresses and keep your ill for your wives.

RHODOPHIL.

Prithee, leave me to my own cogitations; I am thinking over all my sins, to find for which of them it was I married thee.

DORALICE.

Whatever your sin was, mine's the punishment.

RHODOPHIL.

My comfort is thou art not immortal, and when that blessed, that divine day comes of thy departure, I'm resolved I'll make one holy day more in the almanac for thy sake.

DORALICE.

Aye, you had need make a holy day for me, for I am sure you have made me a martyr.

RHODOPHIL.

Then, setting my victorious foot upon thy head, in the first hour of thy silence (that is, the first hour thou art dead, for I despair of it before), I will swear by thy ghost an oath, as terrible to me as Styx is to the Gods, never more to be in danger of the banes[38] of matrimony.

DORALICE.

And I am resolved to marry the very same day thou die'st, if it be but to show how little I'm concerned for thee.

RHODOPHIL.

Prithee Doralice, why do we quarrel thus a-days? Hah? This is but a kind of heathenish life and does not answer the ends of marriage. If I have erred, propound what reasonable atonement may be made before we sleep, and I shall not be refractory. But withal consider I have been married these three years, and be not too tyrannical.

DORALICE.

What should you talk of a peace abed, when you can give no security for performance of articles?

RHODOPHIL.

Then, since we must live together and both of us stand upon our terms as to matter of dying first, let us make ourselves as merry as we can with our misfortunes. Why there's the devil on't! If thou couldst make my enjoying thee but a little less easy or a little more unlawful, thou shouldst see what a termagant lover I would prove. I have taken such pains to enjoy thee, Doralice, that I have fancied thee all the fine women in the town to help me out. But now there's none left for me to think on, my imagination is quite jaded. Thou art a wife, and thou wilt be a wife, and I can make thee another no longer. (*Exit.*)

DORALICE.

Well, since thou art a husband and wilt be a husband, I'll try if I can find out another! 'Tis a pretty time we women have on't, to be made widows while we are married. Our husbands think it reasonable to complain that we are the same, and the same to them, when we have more reason to complain that they are not the same to us. Because they cannot feed on one dish, therefore we must be starved. 'Tis enough that they have a sufficient ordinary provided and a table ready spread for 'em. If they cannot fall to and eat heartily, the fault is theirs, and 'tis pity, methinks, that the good creature should be lost when many a poor sinner would be glad on't.

Enter Melantha and Artemis to her.

MELANTHA.

Dear, my dear, pity me, I am so chagrin today and have had the most signal affront at court! I went this afternoon to do my devoir to Princess Amalthea, found her, conversed with her, and helped to make her court some half an hour, after which she went to take the air, chose out two ladies to go with her that came in after me, and left me most barbarously behind her.

ARTEMIS.

You are the less to be pitied, Melantha, because you subject yourself to these affronts by coming perpetually to court, where you have no business nor employment.

MELANTHA.

I declare, I had rather of the two, be *raillied*,[39] nay, *mal traitée* at court, than be deified in the town. For assuredly, nothing can be so *ridicule*, as a mere town lady.

DORALICE.

Especially at court. How I have seen 'em crowd and sweat in the Drawing Room* on a holiday night! For that's their time to swarm and invade the presence. Oh, how they catch at a bow or any little salute* from a courtier to make show of their acquaintance! And rather than be thought to be quite unknown, they curtsy to one another. But they take true pains to come near the circle and press and peep upon the Princess, to write letters into the country how she was dressed, while the ladies that stand about make their court to her with abusing them.

38 banes] obsolete spelling of banns, the public announcement of a proposed marriage, but also a pun on the modern meanings, poison, death, destruction

39 *raillied*] mocked (Frenglish)

ARTEMIS.

These are sad truths, Melantha. And therefore I would e'en advise you to quit the court and live either wholly in the town or, if you like not that, in the country.

DORALICE.

In the country! Nay, that's to fall beneath the town, for they live there upon our offals here. Their entertainment of wit is only the remembrance of what they had when they were last in town. They live this year upon the last year's knowledge, as their cattle do all night by chewing the cud of what they ate in the afternoon.

MELANTHA.

And they tell, for news, such unlikely stories. A letter from one of us is such a present to 'em that the poor souls wait for the carrier's day with such devotion that they cannot sleep the night before.

ARTEMIS.

No more than I can the night before I am to go a journey.

DORALICE.

Or I, before I am to try on a new gown.

MELANTHA.

A song that's stale here will be new there a twelvemonth hence, and if a man of the town by chance come amongst 'em, he's reverenced for teaching 'em the tune.

DORALICE.

A friend of mine, who makes songs sometimes, came lately out of the west and vowed he was so put out of countenance with a song of his, for at the first country gentleman's he visited, he saw three tailors crosslegged upon the table in the hall, who were tearing as loud as ever they could sing, "After the pangs of a desperate lover,"[40] etcetera, and all the day heard nothing else but the daughters of the house and the maids humming it over in every corner and the father whistling it.

ARTEMIS.

Indeed, I have observed of myself that when I am out of town but a fortnight, I am so humble that I would receive a letter from my tailor or mercer for a favor.

MELANTHA.

When I have been at grass in the summer and am new come up again, methinks I'm to be turned into *ridicule* by all that see me. But when I have been once or twice at court, I begin to value myself again and to despise my country acquaintance.

ARTEMIS.

There are places where all people may be adored, and we ought to know ourselves so well as to choose 'em.

DORALICE.

That's very true. Your little courtier's wife, who speaks to the King but once a month, need but go to a town lady and there she may vapor and cry, "The King and I," at every word. Your town lady, who is laughed at in the circle, takes her coach into the city, and there she's called "your honor" and has a banquet from the merchant's wife, whom she laughs at for her kindness. And, as for my finical cit,* she removes but to her country house and there insults over the country gentlewoman that never comes up, who treats her with frumenty and custard and opens her dear bottle of *mirabilis*[41] beside for a gill glass of it at parting.

ARTEMIS.

At last, I see, we shall leave Melantha where we found her, for by your description of the town and country they are become more dreadful to her than the court where she was affronted. But you forget we are to wait on the Princess Amalthea. Come, Doralice.

DORALICE.

Farewell, Melantha.

MELANTHA.

Adieu, my dear.

ARTEMIS.

You are out of charity with her, and therefore I shall not give your service.

MELANTHA.

Do not omit it, I beseech you, for I have such a tender for the court that I love it even from the Drawing Room to the lobby and can never be *rebutée* by any usage. But hark you, my dears, one thing I had forgot of great concernment.

---

40 After ... lover] a song from Dryden's play *An Evening's Love* (1668)

41 *mirabilis*] *aqua mirabilis*, a cordial distilled from wine and spices

DORALICE.
Quickly then, we are in haste.

MELANTHA.
Do not call it my "service," that's too vulgar, but do my *baisemains*[42] to the Princess Amalthea; that is *spirituelle*![43]

DORALICE.
To do you service then, we will *prendre* the *carosse*[44] to Court, and do your *baisemains* to the Princess Amalthea, in your phrase *spirituelle*.

Exeunt Artemis and Doralice. Enter Philotis, with a paper in her hand.

MELANTHA.
Oh are you there, minion? And well, are you not a most precious* damsel to retard all my visits for want* of language when you know you are paid so well for furnishing me with new words for my daily conversation? Let me die if I have not run the risk already to speak like one of the vulgar. And if I have one phrase left in all my store that is not threadbare and *usé* and fit for nothing but to be thrown to peasants.

PHILOTIS.
Indeed madam, I have been very diligent in my vocation, but you have so drained all the French plays and romances that they are not able to supply you with words for your daily expenses.

MELANTHA.
Drained! what a word's there! *Épuisée*, you sot* you. Come, produce your morning's work.

PHILOTIS. (*Shows the paper.*)
'Tis here, madam.

MELANTHA.
Oh my Venus! Fourteen or fifteen words to serve me a whole day! Let me die, at this rate I cannot last till night. Come, read your works. Twenty to one, half of 'em will not pass muster neither.

PHILOTIS. (*Reads.*)
Sottises.[45]

MELANTHA.
Sottises: *bon*. That's an excellent word to begin withal; as for example, he or she said a thousand *sottises* to me. Proceed.

PHILOTIS.
Figure; as what a figure of a man is there! *Naïve*, and *Naïveté*.

MELANTHA.
Naïve! As how?

PHILOTIS.
Speaking of a thing that was naturally said. It was so *naïve*: or such an innocent piece of simplicity; 'twas such a *naïveté*.

MELANTHA.
Truce with your interpretations; make haste.

PHILOTIS.
Foible, chagrin, grimace, embarrassé, double entendre, équivoque, éclaircissement, suite, bévue,[46] *façon, penchant, coup d'étourdi,*[47] and *ridicule*.

MELANTHA.
Hold, hold, how did they begin?

PHILOTIS.
They began at *sottises* and ended *en ridicule*.

MELANTHA.
Now give me your paper in my hand and hold you my glass* while I practice my postures for the day. (*Melantha laughs in the glass.*) How does that laugh become my face?

PHILOTIS.
Sovereignly well, madam.

MELANTHA.
Sovereignly! Let me die, that's not amiss. That word shall not be yours. I'll invent it and bring it up myself. My new point gorget[48] shall be yours upon't. Not a word of the word, I charge you.

PHILOTIS.
I am dumb, madam.

MELANTHA. (*Looking in the glass again.*)
That glance, how suits it with my face?

PHILOTIS.
'Tis so *languissant*.

MELANTHA.
Languissant! That word shall be mine too, and my

42 do my *baisemains*] kiss the hands of; pay my regards to

43 *spirituelle*] witty

44 *prendre* the *carosse*] take the carriage

45 *sottises*] silly things

46 *bévue*] blunder

47 *coup d'étourdi*] thoughtless act

48 point gorget] lace wimple, a covering for the neck and breast

last Indian gown[49] thine for it. (*Looks again.*) That sigh?

PHILOTIS.

'Twill make many a man sigh, madam. 'Tis a mere* *incendiaire.*

MELANTHA.

Take my gimp petticoat for that truth. If thou hast more of these phrases, let me die but I could give away all my wardrobe and go naked for 'em.

PHILOTIS.

Go naked? Then you would be a Venus, madam. Oh Jupiter! What had I forgot? This paper was given me by Rhodophil's page.

MELANTHA. (*Reading the letter.*)

"Beg the favor from you—gratify my passion—so far—assignation—in the grotto—behind the terrace clock this evening." Well, for the *billets doux* there's no man in Sicily must dispute with Rhodophil. They are so French, so *galant*, and so *tendre*, that I cannot resist the temptation of the assignation. Now go you away, Philotis; it imports me to practice what I shall say to my servant* when I meet him.

Exit Philotis.

"Rhodophil, you'll wonder at my assurance to meet you here; let me die, I am so out of breath with coming that I can render you no reason of it." Then he will make this *repartee*: "Madam, I have no reason to accuse you for that which is so great a favor to me." Then I reply, "But why have you drawn me to this solitary place? Let me die but I am apprehensive of some violence from you." Then, says he, "Solitude, madam, is most fit for lovers, but by this fair hand—" "Nay, now I vow you're rude, sir. Oh fie, fie, fie. I hope you'll be honorable?" "You'd laugh at me if I should, madam—" "What do you mean to throw me down thus? Ah me! ah, ah, ah."

Enter Polydamas, Leonidas, and guards.

Oh Venus! The King and court. Let me die, but I fear they have found my *foible*, and will turn me into *ridicule*. (*Exit running.*)

49 Indian gown] dressing gown made of Indian fabric

LEONIDAS.

Sir, I beseech you.

POLYDAMAS.

Do not urge my patience.

LEONIDAS.

I'll not deny
But what your spies informed you of is true:
I love the fair Palmyra. But I loved her
Before I knew your title to my blood.

Enter Palmyra, guarded.

See, here she comes and looks, amidst her guards,
Like a weak dove under the falcon's grip.
Oh Heav'n, I cannot bear it.

POLYDAMAS.

Maid, come hither.
Have you presumed so far as to receive
My son's affection?

PALMYRA. [*Aside.*]

Alas, what shall I answer? To confess it
Will raise a blush upon a virgin's face.
Yet I was ever taught 'twas base to lie.

POLYDAMAS.

You've been too bold, and you must love no more.

PALMYRA.

Indeed I must; I cannot help my love.
I was so tender when I took the bent
That now I grow that way.

POLYDAMAS.

He is a prince, and you are meanly born.

LEONIDAS.

Love either finds equality or makes it.
Like death, he knows no difference in degrees
But planes and levels all.

PALMYRA.

Alas, I had not rendered up my heart
Had he not loved me first. But he preferred me
Above the maidens of my age and rank,
Still* shunned their company, and still* sought mine.
I was not won by gifts, yet still* he gave.
And all his gifts, though small, yet spoke his love.
He picked the earliest strawberries in woods,
The clustered filberts, and the purple grapes.
He taught a prating stare[50] to speak my name.

50 stare] starling

And when he found a nest of nightingales,
Or callow linnets, he would show 'em me,
And let me take 'em out.

POLYDAMAS.
This is a little mistress, meanly born,
Fit only for a prince's vacant hours,
And then, to laugh at her simplicity,
Not fix a passion there. Now hear my sentence.

LEONIDAS.
Remember ere you give it, 'tis pronounced
Against us both.

POLYDAMAS.
First, in her hand
There shall be placed a player's painted scepter
And on her head a gilded pageant crown.
Thus shall she go,
With all the boys attending on her triumph.
That done, be put alone into a boat
With bread and water only for three days.
So on the sea she shall be set adrift,
And who relieves her, dies.

PALMYRA.
I only beg that you would execute
The last part first. Let me be put to sea.
The bread and water for my three days' life
I give you back; I would not live so long.
But let me 'scape the shame.

LEONIDAS.
Look to me, Piety, and you, oh gods, look to my piety:
Keep me from saying that which misbecomes a son,
But let me die before I see this done.

POLYDAMAS.
If you forever will abjure her sight,
I can be yet a father; she shall live.

LEONIDAS.
Hear, oh you Pow'rs, is this to be a father?
I see 'tis all my happiness and quiet
You aim at, sir. And take 'em.
I will not save ev'n my Palmyra's life
At that ignoble price. But I'll die with her.

PALMYRA.
So had I done by you
Had Fate made me a princess. Death, methinks,
Is not a terror now;
He is not fierce or grim but fawns and soothes me
And slides along, like Cleopatra's aspic,
Off'ring his service to my troubled breast.

LEONIDAS.
Begin what you have purposed when you please.
Lead her to scorn, your triumph shall be doubled.
As holy priests
In pity go with dying malefactors,
So will I share her shame.

POLYDAMAS.
You shall not have your will so much.—First part 'em,
Then execute your office.

LEONIDAS. (*Draws his sword.*)
No, I'll die
In her defense.

PALMYRA.
Ah hold, and pull not on
A curse to make me worthy of my death.
Do not by lawless force oppose your father,
Whom you have too much disobeyed for me.

LEONIDAS. (*Presenting his sword to his father upon his knees.*)
Here, take it, sir, and with it, pierce my heart.
You have done more in taking my Palmyra.
You are my father, therefore I submit.

POLYDAMAS.
Keep him from anything he may design
Against his life, whilst the first fury lasts,
And now perform what I commanded you.

LEONIDAS.
In vain: if sword and poison be denied me,
I'll hold my breath and die.

PALMYRA.
Farewell, my last Leonidas. Yet live,
I charge you live till you believe me dead.
I cannot die in peace if you die first.
If life's a blessing, you shall have it last.

POLYDAMAS.
Go on with her, and lead him after me.

Enter Argaleon hastily, with Hermogenes.

ARGALEON.
I bring you, sir, such news as must amaze you
And such as will prevent you from an action
Which would have rendered all your life unhappy.

Hermogenes kneels.

POLYDAMAS.
Hermogenes, you bend your knees in vain,
My doom's already passed.
HERMOGENES.
I kneel not for Palmyra, for I know
She will not need my pray'rs, but for myself:
With a feigned tale I have abused your ears
And therefore merit death. But since, unforced,
I first accuse myself, I hope your mercy.
POLYDAMAS.
Haste to explain your meaning.
HERMOGENES.
Then in few words, Palmyra is your daughter.
POLYDAMAS.
How can I give belief to this impostor?
He who has once abused me, often may.
I'll hear no more.
ARGALEON.
For your own sake, you must.
HERMOGENES.
A parent's love (for I confess my crime)
Moved me to say Leonidas was yours,
But when I heard Palmyra was to die,
The fear of guiltless blood so stung my conscience
That I resolved, ev'n with my shame, to save
Your daughter's life.
POLYDAMAS.
But how can I be certain but that interest,
Which moved you first to say your son was mine,
Does not now move you too to save your daughter?
HERMOGENES.
You had but then my word; I bring you now
Authentic testimonies. Sir, in short,
(Delivers on his knees a jewel, and a letter.)
If this will not convince you, let me suffer.
POLYDAMAS. (*Looking first on the jewel.*)
I know this jewel well, 'twas once my mother's,
Which, marrying, I presented to my wife.
And this, oh this is my Eudocia's hand.
(*Reads.*)
"This was the pledge of love given to Eudocia,
Who, dying, to her young Palmyra leaves it.
And this when you, my dearest lord, receive,
Own her, and think on me, dying Eudocia."
(*To Argaleon.*)
Take it; 'tis well there is no more to read,
My eyes grow full and swim in their own light.
(*He embraces Palmyra.*)
PALMYRA.
I fear, sir, this is your intended pageant.
You sport yourself at poor Palmyra's cost.
But if you think to make me proud,
Indeed I cannot be so: I was born
With humble thoughts and lowly, like my birth.
A real fortune could not make me haughty,
Much less a feigned.
POLYDAMAS.
This was her mother's temper.
I have too much deserved thou shouldst suspect
That I am not thy father, but my love
Shall henceforth show I am. Behold my eyes,
And see a father there begin to flow:
This is not feigned, Palmyra.
PALMYRA.
I doubt no longer, sir. You are a king
And cannot lie. Falsehood's a vice too base
To find a room in any royal breast.
I know, in spite of my unworthiness,
I am your child, for when you would have killed me,
Methought I loved you then.
ARGALEON.
Sir, we forget the Prince Leonidas,
His greatness should not stand neglected thus.
POLYDAMAS.
Guards, you may now retire. Give him his sword
And leave him free.
LEONIDAS.
Then the first use I make of liberty
Shall be, with your permission, mighty sir,
To pay that reverence to which nature binds me.
(*Kneels to Hermogenes.*)
ARGALEON.
Sure you forget your birth thus to misplace
This act of your obedience; you should kneel
To nothing but to Heav'n and to a king.
LEONIDAS.
I never shall forget what nature owes
Nor be ashamed to pay it. Though my father
Be not a king, I know him brave and honest
And well deserving of a worthier son.
POLYDAMAS.
He bears it gallantly.

LEONIDAS. (*To Hermogenes.*)
Why would you not instruct me, sir, before
Where I should place my duty?
From which, if ignorance have made me swerve,
I beg your pardon for an erring son.

PALMYRA.
I almost grieve I am a princess, since
It makes him lose a crown.

LEONIDAS.
And next, to you, my King, thus low I kneel
T'implore your mercy. If in that small time
I had the honor to be thought your son
I paid not strict obedience to your will,
I thought, indeed, I should not be compelled,
But thought it as your son; so what I took
In duty from you I restored in courage
Because your son should not be forced.

POLYDAMAS.
You have my pardon for it.

LEONIDAS.
To you, fair Princess, I congratulate
Your birth, of which ever I thought you worthy.
And give me leave to add that I am proud
The gods have picked me out to be the man
By whose dejected fate yours is to rise,
Because no man could more desire your fortune
Or franklier part with his to make you great.

PALMYRA.
I know the King, though you are not his son,
Will still regard you as my foster-brother
And so conduct you downward from a throne
By slow degrees, so unperceived and soft
That it may seem no fall, or if it be,
May Fortune lay a bed of down beneath you.

POLYDAMAS.
He shall be ranked with my nobility
And kept from scorn by a large pension giv'n him.

LEONIDAS. (*Bowing.*)
You are all great and royal in your gifts,
But at the donor's feet I lay 'em down.
Should I take riches from you, it would seem
As I did want a soul to bear that poverty
To which the gods designed my humble birth.
And should I take your honors without merit,
It would appear I wanted* manly courage
To hope 'em, in your service, from my sword.

POLYDAMAS.
Still brave and like yourself.
The court shall shine this night in full splendor
And celebrate this new discovery.*
—Argaleon, lead my daughter. As we go
I shall have time to give her my commands,
In which you are concerned.

Exeunt all but Leonidas.

LEONIDAS.
Methinks I do not want
That huge long train of fawning followers
That swept a furlong after me.
'Tis true, I am alone.
So was the Godhead ere he made the world
And better served Himself than served by Nature.
And yet I have a soul
Above this humble fate. I could command,
Love to do good, give largely to true merit,
All that a king should do. But though these are not
My province, I have seen enough within
To exercise my virtue.
All that a heart so fixed as mine can move
Is that my niggard fortune starves my love.

Exit.

Scene ii.

Palamede and Doralice meet: she with a book in her hand, seems to start at sight of him.

DORALICE.
'Tis a strange thing that no warning will serve your turn and that no retirement will secure me from your impertinent addresses! Did not I tell you that I was to be private here at my devotions?

PALAMEDE.
Yes, and you see I have observed my cue exactly. I am come to relieve you from them. Come, shut up, shut up your book; the man's come who is to supply all your necessities.

DORALICE.
Then it seems you are so impudent to think it was an assignation? This, I warrant, was your lewd interpretation of my innocent meaning.

PALAMEDE.
Venus forbid that I should harbor so unreasonable

a thought of a fair young lady that you should lead me hither into temptation. I confess I might think indeed it was a kind of honorable challenge to meet privately without seconds and decide the difference betwixt the two sexes. But Heaven forgive me if I thought amiss.

DORALICE.
You thought too, I'll lay my life on't, that you might as well make love* to me, as my husband does to your mistress.

PALAMEDE.
I was so unreasonable to think so too.

DORALICE.
And then you wickedly inferred that there was some justice in the revenge of it, or at least but little injury for a man to endeavor to enjoy that which he accounts a blessing and which is not valued as it ought by the dull possessor. Confess your wickedness, did you not think so?

PALAMEDE.
I confess I was thinking so, as fast as I could, but you think so much before me that you will let me think nothing.

DORALICE.
'Tis the very thing that I designed. I have forestalled all your arguments and left you without a word more to plead for mercy. If you have anything farther to offer ere sentence pass— Poor animal, I brought you hither only for my diversion.

PALAMEDE.
That you may have if you'll make use of me the right way. But I tell thee, woman, I am now past talking.

DORALICE.
But it may be I came hither to hear what fine things you could say for yourself.

PALAMEDE.
You would be very angry, to my knowledge, if I should lose so much time to say many of 'em. By this hand you would—

DORALICE.
Fie Palamede, I am a woman of honor.

PALAMEDE.
I see you are: you have kept touch with your assignation. And before we part, you shall find that I am a man of honor. Yet I have one scruple of conscience—

DORALICE.
I warrant you will not want* some naughty argument or other to satisfy yourself. I hope you are afraid of betraying your friend?

PALAMEDE.
Of betraying my friend! I am more afraid of being betrayed by you to my friend. You women now are got into the way of telling first yourselves. A man who has any care of his reputation will be loath to trust it with you.

DORALICE.
Oh, you charge your faults upon our sex. You men are like cocks: you never make love* but you clap your wings and crow when you have done.

PALAMEDE.
Nay, rather you women are like hens: you never lay but you cackle an hour after to discover* your nest. But I'll venture it for once.

DORALICE.
To convince you that you are in the wrong, I'll retire into the dark grotto to my devotion and make so little noise that it shall be impossible for you to find me.

PALAMEDE.
But if I find you—

DORALICE.
Aye, if you find me— But I'll put you to search in more corners than you imagine.

She runs in, and he after her. Enter Rhodophil and Melantha.

MELANTHA.
Let me die but this solitude and that grotto are scandalous. I'll go no further; besides, you have a sweet lady of your own.

RHODOPHIL.
But a sweet mistress, now and then, makes my sweet lady so much more sweet.

MELANTHA.
I hope you will not force me?

RHODOPHIL.
But I will, if you desire it.

PALAMEDE. (*Within.*)
Where the devil are you, madam? S'death,* I begin to be weary of this hide and seek. If you stay a little longer till the fit's over, I'll hide in my turn and

put you to the finding me. (*He enters, and sees Rhodophil and Melantha.*)
How! Rhodophil and my mistress!

MELANTHA. [*Aside.*]
My servant* to apprehend me! This is *surprenant au dernier.*[51]

RHODOPHIL. [*Aside.*]
I must on; there's nothing but impudence can help me out.

PALAMEDE.
Rhodophil, how came you hither in so good company?

RHODOPHIL.
As you see, Palamede, an effect of pure friendship: I was not able to live without you.

PALAMEDE.
But what makes my mistress with you?

RHODOPHIL.
Why, I heard you were here alone and could not in civility but bring her to you.

MELANTHA.
You'll pardon the effects of a passion which I may now avow for you, if it transported me beyond the rules of *bienséance.*[52]

PALAMEDE.
But who told you I was here? They that told you that may tell you more, for aught I know.

RHODOPHIL.
Oh for that matter, we had intelligence.

PALAMEDE.
But let me tell you, we came hither so very privately that you could not trace us.

RHODOPHIL.
Us? What us? You are alone.

PALAMEDE. [*Aside.*]
Us! the devil's in me for mistaking.—Me, I meant. Or us. That is, you are me, or I you, as we are friends. That's us.

DORALICE. (*Within.*)
Palamede, Palamede.

RHODOPHIL.
I should know that voice? Who's within there that calls you?

PALAMEDE.
Faith, I can't imagine; I believe the place is haunted.

DORALICE. (*Within.*)
Palamede, Palamede, all cocks hidden.[53]

PALAMEDE.
Lord, Lord, what shall I do? Well, dear friend, to let you see I scorn to be jealous and that I dare trust my mistress with you, take her back, for I would not willingly have her frighted, and I am resolved to see who's there. I'll not be daunted with a bugbear, that's certain. Prithee, dispute it not. It shall be so. Nay, do not put me to swear, but go quickly. There's an effect of pure friendship for you now.

Enter Doralice, and looks amazed, seeing them.

RHODOPHIL.
Doralice! I am thunderstruck to see you here.

PALAMEDE.
So am I! Quite thunderstruck. Was it you that called me within? [*Aside.*] I must be impudent.

RHODOPHIL.
How came you hither, Spouse?

PALAMEDE.
Aye, how came you hither? And what is more, how could you be here without my knowledge?

DORALICE.
(*To her husband.*) Oh gentleman, have I caught you, i'faith? Have I broke forth in ambush upon you? I thought my suspicions would prove true.

RHODOPHIL.
Suspicions! This is very fine, Spouse! Prithee, what suspicions?

DORALICE.
Oh, you feign ignorance. Why, of you and Melantha. Here have I stayed these two hours, waiting with all the rage of a passionate, loving wife, but infinitely jealous, to take you two in the manner, for hither I was certain you would come.

RHODOPHIL.
But you are mistaken, Spouse, in the occasion, for we came hither on purpose to find Palamede, on intelligence he was gone before.

51 *surprenant au dernier*] surprising to the extreme

52 *bienséance*] decorum

53 all cocks hidden] variant of "all hid" in hide and seek, with bawdy connotations

PALAMEDE.

I'll be hanged then if the same party who gave you intelligence I was here did not tell your wife you would come hither. Now I smell the malice on't on both sides.

DORALICE.

Was it so, think you? Nay then, I'll confess my part of the malice too. As soon as ever I spied my husband and Melantha come together, I had a strange temptation to make him jealous in revenge. And that made me call "Palamede, Palamede," as though there had been an intrigue between us.

MELANTHA.

Nay, I avow there was an appearance of an intrigue between us too.

PALAMEDE.

To see how things will come about!

RHODOPHIL. (*Embraces.*)

And was it only thus, my dear Doralice?

DORALICE. (*Embracing him.*)

And did I wrong nown* Rhodophil with a false suspicion?

PALAMEDE. (*Aside.*)

Now am I confident we had all four the same design. 'Tis a pretty odd kind of game this, where each of us plays for double stakes. This is just thrust and parry with the same motion: I am to get his wife and yet to guard my own mistress. But I am vilely suspicious that while I conquer in the right wing, I shall be routed in the left. For both our women will certainly betray their party, because they are each of them for gaining of two, as well as we and I much fear,
If their necessities and ours were known,
They have more need of two than we of one.

Exeunt, embracing one another.

Act IV, scene i.

Enter Leonidas, musing, Amalthea following him.

AMALTHEA.

Yonder he is, and I must speak or die.
And yet 'tis death to speak, yet he must know
I have a passion for him and may know it
With a less blush, because to offer it
To his low fortunes shows I loved before
His person, not his greatness.

LEONIDAS.

First scorned and now commanded from the court!
The King is good, but he is wrought to this
By proud Argaleon's malice.
What more disgrace can Love and Fortune join
T'inflict upon one man? I cannot now
Behold my dear Palmyra. She, perhaps, too
Is grown ashamed of a mean,* ill-placed love.

AMALTHEA. (*Aside.*)

Assist me, Venus, for I tremble when
I am to speak, but I must force myself.
—Sir, I would crave but one short minute with you
And some few words.

LEONIDAS. (*Aside.*)

The proud Argaleon's sister!

AMALTHEA. (*Aside.*)

Alas, it will not out; shame stops my mouth.
—Pardon my error, sir, I was mistaken
And took you for another.

LEONIDAS. (*Aside.*)

In spite of all his guards, I'll see Palmyra.
Though meanly born, I have a kingly soul yet.

AMALTHEA. (*Aside.*)

I stand upon a precipice, where fain
I would retire, but love still thrusts me on.
Now I grow bolder and will speak to him.
—Sir, 'tis indeed to you that I would speak,
And if—

LEONIDAS.

Oh, you are sent to scorn my fortunes.
Your sex and beauty are your privilege,
But should your brother—

AMALTHEA. [*Aside.*]

Now he looks angry, and I dare not speak.
—I had some business with you, sir,
But 'tis not worth your knowledge.

LEONIDAS.

Then 'twill be charity to let me mourn
My griefs alone, for I am much disordered.

AMALTHEA.

'Twill be more charity to mourn 'em with you.
Heav'n knows I pity you.

LEONIDAS.

Your pity, madam,
Is generous, but 'tis unavailable.[54]

---

[54] unavailable] of no avail

AMALTHEA.
You know not till 'tis tried.
Your sorrows are no secret: you have lost
A crown and mistress.
LEONIDAS.
Are not these enough?
Hang two such weights on any other soul
And see if it can bear 'em.
AMALTHEA.
More: you are banished by my brother's means
And ne'er must hope again to see your princess,
Except as pris'ners view fair walks and streets
And careless passengers[55] going by their grates
To make 'em feel the want* of liberty.
But worse than all,
The King this morning has enjoined his daughter
T'accept my brother's love.
LEONIDAS.
Is this your pity?
You aggravate my griefs and print 'em deeper
In new and heavier stamps.
AMALTHEA.
'Tis as physicians show the desperate ill
T'endear their art by mitigating pains
They cannot wholly cure. When you despair
Of all you wish, some part of it, because
Unhoped for, may be grateful, and some other—
LEONIDAS.
What other?
AMALTHEA.
Some other may—
(*Aside.*)
My shame again has seized me, and I can go
No farther—
LEONIDAS.
These often failings, sighs, and interruptions
Make me imagine you have grief like mine.
Have you ne'er loved?
AMALTHEA.
I? Never. (*Aside.*) 'Tis in vain;
I must despair in silence.
LEONIDAS.
You come as I suspected then: to mock,
At least observe my griefs. Take it not ill
That I must leave you. (*Is going.*)
AMALTHEA.
You must not go with these unjust opinions.
Command my life and fortunes. You are wise:
Think, and think well, what I can do to serve you.
LEONIDAS.
I have but one thing in my thoughts and wishes.
If by your means I can obtain the sight
Of my adored Palmyra or, what's harder,
One minute's time to tell her I die hers.
She starts back.
I see I am not to expect it from you
Nor could, indeed, with reason.
AMALTHEA.
Name any other thing. Is Amalthea
So despicable she can serve your wishes
In this alone?
LEONIDAS.
If I should ask of Heav'n,
I have no other suit.
AMALTHEA.
To show you, then, I can deny you nothing,
Though 'tis more hard to me than any other,
Yet I will do't for you.
LEONIDAS.
Name quickly, name the means, speak, my good angel.
AMALTHEA.
Be not so much o'erjoyed, for if you are,
I'll rather die than do it. This night the court
Will be in masquerade.
You shall attend on me; in that disguise
You may both see and speak to her,
If you dare venture it.
LEONIDAS.
Yes, were a god her guardian
And bore in each hand thunder, I would venture.
AMALTHEA.
Farewell then. Two hours hence I will expect you.
[*Aside.*]
My heart's so full that I can stay no longer. (*Exit.*)
LEONIDAS.
Already it grows dusky; I'll prepare
With haste for my disguise. But who are these?

Enter Hermogenes and Eubulus.

[55] passengers] passersby

HERMOGENES.
'Tis he, we need not fear to speak to him.
EUBULUS.
Leonidas.
LEONIDAS.
Sure I have known that voice.
HERMOGENES.
You have some reason, sir, 'tis Eubulus,
Who bred you with the Princess and, departing,
Bequeathed you to my care.
LEONIDAS. (*Kneeling.*)
My foster father! Let my knees express
My joys for your return!
EUBULUS.
Rise, sir, you must not kneel.
LEONIDAS.
E'er since you left me,
I have been wand'ring in a maze of fate,
Led by false fires of a fantastic glory
And the vain luster of imagined crowns.
But ah! Why would you leave me? Or how could you
Absent yourself so long?
EUBULUS.
I'll give you a most just account of both,
And something more I have to tell you which
I know must cause your wonder. But this place,
Though almost hid in darkness, is not safe.

Torches appear.

Already I discern some coming towards us
With lights who may discover me.—Hermogenes,
Your lodgings are hard by and much more private.
HERMOGENES.
There you may freely speak.
LEONIDAS.
Let us make haste,
For some affairs and of no small importance
Call me another way.

Exeunt. Enter Palamede and Rhodophil, with visor masks in their hands and torches before 'em.

PALAMEDE.
We shall have noble sport tonight, Rhodophil: this masquerading is a most glorious invention.

RHODOPHIL.
I believe it was invented first by some jealous lover to discover the haunts of his jilting mistress or perhaps by some distressed servant* to gain an opportunity with a jealous man's wife.

PALAMEDE.
No, it must be the invention of a woman: it has so much of subtlety and love in it.

RHODOPHIL.
I am sure 'tis extremely pleasant, for to go unknown is the next degree to going invisible.

PALAMEDE.
What with our antique[56] habits and feigned voices, do you know me? and I know you? Methinks we move and talk just like so many overgrown puppets.

RHODOPHIL.
Masquerade is only visor-mask improved, a heightening of the same fashion.

PALAMEDE.
No: masquerade is visor-mask in debauch, and I like it the better for't. For with a visor-mask, we fool ourselves into courtship for the sake of an eye that glanced or a hand that stole itself out of the glove sometimes to give us a sample of the skin. But in masquerade there is nothing to be known; she's all terra incognita, and the bold discoverer leaps ashore and takes his lot among the wild Indians and savages without the vile consideration of safety to his person or of beauty or wholesomeness in his mistress.

Enter Beliza.

RHODOPHIL.
Beliza, what make you here?

BELIZA.
Sir, my lady sent me after you to let you know she finds herself a little indisposed so that she cannot be at court but is retired to rest in her own apartment where she shall want* the happiness of your dear embraces tonight.

RHODOPHIL.
A very fine phrase, Beliza, to let me know my wife desires to lie alone.

PALAMEDE.
I doubt,* Rhodophil, you take the pains sometimes to instruct your wife's woman in these elegancies.

---

[56] antique] from earlier times, but also possibly antic

RHODOPHIL.
Tell my dear lady that since I must be so unhappy as not to wait on her tonight, I will lament bitterly for her absence. 'Tis true, I shall be at court, but I will take no divertissement there. And when I return to my solitary bed, if I am so forgetful of my passion as to sleep, I will dream of her and betwixt sleep and waking put out my foot towards her side for midnight consolation and, not finding her, I will sigh and imagine myself a most desolate widower.

BELIZA.
I shall do your commands, sir. (*Exit.*)

RHODOPHIL. (*Aside.*)
She's sick as aptly for my purpose as if she had contrived it so. Well, if ever woman was a helpmeet for man, my spouse is so, for within this hour I received a note from Melantha that she would meet me this evening in masquerade in boy's habit to rejoice with me before she entered into fetters. For I find she loves me better than Palamede only because he's to be her husband. There's something of antipathy in the word "marriage" to the nature of love; marriage is the mere ladle of affection that cools it when 'tis never* so fiercely boiling over.

PALAMEDE.
Dear Rhodophil, I must needs beg your pardon; there is an occasion fallen out which I had forgot. I cannot be at court tonight.

RHODOPHIL.
Dear Palamede, I am sorry we shall not have one course together at the herd. But I find your game lies single. Good fortune to you with your mistress. (*Exit.*)

PALAMEDE.
He has wished me good fortune with his wife. There's no sin in this then; there's fair leave given. Well, I must go visit the sick; I cannot resist the temptations of my charity. Oh what a difference will she find betwixt a dull, resty* husband and a quick,* vigorous lover! He sets out like a carrier's horse, plodding on because he knows he must, with the bells of matrimony chiming so melancholy about his neck, in pain till he's at his journey's end. And despairing to get thither, he is fain to fortify imagination with the thoughts of another woman. I take heat after heat, like a well-breathed courser, and— (*Clashing of swords within.*) But hark, what noise is that? Swords! Nay then, have with you. (*Exit.*)

Reenter Palamede, with Rhodophil, and Doralice in man's habit.

RHODOPHIL.
Friend, your relief was very timely; otherwise, I had been oppressed.

PALAMEDE.
What was the quarrel?*

RHODOPHIL.
What I did was in rescue of this youth.

PALAMEDE.
What cause could he give 'em?

DORALICE.
The cause was nothing but only the common cause of fighting in masquerades: they were drunk, and I was sober.

RHODOPHIL.
Have they not hurt you?

DORALICE.
No, but I am exceeding ill with the fright on't.

PALAMEDE.
Let's lead him to some place where he may refresh himself.

RHODOPHIL.
Do you conduct him then.

PALAMEDE. (*Aside.*)
How cross this happens to my design of going to Doralice! For I am confident she was sick on purpose that I should visit her.—Hark you, Rhodophil, could not you take care of the stripling? I am partly engaged tonight.

RHODOPHIL.
You know I have business.—But come, youth, if it must be so.

DORALICE. (*To Rhodophil.*)
No, good sir, do not give yourself that trouble; I shall be safer and better pleased with your friend here.

RHODOPHIL.
Farewell then, once more I wish you a good adventure.

PALAMEDE.
Damn this kindness! Now must I be troubled with this young rogue and miss my opportunity with Doralice.

Exeunt Rhodophil alone, Palamede with Doralice.

Scene ii.

Enter Polydamas.

POLYDAMAS.
Argaleon counseled well to banish him.
He has I know not what
Of greatness in his looks and of high fate
That almost awes me. But I fear my daughter,
Who hourly moves me for him, and I marked
She sighed when I but named Argaleon to her.
But see, the maskers. Hence, my cares: this night
At least take truce and find me on my pillow.

Enter the Princess in masquerade, with ladies. At the other end, Argaleon and gentlemen in masquerade, then Leonidas leading Amalthea. The King sits. A dance. After the dance.

AMALTHEA. (*To Leonidas.*)
That's the Princess;
I saw the habit ere she put it on.
LEONIDAS.
I know her by a thousand other signs;
She cannot hide so much divinity.
Disguised and silent, yet some graceful motion
Breaks from her and shines round her like a glory. (*Goes to Palmyra.*)
AMALTHEA.
Thus she reveals herself and knows it not.
Like love's dark lantern, I direct his steps,
And yet he sees not that which gives him light.
PALMYRA. (*To Leonidas.*)
I know you. But alas, Leonidas,
Why should you tempt this danger on yourself?
LEONIDAS.
Madam, you know me not, if you believe
I would not hazard greater for your sake.
But you, I fear, are changed.
PALMYRA.
No, I am still the same.
But there are many things became Palmyra
Which ill become the Princess.
LEONIDAS.
I ask nothing
Which honor will not give you leave to grant.
One hour's short audience at my father's house
You cannot sure refuse me.
PALMYRA.
Perhaps I should, did I consult strict virtue.
But something must be given to love and you.
When would you I should come?
LEONIDAS.
This evening, with the speediest opportunity.
I have a secret to discover* to you
Which will surprise and please you.
PALMYRA.
'Tis enough.
Go now, for we may be observed and known.
I trust your honor; give me not occasion
To blame myself or you.
LEONIDAS.
You never shall repent your good opinion. (*Kisses her hand, and exit.*)
ARGALEON.
I cannot be deceived: that is the Princess.
One of her maids betrayed the habit to me.
But who was he with whom she held discourse?
'Tis one she favors, for he kissed her hand.
Our shapes are like, our habits near the same.
She may mistake and speak to me for him.
I am resolved I'll satisfy my doubts
Though to be more tormented. (*Exit.*)

Song.

I.

Whilst Alexis lay pressed
In her arms he loved best,
With his hands round her neck
And his head on her breast,
He found the fierce pleasure too hasty to stay,
And his soul in the tempest just flying away.

2.

When Celia saw this,
With a sigh and a kiss
She cried, "Oh my dear, I am robbed of my bliss;
'Tis unkind to your love and unfaithfully done
To leave me behind you and die* all alone."

3.

The youth, though in haste
And breathing his last,
In pity died slowly, while she died more fast;
Till at length she cried, "Now my dear, now let us go,
Now die, my Alexis, and I will die too."

4.

Thus entranced they did lie,
Till Alexis did try
To recover new breath that again he might die.
Then often they died, but the more they did so,
The nymph died more quick and the shepherd
more slow.

Another dance. After it, Argaleon reenters and stands by the Princess.

PALMYRA. (*To Argaleon.*)
Leonidas, what means this quick return?
ARGALEON. (*Aside.*)
Oh Heav'n! 'Tis what I feared.
PALMYRA.
Is aught of moment happened since you went?
ARGALEON.
No madam, but I understood not fully
Your last commands.
PALMYRA.
And yet you answered to 'em.
Retire, you are too indiscreet a lover.
I'll meet you where I promised. (*Exit.*)
ARGALEON.
Oh my curst fortune! What have I discovered?
But I will be revenged. (*Whispers to the King.*)
POLYDAMAS.
But are you certain you are not deceived?
ARGALEON.
Upon my life.
POLYDAMAS.
Her honor is concerned.
Somewhat I'll do, but I am yet distracted
And I know not where to fix. I wished a child,
And Heav'n, in anger, granted my request.
So blind we are, our wishes are so vain,
That what we most desire proves most our pain.

Exeunt omnes.

Scene iii. An eating house.

Bottles of wine on the table. Palamede, and Doralice in man's habit.

DORALICE. (*Aside.*)
Now cannot I find in my heart to discover* myself, though I long he should know me.

PALAMEDE.
I tell thee, boy, now I have seen thee safe, I must be gone. I have no leisure to throw away on thy raw conversation. I am a person that understand better things, I.

DORALICE.
Were I a woman, oh how you'd admire me! Cry up every word I said and screw your face into a submissive smile, as I have seen a dull gallant act wit and counterfeit pleasantness when he whispers to a great person in a playhouse, smile and look briskly when the other answers, as if something of extraordinary had passed betwixt 'em, when, heaven knows, there was nothing else but, "What o'clock does your lordship think it is?" and my lord's repartee is, "'Tis almost parktime,"[57] or, at most, "Shall we out of the pit and go behind the scenes for an act or two?" And yet such fine things as these would be wit in a mistress's mouth.

PALAMEDE.
Aye boy, there's Dame Nature in the case. He who cannot find wit in a mistress deserves to find nothing else, boy. But these are riddles to thee, child, and I have not leisure to instruct thee; I have affairs to dispatch, great affairs. I am a man of business.

DORALICE.
Come, you shall not go. You have no affairs but what you may dispatch here, to my knowledge.

PALAMEDE.
I find now thou art a boy of more understanding than I thought thee, a very lewd wicked boy. O'my conscience thou wouldst debauch me and hast some evil designs upon my person.

DORALICE.
You are mistaken, sir. I would only have you show me a more lawful reason why you would leave me than I can why you should not, and I'll not stay you. For I am not so young but I understand the necessities of flesh and blood and the pressing occasions of mankind as well as you.

PALAMEDE.
A very forward and understanding boy! Thou art in great danger of a page's wit, to be brisk at

57 parktime] the fashionable time to be in the park

fourteen and dull at twenty. But I'll give thee no further account; I must and will go.

DORALICE.

My life on't, your mistress is not at home.

PALAMEDE. [*Aside.*]

This imp will make me very angry.—I tell thee, young sir, she is at home and at home for me, and what is more, she is abed for me and sick for me.

DORALICE.

For you only?

PALAMEDE.

Aye, for me only.

DORALICE.

But how do you know she's sick abed?

PALAMEDE.

She sent her husband word so.

DORALICE.

And are you such a novice in love, to believe a wife's message to her husband?

PALAMEDE.

Why, what the devil should be her meaning else?

DORALICE.

It may be to go in masquerade as well as you, to observe your haunts and keep you company without your knowledge.

PALAMEDE.

Nay, I'll trust her for that. She loves me too well to disguise herself from me.

DORALICE.

If I were she, I would disguise on purpose to try your wit and come to my servant* like a riddle: "Read me and take me."

PALAMEDE.

I could know her in any shape. My good genius* would prompt me to find out a handsome woman. There's something in her that would attract me to her without my knowledge.

DORALICE.

Then you make a loadstone of your mistress?

PALAMEDE.

Yes, and I carry steel about me which has been so often touched that it never fails to point to the north pole.

DORALICE.

Yet still my mind gives me that you have met her disguised tonight and have not known her.

PALAMEDE.

[*Aside.*] This is the most pragmatical,[58] conceited little fellow. He will needs understand my business better then myself.—I tell thee once more, thou dost not know my mistress.

DORALICE.

And I tell you once more that I know her better than you do.

PALAMEDE. [*Aside.*]

The boy's resolved to have the last word. I find I must go without reply. (*Exit.*)

DORALICE.

Ah mischief, I have lost him with my fooling. Palamede, Palamede.

He returns. She plucks off her peruke, and puts it on again when he knows her.

PALAMEDE.

Oh heavens! Is it you, madam?

DORALICE.

Now, where was your good genius that would prompt you to find me out?

PALAMEDE.

Why, you see I was not deceived; you, yourself, were my good genius.

DORALICE.

But where was the steel that knew the loadstone, hah?

PALAMEDE.

The truth is, madam, the steel has lost its virtue, and therefore, if you please, we'll new touch it.

Enter Rhodophil, and Melantha in boy's habit. Rhodophil sees Palamede kissing Doralice's hand.

RHODOPHIL.

Palamede again! Am I fallen into your quarters? What? Engaging with a boy? Is all honorable?

PALAMEDE.

Oh, very honorable on my side. I was just chastising this young villain. He was running away without paying his share of the reckoning.

RHODOPHIL.

Then I find I was deceived in him.

58 pragmatical] officious

PALAMEDE.

Yes, you are deceived in him. 'Tis the archest rogue if you did but know him.

MELANTHA.

Good Rhodophil, let us get off *à la dérobée*[59] for fear I should be discovered.

RHODOPHIL. [*To Melantha.*]

There's no retiring now; I warrant you for discovery. Now have I the oddest thought: to entertain you before your servant's* face and he never the wiser. 'Twill be the prettiest juggling trick to cheat him when he looks upon us.

MELANTHA.

This is the strangest *caprice* in you.

PALAMEDE. (*To Doralice.*)

This Rhodophil's the unluckiest fellow to me! This is now the second time he has barred the dice when we were just ready to have nicked him, but if ever I get the box again—

DORALICE. [*To Palamede.*]

Do you think he will not know me? Am I like myself?

PALAMEDE. [*To Doralice.*]

No more than a picture in the hangings.

DORALICE. [*To Palamede.*]

Nay, then he can never discover me now the wrong side of the arras is turned towards him.

PALAMEDE. [*To Doralice.*]

At least 'twill be some pleasure to me to enjoy what freedom I can while he looks on; I will storm the outworks of matrimony even before his face.

RHODOPHIL.

What wine have you there, Palamede?

PALAMEDE.

Old Chios,[60] or the rogue's damned that drew it.

RHODOPHIL.

Come: to the most constant of mistresses; that I believe is yours, Palamede.

DORALICE.

Pray spare your seconds, for my part I am but a weak brother.

PALAMEDE.

Now, to the truest of turtles.* That is your wife, Rhodophil, that lies sick at home in the bed of honor.

RHODOPHIL.

Now let's have one common health and so have done.

DORALICE.

Then for once I'll begin it. Here's to him that has the fairest lady of Sicily in masquerade tonight.

PALAMEDE.

This is such an obliging health, I'll kiss thee, dear rogue, for thy invention. (*Kisses her.*)

RHODOPHIL.

He who has this lady is a happy man, without dispute. (*Aside.*) I'm most concerned in this, I am sure.

PALAMEDE.

Was it not well found out, Rhodophil?

MELANTHA.

Aye, this was *bien trouvé*[61] indeed.

DORALICE. (*To Melantha.*)

I suppose I shall do you a kindness to inquire if you have not been in France, sir?

MELANTHA.

To do you service, sir.

DORALICE.

Oh monsieur, *votre valet bien humble.* (*Saluting* her.*)

MELANTHA.

Votre esclave, monsieur, de tout mon coeur. (*Returning the salute.*)

DORALICE.

I suppose, sweet sir, you are the hope and joy of some thriving citizen who has pinched himself at home to breed you abroad, where you have learnt your exercises, as it appears, most awkwardly and are returned with the addition of a new-laced bosom and a clap to your good old father, who looks at you with his mouth while you spout French with your man monsieur.

PALAMEDE.

Let me kiss thee again for that, dear rogue.

MELANTHA.

And you, I imagine, are my young master whom your mother durst not trust upon salt water but left you to be your own tutor at fourteen, to be

59 *à la dérobée*] secretly

60 Old Chios] wine from the Greek island of Chios

61 *bien trouvé*] well put

very brisk and *entreprenant*, to endeavor to be debauched ere you have learnt the knack on't, to value yourself upon a clap before you can get it, and to make it the height of your ambition to get a player for your mistress.

RHODOPHIL. (*Embracing Melantha.*)
Oh dear young bully, thou hast tickled him with a repartee, i'faith.

MELANTHA.
You are one of those that applaud our country plays where drums and trumpets and blood and wounds are wit.

RHODOPHIL.
Again, my boy? let me kiss thee most abundantly.

DORALICE.
You are an admirer of the dull French poetry, which is so thin that it is the very leaf-gold of wit, the very wafers and whipped cream of sense, for which a man opens his mouth and gapes to swallow nothing. And to be an admirer of such profound dullness, one must be endowed with a great perfection of impudence and ignorance.

PALAMEDE.
Let me embrace thee most vehemently.

MELANTHA. (*Advancing.*)
I'll sacrifice my life for French poetry.

DORALICE.
I'll die upon the spot for our country wit.

RHODOPHIL. (*To Melantha.*)
Hold, hold, young Mars. Palamede, draw back your hero.

PALAMEDE.
'Tis time; I shall be drawn in for a second else at the wrong weapon.

MELANTHA.
Oh that I were a man for thy sake!

DORALICE.
You'll be a man as soon as I shall.

Enter a messenger to Rhodophil.

MESSENGER.
Sir, the King has instant business with you. I saw the guard drawn up by your lieutenant before the palace gate, ready to march.

RHODOPHIL.
'Tis somewhat sudden. Say that I am coming.

Exit Messenger.

Now Palamede, what think you of this sport?
This is some sudden tumult. Will you along?

PALAMEDE.
Yes, yes, I will go but the devil take me if ever I was less in humor. Why the pox could they not have stayed their tumult till tomorrow? Then I had done my business and been ready for 'em. Truth is, I had a little transitory crime to have committed first, and I am the worst man in the world at repenting till a sin be thoroughly done. But what shall we do with the two boys?

RHODOPHIL.
Let them take a lodging in the house till the business be over.

DORALICE.
What, lie with a boy? For my part, I own it, I cannot endure to lie with a boy.

PALAMEDE.
The more's my sorrow. I cannot accommodate you with a better bedfellow.

MELANTHA.
Let me die if I enter into a pair of sheets with him that hates the French.

DORALICE.
Pish, take no care for us but leave us in the streets. I warrant you, as late as it is I'll find my lodging as well as any drunken bully of 'em all.

RHODOPHIL. (*Aside.*)
I'll fight in mere* revenge and wreak my passion
On all that spoil this hopeful assignation.

PALAMEDE.
I'm sure we fight in a good quarrel.*
Rogues may pretend religion and the laws,
But a kind* mistress is the Good Old Cause.*

Exeunt.

Scene iv.

Enter Palmyra, Eubulus, Hermogenes.

PALMYRA.
You tell me wonders, that Leonidas
Is Prince Theagenes, the late King's son.

EUBULUS.
It seemed as strange to him as now to you
Before I had convinced him. But besides

His great resemblance to the King his father,
The Queen his mother lives, secured by me
In a religious house, to whom each year
I brought the news of his increasing virtues.
My last long absence from you both was caused
By wounds which in my journey I received
When set upon by thieves; I lost those jewels
And letters which your dying mother left.

HERMOGENES.
The same he means, which, since brought to the King,
Made him first know he had a child alive.
'Twas then my care of Prince Leonidas
Caused me to say he was th'usurper's son
Till, after forced by your apparent danger,
I made the true discovery* of your birth
And once more hid my Prince's.

Enter Leonidas.

LEONIDAS.
Hermogenes and Eubulus, retire.
Those of our party whom I left without
Expect your aid and counsel.

Exeunt Hermogenes and Eubulus.

PALMYRA.
I should, Leonidas, congratulate
This happy change of your exalted fate,
But as my joy, so you my wonder move:
Your looks have more of business than of love,
And your last words some great design did show.

LEONIDAS.
I frame not any to be hid from you.
You in my love all my designs may see.
But what have love and you designed for me?
Fortune, once more, has set the balance right:
First equaled us in lowness then in height.
Both of us have so long like gamesters thrown,
Till Fate comes round and gives to each his own.
As Fate is equal, so may Love appear:
Tell me, at least, what I must hope or fear.

PALMYRA.
After so many proofs, how can you call
My love in doubt? Fear nothing and hope all.
Think what a prince, with honor, may receive
Or I may give without a parent's leave.

LEONIDAS.
You give and then restrain the grace you show,
As ostentatious priests when souls they woo:
Promise their Heav'n to all but grant to few.
But do for me what I have dared for you:
I did no argument from duty bring;
Duty's a name, and love's a real thing.

PALMYRA.
Man's love may, like wild torrents, overflow;
Woman's as deep, but in its banks must go.
My love is mine and that I can impart
But cannot give my person with my heart.

LEONIDAS.
Your love is then no gift:
For when the person it does not convey,
'Tis to give gold and not to give the key.

PALMYRA.
Then ask my father.

LEONIDAS.
He detains my throne.
Who holds back mine will hardly give his own.

PALMYRA.
What then remains?

LEONIDAS.
That I must have recourse
To arms and take my love and crown by force.
Hermogenes is forming the design,
And with him all the brave and loyal join.

PALMYRA.
And is it thus you court Palmyra's bed?
Can she the murd'rer of her parent wed?
Desist from force: so much you well may give
To love and me, to let my father live.

LEONIDAS.
Each act of mine my love to you has shown,
But you who tax my want* of it have none.
You bid me part with you and let him live,
But they should nothing ask who nothing give.

PALMYRA.
I give what virtue and what duty can
In vowing ne'er to wed another man.

LEONIDAS.
You will be forced to be Argaleon's wife.

PALMYRA.
I'll keep my promise though I lose my life.

LEONIDAS.
Then you lose love, for which we both contend.
For life is but the means, but love's the end.
PALMYRA.
Our souls shall love hereafter.
LEONIDAS.
I much fear
That soul which could deny the body here
To taste of love would be a niggard there.
PALMYRA.
Then 'tis past hope: our cruel fate, I see,
Will make a sad divorce 'twixt you and me.
For if you force employ, by Heav'n I swear
And all blessed beings—
LEONIDAS.
Your rash oath forbear.
PALMYRA.
I never—
LEONIDAS.
Hold once more. But yet, as he
Who 'scapes a dang'rous leap looks back to see,
So I desire, now I am past my fear,
To know what was that oath you meant to swear.
PALMYRA.
I meant that, if you hazarded your life
Or sought my father's, ne'er to be your wife.
LEONIDAS.
See now, Palmyra, how unkind you prove!
Could you with so much ease forswear my love?
PALMYRA.
You force me with your ruinous design.
LEONIDAS.
Your father's life is more your care than mine.
PALMYRA.
You wrong me: 'tis not, though it ought to be;
You are my care, Heav'n knows, as well as he.
LEONIDAS.
If now the execution I delay,
My honor and my subjects I betray.
All is prepared for the just enterprise,
And the whole city will tomorrow rise.
The leaders of the party are within,
And Eubulus has sworn that he will bring
To head their arms the person of their King.
PALMYRA.
In telling this, you make me guilty too;
I therefore must discover* what I know.
What honor bids you do, nature bids me prevent.
But kill me first and then pursue your black intent.
LEONIDAS.
Palmyra, no, you shall not need to die,
Yet I'll not trust so strict a piety.
—Within there.

Enter Eubulus.

Eubulus, a guard prepare.
Here, I commit this pris'ner to your care.

Kisses Palmyra's hand, then gives it to Eubulus.

PALMYRA.
Leonidas, I never thought these bands
Could e'er be giv'n me by a lover's hands.
LEONIDAS. (*Kneeling.*)
Palmyra, thus your judge himself arraigns;
He who imposed these bonds, still wears your chains.
When you to love or duty false must be,
Or to your father guilty or to me,
These chains alone remain to set you free.

Noise of swords clashing.

POLYDAMAS. (*Within.*)
Secure these first, then search the inner room.
LEONIDAS.
From whence do these tumultuous clamors come?

Enter Hermogenes, hastily.

HERMOGENES.
We are betrayed, and there remains alone
This comfort, that your person is not known.

Enter the King, Argaleon, Rhodophil, Palamede, guards; some like citizens as prisoners.

POLYDAMAS.
What mean these midnight consultations here,
Where I, like an unsummoned guest, appear?
LEONIDAS.
Sir—
ARGALEON.
There needs no excuse, 'tis understood:
You were all watching for your prince's good.
POLYDAMAS.
My reverend city friends, you are well met!

On what great work were your grave wisdoms set?
Which of my actions were you scanning here?
What French invasion have you found to fear?[62]

LEONIDAS.
They are my friends and come, sir, with intent
To take their leaves before my banishment.

POLYDAMAS. (*Seeing Palmyra.*)
Your exile in both sexes friends can find:
I see the ladies, like the men, are kind.

PALMYRA. (*Kneeling.*)
Alas, I came but—

POLYDAMAS.
Add not to your crime
A lie. I'll hear you speak some other time.
How? Eubulus! Nor time, nor thy disguise
Can keep thee undiscovered from my eyes.
—A guard there, seize 'em all.

RHODOPHIL.
Yield, sir, what use of valor can be shown?

PALAMEDE.
One and unarmed against a multitude!

LEONIDAS.[c]
Oh for a sword!

He reaches at one of the guard's halberds and is seized behind.

I wonnot lose my breath
In fruitless prayers but beg a speedy death.

PALMYRA.
Oh spare Leonidas and punish me.

POLYDAMAS.
Mean* girl, thou want'st* an advocate for thee.
Now the mysterious knot will be untied:
Whether the young King lives or where he died.
Tomorrow's dawn shall the dark riddle clear,
Crown all my joys, and dissipate my fear.

Exeunt omnes.

Act V, scene i.

Palamede, Straton. Palamede with a letter in his hand.

PALAMEDE.
This evening, sayest thou? will they both be here?

STRATON.
Yes, sir, both my old master and your mistress's father. The old gentlemen ride hard this journey. They say it shall be the last time they will see the town, and both of 'em are so pleased with this marriage which they have concluded for you that I am afraid they will live some years longer to trouble you with the joy of it.

PALAMEDE.
But this is such an unreasonable thing, to impose upon me to be married tomorrow. 'Tis hurrying a man to execution without giving him time to say his prayers.

STRATON.
Yet if I might advise you, sir, you should not delay it, for your younger brother comes up with 'em and is got already into their favors. He has gained much upon my old master by finding fault with innkeeper's bills and by starving us and our horses to show his frugality. And he is very well with your mistress's father by giving him receipts* for the spleen, gout, and scurvy and other infirmities of old age.

PALAMEDE.
I'll rout him and his country education. Pox on him, I remember him before I traveled. He had nothing in him but mere jockey,[63] used to talk loud and make matches and was all for the crack of the field.[64] Sense and wit were as much banished from his discourse as they are when the court goes out of town to a horse race. Go now and provide your master's lodgings.

STRATON.
I go, sir. (*Exit.*)

PALAMEDE.
It vexes me to the heart to leave all my designs with Doralice unfinished, to have flown her so often to a mark and still to be bobbed at retrieve.[65] If I had but once enjoyed her, though I could not have satisfied my stomach with the feast, at least I should have relished my mouth a little. But now—

---

[62] reverend city friends...fear] alludes to opposition in the City of London to Charles II's policy of seeking an alliance with France and Louis XIV

[63] jockey] horsemanship; also shrewd dealing with a suggestion of fraud

[64] crack of the field] favorite

[65] to have flown ... bobbed at retrieve] like a bird of prey disappointed at the last moment of its quarry

Enter Philotis.

PHILOTIS.

Oh sir, you are happily met; I was coming to find you.

PALAMEDE.

From your lady, I hope.

PHILOTIS.

Partly from her, but more especially from myself. She has just now received a letter from her father with an absolute command to dispose herself to marry you tomorrow.

PALAMEDE.

And she takes it to the death?

PHILOTIS.

Quite contrary: the letter could never have come in a more lucky minute, for it found her in an ill humor with a rival of yours, that shall be nameless, about the pronunciation of a French word.

PALAMEDE.

Count Rhodophil, never disguise it, I know the amour. But I hope you took the occasion to strike in for me?

PHILOTIS.

It was my good fortune to do you some small service in it. For your sake I discommended him all over: clothes, person, humor,* behavior, everything. And to sum up all, told her it was impossible to find a married man that was otherwise, for they were all so mortified at home with their wives' ill humors that they could never recover themselves to be company abroad.

PALAMEDE.

Most divinely urged!

PHILOTIS.

Then I took occasion to commend your good qualities: as the sweetness of your humor,* the comeliness of your person, your good mien, your valor, but above all your liberality.

PALAMEDE.

I vow to Gad I had like to have forgot that good quality in myself, if thou hadst not remembered me on't. Here are five pieces for thee.

PHILOTIS.

Lord, you have the softest hand, sir! It would do a woman good to touch it. Count Rhodophil's is not half so soft, for I remember I felt it once when he gave me ten pieces for my New Year's gift.

PALAMEDE.

Oh, I understand you, madam. You shall find my hand as soft again as Count Rhodophil's. There are twenty pieces for you. The former was but a retaining fee; now I hope you'll plead for me.

PHILOTIS.

Your own merits speak enough. Be sure only to ply her with French words, and I'll warrant you'll do your business. Here are a list of her phrases for this day. Use 'em to her upon all occasions and foil her at her own weapon. For she's like one of the old Amazons, she'll never marry, except it be the man who has first conquered her.

PALAMEDE.

I'll be sure to follow your advice, but you'll forget to further my design.

PHILOTIS.

What, do you think I'll be ungrateful? But however, if you distrust my memory, put some token on my finger to remember it by. That diamond there would do admirably.

PALAMEDE.

There 'tis and I ask your pardon heartily for calling your memory into question. I assure you I'll trust it another time without putting you to the trouble of another token.

Enter Palmyra and Artemis.

ARTEMIS.

Madam, this way the prisoners are to pass;
Here you may see Leonidas.

PALMYRA.

Then here I'll stay and follow him to death.

Enter Melantha hastily.

MELANTHA.

Oh, here's her Highness! Now is my time to introduce myself and to make my court to her in my new French phrases. Stay, let me read my catalog: *suite, figure, chagrin, naïveté,* and "let me die" for the parenthesis of all.

PALAMEDE. (*Aside.*)

Do, persecute her, and I'll persecute thee as fast in thy own dialect.

MELANTHA.

Madam, the Princess! Let me die but this is a most horrid spectacle, to see a person who makes so grand a figure in the court without the *suite* of a princess and entertaining your *chagrin* all alone. [*Aside.*] *Naïveté* should have been there, but the disobedient word would not come in.

PALMYRA.

What is she, Artemis?

ARTEMIS.

An impertinent lady, madam, very ambitious of being known to your highness.

PALAMEDE. (*To Melantha.*)

Let me die, madam, if I have not waited you here these two long hours without so much as the *suite* of a single servant to attend me, entertaining myself with my own *chagrin* till I had the honor to see your ladyship, who are a person that makes so considerable a figure in the court.

MELANTHA.

Truce with your *douceurs*, good servant;* you see I am addressing to the Princess. Pray do not *embarrass* me—*Embarrass* me! What a delicious French word do you make me lose upon you too! (*To the Princess.*) Your Highness, madam, will please to pardon the *bévue* which I made in not sooner finding you out to be a princess. But let me die if this *éclaircissement* which is made this day of your quality* does not ravish me, and give me leave to tell you—

PALAMEDE.

But first give me leave to tell you, madam, that I have so great a tender for your person and such a *penchant* to do you service, that—

MELANTHA.

What, must I still be troubled with your *sottises*? [*Aside.*] There's another word lost that I meant for the Princess, with a mischief to you.—But your Highness, madam—

PALAMEDE.

But your ladyship, madam—

Enter Leonidas guarded and led over the stage.

MELANTHA.

Out upon him, how he looks, madam! Now he's found no prince, he is the strangest figure of a man. How could I make that *coup d'étourdi* to think him one?

PALMYRA.

Away, impertinent.—My dear Leonidas!

LEONIDAS.

My dear Palmyra!

PALMYRA.

Death shall never part us.
My destiny is yours.

He is led off; she follows.

MELANTHA.

Impertinent! Oh, I am the most unfortunate person this day breathing, that the Princess should thus *rompre en visière*[66] without occasion. Let me die but I'll follow her to death till I make my peace.

PALAMEDE. (*Holding her.*)

And let me die, but I'll follow you to the infernals till you pity me.

MELANTHA. (*Turning towards him angrily.*)

Aye, 'tis long of you that this *malheur*[67] is fallen upon me; your impertinence has put me out of the good graces of the Princess, and all that, which has ruined me, and all that, and, therefore, let me die, but I'll be revenged, and all that.

PALAMEDE.

Façon, façon,[68] you must and shall love me, and all that, for my old man is coming up, and all that, and I am *désespéré au dernier*[69] and will not be disinherited, and all that.

MELANTHA.

How durst you interrupt me so *mal à propos* when you knew I was addressing to the Princess?

PALAMEDE.

But why would you address yourself so much *à contretemps* then?

MELANTHA.

Ah, *mal peste*!

PALAMEDE.

Ah *j'enrage*!

PHILOTIS.

Radoucissez vous, de grâce, madame; vous êtes bien

66 *rompre en visière*] quarrel with openly

67 *malheur*] misfortune

68 *façon*] affectation

69 *désespéré au dernier*] desperate to the last extreme

en colère pour peu de chose. Vous n'entendez pas la raillerie galante.[70]

MELANTHA.

À d'autres, à d'autres. He mocks himself of me; he abuses me. Ah me unfortunate! (*Cries!*)

PHILOTIS.

You mistake him, madam. He does but accommodate his phrase to your refined language. *Ah, qu'il est un cavalier accompli!* (*To him.*) Pursue your point, sir.

PALAMEDE. (*Singing.*)

Ah, qu'il fait beau dans ces boccages;
Ah que le ciel donne un beau jour![71]
There I was with you, with a *menuet.*

MELANTHA. (*Laughs.*)

Let me die now, but this singing is fine and extremely French in him. (*Crying.*) But then, that he should use my own words as it were in contempt of me, I cannot bear it.

PALAMEDE. (*Singing.*)

Ces beaux séjours, ces doux ramages—

MELANTHA. (*Singing after him.*)

Ces beaux séjours, ces doux ramages,
Ces beaux séjours, nous invitent à l'amour![72]
(*Laughing.*)
Let me die, but he sings *en cavalier*, and so humors the cadence.

PALAMEDE. (*Singing again.*)

Vois, ma Climène, vois sous ce chêne,
S'entrebaiser ces oiseaux amoureux![73]
Let me die now, but that was fine. Ah, now for three or four brisk Frenchmen, to be put into masking habits and to sing it on a theater, how witty it would be! and then to dance helter skelter to a *chanson à boire: toute la terre, toute la terre est a moi!*[74] What's matter though it were made and sung two or three years ago in cabarets. How it would attract the admiration, especially of every one that's an *éveillé!*[75]

MELANTHA.

Well I begin to have a tender for you, but yet upon condition that—when we are married, you—

PHILOTIS. [*To Palamede.*]

You must drown her voice. If she makes her French conditions, you are a slave forever.

Palamede sings, while she speaks.

MELANTHA.

First you will engage that—

PALAMEDE. (*Louder.*)

Fa, la, la, la, etc.

MELANTHA.

Will you hear the conditions?

PALAMEDE.

No, I will hear no conditions! I am resolved to win you *en français*: to be very airy, with abundance of noise and no sense. Fa, la, la, la, etc.

MELANTHA.

Hold, hold. I am vanquished with your *gaieté d'esprit.* I am yours and will be yours *sans nulle réservé, ni condition.* And let me die, if I do not think myself the happiest nymph in Sicily. My dear French dear, stay but a *minute,* till I *raccommode* myself with the Princess, and then I am yours *jusqu'à la mort.—Allons donc.*[76]

Exeunt Melantha, Philotis.

PALAMEDE. (*Fanning himself with his hat.*)

I never thought before that wooing was so laborious an exercise. If she were worth a million, I have deserved her. And now, methinks too, with taking all this pains for her I begin to like her. 'Tis so. I have known many who never cared for hare nor partridge but those they caught themselves would eat heartily. The pains, the story a man tells of the taking of 'em, makes the meat go down more pleasantly. Besides, last night I had a sweet dream of her, and Gad, she

70 *Radoucissez ... galante*] Please calm yourself, madam; you've worked yourself into a rage over nothing. You don't understand gallant raillery.

71 *Ah, qu'il...beau jour!*] Ah, how lovely the weather in these thickets: Heaven grants a beautiful day (a song from Molière's *Le Bourgeois gentilhomme*).

72 *Ces beaux ... l'amour*] These beautiful abodes, these gentle birdsongs, these sweet abodes invite us both to love (same song from Molière).

73 *Vois ... amoreux*] See, my Climene, see under the oak the amorous birds coupling (another song from the same play).

74 *Chanson ... moi*] a drinking song: All of the earth, all of the earth is mine.

75 *éveillé*] sharp, bright, alert person

76 *jusqu'à ... donc*] until death.—Let's go, then

I have once dreamed of I am stark mad till I enjoy her, let her be never* so ugly.

Enter Doralice.

DORALICE.
Who's that you are so mad to enjoy, Palamede?

PALAMEDE.
You may easily imagine that, sweet Doralice.

DORALICE.
More easily than you think I can. I met just now with a certain man who came to you with letters from a certain old gentleman, yclept your father, whereby I am given to understand that tomorrow you are to take an oath in the church to be grave henceforward, to go ill-dressed and slovenly, to get heirs for your estate, and to dandle 'em for your diversion, and in short, that love and courtship are to be no more.

PALAMEDE.
Now have I so much shame to be thus apprehended in the manner that I can neither speak nor look upon you. I have abundance of grace in me, that I find. But if you have any spark of true friendship in you, retire a little with me to the next room that has a couch or bed in't and bestow your charity upon a poor dying man. A little comfort from a mistress before a man is going to give himself in marriage is as good as a lusty dose of strong water to a dying malefactor: it takes away the sense of hell and hanging from him.

DORALICE.
No good Palamede, I must not be so injurious to your bride. 'Tis ill drawing from the bank today when all your ready money is payable tomorrow.

PALAMEDE.
A wife is only to have the ripe fruit that falls of itself, but a wise man will always preserve a shaking for a mistress.

DORALICE.
But a wife for the first quarter is a mistress.

PALAMEDE.
But when the second comes—

DORALICE.
When it does come, you are so given to variety that you would make a wife of me in another quarter.

PALAMEDE.
No, never, except I were married to you. Married people can never oblige one another, for all they do is duty, and consequently there can be no thanks. But love is more frank and generous than he is honest. He's a liberal giver, but a cursèd paymaster.

DORALICE.
I declare I will have no gallant. But if I would, he should never be a married man. A married man is but a mistress's half-servant as a clergyman is but the King's half-subject. For a man to come to me that smells o'th'wife! 'Slife,* I would as soon wear her old gown after her as her husband.

PALAMEDE.
Yet 'tis a kind of fashion to wear a princess's cast* shoes. You see the country ladies buy 'em to be fine in them.

DORALICE.
Yes, a princess's shoes may be worn after her because they keep their fashion by being so little used. But generally a married man is the creature of the world the most out of fashion. His behavior is dumpish, his discourse his wife and family, his habit so much neglected it looks as if that were married too. His hat is married, his peruke is married, his breeches are married, and if we could look within his breeches, we should find him married there too.

PALAMEDE.
Am I then to be discarded forever? Pray do but mark how terrible that word sounds. Forever! It has a very damned sound, Doralice.

DORALICE.
Aye, forever! It sounds as hellishly to me as it can do to you, but there's no help for't.

PALAMEDE.
Yet if we had but once enjoyed one another—but then once only is worse than not at all. It leaves a man with such a lingering after it.

DORALICE.
For aught I know 'tis better that we have not. We might upon trial have liked each other less, as many a man and woman that have loved as desperately as we and yet, when they came to possession, have sighed and cried to themselves "Is this all?"

PALAMEDE.
That is only if the servant* were not found a man of this world. But if upon trial we had not liked each other, we had certainly left loving, and faith, that's the greater happiness of the two.

DORALICE.
'Tis better as 'tis. We have drawn off already as much of our love as would run clear; after possessing, the rest is but jealousies and disquiets and quarreling and piecing.[77]

PALAMEDE.
Nay, after one great quarrel there's never any sound piecing; the love is apt to break in the same place again.

DORALICE.
I declare I would never renew a love; that's like him who trims an old coach for ten years together. He might buy a new one better cheap.

PALAMEDE.
Well madam, I am convinced that 'tis best for us not to have enjoyed. But Gad, the strongest reason is because I can't help it.

DORALICE.
The only way to keep us new to one another is never to enjoy, as they keep grapes by hanging 'em upon a line. They must touch nothing if you would preserve 'em fresh.

PALAMEDE.
But then they wither and grow dry in the very keeping. However, I shall have a warmth for you and an eagerness every time I see you, and if I chance to outlive Melantha—

DORALICE.
And if I chance to outlive Rhodophil—

PALAMEDE.
Well, I'll cherish my body as much as I can upon that hope. 'Tis true, I would not directly murder the wife of my bosom, but to kill her civilly, by the way of kindness,* I'll put[78] as fair as another man. I'll begin tomorrow night and be very wrathful with her, that's resolved on.

DORALICE.
Well Palamede, here's my hand: I'll venture to be your second wife for all your threatenings.

PALAMEDE.
In the meantime I'll watch you hourly, as I would the ripeness of a melon, and I hope you'll give me leave now and then to look on you and to see if you are not ready to be cut yet.

[77] piecing] making up, making peace

[78] put] exert myself, thrust (as a weapon)

DORALICE.
No, no, that must not be, Palamede, for fear the gardener should come and catch you taking up the glass.[79]

Enter Rhodophil.

RHODOPHIL. (*Aside.*)
Billing so sweetly! Now I am confirmed in my suspicions. I must put an end to this, ere it go further. (*Aside to Doralice.*) Cry you mercy, Spouse, I fear I have interrupted your recreations.

DORALICE.
What recreations?

RHODOPHIL.
Nay, no excuses, good Spouse. I saw fair hand conveyed to lip and pressed, as though you had been squeezing soft wax together for an indenture. Palamede, you and I must clear this reckoning. Why would you have seduced my wife?

PALAMEDE.
Why would you have debauched my mistress?

RHODOPHIL.
What do you think of that civil couple that played at a game called "Hide and Seek" last evening in the grotto?

PALAMEDE.
What do you think of that innocent pair who made it their pretense to seek for others but came, indeed, to hide themselves there?

RHODOPHIL.
All things considered, I begin vehemently to suspect that the young gentleman I found in your company last night was a certain youth of my acquaintance.

PALAMEDE.
And I have an odd imagination that you could never have suspected my small gallant if your little villainous Frenchman had not been a false brother.

RHODOPHIL.
Farther arguments are needless. Draw off, I shall speak to you now by the way of Bilbo. (*Claps his hand to his sword.*)

PALAMEDE.
And I shall answer you by the way of Dangerfield.[80] (*Claps his hand on his.*)

[79] glass] a protective covering for a young plant

[80] Dangerfield] a sword-carrying bully

DORALICE.

Hold, hold, are not you two a couple of mad, fighting fools to cut one another's throats for nothing?

PALAMEDE.

How, for nothing? He courts the woman I must marry.

RHODOPHIL.

And he courts you whom I have married.

DORALICE.

But you can neither of you be jealous of what you love not.

RHODOPHIL.

Faith I am jealous, and that makes me partly suspect that I love you better then I thought.

DORALICE.

Pish! a mere jealousy of honor.

RHODOPHIL.

Gad I am afraid there's something else in't, for Palamede has wit, and if he loves you, there's something more in ye than I have found, some rich mine, for aught I know, that I have not yet discovered.

PALAMEDE.

'Slife,* what's this? Here's an argument for me to love Melantha, for he has loved her, and he has wit too, and for aught I know, there may be a mine. But if there be, I am resolved I'll dig for't.

DORALICE. (*To Rhodophil.*)

Then I have found my account in raising your jealousy. Oh! 'Tis the most delicate sharp sauce to a cloyed stomach; it will give you a new edge, Rhodophil.

RHODOPHIL.

And a new point too, Doralice, if I could be sure thou art honest.*

DORALICE.

If you are wise, believe me for your own sake. Love and religion have but one thing to trust to: that's a good sound faith. Consider, if I have played false, you can never find it out by any experiment you can make upon me.

RHODOPHIL.

No? Why, suppose I had a delicate screwed gun. If I left her clean and found her foul, I should discover to my cost she had been shot in.

DORALICE.

But if you left her clean and found her only rusty, you would discover to your shame she was only so for want* of shooting.

PALAMEDE.

Rhodophil, you know me too well to imagine I speak for fear, and therefore, in consideration of our past friendship, I will tell you and bind it by all things holy that Doralice is innocent.

RHODOPHIL.

Friend, I will believe you and vow the same for your Melantha. But the devil on't is, how we shall keep 'em so.

PALAMEDE.

What dost think of a blessed community betwixt us four for the solace of the women and relief of the men? Methinks it would be a pleasant kind of life: wife and husband for the standing dish and mistress and gallant for the dessert.

RHODOPHIL.

But suppose the wife and the mistress should both long for the standing dish? How should they be satisfied together?

PALAMEDE.

In such a case they must draw lots. And yet that would not do neither, for they would both be wishing for the longest cut.[d]

RHODOPHIL.

Then I think, Palamede, we had as good make a firm league not to invade each others' propriety.

PALAMEDE.

Content, say I. From henceforth let all acts of hostility cease betwixt us, and that in the usual form of treaties, as well by sea as by land, and in all fresh waters.

DORALICE.

I will add but one proviso: that whoever breaks the league, either by war abroad or by neglect at home, both the women shall revenge themselves by the help of the other party.

RHODOPHIL.

That's but reasonable. Come away, Doralice, I have a great temptation to be sealing articles in private.

PALAMEDE. (*Claps him on the shoulder.*)

Hast thou so? Fall on Macduff, And curst be he that first cries, "Hold, enough."[81]

---

[81] Fall on ... enough] slight misquotation of Macbeth's challenge in Act 5 of Shakespeare's *Macbeth*

Enter Polydamas, Palmyra, Artemis, Argaleon; after them Eubulus and Hermogenes, guarded.

PALMYRA.
Sir, on my knees I beg you.
POLYDAMAS.
Away, I'll hear no more.
PALMYRA.
For my dead mother's sake; you say you loved her,
And tell me I resemble her. Thus she
Had begged.
POLYDAMAS.
And thus had I denied her.
PALMYRA.
You must be merciful.
ARGALEON.
You must be constant.
POLYDAMAS.
Go, bear 'em to the torture.—You have boasted
You have a king to head you. I would know
To whom I must resign.
EUBULUS.
This is our recompense
For serving thy dead queen.
HERMOGENES.
And education
Of thy daughter.
ARGALEON.
You are too modest in not naming all
His obligations to you. Why did you
Omit his son, the Prince Leonidas?
POLYDAMAS.
That imposture
I had forgot; their tortures shall be doubled.
HERMOGENES.
You please me; I shall die the sooner.
EUBULUS.
No, could I live an age and still be racked,
I still would keep the secret.

As they are going off, enter Leonidas, guarded.

LEONIDAS.
Oh whither do you hurry innocence?
If you have any justice, spare their lives,
Or if I cannot make you just, at least
I'll teach you to more purpose to be cruel.
PALMYRA.
Alas, what does he seek!
LEONIDAS.
Make me the object of your hate and vengeance!
Are these decrepit bodies, worn to ruin,
Just ready of themselves to fall asunder
And to let drop the soul,
Are these fit subjects for a rack and tortures?
Where would you fasten any hold upon 'em?
Place pains on me, united fix 'em here.
I have both youth and strength and soul to bear 'em.
And if they merit death, then I much more,
Since 'tis for me they suffer.
HERMOGENES.
Heav'n forbid
We should redeem our pains or worthless lives
By our exposing yours.
EUBULUS.
Away with us.—Farewell, sir.
I only suffer in my fears for you.
ARGALEON. (*Aside.*)
So much concerned for him? Then my
Suspicion's true. (*Whispers the King.*)
PALMYRA.
Hear yet my last request for poor Leonidas,
Or take my life with his.
ARGALEON. (*To the King.*)
Rest satisfied: Leonidas is he.
POLYDAMAS.
I am amazed. What must be done?
ARGALEON.
Command his execution instantly;
Give him not leisure to discover* it;
He may corrupt the soldiers.
POLYDAMAS.
Hence with that traitor, bear him to his death.
Haste there, and see my will performed.
LEONIDAS.
Nay, then I'll die like him the gods have made me.
Hold, gentlemen, I am— (*Argaleon stops his mouth.*)
ARGALEON.
Thou art a traitor; 'tis not fit to hear thee.
LEONIDAS. (*Getting loose a little.*)
I say I am the—
ARGALEON. (*Again stopping his mouth.*)
So, gag him, and lead him off.

Leonidas, Hermogenes, Eubulus, led off. Polydamas and Argaleon follow.

PALMYRA.
  Duty and love by turns possess my soul
  And struggle for a fatal victory.
  I will discover* he's the King. Ah no,
  That will perhaps save him,
  But then I am guilty of a father's ruin.
  What shall I do or not do? Either way
  I must destroy a parent or a lover.
  Break, heart, for that's the least of ills to me,
  And death the only cure. (*Swoons.*)
ARTEMIS.
  Help, help the Princess.
RHODOPHIL.
  Bear her gently hence where she may
  Have more succor.

She is born off, Artemis follows her. Shouts within, and clashing of swords.

PALAMEDE.
  What noise is that?

Enter Amalthea, running.

AMALTHEA.
  Oh gentlemen, if you have loyalty
  Or courage, show it now. Leonidas
  Broke on the sudden from his guards and, snatching
  A sword from one, his back against the scaffold,
  Bravely defends himself and owns aloud
  He is our long lost King, found for this moment
  But, if your valors help not, lost forever.
  Two of his guards, moved by the sense of virtue,
  Are turned for him, and there they stand at bay
  Against an host of foes.
RHODOPHIL.
  Madam, no more,
  We lose time. My command or my example
  May move the soldiers to the better cause.
  (*To Palamede.*) You'll second me?
PALAMEDE.
  Or die with you. No subject e'er can meet
  A nobler fate than at his sovereign's feet.

Exeunt. Clashing of swords within, and shouts. Enter Leonidas, Rhodophil, Palamede, Eubulus, Hermogenes, and their party, victorious; Polydamas and Argaleon, disarmed.

LEONIDAS.
  That I survive the dangers of this day,
  Next to the gods, brave friends, be yours the honor.
  And let Heav'n witness for me that my joy
  Is not more great for this my right restored
  Than 'tis that I have power to recompense
  Your loyalty and valor. Let mean* princes
  Of abject souls fear to reward great actions;
  I mean to show,
  That whatsoe'er subjects like you dare merit,
  A king, like me, dares give.
RHODOPHIL.
  You make us blush; we have deserved so little.
PALAMEDE.
  And yet instruct us how to merit more.
LEONIDAS.
  And as I would be just in my rewards,
  So should I in my punishments: these two,
  This the usurper of my crown, the other
  Of my Palmyra's love, deserve that death
  Which both designed for me.
POLYDAMAS.
  And we expect it.
ARGALEON.
  I have too long been happy to live wretched.
POLYDAMAS.
  And I too long have governed to desire
  A life without an empire.
LEONIDAS.
  You are Palmyra's father and as such,
  Though not a king, shall have obedience paid
  From him who is one. Father: in that name
  All injuries forgot and duty owned. (*Embraces him.*)
POLYDAMAS.
  Oh, had I known you could have been this King,
  Thus godlike, great, and good, I should have wished
  T'have been dethroned before. 'Tis now I live
  And more than reign; now all my joys flow pure,
  Unmixed with cares and undisturbed by conscience.

Enter Palmyra, Amalthea, Artemis, Doralice, and Melantha.

LEONIDAS.
  See, my Palmyra comes, the frighted blood
  Scarce yet recalled to her pale cheeks,
  Like the first streaks of light broke loose from
    darkness

And dawning into blushes. (*To Polydamas.*) Sir, you said
Your joys were full. Oh, would you make mine so!
I am but half restored without this blessing.

POLYDAMAS.
The gods, and my Palmyra, make you happy,
As you make me. (*Gives her hand to Leonidas.*)

PALMYRA.
Now all my prayers are heard:
I may be dutiful and yet may love.
Virtue and patience have at length unraveled
The knots which Fortune tied.

MELANTHA.
Let me die but I'll congratulate his majesty. How admirably well his royalty becomes him! Becomes! That is, *lui sied*,[82] but our damned language expresses nothing.

PALAMEDE.
How? Does it become him already? 'Twas but just now you said he was such a figure of a man.

MELANTHA.
True, my dear, when he was a private man, he was a figure, but since he is a king, methinks he has assumed another figure: he looks so grand and so august. (*Going to the King.*)

PALAMEDE.
Stay, stay, I'll present you when it is more convenient. [*Aside.*] I find I must get her a place at court, and when she is once there, she can be no longer ridiculous. For she is young enough and pretty enough and fool enough and French enough to bring up a fashion there to be affected.

LEONIDAS. (*To Rhodophil.*)
Did she then lead you to this brave attempt?
(*To Amalthea.*)
To you, fair Amalthea, what I am,
And what all these, from me, we jointly owe.
First, therefore, to your great desert, we give
Your brother's life but keep him under guard
Till our new power be settled. What more grace
He may receive shall from his future carriage
Be given, as he deserves.

ARGALEON.
I neither now desire nor will deserve it.
My loss is such as cannot be repaired,
And to the wretched, life can be no mercy.

LEONIDAS.
Then be a prisoner always. Thy ill fate
And pride will have it so. But since in this I cannot,
Instruct me, generous* Amalthea, how
A king may serve you.

AMALTHEA.
I have all I hope
And all I now must wish: I see you happy.
Those hours I have to live, which Heav'n in pity
Will make but few, I vow to spend with vestals:
The greatest part in pray'rs for you; the rest
In mourning my unworthiness.
Press me not farther to explain myself;
'Twill not become me and may cause you trouble.

LEONIDAS. (*Aside.*)
Too well I understand her secret grief
But dare not seem to know it. (*To Palmyra.*) Come my fairest,
Beyond my crown I have one joy in store:
To give that crown to her whom I adore.

Exeunt omnes.

FINIS.

Textual Notes

[a] Copytext is the first edition, a 1673 quarto (Q1). Also consulted: the second edition, a 1684 quarto (Q2); the third edition, a 1691 quarto (Q3); the fourth edition, a 1698 edition (Q4); the first collected edition in 1701 (C1); the second collected edition (Congreve's—C2); and modern editions of 1967 (Beaurline and Bowers—BB), of 1981 (Auburn), and of 1978 (California Edition—CE).

[b] consider,] C1, BB, Auburn; consider Q1-4, C2, CE

[c] LEONIDAS] C1, BB, Auburn, CE; *om.* Q1-4, C2

[d] cut] C1, BB, Auburn, CE; out Q1-4, C2

82 *lui sied*] It becomes him.

The Country Wife[a]

by William Wycherley (1641-1715)

edited by Peggy Thompson

William Wycherley was an aspiring courtier, occasional soldier, and Shropshire heir, whose long life was marred by illness, debt, litigation, and two controversial marriages. At the time he wrote *The Country Wife* (1675), however, he enjoyed the friendship of the Court wits, the admiration of the Court ladies, and the fondness of the King himself. The third of Wycherley's four comedies for the stage, *The Country Wife* was first performed by the King's Company at the Theatre Royal, Drury Lane, probably on January 12, 1675. It featured several original members of the company, including Charles Hart as the deceptive, self-serving Horner, a role that contrasted ironically with the many heroic and tragic parts Hart had previously played. Elizabeth Boutell played Margery Pinchwife, one of the breeches roles for which she was famous and which, with the introduction of actresses after the Restoration, had assumed new significance by publicly exposing the shape of a woman's legs.

The importance of *The Country Wife* in the history of dramatic literature is suggested by both the extensive praise it received for its wit and the increasing censure it incurred for its licentiousness. The play was moderately successful on the stage through the mid-eighteenth century. But it was controversial almost immediately, as evidenced by Wycherley's next play, *The Plain Dealer* (1676), which features a discussion of the offending "china scene." In 1753, *The Country Wife* disappeared from the stage, replaced a few years later by two radical adaptations which claimed to have excised the impropriety of the original: a two-act afterpiece by John Lee (1765) and a full-length play, *The Country Girl*, by David Garrick (1766). Both eliminated what scholars have long seen as the vital center of the play, Horner's character and the Fidget-Squeamish plot of lust and deception. Although Wycherley's own comedy did not reappear on the English stage until 1924, *The Country Wife*, together with *The Plain Dealer*, eventually secured his reputation as a powerful comedic and satiric dramatist.

DRAMATIS PERSONAE

[Men]

Mr. Horner.
Mr. Harcourt.
Mr. Dorilant.
Mr. Pinchwife.
Mr. Sparkish.
Sir Jaspar Fidget.
A boy.
[Dr.] Quack.
[Clasp, a bookseller.]
[A parson.]
Waiters, servants, and attendants.

[Women]

Mrs. Margery Pinchwife.
Mrs.* Alithea.
My Lady Fidget.
Mrs.* Dainty Fidget.
Mrs.* Squeamish.
Old Lady Squeamish.
Lucy, Alithea's maid.

The Scene: London.

The Country Wife.

Indignor quicquam reprehendi, non quia crasse
Compositum illepideve putetur, sed quia nuper,
Nec veniam antiquis, sed honorem et praemia posci.
Horat.[1]

Act I. [Horner's lodging.]

Enter Horner and Quack following him at a distance.

HORNER. (*Aside.*)
A quack is as fit for a pimp as a midwife for a bawd; they are still but in their way both helpers of nature.—Well my dear doctor, hast thou done what I desired?

QUACK.
I have undone you forever with the women and reported you throughout the whole Town* as bad as an eunuch with as much trouble as if I had made you one in earnest.

HORNER.
But have you told all the midwives you know, the orange wenches* at the playhouses, the City* husbands, and old fumbling keepers* of this end of the Town? For they'll be the readiest to report it.

QUACK.
I have told all the chambermaids, waiting women, tirewomen,[2] and old women of my acquaintance, nay, and whispered it as a secret to 'em and to the whisperers of Whitehall,* so that you need not doubt 'twill spread, and you will be as odious to the handsome young women as—

HORNER.
As the small pox. Well—

QUACK.
And to the married women of this end of the Town as—

HORNER.
As the great ones,[3] nay, as their own husbands.

QUACK.
And to the City dames as Aniseed Robin[4] of filthy and contemptible memory, and they will frighten their children with your name, especially their females.

HORNER.
And cry, "Horner's coming to carry you away!" I am only afraid 'twill not be believed. You told 'em 'twas by an English-French disaster and an English-French chirurgeon,[5] who has given me at once, not only a cure, but an antidote for the future against that damned malady and that worse distemper, love, and all other women's evils.

QUACK.
Your late journey into France has made it the more

1 *Indignor* … Horat.] Horace, *Epistles* II.i.76-78: "I am impatient that any work is censured, not because it is thought to be coarse or inelegant in style, but because it is modern, and that what is claimed for the ancients should be, not indulgence, but honour and rewards" (Loeb).

2 tirewomen] ladies' maids in charge of attire

3 the great ones] the great (or French) pox, i.e., syphilis

4 Aniseed Robin] a notorious hermaphrodite

5 English-French disaster … English-French chirurgeon] a French pox caught by an Englishman, treated by an English doctor practicing in France

credible, and your being here a fortnight before you appeared in public looks as if you apprehended the shame, which I wonder you do not. Well, I have been hired by young gallants to belie 'em t'other way, but you are the first would be thought a man unfit for women.

HORNER.
Dear Mr. Doctor, let vain rogues be contented only to be thought abler men than they are; generally 'tis all the pleasure they have, but mine lies another way.

QUACK.
You take, methinks, a very preposterous way to it and as ridiculous as if we operators in physic should put forth bills to disparage our medicaments with hopes to gain customers.

HORNER.
Doctor, there are quacks in love as well as physic who get but the fewer and worse patients for their boasting; a good name is seldom got by giving it one's self, and women no more than honor are compassed by bragging. Come, come, doctor, the wisest lawyer never discovers* the merits of his cause till the trial; the wealthiest man conceals his riches, and the cunning gamester his play; shy husbands and keepers,* like old rooks,* are not to be cheated but by a new unpracticed trick: false friendship will pass now no more than false dice upon 'em, no, not in the City.

Enter boy.

BOY.
There are two ladies and a gentleman coming up.

HORNER.
A pox! some unbelieving sisters of my former acquaintance, who, I am afraid, expect their sense should be satisfied of the falsity of the report.

Enter Sir Jaspar Fidget, Lady Fidget, and Dainty.

No—this formal fool and women!

QUACK.
His wife and sister.

SIR JASPAR.
My coach breaking just now before your door, sir, I look upon as an occasional[6] reprimand to me, sir, for not kissing your hands, sir, since your coming out of France, sir, and so my disaster, sir, has been my good fortune, sir, and this is my wife and sister, sir.

[6] occasional] timely, arising from the occasion

HORNER.
What then, sir?

SIR JASPAR.
My lady and sister, sir.—Wife, this is Master Horner.

LADY FIDGET.
Master Horner, husband!

SIR JASPAR.
My lady, my Lady Fidget, sir.

HORNER.
So, sir.

SIR JASPAR.
Won't you be acquainted with her, sir? (*Aside.*) So the report is true, I find by his coldness or aversion to the sex, but I'll play the wag with him.—Pray salute* my wife, my lady, sir.

HORNER.
I will kiss no man's wife, sir, for him, sir; I have taken my eternal leave, sir, of the sex already, sir.

SIR JASPAR. (*Aside.*)
Ha, ha, ha, I'll plague him yet.—Not know my wife, sir?

HORNER.
I do know your wife, sir: she's a woman, sir, and consequently a monster, sir, a greater monster than a husband, sir.

SIR JASPAR.
A husband! How, sir?

HORNER. (*Makes horns.**)
So, sir. But I make no more cuckholds, sir.

SIR JASPAR.
Ha, ha, ha, Mercury, Mercury.[7]

LADY FIDGET.
Pray Sir Jaspar, let us be gone from this rude fellow.

DAINTY.
Who, by his breeding, would think he had ever been in France?

LADY FIDGET.
Faugh, he's but too much a French fellow, such as

[7] Mercury] god associated with wit (who wears a hat with wings resembling cuckold's horns); also, substance used to treat venereal disease

hate women of quality* and virtue for their love to their husbands, Sir Jaspar; a woman is hated by 'em as much for loving her husband as for loving their money. But pray, let's be gone.

HORNER.
You do well, madam, for I have nothing that you came for. I have brought over not so much as a bawdy picture, new postures,* nor the second part of the *Ecole des filles*,[8] nor—

QUACK. (*Apart to Horner.*)
Hold for shame, sir. What d'ye mean? You'll ruin yourself forever with the sex.

SIR JASPAR.
Ha, ha, ha, he hates women perfectly, I find.

DAINTY.
What pity 'tis he should.

LADY FIDGET.
Aye, he's a base rude fellow for it, but affectation makes not a woman more odious to them than virtue.

HORNER.
Because your virtue is your greatest affectation, madam.

LADY FIDGET.
How, you saucy fellow, would you wrong my honor?

HORNER.
If I could.

LADY FIDGET.
How d'ye mean, sir?

SIR JASPAR.
Ha, ha, ha, no, he can't wrong your ladyship's honor, upon my honor; he, poor man—hark you in your ear—a mere eunuch.

LADY FIDGET.
Oh filthy French beast! Faugh, faugh! Why do we stay? Let's be gone; I can't endure the sight of him.

SIR JASPAR.
Stay but till the chairs* come; they'll be here presently.

LADY FIDGET.
No, no.

SIR JASPAR.
Nor can I stay longer: 'tis—let me see, a quarter and a half quarter of a minute past eleven; the Council[9] will be sat; I must away. Business must be preferred always before love and ceremony with the wise, Mr. Horner.

HORNER.
And the impotent, Sir Jaspar.

SIR JASPAR.
Aye, aye, the impotent Master Horner, ha, ha, ha!

LADY FIDGET.
What, leave us with a filthy man alone in his lodgings?

SIR JASPAR.
He's an innocent man now, you know. Pray stay, I'll hasten the chairs to you.—Mr.Horner, your servant. I should be glad to see you at my house. Pray, come and dine with me and play at cards with my wife after dinner; you are fit for women at that game yet, ha, ha! (*Aside.*) 'Tis as much a husband's prudence to provide innocent diversion for a wife as to hinder her unlawful pleasures, and he had better employ her than let her employ herself.—Farewell. (*Exit.*)

HORNER.
Your servant, Sir Jaspar.

LADY FIDGET.
I will not stay with him, faugh!

HORNER.
Nay madam, I beseech you stay, if it be but to see I can be as civil to ladies yet as they would desire.

LADY FIDGET.
No, no, faugh, you cannot be civil to ladies.

DAINTY.
You as civil as ladies would desire!

LADY FIDGET.
No, no, no, faugh, faugh, faugh!

Exeunt Lady Fidget and Dainty.

QUACK.
Now I think, I, or you yourself rather, have done your business with the women.

HORNER.
Thou art an ass. Don't you see already upon the

[8] *Ecole des filles*] notoriously bawdy dialogues by Michel Millot (1655); the "second part," like the "new postures," was nonexistent

[9] Council] the Privy Council, the King's advisory body

report and my carriage, this grave man of business leaves his wife in my lodgings, invites me to his house and wife, who before would not be acquainted with me out of jealousy?

QUACK.

Nay, by this means you may be the more acquainted with the husbands, but the less with the wives.

HORNER.

Let me alone; if I can but abuse the husbands, I'll soon disabuse the wives. Stay—I'll reckon you up the advantages I am like to have by my strategem: first, I shall be rid of all my old acquaintances, the most insatiable sorts of duns that invade our lodgings in a morning. And next to the pleasure of making a new mistress is that of being rid of an old one and of all old debts: love, when it comes to be so, is paid the most unwillingly.

QUACK.

Well, you may be so rid of your old acquaintances, but how will you get any new ones?

HORNER.

Doctor, thou wilt never make a good chemist,[10] thou art so incredulous and impatient. Ask but all the young fellows of the Town if they do not lose more time, like huntsmen, in starting the game than in running it down; one knows not where to find 'em, who will or will not. Women of quality* are so civil, you can hardly distinguish love from good breeding, and a man is often mistaken. But now I can be sure, she that shows an aversion to me loves the sport, as those women that are gone, whom I warrant to be right. And then the next thing is, your* women of honor, as you call 'em, are only chary of their reputations, not their persons, and 'tis scandal they would avoid, not men. Now may I have by the reputation of an eunuch the privileges of one and be seen in a lady's chamber in a morning as early as her husband, kiss virgins before their parents or lovers, and may be, in short, the passe-partout of the Town. Now, doctor.

QUACK.

Nay, now you shall be the doctor, and your process is so new that we do not know but it may succeed.

[10] chemist] alchemist, who needs both credulity and patience to see his projection through

HORNER.

Not so new neither: *probatum est*,* doctor.

QUACK.

Well, I wish you luck and many patients whilst I go to mine. (*Exit.*)

Enter Harcourt and Dorilant to Horner.

HARCOURT.

Come, your appearance at the play yesterday has, I hope, hardened you for the future against the women's contempt and the men's raillery, and now you'll abroad as you were wont.

HORNER.

Did I not bear it bravely?*

DORILANT.

With a most theatrical impudence, nay, more than the orange wenches show there or a drunken vizard mask* or a great bellied actress, nay, or the most impudent of creatures, an ill poet, or what is yet more impudent, a second-hand critic.

HORNER.

But what say the ladies? Have they no pity?

HARCOURT.

What ladies? The vizard masks, you know, never pity a man when all's gone though in their service.

DORILANT.

And for the women in the boxes, you'd never pity them when 'twas in your power.

HARCOURT.

They say 'tis pity, but all that deal with common women should be served so.

DORILANT.

Nay I dare swear, they won't admit you to play at cards with them, go to plays with 'em, or do the little duties which other shadows of men are wont to do for 'em.

HORNER.

Who do you call shadows of men?

DORILANT.

Half men.

HORNER.

What, boys?

DORILANT.

Aye, your old boys, old *beaux garçons*,[11] who like

[11] *beaux garçons*] fops (literally, pretty boys [Fr.])

superannuated stallions are suffered to run, feed, and whinny with the mares as long as they live, though they can do nothing else.

HORNER.

Well, a pox on love and wenching; women serve but to keep a man from better company. Though I can't enjoy them, I shall you the more. Good fellowship and friendship are lasting, rational, and manly pleasures.

HARCOURT.

For all that, give me some of those pleasures you call effeminate, too; they help to relish one another.

HORNER.

They disturb one another.

HARCOURT.

No, mistresses are like books: if you pore upon them too much, they doze you and make you unfit for company, but if used discreetly, you are the fitter for conversation* by 'em.

DORILANT.

A mistress should be like a little country retreat near the Town, not to dwell in constantly but only for a night and away, to taste the Town the better when a man returns.

HORNER.

I tell you, 'tis as hard to be a good fellow, a good friend, and a lover of women as 'tis to be a good fellow, a good friend, and a lover of money. You cannot follow both; then choose your side. Wine gives you liberty; love takes it away.

DORILANT.

Gad, he's in the right on't.

HORNER.

Wine gives you joy; love, grief and tortures, besides the chirurgeon's. Wine makes us witty; love, only sots.* Wine makes us sleep; love breaks it.

DORILANT.

By the world, he has reason, Harcourt.

HORNER.

Wine makes—

DORILANT.

Aye, wine makes us—makes us princes; love makes us beggars, poor rogues, egad—and wine—

HORNER.

So, there's one converted.—No, no, love and wine, oil and vinegar.

HARCOURT.

I grant it: love will still* be uppermost.

HORNER.

Come, for my part I will have only those glorious manly pleasures of being very drunk and very slovenly.

Enter boy.

BOY.

Mr. Sparkish is below, sir.

HARCOURT.

What, my dear friend! a rogue that is fond of me only, I think, for abusing him.

DORILANT.

No, he can no more think the men laugh at him than that women jilt him, his opinion of himself is so good.

HORNER.

Well, there's another pleasure by drinking, I thought not of: I shall lose his acquaintance because he cannot drink, and you know 'tis a very hard thing to be rid of him, for he's one of those nauseous offerers at wit who, like the worst fiddlers, run themselves into all companies.

HARCOURT.

One that by being in the company of men of sense would pass for one.

HORNER.

And may so to the short-sighted world, as a false jewel amongst true ones is not discerned at a distance; his company is as troublesome to us as a cuckold's when you have a mind to his wife's.

HARCOURT.

No, the rogue will not let us enjoy one another, but ravishes our conversation, though he signifies no more to't than Sir Martin Mar-all's[12] gaping and awkward thrumming upon the lute does to his man's voice and music.

DORILANT.

And to pass for a wit in Town shows himself a fool every night to us that are guilty of the plot.

12 Sir Martin Mar-all] foolish hero of Dryden's play of that name (1667), who mimes a serenade to his mistress even after his hidden servant has stopped singing and playing his lute

HORNER.

Such wits as he are, to a company of reasonable men, like rooks[13] to the gamesters, who only fill a room at the table but are so far from contributing to the play that they only serve to spoil the fancy of those that do.

DORILANT.

Nay, they are used like rooks, too—snubbed, checked, and abused—yet the rogues will hang on.

HORNER.

A pox on 'em and all that force Nature and would be still what she forbids 'em; affectation is her greatest monster.

HARCOURT.

Most men are the contraries to that they would seem: your bully, you see, is a coward with a long sword; the little humbly fawning physician with his ebony cane is he that destroys men.

DORILANT.

The usurer, a poor rogue possessed of moldy bonds and mortgages, and we they call spendthrifts are only wealthy who lay out his money upon daily new purchases of pleasure.

HORNER.

Aye, your arrantest cheat is your trustee or executor; your jealous man, the greatest cuckold; your churchman, the greatest atheist; and your noisy pert rogue of a wit, the greatest fop, dullest ass, and worst company, as you shall see. For here he comes.

Enter Sparkish to them.

SPARKISH.

How is't, sparks, how is't? Well faith, Harry, I must rally thee a little, ha, ha, ha, upon the report in Town of thee, ha, ha, ha. I can't hold i'faith. Shall I speak?

HORNER.

Yes, but you'll be so bitter then.

SPARKISH.

Honest Dick and Frank here shall answer for me; I will not be extreme bitter, by the universe.

HARCOURT.

We will be bound in ten thousand pound bond, he shall not be bitter at all.

DORILANT.

Nor sharp, nor sweet.

HORNER.

What, not downright insipid?

SPARKISH.

Nay then, since you are so brisk and provoke me, take what follows: you must know, I was discoursing and rallying with some ladies yesterday, and they happened to talk of the fine new signs in Town.

HORNER.

Very fine ladies, I believe.

SPARKISH.

Said I, "I know where the best new sign is." "Where?" says one of the ladies. "In Covent Garden,*" I replied. Said another, "In what street?" "In Russell Street," answered I. "Lord," says another, "I'm sure there was ne'er a fine new sign there yesterday." "Yes, but there was," said I again, "and it came out of France and has been there a fortnight."

DORILANT.

A pox, I can hear no more, prithee.

HORNER.

No, hear him out; let him tune his crowd* a while.

HARCOURT.

The worst music, the greatest preparation.

SPARKISH.

Nay faith, I'll make you laugh. "It cannot be," says a third lady. "Yes, yes," quoth I again. Says a fourth lady—

HORNER.

Look to't, we'll have no more ladies.

SPARKISH.

No? Then mark, mark, now. Said I to the fourth, "Did you never see Mr. Horner? He lodges in Russell Street, and he's a sign of a man, you know, since he came out of France." He, ha, he!

HORNER.

But the devil take me if thine be the sign of a jest.

SPARKISH.

With that they all fell a-laughing till they bepissed themselves. What, but it does not move you, methinks? Well, I see one had as good go to law without a witness as break a jest without a laugher on one's side.—Come, come, sparks, but where do we dine? I have left at Whitehall an earl to dine with you.

---

13 rooks] here gulls or foolish victims, rather than the more common meaning, tricksters or cheaters

DORILANT.
Why, I thought thou hadst loved a man with a title better than a suit with a French trimming to't.

HARCOURT.
Go, to him again.

SPARKISH.
No sir, a wit to me is the greatest title in the world.

HORNER.
But go dine with your earl, sir; he may be exceptious. We are your friends and will not take it ill to be left, I do assure you.

HARCOURT.
Nay, faith he shall go to him.

SPARKISH.
Nay, pray gentlemen.

DORILANT.
We'll thrust you out if you wonnot. What, disappoint anybody for us?

SPARKISH.
Nay, dear gentlemen, hear me.

HORNER.
No, no, sir, by no means; pray go, sir.

SPARKISH.
Why, dear rogues—

DORILANT.
No, no.

They all thrust him out of the room.

ALL.
Ha, ha, ha.

Sparkish returns.

SPARKISH.
But sparks, pray hear me. What, d'ye think I'll eat then with gay shallow fops and silent coxcombs? I think wit as necessary at dinner as a glass of good wine, and that's the reason I never have any stomach when I eat alone. Come, but where do we dine?

HORNER.
Ev'n where you will.

SPARKISH.
At Chateline's.[14]

DORILANT.
Yes, if you will.

SPARKISH.
Or at the Cock.[15]

DORILANT.
Yes, if you please.

SPARKISH.
Or at the Dog and Partridge.[16]

HORNER.
Aye, if you have a mind to't, for we shall dine at neither.

SPARKISH.
Pshaw, with your fooling we shall lose the new play, and I would no more miss seeing a new play the first day than I would miss sitting in the wits' row[17]; therefore, I'll go fetch my mistress and away. (*Exit.*)

Enter Pinchwife.

HORNER.
Who have we here, Pinchwife?

PINCHWIFE.
Gentlemen, your humble servant.

HORNER.
Well Jack, by thy long absence from the Town, the grumness[18] of thy countenance, and the slovenliness of thy habit, I should give thee joy, should I not, of marriage?

PINCHWIFE. (*Aside.*)
Death, does he know I'm married, too? I thought to have concealed it from him at least.—My long stay in the country will excuse my dress, and I have a suit of law that brings me up to Town that puts me out of humor; besides, I must give Sparkish tomorrow five thousand pound to lie with my sister.

HORNER.
Nay, you country gentlemen, rather than not purchase, will buy anything, and he is a cracked

---

14 Chateline's] fashionable French restaurant in Covent Garden*

15 the Cock] Out of many taverns by that name, this probably refers to a less fashionable one in Bow Street, Covent Garden, frequented by Wycherley.

16 the Dog and Partridge] an unfashionable tavern in Fleet Street

17 wits' row] near the front of the theater pit

18 grumness] moroseness, gloominess

title,[19] if we may quibble. Well, but am I to give thee joy? I heard thou wert married.

PINCHWIFE.
What then?

HORNER.
Why, the next thing that is to be heard is thou'rt a cuckold.

PINCHWIFE. (*Aside.*)
Insupportable name.

HORNER.
But I did not expect marriage from such a whoremaster as you: one that knew the Town so much and women so well.

PINCHWIFE.
Why, I have married no London wife.

HORNER.
Pshaw, that's all one: that grave circumspection in marrying a country wife is like refusing a deceitful pampered Smithfield[20] jade to go and be cheated by a friend in the country.

PINCHWIFE. (*Aside.*)
A pox on him and his simile.—At least we are a little surer of the breed there, know what her keeping has been, whether foiled[21] or unsound.*

HORNER.
Come, come, I have known a clap gotten in Wales, and there are cozens,[22] justices, clerks, and chaplains in the country; I won't say coachmen. But she's handsome and young?

PINCHWIFE. (*Aside.*)
I'll answer as I should do.—No, no, she has no beauty but her youth, no attraction but her modesty: wholesome, homely, and housewifely, that's all.

DORILANT.
He talks as like a grazier as he looks.

PINCHWIFE.
She's too awkward, ill-favored, and silly* to bring to Town.

HARCOURT.
Then methinks you should bring her to be taught breeding.

PINCHWIFE.
To be taught! No sir, I thank you, good wives and private soldiers should be ignorant. [*Aside.*] I'll keep her from your instructions, I warrant you.

HARCOURT. (*Aside.*)
The rogue is as jealous as if his wife were not ignorant.

HORNER.
Why, if she be ill-favored, there will be less danger here for you than by leaving her in the country: we have such variety of dainties that we are seldom hungry.

DORILANT.
But they have always coarse, constant, swingeing stomachs in the country.

HARCOURT.
Foul feeders indeed.

DORILANT.
And your hospitality is great there.

HARCOURT.
Open house, every man's welcome.

PINCHWIFE.
So, so, gentlemen.

HORNER.
But prithee, why wouldst thou marry her? If she be ugly, ill-bred, and silly, she must be rich then.

PINCHWIFE.
As rich as if she brought me twenty thousand pound out of this Town, for she'll be as sure not to spend her moderate portion as a London baggage would be to spend hers, let it be what it would; so 'tis all one. Then because she's ugly, she's the likelier to be my own, and being ill-bred, she'll hate conversation* and, since silly and innocent, will not know the difference betwixt a man of one-and-twenty and one of forty.

HORNER.
Nine—to my knowledge. But if she be silly, she'll expect as much from a man of forty-nine as from him of one-and-twenty. But methinks wit is more necessary than beauty, and I think no young woman ugly that has it and no handsome woman agreeable without it.

PINCHWIFE.
'Tis my maxim: he's a fool that marries, but he's a

[19] cracked title] Either Sparkish's patrimony or his genealogy is of questionable value.

[20] Smithfield] suburban market, known for its sharp practice

[21] foiled] injured (of a horse), deflowered (of a woman)

[22] cozens] a variant of "cozeners" (q.v.) or possibly an alternate spelling of "cousins"

greater that does not marry a fool. What is wit in a wife good for but to make a man a cuckold?

HORNER.

Yes, to keep it from his knowledge.

PINCHWIFE.

A fool cannot contrive to make her husband a cuckold.

HORNER.

No, but she'll club with a man that can, and what is worse, if she cannot make her husband a cuckold, she'll make him jealous and pass for one, and then 'tis all one.

PINCHWIFE.

Well, well, I'll take care for one: my wife shall make me no cuckold though she had your help, Mr. Horner. I understand the Town, sir.

DORILANT. (*Aside.*)

His help!

HARCOURT. (*Aside.*)

He's come newly to Town, it seems, and has not heard how things are with him.

HORNER.

But tell me, has marriage cured thee of whoring, which it seldom does?

HARCOURT.

'Tis more than age can do.

HORNER.

No, the word is, "I'll marry and live honest.*" But a marriage vow is like a penitent gamester's oath and entering into bonds and penalties to stint himself to such a particular small sum at play for the future, which makes him but the more eager, and not being able to hold out, loses his money again and his forfeit to boot.

DORILANT.

Aye, aye, a gamester will be a gamester whilst his money lasts, and a whoremaster, whilst his vigor.

HARCOURT.

Nay, I have known 'em, when they are broke and can lose no more, keep a-fumbling with the box[23] in their hands to fool with only and hinder other gamesters.

DORILANT.

That had wherewithal to make lusty stakes.

PINCHWIFE.

Well gentlemen, you may laugh at me, but you shall never lie with my wife. I know the Town.

HORNER.

But prithee, was not the way you were in better? Is not keeping* better than marriage?

PINCHWIFE.

A pox on't, the jades would jilt me; I could never keep a whore to myself.

HORNER.

So then you only married to keep a whore to yourself. Well but let me tell you, women, as you say, are, like soldiers, made constant and loyal by good pay rather than by oaths and covenants. Therefore, I'd advise my friends to keep rather than marry since, too, I find by your example it does not serve one's turn, for I saw you yesterday in the eighteen-penny place[24] with a pretty country wench.

PINCHWIFE. (*Aside.*)

How the devil! Did he see my wife then? I sat there that she might not be seen, but she shall never go to a play again.

HORNER.

What, dost thou blush at nine-and-forty for having been seen with a wench?

DORILANT.

No faith, I warrant 'twas his wife, which he seated there out of sight, for he's a cunning rogue and understands the Town.

HARCOURT.

He blushes; then 'twas his wife, for men are now more ashamed to be seen with them in public than with a wench.

PINCHWIFE. (*Aside.*)

Hell and damnation! I'm undone since Horner has seen her and they know 'twas she.

HORNER.

But prithee, was it thy wife? She was exceedingly pretty. I was in love with her at that distance.

PINCHWIFE.

You are like never to be nearer to her. Your servant, gentlemen. (*Offers* to go.*)

23 box] dice cup, with bawdy suggestion

24 the eighteen-penny place] the middle gallery in the theater, away from the gallants in the pit and boxes

HORNER.
Nay, prithee stay.

PINCHWIFE.
I cannot; I will not.

HORNER.
Come, you shall dine with us.

PINCHWIFE.
I have dined already.

HORNER.
Come, I know thou hast not. I'll treat thee, dear rogue; thou shalt spend none of thy Hampshire money today.

PINCHWIFE. (*Aside.*)
Treat me! So he uses me already like his cuckold.

HORNER.
Nay, you shall not go.

PINCHWIFE.
I must, I have business at home. (*Exit.*)

HARCOURT.
To beat his wife: he's as jealous of her as a Cheapside* husband of a Covent Garden* wife.

HORNER.
Why, 'tis as hard to find an old whoremaster without jealousy and the gout as a young one without fear or the pox.
As gout in age from pox in youth proceeds,
So wenching past, then jealousy succeeds:
The worst disease that love and wenching breeds.

[Exeunt.]

Act II. [Pinchwife's lodging.]

Margery Pinchwife and Alithea, Pinchwife peeping behind at the door.

MARGERY.
Pray sister, where are the best fields and woods to walk in in London?

ALITHEA.
A pretty question. Why sister, Mulberry Garden[25] and St. James's Park* and, for close walks, the New Exchange.*

MARGERY.
Pray sister, tell my why my husband looks so grum here in Town and keeps me up so close and will not let me go a-walking nor let me wear my best gown yesterday?

ALITHEA.
Oh, he's jealous, sister.

MARGERY.
Jealous, what's that?

ALITHEA.
He's afraid you should love another man.

MARGERY.
How should he be afraid of my loving another man when he will not let me see any but himself?

ALITHEA.
Did he not carry you yesterday to a play?

MARGERY.
Aye, but we sat amongst ugly people; he would not let me come near the gentry, who sat under us, so that I could not see 'em. He told me none but naughty women sat there, whom they toused and moused, but I would have ventured for all that.

ALITHEA.
But how did you like the play?

MARGERY.
Indeed I was aweary of the play, but I liked hugeously the actors; they are the goodliest, properest men, sister.

ALITHEA.
Oh, but you must not like the actors, sister.

MARGERY.
Ay, how should I help it, sister? Pray sister, when my husband comes in, will you ask leave for me to go a-walking?

ALITHEA. (*Aside.*)
A-walking, ha, ha! Lord, a country gentlewoman's leisure is the drudgery of a foot post, and she requires as much airing as her husband's horses.

Enter Pinchwife.

But here comes your husband; I'll ask, though I'm sure he'll not grant it.

MARGERY.
He says he won't let me go abroad for fear of catching the pox.

ALITHEA.
Fie, the small pox you should say.

25 Mulberry Garden] a fashionable promenade within St. James's Park,* at the site of the current Buckingham Palace

MARGERY.

Oh my dear, dear bud, welcome home. Why dost thou look so froppish?[26] Who has nangered[27] thee?

PINCHWIFE.

You're a fool.

Margery goes aside and cries.

ALITHEA.

Faith so she is, for crying for no fault, poor, tender creature!

PINCHWIFE.

What, you would have her as impudent as yourself, as arrant a jill-flirt,* a gadder, a magpie, and, to say all, a mere* notorious Town woman?

ALITHEA.

Brother, you are my only censurer, and the honor of your family shall sooner suffer in your wife there than in me, though I take the innocent liberty of the Town.

PINCHWIFE.

Hark you, mistress, do not talk so before my wife. The innocent liberty of the Town!

ALITHEA.

Why pray, who boasts of any intrigue with me? What lampoon has made my name notorious? What ill women frequent my lodgings? I keep no company with any women of scandalous reputations.

PINCHWIFE.

No, you keep the men of scandalous reputations company.

ALITHEA.

Where? Would you not have me civil? answer 'em in a box at the plays? in the Drawing Room* at Whitehall?* in St. James's Park? Mulberry Garden? or—

PINCHWIFE.

Hold, hold, do not teach my wife where the men are to be found; I believe she's the worse for your Town documents[28] already. I bid you keep her in ignorance as I do.

MARGERY.

Indeed, be not angry with her, bud; she will tell me nothing of the Town, though I ask her a thousand times a day.

PINCHWIFE.

Then you are very inquisitive to know, I find?

MARGERY.

Not I, indeed, dear. I hate London. Our place-house[29] in the country is worth a thousand of't. Would I were there again!

PINCHWIFE.

So you shall, I warrant, but were you not talking of plays and players when I came in?—You are her encourager in such discourses.

MARGERY.

No indeed, dear, she chid me just now for liking the playermen.

PINCHWIFE. (*Aside.*)

Nay, if she be so innocent as to own to me her liking them, there is no hurt in't.—Come my poor rogue, but thou lik'st none better than me?

MARGERY.

Yes indeed, but I do: the playermen are finer folks.

PINCHWIFE.

But you love none better then me?

MARGERY.

You are mine own dear bud, and I know you; I hate a stranger.

PINCHWIFE.

Aye my dear, you must love me only and not be like the naughty Town women, who only hate their husbands and love every man else, love plays, visits, fine coaches, fine clothes, fiddles, balls, treats, and so lead a wicked Town life.

MARGERY.

Nay, if to enjoy all these things be a Town life, London is not so bad a place, dear.

PINCHWIFE.

How! If you love me, you must hate London.

ALITHEA. [*Aside.*]

The fool has forbid me discovering* to her the pleasures of the Town, and he is now setting her agog upon them himself.

26 froppish] fretful, peevish

27 nangered] angered; Margery tacks on the *n* in her characteristic babytalk with her *bud.*

28 documents] lessons

29 place-house] chief residence of an estate

MARGERY.
But husband, do the Town women love the playermen, too?
PINCHWIFE.
Yes, I warrant you.
MARGERY.
Ay, I warrant you.
PINCHWIFE.
Why, you do not, I hope?
MARGERY.
No, no, bud, but why have we no playermen in the country?
PINCHWIFE.
Hah! Mrs. Minx, ask me no more to go to a play.
MARGERY.
Nay, why, love? I did not care for going, but when you forbid me, you make me, as't were, desire it.
ALITHEA. (*Aside.*)
So 'twill be in other things, I warrant.
MARGERY.
Pray, let me go to a play, dear.
PINCHWIFE.
Hold your peace; I wonnot.
MARGERY.
Why, love?
PINCHWIFE.
Why, I'll tell you.
ALITHEA. (*Aside.*)
Nay, if he tell her, she'll give him more cause to forbid her that place.
MARGERY.
Pray, why, dear?
PINCHWIFE.
First, you like the actors, and the gallants may like you.
MARGERY.
What, a homely country girl? No, bud, nobody will like me.
PINCHWIFE.
I tell you, yes, they may.
MARGERY.
No, no, you jest. I won't believe you; I will go.
PINCHWIFE.
I tell you then that one of the lewdest fellows in Town, who saw you there, told me he was in love with you.
MARGERY.
Indeed! Who, who, pray, who was't?
PINCHWIFE. (*Aside.*)
I've gone too far and slipped before I was aware. How overjoyed she is!
MARGERY.
Was it any Hampshire gallant, any of our neighbors? I promise you, I am beholding to him.
PINCHWIFE.
I promise you, you lie, for he would but ruin you as he has done hundreds. He has no other love for women but that. Such as he look upon women like basilisks, but to destroy 'em.
MARGERY.
Ay, but if he loves me, why should he ruin me? Answer me to that. Methinks he should not; I would do him no harm.
ALITHEA.
Ha, ha, ha.
PINCHWIFE.
'Tis very well, but I'll keep him from doing you any harm, or me either.

Enter Sparkish and Harcourt.

But here comes company. Get you in, get you in.
MARGERY.
But pray, husband, is he a pretty gentleman that loves me?
PINCHWIFE.
In baggage, in. (*Thrusts her in; shuts the door.*) What, all the lewd libertines of the Town brought to my lodging by this easy coxcomb! S'death,* I'll not suffer it.
SPARKISH.
Here Harcourt, do you approve my choice?—Dear little rogue, I told you I'd bring you acquainted with all my friends, the wits, and—

Harcourt salutes her.*

PINCHWIFE.
Aye, they shall know her as well as you yourself will, I warrant you.
SPARKISH.
This is one of those, my pretty rogue, that are to dance at your wedding tomorrow, and him you must bid welcome ever to what you and I have.

PINCHWIFE. (*Aside.*)
Monstrous!
SPARKISH.
Harcourt, how dost thou like her, faith?—Nay dear, do not look down; I should hate to have a wife of mine out of countenance at any thing.
PINCHWIFE.
Wonderful!
SPARKISH.
Tell me, I say, Harcourt, how dost thou like her? Thou hast stared upon her enough to resolve me.
HARCOURT.
So infinitely well that I could wish I had a mistress, too, that might differ from her in nothing but her love and engagement to you.
ALITHEA.
Sir, Master Sparkish has often told me that his acquaintance were all wits and railleurs,[30] and now I find it.
SPARKISH.
No, by the universe, madam, he does not rally now; you may believe him. I do assure you, he is the honestest, worthiest, true-hearted gentleman—a man of such perfect honor, he would say nothing to a lady he does not mean.
PINCHWIFE. [*Aside.*]
Praising another man to his mistress!
HARCOURT.
Sir, you are so beyond expectation obliging, that—
SPARKISH.
Nay, egad, I am sure you do admire her extremely; I see't in your eyes.—He does admire you, madam.—By the world, don't you?
HARCOURT.
Yes, above the world or the most glorious part of it, her whole sex, and till now I never thought I should have envied you, or any man about to marry, but you have the best excuse for marriage I ever knew.
ALITHEA.
Nay, now, sir, I'm satisfied you are of the society of the wits and railleurs since you cannot spare your friend, even when he is but too civil to you, but the surest sign is since you are an enemy to marriage, for that I hear you hate as much as business or bad wine.

[30] railleurs] those who banter or mock; a fashionable French word appealing to Sparkish

HARCOURT.
Truly madam, I never was an enemy to marriage till now because marriage was never an enemy to me before.
ALITHEA.
But why, sir, is marriage an enemy to you now? because it robs you of your friend here? For you look upon a friend married as one gone into a monastery, that is, dead to the world.
HARCOURT.
'Tis indeed because you marry him. I see, madam, you can guess my meaning. I do confess heartily and openly I wish it were in my power to break the match. By heavens, I would!
SPARKISH.
Poor Frank!
ALITHEA.
Would you be so unkind to me?
HARCOURT.
No, no, 'tis not because I would be unkind to you.
SPARKISH.
Poor Frank! No, gad, 'tis only his kindness to me.
PINCHWIFE. (*Aside.*)
Great kindness to you, indeed. Insensible fop, let a man make love* to his wife to his face!
SPARKISH.
Come, dear Frank, for all my wife there that shall be, thou shalt enjoy me sometimes, dear rogue. By my honor, we men of wit condole for our deceased brother in marriage as much as for one dead in earnest. I think that was prettily said of me, hah, Harcourt? But come, Frank, be not melancholy for me.
HARCOURT.
No, I assure you I am not melancholy for you.
SPARKISH.
Prithee Frank, dost think my wife that shall be there a fine person?
HARCOURT.
I could gaze upon her till I became as blind as you are.
SPARKISH.
How, as I am! How?
HARCOURT.
Because you are a lover, and true lovers are blind, stock-blind.[31]

[31] stock-blind] blind as a stock, or log, purblind (cf. stock-still)

SPARKISH.
True, true, but by the world, she has wit, too, as well as beauty. Go, go with her into a corner and try if she has wit; talk to her anything; she's bashful before me.

HARCOURT.
Indeed, if a woman wants* wit in a corner, she has it nowhere.

ALITHEA. (*Aside to Sparkish.*)
Sir, you dispose of me a little before your time.

SPARKISH.
Nay, nay, madam, let me have an earnest of your obedience, or— Go, go, madam

Harcourt courts Alithea aside.

PINCHWIFE.
How, sir! if you are not concerned for the honor of a wife, I am for that of a sister. He shall not debauch her. Be a pander to your own wife, bring men to her, let 'em make love* before your face, thrust 'em into a corner together, then leave 'em in private! Is this your Town wit and conduct?

SPARKISH.
Ha, ha, ha, a silly* wise rogue would make one laugh more than a stark fool, ha, ha! I shall burst. Nay, you shall not disturb 'em. I'll vex thee, by the world. (*Struggles with Pinchwife to keep him from Harcourt and Alithea.*)

ALITHEA.
The writings are drawn, sir, settlements made; 'tis too late, sir, and past all revocation.

HARCOURT.
Then so is my death.

ALITHEA.
I would not be unjust to him.

HARCOURT.
Then why to me so?

ALITHEA.
I have no obligation to you.

HARCOURT.
My love.

ALITHEA.
I had his before.

HARCOURT.
You never had it: he wants,* you see, jealousy, the only infallible sign of it.

ALITHEA.
Love proceeds from esteem; he cannot distrust my virtue. Besides, he loves me, or he would not marry me.

HARCOURT.
Marrying you is no more sign of his love than bribing your woman, that he may marry you, is a sign of his generosity. Marriage is rather a sign of interest than love, and he that marries a fortune, covets a mistress, not loves her. But if you take marriage for a sign of love, take it from me immediately.

ALITHEA.
No, now you have put a scruple in my head. But in short, sir, to end our dispute, I must marry him: my reputation would suffer in the world else.

HARCOURT.
No, if you do marry him, with your pardon, madam, your reputation suffers in the world, and you would be thought in necessity for a cloak.

ALITHEA.
Nay, now you are rude, sir.—Mr. Sparkish, pray come hither; your friend here is very troublesome and very loving.

HARCOURT. (*Aside to Alithea.*)
Hold, hold—

PINCHWIFE.
D'ye hear that?

SPARKISH.
Why, d'ye think I'll seem to be jealous, like a country bumpkin?

PINCHWIFE.
No, rather be a cuckold, like a credulous cit.*

HARCOURT.
Madam, you would not have been so little generous* as to have told him.

ALITHEA.
Yes, since you could be so little generous* as to wrong him.

HARCOURT.
Wrong him! No man can do't; he's beneath an injury: a bubble,* a coward, a senseless idiot, a wretch so contemptible to all the world but you that—

ALITHEA.
Hold, do not rail at him, for since he is like to be my husband, I am resolved to like him. Nay, I

think I am obliged to tell him you are not his friend.—Master Sparkish, Master Sparkish.

SPARKISH.
What, what? Now, dear rogue, has not she wit?

HARCOURT. (*Speaks surlily.*)
Not so much as I thought and hoped she had.

ALITHEA.
Mr. Sparkish, do you bring people to rail at you?

HARCOURT.
Madam—

SPARKISH.
How! No, but if he does rail at me, 'tis but in jest, I warrant, what we wits do for one another and never take any notice of it.

ALITHEA.
He spoke so scurrilously of you I had no patience to hear him; besides, he has been making love* to me.

HARCOURT. (*Aside.*)
True, damned, tell-tale woman.

SPARKISH.
Pshaw, to show his parts.* We wits rail and make love often but to show our parts; as we have no affections, so we have no malice, we—

ALITHEA.
He said you were a wretch, below an injury.

SPARKISH.
Pshaw.

HARCOURT. [*Aside.*]
Damned, senseless, impudent, virtuous jade! Well, since she won't let me have her, she'll do as good: she'll make me hate her.

ALITHEA.
A common bubble.*

SPARKISH.
Pshaw.

ALITHEA.
A coward.

SPARKISH.
Pshaw, pshaw.

ALITHEA.
A senseless, driveling idiot.

SPARKISH.
How! Did he disparage my parts?* Nay, then my honor's concerned. I can't put up that, sir.—By the world, brother, help me to kill him. (*Aside.*) I may draw now, since we have the odds of him; 'tis a good occasion, too, before my mistress. (*Offers* to draw.*)

ALITHEA.
Hold, hold!

SPARKISH.
What, what?

ALITHEA. (*Aside.*)
I must not let 'em kill the gentleman neither, for his kindness* to me. I am so far from hating him that I wish my gallant had his person and understanding. Nay, if my honor—

SPARKISH.
I'll be thy death.

ALITHEA.
Hold, hold! Indeed, to tell the truth, the gentleman said after all that what he spoke was but out of friendship to you.

SPARKISH.
How! Say I am, I am a fool, that is, no wit, out of friendship to me?

ALITHEA.
Yes, to try whether I was concerned enough for you, and made love* to me only to be satisfied of my virtue, for your sake.

HARCOURT. (*Aside.*)
Kind however—

SPARKISH.
Nay, if it were so, my dear rogue, I ask thee pardon, but why would not you tell me so, faith?

HARCOURT.
Because I did not think on't, faith.

SPARKISH.
Come, Horner does not come, Harcourt, let's be gone to the new play.—Come, madam.

ALITHEA.
I will not go if you intend to leave me alone in the box and run into the pit, as you use to do.

SPARKISH.
Pshaw, I'll leave Harcourt with you in the box to entertain you, and that's as good. If I sat in the box, I should be thought no judge but of trimmings.—Come away, Harcourt, lead her down.

Exeunt Sparkish, Harcourt, and Alithea.

PINCHWIFE.
Well, go thy ways, for the flower of the true Town fops, such as spend their estates before they come to 'em and are cuckolds before they're married. But let me go look to my own freehold.—How—

Enter My Lady Fidget, Dainty, and Mistress Squeamish.

LADY FIDGET.
Your servant, sir. Where is your lady? We are come to wait upon her to the new play.

PINCHWIFE.
New play!

LADY FIDGET.
And my husband will wait upon you presently.

PINCHWIFE. (*Aside.*)
Damn your civility.—Madam, by no means, I will not see Sir Jaspar here till I have waited upon him at home, nor shall my wife see you till she has waited upon your ladyship at your lodgings.

LADY FIDGET.
Now we are here, sir—

PINCHWIFE.
No, madam.

DAINTY.
Pray, let us see her.

MRS. SQUEAMISH.
We will not stir till we see her.

PINCHWIFE. (*Aside.*)
A pox on you all. (*Goes to the door and returns.*) She has locked the door and is gone abroad.

LADY FIDGET.
No, you have locked the door, and she's within.

DAINTY.
They told us below she was here.

PINCHWIFE. [*Aside.*]
Will nothing do?—Well it must out then: to tell you the truth, ladies, which I was afraid to let you know before lest it might endanger your lives, my wife has just now the small pox come out upon her. Do not be frightened, but pray, be gone ladies. You shall not stay here in danger of your lives. Pray get you gone, ladies.

LADY FIDGET.
No, no, we have all had 'em.

MRS. SQUEAMISH.
Alack, alack.

DAINTY.
Come, come, we must see how it goes with her. I understand the disease.

LADY FIDGET.
Come.

PINCHWIFE. (*Aside.*)
Well, there is no being too hard for women at their own weapon, lying; therefore, I'll quit the field. (*Exit.*)

MRS. SQUEAMISH.
Here's an example of jealousy.

LADY FIDGET.
Indeed, as the world goes, I wonder there are no more jealous, since wives are so neglected.

DAINTY.
Pshaw, as the world goes, to what end should they be jealous?

LADY FIDGET.
Faugh, 'tis a nasty world.

MRS. SQUEAMISH.
That men of parts,* great acquaintance, and quality* should take up with and spend themselves and fortunes in keeping* little playhouse creatures, faugh!

LADY FIDGET.
Nay, that women of understanding, great acquaintance, and good quality should fall a-keeping, too, of little creatures, faugh!

MRS. SQUEAMISH.
Why, 'tis the men of quality's fault: they never visit women of honor and reputation as they used to do and have not so much as common civility for ladies of our rank but use us with the same indifferency and ill breeding as if we were all married to 'em.

LADY FIDGET.
She says true. 'Tis an arrant shame women of quality should be so slighted; methinks birth, birth, should go for something. I have known men admired, courted, and followed for their titles only.

MRS. SQUEAMISH.
Aye, one would think men of honor should not love, no more than marry, out of their own rank.

DAINTY.
Fie, fie upon 'em, they are come to think crossbreeding for themselves best, as well as for their dogs and horses.

LADY FIDGET.
They are dogs and horses for't.

MRS. SQUEAMISH.
One would think if not for love, for vanity a little.

DAINTY.
Nay, they do satisfy their vanity upon us sometimes and are kind* to us in their report, tell all the world they lie with us.

LADY FIDGET.
Damned rascals, that we should be only wronged by 'em! To report a man has had a person, when he has not had a person, is the greatest wrong in the whole world that can be done to a person.

MRS. SQUEAMISH.
Well, 'tis an arrant shame noble persons should be so wronged and neglected.

LADY FIDGET.
But still 'tis an arranter shame for a noble person to neglect her own honor and defame her own noble person with little inconsiderable fellows, faugh!

DAINTY.
I suppose the crime against our honor is the same with a man of quality as with another.

LADY FIDGET.
How! No, sure the man of quality is likest one's husband, and therefore, the fault should be the less.

DAINTY.
But then the pleasure should be the less.

LADY FIDGET.
Fie, fie, fie, for shame sister! Whither shall we ramble? Be continent in your discourse, or I shall hate you.

DAINTY.
Besides, an intrigue is so much the more notorious for the man's quality.

MRS. SQUEAMISH.
'Tis true, nobody takes notice of a private man, and therefore, with him 'tis more secret, and the crime's the less when 'tis not known.

LADY FIDGET.
You say true. I'faith, I think you are in the right on't. 'Tis not an injury to a husband till it be an injury to our honors, so that a woman of honor loses no honor with a private person, and to say truth—

DAINTY. (*Apart to Mrs. Squeamish.*)
So the little fellow is grown a private person—with her—

LADY FIDGET.
But still my dear, dear honor.

Enter Sir Jaspar, Horner, Dorilant.

SIR JASPAR.
Aye, my dear, dear of honor, thou hast still so much honor in thy mouth—

HORNER. (*Aside.*)
That she has none elsewhere—

LADY FIDGET.
Oh, what d'ye mean to bring in these upon us?

DAINTY.
Faugh, these are as bad as wits!

MRS. SQUEAMISH.
Faugh!

LADY FIDGET.
Let us leave the room.

SIR JASPAR.
Stay, stay, faith, to tell you the naked truth.

LADY FIDGET.
Fie, Sir Jaspar, do not use that word "naked."

SIR JASPAR.
Well, well, in short, I have business at Whitehall* and cannot go to the play with you; therefore, would have you go—

LADY FIDGET.
With those two to a play?

SIR JASPAR.
No, not with t'other, but with Mr. Horner; there can be no more scandal to go with him than with Mr. Tattle or Master Limberham.[32]

LADY FIDGET.
With that nasty fellow! No—no.

SIR JASPAR.
Nay prithee dear, hear me. (*Whispers to Lady Fidget.*)

Horner, Dorilant drawing near Squeamish and Dainty.

32 Mr. Tattle or Master Limberham] obviously, by their names, unthreatening as companions: Tattle is self-explanatory; Limberham implies loose-limbed (we might say "weak-kneed")

HORNER.
Ladies.

DAINTY.
Stand off.

MRS. SQUEAMISH.
Do not approach us.

DAINTY.
You herd with the wits; you are obscenity all over.

MRS. SQUEAMISH.
And I would as soon look upon a picture of Adam and Eve without fig leaves as any of you, if I could help it; therefore, keep off and do not make us sick.

DORILANT.
What a devil are these?

HORNER.
Why, these are pretenders to honor, as critics to wit, only by censuring others, and as every raw, peevish, out-of-humored, affected, dull, tea-drinking, arithmetical[33] fop sets up for a wit by railing at men of sense, so these for honor, by railing at the Court and ladies of as great honor as quality.*

SIR JASPAR.
Come Mr. Horner, I must desire you to go with these ladies to the play, sir.

HORNER.
I, sir!

SIR JASPAR.
Aye, aye, come, sir.

HORNER.
I must beg your pardon, sir, and theirs. I will not be seen in women's company in public again for the world.

SIR JASPAR.
Ha, ha, strange aversion!

MRS. SQUEAMISH.
No, he's for women's company in private.

SIR JASPAR.
He—poor man—he! Ha, ha, ha.

DAINTY.
'Tis a greater shame amongst lewd fellows to be seen in virtuous women's company than for the women to be seen with them.

HORNER.
Indeed madam, the time was I only hated virtuous women, but now I hate the other, too. I beg your pardon, ladies.

LADY FIDGET.
You are very obliging, sir, because we would not be troubled with you.

SIR JASPAR.
In sober sadness he shall go.

DORILANT.
Nay, if he wonnot, I am ready to wait upon the ladies, and I think I am the fitter man.

SIR JASPAR.
You, sir! no, I thank you for that. Master Horner is a privileged man amongst the virtuous ladies; 'twill be a great while before you are so. He, he, he, he's my wife's gallant, he, he, he. No, pray withdraw, sir, for as I take it, the virtuous ladies have no business with you.

DORILANT.
And I am sure, he can have none with them. 'Tis strange a man can't come amongst virtuous women now but upon the same terms as men are admitted into the Great Turk's seraglio, but heavens keep me from being an ombre player with 'em. But where is Pinchwife? (*Exit.*)

SIR JASPAR.
Come, come, man. What, avoid the sweet society of womankind? that sweet, soft, gentle, tame, noble creature woman, made for man's companion—

HORNER.
So is that soft, gentle, tame, and more noble creature a spaniel, and has all their tricks: can fawn, lie down, suffer beating, and fawn the more, barks at your friends when they come to see you, makes your bed hard, gives you fleas and the mange sometimes, and all the difference is, the spaniel's the more faithful animal and fawns but upon one master.

SIR JASPAR.
He, he, he.

MRS. SQUEAMISH.
Oh, the rude beast!

DAINTY.
Insolent brute!

LADY FIDGET.
Brute! Stinking, mortified, rotten French wether, to dare—

---

33 arithmetical] precise

SIR JASPAR.

Hold, an't* please your ladyship.—For shame, Master Horner, your mother was a woman. (*Aside.*) Now shall I never reconcile 'em.—Hark you, madam, take my advice in your anger: you know you often want* one to make up your drolling pack of ombre players, and you may cheat him easily, for he's an ill gamester and consequently loves play. Besides, you know, you have but two old civil gentlemen (with stinking breaths, too) to wait upon you abroad. Take in the third into your service. The other are but crazy, and a lady should have a supernumerary gentleman-usher, as a supernumerary coach-horse, lest sometimes you should be forced to stay at home.

LADY FIDGET.

But are you sure he loves play and has money?

SIR JASPAR.

He loves play as much as you and has money as much as I.

LADY FIDGET.

Then I am contented to make him pay for his scurrility; money makes up in a measure all other wants* in men. (*Aside.*) Those whom we cannot make hold for gallants, we make fine.[34]

SIR JASPAR. (*Aside.*)

So, so, now to mollify, to wheedle him.—Master Horner, will you never keep civil company? Methinks 'tis time now, since you are only fit for them. Come, come, man, you must e'en fall to visiting our wives, eating at our tables, drinking tea with our virtuous relations after dinner, dealing cards to 'em, reading plays and gazettes to 'em, picking fleas out of their shocks* for 'em, collecting receipts,* new songs, women, pages, and footmen for 'em.

HORNER.

I hope they'll afford me better employment, sir.

SIR JASPAR.

He, he, he! 'Tis fit you know your work before you come into your place, and since you are unprovided of a lady to flatter and a good house to eat at, pray frequent mine and call my wife "mistress," and she shall call you "gallant," according to the custom.

[34] fine] pay a penalty

HORNER.

Who, I?

SIR JASPAR.

Faith, thou shalt for my sake; come, for my sake only.

HORNER.

For your sake—

SIR JASPAR.

Come, come, here's a gamester for you; let him be a little familiar sometimes. Nay, what if a little rude? Gamesters may be rude with ladies, you know.

LADY FIDGET.

Yes, losing gamesters have a privilege with women.

HORNER.

I always thought the contrary, that the winning gamester had most privilege with women, for when you have lost your money to a man, you'll lose anything you have, all you have, they say, and he may use you as he pleases.

SIR JASPAR.

He, he, he! Well, win or lose, you shall have your liberty with her.

LADY FIDGET.

As he behaves himself and for your sake, I'll give him admittance and freedom.

HORNER.

All sorts of freedom, madam?

SIR JASPAR.

Aye, aye, aye, all sorts of freedom thou canst take, and so go to her; begin thy new employment. Wheedle her, jest with her, and be better acquainted one with another.

HORNER. (*Aside.*)

I think I know her already, therefore, may venture with her, my secret for hers.

Horner and Lady Fidget whisper.

SIR JASPAR.

Sister, Cuz, I have provided an innocent playfellow for you there.

DAINTY.

Who, he!

MRS. SQUEAMISH.

There's a playfellow indeed.

SIR JASPAR.

Yes, sure. What, he is good enough to play at cards, blindman's buff, or the fool with sometimes.

MRS. SQUEAMISH.
Faugh, we'll have no such playfellows.

DAINTY.
No sir, you shan't choose playfellows for us, we thank you.

SIR JASPAR.
Nay, pray hear me. (*Whispering to them.*)

LADY FIDGET. [*Aside to Horner.*]
But poor gentleman, could you be so generous?* so truly a man of honor, as for the sakes of us women of honor, to cause your self to be reported no man? no man! and to suffer your self the greatest shame that could fall upon a man, that none might fall upon us women by your conversation.* But indeed, sir, as perfectly, perfectly the same man as before your going into France, sir, as perfectly, perfectly, sir?

HORNER.
As perfectly, perfectly, madam. Nay, I scorn you should take my word; I desire to be tried only, madam.

LADY FIDGET.
Well, that's spoken again like a man of honor; all men of honor desire to come to the test. But indeed, generally you men report such things of yourselves one does not know how or whom to believe, and it is come to that pass, we dare not take your words, no more than your tailors,[35] without some staid servant of yours be bound with you. But I have so strong a faith in your honor, dear, dear, noble sir, that I'd forfeit mine for yours at any time, dear sir.

HORNER.
No madam, you should not need to forfeit it for me: I have given you security already to save you harmless, my late reputation being so well known in the world, madam.

LADY FIDGET.
But if upon any future falling out or upon a suspicion of my taking the trust out of your hands to employ some other, you yourself should betray your trust, dear sir? I mean, if you'll give me leave to speak obscenely, you might tell, dear sir.

HORNER.
If I did, nobody would believe me: the reputation of impotency is as hardly recovered again in the world as that of cowardice, dear madam.

LADY FIDGET.
Nay then, as one may say, you may do your worst, dear, dear, sir.

SIR JASPAR.
Come, is your ladyship reconciled to him yet? Have you agreed on matters? For I must be gone to Whitehall.

LADY FIDGET.
Why indeed, Sir Jaspar, Master Horner is a thousand, thousand times a better man than I thought him.—Cousin Squeamish, Sister Dainty, I can name him now. Truly not long ago, you know, I thought his very name obscenity, and I would as soon have lain with him as have named him.

SIR JASPAR.
Very likely, poor madam.

DAINTY.
I believe it.

MRS. SQUEAMISH.
No doubt on't.

SIR JASPAR.
Well, well, that your ladyship is as virtuous as any she, I know, and him all the Town knows, he, he, he. Therefore, now you like him, get you gone to your business together. Go, go, to your business, I say, pleasure, whilst I go to my pleasure, business.

LADY FIDGET.
Come then, dear gallant.

HORNER.
Come away, my dearest mistress.

SIR JASPAR.
So, so, why 'tis as I'd have it. (*Exit.*)

HORNER.
And as I'd have it.

LADY FIDGET.
Who for his business from his wife will run
Takes the best care to have her business done.

Exeunt.

35 tailors] Unpunctuated in the original, "tailors" has three grammatical possibilities: nominative plural, possessive plural, and possessive singular—each with different interpretive possibilities.

Act III, scene i. [Pinchwife's lodging.]

Alithea and Margery.

ALITHEA.

Sister, what ails you, you are grown melancholy?

MARGERY.

Would it not make anyone melancholy to see you go every day fluttering about abroad, whilst I must stay at home like a poor lonely, sullen bird in a cage?

ALITHEA.

Aye sister, but you came young and just from the nest to your cage, so that I thought you liked it and could be as cheerful in't as others that took their flight themselves early and are hopping abroad in the open air.

MARGERY.

Nay, I confess I was quiet enough till my husband told me what pure[36] lives the London ladies live abroad, with their dancing, meetings, and junketings, and dressed every day in their best gowns, and I warrant you, play at ninepins every day of the week, so they do.

Enter Pinchwife.

PINCHWIFE.

Come, what's here to do? You are putting the Town pleasures in her head and setting her a-longing.

ALITHEA.

Yes, after ninepins! You suffer none to give her those longings, you mean, but yourself.

PINCHWIFE.

I tell her of the vanities of the Town like a confessor.

ALITHEA.

A confessor! just such a confessor as he that by forbidding a silly* ostler to grease the horses' teeth,[37] taught him to do't.

PINCHWIFE.

Come Mistress Flippant, good precepts are lost when bad examples are still* before us: the liberty you take abroad makes her hanker after it and out of humor at home, poor wretch! She desired not to come to London; I would bring her.

ALITHEA.

Very well.

PINCHWIFE.

She has been this week in Town and never desired, till this afternoon, to go abroad.

ALITHEA.

Was she not at a play yesterday?

PINCHWIFE.

Yes, but she ne'er asked me; I was myself the cause of her going.

ALITHEA.

Then if she ask you again, you are the cause of her asking, and not my example.

PINCHWIFE.

Well, tomorrow night I shall be rid of you, and the next day before 'tis light, she and I'll be rid of the Town and my dreadful apprehensions.—Come, be not melancholy, for thou shalt go into the country after tomorrow, dearest.

ALITHEA.

Great comfort.

MARGERY.

Pish, what d'ye tell me of the country for?

PINCHWIFE.

How's this! What, pish at the country?

MARGERY.

Let me alone; I am not well.

PINCHWIFE.

Oh, if that be all—what ails my dearest?

MARGERY.

Truly I don't know, but I have not been well since you told me there was a gallant at the play in love with me.

PINCHWIFE.

Hah—

ALITHEA.

That's by my example too.

PINCHWIFE.

Nay, if you are not well but are so concerned because a lewd fellow chanced to lie and say he liked you, you'll make me sick, too.

MARGERY.

Of what sickness?

PINCHWIFE.

Oh, of that which is worse than the plague, jealousy.

---

36 pure] fine, wonderful; a ruralism

37 grease the horses's teeth] a ruse so that the horses cannot eat what the owner has paid for

MARGERY.

Pish, you jeer. I'm sure there's no such disease in our receipt-book* at home.

PINCHWIFE.

No, thou never met'st with it, poor innocent. (*Aside.*) Well, if thou cuckold me, 'twill be my own fault, for cuckolds and bastards are generally makers of their own fortune.

MARGERY.

Well but pray, bud, let's go to a play tonight.

PINCHWIFE.

'Tis just done; she comes from it.—But why are you so eager to see a play?

MARGERY.

Faith dear, not that I care one pin for their talk there, but I like to look upon the playermen and would see, if I could, the gallant you say loves me; that's all, dear bud.

PINCHWIFE.

Is that all, dear bud?

ALITHEA.

This proceeds from my example.

MARGERY.

But if the play be done, let's go abroad, however, dear bud.

PINCHWIFE.

Come, have a little patience, and thou shalt go into the country on Friday.

MARGERY.

Therefore, I would see first some sights to tell my neighbors of. Nay, I will go abroad, that's once.[38]

ALITHEA.

I'm the cause of this desire, too.

PINCHWIFE.

But now I think on't, who was the cause of Horner's coming to my lodging today? That was you.

ALITHEA.

No, you, because you would not let him see your handsome wife out of your lodging.

MARGERY.

Why, oh Lord! Did the gentleman come hither to see me indeed?

PINCHWIFE.

No, no.—You are not cause of that damned question, too, Mistress Alithea? (*Aside.*) Well, she's in the right of it: he is in love with my wife—and comes after her. 'Tis so. But I'll nip his love in the bud, lest he should follow us into the country and break his chariot* wheel near our house on purpose for an excuse to come to't. But I think I know the Town.

MARGERY.

Come, pray bud, let's go abroad before 'tis late, for I will go, that's flat and plain.

PINCHWIFE. (*Aside.*)

So! The obstinacy already of a Town wife, and I must, whilst she's here, humor her like one.—Sister, how shall we do, that she may not be seen or known?

ALITHEA.

Let her put on her mask.

PINCHWIFE.

Pshaw, a mask makes people but the more inquisitive and is as ridiculous a disguise as a stage beard; her shape, stature, habit will be known, and if we should meet with Horner, he would be sure to take acquaintance with us, must wish her joy, kiss her, talk to her, leer upon her, and the devil and all. No, I'll not use her to a mask; 'tis dangerous, for masks have made more cuckolds than the best faces that ever were known.

ALITHEA.

How will you do then?

MARGERY.

Nay, shall we go? The Exchange* will be shut, and I have a mind to see that.

PINCHWIFE.

So—I have it. I'll dress her up in the suit we are to carry down to her brother, little Sir James; nay, I understand the Town tricks. Come, let's go dress her. A mask! No—a woman masked, like a covered dish, gives a man curiosity and appetite, when, it may be, uncovered, 'twould turn his stomach. No, no.

ALITHEA.

Indeed, your comparison is something a greasy one. But I had a gentle gallant used to say, a beauty masked, like the sun in eclipse, gathers together more gazers than if it shined out.

Exeunt.

[38] that's once] that's final, or positive; once and for all

Scene ii. The New Exchange.*

Enter Horner, Harcourt, Dorilant; [Clasp at his booth].

DORILANT.
Engaged to women, and not sup with us?

HORNER.
Aye, a pox on 'em all.

HARCOURT.
You were much a more reasonable man in the morning and had as noble resolutions against 'em as a widower of a week's liberty.

DORILANT.
Did I ever think to see you keep company with women in vain?

HORNER.
In vain! No, 'tis since I can't love 'em, to be revenged on 'em.

HARCOURT.
Now your sting is gone, you looked in the box amongst all those women like a drone in the hive: all upon you, shoved and ill-used by 'em all, and thrust from one side to t'other.

DORILANT.
Yet he must be buzzing amongst 'em still, like other old beetle-headed, lickerish drones. Avoid 'em and hate 'em as they hate you.

HORNER.
Because I do hate 'em and would hate 'em yet more, I'll frequent 'em. You may see by marriage, nothing makes a man hate a woman more than her constant conversation.* In short, I converse with 'em, as you do with rich fools, to laugh at 'em and use 'em ill.

DORILANT.
But I would no more sup with women unless I could lie with 'em, than sup with a rich coxcomb unless I could cheat him.

HORNER.
Yes, I have known thee sup with a fool for his drinking; if he could set out your hand[39] that way only, you were satisfied, and if he were a wine-swallowing mouth, 'twas enough.

HARCOURT.
Yes, a man drinks often with a fool, as he tosses with a marker, only to keep his hand in ure.[40] But do the ladies drink?

HORNER.
Yes sir, and I shall have the pleasure at least of laying 'em flat with a bottle and bring as much scandal that way upon 'em as formerly t'other.

HARCOURT.
Perhaps you may prove as weak a brother amongst 'em that way as t'other.

DORILANT.
Faugh, drinking with women is as unnatural as scolding with 'em, but 'tis a pleasure of decayed fornicators and the basest way of quenching love.

HARCOURT.
Nay, 'tis drowning love instead of quenching it. But leave us for civil women, too!

DORILANT.
Aye, when he can't be the better for 'em. We hardly pardon a man that leaves his friend for a wench, and that's a pretty lawful call.

HORNER.
Faith, I would not leave you for 'em if they would not drink.

DORILANT.
Who would disappoint his company at Lewis's[41] for a gossiping?

HARCOURT.
Faugh, wine and women good apart, together as nauseous as sack* and sugar. But hark you, sir, before you go, a little of your advice; an old maimed general, when unfit for action, is fittest for counsel. I have other designs upon women than eating and drinking with them. I am in love with Sparkish's mistress, whom he is to marry tomorrow. Now how shall I get her?

Enter Sparkish, looking about.

HORNER.
Why, here comes one will help you to her.

HARCOURT.
He! He, I tell you, is my rival and will hinder my love.

39 set out your hand] furnish you

40 tosses … ure] throws dice with a scorekeeper (i.e. one who doesn't play for money) only to keep in practice

41 Lewis's] presumably, a tavern or eating house, though not positively identified

HORNER.

No, a foolish rival and a jealous husband assist their rivals' designs, for they are sure to make their women hate them, which is the first step to their love for another man.

HARCOURT.

But I cannot come near his mistress but in his company.

HORNER.

Still the better for you, for fools are most easily cheated when they themselves are accessories, and he is to be bubbled* of his mistress, as of his money, the common mistress, by keeping him company.

SPARKISH.

Who is that, that is to be bubbled? Faith, let me snack;[42] I han't met with a bubble since Christmas. Gad, I think bubbles are like their brother woodcocks, go out with the cold weather.

HARCOURT. (*Apart to Horner.*)

A pox! He did not hear all, I hope.

SPARKISH.

Come, you bubbling rogues, you. Where do we sup?—Oh Harcourt, my mistress tells me you have been making fierce love* to her all the play long, ha, ha—but I—

HARCOURT.

I make love to her?

SPARKISH.

Nay, I forgive thee, for I think I know thee, and I know her, but I am sure I know myself.

HARCOURT.

Did she tell you so? I see all women are like these of the Exchange, who, to enhance the price of their commodities, report to their fond* customers offers which were never made 'em.

HORNER.

Aye, women are as apt to tell before the intrigue as men after it and so show themselves the vainer sex. But hast thou a mistress, Sparkish? 'Tis as hard for me to believe it as that thou ever hadst a bubble, as you bragged just now.

SPARKISH.

Oh your servant, sir. Are you at your raillery, sir? But we were some of us beforehand with you today at the play. The wits were something bold with you, sir. Did you not hear us laugh?

HARCOURT.

Yes, but I thought you had gone to plays to laugh at the poet's wit, not at your own.

SPARKISH.

Your servant, sir. No, I thank you. Gad, I go to a play as to a country treat: I carry my own wine to one and my own wit to t'other, or else I'm sure I should not be merry at either, and the reason why we are so often louder than the players is because we think we speak more wit and so become the poet's rivals in his audience. For to tell you the truth, we hate the silly rogues, nay, so much that we find fault even with their bawdy upon the stage whilst we talk nothing else in the pit as loud.

HORNER.

But why shouldst thou hate the silly poets? Thou hast too much wit to be one, and they, like whores, are only hated by each other, and thou dost scorn writing, I'm sure.

SPARKISH.

Yes, I'd have you to know, I scorn writing, but women, women, that make men do all foolish things, make 'em write songs, too; everybody does it. 'Tis e'en as common with lovers as playing with fans, and you can no more help rhyming to your Phyllis than drinking to your Phyllis.

HARCOURT.

Nay, poetry in love is no more to be avoided than jealousy.

DORILANT.

But the poets damned your songs, did they?

SPARKISH.

Damn the poets! They turned 'em into burlesque, as they call it; that burlesque is a hocus-pocus trick they have got, which by the virtue of "*hictius doctius,** topsey turvey," they make a wise and witty man in the world a fool upon the stage, you know not how, and 'tis, therefore, I hate 'em too, for I know not but it may be my own case, for they'll put a man into a play for looking asquint. Their predecessors were contented to make serving men only their stage fools, but these rogues must have gentlemen, with a pox to 'em, nay, knights. And indeed, you shall hardly see a fool upon the stage but he's a knight,

[42] snack] share, take part

and to tell you the truth, they have kept me these six years from being a knight in earnest, for fear of being knighted in a play and dubbed a fool.

DORILANT.

Blame 'em not; they must follow their copy, the age.

HARCOURT.

But why shouldst thou be afraid of being in a play, who expose yourself everyday in the playhouses and as public places?

HORNER.

'Tis but being on the stage instead of standing on a bench in the pit.

DORILANT.

Don't you give money to painters to draw you like? And are you afraid of your pictures at length in a playhouse where all your mistresses may see you?

SPARKISH.

A pox! Painters don't draw the small pox or pimples in one's face. Come, damn all your silly authors whatever, all books and booksellers, by the world, and all readers, courteous or uncourteous.

HARCOURT.

But who comes here, Sparkish?

Enter Pinchwife and his wife in man's clothes; Alithea; Lucy, her maid.

SPARKISH.

Oh hide me! There's my mistress, too. (*Hides himself behind Harcourt.*)

HARCOURT.

She sees you.

SPARKISH.

But I will not see her; 'tis time to go to Whitehall,* and I must not fail the Drawing Room.*

HARCOURT.

Pray, first carry me and reconcile me to her.

SPARKISH.

Another time, faith, the King will have supped.

HARCOURT.

Not with the worse stomach for thy absence. Thou art one of those fools that think their attendance at the King's meals as necessary as his physicians', when you are more troublesome to him than his doctors or his dogs.

SPARKISH.

Pshaw, I know my interest, sir. Prithee hide me.

HORNER.

Your servant, Pinchwife.—What, he knows us not!

PINCHWIFE. (*To his wife aside.*)

Come along.

MARGERY.

Pray, have you any ballads? Give me six-penny worth.

CLASP.

We have no ballads.

MARGERY.

Then give me *Covent Garden Drollery*,[43] and a play or two.—Oh here's *Tarugo's Wiles* and *The Slighted Maiden.*[44] I'll have them.

PINCHWIFE. (*Apart to her.*)

No, plays are not for your reading. Come along. Will you discover* yourself?

HORNER.

Who is that pretty youth with him, Sparkish?

SPARKISH.

I believe his wife's brother, because he's something like her, but I never saw her but once.

HORNER.

Extremely handsome. I have seen a face like it, too. Let us follow 'em.

Exeunt Pinchwife, Margery; Alithea, Lucy, Horner, Dorilant following them.

HARCOURT.

Come Sparkish, your mistress saw you and will be angry you go not to her; besides, I would fain be reconciled to her, which none but you can do, dear friend.

SPARKISH.

Well that's a better reason, dear friend. I would not go near her now for hers or my own sake, but I can deny you nothing, for though I have known thee a great while, never go,[45] if I do not love thee as well as a new acquaintance.

---

43 *Covent Garden Drollery*] a miscellany of songs, poems, prologues and epilogues by various writers, including Wycherley, published in 1672

44 *Tarugo's Wiles* and *The Slighted Maiden]* a comedy by Sir Thomas St. Serfe (1668) and a tragicomedy by Sir Robert Staplyton (1663)

45 never go] like "never stir" below, a phrase of reassurance meaning roughly "don't worry"

HARCOURT.
I am obliged to you indeed, dear friend. I would be well with her only to be well with thee still, for these ties to wives usually dissolve all ties to friends. I would be contented she should enjoy you a-nights, but I would have you to my self a-days, as I have had, dear friend.

SPARKISH.
And thou shalt enjoy me a-days, dear, dear friend, never stir, and I'll be divorced from her sooner than from thee. Come along.

HARCOURT. (*Aside.*)
So we are hard put to't when we make our rival our procurer, but neither she nor her brother would let me come near her now. When all's done, a rival is the best cloak to steal to a mistress under without suspicion, and when we have once got to her as we desire, we throw him off like other cloaks.

Exit Sparkish, Harcourt following him. Re-enter Pinchwife, Margery in man's clothes.

PINCHWIFE. (*To Alithea [offstage].*)
Sister, if you will not go, we must leave you. (*Aside.*) The fool, her gallant, and she will muster up all the young saunterers of this place, and they will leave their dear seamstresses to follow us. What a swarm of cuckolds and cuckold-makers are here?—Come let's be gone, Mistress Margery.

MARGERY.
Don't you believe that, I han't half my belly full of sights yet.

PINCHWIFE.
Then walk this way.

MARGERY.
Lord, what a power of brave* signs are here! Stay—the Bull's Head, the Ram's Head, and the Stag's Head, dear—

PINCHWIFE.
Nay, if every husband's proper sign here were visible, they would be all alike.

MARGERY.
What d'ye mean by that, bud?

PINCHWIFE.
'Tis no matter—no matter, bud.

MARGERY.
Pray tell me, nay, I will know.

PINCHWIFE.
They would be all bulls', stags', and rams' heads.

Exeunt Pinchwife, Margery. Re-enter Sparkish, Harcourt, Alithea, Lucy at t'other door.

SPARKISH.
Come dear madam, for my sake, you shall be reconciled to him.

ALITHEA.
For your sake, I hate him.

HARCOURT.
That's something too cruel, madam, to hate me for his sake.

SPARKISH.
Aye indeed, madam, too, too cruel to me to hate my friend for my sake.

ALITHEA.
I hate him because he is your enemy, and you ought to hate him, too, for making love* to me, if you love me.

SPARKISH.
That's a good one! I hate a man for loving you! If he did love you, 'tis but what he can't help, and 'tis your fault not his, if he admires you. I hate a man for being of my opinion! I'll ne'er do't, by the world.

ALITHEA.
Is it for your honor or mine to suffer a man to make love to me, who am to marry you tomorrow?

SPARKISH.
Is it for your honor or mine to have me jealous? That he makes love to you is a sign you are handsome, and that I am not jealous is a sign you are virtuous. That, I think, is for your honor.

ALITHEA.
But 'tis your honor, too, I am concerned for.

HARCOURT.
But why, dearest madam, will you be more concerned for his honor than he is himself? Let his honor alone for my sake and his. He, he, has no honor—

SPARKISH.
How's that?

HARCOURT.
But what my dear friend can guard himself.

SPARKISH.
Oh ho—that's right again.

HARCOURT.

Your care of his honor argues his neglect of it, which is no honor to my dear friend here; therefore, once more, let his honor go which way it will, dear madam.

SPARKISH.

Aye, aye, were it for my honor to marry a woman whose virtue I suspected and could not trust her in a friend's hands?

ALITHEA.

Are you not afraid to lose me?

HARCOURT.

He afraid to lose you, madam! No, no— you may see how the most estimable and most glorious creature in the world is valued by him. Will you not see it?

SPARKISH.

Right, honest Frank, I have that noble value for her that I cannot be jealous of her.

ALITHEA.

You mistake him: he means you care not for me nor who has me.

SPARKISH.

Lord madam, I see you are jealous. Will you wrest a poor man's meaning from his words?

ALITHEA.

You astonish me, sir, with your want* of jealousy.

SPARKISH.

And you make me giddy, madam, with your jealousy and fears and virtue and honor; gad, I see virtue makes a woman as troublesome as a little reading or learning.

ALITHEA.

Monstrous!

LUCY. (*Behind.*)

Well, to see what easy husbands these women of quality* can meet with! A poor chambermaid can never have such ladylike luck. Besides, he's thrown away upon her; she'll make no use of her fortune, her blessing. None to a gentleman for a pure cuckold, for it requires good breeding to be a cuckold.

ALITHEA.

I tell you then plainly: he pursues me to marry me.

SPARKISH.

Pshaw—

HARCOURT.

Come madam, you see you strive in vain to make him jealous of me; my dear friend is the kindest creature in the world to me.

SPARKISH.

Poor fellow.

HARCOURT.

But his kindness only is not enough for me, without your favor; your good opinion, dear madam, 'tis that must perfect my happiness. Good gentleman, he believes all I say; would you would do so. Jealous of me! I would not wrong him nor you for the world.

Alithea walks carelessly to and fro.

SPARKISH.

Look you there, hear him, hear him, and do not walk away so.

HARCOURT.

I love you, madam, so—

SPARKISH.

How's that! Nay—now you begin to go too far indeed.

HARCOURT.

So much, I confess, I say I love you, that I would not have you miserable and cast yourself away upon so unworthy and inconsiderable a thing as what you see here. (*Clapping his hand on his breast, points at Sparkish.*)

SPARKISH.

No, faith, I believe thou wouldst not, now his meaning is plain. But I knew before thou wouldst not wrong me nor her.

HARCOURT.

No, no, heavens forbid the glory of her sex should fall so low as into the embraces of such a contemptible wretch, the last of mankind—my dear friend here—I injure him. (*Embracing Sparkish.*)

ALITHEA.

Very well.

SPARKISH.

No, no, dear friend, I knew it.—Madam, you see he will rather wrong himself than me in giving himself such names.

ALITHEA.

Do not you understand him yet?

SPARKISH.
Yes, how modestly he speaks of himself, poor fellow.

ALITHEA.
Methinks he speaks impudently of yourself, since—before yourself, too, insomuch that I can no longer suffer his scurrilous abusiveness to you, no more than his love to me. (*Offers* to go.*)

SPARKISH.
Nay, nay, madam, pray stay. His love to you! Lord madam, has he not spoke yet plain enough?

ALITHEA.
Yes indeed, I should think so.

SPARKISH.
Well then, by the world, a man can't speak civilly to a woman now but presently* she says he makes love to her. Nay madam, you shall stay, with your pardon, since you have not yet understood him, till he has made an éclaircissement of his love to you, that is, what kind of love it is.—Answer to thy catechism. Friend, do you love my mistress here?

HARCOURT.
Yes, I wish she would not doubt it.

SPARKISH.
But how do you love her?

HARCOURT.
With all my soul.

ALITHEA.
I thank him, methinks he speaks plain enough now.

SPARKISH.
(*To Alithea.*)
You are out[46] still.—But with what kind of love, Harcourt?

HARCOURT.
With the best and truest love in the world.

SPARKISH.
Look you there then: that is with no matrimonial love, I'm sure.

ALITHEA.
How's that, do you say matrimonial love is not best?

SPARKISH. [*Aside.*]
Gad, I went too far ere I was aware.—But speak for thyself, Harcourt: you said you would not wrong me nor her.

HARCOURT.
No, no, madam, e'en take him for Heaven's sake—

SPARKISH.
Look you there, madam.

HARCOURT.
Who should in all justice be yours, he that loves you most. (*Claps his hand on his breast.*)

ALITHEA.
Look you there, Mr. Sparkish. Who's that?

SPARKISH.
Who should it be? Go on, Harcourt.

HARCOURT.
Who loves you more than women, titles, or fortune fools. (*Points at Sparkish.*)

SPARKISH.
Look you there: he means me still, for he points at me.

ALITHEA.
Ridiculous!

HARCOURT.
Who can only match your faith and constancy in love.

SPARKISH.
Aye.

HARCOURT.
Who knows, if it be possible, how to value so much beauty and virtue.

SPARKISH.
Aye.

HARCOURT.
Whose love can no more be equaled in the world than that heavenly form of yours.

SPARKISH.
No—

HARCOURT.
Who could no more suffer a rival than your absence and yet could no more suspect your virtue than his own constancy in his love to you.

SPARKISH.
No—

HARCOURT.
Who, in fine, loves you better than his eyes that first made him love you.

SPARKISH.
Aye.—Nay madam, faith you shan't go till—

46 out] mistaken

ALITHEA.
Have a care lest you make me stay too long—

SPARKISH.
But till he has saluted* you, that I may be assured you are friends after his honest advice and declaration. Come pray, madam, be friends with him.

Enter Pinchwife, Margery.

ALITHEA.
You must pardon me, sir, that I am not yet so obedient to you.

PINCHWIFE.
What, invite your wife to kiss men? Monstrous! Are you not ashamed? I will never forgive you.

SPARKISH.
Are you not ashamed that I should have more confidence in the chastity of your family than you have? You must not teach me: I am a man of honor, sir, though I am frank and free. I am frank, sir—

PINCHWIFE.
Very frank, sir, to share your wife with your friends.

SPARKISH.
He is an humble, menial friend, such as reconciles the differences of the marriage bed. You know man and wife do not always agree. I design him for that use, therefore, would have him well with my wife.

PINCHWIFE.
A menial friend—you will get a great many menial friends by showing your wife as you do.

SPARKISH.
What then, it may be I have a pleasure in't, as I have to show fine clothes at a playhouse the first day and count money before poor rogues.

PINCHWIFE.
He that shows his wife or money will be in danger of having them borrowed sometimes.

SPARKISH.
I love to be envied and would not marry a wife that I alone could love; loving alone is as dull as eating alone. Is it not a frank age, and I am a frank person? And to tell you the truth, it may be I love to have rivals in a wife: they make her seem to a man still* but as a kept* mistress, and so good night, for I must to Whitehall.—Madam, I hope you are now reconciled to my friend, and so I wish you a good night, madam, and sleep if you can, for tomorrow you know I must visit you early with a canonical gentleman.—Good night, dear Harcourt. (*Exit.*)

HARCOURT.
Madam, I hope you will not refuse my visit tomorrow, if it should be earlier, with a canonical gentleman, than Mr. Sparkish's.

PINCHWIFE. (*Coming between Alithea and Harcourt.*)
This gentlewoman is yet under my care; therefore, you must yet forbear your freedom with her, sir.

HARCOURT.
Must, sir—

PINCHWIFE.
Yes, sir, she is my sister.

HARCOURT.
'Tis well she is, sir—for I must be her servant, sir.—Madam—

PINCHWIFE.
Come away, sister. We had been gone if it had not been for you and so avoided these lewd rakehells who seem to haunt us.

Enter Horner, Dorilant to them.

HORNER.
How now, Pinchwife?

PINCHWIFE.
Your servant.

HORNER.
What, I see a little time in the country makes a man turn wild and unsociable and only fit to converse with his horses, dogs, and his herds.

PINCHWIFE.
I have business, sir, and must mind it. Your business is pleasure; therefore, you and I must go different ways.

HORNER.
Well, you may go on, but this pretty young gentleman— (*Takes hold of Margery.*)

HARCOURT.
The lady—

DORILANT.
And the maid—

HORNER.
Shall stay with us, for I suppose their business is the same with ours, pleasure.

PINCHWIFE. (*Aside.*)
'Sdeath,* he knows her, she carries it so sillily,* yet if he does not, I should be more silly to discover* it first.

ALITHEA.
Pray let us go, sir.

PINCHWIFE.
Come, come—

HORNER. (*To Margery.*)
Had you not rather stay with us?—Prithee Pinchwife, who is this pretty young gentleman?

PINCHWIFE.
One to whom I'm a guardian. (*Aside.*) I wish I could keep her out of your hands—

HORNER.
Who is he? I never saw any thing so pretty in all my life.

PINCHWIFE.
Pshaw, do not look upon him so much. He's a poor bashful youth; you'll put him out of countenance. Come away, brother. (*Offers* to take her away.*)

HORNER.
Oh your brother!

PINCHWIFE.
Yes, my wife's brother.—Come, come, she'll stay supper for us.

HORNER.
I thought so, for he is very like her I saw you at the play with, whom I told you I was in love with.

MARGERY. (*Aside.*)
Oh jiminy!* Is this he that was in love with me? I am glad on't, I vow, for he's a curious fine gentleman, and I love him already, too. (*To Mr. Pinchwife.*) Is this he, bud?

PINCHWIFE. (*To his wife.*)
Come away, come away.

HORNER.
Why, what haste are you in? Why won't you let me talk with him?

PINCHWIFE.
Because you'll debauch him. He's yet young and innocent, and I would not have him debauched for anything in the world. (*Aside.*) How she gazes on him! The devil—

HORNER.
Harcourt, Dorilant, look you here: this is the likeness of that dowdy he told us of, his wife. Did you ever see a lovelier creature? The rogue has reason to be jealous of his wife, since she is like him, for she would make all that see her in love with her.

HARCOURT.
And as I remember now, she is as like him here as can be.

DORILANT.
She is indeed very pretty, if she be like him.

HORNER.
Very pretty? a very pretty commendation! She is a glorious creature, beautiful beyond all things I ever beheld.

PINCHWIFE.
So, so.

HARCOURT.
More beautiful than a poet's first mistress of imagination.

HORNER.
Or another man's last mistress of flesh and blood.

MARGERY.
Nay, now you jeer, sir. Pray don't jeer me—

PINCHWIFE.
Come, come. (*Aside.*) By heavens, she'll discover* herself!

HORNER.
I speak of your sister, sir.

PINCHWIFE.
Aye, but saying she was handsome, if like him, made him blush. (*Aside.*) I am upon a rack—

HORNER.
Methinks he is so handsome, he should not be a man.

PINCHWIFE. [*Aside.*]
Oh there 'tis out! He has discovered her! I am not able to suffer any longer. (*To his wife.*) Come, come away, I say—

HORNER.
Nay by your leave, sir, he shall not go yet.—Harcourt, Dorilant, let us torment this jealous rogue a little.

HARCOURT AND DORILANT.
How?

HORNER.
I'll show you.

PINCHWIFE.
Come, pray let him go. I cannot stay fooling any longer. I tell you his sister stays supper for us.

HORNER.
Does she? Come then we'll all go sup with her and thee.

PINCHWIFE.
No, now I think on't, having stayed so long for us, I warrant she's gone to bed. (*Aside.*) I wish she and I were well out of their hands.—Come, I must rise early tomorrow, come.

HORNER.
Well then, if she be gone to bed, I wish her and you a good night.—But pray, young gentleman, present my humble service to her.

MARGERY.
Thank you heartily, sir.

PINCHWIFE. (*Aside.*)
S'death,* she will discover* herself yet in spite of me.—He is something more civil to you, for your kindness to his sister, than I am, it seems.

HORNER.
Tell her, dear sweet little gentleman, for all your brother there, that you have revived the love I had for her at first sight in the playhouse.

MARGERY.
But did you love her indeed and indeed?

PINCHWIFE. (*Aside.*)
So, so.—Away, I say.

HORNER.
Nay, stay. Yes, indeed and indeed, pray do you tell her so and give her this kiss from me. (*Kisses her.*)

PINCHWIFE. (*Aside.*)
Oh heavens! What do I suffer! Now 'tis too plain he knows her and yet—

HORNER.
And this and this— (*Kisses her again.*)

MARGERY.
What do you kiss me for? I am no woman.

PINCHWIFE. (*Aside.*)
So—there 'tis out.—Come, I cannot, nor will stay any longer.

HORNER.
Nay, they shall send your lady a kiss, too. Here Harcourt, Dorilant, will you not?

They kiss her.

PINCHWIFE. (*Aside.*)
How! Do I suffer this? Was I not accusing another just now for this rascally patience in permitting his wife to be kissed before his face? Ten thousand ulcers gnaw away their lips.—Come, come.

HORNER.
Good night, dear little gentleman.—Madam, good night.—Farewell, Pinchwife. (*Apart to Harcourt and Dorilant.*) Did not I tell you I would raise his jealous gall?

Exeunt Horner, Harcourt, and Dorilant.

PINCHWIFE.
So they are gone at last.—Stay, let me see first if the coach be at this door. (*Exit.*)

Horner, Harcourt, Dorilant return.

HORNER.
What, not gone yet? Will you be sure to do as I desired you, sweet sir?

MARGERY.
Sweet sir, but what will you give me then?

HORNER.
Anything. Come away into the next walk.

Exit Horner, haling away Margery.

ALITHEA.
Hold, hold, what d'ye do?

LUCY.
Stay, stay, hold—

Alithea, Lucy struggling with Harcourt and Dorilant.

HARCOURT.
Hold, madam, hold. Let him present[47] him; he'll come presently. Nay, I will never let you go till you answer my question.

LUCY.
For God's sake, sir, I must follow 'em.

DORILANT.
No, I have something to present you with, too. You shan't follow them.

Pinchwife returns.

PINCHWIFE.
Where? how? what's become of—? Gone! Whither?

---

47 present] give him a present

LUCY.
He's only gone with the gentleman, who will give him something, an't* please your worship.

PINCHWIFE.
Something—give him something, with a pox! Where are they?

ALITHEA.
In the next walk only, brother.

PINCHWIFE.
Only! Only! Where? Where? (*Exit and returns presently,* then goes out again.*)

HARCOURT.
What's the matter with him? Why so much concerned?—But dearest madam—

ALITHEA.
Pray let me go, sir. I have said and suffered enough already.

HARCOURT.
Then you will not look upon nor pity my sufferings?

ALITHEA.
To look upon 'em, when I cannot help 'em, were cruelty, not pity; therefore, I will never see you more.

HARCOURT.
Let me then, madam, have my privilege of a banished lover: complaining or railing and giving you but a farewell reason why, if you cannot condescend to marry me, you should not take that wretch my rival.

ALITHEA.
He only, not you, since my honor is engaged so far to him, can give me a reason why I should not marry him, but if he be true and what I think him to me, I must be so to him. Your servant, sir.

HARCOURT.
Have women only constancy when 'tis a vice and, like Fortune, only true to fools?

DORILANT. (*To Lucy, who struggles to get from him.*)
Thou shalt not stir, thou robust creature. You see I can deal with you; therefore, you should stay the rather and be kind.*

Enter Pinchwife.

PINCHWIFE.
Gone, gone, not to be found! quite gone! Ten thousand plagues go with 'em! Which way went they?

ALITHEA.
But into t'other walk, brother.

LUCY.
Their business will be done presently sure, an't* please your worship; it can't be long in doing, I'm sure on't.

ALITHEA.
Are they not there?

PINCHWIFE.
No, you know where they are, you infamous wretch, eternal shame of your family, which you do not dishonor enough yourself, you think, but you must help her to do it, too, thou legion of bawds!

ALITHEA.
Good brother!

PINCHWIFE.
Damned, damned sister!

ALITHEA.
Look you here, she's coming.

Enter Margery in man's clothes, running with her hat under her arm, full of oranges and dried fruit, Horner following.

MARGERY.
Oh dear bud, look you here what I have got! See.

PINCHWIFE. (*Aside, rubbing his forehead.*)
And what I have got here, too, which you can't see.

MARGERY.
The fine gentleman has given me better things yet.

PINCHWIFE.
Has he so? (*Aside.*) Out of breath and colored—I must hold yet.

HORNER.
I have only given your little brother an orange, sir.

PINCHWIFE. (*To Horner.*)
Thank you, sir. (*Aside.*) You have only squeezed my orange, I suppose, and given it me again, yet I must have a City* patience. (*To his wife.*) Come, come away.

MARGERY.
Stay, till I have put up my fine things, bud.

Enter Sir Jaspar Fidget.

SIR JASPAR.
Oh, Master Horner, come, come, the ladies stay for you. Your mistress, my wife, wonders you make not more haste to her.

HORNER.
I have stayed this half hour for you here, and 'tis your fault I am not now with your wife.

SIR JASPAR.
But pray, don't let her know so much; the truth on't is I was advancing a certain project to his Majesty about—I'll tell you.

HORNER.
No, let's go and hear it at your house.—Good night, sweet little gentleman. One kiss more.(*Kisses her.*) You'll remember me now, I hope.

DORILANT.
What, Sir Jaspar, will you separate friends? He promised to sup with us, and if you take him to your house, you'll be in danger of our company, too.

SIR JASPAR.
Alas gentlemen, my house is not fit for you: there are none but civil women there, which are not for your turn. He, you know, can bear with the society of civil women, now, ha, ha, ha. Besides he's one of my family;* he's—he, he, he.

DORILANT.
What is he?

SIR JASPAR.
Faith, my eunuch, since you'll have it, he, he, he.

Exit Sir Jaspar Fidget and Horner.

DORILANT.
I rather wish thou wert his, or my cuckold.—Harcourt, what a good cuckold is lost there for want of a man to make him one; thee and I cannot have Horner's privilege, who can make use of it.

HARCOURT.
Aye, to poor Horner 'tis like coming to an estate at threescore, when a man can't be the better for't.

PINCHWIFE.
Come.

MARGERY.
Presently, bud.

DORILANT.
Come, let us go, too. (*To Alithea.*) Madam, your servant. (*To Lucy.*) Good night, strapper.

HARCOURT.
Madam, though you will not let me have a good day or night, I wish you one, but dare not name the other half of my wish.

ALITHEA.
Good night, sir, forever.

MARGERY.
I don't know where to put this. Here, dear bud, you shall eat it. Nay, you shall have part of the fine gentleman's good things, or treat as you call it, when we come home.

PINCHWIFE.
Indeed I deserve it, since I furnished the best part of it. (*Strikes away the orange.*)
The gallant treats, presents, and gives the ball,
But 'tis the absent cuckold pays for all.

Act IV, scene i. Pinchwife's house in the morning.

Lucy, Alithea dressed in new clothes.

LUCY.
Well madam, now have I dressed you and set you out with so many ornaments and spent upon you ounces of essence and pulvillio,* and all this for no other purpose but as people adorn and perfume a corpse for a stinking second-hand grave, such or as bad I think Master Sparkish's bed.

ALITHEA.
Hold your peace.

LUCY.
Nay madam, I will ask you the reason why you would banish poor Master Harcourt forever from your sight? How could you be so hard-hearted?

ALITHEA.
'Twas because I was not hard-hearted.

LUCY.
No, no, 'twas stark love and kindness, I warrant.

ALITHEA.
It was so: I would see him no more because I love him.

LUCY.
Hey day, a very pretty reason.

ALITHEA.
You do not understand me.

LUCY.
I wish you may yourself.

ALITHEA.
I was engaged to marry, you see, another man, whom my justice will not suffer me to deceive or injure.

LUCY.
Can there be a greater cheat or wrong done to a man than to give him your person without your heart? I should make a conscience of it.

ALITHEA.
I'll retrieve it for him after I am married awhile.

LUCY.
The woman that marries to love better will be as much mistaken as the wencher that marries to live better. No madam, marrying to increase love is like gaming to become rich: alas, you only lose what little stock you had before.

ALITHEA.
I find by your rhetoric you have been bribed to betray me.

LUCY.
Only by his merit that has bribed your heart, you see, against your word and rigid honor. But what a devil is this honor? 'Tis sure a disease in the head, like the megrim or falling sickness,[48] that always hurries people away to do themselves mischief. Men lose their lives by it; women, what's dearer to 'em, their love, the life of life.

ALITHEA.
Come, pray talk you no more of honor nor Master Harcourt. I wish the other would come to secure my fidelity to him and his right in me.

LUCY.
You will marry him then?

ALITHEA.
Certainly, I have given him already my word and will my hand, too, to make it good when he comes.

LUCY.
Well, I wish I may never stick pin more, if he be not an arrant natural* to t'other fine gentleman.

ALITHEA.
I own he wants* the wit of Harcourt, which I will dispense withal for another want he has, which is want of jealousy, which men of wit seldom want.

LUCY.
Lord madam, what should you do with a fool to your husband? You intend to be honest,* don't you? Then that husbandly virtue, credulity, is thrown away upon you.

ALITHEA.
He only that could suspect my virtue should have cause to do it; 'tis Sparkish's confidence in my truth that obliges me to be so faithful to him.

LUCY.
You are not sure his opinion may last.

ALITHEA.
I am satisfied 'tis impossible for him to be jealous after the proofs I have had of him. Jealousy in a husband, Heaven defend me from it! It begets a thousand plagues to a poor woman: the loss of her honor, her quiet, and her—

LUCY.
And her pleasure.

ALITHEA.
What d'ye mean, impertinent?

LUCY.
Liberty is a great pleasure, madam.

ALITHEA.
I say loss of her honor, her quiet, nay, her life sometimes, and what's as bad almost, the loss of this Town; that is, she is sent into the country, which is the last ill usage of a husband to a wife, I think.

LUCY. (*Aside.*)
Oh does the wind lie there?—Then of necessity, madam, you think a man must carry his wife into the country if he be wise. The country is as terrible I find to our young English ladies as a monastery to those abroad. And on my virginity, I think they would rather marry a London gaoler than a high sheriff of a county, since neither can stir from his employment. Formerly women of wit married fools for a great estate, a fine seat, or the like, but now 'tis for a pretty seat only in Lincoln's Inn Fields, St. James's Fields, or the Pall Mall.[49]

Enter to them Sparkish and Harcourt dressed like a parson.

SPARKISH.
Madam, your humble servant, a happy day to you and to us all.

HARCOURT.
Amen.

---

[48] falling sickness] epilepsy

[49] Lincoln's Inns Fields, St. James's Fields, ... the Pall Mall] fashionable places to live in London

ALITHEA.
Who have we here?

SPARKISH.
My chaplain, faith. Oh madam, poor Harcourt remembers his humble service to you and, in obedience to your last commands, refrains coming into your sight.

ALITHEA.
Is not that he?

SPARKISH.
No, fie, no, but to show that he ne'er intended to hinder our match, has sent his brother here to join our hands. When I get me a wife, I must get her a chaplain, according to the custom; this is his brother and my chaplain.

ALITHEA.
His brother?

LUCY. (*Aside.*)
And your chaplain, to preach in your pulpit then.

ALITHEA.
His brother!

SPARKISH.
Nay, I knew you would not believe it.—I told you, sir, she would take you for your brother Frank.

ALITHEA.
Believe it!

LUCY. (*Aside.*)
His brother! Ha, ha, he, he has a trick left still it seems.

SPARKISH.
Come my dearest, pray let us go to church before the canonical hour* is past.

ALITHEA.
For shame! You are abused still.

SPARKISH.
By the world, 'tis strange now you are so incredulous.

ALITHEA.
'Tis strange you are so credulous.

SPARKISH.
Dearest of my life, hear me: I tell you this is Ned Harcourt of Cambridge; by the world, you see he has a sneaking college look. 'Tis true he's something like his brother Frank, and they differ from each other no more than in their age, for they were twins.

LUCY.
Ha, ha, he.

ALITHEA.
Your servant, sir. I cannot be so deceived, though you are. But come let's hear, how do you know what you affirm so confidently?

SPARKISH.
Why, I'll tell you all. Frank Harcourt coming to me this morning to wish me joy and present his service to you, I asked him if he could help me to a parson, whereupon he told me he had a brother in Town who was in orders, and he went straight away and sent him you see there to me.

ALITHEA.
Yes, Frank goes, and puts on a black coat, then tells you he is Ned; that's all you have for't.

SPARKISH.
Pshaw, pshaw, I tell you by the same token, the midwife put her garter about Frank's neck to know 'em asunder, they were so like.

ALITHEA.
Frank tells you this, too.

SPARKISH.
Aye, and Ned there too; nay, they are both in a story.

ALITHEA.
So, so, very foolish.

SPARKISH.
Lord, if you won't believe one, you had best try him by your chambermaid there, for chambermaids must needs know chaplains from other men, they are so used to 'em.[50]

LUCY.
Let's see: nay, I'll be sworn he has the canonical smirk and the filthy, clammy palm of a chaplain.

ALITHEA.
Well, most reverend doctor, pray let us make an end of this fooling.

HARCOURT.
With all my soul, divine, heavenly creature, when you please.

ALITHEA.
He speaks like a chaplain indeed.

---

50 chambermaids ... used to 'em] Alleged promiscuity between chambermaids and the clergy was a standard joke of the time.

SPARKISH.
Why, was there not, "soul," "divine," "heavenly," in what he said?

ALITHEA.
Once more, most impertinent blackcoat, cease your persecution and let us have a conclusion of this ridiculous love.

HARCOURT. (*Aside.*)
I had forgot, I must suit my style to my coat, or I wear it in vain.

ALITHEA.
I have no more patience left; let us make once an end of this troublesome love, I say.

HARCOURT.
So be it, seraphic lady, when your honor shall think it meet and convenient so to do.

SPARKISH.
Gad, I'm sure none but a chaplain could speak so, I think.

ALITHEA.
Let me tell you, sir, this dull trick will not serve your turn. Though you delay our marriage, you shall not hinder it.

HARCOURT.
Far be it from me, munificent patroness, to delay your marriage. I desire nothing more than to marry you presently,* which I might do, if you yourself would, for my noble, good-natured, and thrice generous patron here would not hinder it.

SPARKISH.
No, poor man, not I, faith.

HARCOURT.
And now, madam, let me tell you plainly, nobody else shall marry you, by heavens. I'll die first, for I'm sure I should die* after it.

LUCY. [*Aside.*]
How his love has made him forget his function, as I have seen it in real parsons.

ALITHEA.
That was spoken like a chaplain, too! Now you understand him, I hope.

SPARKISH.
Poor man, he takes it heinously to be refused. I can't blame him; 'tis putting an indignity upon him not to be suffered. But you'll pardon me, madam, it shan't be; he shall marry us. Come away, pray madam.

LUCY.
Ha, ha, he, more ado! 'Tis late.

ALITHEA.
Invincible stupidity, I tell you he would marry me as your rival, not as your chaplain.

SPARKISH. (*Pulling her away.*)
Come, come, madam.

LUCY.
I pray, madam, do not refuse this reverend divine the honor and satisfaction of marrying you, for I dare say, he has set his heart upon't, good doctor.

ALITHEA.
What can you hope or design by this?

HARCOURT. [*Aside.*]
I could answer her, a reprieve for a day only often revokes a hasty doom; at worst, if she will not take mercy on me and let me marry her, I have at least the lover's second pleasure, hindering my rival's enjoyment, though but for a time.

SPARKISH.
Come, madam, 'tis e'en twelve o'clock, and my mother charged me never to be married out of the canonical hours. Come, come. Lord, here's such a deal of modesty, I warrant, the first day.

LUCY.
Yes, an't* please your worship, married women show all their modesty the first day, because married men show all their love the first day.

Exeunt.

Scene [ii]. A bedchamber.

Pinchwife, Margery.

PINCHWIFE.
Come tell me, I say.

MARGERY.
Lord, han't I told it an hundred times over?

PINCHWIFE. (*Aside.*)
I would try, if in the repetition of the ungrateful tale, I could find her altering it in the least circumstance, for if her story be false, she is so too.—Come, how was't, baggage?

MARGERY.
Lord, what pleasure you take to hear it, sure!

PINCHWIFE.
No, you take more in telling it, I find, but speak. How was't?

MARGERY.
He carried me up into the house next to the Exchange.

PINCHWIFE.
So, and you two were only in the room.

MARGERY.
Yes, for he sent away a youth that was there, for some dried fruit and China oranges.*

PINCHWIFE.
Did he so? Damn him for it—and for—

MARGERY.
But presently* came up the gentlewoman of the house.

PINCHWIFE.
Oh 'twas well she did. But what did he do whilst the fruit came?

MARGERY.
He kissed me an hundred times and told me he fancied he kissed my fine sister, meaning me, you know, whom he said he loved with all his soul and bid me be sure to tell her so and to desire her to be at her window by eleven of the clock this morning, and he would walk under it at that time.

PINCHWIFE. (*Aside.*)
And he was as good as his word, very punctual. A pox reward him for't.

MARGERY.
Well, and he said if you were not within, he would come up to her, meaning me, you know, bud, still.

PINCHWIFE. (*Aside.*)
So—he knew her certainly, but for this confession I am obliged to her simplicity.—But what, you stood very still when he kissed you?

MARGERY.
Yes, I warrant you. Would you have had me discovered* myself?

PINCHWIFE.
But you told me he did some beastliness to you, as you called it. What was't?

MARGERY.
Why, he put—

PINCHWIFE.
What?

MARGERY.
Why he put the tip of his tongue between my lips and so muzzled[51] me—and I said I'd bite it.

PINCHWIFE.
An eternal canker seize it, for a dog!

MARGERY.
Nay, you need not be so angry with him neither, for to say truth, he has the sweetest breath I ever knew.

PINCHWIFE.
The devil—you were satisfied with it then and would do it again.

MARGERY.
Not unless he should force me.

PINCHWIFE.
Force you, changeling! I tell you no woman can be forced.

MARGERY.
Yes, but she may sure, by such a one as he, for he's a proper, goodly strong man; 'tis hard, let me tell you, to resist him.

PINCHWIFE. [*Aside.*]
So, 'tis plain she loves him, yet she has not love enough to make her conceal it from me, but the sight of him will increase her aversion for me and love for him, and that love instruct her how to deceive me and satisfy him, all idiot as she is. Love, 'twas he gave women first their craft, their art of deluding; out of Nature's hands they came plain, open, silly,* and fit for slaves, as she and Heaven intended 'em, but damned Love—well—I must strangle that little monster whilst I can deal with him.—Go fetch pen, ink, and paper out of the next room.

MARGERY.
Yes bud. (*Exit.*)

PINCHWIFE.
Why should women have more invention in love than men? It can only be because they have more desires, more soliciting passions, more lust, and more of the Devil.

Margery returns.

Come minx, sit down and write.

MARGERY.
Aye, dear bud, but I can't do't very well.

PINCHWIFE.
I wish you could not at all.

---

[51] muzzled] "to fondle with the mouth close" (Johnson's *Dictionary*); to French kiss

MARGERY.
But what should I write for?

PINCHWIFE.
I'll have you write a letter to your lover.

MARGERY.
Oh Lord, to the fine gentleman a letter!

PINCHWIFE.
Yes, to the fine gentleman.

MARGERY.
Lord, you do but jeer; sure you jest.

PINCHWIFE.
I am not so merry. Come write as I bid you.

MARGERY.
What, do you think I am a fool?

PINCHWIFE. [*Aside.*]
She's afraid I would not dictate any love to him; therefore, she's unwilling.—But you had best begin.

MARGERY.
Indeed and indeed, but I won't, so I won't.

PINCHWIFE.
Why?

MARGERY.
Because he's in Town; you may send for him if you will.

PINCHWIFE.
Very well, you would have him brought to you. Is it come to this? I say take the pen and write, or you'll provoke me.

MARGERY.
Lord, what d'ye make a fool of me for? Don't I know that letters are never writ but from the country to London and from London into the country? Now he's in Town, and I am in Town, too; therefore, I can't write to him, you know.

PINCHWIFE. (*Aside.*)
So, I am glad it is no worse; she is innocent enough yet.—Yes, you may when your husband bids you write letters to people that are in Town.

MARGERY.
Oh may I so! Then I'm satisfied.

PINCHWIFE.
Come begin. (*Dictates.*) "Sir"—

MARGERY.
Shan't I say, "Dear Sir"? You know one says always something more than bare "Sir."

PINCHWIFE.
Write as I bid you, or I will write whore with this penknife in your face.

MARGERY.
Nay, good bud. (*She writes.*) "Sir"—

PINCHWIFE.
"Though I suffered last night your nauseous, loathed kisses and embraces"—Write.

MARGERY.
Nay, why should I say so? You know I told you he had a sweet breath.

PINCHWIFE.
Write!

MARGERY.
Let me but put out "loathed."

PINCHWIFE.
Write I say!

MARGERY.
Well then. (*Writes.*)

PINCHWIFE.
Let's see what have you writ. (*Takes the paper and reads.*) "Though I suffered last night your kisses and embraces"—Thou impudent creature! Where is "nauseous" and "loathed"?

MARGERY.
I can't abide to write such filthy words.

PINCHWIFE. (*Holds up penknife.*)
Once more, write as I'd have you and question it not, or I will spoil thy writing with this. I will stab out those eyes that cause my mischief.

MARGERY.
Oh Lord, I will! [*Writes.*]

PINCHWIFE.
So—so—let's see now! (*Reads.*) "Though I suffered last night your nauseous, loathed kisses, and embraces." Go on: "Yet I would not have you presume that you shall ever repeat them." So—

She writes.

MARGERY.
I have writ it.

PINCHWIFE.
On then: "I then concealed myself from your knowledge to avoid your insolencies."

She writes.

MARGERY.
So—

PINCHWIFE.
"The same reason now I am out of your hands"—

She writes.

MARGERY.
So—

PINCHWIFE.
"Makes me own to you my unfortunate though innocent frolic of being in man's clothes"—

She writes.

MARGERY.
So—

PINCHWIFE.
"That you may forever more cease to pursue her who hates and detests you"—

She writes on.

MARGERY.
So—h— (*Sighs.*)

PINCHWIFE.
What, do you sigh?—"detests you—as much as she loves her husband and her honor."

MARGERY.
I vow, husband, he'll ne'er believe I should write such a letter.

PINCHWIFE.
What, he'd expect a kinder from you? Come now, your name only.

MARGERY.
What, shan't I say "Your most faithful, humble servant till death"?

PINCHWIFE.
No, tormenting fiend. (*Aside.*) Her style, I find, would be very soft.—Come wrap it up now whilst I go fetch wax and a candle and write on the back side "For Mr. Horner." (*Exit.*)

MARGERY.
"For Mr. Horner." So, I am glad he has told me his name. Dear Mr. Horner, but why should I send thee such a letter that will vex thee and make thee angry with me?—Well, I will not send it.—Aye, but then my husband will kill me, for I see plainly he won't let me love Mr. Horner.—But what care I for my husband?—I won't so, I won't send poor Mr. Horner such a letter.—But then my husband— But oh, what if I writ at bottom, "My husband made me write it"?—Aye, but then my husband would see't.—Can one have no shift? Ah, a London woman would have had a hundred presently.* Stay—what if I should write a letter and wrap it up like this and write upon't, too?—Aye, but then my husband would see't.—I don't know what to do.—But yet y'vads[52] I'll try, so I will, for I will not send this letter to poor Mr. Horner, come what will on't. (*She writes and repeats what she hath writ.*) "Dear, sweet Mr. Horner"—so— "My husband would have me send you a base, rude, unmannerly letter, but I won't,"—so—"and would have me forbid you loving me, but I won't,"—so—"and would have me say to you, I hate you, poor Mr. Horner, but I won't tell a lie for him,"—there—"for I'm sure if you and I were in the country at cards together,"—so—"I could not help treading on your toe under the table"—so—"or rubbing knees with you and staring in your face till you saw me"—very well—"and then looking down and blushing for an hour together."—so—"But I must make haste before my husband come, and now he has taught me to write letters, you shall have longer ones from me who am, dear, dear, poor dear Mr. Horner, your most humble friend and servant to command till death, Margery Pinchwife." Stay, I must give him a hint at bottom—so—now wrap it up just like t'other—so—now write "For Mr. Horner."—But oh now what shall I do with it? For here comes my husband.

Enter Pinchwife.

PINCHWIFE. (*Aside.*)
I have been detained by a sparkish coxcomb who pretended a visit to me, but I fear 'twas to my wife.—What, have you done?

MARGERY.
Aye, aye, bud, just now.

PINCHWIFE.
Let's see't. What d'ye tremble for? What, you would not have it go?

52 y'vads] in faith; a rustic expression

MARGERY.
Here. (*Aside.*) No, I must not give him that; so I had been served if I had given him this.

He opens and reads the first letter.

PINCHWIFE.
Come, where's the wax and seal?

MARGERY. (*Aside.*)
Lord, what shall I do now? Nay, then I have it.—Pray let me see't. Lord, you think me so arrant a fool, I cannot seal a letter? I will do't, so I will. (*Snatches the letter from him, changes it for the other, seals it, and delivers it to him.*)

PINCHWIFE.
Nay, I believe you will learn that and other things, too, which I would not have you.

MARGERY.
So, han't I done it curiously?[53] (*Aside.*) I think I have: there's my letter going to Mr. Horner, since he'll needs have me send letters to folks.

PINCHWIFE.
'Tis very well, but I warrant, you would not have it go now?

MARGERY.
Yes indeed, but I would, bud, now.

PINCHWIFE.
Well, you are a good girl then. Come let me lock you up in your chamber till I come back, and be sure you come not within three strides of the window when I am gone, for I have a spy in the street.

Exit Margery. Pinchwife locks the door.

At least 'tis fit she think so. If we do not cheat women, they'll cheat us, and fraud may be justly used with secret enemies, of which a wife is the most dangerous. And he that has a handsome one to keep, and a frontier town, must provide against treachery rather than open force. Now I have secured all within, I'll deal with the foe without with false intelligence.

Holds up the letter and exits.

[53] curiously] skillfully

Scene [iii]. Horner's lodging.

Quack and Horner.

QUACK.
Well sir, how fadges[54] the new design? Have you not the luck of all your brother projectors,* to deceive only yourself at last?

HORNER.
No, good domine[55] doctor, I deceive you, it seems, and others too, for the grave matrons and old rigid husbands think me as unfit for love as they are. But their wives, sisters, and daughters know, some of 'em, better things already.

QUACK.
Already!

HORNER.
Already, I say. Last night I was drunk with half a dozen of your* civil persons, as you call 'em, and people of honor and so was made free of their society and dressing rooms forever hereafter and am already come to the privileges of sleeping upon their pallets, warming smocks, tying shoes and garters, and the like, doctor, already, already, doctor.

QUACK.
You have made use of your time, sir.

HORNER.
I tell thee, I am now no more interruption to 'em when they sing or talk bawdy than a little, squab, French page who speaks no English.

QUACK.
But do civil persons and women of honor drink and sing bawdy songs?

HORNER.
Oh amongst friends, amongst friends. For your bigots in honor are just like those in religion: they fear the eye of the world more than the eye of Heaven and think there is no virtue but railing at vice and no sin but giving scandal. They rail at a poor, little, kept* player and keep themselves some young, modest pulpit comedian to be privy to their sins in their closets,* not to tell 'em of them in their chapels.

QUACK.
Nay, the truth on't is, priests amongst the women

[54] fadges] prospers

[55] domine] master (of a profession)

now have quite got the better of us lay confessors, physicians.

HORNER.
And they are rather their patients, but—

Enter Lady Fidget, looking about her.

Now we talk of women of honor, here comes one. Step behind the screen there and but observe if I have not particular privileges with the women of reputation already, doctor, already.

LADY FIDGET.
Well Horner, am not I a woman of honor? You see I'm as good as my word.

HORNER.
And you shall see, madam, I'll not be behindhand with you in honor, and I'll be as good as my word, too, if you please but to withdraw into the next room.

LADY FIDGET.
But first, my dear sir, you must promise to have a care of my dear honor.

HORNER.
If you talk a word more of your honor, you'll make me incapable to wrong it. To talk of honor in the mysteries of love is like talking of Heaven or the Deity in an operation of witchcraft: just when you are employing the Devil, it makes the charm impotent.

LADY FIDGET.
Nay, fie, let us not be smutty! But you talk of mysteries and bewitching to me; I don't understand you.

HORNER.
I tell you, madam, the word "money" in a mistress's mouth at such a nick of time is not a more disheartening sound to a younger brother than that of "honor" to an eager lover like myself.

LADY FIDGET.
But you can't blame a lady of my reputation to be chary.

HORNER.
Chary! I have been chary of it already by the report I have caused of myself.

LADY FIDGET.
Aye, but if you should ever let other women know that dear secret, it would come out. Nay, you must have a great care of your conduct, for my acquaintance are so censorious (oh 'tis a wicked censorious world, Mr. Horner), I say, are so censorious and detracting that perhaps they'll talk to the prejudice of my honor, though you should not let them know the dear secret.

HORNER.
Nay madam, rather than they shall prejudice your honor, I'll prejudice theirs, and to serve you, I'll lie with 'em all, make the secret their own, and then they'll keep it. I am a Machiavel* in love, madam.

LADY FIDGET.
Oh no, sir, not that way.

HORNER.
Nay, the devil take me if censorious women are to be silenced any other way.

LADY FIDGET.
A secret is better kept, I hope, by a single person than a multitude; therefore, pray do not trust anybody else with it, dear, dear Mr. Horner. (*Embracing him.*)

Enter Sir Jaspar Fidget.

SIR JASPAR.
How now!

LADY FIDGET. (*Aside.*)
Oh my husband—prevented—and what's almost as bad, found with my arms about another man. That will appear too much. What shall I say?—Sir Jaspar, come hither. I am trying if Mr. Horner were ticklish, and he's as ticklish as can be. I love to torment the confounded toad. Let you and I tickle him.

SIR JASPAR.
No, your ladyship will tickle him better without me, I suppose. But is this your buying china? I thought you had been at the china house?

HORNER. (*Aside.*)
China house, that's my cue; I must take it.—A pox, can't you keep your impertinent wives at home? Some men are troubled with the husbands, but I with the wives. But I'd have you to know, since I cannot be your journeyman by night, I will not be your drudge by day, to squire your wife about and be your man of straw, or scarecrow, only to pies and jays that would be nibbling at your

forbidden fruit. I shall be shortly the hackney gentleman-usher of the Town.

SIR JASPAR. (*Aside.*)

He, he, he, poor fellow, he's in the right on't, faith: to squire women about for other folks is as ungrateful an employment as to tell money for other folks.—He, he, he, ben't angry, Horner—

LADY FIDGET.

No, 'tis I have more reason to be angry, who am left by you to go abroad indecently alone or, what is more indecent, to pin myself upon such ill-bred people of your acquaintance, as this is.

SIR JASPAR.

Nay prithee, what has he done?

LADY FIDGET.

Nay, he has done nothing.

SIR JASPAR.

But what d'ye take ill if he has done nothing?

LADY FIDGET.

Ha, ha, ha! Faith, I can't but laugh, however. Why, d'ye think, the unmannerly toad would not come down to me to the coach. I was fain to come up to fetch him or go without him, which I was resolved not to do, for he knows china very well and has himself very good, but will not let me see it, lest I should beg some. But I will find it out and have what I came for yet.

Exit Lady Fidget, and locks the door, followed by Horner to the door.

HORNER. (*Apart to Lady Fidget.*)

Lock the door, madam.— So, she has got into my chamber and locked me out. Oh the impertinency of womankind! Well Sir Jaspar, plain dealing is a jewel: if ever you suffer your wife to trouble me again here, she shall carry you home a pair of horns,* by my Lord Mayor she shall; though I cannot furnish you myself, you are sure yet I'll find a way.

SIR JASPAR. (*Aside.*)

Ha, ha, he, at my first coming in and finding her arms about him, tickling him it seems, I was half jealous, but now I see my folly.—He, he, he, poor Horner.

HORNER.

Nay, though you laugh now, 'twill be my turn ere long. Oh women, more impertinent, more cunning, and more mischievous than their monkeys and to me almost as ugly.—Now is she throwing my things about and rifling all I have, but I'll get into her the back way and so rifle her for it.

SIR JASPAR.

Ha, ha, ha, poor angry Horner.

HORNER.

Stay here a little. I'll ferret her out to you presently, I warrant. (*Exit at t'other door.*)

SIR JASPAR.

Wife, my Lady Fidget, wife, he is coming into you the back way.

Sir Jaspar calls through the door to his wife; she answers from within.

LADY FIDGET.

Let him come, and welcome, which way he will.

SIR JASPAR.

He'll catch you and use you roughly and be too strong for you.

LADY FIDGET.

Don't you trouble yourself; let him if he can.

QUACK. (*Behind.*)

This indeed I could not have believed from him nor any but my own eyes.

Enter Mistress Squeamish.

MRS. SQUEAMISH.

Where's this woman-hater, this toad, this ugly, greasy, dirty sloven?

SIR JASPAR. [*Aside.*]

So the women all will have him ugly. Methinks he is a comely person, but his wants* make his form contemptible to 'em, and 'tis e'en as my wife said yesterday, talking of him, that a proper handsome eunuch was as ridiculous a thing as a gigantic coward.

MRS. SQUEAMISH.

Sir Jaspar, your servant. Where is the odious beast?

SIR JASPAR.

He's within in his chamber with my wife; she's playing the wag with him.

MRS. SQUEAMISH.

Is she so? And he's a clownish* beast: he'll give her no quarter; he'll play the wag with her again, let me tell you. Come, let's go help her. What, the door's locked?

SIR JASPAR.
Aye, my wife locked it.

MRS. SQUEAMISH.
Did she so? Let us break it open then.

SIR JASPAR.
No, no, he'll do her no hurt.

MRS. SQUEAMISH.
No. (*Aside.*) But is there no other way to get into 'em? Whither goes this? I will disturb 'em.

Exit Squeamish at another door. Enter Old Lady Squeamish.

OLD LADY SQUEAMISH.
Where is this harlotry, this impudent baggage, this rambling tomrig?[56]—Oh Sir Jaspar, I'm glad to see you here. Did you not see my vild[57] grandchild come in hither just now?

SIR JASPAR.
Yes.

OLD LADY SQUEAMISH.
Aye, but where is she then? Where is she? Lord, Sir Jaspar, I have e'en rattled myself to pieces in pursuit of her. But can you tell what she makes here? They say below, no woman lodges here.

SIR JASPAR.
No.

OLD LADY SQUEAMISH.
No—what does she here then? Say if it be not a woman's lodging, what makes she here? But are you sure no woman lodges here?

SIR JASPAR.
No, nor no man neither: this is Mr. Horner's lodging.

OLD LADY SQUEAMISH.
Is it so? Are you sure?

SIR JASPAR.
Yes, yes.

OLD LADY SQUEAMISH.
So then there's no hurt in't, I hope. But where is he?

SIR JASPAR.
He's in the next room with my wife.

OLD LADY SQUEAMISH.
Nay, if you trust him with your wife, I may with my Biddy. They say he's a merry, harmless man now, e'en as harmless a man as ever came out of Italy with a good voice and as pretty harmless company for a lady as a snake without his teeth.

SIR JASPAR.
Aye, aye, poor man.

Enter Mrs. Squeamish.

MRS. SQUEAMISH.
I can't find 'em.—Oh are you here, Grandmother? I followed, you must know, my Lady Fidget hither; 'tis the prettiest lodging, and I have been staring on the prettiest pictures.

Enter Lady Fidget with a piece of china in her hand and Horner following.

LADY FIDGET.
And I have been toiling and moiling for the prettiest piece of china, my dear.

HORNER.
Nay, she has been too hard for me, do what I could.

MRS. SQUEAMISH.
Oh Lord, I'll have some china, too. Good Mr. Horner, don't think to give other people china and me none. Come in with me, too.

HORNER.
Upon my honor I have none left now.

MRS. SQUEAMISH.
Nay, nay, I have known you deny your china before now, but you shan't put me off so. Come—

HORNER.
This lady had the last there.

LADY FIDGET.
Yes indeed, madam, to my certain knowledge he has no more left.

MRS. SQUEAMISH.
Oh but it may be he may have some you could not find.

LADY FIDGET.
What, d'ye think if he had had any left, I would not have had it too? For we women of quality* never think we have china enough.

---

56 tomrig] "a strumpet, a romping girl, a tomboy" (*OED*)

57 vild] archaic (as suits Old Lady Squeamish) form of "vile"

HORNER.
Do not take it ill. I cannot make china for you all, but I will have a roll-waggon[58] for you, too, another time.

MRS. SQUEAMISH.
Thank you, dear toad.

LADY FIDGET. (*To Horner, aside.*)
What do you mean by that promise?

HORNER. (*Apart to Lady Fidget.*)
Alas, she has an innocent, literal understanding.

OLD LADY SQUEAMISH.
Poor Mr. Horner. He has enough to do to please you all, I see.

HORNER.
Aye madam, you see how they use me.

OLD LADY SQUEAMISH.
Poor gentleman, I pity you.

HORNER.
I thank you, madam. I could never find pity but from such reverend ladies as you are; the young ones will never spare a man.

MRS. SQUEAMISH.
Come, come, beast, and go dine with us, for we shall want a man at ombre after dinner.

HORNER.
That's all their use of me, madam, you see.

MRS. SQUEAMISH.
Come sloven, I'll lead you to be sure of you. (*Pulls him by the cravat.*)

OLD LADY SQUEAMISH.
Alas, poor man, how she tugs him. Kiss, kiss her! That's the way to make such nice* women quiet.

HORNER.
No madam, that remedy is worse than the torment; they know I dare suffer anything rather than do it.

OLD LADY SQUEAMISH.
Prithee, kiss her, and I'll give you her picture in little[59] that you admired so last night, prithee do.

HORNER.
Well, nothing but that could bribe me. I love a woman only in effigy and good painting as much as I hate them. I'll do't, for I could adore the Devil well painted. (*Kisses Mrs. Squeamish.*)

MRS. SQUEAMISH.
Faugh, you filthy toad! Nay, now I've done jesting.

OLD LADY SQUEAMISH.
Ha, ha, ha, I told you so.

MRS. SQUEAMISH.
Faugh, a kiss of his—

SIR JASPAR.
Has no more hurt in't than one of my spaniel's.

MRS. SQUEAMISH.
Nor no more good neither.

QUACK. (*Behind.*)
I will now believe anything he tells me.

Enter Pinchwife.

LADY FIDGET.
Oh Lord, here's a man, Sir Jaspar! My mask, my mask. I would not be seen here for the world.

SIR JASPAR.
What, not when I am with you?

LADY FIDGET.
No, no, my honor—let's be gone.

MRS. SQUEAMISH.
Oh Grandmother, let us be gone. Make haste, make haste. I know not how he may censure us.

LADY FIDGET.
Be found in the lodging of anything like a man? Away.

Exeunt Sir Jaspar, Lady Fidget, Old Lady Squeamish, Mrs. Squeamish.

QUACK. (*Behind.*)
What's here, another cuckold? He looks like one, and none else sure have any business with him.

HORNER.
Well, what brings my dear friend hither?

PINCHWIFE.
Your impertinency.

HORNER.
My impertinency! Why, you gentlemen that have got handsome wives think you have a privilege of saying anything to your friends and are as brutish as if you were our creditors.

PINCHWIFE.
No sir, I'll ne'er trust you anyway.

[58] roll-waggon] a cylindrically shaped Chinese vase
[59] picture in little] miniature

HORNER.
But why not, dear Jack? Why diffide in[60] me thou knowst so well?

PINCHWIFE.
Because I do know you so well.

HORNER.
Han't I been always thy friend, honest Jack, always ready to serve thee, in love or battle, before thou wert married and am so still?

PINCHWIFE.
I believe so; you would be my second now indeed.

HORNER.
Well then, dear Jack, why so unkind, so grum, so strange to me? Come, prithee kiss me, dear rogue. Gad, I was always, I say, and am still as much thy servant as—

PINCHWIFE.
As I am yours, sir. What, you would send a kiss to my wife, is that it?

HORNER.
So there 'tis. A man can't show his friendship to a married man but presently* he talks of his wife to you. Prithee, let thy wife alone and let thee and I be all one, as we were wont. What, thou art as shy of my kindness as a Lombard Street[61] alderman of a courtier's civility at Locket's.*

PINCHWIFE.
But you are over-kind to me, as kind as if I were your cuckold already, yet I must confess you ought to be kind and civil to me since I am so kind, so civil to you as to bring you this. Look you there, sir. (*Delivers him a letter.*)

HORNER.
What is't?

PINCHWIFE.
Only a love letter, sir.

HORNER.
From whom? (*Reads.*)
How, this is from your wife!—hum—and hum—

PINCHWIFE.
Even from my wife, sir. Am I not wondrous kind and civil to you now, too? (*Aside.*) But you'll not think her so.

[60] diffide in] distrust

[61] Lombard Street] in the City

HORNER. (*Aside.*)
Hah, is this a trick of his or hers?

PINCHWIFE.
The gentleman's surprised, I find. What, you expected a kinder letter?

HORNER.
No faith, not I. How could I?

PINCHWIFE.
Yes, yes, I'm sure you did. A man so well made as you are must needs be disappointed if the women declare not their passion at first sight or opportunity.

HORNER. [*Aside.*]
But what should this mean? Stay, the postscript: "Be sure you love me whatsoever my husband says to the contrary, and let him not see this, lest he should come home and pinch me or kill my squirrel." It seems he knows not what the letter contains.

PINCHWIFE.
Come, ne'er wonder at it so much.

HORNER.
Faith, I can't help it.

PINCHWIFE.
Now I think I have deserved your infinite friendship and kindness and have showed myself sufficiently an obliging kind friend and husband. Am I not so, to bring a letter from my wife to her gallant?

HORNER.
Aye, the devil take me, art thou the most obliging, kind friend and husband in the world, ha, ha.

PINCHWIFE.
Well, you may be merry, sir, but in short I must tell you, sir, my honor will suffer no jesting.

HORNER.
What dost thou mean?

PINCHWIFE.
Does the letter want a comment? Then know, sir, though I have been so civil a husband as to bring you a letter from my wife, to let you kiss and court her to my face, I will not be a cuckold, sir, I will not.

HORNER.
Thou art mad with jealousy. I never saw thy wife in my life but at the play yesterday, and I know not if it were she or no. I court her, kiss her!

PINCHWIFE.
I will not be a cuckold, I say; there will be danger in making me a cuckold.

HORNER.
Why, wert thou not well cured of thy last clap?
PINCHWIFE.
I wear a sword.
HORNER.
It should be taken from thee lest thou shouldst do thyself a mischief with it. Thou art mad, man.
PINCHWIFE.
As mad as I am and as merry as you are, I must have more reason from you ere we part, I say again, though you kissed and courted last night my wife in man's clothes, as she confesses in her letter.
HORNER. (*Aside.*)
Hah!
PINCHWIFE.
Both she and I say you must not design it again, for you have mistaken your woman, as you have done your man.
HORNER. (*Aside.*)
Oh I understand something now.—Was that thy wife? Why wouldst thou not tell me 'twas she? Faith, my freedom with her was your fault, not mine.
PINCHWIFE. (*Aside.*)
Faith, so 'twas.
HORNER.
Fie, I'd never do't to a woman before her husband's face, sure.
PINCHWIFE.
But I had rather you should do't to my wife before my face than behind my back, and that you shall never do.
HORNER.
No, you will hinder me.
PINCHWIFE.
If I would not hinder you, you see by her letter, she would.
HORNER.
Well, I must e'en acquiesce then and be contented with what she writes.
PINCHWIFE.
I'll assure you 'twas voluntarily writ; I had no hand in't, you may believe me.
HORNER.
I do believe thee, faith.
PINCHWIFE.
And believe her too, for she's an innocent creature, has no dissembling in her, and so fare you well, sir.
HORNER.
Pray however, present my humble service to her and tell her I will obey her letter to a tittle and fulfill her desires be what they will or with what difficulty soever I do't, and you shall be no more jealous of me, I warrant her, and you—
PINCHWIFE.
Well then, fare you well, and play with any man's honor but mine, kiss any man's wife but mine, and welcome. (*Exit.*)
HORNER.
Ha, ha, ha, doctor.
QUACK.
It seems he has not heard the report of you or does not believe it.
HORNER.
Ha, ha, now doctor, what think you?
QUACK.
Pray let's see the letter. (*Reads.*) Hum—"for"—"dear"—"love you"—
HORNER.
I wonder how she could contrive it! What say'st thou to't? 'Tis an original.
QUACK.
So are your cuckolds, too, originals, for they are like no other common cuckolds, and I will henceforth believe it not impossible for you to cuckold the Grand Signior[62] amidst his guards of eunuchs, that I say.
HORNER.
And I say for the letter, 'tis the first love letter that ever was without flames, darts, fates, destinies, lying, and dissembling in't.

Enter Sparkish pulling in Pinchwife.

SPARKISH.
Come back! You are a pretty brother-in-law, neither go to church nor to dinner with your sister bride.
PINCHWIFE.
My sister denies her marriage and you see is gone away from you dissatisfied.

62 Grand Signior] the Sultan of Turkey

SPARKISH.

Pshaw, upon a foolish scruple that our parson was not in lawful orders and did not say all the Common Prayer,[63] but 'tis her modesty only, I believe. But let women be never so modest the first day, they'll be sure to come to themselves by night, and I shall have enough of her then. In the meantime, Harry Horner, you must dine with me; I keep my wedding at my aunt's in the Piazza.[64]

HORNER.

Thy wedding! What stale maid has lived to despair of a husband, or what young one of a gallant?

SPARKISH.

Oh your servant, sir. This gentleman's sister then—no stale maid.

HORNER.

I'm sorry for't.

PINCHWIFE. (*Aside.*)

How comes he so concerned for her?

SPARKISH.

You sorry for't! Why, do you know any ill by her?

HORNER.

No, I know none but by thee; 'tis for her sake, not yours, and another man's sake that might have hoped, I thought—

SPARKISH.

Another man, another man, what is his name?

HORNER.

Nay, since 'tis past, he shall be nameless. (*Aside.*) Poor Harcourt, I am sorry thou hast missed her.

PINCHWIFE. (*Aside.*)

He seems to be much troubled at the match.

SPARKISH.

Prithee, tell me.—Nay, you shan't go, brother.

PINCHWIFE.

I must of necessity, but I'll come to you to dinner. (*Exit.*)

SPARKISH.

But Harry, what, have I a rival in my wife already? But with all my heart, for he may be of use to me hereafter, for though my hunger is now my sauce and I can fall on heartily without. But the time will come, when a rival will be as good sauce for a married man to a wife as an orange to veal.

HORNER.

Oh thou damned rogue, thou hast set my teeth on edge with thy orange.

SPARKISH.

Then let's to dinner. There I was with you again. Come.

HORNER.

But who dines with thee?

SPARKISH.

My friends and relations, my brother Pinchwife, you see, of your acquaintance.

HORNER.

And his wife?

SPARKISH.

No, gad, he'll ne'er let her come amongst us good fellows. Your stingy country coxcomb keeps his wife from his friends as he does his little firkin of ale for his own drinking, and a gentleman can't get a smack on't. But his servants, when his back is turned, broach it at their pleasure and dust it away, ha, ha, ha. Gad, I am witty, I think, considering I was married today, by the world, but come—

HORNER.

No, I will not dine with you unless you can fetch her, too.

SPARKISH.

Pshaw, what pleasure canst thou have with women now, Harry?

HORNER.

My eyes are not gone. I love a good prospect yet and will not dine with you unless she does too. Go fetch her, therefore, but do not tell her husband 'tis for my sake.

SPARKISH.

Well, I'll go try what I can do. In the meantime, come away to my aunt's lodging; 'tis in the way to Pinchwife's.

HORNER. [*Apart to Quack.*]

The poor woman has called for aid and stretched forth her hand, doctor; I cannot but help her over the pale out of the briars.

Exeunt.

[63] Common Prayer] the marriage service within the Anglican *Book of Common Prayer*

[64] Piazza] arcade around two sides of Covent Garden*

Scene [iv]. Pinchwife's house.

Margery alone leaning on her elbow. A table, pen, ink, and paper.

MARGERY.
Well 'tis e'en so: I have got the London disease they call love; I am sick of my husband and for my gallant. I have heard this distemper called a fever, but methinks 'tis liker an ague, for when I think of my husband, I tremble and am in a cold sweat and have inclinations to vomit, but when I think of my gallant, dear Mr. Horner, my hot fit comes, and I am all in a fever indeed, and as in other fevers, my own chamber is tedious to me, and I would fain be removed to his, and then methinks I should be well. Ah poor Mr. Horner! Well, I cannot, will not stay here; therefore, I'll make an end of my letter to him, which shall be a finer letter than my last, because I have studied it like anything. Oh sick! sick! (*Takes the pen and writes.*)

Enter Mr. Pinchwife, who, seeing her writing, steals softly behind her and looking over her shoulder, snatches the paper from her.

PINCHWIFE.
What, writing more letters?
MARGERY.
Oh Lord, bud, why d'ye fright me so?

She offers to run out; he stops her and reads.

PINCHWIFE.
How's this! Nay, you shall not stir, madam. "Dear, dear, dear, Mr. Horner"—very well—I have taught you to write letters to good purpose, but let's see't. "First I am to beg your pardon for my boldness in writing to you, which I'd have you to know I would not have done, had not you said first you loved me so extremely, which if you do, you will never suffer me to lie in the arms of another man, whom I loathe, nauseate, and detest." Now you can write these filthy words! But what follows? "Therefore, I hope you will speedily find some way to free me from this unfortunate match, which was never, I assure you, of my choice, but I'm afraid 'tis already too far gone; however, if you love me, as I do you, you will try what you can do, but you must help me away before tomorrow, or else, alas, I shall be forever out of your reach for I can defer no longer our—" (*The letter concludes.*) "Our"? What is to follow "our"? Speak! What? Our journey into the country, I suppose. Oh woman, damned woman! And Love, damned Love, their old tempter! For this is one of his miracles: in a moment he can make those blind that could see and those see that were blind, those dumb that could speak and those prattle who were dumb before, nay, what is more than all, make these dough-baked,[65] senseless, indocile animals, women, too hard for us, their politic lords and rulers, in a moment. But make an end of your letter, and then I'll make an end of you thus and all my plagues together. (*Draws his sword.*)
MARGERY.
Oh Lord, oh Lord, you are such a passionate man, bud!

Enter Sparkish.

SPARKISH.
How now, what's here to do?
PINCHWIFE.
This fool here now!
SPARKISH.
What, drawn upon your wife? You should never do that but at night in the dark when you can't hurt her. This is my sister-in-law, is it not? (*Pulls aside her handkerchief.*) Aye faith, e'en our country Margery, one may know her. Come, she and you must go dine with me; dinner's ready, come. But where's my wife? Is she not come home yet? Where is she?
PINCHWIFE.
Making you a cuckold. 'Tis that they all do as soon as they can.
SPARKISH.
What, the wedding day? No, a wife that designs to make a cully of her husband will be sure to let him win the first stake of love, by the world. But come, they stay dinner for us; come, I'll lead down, our Margery.
MARGERY.
No sir, go, we'll follow you.

---

65 dough-baked] half-baked, foolish

SPARKISH.

I will not wag without you.

PINCHWIFE.

This coxcomb is a sensible torment to me amidst the greatest in the world.

SPARKISH.

Come, come, Madam Margery.

PINCHWIFE.

No, I'll lead her my way. What, would you treat your friends with mine, for want* of your own wife? (*Leads her to t'other door and locks her in and returns. Aside.*) I am contented my rage should take breath.

SPARKISH.

I told Horner this.

PINCHWIFE.

Come now.

SPARKISH.

Lord, how shy you are of your wife, but let me tell you, brother, we men of wit have amongst us a saying that cuckolding, like the small pox, comes with a fear, and you may keep your wife as much as you will out of danger of infection, but if her constitution incline her to't, she'll have it sooner or later, by the world, say they.

PINCHWIFE. (*Aside.*)

What a thing is a cuckold, that every fool can make him ridiculous.—Well sir, but let me advise you, now you are come to be concerned because you suspect the danger, not to neglect the means to prevent it, especially when the greatest share of the malady will light upon your own head, for
Hows'e'er the kind wife's belly comes to swell,
The husband breeds[66] for her and first is ill.

Act V, scene i. Pinchwife's house.

Enter Pinchwife and Margery. A table and candle.

PINCHWIFE.

Come, take the pen and make an end of the letter, just as you intended. If you are false in a tittle, I shall soon perceive it and punish you with this as you deserve. (*Lays his hand on his sword.*) Write what was to follow. Let's see. "You must make haste and help me away before tomorrow, or else I shall be forever out of your reach, for I can defer no longer our—" What follows "our"?

MARGERY.

Must all out then, bud? (*Margery takes the pen and writes.*) Look you there then.

PINCHWIFE.

Let's see. "For I can defer no longer our—wedding. Your slighted Alithea." What's the meaning of this, my sister's name to't? Speak, unriddle!

MARGERY.

Yes indeed, bud.

PINCHWIFE.

But why her name to't? Speak—speak, I say!

MARGERY.

Aye, but you'll tell her then again. If you would not tell her again—

PINCHWIFE.

I will not. I am stunned; my head turns round. Speak.

MARGERY.

Won't you tell her indeed and indeed?

PINCHWIFE.

No. Speak, I say.

MARGERY.

She'll be angry with me, but I had rather she should be angry with me than you, bud, and to tell you the truth, 'twas she made me write the letter and taught me what I should write.

PINCHWIFE. [*Aside.*]

Hah! I thought the style was somewhat better than her own.—But how could she come to you to teach you, since I had locked you up alone?

MARGERY.

Oh, through the keyhole, bud.

PINCHWIFE.

But why should she make you write a letter for her to him, since she can write herself?

MARGERY.

Why, she said because—for I was unwilling to do it.

PINCHWIFE.

Because what? Because?

MARGERY.

Because lest Mr. Horner should be cruel and refuse her, or vain afterwards and show the letter, she might disown it, the hand not being hers.

66 breeds] grows the cuckold's horns

PINCHWIFE. (*Aside.*)

How's this? Hah! Then I think I shall come to myself again. This changeling could not invent this lie. But if she could, why should she? She might think I should soon discover it. Stay—now I think on't, too, Horner said he was sorry she had married Sparkish, and her disowning her marriage to me makes me think she has evaded it for Horner's sake. Yet why should she take this course? But men in love are fools; women may well be so.—But hark you, madam, your sister went out in the morning and I have not seen her within since.

MARGERY.

Alackaday, she has been crying all day above, it seems, in a corner.

PINCHWIFE.

Where is she? Let me speak with her.

MARGERY. (*Aside.*)

Oh Lord, then he'll discover all.—Pray hold, bud. What, d'ye mean to discover* me? She'll know I have told you then. Pray bud, let me talk with her first.

PINCHWIFE.

I must speak with her to know whether Horner ever made her any promise and whether she be married to Sparkish or no.

MARGERY.

Pray dear bud, don't till I have spoken with her and told her that I have told you all, for she'll kill me else.

PINCHWIFE.

Go then, and bid her come out to me.

MARGERY.

Yes, yes, bud.

PINCHWIFE.

Let me see—

MARGERY. [*Aside.*]

I'll go, but she is not within to come to him. I have just got time to know of Lucy, her maid, who first set me on work, what lie I shall tell next, for I am e'en at my wit's end. (*Exit.*)

PINCHWIFE.

Well, I resolve it: Horner shall have her. I'd rather give him my sister than lend him my wife, and such an alliance will prevent his pretensions to my wife, sure. I'll make him of kin to her, and then he won't care for her.

Margery returns.

MARGERY.

Oh Lord, bud, I told you what anger you would make me with my sister.

PINCHWIFE.

Won't she come hither?

MARGERY.

No no, alackaday, she's ashamed to look you in the face, and she says if you go in to her, she'll run away downstairs and shamefully go herself to Mr. Horner, who has promised her marriage, she says, and she will have no other, so she won't—

PINCHWIFE.

Did he so—promise her marriage? Then she shall have no other. Go tell her so, and if she will come and discourse with me a little concerning the means, I will about it immediately. Go.

Exit Margery.

His estate is equal to Sparkish's, and his extraction as much better than his as his parts* are, but my chief reason is I'd rather be of kin to him by the name of brother-in-law than that of cuckold.

Enter Margery.

Well, what says she now?

MARGERY.

Why, she says she would only have you lead her to Horner's lodging—with whom she first will discourse the matter before she talk with you, which yet she cannot do, for, alack poor creature, she says she can't so much as look you in the face; therefore, she'll come to you in a mask, and you must excuse her if she make you no answer to any question of yours till you have brought her to Mr. Horner, and if you will not chide her nor question her, she'll come out to you immediately.

PINCHWIFE.

Let her come. I will not speak a word to her nor require a word from her.

MARGERY.

Oh, I forgot: besides, she says, she cannot look you in the face though through a mask; therefore, would desire you to put out the candle.

PINCHWIFE.

I agree to all; let her make haste.

Exit Margery; [Pinchwife] puts out the candle.

There, 'tis out. My case is something better: I'd rather fight with Horner for not lying with my sister than for lying with my wife, and of the two, I had rather find my sister too forward than my wife. I expected no other from her free education, as she calls it, and her passion for the Town. Well, wife and sister are names which make us expect love and duty, pleasure and comfort, but we find 'em plagues and torments and are equally, though differently, troublesome to their keeper, for we have as much ado to get people to lie with our sisters as to keep 'em from lying with our wives.

Enter Margery masked and in hoods and scarves and a nightgown and petticoat of Alithea's, in the dark.*

What, are you come, sister? Let us go then, but first let me lock up my wife. Mistress Margery, where are you?

MARGERY.
Here, bud.

PINCHWIFE.
Come hither, that I may lock you up.

Margery gives him her hand, but when he lets her go, she steals softly on t'other side of him.

Get you in. (*Locks the door.*) Come, sister, where are you now?

[She] is led away by him for his sister Alithea.

Scene [ii]. Horner's lodging.

Quack, Horner.

QUACK.
What, all alone, not so much as one of your cuckolds here nor one of their wives? They use to take their turns with you as if they were to watch you.

HORNER.
Yes, it often happens that a cuckold is but his wife's spy and is more upon family duty when he is with her gallant abroad hindering his pleasure than when he is at home with her playing the gallant. But the hardest duty a married woman imposes upon a lover is keeping her husband company always.

QUACK.
And his fondness wearies you almost as soon as hers.

HORNER.
A pox, keeping a cuckold company after you have had his wife is as tiresome as the company of a country squire to a witty fellow of the Town when he has got all his money.

QUACK.
And as at first a man makes a friend of the husband to get the wife, so at last you are fain to fall out with the wife to be rid of the husband.

HORNER.
Aye, most cuckold-makers are true courtiers: when once a poor man has cracked his credit for 'em, they can't abide to come near him.

QUACK.
But at first to draw him in, are so sweet, so kind, so dear, just as you are to Pinchwife. But what becomes of that intrigue with his wife?

HORNER.
A pox, he's as surly as an alderman that has been bit,* and since he's so coy, his wife's kindness* is in vain, for she's a silly* innocent.

QUACK.
Did she not send you a letter by him?

HORNER.
Yes, but that's a riddle I have not yet solved. Allow the poor creature to be willing, she is silly, too, and he keeps her up so close—

QUACK.
Yes, so close that he makes her but the more willing and adds but revenge to her love, which two, when met, seldom fail of satisfying each other one way or other.

HORNER.
What, here's the man we are talking of, I think.

Enter Pinchwife leading in his wife masked, muffled, and in her sister's gown.

HORNER.
Pshaw.

QUACK.
Bringing his wife to you is the next thing to bringing a love letter from her.

HORNER.
What means this?

PINCHWIFE.
The last time, you know, sir, I brought you a love

letter; now you see a mistress. I think you'll say I am a civil man to you.

HORNER.
Aye, the devil take me, will I say thou art the civilest man I ever met with, and I have known some. I fancy I understand thee now better than I did the letter, but hark thee in thy ear—

PINCHWIFE.
What?

HORNER.
Nothing but the usual question, man. Is she sound,* on thy word?

PINCHWIFE.
What, you take her for a wench and me for a pimp?

HORNER.
Pshaw, wench and pimp, paw[67] words. I know thou art an honest fellow and hast a great acquaintance among the ladies and perhaps hast made love* for me rather than let me make love to thy wife—

PINCHWIFE.
Come sir, in short, I am for no fooling.

HORNER.
Nor I neither. Therefore, prithee, let's see her face presently;* make her show, man. Art thou sure I don't know her?

PINCHWIFE.
I am sure you do know her.

HORNER.
A pox, why dost thou bring her to me then?

PINCHWIFE.
Because she's a relation of mine.

HORNER.
Is she, faith, man? Then thou art still more civil and obliging, dear rogue.

PINCHWIFE.
Who desired me to bring her to you.

HORNER.
Then she is obliging, dear rogue.

PINCHWIFE.
You'll make her welcome, for my sake, I hope.

HORNER.
I hope she is handsome enough to make herself welcome. Prithee, let her unmask.

[67] paw] "improper, naughty, obscene" (*OED*)

PINCHWIFE.
Do you speak to her; she would never be ruled by me.

HORNER.
Madam—

Margery whispers to Horner.

She says she must speak with me in private. Withdraw, prithee.

PINCHWIFE. (*Aside.*)
She's unwilling, it seems, I should know all her undecent conduct in this business.—Well then, I'll leave you together and hope when I am gone you'll agree; if not, you and I shan't agree, sir.

HORNER. [*Aside.*]
What means the fool?—If she and I agree, 'tis no matter what you and I do.

Whispers to Margery, who makes signs with her hand for [Pinchwife] to be gone.

PINCHWIFE.
In the meantime, I'll fetch a parson and find out Sparkish and disabuse him. You would have me fetch a parson, would you not? [*Aside.*] Well then, now I think I am rid of her and shall have no more trouble with her. Our sisters and daughters, like usurers' money, are safest when put out, but our wives, like their writings, never safe but in our closets* under lock and key. (*Exit.*)

Enter Boy.

BOY.
Sir Jaspar Fidget, sir, is coming up.

HORNER. [*Aside to Quack.*]
Here's the trouble of a cuckold now we are talking of. A pox on him! Has he not enough to do to hinder his wife's sport, but he must other women's, too?—Step in here, madam.

Exit Margery. Enter Sir Jaspar.

SIR JASPAR.
My best and dearest friend.

HORNER. [*Aside to Quack.*]
The old style, doctor.—Well, be short, for I am busy. What would your impertinent wife have now?

SIR JASPAR.

Well guessed i'faith, for I do come from her.

HORNER.

To invite me to supper. Tell her I can't come. Go.

SIR JASPAR.

Nay, now you are out, faith, for my lady and the whole knot of the virtuous gang, as they call themselves, are resolved upon a frolic of coming to you tonight in a masquerade and are all dressed already.

HORNER.

I shan't be at home.

SIR JASPAR.

Lord, how churlish he is to women! Nay, prithee don't disappoint 'em; they'll think 'tis my fault. Prithee, don't. I'll send in the banquet and the fiddles, but make no noise on't, for the poor virtuous rogues would not have it known for the world that they go a-masquerading, and they would come to no man's ball but yours.

HORNER.

Well, well—get you gone and tell 'em if they come, 'twill be at the peril of their honor and yours.

SIR JASPAR.

He, he, he—we'll trust you for that. Farewell. (*Exit.*)

HORNER.

Doctor, anon you too shall be my guest,
But now I'm going to a private feast.

[Exeunt.]

Scene [iii]. The Piazza of Covent Garden.

Sparkish, Pinchwife.

SPARKISH. (*The letter in his hand.*)

But who would have thought a woman could have been false to me? By the world, I could not have thought it.

PINCHWIFE.

You were for giving and taking liberty; she has taken it only, sir, now you find in that letter. You are a frank person, and so is she, you see there.

SPARKISH.

Nay, if this be her hand, for I never saw it.

PINCHWIFE.

'Tis no matter whether that be her hand or no. I am sure this hand, at her desire, led her to Mr. Horner, with whom I left her just now to go fetch a parson to 'em at their desire, too, to deprive you of her forever, for it seems yours was but a mock marriage.

SPARKISH.

Indeed, she would needs have it that 'twas Harcourt himself in a parson's habit that married us, but I'm sure he told me 'twas his brother Ned.

PINCHWIFE.

Oh there 'tis out, and you were deceived, not she, for you are such a frank person. But I must be gone. You'll find her at Mr. Horner's; go and believe your eyes. (*Exit.*)

SPARKISH.

Nay, I'll to her and call her as many crocodiles, sirens, harpies, and other heathenish names as a poet would do a mistress who had refused to hear his suit, nay more, his verses on her. But stay, is not that she following a torch at t'other end of the Piazza, and from Horner's certainly? 'Tis so.

Enter Alithea following a torch and Lucy behind.

You are well met, madam, though you don't think so. What, you have made a short visit to Mr. Horner, but I suppose you'll return to him presently; by that time the parson can be with him.

ALITHEA.

Mr. Horner and the parson, sir!

SPARKISH.

Come madam, no more dissembling, no more jilting, for I am no more a frank person.

ALITHEA.

How's this?

LUCY. (*Aside.*)

So 'twill work, I see.

SPARKISH.

Could you find out no easy country fool to abuse? None but me, a gentleman of wit and pleasure about the Town? But it was your pride to be too hard for a man of parts,* unworthy, false woman, false as a friend that lends a man money to lose, false as dice, who undo those that trust all they have to 'em.

LUCY. (*Aside.*)

He has been a great bubble* by his similes, as they say.

ALITHEA.

You have been too merry, sir, at your wedding dinner, sure.

SPARKISH.
What, d'ye mock me too?

ALITHEA.
Or you have been deluded.

SPARKISH.
By you.

ALITHEA.
Let me understand you.

SPARKISH.
Have you the confidence—I should call it something else, since you know your guilt—to stand my just reproaches? You did not write an impudent letter to Mr. Horner, who I find now has clubbed with you in deluding me with his aversion for women, that I might not, forsooth, suspect him for my rival?

LUCY. (*Aside.*)
D'ye think the gentleman can be jealous now, madam?

ALITHEA.
I write a letter to Mr. Horner!

SPARKISH.
Nay madam, do not deny it; your brother showed it me just now and told me likewise he left you at Horner's lodging to fetch a parson to marry you to him, and I wish you joy, madam, joy, joy, and to him, too, much joy and to myself, more joy for not marrying you.

ALITHEA. (*Aside.*)
So I find my brother would break off the match, and I can consent to't, since I see this gentleman can be made jealous.—Oh Lucy, by his rude usage and jealousy, he makes me almost afraid I am married to him. Art thou sure 'twas Harcourt himself and no parson that married us?

SPARKISH.
No madam, I thank you. I suppose that was a contrivance too of Mr. Horner's and yours to make Harcourt play the parson, but I would as little as you have him one now, no, not for the world, for shall I tell you another truth? I never had any passion for you till now, for now I hate you. 'Tis true I might have married your portion, as other men of parts* of the Town do sometimes, and so, your servant, and to show my unconcernedness, I'll come to your wedding and resign you with as much joy as I would a stale wench to a new cully, nay, with as much joy as I would after the first night, if I had been married to you. There's for you, and so, your servant, servant. (*Exit.*)

ALITHEA.
How was I deceived in a man!

LUCY.
You'll believe, then, a fool may be made jealous now? For that easiness in him that suffers him to be led by a wife will likewise permit him to be persuaded against her by others.

ALITHEA.
But marry Mr. Horner? My brother does not intend it, sure. If I thought he did, I would take thy advice and Mr. Harcourt for my husband, and now I wish that if there be any over-wise woman of the Town, who, like me, would marry a fool for fortune, liberty, or title: first, that her husband may love play and be a cully to all the Town but her and suffer none but Fortune to be mistress of his purse; then, if for liberty, that he may send her into the country under the conduct of some housewifely mother-in-law; and if for title, may the world give 'em none but that of cuckold.

LUCY.
And for her greater curse, madam, may he not deserve it.

ALITHEA.
Away, impertinent!—Is not this my old Lady Lanterlu's?[68]

LUCY.
Yes, madam. (*Aside.*) And here I hope we shall find Mr. Harcourt.

Exeunt.

Scene [iv]. Horner's lodging.

Horner, Lady Fidget, Dainty, Mrs. Squeamish. A table, banquet, and bottles.

HORNER. (*Aside.*)
A pox, they are come too soon—before I have sent back my new mistress! All I have now to do is to lock her in that they may not see her.

---

68 Lady Lanterlu's] lanterloo, or loo, a popular card game; from *lanturelu*, French for twaddle

LADY FIDGET.
That we may be sure of our welcome, we have brought our entertainment with us and are resolved to treat thee, dear toad—
DAINTY.
And that we may be merry to purpose, have left Sir Jaspar and my old Lady Squeamish quarreling at home at backgammon.
MRS. SQUEAMISH.
Therefore, let us make use of our time, lest they should chance to interrupt us.
LADY FIDGET.
Let us sit then.
HORNER.
First that you may be private, let me lock this door and that, and I'll wait upon you presently.
LADY FIDGET.
No sir, shut 'em only and your lips forever, for we must trust you as much as our women.*
HORNER.
You know all vanity's killed in me; I have no occasion for talking.
LADY FIDGET.
Now ladies, supposing we had drank each of us our two bottles, let us speak the truth of our hearts.
DAINTY AND MRS. SQUEAMISH.
Agreed.
LADY FIDGET.
By this brimmer, for truth is nowhere else to be found. (*Aside to Horner.*) Not in thy heart, false man.
HORNER. (*Aside to Lady Fidget.*)
You have found me a true man, I'm sure.
LADY FIDGET. (*Aside to Horner.*)
Not every way.—But let us sit and be merry. (*Sings.*)

I.

Why should our damned tyrants oblige us to live
On the pittance of pleasure which they only give?
    We must not rejoice
    With wine and with noise.
In vain we must wake in a dull bed alone,
Whilst to our warm rival the bottle they're gone.
    Then lay aside charms
    And take up these arms.*

(**The glasses.*)

II.

'Tis wine only gives 'em their courage and wit;
Because we live sober to men, we submit.
    If for beauties you'd pass,
    Take a lick of the glass;
'Twill mend your complexions, and when they are gone,
The best red we have is the red of the grape.
    Then sisters lay't on
    And damn a good shape.

DAINTY.
Dear brimmer! Well, in token of our openness and plain dealing, let us throw our masks over our heads.
HORNER.
So 'twill come to the glasses anon.
MRS. SQUEAMISH.
Lovely brimmer! Let me enjoy him first.
LADY FIDGET.
No, I never part with a gallant till I've tried him. Dear brimmer that mak'st our husbands short-sighted—
DAINTY.
And our bashful gallants bold—
MRS. SQUEAMISH.
And for want* of a gallant, the butler lovely in our eyes. Drink, eunuch.
LADY FIDGET.
Drink, thou representative of a husband. Damn a husband—
DAINTY.
And as it were a husband, an old keeper*—
MRS. SQUEAMISH.
And an old grandmother—
HORNER.
And an English bawd and a French chirurgeon.
LADY FIDGET.
Aye, we have all reason to curse 'em.
HORNER.
For my sake, ladies.
LADY FIDGET.
No, for our own, for the first spoils all young gallant's industry—
DAINTY.
And the other's art makes 'em bold only with common women—

MRS. SQUEAMISH.
And rather run the hazard of the vile distemper amongst them than of a denial amongst us.

DAINTY.
The filthy toads choose mistresses now as they do stuffs, for having been fancied and worn by others—

MRS. SQUEAMISH.
For being common and cheap—

LADY FIDGET.
Whilst women of quality,* like the richest stuffs, lie untumbled and unasked for.

HORNER.
Aye, neat and cheap and new often they think best.

DAINTY.
No sir, the beasts will be known by a mistress longer than by a suit—

MRS. SQUEAMISH.
And 'tis not for cheapness neither—

LADY FIDGET.
No, for the vain fops will take up druggets and embroider 'em. But I wonder at the depraved appetites of witty men; they used to be out of the common road and hate imitation. Pray tell me, beast, when you were a man, why you rather chose to club with a multitude in a common house for an entertainment than to be the only guest at a good table.

HORNER.
Why faith, ceremony and expectation are unsufferable to those that are sharp bent;[69] people always eat with the best stomach at an ordinary, where every man is snatching for the best bit—

LADY FIDGET.
Though he get a cut over the fingers. But I have heard people eat most heartily of another man's meat, that is, what they do not pay for.

HORNER.
When they are sure of their welcome and freedom, for ceremony in love and eating is as ridiculous as in fighting: falling on briskly is all should be done in those occasions.

LADY FIDGET.
Well then, let me tell you, sir, there is nowhere more freedom than in our houses, and we take freedom from a young person as a sign of good breeding, and a person may be as free as he pleases with us, as frolic, as gamesome, as wild as he will.

HORNER.
Han't I heard you all declaim against wild men?

LADY FIDGET.
Yes, but for all that, we think wildness in a man as desirable a quality as in a duck or rabbit. A tame man, faugh!

HORNER.
I know not, but your reputations frightened me as much as your faces invited me.

LADY FIDGET.
Our reputation! Lord, why should you not think that we women make use of our reputation as you men of yours, only to deceive the world with less suspicion? Our virtue is like the stateman's religion, the Quaker's word,[70] the gamester's oath, and the great man's honor: but to cheat those that trust us.

MRS. SQUEAMISH.
And that demureness, coyness, and modesty that you see in our faces in the boxes at plays is as much a sign of a kind* woman as a vizard-mask* in the pit.

DAINTY.
For I assure you, women are least masked when they have the velvet vizard on.

LADY FIDGET.
You would have found us modest women in our denials only—

MRS. SQUEAMISH.
Our bashfulness is only the reflection of the men's—

DAINTY.
We blush when they are shame-faced.

HORNER.
I beg your pardon, ladies, I was deceived in you devilishly. But why that mighty pretense to honor?

LADY FIDGET.
We have told you, but sometimes 'twas for the same reason you men pretend business often: to avoid ill company, to enjoy the better and more privately those you love.

---

[69] sharp bent] hungry

[70] Quaker's word] Quakers do not take oaths.

HORNER.

But why would you ne'er give a friend a wink then?

LADY FIDGET.

Faith, your reputation frightened us as much as ours did you, you were so notoriously lewd—

HORNER.

And you so seemingly honest.*

LADY FIDGET.

Was that all that deterred you?

HORNER.

And so expensive— (You allow freedom, you say?)

LADY FIDGET.

Aye, aye.

HORNER.

That I was afraid of losing my little money, as well as my little time, both which my other pleasures required.

LADY FIDGET.

Money, faugh! You talk like a little fellow now. Do such as we expect money?

HORNER.

I beg your pardon, madam, I must confess I have heard that great ladies, like great merchants, set but the higher prices upon what they have because they are not in necessity of taking the first offer.

DAINTY.

Such as we make sale of our hearts?

MRS. SQUEAMISH.

We bribed for our love? Faugh!

HORNER.

With your pardon, ladies, I know, like great men in offices, you seem to exact flattery and attendance only from your followers, but you have receivers[71] about you and such fees to pay, a man is afraid to pass your grants;[72] besides, we must let you win at cards, or we lose your hearts, and if you make an assignation, 'tis at a goldsmith's, jeweler's, or china house, where for your honor you deposit to him, he must pawn his to the punctual cit,* and so paying for what you take up, pays for what he takes up.

DAINTY.

Would you not have us assured of our gallant's love?

MRS. SQUEAMISH.

For love is better known by liberality than by jealousy—

LADY FIDGET.

For one may be dissembled, the other not. (*Aside.*) But my jealousy can be no longer dissembled, and they are telling-ripe.—Come, here's to our gallants in waiting, whom we must name, and I'll begin: this is my false rogue. (*Claps him on the back.*)

MRS. SQUEAMISH.

How!

HORNER.

So all will out now—

MRS. SQUEAMISH. (*Aside to Horner.*)

Did you not tell me 'twas for my sake only you reported yourself no man?

DAINTY. (*Aside.*)

Oh wretch! Did you not swear to me 'twas for my love and honor you passed for that thing you do?

HORNER.

So, so.

LADY FIDGET.

Come, speak ladies. This is my false villain.*

MRS. SQUEAMISH.

And mine too.

DAINTY.

And mine.

HORNER.

Well then, you are all three my false rogues too, and there's an end on't.

LADY FIDGET.

Well then, there's no remedy, sister sharers. Let us not fall out but have a care of our honor. Though we get no presents, no jewels of him, we are savers of our honor, the jewel of most value and use, which shines yet to the world unsuspected, though it be counterfeit.

HORNER.

Nay and is e'en as good as if it were true, provided the world think so, for honor, like beauty now, only depends on the opinion of others.

LADY FIDGET.

Well Harry Common, I hope you can be true to

71 receivers] servants who must be paid for cooperation and silence

72 pass your grants] accept your favors

three. Swear. But 'tis no purpose to require your oath, for you are as often forsworn as you swear to new women.

HORNER.

Come, faith madam, let us e'en pardon one another, for all the difference I find betwixt we men and you women, we forswear ourselves at the beginning of an amour, you, as long as it lasts.

Enter Sir Jaspar Fidget and Old Lady Squeamish.

SIR JASPAR.

Oh my Lady Fidget, was this your cunning, to come to Mr. Horner without me? But you have been no where else, I hope?

LADY FIDGET.

No, Sir Jaspar.

OLD LADY SQUEAMISH.

And you came straight hither, Biddy?

MRS. SQUEAMISH.

Yes indeed, Lady Grandmother.

SIR JASPAR.

'Tis well, 'tis well. I knew when once they were thoroughly acquainted with poor Horner, they'd ne'er be from him. You may let her masquerade it with my wife and Horner, and I warrant her reputation safe.

Enter boy.

BOY.

Oh sir, here's the gentleman come whom you bid me not suffer to come up without giving you notice, with a lady, too, and other gentlemen.

HORNER.

Do you all go in there, whilst I send 'em away.—And boy, do you desire 'em to stay below till I come, which shall be immediately.

Exeunt Sir Jaspar, [Old] Lady Squeamish, Lady Fidget, Dainty, Mrs. Squeamish.

BOY.

Yes sir. (*Exit.*)

Exit Horner at t'other door, and returns with Margery.

HORNER.

You would not take my advice to be gone home before your husband came back. He'll now discover all, yet pray, my dearest, be persuaded to go home and leave the rest to my management; I'll let you down the back way.

MARGERY.

I don't know the way home, so I don't.

HORNER.

My man shall wait upon you.

MARGERY.

No, don't you believe that I'll go at all. What, are you weary of me already?

HORNER.

No my life, 'tis that I may love you long, 'tis to secure my love and your reputation with your husband; he'll never receive you again else.

MARGERY.

What care I? D'ye think to frighten me with that? I don't intend to go to him again; you shall be my husband now.

HORNER.

I cannot be your husband, dearest, since you are married to him.

MARGERY.

Oh, would you make me believe that? Don't I see every day at London here, women leave their first husbands and go and live with other men as their wives? Pish, pshaw, you'd make me angry, but that I love you so mainly.

HORNER.

So, they are coming up. In again, in, I hear 'em.

Exit Margery.

Well, a silly* mistress is like a weak place, soon got, soon lost; a man has scarce time for plunder. She betrays her husband first to her gallant and then her gallant to her husband.

Enter Pinchwife, Alithea, Harcourt, Sparkish, Lucy, and a parson.

PINCHWIFE.

Come madam, 'tis not the sudden change of your dress, the confidence of your asseverations, and your false witness there shall persuade me I did not bring you hither just now; here's my witness, who cannot deny it, since you must be confronted.—Mr. Horner, did not I bring this lady to you just now?

HORNER. (*Aside.*)
Now must I wrong one woman for another's sake, but that's no new thing with me, for in these cases I am still on the criminal's side against the innocent.

ALITHEA.
Pray speak, sir.

HORNER. (*Aside.*)
It must be so. I must be impudent and try my luck; impudence uses to be too hard for truth.

PINCHWIFE.
What, you are studying an evasion or excuse for her. Speak, sir.

HORNER.
No, faith, I am something backward only to speak in women's affairs or disputes.

PINCHWIFE.
She bids you speak.

ALITHEA.
Aye, pray sir, do, pray satisfy him.

HORNER.
Then truly, you did bring that lady to me just now.

PINCHWIFE.
Oh ho!

ALITHEA.
How, sir!

HARCOURT.
How, Horner!

ALITHEA.
What mean you, sir? I always took you for a man of honor.

HORNER. (*Aside.*)
Aye, so much a man of honor that I must save my mistress, I thank you, come what will on't.

SPARKISH.
So if I had had her, she'd have made me believe, the moon had been made of a Christmas pie.

LUCY. (*Aside.*)
Now could I speak, if I durst, and solve the riddle, who am the author of it.

ALITHEA.
Oh unfortunate woman! [*To Harcourt.*] A combination against my honor, which most concerns me now, because you share in my disgrace, sir, and it is your censure, which I must now suffer, that troubles me, not theirs.

HARCOURT.
Madam, then have no trouble; you shall now see 'tis possible for me to love, too, without being jealous. I will not only believe your innocence myself, but make all the world believe it. (*Apart to Horner.*) Horner, I must now be concerned for this lady's honor.

HORNER.
And I must be concerned for a lady's honor, too.

HARCOURT.
This lady has her honor, and I will protect it.

HORNER.
My lady has not her honor, but has given it me to keep, and I will preserve it.

HARCOURT.
I understand you not.

HORNER.
I would not have you.

MARGERY. (*Peeping in behind.*)
What's the matter with 'em all?

PINCHWIFE.
Come, come, Mr. Horner, no more disputing. Here's the parson; I brought him not in vain.

HARCOURT.
No sir, I'll employ him, if this lady please.

PINCHWIFE.
How, what d'ye mean?

SPARKISH.
Aye, what does he mean?

HORNER.
Why, I have resigned your sister to him; he has my consent.

PINCHWIFE.
But he has not mine, sir. A woman's injured honor, no more than a man's, can be repaired or satisfied by any but him that first wronged it, and you shall marry her presently,* or— (*Lays his hand on his sword.*)

Enter Margery.

MARGERY.
Oh Lord, they'll kill poor Mr. Horner! Besides, he shan't marry her whilst I stand by and look on; I'll not lose my second husband so.

PINCHWIFE.
What do I see?

ALITHEA.
My sister in my clothes!

SPARKISH.
Hah!

MARGERY. (*To Pinchwife.*)
Nay, pray now don't quarrel* about finding work for the parson; he shall marry me to Mr. Horner, for now I believe you have enough of me.

HORNER.
Damned, damned, loving changeling.

MARGERY.
Pray sister, pardon me for telling so many lies of you.

HARCOURT.
I suppose the riddle is plain now.

LUCY.
No, that must be my work, good sir, hear me. *Kneels to Pinchwife, who stands doggedly, with his hat over his eyes.*

PINCHWIFE.
I will never hear woman again, but make 'em all silent thus— (*Offers* to draw upon his wife.*)

HORNER.
No, that must not be.

PINCHWIFE.
You then shall go first; 'tis all one to me. (*Offers* to draw on Horner, stopped by Harcourt.*)

HARCOURT.
Hold—

Enter Sir Jaspar Fidget, Lady Fidget, Old Lady Squeamish, Dainty, Mrs. Squeamish.

SIR JASPAR.
What's the matter, what's the matter, pray what's the matter, sir? I beseech you communicate, sir.

PINCHWIFE.
Why, my wife has communicated, sir, as your wife may have done, too, sir, if she knows him, sir.

SIR JASPAR.
Pshaw, with him, ha, ha, he!

PINCHWIFE.
D'ye mock me, sir? A cuckold is a kind of wild beast, have a care, sir.

SIR JASPAR.
No, sure you mock me, sir. He cuckold you! It can't be, ha, ha, he. Why, I'll tell you, sir. (*Offers to whisper.*)

PINCHWIFE.
I tell you again, he has whored my wife and yours, too, if he knows her, and all the women he comes near. 'Tis not his dissembling, his hypocrisy can wheedle me.

SIR JASPAR.
How! Does he dissemble? Is he a hypocrite? Nay, then—how—wife—sister, is he a hypocrite?

OLD LADY SQUEAMISH.
A hypocrite! A dissembler! Speak, young harlotry, speak. How!

SIR JASPAR.
Nay, then—oh my head too—oh thou libidinous lady!

OLD LADY SQUEAMISH.
Oh thou harloting harlotry, hast thou done't then?

SIR JASPAR.
Speak, good Horner. Art thou a dissembler, a rogue? Hast thou—

HORNER.
Soh—

LUCY. (*Apart to Horner.*)
I'll fetch you off and her too, if she will but hold her tongue.

HORNER. (*Apart to Lucy.*)
Canst thou? I'll give thee—

LUCY. (*To Mr. Pinchwife.*)
Pray have but patience to hear me, sir, who am the unfortunate cause of all this confusion. Your wife is innocent, I only culpable, for I put her upon telling you all these lies concerning my mistress in order to the breaking off the match between Mr. Sparkish and her to make way for Mr. Harcourt.

SPARKISH.
Did you so, eternal rotten tooth? Then it seems my mistress was not false to me; I was only deceived by you.—Brother that should have been, now, man of conduct, who is a frank person now? To bring your wife to her lover—hah!

LUCY.
I assure you, sir, she came not to Mr. Horner out of love, for she loves him no more—

MARGERY.
Hold! I told lies for you, but you shall tell none for me, for I do love Mr. Horner with all my soul, and nobody shall say me nay. Pray don't you go

to make poor Mr. Horner believe to the contrary. 'Tis spitefully done of you, I'm sure.

HORNER. (*Aside to Margery.*)
Peace, dear idiot.

MARGERY.
Nay, I will not peace.

PINCHWIFE.
Not till I make you.

Enter Dorilant, Quack.

DORILANT.
Horner, your servant. I am the doctor's guest; he must excuse our intrusion.

QUACK.
But what's the matter, gentlemen? For Heaven's sake, what's the matter?

HORNER.
Oh 'tis well you are come. 'Tis a censorious world we live in. You may have brought me a reprieve, or else I had died for a crime I never committed, and these innocent ladies had suffered with me; therefore, pray satisfy these worthy, honorable, jealous gentlemen that—(*Whispers.*)

QUACK.
Oh I understand you. Is that all?—Sir Jasper, by heavens and upon the word of a physician, sir,—(*Whispers to Sir Jaspar.*)

SIR JASPAR.
Nay, I do believe you truly.—Pardon me, my virtuous lady and dear of honor.

OLD LADY SQUEAMISH.
What, then all's right again.

SIR JASPAR.
Aye, aye, and now let us satisfy him, too.

They whisper with Pinchwife.

PINCHWIFE.
An eunuch! Pray no fooling with me.

QUACK.
I'll bring half the chirurgeons in Town to swear it.

PINCHWIFE.
They! They'll swear a man that bled to death through his wounds died of an apoplexy.

QUACK.
Pray hear me, sir. Why, all the Town has heard the report of him.

PINCHWIFE.
But does all the Town believe it?

QUACK.
Pray inquire a little and first of all these.

PINCHWIFE.
I'm sure when I left the Town he was the lewdest fellow in't.

QUACK.
I tell you, sir, he has been in France since. Pray ask but these ladies and gentlemen, your friend Mr. Dorilant.—Gentlemen and ladies, han't you all heard the late sad report of poor Mr. Horner?

ALL LADIES.
Aye, aye, aye.

DORILANT.
Why, thou jealous fool, dost thou doubt it? He's an arrant French capon.

MARGERY.
'Tis false, sir, you shall not disparage poor Mr. Horner, for to my certain knowledge—

LUCY.
Oh hold!

MRS.SQUEAMISH. (*Aside to Lucy.*)
Stop her mouth!

LADY FIDGET. (*To Pinchwife.*)
Upon my honor, sir, 'tis as true—

DAINTY.
D'ye think we would have been seen in his company—

MRS. SQUEAMISH.
Trust our unspotted reputations with him?

LADY FIDGET. (*Aside to Horner.*)
This you get and we, too, by trusting your secret to a fool.

HORNER.
Peace, madam. (*Aside to Quack.*) Well Doctor, is not this a good design that carries a man on unsuspected and brings him off safe?

PINCHWIFE. (*Aside.*)
Well, if this were true, but my wife—

Dorilant whispers with Margery.

ALITHEA.
Come brother, your wife is yet innocent, you see, but have a care of too strong an imagination, lest like an over-concerned, timorous gamester, by

fancying an unlucky cast, it should come. Women and Fortune are truest still* to those that trust 'em.

LUCY.

And any wild thing grows but the more fierce and hungry for being kept up and more dangerous to the keeper.

ALITHEA.

There's doctrine for all husbands, Mr. Harcourt.

HARCOURT.

And I edify, madam, so much that I am impatient till I am one.

DORILANT.

And I edify so much by example I will never be one.

SPARKISH.

And because I will not disparage my parts,* I'll ne'er be one.

HORNER.

And I, alas, can't be one.

PINCHWIFE.

But I must be one against my will, to a country wife, with a country murrain to me.

MARGERY. (*Aside.*)

And I must be a country wife still, too, I find, for I can't, like a City* one, be rid of my musty husband and do what I list.

HORNER.

Now sir, I must pronounce your wife innocent, though I blush whilst I do it, and I am the only man by her now exposed to shame, which I will straight drown in wine, as you shall your suspicion, and the ladies' troubles we'll divert with a ballet.—Doctor, where are your maskers?

LUCY.

Indeed, she's innocent, sir. I am her witness, and her end of coming out was but to see her sister's wedding, and what she has said to your face of her love to Mr. Horner was but the usual innocent revenge on a husband's jealousy, was it not? Madam, speak.

MARGERY. (*Aside to Lucy and Horner.*)

Since you'll have me tell more lies.—Yes indeed, bud.

PINCHWIFE.

For my own sake, fain I would all believe:
Cuckolds, like lovers, should themselves deceive.
But— (*Sighs.*)
His honor is least safe (too late I find)
Who trusts it with a foolish wife or friend.

A dance of cuckolds.

HORNER.

Vain fops but court and dress and keep a pother
To pass for women's men with one another,
But he who aims by women to be prized,
First by the men, you see, must be despised.

[Exeunt.]

FINIS.

Textual Notes

[a] Copytext is the first edition, a 1675 quarto (Q1). Also consulted: modern editions of 1924 (Summers), 1967 (Weales), 1975 (Cook and Swannell), 1979 (Friedman), 1981 (Holland), 1991 (Ogden), and 1996 (Dixon).

The Man of Mode; or, Sir Fopling Flutter[a]

by George Etherege (1636-1692)

edited by John H. O'Neill

Etherege's third and last comedy, *The Man of Mode*, debuted on March 11, 1676 at the Duke's Theatre in Dorset Garden, with King Charles II in attendance. According to *Roscius Anglicanus*, the memoirs of John Downes, the prompter of the Duke's Company, the cast for the performance included the following major company actors: Thomas Betterton as Dorimant; Henry Harris as Medley; William Smith as Sir Fopling Flutter; and Anthony Leigh as Old Bellair. Elizabeth Barry, fledgling starlet, apparently played Mrs. Loveit. It is unfortunate that Downes did not remember, or neglected to note, the actress who created the role of Harriet, one of the wittiest parts on the Restoration stage.

The Man of Mode took part in the 1670s' vogue for sexually explicit comedies, such as Betterton's *The Amorous Widow*, Dryden's *Marriage à la Mode* and *Mr. Limberham*, and Wycherley's *The Country Wife*. Early authorities agree that Etherege's comedy, with its accomplished actors and with splendid costumes, was highly successful in its first run—a contemporary letter says that "the entire court went three or four times to see *The Man of Mode*" (*London Stage*)—and that it remained popular with Restoration audiences well after the death of its author. It sustained its popularity on the English stage until the second half of the eighteenth century, when changing tastes made its sexual frankness seem objectionable. After a performance on October 31, 1755, Richard Cross wrote in his diary that the play was "Much dislik'd & Hiss'd" (*London Stage*). Soon thereafter, it was dropped from the repertory. There is no record of its being performed in the nineteenth century. But in the twentieth century it has been the focus of extensive critical interest. Together with Wycherley's *The Country Wife* and Congreve's *The Way of the World*, it is among the best-known comedies of the period.

Although we know that contemporary audiences loved the play, we cannot be sure how they interpreted it. Did they see it as an elegant description of the contemporary beau monde? As a picture of vice and degeneracy? As fantasy and farce? As satire? As social comedy?

The prologue and epilogue to *The Man of Mode* provide significant critical commentary on the play's meaning for contemporaries. In the prologue, the actor warns the gallants in the audience, using the familiar metaphor of satire as a mirror, that the comedy they will see presents a reflection of their own follies. The metaphor is twice repeated in the body of the play—first in Act II, scene i, which opens with Mrs. Loveit looking into her pocket glass and complaining to Pert, "I hate myself, I look so ill today," and second in Act IV, Scene ii, where Fopling asks Dorimant why he does not have a mirror hung up in his chamber so that he can "entertain himself."

The epilogue discusses the artistic problems posed by the creation of the fool character on stage. Many productions present "monstrous fools," which seem completely unreal and are appropriate only to farce. "A substantial ass" must be a realistic fool, incorporating "something of man," so that the character may resemble the gallants in the audience. The character of Sir Fopling, the epilogue continues, is difficult to distinguish from that of a wit, combining as it does elements of nature and artifice. This critical comment reinforces Medley's observation about Fopling in Act I: "Many a fool had been lost to the world, had their indulgent parents wisely bestowed neither learning nor good breeding upon 'em."

The epilogue ends by returning to the idea that the play presents its audience with a perspective on themselves, but now the metaphor is changed. Sir Fopling is a composite figure, comprising details drawn from a variety of individuals, representing the audience as a member of Parliament represents his constituents—"He's knight o' the shire and represents ye all." The prologue and epilogue, then, stress the play's satirical caricatures. The ending of the play, however, promises to put the most energetic young people to bed together, the typical ending of comedy.

PROLOGUE[1]

Like dancers on the ropes poor poets fare:
Most perish young, the rest in danger are.
This, one would think, should make our authors wary,
But gamester-like, the giddy fools miscarry;
A lucky hand or two so tempts 'em on,
They cannot leave off play till they're undone.
With modest fears a muse does first begin,
Like a young wench newly enticed to sin,
But tickled once with praise, by her good will
The wanton fool would never more lie still.
'Tis an old mistress you'll meet here tonight,
Whose charms you once have looked on with delight.
But now, of late, such dirty drabs have known ye,
A muse o'th'better sort's ashamed to own ye.
Nature well-drawn and wit must now give place
To gaudy nonsense and to dull grimace,
Nor is it strange that you should like so much
That kind of wit, for most of yours is such.
But I'm afraid that, while to France we go
To bring you home fine dresses, dance, and show,[2]
The stage, like you, will but more foppish grow.
Of foreign wares why should we fetch the scum,
When we can be so richly served at home?
For Heav'n be thanked, 'tis not so wise an age
But your own follies may supply the stage.
Though often plowed, there's no great fear the soil
Should barren grow by the too-frequent toil,
While at your doors are to be daily found
Such loads of dunghill to manure the ground.
'Tis by your follies that we players thrive,
As the physicians by diseases live,
And as each year some new distemper reigns,
Whose friendly poison helps t'increase their gains,
So among you there starts up every day
Some new, unheard-of fool for us to play.
Then, for your own sakes, be not too severe,
Nor what you all admire at home damn here.
Since each is fond of his own ugly face,
Why should you, when we hold it, break the glass?*

DRAMATIS PERSONAE

GENTLEMEN

Mr. Dorimant.
Mr. Medley.
Old Bellair.
Young Bellair.
Sir Fopling Flutter.
[Other men]
A shoemaker.
Four slovenly bullies.
Two chairmen.*
Mr. Smirk, a parson.
Handy, a valet de chambre.
Pages, footmen, etc.

GENTLEWOMEN

Lady Townley.
Emilia.
Mrs.* Loveit.
Bellinda.

[1] Prologue] probably spoken by Thomas Betterton, the actor who created the role of Dorimant (see lines 19-21, below, and note); written by "Sir Car Scroope, Baronet": Scroope (1649-1680), like Etherege, was a member of the Rochester-Buckingham circle of Whig wits in 1676.

[2] to France … show] Betterton had been sent to France as an official agent of King Charles II to study the French theater and to develop ideas for improving the quality of spectacle—costumes, sets, and machinery—on the English stage.

Lady Woodvill.
Harriet, her daughter.
Waiting women
Pert.
Busy.
[Other women]
An orange-woman.*

The Man of Mode; or, Sir Fopling Flutter.

Act I, scene i. A dressing room.
A table covered with a toilet;[3] clothes laid ready.

Enter Dorimant in his gown and slippers, with a note in his hand made up,[4] repeating verses.

DORIMANT.
"Now, for some ages, had the pride of Spain
Made the sun shine on half the world in vain."[5]
(*Then looking on the note.*) "For Mrs. Loveit." What a dull, insipid thing is a billet-doux written in cold blood, after the heat of the business is over! It is a tax upon good nature which I have here been laboring to pay, and have done it, but with as much regret as ever fanatic[6] paid the Royal Aid[7] or church duties.[8] 'Twill have the same fate, I know, that all my notes to her have had of late: 'twill not be thought kind enough. Faith, women are i'the right when they jealously examine our letters, for in them we always first discover* our decay of passion.—Hey! Who waits?

Enter Handy.

HANDY.
Sir—

DORIMANT.
Call a footman.

HANDY.
None of 'em are come yet.

DORIMANT.
Dogs! Will they ever lie snoring abed till noon?

HANDY.
'Tis all one, sir: if they're up, you indulge 'em so, they're ever poaching after whores all the morning.

DORIMANT.
Take notice henceforward who's wanting* in his duty; the next clap he gets, he shall rot for an example. What vermin are those chattering without?

HANDY.
Foggy[9] Nan, the orange-woman, and swearing Tom, the shoemaker.

DORIMANT.
Go, call in that overgrown jade with the flasket[10] of guts before her. Fruit is refreshing in a morning.

Exit Handy.

"It is not that I love you less,
Than when before your feet I lay—"[11]

Enter [Handy with] orange-woman.

How now, double tripe, what news do you bring?

ORANGE-WOMAN.
News! Here's the best fruit has come to Town* t' year. Gad, I was up before four o'clock this morning and bought all the choice i'the market.

DORIMANT.
The nasty refuse of your shop.

ORANGE-WOMAN.
You need not make mouths at it. I assure you, 'tis all culled ware.

DORIMANT.
The citizens* buy better on a holiday in their walk to Tottenham.[12]

3 toilet] a richly decorated cloth used as a cover for a dressing table

4 made up] written and folded

5 "Now ... vain"] Waller, "Of a War with Spain, and a Fight at Sea," 1-2

6 fanatic] an epithet applied to Dissenters, those who as a matter of conscience rejected the authority of the Crown and the Church of England

7 Royal Aid] "An extraordinary subsidy or tax made by Parliament for the King" (Barnard)

8 Church duties] local taxes charged for services of the parish church

9 foggy] flabby, puffy

10 flasket] a long, shallow basket

11 "It is ... lay"] Waller, "The Self-Banished," 1-2

12 Tottenham] village about 8 miles north of the City of London, now part of metropolitan London

ORANGE-WOMAN.
Good or bad, 'tis all one; I never knew you commend anything. Lord, would the ladies had heard you talk of 'em as I have done. Here— (*Sets down the fruit.*) Bid your man give me an angel.*

DORIMANT.
Give the bawd her fruit again.

ORANGE-WOMAN.
Well, on my conscience, there never was the like of you.—God's my life, I had almost forgot to tell you, there is a young gentlewoman, lately come to Town with her mother, that is so taken with you.

DORIMANT.
Is she handsome?

ORANGE-WOMAN.
Nay,[13] gad, there are few finer women, I tell you but so, and a hugeous fortune, they say. Here, eat this peach, it comes from the stone;[14] 'tis better than any Newington[15] y'ave tasted.

DORIMANT. (*Taking the peach.*)
This fine woman, I'll lay my life, is some awkward, ill-fashioned country toad, who, not having above four dozen of black hairs on her head, has adorned her baldness with a large white fruz,[16] that she may look sparkishly in the forefront of the King's box at an old play.

ORANGE-WOMAN.
Gad, you'd change your note quickly if you did but see her!

DORIMANT.
How came she to know me?

ORANGE-WOMAN.
She saw you yesterday at the Change.* She told me you came and fooled with the woman at the next shop.

DORIMANT.
I remember, there was a mask* observed me, indeed. "Fooled," did she say?

ORANGE-WOMAN.
Aye, I vow she told me twenty things you said, too, and acted with her head[b] and with her body so like you—

Enter Medley.

MEDLEY.
Dorimant, my life, my joy, my darling sin! How dost thou?

ORANGE-WOMAN.
Lord, what a filthy trick these men have got of kissing one another! (*She spits.*)

MEDLEY.
Why do you suffer this cartload of scandal to come near you and make your neighbors think you so improvident to need a bawd?

ORANGE-WOMAN.
Good—now we shall have it! You did but want* him to help you. Come, pay me for my fruit.

MEDLEY.
Make us thankful[17] for it, huswife. Bawds are as much out of fashion as gentlemen-ushers;[18] none but old formal ladies use the one, and none but foppish old stagers employ the other. Go, you are an insignificant brandy bottle.

DORIMANT.
Nay, there you wrong her. Three quarts of canary is her business.

ORANGE-WOMAN.
What you please, gentlemen.

DORIMANT.
To him! Give him as good as he brings.

ORANGE-WOMAN.
Hang him, there is not such another heathen in the Town again, except it be the shoemaker without.

MEDLEY.
I shall see you hold up your hand at the bar next sessions for murder, huswife. That shoemaker can take his oath you are in fee with the doctors to sell green fruit to the gentry, that the crudities[19] may breed diseases.

---

13 Nay] used as an interjection; does not mean "no"

14 comes from the stone] a freestone peach, one in which the fruit does not cling to the stone, or pit

15 Newington] a peach from the southeast of England

16 fruz] a frizzy, rumpled, and uneven wig

17 Make us thankful] "God make us thankful," here said ironically

18 gentlemen-ushers] door-keepers or male attendants on a lady

19 crudities] indigestible matter

ORANGE-WOMAN.
Pray give me my money.

DORIMANT.
Not a penny! When you bring the gentlewoman hither you spoke of, you shall be paid.

ORANGE-WOMAN.
The gentlewoman! The gentlewoman may be as honest* as your sisters, for aught as I know. Pray pay me, Mr. Dorimant, and do not abuse me so. I have an honester way of living; you know it.

MEDLEY.
Was there ever such a resty* bawd?

DORIMANT.
Some jade's tricks she has, but she makes amends when she's in good humor.—Come, tell me the lady's name, and Handy shall pay you.

ORANGE-WOMAN.
I must not; she forbid me.

DORIMANT.
That's a sure sign she would have you.

MEDLEY.
Where does she live?

ORANGE-WOMAN.
They lodge at my house.

MEDLEY.
Nay, then she's in a hopeful way.[20]

ORANGE-WOMAN.
Good Mr. Medley, say your pleasure of me, but take heed how you affront my house. God's my life, in a hopeful way!

DORIMANT.
Prithee, peace. What kind of woman's the mother?

ORANGE-WOMAN.
A goodly, grave gentlewoman. Lord, how she talks against the wild young men o'the Town! As for your part, she thinks you an arrant devil: should she see you, on my conscience she would look if you had not a cloven foot.

DORIMANT.
Does she know me?

ORANGE-WOMAN.
Only by hearsay. A thousand horrid stories have been told her of you, and she believes 'em all.

MEDLEY.
By the character,* this should be the famous Lady Woodvill and her daughter Harriet.

ORANGE-WOMAN. [*Aside.*]
The devil's in him for guessing, I think.

DORIMANT.
Do you know 'em?

MEDLEY.
Both very well. The mother's a great admirer of the forms and civility of the last age.[21]

DORIMANT.
An antiquated beauty may be allowed to be out of humor at the freedoms of the present. This is a good account of the mother. Pray, what is the daughter?

MEDLEY.
Why first, she's an heiress, vastly rich.

DORIMANT.
And handsome?

MEDLEY.
What alteration a twelvemonth may have bred in her, I know not, but a year ago she was the beautifullest creature I ever saw: a fine, easy, clean shape; light brown hair in abundance; her features regular; her complexion clear and lively; large, wanton eyes; but above all, a mouth that has made me kiss it a thousand times in imagination—teeth white and even, and pretty, pouting lips, with a little moisture ever hanging on them, that look like the Provins rose[22] fresh on the bush ere the morning sun has quite drawn up the dew.

DORIMANT.
Rapture, mere* rapture!

ORANGE-WOMAN.
Nay, gad, he tells you true. She's a delicate creature.

DORIMANT.
Has she wit?

MEDLEY.
More than is usual in her sex, and as much malice. Then, she's as wild as you would wish her and has a demureness in her looks that makes it so surprising.

---

20 in a hopeful way] in a situation to give hope of success (presumably, of seduction)

21 forms and civility of the last age] the formal manners of the reign of King Charles I, which ended in 1649

22 Provins rose] *Rosa gallica*, formerly known as *Rosa provinciallis*, that is, Provence Rose

DORIMANT.
Flesh and blood cannot hear this and not long to know her.

MEDLEY.
I wonder what makes her mother bring her up to Town? An old, doting keeper* cannot be more jealous of his mistress.

ORANGE-WOMAN.
She made me laugh yesterday. There was a judge came to visit 'em, and the old man, she told me, did so stare upon her and, when he saluted* her, smacked so heartily—who would think it of 'em?

MEDLEY.
God-a-mercy, Judge!

DORIMANT.
Do 'em right, the gentlemen of the long robe[23] have not been wanting* by their good examples to countenance the crying sin o'the nation.

MEDLEY.
Come, on with your trappings; 'tis later than you imagine.

DORIMANT.
Call in the shoemaker, Handy.

ORANGE-WOMAN.
Good Mr. Dorimant, pay me. Gad, I had rather give you my fruit than stay to be abused by that foul-mouthed rogue. What you gentlemen say, it matters not much, but such a dirty fellow does one more disgrace.

DORIMANT. [*To Handy.*]
Give her ten shillings. [*To orange-woman.*] And be sure you tell the young gentlewoman I must be acquainted with her.

ORANGE-WOMAN.
Now do you long to be tempting this pretty creature. Well, heavens mend you!

MEDLEY.
Farewell, bog[24]—

Exeunt orange-woman and Handy.

Dorimant, when did you see your *pis aller*, as you call her, Mrs. Loveit?

DORIMANT.
Not these two days.

MEDLEY.
And how stand affairs between you?

DORIMANT.
There has been great patching of late, much ado; we make a shift to hang together.

MEDLEY.
I wonder how her mighty spirit bears it?

DORIMANT.
Ill enough, on all conscience. I never knew so violent a creature.

MEDLEY.
She's the most passionate in her love and the most extravagant in her jealousy of any woman I ever heard of. What note is that?

DORIMANT.
An excuse I am going to send her for the neglect I am guilty of.

MEDLEY.
Prithee, read it.

DORIMANT.
No, but if you will take the pains, you may.

MEDLEY. (*Reads.*)
"I never was a lover of business, but now I have a just reason to hate it, since it has kept me these two days from seeing you. I intend to wait upon you in the afternoon, and in the pleasure of your conversation* forget all I have suffered during this tedious absence."—This business of yours, Dorimant, has been with a vizard* at the playhouse; I have had an eye on you. If some malicious body should betray you, this kind note would hardly make your peace with her.

DORIMANT.
I desire no better.

MEDLEY.
Why, would her knowledge of it oblige you?

DORIMANT.
Most infinitely: next to the coming to a good understanding with a new mistress, I love a quarrel with an old one. But the devil's in't, there has been such a calm in my affairs of late, I have not had the pleasure of making a woman so much as break her fan, to be sullen, or forswear herself these three days.

23 gentlemen of the long robe] lawyers and judges, the legal profession

24 bog] term for a fat person

MEDLEY.

A very great misfortune! Let me see, I love mischief well enough to forward this business myself. I'll about it presently,* and though I know the truth of what y'ave done will set her a-raving, I'll heighten it a little with invention, leave her in a fit o'the mother,* and be here again before y'are ready.

DORIMANT.

Pray stay, you may spare yourself the labor. The business is undertaken already by one who will manage it with as much address and, I think, with a little more malice than you can.

MEDLEY.

Who i'the devil's name can this be?

DORIMANT.

Why, the vizard, that very vizard you saw me with.

MEDLEY.

Does she love mischief so well as to betray herself to spite another?

DORIMANT.

Not so, neither, Medley; I will make you comprehend the mystery. This mask,* for a farther confirmation of what I have been these two days swearing to her, made me yesterday at the playhouse make her a promise before her face utterly to break off with Loveit and, because she tenders my reputation and would not have me do a barbarous thing, has contrived a way to give me a handsome occasion.

MEDLEY.

Very good.

DORIMANT.

She intends, about an hour before me this afternoon, to make Loveit a visit, and (having the privilege by reason of a professed friendship between 'em to talk of her concerns)—

MEDLEY.

Is she a friend?

DORIMANT.

Oh, an intimate friend!

MEDLEY.

Better and better! Pray proceed.

DORIMANT.

She means insensibly[25] to insinuate a discourse of me and artificially[26] raise her jealousy to such a height that, transported with the first motions of her passion, she shall fly upon me with all the fury imaginable as soon as ever I enter. The quarrel being thus happily begun, I am to play my part: confess and justify all my roguery, swear her impertinence and ill humor makes her intolerable, tax her with the next fop that comes into my head, and in a huff march away, slight her, and leave her to be taken by whosoever thinks it worth his time to lie down before her.

MEDLEY.

This vizard is a spark and has a genius that makes her worthy of yourself, Dorimant.

Enter Handy, shoemaker, and footman.

DORIMANT. [*To footman.*]

You rogue there, who sneak like a dog that has flung down a dish! If you do not mend your waiting, I'll uncase you[27] and turn you loose to the wheel of fortune.—Handy, seal this and let him run with it presently.*

Exeunt Handy and footman[; Handy returns after a moment].

MEDLEY.

Since y'are resolved on a quarrel, why do you send her this kind note?

DORIMANT.

To keep her at home in order to the business. (*To the shoemaker.*) How now, you drunken sot?

SHOEMAKER.

'Sbud,* you have no reason to talk. I have not had a bottle of sack* of yours in my belly this fortnight.

MEDLEY.

The orange-woman says your neighbors take notice what a heathen you are and design to inform the bishop and have you burned for an atheist.

SHOEMAKER.

Damn her, dunghill! If her husband does not remove her, she stinks so, the parish intend to indict him for a nuisance.

25 insensibly] gradually, imperceptibly

26 artificially] cunningly

27 uncase you] strip you of your livery, fire you

MEDLEY.
I advise you like a friend, reform your life. You have brought the envy of the world upon you by living above yourself. Whoring and swearing are vices too genteel for a shoemaker.

SHOEMAKER.
'Sbud, I think you men of quality* will grow as unreasonable as the women; you would engross the sins o'the nation. Poor folks can no sooner be wicked but th'are railed at by their betters.

DORIMANT.
Sirrah, I'll have you stand i'the pillory for this libel.

SHOEMAKER.
Some of you deserve it, I'm sure. There are so many of 'em that our journeymen nowadays, instead of harmless ballads, sing nothing but your damned lampoons.

DORIMANT.
Our lampoons, you rogue?

SHOEMAKER.
Nay, good master, why should not you write your own commentaries as well as Caesar?[28]

MEDLEY.
The rascal's read, I perceive.

SHOEMAKER.
You know the old proverb, ale and history.[29]

DORIMANT.
Draw on my shoes, sirrah.

SHOEMAKER.
Here's a shoe—

DORIMANT.
Sits with more wrinkles than there are in an angry bully's forehead.

SHOEMAKER.
'Sbud, as smooth as your mistress's skin does upon her. So, strike your foot in home. 'Sbud, if e'er a monsieur of 'em all make more fashionable ware, I'll be content to have my ears whipped off with my own paring knife.

MEDLEY.
And served up in a ragout, instead of coxcombs, to a company of French shoemakers for a collation.

SHOEMAKER.
Hold, hold! Damn 'em, caterpillars! Let 'em feed upon cabbage!—Come master, your health this morning next my heart now.[30]

DORIMANT.
Go, get you home, and govern your family better! Do not let your wife follow you to the alehouse, beat your whore, and lead you home in triumph.

SHOEMAKER.
'Sbud, there's never a man i'the Town lives more like a gentleman with his wife than I do. I never mind her motions; she never inquires into mine. We speak to one another civilly, hate one another heartily, and because 'tis vulgar to lie and soak[31] together, we have each of us our several settle-bed.

DORIMANT. [*To Handy.*]
Give him half a crown.

MEDLEY.
Not without he will promise to be bloody drunk.

SHOEMAKER. [*Taking the coin.*]
Tope's the word i'the eye of the world, for my master's honor, Robin!

DORIMANT.
Do not debauch my servants, sirrah.

SHOEMAKER.
I only tip him the wink; he knows an alehouse from a hovel.

Exit Shoemaker.

DORIMANT. [*To Handy.*]
My clothes, quickly!

MEDLEY.
Where shall we dine today?

Enter Young Bellair.

DORIMANT.
Where you will. Here comes a good third man.

YOUNG BELLAIR.
Your servant, gentlemen.

MEDLEY.
Gentle* sir, how will you answer this visit to your honorable mistress? 'Tis not her interest you should

28 commentaries … Caesar] memoirs, as Caesar's *Gallic Wars*

29 ale and history] "Truth is in ale as in history" (proverbial).

30 your health … now] The shoemaker asks for money to drink to Dorimant's health.

31 soak] drink

keep company with men of sense, who will be talking reason.

YOUNG BELLAIR.
I do not fear her pardon, do you but grant me yours for my neglect of late.

MEDLEY.
Though y'ave made us miserable by the want* of your good company, to show you I am free from all resentment, may the beautiful cause of our misfortune give you all the joys happy lovers have shared ever since the world began.

YOUNG BELLAIR.
You wish me in heaven, but you believe me on my journey to hell.

MEDLEY.
You have a good strong faith, and that may contribute much towards your salvation. I confess I am but of an untoward constitution, apt to have doubts and scruples, and in love they are no less distracting than in religion. Were I so near marriage, I should cry out by fits as I ride in my coach, "Cuckold, cuckold!" with no less fury than the mad fanatic does "Glory!" in Bethlem.[32]

YOUNG BELLAIR.
Because religion makes some run mad, must I live an atheist?

MEDLEY.
Is it not great indiscretion for a man of credit, who may have money enough on his word, to go and deal with Jews, who for little sums make men enter into bonds and give judgments?[33]

YOUNG BELLAIR.
Preach no more on this text; I am determined, and there is no hope of my conversion.

DORIMANT. (*To Handy, who is fiddling about him.*)
Leave your unnecessary fiddling. A wasp that's buzzing about a man's nose at dinner is not more troublesome than thou art.

HANDY.
You love to have your clothes hang just, sir.

DORIMANT.
I love to be well-dressed, sir, and think it no scandal to my understanding.

HANDY.
Will you use the essence or orange-flower water?

DORIMANT.
I will smell as I do today, no offense to the ladies' noses.

HANDY.
Your pleasure, sir. [*Exit.*]

DORIMANT.
That a man's excellency should lie in neatly tying of a ribbon or a cravat! How careful's Nature in furnishing the world with necessary coxcombs!

YOUNG BELLAIR.
That's a mighty pretty suit of yours, Dorimant.

DORIMANT.
I am glad 't has your approbation.

YOUNG BELLAIR.
No man in Town has a better fancy in his clothes than you have.

DORIMANT.
You will make me have an opinion of my genius.

MEDLEY.
There is a great critic, I hear, in these matters lately arrived piping hot from Paris.

YOUNG BELLAIR.
Sir Fopling Flutter, you mean.

MEDLEY.
The same.

YOUNG BELLAIR.
He thinks himself the pattern of modern gallantry.

DORIMANT.
He is indeed the pattern of modern foppery.

MEDLEY.
He was yesterday at the play, with a pair of gloves up to his elbows and a periwig more exactly curled than a lady's head newly dressed for a ball.

YOUNG BELLAIR.
What a pretty lisp he has!

DORIMANT.
Ho, that he affects in imitation of the people of quality* of France.

MEDLEY.
His head stands for the most part on one side, and

32 mad fanatic ... Bethlem] Bethlehem Hospital, commonly known as Bedlam, the mental hospital in London. The "mad fanatic," formerly porter to Oliver Cromwell, was a patient in the hospital (Brett-Smith).

33 enter ... judgments] give security for a loan

his looks are more languishing than a lady's when she lolls at stretch in her coach or leans her head carelessly against the side of a box i'the playhouse.

DORIMANT.

He is a person indeed of great acquired follies.

MEDLEY.

He is, like many others, beholding to his education for making him so eminent a coxcomb. Many a fool had been lost to the world, had their indulgent parents wisely bestowed neither learning nor good breeding on 'em.

YOUNG BELLAIR.

He has been, as the sparkish word is, brisk upon the ladies already. He was yesterday at my Aunt Townley's and gave Mrs. Loveit a catalogue of his good qualities under the character* of a complete gentleman, who, according to Sir Fopling, ought to dress well, dance well, fence well, have a genius for love letters, an agreeable voice for a chamber, be very amorous, something discreet, but not overconstant.

MEDLEY.

Pretty ingredients to make an accomplished person!

DORIMANT.

I am glad he pitched upon Loveit.

YOUNG BELLAIR.

How so?

DORIMANT.

I wanted a fop to lay to her charge, and this is as pat as may be.

YOUNG BELLAIR.

I am confident she loves no man but you.

DORIMANT.

The good fortune were enough to make me vain but that I am in my nature modest.

YOUNG BELLAIR.

Hark you, Dorimant.—With your leave, Mr. Medley, 'tis only a secret concerning a fair lady.

MEDLEY.

Your good breeding, sir, gives you too much trouble. You might have whispered without all this ceremony.

YOUNG BELLAIR. (*To Dorimant.*)

How stand your affairs with Bellinda of late?

DORIMANT.

She's a little jilting baggage.

YOUNG BELLAIR.

Nay, I believe her false enough, but she's ne'er the worse for your purpose. She was with you yesterday in disguise at the play.

DORIMANT.

There we fell out and resolved never to speak to one another more.

YOUNG BELLAIR.

The occasion?

DORIMANT.

Want* of courage to meet me at the place appointed. These young women apprehend loving as much as the young men do fighting at first, but once entered, like them too, they all turn bullies straight.

Enter Handy.

HANDY. (*To Young Bellair.*)

Sir, your man without desires to speak with you.

YOUNG BELLAIR.

Gentlemen, I'll return immediately. (*Exit.*)

MEDLEY.

A very pretty fellow, this.

DORIMANT.

He's handsome, well-bred, and by much the most tolerable of all the young men that do not abound in wit.

MEDLEY.

Ever well-dressed, always complaisant, and seldom impertinent; you and he are grown very intimate, I see.

DORIMANT.

It is our mutual interest to be so. It makes the women think the better of his understanding and judge more favorably of my reputation; it makes him pass upon some for a man of very good sense, and I upon others for a very civil person.

MEDLEY.

What was that whisper?

DORIMANT.

A thing which he would fain have known, but I did not think it fit to tell him. It might have frighted him from his honorable intentions of marrying.

MEDLEY.

Emilia, give her her due, has the best reputation

of any young woman about the Town who has beauty enough to provoke detraction. Her carriage is unaffected, her discourse modest—not at all censorious nor pretending, like the counterfeits of the age.

DORIMANT.

She's a discreet maid, and I believe nothing can corrupt her but a husband.

MEDLEY.

A husband?

DORIMANT.

Yes, a husband. I have known many women make a difficulty of losing a maidenhead, who have afterwards made none of making a cuckold.

MEDLEY.

This prudent consideration, I am apt to think, has made you confirm poor Bellair in the desperate resolution he has taken.

DORIMANT.

Indeed, the little hope I found there was of her, in the state she was in, has made me by my advice contribute something towards the changing of her condition.

Enter Young Bellair.

Dear Bellair, by heavens, I thought we had lost thee! Men in love are never to be reckoned on when we would form a company.

YOUNG BELLAIR.

Dorimant, I am undone. My man has brought the most surprising news i'the world.

DORIMANT.

Some strange misfortune is befallen your love?

YOUNG BELLAIR.

My father came to Town last night and lodges i'the very house where Emilia lies.

MEDLEY.

Does he know it is with her you are in love?

YOUNG BELLAIR.

He knows I love, but knows not whom, without some officious sot* has betrayed me.

DORIMANT.

Your Aunt Townley is your confidante and favors the business.

YOUNG BELLAIR.

I do not apprehend any ill office from her. I have received a letter, in which I am commanded by my father to meet him at my aunt's this afternoon. He tells me farther he has made a match for me and bids me resolve to be obedient to his will or expect to be disinherited.

MEDLEY.

Now's your time, Bellair. Never had lover such an opportunity of giving a generous proof of his passion.

YOUNG BELLAIR.

As how, I pray?

MEDLEY.

Why, hang an estate, marry Emilia out of hand, and provoke your father to do what he threatens. 'Tis but despising a coach, humbling yourself to a pair of galoshes,[34] being out of countenance when you meet your friends, pointed at and pitied wherever you go by all the amorous fops that know you, and your fame will be immortal.

YOUNG BELLAIR.

I could find it in my heart to resolve not to marry at all.

DORIMANT.

Fie, fie! That would spoil a good jest and disappoint the well-natured Town of an occasion of laughing at you.

YOUNG BELLAIR.

The storm I have so long expected hangs o'er my head and begins to pour down upon me. I am on the rack and can have no rest till I'm satisfied in what I fear. Where do you dine?

DORIMANT.

At Long's or Locket's.*

MEDLEY.

At Long's let it be.

YOUNG BELLAIR.

I'll run and see Emilia and inform myself how matters stand. If my misfortunes are not so great as to make me unfit for company, I'll be with you. (*Exit.*)

Enter a footman, with a letter.

FOOTMAN. (*To Dorimant.*)

Here's a letter, sir.

---

34 galoshes] pattens or clogs, wooden attachments to the shoe to raise the walker out of the mud and filth of the street

DORIMANT.
The superscription's right: "For Mr. Dorimant."
MEDLEY.
Let's see—the very scrawl and spelling of a true-bred whore.
DORIMANT.
I know the hand. The style is admirable, I assure you.
MEDLEY.
Prithee, read it.
DORIMANT. (Reads.)
"I told a you you dud not love me, if you dud, you would have seen me again ere now. I have no money and am very mallicolly. Pray send me a guynie to see the operies. Your servant to command, Molly."
MEDLEY.
Pray let the whore have a favorable answer, that she may spark it[35] in a box and do honor to her profession.
DORIMANT.
She shall, and perk up i'the face of quality.* [*To Handy.*] Is the coach at door?
HANDY.
You did not bid me send for it.
DORIMANT.
Eternal blockhead!

Handy offers to go out.

Hey, sot!*
HANDY.
Did you call me, sir?
DORIMANT.
I hope you have no just exception to the name, sir?
HANDY.
I have sense, sir.
DORIMANT.
Not so much as a fly in winter.—How did you come, Medley?
MEDLEY.
In a chair.*
FOOTMAN.
You may have a hackney coach if you please, sir.

[35] spark it] show off, look fashionable

DORIMANT.
I may ride the elephant if I please, sir. Call another chair and let my coach follow to Long's.
"Be calm, ye great parents, [of the floods and the springs,
While each Nereid and Triton plays, revels, and sings"][36]

Exeunt singing.

Act II, scene i. [Lady Townley's house.]

Enter my Lady Townley and Emilia.

LADY TOWNLEY.
I was afraid, Emilia, all had been discovered.*
EMILIA.
I tremble with the apprehension still.
LADY TOWNLEY.
That my brother should take lodgings i'the very house where you lie!
EMILIA.
'Twas lucky we had timely notice to warn the people[37] to be secret. He seems to be a mighty good-humored old man.
LADY TOWNLEY.
He ever had a notable smirking way with him.
EMILIA.
He calls me rogue, tells me he can't abide me, and does so bepat me.
LADY TOWNLEY.
On my word, you are much in his favor, then.
EMILIA.
He has been very inquisitive, I am told, about my family, my reputation, and my fortune.
LADY TOWNLEY.
I am confident he does not i'the least suspect you are the woman his son's in love with.
EMILIA.
What should make him then inform himself so particularly of me?
LADY TOWNLEY.
He was always of a very loving temper himself. It may be he has a doting fit upon him, who knows?

[36] "Be calm ... sings"] from Shadwell's adaptation of *The Tempest* (Act V)

[37] the people] the servants

EMILIA.
It cannot be.

Enter Young Bellair.

LADY TOWNLEY.
Here comes my nephew.—Where did you leave your father?

YOUNG BELLAIR.
Writing a note within.—Emilia, this early visit looks as if some kind jealousy would not let you rest at home.

EMILIA.
The knowledge I have of my rival gives me a little cause to fear your constancy.

YOUNG BELLAIR.
My constancy! I vow—

EMILIA.
Do not vow—Our love is frail as is our life, and full as little in our power, and are you sure you shall outlive this day?

YOUNG BELLAIR.
I am not, but when we are in perfect health, 'twere an idle thing to fright ourselves with the thoughts of sudden death.

LADY TOWNLEY.
Pray, what has passed between you and your father i'the garden?

YOUNG BELLAIR.
He's firm in his resolution, tells me I must marry Mrs.* Harriet, or swears he'll marry himself and disinherit me. When I saw I could not prevail with him to be more indulgent, I dissembled an obedience to his will, which has composed his passion and will give us time—and, I hope, opportunity—to deceive him.

Enter Old Bellair, with a note in his hand.

LADY TOWNLEY.
Peace, here he comes.

OLD BELLAIR.
Harry, take this and let your man carry it for me to Mr. Fourbe's[38] chamber—my lawyer, i'the Temple.*

38 Fourbe] The French word *fourbe* means a cheat or "con artist" or "scam."

[Exit Young Bellair.]

(*To Emilia.*) Neighbor, adod[39] I am glad to see thee here.—Make much of her, sister. She's one of the best of your acquaintance. I like her countenance and her behavior well; she has a modesty that is not common i'this age, adod she has.

LADY TOWNLEY.
I know her value, brother, and esteem her accordingly.

OLD BELLAIR.
Advise her to wear a little more mirth in her face; adod, she's too serious.

LADY TOWNLEY.
The fault is very excusable in a young woman.

OLD BELLAIR.
Nay, adod, I like her ne'er the worse; a melancholy beauty has her charms. I love a pretty sadness in a face which varies now and then, like changeable colors, into a smile.

LADY TOWNLEY.
Methinks you speak very feelingly, brother.

OLD BELLAIR.
I am but five-and-fifty, sister, you know—an age not altogether unsensible! (*To Emilia.*) Cheer up, sweetheart; I have a secret to tell thee may chance to make thee merry. We three will make collation together anon. I'the meantime, mum, I can't abide you; go, I can't abide you—

Enter Young Bellair.

Harry! Come, you must along with me to my Lady Woodvill's.—I am going to slip the boy at a mistress.

YOUNG BELLAIR.
At a wife, sir, you would say.

OLD BELLAIR.
You need not look so glum, sir. A wife is no curse when she brings the blessing of a good estate with her. But an idle Town flirt, with a painted face, a rotten reputation, and a crazy fortune, adod, is the devil and all—and such a one I hear you are in league with.

39 adod] mild oath

YOUNG BELLAIR.
I cannot help detraction, sir.

OLD BELLAIR.
Out, a pize* o'their breeches, there are keeping* fools enough for such flaunting baggages, and they are e'en too good for 'em. (*To Emilia.*) Remember night. Go, y'are a rogue, y'are a rogue. Fare you well, fare you well.—Come, come, come along, sir.

Exeunt Old and Young Bellair.

LADY TOWNLEY.
On my word, the old man comes on apace. I'll lay my life he's smitten.

EMILIA.
This is nothing but the pleasantness of his humor.*

LADY TOWNLEY.
I know him better than you; let it work. It may prove lucky.

Enter a page.

PAGE.
Madam, Mr. Medley has sent to know whether a visit will not be troublesome this afternoon.

LADY TOWNLEY.
Send him word his visits never are so.

[Exit page.]

EMILIA.
He's a very pleasant man.

LADY TOWNLEY.
He's a very necessary man among us women. He's not scandalous i'the least, perpetually contriving to bring good company together, and always ready to stop up a gap at ombre. Then, he knows all the little news o'the Town.

EMILIA.
I love to hear him talk o'the intrigues. Let 'em be never so dull in themselves, he'll make 'em pleasant i'the relation.

LADY TOWNLEY.
But he improves things so much one can take no measure of the truth from him. Mr. Dorimant swears a flea or a maggot is not made more monstrous by a magnifying glass than a story is by his telling it.

Enter Medley.

EMILIA.
Hold, here he comes.

LADY TOWNLEY.
Mr. Medley.

MEDLEY.
Your servant, madam.

LADY TOWNLEY.
You have made yourself a stranger of late.

EMILIA.
I believe you took a surfeit of ombre last time you were here.

MEDLEY.
Indeed I had my bellyful of that termagant, Lady Dealer. There never was so insatiable a carder; an old gleeker[40] never loved to sit to't like her. I have played with her now at least a dozen times, till she's worn out all her fine complexion and her tour[41] would keep in curl no longer.

LADY TOWNLEY.
Blame her not, poor woman. She loves nothing so well as a black ace.

MEDLEY.
The pleasure I have seen her in when she has had hope in drawing for a matadore![42]

EMILIA.
'Tis as pretty sport to her as persuading masks off is to you, to make discoveries.

LADY TOWNLEY.
Pray, where's your friend Mr. Dorimant?

MEDLEY.
Soliciting his affairs. He's a man of great employment—has more mistresses now depending than the most eminent lawyer in England has causes.

EMILIA.
Here has been Mrs. Loveit so uneasy and out of humor these two days.

---

[40] gleeker] one who plays gleek, a card game

[41] tour] from the French expression *tour de cheveaux*, "a tress or border of hair, going round the head, which mingled dextrously with the natural hair, lengthens and thickens it" (*OED*)

[42] matadore] in ombre, the three highest cards are called the matadores, including the two black aces and a trump card.

LADY TOWNLEY.
How strangely love and jealousy rage in that poor woman!

MEDLEY.
She could not have picked out a devil upon earth so proper to torment her. He's made her break a dozen or two of fans already, tear half a score points in pieces, and destroy hoods and knots without number.

LADY TOWNLEY.
We heard of a pleasant serenade he gave her t'other night.

MEDLEY.
A Danish serenade, with kettledrums and trumpets.

EMILIA.
Oh, barbarous!

MEDLEY.
What, you are of the number of the ladies whose ears are grown so delicate since our operas, you can be charmed with nothing but *flûtes douces*[43] and French hautboys?

EMILIA.
Leave your raillery and tell us, is there any new wit come forth, songs or novels?

MEDLEY.
A very pretty piece of gallantry, by an eminent author, called the *Diversions of Brussels*,[44] very necessary to be read by all old ladies who are desirous to improve themselves at Questions and Commands, Blindman's Buff, and the like fashionable recreations.

EMILIA.
Oh, ridiculous!

MEDLEY.
Then there is *The Art of Affectation*,[45] written by a late beauty of quality,* teaching you how to draw up your breasts, stretch up your neck, to thrust out your breech, to play with your head, to toss up your nose, to bite your lips, to turn up your eyes, to speak in a silly soft tone of a voice, and use all the foolish French words that will infallibly make your person and conversation charming, with a short apology at the latter end, in the behalf of young ladies who notoriously wash and paint,[46] though they have naturally good complexions.

EMILIA.
What a deal of stuff you tell us!

MEDLEY.
Such as the Town affords, madam. The Russians, hearing the great respect we have for foreign dancing, have lately sent over some of their best balladines,[47] who are now practicing a famous ballet which will be suddenly* danced at the Bear Garden.*

LADY TOWNLEY.
Pray forbear your idle stories and give us an account of the state of love as it now stands.

MEDLEY.
Truly there has been some revolutions in those affairs: great chopping and changing[48] among the old, and some new lovers, whom malice, indiscretion, and misfortune have luckily brought into play.

LADY TOWNLEY.
What think you of walking into the next room and sitting down before you engage in this business?

MEDLEY.
I wait upon you, and I hope (though women are commonly unreasonable) by the plenty of scandal I shall discover,* to give you very good content, ladies.

Exeunt.

Scene ii. [Mrs. Loveit's lodgings.]

Enter Mrs. Loveit and Pert, Mrs. Loveit putting up a letter, then pulling out her pocket glass and looking in it.*

MRS. LOVEIT.
Pert.

43 *flûtes douces*] "sweet flutes" or recorders (Fr.)— like the Italian opera, a recent import to England in the mid-1670's

44 *Diversions of Brussels*] identified as *A Treatise of the Sports of Wit*, published in 1675 by Richard Flecknoe

45 *The Art of Affectation*] a parodic reference to *The Gentlewoman's Companion* (1675), by Hannah Woolley (Conaghan)

46 wash and paint] use cosmetics

47 balladines] theatrical dancers

48 chopping and changing] originally terms of trade (selling and exchanging), here obviously metaphorical

PERT.
Madam?
MRS. LOVEIT.
I hate myself, I look so ill today.
PERT.
Hate the wicked cause on't, that base man Mr. Dorimant, who makes you torment and vex yourself continually.
MRS. LOVEIT.
He is to blame, indeed.
PERT.
To blame to be two days without sending, writing, or coming near you, contrary to his oath and covenant! 'Twas to much purpose to make him swear! I'll lay my life there's not an article but he has broken: talked to the vizards* i'the pit, waited upon the ladies from the boxes to their coaches, gone behind the scenes and fawned upon those little insignificant creatures, the players. 'Tis impossible for a man of his inconstant temper to forbear, I'm sure.
MRS. LOVEIT.
I know he is a devil, but he has something of the angel yet undefaced in him, which makes him so charming and agreeable that I must love him, be he never so wicked.
PERT.
I little thought, madam, to see your spirit tamed to this degree, who banished poor Mr. Lackwit but for taking up another lady's fan in your presence.
MRS. LOVEIT.
My knowing of such odious fools contributes to the making of me love Dorimant the better.
PERT.
Your knowing of Mr. Dorimant, in my mind, should rather make you hate all mankind.
MRS. LOVEIT.
So it does, besides himself.
PERT.
Pray, what excuse does he make in his letter?
MRS. LOVEIT.
He has had business.
PERT.
Business in general terms would not have been a current excuse for another. A modish man is always very busy when he is in pursuit of a new mistress.
MRS. LOVEIT.
Some fop has bribed you to rail at him. He had business; I will believe it and will forgive him.
PERT.
You may forgive him anything, but I shall never forgive him his turning me into ridicule, as I hear he does.
MRS. LOVEIT.
I perceive you are of the number of those fools his wit had made his enemies.
PERT.
I am of the number of those he's pleased to rally, madam, and if we may believe Mr. Wagfan and Mr. Caperwell, he sometimes makes merry with yourself, too, among his laughing companions.
MRS. LOVEIT.
Blockheads are as malicious to witty men as ugly women are to the handsome; 'tis their interest, and they make it their business to defame 'em.
PERT.
I wish Mr. Dorimant would not make it his business to defame you.
MRS. LOVEIT.
Should he, I had rather be made infamous by him than owe my reputation to the dull discretion of those fops you talk of.

Enter Bellinda.

(*Running to her.*) Bellinda!
BELLINDA.
My dear!
MRS. LOVEIT.
You have been unkind of late.
BELLINDA.
Do not say unkind, say unhappy!
MRS. LOVEIT.
I could chide you. Where have you been these two days?
BELLINDA.
Pity me rather, my dear, where I have been so tired with two or three country gentlewomen, whose conversation has been more insufferable than a country fiddle.
MRS. LOVEIT.
Are they relations?
BELLINDA.
No, Welsh acquaintance I made when I was last

year at St. Winifred's.[49] They have asked me a thousand questions of the modes and intrigues of the Town, and I have told 'em almost as many things for news that hardly were so when their gowns were in fashion.

MRS. LOVEIT.
Provoking creatures, how could you endure 'em?

BELLINDA. (*Aside.*)
Now to carry on my plot; nothing but love could make me capable of so much falsehood. 'Tis time to begin, lest Dorimant should come before her jealousy has stung her. (*Laughs and then speaks on.*) I was yesterday at a play with 'em, where I was fain to show 'em the living, as the man at Westminster does the dead. That is Mrs.* Such-a-one, admired for her beauty; this is Mr. Such-a-one, cried up for a wit; that is sparkish Mr. Such-a-one, who keeps* reverend Mrs. Such-a-one; and there sits fine Mrs. Such-a-one, who was lately cast off by my Lord Such-a-one.

MRS. LOVEIT.
Did you see Dorimant there?

BELLINDA.
I did, and imagine you were there with him and have no mind to own it.

MRS. LOVEIT.
What should make you think so?

BELLINDA.
A lady masked, in a pretty dishabille, whom Dorimant entertained with more respect than the gallants do a common vizard.*

MRS. LOVEIT. (*Aside.*)
Dorimant at the play entertaining a mask!* Oh, heavens!

BELLINDA. (*Aside.*)
Good!

MRS. LOVEIT.
Did he stay all the while?

BELLINDA.
Till the play was done, and then led her out, which confirms me it was you.

MRS. LOVEIT.
Traitor!

PERT.
Now you may believe he had business, and you may forgive him too.

MRS. LOVEIT.
Ungrateful, perjured man!

BELLINDA.
You seem so much concerned, my dear, I fear I have told you unawares what I had better have concealed for your quiet.

MRS. LOVEIT.
What manner of shape had she?

BELLINDA.
Tall and slender. Her motions were very genteel. Certainly she must be some person of condition.

MRS. LOVEIT.
Shame and confusion be ever in her face when she shows it!

BELLINDA.
I should blame your discretion for loving that wild man, my dear, but they say he has a way so bewitching that few can defend their hearts who know him.

MRS. LOVEIT.
I will tear him from mine, or die i'the attempt!

BELLINDA.
Be more moderate.

MRS. LOVEIT.
Would I had daggers, darts, or poisoned arrows in my breast, so I could but remove the thoughts of him from thence!

BELLINDA.
Fie, fie, your transports are too violent, my dear. This may be but an accidental gallantry, and 'tis likely ended at her coach.

PERT.
Should it proceed farther, let your comfort be, the conduct Mr. Dorimant affects will quickly make you know your rival, ten to one let you see her ruined, her reputation exposed to the Town—a happiness none will envy her but yourself, madam.

MRS. LOVEIT.
Whoe'er she be, all the harm I wish her is, may she love him as well as I do, and may he give her as much cause to hate him!

PERT.
Never doubt the latter end of your curse, madam!

[49] St. Winifred's] St. Winifred's Well, at Holywell, Wales

MRS. LOVEIT.
May all the passions that are raised by neglected love—jealousy, indignation, spite, and thirst of revenge—eternally rage in her soul, as they do now in mine! (*Walks up and down with a distracted air.*)

Enter a page.

PAGE.
Madam, Mr. Dorimant—

MRS. LOVEIT.
I will not see him.

PAGE.
I told him you were within, madam.

MRS. LOVEIT.
Say you lied, say I'm busy—shut the door—say anything!

PAGE.
He's here, madam. [*Exit.*]

Enter Dorimant.

DORIMANT.
"They taste of death who do at heaven arrive;
But we this paradise approach alive."[50]
(*To Mrs. Loveit.*) What, dancing the galloping nag[51] without a fiddle? (*Offers to catch her by the hand; she flings away and walks on.*) I fear this restlessness of the body, madam, (*Pursuing her.*) proceeds from an unquietness of the mind. What unlucky accident puts you out of humor? A point ill-washed? Knots spoiled i'the making up? Hair shaded awry? Or some other little mistake in setting you in order?

PERT.
A trifle in my opinion, sir, more inconsiderable than any you mention.

DORIMANT.
Oh, Mrs.* Pert! I never knew you sullen enough to be silent. Come, let me know the business.

PERT.
The business, sir, is the business that has taken you up these two days. How have I seen you laugh at men of business, and now to become a man of business yourself!

DORIMANT.
We are not masters of our own affections; our inclinations daily alter. Now we love pleasure, and anon we shall dote on business. Human frailty will have it so, and who can help it?

MRS. LOVEIT.
Faithless, inhuman, barbarous man—

DORIMANT. [*Aside.*]
Good, now the alarm strikes—

MRS. LOVEIT.
Without sense of love, of honor, or of gratitude! Tell me, for I will know, what devil masked she was, you were with at the play yesterday.

DORIMANT.
Faith, I resolved as much as you, but the devil was obstinate and would not tell me.

MRS. LOVEIT.
False in this as in your vows to me! You do know!

DORIMANT.
The truth is, I did all I could to know.

MRS. LOVEIT.
And dare you own it to my face? Hell and Furies! (*Tears her fan in pieces.*)

DORIMANT.
Spare your fan, madam. You are growing hot and will want it to cool you.

MRS. LOVEIT.
Horror and distraction seize you! Sorrow and remorse gnaw your soul and punish all your perjuries to me! (*Weeps.*)

DORIMANT. (*Turning to Bellinda.*)
"So thunder breaks the cloud in twain,
And makes a passage for the rain."[52]
(*To Bellinda.*) Bellinda, you are the devil that have raised this storm. You were at the play yesterday and have been making discoveries* to your dear.

BELLINDA.
Y'are the most mistaken man i'the world.

DORIMANT.
It must be so, and here I vow revenge—resolve to pursue and persecute you more impertinently than ever any loving fop did his mistress, hunt you i'the

50 "They … alive] Waller, "Of her Chamber," 1-2 (slightly misquoted)

51 galloping nag] a country dance

52 "So … rain"] Matthew Roydon, "An Elegie, or Friend's Passion, for his Astrophill [Sir Philip Sidney]" 34-35 (slightly misquoted)

Park,* trace you i' the Mall,* dog you in every visit you make, haunt you at the plays and i'the Drawing Room,* hang my nose in your neck and talk to you whether you will or no, and ever look upon you with such dying eyes till your friends grow jealous of me, send you out of Town, and the world suspect your reputation. (*He looks kindly on Bellinda. In a lower voice.*) At my Lady Townley's when we go from hence.

BELLINDA.
I'll meet you there.

DORIMANT.
Enough.

MRS. LOVEIT. (*Pushing Dorimant away.*)
Stand off! You shannot stare upon her so.

DORIMANT.
Good! There's one made jealous already.

MRS. LOVEIT.
Is this the constancy you vowed?

DORIMANT.
Constancy at my years? 'Tis not a virtue in season; you might as well expect the fruit the autumn ripens i'the spring.

MRS. LOVEIT.
Monstrous principle!

DORIMANT.
Youth has a long journey to go, madam. Should I have set up my rest at the first inn I lodged at, I should never have arrived at the happiness I now enjoy.

MRS. LOVEIT.
Dissembler, damned dissembler!

DORIMANT.
I am so, I confess. Good nature and good manners corrupt me. I am honest in my inclinations and would not, were't not to avoid offense, make a lady a little in years believe I think her young, wilfully mistake art for nature, and seem as fond of a thing I am weary of as when I doted on't in earnest.

MRS. LOVEIT.
False man!

DORIMANT.
True woman.

MRS. LOVEIT.
Now you begin to show yourself!

DORIMANT.
Love gilds us over and makes us show fine things to one another for a time, but soon the gold wears off, and then again the native brass appears.

MRS. LOVEIT.
Think on your oaths, your vows, and protestations, perjured man!

DORIMANT.
I made 'em when I was in love.

MRS. LOVEIT.
And therefore ought they not to bind? Oh, impious!

DORIMANT.
What we swear at such a time may be a certain proof of a present passion, but to say truth, in love there is no security to be given for the future.

MRS. LOVEIT.
Horrid and ungrateful, be gone! And never see me more!

DORIMANT.
I am not one of those troublesome coxcombs who, because they were once well-received, take the privilege to plague a woman with their love ever after. I shall obey you, madam, though I do myself some violence. (*He offers to go, and Mrs. Loveit pulls him back.*)

MRS. LOVEIT.
Come back, you shannot go! Could you have the ill nature to offer it?

DORIMANT.
When love grows diseased, the best thing we can do is to put it to a violent death. I cannot endure the torture of a lingering and consumptive passion.

MRS. LOVEIT.
Can you think mine sickly?

DORIMANT.
Oh, 'tis desperately ill! What worse symptoms are there than your being always uneasy when I visit you, your picking quarrels with me on slight occasions, and in my absence kindly listening to the impertinences of every fashionable fool that talks to you?

MRS. LOVEIT.
What fashionable fool can you lay to my charge?

DORIMANT.
Why, the very cock-fool of all those fools, Sir Fopling Flutter.

MRS. LOVEIT.
I never saw him in my life but once.

DORIMANT.
The worse woman you, at first sight to put on all your charms, to entertain him with that softness in your voice and all that wanton kindness in your eyes you so notoriously affect when you design a conquest.

MRS. LOVEIT.
So damned a lie did never malice yet invent! Who told you this?

DORIMANT.
No matter. That ever I should love a woman that can dote on a senseless caper, a tawdry French ribbon, and a formal cravat!

MRS. LOVEIT.
You make me mad!

DORIMANT.
A guilty conscience may do much. Go on, be the game-mistress o'the Town and enter[53] all our young fops, as fast as they come from travel.

MRS. LOVEIT.
Base and scurrilous!

DORIMANT.
A fine mortifying reputation 'twill be for a woman of your pride, wit, and quality!*

MRS. LOVEIT.
This jealousy's a mere pretense, a cursed trick of your own devising. I know you.

DORIMANT.
Believe it and all the ill of me you can. I would not have a woman have the least good thought of me that can think well of Fopling. Farewell. Fall to, and much good may do you with your coxcomb.

MRS. LOVEIT.
Stay! Oh stay, and I will tell you all!

DORIMANT.
I have been told too much already. (*Exit.*)

MRS. LOVEIT.
Call him again!

PERT.
E'en let him go, a fair riddance!

MRS. LOVEIT.
Run, I say, call him again. I will have him called!

PERT.
The Devil should carry him away first, were it my concern. (*Exit.*)

BELLINDA.
He's frighted me from the very thoughts of loving men. For Heaven's sake, my dear, do not discover* what I told you. I dread his tongue as much as you ought to have done his friendship.

Enter Pert.

PERT.
He's gone, madam.

MRS. LOVEIT.
Lightning blast him!

PERT.
When I told him you desired him to come back, he smiled, made a mouth at me, flung into his coach, and said—

MRS. LOVEIT.
What did he say?

PERT.
"Drive away," and then repeated verses.

MRS. LOVEIT.
Would I had made a contract to be a witch when first I entertained* this greater devil. Monster, barbarian! I could tear myself in pieces. Revenge, nothing but revenge can ease me. Plague, war, famine, fire, all that can bring universal ruin and misery on mankind—with joy I'd perish to have you in my power but this moment! (*Exit.*)

PERT.
Follow, madam. Leave her not in this outrageous passion. (*Gathers up the things.*)

BELLINDA.
He's given me the proof which I desired of his love, but 'tis a proof of his ill nature too. I wish I had not seen him use her so.
I sigh to think that Dorimant may be
One day as faithless and unkind to me.

Exeunt.

Act III, scene i. Lady Woodvill's lodgings.

Enter Harriet and Busy, her woman.

BUSY.
Dear madam, let me set that curl in order!

---

53 enter] instruct, initiate, train

HARRIET.
Let me alone! I will shake 'em all out of order!

BUSY.
Will you never leave this wildness?

HARRIET.
Torment me not!

BUSY.
Look, there's a knot falling off.

HARRIET.
Let it drop!

BUSY.
But one pin, dear madam.

HARRIET.
How do I daily suffer under thy officious fingers!

BUSY.
Ah, the difference that is between you and my Lady Dapper: how uneasy she is if the least thing be amiss about her.

HARRIET.
She is indeed most exact! Nothing is ever wanting* to make her ugliness remarkable!

BUSY.
Jeering people say so.

HARRIET.
Her powdering, painting, and her patching[54] never fail in public to draw the tongues and eyes of all the men upon her.

BUSY.
She is indeed a little too pretending.

HARRIET.
That women should set up for beauty as much in spite of nature as some men have done for wit!

BUSY.
I hope without offense one may endeavor to make one's self agreeable.

HARRIET.
Not when 'tis impossible. Women then ought to be no more fond of dressing than fools should be of talking. Hoods and modesty, masks and silence, things that shadow and conceal—they should think of nothing else.

BUSY.
Jesu! Madam, what will your mother think is become of you? For Heaven's sake, go in again.

HARRIET.
I won't!

BUSY.
This is the extravagant'st thing that ever you did in your life, to leave her and a gentleman who is to be your husband.

HARRIET.
My husband! Hast thou so little wit to think I spoke what I meant when I overjoyed her in the country with a low curtsy and "What you please, madam; I shall ever be obedient"?

BUSY.
Nay, I know not; you have so many fetches.

HARRIET.
And this was one, to get her up to London. Nothing else, I assure thee.

BUSY.
Well, the man, in my mind, is a fine man.

HARRIET.
The man indeed wears his clothes fashionably and has a pretty, negligent way with him, very courtly and much affected. He bows, and talks, and smiles so agreeably as he thinks.

BUSY.
I never saw anything so genteel.

HARRIET.
Varnished over with good breeding, many a blockhead makes a tolerable show.

BUSY.
I wonder you do not like him.

HARRIET.
I think I might be brought to endure him, and that is all a reasonable woman should expect in a husband, but there is duty i'the case, and like the haughty Merab, I

"Find much aversion in my stubborn mind,"

which[c]

"is bred by being promised and designed."[55]

BUSY.
I wish you do not design your own ruin! I partly

---

54 patching] applying artificial beauty marks, small pieces of black silk, to set off the complexion

55 haughty Merab … designed] Merab, promised by her father Saul to David after his victory over Goliath but given instead to someone else (I Samuel 18:17-19), was portrayed by Cowley in *Davideis* as haughty; the lines from Cowley (Bk. III), slightly misquoted, reveal why.

guess your inclinations, madam—that Mr. Dorimant—

HARRIET.
Leave your prating and sing some foolish song or other.

BUSY.
I will—the song you love so well ever since you saw Mr. Dorimant.

Song.

When first Amintas charmed my heart,
My heedless sheep began to stray;
The wolves soon stole the greatest part,
And all will now be made a prey.

Ah, let not love your thoughts possess,
'Tis fatal to a shepherdess;
The dang'rous passion you must shun,
Or else like me be quite undone.

HARRIET.
Shall I be paid down by a covetous parent for a purchase? I need no land. No, I'll lay myself out all in love. It is decreed—

Enter Young Bellair.

YOUNG BELLAIR.
What generous resolution are you making, madam?

HARRIET.
Only to be disobedient, sir.

YOUNG BELLAIR.
Let me join hands with you in that—

HARRIET.
With all my heart. I never thought I should have given you mine so willingly. Here I, Harriet—

YOUNG BELLAIR.
And I, Harry—

HARRIET.
Do solemnly protest—

YOUNG BELLAIR.
And vow—

HARRIET.
That I with you—

YOUNG BELLAIR.
And I with you—

BOTH.
Will never marry—

HARRIET.
A match!

YOUNG BELLAIR.
And no match! How do you like this indifference now?

HARRIET.
You expect I should take it ill, I see.

YOUNG BELLAIR.
'Tis not unnatural for you women to be a little angry, you miss a conquest—though you would slight the poor man were he in your power.

HARRIET.
There are some, it may be, have an eye like Bartholomew, big enough for the whole fair, but I am not of the number, and you may keep your gingerbread.[56] 'Twill be more acceptable to the lady whose dear image it wears, sir.

YOUNG BELLAIR.
I must confess, madam, you came a day after the fair.

HARRIET.
You own then you are in love?

YOUNG BELLAIR.
I do.

HARRIET.
The confidence is generous, and in return I could almost find in my heart to let you know my inclinations.

YOUNG BELLAIR.
Are you in love?

HARRIET.
Yes—with this dear Town, to that degree I can scarce endure the country in landscapes and in hangings.

YOUNG BELLAIR.
What a dreadful thing 'twould be to be hurried back to Hampshire!

HARRIET.
Ah—name it not!

YOUNG BELLAIR.
As for us, I find we shall agree well enough. Would we could do something to deceive the grave people!

---

56 There are … gingerbread] Bartholomew Cokes in Ben Jonson's *Bartholomew Fair* (1614) is tempted to buy everything for sale at the fair, including gingerbread.

HARRIET.

Could we delay their quick proceeding, 'twere well. A reprieve is a good step towards the getting of a pardon.

YOUNG BELLAIR.

If we give over the game, we are undone. What think you of playing it on booty?[57]

HARRIET.

What do you mean?

YOUNG BELLAIR.

Pretend to be in love with one another! 'Twill make some dilatory excuses we may feign pass the better.

HARRIET.

Let us do't, if it be but for the dear pleasure of dissembling.

YOUNG BELLAIR.

Can you play your part?

HARRIET.

I know not what it is to love, but I have made pretty remarks[58] by being now and then where lovers meet. Where did you leave their Gravities?

YOUNG BELLAIR.

I'th'next room. Your mother was censuring our modern gallant.

Enter Old Bellair and Lady Woodvill.

HARRIET.

Peace! Here they come. I will lean against this wall and look bashfully down upon my fan while you, like an amorous spark, modishly entertain me.

LADY WOODVILL.

Never go about to excuse 'em. Come, come, it was not so when I was a young woman.

OLD BELLAIR.

Adod, they're something disrespectful—

LADY WOODVILL.

Quality* was then considered and not rallied by every fleering fellow.

OLD BELLAIR.

Youth will have its jest, adod it will.

LADY WOODVILL.

'Tis good breeding now to be civil to none but players and Exchange* women. They are treated by 'em as much above their condition as others are below theirs.

OLD BELLAIR.

Out, a pize on 'em! Talk no more; the rogues ha' got an ill habit of preferring beauty, no matter where they find it.

LADY WOODVILL.

See your son and my daughter. They have improved their acquaintance since they were within.

OLD BELLAIR.

Adod, methinks they have! Let's keep back and observe.

YOUNG BELLAIR.

Now for a look and gestures that may persuade 'em I am saying all the passionate things imaginable—

HARRIET.

Your head a little more on one side, ease yourself on your left leg and play with your right hand.

YOUNG BELLAIR.

Thus, is it not?

HARRIET.

Now set your right leg firm on the ground, adjust your belt, then look about you.

YOUNG BELLAIR.

A little exercising will make me perfect.

HARRIET.

Smile, and turn to me again very sparkish.

YOUNG BELLAIR.

Will you take your turn and be instructed?

HARRIET.

With all my heart.

YOUNG BELLAIR.

At one motion play your fan, roll your eyes, and then settle a kind* look upon me.

HARRIET.

So.

YOUNG BELLAIR.

Now spread your fan, look down upon it, and tell the sticks with a finger.

HARRIET.

Very modish.

YOUNG BELLAIR.

Clap your hand up to your bosom, hold down your gown. Shrug a little, draw up your breasts and let 'em fall again, gently, with a sigh or two, etcetera.

57 playing it on booty] having one player lose intentionally in order to draw in others

58 remarks] observations

HARRIET.
By the good instructions you give, I suspect you for one of those malicious observers who watch people's eyes and from innocent looks make scandalous conclusions.
YOUNG BELLAIR.
I know some, indeed, who out of mere* love to mischief are as vigilant as jealousy itself and will give you an account of every glance that passes at a play and i'th'Circle![59]
HARRIET.
'Twill not be amiss now to seem a little pleasant.
YOUNG BELLAIR.
Clap your fan then in both your hands, snatch it to your mouth, smile, and with a lively motion fling your body a little forwards. So—now spread it, fall back on the sudden, cover your face with it, and break out into a loud laughter—take up! Look grave and fall a-fanning of yourself. Admirably well acted!
HARRIET.
I think I am pretty apt at these matters!
OLD BELLAIR.
Adod, I like this well.
LADY WOODVILL.
This promises something.
OLD BELLAIR.
Come, there is love i'th'case, adod there is, or will be.—What say you, young lady?
HARRIET.
All in good time, sir. You expect we should fall to and love as gamecocks fight, as soon as we are set together. Adod, y'are unreasonable!
OLD BELLAIR.
Adod, sirrah, I like thy wit well.

Enter a servant.

SERVANT.
The coach is at the door, madam.
OLD BELLAIR.
Go, get you and take the air together.
LADY WOODVILL.
Will not you go with us?

[59] the Circle] perhaps the Ring,* perhaps the assembly of courtiers and hangers-on at Court

OLD BELLAIR.
Out a pize! Adod, I ha' business and cannot. We shall meet at night at my sister Townley's.
YOUNG BELLAIR. (*Aside.*)
He's going to Emilia. I overheard him talk of a collation.

Exeunt.

Scene ii. [Lady Townley's house.]

Enter Lady Townley, Emilia, and Medley.

LADY TOWNLEY.
I pity the young lovers we last talked of, though to say truth, their conduct has been so indiscreet, they deserve to be unfortunate.
MEDLEY.
Y'ave had an exact account, from the great lady i'th'box down to the little orange-wench.
EMILIA.
Y'are a living libel, a breathing lampoon. I wonder you are not torn in pieces.
MEDLEY.
What think you of setting up an office of intelligence for these matters? The project may get money.
LADY TOWNLEY.
You would have great dealings with country ladies.
MEDLEY.
More than Muddiman[60] has with their husbands!

Enter Bellinda.

LADY TOWNLEY.
Bellinda, what has been become of you? We have not seen you here of late with your friend Mrs. Loveit.
BELLINDA.
Dear creature, I left her but now so sadly afflicted.
LADY TOWNLEY.
With her old distemper, jealousy?
MEDLEY.
Dorimant has played her some new prank.

[60] Muddiman] Henry Muddiman (1629-92), editor of a newsletter of public affairs sent weekly from London to over 140 subscribers in the country

BELLINDA.
Well, that Dorimant is certainly the worst man breathing.

EMILIA.
I once thought so.

BELLINDA.
And do you not think so still?

EMILIA.
No, indeed!

BELLINDA.
Oh, Jesu!

EMILIA.
The Town does him a great deal of injury, and I will never believe what it says of a man I do not know again, for his sake.

BELLINDA.
You make me wonder!

LADY TOWNLEY.
He's a very well-bred man.

BELLINDA.
But strangely ill-natured.

EMILIA.
Then he's a very witty man.

BELLINDA.
But a man of no principles.

MEDLEY.
Your man of principles is a very fine thing, indeed!

BELLINDA.
To be preferred to men of parts* by women who have regard to their reputation and quiet. Well, were I minded to play the fool, he should be the last man I'd think of.

MEDLEY.
He has been the first in many ladies' favors, though you are so severe, madam.

LADY TOWNLEY.
What he may be for a lover, I know not, but he's a very pleasant acquaintance, I am sure.

BELLINDA.
Had you seen him use Mrs. Loveit as I have done, you would never endure him more—

EMILIA.
What! he has quarreled with her again?

BELLINDA.
Upon the slightest occasion. He's jealous of Sir Fopling.

LADY TOWNLEY.
She never saw him in her life but yesterday, and that was here.

EMILIA.
On my conscience, he's the only man in Town that's her aversion. How horribly out of humor she was all the while he talked to her!

BELLINDA.
And somebody has wickedly told him—

Enter Dorimant.

EMILIA.
Here he comes.

MEDLEY.
Dorimant, you are luckily come to justify yourself. Here's a lady—

BELLINDA.
Has a word or two to say to you from a disconsolate person.

DORIMANT.
You tender your reputation too much, I know, madam, to whisper with me before this good company.

BELLINDA.
To serve Mrs. Loveit, I'll make a bold venture.

DORIMANT.
Here's Medley, the very spirit of scandal.

BELLINDA.
No matter!

EMILIA.
'Tis something you are unwilling to hear, Mr. Dorimant.

LADY TOWNLEY.
Tell him, Bellinda, whether he will or no!

BELLINDA. (*Aloud.*)
Mrs. Loveit—

DORIMANT.
Softly, these are laughers; you do not know 'em.

BELLINDA. (*To Dorimant, apart.*)
In a word, y'ave made me hate you, which I thought you never could have done.

DORIMANT.
In obeying your commands?

BELLINDA.
'Twas a cruel part you played! How could you act it?

DORIMANT.
Nothing is cruel to a man who could kill himself

to please you. Remember, five o'clock tomorrow morning.

BELLINDA.
I tremble when you name it.

DORIMANT.
Be sure you come.

BELLINDA.
I shannot.

DORIMANT.
Swear you will.

BELLINDA.
I dare not.

DORIMANT.
Swear, I say.

BELLINDA.
By my life! by all the happiness I hope for—

DORIMANT.
You will.

BELLINDA.
I will.

DORIMANT.
Kind.

BELLINDA.
I am glad I've sworn. I vow I think I should ha' failed you else.

DORIMANT.
Surprisingly kind! In what temper did you leave Loveit?

BELLINDA.
Her raving was prettily[61] over, and she began to be in a brave way of defying you and all your works. Where have you been since you went from thence?

DORIMANT.
I looked in at the play.

BELLINDA.
I have promised and must return to her again.

DORIMANT.
Persuade her to walk in the Mall* this evening.

BELLINDA.
She hates the place and will not come.

DORIMANT.
Do all you can to prevail with her.

BELLINDA.
For what purpose?

DORIMANT.
Sir Fopling will be here anon. I'll prepare him to set upon her there before me.

BELLINDA.
You persecute her too much. But I'll do all you'll ha' me.

DORIMANT. (*Aloud.*)
Tell her plainly, 'tis grown so dull a business I can drudge on no longer.

EMILIA.
There are afflictions in love, Mr. Dorimant.

DORIMANT.
You women make 'em, who are commonly as unreasonable in that as you are at play: without the advantage be on your side, a man can never quietly give over when he's weary.

MEDLEY.
If you would play without being obliged to complaisance, Dorimant, you should play in public places.

DORIMANT.
Ordinaries were a very good thing for that, but gentlemen do not of late frequent 'em. The deep play is now in private houses.

Bellinda offering to steal away.

LADY TOWNLEY.
Bellinda, are you leaving us so soon?

BELLINDA.
I am to go to the Park* with Mrs. Loveit, madam—(*Exit.*)

LADY TOWNLEY.
This confidence[62] will go nigh to spoil this young creature.

MEDLEY.
'Twill do her good, madam. Young men who are brought up under practicing lawyers prove the abler counsel when they come to be called to the bar themselves—

DORIMANT.
The Town has been very favorable to you this afternoon, my Lady Townley. You use to have an

[61] prettily] mostly

[62] confidence] intimate friendship

embarras[63] of chairs* and coaches at your door, an uproar of footmen in your hall, and a noise of fools above here.

LADY TOWNLEY.

Indeed, my house is the general rendezvous and, next to the playhouse, is the common refuge of all the young idle people.

EMILIA.

Company is a very good thing, madam, but I wonder you do not love it a little more chosen.

LADY TOWNLEY.

'Tis good to have an universal taste. We should love wit, but for variety be able to divert ourselves with the extravagancies of those who want* it.

MEDLEY.

Fools will make you laugh.

EMILIA.

For once or twice, but the repetition of their folly after a visit or two grows tedious and insufferable.

LADY TOWNLEY.

You are a little too delicate, Emilia.

Enter a page.

PAGE.

Sir Fopling Flutter, madam, desires to know if you are to be seen.

LADY TOWNLEY.

Here's the freshest fool in Town, and one who has not cloyed you yet.—Page!

PAGE.

Madam?

LADY TOWNLEY.

Desire him to walk up.

[Exit Page.]

DORIMANT.

Do not you fall on him, Medley, and snub him. Soothe him up in his extravagance. He will show the better.

MEDLEY.

You know I have a natural indulgence for fools and need not this caution, sir.

Enter Sir Fopling Flutter, with his page after him.

SIR FOPLING.

Page! Wait without.

[Exit Page.]

(*To Lady Townley.*) Madam, I kiss your hands. I see yesterday was nothing of chance: the *belles assemblées*[64] form themselves here every day. (*To Emilia.*) Lady, your servant.—Dorimant, let me embrace thee. Without lying, I have not met with any of my acquaintance who retain so much of Paris as thou dost—the very air thou hadst when the marquise mistook thee i'th'Tuileries[65] and cried "Hey, chevalier!" and then begged thy pardon.

DORIMANT.

I would fain wear in fashion as long as I can, sir. 'Tis a thing to be valued in men as well as baubles.

SIR FOPLING.

Thou art a man of wit and understands the Town. Prithee let thee and I be intimate. There is no living without making some good man the confidant of our pleasures.

DORIMANT.

'Tis true! But there is no man so improper for such a business as I am.

SIR FOPLING.

Prithee, why hast thou so modest an opinion of thyself?

DORIMANT.

Why first, I could never keep a secret in my life, and then, there is no charm so infallibly makes me fall in love with a woman as my knowing a friend loves her. I deal honestly with you.

SIR FOPLING.

Thy humor's* very gallant, or let me perish. I knew a French count so like thee.

LADY TOWNLEY.

Wit, I perceive, has more power over you than beauty, Sir Fopling, else you would not have let this lady stand so long neglected.

SIR FOPLING. (*To Emilia.*)

A thousand pardons, madam. Some civility's due of course upon the meeting a long absent friend.

63 *embarras*] congestion (Fr.)

64 *belles assemblées*] fashionable gatherings (Fr.)

65 Tuileries] palace in Paris, or the gardens adjacent to it

The éclat of so much beauty, I confess, ought to have charmed me sooner.

EMILIA.
The *brilliant*[66] of so much good language, sir, has much more power than the little beauty I can boast.

SIR FOPLING.
I never saw anything prettier than this high work[67] on your *point d'Espagne*—

EMILIA.
'Tis not so rich as *point de Venise*[68] —

SIR FOPLING.
Not altogether, but looks cooler and is more proper for the season.—Dorimant, is not that Medley?

DORIMANT.
The same, sir.

SIR FOPLING.
Forgive me, sir: in this *embarras* of civilities I could not come to have you in my arms sooner. You understand an equipage the best of any man in Town, I hear.

MEDLEY.
By my own you would not guess it.

SIR FOPLING.
There are critics who do not write, sir.

MEDLEY.
Our peevish poets will scarce allow it.

SIR FOPLING.
Damn 'em, they'll allow no man wit who does not play the fool like themselves and show it! Have you taken notice of the calash I brought over?

MEDLEY.
Oh, yes! 'T has quite another air than th'English makes.

SIR FOPLING.
'Tis as easily known from an English tumbrel as an Inns of Court* man is from one of us.

DORIMANT.
Truly there is a *bel air*[69] in calashes as well as men.

MEDLEY.
But there are few so delicate to observe it.

[66] *brilliant*] sparkle (Fr.)

[67] high work] raised needlework

[68] *point d'Espagne ... Venise*] Spanish and Venetian lace (Fr.)

[69] *bel air*] grace, poise, style (Fr.)

SIR FOPLING.
The world is generally very *grossier*[70] here, indeed.

LADY TOWNLEY. [*To Emilia.*]
He's very fine.

EMILIA.
Extreme proper.

SIR FOPLING.
A slight suit I made to appear in at my first arrival, not worthy your consideration, ladies.

DORIMANT.
The pantaloon is very well mounted.

SIR FOPLING.
The tassels are new and pretty.

MEDLEY.
I never saw a coat better cut.

SIR FOPLING.
It makes me show long-waisted, and I think slender.

DORIMANT.
That's the shape our ladies dote on.

MEDLEY.
Your breech, though, is a handful too high, in my eye, Sir Fopling.

SIR FOPLING.
Peace, Medley, I have wished it lower a thousand times, but a pox on't, 'twill not be!

LADY TOWNLEY.
His gloves are well fringed, large and graceful.

SIR FOPLING.
I was always eminent for being *bien ganté*.[71]

EMILIA.
He wears nothing but what are originals of the most famous hands in Paris.

SIR FOPLING.
You are in the right, madam.

LADY TOWNLEY.
The suit?

SIR FOPLING.
Barroy.

EMILIA.
The garniture?

SIR FOPLING.
Le Gras—

[70] *grossier*] coarse, uncouth (Fr.)

[71] *bien ganté*] well-gloved (Fr.)

MEDLEY.
The shoes?

SIR FOPLING.
Piccar!

DORIMANT.
The periwig?

SIR FOPLING.
Chedreux.[72]

LADY TOWNLEY, EMILIA.
The gloves?

SIR FOPLING.
Orangerie![73] You know the smell, ladies!—Dorimant, I could find in my heart for an amusement to have a gallantry with some of our English ladies.

DORIMANT.
'Tis a thing no less necessary to confirm the reputation of your wit than a duel will be to satisfy the Town of your courage.

SIR FOPLING.
Here was a woman yesterday—

DORIMANT.
Mistress Loveit.

SIR FOPLING.
You have named her!

DORIMANT.
You cannot pitch on a better for your purpose.

SIR FOPLING.
Prithee, what is she?

DORIMANT.
A person of quality,* and one who has a rest of reputation enough to make the conquest considerable. Besides, I hear she likes you, too!

SIR FOPLING.
Methought she seemed, though, very reserved and uneasy all the time I entertained her.

DORIMANT.
Grimace and affectation! You will see her i'th'Mall tonight.

SIR FOPLING.
Prithee, let thee and I take the air together.

DORIMANT.
I am engaged to Medley, but I'll meet you at Saint James's* and give you some information, upon the which you may regulate your proceedings.

SIR FOPLING.
All the world will be in the Park* tonight.—Ladies, 'twere pity to keep so much beauty longer within doors and rob the Ring* of all those charms that should adorn it.—Hey, page!

Enter page.

See that all my people be ready.

[Page] goes out again.

Dorimant, au revoir. [*Exit.*]

MEDLEY.
A fine-mettled coxcomb.

DORIMANT.
Brisk and insipid—

MEDLEY.
Pert and dull.

EMILIA.
However you despise him, gentlemen, I'll lay my life he passes for a wit with many.

DORIMANT.
That may very well be. Nature has her cheats, stums* a brain, and puts sophisticate* dullness often on the tasteless multitude for true wit and good humor.—Medley, come.

MEDLEY.
I must go a little way; I will meet you i'the Mall.

DORIMANT.
I'll walk through the garden thither. (*To the women.*) We shall meet anon and bow.

LADY TOWNLEY.
Not tonight! We are engaged about a business, the knowledge of which may make you laugh hereafter.

MEDLEY.
Your servant, ladies.

DORIMANT.
Au revoir, as Sir Fopling says.

Exeunt Medley and Dorimant.

LADY TOWNLEY.
The old man will be here immediately.

[72] most famous hands in Paris … Chedreux] Presumably the names are those of Parisian artisans, but of these only Chedreux* has been identified.

[73] Orangerie] a scent made from orange-blossoms

EMILIA.
Let's expect him i'th'garden—
LADY TOWNLEY.
Go, you are a rogue!
EMILIA.
I can't abide you!

Exeunt.

Scene iii. The Mall.

Enter Harriet and Young Bellair, she pulling him.

HARRIET.
Come along!
YOUNG BELLAIR.
And leave your mother?
HARRIET.
Busy will be sent with a hue and cry after us, but that's no matter.
YOUNG BELLAIR.
'Twill look strangely in me.
HARRIET.
She'll believe it a freak of mine and never blame your manners.
YOUNG BELLAIR.
What reverend acquaintance is that she has met?
HARRIET.
A fellow beauty of the last king's time, though by the ruins you would hardly guess it.

Exeunt. Enter Dorimant and crosses the stage. Enter Young Bellair and Harriet.

YOUNG BELLAIR.
By this time your mother is in a fine taking.[74]
HARRIET.
If your friend Mr. Dorimant were but here now, that she might find me talking with him!
YOUNG BELLAIR.
She does not know him but dreads him, I hear, of all mankind.
HARRIET.
She concludes if he does but speak to a woman, she's undone—is on her knees every day to pray Heaven defend me from him.

YOUNG BELLAIR.
You do not apprehend him so much as she does.
HARRIET.
I never saw anything in him that was frightful.
YOUNG BELLAIR.
On the contrary, have you not observed something extreme delightful in his wit and person?
HARRIET.
He's agreeable and pleasant, I must own, but he does so much affect being so, he displeases me.
YOUNG BELLAIR.
Lord madam, all he does and says is so easy and so natural.
HARRIET.
Some men's verses seem so to the unskillful, but labor i'the one and affectation i'the other to the judicious plainly appear.
YOUNG BELLAIR.
I never heard him accused of affectation before.

Enter Dorimant and stares upon her.

HARRIET.
It passes on the easy Town, who are favorably pleased in him to call it humor.*

Exeunt Young Bellair and Harriet.

DORIMANT.
'Tis she! It must be she—that lovely hair, that easy shape, those wanton eyes, and all those melting charms about her mouth which Medley spoke of. I'll follow the lottery and put in for a prize with my friend Bellair.

Exit Dorimant, repeating:

"In love the victors from the vanquished fly;
They fly that wound, and they pursue that die."[75]

Enter Young Bellair and Harriet, and after them Dorimant, standing at a distance.

YOUNG BELLAIR.
Most people prefer Hyde Park* to this place.
HARRIET.
It has the better reputation, I confess, but I

---

[74] a fine taking] a disturbed or agitated state of mind

[75] "In love ... that die."] Waller, "To a Friend, of the Different Success of their Loves," 27-28

abominate the dull diversions there—the formal bows, the affected smiles, the silly by-words and amorous tweers[76] in passing. Here one meets with a little conversation now and then.

YOUNG BELLAIR.
These conversations* have been fatal to some of your sex, madam.

HARRIET.
It may be so. Because some who want temper have been undone by gaming, must others who have it wholly deny themselves the pleasure of play?

DORIMANT. (*Coming up gently and bowing to her.*)
Trust me, it were unreasonable, madam.

She starts and looks grave.

HARRIET.
Lord! who's this?

YOUNG BELLAIR.
Dorimant.

DORIMANT. [*To Young Bellair.*]
Is this the woman your father would have you marry?

YOUNG BELLAIR.
It is.

DORIMANT.
Her name?

YOUNG BELLAIR.
Harriet.

DORIMANT.
I am not mistaken; she's handsome.

YOUNG BELLAIR.
Talk to her; her wit is better than her face. We were wishing for you but now.

DORIMANT. (*To Harriet.*)
Overcast with seriousness o'the sudden! A thousand smiles were shining in that face but now. I never saw so quick a change of weather.

HARRIET. (*Aside.*)
I feel as great a change within, but he shall never know it.

DORIMANT.
You were talking of play, madam. Pray, what may be your stint?

HARRIET.
A little harmless discourse in public walks, or at most an appointment in a box, barefaced, at the playhouse. You are for masks and private meetings, where women engage for all they are worth, I hear.

DORIMANT.
I have been used to deep play, but I can make one at small game when I like my gamester well.

HARRIET.
And be so unconcerned you'll ha' no pleasure in't.

DORIMANT.
Where there is a considerable sum to be won, the hope of drawing people in makes every trifle considerable.

HARRIET.
The sordidness of men's natures, I know, makes 'em willing to flatter and comply with the rich, though they are sure never to be the better for 'em.

DORIMANT.
'Tis in their power to do us good, and we despair not but at some time or other they may be willing.

HARRIET.
To men who have fared in this Town like you, 'twould be a great mortification to live on hope. Could you keep a Lent for a mistress?

DORIMANT.
In expectation of a happy Easter, and though time be very precious, think forty days well lost to gain your favor.

HARRIET.
Mr. Bellair! Let us walk, 'tis time to leave him. Men grow dull when they begin to be particular.

DORIMANT.
Y'are mistaken: flattery will not ensue, though I know y'are greedy of the praises of the whole Mall.

HARRIET.
You do me wrong.

DORIMANT.
I do not. As I followed you, I observed how you were pleased when the fops cried, "She's handsome, very handsome, by God she is!" and whispered aloud your name—the thousand several forms you put your face into; then, to make yourself more agreeable, how wantonly you played with your head, flung back your locks, and looked smilingly over your shoulder at 'em.

[76] tweers] glances, leers

HARRIET.
I do not go begging the men's, as you do the ladies', good liking, with a sly softness in your looks and a gentle slowness in your bows as you pass by 'em—as thus, sir—(*Acts him.*) Is not this like you?

Enter Lady Woodvill and Busy.

YOUNG BELLAIR.
Your mother, madam! (*Pulls Harriet. She composes herself.*)

LADY WOODVILL.
Ah, my dear child Harriet!

BUSY.
Now is she so pleased with finding her again, she cannot chide her.

LADY WOODVILL.
Come away!

DORIMANT.
'Tis now but high Mall, madam—the most entertaining time of all the evening.

HARRIET.
I would fain see that Dorimant, Mother, you so cry out of for a monster. He's in the Mall, I hear.

LADY WOODVILL.
Come away, then! The plague is here, and you should dread the infection.

YOUNG BELLAIR.
You may be misinformed of the gentleman.

LADY WOODVILL.
Oh, no! I hope you do not know him. He is the prince of all the devils in the Town—delights in nothing but in rapes and riots.

DORIMANT.
If you did but hear him speak, madam—

LADY WOODVILL.
Oh! he has a tongue, they say, would tempt the angels to a second fall!

Enter Sir Fopling with his equipage, six footmen and a page.

SIR FOPLING.
Hey, Champagne, Norman, La Rose, La Fleur, La Tour, La Verdure!—Dorimant!

LADY WOODVILL.
Here, here he is among this rout! He names him! Come away, Harriet, come away!

Exeunt Lady Woodvill, Harriet, Busy, and Young Bellair.

DORIMANT.
This fool's coming has spoiled all: she's gone. But she has left a pleasing image of herself behind that wanders in my soul. It must not settle there.

SIR FOPLING.
What reverie is this? Speak, man!

DORIMANT.
"Snatched from myself, how far behind
Already I behold the shore!"[77]

Enter Medley.

MEDLEY.
Dorimant, a discovery! I met with Bellair—

DORIMANT.
You can tell me no news, sir. I know all.

MEDLEY.
How do you like the daughter?

DORIMANT.
You never came so near truth in your life as you did in her description.

MEDLEY.
What think you of the mother?

DORIMANT.
Whatever I think of her, she thinks very well of me, I find.

MEDLEY.
Did she know you?

DORIMANT.
She did not. Whether she does now or no, I know not. Here was a pleasant scene towards, when in came Sir Fopling, mustering up his equipage, and at the latter end named me and frighted her away.

MEDLEY.
Loveit and Bellinda are not far off. I saw 'em alight at St. James's.*

DORIMANT.
Sir Fopling, hark you, a word or two. (*Whispers.*) Look you do not want* assurance.

SIR FOPLING.
I never do on these occasions.

77 "Snatched … shore!" Waller, "Of Loving at First Sight," 3-4

DORIMANT.

Walk on; we must not be seen together. Make your advantage of what I have told you. The next turn you will meet the lady.

SIR FOPLING.

Hey! Follow me all. (*Exit with equipage.*)

DORIMANT.

Medley, you shall see good sport anon between Loveit and this Fopling.

MEDLEY.

I thought there was something toward, by that whisper.

DORIMANT.

You know a worthy principle of hers?

MEDLEY.

Not to be so much as civil to a man who speaks to her in the presence of him she professes to love.

DORIMANT.

I have encouraged Fopling to talk to her tonight.

MEDLEY.

Now you are here, she will go nigh to beat him.

DORIMANT.

In the humor she's in, her love will make her do some very extravagant thing, doubtless.

MEDLEY.

What was Bellinda's business with you at my Lady Townley's?

DORIMANT.

To get me to meet Loveit here in order to an éclaircissement. I made some difficulty of it and have prepared this rencounter to make good my jealousy.

Enter Mrs. Loveit, Bellinda, and Pert.

MEDLEY.

Here they come!

DORIMANT.

I'll meet her and provoke her with a deal of dumb civility in passing by, then turn short and be behind her when Sir Fopling sets upon her.

[Bows to Mrs. Loveit.]

"See how unregarded now
That piece of beauty passes."[78]

Exeunt Dorimant and Medley.

BELLINDA.

How wonderful respectfully he bowed!

PERT.

He's always over-mannerly when he has done a mischief.

BELLINDA.

Methought indeed, at the same time he had a strange, despising countenance.

PERT.

The unlucky look he thinks becomes him.

BELLINDA.

I was afraid you would have spoke to him, my dear.

MRS. LOVEIT.

I would have died first. He shall no more find me the loving fool he has done.

BELLINDA.

You love him still!

MRS. LOVEIT.

No.

PERT.

I wish you did not.

MRS. LOVEIT.

I do not, and I will have you think so!—What made you hale me to this odious place, Bellinda?

BELLINDA.

I hate to be hulched[79] up in a coach. Walking is much better.

MRS. LOVEIT.

Would we could meet Sir Fopling now!

BELLINDA.

Lord! would you not avoid him?

MRS. LOVEIT.

I would make him all the advances that may be.

BELLINDA.

That would confirm Dorimant's suspicion, my dear.

MRS. LOVEIT.

He is not jealous, but I will make him so and be revenged a way he little thinks on.

BELLINDA. (*Aside.*)

If she should make him jealous, that may make him fond of her again. I must dissuade her from

---

[78] "See ... passes."] a paraphrase of Suckling, *Sonnets*, I, 1-2

[79] hulched up] bundled up, bent like a hunchback

it.—Lord! My dear, this will certainly make him hate you.

MRS. LOVEIT.
'Twill make him uneasy, though he does not care for me. I know the effects of jealousy on men of his proud temper.

BELLINDA.
'Tis a fantastic remedy: its operations are dangerous and uncertain.

MRS. LOVEIT.
'Tis the strongest cordial we can give to dying love. It often brings it back when there's no sign of life remaining. But I design not so much the reviving his, as my revenge.

Enter Sir Fopling and his equipage.

SIR FOPLING.
Hey! Bid the coachman send home four of his horses and bring the coach to Whitehall.* I'll walk over the Park.* [*To Mrs. Loveit.*] Madam, the honor of kissing your fair hands is a happiness I missed this afternoon at my Lady Townley's.

MRS. LOVEIT.
You were very obliging, Sir Fopling, the last time I saw you there.

SIR FOPLING.
The preference was due to your wit and beauty. [*To Bellinda.*] Madam, your servant. There never was so sweet an evening.

BELLINDA.
'T has drawn all the rabble of the Town hither.

SIR FOPLING.
'Tis pity there's not an order made that none but the beau monde should walk here.

MRS. LOVEIT.
'Twould add much to the beauty of the place. See what a sort of nasty fellows are coming!

Enter four ill-fashioned fellows singing,

"'Tis not for kisses alone,
[So long I have made my address]."

MRS. LOVEIT.
Faugh! Their periwigs are scented with tobacco so strong—

SIR FOPLING.
It overcomes our pulvillio.* Methinks I smell the coffeehouse they come from.

FIRST MAN.
Dorimant's convenient,[80] Madam Loveit.

SECOND MAN.
I like the oily _______* buttock with her.

THIRD MAN.
What spruce prig is that?

FIRST MAN.
A caravan,[81] lately come from Paris.

SECOND MAN.
Peace, they smoke!

All of them coughing, exeunt singing,

"There's something else to be done,
[Which you cannot choose but guess]."[82]

Enter Dorimant and Medley.

DORIMANT.
They're engaged—

MEDLEY.
She entertains him as if she liked him.

DORIMANT.
Let us go forward—seem earnest in discourse and show ourselves. Then you shall see how she'll use him.

BELLINDA.
Yonder's Dorimant, my dear.

MRS. LOVEIT.
I see him. (*Aside.*) He comes insulting, but I will disappoint him in his expectation. (*To Sir Fopling.*) I like this pretty, nice* humor* of yours, Sir Fopling.—With what a loathing eye he looked upon those fellows!

SIR FOPLING.
I sat near one of 'em at a play today and was almost poisoned with a pair of cordovan gloves he wears—

MRS. LOVEIT.
Oh, filthy cordovan! How I hate the smell! (*Laughs in a loud, affected way.*)

---

80 convenient] mistress or whore

81 caravan] a prospective victim of plunder, evidenced by his equipage

82 "'Tis not for kisses ... [choose but guess]."] lines from a popular song, first published in 1676, beginning "Tell me no more you love, / Unless you will grant my desire."

SIR FOPLING.
Did you observe, madam, how their cravats hung loose an inch from their neck, and what a frightful air it gave 'em?

MRS. LOVEIT.
Oh! I took particular notice of one that is always spruced up with a deal of dirty, sky-colored ribbon.

BELLINDA.
That's one of the walking flageolets[83] who haunt the Mall o'nights—

MRS. LOVEIT.
Oh! I remember him! H'as a hollow tooth, enough to spoil the sweetness of an evening.

SIR FOPLING.
I have seen the tallest walk the streets with a dainty pair of boxes,[84] neatly buckled on.

MRS. LOVEIT.
And a little footboy at his heels, pocket-high, with a flat cap,[85] a dirty face—

SIR FOPLING.
And a snotty nose—

MRS. LOVEIT.
Oh—odious! There's many of my own sex with that Holborn[86] equipage trig[87] to Gray's Inn Walks, and now and then travel hither on a Sunday.

MEDLEY. [*To Dorimant.*]
She takes no notice of you.

DORIMANT.
Damn her! I am jealous of a counterplot!

MRS. LOVEIT.
Your liveries are the finest, Sir Fopling—Oh, that page! That page is the prettilly'st dressed—they are all Frenchmen?

SIR FOPLING.
There's one damned English blockhead among 'em. You may know him by his mien.

MRS. LOVEIT.
Oh, that's he, that's he! What do you call him?

SIR FOPLING.
Hey—I know not what to call him—

MRS. LOVEIT.
What's your name?

FOOTMAN.
John Trott, madam.

SIR FOPLING.
Oh, insufferable! Trott, Trott, Trott! There's nothing so barbarous as the names of our English servants. What countryman are you, sirrah?

FOOTMAN.
Hampshire, sir.

SIR FOPLING.
Then Hampshire be your name. Hey, Hampshire!

MRS. LOVEIT.
Oh, that sound! That sound becomes the mouth of a man of quality!*

MEDLEY.
Dorimant, you look a little bashful on the matter!

DORIMANT.
She dissembles better than I thought she could have done.

MEDLEY.
You have tempted her with too luscious a bait. She bites at the coxcomb.

DORIMANT.
She cannot fall from loving me to that?

MEDLEY.
You begin to be jealous in earnest.

DORIMANT.
Of one I do not love—

MEDLEY.
You did love her.

DORIMANT.
The fit has long been over—

MEDLEY.
But I have known men fall into dangerous relapses when they have found a woman inclining to another.

DORIMANT (*To himself.*)
He guesses the secret of my heart! I am concerned but dare not show it, lest Bellinda should mistrust all I have done to gain her.

---

83 flageolet] a small wind instrument similar to a recorder

84 boxes] probably galoshes again, platform shoes

85 flat cap] a round cap with a low, flat crown, worn in the 16th-17th c. by London citizens, particularly apprentices

86 Holborn] a borough in the commercial district of London, which includes several of the Inns of Court, including Gray's Inn

87 trig] walk briskly, trip

BELLINDA. (*Aside.*)
I have watched his look and find no alteration there. Did he love her, some signs of jealousy would have appeared.

DORIMANT. [*To Mrs. Loveit.*]
I hope this happy evening, madam, has reconciled you to the scandalous Mall. We shall have you now hankering[88] here again.

MRS. LOVEIT.
Sir Fopling, will you walk?

SIR FOPLING.
I am all obedience, madam—

MRS. LOVEIT.
Come along, then—and let's agree to be malicious on all the ill-fashioned things we meet.

SIR FOPLING.
We'll make a critique on the whole Mall, madam.

MRS. LOVEIT.
Bellinda, you shall engage—

BELLINDA.
To the reserve of our friends, my dear.

MRS. LOVEIT.
No! No exceptions—

SIR FOPLING.
We'll sacrifice all to our diversion—

MRS. LOVEIT.
All—all—

SIR FOPLING.
All!

BELLINDA.
All? Then let it be.

Exeunt Sir Fopling, Mrs. Loveit, Bellinda, and Pert, laughing.

MEDLEY.
Would you had brought some more of your friends, Dorimant, to have been witnesses of Sir Fopling's disgrace and your triumph!

DORIMANT.
'Twere unreasonable to desire you not to laugh at me, but pray do not expose me to the Town this day or two.

MEDLEY.
By that time you hope to have regained your credit.

DORIMANT.
I know she hates Fopling and only makes use of him in hope to work me on again. Had it not been for some powerful considerations which will be removed tomorrow morning, I had made her pluck off this mask and show the passion that lies panting under.

Enter a footman.

MEDLEY.
Here comes a man from Bellair, with news of your last adventure.

DORIMANT.
I am glad he sent him. I long to know the consequence of our parting.

FOOTMAN.
Sir, my master desires you to come to my Lady Townley's presently and bring Mr. Medley with you. My Lady Woodvill and her daughter are there.

MEDLEY.
Then all's well, Dorimant.

FOOTMAN.
They have sent for the fiddles and mean to dance. He bid me tell you, sir, the old lady does not know you, and would have you own yourself to be Mr. Courtage. They are all prepared to receive you by that name.

DORIMANT.
That foppish admirer of quality,* who flatters the very meat at honorable tables and never offers love to a woman below a lady-grandmother!

MEDLEY.
You know the character you are to act, I see.

DORIMANT.
This is Harriet's contrivance—wild, witty, lovesome, beautiful and young!—Come along, Medley.

MEDLEY.
This new woman would well supply the loss of Loveit.

DORIMANT.
That business must not end so. Before tomorrow sun is set, I will revenge and clear it.
And you and Loveit, to her cost, shall find
I fathom all the depths of womankind.

Exeunt.

[88] hankering] loitering, "hanging out"

Act IV, scene i. [Lady Townley's house.]

The scene opens with the fiddles playing a country dance. Enter Dorimant [and] Lady Woodvill, Young Bellair and Mrs. Harriet, Old Bellair and Emilia, Mr. Medley and Lady Townley, as having just ended the dance.

OLD BELLAIR.
So, so, so! A smart bout, a very smart bout, adod!

LADY TOWNLEY.
How do you like Emilia's dancing, brother?

OLD BELLAIR.
Not at all, not at all!

LADY TOWNLEY.
You speak not what you think, I am sure.

OLD BELLAIR.
No matter for that—go, bid her dance no more. It don't become her, it don't become her. Tell her I say so. (*Aside.*) Adod, I love her.

DORIMANT. (*To Lady Woodvill.*)
All people mingle nowadays, madam. And in public places women of quality* have the least respect showed 'em.

LADY WOODVILL.
I protest you say the truth, Mr. Courtage.

DORIMANT.
Forms and ceremonies, the only things that uphold quality* and greatness, are now shamefully laid aside and neglected.

LADY WOODVILL.
Well, this is not the women's age, let 'em think what they will. Lewdness is the business now; love was the business in my time.

DORIMANT.
The women, indeed, are little beholding to the young men of this age. They're generally only dull admirers of themselves and make their court to nothing but their periwigs and their cravats—and would be more concerned for the disordering of 'em, though on a good occasion, than a young maid would be for the tumbling of her head or handkercher.[89]

LADY WOODVILL.
I protest you hit 'em.

DORIMANT.
They are very assiduous to show themselves at Court, well-dressed, to the women of quality,* but their business is with the stale mistresses of the Town, who are prepared to receive their lazy addresses by industrious old lovers who have cast 'em off and made 'em easy.

HARRIET.
He fits my mother's humor* so well, a little more and she'll dance a kissing dance[90] with him anon.

MEDLEY.
Dutifully observed, madam.

DORIMANT.
They pretend to be great critics in beauty: by their talk you would think they liked no face—and yet can dote on an ill one if it belongs to a laundress or a tailor's daughter. They cry a woman's past her prime at twenty, decayed at four-and-twenty, old and insufferable at thirty.

LADY WOODVILL.
Insufferable at thirty! That they are in the wrong, Mr. Courtage. At five-and-thirty there are living proofs enough to convince 'em.

DORIMANT.
Aye, madam! there's Mrs. Setlooks, Mrs. Droplip, and my Lady Lowd! Show me among all our opening buds a face that promises so much beauty as the remains of theirs.

LADY WOODVILL.
The depraved appetite of this vicious age tastes nothing but green fruit and loathes it when 'tis kindly[91] ripened.

DORIMANT.
Else so many deserving women, madam, would not be so untimely neglected.

LADY WOODVILL.
I protest, Mr. Courtage, a dozen such good men as you would be enough to atone for that wicked Dorimant and all the under-debauchees of the Town.

89 head ... handkercher] hairdo and a kerchief worn as a head-covering

90 kissing dance] cushion dance, a round dance, formerly danced at weddings, in which the women and men alternately knelt on a cushion to be kissed (*OED*)

91 kindly] naturally

Harriet, Emilia, Young Bellair, Medley, and Lady Townley break out into a laughter.

What's the matter there?

MEDLEY.

A pleasant mistake, madam, that a lady has made occasions a little laughter.

OLD BELLAIR.

Come, come, you keep 'em idle! They are impatient till the fiddles play again.

DORIMANT.

You are not weary, madam?

LADY WOODVILL.

One dance more! I cannot refuse you, Mr. Courtage.

They dance. After the dance, Old Bellair singing and dancing up to Emilia.

EMILIA.

You are very active, sir.

OLD BELLAIR.

Adod, sirrah, when I was a young fellow, I could ha' capered up to my woman's gorget.

DORIMANT. [*To Lady Woodvill.*]

You are willing to rest yourself, madam?

LADY TOWNLEY.

We'll walk into my chamber and sit down.

MEDLEY.

Leave us Mr. Courtage: he's a dancer, and the young ladies are not weary yet.

LADY WOODVILL.

We'll send him out again.

HARRIET.

If you do not quickly, I know where to send for Mr. Dorimant.

LADY WOODVILL.

This girl's head, Mr. Courtage, is ever running on that wild fellow.

DORIMANT.

'Tis well you have got her a good husband, madam. That will settle it.

Exeunt Lady Townley, Lady Woodvill, and Dorimant.

OLD BELLAIR (*To Emilia.*)

Adod, sweetheart, be advised and do not throw thyself away on a young, idle fellow.

EMILIA.

I have no such intention, sir.

OLD BELLAIR.

Have a little patience! Thou shalt have the man I spake of. Adod, he loves thee and will make a good husband. But no words—

EMILIA.

But sir—

OLD BELLAIR.

No answer—out a pize!* Peace! and think on't.

Enter Dorimant.

DORIMANT.

Your company is desired within, sir.

OLD BELLAIR.

I go, I go, good Mr. Courtage. (*To Emilia.*) Fare you well. Go, I'll see you no more!

EMILIA.

What have I done, sir?

OLD BELLAIR.

You are ugly, you are ugly!—Is she not, Mr. Courtage?

EMILIA.

Better words, or I shan't abide you!

OLD BELLAIR.

Out a pize! Adod, what does she say?—Hit her a pat for me there. (*Exit.*)

MEDLEY. [*To Emilia.*]

You have charms for the whole family.

DORIMANT.

You'll spoil all with some unseasonable jest, Medley.

MEDLEY.

You see I confine my tongue and am content to be a bare spectator, much contrary to my nature.

EMILIA.

Methinks, Mr. Dorimant, my Lady Woodvill is a little fond of you.

DORIMANT.

Would her daughter were.

MEDLEY.

It may be you may find her so. Try her. You have an opportunity.

DORIMANT.

And I will not lose it.—Bellair, here's a lady has something to say to you.

YOUNG BELLAIR.
I wait upon her.—Mr. Medley, we have both business with you.

DORIMANT.
Get you all together, then.

[He approaches Harriet and bows; she curtsies.]

(*To Harriet.*) That demure curtsy is not amiss in jest, but do not think in earnest it becomes you.

HARRIET.
Affectation is catching, I find; from your grave bow I got it.

DORIMANT.
Where had you all that scorn and coldness in your look?

HARRIET.
From nature, sir; pardon my want* of art. I have not learnt those softnesses and languishings which now in faces are so much in fashion.

DORIMANT.
You need 'em not. You have a sweetness of your own, if you would but calm your frowns and let it settle.

HARRIET.
My eyes are wild and wandering like my passions and cannot yet be tied to rules of charming.

DORIMANT.
Women, indeed, have commonly a method of managing those messengers of love. Now they will look as if they would kill, and anon they will look as if they were dying. They point and rebate their glances, the better to invite us.

HARRIET.
I like this variety well enough, but hate the set face that always looks as it would say, "Come love me"— a woman who at plays makes the *doux yeux*[92] to a whole audience and at home cannot forbear 'em to her monkey.

DORIMANT.
Put on a gentle smile and let me see how well it will become you.

HARRIET.
I am sorry my face does not please you as it is, but I shall not be complaisant and change it.

DORIMANT.
Though you are obstinate, I know 'tis capable of improvement and shall do you justice, madam, if I chance to be at Court when the critics of the Circle pass their judgment, for thither you must come.

HARRIET.
And expect to be taken in pieces, have all my features examined, every motion censured, and on the whole be condemned to be but pretty, or a beauty of the lowest rate. What think you?

DORIMANT.
The women—nay, the very lovers who belong to the Drawing Room*—will maliciously allow you more than that. They always grant what is apparent, that they may the better be believed when they name concealed faults they cannot easily be disproved in.

HARRIET.
Beauty runs as great a risk exposed at Court as wit does on the stage, where the ugly and the foolish are all free to censure.

DORIMANT (*Aside.*)
I love her and dare not let her know it. I fear sh'as an ascendant o'er me and may revenge the wrongs I have done her sex. (*To her.*) Think of making a party, madam; love will engage.

HARRIET.
You make me start! I did not think to have heard of love from you.

DORIMANT.
I never knew what 'twas to have a settled ague yet, but now and then have had irregular fits.

HARRIET.
Take heed—sickness after long health is commonly more violent and dangerous.

DORIMANT. (*Aside.*)
I have took the infection from her and feel the disease now spreading in me. (*To her.*) Is the name of love so frightful that you dare not stand it?

HARRIET.
'Twill do little execution out of your mouth on me, I am sure.

DORIMANT.
It has been fatal—

HARRIET.
To some easy women, but we are not all born to

92 *doux yeux*] flirtatious glances (Fr.)

one destiny. I was informed you use to laugh at love, and not make it.*

DORIMANT.

The time has been, but now I must speak—

HARRIET.

If it be on that idle subject, I will put on my serious look, turn my head carelessly from you, drop my lip, let my eyelids fall and hang half o'er my eyes—thus—while you buzz a speech of an hour long in my ear and I answer never a word. Why do you not begin?

DORIMANT.

That the company may take notice how passionately I make advances of love and how disdainfully you receive 'em.

HARRIET.

When your love's grown strong enough to make you bear being laughed at, I'll give you leave to trouble me with it. Till when, pray forbear, sir.

Enter Sir Fopling and others in masks.

DORIMANT.

What's here, masquerades?

HARRIET.

I thought that foppery had been left off, and people might have been in private with a fiddle.

DORIMANT.

'Tis endeavored to be kept on foot still by some who find themselves the more acceptable, the less they are known.

YOUNG BELLAIR.

This must be Sir Fopling.

MEDLEY.

That extraordinary habit shows it.

YOUNG BELLAIR.

What are the rest?

MEDLEY.

A company of French rascals whom he picked up in Paris and has brought over to be his dancing equipage on these occasions. Make him own himself; a fool is very troublesome when he presumes he is incognito.

SIR FOPLING. (*To Harriet.*)

Do you know me?

HARRIET.

Ten to one but I guess at you.

SIR FOPLING.

Are you women as fond of a vizard as we men are?

HARRIET.

I am very fond of a vizard that covers a face I do not like, sir.

YOUNG BELLAIR.

Here are no masks, you see, sir, but those which came with you. This was intended a private meeting, but because you look like a gentleman, if you will discover* yourself and we know you to be such, you shall be welcome.

SIR FOPLING. (*Pulling off his mask.*)

Dear Bellair.

MEDLEY.

Sir Fopling! How came you hither?

SIR FOPLING.

Faith, as I was coming late from Whitehall,* after the King's *couchée*,[93] one of my people told me he had heard fiddles at my Lady Townley's, and—

DORIMANT.

You need not say any more, sir.

SIR FOPLING.

Dorimant, let me kiss thee.

DORIMANT.

Hark you, Sir Fopling—(*Whispers.*)

SIR FOPLING.

Enough, enough, Courtage. [*Indicates Harriet.*] A pretty kind of young woman that, Medley. I observed her in the Mall, more *éveillée*[94] than our English women commonly are. Prithee, what is she?

MEDLEY.

The most noted coquette in Town; beware of her.

SIR FOPLING.

Let her be what she will, I know how to take my measures. In Paris the mode is to flatter the *prude*, laugh at the *faux-prude*, make serious love to the *demi-prude*, and only rally with the coquette. Medley, what think you?

MEDLEY.

That for all this smattering of the mathematics, you may be out in your judgment at tennis.

---

93 *couchée*] the formal ceremony accompanying the king's going to bed (Fr.)

94 *eveillée*] lively, sprightly, intelligent (Fr.)

SIR FOPLING.

What *coq-à-l'âne*[95] is this? I talk of women and thou answer'st tennis.

MEDLEY.

Mistakes will be, for want of apprehension.

SIR FOPLING.

I am very glad of the acquaintance I have with this family.

MEDLEY.

My lady truly is a good woman.

SIR FOPLING.

Ah, Dorimant—Courtage, I would say—would thou hadst spent the last winter in Paris with me. When thou wert there, La Corneus and Sallyes[96] were the only habitudes we had; a comedian would have been a *bonne fortune*. No stranger ever passed his time so well as I did some months before I came over. I was well received in a dozen families, where all the women of quality* used to visit. I have intrigues to tell thee more pleasant than ever thou read'st in a novel.

HARRIET.

Write 'em, sir, and oblige us women. Our language wants* such little stories.

SIR FOPLING.

Writing, madam, 's a mechanic part of wit. A gentleman should never go beyond a song or a *billet*.

HARRIET.

Bussy was a gentleman.

SIR FOPLING.

Who, d'Ambois?[97]

MEDLEY. [*Aside*.]

Was there ever such a brisk blockhead?

HARRIET.

Not d'Ambois, sir, but Rabutin.[98] He who writ the *Loves of France*.

SIR FOPLING.

That may be, madam! many gentlemen do things that are below 'em.—Damn your authors, Courtage, women are the prettiest things we can fool away our time with.

HARRIET.

I hope ye have wearied yourself tonight at Court, sir, and will not think of fooling with anybody here.

SIR FOPLING.

I cannot complain of my fortune there, madam.—Dorimant—

DORIMANT.

Again!

SIR FOPLING.

Courtage, a pox on't! I have something to tell thee. When I had made my court within, I came out and flung myself upon the mat under the state[99] i'th'outward room, i'th'midst of half a dozen beauties who were withdrawn to jeer among themselves, as they called it.

DORIMANT.

Did you know 'em?

SIR FOPLING.

Not one of 'em, by heavens! not I. But they were all your friends.

DORIMANT.

How are you sure of that?

SIR FOPLING.

Why, we laughed at all the Town—spared nobody but yourself. They found me a man for their purpose.

DORIMANT.

I know you are malicious to your power.

SIR FOPLING.

And faith, I had occasion to show it, for I never saw more gaping fools at a ball or on a birthday.*

DORIMANT.

You learned who the women were?

SIR FOPLING.

No matter! they frequent the Drawing Room.*

DORIMANT.

And entertain themselves pleasantly at the expense of all the fops who come there.

---

95 *coq-à-l'âne*] cock-and-bull story, nonsense (Fr.)

96 Corneus and Sallyes] Mmes. Corneul and Selles, keepers of Parisian salons (Verity)

97 d'Ambois] Bussy d'Ambois, hero and title character of the 1604 tragedy by the English playwright George Chapman, seen in revival on the Restoration stage

98 Rabutin] Roger de Rabutin, Comte de Bussy (1618-1693), author of the *Histoire Amoureuse des Gaules*, whose title Harriet translates into English in this sentence.

99 state] ceremonial canopy

SIR FOPLING.
That's their business. Faith, I sifted 'em and find they have a sort of wit among them—(*Pinches a tallow candle.*) Ah, filthy!

DORIMANT.
Look, he has been pinching the tallow candle.

SIR FOPLING.
How can you breathe in a room where there's grease frying? Dorimant, thou art intimate with my lady; advise her, for her own sake and the good company that comes hither, to burn wax lights.

HARRIET.
What are these masquerades who stand so obsequiously at a distance?

SIR FOPLING.
A set of balladines, whom I picked out of the best in France and brought over with a *flûte douce* or two, my servants. They shall entertain you.

HARRIET.
I had rather see you dance yourself, Sir Fopling.

SIR FOPLING.
And I had rather do it—all the company knows it—but, madam—

MEDLEY.
Come, come! No excuses, Sir Fopling.

SIR FOPLING.
By heavens, Medley—

MEDLEY.
Like a woman, I find, you must be struggled with before one brings you to[d] what you desire.

HARRIET. (*Aside.*)
Can he dance?

EMILIA.
And fence and sing too, if you'll believe him.

DORIMANT.
He has no more excellence in his heels than in his head. He went to Paris a plain, bashful English blockhead and is returned a fine, undertaking[100] French fop.

MEDLEY.
I cannot prevail.

SIR FOPLING.
Do not think it want* of complaisance, madam.

HARRIET.
You are too well-bred to want that, Sir Fopling. I believe it want of power.

SIR FOPLING.
By heavens, and so it is! I have sat up so damned late and drunk so cursed hard since I came to this lewd Town that I am fit for nothing but low dancing now—a *courante*, a *bourrée*, or a *menuet.*[101] But St. André[102] tells me, if I will but be regular, in one month I shall rise again. (*Endeavors at a caper.*) Pox on this debauchery!

EMILIA.
I have heard your dancing much commended.

SIR FOPLING.
It had the good fortune to please in Paris. I was judged to rise within an inch as high as the Basque[103] in an entry[104] I danced there.

HARRIET. [*To Emilia.*]
I am mightily taken with this fool. Let us sit.—Here's a seat, Sir Fopling.

SIR FOPLING.
At your feet, madam. I can be nowhere so much at ease. By your leave, gown. [*Sits.*]

HARRIET, EMILIA.
Ah, you'll spoil it!

SIR FOPLING.
No matter, my clothes are my creatures. I make 'em to make my court to you ladies.—Hey, *qu'on commence!*[105]

Dance. [Sir Fopling points] to an English dancer.[e]

English motions! I was forced to entertain* this fellow, one of my set miscarrying.—Oh, horrid! Leave your damned manner of dancing and put on the French air. Have you not a pattern before you?—Pretty well! Imitation in time may bring him to something.

100 undertaking] enterprising

101 low dancing … *menuet*] Fopling calls such dances "low" because they do not require capers.

102 St. André] a well-known French dancing master and choreographer for the English stage

103 the Basque] probably "le Basque sauter," a French dancer (Barnard)

104 entry] a dance performed as an interlude in an entertainment

105 *qu'on commence*] begin! (Fr.)

After the dance, enter Old Bellair, Lady Woodvill, and Lady Townley.

OLD BELLAIR.
Hey, adod, what have we here? A mumming?

LADY WOODVILL.
Where's my daughter? Harriet!

DORIMANT.
Here, here, madam! I know not but under these disguises there may be dangerous sparks. I gave the young lady warning.

LADY WOODVILL.
Lord! I am so obliged to you, Mr. Courtage.

HARRIET.
Lord! How you admire this man!

LADY WOODVILL.
What have you to except against him?

HARRIET.
He's a fop.

LADY WOODVILL.
He's not a Dorimant, a wild, extravagant fellow of the times.

HARRIET.
He's a man made up of forms and commonplaces, sucked out of the remaining lees of the last age.

LADY WOODVILL.
He's so good a man that were you not engaged—

LADY TOWNLEY.
You'll have but little night to sleep in.

LADY WOODVILL.
Lord, 'tis perfect day!

DORIMANT. (*Aside.*)
The hour is almost come I appointed Bellinda, and I am not so foppishly in love here to forget. I am flesh and blood yet.

LADY TOWNLEY.
I am very sensible, madam.

LADY WOODVILL.
Lord, madam—

HARRIET.
Look, in what a struggle is my poor mother yonder!

YOUNG BELLAIR.
She has much ado to bring out the compliment.

DORIMANT.
She strains hard for it.

HARRIET.
See, see! her head tottering, her eyes staring, and her underlip trembling—

DORIMANT.
Now, now she's in the very convulsions of her civility. (*Aside.*) 'Sdeath, I shall lose Bellinda! I must fright her hence. She'll be an hour in this fit of good manners else. (*To Lady Woodvill.*) Do you not know Sir Fopling, madam?

LADY WOODVILL.
I have seen that face—Oh Heaven, 'tis the same we met in the Mall! How came he here?

DORIMANT.
A fiddle in this Town is a kind of fop-call. No sooner it strikes up, but the house is besieged with an army of masquerades straight.

LADY WOODVILL.
Lord, I tremble, Mr. Courtage. For certain Dorimant is in the company.

DORIMANT.
I cannot confidently say he is not. You had best be gone. I will wait upon you. Your daughter is in the hands of Mr. Bellair.

LADY WOODVILL.
I'll see her before me.—Harriet, come away!

YOUNG BELLAIR. [*Calling to servants offstage.*]
Lights, lights!

LADY TOWNLEY.
Light, down there!

OLD BELLAIR.
Adod, it needs not—

DORIMANT.
Call my Lady Woodvill's coach to the door quickly!

[Exeunt Emilia, Young Bellair, Lady Woodvill, Harriet, Lady Townley, and Dorimant.]

OLD BELLAIR.
Stay, Mr. Medley; let the young fellows do that duty. We will drink a glass of wine together. 'Tis good after dancing. What mumming spark is that?

MEDLEY.
He is not to be comprehended in few words.

SIR FOPLING.
Hey, La Tour!

MEDLEY.
Whither away, Sir Fopling?

SIR FOPLING.
I have business with Courtage.

MEDLEY.
He'll but put the ladies into their coach and come up again.

OLD BELLAIR.
In the meantime I'll call for a bottle. (*Exit.*)

Enter Young Bellair.

MEDLEY.
Where's Dorimant?

YOUNG BELLAIR.
Stol'n home. He has had business waiting for him there all this night, I believe, by an impatience I observed in him.

MEDLEY.
Very likely. 'Tis but dissembling drunkenness, railing at his friends, and the kind* soul will embrace the blessing and forget the tedious expectation.

SIR FOPLING.
I must speak with him before I sleep.

YOUNG BELLAIR. [*To Medley.*]
Emilia and I are resolved on that business.

MEDLEY.
Peace, here's your father.

Enter Old Bellair and butler with a bottle of wine.

OLD BELLAIR.
The women are all gone to bed.—Fill, boy!—Mr. Medley, begin a health.

MEDLEY.
To Emilia.

OLD BELLAIR.
Out a pize!* She's a rogue, and I'll not pledge you.

MEDLEY. (*Whispers.*)
I know you will.[f]

OLD BELLAIR.
Adod, drink it, then!

SIR FOPLING.
Let us have the new *bachique.*

OLD BELLAIR.
Adod, that is a hard word! What does it mean, sir?

MEDLEY.
A catch or drinking song.

OLD BELLAIR.
Let us have it, then.

SIR FOPLING.
Fill the glasses round and draw up in a body.—Hey! music!

They sing.

The pleasures of love and the joys of good wine,
To perfect our happiness wisely we join.
We to beauty all day
Give the sovereign sway
And her favorite nymphs devoutly obey.
At the plays we are constantly making our court,
And when they are ended, we follow the sport
To the Mall* and the Park,*
Where we love till 'tis dark;
Then sparkling champagne
Puts an end to their reign;
It quickly recovers
Poor languishing lovers,
Makes us frolic and gay, and drowns all our sorrow;
But alas! we relapse again on the morrow.
    Let every man stand
    With his glass in his hand,
And briskly discharge at the word of command.
    Here's a health to all those
    Whom tonight we depose.
Wine and beauty by turns great souls should inspire;
Present all together; and now, boys, give fire!

OLD BELLAIR.
Adod, a pretty business and very merry!

SIR FOPLING.
Hark you, Medley, let you and I take the fiddles and go waken Dorimant.

MEDLEY.
We shall do him a courtesy, if it be as I guess. For after the fatigue of this night, he'll quickly have his belly full and be glad of an occasion to cry, "Take away, Handy!"

YOUNG BELLAIR.
I'll go with you, and there we'll consult about affairs, Medley.

OLD BELLAIR. (*Looks on his watch.*)
Adod, 'tis six o'clock!

SIR FOPLING.
Let's away, then.

OLD BELLAIR.
Mr. Medley, my sister tells me you are an honest

man. And adod, I love you. Few words and hearty, that's the way with old Harry, old Harry.

SIR FOPLING.
Light your flambeaux! Hey!

OLD BELLAIR.
What does the man mean?

MEDLEY.
'Tis day, Sir Fopling.

SIR FOPLING.
No matter. Our serenade will look the greater.

Exeunt omnes.

Scene ii. Dorimant's lodging, a table, a candle, a toilet, etc.

Handy tying up linen. Enter Dorimant in his gown, and Bellinda.

DORIMANT.
Why will you be gone so soon?

BELLINDA.
Why did you stay out so late?

DORIMANT.
Call a chair,* Handy!

[Exit Handy.]

What makes you tremble so?

BELLINDA.
I have a thousand fears about me. Have I not been seen, think you?

DORIMANT.
By nobody but myself and trusty Handy.

BELLINDA.
Where are all your people?

DORIMANT.
I have dispersed 'em on sleeveless[106] errands. What does that sigh mean?

BELLINDA.
Can you be so unkind to ask me?—Well—(*Sighs.*) were it to do again—

DORIMANT.
We should do it, should we not?

BELLINDA.
I think we should: the wickeder man you, to make me love so well. Will you be discreet now?

DORIMANT.
I will—

BELLINDA.
You cannot.

DORIMANT.
Never doubt it.

BELLINDA.
I will not expect it.

DORIMANT.
You do me wrong.

BELLINDA.
You have no more power to keep the secret than I had not to trust you with it.

DORIMANT.
By all the joys I have had and those you keep in store—

BELLINDA.
You'll do for my sake what you never did before—

DORIMANT.
By that truth thou hast spoken, a wife shall sooner betray herself to her husband—

BELLINDA.
Yet I had rather you should be false in this than in another thing you promised me.

DORIMANT.
What's that?

BELLINDA.
That you would never see Loveit more but in public places—in the Park,* at Court and plays.

DORIMANT.
'Tis not likely a man should be fond of seeing a damned old play when there is a new one acted.

BELLINDA.
I dare not trust your promise.

DORIMANT.
You may—

BELLINDA.
This does not satisfy me. You shall swear you never will see her more.

DORIMANT.
I will! a thousand oaths—by all—

BELLINDA.
Hold—you shall not, now I think on't better.

DORIMANT.
I will swear—

106 sleeveless] useless

BELLINDA.
I shall grow jealous of the oath and think I owe your truth to that, not to your love.

DORIMANT.
Then, by my love! No other oath I'll swear.

(Enter Handy.)

HANDY.
Here's a chair.

BELLINDA.
Let me go.

DORIMANT.
I cannot.

BELLINDA.
Too willingly, I fear.

DORIMANT.
Too unkindly feared. When will you promise me again?

BELLINDA.
Not this fortnight.

DORIMANT.
You will be better than your word.

BELLINDA.
I think I shall. Will it not make you love me less?

Fiddles without.

(*Starting.*) Hark! what fiddles are these?

DORIMANT.
Look out, Handy.

Exit Handy and returns.

HANDY.
Mr. Medley, Mr. Bellair, and Sir Fopling. They are coming up.

DORIMANT.
How got they in?

HANDY.
The door was open for the chair.

BELLINDA.
Lord! let me fly!

DORIMANT.
Here, here—down the back stairs. I'll see you into your chair.

BELLINDA.
No, no! stay and receive 'em. And be sure you keep your word and never see Loveit more. Let it be a proof of your kindness.*

DORIMANT.
It shall.—Handy, direct her. (*Kissing her hand.*) Everlasting love go along with thee.

Exeunt Bellinda and Handy. Enter Young Bellair, Medley, and Sir Fopling.

YOUNG BELLAIR.
Not abed yet?

MEDLEY.
You have had an irregular fit, Dorimant.

DORIMANT.
I have.

YOUNG BELLAIR.
And is it off already?

DORIMANT.
Nature has done her part, gentlemen. When she falls kindly to work, great cures are effected in little time, you know.

SIR FOPLING.
We thought there was a wench in the case, by the chair that waited. Prithee, make us a *confidence.*

DORIMANT.
Excuse me.

SIR FOPLING.
Le sage[107] Dorimant—was she pretty?

DORIMANT.
So pretty she may come to keep her coach and pay parish duties, if the good humor of the age continue.

MEDLEY.
And be of the number of the ladies kept by public-spirited men for the good of the whole Town.

SIR FOPLING.
Well said, Medley. (*Dancing by himself.*)

YOUNG BELLAIR.
See Sir Fopling dancing.

DORIMANT.
You are practicing and have a mind to recover, I see.

SIR FOPLING.
Prithee, Dorimant, why hast not thou a glass* hung up here? A room is the dullest thing without one!

YOUNG BELLAIR.
Here is company to entertain you.

---

107 *sage*] wise, discreet (Fr.)

SIR FOPLING.
But I mean in case of being alone. In a glass a man may entertain himself—
DORIMANT.
The shadow of himself, indeed.
SIR FOPLING.
Correct the errors of his motions and his dress.
MEDLEY.
I find, Sir Fopling, in your solitude you remember the saying of the wise man, and study yourself.
SIR FOPLING.
'Tis the best diversion in our retirements. Dorimant, thou art a pretty fellow and wear'st thy clothes well, but I never saw thee have a handsome cravat. Were they made up like mine, they'd give another air to thy face. Prithee, let me send my man to dress thee but one day. By heavens, an Englishman cannot tie a ribbon!
DORIMANT.
They are something clumsy-fisted—
SIR FOPLING.
I have brought over the prettiest fellow that ever spread a toilet. He served some time under Merrille, the greatest *génie* in the world for a valet de chambre.
DORIMANT.
What, he who formerly belonged to the duke of Candale?[108]
SIR FOPLING.
The same, and got him his immortal reputation.
DORIMANT.
Y'ave a very fine brandenburgh[109] on, Sir Fopling.
SIR FOPLING.
It serves to wrap me up, after the fatigue of a ball.
MEDLEY.
I see you often in it, with your periwig tied up.
SIR FOPLING.
We should not always be in a set dress. 'Tis more *en cavalier* to appear now and then in a dishabille.
MEDLEY.
Pray, how goes your business with Loveit?

[108] the Duke of Candale] Louis-Charles Gaston de Nogaret de Foix, Duc de Candale (1627-58), a French general admired for his elegance of dress

[109] brandenburgh] woolen morning gown

SIR FOPLING.
You might have answered yourself in the Mall last night.—Dorimant! did you not see the advances she made me? I have been endeavoring at a song!
DORIMANT.
Already!
SIR FOPLING.
'Tis my *coup d'essai*[110] in English. I would fain have thy opinion of it.
DORIMANT.
Let's see it.
SIR FOPLING.
Hey, page, give me my song.—Bellair, here. Thou hast a pretty voice: sing it.
YOUNG BELLAIR.
Sing it yourself, Sir Fopling.
SIR FOPLING.
Excuse me.
YOUNG BELLAIR.
You learnt to sing in Paris.
SIR FOPLING.
I did—of Lambert,[111] the greatest master in the world. But I have his own fault, a weak voice, and care not to sing out of a *ruelle*.[112]
DORIMANT.
A *ruelle* is a pretty cage for a singing fop, indeed.

Young Bellair reads the song.

How charming Phillis is, how fair!
    Ah, that she were as willing
To ease my wounded heart of care
    And make her eyes less killing.
I sigh! I sigh! I languish now,
    And love will not let me rest;
I drive about the Park* and bow
    Still as I meet my dearest.

SIR FOPLING.
Sing it, sing it, man! It goes to a pretty new tune which I am confident was made by Baptiste.[113]

[110] *coup d'essai*] first attempt (Fr.)

[111] Lambert] Michel Lambert (1610-96), French lutenist and singer

[112] *ruelle*] a space in a bedchamber, where fashionable visitors attended women of quality at their levees

[113] Baptiste] probably Jean-Baptiste Lully (1632-87),

MEDLEY.
Sing it yourself, Sir Fopling. He does not know the tune.

SIR FOPLING.
I'll venture. (*Sings.*)

DORIMANT.
Aye, marry,* now 'tis something. I shall not flatter you, Sir Fopling; there is not much thought in't. But 'tis passionate and well-turned.

MEDLEY.
After the French way.

SIR FOPLING.
That I aimed at—does it not give you a lively image of the thing? Slap, down goes the glass,[114] and thus we are at it.

DORIMANT.
It does indeed. I perceive, Sir Fopling, you'll be the very head of the sparks who are lucky in compositions of this nature.

Enter Sir Fopling's footman.

SIR FOPLING.
La Tour, is the bath ready?

FOOTMAN.
Yes, sir.

SIR FOPLING.
Adieu donc, mes chers.[115]

Exeunt Sir Fopling and footman.

MEDLEY.
When have you your revenge on Loveit, Dorimant?

DORIMANT.
I will but change my linen and about it.

MEDLEY.
The powerful considerations which hindered have been removed, then?

DORIMANT.
Most luckily, this morning. You must along with me; my reputation lies at stake there.

MEDLEY.
I am engaged to Bellair.

DORIMANT.
What's your business?

MEDLEY.
Ma-tri-mony, an't* like you.

DORIMANT.
It does not, sir.

YOUNG BELLAIR.
It may in time, Dorimant. What think you of Mrs. Harriet?

DORIMANT.
What does she think of me?

YOUNG BELLAIR.
I am confident she loves you.

DORIMANT.
How does it appear?

YOUNG BELLAIR.
Why, she's never well but when she's talking of you, but then she finds all the faults in you she can. She laughs at all who commend you, but then she speaks ill of all who do not.

DORIMANT.
Women of her temper betray themselves by their over-cunning. I had once a growing love with a lady who would always quarrel with me when I came to see her and yet was never quiet if I stayed a day from her.

YOUNG BELLAIR.
My father is in love with Emilia.

DORIMANT.
That is a good warrant for your proceedings. Go on and prosper; I must to Loveit.—Medley, I am sorry you cannot be a witness.

MEDLEY.
Make her meet Sir Fopling again in the same place and use him ill before me.

DORIMANT.
That may be brought about, I think.—I'll be at your aunt's anon and give you joy, Mr. Bellair.

YOUNG BELLAIR.
You had not best think of Mrs. Harriet too much. Without church security, there's no taking up there.

---

master of court music to Louis XIV; possibly Giovanni Battista Draghi (c. 1640-1710), Italian harpsichordist and composer living in England and writing for the stage

114 down goes the glass] perhaps a window glass, perhaps a wine glass, perhaps a mirror—in that order of probability

115 *Adieu donc, mes chers*] Good-bye, then, my dears (Fr.)

DORIMANT.
I may fall into the snare, too. But—
The wise will find a difference in our fate:
You wed a woman, I a good estate.

Exeunt.

Scene iii. [The Mall.]

Enter the chair with Bellinda; the men set it down and open it. Bellinda starting.*

BELLINDA. (*Surprised.*)
Lord! where am I? In the Mall! Whither have you brought me?
FIRST CHAIRMAN.
You gave us no directions, madam.
BELLINDA. (*Aside.*)
The fright I was in made me forget it.
FIRST CHAIRMAN.
We use to carry a lady from the squire's hither.
BELLINDA. (*Aside.*)
This is Loveit! I am undone if she sees me.—Quickly, carry me away!
FIRST CHAIRMAN.
Whither, an't* like your honor?
BELLINDA.
Ask no questions—

Enter Mrs. Loveit's footman.

FOOTMAN.
Have you seen my lady, madam?
BELLINDA.
I am just come to wait upon her.
FOOTMAN.
She will be glad to see you, madam. She sent me to you this morning to desire your company, and I was told you went out by five o'clock.
BELLINDA. (*Aside.*)
More and more unlucky!
FOOTMAN.
Will you walk in, madam?
BELLINDA.
I'll discharge my chair and follow. Tell your mistress I am here.

Exit footman. [Bellinda] gives the chairmen money.

Take this, and if ever you should be examined, be sure you say you took me up in the Strand,* over against the Exchange,* as you will answer it to Mr. Dorimant.
CHAIRMEN.
We will, an't like your honor.

Exeunt chairmen.

BELLINDA.
Now to come off, I must on—
In confidence and lies some hope is left;
'Twere hard to be found out in the first theft.

Exit.

Act V, scene i. [*Mrs. Loveit's lodgings.*]

Enter Mrs. Loveit and Pert.

PERT.
Well! In my eyes, Sir Fopling is no such despicable person.
MRS. LOVEIT.
You are an excellent judge.
PERT.
He's as handsome a man as Mr. Dorimant, and as great a gallant.
MRS. LOVEIT.
Intolerable! Is't not enough I submit to his impertinences, but must I be plagued with yours, too?
PERT.
Indeed, madam—
MRS. LOVEIT.
'Tis false, mercenary malice—

Enter her footman.

FOOTMAN.
Mrs.* Bellinda, madam—
MRS. LOVEIT.
What of her?
FOOTMAN.
She's below.
MRS. LOVEIT.
How came she?
FOOTMAN.
In a chair; ambling Harry brought her.
MRS. LOVEIT.
He bring her! His chair stands near Dorimant's door and always brings me from thence—run and ask him where he took her up. Go!

[Exit footman.]

There is no truth in friendship neither. Women as well as men, all are false, or all are so to me, at least.

PERT.

You are jealous of her, too?

MRS. LOVEIT.

You had best tell her I am. 'Twill become the liberty you take of late. This fellow's bringing of her, her going out by five o'clock—I know not what to think.

Enter Bellinda.

Bellinda, you are grown an early riser, I hear.

BELLINDA.

Do you not wonder, my dear, what made me abroad so soon?

MRS. LOVEIT.

You do not use to be so.

BELLINDA.

The country gentlewomen I told you of (Lord! They have the oddest diversions!) would never let me rest till I promised to go with them to the markets this morning to eat fruit and buy nosegays.

MRS. LOVEIT.

Are they so fond of a filthy nosegay?

BELLINDA.

They complain of the stinks of the Town and are never well but when they have their noses in one.

MRS. LOVEIT.

There are essences and sweet waters.

BELLINDA.

Oh, they cry out upon perfumes, they are unwholesome. One of 'em was falling into a fit with the smell of these neroli.

MRS. LOVEIT.

Methinks in complaisance you should have had a nosegay too.

BELLINDA.

Do you think, my dear, I could be so loathsome to trick myself up with carnations and stock-gillyflowers?[116] I begged their pardon and told them I never wore anything but orange-flowers and tuberose. That which made me willing to go was a strange desire I had to eat some fresh nectarines.

MRS. LOVEIT.

And had you any?

BELLINDA.

The best I ever tasted.

MRS. LOVEIT.

Whence came you now?

BELLINDA.

From their lodgings, where I crowded out of a coach and took a chair* to come and see you, my dear.

MRS. LOVEIT.

Whither did you send for that chair?

BELLINDA.

'Twas going by empty.

MRS. LOVEIT.

Where do these country gentlewomen lodge, I pray?

BELLINDA.

In the Strand,* over against the Exchange.*

PERT.

That place is never without a nest of 'em. They are always, as one goes by, fleering in balconies or staring out of windows.

Enter footman.

MRS. LOVEIT. (*To the Footman.*)

Come hither. (*Whispers.*)

BELLINDA. (*Aside.*)

This fellow by her order has been questioning the chairmen! I threatened 'em with the name of Dorimant. If they should have told truth, I am lost forever.

MRS. LOVEIT.

In the Strand, said you?

FOOTMAN.

Yes, madam, over against the Exchange. (*Exit.*)

MRS. LOVEIT. [*Aside.*]

She's innocent, and I am much to blame.

BELLINDA. (*Aside.*)

I am so frighted, my countenance will betray me.

MRS. LOVEIT.

Bellinda! what makes you look so pale?

---

[116] stock-gillyflowers] a kind of carnation: The plant *Matthiola incana*; so called as having a woody stem, in distinction from clove-gillyflower (*OED*)

BELLINDA.

Want* of my usual rest and jolting up and down so long in an odious hackney.

Footman returns.

FOOTMAN.

Madam, Mr. Dorimant.

MRS. LOVEIT.

What makes him here?

BELLINDA. (*Aside.*)

Then I am betrayed indeed. He's broke his word, and I love a man that does not care for me.

MRS. LOVEIT.

Lord, you faint, Bellinda!

BELLINDA.

I think I shall! Such an oppression here on the sudden.

PERT.

She has eaten too much fruit, I warrant you.

MRS. LOVEIT.

Not unlikely.

PERT.

'Tis that lies heavy on her stomach.

MRS. LOVEIT.

Have her into my chamber, give her some surfeit-water, and let her lie down a little.

PERT.

Come, madam. I was a strange devourer of fruit when I was young—so ravenous.

Exeunt Bellinda and Pert, leading her off.

MRS. LOVEIT.

Oh, that my love would be but calm awhile, that I might receive this man with all the scorn and indignation he deserves!

Enter Dorimant.

DORIMANT.

Now for a touch of Sir Fopling to begin with. Hey—page— Give positive order than none of my people stir—Let the canaille wait, as they should do.
—Since noise and nonsense have such pow'rful
  charms,
"I, that I may successful prove,
Transform myself to what you love."[117]

[117] "I ... love"] Waller, "To the Mutable Fair," 5-6 (slightly altered)

MRS. LOVEIT.

If that would do, you need not change from what you are; you can be vain and loud enough.

DORIMANT.

But not with so good a grace as Sir Fopling.—Hey, Hampshire!—Oh, that sound! That sound becomes the mouth of a man of quality.*

MRS. LOVEIT.

Is there a thing so hateful as a senseless mimic?

DORIMANT.

He's a great grievance, indeed, to all who, like yourself, madam, love to play the fool in quiet.

MRS. LOVEIT.

A ridiculous animal, who has more of the ape than the ape has of the man in him.

DORIMANT.

I have as mean an opinion of a sheer mimic as yourself, yet were he all ape, I should prefer him to the gay, the giddy, brisk, insipid, noisy fool you dote on.

MRS. LOVEIT.

Those noisy fools, however you despise 'em, have good qualities which weigh more (or ought, at least) with us women than all the pernicious wit you have to boast of.

DORIMANT.

That I may hereafter have a just value for their merit, pray do me the favor to name 'em.

MRS. LOVEIT.

You'll despise 'em as the dull effects of ignorance and vanity, yet I care not if I mention some. First, they really admire us, while you at best but flatter us well.

DORIMANT.

Take heed! fools can dissemble, too—

MRS. LOVEIT.

They may, but not so artificially as you—there is no fear they should deceive us. Then, they are assiduous, sir. They are ever offering us their service and always waiting on our will.

DORIMANT.

You owe that to their excessive idleness. They know not how to entertain themselves at home, and find so little welcome abroad, they are fain to fly to you who countenance 'em as a refuge against the solitude they would be otherwise condemned to.

MRS. LOVEIT.

Their conversation,* too, diverts us better.

DORIMANT.
Playing with your fan, smelling to your gloves, commending your hair, and taking notice how 'tis cut and shaded after the new way—

MRS. LOVEIT.
Were it sillier than you can make it, you must allow 'tis pleasanter to laugh at others than to be laughed at ourselves, though never so wittily. Then, though they want* skill to flatter us, they flatter themselves so well, they save us the labor. We need not take that care and pains to satisfy 'em of our love, which we so often lose on you.

DORIMANT.
They commonly, indeed, believe too well of themselves and always better of you than you deserve.

MRS. LOVEIT.
You are in the right. They have an implicit faith in us, which keeps 'em from prying narrowly into our secrets and saves us the vexatious trouble of clearing doubts which your subtle and causeless jealousies every moment raise.

DORIMANT.
There is an inbred falsehood in women which inclines 'em still* to them whom they may most easily deceive.

MRS. LOVEIT.
The man who loves above his quality* does not suffer more from the insolent impertinence of his mistress than the woman who loves above her understanding does from the arrogant presumptions of her friend.

DORIMANT.
You mistake the use of fools: they are designed for properties and not for friends. You have an indifferent stock of reputation left yet. Lose it all like a frank gamester on the square. 'Twill then be time enough to turn rook* and cheat it up again on a good, substantial bubble.*

MRS. LOVEIT.
The old and the ill-favored are only fit for properties, indeed, but young and handsome fools have met with kinder fortunes.

DORIMANT.
They have, to the shame of your sex be it spoken. 'Twas this, the thought of this, made me by a timely jealousy endeavor to prevent the good fortune you are providing for Sir Fopling—but against a woman's frailty all our care is vain.

MRS. LOVEIT.
Had I not with a dear experience bought the knowledge of your falsehood, you might have fooled me yet. This is not the first jealousy you have feigned to make a quarrel with me and get a week to throw away on some such unknown, inconsiderable slut as you have been lately lurking with at plays.

DORIMANT.
Women, when they would break off with a man, never want* th'address to turn the fault on him.

MRS. LOVEIT.
You take a pride of late in using of me ill, that the Town may know the power you have over me, which now (as unreasonably as yourself) expects that I (do me all the injuries you can) must love you still.

DORIMANT.
I am so far from expecting that you should, I begin to think you never did love me.

MRS. LOVEIT.
Would the memory of it were so wholly worn out in me that I did doubt it too! What made you come to disturb my growing quiet?

DORIMANT.
To give you joy of your growing infamy.

MRS. LOVEIT.
Insupportable! Insulting devil! This from you, the only author of my shame! This from another had been but justice, but from you, 'tis a hellish and inhuman outrage. What have I done?

DORIMANT.
A thing that puts you below my scorn and makes my anger as ridiculous as you have made my love.

MRS. LOVEIT.
I walked last night with Sir Fopling.

DORIMANT.
You did, madam, and you talked and laughed aloud—Ha, ha, ha—Oh, that laugh, that laugh becomes the confidence of a woman of quality.*

MRS. LOVEIT.
You, who have more pleasure in the ruin of a woman's reputation than in the endearments of her love, reproach me not with yourself and I defy you to name the man can lay a blemish on my fame.

DORIMANT.

To be seen publicly so transported with the vain follies of that notorious fop to me is an infamy below the sin of prostitution with another man.

MRS. LOVEIT.

Rail on! I am satisfied in the justice of what I did; you had provoked me to't.

DORIMANT.

What I did was the effect of a passion whose extravagancies you have been willing to forgive.

MRS. LOVEIT.

And what I did was the effect of a passion you may forgive if you think fit.

DORIMANT.

Are you so indifferent grown?

MRS. LOVEIT.

I am.

DORIMANT.

Nay, then 'tis time to part. I'll send you back your letters you have so often asked for. I have two or three of 'em about me.

MRS. LOVEIT.

Give 'em me.

DORIMANT.

You snatch as if you thought I would not—there—and may the perjuries in 'em be mine if e'er I see you more. (*Offers to go; she catches him.*)

MRS. LOVEIT.

Stay!

DORIMANT.

I will not.

MRS. LOVEIT.

You shall!

DORIMANT.

What have you to say?

MRS. LOVEIT.

I cannot speak it yet.

DORIMANT.

Something more in commendation of the fool. Death! I want* patience! Let me go.

MRS. LOVEIT.

I cannot. (*Aside.*) I can sooner part with the limbs that hold him.—I hate that nauseous fool, you know I do.

DORIMANT.

Was it the scandal you were fond of, then?

MRS. LOVEIT.

Y'ad raised my anger equal to my love, a thing you ne'er could do before, and in revenge I did—I know not what I did. Would you would not think on't any more.

DORIMANT.

Should I be willing to forget it, I shall be daily minded of it. 'Twill be a commonplace for all the Town to laugh at me, and Medley, when he is rhetorically drunk, will ever be declaiming it on my ears.

MRS. LOVEIT.

'Twill be believed a jealous spite. Come, forget it.

DORIMANT.

Let me consult my reputation; you are too careless of it. (*Pauses.*) You shall meet Sir Fopling in the Mall again tonight.

MRS. LOVEIT.

What mean you?

DORIMANT.

I have thought on it, and you must. 'Tis necessary to justify my love to the world. You can handle a coxcomb as he deserves when you are not out of humor, madam.

MRS. LOVEIT.

Public satisfaction for the wrong I have done you? This is some new device to make me more ridiculous!

DORIMANT.

Hear me!

MRS. LOVEIT.

I will not.

DORIMANT.

You will be persuaded.

MRS. LOVEIT.

Never.

DORIMANT.

Are you so obstinate?

MRS. LOVEIT.

Are you so base?

DORIMANT.

You will not satisfy my love?

MRS. LOVEIT.

I would die to satisfy that, but I will not, to save you from a thousand racks, do a shameless thing to please your vanity.

DORIMANT.
Farewell, false woman.
MRS. LOVEIT.
Do! Go!
DORIMANT.
You will call me back again.
MRS. LOVEIT.
Exquisite fiend! I knew you came but to torment me.

Enter Bellinda and Pert.

DORIMANT. (*Surprised.*)
Bellinda here!
BELLINDA. (*Aside.*)
He starts and looks pale! The sight of me has touched his guilty soul.
PERT.
'Twas but a qualm, as I said, a little indigestion. The surfeit-water did it, madam, mixed with a little mirabilis.[118]
DORIMANT. [*Aside*].
I am confounded and cannot guess how she came hither!
MRS. LOVEIT.
'Tis your fortune, Bellinda, ever to be here when I am abused by this prodigy of ill nature.
BELLINDA.
I am amazed to find him here! How has he the face to come near you?
DORIMANT. (*Aside.*)
Here is fine work towards! I never was at such a loss before.
BELLINDA.
One who makes a public profession of breach of faith and ingratitude! I loathe the sight of him.
DORIMANT. [*Aside*].
There is no remedy. I must submit to their tongues now and some other time bring myself off as well as I can.
BELLINDA.
Other men are wicked, but then they have some sense of shame! He is never well but when he triumphs—nay, glories—to a woman's face in his villainies.
MRS. LOVEIT.
You are in the right, Bellinda, but methinks your kindness for me makes you concern yourself too much with him.
BELLINDA.
It does indeed, my dear. His barbarous carriage to you yesterday made me hope you ne'er would see him more, and the very next day to find him here again provokes me strangely. But because I know you love him, I have done.
DORIMANT.
You have reproached me handsomely, and I deserve it for coming hither, but—
PERT.
You must expect it, sir. All women will hate you for my lady's sake!
DORIMANT.
Nay, if she begins too, 'tis time to fly. I shall be scolded to death, else. (*Aside to Bellinda.*) I am to blame in some circumstances, I confess, but as to the main, I am not so guilty as you imagine.—I shall seek a more convenient time to clear myself.
MRS. LOVEIT.
Do it now! What impediments are here?
DORIMANT.
I want* time, and you want* temper.
MRS. LOVEIT.
These are weak pretenses.
DORIMANT.
You were never more mistaken in your life—and so farewell. (*Flings off.*)
MRS. LOVEIT.
Call a footman, Pert! Quickly! I will have him dogged.
PERT.
I wish you would not, for my quiet and your own.
MRS. LOVEIT.
I'll find out the infamous cause of all our quarrels, pluck her mask off, and expose her bare-faced to the world!

118 mirabilis] *aqua mirabilis*, literally, wonderful water (Latin), a medicinal potion, "prepared of cloves, galangals, cubebs, mace, cardomums, nutmegs, ginger, and spirit of wine, digested twenty-four hours, then distilled" (Johnson's *Dictionary*)

BELLINDA. (*Aside.*)
Let me but escape this time, I'll never venture more.

MRS. LOVEIT.
Bellinda, you shall go with me.

BELLINDA.
I have such a heaviness hangs on me with what I did this morning, I would fain go home and sleep, my dear.

MRS. LOVEIT.
Death and eternal darkness! I shall never sleep again. Raging fevers seize the world and make mankind as restless all as I am! (*Exit.*)

BELLINDA.
I knew him false and helped to make him so. Was not her ruin enough to fright me from the danger? It should have been, but love can take no warning.

Exit.

Scene ii. Lady Townley's house.

Enter Medley, Young Bellair, Lady Townley, Emilia, and chaplain [Mr. Smirk].

MEDLEY.
Bear up, Bellair, and do not let us see that repentance in thine we daily do in married faces.

LADY TOWNLEY.
This wedding will strangely surprise my brother when he knows it.

MEDLEY.
Your nephew ought to conceal it for a time, madam. Since marriage has lost its good name, prudent men seldom expose their own reputations till 'tis convenient to justify their wives'.

OLD BELLAIR. (*Without.*)
Where are you all there? Out, adod, will nobody hear?

LADY TOWNLEY.
My brother! Quickly, Mr. Smirk, into this closet.* You must not be seen yet.

[Smirk] goes into the closet. Enter Old Bellair and Lady Townley's page.

OLD BELLAIR. [*To page.*]
Desire Mr. Fourbe to walk into the lower parlor. I will be with him presently.

[Exit Page.]

(*To Young Bellair.*) Where have you been, sir, you could not wait on me today?

YOUNG BELLAIR.
About a business.

OLD BELLAIR.
Are you so good at business? Adod, I have a business too, you shall dispatch out of hand, sir.—Send for a parson, sister. My Lady Woodvill and her daughter are coming.

LADY TOWNLEY.
What need you huddle up things thus?

OLD BELLAIR.
Out a pize!* Youth is apt to play the fool, and 'tis not good it should be in their power.

LADY TOWNLEY.
You need not fear your son.

OLD BELLAIR.
He's been idling this morning, and adod, I do not like him. (*To Emilia.*) How dost thou do, sweetheart?

EMILIA.
You are very severe, sir. Married in such haste!

OLD BELLAIR.
Go to,* thou'rt a rogue, and I will talk with thee anon.

Enter Lady Woodvill, Harriet, and Busy.

Here's my Lady Woodvill come.—Welcome, madam. Mr. Fourbe's below with the writings.[119]

LADY WOODVILL.
Let us down and make an end, then.

OLD BELLAIR.
Sister, show the way. (*To Young Bellair, who is talking to Harriet.*) Harry, your business lies not there yet!—Excuse him till we have done, lady, and then, adod, he shall be for thee.—Mr. Medley, we must trouble you to be a witness.

MEDLEY.
I luckily came for that purpose, sir.

Exeunt Old Bellair, Medley, Young Bellair, Lady Townley, and Lady Woodvill.

BUSY.
What will you do, madam?

---

[119] writings] the contracts and documents of the marriage settlement

HARRIET.
Be carried back and mewed up in the country again, run away here—anything rather than be married to a man I do not care for.—Dear Emilia, do thou advise me!
EMILIA.
Mr. Bellair is engaged, you know.
HARRIET.
I do, but know not what the fear of losing an estate may fright him to.
EMILIA.
In the desperate condition you are in, you should consult with some judicious man. What think you of Mr. Dorimant?
HARRIET.
I do not think of him at all.
BUSY. [*Aside.*]
She thinks of nothing else, I am sure—
EMILIA.
How fond your mother was of Mr. Courtage!
HARRIET.
Because I contrived the mistake to make a little mirth, you believe I like the man.
EMILIA.
Mr. Bellair believes you love him.
HARRIET.
Men are seldom in the right when they guess at a woman's mind. Would she whom he loves loved him no better!
BUSY. (*Aside.*)
That's e'en well enough, on all conscience.
EMILIA.
Mr. Dorimant has a great deal of wit.
HARRIET.
And takes a great deal of pains to show it.
EMILIA.
He's extremely well fashioned.
HARRIET.
Affectedly grave, or ridiculously wild and apish.
BUSY.
You defend him still* against your mother.
HARRIET.
I would not, were he justly rallied, but I cannot hear anyone undeservedly railed at.
EMILIA.
Has your woman learnt the song you were so taken with?
HARRIET.
I was fond of a new thing. 'Tis dull at second hearing.
EMILIA.
Mr. Dorimant made it.
BUSY.
She knows it, madam, and has made me sing it at least a dozen times this morning.
HARRIET.
Thy tongue is as impertinent as thy fingers.
EMILIA. [*To Busy.*]
You have provoked her.
BUSY.
'Tis but singing the song and I shall appease her.
EMILIA.
Prithee, do.
HARRIET.
She has a voice will grate your ears worse than a catcall and dresses so ill she's scarce fit to trick up a yeoman's daughter on a holiday.

Busy sings.

Song.[120]

As Amoret with Phillis sat
One evening on the plain,
And saw the charming Strephon wait
To tell the nymph his pain,

The threat'ning danger to remove,
She whispered in her ear,
"Ah, Phillis, if you would not love,
This shepherd do not hear.

None ever had so strange an art,
His passion to convey
Into a list'ning virgin's heart
And steal her soul away.

Fly, fly betimes, for fear you give
Occasion for your fate."
"In vain," said she, "in vain I strive,
Alas! 'tis now too late."

---

120 Song] author identified in the text as "Sir C. S.," probably Sir Car Scroope again

Enter Dorimant.

DORIMANT.

"Music so softens and disarms the mind—"

HARRIET.

"That not one arrow does resistance find."[121]

DORIMANT.

Let us make use of the lucky minute, then.

HARRIET. (*Aside, turning from Dorimant.*)

My love springs with my blood into my face. I dare not look upon him yet.

DORIMANT.

What have we here, the picture of celebrated Beauty giving audience in public to a declared Lover?

HARRIET.

Play the dying Fop and make the piece complete, sir.

DORIMANT.

What think you if the hint were well improved? The whole mystery of making love pleasantly designed and wrought in a suite of hangings?

HARRIET.

'Twere needless to execute fools in effigy who suffer daily in their own persons.

DORIMANT. (*To Emilia, aside.*)

Mrs. Bride, for such I know this happy day has made you—

EMILIA.

Defer the formal joy you are to give me, and mind your business with her. (*Aloud.*) Here are the dreadful preparations, Mr. Dorimant—writings sealing, and a parson sent for—

DORIMANT.

To marry this lady—

BUSY.

Condemned she is, and what will become of her I know not, without you generously engage in a rescue.

DORIMANT.

In this sad condition, madam, I can do no less than offer you my service.

HARRIET.

The obligation is not great; you are the common sanctuary for all young women who run from their relations.

DORIMANT.

I have always my arms open to receive the distressed. But I will open my heart and receive you where none yet did ever enter. You have filled it with a secret, might I but let you know it—

HARRIET.

Do not speak it if you would have me believe it. Your tongue is so famed for falsehood, 'twill do the truth an injury. (*Turns away her head.*)

DORIMANT.

Turn not away, then, but look on me and guess it.

HARRIET.

Did you not tell me there was no credit to be given to faces? That women nowadays have their passions as much at will as they have their complexions and put on joy and sadness, scorn and kindness with the same ease they do their paint and patches— Are they the only counterfeits?

DORIMANT.

You wrong your own while you suspect my eyes. By all the hope I have in you, the inimitable color in your cheeks is not more free from art than are the sighs I offer.

HARRIET.

In men who have been long hardened in sin, we have reason to mistrust the first signs of repentance.

DORIMANT.

The prospect of such a heaven will make me persevere and give you marks that are infallible.

HARRIET.

What are those?

DORIMANT.

I will renounce all the joys I have in friendship and in wine, sacrifice to you all the interest I have in other women—

HARRIET.

Hold! Though I wish you devout, I would not have you turn fanatic. Could you neglect these a while and make a journey into the country?

DORIMANT.

To be with you, I could live there and never send one thought to London.

[121] "Music … find"] Waller, "Of my Lady Isabella, Playing on the Lute," 11-12 (slightly misquoted)

HARRIET.
What'er you say, I know all beyond Hyde Park's a desert to you, and that no gallantry can draw you farther.

DORIMANT.
That has been the utmost limit of my love—but now my passion knows no bounds, and there's no measure to be taken of what I'll do for you from anything I ever did before.

HARRIET.
When I hear you talk thus in Hampshire, I shall begin to think there may be some little truth enlarged upon.

DORIMANT.
Is this all? Will you not promise me—

HARRIET.
I hate to promise. What we do then is expected from us and wants* much of the welcome it finds when it surprises.

DORIMANT.
May I not hope?

HARRIET.
That depends on you and not on me, and 'tis to no purpose to forbid it. (*Turns to Busy.*)

BUSY.
Faith, madam, now I perceive the gentleman loves you, too, e'en let him know your mind and torment yourselves no longer.

HARRIET.
Dost think I have no sense of modesty?

BUSY.
Think, if you lose this, you may never have another opportunity.

HARRIET.
May he hate me (a curse that frights me when I speak it!) if ever I do a thing against the rules of decency and honor.

DORIMANT. (*To Emilia.*)
I am beholding to you for your good intentions, madam.

EMILIA.
I thought the concealing of our marriage from her might have done you better service.

DORIMANT.
Try her again.

EMILIA.
What have you resolved, madam? The time draws near.

HARRIET.
To be obstinate and protest against this marriage.

Enter Lady Townley in haste.

LADY TOWNLEY. (*To Emilia.*)
Quickly, quickly, let Mr. Smirk out of the closet!

Smirk comes out of the closet.

HARRIET.
A parson! Had you laid him in here?

DORIMANT.
I knew nothing of him.

HARRIET.
Should it appear you did, your opinion of my easiness may cost you dear.

Enter Old Bellair, Young Bellair, Medley, and Lady Woodvill.

OLD BELLAIR.
Out a pize,* the canonical hour* is almost past! Sister, is the man of God come?

LADY TOWNLEY.
He waits your leisure.

OLD BELLAIR.
By your favor, sir.—Adod, a pretty spruce fellow! What may we call him?

LADY TOWNLEY.
Mr. Smirk, my Lady Biggot's chaplain.

OLD BELLAIR.
A wise woman, adod she is. The man will serve for the flesh as well as the spirit.—Please you, sir, to commission a young couple to go to bed together a God's name?—Harry!

YOUNG BELLAIR.
Here, sir—

OLD BELLAIR.
Out a pize! Without your mistress in your hand?

SMIRK.
Is this the gentleman?

OLD BELLAIR.
Yes, sir.

SMIRK.
Are you not mistaken, sir?

OLD BELLAIR.
Adod, I think not, sir!

SMIRK.
Sure you are, sir.

OLD BELLAIR.
You look as if you would forbid the banns, Mr. Smirk. I hope you have no pretension to the lady.

SMIRK.
Wish him joy, sir! I have done him the good office today already.

OLD BELLAIR.
Out a pize! What do I hear?

LADY TOWNLEY.
Never storm, brother. The truth is out.

OLD BELLAIR.
How say you, sir? Is this your wedding day?

YOUNG BELLAIR.
It is, sir.

OLD BELLAIR.
And adod, it shall be mine, too! (*To Emilia.*) Give me thy hand, sweetheart. [*She declines to give her hand.*] What dost thou mean? Give me thy hand, I say!

Emilia kneels and Young Bellair.

LADY TOWNLEY.
Come, come, give her your blessing. This is the woman your son loved and is married to.

OLD BELLAIR.
Hah! Cheated! Cozened! And by your contrivance, sister!

LADY TOWNLEY.
What would you do with her? She's a rogue, and you can't abide her.

MEDLEY.
Shall I hit her a pat for you, sir?

OLD BELLAIR.
Adod, you are all rogues, and I never will forgive you.

LADY TOWNLEY.
Whither? Whither away?

MEDLEY.
Let him go and cool awhile.

LADY WOODVILL. (*To Dorimant.*)
Here's a business broke out now, Mr. Courtage. I am made a fine fool of.

DORIMANT.
You see the old gentleman knew nothing of it.

LADY WOODVILL.
I find he did not. I shall have some trick put upon me, if I stay in this wicked Town any longer.—Harriet! Dear child, where art thou? I'll into the country straight.

OLD BELLAIR.
Adod, madam, you shall hear me first.

Enter Mrs. Loveit and Bellinda.

MRS. LOVEIT.
Hither my man dogged him.

BELLINDA.
Yonder he stands, my dear.

MRS. LOVEIT.
I see him—(*Aside.*) and with him the face that has undone me! Oh, that I were but where I might throw out the anguish of my heart! Here it must rage within and break it.

LADY TOWNLEY.
Mrs. Loveit! Are you afraid to come forward?

MRS. LOVEIT.
I was amazed to see so much company here in a morning. The occasion sure is extraordinary.

DORIMANT. (*Aside.*)
Loveit and Bellinda! The Devil owes me a shame today and I think never will have done paying it.

MRS. LOVEIT.
Married! Dear Emilia! How am I transported with the news!

HARRIET. (*To Dorimant.*)
I little thought Emilia was the woman Mr. Bellair was in love with. I'll chide her for not trusting me with the secret.

DORIMANT.
How do you like Mrs. Loveit?

HARRIET.
She's a famed mistress of yours, I hear.

DORIMANT.
She has been, on occasion.

OLD BELLAIR. (*To Lady Woodvill.*)
Adod, madam, I cannot help it.

LADY WOODVILL.
You need make no more apologies, sir.

EMILIA. (*To Mrs. Loveit.*)
The old gentleman's excusing himself to my Lady Woodvill.

MRS. LOVEIT.
Ha, ha, ha! I never heard of anything so pleasant.

HARRIET. (*To Dorimant.*)
She's extremely overjoyed at something.

DORIMANT.
At nothing. She is one of those hoiting[122] ladies who gaily fling themselves about and force a laugh when their aching hearts are full of discontent and malice.

MRS. LOVEIT.
Oh Heaven, I was never so near killing myself with laughing.—Mr. Dorimant! are you a brideman?

LADY WOODVILL.
Mr. Dorimant! Is this Mr. Dorimant, madam?

MRS. LOVEIT.
If you doubt it, your daughter can resolve you, I suppose.

LADY WOODVILL.
I am cheated, too, basely cheated!

OLD BELLAIR.
Out a pize, what's here? More knavery yet?

LADY WOODVILL.
Harriet! On my blessing, come away, I charge you.

HARRIET.
Dear mother, do but stay and hear me.

LADY WOODVILL.
I am betrayed, and thou art undone, I fear.

HARRIET.
Do not fear it. I have not, nor never will, do anything against my duty. Believe me, dear mother, do!

DORIMANT. (*To Mrs. Loveit.*)
I had trusted you with this secret but that I knew the violence of your nature would ruin my fortune—as now unluckily it has. I thank you, madam.

MRS. LOVEIT.
She's an heiress, I know, and very rich.

DORIMANT.
To satisfy you, I must give up my interest wholly to my love. Had you been a reasonable woman, I might have secured 'em both and been happy.

MRS. LOVEIT.
You might have trusted me with anything of this kind; you know you might. Why did you go under a wrong name?

DORIMANT.
The story is too long to tell you now. Be satisfied—this is the business; this is the mask* has kept me from you.

BELLINDA. (*Aside.*)
He's tender of my honor, though he's cruel to my love.

MRS. LOVEIT.
Was it no idle mistress, then?

DORIMANT.
Believe me, a wife, to repair the ruins of my estate that needs it.

MRS. LOVEIT.
The knowledge of this makes my grief hang lighter on my soul, but I shall never more be happy.

DORIMANT.
Bellinda—

BELLINDA.
Do not think of clearing yourself with me. It is impossible—Do all men break their words thus?

DORIMANT.
Th'extravagant words they speak in love. 'Tis as unreasonable to expect we should perform all we promise then, as do all we threaten when we are angry. When I see you next—

BELLINDA.
Take no notice of me, and I shall not hate you.

DORIMANT.
How came you to Mrs. Loveit?

BELLINDA.
By a mistake the chairmen* made for want* of my giving them directions.

DORIMANT.
'Twas a pleasant one. We must meet again.

BELLINDA.
Never.

DORIMANT.
Never?

BELLINDA.
When we do, may I be as infamous as you are false.

LADY TOWNLEY.
Men of Mr. Dorimant's character always suffer in the general opinion of the world.

[122] hoiting] given to noisy and silly mirth

MEDLEY.
You can make no judgment of a witty man from common fame, considering the prevailing faction, madam.

OLD BELLAIR.
Adod, he's in the right.

MEDLEY.
Besides, 'tis a common error among women to believe too well of them they know and too ill of them they don't.

OLD BELLAIR.
Adod, he observes well.

LADY TOWNLEY.
Believe me, madam, you will find Mr. Dorimant as civil a gentleman as you thought Mr. Courtage.

HARRIET.
If you would but know him better—

LADY WOODVILL.
You have a mind to know him better? Come away—You shall never see him more.

HARRIET.
Dear mother, stay!

LADY WOODVILL.
I wonnot be consenting to your ruin.

HARRIET.
Were my fortune in your power—

LADY WOODVILL.
Your person is.

HARRIET.
Could I be disobedient, I might take it out of yours and put it into his.

LADY WOODVILL.
'Tis that you would be at: you would marry this Dorimant.

HARRIET.
I cannot deny it! I would, and never will marry any other man.

LADY WOODVILL.
Is this the duty that you promised?

HARRIET.
But I will never marry him against your will.

LADY WOODVILL. (*Aside.*)
She knows the way to melt my heart. (*To Harriet.*) Upon yourself light your undoing.

MEDLEY. (*To Old Bellair.*)
Come sir, you have not the heart any longer to refuse your blessing.

OLD BELLAIR.
Adod, I ha' not.—Rise, and God bless you both. Make much of her, Harry; she deserves thy kindness.* (*To Emilia.*) Adod sirrah, I did not think it had been in thee.

Enter Sir Fopling and his page.

SIR FOPLING.
'Tis a damned windy day! Hey, page! Is my periwig right?

PAGE.
A little out of order, sir.

SIR FOPLING.
Pox o'this apartment! It wants* an antechamber to adjust oneself in. (*To Mrs. Loveit.*) Madam, I came from your house, and your servants directed me hither.

MRS. LOVEIT.
I will give order hereafter they shall direct you better.

SIR FOPLING.
The great satisfaction I had in the Mall last night has given me much disquiet since.

MRS. LOVEIT.
'Tis likely to give me more than I desire.

SIR FOPLING. [*Aside.*]
What the devil makes her so reserved?—Am I guilty of an indiscretion, madam?

MRS. LOVEIT.
You will be of a great one, if you continue your mistake, sir.

SIR FOPLING.
Something puts you out of humor.

MRS. LOVEIT.
The most foolish, inconsiderable thing that ever did.

SIR FOPLING.
Is it in my power?

MRS. LOVEIT.
To hang or drown it. Do one of 'em, and trouble me no more.

SIR FOPLING.
So *fière? Serviteur*, madam.[123]—Medley, where's Dorimant?

---

123 So *fière? Serviteur*, madam] So haughty? Your servant, madam (Fr.)

MEDLEY.
Methinks the lady has not made you those advances today she did last night, Sir Fopling.

SIR FOPLING.
Prithee, do not talk of her.

MEDLEY.
She would be a *bonne fortune.*

SIR FOPLING.
Not to me at present.

MEDLEY.
How so?

SIR FOPLING.
An intrigue now would be but a temptation to me to throw away that vigor on one which I mean shall shortly make my court to the whole sex in a ballet.

MEDLEY.
Wisely considered, Sir Fopling.

SIR FOPLING.
No one woman is worth the loss of a cut* in a caper.

MEDLEY.
Not when 'tis so universally designed.

LADY WOODVILL.
Mr. Dorimant, everyone has spoke so much in your behalf that I can no longer doubt but I was in the wrong.

MRS. LOVEIT.
There's nothing but falsehood and impertinence in this world! All men are villains or fools. Take example from my misfortunes. Bellinda, if thou wouldst be happy, give thyself wholly up to goodness.

HARRIET. (*To Mrs. Loveit.*)
Mr. Dorimant has been your God almighty long enough. 'Tis time to think of another.

MRS. LOVEIT.
Jeered by her! I will lock myself up in my house and never see the world again.

HARRIET.
A nunnery is the more fashionable place for such a retreat and has been the fatal consequence of many a *belle passion.*

MRS. LOVEIT.
Hold, heart, till I get home! Should I answer, 'twould make her triumph greater. (*Going out.*)

DORIMANT.
Your hand, Sir Fopling—

SIR FOPLING.
Shall I wait upon you, madam?

MRS. LOVEIT.
Legion of fools,[124] as many devils take thee! (*Exit.*)

MEDLEY.
Dorimant, I pronounce thy reputation clear—and henceforward, when I would know anything of woman, I will consult no other oracle.

SIR FOPLING.
Stark mad, by all that's handsome!—Dorimant, thou hast engaged me in a pretty business.

DORIMANT.
I have not leisure now to talk about it.

OLD BELLAIR.
Out a pize, what does this man of mode do here again?

LADY TOWNLEY.
He'll be an excellent entertainment within, brother, and is luckily come to raise the mirth of the company.

LADY WOODVILL.
Madam, I take my leave of you.

LADY TOWNLEY.
What do you mean, madam?

LADY WOODVILL.
To go this afternoon part of my way to Hartly—[125]

OLD BELLAIR.
Adod, you shall stay and dine first! Come, we will all be good friends, and you shall give Mr. Dorimant leave to wait upon you and your daughter in the country.

LADY WOODVILL.
If his occasions bring him that way, I have now so good an opinion of him, he shall be welcome.

HARRIET.
To a great, rambling, lone house that looks as it were not inhabited, the family's* so small. There

124 legion] a multitude, with an allusion to the devils exorcised by Jesus in Mark 5:9: "My name is Legion: for we are many."

125 Hartly] "Hartley Row, Hampshire, about half-way between London and Salisbury" (NCS)

you'll find my mother, an old lame aunt, and myself, sir, perched up on chairs at a distance in a large parlor, sitting moping like three or four melancholy birds in a spacious volary—[126] Does not this stagger your resolution?

DORIMANT.

Not at all, madam! The first time I saw you, you left me with the pangs of love upon me, and this day my soul has quite given up her liberty.

HARRIET.

This is more dismal than the country!—Emilia, pity me, who am going to that sad place. Methinks I hear the hateful noise of rooks already—kaw, kaw, kaw!—There's music in the worst cry in London: "My dill and cucumbers to pickle."

OLD BELLAIR.

Sister, knowing of this matter, I hope you have provided us some good cheer.

LADY TOWNLEY.

I have, brother, and the fiddles too—

OLD BELLAIR.

Let 'em strike up, then. The young lady shall have a dance before she departs.

Dance.

(*After the dance.*) So now we'll in, and make this an arrant wedding day. (*To the pit.**)
And if these honest gentlemen rejoice,
Adod, the boy has made a happy choice.

Exeunt omnes.

EPILOGUE[127]

Most modern wits such monstrous fools have shown,
They seemed not of Heav'n's making, but their own.
Those nauseous harlequins in farce may pass,
But there goes more to a substantial ass!
Something of man must be exposed to view,
That, gallants, they may more resemble you.
Sir Fopling is a fool so nicely* writ,
The ladies would mistake him for a wit
And (when he sings, talks loud, and cocks) would cry:
"I vow, methinks he's pretty company—
So brisk, so gay, so traveled, so refined,
As he took pains to graft upon his kind."[128]
True fops help Nature's work, and go to school
To file and finish God a'mighty's fool.
Yet none Sir Fopling him, or him, can call;
He's knight o'th'shire[129] and represents ye all.
From each he meets, he culls whate'er he can;
Legion's his name, a people in a man.
His bulky folly gathers as it goes,
And, rolling o'er you, like a snowball grows.
His various modes from various fathers follow:
One taught the toss,[130] and one the new French wallow.[131]
His sword-knot,[132] this; his cravat, this designed;
And this, the yard-long snake[133] he twirls behind.
From one, the sacred periwig he gained,
Which wind ne'er blew, nor touch of hat profaned;
Another's diving bow he did adore,
Which with a shog[134] casts all the hair before,
Till he with full decorum brings it back
And rises with a water spaniel shake.
As for his songs (the ladies' dear delight),
Those sure he took from most of you who write.
Yet every man is safe from what he feared,
For no one fool is hunted from the herd.

FINIS.

126 volary] a large bird-cage or aviary

127 Epilogue] written by Dryden, spoken by William Smith, who played Sir Fopling

128 graft upon his kind] to improve his natural qualities

129 knight o'th'shire] local representative in Parliament

130 toss] toss of the head

131 wallow] rolling walk or gait

132 sword-knot] a ribbon or tassel tied to the hilt of a sword for ornament

133 snake] a long curl or tail attached to a wig

134 shog] shake, jerk

Textual Notes

[a] Copytext is the first edition, the 1676 quarto (Q1), incorporating stop-press corrections. Also consulted were the 1684 quarto edition (Q2) and the modern editions of 1888 (Verity); 1927 (Brett-Smith); 1939, revised 1969 (Nettleton, Case, and Stone—NCS); 1953 (Harris); 1959 (Wilson); 1966 (Carnochan); 1973 (Conaghan); 1979 (Barnard); 1982 (Cordner); and 1994 (Lawrence). For readings in the posthumous early editions, including the 1693 quarto edition (Q3), the 1704 *Works of Sir George Etherege* (W), the 1711 *Collection of the Best English Plays* (CBEP), and the 1711 octavo edition (O), I have used the tables of variants printed in some of the modern editions listed above.

[b] with her head] W, Verity, Brett-Smith, NCS, Wilson, Carnochan, Barnard, Lawrence; with head Q1, Q2, Q3, Harris, Conaghan, Cordner

[c] which] In Q1, printed as the catchword at the bottom of p. 32 but not in the text. In Q2, Q3, W, Verity, and Lawrence it is added to the succeeding line. Except for Lawrence, editors since Brett-Smith have printed the word as Harriet's link between the two lines, as here.

[d] you to what] W, Verity, Brett-Smith, NCS, Harris, Wilson, Carnochan, Conaghan, Barnard, Cordner, Lawrence; you what Q1, Q2, Q3

[e] *to an English dancer* (s.d.)] Conaghan, Barnard; *om.* Q1 (uncorrected); to an English dancer (text) Q1 (corrected), Q2, Verity, Brett-Smith, NCS, Harris, Wilson, Carnochan, Cordner, Lawrence

[f] will] CBEP, Verity, Brett-Smith, NCS, Harris, Wilson, Carnochan, Barnard, Lawrence; well Q1, Q2, Q3, W, O, Conaghan, Cordner

The Rover; or, The Banished Cavaliers[a]

by Aphra Behn (1640?-1689)
edited by Anne Russell

Almost nothing is known with certainty of Aphra Behn's early life. From 1671 until her death in 1689, Behn earned her living as a prolific playwright, translator, editor, poet, and novelist. Behn's plays were a significant part of the theatrical repertoire until the middle of the eighteenth century.

The Rover, or The Banish'd Cavaliers (1677) was one of Behn's most popular plays. Like many of her contemporaries, Behn adapted an earlier play, Thomas Killigrew's *Thomaso, or The Wanderer*. In *The Rover*, Behn examines contemporary issues such as forced marriage and double sexual standards with particular focus on the perspectives of women characters. The complex plot, relying on disguise and mistaken identity, includes many parallels of character and situation. The virginal sisters Hellena and Florinda complain that their brother has arranged Florinda's marriage to an old man and Hellena's admission to a nunnery. In another plot the courtesan Angellica Bianca argues that wives and prostitutes are treated similarly as commodities. Her thoughtful analysis points to a recurring plot motif—the male characters' difficulty in distinguishing "a maid of quality" from a "harlot."

The Rover is set during the Commonwealth, when Parliament under Oliver Cromwell ruled England and many of the supporters of the monarchy lived in exile; it was performed, however, after the restoration of the monarchy. The Rover of the title, the aptly named Willmore, is a rake and libertine. He and other "Banish'd Cavaliers" arrive in Naples during carnival, eager to take advantage of the sexual opportunities allowed by the temporary freedom of masks and disguises. In a long scene, Willmore and Angellica Bianca debate the relations between love and money. Succumbing to Willmore's argument that love ought to be given rather than sold, she gives her love and her money to Willmore, who immediately shifts his attention to the pursuit of the witty Hellena, who is in carnival disguise.

Other characters include Willmore's friend Belvile, who is in love with Florinda. Blunt, a dim-witted comic butt during most of the play, is attracted to a prostitute he thinks to be a young wife; however, she and her pimp rob and humiliate him. Blunt's desire to take revenge by beating and raping other women endangers Florinda, and also moves the many plots towards closure.

As this brief summary suggests, there are many inconsistencies of tone in this comedy. The plot includes duels, robberies, and rape attempts; many characters make casual anti-semitic and anti-catholic slurs. Women characters complain about their subjection to male control, yet seem indulgently tolerant of the men who threaten them. Sexual double standards are criticized in the early parts of the play but deflected in the conclusion. The eloquent Angellica Bianca is silenced; Willmore, the proselytizer of free love, accepts marriage (which conveniently comes with Hellena's fortune); and the attempted rapes by Willmore, Blunt and others are instantly forgiven and forgotten.

Critics are divided on how to interpret the conventional round of marriages and forgiveness with which *The Rover* ends. Does the conclusion portray imperfect, but pragmatic, strategies needed for survival in a violent and ruthless society? Or do the final scenes endorse a return to the socio-economic order, socializing the great sexual energy of its lead character? Behn did not let the question settle. The character of Willmore was so popular that she wrote a sequel in 1681. As it opens, Willmore offhandedly notes that Hellena has died and that he has spent her money. He then proceeds to pursue free love, as he had done in *The Rover*.

[I.i]

DRAMATIS PERSONAE

[MEN]

Don Antonio, the Viceroy's son.
Don Pedro, a noble Spaniard, his friend.
Belvile, an English colonel in love with Florinda.
Willmore, the Rover.[1]
Frederick, an English gentleman and friend to Belvile and Blunt.[b]
Blunt, an English country gentleman.
Stephano, servant to Don Pedro.
Phillippo, Lucetta's gallant.
Sancho, pimp to Lucetta.
Biskey, and Sebastian, two bravoes[2] to Angellica.
Officers and Soldiers.
[Diego,] Page to Don Antonio.
Boy.

WOMEN.

Florinda, sister to Don Pedro.
Hellena, a gay young woman designed for a nun, and sister to Florinda.
Valeria, a kinswoman to Florinda.
Angellica Bianca, a famous courtesan.
Moretta, her woman.
Callis, governess to Florinda and Hellena.
Lucetta, a jilting wench.
Servants, other masqueraders, men and women.

THE SCENE: NAPLES, IN CARNIVAL TIME.

The Rover; or, The Banished Cavaliers.[3]

Act I, scene i. A chamber.

Enter Florinda and Hellena.

FLORINDA.
What an impertinent thing is a young girl bred in a nunnery! How full of questions! Prithee no more Hellena; I have told thee more than thou understand'st already.

HELLENA.
The more's my grief. I would fain know as much as you, which makes me so inquisitive; nor is't enough I know you're a lover, unless you tell me too, who 'tis you sigh for.

FLORINDA.
When you're a lover, I'll think you fit for a secret of that nature.

HELLENA.
'Tis true, I never was a lover yet, but I begin to have a shrewd guess what it is to be so and fancy it very pretty to sigh, and sing, and blush, and wish, and dream, and wish, and long and wish to see the man, and when I do, look pale and tremble; just as you did when my brother brought home the fine English colonel to see you. What do you call him, Don Belvile?

FLORINDA.
Fie, Hellena.

HELLENA.
That blush betrays you. I am sure 'tis so—or is it Don Antonio the viceroy's son? or perhaps the rich old Don Vincentio whom my father designs you for a husband? Why do you blush again?

FLORINDA.
With indignation, and how near soever my father thinks I am to marrying that hated object, I shall let him see I understand better what's due to my beauty, birth and fortune, and more to my soul, than to obey those unjust commands.

HELLENA.
Now hang me if I don't love thee for that dear disobedience. I love mischief strangely, as most of our sex do, who are come to love nothing else. But tell me dear Florinda, don't you love that fine *Anglese*?[4] For I vow, next to loving him myself, 'twill please me most that you do so, for he is so gay and so handsome.

FLORINDA.
Hellena, a maid designed for a nun ought not to be so curious in a discourse of love.

HELLENA.
And dost thou think that ever I'll be a nun? or at least till I'm so old, I'm fit for nothing else? Faith

[1] Rover] wanderer; also pirate

[2] bravoes] hired soldiers; bodyguards

[3] *Cavaliers*] Supporters of the English monarchy during the English Civil War; many cavaliers left England after the execution of King Charles I in 1649.

[4] *Anglese*] Englishman (It.)

no, sister. And that which makes me long to know whether you love Belvile is because I hope he has some mad companion or other that will spoil my devotion. Nay, I'm resolved to provide myself this carnival, if there be e'er a handsome proper fellow of my humor* above ground, though I ask first.

FLORINDA.
Prithee, be not so wild.

HELLENA.
Now you have provided yourself of a man, you take no care for poor me. Prithee, tell me, what dost thou see about me that is unfit for love? Have I not a world of youth? a humor* gay? a beauty passable? a vigor desirable? well shaped? clean limbed? sweet breathed? and sense enough to know how all these ought to be employed to the best advantage? Yes, I do and will; therefore, lay aside your hopes of my fortune by my being a devote,[5] and tell me how you came acquainted with this Belvile, for I perceive you knew him before he came to Naples.

FLORINDA.
Yes, I knew him at the siege of Pamplona.[6] He was then a colonel of French horse, who when the town was ransacked, nobly treated my brother and myself, preserving us from all insolences, and I must own (besides great obligations) I have I know not what that pleads kindly for him about my heart, and will suffer no other to enter.—But see, my brother.

Enter Don Pedro, Stephano with a masquing habit,[7] and Callis.

PEDRO.
Good morrow, sister. Pray, when saw you your lover Don Vincentio?

FLORINDA.
I know not, sir. Callis, when was he here? For I consider it so little, I know not when it was.

PEDRO.
I have a command from my father here to tell you, you ought not to despise him, a man of so vast a fortune, and such a passion for you.—Stephano, my things.

Puts on his masquing habit.

FLORINDA.
A passion for me, 'tis more than e'er I saw, or he had a desire should be known. I hate Vincentio, sir, and I would not have a man so dear to me as my brother follow the ill customs of our country and make a slave of his sister. And sir, my father's will I'm sure you may divert.

PEDRO.
I know not how dear I am to you, but I wish only to be ranked in your esteem equal with the English Colonel Belvile. Why do you frown and blush? Is there any guilt belongs to the name of that cavalier?

FLORINDA.
I'll not deny I value Belvile. When I was exposed to such dangers as the licensed lust of common soldiers threatened, when rage and conquest flew through the city, then Belvile, this criminal for my sake, threw himself into all dangers to save my honor. And will you not allow him my esteem?

PEDRO.
Yes, pay him what you will in honor, but you must consider Don Vincentio's fortune and the jointure he'll make you.

FLORINDA.
Let him consider my youth, beauty and fortune, which ought not to be thrown away on his age and jointure.

PEDRO.
'Tis true, he's not so young and fine a gentleman as that Belvile, but what jewels will that cavalier present you with? those of his eyes and heart?

HELLENA.
And are not those better than any Don Vincentio has brought from the Indies?

PEDRO.
Why, how now! Has your nunnery breeding taught you to understand the value of hearts and eyes?

HELLENA.
Better than to believe Vincentio's deserve value from any woman. He may perhaps increase her bags,[8] but not her family.

---

5 devote] a nun or religious person, devotee

6 Pamplona] a fortified town in Navarre in the north of Spain, disputed by France

7 *masquing habit*] costume worn at carnival

8 bags] wealth

PEDRO.

This is fine. Go—up to your devotion; you are not designed for the conversation* of lovers.

HELLENA. (*Aside.*)

Nor saints yet a while, I hope. Is't not enough you make a nun of me, but you must cast my sister away too, exposing her to a worse confinement than a religious life?

PEDRO.

The girl's mad! It is a confinement to be carried into the country, to an ancient villa belonging to the family of the Vincentios these five hundred years, and have no other prospect than that pleasing one of seeing all her own that meets her eyes—a fine air, large fields and gardens, where she may walk and gather flowers.

HELLENA.

When, by moonlight? For I am sure she dares not encounter with the heat of the sun; that were a task only for Don Vincentio and his Indian breeding,[9] who loves it in the dog days. And if these be her daily divertissements, what are those of the night, to lie in a wide moth-eaten bed chamber, with furniture in fashion in the reign of King Sancho the First;[10] the bed, that which his forefathers lived and died in.

PEDRO.

Very well.

HELLENA.

This apartment (new furbished and fitted out for the young wife) he (out of freedom) makes his dressing room, and being a frugal and jealous coxcomb, instead of a valet to uncase his feeble carcass, he desires you to do that office—signs of favor I'll assure you, and such as you must not hope for, unless your woman be out of the way.

PEDRO.

Have you done yet?

HELLENA.

That honor being past, the giant stretches itself, yawns and sighs a belch or two, loud as a musket, throws himself into bed, and expects you in his foul sheets, and ere you can get yourself undressed, calls you with a snore or two. And are not these fine blessings to a young lady?

PEDRO.

Have you done yet?

HELLENA.

And this man you must kiss, nay you must kiss none but him, too, and nuzzle through his beard to find his lips. And this you must submit to for threescore years, and all for a jointure.

PEDRO.

For all your character* of Don Vincentio, she is as like to marry him as she was before.

HELLENA.

Marry Don Vincentio! Hang me, such a wedlock would be worse than adultery with another man. I had rather see her in the Hotel de Dieu,[11] to waste her youth there in vows and be a handmaid to lazars and cripples, than to lose it in such a marriage.

PEDRO.

You have considered, sister, that Belvile has no fortune to bring you to—banished his country, despised at home, and pitied abroad.

HELLENA.

What then? The viceroy's son is better than that old Sir Fifty. Don Vincentio! Don Indian! He thinks he's trading to Gambo[12] still and would barter himself (that bell and bauble[13]) for your youth and fortune.

PEDRO.

Callis, take her hence, and lock her up all this Carnival, and at Lent she shall begin her everlasting penance in a monastery.

HELLENA.

I care not; I had rather be a nun than be obliged to marry as you would have me, if I were designed for't.

PEDRO.

Do not fear the blessing of that choice. You shall be a nun.

---

[9] Indian breeding] presumably Don Vincentio was raised in the Indies

[10] King Sancho the First] a king from long ago

[11] Hotel de Dieu] hospital run by nuns for the care of the destitute and outcast

[12] Gambo] Gambia, on the Slave Coast of Africa

[13] bell and bauble] trifles, but also the signs of a professional fool

HELLENA.

Shall I so? You may chance to be mistaken in my way of devotion. A nun! Yes, I am like to make a fine nun! I have an excellent humor* for a grate.[14] (*Aside.*) No, I'll have a saint of my own to pray to shortly, if I like any that dares venture on me.

PEDRO.

Callis, make it your business to watch this wild cat. As for you, Florinda, I've only tried you all this while and urged my father's will; but mine is that you would love Antonio. He is brave and young, and all that can complete the happiness of a gallant maid. This absence of my father will give us opportunity to free you from Vincentio by marrying here, which you must do tomorrow.

FLORINDA.

Tomorrow!

PEDRO.

Tomorrow, or 'twill be too late. 'Tis not my friendship to Antonio which makes me urge this, but love to thee and hatred to Vincentio. Therefore, resolve upon tomorrow.

FLORINDA.

Sir, I shall strive to do as shall become your sister.

PEDRO.

I'll both believe and trust you. Adieu.

Exeunt Pedro and Stephano.

HELLENA.

As becomes his sister! That is to be as resolved your way, as he is his—(*Hellena goes to Callis.*)

FLORINDA.

I ne'er till now perceived my ruin near.
I've no defense against Antonio's love,
For he has all the advantages of nature,
The moving arguments of youth and fortune.

HELLENA.

But hark you, Callis, you will not be so cruel to lock me up indeed, will you?

CALLIS.

I must obey the commands I have. Besides, do you consider what a life you are going to lead?

HELLENA.

Yes, Callis, that of a nun; and till then I'll be indebted a world of prayers to you if you'll let me now see what I never did, the divertissements of a carnival.

CALLIS.

What, go in masquerade? 'Twill be a fine farewell to the world, I take it. Pray, what would you do there?

HELLENA.

That which all the world does, as I am told: be as mad as the rest and take all innocent freedoms. Sister, you'll go too, will you not? Come, prithee be not sad. We'll outwit twenty brothers if you'll be ruled by me. Come, put off this dull humor* with your clothes and assume one as gay and as fantastic, as the dress my cousin Valeria and I have provided, and let's ramble.

FLORINDA.

Callis, will you give us leave to go?

CALLIS. (*Aside.*)

I have a youthful itch of going myself.—Madam, if I thought your brother might not know it, and I might wait on you; for by my troth I'll not trust young girls alone.

FLORINDA.

Thou seest my brother's gone already, and thou shalt attend and watch us.

Enter Stephano.

STEPHANO.

Madam, the habits are come, and your cousin Valeria is dressed and stays for you.

FLORINDA.

'Tis well. I'll write a note, and if I chance to see Belvile and want an opportunity to speak to him, that shall let him know what I've resolved in favor of him.

HELLENA.

Come, let's in and dress us.

Exeunt.

Scene ii. A long street.

Enter Belvile melancholy, Blunt and Frederick.

FREDERICK.

Why,[c] what the devil ails the colonel? In a time when all the world is gay, to look like mere* Lent thus? Had'st thou been long enough in Naples to

[14] grate] bars in the door of a convent, marking the separation of the nun from the world

have been in love, I should have sworn some such judgment had befallen thee.

BELVILE.

No, I have made no new amours since I came to Naples.

FREDERICK.

You have left none behind you in Paris?

BELVILE.

Neither.

FREDERICK.

I cannot divine the cause, then, unless the old cause, the want of money.

BLUNT.

And another old cause, the want of a wench. Would not that revive you?

BELVILE.

You are mistaken, Ned.

BLUNT.

Nay, 'sheartlikins,[15] then thou'rt past cure.

FREDERICK.

I have found it out; thou hast renewed thy acquaintance with the lady that cost thee so many sighs at the siege of Pamplona—pox on't, what d'ye call her—her brother's a noble Spaniard—nephew to the dead general—Florinda—ay Florinda—and will nothing serve thy turn but that damned virtuous woman? whom on my conscience thou lovest in spite too, because thou seest little or no possibility of gaining her.

BELVILE.

Thou art mistaken. I have int'rest enough in that lovely virgin's heart to make me proud and vain, were it not abated by the severity of a brother, who perceiving my happiness—

FREDERICK.

Has civilly forbid thee the house?

BELVILE.

'Tis so; to make way for a powerful rival, the viceroy's son, who has the advantage of me in being a man of fortune, a Spaniard, and her brother's friend; which gives him liberty to make his court, whilst I have recourse only to letters and distant looks from her window, which are as soft and kind as those which Heaven sends down on penitents.

BLUNT.

Heyday! 'Sheartlikins, simile! By this light, the man is quite spoiled. Fred, what the devil are we made of that we cannot be thus concerned for a wench? 'Sheartlikins, our cupids are like the cooks of the camp, they can roast or boil a woman, but they have none of the fine tricks to set 'em off, no hogoes* to make the sauce pleasant and the stomach sharp.

FREDERICK.

I dare swear I have had a hundred as young, kind and handsome as this Florinda, and dogs eat me, if they were not as troublesome to me i'the morning as they were welcome o'er night.

BLUNT.

And yet I warrant he would not touch another woman if he might have her for nothing.

BELVILE.

That's thy joy, a cheap whore.

BLUNT.

Why, ay, 'sheartlikins, I love a frank soul. When did you ever hear of an honest woman that took a man's money? I warrant 'em good ones. But gentlemen, you may be free, you have been kept so poor with Parliaments and Protectors,[16] that the little stock you have is not worth preserving. But I thank my stars, I had more grace than to forfeit my estate by cavaliering.[17]

BELVILE.

Methinks only following the Court[18] should be sufficient to entitle 'em to that.

BLUNT.

'Sheartlikins, they know I follow it to do it no good, unless they pick a hole in my coat for

---

[15] 'sheartlikins] God's little heart; a "minced oath" combining "God's heart" and "bodikin." Also "heartikin," "adsheartlikins."

[16] Protectors] During the period of Parliamentary rule, Oliver Cromwell used the title of Protector of England.

[17] cavaliering] During the protectorate, cavaliers who left England could have their estates confiscated. Blunt boasts that he has managed to travel overseas without identifying himself, or being identified, as a cavalier, and hence is not liable to lose his property. There is the connotation that Blunt refused to fight as well.

[18] Court] retinue of the exiled Charles II

lending you money now and then, which is a greater crime to my conscience, gentlemen, than to the Commonwealth.[19]

Enter Willmore.

WILLMORE.
Hah! Dear Belvile! Noble colonel!

BELVILE.
Willmore! Welcome ashore, my dear rover! What happy wind blew us this good fortune?

WILLMORE.
Let me salute* my dear Frederick and then command me. How is't, honest lad?

FREDERICK.
Faith, sir, the old compliment, infinitely the better to see my dear mad Willmore again. Prithee, why camest thou ashore? And where's the Prince?[20]

WILLMORE.
He's well, and reigns still lord of the watery element. I must aboard again within a day or two, and my business ashore was only to enjoy myself a little this carnival.

BELVILE.
Pray, know our new friend, sir; he's but bashful, a raw traveller, but honest, stout and one of us.

WILLMORE. (*Embraces Blunt.*)
That you esteem him gives him an int'rest here.

BLUNT.
Your servant, sir.

WILLMORE.
But well—faith, I'm glad to meet you again in a warm climate, where the kind sun has its god-like power still over the wine and women. Love and mirth are my business in Naples, and if I mistake not the place, here's an excellent market for chapmen of my humor*.

BELVILE.
See, here be those kind merchants of love you look for.

Enter several men in masquing habits, some playing on music, others dancing after; women dressed like courtesans, with papers pinned on their breasts, and baskets of flowers in their hands.

BLUNT.
'Sheartlikins, what have we here?

FREDERICK.
Now the game begins.

WILLMORE.
Fine pretty creatures! May a stranger have leave to look and love? What's here? (*Reads the papers.*) "Roses for every month"?

BLUNT.
Roses for every month? What means that?

BELVILE.
They are, or would have you think, they're courtesans, who here in Naples, are to be hired by the month.

WILLMORE.
Kind and obliging to inform us. Pray, where do these roses grow? I would fain plant some of 'em in a bed of mine.

WOMEN.
Beware such roses, sir.

WILLMORE.
A pox of fear: I'll be baked with thee between a pair of sheets, and that's thy proper still;[21] so I might but strew such roses over me, and under me.—Fair one, would you would give me leave to gather at your bush this idle month; I would go near to make some body smell of it all the year after.

BELVILE.
And thou hast need of such a remedy, for thou stink'st of tar and rope's ends, like a dock or pest-house.[22]

The woman puts herself into the hands of a man and exeunt.

WILLMORE.
Nay, nay, you shall not leave me so.

BELVILE.
By all means use no violence here.

[19] Commonwealth] name for England during Parliamentary rule

[20] Prince] Charles II

[21] baked ... still] Willmore's double entendre refers to the process by which rose petals are distilled to make rosewater.

[22] pest-house] hospital for plague victims

WILLMORE.
Death! Just as I was going to be damnably in love, to have her led off! I could pluck that rose out of his hand, and even kiss the bed the bush grew in.

FREDERICK.
No friend to love like a long voyage at sea.

BLUNT.
Except a nunnery, Frederick.

WILLMORE.
Death! But will they not be kind? quickly be kind? Thou know'st I'm no tame fighter, but a rampant lion of the forest.

Advance from the farther end of the scenes two men dressed all over with horns of several sorts, making grimaces at one another, with papers pinned on their backs.*

BELVILE.
Oh the fantastical rogues, how they're dressed! 'Tis a satire against the whole sex.

WILLMORE.
Is this a fruit that grows in this warm country?

BELVILE.
Yes, 'tis pretty to see these Italians start, swell and stab at the word "cuckold," and yet stumble at horns on every threshold.

WILLMORE.
See what's on their back. (*Reads.*) "Flowers of every night." Ah, rogue! and more sweet than roses of every month! This is a gardener of Adam's own breeding.

They dance.

BELVILE.
What think you of those grave people? Is a wake in Essex half so mad or extravagant?

WILLMORE.
I like their sober grave way; 'tis a kind of legal authorized fornication, where the men are not chid for't, nor the women despised, as amongst our dull English even the monsieurs want that part of good manners.

BELVILE.
But here in Italy a monsieur is the humblest, best-bred gentleman; duels are so baffled by bravoes, that an age shows not one but between a Frenchman and a hangman, who is as much too hard for him on the piazza, as they are for a Dutchman on the New Bridge.[23]—But see, another crew.

Enter Florinda, Hellena and Valeria, dressed like gypsies; Callis and Stephano; Lucetta, Phillipo and Sancho in masquerade.

HELLENA.
Sister, there's your Englishman, and with him a handsome proper fellow. I'll to him, and instead of telling him his fortune, try my own.

WILLMORE.
Gypsies, on my life. Sure these will prattle if a man cross their hands.[24] (*Goes to Hellena.*) Dear, pretty (and I hope) young devil, will you tell an amorous stranger what luck he's like to have?

HELLENA.
Have a care how you venture with me, sir, lest I pick your pocket, which will more vex your English humor* than an Italian fortune will please you.

WILLMORE.
How the devil cam'st thou to know my country and humor*?

HELLENA.
The first I guess by a certain forward impudence, which does not displease me at this time; and the loss of your money will vex you because I hope you have but very little to lose.

WILLMORE.
Egad, child, thou'rt i'th' right; it is so little, I dare not offer it thee for a kindness. But cannot you divine what other things of more value I have about me, that I would more willingly part with?

HELLENA.
Indeed no, that's the business of a witch, and I am but a Gypsy yet. Yet without looking in your hand, I have a parlous guess 'tis some foolish heart you mean, an inconstant English heart, as little worth stealing as your purse.

WILLMORE.
Nay, then thou dost deal with the devil, that's

23 Dutchman on the New Bridge] an anachronistic reference to the French defeat of the Dutch at Niuewerbrug in 1673.

24 cross their hands] with silver, as payment for telling a fortune

certain. Thou hast guessed as right as if thou had'st been one of that number it has languished for. I find you'll be better acquainted with it, nor can you take it in a better time; for I am come from the sea, child, and Venus not being propitious to me in her own element,[25] I have a world of love in store. Would you would be good-natured and take some on't off my hands.

HELLENA.
Why, I could be inclined that way, but for a foolish vow I am going to make—to die a maid.

WILLMORE.
Then thou art damned without redemption, and as I am a good Christian, I ought in charity to divert so wicked a design; therefore prithee, dear creature, let me know quickly when and where I shall begin to set a helping hand to so good a work.

HELLENA.
If you should prevail with my tender heart (as I begin to fear you will, for you have horrible loving eyes), there will be difficulty in't, that you'll hardly undergo for my sake.

WILLMORE.
Faith, child, I have been bred in dangers and wear a sword that has been employed in a worse cause than for a handsome kind woman. Name the danger. Let it be anything but a long siege, and I'll undertake it.

HELLENA.
Can you storm?

WILLMORE.
Oh most furiously.

HELLENA.
What think you of a nunnery wall? For he that wins me must gain that first.

WILLMORE.
A nun! Oh how I love thee for't! There's no sinner like a young saint. Nay, now there's no denying me, the old law[26] had no curse (to a woman) like dying a maid; witness Jepthah's daughter.[27]

HELLENA.
A very good text this, if well handled, and I perceive, Father Captain, you would impose no severe penance on her who were inclined to console herself, before she took orders.

WILLMORE.
If she be young and handsome.

HELLENA.
Ay, there's it. But if she be not—

WILLMORE.
By this hand, child, I have an implicit faith, and dare venture on thee with all faults. Besides, 'tis more meritorious to leave the world when thou hast tasted and proved the pleasure on't. Then, 'twill be a virtue in thee, which now will be pure ignorance.

HELLENA.
I perceive, good Father Captain, you design only to make me fit for heaven, but if on the contrary, you should quite divert me from it and bring me back to the world again, I should have a new man to seek, I find; and what a grief that will be, for when I begin, I fancy I shall love like anything. I never tried yet.

WILLMORE.
Egad and that's kind.—Prithee, dear creature, give me credit for a heart, for faith, I'm a very honest fellow. Oh, I long to come first to the banquet of love! And such a swingeing appetite I bring—oh, I'm impatient—thy lodging, sweetheart, thy lodging, or I'm a dead man!

HELLENA.
Why must we be either guilty of fornication or murder if we converse with you men? And is there no difference between leave to love me, and leave to lie with me?

WILLMORE.
Faith, child, they were made to go together.

LUCETTA.
Are you sure this is the man? (*Pointing to Blunt.*)

SANCHO.
When did I mistake your game?

LUCETTA.
This is a stranger, I know by his gazing; if he be brisk, he'll venture to follow me, and then, if I understand my trade, he's mine. He's English too,

25 Venus ... element] Venus, goddess of love, emerged from the sea.

26 old law] Old Testament law

27 Jephthah's daughter] Jephthah delayed the sacrifice of his virginal daughter for two months while she "bewailed her virginity"; see Judges 11: 30-40.

and they say that's a sort of good-natured loving people, and have generally so kind an opinion of themselves, that a woman of any wit may flatter 'em into any sort of fool she pleases.

She often passes by Blunt and gazes on him; he struts and cocks, and walks and gazes on her.

BLUNT. [*Aside.*]
'Tis so. She is taken. I have beauties which my false glass* at home did not discover.

FLORINDA. [*Aside.*]
This woman watches me so, I shall get no opportunity to discover myself to him and so miss the intent of my coming.—But as I was saying, sir (*Looking in his hand.*), by this line you should be a lover.

BELVILE.
I thought how right you guessed, all men are in love, or pretend to be so. Come, let me go, I'm weary of this fooling.

[He] walks away. She holds him, he strives to get from her.

FLORINDA.
I will not, till you have confessed whether the passion that you have vowed Florinda be true or false.

BELVILE. (*Turns quick towards her.*)
Florinda!

FLORINDA.
Softly.

BELVILE.
Thou hast named one will fix me here for ever.

FLORINDA.
She'll be disappointed, then, who expects you this night at the garden gate, and if you fail not, as—let me see the other hand—you will go near to do, she vows to die or make you happy. (*Looks on Callis, who observes 'em.*)

BELVILE.
What canst thou mean?

FLORINDA.
That which I say. Farewell. (*Offers to go.*)

BELVILE.
Oh charming sibyl, stay, complete that joy which as it is will turn into distraction! Where must I be? At the garden gate? I know it. At night you say? I'll sooner forfeit heaven than disobey.

Enter Don Pedro and other masquers, and pass over the stage.

CALLIS.
Madam, your brother's here.

FLORINDA.
Take this to instruct you farther. (*Gives him a letter and goes off.*)

FREDERICK.
Have a care, sir, what you promise; this may be a trap laid by her brother to ruin you.

BELVILE.
Do not disturb my happiness with doubts. (*Opens the letter.*)

WILLMORE.
My dear pretty creature, a thousand blessings on thee! Still in this habit, you say? and after dinner at this place?

HELLENA.
Yes, if you will swear to keep your heart and not bestow it between this and that.

WILLMORE.
By all the little gods of love, I swear I'll leave it with you, and if you run away with it, those deities of justice will revenge me.

Exeunt all the women.

FREDERICK.
Do you know the hand?

BELVILE.
'Tis Florinda's.
All blessings fall upon the virtuous maid.

FREDERICK.
Nay, no idolatry; a sober sacrifice I'll allow you.

BELVILE.
Oh friends, the welcom'st news! the softest letter! Nay, you shall all see it! And could you now be serious, I might be made the happiest man the sun shines on!

WILLMORE.
The reason of this mighty joy?

BELVILE.
See how kindly she invites me to deliver her from the threatened violence of her brother. Will you not assist me?

WILLMORE.
I know not what thou mean'st, but I'll make one at any mischief where a woman's concerned. But she'll be grateful to us for the favor, will she not?
BELVILE.
How mean you?
WILLMORE.
How should I mean? Thou know'st there's but one way for a woman to oblige me.
BELVILE.
Do not profane. The maid is nicely virtuous.
WILLMORE.
Whoo, pox, then she's fit for nothing but a husband; let her e'en go, Colonel.
FREDERICK.
Peace, she's the colonel's mistress, sir.
WILLMORE.
Let her be the devil; if she be thy mistress, I'll serve her. Name the way.
BELVILE.
Read here this postscript. (*Gives him a letter.*)
WILLMORE. (*Reads.*)
"At ten at night—at the garden gate—of which, if I cannot get the key, I will contrive a way over the wall—come attended with a friend or two." Kind heart, if we three cannot weave a string to let her down a garden wall, 'twere pity but the hangman wove one for us all.
FREDERICK.
Let her alone for that. Your woman's wit, your fair kind woman, will out-trick a broker or a Jew, and contrive like a Jesuit in chains.—But see, Ned Blunt is stolen out after the lure of a damsel.

Exeunt Blunt and Lucetta.

BELVILE.
So he'll scarce find his way home again, unless we get him cried by the bellman in the market-place, and 'twould sound prettily—a lost English boy of thirty.
FREDERICK.
I hope 'tis some common crafty sinner, one that will fit* him; it may be she'll sell him for Peru;[28] the rogue's sturdy and would work well in a mine; at least I hope she'll dress him for our mirth, cheat him of all, then have him well-favoredly hanged and turned out naked at midnight.
WILLMORE.
Prithee, what humor* is he of that you wish him so well?
BELVILE.
Why of an English elder brother's humor*, educated in a nursery, with a maid to tend him till fifteen, and lies with his grandmother till he's of age: one that knows no pleasure beyond riding to the next fair, or going up to London with his right worshipful father in Parliament-time, wearing gay clothes, or making honorable love to his lady mother's laundry-maid; gets drunk at a hunting-match, and ten to one then gives some proofs of his prowess. A pox upon him, he's our banker and has all our cash about him, and if he fail, we are all broke.
FREDERICK.
Oh let him alone for that matter, he's of a damned stingy quality that will secure our stock. I know not in what danger it were indeed if the jilt should pretend she's in love with him, for 'tis a kind believing coxcomb; otherwise, if he part with more than a piece of eight—geld[29] him: for which offer he may chance to be beaten, if she be a whore of the first rank.
BELVILE.
Nay, the rogue will not be easily beaten, he's stout enough. Perhaps if they talk beyond his capacity, he may chance to exercise his courage upon some of them; else I'm sure they'll find it as difficult to beat as to please him.
WILLMORE.
'Tis a lucky devil to light upon so kind a wench!
FREDERICK.
Thou had'st a great deal of talk with thy little Gypsy; could'st thou do no good upon her? For mine was hard-hearted.

[28] Peru] known for its many mines using slave labor

[29] geld] Behn (whose spelling is "gueld") puns on near homynyms: geld] to castrate; gild] to overlay with gold. The second is latent because Frederick has just referred to pieces of eight. There is a third possible pun in the archaic sense of gild] to make bloody. Both the second and third meanings seem picked up in Frederick's subsequent "beaten."

WILLMORE.

Hang her, she was some damned honest person of quality,* I'm sure, she was so very free and witty. If her face be but answerable to her wit and humor*, I would be bound to constancy this month to gain her. In the meantime, have you made no kind acquaintance since you came to town? You do not use to be honest so long, gentlemen.

FREDERICK.

Faith, love has kept us honest; we have been all fired with a beauty newly come to town, the famous Paduana,[30] Angellica Bianca.

WILLMORE.

What, the mistress of the dead Spanish general?

BELVILE.

Yes, she's now the only adored beauty of all the youth in Naples, who put on all their charms to appear lovely in her sight, their coaches, liveries, and themselves, all gay as on a monarch's birthday, to attract the eyes of this fair charmer, while she has the pleasure to behold all languish for her that see her.

FREDERICK.

'Tis pretty to see with how much love the men regard her, and how much envy the women.

WILLMORE.

What gallant has she?

BELVILE.

None, she's exposed to sale, and four days in the week she's yours—for so much a month.

WILLMORE.

The very thought of it quenches all manner of fire in me. Yet prithee, let's see her.

BELVILE.

Let's first to dinner, and after that we'll pass the day as you please. But at night ye must all be at my devotion.

WILLMORE.

I will not fail you.

Act II, scene i. The long street.

Enter Belvile and Frederick in masquing habits, and Willmore in his own clothes, with a vizard in his hand.

WILLMORE.

But why thus disguised and muzzled?

BELVILE.

Because whatever extravagances we commit in these faces, our own may not be obliged to answer 'em.

WILLMORE.

I should have changed my eternal buff too; but no matter, my little Gypsy would not have found me out then, for if she should change hers, it is impossible I should know her, unless I should hear her prattle. A pox on't, I cannot get her out of my head. Pray Heaven, if ever I do see her again, she prove damnably ugly, that I may fortify myself against her tongue.

BELVILE.

Have a care of love, for o'my conscience, she was not of a quality to give thee any hopes.

WILLMORE.

Pox on 'em, why do they draw a man in then? She has played with my heart so, that 'twill never lie still till I have met with some kind wench that will play the game out with me. Oh, for my arms full of soft, white, kind—woman! such as I fancy Angellica.

BELVILE.

This is her house, if you were but in stock[31] to get admittance. They have not dined yet; I perceive the picture is not out.

Enter Blunt.

WILLMORE.

I long to see the shadow of the fair substance; a man may gaze on that for nothing.

BLUNT.

Colonel, thy hand—and thine, Fred. I have been an ass, a deluded fool, a very coxcomb from my birth till this hour, and heartily repent my little faith.

BELVILE.

What the devil's the matter with thee, Ned?

BLUNT.

Oh such a mistress, Fred, such a girl!

WILLMORE.

Ha! where?

FREDERICK.

Ay, where!

[30] Paduana] a woman from Padua

[31] in stock] supplied with funds

BLUNT.

So fond, so amorous, so toying and so fine! and all for sheer love, ye rogue! Oh how she looked and kissed! and soothed my heart from my bosom. I cannot think I was awake, and yet methinks I see and feel her charms still. Fred, try if she have not left the taste of her balmy kisses upon my lips. (*Kisses him.*)

BELVILE.

Ha! Ha! Ha!

WILLMORE.

Death, man, where is she?

BLUNT.

What a dog was I to stay in dull England so long. How have I laughed at the colonel when he sighed for love! But now the little archer[32] has revenged him! And by this one dart, I can guess at all his joys, which then I took for fancies, mere dreams and fables. Well, I'm resolved to sell all in Essex, and plant here for ever.

BELVILE.

What a blessing 'tis thou hast a mistress thou dar'st boast of, for I know thy humor* is rather to have a proclaimed clap than a secret amour.

WILLMORE.

Dost know her name?

BLUNT.

Her name? No, 'sheartlikins, what care I for names? She's fair! young! brisk and kind! even to ravishment! And what a pox care I for knowing her by any other title?

WILLMORE.

Didst give her anything?

BLUNT.

Give her! Ha, ha, ha! Why she's a person of quality.* That's a good one, give her! 'Sheartlikins, dost think such creatures are to be bought? Or are we provided for such a purchase? Give her, quoth ye? Why, she presented me with this bracelet for the toy of a diamond I used to wear. No, gentlemen, Ned Blunt is not everybody. She expects me again tonight.

WILLMORE.

Egad, that's well; we'll all go.

[32] little archer] Cupid

BLUNT.

Not a soul. No, gentlemen, you are wits; I am a dull country rogue, I.

FREDERICK.

Well, sir, for all your person of quality, I shall be very glad to understand your purse be secure; 'tis our whole estate at present, which we are loath to hazard in one bottom. Come, sir, unlade.

BLUNT.

Take the necessary trifle, useless now to me that am beloved by such a gentlewoman. 'Sheartlikins, money! Here, take mine too.

FREDERICK.

No, keep that to be cozened, that we may laugh.

WILLMORE.

Cozened! Death! Would I could meet with one that would cozen me of all the love I could spare tonight.

FREDERICK.

Pox, 'tis some common whore, upon my life.

BLUNT.

A whore! Yes, with such clothes! such jewels! such a house! such furniture, and so attended! A whore!

BELVILE.

Why yes, sir, they are whores, though they'll neither entertain you with drinking, swearing, or bawdry; are whores in all those gay clothes and right jewels; are whores with those great houses richly furnished with velvet beds, store of plate, handsome attendance and fine coaches; are whores, and arrant ones.

WILLMORE.

Pox on't, where do these fine whores live?

BELVILE.

Where no rogues in office yclept constables dare give 'em laws, nor the wine-inspired bullies of the town break their windows; yet they are whores, though this Essex calf[33] believe 'em persons of quality.

BLUNT.

'Sheartlikins, y'are all fools; there are things about this Essex calf that shall take with the ladies, beyond all your wit and parts. This shape and size,

[33] Essex calf] fool; a native of Essex. Blunt's home county of Essex was famous for its calves.

gentlemen, are not to be despised—my waist too, tolerably long, with other inviting signs, that shall be nameless.

WILLMORE.

Egad, I believe he may have met with some person of quality that may be kind to him.

BELVILE.

Dost thou perceive any such tempting things about him that should make a fine woman, and of quality, pick him out from all mankind to throw away her youth and beauty upon, nay and her dear heart too! No, no, Angellica has raised the price too high.

WILLMORE.

May she languish for mankind till she die, and be damned for that one sin alone.

Enter two bravoes, and hang up a great picture of Angellica's against the balcony, and two little ones at each side of the door.

BELVILE.

See there, the fair sign to the inn where a man may lodge that's fool enough to give her price.

Willmore gazes on the picture.

BLUNT.

'Sheartlikins, gentlemen, what's this!

BELVILE.

A famous courtesan, that's to be sold.

BLUNT.

How? To be sold! Nay then, I have nothing to say to her. Sold! What impudence is practiced in this country? With what order and decency whoring's established here by virtue of the Inquisition. Come, let's be gone, I'm sure we're no chapmen for this commodity.

FREDERICK.

Thou art none, I'm sure, unless thou could'st have her in thy bed at a price of a coach in the street.

WILLMORE.

How wondrous fair she is. A thousand crowns a month! By heaven, as many kingdoms were too little. A plague of this poverty—of which I ne'er complain but when it hinders my approach to beauty which virtue ne'er could purchase. (*Turns from the picture.*)

BLUNT.

What's this? (*Reads.*) "A thousand crowns a month"!—'Sheartlikins, here's a sum! Sure 'tis a mistake.—Hark you friend, does she take or give so much by the month?

FREDERICK.

A thousand crowns! Why 'tis a portion for the Infanta.

BLUNT.

Hark ye, friends, won't she trust?

BRAVO.

This is a trade, sir, that cannot live by credit.

Enter Don Pedro in masquerade, followed by Stephano.

BELVILE.

See, here's more company. Let's walk off a while.

Exeunt English. Pedro reads. Enter Angellica and Moretta in the balcony, and draw a silk curtain.

PEDRO.

Fetch me a thousand crowns, I never wished to buy this beauty at an easier rate. (*Passes off.*)

ANGELLICA.

Prithee, what said those fellows to thee?

BRAVO.

Madam, the first were admirers of beauty only, but no purchasers; they were merry with your price and picture, laughed at the sum, and so passed off.

ANGELLICA.

No matter, I'm not displeased with their rallying; their wonder feeds my vanity, and he that wishes but to buy gives me more pride than he that gives my price can make my pleasure.

BRAVO.

Madam, the last I knew through all his disguises to be Don Pedro, nephew to the general, and who was with him in Pamplona.

ANGELLICA.

Don Pedro! My old gallant's nephew. When his uncle died he left him a vast sum of money; it is he who was so in love with me at Padua, and who used to make the general so jealous.

MORETTA.

Is this he that used to prance before our window and take such care to show himself an amorous ass? If I am not mistaken, he is the likeliest man to give your price.

ANGELLICA.

The man is brave and generous, but of an humor* so uneasy and inconstant, that the victory over his heart is as soon lost as won, a slave that can add little to the triumph of the conqueror. But inconstancy's the sin of all mankind; therefore, I'm resolved that nothing but gold shall charm my heart.

MORETTA.

I'm glad on't; 'tis only interest that women of our profession ought to consider, though I wonder what has kept you from that general disease of our sex so long, I mean that of being in love.

ANGELLICA.

A kind but sullen star under which I had the happiness to be born. Yet I have had no time for love; the bravest and noblest of mankind have purchased my favors at so dear a rate as if no coin but gold were current with our trade.—But here's Don Pedro again, fetch me my lute, for 'tis for him or Don Antonio the viceroy's son that I have spread my nets.

Enter at one door Don Pedro, Stephano; Don Antonio and Diego [Page] at the other door, with people following him in masquerade, antically attired, some with music; they both go up to the picture.

ANTONIO.

A thousand crowns! Had not the painter flattered her, I should not think it dear.

PEDRO.

Flattered her! By Heav'n, he cannot; I have seen the original, nor is there one charm here more than adorns her face and eyes; all this soft and sweet, with a certain languishing air, that no artist can represent.

ANTONIO.

What I heard of her beauty before had fired my soul, but this confirmation of it has blown it to a flame.

PEDRO.

Hah!

PAGE.

Sir, I have known you throw away a thousand crowns on a worse face, and though y'are near your marriage, you may venture a little love here. Florinda will not miss it.

PEDRO. (*Aside.*)

Hah! Florinda! Sure 'tis Antonio.

ANTONIO.

Florinda! Name not those distant joys; there's not one thought of her will check my passion here.

PEDRO.

Florinda scorned! (*A noise of a lute above.*) and all my hopes defeated of the possession of Angellica. (*Antonio gazes up.*) Her injuries, by Heaven, he shall not boast of.

Song (*to a lute above.*)

When Damon first began to love
He languished in a soft desire,
And knew not how the gods to move,
To lessen or increase his fire.
For Caelia in her charming eyes
Wore all love's sweets, and all his cruelties.

II.

But as beneath a shade he lay,
Weaving of flow'rs for Caelia's hair,
She chanced to lead her flock that way,
And saw the am'rous shepherd there.
She gazed around upon the place,
And saw the grove (resembling night)
To all the joys of love invite,
Whilst guilty smiles and blushes dressed her face.
At this the bashful youth all transport grew,
And with kind force he taught the virgin how
To yield what all his sighs could never do.

Angellica throws open the curtains and bows to Antonio, who pulls off his vizard and bows and blows up kisses. Pedro unseen looks in's face.

ANTONIO.

By Heav'n, she's charming fair!

PEDRO.

'Tis he; the false Antonio!

ANTONIO. (*To the bravo.*)

Friend, where must I pay my offering of love?
My thousand crowns I mean.

PEDRO.

That offering I have designed to make.
And yours will come too late.

ANTONIO.

Prithee, be gone, I shall grow angry else.
And then thou art not safe.

PEDRO.
My anger may be fatal, sir, as yours,
And he that enters here may prove this truth.
ANTONIO.
I know not who thou art, but I am sure thou'rt worth my killing, for aiming at Angellica.

They draw and fight. Enter Willmore and Blunt who draw and part 'em.

BLUNT.
'Sheartlikins, here's fine doings.
WILLMORE.
Tilting for the wench, I'm sure. Nay, gad, if that would win her, I have as good a sword as the best of ye. Put up—put up, and take another time and place, for this is designed for lovers only.

They all put up.

PEDRO.
We are prevented; dare you meet me tomorrow
on the Molo?[34]
For I've a title to a better quarrel,*
That of Florinda, in whose credulous heart
Thou'st made an int'rest and destroyed my hopes.
ANTONIO.
Dare!
I'll meet thee there as early as the day.
PEDRO.
We will come thus disguised that whosoever chance to get the better, he may escape unknown.
ANTONIO.
It shall be so.

Exeunt Pedro and Stephano.

Who should this rival be? unless the English colonel, of whom I've often heard Don Pedro speak; it must be he, and time he were removed, who lays claim to all my happiness.

Willmore having gazed all this while on the picture, pulls down a little one.

WILLMORE.
This posture's loose and negligent,
The sight on't would beget a warm desire
In souls whom impotence and age had chilled.
—This must along with me.
BRAVO.
What means this rudeness, sir? Restore the picture.
ANTONIO.
Hah! Rudeness committed to the fair Angellica!
Restore the picture, sir—
WILLMORE.
Indeed I will not, sir.
ANTONIO.
By Heaven, but you shall.
WILLMORE.
Nay, do not show your sword; if you do, by this dear beauty—I will show mine too.
ANTONIO.
What right can you pretend to't?
WILLMORE.
That of possession, which I will maintain. You perhaps have a thousand crowns to give for the original.
ANTONIO.
No matter, sir, you shall restore the picture.

Angellica and Moretta above.

ANGELLICA.
Oh Moretta! What's the matter?
ANTONIO.
Or leave your life behind.
WILLMORE.
Death! You lie. I will do neither.

They fight; the Spaniards join with Antonio; Blunt laying on like mad.

ANGELLICA.
Hold, I command you, if for me you fight.

They leave off and bow.

WILLMORE.
How heavenly fair she is! Ah, plague of her price.
ANGELLICA.
You sir, in buff, you that appear a soldier, that first began this insolence—
WILLMORE.
'Tis true, I did so, if you call it insolence for a man to preserve himself. I saw your charming picture and was wounded; quite through my soul each pointed

[34] the Molo] pier; from French *môle*

beauty ran, and wanting a thousand crowns to procure my remedy, I laid this little picture to my bosom—which if you cannot allow me, I'll resign.

ANGELLICA.
No, you may keep the trifle.

ANTONIO.
You shall first ask me leave, and this. (*Fight again as before.*)

Enter Belvile and Frederick who join with the English.

ANGELLICA.
Hold! Will you ruin me? Biskey—Sebastian—part 'em.

The Spaniards are beaten off.

MORETTA.
Oh madam, we're undone. A pox upon that rude fellow, he's set on to ruin us. We shall never see good days till all these fighting poor rogues are sent to the galleys.

Enter Belvile, Blunt, Frederick, and Willmore with's shirt bloody.

BLUNT.
'Sheartlikins, beat me at this sport, and I'll ne'er wear sword more.

BELVILE.
The devil's in thee for a mad fellow; thou art always one at an unlucky adventure. Come, let's be gone whilst we're safe, and remember these are Spaniards, a sort of people that know how to revenge an affront.

FREDERICK. (*To Willmore.*)
You bleed! I hope you are not wounded.

WILLMORE.
Not much. A plague on your dons; if they fight no better, they'll ne'er recover Flanders.* What the devil was't to them that I took down the picture?

BLUNT.
Took it! 'Sheartlikins, we'll have the great one too; 'tis ours by conquest. Prithee, help me up and I'll pull it down—

ANGELLICA.
Stay, sir, and ere you affront me farther, let me know how you durst commit this outrage. To you I speak, sir, for you appear a gentleman.

WILLMORE.
To me, madam?—Gentlemen, your servant.

Belvile stays him.

BELVILE.
Is the devil in thee? Dost know the danger of entering the house of an incensed courtesan?

WILLMORE.
I thank you for your care, but there are other matters in hand, there are, though we have no great temptation.—Death! Let me go.

FREDERICK.
Yes, to your lodging if you will, but not in here.—Damn these gay harlots. By this hand I'll have as sound and handsome a whore for a patacoon.[35]—Death, man, she'll murder thee.

WILLMORE.
Oh! Fear me not. Shall I not venture where a beauty calls? a lovely, charming beauty! for fear of danger! when, by Heaven, there's none so great as to long for her whilst I want money to purchase her.

FREDERICK.
Therefore, 'tis loss of time unless you had the thousand crowns to pay.

WILLMORE.
It may be she may give a favor; at least I shall have the pleasure of saluting her when I enter, and when I depart.

BELVILE.
Pox, she'll as soon lie with thee as kiss thee, and sooner stab than do either. You shall not go.

ANGELLICA.
Fear not, sir, all I have to wound with is my eyes.

BLUNT.
Let him go. 'Sheartlikins, I believe the gentlewoman means well.

BELVILE.
Well, take thy fortune; we'll expect you in the next street. Farewell, fool—farewell—

WILLMORE.
Bye, Colonel. (*Goes in.*)

---

[35] patacoon] Spanish coin; value in seventeenth century, ca. one fourth of an English pound

FREDERICK.
The rogue's stark mad for a wench.

Exeunt.

Scene ii. A fine chamber.

Enter Willmore, Angellica and Moretta.

ANGELLICA.
Insolent sir, how durst you pull down my picture?

WILLMORE.
Rather, how durst you set it up, to tempt poor amorous mortals with so much excellence, which I find you have but too well consulted by the unmerciful price you set upon't? Is all this heaven of beauty shown to move despair in those that cannot buy? And can you think th'effects of that despair should be less extravagant than I have shown?

ANGELLICA.
I sent for you to ask my pardon, sir, not to aggravate your crime. I thought I should have seen you at my feet imploring it.

WILLMORE.
You are deceived; I came to rail at you, and rail such truths too, as shall let you see the vanity of that pride which taught you how to set such price on sin. For such it is, whilst that which is love's due is meanly bartered for.

ANGELLICA.
Ha! ha! ha! Alas, good captain, what pity 'tis your edifying doctrine will do no good upon me.—Moretta! Fetch the gentleman a glass, and let him survey himself, to see what charms he has—(*Aside in a soft tone.*) and guess my business.

MORETTA.
He knows himself of old; I believe those breeches and he have been acquainted ever since he was beaten at Worcester.[36]

ANGELLICA.
Nay, do not abuse the poor creature—

MORETTA.
Good weather-beaten corporal, will you march off? We have no need of your doctrine, though you have of our charity, but at present we have no scraps, we can afford no kindness for God's sake. In fine, sirrah, the price is too high i'th'mouth[37] for you; therefore, troop, I say.

WILLMORE.
Here, good forewoman of the shop, serve me, and I'll be gone.

MORETTA.
Keep it to pay your laundress, your linen stinks of the gunroom, for here's no selling by retail.

WILLMORE.
Thou hast sold plenty of thy stale ware at a cheap rate.

MORETTA.
Ay, the more silly,* kind heart I, but this is an age wherein beauty is at higher rates. In fine, you know the price of this.

WILLMORE.
I grant you 'tis here set down, a thousand crowns a month. Pray, how much may come to my share for a pistole? Bawd, take your black lead and sum it up, that I may have a pistole's worth of this vain gay thing, and I'll trouble you no more.

MORETTA.
Pox on him, he'll fret me to death.—Abominable fellow, I tell thee, we only sell by the whole piece.

WILLMORE.
'Tis very hard, the whole cargo or nothing. Faith, madam, my stock will not reach it; I cannot be your chapman. Yet I have countrymen in town, merchants of love like me; I'll see if they'll put in for a share. We cannot lose much by it, and what we have no use for, we'll sell upon the Friday's mart at "Who gives more?"—I am studying, madam, how to purchase you, though at present I am unprovided of money.

ANGELLICA. [*Aside.*]
Sure, this from any other man would anger me, nor shall he know the conquest he has made.—Poor angry man, how I despise this railing.

WILLMORE.
Yes, I am poor—but I'm a gentleman,
And one that scorns this baseness which you practice;
Poor as I am, I would not sell myself,

---

[36] Worcester] The Battle of Worcester (1651) was the final defeat of Charles II by the Parliamentary forces, after which he fled to the continent.

[37] high i'th'mouth] elevated

No, not to gain your charming, high-prized person.
Though I admire you strangely for your beauty,
Yet I contemn your mind.—
And yet I would at any rate enjoy you
At your own rate—but cannot. See here
The only sum I can command on earth;
I know not where to eat when this is gone.
Yet such a slave I am to love and beauty
This last reserve I'll sacrifice to enjoy you.
—Nay, do not frown, I know you're to be bought,
And would be bought by me, by me,
For a mean trifling sum if I could pay it down;
Which happy knowledge I will still repeat,
And lay it to my heart; it has a virtue in't,
And soon will cure those wounds your eyes have made.
—And yet—there's something so divinely powerful there—
Nay, I will gaze—to let you see my strength.

Holds her, looks on her, and pauses and sighs.

By Heav'n, bright creature—I would not for the world
Thy fame were half so fair as is thy face.

Turns her away from him.

ANGELLICA. (*Aside.*)
His words go through me to the very soul.
—If you have nothing else to say to me—
WILLMORE.
Yes, you shall hear how infamous you are—
For which I do not hate thee—
But that secures my heart, and all the flames it feels
Are but so many lusts—
I know it by their sudden bold intrusion.
The fire's impatient and betrays, 'tis false—
For had it been the purer flame of love,
I should have pined and languished at your feet,
Ere found the impudence to have discovered it.
I now dare stand your scorn, and your denial.
MORETTA.
Sure she's bewitched, that she can stand thus tamely and hear his saucy railing.—Sirrah, will you be gone?
ANGELLICA. (*To Moretta.*)
How dare you take this liberty? Withdraw.—Pray tell me, sir, are not you guilty of the same mercenary crime? When a lady is proposed to you for a wife, you never ask how fair, discreet, or virtuous she is, but what's her fortune—which if but small, you cry, "She will not do my business" and basely leave her, though she languish for you. Say, is not this as poor?
WILLMORE.
It is a barbarous custom, which I will scorn to defend in our sex, and do despise in yours.
ANGELLICA.
Thou'rt a brave fellow! Put up thy gold, and know,
That were thy fortune large as is thy soul,
Thou should'st not buy my love.
Couldst thou forget those mean effects of vanity
Which set me out to sale, and, as a lover, prize my yielding joys?
Canst thou believe they'll be entirely thine,
Without considering they were mercenary?
WILLMORE.
I cannot tell, I must bethink me first. (*Aside.*) Hah!
Death, I'm going to believe her.
ANGELLICA.
Prithee, confirm that faith—or if thou canst not—
flatter me a little, 'twill please me from thy mouth.
WILLMORE. (*Aside.*)
Curse on thy charming tongue!—Dost thou return
My feigned contempt with so much subtlety?
Thou'st found the easiest way into my heart,
Though I yet know that all thou say'st is false.

Turning from her in rage.

ANGELLICA.
By all that's good, 'tis real;
I never loved before, though oft a mistress.
Shall my first vows be slighted?
WILLMORE. (*Aside.*)
What can she mean?
ANGELLICA. (*In an angry tone.*)
I find you cannot credit me.
WILLMORE.
I know you take me for an arrant ass,
An ass that may be soothed into belief
And then be used at pleasure—
But madam, I have been so often cheated
By perjured, soft, deluding hypocrites,

That I've no faith left for the cozening sex;
Especially for women of your trade.

ANGELLICA.
The low esteem you have of me, perhaps
May bring my heart again—
For I have pride that yet surmounts my love.

She turns with pride; he holds her.

WILLMORE.
Throw off this pride, this enemy to bliss,
And show the pow'r of love; 'tis with those arms
I can be only vanquished, made a slave.

ANGELLICA.
Is all my mighty expectation vanished?
—No, I will not hear thee talk. Thou hast a charm
In every word that draws my heart away.
And all the thousand trophies I designed
Thou hast undone—Why art thou soft?
Thy looks are bravely rough, and meant for war.
Could'st thou not storm on still?
I then perhaps had been as free as thou.

WILLMORE. (*Aside.*)
Death, how she throws her fire about my soul!
—Take heed, fair creature, how you raise my hope,
Which, once assumed, pretends to all dominion.
There's not a joy thou hast in store,
I shall not then command—
For which I'll pay thee back my soul! my life!
—Come, let's begin th'account this happy minute!

ANGELLICA.
And will you pay me then the price I ask?

WILLMORE.
Oh, why dost thou draw me from an awful worship,
By showing thou art no divinity?
Conceal the fiend, and show me all the angel!
Keep me but ignorant, and I'll be devout
And pay my vows forever at this shrine.

Kneels and kisses her hand.

ANGELLICA.
The pay I mean is but thy love for mine.
Can you give that?—

WILLMORE.
Entirely. Come, let's withdraw! where I'll renew my vows—and breathe 'em with such ardor thou shalt not doubt my zeal.

ANGELLICA.
Thou hast a pow'r too strong to be resisted.

Exeunt Willmore and Angellica.

MORETTA.
Now my curse go with you. Is all our project fallen to this? to love the only enemy to our trade? Nay, to love such a shameroon,[38] a very beggar, nay a pirate beggar, whose business is to rifle, and be gone, a no-purchase, no-pay tatterdemalion and English picaroon, a rogue that fights for daily drink and takes a pride in being loyally lousy. Oh, I could curse now, if I durst. This is the fate of most whores.
Trophies, which from believing fops we win,
Are spoils to those who cozen us again.

Act III, scene i. A street.

Enter Florinda, Valeria, Hellena, in antic different dresses from what they were in before. Callis attending.

FLORINDA.
I wonder what should make my brother in so ill a humor*? I hope he has not found out our ramble this morning.

HELLENA.
No, if he had, we should have heard on't at both ears, and have been mewed up this afternoon, which I would not for the world should have happened.—Hey ho, I'm as sad as a lover's lute.

VALERIA.
Well, methinks we have learnt this trade of gypsies as readily as if we have been bred upon the road to Loretto,[39] and yet I did so fumble when I told the stranger his fortune that I was afraid I should have told my own and yours by mistake. But methinks Hellena has been very serious ever since.

FLORINDA.
I would give my garters she were in love to be revenged upon her for abusing me.—How is't, Hellena?

HELLENA.
Ah—would I had never seen my mad monsieur—and yet for all your laughing, I am not in love—

[38] shameroon] one who deceives or uses false pretenses

[39] Loretto] a city in Italy famous as a place of pilgrimage

and yet this small acquaintance, o'my conscience, will never out of my head.

VALERIA.

Ha, ha, ha! I laugh to think how thou art fitted with a lover, a fellow that I warrant loves every new face he sees.

HELLENA.

Hum—he has not kept his word with me here—and may be taken up. That thought is not very pleasant to me. What the deuce should this be, now, that I feel?

VALERIA.

What is't like?

HELLENA.

Nay, the lord knows. But if I should be hanged, I cannot choose but be angry and afraid when I think that mad fellow should be in love with anybody but me. What to think of myself, I know not. Would I could meet with some true damned Gypsy, that I might know my fortune.

VALERIA.

Know it! Why there's nothing so easy; thou wilt love this wandering inconstant till thou find'st thyself hanged about his neck, and then be as mad to get free again.

FLORINDA.

Yes, Valeria, we shall see her bestride his baggage horse, and follow him to the campaign.

HELLENA.

So, so, now you are provided for, there's no care taken of poor me. But since you have set my heart a-wishing, I am resolved to know for what. I will not die of the pip, so I will not.

FLORINDA.

Art thou mad to talk so? Who will like thee well enough to have thee that hears what a mad wench thou art?

HELLENA.

Like me! I don't intend every he that likes me shall have me, but he that I like; I should have stayed in the nunnery still, if I had liked my lady Abbess as well as she liked me. No, I came thence not (as my wise brother imagines) to take an eternal farewell of the world, but to love and to be beloved, and I will be beloved, or I'll get one of your men, so I will.

VALERIA.

Am I put into the number of lovers?

HELLENA.

You? Why, coz, I know thou'rt too good-natured to leave us in any design; thou wouldst venture a cast, though thou comest off a loser, especially with such a gamester. I observe your man and your willing ear incline that way; and if you are not a lover, 'tis an art soon learnt, that I find. (*Sighs.*)

FLORINDA.

I wonder how you learnt to love so easily; I had a thousand charms to meet my eyes and ears ere I could yield, and 'twas the knowledge of Belvile's merit, not the surprising person, took my soul. Thou art too rash to give a heart at first sight.

HELLENA.

Hang your considering lover; I never thought beyond the fancy that 'twas a very pretty, idle, silly kind of pleasure to pass one's time with, to write little soft nonsensical billets, and with great difficulty and danger receive answers in which I shall have my beauty praised, my wit admired (though little or none), and have the vanity and power to know I am desirable; then I have the more inclination that way, because I am to be a nun, and so shall not be suspected to have any such earthly thoughts about me. But when I walk thus—and sigh thus—they'll think my mind's upon my monastery and cry how happy 'tis she's so resolved. But not a word of man.

FLORINDA.

What a mad creature's this?

HELLENA.

I'll warrant, if my brother hears either of you sigh, he cries (gravely), "I fear you have the indiscretion to be in love, but take heed of the honor of our house, and your own unspotted fame," and so he conjures on till he has laid the soft-winged god in your hearts, or broke the bird's nest.—But see, here comes your lover, but where's my inconstant? Let's step aside, and we may learn something. (*Go aside.*)

Enter Belvile, Frederick and Blunt.

BELVILE.

What means this! The picture's taken in.

BLUNT.
It may be the wench is good-natured and will be kind gratis. Your friend's a proper handsome fellow.
BELVILE.
I rather think she has cut his throat and is fled: I am mad he should throw himself into dangers. Pox on't, I shall want him too at night. Let's knock and ask for him.
HELLENA.
My heart goes a-pit a-pat, for fear 'tis my man they talk of.

Knock; Moretta above.

MORETTA.
What would you have!
BELVILE.
Tell the stranger that entered here about two hours ago that his friends stay here for him.
MORETTA.
A curse upon him for Moretta; would he were at the devil. But he's coming to you.

Enter Willmore.

HELLENA.
Aye, aye, 'tis he! Oh how this vexes me.
BELVILE.
And how and how dear lad, has fortune smiled? Are we to break her windows? Or raise up altars to her, hah?
WILLMORE.
Does not my fortune sit triumphant on my brow? Dost not see the little wanton god there all gay and smiling? Have I not an air about my face and eyes that distinguish me from the crowd of common lovers? By Heaven, Cupid's quiver has not half so many darts as her eyes! Oh, such a bona roba*! To sleep in her arms is lying in fresco,[40] all perfumed air about me.
HELLENA. (*Aside.*)
Here's fine encouragement for me to fool on.
WILLMORE.
Hark ye, where didst thou purchase that rich canary we drank today! Tell me, that I may adore the spigot and sacrifice to the butt! The juice was divine! into which I must dip my rosary and then bless all things that I would have bold or fortunate.
BELVILE.
Well, sir, let's go take a bottle and hear the story of your success.
FREDERICK.
Would not French wine do better?
WILLMORE.
Damn the hungry balderdash,[41] cheerful sack* has a generous virtue in't inspiring a successful confidence, gives eloquence to the tongue, and vigor to the soul, and has in a few hours completed all my hopes and wishes! There's nothing left to raise a new desire in me. Come, let's be gay and wanton—and gentlemen, study, study what you want, for here [*Jingles a purse.*] are friends that will supply, gentlemen. Hark! What a charming sound they make—'tis he and she gold whilst here, and shall beget new pleasures every moment.
BLUNT.
But hark ye sir, you are not married, are you?
WILLMORE.
All the honey of matrimony, but none of the sting, friend.
BLUNT.
'Sheartlikins, thou'rt a fortunate rogue!
WILLMORE.
I am so, sir, let these [*Jingles again.*] inform you! Hah, how sweetly they chime! Pox of poverty, it makes a man a slave, makes wit and honor sneak. My soul grew lean and rusty for want of credit.
BLUNT.
'Sheartlikins, this I like well, it looks like my lucky bargain! Oh how I long for the approach of my squire that is to conduct me to her house again. Why, here's two provided for.
FREDERICK.
By this light, y'are happy men.
BLUNT.
Fortune is pleased to smile on us, gentlemen—to smile on us.

Enter Sancho and pulls down Blunt by the sleeve.

40 in fresco] alfresco

41 balderdash] a mixture of alcoholic drinks

SANCHO.

Sir, my lady expects you— (*They go aside.*) She has removed all that might oppose your will and pleasure—and is impatient till you come.

BLUNT.

Sir, I'll attend you.—Oh, the happiest rogue! I'll take no leave, lest they either dog me, or stay me.

Exit with Sancho.

BELVILE.

But then the little Gypsy is forgot?

WILLMORE.

A mischief on thee for putting her into my thoughts. I had quite forgot her else, and this night's debauch had drunk her quite down.

HELLENA.

Had it so, good captain! (*Claps him on the back.*)

WILLMORE. (*Aside.*)

Hah! I hope she did not hear me.

HELLENA.

What, afraid of such a champion?

WILLMORE.

Oh! You're a fine lady of your word, are you not? To make a man languish a whole day—

HELLENA.

In tedious search of me.

WILLMORE.

Egad child, thou'rt in the right; had'st thou seen what a melancholy dog I have been ever since I was a lover, how I have walked the streets like a Capuchin with my hands in my sleeves, faith, sweetheart, thou wouldst pity me.

HELLENA. [*Aside.*]

Now if I should be hanged I can't be angry with him, he dissembles so heartily.—Alas, good captain, what pains you have taken. Now were I ungrateful not to reward so true a servant.

WILLMORE.

Poor soul! That's kindly said; I see thou bearest a conscience. Come then, for a beginning show me thy dear face.

HELLENA.

I'm afraid, my small acquaintance, you have been staying that swingeing stomach you boasted this morning; I then remember my little collation would have gone down with you, without the sauce of a handsome face. Is your stomach so queasy now?

WILLMORE.

Faith, long fasting, child, spoils a man's appetite—yet if you durst treat, I could so lay about me still—

HELLENA.

And would you fall to, before a priest says grace?

WILLMORE.

Oh fie, fie, what an old, out of fashioned thing hast thou named? Thou couldst not dash me more out of countenance shouldst thou show me an ugly face.

Whilst he is seemingly courting Hellena, enter Angellica, Moretta, Biskey and Sebastian, all in masquerade; Angellica sees Willmore and stares.

ANGELLICA.

Heavens, 'tis he! and passionately fond to see another woman.

MORETTA.

What could you less expect from such a swaggerer?

ANGELLICA.

Expect! As much as I paid him, a heart entire
Which I had pride enough to think when ere I gave,
It would have raised the man above the vulgar,
Made him all soul! and that all soft and constant.

HELLENA.

You see, Captain, how willing I am to be friends with you, till time and ill luck make us lovers, and ask you the question first, rather than put your modesty to the blush by asking me (for alas!) I know you captains are such strict men and such severe observers of your vows to chastity, that 'twill be hard to prevail with your tender conscience to marry a young willing maid.

WILLMORE.

Do not abuse me, for fear I should take thee at thy word, and marry thee indeed, which I'm sure will be revenge sufficient.

HELLENA.

O' my conscience, that will be our destiny, because we are both of one humor*; I am as inconstant as you, for I have considered, Captain, that a handsome woman has a great deal to do whilst her face is good, for then is our harvest-time to gather friends; and should I in these days of my youth catch a fit of foolish constancy, I were undone; 'tis loitering by daylight in our great journey. Therefore, I declare I'll allow but one year for love, one year for indifference, and one year for hate—and then—go hang yourself! For I profess myself the gay, the kind, and the inconstant. The devil's in't if this won't please you.

WILLMORE.

Oh most damnably! I have a heart with a hole quite through it too: no prison mine to keep a mistress in.

ANGELLICA. (*Aside.*)

Perjured man! How I believe thee now.

HELLENA.

Well, I see our business as well as humors* are alike; yours to cozen as many maids as will trust you, and I as many men as have faith. See if I have not as desperate a lying look as you can have for the heart of you. (*Pulls off her vizard: he starts.*) How do you like it, captain?

WILLMORE.

Like it! By Heaven, I never saw so much beauty! Oh the charms of those sprightly black eyes! that strangely fair face, full of smiles and dimples! those soft round melting cherry lips! and small even white teeth! not to be expressed, but silently adored! Oh, one look more! and strike me dumb, or I shall repeat nothing else till I'm mad.

He seems to court her to pull off her vizard: she refuses.

ANGELLICA.

I can endure no more, nor is it fit to interrupt him, for if I do, my jealousy has so destroyed my reason, I shall undo him; therefore, I'll retire. (*To one of her bravoes.*) And you, Sebastian, follow that woman and learn who 'tis, (*To the other bravo.*) while you tell the fugitive, I would speak to him instantly.

Exit. This while Florinda is talking to Belvile, who stands sullenly. Frederick courting Valeria.

VALERIA. [*To Belvile.*]

Prithee, dear stranger, be not so sullen, for though you have lost your love, you see my friend frankly offers you hers to play with in the meantime.

BELVILE.

Faith, madam, I am sorry I can't play at her game.

FREDERICK.

Pray, leave your intercession and mind your own affair. They'll better agree apart; he's a modest sigher in company, but alone no woman scapes him.

FLORINDA.

[*Aside.*] Sure he does but rally, yet if it should be true—I'll tempt him farther.—Believe me, noble stranger, I'm no common mistress, and for a little proof on't, wear this jewel—nay, take it, sir, 'tis right, and bills of exchange may sometimes miscarry.

BELVILE.

Madam, why am I chose out of all mankind to be the object of your bounty?

VALERIA.

There's another civil question asked.

FREDERICK.

Pox of's modesty, it spoils his own markets and hinders mine.

FLORINDA.

Sir, from my window, I have often seen you, and women of my quality have so few opportunities for love that we ought to lose none.

FREDERICK.

Aye, this is something! Here's a woman! When shall I be blessed with so much kindness from your fair mouth?

(*Aside to Belvile.*)—Take the jewel, fool.

BELVILE.

You tempt me strangely, madam, every way—

FLORINDA. (*Aside.*)

So, if I find him false, my whole repose is gone.

BELVILE.

And but for a vow I've made to a very fair[d] lady, this goodness had subdued me.

FREDERICK.

Pox on't, be kind, in pity to me be kind, for I am to thrive here but as you treat her friend.

HELLENA.

Tell me what you did in yonder house, and I'll unmask.

WILLMORE.

Yonder house—oh—I went to—a—to—why, there's a friend of mine lives there.

HELLENA.

What, a she, or a he friend?

WILLMORE.
A man, upon honor! a man. A she friend? No, no, madam, you have done my business, I thank you.

HELLENA.
And was't your man friend that had more darts in's eyes than Cupid carries in's whole budget of arrows?

WILLMORE.
So—

HELLENA.
Ah, such a bona roba*! to be in her arms is lying alfresco, all perfumed air about me—was this your man friend too?

WILLMORE.
So—

HELLENA.
That gave you the he and the she gold that begets young pleasures?

WILLMORE.
Well, well, madam, then you see there are ladies in the world that will not be cruel—there are, madam, there are—

HELLENA.
And there be men too, as fine, wild, inconstant fellows as yourself, there be, Captain, there be, if you go to that now. Therefore, I'm resolved—

WILLMORE.
Oh!

HELLENA.
To see your face no more—

WILLMORE.
Oh!

HELLENA.
Till tomorrow.

WILLMORE.
Egad, you frighted me.

HELLENA.
Nor then neither, unless you'll swear never to see that lady more.

WILLMORE.
See her! Why, never to think of womankind again.

HELLENA.
Kneel—and swear—

Kneels, she gives him her hand.

WILLMORE.
I do, never to think—to see—to love—nor lie—with any but thy self.

HELLENA.
Kiss the book.

WILLMORE.
Oh, most religiously. (*Kisses her hand.*)

HELLENA.
Now what a wicked creature am I, to damn a proper fellow.

CALLIS. (*To Florinda.*)
Madam, I'll stay no longer, 'tis e'en dark.

FLORINDA.
However, sir, I'll leave this with you—that when I'm gone, you may repent the opportunity you have lost by your modesty.

Gives him the jewel which is her picture, and exits. He gazes after her.

WILLMORE.
'Twill be an age till tomorrow—and till then I will most impatiently expect you. Adieu, my dear pretty angel.

Exeunt all the women.

BELVILE.
Hah! Florinda's picture—'twas she herself—what a dull dog was I! I would have given the world for one minute's discourse with her.

FREDERICK.
This comes of your modesty! Ah, pox o' your vow, 'twas ten to one, but we had lost the jewel by't.

BELVILE.
Willmore! The blessed'st opportunity lost! Florinda! Friends! Florinda!

WILLMORE.
Ah rogue! such black eyes! such a face! such a mouth! such teeth! and so much wit!

BELVILE.
All, all, and a thousand charms besides.

WILLMORE.
Why, dost thou know her?

BELVILE.
Know her! Aye, aye, and a pox take me with all my heart for being modest.

WILLMORE.
But hark ye, friend of mine, are you my rival? And have I been only beating the bush all this while?

BELVILE.
I understand thee not. I'm mad. See here— (*Shows the picture.*)

WILLMORE.
Hah! Whose picture's this? 'Tis a fine wench!

FREDERICK.
The colonel's mistress, sir.

WILLMORE.
Oh, oh, here—I thought't had been another prize. Come, come, a bottle will set thee right again. (*Gives the picture back.*)

BELVILE.
I am content to try, and by that time 'twill be late enough for our design.

WILLMORE.
Agreed.
Love does all day the soul's great empire keep,
But wine at night lulls the soft god asleep.

Exeunt.

Scene ii. Lucetta's house.

Enter Blunt and Lucetta with a light.

LUCETTA.
Now we are safe and free; no fears of the coming home of my old jealous husband, which made me a little thoughtful when you came in first. But now love is all the business of my soul.

BLUNT. (*Aside.*)
I am transported! Pox on't, that I had but some fine things to say to her, such as lovers use. I was a fool not to learn of Frederick a little by heart before I came. Something I must say.—'Sheartlikins, sweet soul! I am not used to compliment, but I'm an honest gentleman, and thy humble servant.

LUCETTA.
I have nothing to pay for so great a favor, but such a love as cannot but be great, since at first sight of that sweet face and shape, it made me your absolute captive.

BLUNT.
Kind heart! (*Aside.*) How prettily she talks! Egad, I'll show her husband a Spanish trick: send him out of the world and marry her. She's damnably in love with me and will ne'er mind settlements, and so there's that saved.

LUCETTA.
Well, sir, I'll go and undress me and be with you instantly.

BLUNT.
Make haste, then, for 'sheartlikins, dear soul, thou canst not guess at the pain of a longing lover, when his joys are drawn within the compass of a few minutes.

LUCETTA.
You speak my sense, and I'll make haste to prove it.

Exit.

BLUNT.
'Tis a rare girl! And this one night's enjoyment with her will be worth all the days I ever passed in Essex. Would she would go with me into England; though to say truth, there's plenty of whores already. But a pox on 'em, they are such mercenary, prodigal whores, that they want such a one as this that's free and generous to give 'em good examples. Why, what a house she has, how rich and fine!

Enter Sancho.

SANCHO.
Sir, my lady has sent me to conduct you to her chamber.

BLUNT.
Sir, I shall be proud to follow.—Here's one of her servants too! 'Sheartlikins, by this garb and gravity, he might be a justice of peace in Essex and is but a pimp here.

Exeunt.

Scene iii.

The scene changes to a chamber with an alcove bed in't, a table, etc. Lucetta in bed. Enter Sancho and Blunt, who takes the candle of Sancho at the door.

SANCHO.
Sir, my commission reaches no farther.

BLUNT.
Sir, I'll excuse your compliment.

[Exit Sancho.]

What, in bed my sweet mistress?

LUCETTA.
You see, I still outdo you in kindness.

BLUNT.
And thou shalt see what haste I'll make to quit scores. —Oh, the luckiest rogue! (*He undresses himself.*)

LUCETTA.
Should you be false or cruel now!

BLUNT.
False! 'Sheartlikins, what dost thou take me for? a Jew? an insensible heathen? A pox of thy old jealous husband; an he were dead, egad, sweet soul, it should be none of my fault if I did not marry thee.

LUCETTA.
It never should be mine.

BLUNT.
Good soul! [*Aside.*] I'm the fortunatest dog!

LUCETTA.
Are you not undressed yet?

BLUNT.
As much as my impatience will permit.

Goes toward the bed in his shirt, drawers, etc.

LUCETTA.
Hold, sir, put out the light, it may betray us else.

BLUNT.
Anything, I need no other light but that of thine eyes! —'Sheartlikins, there I think I had it.

Puts out the candle; the bed descends [presumably through a trap door]; he gropes about to find it.

Why—why—where am I got? What, not yet? Where are you sweetest?Ah, the rogue's silent now—a pretty love-trick this. How she'll laugh at me anon!—You need not, my dear rogue! You need not! I'm all on fire already. Come, come, now call me in pity.—Sure I'm enchanted! I have been round the chamber and can find neither woman nor bed. I locked the door. I'm sure she cannot go that way, or if she could, the bed could not.—Enough, enough, my pretty wanton, do not carry the jest too far— (*Lights on a trap and is let down.*) Hah, betrayed! Dogs! Rogues! Pimps! Help! Help!

Enter Lucetta, Phillippo, and Sancho with a light.

PHILLIPPO.
Ha, ha, ha, he's dispatched finely.

LUCETTA.
Now, sir, had I been coy, we had missed of this booty.

PHILLIPPO.
Nay, when I saw't was a substantial fool, I was mollified; but when you dote upon a serenading coxcomb, upon a face, fine clothes, and a lute, it makes me rage.

LUCETTA.
You know I was never guilty of that folly, my dear Phillippo, but with yourself. But come, let's see what we have got by this.

PHILLIPPO.
A rich coat! Sword and hat—these breeches, too, are well lined. See here, a gold watch! a purse—hah! Gold! at least two hundred pistoles! a bunch of diamond rings! and one with the family arms! a gold box—with a medal of his king! and his lady mother's picture! These were sacred relics, believe me. See, the waistband of his breeches have a mine of gold! Old Queen Bess's,[42] we have a quarrel* to her ever since eighty-eight,[43] and may therefore justify the theft; the Inquisition might have committed it.

LUCETTA.
See, a bracelet of bowed[44] gold! These his sisters tied about his arm at parting. But well—for all this, I fear his being a stranger may make a noise and hinder our trade with them hereafter.

PHILLIPPO.
That's our security; he is not only a stranger to us, but to the country too. The common shore* into which he is descended, thou knowst conducts him into another street, which this light will hinder him from ever finding again. He knows neither your name, nor that of the street where your house is, nay, nor the way to his own lodgings.

---

[42] old Queen Bess] Queen Elizabeth I, who reigned from 1558-1603

[43] eighty-eight] 1588, year of the defeat of the Spanish Armada

[44] bowed] bent, braided

LUCETTA.

And art not thou an unmerciful rogue! not to afford him one night for all this? I should not have been such a Jew.

PHILLIPPO.

Blame me not, Lucetta, to keep as much of thee as I can to myself. Come, that thought makes me wanton! Let's to bed!—Sancho, lock up these.
This is the fleece which fools do bear,
Designed for witty men to shear.

Exeunt.

Scene iv

The scene changes and discovers Blunt, creeping out of a common shore, his face, etc. all dirty.

BLUNT.

Oh lord! (*Climbing up.*) I am got out at last, and (which is a miracle) without a clue—and now to damning and cursing—but if that would ease me, where shall I begin? With my fortune, myself, or the quean that cozened me? What a dog was I to believe in woman! Oh coxcomb! Ignorant conceited coxcomb! To fancy she could be enamoured with my person! At first sight enamoured! Oh, I'm a cursed puppy! 'Tis plain, "fool" was writ upon my forehead! She perceived it—saw the Essex calf there—for what allurements could there be in this countenance, which I can endure, because I'm acquainted with it—oh, dull, silly dog! To be thus soothed into a cozening! Had I been drunk, I might fondly have credited the young quean! But as I was in my right wits, to be thus cheated confirms it I am a dull, believing, English country fop—but my comrades! Death and the devil! There's the worst of all—then a ballad will be sung tomorrow on the *prado*,[45] to a lousy tune of "The Enchanted 'Squire, and the Annihilated Damsel"—but Frederick, that rogue, and the colonel, will abuse me beyond all Christian patience—had she left me my clothes, I have a bill of exchange at home would have saved my credit—but now all hope is taken from me—well, I'll home (if I can find the way) with this consolation, that I am not the first kind, believing coxcomb; but there are, gallants, many such good natures amongst ye.
And though you've better arts to hide your follies,
Adsheartlikins y'are all as arrant cullies.

Exit.

Scene v. The garden in the night.

Enter Florinda in an undress, with a key and a little box.

FLORINDA.

Well, thus far I'm on my way to happiness. I have got myself free from Callis; my brother, too, I find by yonder light, is got into his cabinet and thinks not of me; I have by good fortune got the key of the garden back door. I'll open it to prevent Belvile's knocking—a little noise will now alarm my brother. Now am I as fearful as a young thief. (*Unlocks the door.*) Hark—what noise is that? Oh, 'twas the wind that played amongst the boughs.—Belvile stays long, methinks—it's time—stay—for fear of a surprise, I'll hide these jewels in yonder jessamine. (*She goes to lay down the box.*)

Enter Willmore drunk.

WILLMORE.

What the devil is become of these fellows, Belvile and Frederick? They promised to stay at the next corner for me, but who the devil knows the corner of a full moon? Now, whereabouts am I? Hah—what have we here? a garden! a very convenient place to sleep in. Hah—what has God sent us here? a female! by this light, a woman! I'm a dog if it be not a very wench!

FLORINDA.

He's come! Hah—who's there?

WILLMORE.

Sweet soul! Let me salute* thy shoestring.

FLORINDA.

'Tis not my Belvile. Good heavens! I know him not.—Who are you, and from whence come you?

WILLMORE.

Prithee, prithee child—not so many questions. Let it suffice I am here, child. Come, come kiss me.

FLORINDA.

Good gods! what luck is mine?

[45] *prado*] field, lawn, meadow (Sp.)

WILLMORE.

Only good luck, child, parlous good luck. Come hither. —'Tis a delicate, shining wench—by this hand she's perfumed and smells like any nosegay.— Prithee, dear soul, let's not play the fool and lose time, precious time, for as Gad shall save me, I'm as honest a fellow as breathes, though I'm a little disguised* at present. Come, I say. Why, thou may'st be free with me, I'll be very secret. I'll not boast who 'twas obliged me, not I—for hang me if I know thy name.

FLORINDA.

Heavens! What a filthy beast is this?

WILLMORE.

I am so, and thou ought'st the sooner to lie with me for that reason—for look you child, there will be no sin in't, because 'twas neither designed nor premeditated. 'Tis pure accident on both sides—that's a certain thing now. Indeed, should I make love to you, and to[e]you vow fidelity—and swear and lie till you believed and yielded—that were to make it wilful fornication, the crying sin of the nation. Thou art therefore (as thou art a good Christian) obliged in conscience to deny me nothing. Now—come be kind without any more idle prating.

FLORINDA.

Oh I am ruined.—Wicked man, unhand me.

WILLMORE.

Wicked! Egad child, a judge, were he young and vigorous and saw those eyes of thine, would know 'twas they gave the first blow—the first provocation. Come prithee, let's lose no time, I say—this is a fine convenient place.

FLORINDA.

Sir, let me go, I conjure you, or I'll call out.

WILLMORE.

Aye, aye, you were best to call witness to see how finely you treat me—do—

FLORINDA.

I'll cry murder! rape! or anything! if you do not instantly let me go.

WILLMORE.

A rape! Come, come, you lie, you baggage, you lie. What, I'll warrant you would fain have the world believe now that you are not so forward as I. No, not you. Why, at this time of night, was your cobweb door set open, dear spider—but to catch flies? Hah—come—or I shall be damnably angry. Why, what a coil is here—

FLORINDA.

Sir, can you think—

WILLMORE.

That you would do't for nothing—oh, oh, I find what you would be at—look, here's a pistole for you—here's a work indeed—here—take it I say—

FLORINDA.

For Heaven's sake, sir, as you're a gentleman—

WILLMORE.

So—now—now—she would be wheedling me for more—what, you will not take it then—you are resolved you will not? Come, come take it or I'll put it up again—for look ye, I never give more. Why how now, mistress, are you so high i'th'mouth a pistole won't down with you? Hah—why, what a work's here—in good time—come, no struggling to be gone—but an y'are good at a dumb wrestle I'm for ye—look ye—I'm for ye— (*She struggles with him.*)

Enter Belvile and Frederick.

BELVILE.

The door is open. A pox of this mad fellow; I'm angry that we've lost him; I durst have sworn he had followed us.

FREDERICK.

But you were so hasty, Colonel, to be gone.

FLORINDA.

Help! Help! Murder! Help—oh, I am ruined.

BELVILE.

Hah! Sure that's Florinda's voice. (*Comes up to them.*) A man!—Villain, let go that lady!

Willmore turns and draws, Frederick interposes.

FLORINDA.

Belvile! (*A noise.*) Heavens! My brother too is coming, and 'twill be impossible to escape.— Belvile, I conjure you to walk under my chamber window, from whence I'll give you some instructions what to do. This rude man has undone us.

Exit.

WILLMORE.
Belvile!

Enter Pedro, Stephano, and other servants with lights.

PEDRO.
I'm betrayed! Run, Stephano, and see if Florinda be safe.

Exit Stephano.

So, whoe'er they be, all is not well. I'll to Florinda's chamber.

They fight and Pedro's party beats 'em out. Going out, meets Stephano.

STEPHANO.
You need not, sir; the poor lady's fast asleep and thinks no harm. I would not awake her, sir, for fear of frighting her with your danger.

PEDRO.
I'm glad she's there.—Rascals, how came the garden door open?

STEPHANO.
That question comes too late, sir; some of my fellow servants masquerading, I'll warrant.

PEDRO.
Masquerading! a lewd custom to debauch our youth. There's something more in this than I imagine.

Exeunt.

Scene vi. Scene changes to the street.

Enter Belvile in rage, Frederick holding him, and Willmore melancholy.

WILLMORE.
Why, how the devil should I know Florinda?

BELVILE.
A plague of your ignorance! If it had not been Florinda, must you be a beast? a brute? a senseless swine?

WILLMORE.
Well, sir, you see I am endued with patience—I can bear—though egad, y'are very free with me, methinks. I was in good hopes the quarrel* would have been on my side, for so uncivilly interrupting me.

BELVILE.
Peace, brute! whilst thou'rt safe.—Oh, I'm distracted.

WILLMORE.
Nay, nay, I'm an unlucky dog, that's certain.

BELVILE.
Ah, curse upon the star that ruled my birth! or whatsoever other influence that makes me still* so wretched.

WILLMORE.
Thou break'st my heart with these complaints. There is no star in fault, no influence but sack,* the cursed sack I drunk.

FREDERICK.
Why, how the devil came you so drunk?

WILLMORE.
Why, how the devil came you so sober?

BELVILE.
A curse upon his thin skull, he was always beforehand that way.

FREDERICK.
Prithee, dear Colonel, forgive him, he's sorry for his fault.

BELVILE.
He's always so after he has done a mischief—a plague on all such brutes.

WILLMORE.
By this light, I took her for an arrant harlot.

BELVILE.
Damn your debauched opinion! Tell me sot, had'st thou so much sense and light about thee to distinguish her woman, and could'st not see something about her face and person to strike an awful reverence into thy soul?

WILLMORE.
Faith no, I considered her as mere* a woman as I could wish.

BELVILE.
'Sdeath,* I have no patience.—Draw, or I'll kill you.

WILLMORE.
Let that alone till tomorrow, and if I set not all right again, use your pleasure.

BELVILE.
Tomorrow! Damn it.
The spiteful light will lead me to no happiness.

Tomorrow is Antonio's and perhaps
Guides him to my undoing. Oh, that I could meet
This rival! This pow'rful fortunate!

WILLMORE.
What then?

BELVILE.
Let thy own reason, or my rage, instruct thee.

WILLMORE.
I shall be finely informed, then, no doubt. Hear me, Colonel—hear me—show me the man and I'll do his business.

BELVILE.
I know him no more than thou, or if I did, I should not need thy aid.

WILLMORE.
This, you say, is Angellica's house. I promised the kind baggage to lie with her tonight. (*Offers* to go in.*)

Enter Antonio and his page. Antonio knocks on the hilt of's sword.

ANTONIO.
You paid the thousand crowns I directed?

PAGE.
To the lady's old woman, sir, I did.

WILLMORE.
Who the devil have we here!

BELVILE.
I'll now plant myself under Florinda's window, and if I find no comfort there, I'll die.

Exeunt Belvile and Frederick. Enter Moretta.

MORETTA.
Page!

PAGE.
Here's my lord.

WILLMORE.
How is this! a picaroon going to board my frigate? Here's one chase gun[46] for you.

Drawing his sword, jostles Antonio who turns and draws. They fight, Antonio falls.

MORETTA.
Oh bless us! We're all undone! (*Runs in and shuts the door.*)

[46] chase gun] swivel gun on bow or stern used in pursuit

PAGE.
Help! Murder!

Belvile returns at the noise of the fighting.

BELVILE.
Hah! The mad rogue's engaged in some unlucky adventure again.

Enter two or three masqueraders.

MASQUERADERS.
Hah! A man killed!

WILLMORE.
How! a man killed! Then I'll go home to sleep.

Puts up and reels out. Exeunt masqueraders another way.

BELVILE.
Who should it be! Pray Heaven the rogue is safe, for all my quarrel* to him.

As Belvile is groping about, enter an officer and six soldiers.

SOLDIER.
Who's there?

OFFICER.
So here's one dispatched.—Secure the murderer.

Soldiers seize on Belvile.

BELVILE.
Do not mistake my charity for murder!
I came to his assistance.

OFFICER.
That shall be tried, sir.—St. Jago,[47] swords drawn in Carnival time! (*Goes to Antonio.*)

ANTONIO.
Thy hand, prithee.

OFFICER.
Hah! Don Antonio!—Look well to the villain there.—How is it, sir?

ANTONIO.
I'm hurt.

BELVILE.
Has my humanity made me a criminal?

OFFICER.
Away with him.

[47] St. Jago] Santiago (St. James the Apostle), patron saint of Spain

BELVILE.

What a cursed chance is this!

Exeunt soldiers with Belvile.

ANTONIO.

This is the man that has set upon me twice.—(*To the officer.*) Carry him to my apartment, till you have farther orders from me.

Exit Antonio led.

Act IV, scene i. A fine room.

Discovers Belvile as by dark alone.

BELVILE.

When shall I be weary of railing on Fortune, who is resolved never to turn with smiles upon me? Two such defeats in one night none but the devil and that mad rogue could have contrived to have plagued me with. I am here a prisoner—but where, Heaven knows—and if there be murder done, I can soon decide[48] the fate of a stranger in a nation without mercy. Yet this is nothing to the torture my soul bows with when I think of losing my fair, my dear, Florinda.—Hark, my door opens—a light—a man—and seems of quality*—armed too! Now shall I die like a dog without defense.

Enter Antonio in a nightgown with a light; his arm in a scarf, and a sword under his arm. He sets the candle on the table.*

ANTONIO.

Sir, I come to know what injuries I have done you that could provoke you to so mean an action as to attack me basely, without allowing time for my defense?

BELVILE.

Sir, for a man in my circumstances to plead innocence would look like fear, but view me well, and you will find no marks of coward on me, nor anything that betrays that brutality you accuse me with.

ANTONIO.

In vain, sir, you impose upon my sense.
You are not only he who drew on me last night,
But yesterday before the same house, that of
Angellica.
Yet there is something in your face and mien
That makes me wish I were mistaken.

BELVILE.

I own I fought today in the defense of a friend of mine with whom you (if you're the same) and your party were first engaged.
Perhaps you think this crime enough to kill me,
But if you do, I cannot fear you'll do it basely.

ANTONIO.

No, sir, I'll make you fit for a defense with this. (*Gives him the sword.*)

BELVILE.

This gallantry surprises me—nor know I how to use this present, sir, against a man so brave.

ANTONIO.

You shall not need.
For know, I come to snatch you from a danger
That is decreed against you:
Perhaps your life or long imprisonment;
And 'twas with so much courage you offended,
I cannot see you punished.

BELVILE.

How shall I pay this generosity?

ANTONIO.

It had been safer to have killed another
Than have attempted me.
To show your danger, sir, I'll let you know my
quality;
And 'tis the viceroy's son whom you have wounded.

BELVILE.

The viceroy's son! (*Aside.*)
Death and confusion! Was this plague reserved
To complete all the rest? Obliged by him!
The man of all the world I would destroy.

ANTONIO.

You seem disordered, sir.

BELVILE.

Yes, trust me, sir, I am, and 'tis with pain
That man receives such bounties
Who wants the pow'r to pay 'em back again.

ANTONIO.

To gallant spirits 'tis indeed uneasy;
But you may quickly overpay me, sir.

BELVILE. (*Aside.*)

Then I am well.—Kind Heav'n, but set us even,
That I may fight with him and keep my honor safe.

[48] decide] determine

—Oh, I'm impatient, sir, to be discounting
The mighty debt I owe you. Command me quickly—

ANTONIO.
I have a quarrel* with a rival, sir,
About the maid we love.

BELVILE. (*Aside.*)
Death, 'tis Florinda he means—
That thought destroys my reason,
And I shall kill him—

ANTONIO.
My rival, sir,
Is one has all the virtues man can boast of.

BELVILE. (*Aside.*)
Death! Who should this be?

ANTONIO.
He challenged me to meet him on the Molo
As soon as day appeared; but last night's quarrel*
Has made my arm unfit to guide a sword.

BELVILE.
I apprehend you, sir; you'd have me kill the man
That lays a claim to the maid you speak of.
I'll do't—I'll fly to do't!

ANTONIO.
Sir, do you know her?

BELVILE.
No, sir, but 'tis enough she is admired by you.

ANTONIO.
Sir, I shall rob you of the glory on't,
For you must fight under my name and dress.

BELVILE.
That opinion must be strangely obliging that makes
You think I can personate the brave Antonio,
Whom I can but strive to imitate.

ANTONIO.
You say too much to my advantage.
Come, sir, the day appears that calls you forth.
Within, sir, is the habit.

Exit Antonio.

BELVILE.
Fantastic Fortune, thou deceitful light,
That cheats the wearied traveller by night,
Though on a precipice each step you tread,
I am resolved to follow where you lead.

Exit.

Scene ii. The Molo.

Enter Florinda and Callis in masks with Stephano.

FLORINDA. (*Aside.*)
I'm dying with my fears; Belvile's not coming as I expected under my window makes me believe that all those fears are true.—
Canst thou not tell with whom my brother fights?

STEPHANO.
No, madam, they were both in masquerade. I was by when they challenged one another, and they had decided the quarrel* then, but were prevented by some cavaliers, which made 'em put it off till now—but I am sure 'tis about you they fight.

FLORINDA. (*Aside.*)
Nay, then 'tis with Belvile, for what other lover have I that dares fight for me, except Antonio? And he is too much in favor with my brother. If it be he, for whom shall I direct my prayers to heaven?

STEPHANO.
Madam, I must leave you, for if my master see me, I shall be hanged for being your conductor. I escaped narrowly for the excuse I made for you last night i'th'garden.

FLORINDA.
And I'll reward thee for't. Prithee no more.

Exit Stephano. Enter Don Pedro in his masquing habit.

PEDRO.
Antonio's late today; the place will fill, and we may be prevented. (*Walks about.*)

FLORINDA. (*Aside.*)
"Antonio"—sure I heard amiss.

PEDRO.
But who will not excuse a happy lover
When soft fair arms confine the yielding neck,
And the kind whisper languishingly breathes,
"Must you be gone so soon?"
Sure I had dwelt for ever on her bosom.
But stay, he's here.

Enter Belvile dressed in Antonio's clothes.

FLORINDA.
'Tis not Belvile; half my fears are vanished.

PEDRO.
Antonio!

BELVILE. (*Aside.*)
This must be he.—You're early, sir. I do not use to be outdone this way.
PEDRO.
The wretched, sir, are watchful, and 'tis enough
You've the advantage of me in Angellica.
BELVILE. (*Aside.*)
Angellica! Or I've mistook my man or else Antonio.
Can he forget his int'rest in Florinda,
And fight for common prize?
PEDRO.
Come, sir, you know our terms—
BELVILE. (*Aside.*)
By Heav'n not I.—
No talking, I am ready, sir. (*Offers to fight, Florinda runs in.*)
FLORINDA. (*To Belvile.*)
Oh hold! Whoe'er you be, I do conjure you hold!
If you strike here—I die.
PEDRO.
Florinda!
BELVILE. [*Aside.*]
Florinda imploring for my rival!
PEDRO.
Away, this kindness is unseasonable.

Puts her by; they fight; she runs in just as Belvile disarms Pedro.

FLORINDA.
Who are you, sir, that dares deny my prayers?
BELVILE.
Thy prayers destroy him; if thou would'st preserve him,
Do that thou'rt unacquainted with and curse him.

She holds him.

FLORINDA.
By all you hold most dear, by her you love,
I do conjure you, touch him not.
BELVILE.
By her I love!
See—I obey—and at your feet resign
The useless trophy of my victory.

Lays his sword at her feet.

PEDRO.
Antonio, you've done enough to prove you love Florinda.
BELVILE.
Love Florinda! Does Heav'n love adoration, prayer or penitence! Love her! Here, sir—your sword again. (*Snatches up the sword and gives it him.*)
Upon this truth I'll fight my life away.
PEDRO.
No, you've redeemed my sister, and my friendship!

He gives him Florinda and pulls off his vizard to show his face and puts it on again.

BELVILE.
Don Pedro!
PEDRO.
Can you resign your claims to other women,
And give your heart entirely to Florinda?
BELVILE.
Entire! as dying saints' confessions are!
I can delay my happiness no longer.
This minute let me make Florinda mine!
PEDRO.
This minute let it be—no time so proper.
This night my father will arrive from Rome
And possibly may hinder what we purpose!
FLORINDA.
Oh heavens! this minute!

Enter masqueraders and pass over.

BELVILE.
Oh, do not ruin me!
PEDRO.
The place begins to fill, and that we may not be observed, do you walk off to St. Peter's Church, where I will meet you and conclude your happiness.
BELVILE.
I'll meet you there—(*Aside.*) if there be no more saints' churches in Naples.
FLORINDA.
Oh, stay sir, and recall your hasty doom!
Alas, I have not yet prepared my heart
To entertain* so strange a guest.
PEDRO.
Away, this silly* modesty is assumed too late.
(*Pedro talks to Callis this while.*)

BELVILE.
Heaven, madam! What do you do?
FLORINDA.
Do! Despise the man that lays a tyrant's claim
To what he ought to conquer by submission.
BELVILE.
You do not know me. Move a little this way.
(*Draws her aside.*)
FLORINDA.
Yes, you may force me even to the altar,
But not the holy man that offers there
Shall force me to be thine.
BELVILE.
Oh do not lose so blest an opportunity—
See—'tis your Belvile—not Antonio,
Whom your mistaken scorn and anger ruins.
(*Pulls off his vizard.*)
FLORINDA.
Belvile!
Where was my soul it could not meet thy voice
And take this knowledge in?

As they are talking, enter Willmore, finely dressed, and Frederick.

WILLMORE.
No intelligence, no news of Belvile yet! Well, I am the most unlucky rascal in nature. Hah—am I deceived? or is it he? Look, Fred—'tis he—my dear Belvile!

Runs and embraces him. Belvile's vizard falls out on's hand.

BELVILE.
Hell and confusion seize thee!
PEDRO.
Hah! Belvile! I beg your pardon sir.

Takes Florinda from him.

BELVILE.
Nay, touch her not. She's mine by conquest, sir;
I won her by my sword.
WILLMORE.
Didst thou so! And egad, child, we'll keep her by the sword.

Draws on Pedro. Belvile goes between.

BELVILE.
Stand off!
Thou'rt so profanely lewd, so curst by Heaven,
All quarrels* thou espousest must be fatal.
WILLMORE.
Nay, an you be so hot, my valor's coy, and shall be courted when you want it next. (*Puts up his sword.*)
BELVILE. (*To Pedro.*)
You know I ought to claim a victor's right.
But you're the brother to divine Florinda,
To whom I'm such a slave—to purchase her,
I durst not hurt the man she holds so dear.
PEDRO.
'Twas by Antonio's, not by Belvile's sword
This question should have been decided, sir.
I must confess, much to your bravery's due,
Both now, and when I met you last in arms.
But I am nicely punctual in my word,
As men of honor ought, and beg your pardon.
For this mistake another time shall clear.
(*Aside to Florinda as they are going out.*)
This was some plot between you and Belvile.
But I'll prevent you.

Belvile looks after her and begins to walk up and down in rage.

WILLMORE.
Do not be modest now and lose the woman, but if we shall fetch her back so—
BELVILE.
Do not speak to me—
WILLMORE.
Not speak to you? Egad, I'll speak to you, and will be answered, too.
BELVILE.
Will you, sir—
WILLMORE.
I know I've done some mischief, but I'm so dull a puppy, that I'm the son of a whore if I know how, or where—prithee inform my understanding—
BELVILE.
Leave me, I say, and leave me instantly.
WILLMORE.
I will not leave you in this humor*, nor till I know my crime.

BELVILE.
Death, I'll tell you sir—

Draws and runs at Willmore. He runs out, Belvile after him; Frederick interposes. Enter Angellica, Moretta and Sebastian.

ANGELLICA.
Hah—Sebastian—
Is not that Willmore? Haste—haste and bring him back.

FREDERICK.
The colonel's mad—I never saw him thus before. I'll after 'em lest he do some mischief, for I am sure Willmore will not draw on him.

Exit.

ANGELLICA.
I am all rage! my first desires defeated!
For one for aught he knows that has no
Other merit than her quality,
Her being Don Pedro's sister—he loves her!
I know 'tis so—dull, dull, insensible—
He will not see me now though oft invited,
And broke his word last night—false perjured man!
He that but yesterday fought for my favors
And would have made his life a sacrifice
To've gained one night with me
Must now be hired and courted to my arms.

MORETTA.
I told you what would come on't, but Moretta's an old doting fool. Why did you give him five hundred crowns, but to set himself out for other lovers! You should have kept him poor if you had meant to have had any good from him.

ANGELLICA.
Oh, name not such mean trifles; had I given him all
My youth has earned from sin,
I had not lost a thought, nor sigh upon't.
But I have given him my eternal rest,
My whole repose, my future joys, my heart!
My virgin heart, Moretta! Oh, 'tis gone!

MORETTA.
Curse on him, here he comes; how fine she has made him too.

Enter Willmore and Sebastian; Angellica turns and walks away.

WILLMORE.
How now, turned shadow!
Fly when I pursue and follow when I fly! (*Sings.*)
Stay, gentle shadow of my dove
And tell me ere I go,
Whether the substance may not prove
A fleeting thing like you.

As she turns she looks on him.

There's a soft kind look remaining yet.

ANGELLICA.
Well sir, you may be gay; all happiness, all joys, pursue you still. Fortune's your slave and gives you every hour choice of new hearts and beauties, till you are cloyed with the repeated bliss which others vainly languish for. (*Turns away in rage.*) But know, false man, that I shall be revenged.

WILLMORE.
So, gad, there are of those faint-hearted lovers whom such a sharp lesson next their hearts would make as impotent as fourscore. Pox o' this whining. My business is to laugh and love. A pox on't, I hate your sullen lover. A man shall lose as much time to put you in humor now, as would serve to gain a new woman.

ANGELLICA.
I scorn to cool that fire I cannot raise,
Or do the drudgery of your virtuous mistress.

WILLMORE.
A virtuous mistress! Death, what a thing thou hast found out for me! Why, what the devil should I do with a virtuous woman? a sort of ill-natured creatures, that take a pride to torment a lover. Virtue is but an infirmity in woman, a disease that renders even the handsome ungrateful; whilst the ill-favored, for want of solicitations and address, only fancy themselves so. I have lain with a woman of quality,* who has all the while been railing at whores.

ANGELLICA.
I will not answer for your mistress's virtue,
Though she be young enough to know no guilt;
And I could wish you would persuade my heart
'Twas the two hundred thousand crowns you courted.

WILLMORE.
Two hundred thousand crowns! What story's this?
What trick? What woman? Hah!

ANGELLICA.
How strange you make it; have you forgot the creature you entertained on the piazza last night?

WILLMORE. (*Aside.*)
Hah! My Gypsy worth two hundred thousand crowns! Oh, how I long to be with her. Pox, I knew she was of quality.*

ANGELLICA.
False man! I see my ruin in thy face.
How many vows you breathed upon my bosom,
Never to be unjust—have you forgot so soon?

WILLMORE.
Faith no, I was just coming to repeat 'em—but here's a humor indeed would make a man a saint. (*Aside.*) Would she would be angry enough to leave me and command me not to wait on her.

Enter Hellena dressed in man's clothes.

HELLENA.
This must be Angellica! I know it by her mumping* matron here. Aye, aye, 'tis she! My mad captain's with her too, for all his swearing—how this unconstant humor* makes me love him!—Pray, good grave gentlewoman, is not this Angellica?

MORETTA.
My too young sir, it is.—I hope 'tis one from Don Antonio. (*Goes to Angellica.*)

HELLENA. (*Aside.*)
Well, something I'll do to vex him for this.

ANGELLICA.
I will not speak with him; am I in humor to receive a lover?

WILLMORE.
Not speak with him! Why, I'll be gone and wait your idler minutes. Can I show less obedience to the thing I love so fondly? (*Offers to go.*)

ANGELLICA.
A fine excuse this! Stay—

WILLMORE.
And hinder your advantage! Should I repay your bounties so ungratefully?

ANGELLICA.
Come hither, boy—that I may let you see
How much above the advantages you name
I prize one minute's joy with you.

WILLMORE.
Oh, you destroy me with this endearment. (*Impatient to be gone.*) Death! How shall I get away?—Madam, 'twill not be fit I should be seen with you; besides, it will not be convenient—and I've a friend—that's dangerously sick.

ANGELLICA.
I see you're impatient—yet you shall stay.

WILLMORE. (*Aside, and walks about impatiently.*)
And miss my assignation with my Gypsy.

Moretta brings Hellena, who addresses herself to Angellica.

HELLENA.
Madam, you'll hardly pardon my intrusion
When you shall know my business,
And I'm too young to tell my tale with art;
But there must be a wondrous store of goodness,
Where so much beauty dwells.

ANGELLICA.
A pretty advocate, whoever sent thee.
Prithee proceed—(*To Willmore, who is stealing off.*) Nay, sir, you shall not go.

WILLMORE. (*Aside.*)
Then I shall lose my dear Gypsy for ever. Pox on't, she stays me out of spite.

HELLENA.
I am related to a lady, madam,
Young, rich, and nobly born, but has the fate
To be in love with a young English gentleman.
Strangely she loves him, at first sight she loved him,
But did adore him when she heard him speak;
For he, she said, had charms in every word,
That failed not to surprise, to wound and conquer.

WILLMORE. (*Aside.*)
Hah! Egad, I hope this concerns me.

ANGELLICA. [*Aside.*]
'Tis my false man, he means—would he were gone.
This praise will raise his pride and ruin me— (*To Willmore.*) Well
Since you are so impatient to be gone,
I will release you, sir.

WILLMORE. (*Aside.*)
Nay, then, I'm sure 'twas me he spoke of; this cannot be the effects of kindness in her.—No, madam, I've considered better on't and will not give you cause of jealousy.

ANGELLICA.
But, sir, I've—business, that—
WILLMORE.
This shall not do; I know 'tis but to try me.
ANGELLICA.
Well, to your story, boy— (*Aside.*) though 'twill undo me.
HELLENA.
With this addition to his other beauties,
He won her unresisting tender heart.
He vowed, and sighed, and swore he loved her dearly;
And she believed the cunning flatterer
And thought herself the happiest maid alive.
Today was the appointed time by both
To consummate their bliss,
The virgin, altar, and the priest were dressed
And whilst she languished for th'expected bridegroom,
She heard he paid his broken vows to you.
WILLMORE.
So, this is some dear rogue that's in love with me and this way lets me know it, or if it be not me, he means someone whose place I may supply.
ANGELLICA.
Now I perceive
The cause of thy impatience to be gone
And all the business of this glorious dress.
WILLMORE.
Damn the young prater, I know not what he means.
HELLENA.
Madam,
In your fair eyes I read too much concern
To tell my farther business.
ANGELLICA.
Prithee, sweet youth, talk on, thou mayest perhaps
Raise here a storm that may undo my passion,
And then I'll grant thee anything.
HELLENA.
Madam, 'tis to entreat you (oh unreasonable)
You would not see this stranger;
For if you do, she vows you are undone,
Though nature never made a man so excellent,
And sure he'd been a god, but for inconstancy.
WILLMORE. (*Aside.*)
Ah, rogue, how finely he's instructed! 'Tis plain; some woman that has seen me *en passant.*
ANGELLICA.
Oh, I shall burst with jealousy! Do you know the man you speak of?
HELLENA.
Yes, madam, he used to be in buff and scarlet.
ANGELLICA. (*To Willmore.*)
Thou, false as hell, what canst thou say to this?
WILLMORE.
By Heaven— (*He walks about, they follow.*)
ANGELLICA.
Hold, do not damn thyself—
HELLENA.
Nor hope to be believed.
ANGELLICA.
Oh perjured man!
Is't thus you pay my generous passion back?
HELLENA.
Why would you, sir, abuse my lady's faith?
ANGELLICA.
And use me so unhumanely.
HELLENA.
A maid so young, so innocent—
WILLMORE.
Ah, young devil.
ANGELLICA.
Dost thou know thy life is in my power?
HELLENA.
Or think my lady cannot be revenged?
WILLMORE. (*Aside.*)
So, so, the storm comes finely on.
ANGELLICA.
Now thou art silent, guilt has struck thee dumb.
Oh, hadst thou still been so, I'd lived in safety.
(*She turns away and weeps.*)
WILLMORE. (*Aside to Hellena; looks toward Angellica to watch her turning and as she comes towards them he meets her.*)
Sweetheart, the lady's name and house—quickly, I'm impatient to be with her.
HELLENA. (*Aside.*)
So, now is he for another woman.
WILLMORE.
The impudent'st young thing in nature,
I cannot persuade him out of his error, madam.
ANGELLICA.
I know he's in the right—yet thou'st a tongue

That would persuade him to deny his faith. (*In rage walks away.*)

WILLMORE.
Her name, her name, dear boy— (*Said softly to Hellena.*)

HELLENA.
Have you forgot it, sir?

WILLMORE. (*Aside.*)
Oh, I perceive he's not to know I am a stranger to this lady.—Yes, yes, I do know—but I have forgot the—

Angellica turns.

—By heaven such early confidence I never saw.

ANGELLICA.
Did I not charge you with this mistress, sir?
Which you denied, though I beheld your perjury.
This little generosity of thine has rendered back my heart. (*Walks away.*)

WILLMORE.
So, you have made sweet work here, my little mischief; look your lady be kind and good-natured now, or I shall have but a cursed bargain on't.

Angellica turns toward them.

—The rogue's bred up to mischief;
Art thou so great a fool to credit him?

ANGELLICA.
Yes, I do, and you in vain impose upon me.
—Come hither, boy. Is not this he you spake of?

HELLENA.
I think—it is; I cannot swear, but I vow he has just such another lying lover's look. (*Hellena looks in his face, he gazes on her.*)

WILLMORE. (*Aside.*)
Hah! Do not I know that face? By Heaven, my little Gypsy! what a dull dog was I! Had I but looked that way I'd known her. Are all my hopes of a new woman banished?—Egad, if I do not fit thee for this, hang me.— Madam, I have found out the plot.

HELLENA. [*Aside.*]
Oh lord, what does he say? Am I discovered now?

WILLMORE.
Do you see this young spark here?

HELLENA. [*Aside.*]
He'll tell her who I am.

WILLMORE.
Who do you think this is?

HELLENA. [*Aside.*]
Aye, aye, he does know me.—Nay, dear Captain! I am undone if you discover me.

WILLMORE.
Nay, nay, no cogging; she shall know what a precious* mistress I have.

HELLENA.
Will you be such a devil?

WILLMORE.
Nay, nay, I'll teach you to spoil sport you will not make.—This small ambassador comes not from a person of quality,* as you imagine and he says, but from a very arrant Gypsy, the talkingest, pratingest, cantingest little animal thou ever saw'st.

ANGELLICA.
What news you tell me, that's the thing I mean.

HELLENA. (*Aside.*)
Would I were well off the place; if ever I go a captain-hunting again—

WILLMORE.
Mean that thing? that Gypsy thing? Thou may'st as well be jealous of thy monkey or parrot, as of her; a German motion* were worth a dozen of her, and a dream were a better enjoyment, a creature of a constitution fitter for heaven than man.

HELLENA. (*Aside.*)
Though I'm sure he lies, yet this vexes me.

ANGELLICA.
You are mistaken, she's a Spanish woman
Made up of no such dull materials.

WILLMORE.
Materials, egad, an she be made of any that will either dispense or admit of love, I'll be bound to continence.

HELLENA. (*Aside to him.*)
Unreasonable man, do you think so?

WILLMORE.
You may return, my little brazen head,[49] and tell your lady that till she be handsome enough to be beloved, or I dull enough to be religious, there will be small hopes of me.

---

[49] brazen head] a brazen (brass) head which can speak or prophesy

ANGELLICA.
Did you not promise then to marry her?

WILLMORE.
Not I, by Heaven.

ANGELLICA.
You cannot undeceive my fears and torments till you have vowed you will not marry her.

HELLENA. (*Aside.*)
If he swears that, he'll be revenged on me indeed for all my rogueries.

ANGELLICA.
I know what arguments you'll bring up against me—fortune, and honor—

WILLMORE.
Honor, I tell you, I hate it in your sex, and those that fancy themselves possessed of that foppery are the most impertinently troublesome of all womankind and will transgress nine commandments to keep one, and to satisfy your jealousy, I swear—

HELLENA. (*Aside to him.*)
Oh, no swearing, dear Captain.

WILLMORE.
If it were possible I should ever be inclined to marry, it should be some kind young sinner, one that has generosity enough to give a favor handsomely to one that can ask it discreetly, one that has wit enough to manage an intrigue of love—oh, how civil such a wench is, to a man that does her the honor to marry her.

ANGELLICA.
By Heaven, there's no faith in anything he says.

Enter Sebastian.

SEBASTIAN.
Madam, Don Antonio—

ANGELLICA.
Come hither.

HELLENA. [*Aside.*]
Hah! Antonio! He may be coming hither, and he'll certainly discover me. I'll therefore retire without a ceremony.

Exit Hellena.

ANGELLICA.
I'll see him; get my coach ready.

SEBASTIAN.
It waits you, madam.

WILLMORE.
This is lucky.—What, madam, now I may be gone and leave you to the enjoyment of my rival?

ANGELLICA.
Dull man, that canst not see how ill, how poor,
That false dissimulation looks. Be gone,
And never let me see thy cozening face again,
Lest I relapse and kill thee.

WILLMORE.
Yes, you can spare me now— Farewell, till you're in better humor.—I'm glad of this release—
Now for my Gypsy:
For though to worse we change, yet still we find
New joys, new charms, in a new miss that's kind.

Exit Willmore.

ANGELLICA.
He's gone, and in this ague of my soul,
The shivering fit returns;
Oh, with what willing haste he took his leave,
As if the longed-for minute were arrived
Of some blest assignation.
In vain I have consulted all my charms,
In vain this beauty prized, in vain believed
My eyes could kindle any lasting fires.
I had forgot my name, my infamy,
And the reproach that honor lays on those
That dare pretend a sober passion here.
Nice* reputation, though it leave behind
More virtues than inhabit where that dwells,
Yet that once gone, those virtues shine no more.
Then since I am not fit to be beloved,
I am resolved to think on a revenge
On him that soothed me thus to my undoing.

Exeunt.

Scene iii. A street.

Enter Florinda and Valeria in habits different from what they have been seen in.

FLORINDA.
We're happily escaped, and yet I tremble still.

VALERIA.
A lover and fear! Why, I am but half an one, and

yet I have courage for any attempt. Would Hellena were here, I would fain have had her as deep in this mischief as we; she'll fare but ill else, I doubt.

FLORINDA.
She pretended a visit to the Augustine nuns, but I believe some other design carried her out. Pray Heaven we light on her. Prithee, what didst do with Callis?

VALERIA.
When I saw no reason would do good on her, I followed her into the wardrobe, and as she was looking for something in a great chest, I toppled her in by the heels, snatched the key of the apartment where you were confined, locked her in, and left her bawling for help.

FLORINDA.
'Tis well you resolve to follow my fortunes, for thou darest never appear at home again after such an action.

VALERIA.
That's according as the young stranger and I shall agree. But to our business: I delivered your letter, your note to Belvile, when I got out under pretence of going to mass. I found him at his lodging, and believe me it came seasonably, for never was a man in so desperate a condition. I told him of your resolution of making your escape today if your brother would be absent long enough to permit you; if not, to die rather than be Antonio's.

FLORINDA.
Thou shouldst have told him I was confined to my chamber upon my brother's suspicion that the business on the Molo was a plot laid between him and I.

VALERIA.
I said all this, and told him your brother was now gone to his devotion, and he resolves to visit every church till he find him and not only undeceive him in that, but caress him so as shall delay his return home.

FLORINDA.
Oh heavens! He's here, and Belvile with him too.

They put on their vizards. Enter Don Pedro, Belvile, Willmore; Belvile and Don Pedro seeming in serious discourse.

VALERIA.
Walk boldly by them, and I'll come at distance, lest he suspect us. (*She walks by them, and looks back on them.*)

WILLMORE.
Hah! A woman, and of an excellent mien.

PEDRO.
She throws a kind look back on you.

WILLMORE.
Death, 'tis a likely wench, and that kind look shall not be cast away—I'll follow her.

BELVILE.
Prithee do not.

WILLMORE.
Do not? By heavens, to the antipodes with such an invitation.

She goes out, and Willmore follows her.

BELVILE.
'Tis a mad fellow for a wench.

Enter Frederick.

FREDERICK.
Oh Colonel, such news!

BELVILE.
Prithee what?

FREDERICK.
News that will make you laugh in spite of Fortune.

BELVILE.
What, Blunt has had some damned trick put upon him: Cheated, banged or clapped?[50]

FREDERICK.
Cheated sir, rarely cheated of all but his shirt and drawers. The unconscionable whore, too, turned him out before consummation, so that traversing the streets at midnight, the watch found him in this fresco, and conducted him home. By Heaven, 'tis such a sight, and yet I durst as well been hanged as laugh at him or pity him; he beats all that do but ask him a question, and is in such an humor.

PEDRO.
Who is't has met with this ill usage, sir?

50 clapped] hit, struck; also, to get the clap (venereal disease)

BELVILE.
A friend of ours whom you must see for mirth's sake. (*Aside.*) I'll employ him to give Florinda time for an escape.

PEDRO.
What is he?

BELVILE.
A young countryman of ours, one that has been educated at so plentiful a rate, he yet ne'er knew the want of money, and 'twill be a great jest to see how simply he'll look without it. For my part, I'll lend him none, an the rogue know not how to put on a borrowing face and ask first; I'll let him see how good 'tis to play our parts whilst I play his.— Prithee Frederick, do you go home and keep him in that posture till we come.

Exeunt. Enter Florinda from the farther end of the scene, looking behind her.

FLORINDA.
I am followed still— Hah! my brother too, advancing this way. Good heavens, defend me from being seen by him.

She goes off. Enter Willmore, and after him Valeria, at a little distance.

WILLMORE.
Ah! There she sails; she looks back as she were willing to be boarded. I'll warrant her prize.[51]

He goes out, Valeria following. Enter Hellena, just as he goes out, with a page.

HELLENA.
Hah, is not that my captain that has a woman in chase? 'Tis not Angellica. Boy, follow those people at a distance, and bring me an account where they go in.—I'll find his haunts and plague him everywhere.—Hah, my brother—

Exit page; Belvile, Willmore, Pedro cross the stage; Hellena runs off.

[51] sails ... boarded ... prize] In sea battles and piracy, captured ships, called prizes, were seized as the property of those who boarded them.

Scene iv. Scene changes to another street.

Enter Florinda.

FLORINDA.
What shall I do, my brother now pursues me. Will no kind pow'r protect me from his tyranny? Hah, here's a door open; I'll venture in, since nothing can be worse than to fall into his hands. My life and honor are at stake, and my necessity has no choice.

She goes in. Enter Valeria and Hellena's page peeping after Florinda.

PAGE.
Here she went in; I shall remember this house.

Exit Boy.

VALERIA.
This is Belvile's lodging; she's gone in as readily as if she knew it.—Hah! here's that mad fellow again. I dare not venture in. I'll watch my opportunity.

Goes aside. Enter Willmore, gazing about him.

WILLMORE.
I have lost her hereabouts. Pox on't, she must not scape me so. (*Goes out.*)

Scene v. Blunt's chamber.

Blunt discovered sitting on a couch in his shirt and drawers, reading.

BLUNT.
So, now my mind's a little at peace, since I have resolved revenge. A pox on this tailor though, for not bringing home the clothes I bespoke. And a pox of all poor cavaliers, a man can never keep a spare suit for 'em, and I shall have these rogues come in and find me naked. And then I'm undone. But I'm resolved to arm myself—the rascals shall not insult over me too much. (*Puts on an old rusty sword and buff belt.*) Now, how like a morris dancer I am equipped. A fine lady-like whore to cheat me thus, without affording me a kindness for my money. A pox light on her, I shall never be reconciled to the sex more; she has made me as faithless as a physician, as uncharitable as a

churchman, and as ill-natured as a poet. Oh, how I'll use all womankind hereafter! What would I give to have one of 'em within my reach now! Any mortal thing in petticoats, kind Fortune, send me, and I'll forgive thy last night's malice. Here's a cursed book too (a warning to all young travellers) that can instruct me how to prevent such mischiefs now 'tis too late; well, 'tis a rare convenient thing to read a little now and then, as well as hawk and hunt. (*Sits down again and reads.*)

Enter to him Florinda.

FLORINDA.

This house is haunted sure; 'tis well furnished and no living thing inhabits it.—Hah, a man! Heavens, how he's attired! Sure 'tis some ropedancer or fencing master;[52] I tremble now for fear, and yet I must venture now to speak to him.—Sir, if I may not interrupt your meditations—

He starts up and gazes.

BLUNT.

Hah, what's here! Are my wishes granted? and is not that a she creature? 'Sheartlikins, 'tis! What wretched thing art thou—hah!

FLORINDA.

Charitable sir, you've told yourself already what I am, a very wretched maid, forced by a strange unlucky accident to seek safety here,
And must be ruined, if you do not grant it.

BLUNT.

Ruined! Is there any ruin so inevitable as that which now threatens thee? Dost thou know, miserable woman, into what den of mischiefs thou art fallen? what abyss of confusion—hah! Dost not see something in my looks that frights thy guilty soul and makes thee wish to change that shape of woman for any humble animal or devil? For those were safer for thee, and less mischievous.

FLORINDA.

Alas, what mean you, sir? I must confess, your looks have something in 'em makes me fear, but I beseech you, as you seem a gentleman, pity a harmless virgin that takes your house for sanctuary.

BLUNT.

Talk on, talk on, and weep too, till my faith return. Do, flatter me out of my senses again—a harmless virgin with a pox, as much one as t'other, 'sheartlikins. Why, what the devil, can I not be safe in my house for you, not in my chamber, nay, even being naked too cannot secure me; this is an impudence greater than has invaded me yet. (*Pulls her rudely.*) Come, no resistance.

FLORINDA.

Dare you be so cruel?

BLUNT.

Cruel? 'Sheartlikins, as a galley slave, or a Spanish whore. Cruel? Yes, I will kiss and beat thee all over, kiss and see thee all over; thou shalt lie with me too, not that I care for the enjoyment, but to let thee see I have ta'en deliberated malice to thee and will be revenged on one whore for the sins of another. I will smile and deceive thee, flatter thee, and beat thee, kiss and swear and lie to thee, embrace thee and rob thee, as she did me; fawn on thee and strip thee stark naked; then hang thee out at my window by the heels, with a paper of scurvy verses fastened to thy breast, in praise of damnable women. Come, come along.

FLORINDA.

Alas, sir, must I be sacrificed for the crimes of the most infamous of my sex? I never understood the sins you name.

BLUNT.

Do, persuade the fool you love him, or that one of you can be just or honest; tell me I was not an easy coxcomb, or any strange impossible tale. It will be believed sooner than thy false showers or protestations. A generation of damned hypocrites to flatter my very clothes from my back! Dissembling witches! Are these the returns you make an honest gentleman, that trusts, believes, and loves you? But if I be not even with you—(*Pulls her again.*) Come along—or I shall—

Enter Frederick.

FREDERICK.

Hah! What's here to do?

[52] ropedancer or fencing-master] like a morris dancer, a ropedancer or fencing master would wear loose, light clothing.

BLUNT.

'Sheartlikins, Fred. I am glad thou art come to be a witness of my dire revenge.

FREDERICK.

What's this, a person of quality* too, who is upon the ramble to supply the defects of some grave impotent husband?

BLUNT.

No, this has another pretence; some very unfortunate accident brought her hither to save a life pursued by I know not who, or why, and forced to take sanctuary here at Fool's Haven. 'Sheartlikins, to me of all mankind for protection? Is the ass to be cajoled again, think ye? No, young one, no prayers or tears shall mitigate my rage; therefore, prepare for both my pleasures of enjoyment and revenge, for I am resolved to make up my loss here on thy body; I'll take it out in kindness and in beating.

FREDERICK.

Now, mistress of mine, what do you think of this?

FLORINDA.

I think he will not—dares not—be so barbarous.

FREDERICK.

Have a care, Blunt, she fetched a deep sigh; she is enamored with thy shirt and drawers. She'll strip thee even of that. There are of her calling such unconscionable baggages, and such dextrous thieves, they'll flay a man and he shall ne'er miss his skin till he feels the cold. There was a countryman of ours robbed of a row of teeth whilst he was a-sleeping, which the jilt made him buy again when he waked. You see, lady, how little reason we have to trust you.

BLUNT.

'Sheartlikins, why this is most abominable.

FLORINDA.

Some such devils there may be, but by all that's holy, I am none such; I entered here to save a life in danger.

BLUNT.

For no goodness, I'll warrant her.

FREDERICK.

Faith, damsel, you had e'en confessed the plain truth, for we are fellows not to be caught twice in the same trap. Look on that wreck, a tight vessel when he set out of haven, well trimmed and laden, and see how a female picaroon of this island of rogues has shattered him, and canst thou hope for any mercy?

BLUNT.

No, no, gentlewoman, come along; 'sheartlikins, we must be better acquainted.—We'll both lie with her, and then let me alone to bang her.

FREDERICK.

I'm ready to serve you in matters of revenge that has a double pleasure in't.

BLUNT.

Well said. You hear, little one, how you are condemned by public vote to the bed within. (*Pulls her.*) There's no resisting your destiny, sweetheart.

FLORINDA.

Stay, sir, I have seen you with Belvile, an English cavalier; for his sake use me kindly. You know him, sir.

BLUNT.

Belvile, why yes, sweeting, we do know Belvile, and wish he were with us now; he's a cormorant at whore and bacon; he'd have a limb or two of thee, my virgin pullet, but 'tis no matter, we'll leave him the bones to pick.

FLORINDA.

Sir, if you have any esteem for that Belvile, I conjure you to treat me with more gentleness; he'll thank you for the justice.

FREDERICK.

Hark ye, Blunt, I doubt we are mistaken in this matter.

FLORINDA.

Sir, if you find me not worth Belvile's care, use me as you please, and that you may think I merit better treatment than you threaten—pray take this present—

Gives him a ring; he looks on it.

BLUNT.

Hum—a diamond! Why, 'tis a wonderful virtue now that lies in this ring, a mollifying virtue; 'sheartlikins, there's more persuasive rhetoric in't than all her sex can utter.

FREDERICK.

I begin to suspect something; and 'twould anger us vilely to be trussed up for a rape upon a maid of quality,* when we only believe we ruffle a harlot.

BLUNT.

Thou art a credulous fellow, but 'sheartlikins, I have no faith yet. Why, my saint prattled as parlously as this does, she gave me a bracelet too, a devil on her, but I sent my man to sell it today for necessaries, and it proved as counterfeit as her vows of love.

FREDERICK.

However, let it reprieve her till we see Belvile.

BLUNT.

That's hard, yet I will grant it.

Enter a servant.

SERVANT.

Oh, sir, the colonel is just come in with his new friend and a Spaniard of quality, and talks of having you to dinner with 'em.

BLUNT.

'Sheartlikins, I'm undone—I would not see 'em for the world. Hark ye, Fred, lock up the wench in your chamber.

FREDERICK.

Fear nothing, madam; whate'er he threatens, you are safe whilst in my hands.

Exeunt Frederick and Florinda.

BLUNT.

And, sirrah, upon your life, say—I am not at home—or that I'm asleep—or—or anything—away—I'll prevent their coming this way.

Locks the door and exeunt.

Act V, scene i. Blunt's Chamber.

After a great knocking as at his chamber door, enter Blunt softly crossing the stage, in his shirt and drawers as before.

[VOICES.] (*Call and knocking within.*)

Ned, Ned Blunt, Ned Blunt.

BLUNT.

The rogues are up in arms. 'Sheartlikins, this villainous Frederick has betrayed me; they have heard of my blessed fortune—

[VOICES.]

Ned Blunt, Ned, Ned—

BELVILE. [*Within.*]

Why, he's dead, sir, without dispute dead, he has not been seen today; let's break open the door—here—boy—

BLUNT.

Hah, break open the door! 'Sheartlikins, that mad fellow will be as good as his word.

BELVILE. [*Within.*]

Boy, bring something to force the door.

A great noise within, at the door again.

BLUNT.

So, now must I speak in my own defense; I'll try what rhetoric will do.—Hold, hold, what do you mean gentlemen, what do you mean?

BELVILE. (*Within.*)

Oh rogue, art alive? Prithee, open the door and convince us.

BLUNT.

Yes, I am alive gentlemen—but at present a little busy.

BELVILE. (*Within.*)

How, Blunt grown a man of business? Come, come, open and let's see this miracle.

BLUNT.

No, no, no, no, gentlemen, 'tis no great business—but—I am—at—my devotion—'sheartlikins, will you not allow a man time to pray?

BELVILE. (*Within.*)

Turned religious! a greater wonder than the first! Therefore, open quickly, or we shall unhinge, we shall.

BLUNT.

This won't do—why hark ye, Colonel, to tell you the plain truth, I am about a necessary affair of life—I have a wench with me—you apprehend me?—The devil's in't if they be so uncivil as to disturb me now.

WILLMORE. [*Within.*]

How, a wench! Nay then, we must enter and partake. No resistance—unless it be your lady of quality,* and then we'll keep our distance.

BLUNT.

So, the business is out.

WILLMORE. [*Within.*]

Come, come, lend's more hands to the door—now heave altogether—so, well done, my boys—(*Breaks open the door.*)

[V.i]

Enter Belvile, Willmore, Frederick, Pedro [and Boy]. Blunt looks simply, they all laugh at him, he lays his hand on his sword, and comes up to Willmore.

BLUNT.

Hark ye sir, laugh out your laugh quickly, d'ye hear, and be gone. I shall spoil your sport else, 'sheartlikins sir, I shall—the jest has been carried on too long. (*Aside.*) A plague upon my tailor.

WILLMORE.

'Sdeath,* how the whore has dressed him. Faith, sir, I'm sorry.

BLUNT.

Are you so, sir; keep't to yourself then, sir, I advise you, d'ye hear, for I can as little endure your pity as his mirth. (*Lays his hand on's sword.*)

BELVILE.

Indeed, Willmore, thou wert a little too rough with Ned Blunt's mistress. Call a person of quality* whore? and one so young, so handsome, and so eloquent—ha, ha, he—

BLUNT.

Hark ye sir, you know me, and know I can be angry; have a care—for, 'sheartlikins, I can fight too—I can, sir—do you mark me? No more—

BELVILE.

Why so peevish, good Ned? Some disappointments I'll warrant. What, did the jealous count her husband return just in the nick?

BLUNT.

Or the devil, sir. (*They laugh.*) D'ye laugh? Look ye settle me a good sober countenance, and that quickly too, or you shall know Ned Blunt is not—

BELVILE.

Not everybody, we know that.

BLUNT.

Not an ass to be laughed at, sir.

WILLMORE.

Unconscionable sinner, to bring a lover so near his happiness, a vigorous, passionate lover, and then not only cheat him of his movables, but his very desires too.

BELVILE.

Ah! Sir, a mistress is a trifle with Blunt. He'll have a dozen the next time he looks abroad. His eyes have charms not to be resisted; there needs no more than to expose that taking person to the view of the fair, and he leads 'em all in triumph.

PEDRO.

Sir, though I'm a stranger to you, I am ashamed at the rudeness of my nation and, could you learn who did it, would assist you to make an example of 'em.

BLUNT.

Why, aye, there's one speaks sense now, and han'somely; and let me tell you, gentlemen, I should not have showed myself like a Jack Pudding,[53] thus to have made you mirth, but that I have revenge within my power. For know, I have got into my possession a female who had better have fallen under any curse than the ruin I design her; 'sheartlikins, she assaulted me here in my own lodgings, and had doubtless committed a rape upon me, had not this sword defended me.

FREDERICK.

I know not that, but o'my conscience, thou had ravished her, had she not redeemed herself with a ring. Let's see't, Blunt. (*Blunt shows the ring.*)

BELVILE. [*Aside.*]

Hah, the ring I gave Florinda, when we exchanged our vows!—Hark ye Blunt— (*Goes to whisper to him.*)

WILLMORE.

No whispering, good Colonel, there's a woman in the case; no whispering.

BELVILE.

Hark ye fool, be advised, and conceal both the ring and the story for your reputation's sake. Do not let people know what despised cullies we English are, to be cheated and abused by one whore, and another rather bribe thee than be kind to thee, is an infamy to our nation.

WILLMORE.

Come, come, where's the wench? We'll see her, let her be what she will; we'll see her.

PEDRO.

Aye, aye, let us see her. I can soon discover whether she be of quality,* or for your diversion.

BLUNT.

She's in Fred's custody.

---

[53] Jack Pudding] a clown or buffoon; clowning assistant to a mountebank or street performer

WILLMORE.
Come, come, the key. (*To Frederick who gives him the key; they are going.*)

BELVILE.
Death, what shall I do?—Stay gentlemen.—Yet if I hinder 'em, I shall discover* all.—Hold, let's go at once. Give me the key.

WILLMORE.
Nay, hold there, Colonel. I'll go first.

FREDERICK.
Nay, no dispute, Ned and I have the propriety of her.

WILLMORE.
Damn propriety. Then we'll draw cuts. (*Belvile goes to whisper Willmore.*) Nay, no corruption, good Colonel. Come, the longest sword carries her—

They all draw, forgetting Don Pedro, being as a Spaniard, had the longest.

BLUNT.
I yield up my interest to you, gentlemen, and that will be revenge sufficient.

WILLMORE. (*To Pedro.*)
The wench is yours— [*Aside.*] Pox of his Toledo,* I had forgot that.

FREDERICK.
Come sir, I'll conduct you to the lady.

Exeunt Frederick and Pedro.

BELVILE. (*Aside.*)
To hinder him will certainly discover* her.—Dost know, dull beast, what mischief thou hast done?

Willmore walking up and down out of humor.

WILLMORE.
Aye, aye, to trust our fortune to lots, a devil on't; 'twas madness, that's the truth on't.

BELVILE.
Oh intolerable sot—

Enter Florinda running masked, Pedro after her; Willmore gazing round her.

FLORINDA. (*Aside.*)
Good Heaven, defend me from discovery.

PEDRO.
'Tis but in vain to fly me, you're fallen to my lot.

BELVILE.
Sure she's undiscovered yet, but now I fear there is no way to bring her off.

WILLMORE.
Why, what a pox; is not this my woman, the same I followed but now?

Pedro talking to Florinda, who walks up and down.

PEDRO.
As if I did not know ye, and your business here.

FLORINDA. (*Aside.*)
Good Heaven, I fear he does indeed—

PEDRO.
Come, pray be kind; I know you meant to be so when you entered here, for these are proper gentlemen.

WILLMORE.
But sir—perhaps the lady will not be imposed upon. She'll choose her man.

PEDRO.
I am better bred, than not to leave her choice free.

Enter Valeria, and is surprised at sight of Don Pedro.

VALERIA. (*Aside.*)
Don Pedro here! There's no avoiding him.

FLORINDA. (*Aside.*)
Valeria! Then I'm undone—

VALERIA. (*To Pedro, running to him.*)
Oh! Have I found you, sir. The strangest accident—if I had breath—to tell it.

PEDRO.
Speak: Is Florinda safe? Hellena well?

VALERIA.
Aye, aye, sir—Florinda—is safe—from any fears of you.

PEDRO.
Why, where's Florinda? Speak—

VALERIA.
Ay, where indeed, sir, I wish I could inform you—but to hold you no longer in doubt—

FLORINDA. (*Aside.*)
Oh, what will she say—

VALERIA.
She's fled away in the habit—of one of her pages, sir—but Callis thinks you may retrieve her yet. If you make haste away, she'll tell you, sir, the rest—

(*Aside.*) if you can find her out.

PEDRO.

Dishonorable girl, she has undone my aim.—Sir, you see my necessity of leaving you, and I hope you'll pardon it; my sister, I know, will make her flight to you; and if she do, I shall expect she should be rendered back.

BELVILE.

I shall consult my love and honor, sir.

Exit Pedro.

FLORINDA. (*To Valeria.*)

My dear preserver, let me embrace thee.

WILLMORE.

What the devil's all this?

BLUNT.

Mystery by this light.

VALERIA.

Come, come, make haste and get yourselves married quickly, for your brother will return again.

BELVILE.

I'm so surprised with fears and joys, so amazed to find you here in safety, I can scarce persuade my heart into a faith of what I see.

WILLMORE.

Hark ye, Colonel, is this that mistress who has cost you so many sighs, and me so many quarrels* with you?

BELVILE.

It is— (*To Florinda.*) Pray give him the honor of your hand.

WILLMORE.

Thus it must be received then. (*Kneels and kisses her hand.*)

And with it give your pardon, too.

FLORINDA.

The friend to Belvile may command me anything.

WILLMORE. (*Aside.*)

Death, would I might; 'tis a surprising beauty.

BELVILE.

Boy, run and fetch a father instantly.

Exit Boy.

FREDERICK.

So, now do I stand like a dog and have not a syllable to plead my own cause with. By this hand, madam, I was never thoroughly confounded before, nor shall I ever more dare look up with confidence, till you are pleased to pardon me.

FLORINDA.

Sir, I'll be reconciled to you on one condition, that you'll follow the example of your friend, in marrying a maid that does not hate you and whose fortune (I believe) will not be unwelcome to you.

FREDERICK.

Madam, had I no inclinations that way, I should obey your kind commands.

BELVILE.

Who, Frederick marry? He has so few inclinations for womankind, that had he been possessed of paradise he might have continued there to this day, if no crime but love could have disinherited him.

FREDERICK.

Oh, I do not use to boast of my intrigues.

BELVILE.

Boast, why thou dost nothing but boast; and I dare swear, wert thou as innocent from the sin of the grape, as thou art from the apple, thou might'st yet claim that right in Eden which our first parents lost by too much loving.

FREDERICK.

I wish this lady would think me so modest a man.

VALERIA.

She would be sorry, then, and not like you half so well, and I should be loath to break my word with you, which was, that if your friend and mine agreed, it should be a match between you and I. (*She gives him her hand.*)

FREDERICK.

Bear witness, Colonel, 'tis a bargain. (*Kisses her hand.*)

BLUNT. (*To Florinda.*)

I have a pardon to beg too, but 'sheartlikins, I am so out of countenance that I'm a dog if I can say anything to purpose.

FLORINDA.

Sir, I heartily forgive you all.

BLUNT.

That's nobly said, sweet lady.—Belvile, prithee present her her ring again; for I find I have not courage to approach her myself.

Gives him the ring; he gives it to Florinda. Enter Boy.

BOY.

Sir, I have brought the father that you sent for. [*Exit.*]

BELVILE.

'Tis well, and now my dear Florinda, let's fly to complete that mighty joy we have so long wished and sighed for.—Come, Fred—you'll follow?

FREDERICK.

Your example, sir, 'twas ever my ambition in war, and must be so in love.

WILLMORE.

And must not I see this juggling* knot tied?

BELVILE.

No, thou shalt do us better service, and be our guard, lest Don Pedro's sudden return interrupt the ceremony.

WILLMORE.

Content. I'll secure this pass.

Exeunt Belvile, Florinda, Frederick and Valeria. Enter Boy.

BOY. (*To Willmore.*)

Sir, there's a lady without would speak to you.

WILLMORE.

Conduct her in, I dare not quit my post.

BOY.

And sir, your tailor waits you in your chamber.

BLUNT.

Some comfort yet, I shall not dance naked at the wedding.

Exeunt Blunt and Boy. Enter again the Boy, conducting in Angellica in a masquing habit and a vizard. Willmore runs to her.

WILLMORE.

This can be none but my pretty Gypsy.—Oh, I see you can follow as well as fly. Come, confess thyself the most malicious devil in nature; you think you have done my business with Angellica—

ANGELLICA.

Stand off, base villain— (*She draws a pistol, and holds it to his breast.*)

WILLMORE.

Hah, 'tis not she.—Who art thou? and what's thy business?

ANGELLICA.

One thou hast injured and who comes to kill thee for't.

WILLMORE.

What the devil canst thou mean?

ANGELLICA.

By all my hopes to kill thee— (*Holds still the pistol to his breast, he going back, she following still.*)

WILLMORE.

Prithee, on what acquaintance? For I know thee not.

ANGELLICA.

Behold this face—so lost to thy remembrance,
And then call all thy sins about thy soul, (*Pulls off her vizard.*)
And let 'em die with thee.

WILLMORE.

Angellica!

ANGELLICA.

Yes, traitor,
Does not thy guilty blood run shivering through thy veins?
Hast thou no horror at this sight that tells thee
Thou hast not long to boast thy shameful conquest?

WILLMORE.

Faith, no, child, my blood keeps its old ebbs and flows still and that usual heat too that could oblige thee with a kindness, had I but opportunity.

ANGELLICA.

Devil! Dost wanton with my pain? Have at thy heart.

WILLMORE.

Hold, dear virago! Hold thy hand a little; I am not now at leisure to be killed—hold and hear me—(*Aside.*) Death, I think she's in earnest.

ANGELLICA. (*Aside, turning from him.*)

Oh, if I take not heed,
My coward heart will leave me to his mercy.
—What have you, sir, to say? But should I hear thee,
Thou'dst talk away all that is brave about me:
(*Follows him with the pistol to his breast.*)
And I have vowed thy death, by all that's sacred.

WILLMORE.

Why, then there's an end of a proper handsome fellow,
That might 'a lived to have done good service yet;
That's all I can say to't.

ANGELLICA. (*Pausingly.*)

Yet—I would give thee—time for—penitence.

WILLMORE.
Faith child, I thank God I have ever took
Care to lead a good, sober, hopeful life, and am of a religion
That teaches me to believe I shall depart in peace.

ANGELLICA.
So will the devil! Tell me,
How many poor believing fools thou hast undone?
How many hearts thou hast betrayed to ruin?
Yet these are little mischiefs to the ills
Thou'st taught mine to commit: thou'st taught it love.

WILLMORE.
Egad, 'twas shrewdly hurt the while.

ANGELLICA.
Love, that has robbed it of its unconcern,
Of all that pride that taught me how to value it.
And in its room
A mean submissive passion was conveyed,
That made me humbly bow, which I ne'er did
To any thing but Heaven.
Thou, perjured man, didst this, and with thy oaths,
Which on thy knees, thou didst devoutly make,
Softened my yielding heart—and then, I was a slave—
Yet still had been content to've worn my chains,
Worn 'em with vanity and joy forever,
Hadst thou not broke those vows that put them on.
'Twas then I was undone. (*All this while follows him with the pistol to his breast.*)

WILLMORE.
Broke my vows! Why, where hast thou lived?
Amongst the gods? For I never heard of mortal man
That has not broke a thousand vows.

ANGELLICA.
Oh impudence!

WILLMORE.
Angellica! That beauty has been too long tempting
Not to have made a thousand lovers languish,
Who in the amorous fever[f] no doubt have sworn
Like me. Did they all die in that faith? still adoring?
I do not think they did.

ANGELLICA.
No, faithless man; had I repaid their vows, as I did thine,
I would have killed the ingrateful that had abandoned me.

WILLMORE.
This old general has quite spoiled thee; nothing makes a woman so vain as being flattered. Your old lover ever supplies the defects of age, with intolerable dotage, vast charge, and that which you call constancy; and attributing this to your own merits, you domineer, and throw your favors in's teeth, upbraiding him still with the defects of age, and cuckold him as often as he deceives your expectations. But the gay, young, brisk lover that brings his equal fires, and can give you dart for dart, will be as nice as you sometimes.

ANGELLICA.
All this thou'st made me know, for which I hate thee.
Had I remained in innocent security,
I should have thought all men were born my slaves,
And worn my pow'r like lightning in my eyes,
To have destroyed at pleasure when offended.
But when love held the mirror, the undeceiving glass
Reflected all the weakness of my soul, and made me know
My richest treasure being lost, my honor,
All the remaining spoil could not be worth
The conqueror's care or value.
Oh how I fell, like a long worshipped idol
Discovering all the cheat.
Would not the incense and rich sacrifice,
Which blind devotion offered at my altars,
Have fall'n to thee?
Why wouldst thou then destroy my fancied pow'r?

WILLMORE.
By Heaven, thou'rt brave, and I admire thee strangely.
I wish I were that dull, that constant thing
Which thou wouldst have and nature never meant me.
I must, like cheerful birds, sing in all groves
And perch on every bough,
Billing the next kind she that flies to meet me;
Yet after all could build my nest with thee,
Thither repairing when I'd loved my round,
And still reserve a tributary flame.

To gain your credit, I'll pay you back your charity
And be obliged for nothing but for love. (*Offers her a purse of gold.*)

ANGELLICA.
Oh that thou wert in earnest!
So mean a thought of me
Would turn my rage to scorn, and I should pity thee
And give thee leave to live;
Which for the public safety of our sex
And my own private injuries I dare not do.
Prepare— (*Follows still, as before.*)
I will no more be tempted with replies.

WILLMORE.
Sure—

ANGELLICA.
Another word will damn thee! I've heard thee talk too long.

She follows him with the pistol ready to shoot; he retires still amazed. Enter Don Antonio, his arm in a scarf, and lays hold on the pistol.

ANTONIO.
Hah! Angellica!

ANGELLICA.
Antonio! What devil brought thee hither?

ANTONIO.
Love and curiosity, seeing your coach at door.
Let me disarm you of this unbecoming instrument of death—
(*Takes away the pistol.*) Amongst the number of your slaves, was there not one worthy the honor to have fought your quarrel*?
—Who are you, sir, that are so very wretched
To merit death from her?

WILLMORE.
One, sir, that could have made a better end of an amorous quarrel without you than with you.

ANTONIO.
Sure 'tis some rival. Hah, the very man took down her picture yesterday, the very same that set on me last night. Blest opportunity— (*Offers to shoot him.*)

ANGELLICA.
Hold, you're mistaken sir.

ANTONIO.
By Heaven, the very same!
—Sir, what pretensions have you to this lady?

WILLMORE.
Sir, I do not use to be examined and am ill at all disputes but this— (*Draws; Antonio offers to shoot.*)

ANGELLICA. (*To Willmore.*)
Oh hold! You see he's armed with certain death.
—And you Antonio, I command you hold,
By all the passion you've so lately vowed me.

Enter Don Pedro, sees Antonio and stays.

PEDRO. (*Aside.*)
Hah, Antonio! and Angellica!

ANTONIO.
When I refuse obedience to your will,
May you destroy me with your mortal hate.
By all that's holy I adore you so,
That even my rival, who has charms enough
To make him fall a victim to my jealousy,
Shall live, nay and have leave to love on still.

PEDRO. (*Aside.*)
What's this I hear?

ANGELLICA. (*Pointing to Willmore.*)
Ah thus! 'Twas thus he talked, and I believed.
—Antonio, yesterday,
I'd not have sold my interest in his heart
For all the sword has won and lost in battle.
—But now to show my utmost of contempt,
I give thee life, which if thou wouldst preserve,
Live where my eyes may never see thee more,
Live to undo someone whose soul may prove
So bravely constant to revenge my love.

Goes out, Antonio follows, but Pedro pulls him back.

PEDRO.
Antonio—stay.

ANTONIO.
Don Pedro—

PEDRO.
What coward fear was that prevented thee
From meeting me this morning on the Molo?

ANTONIO.
Meet thee?

PEDRO.
Yes me; I was the man that dared thee to't.

ANTONIO.
Hast thou so often seen me fight in war

To find no better cause to excuse my absence?
I sent my sword and one to do thee right,
Finding myself uncapable to use a sword.

PEDRO.
But 'twas Florinda's quarrel* we fought,
And you, to show how little you esteemed her,
Sent me your rival, giving him your interest.
But I have found the cause of this affront,
And when I meet you fit for the dispute,
I'll tell you my resentment.

ANTONIO.
I shall be ready, sir, ere long, to do you reason.

Exit Antonio.

PEDRO.
If I could find Florinda now whilst my anger's high, I think I should be kind and give her to Belvile in revenge.

WILLMORE.
Faith, sir, I know not what you would do, but I believe the priest within has been so kind.

PEDRO.
How! My sister married?

WILLMORE.
I hope by this time he is, and bedded too, or he has not my longings about him.

PEDRO.
Dares he do this! Does he not fear my power?

WILLMORE.
Faith, not at all. If you will go in, and thank him for the favor he has done your sister, so; if not, sir, my power's greater in this house than yours. I have a damned surly crew here, that will keep you till the next tide, and then clap you on board for prize;[g] my ship lies but a league off the Molo, and we shall show your donship a damned tramontane rover's trick.

Enter Belvile.

BELVILE.
This rogue's in some new mischief—hah, Pedro returned!

PEDRO.
Colonel Belvile, I hear you have married my sister?

BELVILE.
You have heard the truth then, sir.

PEDRO.
Have I so; then, sir, I wish you joy.

BELVILE.
How!

PEDRO.
By this embrace I do, and I am glad on't.

BELVILE.
Are you in earnest?

PEDRO.
By our long friendship and my obligations to thee, I am,
The sudden change I'll give you reasons for anon.
Come lead me to my sister,
That she may know I now approve her choice.

Exeunt Belvile with Pedro. Willmore goes to follow them. Enter Hellena as before in boy's clothes, and pulls him back.

WILLMORE.
Hah! My Gypsy!—Now a thousand blessings on thee for this kindness. Egad child, I was e'en in despair of ever seeing thee again; my friends are all provided for within, each man his kind woman.

HELLENA.
Hah! I thought they had served me some such trick!

WILLMORE.
And I was e'en resolved to go aboard and condemn myself to my lone cabin and the thoughts of thee.

HELLENA.
And could you have left me behind, would you have been so ill natured?

WILLMORE.
Why, 'twould have broke my heart, child. But since we are met again, I defy foul weather to part us.

HELLENA.
And would you be a faithful friend now, if a maid should trust you?

WILLMORE.
For a friend I cannot promise; thou art of a form so excellent, a face and humor* too good for cold dull friendship. I am parlously afraid of being in love, child, and you have not forgot how severely you have used me?

HELLENA.
That's all one; such usage you must still look for,

to find out all your haunts, to rail at you to all that love you, till I have made you love only me in your own defense, because nobody else will love you.

WILLMORE.

But hast thou no better quality to recommend thyself by?

HELLENA.

Faith, none, Captain. Why, 'twill be the greater charity to take me for thy mistress. I am a lone child, a kind of orphan lover, and why I should die a maid, and in a captain's hands too, I do not understand.

WILLMORE.

Egad, I was never clawed away with broadsides from any female before. Thou hast one virtue I adore, good nature. I hate a coy, demure mistress, she's as troublesome as a colt; I'll break none. No, give me a mad mistress when mewed and, in flying, one I dare trust upon the wing, that whilst she's kind will come to the lure.

HELLENA.

Nay, as kind as you will, good Captain, whilst it lasts, but let's lose no time.

WILLMORE.

My time's as precious to me as thine can be; therefore, dear creature, since we are so well agreed, let's retire to my chamber, and if ever thou wert treated with such savory love—Come, my bed's prepared for such a guest, all clean and sweet as thy fair self. I love to steal a dish and a bottle with a friend, and hate long graces. Come let's retire and fall to.

HELLENA.

'Tis but getting my consent, and the business is soon done. Let but old gaffer Hymen and his priest say amen to't, and I dare lay my mother's daughter by as proper a fellow as your father's son, without fear or blushing.

WILLMORE.

Hold, hold, no bug* words, child. Priest and Hymen! Prithee, add a hangman to 'em to make up the consort. No, no, we'll have no vows but love, child, nor witness but the lover; the kind deity enjoins naught but love and enjoy! Hymen and priest wait still upon portion and jointure; love and beauty have their own ceremonies. Marriage is as certain a bane to love as lending money is to friendship. I'll neither ask nor give a vow—though I could be content to turn Gypsy, and become a left-handed bridegroom[54] to have the pleasure of working that great miracle of making a maid a mother, if you durst venture; 'tis upse[55] Gypsy that, and if I miss, I'll lose my labor.

HELLENA.

And if you do not lose, what shall I get? a cradle full of noise and mischief, with a pack of repentance at my back? Can you teach me to weave inkle to pass my time with? 'Tis upse Gypsy that too.

WILLMORE.

I can teach thee to weave a true love's knot better.

HELLENA.

So can my dog.

WILLMORE.

Well, I see we are both upon our guards, and I see there's no way to conquer good nature, but by yielding—here—give me thy hand—one kiss and I am thine—

HELLENA.

One kiss! How like my page he speaks; I am resolved you shall have none, for asking such a sneaking sum. He that will be satisfied with one kiss, will never die of that longing. Good friend single kiss, is all your talking come to this? a kiss, a caudle! Farewell, captain single kiss. (*Going out; he stays her.*)

WILLMORE.

Nay, if we part so, let me die like a bird upon a bough, at the sheriff's charge.[56] By Heaven, both the Indies shall not buy thee from me. I adore thy humor* and will marry thee, and we are so of one humor*, it must be a bargain. Give me thy hand—(*Kisses her hand.*) And now let the blind ones (Love and Fortune) do their worst.

HELLENA.

Why, God-a-mercy, Captain!

WILLMORE.

But hark ye, the bargain is now made, but is it not

---

54 left-handed bridegroom] one married in a morganatic ceremony, leading to no inheritance

55 upse] in the manner or fashion of

56 let me ... at the sheriff's charge] let me be hanged (Spencer)

fit we should know each other's names, that when we have reason to curse one another hereafter (and people ask me who 'tis I give to the devil) I may at least be able to tell what family you came of.

HELLENA.
Good reason, Captain; and where I have cause (as I doubt not but I shall have plentiful) that I may know at whom to throw my—blessings—I beseech ye your name.

WILLMORE.
I am called Robert the Constant.

HELLENA.
A very fine name; pray was it your falconer or butler that christened you? Do they not use to whistle when they call you?

WILLMORE.
I hope you have a better, that a man may name without crossing himself, you are so merry with mine.

HELLENA.
I am called Hellena the Inconstant.

Enter Pedro, Belvile, Florinda, Frederick, Valeria.

PEDRO. [*Aside.*]
Hah! Hellena!

FLORINDA.
Hellena!

HELLENA.
The very same.—Hah, my brother!—Now Captain, show your love and courage; stand to your arms, and defend me bravely, or I am lost forever.

PEDRO.
What's this I hear! False girl, how came you hither and what's your business? Speak. (*Goes roughly to her.*)

WILLMORE.
Hold off, sir, you have leave to parley only. (*Puts himself between.*)

HELLENA.
I had e'en as good tell it, as you guess it; faith, brother, my business is the same with all living creatures of my age, to love, and be beloved, and here's the man.

PEDRO.
Perfidious maid, hast thou deceived me too? deceived thyself and Heaven?

HELLENA.
'Tis time enough to make my peace with that.
Be you but kind; let me alone with Heaven.

PEDRO.
Belvile, I did not expect this false play from you. Was't not enough you'd gain Florinda (which I pardoned) but your lewd friends too must be enriched with the spoils of a noble family?

BELVILE.
Faith, sir, I am as much surprised at this as you can be. Yet sir, my friends are gentlemen, and ought to be esteemed for their misfortunes, since they have the glory to suffer with the best of men and kings; 'tis true, he's a rover of fortune, yet a prince aboard his little wooden world.

PEDRO.
What's this to the maintenance of a woman of her birth and quality?*

WILLMORE.
Faith, sir, I can boast of nothing but a sword which does me right where'er I come and has defended a worse cause than a woman's; and since I loved her before I either knew her birth or name, I must pursue my resolution and marry her.

PEDRO.
And is all your holy intent of becoming a nun debauched into a desire of man?

HELLENA.
Why, I have considered the matter, brother, and find the three hundred thousand crowns my uncle left me (and you cannot keep from me) will be better laid out in love than in religion, and turn to as good an account. Let most voices carry it, for Heaven or the captain?

ALL CRY.
A captain! A captain!

HELLENA.
Look ye, sir, 'tis a clear case.

PEDRO. (*Aside.*)
Oh I am mad. If I refuse, my life's in danger.—Come. There's one motive induces me. Take her. I shall now be free from fears of her honor. Guard it you now, if you can; I have been a slave to't long enough. (*Gives her to him.*)

WILLMORE.
Faith, sir, I am of a nation that are of opinion a

woman's honor is not worth guarding when she has a mind to part with it.

HELLENA.

Well said, Captain.

PEDRO. (*To Valeria.*)

This was your plot, mistress, but I hope you have married one that will revenge my quarrel to you—

VALERIA.

There's no altering destiny, sir.

PEDRO.

Sooner than a woman's will. Therefore, I forgive you all—and wish you may get my father's pardon as easily, which I fear.

Enter Blunt dressed in a Spanish habit, looking very ridiculously; his man adjusting his band.

MAN.

'Tis very well, sir—

BLUNT.

Well sir, 'sheartlikins, I tell you 'tis damnable ill, sir—a Spanish habit, good lord! Could the devil and my tailor devise no other punishment for me, but the mode of a nation I abominate?

BELVILE.

What's the matter, Ned?

BLUNT.

Pray view me round, and judge— (*Turns round.*)

BELVILE.

I must confess thou art a kind of an odd figure.

BLUNT.

In a Spanish habit with a vengeance! I had rather be in the Inquisition for Judaism, than in this doublet and breeches; a pillory were an easy collar to this, three handfuls high; and these shoes too, are worse than the stocks, with the sole an inch shorter than my foot. In fine, gentlemen, methinks I look altogether like a bag of bays[57] stuffed full of fool's flesh.

BELVILE.

Methinks 'tis well, and makes thee look *en cavalier.** Come, sir, settle your face and salute* our friends.—Lady—

BLUNT.

Hah! Say'st thou so, my little rover— (*To Hellena.*) Lady (if you be one), give me leave to kiss your hand, and tell you, 'sheartlikins, for all I look so, I am your humble servant.—A pox of my Spanish habit.

Music is heard to play. Enter Boy.

WILLMORE.

Hark—what's this?

BOY.

Sir, as the custom is, the gay people in masquerade who make every man's house their own are coming up.

Enter several men and women in masquing habits with music; they put themselves in order and dance.

BLUNT.

'Sheartlikins, would 'twere lawful to pull off their false faces, that I might see if my doxy were not among'st 'em.

BELVILE. (*To the masquers.*)

Ladies and gentlemen, since you are come so apropos, you must take a small collation with us.

WILLMORE.

Whilst we'll to the good man within, who stays to give us a cast of his office. (*To Hellena.*) Have you no trembling at the near approach?

HELLENA.

No more than you have in an engagement or a tempest.

WILLMORE.

Egad thou'rt a brave girl, and I admire thy love and courage.

Lead on, no other dangers they can dread,
Who venture in the storms o'th' marriage bed.

Exeunt.

THE END.

[57] bag of bays] a bag of bay leaves used in cooking

Textual Notes

[a] The copytext is the first edition, a 1667 quarto (Q1), which exists in three issues. Although the title pages of the first two issues do not name the author, the "Prologue" of all three issues refers to the author as "he." The third issue, however, adds "written by Mrs. A. Behn" to the title page. In some copies of the second issue, and in the third issue, the author's "Postscript" is printed with the addition of the phrase "especially of our sex," an acknowledgment that the author is a woman.

Other editions consulted include quartos from 1697 (Q2) and 1709 (Q3); collections of Behn's works published in 1702 (A) and 1724 (B); and modern editions of 1915 (Summers); 1967 (Link); 1995 (Spencer); and 1995 (Todd).

[b] Blunt] Q2, A, B, Summers, Link, Spencer; Fred. Q1, Q3, Todd

[c] Why] The first edition reads "whe," an exclamation used for emphasis or to demand attention; variant of archaic "we" (OED). Since there is no satisfactory modern equivalent for this now-archaic expression, I have followed the examples of previous editors and changed "whe" to "why" throughout.

[d] fair] Q3, Link, Spencer, Todd; *om.* Q2, A, and some copies of Q1; fine B, Summers

[e] to] *om.* Q1, Q2, Q3, A, B, Summers, Link; vow you Spencer, Todd

[f] fever] Q3, Link, Spencer, Todd; favour Q1, Q2, A, B, Summers

[g] for prize] Q3, Link, Spencer; for prise Q1, Todd; my prize Q2, A, B, Summers

All for Love; or, The World Well Lost[a]

by John Dryden (1631-1700)

edited by Tanya Caldwell

Dryden once claimed that he "never writ anything for myself but *Anthony and Cleopatra.*" Whatever the sentiments of the poet laureate during the two years over which he supposedly composed the play, *All for Love* was a dramatic and a literary success from its appearance in 1677. The second of three Shakespeare adaptations that Dryden wrote (though he also looked to historical accounts and other English dramatizations of the lives and loves of Antony and Cleopatra), *All for Love* appealed to Restoration and eighteenth-century audiences in a number of ways. First, the so-called neoclassical neatness of the play went down much better than the perceived messiness of Shakespeare's *Antony and Cleopatra,* with its many scenes, widely scattered geographical locations, and ten-year time span. While Dryden's 1668 *Essay of Dramatick Poesy* had defended English drama against charges that it did not adhere to the classical unities, *All for Love* observes unity of time, place, and action—"more exactly," Dryden admits in the preface, "than, perhaps, the English theater requires." All the same, he insists in the title page and preface that the play imitates the "style" of the "divine Shakespeare," which in order best to do he has abandoned the rhyming couplets to which his audiences had become accustomed. Dryden expresses his nervousness over this switch in a prologue. Also a sign of the times in which the play was written are the themes of love vs. honor and public duty vs. private passion. The play was first performed during great political unrest and opposition to Charles II's government, and critics noticed the parallel between Antony and Charles as rulers with foreign mistresses that threatened their political stability.

The play's staging contributed to its great success right to the end of the eighteenth century (it kept *Antony and Cleopatra* from the stage and was performed 123 times between 1700 and 1800). The King's Company production of the play, which debuted on February 12, 1677, put the popular and charismatic Charles Hart and Elizabeth Boutell in the lead roles. The cat-fight between Cleopatra and Octavia must have especially delighted audiences since the aging Katherine Corey, known for her shrewish roles, played against the young, attractive Boutell. (In his preface Dryden in fact regrets bringing Octavia on stage, for this "must lessen the favor of the audience" to the love of Antony and Cleopatra.) In the eighteenth century such powerful acting teams as Barton Booth and Anne Oldfield, Spranger Barry and Peg Wolfington took over the lead roles.

[I]

DRAMATIS PERSONAE

[MEN]

Marc Antony.
Ventidius, his general.
Dollabella, his friend.
Alexas, the Queen's eunuch.
Serapion, priest of Isis.
Another priest.
Servants to Antony.

[WOMEN]

Cleopatra, Queen of Egypt.
Octavia, Antony's wife.
Charmion, Iras, Cleopatra's maids.
Antony's two little daughters.

Scene: Alexandria.

All for Love; or, The World Well Lost.

Facile est [enim] verbum aliquod ardens (ut ita dicam) notare: idque restinctis [iam] animorum incendiis irridere. Cicero[1]

Act I. Scene: the Temple of Isis.

Enter Serapion, Myris, priests of Isis.

SERAPION.
Portents and prodigies are grown so frequent
That they have lost their name. Our fruitful Nile
Flowed ere the wonted season with a torrent
So unexpected and so wondrous fierce
That the wild deluge overtook the haste
Ev'n of the hinds that watched it: men and beasts
Were borne above the tops of trees that grew
On th'utmost margin of the watermark.
Then with so swift an ebb the flood drove backward,
It slipped from underneath the scaly herd:
Here monstrous phocae[2] panted on the shore;
Forsaken dolphins there, with their broad tails,
Lay lashing the departing waves; hard by 'em,
Sea-horses[3] flound'ring in the slimy mud
Tossed up their heads and dashed the ooze about 'em.

Enter Alexas behind them.

MYRIS.
Avert these omens, Heav'n.
SERAPION.
Last night, between the hours of twelve and one,
In a lone isle o'th' temple while I walked,
A whirlwind rose, that with a violent blast
Shook all the dome. The doors around me clapped;
The iron wicket, that defends the vault
Where the long race* of Ptolemies is laid,
Burst open, and disclosed the mighty dead.
From out each monument, in order placed,
An armed ghost start[4] up; the boy-king[5] last
Reared his inglorious head. A peal of groans
Then followed, and a lamentable voice
Cried, "Egypt is no more." My blood ran back,
My shaking knees against each other knocked;
On the cold pavement down I fell entranced
And so unfinished left the horrid scene.
ALEXAS. (*Showing himself.*)
And dreamed you this? or did invent the story
To frighten our Egyptian boys withal
And train 'em up betimes in fear of priesthood?
SERAPION.
My lord, I saw you not,
Nor meant my words should reach your ears, but what
I uttered was most true.
ALEXAS.
A foolish dream,
Bred from the fumes of indigested feasts[6]
And holy luxury.
SERAPION.
I know my duty:
This goes no farther.

---

[1] *Facile* ... Cicero] Cicero, *Orator* viii, 27: "It is easy, indeed, to criticize some flaming word, if I may use this expression, and to laugh at it when the passion of the moment has cooled" (Loeb).

[2] phocae] seals

[3] sea-horses] hippopotami

[4] start] started (an obsolete past tense form)

[5] boy-king] Ptolemy XIV, last of the kings of Egypt and Cleopatra's half-brother, whom, according to common practice, she married when he was just eleven years old. He died in 44 BCE, probably poisoned or done away with by Cleopatra.

[6] indigested feasts] a common explanation for bad dreams

ALEXAS.

'Tis not fit it should.
Nor would the times now bear it, were it true.
All southern, from yon hills, the Roman camp
Hangs o'er us black and threat'ning, like a storm
Just breaking on our heads.

SERAPION.

Our faint Egyptians pray for Antony,
But in their servile hearts they own Octavius.[7]

MYRIS.

Why then does Antony dream out his hours
And tempts not Fortune for a noble day
Which might redeem what Actium[8] lost?

ALEXAS.

He thinks 'tis past recovery.

SERAPION.

Yet the foe
Seems not to press the siege.

ALEXAS.

Oh, there's the wonder.
Maecenas and Agrippa,[9] who can most[10]
With Caesar, are his foes. His wife Octavia,[11]
Driv'n from his house, solicits her revenge,
And Dollabella, who was once his friend,
Upon some private grudge now seeks his ruin:
Yet still war seems on either side to sleep.

SERAPION.

'Tis strange that Antony, for some days past,
Has not beheld the face of Cleopatra,
But here in Isis' temple lives retired
And makes his heart a prey to black despair.

ALEXAS.

'Tis true, and we much fear he hopes by absence
To cure his mind of love.

SERAPION.

If he be vanquished
Or make his peace, Egypt is doomed to be
A Roman province, and our plenteous harvests
Must then redeem the scarceness of their soil.
While Antony stood firm, our Alexandria
Rivaled proud Rome (Dominion's other seat),
And Fortune, striding like a vast Colossus,[12]
Could fix an equal foot of empire here.

ALEXAS.

Had I my wish, these tyrants of all Nature
Who lord it o'er mankind, should perish, perish
Each by the other's sword, but since our will
Is lamely followed by our pow'r, we must
Depend on one, with him to rise or fall.

SERAPION.

How stands the queen affected?

ALEXAS.

Oh, she dotes,
She dotes, Serapion, on this vanquished man
And winds herself about his mighty ruins,
Whom would she yet forsake, yet yield him up,
This hunted prey, to his pursuer's hands,
She might preserve us all, but 'tis in vain—
This changes my designs, this blasts my counsels
And makes me use all means to keep him here,
Whom I could wish divided from her arms
Far as the earth's deep center. Well, you know
The state of things; no more of your ill omens
And black prognostics; labor to confirm
The people's hearts.

Enter Ventidius, talking aside with a gentleman of Antony's.

SERAPION.

These Romans will o'erhear us.
But who's that stranger? By his warlike port,

[7] Octavius] Also referred to throughout the play as "Caesar," Octavius Caesar was the nephew and adopted son of Julius Caesar. At the time of the events described in the play he was one of the three rulers of Rome, or triumvirs, along with Antony and Lepidus. When Octavius became sole ruler on Antony's death, he changed his name to Augustus.

[8] Actium] the famous naval battle of Actium, in which Octavius defeated Antony, took place in 31 BCE, the year before the events portrayed in this play

[9] Maecenas and Agrippa] Gaius Maecenas (70-8 BCE) was Octavius' friend, political advisor, and later propaganda agent; Marcus Agrippa, famed for his military genius, commanded Octavius' troops at Actium.

[10] can most] can do most

[11] Octavia] Antony married Octavius' sister after the death of his wife, Fulvia, in order to strengthen his political standing in the triumvirate.

[12] like a vast Colossus] The Colossus of Rhodes, a giant statue of Apollo, straddled the entrance to the harbor.

His fierce demeanor, and erected look,
He's of no vulgar* note.

ALEXAS.
Oh 'tis Ventidius,[13]
Our emp'ror's great lieutenant in the East,
Who first showed Rome that Parthia[14] could be conquered.
When Antony returned from Syria last,
He left this man to guard the Roman frontiers.

SERAPION.
You seem to know him well.

ALEXAS.
Too well. I saw him in Cilicia[15] first,
When Cleopatra there met Antony:
A mortal foe he was to us, and Egypt.
But, let me witness to the worth I hate,
A braver Roman never drew a sword.
Firm to his prince, but as a friend, not slave.
He ne'er was of his pleasures, but presides
O'er all his cooler hours and morning counsels;
In short, the plainness, fierceness, rugged virtue
Of an old true-stamped Roman lives in him.
His coming bodes I know not what of ill
To our affairs. Withdraw, to mark him better,
And I'll acquaint you why I sought you here
And what's our present work.

They withdraw to a corner of the stage, and Ventidius with the other comes forward to the front.

VENTIDIUS.
Not see him, say you?
I say I must, and will.

GENTLEMAN.
He has commanded,
On pain of death, none should approach his presence.

VENTIDIUS.
I bring him news will raise his drooping spirits,
Give him new life.

GENTLEMAN.
He sees not Cleopatra.

VENTIDIUS.
Would he had never seen her.

GENTLEMAN.
He eats not, drinks not, sleeps not, has no use
Of anything but thought, or if he talks,
'Tis to himself, and then 'tis perfect raving.
Then he defies the world and bids it pass;
Sometimes he gnaws his lip and curses loud
The boy Octavius;[16] then he draws his mouth
Into a scornful smile and cries, "Take all,
The world's not worth my care."

VENTIDIUS.
Just, just his nature.
Virtue's his path, but sometimes 'tis too narrow
For his vast soul, and then he starts out wide
And bounds into a vice that bears him far
From his first course and plunges him in ills.
But, when his danger makes him find his fault,
Quick to observe and full of sharp remorse,
He censures eagerly his own misdeeds,
Judging himself with malice to himself
And not forgiving what as man he did
Because his other parts are more than man.
He must not thus be lost.

Alexas and the priests come forward.

ALEXAS.
You have your full instructions, now advance;
Proclaim your orders loudly.

SERAPION.
Romans, Egyptians, hear the Queen's command.
Thus Cleopatra bids, "Let labor cease.
To pomp and triumphs give this happy day
That gave the world a lord: 'tis Antony's."

[13] Ventidius] The historical Publius Ventidius, a talented general, in fact died in 38 BCE–before the events of this play.

[14] Parthia] a country in ancient Asia, south-east of the Caspian sea; Ventidius conquered the Parthians in 39 and 38 BCE.

[15] Cilicia] southeastern section of what is now Turkey; after the Battle at Philippi, Antony summoned Cleopatra hither to account for her actions during the civil war precipitated by Julius Caesar's assassination. This was not their first meeting, for Cleopatra had been Caesar's mistress in Rome; below, Antony and Cleopatra remember an earlier meeting yet.

[16] boy Octavius] Antony was twenty years older than the thirty-three year old Octavius.

Live, Antony, and Cleopatra live.
Be this the general voice sent up to Heav'n,
And every public place repeat this echo.
VENTIDIUS. (*Aside.*)
Fine pageantry!
SERAPION.
Set out before your doors
The images of all your sleeping fathers[17]
With laurels crowned; with laurels wreathe your posts
And strow with flow'rs the pavement; let the priests
Do present sacrifice; pour out the wine,
And call the gods to join with you in gladness.
VENTIDIUS.
Curse on the tongue that bids this general joy.
Can they be friends of Antony who revel
When Antony's in danger? Hide, for shame,
You Romans, your great grandsires' images,
For fear their souls should animate their marbles
To blush at their degenerate progeny.
ALEXAS.
A love which knows no bounds to Antony
Would mark the day with honors, when all Heaven
Labored for him, when each propitious star
Stood wakeful in his orb to watch that hour
And shed his better influence.* Her own birthday
Our Queen neglected, like a vulgar fate
That passed obscurely by.
VENTIDIUS.
Would it had slept
Divided far from his, till some remote
And future age had called it out to ruin
Some other prince, not him.
ALEXAS.
Your Emperor,
Though grown unkind, would be more gentle than
T'upbraid my Queen for loving him too well.
VENTIDIUS.
Does the mute sacrifice upbraid the priest?
He knows him not his executioner.
Oh, she has decked his ruin with her love,
Led him in golden bands to gaudy slaughter,
And made perdition pleasing: She has left him
The blank of what he was.
I tell thee, eunuch, she has quite unmanned him:
Can any Roman see and know him now,
Thus altered from the lord of half mankind,
Unbent, unsinewed, made a woman's toy,
Shrunk from the vast extent of all his honors,
And cramped within a corner of the world?
Oh Antony!
Thou bravest soldier, and thou best of friends!
Bounteous as Nature; next to Nature's God!
Couldst thou but make new worlds, so wouldst thou give 'em,
As bounty were thy being. Rough in battle
As the first Romans when they went to war,
Yet, after victory, more pitiful
Than all their praying virgins left at home!
ALEXAS.
Would you could add to those more shining virtues
His truth to her who loves him.
VENTIDIUS.
Would I could not.
But wherefore waste I precious hours with thee?
Thou art her darling mischief, her chief engine,*
Antony's other fate. Go, tell thy queen
Ventidius is arrived to end her charms.
Let your Egyptian timbrels play alone,
Nor mix effeminate sounds with Roman trumpets.
You dare not fight for Antony; go pray,
And keep your coward's holy day in temples.

Exeunt Alexas and Serapion. Enter second gentleman[b] *of Antony.*

SECOND GENTLEMAN.
The Emperor approaches and commands,
On pain of death, that none presume to stay.
FIRST GENTLEMAN.
I dare not disobey him. (*Going out with the other.*)
VENTIDIUS.
Well, I dare.
But I'll observe him first unseen and find
Which way his humor drives: the rest I'll venture.
(*Withdraws.*)

Enter Antony walking with a disturbed motion before he speaks.

17 images of all your sleeping fathers] the *imagines* or masks of distinguished ancestors, which were kept in noble Roman families

[I]

ANTONY.
They tell me 'tis my birthday, and I'll keep it
With double pomp of sadness.
'Tis what the day deserves, which gave me breath.
Why was I raised the meteor of the world,
Hung in the skies, and blazing as I traveled,
Till all my fires were spent, and then cast downward
To be trod out by Caesar?
VENTIDIUS. (*Aside.*)
On my soul,
'Tis mournful, wondrous mournful!
ANTONY.
Count thy gains.
Now, Antony, wouldst thou be born for this?
Glutton of Fortune, thy devouring youth
Has starved thy wanting age.
VENTIDIUS. (*Aside.*)
How sorrow shakes him!
So, now the tempest tears him up by th'roots
And on the ground extends the noble ruin.
ANTONY. (*Having thrown himself down.*)
Lie there, thou shadow of an emperor;
The place thou pressest on thy mother earth
Is all thy empire now. Now it contains thee;
Some few days hence, and then 'twill be too large,
When thou'rt contracted in thy narrow urn,
Shrunk to a few cold ashes. Then Octavia
(For Cleopatra will not live to see it),
Octavia then will have thee all her own
And bear thee in her widowed hand to Caesar;
Caesar will weep, the crocodile will weep,
To see his rival of the universe
Lie still and peaceful there. I'll think no more on't.
Give me some music; look that it be sad.
I'll soothe my melancholy till I swell
And burst myself with sighing–

Soft music.

'Tis somewhat to my humor. Stay, I fancy
I'm now turned wild, a commoner of Nature;
Of all forsaken, and forsaking all,
Live in a shady forest's sylvan scene,
Stretched at my length beneath some blasted oak.
I lean my head upon the mossy bark,
And look just of a piece, as I grew from it:
My uncombed locks, matted like mistletoe,
Hang o'er my hoary face; a murm'ring brook
Runs at my foot.
VENTIDIUS.
Methinks I fancy
Myself there too.
ANTONY.
The herd come jumping by me
And, fearless, quench their thirst while I look on
And take me for their fellow-citizen.
More of this image, more; it lulls my thoughts.

Soft music again.

VENTIDIUS.
I must disturb him; I can hold no longer. (*Stands before him.*)
ANTONY. (*Starting up.*)
Art thou Ventidius?
VENTIDIUS.
Are you Antony?
I'm liker what I was, than you to him
I left you last.
ANTONY.
I'm angry.
VENTIDIUS.
So am I.
ANTONY.
I would be private: leave me.
VENTIDIUS.
Sir, I love you,
And therefore will not leave you.
ANTONY.
Will not leave me?
Where have you learnt that answer? Who am I?
VENTIDIUS.
My Emperor; the man I love next heaven:
If I said more, I think 'twere scarce a sin;
Y'are all that's good, and god-like.[c]
ANTONY.
All that's wretched.
You will not leave me then?
VENTIDIUS.
'Twas too presuming
To say I would not, but I dare not leave you,
And 'tis unkind in you to chide me hence
So soon, when I so far have come to see you.
ANTONY.
Now thou hast seen me, art thou satisfied?
For, if a friend, thou hast beheld enough;
And, if a foe, too much.

VENTIDIUS. (*Weeping.*)
Look, Emperor, this is no common dew.
I have not wept this forty year, but now
My mother comes afresh into my eyes;
I cannot help her softness.

ANTONY.
By Heav'n, he weeps, poor good old man, he weeps!
The big round drops course one another down
The furrows of his cheeks. Stop 'em, Ventidius,
Or I shall blush to death: they set my shame,
That caused 'em, full before me.

VENTIDIUS.
I'll do my best.

ANTONY.
Sure there's contagion in the tears of friends:
See, I have caught it too. Believe me, 'tis not
For my own griefs, but thine—Nay, father.

VENTIDIUS.
Emperor.

ANTONY.
Emperor? Why, that's the style of victory.[18]
The conqu'ring soldier, red with unfelt wounds,
Salutes his general so, but never more
Shall that sound reach my ears.

VENTIDIUS.
I warrant you.

ANTONY.
Actium, Actium! Oh—

VENTIDIUS.
It sits too near you.

ANTONY.
Here, here it lies, a lump of lead by day,
And in my short, distracted nightly slumbers,
The hag that rides my dreams–[19]

VENTIDIUS.
Out with it; give it vent.

ANTONY.
Urge not my shame.
I lost a battle.

VENTIDIUS.
So has Julius[20] done.

ANTONY.
Thou favor'st me and speak'st not half thou think'st,
For Julius fought it out and lost it fairly,
But Antony—

VENTIDIUS.
Nay, stop not.

ANTONY.
Antony—
(Well, thou wilt have it) like a coward, fled,
Fled while his soldiers fought; fled first, Ventidius.
Thou long'st to curse me, and I give thee leave.
I know thou cam'st prepared to rail.

VENTIDIUS.
I did.

ANTONY.
I'll help thee–I have been a man, Ventidius—

VENTIDIUS.
Yes, and a brave one, but—

ANTONY.
I know thy meaning.
But I have lost my reason, have disgraced
The name of soldier with inglorious ease.
In the full vintage of my flowing honors,
Sat still, and saw it pressed by other hands.
Fortune came smiling to my youth, and wooed it,
And purple greatness[21] met my ripened years.
When first I came to empire, I was borne
On tides of people, crowding to my triumphs,[22]
The wish of nations, and the willing world
Received me as its pledge of future peace.
I was so great, so happy, so beloved,
Fate could not ruin me, till I took pains
And worked against my Fortune, chid her from me,
And turned her loose; yet still she came again.
My careless days and my luxurious nights
At length have wearied her, and now she's gone,
Gone, gone, divorced forever. Help me, soldier,

---

[18] Emperor … victory.] Antony has in mind the Roman word *imperator*, which was bestowed upon a Roman general after an important victory.

[19] hag that rides my dreams] the evil spirit that, it was believed, haunts dreams, as if riding the body of the dreamer: hence, nightmare

[20] Julius] Julius Caesar

[21] purple greatness] The purple cloak or toga was worn only by those of the highest ranks in Roman society.

[22] triumphs] A victorious Roman general was permitted a "triumph" or procession of his army and prisoners through Rome.

To curse this madman, this industrious fool,
Who labored to be wretched: prithee, curse me.

VENTIDIUS.
No.

ANTONY.
Why?

VENTIDIUS.
You are too sensible already
Of what y'have done, too conscious of your failings,
And like a scorpion, whipped by others first
To fury, sting yourself in mad revenge.
I would bring balm and pour it in your wounds,
Cure your distempered mind, and heal your fortunes.

ANTONY.
I know thou wouldst.

VENTIDIUS.
I will.

ANTONY.
Ha, ha, ha, ha.

VENTIDIUS.
You laugh.

ANTONY.
I do, to see officious love
Give cordials to the dead.

VENTIDIUS.
You would be lost then?

ANTONY.
I am.

VENTIDIUS.
I say, you are not. Try your fortune.

ANTONY.
I have, to th'utmost. Dost thou think me desperate
Without just cause? No, when I found all lost
Beyond repair, I hid me from the world
And learnt to scorn it here, which now I do
So heartily, I think it is not worth
The cost of keeping.

VENTIDIUS.
Caesar thinks not so:
He'll thank you for the gift he could not take.
You would be killed like Tully,[23] would you? Do,
Hold out your throat to Caesar and die tamely.

ANTONY.
No, I can kill myself, and so resolve.

VENTIDIUS.
I can die with you, too, when time shall serve,
But Fortune calls upon us now to live,
To fight, to conquer.

ANTONY.
Sure thou dream'st, Ventidius.

VENTIDIUS.
No, 'tis you dream; you sleep away your hours
In desperate sloth, miscalled philosophy.
Up, up, for honor's sake; twelve legions wait you
And long to call you chief. By painful journeys
I led 'em, patient both of heat and hunger,
Down from the Parthian marches[24] to the Nile.
'Twill do you good to see their sunburnt faces,
Their scarred cheeks, and chapped hands; there's virtue in 'em.
They'll sell those mangled limbs at dearer rates
Than yon trim bands[25] can buy.

ANTONY.
Where left you them?

VENTIDIUS.
I said in Lower Syria.[26]

ANTONY.
Bring 'em hither;
There may be life in these.

VENTIDIUS.
They will not come.

ANTONY.
Why didst thou mock my hopes with promised aids
To double my despair? They're mutinous.

VENTIDIUS.
Most firm and loyal.

ANTONY.
Yet they will not march
To succor me. Oh trifler!

VENTIDIUS.
They petition
You would make haste to head 'em.

23 Tully] Marcus Tullius Cicero, Antony's long-time enemy, was captured and killed by Antony's soldiers in Caieta in 43 BCE.

24 marches] borders

25 yon trim bands] Octavius' troops

26 Lower Syria] During Antony's time both Phoenicia and Judea were included in Syria.

ANTONY.
I'm besieged.
VENTIDIUS.
There's but one way shut up: How came I hither?
ANTONY.
I will not stir.
VENTIDIUS.
They would perhaps desire
A better reason.
ANTONY.
I have never used[27]
My soldiers to demand a reason of
My actions. Why did they refuse to march?
VENTIDIUS.
They said they would not fight for Cleopatra.
ANTONY.
What was't they said?
VENTIDIUS.
They said they would not fight for Cleopatra.
Why should they fight indeed, to make her conquer
And make you more a slave? to gain you kingdoms,
Which, for a kiss at your next midnight feast,
You'll sell to her? Then she new-names her jewels
And calls this diamond such or such a tax;
Each pendant in her ear shall be a province.
ANTONY.
Ventidius, I allow your tongue free license
On all my other faults, but on your life,
No word of Cleopatra: She deserves
More worlds than I can lose.
VENTIDIUS.
Behold, you Pow'rs,
To whom you have intrusted humankind;
See Europe, Afric, Asia put in balance
And all weighed down by one light, worthless woman!
I think the gods are Antonys, and give,
Like prodigals, this nether world away
To none but wasteful hands.
ANTONY.
You grow presumptuous.
VENTIDIUS.
I take the privilege of plain love to speak.
ANTONY.
Plain love! Plain arrogance, plain insolence:
Thy men are cowards; thou an envious traitor,
Who, under seeming honesty, hast vented
The burden of thy rank, o'erflowing gall.
Oh that thou wert my equal, great in arms
As the first Caesar was, that I might kill thee
Without a stain to honor!
VENTIDIUS.
You may kill me.
You have done more already: called me traitor.
ANTONY.
Art thou not one?
VENTIDIUS.
For showing you yourself,
Which none else durst have done? But had I been
That name, which I disdain to speak again,
I needed not have sought your abject fortunes,
Come to partake your fate, to die with you.
What hindered me t'have led my conqu'ring eagles[28]
To fill Octavius' bands? I could have been
A traitor then, a glorious, happy traitor,
And not have been so called.
ANTONY.
Forgive me, soldier:
I've been too passionate.
VENTIDIUS.
You thought me false;
Thought my old age betrayed you. Kill me, sir;
Pray, kill me. Yet you need not; your unkindness
Has left your sword no work.
ANTONY.
I did not think so;
I said it in my rage: prithee forgive me.
Why didst thou tempt my anger by discovery
Of what I would not hear?
VENTIDIUS.
No prince but you
Could merit that sincerity I used,
Nor durst another man have ventured it,
But you, ere love misled your wand'ring eyes,
Were sure the chief and best of human race,

27 used] accustomed

28 my conqu'ring eagles] The eagle was the principal standard carried before a Roman legion.

Framed in the very pride and boast of Nature,
So perfect, that the gods who formed you wondered
At their own skill, and cried, "A lucky hit
Has mended our design." Their envy hindered,
Else you had been immortal and a pattern,
When Heav'n would work for ostentation sake,
To copy out again.

ANTONY.
But Cleopatra—
Go on, for I can bear it now.

VENTIDIUS.
No more.

ANTONY.
Thou dar'st not trust my passion, but thou mayst:
Thou only lov'st; the rest have flattered me.

VENTIDIUS.
Heav'n's blessing on your heart for that kind word.
May I believe you love me? Speak again.

ANTONY.
Indeed I do. Speak this, and this, and this.
(*Hugging him.*)
Thy praises were unjust, but I'll deserve 'em,
And yet mend all. Do with me what thou wilt;
Lead me to victory. Thou know'st the way.

VENTIDIUS.
And, will you leave this—

ANTONY.
Prithee do not curse her,
And I will leave her; though Heav'n knows, I love
Beyond life, conquest, empire, all but honor.
But I will leave her.

VENTIDIUS.
That's my royal master.
And, shall we fight?

ANTONY.
I warrant thee, old soldier,
Thou shalt behold me once again in iron
And at the head of our old troops that beat
The Parthians cry aloud, "Come, follow me."

VENTIDIUS.
Oh now I hear my Emp'ror! In that word
Octavius fell. Gods, let me see that day
And, if I have ten years behind, take all;
I'll thank you for th'exchange.

ANTONY.
Oh Cleopatra!

VENTIDIUS.
Again?

ANTONY.
I've done: in that last sigh, she went.
Caesar shall know what 'tis to force a lover
From all he holds most dear.

VENTIDIUS.
Methinks you breathe
Another soul: your looks are more divine;
You speak a hero, and you move a god.

ANTONY.
Oh, thou hast fired me; my soul's up in arms
And mans each part about me. Once again,
That noble eagerness of fight has seized me:
That eagerness with which I darted upward
To Cassius' camp.[29] In vain the steepy hill
Opposed my way; in vain a war of spears
Sung round my head and planted all my shield.
I won the trenches while my foremost men
Lagged on the plain below.

VENTIDIUS.
Ye gods, ye gods,
For such another hour!

ANTONY.
Come on, my soldier!
Our hearts and arms are still the same: I long
Once more to meet our foes, that thou and I,
Like Time and Death, marching before our troops,
May taste fate[30] to 'em; mow 'em out a passage
And, ent'ring where the foremost squadrons yield,
Begin the noble harvest of the field.

Exeunt.

Act II.

Cleopatra, Iras, and Alexas.

CLEOPATRA.
What shall I do, or whither shall I turn?
Ventidius has o'ercome, and he will go.

ALEXAS.
He goes to fight for you.

---

29 Cassius' camp] Antony and Octavius defeated Cassius and Brutus at Philippi in 42 BCE.

30 taste fate] as an official taster would test food and drink for a monarch

CLEOPATRA.
Then he would see me ere he went to fight.
Flatter me not: if once he goes, he's lost,
And all my hopes destroyed.
ALEXAS.
Does this weak passion
Become a mighty queen?
CLEOPATRA.
I am no queen.
Is this to be a queen, to be besieged
By yon insulting Roman, and to wait
Each hour the victor's chain? These ills are small,
For Antony is lost, and I can mourn
For nothing else but him. Now come, Octavius,
I have no more to lose; prepare thy bands;
I'm fit to be a captive: Antony
Has taught my mind the fortune of a slave.
IRAS.
Call reason to assist you.
CLEOPATRA.
I have none,
And none would have: my love's a noble madness,
Which shows the cause deserved it. Moderate sorrow
Fits vulgar love, and for a vulgar man,
But I have loved with such transcendent passion,
I soared, at first, quite out of reason's view,
And now am lost above it. No, I'm proud
'Tis thus. Would Antony could see me now.
Think you he would not sigh? Though he must leave me,
Sure he would sigh, for he is noble-natured
And bears a tender heart: I know him well.
Ah, no, I know him not; I knew him once,
But now 'tis past.
IRAS.
Let it be past with you:
Forget him, madam.
CLEOPATRA.
Never, never, Iras.
He once was mine; and once, though now 'tis gone,
Leaves a faint image of possession still.
ALEXAS.
Think him unconstant, cruel, and ungrateful.
CLEOPATRA.
I cannot. If I could, those thoughts were vain;
Faithless, ungrateful, cruel though he be,
I still must love him.

Enter Charmion.

Now, what news, my Charmion?
Will he be kind? and will he not forsake me?
Am I to live, or die? Nay, do I live?
Or am I dead? for, when he gave his answer,
Fate took the word, and then I lived or died.
CHARMION.
I found him, madam—
CLEOPATRA.
A long speech preparing?
If thou bring'st comfort, haste, and give it me,
For never was more need.
IRAS.
I know he loves you.
CLEOPATRA.
Had he been kind, her eyes had told me so
Before her tongue could speak it. Now she studies
To soften what he said, but give me death
Just as he sent it, Charmion, undisguised
And in the words he spoke.
CHARMION.
I found him then
Incompassed round, I think, with iron statues,
So mute, so motionless his soldiers stood
While awfully he cast his eyes about,
And ev'ry leader's hopes or fears surveyed:
Methought he looked resolved, and yet not pleased.
When he beheld me struggling in the crowd,
He blushed, and bade make way.
ALEXAS.
There's comfort yet.
CHARMION.
Ventidius fixed his eyes upon my passage,
Severely, as he meant to frown me back,
And sullenly gave place. I told my message,
Just as you gave it, broken and disordered;
I numbered in it all your sighs and tears,
And while I moved your pitiful request
That you but only begged a last farewell,
He fetched an inward groan and, ev'ry time
I named you, sighed as if his heart were breaking,
But shunned my eyes, and guiltily looked down.
He seemed not now that awful[31] Antony

[31] awful] awe-inspiring

Who shook an armed assembly with his nod,
But making show as he would rub his eyes,
Disguised and blotted out a falling tear.

CLEOPATRA.
Did he then weep? and was I worth a tear?
If what thou hast to say be not as pleasing,
Tell me no more, but let me die contented.

CHARMION.
He bid me say, he knew himself so well,
He could deny you nothing if he saw you,
And therefore—

CLEOPATRA.
Thou wouldst say, he would not see me?

CHARMION.
And therefore begged you not to use a power
Which he could ill resist, yet he should ever
Respect you as he ought.

CLEOPATRA.
Is that a word
For Antony to use to Cleopatra?
Oh that faint word, "respect"! How I disdain it!
Disdain myself, for loving after it!
He should have kept that word for cold Octavia.
Respect is for a wife: Am I that thing,
That dull, insipid lump, without desires,
And without pow'r to give 'em?

ALEXAS.
You misjudge;
You see through love, and that deludes your sight,
As what is straight seems crooked through the water.
But I, who bear my reason undisturbed,
Can see this Antony, this dreaded man,
A fearful slave, who fain would run away,
And shuns his master's eyes: if you pursue him,
My life on't, he still drags a chain along
That needs must clog his flight.

CLEOPATRA.
Could I believe thee!

ALEXAS.
By ev'ry circumstance I know he loves.
True, he's hard pressed by int'rest and by honor;
Yet he but doubts and parleys and casts out
Many a long look for succor.

CLEOPATRA.
He sends word
He fears to see my face.

ALEXAS.
And would you more?
He shows his weakness who declines the combat,
And you must urge your fortune. Could he speak
More plainly? To my ears the message sounds,
"Come to my rescue, Cleopatra, come;
Come, free me from Ventidius, from my tyrant;
See me, and give me a pretense to leave him."
I hear his trumpets. This way he must pass.
Please you, retire a while; I'll work him first,
That he may bend more easy.

CLEOPATRA.
You shall rule me,
But all, I fear, in vain.

Exit with Charmion and Iras.

ALEXAS.
I fear so too,
Though I concealed my thoughts to make her bold.
But 'tis our utmost means, and Fate befriend it!
(*Withdraws.*)

Enter lictors with fasces, one bearing the eagle; then enter Antony with Ventidius, followed by other commanders.

ANTONY.
Octavius is the minion of blind Chance,
But holds from Virtue nothing.

VENTIDIUS.
Has he courage?

ANTONY.
But just enough to season him from coward.
Oh, 'tis the coldest youth upon a charge,
The most deliberate fighter! If he ventures
(As in Illyria once they say he did
To storm a town) 'tis when he cannot choose,
When all the world have fixed their eyes upon him,
And then he lives on that for seven years after,
But at a close revenge he never fails.

VENTIDIUS.
I heard you challenged him.

ANTONY.
I did, Ventidius.
What think'st thou was his answer? 'Twas so tame—
He said he had more ways than one to die,
I had not.

VENTIDIUS.
Poor!
ANTONY.
He has more ways than one,
But he would choose 'em all before that one.
VENTIDIUS.
He first would choose an ague or a fever.
ANTONY.
No, it must be an ague, not a fever;
He has not warmth enough to die by that.
VENTIDIUS.
Or old age and a bed.
ANTONY.
Aye, there's his choice.
He would live, like a lamp, to the last wink,
And crawl upon the utmost verge of life.
Oh Hercules! Why should a man like this,
Who dares not trust his fate for one great action,
Be all the care of Heav'n? Why should he lord it
O'er fourscore thousand men, of whom each one
Is braver than himself?
VENTIDIUS.
You conquered for him:
Philippi[32] knows it; there you shared with him
That empire, which your sword made all your own.
ANTONY.
Fool that I was, upon my eagle's wings
I bore this wren till I was tired with soaring,[33]
And now he mounts above me.
Good heav'ns, is this, is this the man who braves me?
Who bids my age make way, drives me before him
To the world's ridge, and sweeps me off like rubbish?
VENTIDIUS.
Sir, we lose time; the troops are mounted all.
ANTONY.
Then give the word to march:
I long to leave this prison of a town,
To join thy legions, and in open field,
Once more to show my face. Lead, my deliverer.

Enter Alexas.

ALEXAS.
Great Emperor,
In mighty arms renowned above mankind,
But, in soft pity to th'oppressed, a god,
This message sends the mournful Cleopatra
To her departing lord.
VENTIDIUS.
Smooth sycophant!
ALEXAS.
A thousand wishes and ten thousand prayers,
Millions of blessings wait you to the wars;
Millions of sighs and tears she sends you too,
And would have sent
As many dear embraces to your arms,
As many parting kisses to your lips,
But those, she fears, have wearied you already.
VENTIDIUS. (*Aside.*)
False crocodile!
ALEXAS.
And yet she begs not now you would not leave her;
That were a wish too mighty for her hopes,
Too presuming
For her low fortune and your ebbing love;[d]
That were a wish for her more prosp'rous days,
Her blooming beauty, and your growing kindness.
ANTONY. (*Aside.*)
Well, I must man it out. What would the Queen?
ALEXAS.
First, to these noble warriors, who attend
Your daring courage in the chase of fame
(Too daring and too dang'rous for her quiet)
She humbly recommends all she holds dear,
All her own cares and fears, the care of you.
VENTIDIUS.
Yes, witness Actium.
ANTONY.
Let him speak, Ventidius.
ALEXAS.
You, when his matchless valor bears him forward,
With ardor too heroic, on his foes,
Fall down, as she would do, before his feet;
Lie in his way and stop the paths of death.
Tell him, this god is not invulnerable,
That absent Cleopatra bleeds in him,
And, that you may remember her petition,
She begs you wear these trifles as a pawn,

32 Philippi] the battle of Philippi 42 BCE in which Antony's troops saved Octavius' troops from being overrun by Brutus

33 upon my eagle's wings … soaring] Aesop's fable of the wren who was carried on the back of an eagle and then flew higher than the eagle

Which, at your wished return, she will redeem
(*Gives jewels to the commanders.*)
With all the wealth of Egypt:
This to the great Ventidius she presents,
Whom she can never count her enemy,
Because he loves her lord.

VENTIDIUS.
Tell her I'll none on't.
I'm not ashamed of honest poverty:
Not all the diamonds of the East can bribe
Ventidius from his faith. I hope to see
These, and the rest of all her sparkling store,
Where they shall more deservingly be placed.

ANTONY.
And who must wear 'em then?

VENTIDIUS.
The wronged Octavia.

ANTONY.
You might have spared that word.

VENTIDIUS.
And he that bribe.

ANTONY.
But have I no remembrance?

ALEXAS.
Yes, a dear one:
Your slave, the Queen—

ANTONY.
My mistress.

ALEXAS.
Then your mistress;
Your mistress would, she says, have sent her soul,
But that you had long since; she humbly begs
This ruby bracelet, set with bleeding hearts,
(The emblems of her own) may bind your arm.
(*Presenting a bracelet.*)

VENTIDIUS.
Now, my best lord, in honor's name I ask you,
For manhood's sake, and for her own dear safety,
Touch not these poisoned gifts,
Infected by the sender; touch 'em not.
Myriads of bluest plagues lie underneath 'em,
And more than aconite has dipped the silk.[34]

ANTONY.
Nay, now you grow too cynical, Ventidius.
A lady's favors may be worn with honor.
What, to refuse her bracelet! On my soul,
When I lie pensive in my tent alone,
'Twill pass the wakeful hours of winter nights
To tell these pretty beads upon my arm,
To count for every one a soft embrace,
A melting kiss at such and such a time,
And now and then the fury of her love.
When–And what harm's in this?

ALEXAS.
None, none, my lord,
But what's to her, that now 'tis past forever.

ANTONY. (*Going to tie it.*)
We soldiers are so awkward–help me tie it.

ALEXAS.
In faith, my lord, we courtiers too are awkward
In these affairs. So are all men indeed;
Ev'n I, who am not one. But shall I speak?

ANTONY.
Yes, freely.

ALEXAS.
Then, my lord, fair hands alone
Are fit to tie it; she who sent it can.

VENTIDIUS.
Hell, Death! this eunuch pander ruins you.
You will not see her?

Alexas whispers an attendant, who goes out.

ANTONY.
But to take my leave.

VENTIDIUS.
Then I have washed an Ethiop.[35] Y'are undone;
Y'are in the toils; y'are taken; y'are destroyed:
Her eyes do Caesar's work.

ANTONY.
You fear too soon.
I'm constant to myself: I know my strength,
And yet she shall not think me barbarous neither,
Born in the depths of Afric. I'm a Roman,
Bred to the rules of soft humanity.
A guest, and kindly used, should bid farewell.

---

34 aconite … silk.] Aconite was supposedly the fastest acting poison; Ventidius perhaps alludes here to the death of Hercules, who was poisoned when he put on the bloody shirt of the centaur Nessus given him by Deianira who hoped to gain his love.

35 washed an Ethiop] proverbial for a futile task

VENTIDIUS.
You do not know
How weak you are to her, how much an infant;
You are not proof against a smile or glance;
A sigh will quite disarm you.

ANTONY.
See, she comes!
Now you shall find your error. Gods, I thank you:
I formed the danger greater than it was,
And now 'tis near, 'tis lessened.

VENTIDIUS.
Mark the end yet.

Enter Cleopatra, Charmion, and Iras.

ANTONY.
Well, madam, we are met.

CLEOPATRA.
Is this a meeting?
Then we must part?

ANTONY.
We must.

CLEOPATRA.
Who says we must?

ANTONY.
Our own hard fates.

CLEOPATRA.
We make those fates ourselves.

ANTONY.
Yes, we have made 'em; we have loved each other
Into our mutual ruin.

CLEOPATRA.
The gods have seen my joys with envious eyes;
I have no friends in heav'n, and all the world
(As 'twere the bus'ness of mankind to part us)
Is armed against my love: ev'n you yourself
Join with the rest; you, you are armed against me.

ANTONY.
I will be justified in all I do
To late posterity, and therefore hear me.
If I mix a lie
With any truth, reproach me freely with it;
Else favor me with silence.

CLEOPATRA.
You command me,
And I am dumb.

VENTIDIUS.
I like this well: he shows authority.

ANTONY.
That I derive my ruin
From you alone—

CLEOPATRA.
Oh heav'ns! I ruin you!

ANTONY.
You promised me your silence, and you break it
Ere I have scarce begun.

CLEOPATRA.
Well, I obey you.

ANTONY.
When I beheld you first, it was in Egypt,
Ere Caesar saw your eyes. You gave me love
And were too young to know it; that I settled
Your father in his throne was for your sake.[36]
I left th'acknowledgment for time to ripen.
Caesar stepped in, and with greedy hand
Plucked the green fruit, ere the first blush of red,
Yet cleaving to the bough. He was my lord
And was, beside, too great for me to rival,
But I deserved you first, though he enjoyed you.
When, after, I beheld you in Cilicia
An enemy to Rome, I pardoned you.

CLEOPATRA.
I cleared myself—

ANTONY.
Again you break your promise.
I loved you still and took your weak excuses,
Took you into my bosom, stained by Caesar,
And not half mine: I went to Egypt with you
And hid me from the bus'ness of the world,
Shut out enquiring nations from my sight,
To give whole years to you.

VENTIDIUS. (*Aside.*)
Yes, to your shame be't spoken.

ANTONY.
How I loved,
Witness ye days and nights and all your hours
That danced away with down upon your feet,
As all your bus'ness were to count my passion.
One day passed by and nothing saw but love;

---

[36] When … your sake.] Antony arrived in Egypt in 55 BCE as part of a Roman army imported to restore Cleopatra's father to his throne (Cleopatra was only fourteen); Caesar first arrived in Alexandria in 48 BCE.

Another came, and still 'twas only love.
The suns were wearied out with looking on,
And I untired with loving.
I saw you ev'ry day, and all the day,
And ev'ry day was still but as the first,
So eager was I still to see you more.

VENTIDIUS.
'Tis all too true.

ANTONY.
Fulvia, my wife,[37] grew jealous,
As she indeed had reason, raised a war
In Italy to call me back.

VENTIDIUS.
But yet
You went not.

ANTONY.
While within your arms I lay,
The world fell mold'ring from my hands each hour
And left me scarce a grasp (I thank your love for't.)

VENTIDIUS.
Well pushed: that last was home.

CLEOPATRA.
Yet may I speak?

ANTONY.
If I have urged a falsehood, yes; else, not.
Your silence says I have not. Fulvia died
(Pardon, you gods, with my unkindness died).
To set the world at peace I took Octavia,
This Caesar's sister; in her pride of youth
And flow'r of beauty did I wed that lady,
Whom blushing I must praise, because I left her.
You called; my love obeyed the fatal summons;
This raised the Roman arms; the cause was yours.
I would have fought by land, where I was stronger;
You hindered it, yet when I fought at sea,
Forsook me fighting, and (Oh stain to honor!
Oh lasting shame!) I knew not that I fled,
But fled to follow you.

VENTIDIUS.
What haste she made to hoist her purple sails!
And, to appear magnificent in flight,
Drew half our strength away.

ANTONY.
All this you caused,
And would you multiply more ruins on me?
This honest man, my best, my only friend,
Has gathered up the shipwrack of my fortunes;
Twelve legions I have left, my last recruits,
And you have watched the news and bring your eyes
To seize them too. If you have aught to answer,
Now speak, you have free leave.

ALEXAS. (*Aside.*)
She stands confounded:
Despair is in her eyes.

VENTIDIUS.
Now lay a sigh i'th'way to stop his passage:
Prepare a tear and bid it for his legions;
'Tis like they shall be sold.

CLEOPATRA.
How shall I plead my cause when you, my judge,
Already have condemned me? Shall I bring
The love you bore me for my advocate?
That now is turned against me, that destroys me,
For, love once past is, at the best, forgotten,
But oft'ner sours to hate: 'twill please my lord
To ruin me, and therefore I'll be guilty.
But could I once have thought it would have pleased you,
That you would pry with narrow searching eyes
Into my faults, severe to my destruction,
And watching all advantages with care
That serve to make me wretched? Speak, my lord,
For I end here. Though I deserve this usage,
Was it like you to give it?

ANTONY.
Oh you wrong me
To think I sought this parting, or desired
To accuse you more than what will clear myself
And justify this breach.

CLEOPATRA.
Thus low I thank you,
And since my innocence will not offend,
I shall not blush to own it.

VENTIDIUS.
After this,
I think she'll blush at nothing.

CLEOPATRA.
You seem grieved
(And therein you are kind) that Caesar first
Enjoyed my love, though you deserved it better.

[37] Fulvia] Antony married Fulvia in 46 BCE; she died in 40 BCE.

I grieve for that, my lord, much more than you,
For had I first been yours, it would have saved
My second choice: I never had been his,
And ne'er had been but yours. But Caesar first,
You say, possessed my love. Not so, my lord:
He first possessed my person, you my love;
Caesar loved me, but I loved Antony.
If I endured him after, 'twas because
I judged it due to the first name of men,
And half constrained, I gave, as to a tyrant,
What he would take by force.

VENTIDIUS.
Oh siren! siren!
Yet grant that all the love she boasts were true,
Has she not ruined you? I still urge that,
The fatal consequence.

CLEOPATRA.
The consequence indeed,
For I dare challenge him, my greatest foe,
To say it was designed: 'tis true I loved you
And kept you far from an uneasy wife
(Such Fulvia was).
Yes, but he'll say you left Octavia for me—
And can you blame me to receive that love
Which quitted such desert for worthless me?
How often have I wished some other Caesar,
Great as the first, and as the second young,
Would court my love, to be refused for you!

VENTIDIUS.
Words, words; but Actium, sir, remember Actium.

CLEOPATRA.
Ev'n there I dare his malice. True, I counseled
To fight at sea, but I betrayed you not.
I fled, but not to the enemy. 'Twas fear.
Would I had been a man, not to have feared,
For none would then have envied me your friendship,
Who envy me your love.

ANTONY.
We're both unhappy:
If nothing else, yet our ill fortune parts us.
Speak: Would you have me perish by my stay?

CLEOPATRA.
If as a friend you ask my judgment, go;
If as a lover, stay. If you must perish—
'Tis a hard word–but stay.

VENTIDIUS.
See now th'effects of her so boasted love!
She strives to drag you down to ruin with her,
But could she 'scape without you, oh how soon
Would she let go her hold and haste to shore
And never look behind!

CLEOPATRA.
Then judge my love by this.
(*Giving Antony a writing.*)
Could I have borne
A life or death, a happiness or woe
From yours divided, this had giv'n me means.

ANTONY.
By Hercules, the writing of Octavius!
I know it well; 'tis that proscribing hand,[38]
Young as it was, that led the way to mine
And left me but the second place in murder.—
See, see, Ventidius! here he offers Egypt,
And joins all Syria to it as a present,
So, in requital, she forsake my fortunes
And join her arms with his.

CLEOPATRA.
And yet you leave me!
You leave me, Antony, and yet I love you.
Indeed I do. I have refused a kingdom;
That's a trifle:
For I could part with life, with anything
But only you. Oh, let me die but with you!
Is that a hard request?

ANTONY.
Next living with you,
'Tis all that Heav'n can give.

ALEXAS. (*Aside.*)
He melts; we conquer.

CLEOPATRA.
No; you shall go. Your int'rest calls you hence.
Yes; your dear int'rest pulls too strong for these
Weak arms to hold you here.– (*Takes his hand.*)
Go, leave me, soldier
(For you're no more a lover), leave me dying:
Push me all pale and panting from your bosom,
And when your march begins, let one run after,

---

38 proscribing hand] After the assassination of Julius Caesar, Octavius and Antony drew up proscription lists of enemies who should die.

Breathless almost for joy, and cry, "She's dead."
The soldiers shout; you then perhaps may sigh
And muster all your Roman gravity.
Ventidius chides, and straight your brow clears up,
As I had never been.

ANTONY.
Gods, 'tis too much; too much for man to bear!

CLEOPATRA.
What is't for me, then,
A weak, forsaken woman? and a lover?
Here let me breathe my last. Envy me not
This minute in your arms: I'll die apace,
As fast as e'er I can, and end your trouble.

ANTONY.
Die! Rather let me perish: loosened Nature
Leap from its hinges. Sink the props of heav'n,
And fall the skies to crush the nether world.
My eyes, my soul, my all!– (*Embraces her.*)

VENTIDIUS.
And what's this toy
In balance with your fortune, honor, fame?

ANTONY.
What is't, Ventidius? It outweighs 'em all;
Why, we have more than conquered Caesar now:
My queen's not only innocent, but loves me.
This, this is she who drags me down to ruin!
"But could she 'scape without me, with what haste
Would she let slip her hold, and make to shore,
And never look behind!"
Down on thy knees, blasphemer as thou art,
And ask forgiveness of wronged innocence.

VENTIDIUS.
I'll rather die than take it. Will you go?

ANTONY.
Go! Whither? Go from all that's excellent!
Faith, honor, virtue, all good things forbid
That I should go from her who sets my love
Above the price of kingdoms. Give, you gods,
Give to your boy, your Caesar,
This rattle of a globe to play withal,
This gewgaw world, and put him cheaply off;
I'll not be pleased with less than Cleopatra.

CLEOPATRA.
She's wholly yours. My heart's so full of joy
That I shall do some wild extravagance
Of love in public, and the foolish world,
Which knows not tenderness, will think me mad.

VENTIDIUS.
Oh women! Women! Women! All the gods
Have not such pow'r of doing good to man
As you of doing harm. (*Exit.*)

ANTONY.
Our men are armed.
Unbar the gate that looks to Caesar's camp.
I would revenge the treachery he meant me,
And long security makes conquest easy.
I'm eager to return before I go,
For all the pleasures I have known beat thick
On my remembrance: how I long for night!
That both the sweets of mutual love may try
And once triumph o'er Caesar ere[e] we die. (*Exeunt.*)

Act III.

At one door enter Cleopatra, Charmion, Iras, and Alexas, a train of Egyptians; at the other, Antony and Romans. The entrance on both sides is prepared by music, the trumpets first sounding on Antony's part, then answered by timbrels etc. on Cleopatra's. Charmion and Iras hold a laurel wreath betwixt them. A dance of Egyptians. After the ceremony, Cleopatra crowns Antony.

ANTONY.
I thought how those white arms would fold me in
And strain me close and melt me into love;
So pleased with that sweet image, I sprung forwards
And added all my strength to every blow.

CLEOPATRA.
Come to me, come my soldier, to my arms.
You've been too long away from my embraces,
But when I have you fast, and all my own,
With broken murmurs and with amorous sighs,
I'll say you were unkind and punish you
And mark you red with many an eager kiss.

ANTONY.
My brighter Venus!

CLEOPATRA.
Oh my greater Mars!

ANTONY.
Thou join'st us well, my love!
Suppose me come from the Phlegraean plains,[39]

39 Phlegraean plains] where Hercules helped the gods defeat the giants in battle and bury them beneath the earth

Where gasping giants lay, cleft by my sword,
And mountain tops pared off each other blow
To bury those I slew. Receive me, goddess:
Let Caesar spread his subtle nets, like Vulcan;[40]
In thy embraces I would be beheld
By heav'n and earth at once,
And make their envy what they meant their sport.
Let those who took us blush; I would love on
With awful state, regardless of their frowns,
As their superior god.
There's no satiety of love in thee:
Enjoyed, thou still art new; perpetual spring
Is in thy arms; the ripened fruit but falls,
And blossoms rise to fill its empty place,
And I grow rich by giving.

Enter Ventidius and stands apart.

ALEXAS.
Oh, now the danger's past, your general comes.
He joins not in your joys, nor minds your triumphs,
But, with contracted brows, looks frowning on,
As envying your success.

ANTONY.
Now, on my soul, he loves me, truly loves me.
He never flattered me in any vice,
But awes me with his virtue: ev'n this minute,
Methinks he has a right of chiding me.
Lead to the temple: I'll avoid his presence;
It checks too strong upon me.

Exeunt the rest. As Antony is going, Ventidius pulls him by the robe.

VENTIDIUS.
Emperor.

ANTONY. (*Looking back.*)
'Tis the old argument; I prithee spare me.

VENTIDIUS.
But this one hearing, emperor.

ANTONY.
Let go
My robe, or by my father Hercules—

VENTIDIUS.
By Hercules his father, that's yet greater,
I bring you somewhat you would wish to know.

ANTONY.
Thou see'st we are observed; attend me here,
And I'll return. (*Exit.*)

VENTIDIUS.
I'm waning in his favor, yet I love him;
I love this man, who runs to meet his ruin,
And sure the gods, like me, are fond of him:
His virtues lie so mingled with his crimes,
As would confound their choice to punish one
And not reward the other.

Enter Antony.

ANTONY.
We can conquer,
You see, without your aid.
We have dislodged their troops;
They look on us at distance, and, like curs
'Scaped from the lion's paws, they bay far off
And lick their wounds and faintly threaten war.
Five thousand Romans with their faces upward
Lie breathless on the plain.

VENTIDIUS.
'Tis well: and he
Who lost 'em could have spared ten thousand more.
Yet if, by this advantage, you could gain
An easier peace, while Caesar doubts the chance
Of arms!—

ANTONY.
Oh think not on't, Ventidius.
The boy pursues my ruin, he'll no peace:
His malice is considerate in advantage.
Oh, he's the coolest murderer, so staunch,
He kills and keeps his temper.

VENTIDIUS.
Have you no friend
In all his army who has pow'r to move him?
Maecenas or Agrippa might do much.

ANTONY.
They're both too deep in Caesar's interests.
We'll work it out by dint of sword, or perish.

VENTIDIUS.
Fain I would find some other.

ANTONY.
Thank thy love.

40 like Vulcan] When Vulcan discovered that his wife Venus was committing adultery with Mars, he ensnared them in bed in a fine, unbreakable net, inviting the other gods to come laugh at them.

Some four or five such victories as this
Will save thy farther pains.

VENTIDIUS.
Expect no more; Caesar is on his guard.
I know, sir, you have conquered against odds,
But still you draw supplies from one poor town,
And of Egyptians; he has all the world,
And at his back nations come pouring in
To fill the gaps you make. Pray think again.

ANTONY.
Why dost thou drive me from myself, to search
For foreign aids? to hunt my memory
And range all o'er a waste and barren place
To find a friend? The wretched have no friends.—
Yet I had one, the bravest youth of Rome,
Whom Caesar loves beyond the love of women;
He could resolve his mind as fire does wax,
From that hard, rugged image melt him down
And mold him in what softer form he pleased.

VENTIDIUS.
Him would I see, that man of all the world:
Just such a one we want.*

ANTONY.
He loved me too:
I was his soul; he lived not but in me.
We were so closed within each other's breasts,
The rivets were not found that joined us first.
That does not reach us yet: we were so mixed,
As meeting streams, both to ourselves were lost;
We were one mass; we could not give or take
But from the same, for he was I, I he.

VENTIDIUS. (*Aside.*)
He moves as I would wish him.

ANTONY.
After this,
I need not tell his name: 'twas Dollabella.

VENTIDIUS.
He's now in Caesar's camp.

ANTONY.
No matter where,
Since he's no longer mine. He took unkindly
That I forbade him Cleopatra's sight
Because I feared he loved her. He confessed
He had a warmth which, for my sake, he stifled;
For 'twere impossible that two, so one,
Should not have loved the same. When he departed,
He took no leave, and that confirmed my thoughts.

VENTIDIUS.
It argues that he loved you more than her,
Else he had stayed. But he perceived you jealous
And would not grieve his friend; I know he loves you.

ANTONY.
I should have seen him, then, ere now.

VENTIDIUS.
Perhaps
He has thus long been lab'ring for your peace.

ANTONY.
Would he were here.

VENTIDIUS.
Would you believe he loved you?
I read your answer in your eyes: you would.
Not to conceal it longer, he has sent
A messenger from Caesar's camp with letters.

ANTONY.
Let him appear.

VENTIDIUS.
I'll bring him instantly.

Exit Ventidius and re-enters immediately with Dollabella.

ANTONY.
'Tis he himself, himself, by holy friendship! (*Runs to embrace him.*)
Art thou returned at last, my better half?
Come, give me all myself. Let me not live,[f]
If the bridegroom, longing for his night,
Was ever half so fond.

DOLLABELLA.
I must be silent, for my soul is busy
About a nobler work: she's new come home,
Like a long-absent man, and wanders o'er
Each room, a stranger to her own, to look
If all be safe.

ANTONY.
Thou hast what's left of me;
For I am now so sunk from what I was,
Thou find'st me at my lowest watermark.
The rivers that ran in and raised my fortunes
Are all dried up or take another course:
What I have left is from my native spring;
I've still a heart that swells in scorn of Fate
And lifts me to my banks.

DOLLABELLA.
Still you are lord of all the world to me.

ANTONY.
Why, then I yet am so; for thou art all.
If I had any joy when thou wert absent,
I grudged it to myself; methought I robbed
Thee of thy part. But oh my Dollabella!
Thou hast beheld me other than I am.
Hast thou not seen my morning chambers filled
With sceptered slaves who waited to salute* me?
With eastern monarchs, who forgot the sun
To worship my uprising? Menial kings
Ran coursing up and down my palace-yard,
Stood silent in my presence, watched my eyes,
And, at my least command, all started out
Like racers to the goal.

DOLLABELLA.
Slaves to your fortune.

ANTONY.
Fortune is Caesar's now, and what am I?

VENTIDIUS.
What you have made yourself; I will not flatter.

ANTONY.
Is this friendly done?

DOLLABELLA.
Yes, when his end is so, I must join with him;
Indeed I must, and yet you must not chide:
Why am I else your friend?

ANTONY.
Take heed, young man,
How thou upbraid'st my love: the Queen has eyes,
And thou too hast a soul. Canst thou remember
When, swelled with hatred, thou beheld'st her first,
As accessary to thy brother's death?

DOLLABELLA.
Spare my remembrance; 'twas a guilty day,
And still the blush hangs here.

ANTONY.
To clear herself
For sending him no aid, she came from Egypt.
Her galley down the silver Cydnos[41] rowed,
The tackling silk, the streamers waved with gold;
The gentle winds were lodged in purple sails.
Her nymphs, like Nereids,[42] round her couch were placed,
Where she, another sea-born Venus, lay.

DOLLABELLA.
No more; I would not hear it.

ANTONY.
Oh, you must!
She lay, and leant her cheek upon her hand
And cast a look so languishingly sweet
As if, secure of all beholders' hearts,
Neglecting she could take 'em. Boys, like cupids,
Stood fanning, with their painted wings, the winds
That played about her face, but if she smiled,
A darting glory seemed to blaze abroad,
That men's desiring eyes were never wearied,
But hung upon the object. To soft flutes
The silver oars kept time, and while they played,
The hearing gave new pleasure to the sight,
And both to thought: 'twas heav'n, or somewhat more,
For she so charmed all hearts, that gazing crowds
Stood panting on the shore and wanted* breath
To give their welcome voice.
Then, Dollabella, where was then thy soul?
Was not thy fury quite disarmed with wonder?
Didst thou not shrink behind me from those eyes
And whisper in my ear, "Oh tell her not
That I accused her of my brother's death"?

DOLLABELLA.
And should my weakness be a plea for yours?
Mine was an age when love might be excused,
When kindly warmth and when my springing youth
Made it a debt to Nature. Yours—

VENTIDIUS.
Speak boldly.
Yours, he would say, in your declining age,
When no more heat was left but what you forced,
When all the sap was needful for the trunk,
When it went down, then you constrained the course
And robbed from Nature to supply desire;
In you (I would not use so harsh a word)
But 'tis plain dotage.

ANTONY.
Hah!

DOLLABELLA.
'Twas urged too home.
But yet the loss was private that I made;
'Twas but myself I lost. I lost no legions;

[41] Cydnos] The river Cydnus flowed through Tarsus in Cilicia.

[42] Nereids] the 50 sea nymphs who were the daughters of the sea god Nereus in Greek mythology

I had no world to lose, no people's love.
ANTONY.
This from a friend?
DOLLABELLA.
Yes, Antony, a true one;
A friend so tender that each word I speak
Stabs my own heart before it reach your ear.
Oh, judge me not less kind because I chide.
To Caesar I excuse you.
ANTONY.
Oh ye gods!
Have I then lived to be excused to Caesar?
DOLLABELLA.
As to your equal.
ANTONY.
Well, he's but my equal;
While I wear this, he never shall be more.
DOLLABELLA.
I bring conditions from him.
ANTONY.
Are they noble?
Methinks thou shouldst not bring 'em else. Yet he
Is full of deep dissembling, knows no honor
Divided from his int'rest. Fate mistook him,
For Nature meant him for an usurer;
He's fit indeed to buy, not conquer, kingdoms.
VENTIDIUS.
Then, granting this,
What pow'r was theirs who wrought so hard a temper
To honorable terms!
ANTONY.
It was my Dollabella, or some god.
DOLLABELLA.
Nor I, nor yet Maecenas nor Agrippa:
They were your enemies, and I a friend
Too weak alone. Yet 'twas a Roman's deed.
ANTONY.
'Twas like a Roman done. Show me that man
Who has preserved my life, my love, my honor;
Let me but see his face.
VENTIDIUS.
That task is mine,
And, Heav'n, thou know'st how pleasing. (*Exit.*)
DOLLABELLA.
You'll remember
To whom you stand obliged?
ANTONY.
When I forget it,
Be thou unkind, and that's my greatest curse.
My queen shall thank him too.
DOLLABELLA.
I fear she will not.
ANTONY.
But she shall do't–the Queen, my Dollabella!
Hast thou not still some grudgings of thy fever?
DOLLABELLA.
I would not see her lost.
ANTONY.
When I forsake her,
Leave me, my better stars, for she has truth
Beyond her beauty. Caesar tempted her,
At no less price than kingdoms, to betray me,
But she resisted all, and yet thou chid'st me
For loving her too well. Could I do so?
DOLLABELLA.
Yes, there's my reason.

Re-enter Ventidius with Octavia, leading Antony's two little daughters.

ANTONY. (*Starting back.*)
Where?–Octavia there!
VENTIDIUS.
What, is she poison to you? a disease?
Look on her, view her well, and those she brings:
Are they all strangers to your eyes? has Nature
No secret call, no whisper they are yours?
DOLLABELLA.
For shame, my lord, if not for love, receive 'em
With kinder eyes. If you confess a man,
Meet 'em, embrace 'em, bid 'em welcome to you.
Your arms should open, ev'n without your knowledge,
To clasp 'em in; your feet should turn to wings
To bear you to 'em and your eyes dart out
And aim a kiss ere you could reach the lips.
ANTONY.
I stood amazed to think how they came hither.
VENTIDIUS.
I sent for 'em; I brought 'em in, unknown
To Cleopatra's guards.
DOLLABELLA.
Yet are you cold?

OCTAVIA.
Thus long I have attended for my welcome,
Which, as a stranger, sure I might expect.
Who am I?
ANTONY.
Caesar's sister.
OCTAVIA.
That's unkind!
Had I been nothing more than Caesar's sister,
Know, I had still remained in Caesar's camp,
But your Octavia, your much injured wife,
Though banished from your bed, driv'n from your house,
In spite of Caesar's sister, still is yours.
'Tis true, I have a heart disdains your coldness
And prompts me not to seek what you should offer,
But a wife's virtue still surmounts that pride:
I come to claim you as my own, to show
My duty first, to ask, nay beg, your kindness.
Your hand, my lord: 'tis mine, and I will have it.
(*Taking his hand.*)
VENTIDIUS.
Do, take it; thou deserv'st it.
DOLLABELLA.
On my soul,
And so she does: she's neither too submissive,
Nor yet too haughty, but so just a mean
Shows, as it ought, a wife and Roman too.
ANTONY.
I fear, Octavia, you have begged my life.
OCTAVIA.
Begged it, my lord?
ANTONY.
Yes, begged it, my ambassadress;
Poorly and basely begged it of your brother.
OCTAVIA.
Poorly and basely I could never beg;
Nor could my brother grant.
ANTONY.
Shall I, who to my kneeling slave could say,
"Rise up, and be a king," shall I fall down
And cry, "Forgive me, Caesar"? Shall I set
A man, my equal, in the place of Jove,
As he could give me being? No; that word
"Forgive" would choke me up
And die upon my tongue.
DOLLABELLA.
You shall not need it.
ANTONY.
I will not need it. Come, you've all betrayed me
(My friend too!) to receive some vile conditions.
My wife has bought me with her prayers and tears,
And now I must become her branded slave.
In every peevish mood she will upbraid
The life she gave: if I but look awry,
She cries, "I'll tell my brother."
OCTAVIA.
My hard fortune
Subjects me still to your unkind mistakes.
But the conditions I have brought are such
You need not blush to take: I love your honor
Because 'tis mine; it never shall be said
Octavia's husband was her brother's slave.
Sir, you are free–free ev'n from her you loathe,
For though my brother bargains for your love,
Makes me the price and cement of your peace,
I have a soul like yours: I cannot take
Your love as alms, nor beg what I deserve.
I'll tell my brother we are reconciled;
He shall draw back his troops, and you shall march
To rule the East: I may be dropped at Athens—
No matter where, I never will complain,
But only keep the barren name of wife
And rid you of the trouble.
VENTIDIUS.
Was ever such a strife of sullen honor!
Both scorn to be obliged.
DOLLABELLA.
Oh, she has touched him in the tender'st part;
See how he reddens with despite and shame
To be outdone in generosity!
VENTIDIUS.
See how he winks! how he dries up a tear
That fain would fall!
ANTONY.
Octavia, I have heard you and must praise
The greatness of your soul,
But cannot yield to what you have proposed,
For I can ne'er be conquered but by love,
And you do all for duty. You would free me
And would be dropped at Athens: Was't not so?
OCTAVIA.
It was, my lord.

ANTONY.
Then I must be obliged
To one who loves me not, who, to herself,
May call me thankless and ungrateful man.
I'll not endure it, no.
VENTIDIUS.
I'm glad it pinches there.
OCTAVIA.
Would you triumph o'er poor Octavia's virtue?
That pride was all I had to bear me up,
That you might think you owed me for your life
And owed it to my duty, not my love.
I have been injured, and my haughty soul
Could brook but ill the man who slights my bed.
ANTONY.
Therefore you love me not.
OCTAVIA.
Therefore, my lord,
I should not love you.
ANTONY.
Therefore you would leave me?
OCTAVIA.
And therefore I should leave you–if I could.
DOLLABELLA.
Her soul's too great, after such injuries,
To say she loves, and yet she lets you see it.
Her modesty and silence plead her cause.
ANTONY.
Oh, Dollabella, which way shall I turn?
I find a secret yielding in my soul,
But Cleopatra, who would die with me,
Must she be left? Pity pleads for Octavia,
But does it not plead more for Cleopatra?
VENTIDIUS.
Justice and pity both plead for Octavia,
For Cleopatra, neither.
One would be ruined with you, but she first
Had ruined you; the other you have ruined,
And yet she would preserve you.
In everything their merits are unequal.
ANTONY.
Oh, my distracted soul!
OCTAVIA.
Sweet Heav'n compose it!
Come, come, my lord, if I can pardon you,
Methinks you should accept it. Look on these:
Are they not yours? or stand they thus neglected
As they are mine? Go to him, children, go;
Kneel to him, take him by the hand, speak to him,
For you may speak, and he may own you, too,
Without a blush, and so he cannot all
His children.[43] Go, I say, and pull him to me,
And pull him to yourselves from that bad woman.
You, Agrippina, hang upon his arms,
And you, Antonia, clasp about his waist.
If he will shake you off, if he will dash you
Against the pavement, you must bear it, children,
For you are mine, and I was born to suffer.

Here the children go to him, etc.

VENTIDIUS.
Was ever sight so moving! Emperor!
DOLLABELLA.
Friend!
OCTAVIA.
Husband!
BOTH CHILDREN.
Father!
ANTONY.
I am vanquished: take me,
Octavia; take me, children; share me all.
(*Embracing them.*)
I've been a thriftless debtor to your loves
And run out much, in riot, from your stock,
But all shall be amended.
OCTAVIA.
Oh blest hour!
DOLLABELLA.
Oh happy change!
VENTIDIUS.
My joy stops at my tongue,
But it has found two channels here for one
And bubbles out above.
ANTONY. (*To Octavia.*)
This is thy triumph; lead me where thou wilt,
Ev'n to thy brother's camp.
OCTAVIA.
All there are yours.

Enter Alexas hastily.

---

43 he cannot … children.] Antony had three children with Cleopatra.

ALEXAS.
The Queen, my mistress, sir, and yours—
ANTONY.
'Tis past.[g]
—Octavia, you shall stay this night; tomorrow
Caesar and we are one.

Exit leading Octavia; Dollabella and the children follow.

VENTIDIUS.
There's news for you; run my officious eunuch,[h]
Be sure to be the first; haste forward;
Haste, my dear eunuch, haste! (*Exit.*)
ALEXAS.
This downright fighting fool, this thick-skulled hero,
This blunt, unthinking instrument of death,
With plain dull virtue has outgone my wit.
Pleasure forsook my earliest infancy;
The luxury of others robbed my cradle
And ravished thence the promise of a man:
Cast out from Nature, disinherited
Of what her meanest children claim by kind,
Yet greatness kept me from contempt. That's gone.
Had Cleopatra followed my advice,
Then he had been betrayed who now forsakes.
She dies for love, but she has known its joys.
Gods, is this just that I, who know no joys,
Must die because she loves?
Enter Cleopatra, Charmion, Iras, train.
Oh, madam, I have seen what blasts my eyes!
Octavia's here!
CLEOPATRA.
Peace with that raven's note.
I know it, too, and now am in
The pangs of death.
ALEXAS.
You are no more a queen;
Egypt is lost.
CLEOPATRA.
What tell'st thou me of Egypt?
My life, my soul is lost! Octavia has him!
Oh fatal name to Cleopatra's love!
My kisses, my embraces now are hers,
While I– But thou hast seen my rival: speak,
Does she deserve this blessing? Is she fair,
Bright as a goddess? and is all perfection
Confined to her? It is. Poor I was made
Of that coarse matter which, when she was finished,
The gods threw by for rubbish.
ALEXAS.
She's indeed a very miracle.
CLEOPATRA.
Death to my hopes, a miracle!
ALEXAS. (*Bowing.*)
A miracle—
I mean, of goodness; for in beauty, madam,
You make all wonders cease.
CLEOPATRA.
I was too rash.
Take this in part of recompense. But, oh, (*Giving a ring.*)
I fear thou flatter'st me.
CHARMION.
She comes! she's here!
IRAS.
Fly, madam, Caesar's sister!
CLEOPATRA.
Were she the sister of the thund'rer Jove[44]
And bore her brother's lightning in her eyes,
Thus would I face my rival.

Meets Octavia with Ventidius. Octavia bears up to her. Their trains come up on either side.

OCTAVIA.
I need not ask if you are Cleopatra:
Your haughty carriage—
CLEOPATRA.
Shows I am a queen.
Nor need I ask who you are.
OCTAVIA.
A Roman:
A name that makes, and can unmake, a queen.
CLEOPATRA.
Your lord, the man who serves me, is a Roman.
OCTAVIA.
He was a Roman, till he lost that name
To be a slave in Egypt, but I come
To free him thence.
CLEOPATRA.
Peace, peace, my lover's Juno.

[44] sister of ... Jove] Juno, Jove's wife and sister, frequently punished her husband's lovers.

When he grew weary of that household clog,*
He chose my easier bonds.

OCTAVIA.
I wonder not
Your bonds are easy. You have long been practised
In that lascivious art: he's not the first
For whom you spread your snares. Let Caesar witness.

CLEOPATRA.
I loved not Caesar; 'twas but gratitude
I paid his love: the worst your malice can
Is but to say the greatest of mankind
Has been my slave. The next, but far above him
In my esteem, is he whom law calls yours,
But whom his love made mine.

OCTAVIA. (*Coming up close to her.*)
I would view nearer
That face which has so long usurped my right
To find th'inevitable charms that catch
Mankind so sure, that ruined my dear lord.

CLEOPATRA.
Oh, you do well to search, for had you known
But half these charms, you had not lost his heart.

OCTAVIA.
Far be their knowledge from a Roman lady,
Far from a modest wife. Shame of our sex,
Dost thou not blush to own those black endearments[45]
That make sin pleasing?

CLEOPATRA.
You may blush, who want* 'em.
If bounteous Nature, if indulgent Heav'n
Have giv'n me charms to please the bravest man,
Should I not thank 'em? Should I be ashamed
And not be proud? I am, that he has loved me,
And when I love not him, Heav'n change this face
For one like that.

OCTAVIA.
Thou lov'st him not so well.

CLEOPATRA.
I love him better and deserve him more.

OCTAVIA.
You do not–cannot: you have been his ruin.
Who made him cheap at Rome, but Cleopatra?
Who made him scorned abroad, but Cleopatra?
At Actium, who betrayed him? Cleopatra.
Who made his children orphans? and poor me
A wretched widow? Only Cleopatra.

CLEOPATRA.
Yet she who loves him best is Cleopatra.
If you have suffered, I have suffered more.
You bear the specious title of a wife
To gild your cause and draw the pitying world
To favor it; the world contemns poor me,
For I have lost my honor, lost my fame,
And stained the glory of my royal house,
And all to bear the branded name of mistress.
There wants but life, and that too I would lose
For him I love.

OCTAVIA.
Be't so, then; take thy wish.
(*Exit with her train.*)

CLEOPATRA.
And 'tis my wish,
Now he is lost for whom alone I lived.
My sight grows dim, and every object dances
And swims before me in the maze of death.
My spirits, while they were opposed, kept up;
They could not sink beneath a rival's scorn.
But now she's gone, they faint.

ALEXAS.
Mine have had leisure
To recollect their strength and furnish counsel
To ruin her who else must ruin you.

CLEOPATRA.
Vain promiser!
Lead me, my Charmion; nay, your hand too, Iras:
My grief has weight enough to sink you both.
Conduct me to some solitary chamber
And draw the curtains round;
Then leave me to myself, to take alone
My fill of grief.
There I till death will his unkindness weep,
As harmless infants moan themselves asleep.

Act IV.

Antony, Dollabella.

DOLLABELLA.
Why would you shift it from yourself on me?
Can you not tell her you must part?

[45] charms … black endearments] Cleopatra was thought to have authored a treatise on cosmetics.

ANTONY.
I cannot.
I could pull out an eye and bid it go,
And t'other should not weep. Oh, Dollabella,
How many deaths are in this word "Depart"!
I dare not trust my tongue to tell her so:
One look of hers would thaw me into tears,
And I should melt till I were lost again.

DOLLABELLA.
Then let Ventidius;
He's rough by nature.

ANTONY.
Oh, he'll speak too harshly;
He'll kill her with the news. Thou, only thou.

DOLLABELLA.
Nature has cast me in so soft a mold
That but to hear a story feigned for pleasure
Of some sad lover's death moistens my eyes,
And robs me of my manhood.–I should speak
So faintly, with such fear to grieve her heart,
She'd not believe it earnest.

ANTONY.
Therefore, therefore
Thou only, thou art fit. Think thyself me,
And when thou speak'st (but let it first be long),
Take off the edge from every sharper sound
And let our parting be as gently made
As other loves begin. Wilt thou do this?

DOLLABELLA.
What you have said so sinks into my soul
That if I must speak, I shall speak just so.

ANTONY.
I leave you then to your sad task. Farewell.
I sent her word to meet you.
(*Goes to the door and comes back.*)
I forgot;
Let her be told I'll make her peace with mine.
Her crown and dignity shall be preserved,
If I have pow'r with Caesar. –Oh, be sure
To think on that.

DOLLABELLA.
Fear not, I will remember.

Antony goes again to the door and comes back.

ANTONY.
And tell her, too, how much I was constrained;
I did not this but with extremest force.
Desire her not to hate my memory,
For I still cherish hers. –Insist on that.

DOLLABELLA.
Trust me, I'll not forget it.

ANTONY.
Then that's all.
(*Goes out and returns again.*)
Wilt thou forgive my fondness this once more?
Tell her, though we shall never meet again,
If I should hear she took another love,
The news would break my heart. –Now I must go,
For every time I have returned, I feel
My soul more tender, and my next command
Would be to bid her stay, and ruin both. (*Exit.*)

DOLLABELLA.
Men are but children of a larger growth;
Our appetites as apt to change as theirs
And full as craving, too, and full as vain.
And yet the soul, shut up in her dark room,
Viewing so clear abroad, at home sees nothing,
But like a mole in earth, busy and blind,
Works all her folly up and casts it outward
To the world's open view. Thus I discovered
And blamed the love of ruined Antony,
Yet wish that I were he, to be so ruined.

Enter Ventidius above.

VENTIDIUS.
Alone? and talking to himself? concerned too?
Perhaps my guess is right; he loved her once
And may pursue it still.

DOLLABELLA.
Oh friendship! friendship!
Ill canst thou answer this; and reason, worse.
Unfaithful in th'attempt; hopeless to win;
And, if I win, undone: mere* madness all.
And yet th'occasion's fair. What injury
To him, to wear the robe which he throws by?

VENTIDIUS.
None, none at all. This happens as I wish,
To ruin her yet more with Antony.

Enter Cleopatra, talking with Alexas, Charmion; Iras on the other side.

DOLLABELLA.
She comes! What charms have sorrow on that face!

Sorrow seems pleased to dwell with so much sweetness,
Yet, now and then, a melancholy smile
Breaks loose, like lightning in a winter's night,
And shows a moment's day.

VENTIDIUS.
If she should love him too! Her eunuch there!
That porc'pisce bodes ill weather.[46] Draw, draw nearer,
Sweet devil, that I may hear.

Dollabella goes over to Charmion and Iras; seems to talk with them.

ALEXAS.
Believe me; try
To make him jealous. Jealousy is like
A polished glass held to the lips when life's in doubt:
If there be breath, 'twill catch the damp and show it.

CLEOPATRA.
I grant you, jealousy's a proof of love,
But 'tis a weak and unavailing med'cine;
It puts out the disease and makes it show,
But has no pow'r to cure.

ALEXAS.
'Tis your last remedy, and strongest too.
And then this Dollabella: Who so fit
To practice on? He's handsome, valiant, young,
And looks as he were laid for Nature's bait
To catch weak women's eyes.
He stands already more than half suspected
Of loving you. The least kind word or glance
You give this youth will kindle him with love;
Then, like a burning vessel set adrift,
You'll send him down amain before the wind
To fire the heart of jealous Antony.

CLEOPATRA.
Can I do this? Ah, no; my love's so true
That I can neither hide it where it is,
Nor show it where it is not. Nature meant me
A wife, a silly, harmless, household dove,
Fond without art and kind* without deceit,
But Fortune, that has made a mistress of me,
Has thrust me out into the wide world, unfurnished
Of falsehood to be happy.

ALEXAS.
Force yourself.
Th'event will be, your lover will return
Doubly desirous to possess the good
Which once he feared to lose.

CLEOPATRA.
I must attempt it,
But oh, with what regret!

Exit Alexas. She comes up to Dollabella.

VENTIDIUS.
So, now the scene draws near; they're in my reach.

CLEOPATRA. (*To Dollabella.*)
Discoursing with my women! Might not I
Share in your entertainment?

CHARMION.
You have been
The subject of it, madam.

CLEOPATRA.
How! and how?

IRAS.
Such praises of your beauty!

CLEOPATRA.
Mere poetry.
Your Roman wits, your Gallus and Tibullus,
Have taught you this from Cytheris and Delia.[47]

DOLLABELLA.
Those Roman wits have never been in Egypt;
Cytheris and Delia else had been unsung.
I who have seen–had I been a poet—
Should choose a nobler name.

CLEOPATRA.
You flatter me.
But 'tis your nation's vice: all of your country
Are flatt'rers and all false. Your friend's like you.
I'm sure he sent you not to speak these words.

DOLLABELLA.
No, madam, yet he sent me—

CLEOPATRA.
Well, he sent you—

[46] porc'pisce bodes ill weather.] The porpoise (literally, pigfish) was thought to be a harbinger of storms.

[47] Gallus ... Delia.] Gaius Cornelius Gallus (c. 69-26 BCE) and Albius Tibullus (48?-19 BCE) were love poets who wrote for and about their faithless mistresses Cytheris and Delia respectively.

DOLLABELLA.
Of a less pleasing errand.
CLEOPATRA.
How less pleasing?
Less to yourself, or me?
DOLLABELLA.
Madam, to both,
For you must mourn, and I must grieve to cause it.
CLEOPATRA.
You, Charmion, and your fellow, stand at a distance.
(*Aside.*) Hold up, my spirits.–Well, now your mournful matter,
For I'm prepared, perhaps can guess it too.
DOLLABELLA.
I wish you would, for 'tis a thankless office
To tell ill news, and I, of all your sex
Most fear displeasing you.
CLEOPATRA.
Of all your sex,
I soonest could forgive you, if you should.
VENTIDIUS.
Most delicate advances! Woman! Woman!
Dear, damned, inconstant sex!
CLEOPATRA.
In the first place,
I am to be forsaken. Is't not so?
DOLLABELLA.
I wish I could not answer to that question.
CLEOPATRA.
Then pass it o'er because it troubles you:
I should have been more grieved another time.
Next, I'm to lose my kingdom. –Farewell, Egypt.
Yet, is there any more?
DOLLABELLA.
Madam, I fear
Your too deep sense of grief has turned your reason.
CLEOPATRA.
No, no, I'm not run mad; I can bear fortune,
And love may be expelled by other love,
As poisons are by poisons.
DOLLABELLA.
You o'erjoy me, madam,
To find your griefs so moderately borne.
You've heard the worst; all are not false like him.
CLEOPATRA.
No: Heav'n forbid they should.
DOLLABELLA.
Some men are constant.
CLEOPATRA.
And constancy deserves reward, that's certain.
DOLLABELLA.
Deserves it not, but gives it leave to hope.
VENTIDIUS.
I'll swear thou hast my leave. I have enough.
But how to manage this! Well, I'll consider. (*Exit.*)
DOLLABELLA.
I came prepared
To tell you heavy news: news which, I thought,
Would fright the blood from your pale cheeks to hear.
But you have met it with a cheerfulness
That makes my task more easy, and my tongue,
Which on another's message was employed,
Would gladly speak its own.
CLEOPATRA.
Hold, Dollabella.
First tell me, were you chosen by my lord,
Or sought you this employment?
DOLLABELLA.
He picked me out, and as his bosom friend,
He charged me with his words.
CLEOPATRA.
The message then
I know was tender, and each accent smooth,
To mollify that rugged word, "Depart."
DOLLABELLA.
Oh, you mistake: he chose the harshest words;
With fiery eyes and with contracted brows,
He coined his face in the severest stamp,
And fury shook his fabric like an earthquake.
He heaved for vent and burst like bellowing Etna
In sounds scarce human, "Hence, away forever.
Let her be gone, the blot of my renown
And bane of all my hopes.
All the time of this speech, Cleopatra seems more and more concerned till she sinks quite down.
Let her be driv'n as far as men can think
From man's commerce. She'll poison to the center."
CLEOPATRA.
Oh, I can bear no more!
DOLLABELLA.
Help, help. Oh wretch! Oh cursèd, cursèd wretch!
What have I done?

CHARMION.

Help, chafe her temples, Iras.

IRAS.

Bend, bend her forward quickly.

CHARMION.

Heav'n be praised;

She comes again.

CLEOPATRA.

Oh, let him not approach me.

Why have you brought me back to this loathed being,
Th'abode of falsehood, violated vows,
And injured love? For pity, let me go,
For if there be a place of long repose,
I'm sure I want it. My disdainful lord
Can never break that quiet, nor awake
The sleeping soul with hollowing in my tomb
Such words as fright her hence. Unkind, unkind!

DOLLABELLA. (*Kneeling.*)

Believe me, 'tis against myself I speak;
That sure deserves belief. I injured him:
My friend ne'er spoke those words. Oh, had you seen
How often he came back and every time
With something more obliging and more kind
To add to what he said. What dear farewells!
How almost vanquished by his love he parted
And leaned to what unwillingly he left.
I, traitor as I was, for love of you
(But what can you not do, who made me false!)
I forged that lie, for whose forgiveness kneels
This self-accused, self-punished criminal.

CLEOPATRA.

With how much ease believe we what we wish!
Rise, Dollabella; if you have been guilty,
I have contributed, and too much love
Has made me guilty too.
Th'advance of kindness which I made was feigned
To call back fleeting love by jealousy,
But 'twould not last. Oh, rather let me lose
Than so ignobly trifle with his heart.

DOLLABELLA.

I find your breast fenced round from human reach,
Transparent as a rock of solid crystal,
Seen through, but never pierced. My friend, my friend!
What endless treasure hast thou thrown away
And scattered, like an infant, in the ocean,
Vain sums of wealth which none can gather thence!

CLEOPATRA.

Could you not beg
An hour's admittance to his private ear?
Like one who wanders through long barren wilds
And yet foreknows no hospitable inn
Is near to succor hunger,
Eats his fill, before his painful march:
So would I feed a while my famished eyes
Before we part, for I have far to go,
If death be far, and never must return.

Ventidius with Octavia behind.

VENTIDIUS.

From hence you may discover—

[Dollabella] takes [Cleopatra's] hand.

Oh, sweet, sweet!

Would you indeed? the pretty hand in earnest?

DOLLABELLA.

I will, for this reward. Draw it not back,
'Tis all I e'er will beg.

VENTIDIUS.

They turn upon us.

OCTAVIA.

What quick eyes has guilt!

VENTIDIUS.

Seem not to have observed 'em and go on.

They enter.

DOLLABELLA.

Saw you the Emperor, Ventidius?

VENTIDIUS.

No.

I sought him, but I heard that he was private,
None with him but Hipparchus, his freedman.

DOLLABELLA.

Know you his bus'ness?

VENTIDIUS.

Giving him instructions

And letters to his brother Caesar.

DOLLABELLA.

Well,

He must be found.

Exeunt Dollabella and Cleopatra.

OCTAVIA.
Most glorious impudence!
VENTIDIUS.
She looked, methought,
As she would say, "Take your old man, Octavia;
Thank you, I'm better here." Well, but what use[i]
Make we of this discovery?
OCTAVIA.
Let it die.
VENTIDIUS.
I pity Dollabella, but she's dangerous:
Her eyes have pow'r beyond Thessalian charms[48]
To draw the moon from heav'n; for eloquence,
The sea-green sirens taught her voice their flatt'ry,
And while she speaks, night steals upon the day,
Unmarked of those that hear. Then she's so charming
Age buds at sight of her and swells to youth.
The holy priests gaze on her when she smiles,
And with heaved hands, forgetting gravity,
They bless her wanton eyes. Even I, who hate her,
With a malignant joy behold such beauty
And, while I curse, desire it. Antony
Must needs have some remains of passion still,
Which may ferment into a worse relapse
If now not fully cured. I know, this minute,
With Caesar he's endeavoring her peace.
OCTAVIA.
You have prevailed. (*Walks off.*) But for a farther purpose
I'll prove how he will relish this discovery.
What, make a strumpet's peace! It swells my heart;
It must not, shannot be.
VENTIDIUS.
His guards appear.
Let me begin, and you shall second me.

Enter Antony.

ANTONY.
Octavia, I was looking for you, my love.
What, are your letters ready? I have giv'n
My last instructions.
OCTAVIA.
Mine, my lord, are written.
ANTONY.
Ventidius! (*Drawing him aside.*)
VENTIDIUS.
My lord?
ANTONY.
A word in private.
When saw you Dollabella?
VENTIDIUS.
Now, my lord,
He parted hence, and Cleopatra with him.
ANTONY.
Speak softly. 'Twas by my command he went,
To bear my last farewell.
VENTIDIUS. (*Aloud.*)
It looked indeed
Like your farewell.
ANTONY.
More softly. –My farewell?
What secret meaning have you in those words
Of "my farewell"? He did it by my order.
VENTIDIUS. (*Aloud.*)
Then he obeyed your order. I suppose
You bid him do it with all gentleness,
All kindness, and all–love.
ANTONY.
How she mourned, the poor forsaken creature![j]
VENTIDIUS.
She took it as she ought; she bore your parting
As she did Caesar's, as she would another's
Were a new love to come.
ANTONY. (*Aloud.*)
Thou dost belie her,
Most basely and maliciously belie her.
VENTIDIUS.
I thought not to displease you; I have done.
OCTAVIA. (*Coming up.*)
You seem disturbed, my lord.
ANTONY.
A very trifle.
Retire, my love.
VENTIDIUS.
It was indeed a trifle.
He sent—
ANTONY. (*Angrily.*)
No more. Look how thou disobey'st me;
Thy life shall answer it.

---

48 Thessalian charms] In the Ancient world, Thessaly was famous for as a center of witchcraft and sorcery.

OCTAVIA.
Then 'tis no trifle.
VENTIDIUS. (*To Octavia.*)
'Tis less, a very nothing: you too saw it,
As well as I, and therefore 'tis no secret.
ANTONY.
She saw it!
VENTIDIUS.
Yes. She saw young Dollabella—
ANTONY.
Young Dollabella!
VENTIDIUS.
Young, I think him young,
And handsome too, and so do others think him.
But what of that? He went by your command,
Indeed 'tis probable, with some kind message,
For she received it graciously. She smiled,
And then he grew familiar with her hand,
Squeezed it, and worried it with ravenous kisses.
She blushed, and sighed, and smiled, and blushed again.
At last she took occasion to talk softly,
And brought her cheek up close and leaned on his;
At which, he whispered kisses back on hers,
And then she cried aloud that constancy
Should be rewarded.
OCTAVIA.
This I saw and heard.
ANTONY.
What woman was it, whom you heard and saw
So playful with my friend! Not Cleopatra?[k]
VENTIDIUS.
Ev'n she, my lord!
ANTONY.
My Cleopatra?
VENTIDIUS.
Your Cleopatra;
Dollabella's Cleopatra;
Every man's Cleopatra.
ANTONY.
Thou lie'st.
VENTIDIUS.
I do not lie, my lord.
Is this so strange? Should mistresses be left
And not provide against a time of change?
You know she's not much used to lonely nights.
ANTONY.
I'll think no more on't.
I know 'tis false and see the plot betwixt you.
You needed not have gone this way, Octavia.
What harms it you that Cleopatra's just?
She's mine no more. I see, and I forgive;
Urge it no farther, love.
OCTAVIA.
Are you concerned
That she's found false?
ANTONY.
I should be, were it so,
For though 'tis past, I would not that the world
Should tax my former choice, that I loved one
Of so light note. But I forgive you both.
VENTIDIUS.
What has my age deserved, that you should think
I would abuse your ears with perjury?
If Heav'n be true, she's false.
ANTONY.
Though heav'n and earth
Should witness it, I'll not believe her tainted.
VENTIDIUS.
I'll bring you, then, a witness
From hell to prove her so. (*Seeing Alexas just entering and starting back.*)
Nay, go not back;
For stay you must, and shall.
ALEXAS.
What means my lord?
VENTIDIUS.
To make you do what you most hate: speak truth.
You are of Cleopatra's private counsel,
Of her bed-counsel, her lascivious hours;
Are conscious of each nightly change she makes,
And watch her, as Chaldeans do the moon;[49]
Can tell what signs she passes through, what day.
ALEXAS.
My noble lord!
VENTIDIUS.
My most illustrious pander,
No fine set speech, no cadence, no turned periods,

[49] as Chaldeans do the moon] Astrology was central to the worship of the Chaldeans, whose beliefs spread through Persia and Arabia.

But a plain homespun truth is what I ask.
I did, myself, o'erhear your queen make love
To Dollabella. Speak, for I will know,
By your confession, what more passed betwixt 'em:
How near the bus'ness draws to your employment,
And when the happy hour.

ANTONY.
Speak truth, Alexas. Whether it offend
Or please Ventidius, care not; justify
Thy injured queen from malice; dare his worst.

OCTAVIA. (*Aside.*)
See how he gives him courage! how he fears
To find her false! and shuts his eyes to truth,
Willing to be misled!

ALEXAS.
As far as love may plead for woman's frailty,
Urged by desert and greatness of the lover;
So far (divine Octavia!) may my queen
Stand ev'n excused to you for loving him
Who is your lord; so far, from brave Ventidius,
May her past actions hope a fair report.

ANTONY.
'Tis well and truly spoken. Mark, Ventidius.

ALEXAS.
To you, most noble Emperor, her strong passion
Stands not excused, but wholly justified.
Her beauty's charms alone, without her crown,
From Ind and Meroe[50] drew the distant vows
Of sighing kings, and at her feet were laid
The scepters of the earth, exposed on heaps,
To choose where she would reign.
She thought a Roman only could deserve her,
And, of all Romans, only Antony;
And, to be less than wife to you, disdained
Their lawful passion.

ANTONY.
'Tis but truth.

ALEXAS.
And yet, though love and your umatched desert
Have drawn her from the due regard of honor,
At last, Heav'n opened her unwilling eyes
To see the wrongs she offered fair Octavia,
Whose bed she lawlessly usurped.
The sad effects of this improsperous war
Confirmed those pious thoughts.

VENTIDIUS. (*Aside.*)
Oh, wheel you there?
Observe him now; the man begins to mend
And talk substantial reason. Fear not, eunuch;
The Emperor has giv'n thee leave to speak.

ALEXAS.
Else I had never dared t'offend his ears
With what the last necessity has urged
On my forsaken mistress. Yet I must not
Presume to say her heart is wholly altered.

ANTONY.
No, dare not for thy life, I charge thee dare not
Pronounce that fatal word!

OCTAVIA. (*Aside.*)
Must I bear this? Good Heav'n, afford me patience.

VENTIDIUS.
On, sweet eunuch; my dear half-man, proceed.

ALEXAS.
Yet Dollabella
Has loved her long. He, next my godlike lord,
Deserves her best, and should she meet his passion,
Rejected, as she is, by him she loved—

ANTONY.
Hence, from my sight, for I can bear no more.
Let Furies drag thee quick to hell; let all
The longer damned have rest; each torturing hand
Do thou employ, till Cleopatra comes,
Then join thou too and help to torture her.

Exit Alexas, thrust out by Antony.

OCTAVIA.
'Tis not well;
Indeed, my lord, 'tis much unkind to me
To show this passion, this extreme concernment
For an abandoned, faithless prostitute.

ANTONY.
Octavia, leave me. I am much disordered.
Leave me, I say.

OCTAVIA.
My lord?

ANTONY.
I bid you leave me.

VENTIDIUS.
Obey him, madam: best withdraw a while
And see how this will work.

50 Ind and Meroe] India and an island in the Nile in Ethiopia

OCTAVIA.
Wherein have I offended you, my lord,
That I am bid to leave you? Am I false
Or infamous? Am I a Cleopatra?
Were I she,
Base as she is, you would not bid me leave you,
But hang upon my neck, take slight excuses,
And fawn upon my falsehood.
ANTONY.
'Tis too much,
Too much, Octavia; I am pressed with sorrows
Too heavy to be borne, and you add more.
I would retire and recollect what's left
Of man within to aid me.
OCTAVIA.
You would mourn
In private for your love, who has betrayed you.
You did but half return to me: your kindness
Lingered behind with her. I hear, my lord,
You make conditions for her,
And would include her treaty. Wondrous proofs
Of love to me!
ANTONY.
Are you my friend, Ventidius?
Or are you turned a Dollabella, too,
And let this Fury loose?
VENTIDIUS.
Oh, be advised,
Sweet madam, and retire.
OCTAVIA.
Yes, I will go, but never to return.
You shall no more be haunted with this Fury.
My lord, my lord, love will not always last
When urged with long unkindness and disdain.
Take her again whom you prefer to me:
She stays but to be called. Poor cozened man!
Let a feigned parting give her back your heart,
Which a feigned love first got. For injured me,
Though my just sense of wrongs forbid my stay,
My duty shall be yours.
To the dear pledges of our former love
My tenderness and care shall be transferred,
And they shall cheer, by turns, my widowed nights.
So, take my last farewell, for I despair
To have you whole, and scorn to take you half.
(*Exit.*)

VENTIDIUS.
I combat Heav'n, which blasts my best designs:
My last attempt must be to win her back,
But oh, I fear, in vain. (*Exit.*)
ANTONY.
Why was I framed with this plain honest heart,
Which knows not to disguise its griefs and weakness,
But bears its workings outward to the world?
I should have kept the mighty anguish in
And forced a smile at Cleopatra's falsehood:
Octavia had believed it and had stayed.
But I am made a shallow-forded stream,
Seen to the bottom, all my clearness scorned,
And all my faults exposed!–See where he comes

Enter Dollabella.

Who has profaned the sacred name of friend
And worn it into vileness!
With how secure a brow and specious form
He gilds the secret villain! Sure that face
Was meant for honesty, but Heav'n mismatched it
And furnished treason out with Nature's pomp
To make its work more easy.
DOLLABELLA.
Oh my friend!
ANTONY.
Well, Dollabella, you performed my message?
DOLLABELLA.
I did, unwillingly.
ANTONY.
Unwillingly?
Was it so hard for you to bear our parting?
You should have wished it.
DOLLABELLA.
Why?
ANTONY.
Because you love me.
And she received my message with as true,
With as unfeigned a sorrow as you brought it?
DOLLABELLA.
She loves you, ev'n to madness.
ANTONY.
Oh, I know it.
You, Dollabella, do not better know
How much she loves me. And should I
Forsake this beauty, this all-perfect creature?

DOLLABELLA.
I could not, were she mine.
ANTONY.
And yet you first
Persuaded me: How come you altered since?
DOLLABELLA.
I said at first I was not fit to go;
I could not hear her sighs and see her tears,
But pity must prevail. And so perhaps
It may again for you, for I have promised
That she should take her last farewell: and see,
She comes to claim my word.

Enter Cleopatra.

ANTONY.
False Dollabella!
DOLLABELLA.
What's false, my lord?
ANTONY.
Why, Dollabella's false,
And Cleopatra's false; both false and faithless.
Draw near, you well-joined wickedness, you serpents
Whom I have, in my kindly bosom, warmed
Till I am stung to death.
DOLLABELLA.
My lord, have I
Deserved to be thus used?
CLEOPATRA.
Can Heav'n prepare
A newer torment? Can it find a curse
Beyond our separation?
ANTONY.
Yes, if Fate
Be just, much greater: Heav'n should be ingenious
In punishing such crimes. The rolling stone
And gnawing vulture were slight pains, invented
When Jove was young,[51] and no examples known
Of mighty ills, but you have ripened sin
To such a monstrous growth, 'twill pose[52] the gods
To find an equal torture. Two, two such—
Oh, there's no farther name! two such–to me,
To me, who locked my soul within your breasts,
Had no desires, no joys, no life, but you.
When half the globe was mine, I gave it you
In dowry with my heart; I had no use,
No fruit of all, but you; a friend and mistress
Was what the world could give. Oh Cleopatra!
Oh Dollabella! how could you betray
This tender heart, which with an infant fondness
Lay lulled betwixt your bosoms and there slept
Secure of[53] injured faith?
DOLLABELLA.
If she has wronged you,
Heav'n, Hell, and you revenge it.
ANTONY.
If she wronged me!
Thou wouldst evade thy part of guilt. But swear
Thou lov'st not her.
DOLLABELLA.
Not so as I love you.
ANTONY.
Not so! Swear, swear, I say, thou dost not love her.
DOLLABELLA.
No more than friendship will allow.
ANTONY.
No more?
Friendship allows thee nothing: thou art perjured—
And yet thou didst not swear thou lov'dst her not,
But not so much, no more. Oh trifling hypocrite,
Who dar'st not own to her thou dost not love,
Nor own to me thou dost! Ventidius heard it;
Octavia saw it.
CLEOPATRA.
They are enemies.
ANTONY.
Alexas is not so. He, he confessed it;
He who, next Hell, best knew it, he avowed it.
(*To Dollabella.*) Why do I seek a proof beyond yourself?
You, whom I sent to bear my last farewell,
Returned to plead her stay.
DOLLABELLA.
What shall I answer?
If to have loved be guilt, then I have sinned,

51 The rolling stone … young] Sisyphus' punishment in the underworld was forever to roll a stone up a hill only to have it roll down again; the giant Tityus was bound to a rock where two vultures gnawed at his liver.

52 pose] pose a challenge to

53 Secure of] safe from

But if to have repented of that love
Can wash away my crime, I have repented.
Yet, if I have offended past forgiveness,
Let not her suffer: she is innocent.

CLEOPATRA.
Ah, what will not a woman do who loves!
What means will she refuse to keep that heart
Where all her joys are placed! 'Twas I encouraged,
'Twas I blew up the fire that scorched his soul
To make you jealous and by that regain you.
But all in vain: I could not counterfeit;
In spite of all the dams, my love broke o'er
And drowned my heart again. Fate took th'occasion,
And thus one minute's feigning has destroyed
My whole life's truth.

ANTONY.
Thin cobweb arts of falsehood,
Seen and broke through at first.

DOLLABELLA.
Forgive your mistress.

CLEOPATRA.
Forgive your friend.

ANTONY.
You have convinced yourselves;
You plead each other's cause. What witness have you
That you but meant to raise my jealousy?

CLEOPATRA.
Ourselves, and Heav'n.

ANTONY.
Guilt witnesses for guilt. Hence, love and friendship.
You have no longer place in human breasts;
These two have driv'n you out. Avoid my sight.
I would not kill the man whom I have[1] loved
And cannot hurt the woman, but avoid me.
I do not know how long I can be tame,
For if I stay one minute more to think
How I am wronged, my justice and revenge
Will cry so loud within me that my pity
Will not be heard for either.

DOLLABELLA.
Heav'n has but
Our sorrow for our sins and then delights
To pardon erring man. Sweet mercy seems
Its darling attribute, which limits justice,
As if there were degrees in infinite
And infinite would rather want perfection
Than punish to extent.

ANTONY.
I can forgive
A foe, but not a mistress and a friend:
Treason is there in its most horrid shape
Where trust is greatest and the soul resigned
Is stabbed by its own guards. I'll hear no more;
Hence from my sight forever.

CLEOPATRA.
How? Forever!
I cannot go one moment from your sight,
And must I go forever?
My joys, my only joys, are centered here:
What place have I to go to? my own kingdom?
That I have lost for you. Or to the Romans?
They hate me for your sake. Or must I wander
The wide world o'er, a helpless, banished woman,
Banished for love of you, banished from you.
Aye, there's the banishment! Oh, hear me, hear me
With strictest justice, for I beg no favor,
And if I have offended you, then kill me,
But do not banish me.

ANTONY.
I must not hear you.
I have a fool within me takes your part,
But honor stops my ears.

CLEOPATRA.
For pity hear me!
Would you cast off a slave who followed you,
Who crouched beneath your spurn?–He has no pity!
See if he gives one tear to my departure,
One look, one kind farewell. Oh iron heart!
Let all the gods look down and judge betwixt us
If he did ever love!

ANTONY.
No more: Alexas!

DOLLABELLA.
A perjured villain!

ANTONY. (*To Cleopatra.*)
Your Alexas, yours.

CLEOPATRA.
Oh, 'twas his plot, his ruinous design,
T'engage you in my love by jealousy.
Hear him; confront him with me; let him speak.

ANTONY.
I have, I have.

CLEOPATRA.
And if he clear me not—
ANTONY.
Your creature! one who hangs upon your smiles!
Watches your eye to say or to unsay
Whate'er you please! I am not to be moved.
CLEOPATRA.
Then must we part? Farewell, my cruel lord,
Th'appearance is against me and I go,
Unjustified, forever from your sight.
How I have loved, you know; how yet I love,
My only comfort is, I know myself.
I love you more, ev'n now you are unkind,
Than when you loved me most; so well, so truly,
I'll never strive against it, but die pleased
To think you once were mine.
ANTONY. [*Aside.*]
Good Heav'n, they weep at parting.
Must I weep too? That calls 'em innocent.
I must not weep, and yet I must, to think
That I must not forgive.—
Live, but live wretched; 'tis but just you should,
Who made me so. Live from each other's sight.
Let me not hear you meet: set all the earth
And all the seas betwixt your sundered loves;
View nothing common but the sun and skies.
Now, all take several ways,
And each your own sad fate with mine deplore:
That you were false, and I could trust no more.

Exeunt severally.

Act V.

Cleopatra, Charmion, Iras.

CHARMION.
Be juster, Heav'n: such virtue punished thus
Will make us think that Chance rules all above
And shuffles, with a random hand, the lots
Which man is forced to draw.
CLEOPATRA.
I could tear out these eyes, that gained his heart
And had not pow'r to keep it. Oh the curse
Of doting on, ev'n when I find it dotage!
Bear witness, gods, you heard him bid me go,
You, whom he mocked with imprecating vows
Of promised faith.–I'll die. I will not bear it.
(*She pulls out her dagger, and they hold her.*) You may hold me—
But I can keep my breath; I can die inward
And choke this love.

Enter Alexas.

IRAS.
Help, oh Alexas, help!
The Queen grows desperate; her soul struggles in her
With all the agonies of love and rage
And strives to force its passage.
CLEOPATRA.
Let me go.
Art thou there, traitor! –Oh,
Oh, for a little breath, to vent my rage!
Give, give me way, and let me loose upon him.
ALEXAS.
Yes, I deserve it, for my ill-timed truth.
Was it for me to prop
The ruins of a falling majesty?
To place myself beneath the mighty flaw,
Thus to be crushed and pounded into atoms
By its o'erwhelming weight? 'Tis too presuming
For subjects to preserve that willful pow'r
Which courts its own destruction.
CLEOPATRA.
I would reason
More calmly with you. Did not you o'errule
And force my plain, direct, and open love
Into these crooked paths of jealousy?
Now, what's th'event? Octavia is removed,
But Cleopatra's banished. Thou, thou villain,
Hast pushed my boat to open sea, to prove,
At my sad cost, if thou canst steer it back.
It cannot be; I'm lost too far; I'm ruined.
Hence, thou imposter, traitor, monster, devil—
I can no more: thou and my griefs have sunk
Me down so low that I want voice to curse thee.
ALEXAS.
Suppose some shipwrecked seaman near the shore,
Dropping and faint with climbing up the cliff:
If, from above, some charitable hand
Pull him to safety, hazarding himself
To draw the other's weight, would he look back
And curse him for his pains? The case is yours:
But one step more and you have gained the height.

CLEOPATRA.
Sunk, never more to rise.
ALEXAS.
Octavia's gone, and Dollabella banished.
Believe me, madam, Antony is yours.
His heart was never lost, but started off
To jealousy, love's last retreat and covert,
Where it lies hid in shades, watchful in silence,
And list'ning for the sound that calls it back.
Some other, any man ('tis so advanced),
May perfect this unfinished work, which I
(Unhappy only to myself) have left
So easy to his hand.
CLEOPATRA.
Look well thou do't; else—
ALEXAS.
Else what your silence threatens.–Antony
Is mounted up the Pharos,[54] from whose turret
He stands surveying our Egyptian galleys
Engaged with Caesar's fleet: now death or conquest.
If the first happen, Fate acquits my promise;
If we o'ercome, the conqueror is yours.

A distant shout within.

CHARMION.
Have comfort, madam: Did you mark that shout?

Second shout nearer.

IRAS.
Hark! they redouble it.
ALEXAS.
'Tis from the port.
The loudness shows it near: good news, kind heavens!
CLEOPATRA.
Osiris make it so!

Enter Serapion.

SERAPION.
Where, where's the Queen?
ALEXAS.
How frightfully the holy coward stares!
As if not yet recovered of th'assault,
When all his gods, and what's more dear to him,
His offerings, were at stake.
SERAPION.
Oh horror, horror!
Egypt has been; our latest hour is come;
The queen of nations from her ancient seat
Is sunk forever in the dark abyss;
Time has unrolled her glories to the last
And now closed up the volume.
CLEOPATRA.
Be more plain:
Say whence thou cam'st (though Fate is in thy face,
Which from thy haggard eyes looks wildly out
And threatens ere thou speak'st).
SERAPION.
I came from Pharos,
From viewing (spare me and imagine it)
Our land's last hope, your navy—
CLEOPATRA.
Vanquished?
SERAPION.
No.
They fought not.
CLEOPATRA.
Then they fled?
SERAPION.
Nor that. I saw,
With Antony, your well-appointed fleet
Row out, and thrice he waved his hand on high,
And thrice with cheerful cries they shouted back.
'Twas then false Fortune, like a fawning strumpet
About to leave the bankrupt prodigal,
With a dissembled smile would kiss at parting
And flatter to the last. The well-timed oars
Now dipped from every bank, now smoothly run
To meet the foe. And soon indeed they met,
But not as foes. In few, we saw their caps
On either side thrown up; th'Egyptian galleys
(Received like friends) passed through and fell behind
The Roman rear, and now they all come forward
And ride within the port.
CLEOPATRA.
Enough, Serapion:
I've heard my doom. This needed not, you gods.
When I lost Antony, your work was done;
'Tis but superfluous malice. Where's my lord?
How bears he this last blow?

[54] Pharos] the lighthouse at Alexandria

SERAPION.
His fury cannot be expressed by words.
Thrice he attempted headlong to have fall'n
Full on his foes and aimed at Caesar's galley;
Withheld, he raves on you, cries he's betrayed.
Should he now find you—
ALEXAS.
Shun him; seek your safety
Till you can clear your innocence.
CLEOPATRA.
I'll stay.
ALEXAS.
You must not. Haste you to your monument,
While I make speed to Caesar.
CLEOPATRA.
Caesar! No,
I have no business with him.
ALEXAS.
I can work him
To spare your life and let this madman perish.
CLEOPATRA.
Base, fawning wretch! wouldst thou betray him too?
Hence from my sight. I will not hear a traitor;
'Twas thy design brought all this ruin on us.
Serapion, thou art honest. Counsel me,
But haste, each moment's precious.
SERAPION.
Retire; you must not yet see Antony.
He who began this mischief,
'Tis just he tempt the danger; let him clear you,
And since he offered you his servile tongue
To gain a poor precarious life from Caesar,
Let him expose the fawning eloquence
And speak to Antony.
ALEXAS.
Oh heavens! I dare not;
I meet my certain death.
CLEOPATRA.
Slave, thou deserv'st it.
Not that I fear my lord will I avoid him.
I know him noble: when he banished me
And thought me false, he scorned to take my life.
But I'll be justified, and then die with him.
ALEXAS.
Oh pity me and let me follow you.
CLEOPATRA.
To death, if thou stir hence. Speak, if thou canst,
Now for thy life, which basely thou wouldst save,
While mine I prize at this. Come, good Serapion.

Exeunt Cleopatra, Serapion, Charmion, Iras.

ALEXAS.
Oh that I less could fear to lose this being,
Which, like a snowball in my coward hand,
The more 'tis grasped, the faster melts away.
Poor reason! what a wretched aid art thou!
For still, in spite of thee,
These two long lovers, soul and body, dread
Their final separation. Let me think:
What can I say to save myself from death
No matter what becomes of Cleopatra?
ANTONY. (*Within.*)
Which way? where?
VENTIDIUS. (*Within.*)
This leads to th'monument.
ALEXAS.
Ah me! I hear him, yet I'm unprepared.
My gift of lying's gone,
And this court-devil, which I so oft have raised,
Forsakes me at my need. I dare not stay,
Yet cannot far go hence. (*Exit.*)

Enter Antony and Ventidius.

ANTONY.
Oh happy Caesar! Thou hast men to lead:
Think not 'tis thou hast conquered Antony,
But Rome has conquered Egypt. I'm betrayed.
VENTIDIUS.
Curse on this treach'rous train!
Their soil and heav'n infect 'em all with baseness,
And their young souls come tainted to the world
With the first breath they draw.
ANTONY.
Th'original villain sure no god created;
He was a bastard of the sun by Nile,
Aped into man, with all his mother's mud
Crusted about his soul.[55]

[55] He was a bastard ... soul.] The muddy banks of the Nile were frequently thought a place where creatures were generated from the earth.

VENTIDIUS.
The nation is
One universal traitor, and their queen
The very spirit and extract of 'em all.
ANTONY.
Is there yet left
A possibility of aid from valor?
Is there one god unsworn to my destruction?
The least unmortgaged hope? for if there be,
Methinks I cannot fall beneath the fate
Of such a boy as Caesar.
The world's one half is yet in Antony,
And from each limb of it that's hewed away
The soul comes back to me.[56]
VENTIDIUS.
There yet remain
Three legions in the town; the last assault
Lopped off the rest. If death be your design,
As I must wish it now, these are sufficient
To make a heap about us of dead foes,
An honest pile for burial.
ANTONY.
They're enough.
We'll not divide our stars, but side by side
Fight emulous, and with malicious eyes
Survey each other's acts; so every death
Thou givest, I'll take on me as a just debt,
And pay thee in a soul.
VENTIDIUS.
Now you shall see I love you. Not a word
Of chiding more. By my few hours of life,
I am so pleased with this brave Roman fate
That I would not be Caesar to outlive you.
When we put off this flesh and mount together,
I shall be shown to all th'ethereal crowd:
"Lo, this is he who died with Antony."
ANTONY.
Who knows but we may pierce through all their troops
And reach my veterans yet? 'Tis worth the tempting
T'o'erleap this gulf of fate
And leave our wond'ring destinies behind.

Enter Alexas trembling.

VENTIDIUS.
See, see that villain:
See Cleopatra stamped upon that face,
With all her cunning, all her arts of falsehood!
How she looks out through those dissembling eyes!
How he has set his count'nance for deceit
And promises a lie before he speaks!
Let me dispatch him first. (*Drawing.*)
ALEXAS.
Oh spare me, spare me.
ANTONY.
Hold, he's not worth your killing. On thy life
(Which thou mayst keep because I scorn to take it),
No syllable to justify thy Queen;
Save thy base tongue its office.
ALEXAS.
Sir, she's gone
Where she shall never be molested more
By love, or you.
ANTONY.
Fled to Dollabella!
Die, traitor; I revoke my promise; die. (*Going to kill him.*)
ALEXAS.
Oh hold! she is not fled.
ANTONY.
She is; my eyes
Are open to her falsehood. My whole life
Has been a golden dream of love and friendship.
But now I wake, I'm like a merchant roused
From soft repose to see his vessel sinking
And all his wealth cast o'er. Ingrateful woman!
Who followed me but as the swallow summer,
Hatching her young ones in my kindly beams,
Singing her flatt'ries to my morning wake,
But now my winter comes, she spreads her wings
And seeks the spring of Caesar.
ALEXAS.
Think not so:
Her fortunes have, in all things, mixed with yours.
Had she betrayed her naval force to Rome,
How easily might she have gone to Caesar,
Secure by such a bribe!

56 The world's … me]The metaphor depends on the traditional theory of the soul's inhabiting every part of the body, but in case of non-mortal amputations, retreating to the remainder.

VENTIDIUS.
She sent it first,
To be more welcome after.
ANTONY.
'Tis too plain;
Else she would have appeared to clear herself.
ALEXAS.
Too fatally she has: she could not bear
To be accused by you, but shut herself
Within her monument, looked down and sighed,
While from her unchanged face the silent tears
Dropped, as they had not leave, but stole their parting.
Some undistinguished words she inly murmured;
At last she raised her eyes, and with such looks
As dying Lucrece* cast–[57]
ANTONY.
My heart forebodes—
VENTIDIUS.
All for the best; go on.
ALEXAS.
She snatched her poniard,
And, ere we could prevent the fatal blow,
Plunged it within her breast, then turned to me:
"Go, bear my lord," said she, "my last farewell,
And ask him if he yet suspect my faith."
More she was saying, but death rushed betwixt.
She half pronounced your name with her last breath
And buried half within her.
VENTIDIUS.
Heav'n be praised!
ANTONY.
Then art thou innocent, my poor dear love,
And art thou dead?
Oh those two words! their sound should be divided:
Hadst thou been false, and died; or hadst thou lived,
And hadst been true– But innocence and death!
This shows not well above. Then what am I,
The murderer of this truth, this innocence!
Thoughts cannot form themselves in words so horrid
As can express my guilt!

57 As dying Lucrece] Lucrece stabbed herself after she had been raped.

VENTIDIUS.
Is't come to this? The gods have been too gracious,
And thus you thank 'em for't?
ANTONY. (*To Alexas.*)
Why stay'st thou here?
Is it for thee to spy upon my soul
And see its inward mourning? Get thee hence;
Thou art not worthy to behold what now
Becomes a Roman emperor to perform.
ALEXAS. (*Aside.*)
He loves her still:
His grief betrays it. Good! The joy to find
She's yet alive completes the reconcilement.
I've saved myself and her. But, oh! the Romans!
Fate comes too fast upon my wit,
Hunts me too hard, and meets me at each double.[58] (*Exit.*)
VENTIDIUS.
Would she had died a little sooner, though,
Before Octavia went; you might have treated.
Now 'twill look tame and would not be received.
Come, rouse yourself, and let's die warm together.
ANTONY.
I will not fight: there's no more work for war.
The bus'ness of my angry hours is done.
VENTIDIUS.
Caesar is at your gates.
ANTONY.
Why, let him enter;
He's welcome now.
VENTIDIUS.
What lethargy has crept into your soul?
ANTONY.
'Tis but a scorn of life and just desire
To free myself from bondage.
VENTIDIUS.
Do it bravely.
ANTONY.
I will, but not by fighting. Oh Ventidius!
What should I fight for now? My queen is dead.
I was but great for her; my pow'r, my empire
Were but my merchandise to buy her love,
And conquered kings, my factors. Now she's dead,
Let Caesar take the world—

58 double] doubling back (like a hunted animal)

An empty circle since the jewel's gone
Which made it worth my strife; my being's nauseous,
For all the bribes of life are gone away.

VENTIDIUS.
Would you be taken?

ANTONY.
Yes, I would be taken,
But as a Roman ought, dead, my Ventidius,
For I'll convey my soul from Caesar's reach
And lay down life myself. 'Tis time the world
Should have a lord and know whom to obey.
We two have kept its homage in suspense
And bent the globe, on whose each side we trod,
Till it was dinted inwards. Let him walk
Alone upon't; I'm weary of my part.
My torch is out, and the world stands before me
Like a black desert at th'approach of night.
I'll lay me down and stray no farther on.

VENTIDIUS.
I could be grieved,
But that I'll not outlive you: choose your death,
For I have seen him in such various shapes,
I care not which I take. I'm only troubled,
The life I bear is worn to such a rag,
'Tis scarce worth giving. I could wish, indeed,
We threw it from us with better grace;
That, like two lions taken in the toils,
We might at least thrust out our paws and wound
The hunters that inclose us.

ANTONY.
I have thought on't.
Ventidius, you must live.

VENTIDIUS.
I must not, sir.

ANTONY.
Wilt thou not live to speak some good of me?
To stand by my fair fame and guard th'approaches
From the ill tongues of men?

VENTIDIUS.
Who shall guard mine,
For living after you?

ANTONY.
Say, I command it.

VENTIDIUS.
If we die well, our deaths will speak themselves
And need no living witness.

ANTONY.
Thou hast loved me,
And fain I would reward thee. I must die:
Kill me, and take the merit of my death
To make thee friends with Caesar.

VENTIDIUS.
Thank your kindness.
You said I loved you, and in recompense
You bid me turn a traitor. Did I think
You would have used me thus? that I should die
With a hard thought of you?

ANTONY.
Forgive me, Roman.
Since I have heard of Cleopatra's death,
My reason bears no rule upon my tongue
But lets my thoughts break all at random out.
I've thought better; do not deny me twice.

VENTIDIUS.
By Heav'n, I will not.
Let it not be t'outlive you.

ANTONY.
Kill me first,
And then die thou, for 'tis but just you serve
Thy friend before thyself.

VENTIDIUS.
Give me your hand.
We soon shall meet again. Now farewell,
Emperor. (*Embrace.*)
Methinks that word's too cold to be my last:
Since death sweeps all distinctions, farewell,
friend.
That's all.—
I will not make a bus'ness of a trifle,
And yet I cannot look on you and kill you;
Pray turn your face.

ANTONY.
I do. Strike home, be sure.

VENTIDIUS.
Home, as my sword will reach. (*Kills himself.*)

ANTONY.
Oh, thou mistak'st.
That wound was none of thine; give it me back:
Thou robb'st me of my death.

VENTIDIUS.
I do, indeed.
But think, 'tis the first time I e'er deceived you,

If that may plead my pardon. And you, gods,
Forgive me if you will, for I die perjured
Rather than kill my friend. (*Dies.*)

ANTONY.
Farewell. Ever my leader, ev'n in death!
My queen and thou have got the start of me,
And I'm the lag of honor.–Gone so soon?
Is death no more? He used him carelessly,
With a familiar kindness; ere he knocked,
Ran to the door and took him in his arms,
As who should say, "Y'are welcome at all hours,
A friend need give no warning." Books had spoiled him,
For all the learned are cowards by profession.
'Tis not worth
My farther thought, for death, for aught I know,
Is but to think no more. Here's to be satisfied.
(*Falls on his sword.*)
I've missed my heart. Oh unperforming hand!
Thou never couldst have erred in a worse time.
My fortune jades me to the last, and death,
Like a great man, takes state, and makes me wait
For my admittance– (*Trampling within.*)
Some, perhaps, from Caesar.
If he should find me living, and suspect
That I played booty with my life! I'll mend
My work ere they can reach me. (*Rises upon his knees.*)

Enter Cleopatra, Charmion, Iras.

CLEOPATRA.
Where is my lord? where is he?

CHARMION.
There he lies,
And dead Ventidius by him.

CLEOPATRA.
My fears were prophets; I am come too late.
Oh that accursed Alexas! (*Runs to [Antony].*)

ANTONY.
Art thou living?
Or am I dead before I knew, and thou
The first kind ghost that meets me?

CLEOPATRA.
Help me seat him.
Send quickly, send for help.

They place him in a chair.

ANTONY.
I am answered.
We live both. Sit thee down, my Cleopatra;
I'll make the most I can of life, to stay
A moment more with thee.

CLEOPATRA.
How is it with you?

ANTONY.
'Tis as with a man
Removing in a hurry, all packed up
But one dear jewel that his haste forgot,
And he, for that, returns upon the spur:
So I come back for thee.

CLEOPATRA.
Too long, you heav'ns, you have been cruel to me;
Now show your mended faith, and give me back
His fleeting life.

ANTONY.
It will not be, my love.
I keep my soul by force.
Say but thou art not false.

CLEOPATRA.
'Tis now too late
To say I'm true: I'll prove it, and die with you.
Unknown to me, Alexas feigned my death,
Which when I knew, I hastened to prevent
This fatal consequence. My fleet betrayed
Both you and me.

ANTONY.
And Dollabella—

CLEOPATRA.
Scarce
Esteemed before he loved, but hated now.[m]

ANTONY.
Enough: my life's not long enough for more.
Thou say'st thou wilt come after: I believe thee,
For I can now believe whate'er thou say'st,
That we may part more kindly.

CLEOPATRA.
I will come.
Doubt not, my life, I'll come, and quickly too:
Caesar shall triumph o'er no part of thee.

ANTONY.
But grieve not, while thou stay'st
My last disastrous times:
Think we have had a clear and glorious day,

And Heav'n did kindly to delay the storm
Just till our close of ev'ning. Ten years' love,
And not a moment lost, but all improved
To th'utmost joys: What ages have we lived?
And now to die each other's, and so dying,
While hand in hand we walk in groves below,
Whole troops of lovers' ghosts shall flock about us,
And all the train be ours.

CLEOPATRA.
Your words are like the notes of dying swans,
Too sweet to last. Were there so many hours
For your unkindness, and not one for love?

ANTONY.
No, not a minute. –This one kiss–more worth
Than all I leave to Caesar. (*Dies.*)

CLEOPATRA.
Oh, tell me so again
And take ten thousand kisses for that word.
My lord, my lord. Speak, if you yet have being.
Sigh to me, if you cannot speak, or cast
One look. Do anything that shows you live.

IRAS.
He's gone too far to hear you,
And this you see, a lump of senseless clay,
The leavings of a soul.

CHARMION.
Remember, madam,
He charged you not to grieve.

CLEOPATRA.
And I'll obey him.
I have not loved a Roman not to know
What should become his wife; his wife, my Charmion,
For 'tis to that high title I aspire,
And now I'll not die less. Let dull Octavia
Survive, to mourn him dead; my nobler fate
Shall knit our spousals with a tie too strong
For Roman laws to break.

IRAS.
Will you then die?

CLEOPATRA.
Why shouldst thou make that question?

IRAS.
Caesar is merciful.

CLEOPATRA.
Let him be so
To those that want his mercy; my poor lord
Made no such cov'nant with him to spare me
When he was dead. Yield me to Caesar's pride?
What! to be led in triumph through all the streets,
A spectacle to base plebeian eyes,
While some dejected friend of Antony's,
Close in a corner, shakes his head and mutters
A secret curse on her who ruined him?
I'll none of that.

CHARMION.
Whatever you resolve,
I'll follow ev'n to death.

IRAS.
I only feared
For you, but more should fear to live without you.

CLEOPATRA.
Why, now 'tis as it should be. Quick, my friends,
Dispatch; ere this, the town's in Caesar's hands.
My lord looks down concerned and fears my stay,
Lest I should be surprised;
Keep him not waiting for his love too long.
You, Charmion, bring my crown and richest jewels,
With 'em, the wreath of victory I made
(Vain augury!) for him who now lies dead.
You, Iras, bring the cure of all our ills.

IRAS.
The aspics, madam?

CLEOPATRA.
Must I bid you twice?

Exeunt Charmion and Iras.

'Tis sweet to die when they would force life on me,
To rush into the dark abode of Death,
And seize him first. If he be like my love,
He is not frightful, sure.
We're now alone, in secrecy and silence,
And is not this like lovers? I may kiss
These pale, cold lips; Octavia does not see me,
And, oh! 'tis better far to have him thus
Than see him in her arms.–Oh welcome, welcome.

Enter Charmion and Iras.

CHARMION.
What must be done?

CLEOPATRA.
Short ceremony, friends,
But yet it must be decent. First, this laurel

Shall crown my hero's head: he fell not basely,
Nor left his shield behind him. Only thou
Couldst triumph o'er thyself, and thou alone
Wert worthy so to triumph.

CHARMION.
To what end
These ensigns of your pomp and royalty?

CLEOPATRA.
Dull that thou art! Why, 'tis to meet my love
As when I saw him first on Cydnos' bank,
All sparkling like a goddess. So adorned,
I'll find him once again; my second spousals
Shall match my first in glory. Haste, haste, both,
And dress the bride of Antony.

CHARMION.
'Tis done.

CLEOPATRA.
Now seat me by my lord. I claim this place,
For I must conquer Caesar too, like him,
And win my share o'th'world. Hail, you dear relics
Of my immortal love!
Oh, let no impious hand remove you hence,
But rest forever here. Let Egypt give
His death that peace, which it denied his life.
Reach me the casket.

IRAS.
Underneath the fruit the aspic lies.

CLEOPATRA. (*Putting aside the leaves.*)
Welcome, thou kind deceiver!
Thou best of thieves, who, with an easy key,
Dost open life, and unperceived by us,
Ev'n steal us from ourselves, discharging so
Death's dreadful office better than himself,
Touching our limbs so gently into slumber
That Death stands by, deceived by his own image,
And thinks himself but sleep.

SERAPION. (*Within.*)
The Queen, where is she?
The town is yielded, Caesar's at the gates.

CLEOPATRA.
He comes too late t'invade the rights of death.
Haste, bare my arm, and rouse the serpent's fury.
(*Holds out her arm and draws it back.*)
Coward flesh—
Wouldst thou conspire with Caesar to betray me,
As thou wert none of mine? I'll force thee to't
And not be sent by him,
But bring, myself, my soul to Antony. (*Turns aside and then shows her arm bloody.*)
Take hence; the work is done.

SERAPION. (*Within.*)
Break ope the door,
And guard the traitor well.

CHARMION.
The next is ours.

IRAS.
Now, Charmion, to be worthy
Of our great queen and mistress.

They apply the aspics.

CLEOPATRA.
Already, Death, I feel thee in my veins.
I go with such a will to find my lord
That we shall quickly meet.
A heavy numbness creeps through every limb,
And now 'tis at my head; my eyelids fall,
And my dear love is vanished in a mist.
Where shall I find him, where? Oh turn me to him,
And lay me on his breast.–Caesar, thy worst.
Now part us, if thou canst. (*Dies.*)

Iras sinks down at her feet and dies; Charmion stands behind her chair as dressing her head. Enter Serapion, two priests, Alexas bound, Egyptians.

TWO PRIESTS.
Behold, Serapion, what havoc death has made!

SERAPION.
'Twas what I feared. Charmion, is this well done?[n]

CHARMION.
Yes, 'tis well done, and like a queen, the last
Of her great race.* I follow her. (*Sinks down; dies.*)

ALEXAS.
'Tis true,
She has done well: much better thus to die
Than live to make a holy-day in Rome.

SERAPION.
See, see how the lovers sit in state together,
As they were giving laws to half mankind.
Th'impression of a smile left in her face
Shows she died pleased with him for whom she lived
And went to charm him in another world.
Caesar's just ent'ring; grief has now no leisure.

Secure that villain, as our pledge of safety
To grace th'imperial triumph. Sleep, blest pair,
Secure from human chance, long ages out,
While all the storms of Fate fly o'er your tomb,
And fame to late posterity shall tell,
No lovers lived so great, or died so well.

[Exeunt.]

Finis.

Textual Notes

[a] The copytext is the 1678 first quarto (Q1). Also consulted were the 1692 quarto (Q2), the 1696 third quarto (Q3), the 1717 collected works (W1), the 1717 collected works (W2), and the 1984 California Edition (CE).

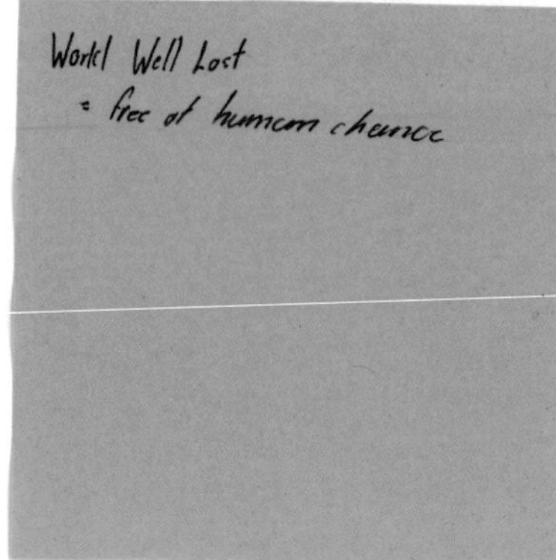

[b] *Enter second gentleman*] CE; Re-enter the Gentleman Q1, Q2; Gentlemen Q3, W1, W2

[c] god-like] W2, CE; good-like Q1, Q2, Q3, W1

[d] Too presuming ... love] CE; *run-on in all early editions*

[e] ere] Q2, Q3, W1, W2, CE; *om.* Q1

[f] Come ... live] CE; *all early editions separate into two lines.*

[g] 'Tis past] CE; *all early editions print as part of following line.*

[h] my ... eunuch] CE; *all early editions print as a separate line.*

[i] Well ... use] CE; *all early editions print as a separate line.*

[j] the ... creature] CE; *all early editions print as a separate line.*

[k] Not Cleopatra] CE; *all early editions print as a separate line.*

[l] have] W2, CE; *om.* Q1, Q2, Q3, W1

[m] Scarce ... now] CE; *all early editions print as one line.*

[n] Charmion ... done] CE; *all early editions print as a separate line.*

A True Widow[a]

by Thomas Shadwell (c. 1641-1692)
edited by Christopher J. Wheatley

Thomas Shadwell was the victim of one of the most effective personal attacks in the English language: John Dryden's *MacFlecknoe.* Consequently Shadwell is remembered not as his contemporaries regarded him—Rochester, for instance, paired him with Wycherley as the two writers of true comedy—but as the heir to the throne of dullness. Dryden and Shadwell's literary and political rupture was not open at the time of *A True Widow*, since Dryden contributed a prologue; that does not demonstrate that *Macflecknoe* was not in circulation yet. It is not clear when, but at some point Shadwell confronted Dryden with *MacFlecknoe*, and Dryden denied authorship. Shadwell was the most talented of the comparatively few Whig playwrights, while Dryden was only the most prominent of the numerous Tory playwrights. Shadwell succeeded Dryden as poet-laureate in 1688 after the Glorious Revolution, and there has been no shortage of critics who have made Dryden a sympathetic victim of political forces. What is more rarely mentioned is that Dryden helped to bar Shadwell from the stage from 1681 until the Glorious Revolution and that Shadwell was a supporter of parliamentary restrictions upon Stuart absolutism.

But Shadwell was also at odds with his age in that he favored instructive humors comedy over the comedy of wit (although his own conversation was highly regarded for its wit). He had engaged in a lengthy public debate with Dryden, carried on in introductions to plays, over the relative importance of wit and judgment, and was also consistently a satirist of the libertine ethos of some Restoration drama. *A True Widow*, which probably premiered on March 21, 1678, failed miserably, according to Shadwell because of "the calamity of the time, which made people not care for diversions, or through the anger of a great many, who thought themselves concerned in the satyr." In short, Shadwell's political affiliation and satirical impulses combined to doom a play of which Shadwell was justly proud.

The play itself attacks numerous social abuses. Selfish's vanity bars him from knowing himself, Gartrude's idiocy makes her prefer Selfish to the gentlemanly (albeit waspish) Stanmore, Young Maggot pretends to wit though unfitted for it, and Prig makes the recreations of a gentleman the work of his life. Above all, Lady Cheatly trades on traditional assumptions about aristocratic honor to cheat the citizens, who, because of religious hypocrisy, richly deserve it. The play within a play, a terrifically funny parody of the comic sublime in sex comedies of the late 1670s (in particular Tom Durfey's *A Fond Husband*) derides the current taste for farce, a genre that avoids the theater's obligation to hold the mirror up to social vice. Only Carlos, Isabella, and the converted Bellamour believe not everything should be for sale in a world turned upside down.

Despite the satire, *A True Widow* has a comic plenitude matched by few plays of the period, and Shadwell was justified in saying in his own defense, "till I see more variety of new humor, than I have produced in my comedies, and more naturally drawn, I shall not despair of bearing up near my contemporaries of the first rate, who write comedy, and of always surmounting the little poetasters of the fourth rate, who condemn me."

[I.i]

DRAMATIS PERSONAE

[MEN]

Bellamour, a gentleman of the Town,* who had retired some time into the country.

Carlos, a gentleman returned from travel, with wit enough left to love his own country.

Stanmore, a gentleman of the Town.

Selfish, a coxcomb conceited of his beauty, wit, and breeding, thinking all women in love with him, always admiring and talking of himself.

Old Maggot, an old credulous fellow, a great enemy to wit, and a great lover of business for business' sake.

Young Maggot, his nephew: an Inns of Court* man, who neglects his law and runs mad after wit, pretending much to love, and both in spite of nature, since his face makes him unfit for one and his brains for the other.

Prig, a coxcomb that never talks or thinks of anything but dogs, horses, hunting, hawking, bowls, tennis, and gaming; a rook,* a most noisy jockey.[1]

Lump, a methodical blockhead, as regular as a clock and goes as true as a pendulum, one that knows what he shall do every day of his life by his almanac, where he sets down all his actions beforehand, a mortal enemy to wit.

[WOMEN]

Lady Cheatly, the true widow, that comes to Town and makes a show of a fortune to put off herself and her two daughters.

Isabella, her eldest, a woman of wit and virtue.

Gartrude, her youngest, very foolish and whorish.

Theodosia, a young lady of wit and fortune, beloved by Carlos.[b]

Lady Busy, a woman of intrigue, very busy in love matters of all kinds, too old for love of her own, always charitably helping forward that of others, very fond of young women, very wise and discreet, half bawd, half matchmaker.

Steward to Lady Cheatly.

Players, doorkeepers, and many other persons, the audience to the play in the play.

Scene: London.

A True Widow.

Odi profanum Vulgus & arceo.[2]

Act I, [scene i. Bellamour's chamber.]

Enter Bellamour and Stanmore.

STANMORE.
Come Bellamour, what not dressed yet? Methinks after so long a fast from wit and fine women as you have had in the country, you should be sharper set after both than to fool away a morning thus in your chamber.

BELLAMOUR.
There is a respect due from a country gentleman to a new suit and peruke: they must not be hastily put on. And the women of this Town, if you don't take care of your own outside, will never let you be acquainted with their insides.

STANMORE.
Thou art mistaken: men succeed now according to the clothes they give, not those they wear.

BELLAMOUR.
Amongst your little whores, Stanmore.

STANMORE.
And amongst your great whores too Bellamour. I knew a gentleman who was so ugly, a modish spark would scarce have given him a livery, yet by a correspondence he kept with a tailor and shoemaker at Paris and two or three of that sort, got one of the finest women in England.

BELLAMOUR.
How so?

STANMORE.
Why, she had always the fashion a month before any of the court-ladies, never wore anything made in England, scarce washed there, and had all the affected new words sent her before they were in

---

[1] jockey] cant term for one who cheats at games

[2] *Odi ... arceo*] Horace, *Odes*, 3.1.1: I hate the uninitiate crowd and keep them far away.

print, which made her pass among fops for a kind of French wit.

BELLAMOUR.

But were not these French petticoats, though given by one man, taken up by many?

STANMORE.

'Faith I think not, she considered her own vanity above any man's address, though one lord made coaches at her, another squeezed in his fat sides at her, till he looked like a full sack; a third writ lamentable sonnets to her; a fourth observed her motions in the park, which, by the way, is the new method of making love.*

BELLAMOUR.

What, do they make love without speaking to one another?

STANMORE.

A great many very fine gentlemen, to look at, better than with it: your side glass[3] let down hastily, when the party goes by, is very passionate if she side-glass you again, for that's the new word. Ply her next day with a billet-doux and you have her sure.

BELLAMOUR.

What if we chance to go the same way, or she won't receive my billet-doux, as you call it?

STANMORE.

For the first, it must never chance; you must instruct your coachman. And for the second, after such an advance as side-glassing of you, if she refuse your billet, she is a jilt, and you must rail at her in all companies.

BELLAMOUR.

I am pretty good at railing, but not so good as thou art, Stanmore.

STANMORE.

I had forgotten half: you must turn as she turns, quit the Park* when she goes out, pass by her twice or thrice between that and St. James's,* talk to her at night in the Drawing Room*—

BELLAMOUR.

Before forty coxcombs, and then the business is sufficiently proclaimed, is it not, think you?

STANMORE.

'Tis all one, it must be so, or you will pass for an old-fashioned lover and never succeed beyond a chambermaid.

BELLAMOUR.

This is a folly of our own growth: it came not to us out of France.

STANMORE.

That nation has at this time no folly so harmless.

BELLAMOUR.

But if there be any stirring of what kind soever, our empty young fellows will be sure to fill themselves with it and prefer it to all the sense and good breeding of their own country. But now we talk of France, I wonder we see not Carlos; he was expected from thence two or three nights since.

Enter Carlos.

STANMORE.

See where he comes. Dear Carlos, I could not run more hastily upon my mistress after a long absence; thou art the delight of all thy friends, and even thy enemies take a malignant pleasure to behold that shape, that feature, and that mien.

CARLOS.

Hold Stanmore, I think thou takest me for a mistress indeed by thy compliments, which I know not how to return.

STANMORE.

Thou art so improved, a man must love as I do not to envy thee.

CARLOS.

Enough Stanmore, your friendship blinds you— (*Aside.*) I never knew any of these loving rogues good for anything.—Bellamour, I am overjoyed to see thee here! I heard thou hadst forsworn the Town.

BELLAMOUR.

Now I see Carlos here, methinks I am a perfect man of the Town again; I only forswore it for a time. 'Faith, money is a thing gotten in ill company and spent in good; I have been laying up.

CARLOS.

Men-of-war after a warm engagement must into the docks to be new built for fight.

BELLAMOUR.

Right, but how goes matters in France? What new foppery is turned up trump there?

[3] side glass] coach window, often opaque

CARLOS.
What with governors, ladies' eldest sons, ambassadors and envoys, you have 'em here almost as soon as the French themselves.

STANMORE.
No alteration since we were there?

CARLOS.
Wit and women are quite out of fashion, so are *flûtes douces*[4] and fiddlers: drums and trumpets are their only music.

BELLAMOUR.
'Tis but ill music for their neighbors.

CARLOS.
At home they are always roaring out *Te Deums* for stealing[5] of some town or other: war and equipage is their discourse, which, by the way, is so pompous, that, should they conquer Europe, they should scarce be savers.

STANMORE.
How came wit and women out of fashion?

CARLOS.
Why, in camps they learn to live without women, and for wit, great men that love to play the fool in quiet find it troublesome.

BELLAMOUR.
'Faith the latter of these is a great grievance here; our great men hate wit, but love damned flattery, though never so fulsome.

CARLOS.
Pray what fools does this Town afford?

STANMORE.
Very choice ones, we'll bring you where you shall enjoy 'em. There is a widow lately come to Town who sets up for a great fortune, has taken a good house, and lives very splendidly, I suppose with intention to put off herself and two daughters, who are very pretty, one of which Bellamour is in love with.

BELLAMOUR.
I make love* to her, I confess, but 'tis a harmless, lambent flame and aims but at fornication. But Stanmore is in love with the other, and Heaven knows what that may end in.

STANMORE.
I have no designs upon her fortune, I aim only at her person; I yet run at the whole herd.

CARLOS.
Come, you know your own tempers no more in love than in play, where those who are very stingy at first will bleed deeply at last.

BELLAMOUR.
This widow, by name the Lady Cheatly, has made her house the rendezvouz of fools, knaves, whoremasters, ladies of all sorts, and young heirs. Amongst the rest of fops, there is Young Maggot, one whom his uncle, whose heir he is, bred at the Inns of Court* and intended for the law. But he has left that and is run wit-mad, thinks of nothing, endeavors at nothing but to be a wit and a lover, and both in spite of nature.

STANMORE.
And though he has made love and wit his whole business, he is gotten no further yet than to be thought a wit by the fools and an ass by the witty men.

CARLOS.
This is a choice spirit. Indeed, 'tis a general folly, for wit is a common idol that every coxcomb worships in his heart, though some blockheads of business dissemble it.

BELLAMOUR.
But there is another coxcomb of that extreme vanity that Nature amongst all her variety of fops has not produced the like: he draws all lines of discourse to the center of his own person and never was known to speak but "I did" or "I said" was at the beginning or end of it.

STANMORE.
He is lean as a skeleton and yet sets up for shape; he changed his tailor twice, because his shoulder bone sticks out.

BELLAMOUR.
He thinks all women in love with him and all men his intimate friends; he will make *doux yeux*[6] to a judge upon the bench and not despair of getting a widow at her husband's funeral; thinks

---

4 *flûtes douces*] gentle or soft flutes (Fr.)

5 stealing] In the 1670s under Louis XIV, the "chamber of reunion" was established to find legal grounds for French claims on cities, which Louis would promptly annex.

6 *doux yeux*] loving glances, sheep's eyes (Fr.)

himself very well bred and welcome at all times to all people, though sober among drunkards and without a penny in his pocket to men deep at play.

CARLOS.

Oh! I remember this coxcomb, he has no fortune and yet is always talking of equipage and dressing: 'tis Selfish. But do any women favor that fop?

STANMORE.

Oh yes! There is no more account to be given of their love before they know man than their longings after, but both are most commonly for nauseous, nasty things.

CARLOS.

They do most things by chance, but when they choose, 'tis ever for the worst.

Enter footman.

FOOTMAN.

Mr. Selfish is combing his peruke below stairs and will be here instantly.

BELLAMOUR.

Retire while I show him.

[Exit footman. Carlos and Stanmore] retire. Enter Selfish, sets his peruke, and bows to the glass. *

SELFISH.

How dost thou do, Bellamour? You fat fellows have always glasses that make one look so thin.

BELLAMOUR.

You look in it much as you do out on't.

SELFISH.

Sure I am not so lean; I was told I looked pretty plump today.—Hah! My damned rogue has put me into the most bustling stuff. Bellamour, I like thy breeches well.

BELLAMOUR.

Why, you don't see 'em.

SELFISH.

Yes, I see 'em in the glass. Your tailor shall make mine! A pox on my *valet de chambre*, how he has tied my cravat up today; a man cannot get a good *valet de chambre*, French or English.

BELLAMOUR.

A French one is fittest for him, because he can fast best.

SELFISH.

I begin to belly, I think, very much: I must go into France and flux; 'twill do my complexion good as well as my shape.

BELLAMOUR.

Why, thou art fit to be hung up at Barber-Surgeons-Hall[7] for a skeleton; a woman had as good lie with a fagot.

SELFISH.

Thou art envious; the ladies are of another mind. I am sure you are above whoremasters' weight, and a woman had as good lie with a pound of candles.[8]

BELLAMOUR.

Enough of this. There is a friend of mine, one Carlos, lately come from France, that understands dressing; I must bring you together.

SELFISH.

You talk of my leanness, I had the most lucky adventure: I was happy in the conversation* of a pretty person of quality,* young and witty; I went in a coach with my hand in her neck from the Duke's Playhouse[9] to the Pall Mall,* kissing her all the way.

BELLAMOUR.

There is a thing happened to me, in which I have occasion for your assistance and advice.

SELFISH.

I have lately succeeded in the affections of so many pretty creatures, faith, I know not how to turn my hands to 'em, poor rogues. If you did but see the advances that all the ladies that come to the widow's and her daughters make to me, you would stand amazed, and so should I, but that I am used to those things.

CARLOS.

This fool is much improved since I went into France.

STANMORE.

Fools always improve in folly, as witty men in understanding.

---

7 Barber-Surgeons-Hall] home of the guild for barber-surgeons, who both cut hair and practiced a primitive form of medicine

8 candles] Inexpensive candles were made with tallow (fat).

9 Duke's Playhouse] Dorset Garden, where this play was itself produced

CARLOS.

Indeed, he has great acquired parts.*

SELFISH.

Bellamour, fare thee well, I must go home and answer two or three billet-doux from persons of quality; I have a bushel in a year. Adieu. (*Exit.*)

CARLOS.

A most admirable coxcomb: he is so full of himself, he ne'er minds another man and so answers quite from the purpose.

BELLAMOUR.

He never answers any man nor cares to be answered; he desires but to be heard. But come Carlos, let's take the air and while away a dining time.

CARLOS.

I hate a dinner: 'tis a good meal for a dull plodding fellow of business that must bait like a carrier's horse and then to plodding again, but the supper is the meal of pleasure and enjoyment.

STANMORE.

Supping indeed is a solemn thing and should be used but with few; every blockhead can dine.

BELLAMOUR.

That is, fill a belly, but there are few men fit to sup: there's more than eating required for that mystery; there must be wit and sense.

Enter Young Maggot.

YOUNG MAGGOT.

Your servant gentlemen. I see, Bellamour, you are going abroad. I only come to show you my last verses.

BELLAMOUR.

Your last verses! I would I could be so happy as to see them.

YOUNG MAGGOT.

You have company, and I have business; some other time.

BELLAMOUR.

What business?

YOUNG MAGGOT.

Why, wit and beauty, I know no other. I am longed for by the ladies now to give account of the play, for the poets will not write, the players act, nor the ladies censure without my judgment first.

BELLAMOUR.

The ladies are indeed your finger watches, that go just as you set them.

YOUNG MAGGOT.

Faith, that's very well imagined, well said. I think thou hast near[c] as much wit as one of us writers.

CARLOS.

What is your opinion of the play?

YOUNG MAGGOT.

I saw it scene by scene and helped him in the writing. It breaks well, the *protasis* good, the *catastasis* excellent, there's no *episode*, but the *catastrophe*[10] is admirable—I lent him that and the love parts and the songs. There are a great many sublimes[11] that are very poetical.

STANMORE.

Poetical, in his judgment, is always fustian and nonsense in another's. I warrant 'tis some roaring, ranting play that's upon the fret all the while.

BELLAMOUR.

Will you carry us to a rehearsal?

YOUNG MAGGOT.

'Tis a familiarity among us writers to see one another naked. You are men of wit and desperate critics, and we poets fear you as singing birds do a hawk.

CARLOS.

Thank you for your hawk.

YOUNG MAGGOT.

Aye, was it not well said?

CARLOS.

But methinks fools should be your only enemies.

YOUNG MAGGOT.

They can't hurt us; besides, a dedication, writing

---

10 *protasis ... catastrophe*] As Montague Summers suggests, Shadwell probably derives this passage from Dryden's *Of Dramatick Poesie*, where Eugenius describes the parts of a play as the "*Protasis*, or entrance, which gives light only to the characters of the persons"; the "*Epitasis*, or working up of the plot"; "the *Catastasis*, called by the Romans, *Status*, the height and full growth of the play"; and "Lastly, the *Catastrophe* . . . the discovery, or unravelling of the plot." Eugenius does not mention the *episode*, which means an incidental narration or digression.

11 sublimes] instances of elevated style, especially as recently made fashionable through Boileau's translation of Longinus's treatise *On the Sublime*

songs for their mistresses, or showing them a play before hand will take them off.

Enter footman.

FOOTMAN.

Sir, Mr. Prig is coming up. [*Exit.*]

YOUNG MAGGOT.

Now shall we be troubled with fools; a man can never enjoy thee half an hour to himself, thou art so haunted with fops.

BELLAMOUR.

How insupportable the rogues are to one another.

CARLOS.

What is this Prig?

STANMORE.

He is an universal gamester, an admirable horse and dog herald, knows all the remarkable ones, their families, and alliances, is indeed more intimately acquainted with beasts than men, and 'tis fit he should be so.

BELLAMOUR.

He is, in short, a led-eater,[12] intelligencer, and dry-jester[13] to gaming- and jockey-lords; flatters, rooks, and passes for a jolly companion amongst 'em; and makes those things which are but the recreations of men of sense his whole business.

Enter Prig.

PRIG.

Gentlemen good morrow, though I think 'tis almost noon. Where were you last night? If you had been at my Lord Squanders, you had seen the best play you had seen this month. My lord lost a thousand pound, Jack Sharper won three hundred, Tom Whiskin an hundred, my Lord Whimsey lost five hundred, Sir Thomas Rantipol lost six hundred, Sir Nicholas Wachum won two hundred, and the rooks were very busy.

STANMORE.

Then you were not idle?

PRIG.

No, faith. But I am come to get you to look upon the best bred horse in England. Woodcock was his grandfather; he is the son of Bay-lusty and the brother of Red Rose; his sister is the white mare, the cousin-german of Crack-a-fart, cousin once removed to Nutmeg, third cousin to my Lord Squander's colt, allied to Flea-bitten by the second venter. In short he is of an excellent family, and I am going to make a civil visit to him. He's to run for the plate at Brackley, Stamford, and Newmarket,[14] and goes out of Town tomorrow.

BELLAMOUR.

We cannot see him, we're engaged.

PRIG.

Engaged! No, faith, let's make a match at tennis today. I was invited to dine by two or three lords, but if you will let me have pen, ink, and paper, I'll send my dispatches and disengage myself. How, will that gentleman and you play with Stanmore, and* I keep his back hand at Gibbons'?[15]

BELLAMOUR.

I do not know his play.

PRIG.

We'll take a bisque of you.

BELLAMOUR.

No, you shan't.

PRIG.

You're half fifteen better than I to a grain.[16]

STANMORE.

No, that he is not.

PRIG.

I never heard the like in my life. Gad, you'll never let me make a reasonable match with you; you beat Sharper at a bisque, and he beats me. What will Stanmore and you give Maggot and me at Whitehall[17] and play the best of your play? hah?

YOUNG MAGGOT.

I never play, I stay at home and write.

PRIG.

Pish, 'tis all one for that: we'll play with you at a bisque and a fault for twenty pound.

YOUNG MAGGOT.

I will not, sir.

12 led-eater] a parasite or sychophant

13 dry-jester] one whose jokes fall flat

14 Brackley … Newmarket] sites of racetracks all round England

15 Gibbons'] tennis court

16 bisque … grain] Prig seeks a handicap.

17 Whitehall] Whitehall* contained tennis courts, a cock-pit, and grounds for tilting and bear-baiting.

PRIG.
Come, I'll hold you twenty pound you do not make a fairer match. Let me see—hold—anon—hum—hah—aye—'tis just so to a hair's breadth. Come, we'll play it.[18]

BELLAMOUR.
I tell you I am engaged today.

PRIG.
We'll play or pay tomorrow at ten. Where shall we sup?

STANMORE.
Nowhere, you cannot sup.

PRIG.
Not sup?

BELLAMOUR.
No, you are not fit to sup.

PRIG.
No? I am sure I have as good a stomach and will eat two meals a day with any man that wears a head.

CARLOS.
That will not do.

PRIG.
No? I'll eat three then. What say you, Maggot, will you play?

YOUNG MAGGOT.
I will never play as long as I live at that or any thing else while I can have pen, ink, and paper.

PRIG.
Oh Lord! Oh Lord! I would not say so for all the world.

BELLAMOUR.
A man must use exercise to keep himself down, he will belly else, and the ladies will not like him.

YOUNG MAGGOT.
I have another way to bring down my belly.

STANMORE.
Another? What's that?

YOUNG MAGGOT.
Why, I study, I study and write. 'Tis exercise of the mind does it. I have none of the worst shapes or complexions. 'Tis writing and inventing does my business.

[18] Let ... it] Unclear, but perhaps Prig is measuring Bellamour's rooms for a tennis court; tennis was played indoors and does not much resemble the modern game.

CARLOS.
Will that do't, sir?

PRIG.
Think? What a pox should a gentleman think of but dogs, horses, dice, tennis, bowls, races, or cockfighting? The devil take me, I never think of anything else, but now and then of a whore (when I have a mind to her).

CARLOS.
This is strange, Mr. Maggot, and very curious. How do you know how much you fall away in a day's time?

YOUNG MAGGOT.
I have an engine* to weigh myself when I sit down to write or think and when I unbend myself again.

PRIG.
How do you unbend?

YOUNG MAGGOT.
Why, I unbend my imagination, my intellect.

PRIG.
Your intellect? Pray sir, what's that? Is't a new word for a crossbow?

YOUNG MAGGOT.
How I scorn fops! Why, I have been in love these two months, and I have wasted above fourteen pound. Love is a great preserver of the shape, a very great one. You know my mistress, the widow's youngest daughter.

CARLOS.
This is a curious coxcomb.

PRIG.
Love! Aye, if a man gets a clap, 'twill take him down.

YOUNG MAGGOT.
May it take down your nose,* you unthinking animal.

PRIG.
What a devil does he mean?

YOUNG MAGGOT.
Why, I weighed myself when I writ my last song, and I wasted six ounces *aver du pois*[19] weight in the writing. And I was not above twelve hours about it.

[19] *aver du pois*] avoirdupois; the spelling indicates the Anglicization of pronunciation.

CARLOS.
I beseech you, let's hear it, sir.

YOUNG MAGGOT.
With all my heart.

Damon see how charming Chloris,
Who gives love to all that see her,
Burning us yet in coldness, glories
And is never, never freer.
Though darts and flames from her eye fly, sir,
And her breast is warm and spicy,
Yet there is coldness in her eye, sir,
And her heart's all over icy.
By coldness I am more inflamed,
As in winter is springwater;
My love by scorn cannot be tamed,
But I the rather would be at her.

PRIG.
Did this make you waste six ounces? I writ a song t'other day, and it did not make me waste at all.

BELLAMOUR.
Prithee Prig, let's hear it.

PRIG. (Sings.)

One night walking in a wood
I met one was a maid as good
As e're she could,
But she fired my blood,
And to her I stood.
With a hey boys, ding, ding, ding boys hey,
With a hey boys, ding, ding, ding.

Quoth I, my pretty buxom lass,
From me this time thou shalt not pass.
In any case,
For the sake of thy face!
I'll lay thee on the grass.
With a hey boys, ding, etc.

YOUNG MAGGOT.
Oh what violence does he to my ears.

PRIG.
What, he does not like it? Pox! These wits like nothing but what they do themselves. I love a tavern song that will roar and make one merry. A pox of his Strephons and Phillises.

BELLAMOUR.
What will become of you, Young Maggot? Your Uncle Maggot, that common foe to wit, is coming up.

YOUNG MAGGOT.
Hide me, gentlemen, hide me. I am undone if he finds me in your company.

BELLAMOUR.
Step in there.

Young Maggot retires. Enter Maggot.

MAGGOT.
Gentlemen, I come to look out an ungracious nephew of mine, who I hear by virtue of your company sets up for a wit. Will any of you keep him when you have made him good for nothing?

BELLAMOUR.
Good for nothing! Why, he is the darling of the ladies: they dote on him for his songs and fear him for his lampoons. And the men think no debauch perfect without him.

MAGGOT.
Yes, I hear he writ a libel. I shall have him scribble away his ears or write himself so far into the ladies' favors to lose his nose* or be knocked o'th'head. These are the fruits of wit.

CARLOS.
The disasters rather.

MAGGOT.
The world will bear with you that have estates, though you have a little, but 'tis enough to undo a man that is to make his fortune. My roguy nephew must leave Cook upon Littleton for Beaumont and Fletcher.[20]

STANMORE.
Poetry is an ornament to a man of any profession.

MAGGOT.
'Tis a damned weed and will let nothing good or profitable grow by it; 'tis the language of the Devil and begun with oracles. Where did you know a wit thrive or indeed keep his own?

---

20 Cook ... Fletcher] Coke upon Littleton, that is, Sir Edward Coke's (1552-1634) commentary on Sir Thomas Littleton's (1422-1481) treatise on tenures, would have been a law student's first book. Francis Beaumont (1584-1616) and John Fletcher (1579-1625) collaborated on numerous plays in the early seventeenth century.

CARLOS.
They part with their money for pleasure, and fools part with their pleasure for money; the one will make a better last will and testament, but the other lead a happier life.

YOUNG MAGGOT.
Profit be gone, what art thou but a breath.
I'll live proud of my infamy and shame,
Graced with the triumphs of a poet's name;
Men can but say, wit did my reason blind,
And wit's the noblest frailty of the mind.
Methinks it runs well thus.

MAGGOT.
What noise is that? Hah! My ungracious nephew repeating verses. Come out you rascal. Dost thou not tremble at my anger? Thou that mightest have been a judge in time, to make a wit of thyself thus!

BELLAMOUR.
Good sir, be patient. Did not the great pleader Cicero make verses?

MAGGOT.
And you see what came on't: he died a beggar and of a violent death.

YOUNG MAGGOT.
Sir, the verses were not my own.

MAGGOT.
Sir, be gone to the Temple,* and let me once more find you at wit, and I'll disinherit you.

YOUNG MAGGOT.
Good sir, hear me.

MAGGOT.
Be gone, I say.

CARLOS.
This is ridiculous enough and odd.

BELLAMOUR.
There is a powerful faction against wit.

STANMORE.
Come, let's take the air.

Exeunt omnes.

[Scene ii. Lady Cheatly's lodgings.]

Enter Lady Cheatly and Mr. Lump, her brother.

LUMP.
I see, lady sister, you are resolved to push on the remnant of your estate and make the snuff* of your fortune burn clearest.

LADY CHEATLY.
As my fortune was, it would do us no good. But this Town, and the way I take, may advance it, or at least dispose of my own person.

LUMP.
You shall not want* my money, so long as I have deeds of trust from you; you shall have the name on't. I have helped you to sober, solid, godly men, who will help to carry on your design.

LADY CHEATLY.
Some cautious old fellow or other (who is wise enough to have his own wisdom contribute to the cheating of him) may snap at me, and some rash, amorous, young fellows may catch at my daughters.

LUMP.
I wish you had set up in the City* among our party and gone to meetings; it might have been a great advantage. I myself have made much benefit of religion, as to my temporal concerns, and (so long as it be directed to a good end) it is a pious fraud and very lawful.

LADY CHEATLY.
No, brother, the godly have two qualities which would spoil my design: great covetousness (which would make 'em pry too narrowly into our fortune) and much eating (which would too soon devour what I have left).

LUMP.
Reproach not the godly, lady sister, I do not like it.

LADY CHEATLY.
Where is there a better market for beauty than near the Court? And who will more likely snap at the shadow of a good fortune than the gentlemen of this end of the Town, who are most of 'em in debt? And I have chosen the best instrument in the world to make 'em believe me rich.

LUMP.
Who is that?

LADY CHEATLY.
A very busy old gentleman and very credulous, that loves to tell news and always magnifies a true story till it becomes a lie, one Mr. Maggot.

LUMP.
I know he is a person of parts,* but he is not solid, he's hot-brained and has not method in him. For my own part, I think not anyone wise who does

not know what he shall do this day fifty years, if he lives. I for my part do.

LADY CHEATLY.
I hope 'tis dining with me, brother.

LUMP.
No, upon the one and twentieth of March I shall fifty years hence dine with Mr. Ananias Felt, an elder of our church, if we live and he observe his method. My journal tells what I shall do each day of my life.

LADY CHEATLY.
Can you tell what you shall do next Midsummer Day fifty years?

LUMP.
I shall go down to my house in Kent.

LADY CHEATLY.
Do you never alter your day?

LUMP.
By no means: if one link of the chain be broken, wisdom falls to the ground.

LADY CHEATLY.
What do you do upon the sixth of May come fifty year?

LUMP.
This book will tell you—May—May—6th—6th. Let me see—6th—I take physic and shave myself.

LADY CHEATLY.
What, sick or well, beard or no beard?

LUMP.
'Tis all one for that, I never break my method—Let me see—the next day—I walk to Hampstead, dine at the Queens Head, come back in my coach, visit Sir Formal Trifle,[21] and at night I do communicate with my wife.

LADY CHEATLY.
Not fifty years hence; you'll go near to break that method.

LUMP.
I never break any—no man can be wise without this principle—but sister, I am to give you a main caution: have a care of wits at this end of the Town; wits are good for nothing, of no use in a commonwealth, they understand not business.

LADY CHEATLY.
The better for my purpose. They value pleasure and will bid high for't.

LUMP.
I say they are good for nothing; they are not men of method and business.

LADY CHEATLY.
So fools say, who seem to be excellent men of business, because they always make a business of what is none and seem to be always very industrious, because they take great pains for what a witty man does with ease.

LUMP.
You are out, you are out. Hang 'em wits, when did you see any of 'em rise?

LADY CHEATLY.
No, because the fools are so numerous and strong, they keep 'em down, or rather, because men of wit (that have fortunes) know what a senseless thing the drudgery of business and authority is, and those that have none, want* the impudence, flattery, and importunity of blockheads.

LUMP.
I fear you are tainted, vilely tainted with wit. If you had fixed in the City, you might have 'scaped the infection; nobody would have put you in the head of wit there. But hold, my hour is come: At three a clock I will throw away a quarter of an hour upon you. Farewell. (*Exit.*)

LADY CHEATLY.
Who waits there?

Enter steward.

Oh my good steward! Are the scriveners come?

STEWARD.
Yes madam, your design prospers beyond our hopes; it has taken fire like a train[22] and run through all the Town, and all believe you to be a great fortune.

LADY CHEATLY.
I have chosen as proper an engine* for my business as can be, my Lady Busy, a perpetual gossiper and

---

21 Sir Formal Trifle] an "Orator, a florid Coxcomb" in Shadwell's *The Virtuoso*, played by Tony Leigh very successfully just two years before this play. Did Leigh play Lump? If so, the reflexivity is multiple.

22 train] a trail of gunpowder

visiter in all families, a very wise lady, a great tattle and newsmonger, who, being something too old for an intrigue of her own, is as good a body to help on those of others as can be and is glad to bring lovers of any kind together.

STEWARD.

Already the belief of your wealth has spread so far that I have had two of the City this morning with me (who having been shrewdly bitten* by goldsmiths) are very desirous to trust their money in your hands, hearing what mortgages you have and believing you can employ it better than anybody.

LADY CHEATLY.

You did not, sure, refuse 'em?

STEWARD.

No, I'll warrant you, madam, they will bring their money presently. Mr. Maggot too entreats me that I will be very importunate with your ladyship to employ a thousand pound of his for him.

LADY CHEATLY.

There needs no importunity, subtle rogue. He thinks to lay it here for a nest egg and that I shall lay many more to it, which he hopes he may have again together with my person.

STEWARD.

No madam, 'tis held in mortmain, never to return again. Besides, we have presents enough to keep your house this month brought in this morning: a red deer potted, a brace of fat does, hams of Bayonne bacon, a brace of swans, potted chars, brant geese, and (besides all this) a piece[23] of the best wine in England. Here are the names of the presenters.

LADY CHEATLY.

Let me see: all well-willers to myself or daughters; cunning fools—how very politic they are! Well, policy is most commonly the foolishest thing in the world.

STEWARD.

Madam, there are a great many waiting about money-business without. Shall I call any of 'em in?

LADY CHEATLY.

By no means when I am alone. When company is with me, they are of use and spread my fame abroad. Entertain 'em well and bid 'em hasten dinner.

Exeunt omnes.

Act II, [scene i. Lady Cheatly's lodgings.]

Enter Lady Cheatly and Lady Busy.

LADY CHEATLY.

Madam, I am so infinitely obliged to your ladyship, who can be so careful of my whole family.

LADY BUSY.

Why truly madam, I love to do good offices. We are bound in Christian charity to one another, and I wished Mr. Maggot to your ladyship, if he be not somewhat too old for the vigor of your ladyship: he is rich and is discreet, and his other defects may be supplied elsewhere.

LADY CHEATLY.

Your ladyship's very obliging.

LADY BUSY.

If not, there's Mr. Prig, an ingenious gentleman of a pretty fortune, whom I wished to you. He is in great favor with lords; I warrant you, you shall seldom take him without a lord in his mouth, they do so court him: they love him mightily.

LADY CHEATLY.

And he loves lords mightily for being so.

LADY BUSY.

Oh mightily! Well madam, your two daughters are accounted the beauties of the Drawing Room;* there's nobody while they are there[d] will vouchsafe to look upon a maid of honor, no, not they, and they are as mad at it.

LADY CHEATLY.

'Tis not the beauty of my daughters makes 'em look at 'em so, but they like an indifferent new face better than those faces they are used to every night. They are weary of 'em.

LADY BUSY.

Oh no, really, your daughters are the prettiest creatures in Town, and I would fain have 'em well settled, one way or other. I have had several offers of husbands for 'em, but I do not think I have yet met with fortunes good enough. But that great lord I told you of is very pressing to enjoy your eldest, and as I said, he offers a thousand pounds

23 piece] a cask of wine equivalent to the butt, holding between 108 and 140 gallons

down and three hundred per annum during life. But that I know your ladyship is discreet and one that has seen the world, I dared not have propounded this to you.

LADY CHEATLY.
My daughters have fortunes enough to marry 'em to good estates, but your ladyship is wise: 'tis good to treat with all persons, and all ways, to settle a young—girl in the world.

LADY BUSY.
Why madam, this will be a great addition to her fortune, and besides, you do not know how he may prefer her, or for ought we know, after he has tried her, he may like her so well as to own her—who knows? Be pleased to consider how marriage is cried down and that there are few that are good for anything will think on't nowadays; besides, custom alters all things mightily: mothers very frequently do this for their daughters now, and if it be a fashion, you know—

LADY CHEATLY.
I am very much obliged to your ladyship's advice. I have propounded it to my daughter, but she is so perverse, she will not listen to me but says she had rather marry a groom than be mistress to a prince.

LADY BUSY.
Oh fie, she has a wrong notion of the thing. I will try to advise her better.

LADY CHEATLY.
Your ladyship will do me a great favor. Here they come both.

Enter Isabella and Gartrude.

LADY BUSY.
Ladies, your servant.

ISABELLA, GARTRUDE.
Your ladyship's most humble servant.

LADY BUSY.
Mrs.* Isabella, I have something to advise you for your good.

ISABELLA.
For my good, madam?

LADY BUSY.
Yes madam, and therefore be pleased to give attention to me.

ISABELLA.
Good manners will make me do that.

LADY BUSY.
Why look you, you are young, I am in years, an ancient woman, and have seen the world, as they say.

ISABELLA.
Ancient? Your ladyship looks very youthfully.

LADY BUSY.
No, no, you are pleased to compliment me, but as I said, my lady and myself have known the world, as the saying is.

ISABELLA. (*Aside.*)
And you the flesh and the devil,[24] as the saying is.

LADY BUSY.
And 'tis fit the young should submit themselves to the gravity and discretion of the old.

ISABELLA.
Yes, where they can find it.

LADY BUSY.
Go to*—my lady is a person whose aim is to settle you well in the world—do you conceive me—and she knows what's fittest and most convenient for you—and obedience is the best virtue.

ISABELLA.
Very well, madam.

LADY BUSY.
Now there is a certain lord, whom my lady has mentioned to you.

ISABELLA.
A lord? a beast, and one that would make me as bad as himself.

LADY CHEATLY.
Good Mrs. Pert, keep in that foolish instrument, your tongue. A beast? There are a great many like him.

LADY BUSY.
Be not so forward, all things have two faces—-do not look upon the wrong one—go to—you are a fine young lady and are brought by your lady mother to Town, the general mart for beauty. Well—you would be so settled in the world, as to

[24] world … devil] "The world, the flesh, and the devil" was a common, proverbial phrase.

have a certain fund[e] whereon you may rely, which in age may secure you from contempt—-good.

ISABELLA.

I hope I shall have enough to keep me honest.*

LADY BUSY.

Nay, Heaven forbid I should persuade you to be dishonest. Virtue is a rare thing, a heavenly thing. But I say still, be mindful of the main:* alas, a woman is a solitary, helpless creature without a man, God knows—good. How may this man be had in marriage say you? Very well if you could get a fine gentleman with money enough, but alas! those do not marry, they have left it off. The customs of the world change in all ages.

ISABELLA.

In ours for the worse.

LADY BUSY.

Very well said, but yet the wisest must obey 'em as they change—Do you conceive, madam?

ISABELLA. (*Aside.*)

Yes, I do conceive you to be doing a very reverend office.

GARTRUDE.

Methinks her ladyship speaks a great deal of reason; she's a fine spoken lady truly.

LADY BUSY.

Now I say, since custom has so run down wedlock, what remains but that we should make use of the next thing to it? Good. Nay, not but that virtue is a rare thing—Heaven forbid I should detract from that—but I say, the main* is to be respected: a good deal of money, there's the point.

ISABELLA.

With little or no reputation, there's the point.

LADY CHEATLY.

Money brings reputation, fool, or at least puts one into that condition that fellows dare not question it.

LADY BUSY.

Nay, Heaven forbid you should lose that, but I say the next thing to marriage is being kind* to a noble lord, etcetera. And if good terms be made and you be well settled in the world—

ISABELLA.

That would be to be settled out of the world, for I should never dare to show my face again.

LADY CHEATLY.

There are as good faces as yours, and better, my nimble chaps, that are shown everyday in the playhouse after it and with the best quality* too.

LADY BUSY.

Yes, and in front of boxes—nay, nay, not but that a good wealthy marriage is beyond it.

ISABELLA.

A very comfortable thing for a gentlewoman to bring herself into a condition of never conversing with a woman of quality,* who has wit and honor, again, but must sort with those tawdry painted things of the Town.

GARTRUDE.

Can't you keep company with my mother and me?

LADY BUSY.

Look you madam, you are under a great mistake, for do not ladies of wit and honor keep daily company with those things as you call them? But d'ye conceive me, the finest things, the gayest things, and some the richest things, I say no more, I pray conceive me—as long as you are true to one man, madam, you are in a manner his lady, I say in a manner his lady; 'tis a kind of marriage, and great persons most commonly cohabit longer with mistresses than they used to do with wives.

LADY CHEATLY.

My lady says right, 'tis nowadays more like marriage than marriage itself.

GARTRUDE.

Oh sister! Do what my lady says, she's a rare person.

LADY BUSY.

A thousand pound, and three hundred pound per annum—say we bring him to four hundred pound, good—a great lord—that is in the way to prefer you, very good—or maybe, may like you so well, as to own you—best of all. Consider.—'Tis enough, madam, at once. Let her ruminate upon this.

GARTRUDE.

Oh Lord, pray sister do. Why, we shall be all made, prithee do.

ISABELLA.

Go you to your Mr. Maggot that dies and makes songs for you.

GARTRUDE.

No, I'll swear he's a fine witty person, but he has

such a grievous face, I can't abide it. But there's Mr. Selfish is the most gentile, well-bred gentleman and has the finest ways among ladies. He will tell you such pretty things of himself, he talks of himself always so prettily and says such neat, gentile, well-bred things to one.

Enter steward.

STEWARD.
Madam, some gentlemen are coming in.

LADY CHEATLY.
Bid the scriveners and the rest of the people come in.

[Exit steward.]

—Daughters go, and walk in the garden.

Exeunt daughters.

—I hope your ladyship will pardon me; this money-business must be minded.

LADY BUSY.
By all means, madam. I'll go make a visit. Your servant. (*Exit.*)

Enter scriveners and several others [including counsel and steward].

SCRIVENER.
I have brought the mortgage, and the mortgager is here ready to seal upon the payment of the within-named sum.

LADY CHEATLY.
Has my counsel perused it?

COUNSEL.
Yes, and find it to be very well drawn.

LADY CHEATLY.
Let me read it.

Enter Stanmore, Bellamour, Carlos, and Maggot.

STEWARD.
The company is come.

LADY CHEATLY.
Peace, I see 'em.

MAGGOT.
Look you, did I not tell you? she's always thus busy, I warrant upon a mortgage or a purchase. She's a vast fortune. I know where her money lies and in what hands. She has a vast deal. Do not interrupt her, you shall hear.

BELLAMOUR.
Then you know all?

MAGGOT.
Know all? Aye. Why Sir William, her late husband, was my intimate friend. Know? Why, I hired this house and bought all the furniture for her. Her daughters will be worth ten thousand pound apiece, at least, to my knowledge—

STANMORE.
This fellow will outlie any traveler.

MAGGOT.
I knew her father as well as any man in the world. Know? Why, I know all.

CARLOS.
This lady must be a cheat, by doing her business so publicly.

MAGGOT.
Mr. Carlos, I knew your father as well as any man in England. Honest James, his keeper: I have had many a buck of him.

BELLAMOUR.
Did you know my father?

MAGGOT.
Did I? No flesh alive better. I did more for him than any man in England. I was a father to him.

BELLAMOUR.
Ay! Then you are my grandfather! But how were you a father to him?

MAGGOT.
How? Why, I gave him his second wife.

COUNSEL. (*Reads.*)
"To have and to hold."

LADY CHEATLY.
'Tis very well: five thousand pound is the sum.— Steward, pay him the money and take the writings.

MAGGOT.
Look you there, did not I tell you?

FIRST CITIZEN.
Well, she's a rare woman at business.

SECOND CITIZEN.
As ever I saw.

STEWARD.
Here are the two gentlemen I spoke of, who humbly desire to place some money in your ladyship's hands.

LADY CHEATLY.

I do not love to meddle with other people's money, you know; besides, I shall have no occasion. I have a great sum to be paid in within this fortnight.

STEWARD.

I know it, madam, but if a purchase should be offered in the mean time—

FIRST CITIZEN.

I beseech your ladyship, take our money. We have been so cheated by base goldsmiths,[25] we are afraid to trust anybody but your ladyship.

LADY CHEATLY.

I do not love to stand charged for other people's money.—Oh me, gentlemen! I was so busy I did not see you. You have not waited long, I hope. Pray forgive my rudeness.

BELLAMOUR.

The rudeness is on our side, to intrude into your ladyship's privacies.

LADY CHEATLY.

By no means. You do me honor.

STANMORE.

Madam, we take the liberty to present Mr. Carlos, a friend of ours lately come out of France, to your ladyship.

LADY CHEATLY.

Sir, I have heard of your noble family, and you'll honor mine in your acquaintance with it.—Sweet Mr. Maggot, your servant.—Gentlemen, have but a little patience till I have dispatched some business, and I'll wait on you.

MAGGOT.

God, she's the finest person in the world and a vast fortune. I would my ungracious nephew had one of her daughters.

Enter Prig.

PRIG.

Madam, your most humble servant.

LADY CHEATLY.

Your servant, sweet Mr. Prig.

PRIG.

Sweet Mr. Prig! Good: matters go on well.—Come gentlemen, since my lady's busy, let's go to langtriloo[26] or ombre.

CARLOS.

Is there no way of spending our time but playing?

PRIG.

None so good. Why, what a pox should one do?

CARLOS.

Read, it is a manly diversion.

PRIG.

Read? So I have read *Markham, The Compleat Farrier*,[27] and two or three books about horses; a book that's written about ombre and that about piquet; and for other books, pox there's nothing in 'em at all.—What think you Bellamour?

BELLAMOUR.

You are in the right.

PRIG.

Look you there, there's nothing in 'em, hah.

STANMORE.

Methinks discourse is a pretty good way of passing one's time.

PRIG.

Gad, so it is: I talk as much as any man in England; my tongue seldom lies still. Oh! I love discourse mightily, and though I say it, I am able to run down all I meet about dogs and horses. Now I think on't, have you ever hunted with my Lord Squander's fox-dogs, Bellamour?

BELLAMOUR.

No. [*Aside.*] Now he's in.

PRIG.

They are the best in England. But there is one dog we call Ranter, I christened him, I was his godfather. He was gotten upon my lord's famous bitch, Lady. You remember what a bitch she was. Oh poor Lady! I was not sorrier when my sister died than when poor Lady died. But let that pass. Ranter was gotten by your father's dog, Rockwood.

BELLAMOUR.

Did you know Rockwood?

---

25 goldsmiths] who dominated banking in seventeenth-century London; the Bank of England was not established until 1694, and even then was primarily a source of funds for William III's continental military operations.

26 langtriloo] or lanterloo, an older form of loo (q.v.)

27 *Markham … Farrier*] two books on horses, *Markham's Masterpiece* (there was an edition in 1675) and *The English Horseman and Compleat Farrier* (1673)

PRIG.

Know him? As well as any man in the world. His father was a dog of my father's, called Jowler; his mother was my noble Lord Squander's father's famous bitch, Venus, which you have heard of.—I remember, Mr. Carlos, Venus was sister to your father's dog, Ringwood.—Rockwood? I knew him as well as I knew your father. Well, rest their souls of a dog and a man, I shall never see two better in the field than Rockwood and your father.

CARLOS.

How the rogue has coupled them.

PRIG.

Yet Ranter's an admirable dog, the best at a cold scent that ever I saw. If there be any forty couple in the field, I'll hold an hundred pound he works it out soonest and leads 'em all when he has done. I love and honor Ranter, I care not who knows it. I made a song of him and have his picture by my bed-side and some of his hair here in a crystal locket.

MAGGOT.

I beseech your ladyship, accept of my thousand pound, 'twill make up the money for that purchase, sweet madam.

LADY CHEATLY.

Well sir, since you will have it so, I'll give my bond for it.

MAGGOT.

Oh madam! I scorn it, I'll have nothing under hand for it.

LADY CHEATLY.

Then I will not take it; nay, I have sworn first.

MAGGOT.

Well, I'll go and fetch it, and your ladyship and I will agree upon that. (*Exit.*)

PRIG.

Hah! The young ladies are in the garden.

BELLAMOUR.

Say you so? Prithee, let's steal down to 'em.

PRIG.

Do, and leave me with the widow.

Exeunt Bellamour, Stanmore, Carlos.

LADY CHEATLY.

Steward, do you take care of all the rest, while I retire from (what I do not care for) business.

[Exit steward.]

—Now I am at leisure. Are the gentlemen gone?

PRIG.

They are gone but into the garden and will wait on your ladyship presently. They have left me that happy opportunity I wished for to renew the suit I have so often made to your ladyship: I beseech you, madam, be pleased to consider my passion, which is so violent to your ladyship, I cannot rest since first I saw your ladyship, for it has indeed put me besides myself. I have not the heart to ride so much as one heat at Newmarket since, and I used to go once in ten days down on purpose, nor have I been able to ride a fox chase since I have had your ladyship in chase. I shall be undone if your la'ship don't quiet my mind with some assurances: I overset[f 28] at trictrac, dealt my self ten at ombre, and all through my passion for your dear self.

LADY CHEATLY.

Sir, though I have a great esteem for your person, yet we widows that have some fortune are to consider something besides passion.

PRIG.

As I have told you before, my estate is not inconsiderable, besides the great favor I have with the gaming and jockey lords, and besides, if the king frequents Newmarket, I doubt not but in a short time to rise.

LADY CHEATLY.

But you are a gamester.

PRIG.

Aye madam, but I never play, I do but rook.

LADY CHEATLY.

Rook? What's that? Cheat?

PRIG.

No madam, I go to twelve and the better of the lay;[29] besides, I get five hundred pound a year at

---

28 overset] to not take a possible point through carelessness

29 twelve ... lay] Unclear. Twelve penny ordinaries (see act V) served a complete meal for a shilling at twelve. After the meal the tables would be cleared and gambling would commence. Alternately, one ruse of rooks dealing with gulls was to bet that they could roll a seven before the gull could role a twelve; the gull would

horse races and cock matches by being in fee with the grooms and cock keepers.[30] And madam, I play as well at tennis, ombre, backgammon, trictrac, and crimp,[31] as any man, which is no small addition to my estate. I gave you these things in my particular, if your ladyship please to remember.

LADY CHEATLY.
But you cannot make a jointure of these things, and therefore, I must consider a little longer.

PRIG.
With all my heart, madam, but in the meantime let you and I play a set at trictrac, and when the rest come in, we'll make a match at ombre.

Enter steward.

STEWARD.
Madam, there are some tenants wait without to speak with you.

LADY CHEATLY.
You'll pardon me, I must go to 'em. (*Exit.*)

PRIG.
Come on, Mr. Steward, what say you to a game at backgammon?

STEWARD.
If you'll retire to my chamber, have at you.

PRIG.
With all my heart.

Exeunt.

[Scene ii. The garden at Lady Cheatly's.]

Enter Theodosia, Isabella, Bellamour, Carlos, Stanmore.

CARLOS.
Who's there, the Lady Pleasant's daughter, Theodosia?

BELLAMOUR.
It is: she's young and handsome, has a great deal of wit, and a very good fortune, which makes her set up for marriage and is impregnable to anything else.

CARLOS.
She's extreme pretty; I loved her violently before I went into France, but now she's a thousand times more beautiful.

STANMORE.
Ladies, your humble servant.

BELLAMOUR.
A gentleman, a friend of ours, lately come out of France. (*He salutes* 'em.*)

CARLOS.
And glad I am so, for all that nation could not show me so much beauty.

THEODOSIA.
I see, sir, you have not been in France for nothing; you have imported French goods, I mean compliments. They are a nation full of complimenters.

CARLOS.
They are so, madam, and the tailor does it full as well as the gentleman; 'tis a road of speaking which all of 'em have. I was not dull enough to get it of 'em, nor would I bring so common a thing as a compliment to you, madam.

THEODOSIA.
You can bring it to nobody that dislikes it more.

CARLOS.
Or needs it less.

THEODOSIA.
Thus I have heard a very rhetorical oration against eloquence.

Enter Gartrude.

GARTRUDE.
Oh Lord, Mr. Stanmore here. (*Runs out.*)

BELLAMOUR.
Run Stanmore, your business is more than half done; 'tis a certain sign when a woman seeks corners that she means some good by it.

STANMORE.
I'll try that. (*Exit.*)

BELLAMOUR. [*To Isabella.*]
I see my friend's caught again, for all his travel. I have a fellow-feeling of his case; let's retire and give him opportunity.

apparently not realize how much the odds were against him. Thus Prig would have the better part of the wager or lay, which could also mean a trick.

30 in fee … cock keepers] Prig bribes grooms and cock keepers for inside information.

31 crimp] a card game

ISABELLA.

With all my heart; opportunity is safe in the beginning of an amour, though it may be dangerous afterwards.

They retire.

THEODOSIA.

I hear never a French word from you, and that's strange: for all our sparks are so refined, they scarce speak a sentence without one, and though they seldom arrive at good French, yet they get enough to spoil their English.

CARLOS.

If a man means nothing, he cannot choose a better language, for it makes a pretty noise without any manner of thought.

THEODOSIA.

You have scarce brought one substantial vanity over with you. What have you learnt there?

CARLOS.

To love my own country and to think that none can show us so fine women. In France they buy their beauty and sell their love.

THEODOSIA.

That fashion is coming up apace here.

CARLOS.

True beauty, madam, can no more be bought than true love; in me behold the one, while I admire the other in yourself.

THEODOSIA.

How many French ladies have you said as much to?

CARLOS.

I went thither to be cured of love, not to make* it.

THEODOSIA.

What love?

CARLOS.

My love of you, which began so early in my heart, self-love was scarce before it. When your disdain could not remove it, I tried absence but in vain too.

THEODOSIA.

'Tis impossible you could bring a heart unhurt from France.

CARLOS.

My love to you preserved me from all foreign invasion.

THEODOSIA.

If you make love, you'll grow dull; it spoils a man of wit, as much as business.

CARLOS.

If love be predominant in conversation,* I confess it, but a little relish of it does well.

THEODOSIA.

The imitation of it may be born, but the thing itself is a dead weight upon the mind, and a man can no more please under that disadvantage than a horse can run a race with a pair of panniers on his back.

CARLOS.

And yet that horse may do it, if the match be well made.

THEODOSIA.

I must have my servant all wit, all gaiety, and the ladies of the Town run mad for him. I would not only triumph over him, but over my whole sex in him.

CARLOS.

This is hard doctrine for a man of my sincerity and truth in love.

THEODOSIA.

Make Isabella slight Bellamour, little Gartrude sacrifice Selfish, be the third word in every lady's mouth from fifteen to five and thirty, and you shall find what I'll say to you.

CARLOS.

To attempt this were great vanity and no less dishonesty to my friend Bellamour.

THEODOSIA.

If you love, you'll think anything lawful.[32] This must be done: I dare not trust my own judgment; I will have you in vogue, ere I favor you in the least.

CARLOS.

Well, since these ladies are your outworks, I will on and, by the force of imagination, make every one Theodosia. But if I fail, think on my constant love, which will not suffer me to use deceit.

THEODOSIA.

Suppose I should answer you in your whining strain and say my love were true as yours, my flame as great, and all your wishes mine.

---

32 love … lawful] alluding to the proverb, all's fair in love and war

CARLOS.
Then were Carlos the happiest man on earth.

THEODOSIA.
No, then the game were up betwixt us and there were no more to do but pay the stakes and then to something else.

CARLOS.
We might play set after set forever.

THEODOSIA.
No, one of us would be broke. Go get you about your task, I say.

Exeunt Carlos and Theodosia. Enter Selfish and Young Maggot.

YOUNG MAGGOT.
Did you see how the ladies flocked about me at court when I made a relation of the rehearsal and afterwards when I read my song to 'em?

SELFISH.
I think I am as well with the ladies there as any man, and they like my songs too; they say they're so easy, so gentile, and well-bred and so pat to the women's understandings. The men say they're silly, but they are envious.

YOUNG MAGGOT.
I'll secure you the play takes; I have done the poet's business with the ladies, who, you know, govern the men, as the moon does the sea.

SELFISH.
There is a pretty creature not past eighteen, whom I have formerly enjoyed, has to oblige me taken upon her the figure of a procurer and is to bring me a maidenhead anon, which fell in love with me at a play.

YOUNG MAGGOT.
But I'll show you my song.

SELFISH.
Of late I have had no leisure to make a song, I am so overrun with new acquaintances.

YOUNG MAGGOT. (*Reads.*)
"Damon see how charming Chloris, etc." How do you like it?

SELFISH.
'Tis soft and very much after my own way, and I like it well. But how like you this peruke?

YOUNG MAGGOT.
'Tis very proper.

SELFISH.
I have five as good by me; I have an hundred pound I got at ombre; Mr. Whimsey owes me two hundred; I have a pad or two, and when I get this debt in, I will buy a chariot,* and perhaps have as good equipage as any man, if I can get an hundred pound Sir Nicholas Wachum owes me. I only want* a couple of hunters for Windsor,[33] and then—

YOUNG MAGGOT.
You don't mind my song, 'tis to my mistress.

SELFISH.
Yes, but I was saying, now I am at ease in my fortune till next Michaelmas.[34]

YOUNG MAGGOT.
But to go on.

SELFISH.
I have lately got a conquest over a lady, the prettiest creature; I snatched a rose from her soft bosom. She is of quality,* all the Town were mad after her, and she threw herself into my arms, and I am the happy man.

YOUNG MAGGOT.
Well, to be in love is the greatest pleasure in the world: it makes one so sweetly melancholy and composed and so fit to write; besides, it keeps one in shape.

SELFISH.
I have not much occasion for love; the ladies follow me and love me so, I have no time for't. Why, I have had three maidenheads this week.

YOUNG MAGGOT.
I would not be without love and writing for all the world. I had a billet from the prettiest creature of sixteen today, I'll tell you.

Enter Carlos, Bellamour, Theodosia and Isabella.

YOUNG MAGGOT.
I have an amour.

SELFISH.
I—

YOUNG MAGGOT.
I—

[33] hunters ... Windsor] horses for a royal fox hunt

[34] Michaelmas] September 29, one of the four quarter ending days of the English business year, when revenues—and bills—were due

SELFISH.
I—
YOUNG MAGGOT.
I—
SELFISH.
This fellow is always talking of himself; one can't speak to him, but he is always at I, I. I wonder at the impertinence of such people.
THEODOSIA.
These fools are always talking of themselves.
ISABELLA.
They are the worst things they can talk of.
CARLOS.
Or we either; therefore, madam, hear me on the last subject.
THEODOSIA.
That's as bad.
BELLAMOUR.
He went a mile to put on that fair peruke for the sake of his complexion.
THEODOSIA.
Prithee Isabella, let's find fault with 'em both and break his heart.

Enter Stanmore and Gartrude.

GARTRUDE.
Fie upon you Mr. Stanmore, I'll ne'er come near you again if you use me so. You nothing but kiss one, and ruffle one, and spoil one's things, that you do.
STANMORE.
Why are you so pretty then, to provoke a man beyond all patience?
GARTRUDE.
Why, how do I provoke you? I have done nothing to anger you, have I?
BELLAMOUR.
What, are you fallen out with your mistress?
STANMORE.
No, but since she's insensible of all I can speak to her and yet so pretty, I cannot but love her; if words won't move her, actions must.
SELFISH.
Oh! Here are the ladies; now you shall see what advances they will make to me, but especially Gartrude, that pretty creature.
YOUNG MAGGOT.
This is a very conceited fellow and would call a gypsy that liked him pretty creature.
SELFISH.
Ladies, your most humble servant.—Now you shall see, Maggot.—Dear pretty creature, let me kiss that nosegay. Well, 'tis a thousand times sweeter in that pretty bosom than in its own bed, though at the sun rising when the morning dew is in drops upon it, sweet madam. Let me kiss that hand that gathered it.
GARTRUDE.
Oh fine, what rare words are these! He uses me like a princess. Sir, 'tis more your goodness than my desert.—Sister, this is a rare man. Mr. Stanmore is a wit they say, but I don't understand him half so well. I always think they jeer one.
ISABELLA.
Indeed, 'tis a hard thing for wit to descend to your capacity.
SELFISH.
I was with some ladies last night did so commend you and said you were the most delicate creature. They did me the favor to say your eyes were black and sparkling like mine, and your nose very much resembling mine, and that you have a pretty pouting about the mouth like me, and fine little blub[35]-lips. I am very well with the ladies at Court, but I see none like you.
STANMORE.
Do you know I love that lady?
SELFISH.
If you do, I pity you; she is otherwise engaged, to my knowledge.

Enter Prig.

PRIG.
Come, faith, since we are all together, let's go to ombre, two companies, and make an afternoon on't.
YOUNG MAGGOT.
I desire you will not interrupt me; I am singing the ladies a new song.
PRIG.
Song? Pish, is not gaming better than hearing of songs? Here's such a stir with these wits.

---

35 blub] full, swelling

ISABELLA.
No, pray let's hear it.

Young Maggot sings Damon, etc.

PRIG.
I observe you wits are always making songs of the love of shepherds and shepherdesses, a company of blockheaded, clownish,* ugly, tawny, sunburnt people. I had e'en as lief hear songs upon the love of their sheep as their own.

CARLOS.
I see these fools need nobody to show 'em; they show themselves well enough.

PRIG.
Methinks that old song is very pretty: "My Mistress is a Tennis Ball, etc."

YOUNG MAGGOT.
This rogue has nothing but tennis courts and bowling greens in his head.

BELLAMOUR.
Prithee Prig, sing one of your own making.

PRIG.
With all my heart.

Enter Lady Cheatly.

LADY CHEATLY.
Mrs.* Theodosia, your humble servant.—Gentlemen, I hope you'll pardon me, I could not neglect business. I think one had better be poor than be troubled with money thus. But if you please to walk in, there's a small banquet waits, and fiddles, to dance, if you please.

ISABELLA.
Pray madam, let's hear Mr. Prig's song first; 'tis his own.

PRIG.
I am glad your ladyship is come to hear it. (*Sings.*)

Hey ho, hey ho,
The merry horn does blow.
'Tis broad day,
Come away.
Twivee, twivee, twivee, hey,
Do not stay.
Then have at the hare,
Let old puss[36] beware.
Twivee, twivee, twivee, ho,
The merry horn does blow.
Come away.

YOUNG MAGGOT.
What a happy thing 'tis to have wit.

PRIG.
Hang wit, give me mirth. This is a catch that I made, and my Lord Squander and I always roar it out after a fox chase. Pox, I hate your swains and your nymphs.

SELFISH.
Do they wear breeches thus cut in France?

CARLOS.
Yes sir.

SELFISH.
What blockheads are our English tailors. I must have some new clothes made immediately in this fashion; I cannot rest till I bespeak 'em.

ISABELLA.
Pray madam, join with us, we shall have very good sport.—Are you well, Mr. Selfish? Sure you are not. I never saw you look so ill before.

THEODOSIA.
He looks extreme ill.—Your complexion seems to have too much of the olive in it today.

SELFISH.
Pardon me, ladies, I think my complexion is well enough, or my glass* is false: I never looked clearer.

CARLOS.
That trimming too, with your favor, is very disagreeable and does not cohere with your complexion at all.

SELFISH.
I assure you, sir, all the ladies I saw today are of another opinion: they said my complexion was much like pretty Mrs.* Gartrude's here.

LADY CHEATLY.
Methinks you look mighty lean and thin. I fear you are going into a consumption, sir.

SELFISH.
Oh no, madam! I am very plump, I am only afraid of being too gross and bellying. I am very fat, I assure your ladyship. Pray feel my ribs, madam.

PRIG.
They laugh at him. The devil take me, I never saw a fellow so altered in my life.—Thou canst not live long, thou smell'st of earth, faugh.

36 puss] the hare (baby hares and rabbits are sometimes called kittens)

SELFISH.
You mistake, I am one of the vigorest fellows, the strongest bodies in England. I was taken for Mr. Carlos today at a little distance.

BELLAMOUR.
Prithee Selfish, do not play the fool with thyself. Get a physician: I never saw your complexion so sallow; thou look'st prodigiously ill.

SELFISH.
Good sir, I know what I am: my cheeks are as plump and my complexion as fresh as any here, my eyes and mouth as cheerful, and everything.

CARLOS.
Nothing will mortify the rogue. He thinks so well of Selfish that he thinks Selfish can never look ill, nor be ill. I believe he thinks Selfish can never die.

SELFISH.
I have a face that will not alter. If I were a-dying, 'twould look well; indeed, my complexion changes sometimes, but never looks ill, I assure you.

GARTRUDE.
I wonder you should be so mistaken all. Methinks he looks very neatly.

BELLAMOUR.
This is a damned peruke. Why did you put it on today?

CARLOS.
But indeed that suit is an odious thing and the trimming the worst I ever saw. 'Tis your tailor's fancy; it becomes you very ill.

SELFISH.
Methinks it is very pretty.—I think they are all out of their wits.

LADY CHEATLY.
'Tis enough: we shall make the man hang himself.

YOUNG MAGGOT.
Do you think I'll suffer you forever to cross me with your damned insipid songs? Let me tell you, it is a grand impertinence.

PRIG.
Gad, I do not know what you mean by your gibberish, but I suppose you call me impertinent, and therefore, I'll be beforehand with you: you are a son of a whore. (*Gives Young Maggot a box on the ear. They draw, the ladies run out shrieking.*)

SELFISH.
I will wait upon the ladies.

BELLAMOUR.
Hold, hold.

CARLOS.
Let 'em alone. If you offer to part 'em, they'll hurt one another.

YOUNG MAGGOT.
I'll not be brutal.* You shall answer for it.—Sir, you are lately come out of France and cannot deny a man of honor your assistance.

PRIG.
Prithee Stanmore, be my second. I'll wit him, with a pox to him.

YOUNG MAGGOT.
Tomorrow morning, done.

PRIG.
Let my second appoint the place.

YOUNG MAGGOT.
With all my heart.—Monsieur Carlos, agree with him.

STANMORE.
Come, let's in, and put it off to the ladies as if you were friends.

PRIG.
Aye, with all my heart. What care I?

YOUNG MAGGOT.
Morbleu,[37] brutal.

Act III, [scene i. Lady Cheatly's lodgings.]

Enter Lady Cheatly, Carlos, Bellamour, Stanmore, Isabella, Theodosia, Gartrude, Lady Busy, Young Maggot, Selfish, Prig, Maggot, Lump.

LUMP.
Lady sister, I am much offended to see you take this course of vanity: Would any wise woman make use of fiddlers, minstrels, and singers? I am very much ashamed of it. It is folly, great folly, not becoming the blood of the Lumps.

ISABELLA.
Let's withdraw, we shall have a lesson from this formal uncle.

GARTRUDE.
I can't abide him.

---

37 Morbleu] French euphemism for *Mort dieu*, by God's (Christ's) death, similar to English *'sdeath**

Exeunt all but Lady Cheatly, Lump, Prig, and Old Maggot.

LUMP.
What pleasure can there be to hear fellows scrape upon cats-guts? There's nothing in't.

LADY CHEATLY.
'Tis the way to get credit at our end of the Town, as singing psalms and praying loud in a foreroom[38] is at yours.

LUMP.
You talk not wisely. Do not several godly men by those means and by frequenting meetings get credit enough to break[39] for a hundred thousand pound and are made by it forever.

MAGGOT.
He is one of the wisest men of the Nation; he is a mighty sober, solid fellow and a rare man at business and loves business mightily.

LUMP.
And for the wits that come hither, I doubt not but these gentlemen are of my opinion: I say they are dangerous, scandalous, and good for nothing.

MAGGOT.
'Tis true, madam, they are a company of flashy, frothy fellows and have no solidity in them.

LADY CHEATLY. (*Aside.*)
I find these coxcombs mistake dullness for solidity.

PRIG.
They talk of wit and this and that and keep a coil and a pother about wit. There's nothing at all in't. What a pox is't good for? I would not give a farthing for wit. Here's Young Maggot and Selfish: why, they don't know how to bet at a horse race or make a good match at tennis and are cross-bitten* at bowls. Hang wit.

MAGGOT.
Wit is one of the grievances of the Nation.

LUMP.
It is, as this gentleman has wisely observed, a grievance, a sore grievance, and I would have an Act of Parliament against it.

MAGGOT.
Let me take a wit at business, see how I'll handle him; I would not be a wit for all the world.

PRIG.
Nor I neither, I hate it; they are a company of fleering, jeering, ill-natured fellows to boot too.

LADY CHEATLY.
Be comforted, gentlemen, you are in no danger.

LUMP.
I say they are in danger, and you too, of catching it, if you suffer them to come amongst ye. I have known solid men, by keeping that base company, become witty and have ruined themselves. For my own part, I would as soon catch the plague as that disease of wit.

LADY CHEATLY.
Oh brother! You have a strong antidote against it.

LUMP.
Thanks be to Heaven, I hate[g] wits! Out upon 'em. They write satires upon good men and will laugh at wise men.

LADY CHEATLY.
Why truly, brother, sometimes wise men will provoke 'em very much.

LUMP.
You are i'th wrong.

Enter steward.

STEWARD.
Here is your scrivener, Mr. Lump, and several others met upon money business.

LUMP.
I ordered mine to come to you. I have four thousand pound paid in this day, which you may use. I will leave my scrivener to take your assignments, either of bonds, judgments, or mortgages, as it shall happen to be disposed by you.

LADY CHEATLY.
But will the scrivener be true and publish it to be my money?

LUMP.
I warrant you, he's a godly man, and you may trust him. He has contributed more to your fame than anyone. I myself have brought in Ananias, and he will send money to you to put out[40] for him. 'Tis

38 foreroom] front room, nearest the street, whence such praying would be audible as desired

39 break] something like our modern sense of "spring for," here to come up with venture capital

40 put out] invest

near four, I must be gone. Though haste does not become a wise man, yet at the present I have some upon me.

LADY CHEATLY.
The haste of a fool is the slowest thing in the world.

LUMP.
It is my hour of walking.

LADY CHEATLY.
Will you not stay and take the assignments?

LUMP.
I will not break my method for the world. I have these twenty years walked through Turnstile Alley to Holborn Fields[41] at four. All the good women observe me and set their bread into the oven by me and by no other clock. When I go by, I hear 'em call, "Carry the bread to the oven, the old gentleman is going by." I do love to be taken notice of for my method. Farewell. (*Exit.*)

LADY CHEATLY.
Let's into the garden.

Exeunt omnes.

[Scene ii. The garden.]

Enter Bellamour and Isabella.

BELLAMOUR.
By Heaven, I love thee more than light or liberty, joy of my heart.

ISABELLA.
Such hearts as yours are seldom near their mouths.

BELLAMOUR.
A kiss of this fair hand will bring mine thither. 'Tis there. But if it were your lips, where would it be?

ISABELLA.
Raptures in love have no more meaning in 'em than rants in poetry, mere fustian; 'tis the stum* of love that makes it fret and fume and fly and never good.

BELLAMOUR.
Can a young lady in so warm an age be insensible of love?

ISABELLA.
A virtuous woman is ever insensible of such a love as is unfit for her. But you sparks, like wolves after many battles, by often preying on carcasses, come at last to venture upon the living: modest or not, 'tis all one to you, you are so well fleshed.

BELLAMOUR.
Not so, madam. I know my duty and your worth, and would time stand still, I could be content to gaze upon that face and not tempt you. But our love is frail, and we must take our pleasure while we may.

ISABELLA.
I must consider while I may and on the shore think on the ruins of a shipwrecked fame.

BELLAMOUR.
We shall never reach love's Indies, if we fear tempests already.

ISABELLA.
Think not to conquer me by dint of simile. I'll never venture the pain and peril of such a bold voyage.

BELLAMOUR.
As tender barks make it daily and return home richly fraught, keep coaches, and live splendidly the rest of their lives.

ISABELLA.
Infamously rather.

BELLAMOUR.
I know not that, but they have their days of visiting, play at ombre, make treats as high and as often as the persons of quality,* wear as good clothes, and want* no fashionable folly that woman's heart can wish for. And of all such my Isabella shall ride admiral.

ISABELLA.
Can you pretend to love and tempt me from my honor? Coaches and clothes! So rogues will rob to live like gentlemen.

BELLAMOUR.
'Tis no dishonor, custom has made it otherwise.

ISABELLA.
When a man of honor can turn coward, you may prevail on me; the case is equal.

BELLAMOUR.
On the contrary, kindness* in women is like courage in men.

ISABELLA.
Did not the general license of the time excuse you, I ne'er would see you more.

41 Holborn Fields] at this time a poor suburb of the City

BELLAMOUR.
What, will nothing down but to have and to hold? I'll marry nobody else, and when my inclination dies, leave you its wealthy widow; you may marry after it.

ISABELLA.
I'll bring no infamy where I bring my person.

BELLAMOUR.
This coldness inflames me more. Consent to my desires, and none of all the ladies shall outshine, no equipage exceed yours.

ISABELLA.
And I the while shall be but a part of your equipage, to be kept.* What is it but to wear your livery and take board-wages?

BELLAMOUR.
I love you well enough to marry you but dare not put my self into your hands, knowing what a jade I am at a long journey.

ISABELLA.
If you ever loved, you can never hate, and I can be content, where I have had the best, to keep the rest and, if you love me less, shall lay the fault on Nature, not on you.

BELLAMOUR.
It goes more against a man's heart to fall in his love than his expense, and they that do either most commonly remove for it; there is no enduring it in the same place. Think on my love, my fortune shall be yours.

ISABELLA.
I scorn a fortune with the ruin of my honor.

BELLAMOUR.
It is but heading with another sort of people, leaving the melancholy hypocrites for the gay cheerful sinners, the envious for the envied.

ISABELLA.
These tales may catch unheedful silly* creatures, whom nature half debauches to your hands, but for myself I swear—

Lady Busy appears to 'em.

LADY BUSY.
Swear not, ungracious child, I have heard all your discourse. The gentleman is a fine gentleman, and his proposals are as reasonable as any lady can wish for; every man cannot bring himself to marry and yet may love better and longer than those that do.

BELLAMOUR.
Right, madam.—This is an unexpected assistance.

LADY BUSY.
There's Mr. Maggot kept* Mrs. Wagtail, after the whole Town had done with her, and loves her very well still. Nay, some have not grudged to spend ten thousand pounds upon a mistress, though they have starved their wives and children.

ISABELLA.
Have you feed this lady to plead for you, or is it the baseness of her own nature?

LADY BUSY.
Is my charity thus rewarded? My honor questioned? I that am companion to the ladies of the best quality?* The jealousest lord thinks his lady safe in my company. My honor is dearer to me than all the world, and but for endeavoring to have you well settled in the world, as I have my daughters, do I deserve this?

ISABELLA.
She is as silly as she's naught.* When you see me next, bring nobler thoughts and better purposes. And so farewell. (*Exit.*)

BELLAMOUR.
What a devil shall I do? She's virtuous and fit enough for a wife. 'Ounds,* how that word makes me start! But all this may be a copy of her countenance,[42] there may by huffs in virtue as well as courage.

LADY BUSY.
I hope, sir, you'll not conceive amiss for what she says.

BELLAMOUR.
No, madam.—Pox on this bawd, I love the treason, but I hate the traitor. (*Exit.*)

Enter Stanmore.

STANMORE.
Your humble servant, madam. Has your ladyship had the goodness to mind my affair?

LADY BUSY.
I have, sir; I see her coming. Retire and let me alone.—Come, pretty Mrs. Gatty.

Exit Stanmore. Enter Mrs. Gartrude.

---

42 copy … countenance] a deceptive appearance

GARTRUDE.

Your servant, madam.

LADY BUSY.

Thou art a pretty creature! Ah, 'twould do a man good to lie by such flesh and blood as thou art. All the matter is to choose a good bedfellow, and for that trust me: there is the prettiest man and the finest gentleman not far off.

GARTRUDE.

Aye, so there is really. Mr. Selfish is the finest person, so civil and well-bred, and is very ingenious too. I vow 'twould do one good to have such a bedfellow.

LADY BUSY.

You are out: 'tis Mr. Stanmore is the man and will make a good settlement, go to,* which the other cannot.

GARTRUDE.

He is a fine gentleman indeed, but really I don't care for a wit: I do not know what to say before 'em. But I can talk with Mr. Selfish all the day long. Oh, he does tell such pretty stories of himself! He is a very fair-spoken man, and I'll swear he is the purest company for a lady that ever was, and so handsome.

LADY BUSY.

Not comparable to Stanmore.

GARTRUDE.

Oh jiminy!* That your ladyship should say so.

LADY BUSY.

I have experience in the world. I know what I say. Your lady mother has desired me to take care to put you into the world. Youth is indiscreet and unwary. Trust us, and 'twill be your own another day. I say, Mr. Stanmore will settle ten times more upon you than the other is worth.

GARTRUDE.

But really, madam, I must confess I don't love a wit. They say they are not good-natured, and they don't admire one half so much as others do, neither.

LADY BUSY.

Come, come madam, if a wit will keep,* he will serve as well as a fool (let 'em say what they will), and you have a way to be too hard for the best of 'em for all their wits.

Enter Selfish.

GARTRUDE.

Oh Lord, here he is! I wonder you should say Mr. Stanmore is as handsome as he. Well, he's a lovely man.

SELFISH.

Ladies, I kiss both your hands. Methinks I see the freshness of the spring in one, and the fruitfulness of the autumn in the other.

GARTRUDE.

Oh rare, what a saying that is, and so like a gentleman!

Stanmore enters.

STANMORE. [*Aside.*]

Now 'tis time to speak for myself: she is very pretty, but why should I love a fool that loves a fool? I see I am a devilish carnal fellow and mind nothing but the body.

LADY BUSY.

I'll steal out to my lady and leave you. We have business of consequence. (*Exit.*)

STANMORE.

Madam, your humble servant.

SELFISH.

Mr. Stanmore, your servant. Were you not at the audience this afternoon?

STANMORE.

No, sir.

SELFISH.

Indeed, I have committed a great fault, to wait upon these ladies when the Court was to appear in all the splendor it could be with all the well-dressed and well-bred men about it, and I was not there. I wish it be not taken ill.

STANMORE.

Oh vanity, vanity!

SELFISH.

I know I was missed and asked for there, but I can mind nothing when ladies are in the way, especially such pretty creatures as Mrs. Gatty.

GARTRUDE.

You are pleased to say so.

STANMORE.

Well, my dear little one, I am resolved to be revenged upon this beauty of yours for making me so mad in love with you.

GARTRUDE.
Why, what will you do with it?

STANMORE.
I'll have no mercy on't, I'll never spare it, faith, you shan't think to make me in love with you for nothing.

SELFISH.
I shall have a new suit come home tomorrow morning in Mr. Carlos his* fashion, but I assure you 'tis something better fancied, both for the color and the garniture.

GARTRUDE.
Really, sir, methinks Mr. Selfish is the prettiest modish person and so gentile, is not he?

STANMORE. [*Aside.*]
'Sheart,* what an entertainment is this to me that I should love such a thing?—Don't mistake him, he is an ass, I assure you.

GARTRUDE.
Oh Lord, that you should say so now! He does everything so like a gentleman, as my Lady Busy says, and is so well-bred.

STANMORE.
Well-bred? Hang him, he is a finical clown,* he has not breeding enough for a *valet de chambre.*

GARTRUDE.
What a strange man are you! Well, you wits never speak well of one another, I vow.

STANMORE.
'Ounds,* what a pretty fool she is! But I am vigorous still; her folly cannot thrust me off, so much as her beauty pulls me to.

SELFISH.
I am going to buy me a pretty, convenient coach. What color do you fancy, dear Mrs. Gatty? I think purple will suit best with my complexion.

GARTRUDE.
Oh yes, purple will be very pretty.

SELFISH.
Nay, I'll say that for myself, my fancy always pleases the ladies. Pretty miss, let me see that delicate busk;[43] I will write a distich upon it and present it to you.

GARTRUDE.
Pray do.

[43] busk] a corset stay

SELFISH.
Let me kiss that happy busk that goes so near your lovely body, and that delicate, sweet, white, soft hand that gave it me.

GARTRUDE.
Well, he's a rare man and is so full of fine courtship.

STANMORE.
Do you know that I will not suffer you to smile and cringe and play the monkey[44] here?

SELFISH.
I cannot help it. If ladies will love me and be affected with my person, what is it to me?

STANMORE.
Get you gone, you coxcomb, I'll endure it no longer. (*He fillips him and pulls off his peruke.*)

GARTRUDE.
Nay, what have you done to poor Mr. Selfish?

SELFISH.
I wonder you should have no more breeding; one would have thought I might have taught you more in this time.

GARTRUDE.
Pray let me help you, I'll set it right again.

STANMORE.
Death and damnation! What's this?

SELFISH.
The devil take me if I could not find in my heart to ruffle your cravat before the lady for this outrage of yours.

STANMORE.
Do you hear, sir? Be gone and leave us, or by Heaven I will cut your throat.

SELFISH.
Well, I cannot be ill-bred, though you can, and therefore I take my leave. (*Exit.*)

GARTRUDE.
Nay, look you now, 'udds* fiddles, what have you done? You have made Mr. Selfish go away. I'll follow him, that I will.

Enter Lady Cheatly and Maggot.

[44] monkey] Monkeys had become fashionable pets among the aristocracy.

LADY CHEATLY.

Do you hear, minx? Be civiller than I hear you are to Mr. Stanmore, and know, I'll turn you out of my house, if you think on Selfish.—Sir, your servant.

GARTRUDE.

Oh lack! What does she say?

STANMORE.

Nay, I'll follow you.

Exit Gartrude and Stanmore.

MAGGOT.

Catch her, man, she'll be a vast fortune: my lady wallows in money, she knows not what to do with it.—But good madam, let me humbly petition you to consider my passion and have some regard to my estate, which is a plentiful one. And then madam, for business, you see a proof: Did you ever see a man tell money better than I do? I do all the ladies' business hereabouts, and great persons', etcetera.

LADY CHEATLY.

I must first consider of reducing my estate into some order before I think of disposing my person.

MAGGOT.

If any man solicits your business like me—try me, madam. I do everything for the ladies.

Enter steward.

STEWARD.

Madam, I have private business for your ladyship's ear.

MAGGOT.

Your servant, madam, I will retire. Be pleased to consider me. (*Exit.*)

STEWARD.

My business concerns your ladyship and myself so nearly that you must pardon me if I urge it home.

LADY CHEATLY. (*Aside.*)

What means he?

STEWARD.

That I have served you faithfully, yourself can witness.

LADY CHEATLY.

I can, and I'll reward you largely.

STEWARD.

'Tis that I ask. Think, madam, I have in your service lost my honesty, laid by my conscience, and while I contribute to your fraud or others, I must not be deceived myself.

LADY CHEATLY. (*Aside.*)

What will he drive at?—I am sorry you ask for what I intended to give you; I did resolve to give you a thousand pound.

STEWARD.

Do not I know that all the bonds you have given to people and the assignments and declarations of trust to your brother are written with the ink I bought of a great artist and that within a month it will wear out, and nothing will remain but blanks?

LADY CHEATLY.

What then? My husband was cheated of his estate by my brother and other rascals, and 'tis fit I should take letters of reprisal.[45]

STEWARD.

No doubt. Your bonds you have taken from others are written with ink I had of the same man, which (rubbed over with a spirit) makes impressions into many sheets, so that you have many bonds for one; the sums are easily altered.

LADY CHEATLY. (*Aside.*)

What would this rascal have?

STEWARD.

A thousand pound! I scorn it: I aim at higher things; I am a gentleman by[h] birth, your equal.

LADY CHEATLY. [*Aside.*]

Heaven and earth! What have I brought myself to?—When my estate is out of dispute, I will increase your reward.

STEWARD.

No madam, I have long honored and loved your ladyship, and nothing less than your person can ever satisfy me.

LADY CHEATLY.

How sir!

STEWARD.

Hold madam, if you use me roughly, I in a moment will blast all your fortunes, and you shall fly from hence as naked as you came. But if you'll marry me, I'll be as humble a servant as I have been before.

---

45 letters of reprisal] letters of marque (q.v.)

LADY CHEATLY. (*Aside.*)
Insolent villain. (*To him.*) Sure thou art not in earnest.
STEWARD.
By Heaven I am, and I will perish or attain my ends.
LADY CHEATLY. (*Aside.*)
He may undo me. Oh that I should lay my plots so shallow! I must have a trick for the rogue.—Give me time to consider of it.
STEWARD.
I can give none, nor will.
LADY CHEATLY.
Marriage would stop my business, and I shall get no more money of my brother or others.
STEWARD.
We'll keep it private.
LADY CHEATLY.
Though modesty would not let me propose it to you, and I would rather have died than done it, I must confess the thing I wished for upon earth.
STEWARD.
Then I am happy and will serve you 'till my death.
LADY CHEATLY.
Forgive this frailty and use me well. Shame and blushes will confound me.
STEWARD.
Dear madam! There's no shame in love and marriage. (*Aside.*) I see she loves me.
LADY CHEATLY.
There yet remains one difficulty: you are my main witness, and (when we are married) you can be none; therefore, if you will go to a Master[46] in Chancery and swear to all my deeds and make affidavit to my false estate, the next hour shall make you master of me and mine.
STEWARD. (*Aside.*)
Hah! I may be catched, and after I have sworn to that, I have no hank upon her.—Before, madam, I never will, but after, for my own sake, I must. I'll get a parson (whom I can trust) and none shall know of the marriage but himself.
LADY CHEATLY. (*Aside.*)
This will not do, I must have another trick for the rascal.—You have convinced me, but I am engaged to a parson already, whom I promised that office to. I'll send for him presently.*
STEWARD.
I am transported with my happiness.
LADY CHEATLY.
Withdraw, sir, I'll come to you instantly.

[Exit Steward.] Enter Prig.

Hah! This fellow shall be my engine,* and I must lose no time.—I am glad you are come: I have a business to communicate to you that concerns you nearly, in which you must be secret.
PRIG.
Does it concern my honor? Madam, I'll cut their throats.
LADY CHEATLY.
No sir, it concerns your love.
PRIG.
Then I'll cut their throats too.
LADY CHEATLY.
No, it is not come to that. But just as I was resolved (having considered your passion) to bestow myself upon you—
PRIG.
Oh dear madam! Let me kiss your fair hand.
LADY CHEATLY.
Would you believe it? This villainous steward, having writings in his hands for the greatest part of my estate, is arrived to that insolence, he threatens to burn 'em unless I will instantly marry him.
PRIG.
Oh dog! Rogue! Your servant, madam: I'll cut his throat immediately.
LADY CHEATLY.
Hold, sir, he's an odd, humorous fellow and will not have his throat cut.
PRIG.
Will he not? Why then I won't.
LADY CHEATLY.
I have designed a better way: to put a false marriage upon him, and you shall be my chaplain. You can get the habit of a parson?
PRIG.
Aye, aye, this is very pretty. I your chaplain? Ha, ha! If my face would but look solid enough for a divine.

[46] Master] an officer of the court who acts as assistant to the judge

LADY CHEATLY.

I warrant you, 'tis a very judicious face and will be very parsonical.

PRIG.

Not so, a gamester's at your service.

LADY CHEATLY.

And you can read the Common Prayer,[47] that's material, for some gentleman can scarce read nowadays.

PRIG.

I warrant you, madam. This will be the prettiest trick.

LADY CHEATLY.

When you have married him and me about an hour hence (nobody else being by), I'll take care to pack him far enough afterwards and thus reserve myself for you. Get a habit quickly and lay it in the closet. Here's the key, there you shall shift. I must be gone. (*Exit.*)

PRIG.

Oh happy man! I shall never need to sneak after a lord, to sing catches, break jests, to eat and rook with him. Well, I'll go no more to twelve, that's certain. I'll get me a pack of fox dogs, hunt every day, and play at the groom-porter's* at night. (*Exit.*)

[Scene iii.] In the garden.

Enter Theodosia and Isabella.

THEODOSIA.

Dear Isabella, how I love these solitary walks, free from the noise and importunity of men.

ISABELLA.

So much the contrary, that should you hear the rattling of a coach, you'd be ready to leap over the wall.

THEODOSIA.

If it were Bellamour's.

ISABELLA.

Why Bellamour's? No, though you knew it to be a tired hackney with six dusty passengers in't. Thou art the giddiest creature.

[47] Common Prayer] i.e. the marriage service in the Anglican Book of Common Prayer

THEODOSIA.

I do not love to be solid as you are and fix upon one man; 'tis better to like all, and love none.

ISABELLA.

Thou hypocrite; do not I know that none but Carlos can please you? He has caught you fast.

THEODOSIA.

No, never think so. Do but hear the men talk of another, and 'tis antidote enough against 'em. They are as malicious as we women and would quarrel as often, if it were not for fear of fighting.

ISABELLA.

Of all men I wonder Stanmore 'scapes it; he speaks well of no man.

THEODOSIA.

'Tis fit to speak ill of fops, who were lost to the world if men of wit might not show 'em.

ISABELLA.

For ought I see, laughing at them does no hurt, for they rise and get fortunes for all that. Fools are lawful prize, but Stanmore speaks ill of witty men.

THEODOSIA.

When the witty men fall upon one another, they make sport for the fools, and so laughing goes round, no matter how.

ISABELLA.

Stanmore says Carlos has an ill breath and takes physic of a French surgeon and that Bellamour keeps* a player and will run out his estate.

THEODOSIA.

And yet you see how dear they are one to another when they meet: 'tis the fashion.

Enter Gartrude.

GARTRUDE.

Oh sister, come hither! Here are four men measuring of swords. I believe they are going to fight in the next field.

Exeunt.

[Scene iv.] In the field.

Carlos, Prig, Stanmore, and Young Maggot.

YOUNG MAGGOT.

How shall I kill this Prig? He wants* two of his vital parts, a brain and a heart.

PRIG.
I'll spoil your writing: have at your madrigal arm, you wit you. (*Prig disarms Young Maggot and comes up to Carlos.*)

STANMORE.
Carlos, you see our advantage.

CARLOS.
And scorn it. Have at you first. (*Disarms Prig. To Stanmore.*) Now, sir, for you.

STANMORE.
We are friends, I love thee, prithee let it alone.

CARLOS.
Not so great friends: I overheard you speaking ill of me to my mistress.

STANMORE.
Prithee Carlos, that's nothing: we all speak ill of one another, and it goes for nothing.

CARLOS.
I am not of your opinion. Have at you.

STANMORE.
At you!

Carlos disarms Stanmore.

Well, you have it, and I am glad I had to do with a brave man.

CARLOS.
You are men of honor and may be trusted with your swords. Let's in amongst the ladies, as if nothing had passed between us.

PRIG. [*Aside.*]
You may do what you will, but the valiant Prig desires his widow may hear of his prowess at least.

YOUNG MAGGOT.
That I should be worsted by an ass.

Exeunt.

[Scene v. The garden.]

The Ladies reenter.

GARTRUDE.
I am afraid Carlos has hurt honest Mr. Stanmore, but Carlos is a fine gentleman and fights so like a gentleman. He said the prettiest things to me in an arbor. Mr. Selfish could not have courted me at a higher rate. I vow I begin to like him strangely. I like a wit better than I did.

ISABELLA.
Thou'lt like any body.

THEODOSIA.
Pray Heaven Carlos be not hurt.

ISABELLA.
You seem disordered.

THEODOSIA.
No, no, what makest thou think so?

ISABELLA.
I am confident Carlos is not hurt.

THEODOSIA.
I think not of him.

ISABELLA.
I cannot blame you. I believe he has honesty to his wit, and honor to his courage; I never saw a finer gentleman.

GARTRUDE.
He has almost as taking a way with him as Mr. Selfish.

THEODOSIA.
I don't like his face, 'tis too serious; his mien is stiff, and he dances ill.

ISABELLA.
You are too nice:* his looks and mien are manly, and he dances like a person of quality;* you are for a page's face and a dancing master's legs, and I hate both.

THEODOSIA.
Nay, never let's fall out about him.

ISABELLA.
If we should, he's here to part us.

Enter Carlos, Prig, and Young Maggot.

THEODOSIA.
He goes on faster with his task than I'd have him.

YOUNG MAGGOT.
There is no living two hours out of the beau monde: I am out of the lady's company like a fish out of the water. Is not that well said, Prig?

PRIG.
Not at all, the devil take me.

THEODOSIA.
Not so mute as a fish, I hope.

YOUNG MAGGOT.
No, we witty men are always talking, now and then two or three of us at a time, invention does

so flow, but I had rather say one fine thing to a lady than twenty to the best wits in Town.

PRIG.
Say fine things! What a pox! Don't we all speak alike? Don't we all speak English?

THEODOSIA.
Had you never a mistress that was a fool?

YOUNG MAGGOT.
None are so gross but they guess when a man says a witty thing; when I say it, I am sure.

PRIG.
Pox on saying, I love doing a witty thing: to win a man's money is to outwit him, I think, and I'll undertake to win yours at ten several games.

YOUNG MAGGOT.
What, cheat me?

PRIG.
No, upon the square, by mere* judgment. A wit is like a running horse, good for no earthly thing beside. When did you ever know any of 'em well with a great man or so much as taken down to a lord's house a-buck-hunting? They can drink some of 'em, but then they talk of philosophy, history, poetry, as if they came into company to study. This is stuff the Devil would not hear.

THEODOSIA.
What would you have 'em talk of?

PRIG.
Why dogs, hawks and horses, crimp, trictrac, and primero. Make me a match at bowls or tennis over a bottle; come, even or odd for two pieces, I hate to be idle.

ISABELLA.
What an intolerable fool is this!

PRIG.
There are three matches to be run at Newmarket, I'll bet money on every one of 'em: I'll hold you six to four of the gelding against the mare; gold to silver on the bay stone-horse[48] against the fleabitten; and an even fifty pound, or what you will—

YOUNG MAGGOT.
You need not run your self out of breath. I will never bet while I live.

PRIG.
Ladies, what think you of five merry guineas? Will either of you bet?

THEODOSIA. [*Aside.*]
I do not like Carlos his talking so long with that fool: she is young and handsome, she has beauty enough to invite, and folly enough to grant.

PRIG.
I hold five pound I make a tennis ball lie upon that stand once in thrice.

ISABELLA.
This fellow has no genius but to play nor no argument but a wager.

YOUNG MAGGOT.
One that wants* wit deserves not to bear the figure of a man.

THEODOSIA.
Such fellows are but ciphers to you men of wit; they make you of greater value.

YOUNG MAGGOT.
I'll swear, that's well said. I don't think I could have said better myself.

PRIG.
What will you give me for this ring at the day of marriage?

CARLOS. [*To Gartrude.*]
You are so pretty and so obliging, there's no resisting both. But will you come and see my lodgings? I have the finest French things.

GARTRUDE.
Really sir, you are so courteous and well-behaved, I cannot deny you coming. You put me so in mind of Mr. Selfish: you have his way with you to a hair. Do you write too? He is a very pretty poet.

CARLOS. [*Aside.*]
Were I not sharp set, this would turn my stomach.—Selfish steals all he writes out of French poetry; he has neither wit nor money but what he borrows. Forget him, and I'll be your servant.

GARTRUDE.
You shall promise to be very civil when I come.

CARLOS. (*Aside.*)
She is very easy, pray Heaven she be sound.* I'll promise anything. Well, Theodosia, if I be false, 'tis your command has pushed me into temptation.

48 stone-horse] a horse that retains its stones or testicles: a stallion

PRIG.

Come, here's ten guineas, I'll lay 'em upon my toe and in six times kick 'em all into my mouth.

ISABELLA.

And what if you do?

PRIG.

Talk of wit! I'll play at prick-penny[49] for twenty pound with anyone here.

CARLOS.

I am for you at tennis.

PRIG.

I'll give you a bisk at Longs[50] for ten pound.

THEODOSIA.

Bowling methinks is better.

PRIG.

I'll give him one in seven for fifty pound.[i]

CARLOS.

We had better reserve our strength; I'll hunt tomorrow.

PRIG.

With all my heart. Halloo, hey Ringwood, Rockwood Jowler, hey. Well, I'll go and play in the meantime.—Pox, this is the basest company, there's no money stirring. (*Exit.*)

THEODOSIA.

What could you do with that fool all this while?

CARLOS.

In obedience to your command, I suffered her impertinence. You are a very* tyrant: your beauty obliges me to love none but you, and yet you'll have me make love to all. Flesh and blood is not able to bear it.

THEODOSIA.

Not so: I would have you gain their esteem and be cried up among 'em. Using us scurvily often does that. Women love the careless, insolent, and loud.

CARLOS.

Faith madam, I am a moral man, I do as I would be done by.

THEODOSIA.

I would not be in love with you for a million: 'twould tempt you horribly.

CARLOS.

It would tempt me to vanity, but never to ingratitude.

THEODOSIA.

Vanity and ingratitude are as inseparable as old age and ugliness. They that think too well of themselves, ever think too ill of others, and I will give you no temptation of any kind.

CARLOS.

You are nothing but temptation: your face, your shape, your voice, nay, your very coldness is a tempter, and therefore have a care on't.

ISABELLA.

You have met with the greatest tyrant of our sex.

CARLOS.

The greatest conqueror, but she has too much goodness for a tyrant; however, I'll tire her cruelty with my patience, and I'll hold her the greatest wager in the world that I get her heart at last.

THEODOSIA.

You have a pretty confidence. Pray what's your wager?

CARLOS.

A wedding night.

THEODOSIA.

Who shall be judge?

CARLOS.

Your friend here.

THEODOSIA.

I can't have a better. Done.

CARLOS.

Done, madam. I am sure good service and perseverance will gain a reasonable woman, where there is not a downright antipathy, and I am resolved never to give you over.

THEODOSIA.

Love in this age is as well counterfeited as complexion: what with the men's lying and swearing, and the women's waters and washes,[51] we know not what to make of one another.

CARLOS.

Try me with commands.

THEODOSIA.

I must have you poetical: that's a great sign of love in a man of wit. I must have songs and sonnets plenty.

49 prick-penny] a game of dice involving legerdemain

50 Longs] Summers suggests the famous ordinary (tavern with food) in the Haymarket, although another of the same name existed in Convent Garden,* and a place with a tennis court would seem to be indicated.

51 waters and washes] colognes and cosmetics

CARLOS.
Very well.

THEODOSIA.
I must never have you see a play but when I am there.

CARLOS.
That is, I must see none at all, for when you are there, I can see nothing but yourself.

THEODOSIA.
Then upon no pretence whatsoever must you go behind the scenes.

CARLOS.
That's grown the sign of a fop, and for my own sake I'll avoid it.

THEODOSIA.
But the women have beauty and wit enough to hearken to a keeper.*

CARLOS.
Some of 'em are so far from having wit of their own that they spoil that little the poets put into 'em by base utterance, and for beauty they lay it on so, that 'tis much alike from fifteen to five and forty.

THEODOSIA.
Item, you must not talk with visors* in the pit,* though they look never* so like women of quality* and are never* so coming.

CARLOS.
Be it so. I never knew any good come of that way of fooling yet, for if they were afraid of me, I was ever more afraid of them. But how shall I arrive at the general fame and reputation you spoke of, with these restraints? The men in vogue forbear none of all these things; they dive like ducks at one end of the pit and rise at the other, then whisk into the whore-boxes, then into the scenes, and always hurry up and down.[52] The devils in an opera are not so busy.[53]

THEODOSIA.
You must take other courses.

CARLOS.
I have bespoken a play for you and all the good company of this house; when the other is done, I hope, madam, you will honor it with your presence.

THEODOSIA.
I'll do as the rest do.

ISABELLA.
This is a new piece of gallantry, Theodosia.

THEODOSIA.
The invitation's general.

GARTRUDE. [*Aside.*]
How mad would they be, if they knew this were meant to me?

Enter Maggot, unseen by the rest.

YOUNG MAGGOT.
Now pretty Mrs. Gartrude and the rest of the good company, I have the poem about me which I told you I writ upon beauty. 'Tis elaborate. I kept my chamber about it as long as a spark does of a clap or a lady of a child; I purged and bled and entered into a diet about it, and that made me have so clear a complexion and write so well, and brought down my belly too.

MAGGOT.
How now, wit! Let me see that damned poem you lay in of so long when you should have studied the law.

YOUNG MAGGOT.
Oh Heaven! I am undone.

MAGGOT.
I shall spoil that month's work.

YOUNG MAGGOT.
Ladies, pray intercede for me and save my poem.

THEODOSIA.
Hold sir, reprieve it.

YOUNG MAGGOT.
'Tis not mine, 'tis a friend's of mine.

MAGGOT.
Ah graceless fool! The worst friend thou hast: thyself thou meanest. (*He tears it and scatters it.*)

YOUNG MAGGOT.
Save this, and I will never be witty again.

MAGGOT.
No sir, there, there, so, 'tis done.

52 scenes … down] Rakehells were notorious for actually going on stage during a performance.

53 devils … busy] a reference to Shadwell's 1674 operatic version of Dryden and Davenant's revision of Shakespeare's *Tempest*

Young Maggot goes to gather up the pieces.

By Heaven, touch a piece on't, and I'll disinherit you.

CARLOS.

Let me intercede for him. He'll mend, and be less witty everyday.

YOUNG MAGGOT.

Forgive me once, and I'll mend and be as dull as an old fat alderman that sleeps over justice at the Old Bailey.[54]

MAGGOT.

At your similes again? Oh you incorrigible wit! Let me see what poetry you have about you.

YOUNG MAGGOT.

Ladies, for Heaven's sake, plead for me, or I am utterly ruined.—Sir, will you disgrace me before my mistress Gartrude?

MAGGOT.

Hang you, coxcomb. She hates wit, because she's a fool, as I do, because I am wise. Stand still. (*He pulls out bundles of papers.*)

YOUNG MAGGOT.

Mercy upon me! What will become of me?

ISABELLA.

Good Mr. Maggot, be more merciful.

MAGGOT.

What's here? A poem called, "A Posy for the Ladies' Delight." A second, "The Flower of Love's Constancy." An "Answer" to it. "Distichs to Write upon Lady's Busks." "Epigram Written in a Lady's Bible in Covent-Garden-Church." Oh wicked wit! "Posies for Wedding Rings." Oh idle rakehell! I shall have you come to write to tobacco boxes and swordblades and knives and to all the ironwork at Sheffield: all these go to it.

YOUNG MAGGOT.

Hold good sir, hold, upon my knees I beg you'll hold. Here cut off this joint, this, this, any joint about me, so you'll spare my poetry.

THEODOSIA.

Have pity on the poor gentleman.

GARTRUDE.

Oh pray, give me those upon the busks.

MAGGOT.

Not one shall live to make him infamous.[j] Must you needs be a wit to the dishonor of your family and the disturbance of your good old father's ashes? I never knew one of our family a wit[k] before. I'll alter my will instantly. (*Exit.*)

YOUNG MAGGOT.

Nay, now you may hang me an* you will, now you have torn my poetry. I have never a copy of any of 'em. I will go hide my self in a hole and never show my head again. (*Exit.*)

CARLOS.

Come ladies, shall we prepare for the play after this farce?

ISABELLA.

With all our hearts.

Act IV, [scene i]. The playhouse.

Enter Carlos, Theodosia, Prig, Lady Cheatly, Maggot, Lady Busy, Bellamour, Isabella, Stanmore, Gartrude, Young Maggot, and Selfish and others coming into the playhouse, seating themselves.

ISABELLA.

By being masked, I shall observe Bellamour's actions.

GARTRUDE.

Now nobody will know me; they'll take me for you in this petticoat.

ISABELLA.

If you hold your tongue, sister. But that makes a great difference betwixt us.

GARTRUDE.

Aye, but I'll whisper, and they shall not know my voice.

ISABELLA.

But they'll soon discover your sense.

CARLOS.

My dear mistress, since you accept my service, I am resolved to ply you so that I must win at last.

THEODOSIA.

You are very resolute and shall find me so. You think to go on like the French king: we shall have you do as he does by a town in Flanders,* set a day when you will take me.[l]

CARLOS.

I hope to corrupt you within with love and make my conquest easier.

[54] Old Bailey] central criminal court, beside Newgate prison

BELLAMOUR.

I wonder Isabella is not here, Stanmore. I am so damnably in love, I am afraid thou'lt never own me; I am a very recreant.

STANMORE.

My mistress is not here neither. Her folly has a little cooled my love, but I have a most abominable lust to her, the wiser passion of the two, and no despair: though that rogue Selfish has her mind, I do not doubt but to get her body, which is worth two of it for my use.

YOUNG MAGGOT.

I wonder pretty Mrs. Gartrude is not here.

SELFISH.

I am amazed at it, for she knew I was to come.

A great knocking at the door. Enter doorkeeper.

CARLOS.

How now! What means that knocking?

DOORKEEPER.

Sir, ladies and several gentlemen knock to get in.

CARLOS.

Let the ladies in for nothing, but make the men pay.

Exit doorkeeper.

PRIG.

Had you ever such a chaplain? I was so disguised, he could not suspect me; methinks I dispatched the business as well as if I had been used to be married myself.

LADY CHEATLY.

'Twas very well. I have since gotten my deeds from him, and because he was a main witness to many of my bonds and mortgages, I have made him swear to 'em all before a Master in Chancery, upon pretence that when it should be known he was my husband, his testimony would not be good.

PRIG.

Ha! Ha! Ha! This was the prettiest invention and will make well for us. But where is the fool?

LADY CHEATLY.

There is a kinsman of mine going for the Indies: I sent him to him with an hundred pound for a venture and have taken care he shall not come back again, for he'll clap him under hatches, carry him away, and sell him for a rogue[55] as he is. He sails this tide.

Several more come in [including several doorkeepers], women masked and men of several sorts. Several young coxcombs fool with the orange women. *

ORANGE WOMAN.

Oranges, will you have any oranges?

FIRST BULLY.

What play do they play? Some confounded play or other.

PRIG.

A pox on't, madam! What should we do at this damned playhouse? Let's send for some cards, and play at langtriloo in the box. Pox on 'em! I ne'er saw a play had anything in't; some of 'em have wit now and then, but what care I for wit?

SELFISH.

Does my cravat sit well? I take all the care I can it should. I love to appear well. What ladies are here in the boxes? Really I never come to a play, but upon account of seeing the ladies.

CARLOS.

Doorkeeper, are they ready to begin?

DOORKEEPER.

Yes, immediately.

SELFISH.

Now you shall see the ladies make up to me; where e're I am, they flock about me. I think I am one of the happiest men on earth! I thank Heaven every day for making me just as I am, Bellamour.

BELLAMOUR. [*Aside.*]

That's Isabella, I am sure, I know the petticoat; what a devil makes her talk to that rogue?

Gartrude chooses to sit by Selfish.

YOUNG MAGGOT.

You'll find it an admirable plot; there's great force and fire in the writing; so full of business and trick, and very fashionable; it passed through my hands; some of us helped him in it.

55 sell … rogue] criminals and the poor were often transported or "spirited" (shanghaied) to the colonies, where they were "indentured"—or virtually enslaved; the steward has been spirited but will be passed off as a transported criminal

FIRST BULLY.
Dam'me! When will these fellows begin? Plague on't! here's a staying.

SECOND MAN.
Whose play is this?

THIRD MAN.
One Prickett's, poet Prickett.

FIRST MAN.
Oh hang him! Pox on him! He cannot write. Prithee let's to Whitehall.*

YOUNG MAGGOT.
Not write, sir? I am one of his patrons. I know the wits don't like him, but he shall write with any of 'em all for an hundred pound.

PRIG.
Aye that he shall. They say, he puts no wit in his plays, but 'tis all one for that, they do the business. He is my poet too, I hate wit.

Enter several ladies and several men.

DOORKEEPER.
Pray sir, pay me, my masters will make me pay it.

THIRD MAN.
Impudent rascal! Do you ask me for money? Take that, sirrah. [*Strikes him.*]

SECOND DOORKEEPER.
Will you pay me, sir?

FOURTH MAN.
No: I don't intend to stay.

SECOND DOORKEEPER.
So you say every day and see two or three acts for nothing.

FOURTH MAN.
I'll break your head, you rascal.

FIRST DOORKEEPER.
Pray sir, pay me.

THIRD MAN.
Set it down, I have no silver about me, or bid my man pay you.

THEODOSIA.
What, do gentlemen run on tick for plays?

CARLOS.
As familiarly as with their tailors.

THIRD DOORKEEPER.
Pox on you, sirrah! Go and bid 'em begin quickly.

Exit [first] doorkeeper. The [company] play[s during] the curtain-time, then take their places.

CARLOS.
Now they'll begin.

Selfish and Young Maggot go to sit down.

YOUNG MAGGOT.[m]
Don't come to us, let you wits sit together. [*To Lady Cheatly.*] These fellows will be witty and trouble us.—Go to your brother wits and make a noise among yourselves, brother wits.

They go on the other side.

SELFISH.
I am always hated by the fools, but I think it rather out of envy than malice.

BELLAMOUR.
Faith! you shan't sit by us.

STANMORE.
Gentlemen, do not mistake yourselves, for you are no wits, though y'are poets, and we will not own you of our party.

YOUNG MAGGOT.
This is mere* envy against us writers, Selfish.

SELFISH.
It is so. I for my part will throw myself at a lady's feet, play with her fan, and fan her gently with it.

The play begins. Enter lover and wife.

LOVER.
Dear madam, let us not omit any occasion but take every opportunity by the hand to improve those amours, which have rendered us so happy to be elevated above the reach of envy.

WIFE.
Sir, I should not entertain a thought that might in any wise be prejudicial to our amours or the improvement thereof, if I were not so extremely obnoxious to* the great infelicity of being subject to a husband, whose jealousy has so much the ascendant over him that it renders him so vigilant not seldom to interrupt our happiest hours.

LOVER.
That turbulent temper does too often disorder the fair quiet of his own mind, as well as discompose ours, and jealousy proves as often an obstruction to his own tranquility as it does an impediment to our fruition.

WIFE.
It is a privilege too absolutely imperious, which, by a seeming conjugal right, our husbands claim over us to make so subtle a scrutiny into all our enterprizes, since they with too great a regret entertain the least motion of ours whereby we would insinuate into their affairs.

LOVER.
But since Fortune (by so many frequent signalizations) has demonstrated how much she is a friend to us in assisting us with so many subterfuges when most we have needed them, it will be a heinous tergiversation from her to abandon that trust we formerly have reposed in her, and she may justly take a pique at our infidelity and, in that caprice, may contrive a revenge suitable to our delinquency.

WIFE.
Rather, Fortune may be apt to believe us too audacious in tempting her with so much importunity that it must needs be more vexatious than agreeable, and while we make such vigorous addresses to another deity, for ought we know, Love may wax jealous of our applications to it: for though he's blind, he can descry and will greatly resent our dereliction, and, when he is incensed, his nature is highly vindicative.

LOVER.
When Fortune takes such pains to assist us in our amours, Love will certainly be very sensible of our omission, and when he is once provoked, he seldom buries injuries in the grave of oblivion.

THEODOSIA.
This is very lewd stuff! Is this the new way of writing?

CARLOS.
A man would think these lovers in plays did not care a farthing for one another, when they find nothing to do but to be florid and talk impertinently when they are alone.

YOUNG MAGGOT.
This is a very strong, sinewy, and correct style, and yet neat, and florid.

SELFISH.
I have taught 'em all this way of writing; I always strive to write like a gentleman, so easy, and well-bred.

PRIG.
These are very good lines, faith.

YOUNG MAGGOT.
Nay, 'tis admirably worded, that's the truth on't.

FIRST MAN.
Dam'me! I don't like it.

SECOND MAN.
Pox on the coxcomb that writ it! There's nothing in't.

FIRST MAN.
God I love drums and trumpets and much ranting, roaring, huffing, and fretting and good store of noise in a play.

LOVER.
I have sufficiently confuted all your argumentation, and nothing then remains but that I should humbly petition to hold the honor of your fair embraces.

WIFE.
The motion is so civil and savors so much of a sincere affection that I can no longer resist it.

LOVER.
Let us retire.

WIFE.
Come.

Exit Lover and Wife.

BELLAMOUR.
So, now they are come to the matter in hand. But here comes the husband.

The husband knocks at the door and turns his back. The lover kicks him several times and retires.

YOUNG MAGGOT.
Now it begins to warm; 'tis an admirable plot.

SELFISH.
Bellamour, see how kind the ladies are to me.—Pretty rogue! Let me repose my head in thy soft bosom.

BELLAMOUR.
'Sdeath!* What's this? She will not speak to me yet suffers that familiarity with that rascal as if it were on purpose to provoke me.

CARLOS.
Why does not the fool look where the blows come?

THEODOSIA.
Oh! That would spoil the plot.

HUSBAND.

This must be the Devil that strikes me. Some whoring rogue or other is gotten with my wife, and the Devil pimps for him. But I have a key to a back door and will surprise him. (*Exit.*)

STANMORE.

I cannot find my mistress, but I'll divert myself with a vizard* in the meantime.

FIRST MAN.

What, not a word? All over in disguise: silence for your folly and a vizard for your ill face?

SECOND MAN. (*To a vizard.*)

Gad! Some whore, I warrant you, or chambermaid, in her lady's old clothes. (*He sits down and lolls in the orange-wench's lap.*)

THIRD MAN.

She must be a woman of quality;* she has right point.[56]

FOURTH MAN.

Faith! She earns all the clothes on her back by lying on't: some punk* lately turned out of keeping,* her livery not quite worn out.

ISABELLA.

I deserve this by coming in a mask, and if I should now discover* myself, 'twould make a quarrel.*

PRIG.

You shall see what tricks I'll play. Faith! I love to be merry. (*Raps people on the backs and twirls their hats and then looks demurely as if he did not do it.*)

Enter two lovers, and wife.

SECOND LOVER.

Have I catcht them? I was jealous of this before, but now I will make further discovery. (*Goes under the table.*)

FIRST LOVER.

In verity it savors of incivility to interrupt our joys in the middle of our felicity, but since the barbarous intruder is defeated, let us embrace the present occasion, which seems to court us.

WIFE.

If anything which I can do can felicitate you, you may command my person.

SECOND LOVER.

Oh damned jade!

Enter husband.

WIFE.

Oh God! My husband.

FIRST LOVER.

'Sdeath!* What shall we do?

YOUNG MAGGOT.

Now it thickens, an admirable plot.

HUSBAND. (*Falls over a form and breaks his shins and puts out the candle.*)

Oh my shins, my shins!

WIFE.

'Tis as we wished.

[The husband] takes up the candle and blows it in again.

YOUNG MAGGOT.

There's a turn. Who would expect that? As great a turn as can be, from darkness to light: Can anything be greater?

FIRST LOVER.

Now we are undone again.

HUSBAND.

Now tremble at my vengeance, thou most perfidious strumpet, for I will kill thee before thou prayest.

WIFE.

What means my dearest honey?

HUSBAND.

Oh thou salacious jade! Canst thou ask, when that stallion-rogue is there.

WIFE.

What rogue? Art thou mad? Here's nobody.

HUSBAND.

Nobody? Why, who's that? Thou most lascivious quean!

WIFE.

Where?

HUSBAND.

There.

WIFE.

I see nobody. Thou art distracted.

FIRST LOVER.

How I adore her for her wit.

HUSBAND.

What fellow's that, huswife?

WIFE.

Which? I see none.

---

[56] right point] genuine lace

HUSBAND.
But I do, and have at him first.

WIFE.
Hold, my dear, if thou seest anybody, it is the Devil, and if thou strik'st it, it will tear thee in pieces.

HUSBAND.
Are you mad? Do you see nobody there?

WIFE.
No, Heaven knows, not I. Oh Heaven! The house is haunted. What does it look like?

HUSBAND.
Oh Lord! It looks like a man. Hah! Methinks he has glaring eyes. Oh! oh! I see his cloven foot: this is that that struck me just now. Oh, Heaven help me!

WIFE.
Oh help! I swound, I swound.

HUSBAND.
Oh my dear wife! Oh the Devil!

First lover goes under the table.

SECOND LOVER.
Have I caught you, sir?

FIRST LOVER.
Since you have, for the lady's sake, don't discover* me.

WIFE.
Oh! Is it there still, my dear?

HUSBAND.
No, I think 'tis gone. Hah! 'tis vanished.

YOUNG MAGGOT.
Well, it concerns me so, I am not able to bear it.

HUSBAND.
My poor dear! I have wronged thee. Prithee forgive me.

WIFE.
I am always abused thus by you. I am too honest.*

HUSBAND.
Prithee forgive me, I will never tax thee more, but I must change my house if it be thus haunted.

WIFE.
I am afraid to live here any longer. Do, my dear.

ISABELLA.
I see Bellamour minds no woman but my foolish sister (whom, I fear, he takes for me), yet she is so ridiculously fond of that fool that he cannot reasonably imagine I would be.

SELFISH.
Do you not see how fond that pretty creature is of me? I make no doubt but I shall enjoy her person.

BELLAMOUR.
Damnation on this rascal! Can a woman of so much wit like him? I'll watch her. Women have odd, fantastic appetites, and there's no trusting of 'em.

SECOND LOVER.
'Tis too apparent that she's false to me, and I'll revenge it by discovering* her to her husband, for all her trick.

FIRST LOVER.
I will cut your throat if you offer it.

SECOND LOVER.
Nay then, you rascal, have at you.

They scuffle under the table, rise with it on their backs; the table falls down; they draw their swords and fight.

HUSBAND.
Oh villainous woman! Are these spirits? Now I am convinced. I know one whoremaster too well to believe it.

Prig strikes a bully over the back; he takes it to be another and strikes him. They fight.

FIRST MAN.
Zounds you rogue! Do you play your tricks with me?

SECOND MAN.
Have at you, dog.

CARLOS.
Impudent rascals! Have at you all.

Bellamour, Stanmore, Carlos beat the bullies out of the house; the actors run off; ladies run out shrieking.

SELFISH.
I will make good the ladies retreat. (*He retreats behind the ladies, with his sword drawn.*)

BELLAMOUR.
Where is this Selfish gone? I must watch him and the lady. (*Exit.*)

CARLOS.
What rascals and cowards are these bullies! Where are the ladies? Boy, go out and bid the players go on.

Enter Theodosia and Isabella.

Oh madam! I am ashamed of this disorder.

THEODOSIA.
Are you not hurt, sir?
CARLOS.
Only a little in the hand.
THEODOSIA.
Come tomorrow, and my shock dog shall lick you whole. A hurt in the hand? Why, 'tis gotten with opening of oysters and cured with a cobweb.[57]
CARLOS.
If you will but pity the wounds you give yourself, I'll ne'er complain to you of any other.
ISABELLA.
Theodosia may affect ill nature, which perhaps her heart is no more guilty of than mine. But I am sure I am extremely troubled at your hurt and would not have you neglect it.
CARLOS.
You are too obliging, 'tis slight and worth neither of your[n] cares.
GARTRUDE.
Oh Lord! Mr. Carlos is hurt, I shall swoon. Oh dear sir! My heart went pit a pat all the while you were fighting.
CARLOS.
That pretty heart should only leap for joy.
LADY BUSY.
Sir, pray let me be so happy as to apply my white ointment; 'tis very sovereign for a green wound.
LADY CHEATLY.
I have a balsam that never fails, and I were most unhappy if one I esteem so well should miscarry for want of it.
THEODOSIA.
Here's a do about a slight hurt; a butcher at the Bear Garden* makes nothing of forty such. I would have the sun shine through my servant now and then.
CARLOS.
You would have one serve you as they do a mountebank, to be run through for him.
ISABELLA.
I cannot rest till I see if Bellamour be wounded. (*Exit.*)

Enter one of the actors.

ACTOR.
Sir, we cannot go on with our play: one of our young women, being frighted with the swords, is fallen into a fit and carried home sick.
CARLOS.
Boy, go and find the company. I have prepared an entertainment upon the stage: we'll have an entry, a song, or some music. There is no loss of the play. This Prickett can write none but low farce, and his fools are rather odious than ridiculous.
THEODOSIA.
You are once in the right.
CARLOS.
My cruel mistress! You see I had some favor from every one but yourself.
THEODOSIA.
I believe it has cost you five pound in penny gleek[58] to get the good will of the old ladies, and the hopes of marriage has prevailed upon the young ones.
CARLOS.
I was never so serious as that comes to with any but yourself.
THEODOSIA.
No more of this. I accept your entertainment.

[Exeunt.]

[Scene ii.] The stage and scenes [of the play-within-the-play].

Enter Selfish and Gartrude.

SELFISH.
Now if your love has any resolution, you may enjoy me and make yourself the happiest lady in Town and please me too.
GARTRUDE.
Indeed you are so well-bred and so much a gentleman, the ladies cannot but love you.
SELFISH.
I have no reason to complain.
GARTRUDE.
And then you dress so finely.

[57] cured … cobweb] traditional folk cure, but listed in Schroeder's *Compleat Chymical Dispensatory* (1669)

[58] gleek] a three-handed card game played with a forty-four card deck

SELFISH.
Indeed, most young fellows when they come to Town, dress at me. But pretty creature, let us retire.

GARTRUDE.
What you please, dear sir, if you'll be civil.

SELFISH. [*Aside.*]
Pretty soul! How she loves me! I am a rogue to be false to these poor creatures.—While they divert themselves with the vulgar entertainments of music and dancing, I will steal the happiest minute that love and beauty can afford.

GARTRUDE.
You shall not need to steal; I'll give you anything. But will you make a song on me?

SELFISH.
Thou shalt be my Chloris, my Phyllis, CÆlia, my all. Let's away my dear.

Exit Selfish and Gartrude. Enter Bellamour.

BELLAMOUR.
Whither is that rascal carrying Isabella? She must do this on purpose to make me mad, for I can never believe she can like Selfish. I'll follow. (*Exit.*)

Enter Stanmore and Isabella.

STANMORE.
Well, you must be my mistress: my heart beats, and I have a thousand disorders upon me which none but she can cause.

ISABELLA.
It beats a false alarm for once. [*Lifts and replaces mask.*] You see I am not she, but she is somewhere behind the scenes. Pray go and look after her.

Exit Stanmore. Enter Carlos and Theodosia.

THEODOSIA.
Prithee pull off thy mask and conceal thyself no longer.

ISABELLA.
Do not discover* me. I hear Bellamour keeps a player; I am resolved to watch him and see if I can make any discovery. [*Exit.*]

Enter Lady Cheatly, Lady Busy, Prig, Maggot, [and carpenter].

MAGGOT.
Madam, your ladyship is so pestered with this gamester Prig that I cannot have time to talk with you.

LADY CHEATLY.
I am so, and I have business of great concernment to confer with you about. Would I were rid of him.

MAGGOT.
I'll have a trick for him.

PRIG.
Sirrah Maggot! I will not suffer you to talk to my lady; she is mine, you old fool.

MAGGOT.
Come out, you young blockhead, and let our swords try whose she is.

PRIG.
Let's fight here. I would have my mistress see how I put in my pass and what a yerk I give it.

MAGGOT.
Thou o'ergrown coward!

LADY CHEATLY.
Gentlemen, I must not suffer quarreling* before me. Mr. Prig, be more temperate.

PRIG.
I will, madam, though 'tis hard when love or honor bids me draw.

Enter Young Maggot.

YOUNG MAGGOT.
Gentlemen, be not so much troubled that the play was interrupted by the bullies, for I have a poem about me, which I'll entertain you with, that perhaps may be more agreeable. I will read it to you.

CARLOS.
But first let's have a dance.

YOUNG MAGGOT.
With all my heart.

LADY CHEATLY.
Do you hear, carpenter? Can you make the machines work? I shall have use of 'em.

CARPENTER.
Yes, madam.

LADY CHEATLY.
Pray be ready when I give you order, do you hear? Thus. Let us all sit and see this dance.

An entry of clowns. Enter Lump.*

LADY CHEATLY.
My brother's here. What shall we do now?
LUMP.
I am ashamed, sister, of your sin and vanity and cannot in conscience let you alone in your evil ways. What makes you in this wicked place? this sink of sin? this house of abominations, where wise men and godly men are abused? It is great wickedness, and I cannot be silent; my zeal and wisdom will not let me be silent.
LADY CHEATLY.
Brother, have a little breeding, as well as zeal and wisdom, and do not disturb the gentlemen.
LUMP.
I care not for breeding. Shall zeal and wisdom give place to that? I say, 'tis not lawful, 'tis sinful, 'tis abominable, to come under the roof with these hornets. There is wit, flashy wit stirring here, and I would as soon be in a pesthouse.
LADY CHEATLY.
I must comply with those I have designs upon for my fortune's sake and for my daughters'.
LUMP.
That does something mollify the sin, but it is too great, and I cannot bear it. Cannot you take religious courses in order to your design? And then you may serve Heaven and yourself together. You are foolish, very foolish, and have no method in you.
CARLOS.
This gentleman is going to read a pious poem to us. Pray, do not interrupt him.
LUMP.
Sir, I must interrupt him, I have a call, a great call to it. All poetry is abominable, and all wit is an idol, a very* Dagon,[59] I will down with it. All the wise and godly party of the Nation hate wit.
YOUNG MAGGOT.
None but fools hate wit, and those that cannot think. For my part, I will venture my blood in defense of poetry.
LUMP.
I will preach against it while I have breath.

[59] Dagon] or Dagan, west Semitic god of fertility, particularly for the Philistines, whose temple to Dagon Samson destroyed (Judges 16)

YOUNG MAGGOT.
Peace, fool! I will read on.
LUMP.
Sister, you shall not hear it: 'tis profane, abominable, a grace-resisting, soul-destroying, conscience-choking, most unutterably sin-nourishing thing, and I cannot bear it, I cannot suffer it.

Lady Cheatly whistles: two mock-devils descend and fly up with Lump.

Murder, murder, what dost thou do, Satan? Whither dost thou fly with me?
YOUNG MAGGOT.
This is very well. Ha! Ha! Ha! Now I may read in quiet.
PRIG.
Pray my dear, let's be going. I hate this wit. I think Mr. Lump is in the right.
LADY CHEATLY.
Sit but a while, and I'll go.
YOUNG MAGGOT. (*Reads.*)
"Beauty, thou great preserver of the world,
By which into dead lumps, quick* life is hurled—"

Prig and Young Maggot are carried up in their chairs and hang in the air.

LADY CHEATLY.
So, now I shall have time to speak with you.

Exit Maggot, Lady Cheatly, Lady Busy.

PRIG.
Hold! Hold! Murder! Murder! What a devil do you mean? My dear! Honey! Where is my lady? Madam! Madam!
YOUNG MAGGOT.
What can this mean? But hold, I'll read on, if you will. "Beauty thou great, etc."

All go out, and leave 'em hanging.

PRIG.
They are all gone. What shall I do? Pox on your wit, sirrah! This is your wit, you damned wit, you.
YOUNG MAGGOT.
You lie, fool! 'Tis a wheadle,[60] a crossbite* of the widow's.

[60] wheadle] a sharper's trick using wheedling (q.v.) (Partridge)

PRIG.
Oh, you damned, scribbling, senseless, singsong wit!

YOUNG MAGGOT.
Oh you damned, gaming, jockey, hunting, tennis fool.

Enter Bellamour.

BELLAMOUR.
Hell and damnation! What have I seen? A curse on all the sex! Is this the virtue she pretended to? To be lewd with so despicable a coxcomb as Selfish, so nauseous a fellow! Death and Hell!

PRIG.
Hark you, Bellamour, prithee help me down.

YOUNG MAGGOT.
Pray let me down.

BELLAMOUR.
Pox on you both.

Enter Selfish.

SELFISH.
Ah Bellamour! I am the happiest man, I think, that ever the sun shined on: I have enjoyed the prettiest creature, just now, in a room behind the scenes. I cannot help telling of thee because thou art my friend. Faith! telling is half the pleasure to me, for I confess to thee, I think, we that are happy in ladies' affections make love as much for vanity as anything else. You know the lady.

BELLAMOUR. (*Aside.*)
Damn the dog.—'Twas one of my lady Cheatly's daughters. Which of 'em was it?

SELFISH.
Well, I can keep nothing from thee: it was one of 'em, but upon your honor, keep it secret. Guess which—they are both desperately in love with me, hah!

BELLAMOUR.
Impudent rascal and coxcomb! (*He strikes him, then beats him with his sword.*)

SELFISH.
What ill breeding is this? Are you distracted?

[Enter Isabella.]

ISABELLA.
Heaven! What's the matter? Hold, hold.

BELLAMOUR.
Be gone, rascal, or I'll run you through.

SELFISH.
I will not be uncivil before a lady. Another time I shall call you to an account.—An ill-bred fellow! (*Exit.*)

ISABELLA.
What's the reason of this quarrel?*

BELLAMOUR.
Here, carpenter.

[Enter carpenter.]

CARPENTER.
Here, sir.

BELLAMOUR.
Let down those fools and dispose of 'em so they may not trouble us.

Carpenter lets 'em down, and presently they sink down and roar out.*

PRIG.
So, this is well.

YOUNG MAGGOT.
Bellamour, I thank you.

BELLAMOUR.
You know too well the occasion of the quarrel.

ISABELLA.
What do you mean?

BELLAMOUR.
Is all your pretense of virtue come to this? and must my love be thus rewarded?

ISABELLA.
This rudeness of yours amazes me.

BELLAMOUR.
'Tis I have cause to be amazed: to be refused the favor, and you grant it to that filthy fool, Selfish. There's nothing but dissembling, treachery, and ingratitude in your whole sex.

ISABELLA.
A favor to Selfish? The fool of all the world I scorn and hate the most? But now I see you'll give me occasion to rank you with him.

BELLAMOUR.
No, you shall never rank me with him. I scorn to be obliged to one who is so free to lay out herself upon such an ass.

ISABELLA.
Has that vain rascal lied on me? and do you believe him?

BELLAMOUR.
My eyes will not lie, madam, I will trust them. And though you have let down your skirt, I know the petticoat too well.

ISABELLA.
Unworthy man! I could stab thee for this affront, but that thou art not worthy of a serious thought. Is this the petticoat you mean?—What has my foolish sister done?

BELLAMOUR.
How? This is not the petticoat.

Enter Stanmore and Gartrude barefaced.

Heaven and earth! 'twas Gartrude I see now.

ISABELLA.
I scorn and hate thee, for thy base suspicion, more than all mankind.

BELLAMOUR.
Madam, I am a dog, a villain,* not fit to live. Kill me, for if you forgive me not, I'll do't myself.

ISABELLA.
I'll never see thy odious face again, do what thou wilt. Farewell, base man. (*Exit.*)

BELLAMOUR.
Hell and devils! What has my rashness brought me to? (*Exit.*)

STANMORE.
Pretty miss! Be not so troubled. I have used thee kindly, very kindly.

GARTRUDE.
Kindly? Oh sad! I'll tell my mother what you have done to me, so I will.

STANMORE.
Thou art not mad, child!* Prithee don't.

GARTRUDE.
But I was mad to let you be so uncivil, and I will tell her. Here she is.

Enter Lady Busy, Lady Cheatly, and Maggot.

STANMORE.
'Sheart!* What a fool she is! I'll not stand the brunt. (*Exit.*)

MAGGOT.
Well madam, I'll dispatch the business and wait on you again. (*Exit.*)

GARTRUDE.
Oh madam! What shall I do? What shall I do?

LADY CHEATLY.
What's the matter?

GARTRUDE.
I thought what 'twould come to: you charged me to be civil to Stanmore, and I am deflowered, so I am.

LADY CHEATLY.
Oh Heaven! What, did he ravish you?

GARTRUDE.
No, because you bid me be civil to him, I consented. I was afraid to anger you, madam.

LADY CHEATLY.
Civil? That was civil with a vengeance! Let me come, I'll knock her on the head, filthy creature.

LADY BUSY.
Hold madam, be wise and make the best on't. Let me alone to manage this affair.—Come pretty Mrs. Gartrude, has he made no settlement upon thee?

GARTRUDE.
He settled nothing but himself upon me, that I know.

LADY CHEATLY.
No, that's the plague: I knew there was no settlement; if that had been done, it had been somewhat.

LADY BUSY.
Go to,* be patient. Let me alone; withdraw, good madam, and trust me.

Exit Lady Cheatly. Enter Stanmore.

Come on, Mr. Stanmore, I must talk with you a little.

STANMORE.
Now for a wise lecture.

LADY BUSY.
Look up, pretty miss, come on.—Sir, my lady Cheatly is a worthy person and of good quality*—right. Mrs. Gartrude is a very pretty young lady—-true. Nor is it fit my lady (who has entertained you so often and so nobly in her house) should be abused—-do you conceive me? Nor is it fit that this pretty young thing should be injured—-you understand me?

STANMORE.
Your ladyship speaks like an oracle.

LADY BUSY.

Very good. This pretty thing, I understand, has been very kind* to you—very well—-

STANMORE.

Fie miss! Fie! Tell tales out of school?—If she has, I am sure I was as kind as she could be for her heart.

LADY BUSY.

Very good—-come, I understand you—-ah, what pleasure 'tis to lie by such a sweet bedfellow! such pretty little swelling breasts! such delicate, black, sparkling eyes! such a fresh complexion! such red, pouting lips! and such a skin! I say no more—in short, she would make a husband very happy. Come, let it be so, and let no more words be made of this matter.

STANMORE.

I'll do what I can to help her to one.

LADY BUSY.

Go to—-that's well said—-yourself then be the man—-oh how the Town will envy you the enjoyment of so fine a lady!

STANMORE.

'Sheart, madam, what do you take me for? If you knew all, what need I marry for the matter?

LADY BUSY.

Go to, she may make as good a wife as can be for all that. Have you not many examples?

STANMORE.

No madam, I have made a vow of chastity that way, which I will never break.

LADY BUSY.

I would not my lady should know this for the world; she would be revenged to the last degree. Let me tell you, you have been very uncivil.

STANMORE.

Faith madam, I think not.

GARTRUDE.

Yes, but you have been uncivil though, that you have.

LADY BUSY.

Go to.—-Do you mind? Do you think a family is to be dishonored? Is that like a gentleman? Nay, not but that human frailty must be passed by, for young people, when they meet, are apt and liable—'tis confessed—but then—Aye, what then? Why, your* gentlemen and your worthy persons strive to make it good—very well. But how is it to be made good? Hmm—-why, either by marriage or settlement.

STANMORE.

I have a private reason must keep me from doing either.

LADY BUSY.

No, no, that won't pass: I know you are too much a gentleman; besides, you made me a° promise you would keep;* and let me tell you, my honor is concerned in it, and I would not have my honor touched for the world.

STANMORE.

I did not promise to keep for another, as I must if I keep her.

GARTRUDE.

You do not say true then.

LADY BUSY.

Fie Mr. Stanmore, that you should say such an ungenteel thing!—Come miss, bear up, and do not cry.—How can you endure to see a young lady's tears and not melt?—Come on, pretty miss, I am sure you will be kind* and constant to Mr. Stanmore, will you not?

GARTRUDE.

Yes, yes.

LADY BUSY.

Good.—Why look you, sir, I know you are a worthy gentleman and will consider of a settlement such as befits a gentlewoman.

STANMORE.

No, madam. Selfish, this evening, in a greenroom behind the scenes, was beforehand with me. She ne'er tells of that. Can I love one that prostitutes herself to that fellow?

LADY BUSY.

How's this?

GARTRUDE.

Oh sad, that you should say such a thing! I am sure he will not say so for the world. Would I might ne'er stir out of this place alive now if I did.

STANMORE.

I had it from his own mouth.

GARTRUDE.

Oh Lord, I'll be far enough,[61] if you had! I'm sure

[61] far enough] colloquial expression expressing absolute negation (Partridge), as in "I'll be hornswoggled"

he's too fine a gentleman and too well-bred to tell such a grievous lie of a lady. I am sure he did not say so, that he did not.

STANMORE.
How she commends him!

LADY BUSY.
You know, Selfish is the vainest fellow that ever was born. Can you believe that coxcomb? It is not generous.

STANMORE.
Shall I believe Bellamour's eyes? He saw it. Good madam, be pleased to forbear your tricks upon me. Farewell. I hate the leavings of a fool; I'll as soon eat the meat he has chewed or wear his foul linen after him. Adieu, good madam. (*Exit.*)

LADY BUSY.
Now see what your indiscretion has done. Did I not tell you Selfish would undo you?

GARTRUDE.
Oh what shall I do! What shall I do! Does your ladyship think you could not get Mr. Selfish to marry me? Oh, he's the prettiest man: I could live and die with him.

LADY BUSY.
Go to, you will utterly ruin yourself. Do you think a fellow that has been so base to boast of your kindness* will marry you? Peace, I say. I will try another: Young Maggot shall be the man.

GARTRUDE.
I can't abide him.

LADY BUSY.
I say go to—-you must marry him, if he will, and be glad on't too. Stanmore has forsaken you; Selfish can't keep* you; your mother will turn you out of doors; and you will starve. Come, come along with me and be better advised.

Exeunt.

Act V, [scene i. Lady Cheatly's lodgings.]

Enter Prig and Lady Cheatly.

PRIG.
Now madam, I hope you will be persuaded to dispatch this business of wedlock this morning; 'twould be much more convenient for me than tomorrow, because I am to go to Newmarket to a cock match. I have laid fifty pound upon Jackanapes against Tom Prig's Boxen Beak; my Dun fights a battle with Tom Whiskin's Duckwing for fifty pound. 'Twill be the best sport in the world. I would fain marry today and go thither tomorrow. Will your ladyship go and see it?

LADY CHEATLY.
No, pray sir, if that be the best sport in the world, see that first and marry afterwards.

PRIG.
Newmarket's a rare place! There a man's never idle: we make visits to horses and talk with grooms, riders, and cock keepers and saunter in the heath all the forenoon; then we dine and never talk a word but of dogs, cocks, and horses; then we saunter into the heath again; then to a cock match; then to a play in a barn; then to supper and never speak a word but of dogs, cocks, and horses again; then to the groom-porter's,* where you may play all night. Oh, 'tis a heavenly life! We are never idle.

LADY CHEATLY.
For ought I see, you are never otherwise.

Enter steward.

Heaven! Is this villain returned?

STEWARD.
Yes, perfidious woman! I am returned, and will make you know that I am not to be used so. What? to be clapped under hatches and carried to the Indies to be sold for a slave? A fine design, truly. But come, madam, I will make you know your lord and master.

LADY CHEATLY.
What means your impudence?

STEWARD.
Impudence! to command my wife? Know your duty.

PRIG.
Your wife? Why, you are her man, are you not?

STEWARD.
What fellow's this? I must have new orders: I must have no such customers about my house.

LADY CHEATLY.
Call a constable, the poor fellow's distracted.

STEWARD.
No, but I may make the lady so, if she persists in her impudence.

PRIG.
Thou art very saucy to thy lady and mistress.

STEWARD.
Peace, fool! Saucy to my wife?

PRIG.
Fool? Hah, fool! What a pox would you be at?

LADY CHEATLY.
Impudent villain!* Thy wife?

STEWARD.
Most audacious woman! Darest thou deny it? Was I not married to you yesterday in your own chamber by a parson of your own choosing?

LADY CHEATLY.
How dar'st thou affirm so impudent a lie? Where didst thou dream this?

PRIG.
I have my cue: I'll have my hand in the plot. (*Exit.*)

STEWARD.
Why, thou most infamous of women! Canst thou deny this?

LADY CHEATLY.
Yes, thou most impudent of rascals, I will deny it to all the world, and I have taken care that thou shalt never prove it.

STEWARD.
Hell and devils! Is there one amongst you like this woman?

LADY CHEATLY.
Well, if you will be quiet and stir no farther in this business, a thousand pound is yours; if not, you never shall have me nor anything of mine. Marry such a fellow?

STEWARD.
No, base woman! I'll undo thee.

LADY CHEATLY.
'Tis out of your power, fool: you have sworn to all my bonds and deeds already.

STEWARD.
Most vile of cheats! I'll find your parson, if he be in England.

Enter Prig in the habit of a parson.

Oh happy fortune! Here he is.

LADY CHEATLY. [*Aside.*]
What means this coxcomb Prig?

STEWARD.
Now, madam.—Did not you marry me to this lady yesterday? Speak, upon the word of a priest.

PRIG.
Yes, I did.

STEWARD.
Now, what says your impudence? I thought I should catch you. Were you so cunning to deny it?—Where do you live, sir?

PRIG.
Madam, pray help me off with my habit.

LADY CHEATLY.
This is well enough.

STEWARD.
Hah! What a devil's this? Were you the parson?

PRIG.
Yes, good sir.

LADY CHEATLY.
Yes, this was my chaplain, you saucy fool! Could you think I would marry such a filthy fellow as you are?

STEWARD.
I will give you to understand, madam, that 'tis a good marriage.—And I'll bring you into the court to swear it, sir.

PRIG.
If you do, sir, I'll hold six to four, I forswear it, sir.

STEWARD.
Why, sure you dare not.

PRIG.
By Heaven, I dare, and will forswear[P] myself for such a widow; gentlemen forswear themselves to get whores and make nothing on't. Be gone out of my house, she is mine. Fellow, be gone, I say.

STEWARD.
Curse on my shallow head! that I should be so credulous to believe her to be true to me when I was an hourly witness of her falsehood to others.—I will have you my wife or be revenged to that degree you shall repent this treachery your whole life. I am going to visit all those you have had business with this month, and I shall tell 'em such a tale. (*Exit.*)

PRIG.
I'll cut his throat; say no more.

LADY CHEATLY.
Pray hasten after this malicious, clamorous rascal and stop him some way or other. He'll invent a thousand lies of me. Get him arrested upon an action of ten thousand pound at my suit.

PRIG.
Let me alone, I'll do as becomes a gentleman. (*Exit.*)
LADY CHEATLY.
This trouble, joined with that fool my daughter, will undo me, but I will find out Maggot, and he shall help to salve up all.

Enter Maggot.

Oh Mr. Maggot! I have business to communicate to you of the greatest concernment to me that ever happened.
MAGGOT.
Gad madam, do! If any man in England understands business or loves it better than I do, I'll be burnt.
LADY CHEATLY.
Every man loves what he is good at. Give me a man of business for my friend. The fine gentlemen of the Town are like fiddlers, only good at idle hours.
MAGGOT.
There are no great persons at this end of the Town have any business but I do it for 'em. I am the busiest man in England, and I hope, madam, you'll consider of my love to business, and to your ladyship.
LADY CHEATLY.
Why, that is part of the business I am to confer with you about.

Enter Lady Busy and Young Maggot.

LADY BUSY.
Madam, I beg you will retire. I have an affair with Young Mr. Maggot that concerns you and Mrs. Gartrude.

Exeunt Lady Cheatly and Maggot.

Mr. Maggot, I can never enough admire your Uncle Maggot's aversion to wit and breeding, nor can I choose but pity you, who are like to be so great a sufferer for your love to both.
YOUNG MAGGOT.
I glory in my suffering for so good a cause.
LADY BUSY.
Well, many a man would be proud of such a nephew. But is it true that you are like to be disinherited?
YOUNG MAGGOT.
It is as true as I myself will ever be to wit and beauty, unless I will recant my works and for the future renounce tropes, figures, similes, and all ornaments of speech.
LADY BUSY.
These are hard conditions.
YOUNG MAGGOT.
A man of my vigorous imagination had as good have been born dumb. I will sing, and starve to death like a grasshopper, ere I submit.
LADY BUSY.
Go to,* suppose some friend of yours, more careful of you than you are of yourself, should find a way to compose this matter without prejudice to your poetry.
YOUNG MAGGOT.
That friend should be another Apollo, if a man, and a tenth muse to me, if a woman.
LADY BUSY.
Good. There is a woman, a pretty one, young and rich too in the case—very well. But how shall I come by this woman, say you? Go to, let me alone: a fine woman, with a good fortune, were no ill refuge from the anger of your uncle, hah?
YOUNG MAGGOT.
But if I should marry, what will the world say of my wit? I had rather lose my honor and starve than lose the name of a wit.
LADY BUSY.
Your reputation is established already. Go to, consider.
YOUNG MAGGOT.
But madam, my heart is engaged, and the poor soul loves me again to madness. I did but kiss my hand to a lady in a window t'other day, and the poor thing fell into a fit; she will never outlive such a heinous tergiversation.
LADY BUSY.
Come, come, you know not the world. This is some soft-hearted fool that will be as fond of another in three days. Go to, I know the sex better than you. But such a reputation, such a face, and such a fortune!
YOUNG MAGGOT.
Nay, if she have a better face and reputation than

my Gartrude, I will forswear poetry and write shorthand at conventicles all the rest of my life.

LADY BUSY.
Is she the woman? My lady Cheatly looks very high for her daughter: Stanmore and several fortunes are about her. Do you conceive me?

YOUNG MAGGOT.
That's all one.
As for my part I have chosen one,
And I'll have my love, or I'll have none.

LADY BUSY.
Hold: a lady of fortune, beauty, and one that loves you, and admires you for your wit, is not to be neglected.

YOUNG MAGGOT.
How? Then she has wit too.

LADY BUSY.
How else should she admire it in you?

YOUNG MAGGOT.
Since she has wit, I will see her, that's certain, and love her, if I can; if not, I'll make her some handsome excuse for't in my next song.

Enter Gartrude.

LADY BUSY.
Well then, here she comes. It is this pretty Gartrude: Ah! what a bedfellow is this, with above ten thousand pound too.

YOUNG MAGGOT.
Pretty creature! Are you she?

GARTRUDE.
Yes, that I am.

YOUNG MAGGOT.
But madam, do you not think marriage will spoil my poetry?

GARTRUDE.
I would not marry you if I thought it would, for I love your verses dearly.

LADY BUSY.
Stanmore and Selfish will hang themselves when they hear of your good fortune.

YOUNG MAGGOT.
Aye, so they will.

GARTRUDE.
Everybody says they love one to one's face, but you said so behind my back: I heard you tell my lady so, and I am resolved I will have you, though my mother turn me out of doors, that I will.

LADY BUSY.
Go, get you together, loving rogues, and let me alone to make your peace with my Lady Cheatly.

Exeunt.

[Scene ii. The same.]

Enter Selfish and Isabel.

SELFISH.
Consider my person and my breeding. Think not of Bellamour, he has two ladies with child by him, and one claims marriage.

ISABELLA.
You had best marry her for him; he'll give a good portion.

SELFISH.
I did not think so harsh a repartee could have come out of that pretty mouth: sure you take something ill from me; my conduct among the ladies does not please you. I confess, I have been somewhat too general in my addresses, but I am resolved to apply myself to you and be less gallant hereafter.

ISABELLA.
Be less vain and less a coxcomb, and know that nothing you forbear or do can please or trouble me.

SELFISH.
Were I not skilled in the various dispositions of your soft sex, these words would make me despair, but I have often known such peevishness the child of love.

ISABELLA.
Were I a man, I'd cudgel you out of this conceit of yourself, but as I am, I can only despise and laugh at you.

SELFISH.
Ha! ha! ha! You are pleasant, and I am glad to find you so. I often discover ladies' affections to me that way, for I am sure they love me, when they are so familiar with me, my pretty *railleur.*[62]

ISABELLA.
Monster of vanity! be gone.

---

62 *railleur*] joker, kidder (Fr.)

[V.ii]

Enter Bellamour.

BELLAMOUR.
I beg upon my knees you will once more hear me.

ISABELLA.
I never will. [*Exit.*]

SELFISH.
It is in vain: Give her over, Bellamour. What would you have her do, poor lady? she loves me. Dost thou think ever to get a lady where I am? Why, my mother has often told me I was born with a caul[63] upon my head, and she wrapped me up in her shift to make me lucky to ladies.

BELLAMOUR.
Impudent coxcomb! I will not disturb the house, but follow me or I'll cut your throat here. You are the occasion of this storm.

SELFISH.
With all my heart. I did intend to demand satisfaction for your ill breeding at the playhouse, and you shall find I can fight as well as I can make love.*

BELLAMOUR.
Come on, vanity.

Exeunt.

[Scene iii. The same.]

Enter Carlos and Theodosia.

THEODOSIA.
I see you are resolved to watch me, to make me confess love as they do witches to make 'em own their contracts with the Devil.

CARLOS.
If you would but look a little guiltily, I would take you upon suspicion.

THEODOSIA.
And so hurry me away to execution. Alas, poor Carlos! Don't I look as if I died for thee? Are not my eyes languishing enough?

CARLOS.
You are pleasant, madam, as becomes a winning gamester.

THEODOSIA.
If I should play on, luck may turn; I think 'tis best to give over as I am.

CARLOS.
But consider how entirely I love you.

THEODOSIA.
Consider how little I care for you.

CARLOS.
The greatest beauties are not always most sincerely loved.

THEODOSIA.
No, they are commonly like great places: courted and won by vain designing knaves. And were I such, I should be yet more suspicious.

CARLOS.
A man that's ready to die a martyr need make no other professions; I should else—

THEODOSIA.
Talk like an ass of charms and tyranny of mine, of chains and slavery of yours. A man that should overhear you would think you had been taken by the Turk.

CARLOS.
'Tis not in your power to make me leave loving you.

THEODOSIA.
'Tis very unreasonable that my indifference should not make you love me less.

CARLOS.
'Tis very unreasonable that my perseverance should not make you love me more. But I will yet hope.

THEODOSIA.
Hope is a thin diet and may be allowed in your feverish condition and, indeed, is the only food that love can live on.

CARLOS.
Oh madam, marriage—

THEODOSIA.
Is to love as the Jesuit's powder* to an ague: it stops the fit and in a little time wears it quite off.

Enter Isabella.

ISABELLA.
My dear, how dost thou?—Carlos, will you forgive me? Lovers take it as ill to be parted as men of honor.

63 caul] To be born with this membrane around the head was considered a good omen.

CARLOS.
I was just upon the point of yielding.

THEODOSIA.
I scorn to take advantages, but I had reduced him to offer marriage.

ISABELLA.
Then it seems he is weary of being your slave and would make you his.

CARLOS.
Madam, you should be generous and take the weakest side. No, I am resolved ever to be her servant, but would be glad of a nearer employment about her person.

THEODOSIA.
Come, prithee Isabella, let's take a turn in the garden and see if we can talk of something else.

CARLOS.
Where'er I go, I shall carry my love with me, and that will not suffer me to talk or think of anything but your dear self.

Exeunt.

[Scene iv. The field.]

Enter Bellamour and Selfish.

BELLAMOUR.
Come sir, I hope you like this place. You are very nice* in choosing one.

SELFISH.
Yes, I like this, for here I ran one man through and gave another his life.

BELLAMOUR.
Let me see if you be armed or not.

SELFISH.
No, I am too well-bred for that.

BELLAMOUR.
Make ready.

SELFISH. [*Aside.*]
And yet I am damnably afraid, but if I should not fight, the ladies will not be so apt to love me as they are.

BELLAMOUR.
Come, will you never have done?

SELFISH.
Yes sir. What great haste are you in?
Beauty, what art thou? But a fading flower.

BELLAMOUR.
Beauty? What a devil hast thou to do with beauty? You are a damned ugly, ill-bred coxcomb, and the ladies care not one jot for you. Draw.

SELFISH.
Come on, I will vindicate myself and the ladies. Now for the ladies.

They fight. Bellamour throws Selfish down and takes his sword.

Do not kill me! Consider how the ladies will hate you if you should.

BELLAMOUR.
No, prithee live, and be an ass still, but trouble me no more.

SELFISH.
Thou art a strange, rough, ill-bred fellow to fight so: to fling a man down and spoil his clothes. You have dirtied all my garniture and spoiled my cravat. Could you not have fought easily, handsomely, and like a gentleman? You were never bred in an academy: they never fight thus brutally in France.

BELLAMOUR.
This is ridiculous enough.

SELFISH.
I warrant, you have done me ten pounds worth of hurt with fighting with me. I do not know how to appear before the ladies. I can't abide such tricks.

BELLAMOUR.
Fare thee well.—If I were not extremely troubled about Isabella, I would divert myself with this coxcomb. (*Exit.*)

SELFISH.
A brutal* fellow! to spoil one's things thus. But I'll go home and dress me. (*Exit.*)

[Scene v. Lady Cheatly's lodgings.]

Enter Lady Cheatly and Maggot.

LADY CHEATLY.
You see I have considered your passion and how apt you are for business. I am afraid of a suit or two in law, which I know you can manage.

MAGGOT.
As well as any man in the world.

LADY CHEATLY.
I have told you of the insolence of the steward and the artifice I used to get rid of him.

MAGGOT.
That shows your ladyship understands business. How happy shall I be! How I shall laugh at and triumph over all my rivals!

LADY CHEATLY.
Not a word of what has passed betwixt us till a fitter opportunity.

Enter Prig, with a plaster upon his face.

How now, Mr. Prig. What ails your face?

PRIG.
Be not frightened my dear, 'tis no great hurt.

MAGGOT.
My dear! Poor fool, how I pity him!

PRIG.
I went to stop that rogue, your steward, and demand satisfaction, as becomes a gentleman, and in fine, we drew, and after some two or three and thirty passes, I found myself run into the arm, and the face, but I worsted him. Yet when I was at a surgeon's the rascal got away.

LADY CHEATLY.
I am sorry you should venture so much for me.

PRIG.
Oh, madam! 'Twas for myself, for we are to be all one flesh. Now nothing troubles me but that this hurt will hinder my journey to Newmarket tomorrow.

MAGGOT.
He, all one flesh with her? Poor coxcomb!

Enter two scriveners.

FIRST SCRIVENER.
Madam, I wonder a lady of quality* should be guilty of such fraud and covin[64] to write bonds with ink that will wear out in a month.

SECOND SCRIVENER.
Other ink you have, too, that with a spirit rubbed upon the paper will make impression through a whole quire.

LADY CHEATLY.
What mean these fellows? Are you mad?

FIRST SCRIVENER.
No, but this is enough to make us mad, for ourselves and our clients to be cheated of such sums.

SECOND SCRIVENER.
Pray madam, give us security and let me renew the bonds with my own ink.

LADY CHEATLY.
Go home and sleep and be sober.

MAGGOT.
What's the meaning of this? Is my lady a cheat?

PRIG.
This is the rogue, your steward's lie.

LADY CHEATLY.
Oh, gentlemen! You have been with that rascal, my steward, the most impudent villain, who, having most of the writings that concern my estate in his hands, had the impudence to threaten to burn 'em, unless I would marry him.

PRIG.
'Tis very true, upon my honor.

LADY CHEATLY.
I, by a wile, got 'em out of his hands, and he, out of revenge for being so disappointed, has invented these malicious lies. But I shall lay him fast enough.

Enter two citizens.

FIRST CITIZEN.
Madam, we did not think your ladyship would put such things upon us to give us false notes for our money.

SECOND CITIZEN.
Notes written with ink that will wear out: we shall have nothing but blanks for our money.

FIRST CITIZEN.
Pray let me have my five hundred pound again.

SECOND CITIZEN.
And me, mine. You have not laid it out yet.

LADY CHEATLY.
What! my rogue of a[q] steward has been with you too, has he?

SECOND CITIZEN.
Rogue! He's an honest man to give us notice of this deceit. Madam, I wonder your ladyship is not ashamed.

PRIG.
How now, impudence! I tell you the steward is the

[64] covin] criminal conspiracy

cheat and rogue. He has lied and abused you. My lady is a person of honor.

MAGGOT.

Hah! There must be something in this: he would not be so foolish to tell so silly a lie.

SECOND SCRIVENER.

My lady is a worthy person, and the steward has invented these lies out of revenge because he had the impudence to pretend* to marry my lady and would have kept all her writings. He'd force her to do it, but she was too hard for him. We know all.

SECOND CITIZEN.

This is strange.

Enter Lump.

LUMP.

Oh thou vile woman! thou reprobate! thou most audacious, seared-conscienced creature! Could such a wicked branch spring from our family, who are precious, godly men and women, all but thyself?

LADY CHEATLY.

Are you mad, brother?

Enter steward.

LUMP.

I knew you would cheat the rest. But must you betray me and give me false deeds? Must I have nothing but blanks for my money?

FIRST SCRIVENER.

What ails thee?[r]

FIRST CITIZEN.

How, are we cheated?

MAGGOT.

'Sdeath!* There must be some fire under all this smoke.

LUMP.

Had it not been for this honest man, who was troubled in conscience and could no longer conceal your fraud, I had ne'er known it, but now I will make an example of you.

FIRST CITIZEN.

How, sir? Are you a precious, godly man and knew of a cheat and would not discover* it?

SECOND CITIZEN.

One of our own church to suffer us to be betrayed?

LUMP.

I had no call to it, till now I am myself concerned.

LADY CHEATLY.

Will you believe this most infamous rascal, that would have dishonored your family and, having all my writings, would have married me or have burnt 'em? I, by seeming to consent to his desires, got 'em out of his hands, made him swear to 'em before a Master in Chancery; then I turned him away for a villain, as he is.

LUMP.

What say you, sir?

PRIG.

Say? I'll hold six to four, he cannot say a word. Upon my honor, this is all true, to my knowledge.

STEWARD.

She caused me to be clapped under hatches in a ship going to the Indies because I knew this secret, and I do assure you, ye are all cheated and in less than a month will have nothing to show for all your money. I cannot in conscience but reveal this.

LADY CHEATLY.

Impudent, lying varlet! How darest thou affirm so devilish a lie?

STEWARD. (*Whispers.*)

Will you marry me yet, and I will retrieve all.

LADY CHEATLY.

Oh heaven and earth! The villain whispers me in the ear now and tells me, if I will marry him, he will deny all.

STEWARD.

Mercy upon me! Will your ladyship's conscience give you leave to say that? Pray madam, consider your soul.

FIRST CITIZEN.

Aye madam, consider your soul.

SECOND CITIZEN.

And the payment of my money.

LADY CHEATLY.

Heaven can witness what I say is true: even just now he asked me to marry him.

LUMP.

If this be true, lady sister, I will ask your pardon.

STEWARD.

What need I ask that which I have already? I am married to her.

ALL.

How!

STEWARD.
And her great anger and the reason she would have sold me to Jamaica was because I could not in conscience conceal these deceits though I might have had the benefit of 'em.

LADY CHEATLY.
This is so extravagantly ridiculous, it makes me laugh. I will not give a serious answer to it.

MAGGOT.
Hah! Married? You did not consummate, I hope. Who married you?

STEWARD.
Why, the truth is, she thought to put a false marriage upon me: when she discovered my intention of making a restitution to those she had injured, she dressed that fellow Prig in the disguise of a parson, and he married us in her bedchamber. But I'll make her know, 'tis a good marriage.

MAGGOT.
Did you know him in the disguise?

STEWARD.
No, till this day he appeared in it to me and then pulled it off to show me 'twas a mock marriage, as they thought. But I will make 'em know otherwise.

LADY CHEATLY.
This is the most amazing impudence. Mr. Prig, declare yourself. (*Aside.*) Deny it, or we are undone.

PRIG.
Is there ever a magistrate here? I will swear that there is not one word of all this true. I know not what he means. I hold gold to silver he's mad.

LADY CHEATLY.
Do you see, brother, what a rascal you have believed? and how you have injured me?

LUMP.
Why thou wicked locust! thou spawn of a serpent! to invent such cursed lies. I'll lay thee within four walls.

STEWARD.
By Heaven, 'tis all true! I'll swear it; nay, I'll swear with you for a thousand pound.

MAGGOT.
Let him swear it, that we may have his ears.*

FIRST CITIZEN.
Madam, we ask your pardon with all our hearts.

SECOND CITIZEN.
Impudent fellow! to abuse my lady so.

STEWARD.
Let me but speak.

FIRST SCRIVENER.
No, base fellow! thou shalt not speak.

SECOND SCRIVENER.
Abuse so worthy a lady? Out, thou wicked fellow!

STEWARD.
'Tis very fine.

LUMP.
Lay an action of ten thousand pound upon him; see who will bail him. To my certain knowledge, she has a great estate and has been always a very conscientious woman; indeed, I was something amazed at this story.

FIRST CITIZEN.
Aye sir, we believe your worship.

SECOND CITIZEN.
We know you are a precious, godly man.

STEWARD.
Are you distracted? Well, be all cheated, an* you will, I have discharged my conscience.

LUMP.
Conscience? thou seed of Beelzebub!

PRIG.
Conscience? An impudent rogue, that offers to forswear himself! I offered to lay him ten to one 'twas all false, and you saw he durst not bet.

FIRST SCRIVENER.
Hang him!

SECOND SCRIVENER.
Base, lying rogue!

Enter sergeants.

FIRST SERGEANT.
I arrest you at the suit of my Lady Cheatly, in an action of ten thousand pounds.

STEWARD.
Oh vile woman!

LADY CHEATLY.
Away with him.

SECOND CITIZEN.
Away with him.

ALL.
Away with the rogue.

LUMP.

I do beseech your pardon, sister: I was mistaken, which I do not use to be, yet that trick at the playhouse was base.

LADY CHEATLY.

I could not help it; I knew not of it.

Enter two creditors.

FIRST CREDITOR.

Madam, you have undone us: you gave us bonds for two hundred pound apiece above six weeks since, and we have nothing but the seals left.

SECOND CREDITOR.

All the ink is worn out: behold here, madam. (*Shows a paper.*)

LADY CHEATLY.

Impostors! lying rogues! I owe you nothing.

LUMP.

These are instruments of this rascally steward's. How come they by the seal?

LADY CHEATLY.

From the steward.

FIRST CREDITOR.

Are ye all mad? We had it from you, for which you had two hundred pounds apiece from us.

PRIG.

Out, you impudent rogue! Get you gone.

FIRST CITIZEN.

Away, lying fellows!

LUMP.

Be gone, ye vipers!

They thrust 'em out.

LADY CHEATLY.

Now gentlemen, I desire you that remain to take part of a collation with me, and I will show all the evidences of my estate to you.

Exeunt.

[Scene vi. The garden.]

Enter Isabella and Bellamour.

ISABELLA.

There can be no defense to suspect me, and with that wretch Selfish too.

BELLAMOUR.

Jealousy, like the smallpox if it comes out kindly, is never mortal, and my love will be the stronger and the more vigorous for this short distemper.

ISABELLA.

It may relapse again.

BELLAMOUR.

'Tis past all danger now.

ISABELLA.

And will you still give a thousand pounds down and three hundred pounds a year for this tenement, notwithstanding the encumbrance of Selfish upon it?

BELLAMOUR.

When I made these offers, I did not know half your worth: I was a fair chapman for your beauty, but your virtue and other perfections are inestimable.

ISABELLA.

And shall I flaunt it in the Park* with my gray Flanders,* crowd the walk with my equipage, and be the envy of all the butterflies in Town?

BELLAMOUR.

Forget that vain discourse, as I have done, and take me and all I have forever.

ISABELLA.

Sure a man of your wit will never marry. Every rich fool can get a woman that way.

BELLAMOUR.

Do not insult, but take me quickly to your mercy.

ISABELLA.

I'll not deceive you: whatever show my mother makes, I have no portion, nor was ever troubled at the thought of it till now.

BELLAMOUR.

I am glad of it, for now my love will be the more easily believed and better taken.

ISABELLA.

No, Bellamour.

BELLAMOUR.

How, madam?

ISABELLA.

No, I say—for were I Queen of Europe, your love would be as well accepted as 'tis now.

BELLAMOUR.

You surprise me with an honor too great to bear.

Enter Lady Cheatly

LADY CHEATLY.

What? Are you agreed yet? She is a foolish girl, sir, and looks as high as better women.

BELLAMOUR.
She's very humble and is pleased to accept me for a husband, and there wants* only your consent and a few words from a parson to complete my happiness.

LADY CHEATLY.
You honor our family and cannot doubt of my consent: she is yours.

Enter Lady Busy, Young Maggot, and Gartrude.

LADY BUSY.
I present you here with a son and daughter: I saw 'em married. Give 'em your blessing.

LADY CHEATLY.
Heaven bless you!—Madam, I can never thank you enough; you have made me happy in removing my greatest affliction.

Enter Selfish and Stanmore.

LADY BUSY.
I love to put lovers together: virtuous actions reward themselves.

STANMORE.
Young Maggot married? Give you joy, sir: your love to wit and beauty is at length rewarded.

YOUNG MAGGOT.
I will now keep company with none but the top wits and write plays, songs, and lampoons in defiance of the fop, my uncle.

LADY BUSY.
Not so fast: get him to settle first.

LADY CHEATLY.
I'll call my brother and the rest of my company to be witnesses to my happiness. (*Exit.*)

SELFISH.
Pretty mistress! You look today like a delicate picture, and Young Maggot your foil.

GARTRUDE.
I vow, you court me so genteelly I shall die to part with you: I cried in the church, that I did, and had like to have spoiled all.

SELFISH.
But will you promise me a meeting.

YOUNG MAGGOT.
Stand off: she's mine.

SELFISH.
You are to have her ever after; methinks you should allow her one day to take leave of her friends.

Enter Lady Cheatly, Lump, Maggot, Prig, etc.

YOUNG MAGGOT.
Uncle, your unkindness has made me look about me, and Heaven has blest my wit and poetry with a rich wife here, Mrs. Gartrude: I won her by 'em.

MAGGOT.
Aye boy, I know it and know her fortune as well as my own. Thou art a mettled lad, and I like thy humor* well. Give me a Phillis with ten thousand pounds, I could sing one of thy own songs myself, I am so taken with this match.

YOUNG MAGGOT.
I hope then you will settle your estate, as you always promised, if I married to your liking.

MAGGOT.
If I have no children by my dear wife, her mother here.

PRIG.
Lady Cheatly your wife! She has promised me marriage.

MAGGOT.
Whate'er she has promised you, she has performed marriage with me this morning. Be gone, rook, they stay for thee at the twelve-penny ordinary.

PRIG.
What say you, madam?

LADY CHEATLY.
'Tis very true.

PRIG.
Then you are very false.

MAGGOT.
As your dice. Gamester, I'll hold you cockpit lay, ten pound to a crown, she's bone of my bone and flesh of my flesh.

LADY CHEATLY.
This is the gentleman I'll live and die with.

PRIG.
Death and hell! I'll declare all I know.

LADY CHEATLY. (*Aside.*)
You will declare yourself a perjured knave if you do. Hark here.

MAGGOT.
What do they whisper for?

LADY CHEATLY.
All the steward says is true: I am worth little or nothing; my whole fortune a cheat; this old

gentleman I chose because he is governable and loves business, of which my broken fortune will give him enough.

PRIG.

What a crossbite* have I 'scaped? This sham was well carried on, madam. Did you hear, old fool?

MAGGOT.

'Ounds!* I am cheated, undone, and my nephew ruined and married to a beggar.

YOUNG MAGGOT.

I must even write hard for the playhouse. I may get the reversion of the Poet Laureate's place. I thought, uncle, you had known every foot of her estate.

PRIG.

Well, I'll go to Newmarket and never have to do with a two-legged jade more. I shall rook, and go to twelve, let what will come on't.

MAGGOT.

Since she has no fortune, I shall have no business neither.

YOUNG MAGGOT.

None but that which I am afraid you can't do, uncle.

MAGGOT.

Is this a time for wit, you rascal, when we are both undone.

He beats Young Maggot's perriwig off; from under it drop several copies of verses.

STANMORE.

A muss, a muss. A copy of verses upon a flea, presented to his mistress in a gold chain. [*Reads.*]

"Oh happy Flea! that mayst both kiss and bite,
Like lovers in their height of appetite,
  Her neck so white.
Pretty black alderman, in golden chain,
Who suck'st her blood yet putt'st her to no pain,
  Whil'st I in vain."[65]

MAGGOT.

What would become of the writing coxcombs, if it were not for reading ones? I'll hear no more.

LADY CHEATLY.

If you will go on and maintain what I have done, I shall have a good estate yet, though it belongs of right to other people.

MAGGOT.

Right? 'Tis no matter for right: I'll show 'em law.

THEODOSIA.

The plague of marriage rages in this house; let us fly from the infection.

CARLOS.

I am so far gone, 'tis to no purpose to remove. Well, if you continue to be so unkind, you will ruin my soul, body, and estate.

THEODOSIA.

How so?

CARLOS.

Why, I can never marry any other, and in despair of you, I shall turn the most debauched whoring rogue, 'twould grieve your heart to see it. I shall never be able to sleep without my three bottles and a fresh woman every night.

ISABELLA.

'Tis an act of charity to redeem him.

THEODOSIA.

The Devil seldom loses anything by matrimony; they most commonly grow worse for't.

CARLOS.

I will lead a solid, sober, husbandly life, if you will marry me; if not, whoring and drinking will ensue.

ISABELLA.

Nay, now I must judge against you: you have lost your wager, and you must pay it; you have confessed to me you loved him infinitely.

THEODOSIA.

Believe her not, I deny it.

CARLOS.

Though I distrust myself, I must believe my fair judge: I will have a canonical bom-baily[66] and arrest you upon execution.

THEODOSIA.

I will have a month's time. You shall be so long a probationer before you enter in the order.

---

65 "Oh … vain."] Maggot's poem invites comparison with John Donne's "The Flea," which would have been regarded as false wit by most Restoration poets.

66 canonical bom-baily] bumbailiff, a bailiff of the lowest kind, one employed in arrests (*OED*), here an officer of the ecclesiastical court, which would enforce the wager through marriage.

CARLOS.

In hope of your good nature, I will press no farther at this time.—Now, you that have reached at your Inn of Matrimony will pray for us travelers upon the road.

STANMORE.

So, gentlemen, we have lost ye: ye are not men of this world. Now make much of your matrimonial bonds; I am glad I have done my business without 'em.

SELFISH.

Ladies are so kind to me, I need never marry one for the matter. Well, I will go home and put on a very delicate, neat, convenient suit to dance with the brides in here.

LUMP.

I give you all joy. You see, sister, how things prosper when godly men are the instruments. I say to all, to all of you I say,
Be godly, observe method, and be wise;

CARLOS.

Most excellent means to cover cheats and lies.

[Exeunt.]

FINIS.

Textual Notes

[a] Copytext is the 1679 first quarto (Q). The quarto of 1689 is in fact the 1679 printing with a new title page etc. The 1693 *Works* of Shadwell are separate printings of plays bound together, *A True Widow* being the "1689" quarto. In 1720 an entirely new edition appeared in *The Works of Thomas Shadwell, Esq.* (W). Shadwell's son John wrote a dedication for the four volume set to George I and may have exercised some editorial control, perhaps working from earlier editions with corrections marked by his father.

In 1903 George Saintsbury edited a collection of four of Shadwell's plays including *A True Widow*; the copy text is W and Saintsbury has introduced no new material, nor are there any useful notes. Montague Summers' edition of Shadwell's complete works in 1927 is of interest for the lengthy introduction to the collection as a whole and Summers' quirky notes. His text, however, is unreliable; although it claims to be derived from Q with few changes, it differs in numerous places.

Contrary to accepted editorial practice, I have adopted numerous readings and a great many punctuation changes from the posthumous W. First, Shadwell complained in a note to Q about numerous errors in the text, particularly in the third and fourth acts, and W corrects the errors that Shadwell specifically pointed out, as well as other obvious misprints. Second, the punctuation of W is closer to modern usage, particularly in the use of commas.

[b] Theodosia ... Carlos] W; *om.* Q

[c] near] W; ne're Q

[d] they are there] W; they there Q

[e] fund] W; fond Q

[f] overset] W; over-see Q

[g] hate] W; have Q

[h] by] W; in Q

[i] fifty pound] W; five shilling Q

[j] infamous] W; in favour Q

[k] a wit] W; *om.* Q

[l] me] W; it Q

[m] YOUNG MAGGOT] Q, W (though the line may be more suitable for Prig)

[n] your] W; our Q

[o] a] W; *om.* Q

[p] will forswear] W; will not forswear Q

[q] of a] W; *om.* Q

[r] thee] the Q; she W, Summers

Venice Preserved; or, A Plot Discovered[a]

by Thomas Otway (1652-1685)

edited by Jessica Munns

Venice Preserved was first performed at the Duke's playhouse in February 1682. The Whig political ascendancy of the Exclusion Crisis had been broken by Charles II's dissolution of the Parliament he called in Oxford in March 1681. This event was swiftly followed by the arrest of the earl of Shaftesbury. *Venice Preserved*, probably written and certainly performed during the time of the "Tory revenge," seems to have been taken by its first audiences as a triumphant Tory play. And Otway's dedication to Louise Kéroualle, the duchess of Portsmouth and Charles II's chief mistress at the time, and his prologue and epilogue (included below) are certainly royalist. However, the play's political sympathies are notoriously unclear.

Set in the Republic of Venice, a state much admired by Whig ideologues and detested by Tories, the play depicts a conspiracy against the Senate. Were the conspiracy royalist, or were the senators noble, a clear political reading could emerge, either condemning or endorsing republicanism, or endorsing or condemning political revolt. However, the Senate and conspiracy are equally morally and politically bankrupt. Neither of the groups can be admired, and their conflict is acted out with both savage and comic intensity. Otway intensifies the sense of equality between the two groups and constantly undercuts his tragic materials with scenes of perverse comedy. Belvidera pleads with her harsh father for the lives of the conspirators, and in the scene immediately following the courtesan Aquilina similarly pleads with the perverse senator, Antonio, while he lies at her feet begging her to kick him. Politics in general emerge as an absurd, degrading, and corrupting activity.

Apart from contemporary politics, Otway's main source was a novella by César Vischard, l'abbé de Saint Réal, *La Conjuration des Espagnols contre la République de Vénise* (1674), translated into English as *A Conspiracy of the Spaniards Against the State of Venice* in 1675 and reissued in 1679. Saint Réal's narrative is also ambiguous, depicting the Senate as corrupt and the conspirators as debased yet touched by moments of nobility. Otway drew on Saint Réal's material, collapsing the timescale and adding in the characters of Belvidera, the sensual wife of Jaffeir, and the perverse senator Antonio. He greatly expanded the role of Aquilina, and the famous "Nicky Nacky" scenes[1] between Aquilina and Antonio are all his own.

Otway had the benefit of the great actors of the Duke's Company in their prime. Thomas Betterton and William Smith played Jaffeir and Pierre, respectively, and Elizabeth Barry played Belvidera. But the actors who perhaps stole the show were Tony Leigh as Antonio and Elizabeth Currer as Aquilina. And although the play entered the permanent repertoire and remained one of the half-dozen most popular tragedies in the eighteenth century, outside of Shakespeare's, it was only as a version sanitized by the excision of the Nicky-Nacky scenes.

Venice Preserved is an unusual form, a tragic political satire. In Jaffeir and Belvidera, Otway created passionate and confused lovers who are destroyed even as Venice is "preserved," but for whose benefit? The only surviving major characters are Antonio and Aquilina.

---

[1] Nicky Nacky scenes] these scenes were very popular with Tories, and an anonymous Whig "Satyr," c. 1682, complained they were more popular than Shadwell's comedies. In the eighteenth century the scenes came to be regarded as obscene (indeed, nicky-nacky was a slang term for female sexual organs) and pointless and were excised.

PROLOGUE

In these distracted times, when each man dreads
The bloody stratagems of busy heads;
When we have feared three years we know not what,[2]
Till witnesses begin to die o'th'rot,
What made our poet meddle with a plot?
Was't that he fancied, for the very sake
And name of plot, his trifling play might take?
For there's not in't one inch-board evidence,[3]
But 'tis, he says, to reason plain and sense,
And that he thinks a plausible defense.
Were truth by sense and reason to be tried,
Sure all our swearers might be laid aside:
No, of such tools our author has no need
To make his plot or make[b] his play succeed;
He of black bills has no prodigious tales[4]
Or Spanish pilgrims cast ashore in Wales;[5]
Here's not one murthered magistrate at least,
Kept rank like venison for a city feast,
Grown four days stiff, the better to prepare
And fit his pliant limbs to ride in chair:*[6]
Yet here's an army raised, though under ground,
But no man seen nor one commission found;
Here is a traitor too, that's very old,
Turbulent, subtle, mischievous and bold,
Bloody, revengeful, and to crown his part,
Loves fumbling with a wench with all his heart,[7]
Till after having many changes passed,
In spight of age (thanks Heaven) is hanged at last.
Next is a Senator that keeps a whore;[8]
In Venice none a higher office bore.
To lewdness every night the lecher ran;
Show me, all London, such another man,
Match him at Mother Creswold's if you can.[9]
Oh Poland, Poland! had it been thy lot
T'have heard in time of this Venetian plot,
Thou surely chosen hadst one king from thence
And honored them as thou hast England since.[10]

DRAMATIS PERSONAE

[MEN]

Duke of Venice.
Priuli, father to Belvidera, a senator.
Antonio, a fine speaker in the Senate.
Jaffeir.
Pierre.
Renault,
Bedamar,
Spinosa,
Theodore,
Eliot,
Revillido,
Durand,
Mezzana,
Bramveil,
Ternon,
Brabe,
[Retrossi,] conspirators.
The Council of Ten.
Officer.
Guards.
Friar.
Executioner and rabble.

---

[2] three years] from the Popish Plot through the Exclusion Crisis (1678-81)

[3] inch-board evidence] "to swear through an inch-board" is to "swear home and hard," presumably hard enough to go through a board an inch thick (*OED*)

[4] black bills ... tales] Oates's testimony included reference to raising an army in Ireland armed with black bills (q.v.).

[5] Spanish pilgrims ... Wales.] William Bedloe, a Popish Plot informer, claimed evidence of a plot to land Irish soldiers, disguised as Spanish pilgrims, in Wales.

[6] murthered magistrate ... chair] Sir Edmund Berry Godfrey, whose body, it was alleged, was removed to Somerset House in a sedan chair* and kept there for tfour days

[7] traitor ... all his heart] the character Renault (probably based on Anthony Ashley Cooper, first earl of Shaftesbury and leader of the movement to exclude James Stuart)

[8] Senator that keeps a whore] the character Antonio (perhaps also based on Shaftesbury, whose first name was Anthony; however, this was also the name of the famous comic actor who created the role, Anthony Leigh)

[9] Mother Creswold's] also spelled Creswell, a notorious London procuress

[10] Poland ... since] Poland had an elective monarchy in the seventeenth century, and Tory satires claimed that Shaftesbury had put himself forward for the election of 1675.

[Women]

Belvidera.
Aquilina.
Two women, attendants on Belvidera.
Two women, servants to Aquilina.

Venice Preserved; or, A Plot Discovered.

Act I.

Enter Priuli and Jaffeir.

PRIULI.
No more! I'll hear no more. Be gone and leave.
JAFFEIR.
Not hear me! By my sufferings but you shall!
My lord, my lord, I'm not that abject wretch
You think me. Patience! Where's the distance throws
Me back so far, but I may boldly speak
In right, though proud oppression will not hear me!
PRIULI.
Have you not wronged me?
JAFFEIR.
Could my nature e'er
Have brooked injustice or the doing wrongs,
I need not now thus low have bent myself
To gain a hearing from a cruel father!
Wronged you?
PRUILI.
Yes! wronged me, in the nicest* point:
The honor of my house. You have done me wrong.
You may remember (for I now will speak,
And urge its baseness) when you first came home
From travel with such hopes as made you looked on
By all men's eyes, a youth of expectation,
Pleased with your growing virtue, I received you,
Courted, and sought to raise you to your merits.
My house, my table, nay my fortune too,
My very self, was yours. You might have used me
To your best service. Like an open friend,
I treated, trusted you, and thought you mine,
When in requital of my best endeavors
You treacherously practiced to undo me,
Seduced the weakness of my age's darling,
My only child, and stole her from my bosom.
Oh Belvidera!
JAFFEIR.
'Tis to me you owe her,
Childless you had been else and in the grave,
Your name extinct nor no more Priuli heard of.
You may remember, scarce five years are past
Since in your brigantine you sailed to see
The Adriatic wedded by our Duke,[11]
And I was with you. Your unskillful pilot
Dashed us upon a rock, when to your boat
You made for safety, entered first yourself.
The affrighted Belvidera following next,
As she stood trembling on the vessel side,
Was by a wave washed off into the deep,
When instantly I plunged into the sea,
And buffeting the billows to her rescue,
Redeemed her life with half the loss of mine.
Like a rich conquest in one hand I bore her
And with the other dashed the saucy waves
That thronged and pressed to rob me of my prize.
I brought her, gave her to your despairing arms.
Indeed you thanked me, but a nobler gratitude
Rose in her soul: for from that hour she loved me,
Till for her life she paid me with herself.
PRIULI.
You stole her from me, like a thief you stole her,
At dead of night; that cursèd hour you chose
To rifle me of all my heart held dear.
May all your joys in her prove false like mine;
A sterile fortune and a barren bed
Attend you both; continual discord make
Your days and nights bitter and grievous; still*
May the hard hand of a vexatious need
Oppress and grind you till at last you find
The curse of disobedience all your portion.
JAFFEIR.
Half of your curse you have bestowed in vain:
Heav'n has already crowned our faithful loves
With a young boy, sweet as his mother's beauty.
May he live to prove more gentle than his grandsire
And happier than his father!

---

[11] Adriatic wedded … Duke] On Ascension Day, August 15, the Doge would cast a ring into the Adriatic Sea to signify the marriage of Venice to the source of its wealth and maritime empire.

PRIULI.

Rather live
To bait thee for his bread and din your ears
With hungry cries whilst his unhappy mother
Sits down and weeps in bitterness of want.*

JAFFEIR.

You talk as if it would please you.

PRIULI.

'Twould, by Heav'n.
Once she was dear indeed: the drops that fell
From my sad heart when she forgot her duty,
The fountain of my life was not so precious.
But she is gone, and if I am a man,
I will forget her.

JAFFEIR.

Would I were in my grave.

PRIULI.

And she too with thee.
For living here, you're but my cursed remembrancers
I once was happy.

JAFFEIR.

You use me thus because you know my soul
Is fond of Belvidera. You perceive
My life feeds on her; therefore, thus you treat me.
Oh! could my soul ever have known satiety.
Were I that thief, the doer of such wrongs
As you upbraid me with, what hinders me
But I might send her back to you with contumely
And court my fortune where she would be kinder!

PRIULI.

You dare not do't.

JAFFEIR.

Indeed my lord, I dare not.
My heart that awes me is too much my master.
Three years are past since first our vows were plighted,
During which time, the world must bear me witness,
I have treated Belvidera like your daughter,
The daughter of a senator of Venice:
Distinction, place, attendance, and observance,
Due to her birth, she always has commanded.
Out of my little fortune I have done this
Because (though hopeless e'er to win your nature)
The world might see I loved her for herself,
Not as the heiress of the great Priuli—

PRIULI.

No more!

JAFFEIR.

Yes! all, and then adieu forever.
There's not a wretch that lives on common charity
But's happier than me, for I have known
The luscious sweets of plenty, every night
Have slept with soft content about my head
And never waked but to a joyful morning,
Yet now must fall like a full ear of corn,
Whose blossom 'scaped yet's withered in the ripening.

PRIULI.

Home and be humble; study to retrench;
Discharge the lazy vermin of thy hall,
Those pageants of thy folly;
Reduce the glittering trappings of thy wife
To humble weeds, fit for thy little state;
Then to some suburb cottage both retire;
Drudge to feed loathsome life; get brats; and starve—
Home, home, I say. (*Exit.*)

JAFFEIR.

Yes, if my heart would let me—
This proud, this swelling heart—home I would go,
But that my doors are hateful to my eyes,
Filled and dammed up with gaping creditors,
Watchful as fowlers when their game will spring.
I have now not fifty ducats in the world,
Yet still I am in love and pleased with ruin.
Oh Belvidera! oh she's my wife,
And we will bear our wayward fate together
But ne'er know comfort more.

Enter Pierre.

PIERRE.

My friend, good morrow!
How fares the honest partner of my heart?
What, melancholy! not a word to spare me?

JAFFEIR.

I'm thinking, Pierre, how that damned starving quality
Called honesty got footing in the world.

PIERRE.

Why, pow'rful villainy first set it up
For its own ease and safety. Honest men

Are the soft, easy cushions on which knaves
Repose and fatten. Were all mankind villains,
They'd starve each other; lawyers would want*
practice,
Cut-throats rewards; each man would kill his brother
Himself, none would be paid or hanged for murder.
Honesty was a cheat invented first
To bind the hands of bold deserving rogues
That fools and cowards might sit safe in power
And lord it uncontrolled above their betters.

JAFFEIR.
Then honesty is but a notion.

PIERRE.
Nothing else:
Like wit, much talked of, not to be defined;
He that pretends to most, too, has least share in't;
'Tis a ragged virtue. Honesty! No more on't.

JAFFEIR.
Sure thou art honest?

PIERRE.
So indeed men think me.
But they're mistaken, Jaffeir: I am a rogue
As well as they—
A fine, gay, bold-faced villain,[12] as thou seest me.
'Tis true, I pay my debts when they're contracted;
I steal from no man, would not cut a throat
To gain admission to a great man's purse
Or a whore's bed; I'd not betray my friend
To get his place or fortune; I scorn to flatter
A blown-up fool above me or crush the wretch
beneath me,
Yet Jaffeir, for all this, I am a villain!

JAFFEIR.
A villain?

PIERRE.
Yes, a most notorious villain:
To see the suff'rings of my fellow creatures
And own myself a man; to see our senators
Cheat the deluded people with a show
Of liberty which yet they ne'er must taste of.
They say, by them our hands are free from fetters,
Yet whom they please they lay in basest bonds,

[12] villain] Throughout this scene, Pierre plays off both meanings of *villain*, base-born villager (even slave) and scoundrel (his *noblesse* should *oblige*).

Bring whom they please to infamy and sorrow,
Drive us like wracks down the rough tide of power
Whilst no hold's left to save us from destruction.
All that bear this are villains, and I one,
Not to rouse up at the great call of Nature
And check the growth of these domestic spoilers
That make us slaves and tell[c] us 'tis our charter.

JAFFEIR.
Oh Aquilina! Friend, to lose such beauty,
The dearest purchase of thy noble labors:
She was thy right by conquest, as by love.

PIERRE.
Oh Jaffeir! I'd so fixed my heart upon her,
That wheresoe'er I framed a scheme of life
For time to come, she was my only joy
With which I wished to sweeten future cares.
I fancied pleasures, none but one that loves
And dotes as I did can imagine like 'em.
When in the extremity of all these hopes,
In the most charming hour of expectation,
Then when our eager wishes soar the highest,
Ready to stoop and grasp the lovely game,
A haggard owl, a worthless kite of prey,
With his foul wings sailed in and spoiled my quarry.

JAFFEIR.
I know the wretch and scorn him as thou hat'st
him.

PIERRE.
Curse on the common good that's so protected,
Where every slave that heaps up wealth enough
To do much wrong becomes a lord of right.
I, who believed no ill could e'er come near me,
Found in embraces of my Aquilina
A wretched old but itching senator,
A wealthy fool that had bought out my title,
A rogue that uses beauty like a lambskin,
Barely to keep him warm. That filthy cuckoo too
Was in my absence crept into my nest
And spoiling all my brood of noble pleasure.

JAFFEIR.
Didst thou not chase him thence?

PIERRE.
I did and drove
The rank old bearded hirco[13] stinking home.

[13] hirco] he-goat

The matter was complained of in the Senate,
I summoned to appear and censured basely
For violating something they call privilege—
This was the recompense of my service.
Would I'd been rather beaten by a coward!
A soldier's mistress, Jaffeir, 's his religion.
When that's profaned, all other ties are broken,
That even dissolves all former bonds of service,
And from that hour I think my self as free
To be the foe as e'er the friend of Venice—
Nay, dear Revenge, whene'er thou call'st, I am
ready.

JAFFEIR.
I think no safety can be here for virtue
And grieve, my friend, as much as thou to live
In such a wretched state as this of Venice
Where all agree to 'spoil the public good
And villains fatten with the brave man's labors.

PIERRE.
We have neither safety, unity, nor peace,
For the foundation's lost of common good;
Justice is lame as well as blind amongst us;
The laws (corrupted to their ends that make 'em)
Serve but for instruments of some new tyranny
That every day starts up to enslave us deeper.
Now could this glorious cause but find out friends
To do it right! oh Jaffeir ! then might'st thou
Not wear these seals of woe upon thy face;[14]
The proud Priuli should be taught humanity
And learn to value such a son as thou art.
I dare not speak! But my heart bleeds this
moment!

JAFFEIR.
Curst be the cause, though I thy friend be part on't.
Let me partake the troubles of thy bosom,
For I am used to misery and perhaps
May find a way to sweeten't to thy spirit.

PIERRE.
Too soon it will reach thy knowledge—

JAFFEIR.
Then from thee
Let it proceed. There's virtue in thy friendship
Would make the saddest tale of sorrow pleasing,
Strengthen my constancy, and welcome ruin.

PIERRE.
Then, thou art ruined!

JAFFEIR.
That I long since knew,
I and ill fortune have been long acquaintance.

PIERRE.
I passed this very moment by thy doors
And found them guarded by a troop of villains;
The sons of public rapine were destroying.
They told me, by the sentence of the law,
They had commission to seize all thy fortune,
Nay more, Priuli's cruel hand hath signed it.
Here stood a ruffian with a horrid face
Lording it o'er a pile of massy plate*
Tumbled into a heap for public sale;
There was another, making villainous* jests
At thy undoing. He had ta'en possession
Of all thy ancient, most domestic ornaments:
Rich hangings, intermixed and wrought with gold;
The very bed which on thy wedding night
Received thee to the arms of Belvidera,
The scene of all thy joys, was violated
By the coarse hands of filthy dungeon villains
And thrown amongst the common lumber.*

JAFFEIR.
Now thanks, Heav'n—

PIERRE.
Thank Heav'n! For what?

JAFFEIR.
That I am not worth a ducat.

PIERRE.
Curse thy dull stars and the worse fate of Venice,
Where brothers, friends, and fathers, all are false;
Where there's no trust, no truth; where innocence
Stoops under vile oppression, and vice lords it.
Hadst thou but seen, as I did, how at last
Thy beauteous Belvidera, like a wretch
That's doomed to banishment, came weeping
forth,
Shining through tears, like April suns in showers
That labor to o'ercome the cloud that loads 'em,
Whilst two young virgins, on whose arms she
leaned,
Kindly looked up and at her grief grew sad,
As if they catched the sorrows that fell from her.
Even the lewd rabble that were gathered round

[14] seals of woe] as in the imprint of a signet; marks or signs

To see the sight stood mute when they beheld her,
Governed their roaring throats, and grumbled pity.
I could have hugged the greasy rogues; they pleased me.

JAFFEIR.
I thank thee for this story from my soul,
Since now I know the worst that can befall me.
Ah Pierre! I have a heart that could have born
The roughest wrong my fortune could have done me,
But when I think what Belvidera feels,
The bitterness her tender spirit tastes of,
I own myself a coward. Bear my weakness,
If, throwing thus my arms about thy neck,
I play the boy and blubber in thy bosom.
Oh! I shall drown thee with my sorrows!

PIERRE.
Burn!
First burn and level Venice to thy ruin!
What, starve like beggars' brats in frosty weather
Under a hedge and whine our selves to death!
Thou or thy cause shall never want* assistance
Whilst I have blood or fortune fit to serve thee.
Command my heart: thou art every way its master.

JAFFEIR.
No: there's a secret pride in bravely dying.

PIERRE.
Rats die in holes and corners; dogs run mad;
Man knows a braver remedy for sorrow:
Revenge, the attribute of gods! They stamped it
With their great image on our natures. Die?
Consider well the cause that calls upon thee,
And if thou art base enough, die then. Remember,
Thy Belvidera suffers. Belvidera!
Die? Damn first! What, be decently interred
In a churchyard and mingle thy brave* dust
With stinking rogues that rot in dirty winding sheets,
Surfeit-slain fools, the common dung o'th soil?

JAFFEIR.
Oh!

PIERRE.
Well said, out with't, swear a little—

JAFFEIR.
Swear!
By sea and air! by earth, by heaven and hell,
I will revenge my Belvidera's tears!
Hark thee, my friend: Priuli—is—a senator!

PIERRE.
A dog!

JAFFEIR.
Agreed.

PIERRE.
Shoot him.

JAFFEIR.
With all my heart.
No more. Where shall we meet at night?

PIERRE.
I'll tell thee:
On the Rialto every night at twelve
I take my evening's walk of meditation.
There we two will meet and talk of precious* Mischief.

JAFFEIR.
Farewell.

PIERRE.
At twelve.

JAFFEIR.
At any hour, my plagues
Will keep me waking.

Exit Pierre.

Tell me why, good Heav'n,
Thou mad'st me what I am, with all the spirit,
Aspiring thoughts, and elegant desires
That fill the happiest man? Ah rather, why
Did'st thou not form me sordid as my fate,
Base minded, dull, and fit to carry burdens?
Why have I sense to know the curse that's on me?
Is this just dealing, Nature?—Belvidera!

Enter Belvidera [with two women attending her].

Poor Belvidera!

BELVIDERA.
Lead me, lead me, my virgins!
To that kind voice.—My lord, my love, my refuge!
Happy my eyes when they behold thy face.
My heavy heart will leave its doleful beating
At sight of thee and bound with sprightful joys.
Oh smile, as when our loves were in their spring,
And cheer my fainting soul.

JAFFEIR.
As when our loves
Were in their spring? Has then my fortune changed?
Art thou not Belvidera, still the same,
Kind, good, and tender, as my arms first found thee?
If thou art altered, where shall I have harbor?
Where ease my loaded heart? Oh! where complain?

BELVIDERA.
Does this appear like change or love decaying
When thus I throw my self into thy bosom
With all the resolution of a strong truth?
Beats not my heart as 'twould alarm thine
To a new charge of bliss? I joy more in thee
Than did thy mother when she hugged thee first
And blessed the gods for all her travail past.

JAFFEIR.
Can there in woman be such glorious faith?
Sure all ill stories of thy sex are false.
Oh woman! lovely woman! Nature made thee
To temper man: we had been brutes without you;
Angels are painted fair to look like you;
There's in you all that we believe of Heav'n,
Amazing brightness, purity and truth,
Eternal joy and everlasting love.

BELVIDERA.
If love be treasure, we'll be wondrous rich:
I have so much, my heart will surely break with't.
Vow's cannot express it when I would declare
How great's my joy. I am dumb with the big thought:
I swell and sigh and labor with my longing.
Oh lead me to some desert wide and wild,
Barren as our misfortunes, where my soul
May have its vent, where I may tell aloud
To the high heavens and every list'ning planet
With what a boundless stock my bosom's fraught;
Where I may throw my eager arms about thee,
Give loose to love with kisses, kindling joy,
And let off all the fire that's in my heart.

JAFFEIR.
Oh Belvidera! double I am a beggar,
Undone by fortune and in debt to thee.
Want!* worldly want! that hungry, meager fiend
Is at my heels and chases me in view.
Canst thou bear cold and hunger? Can these limbs,
Framed for the tender offices of love,
Endure the bitter gripes of smarting poverty?
When banished by our miseries abroad
(As suddenly we shall be) to seek out
(In some far climate where our names are strangers)
For charitable succor, wilt thou then,
When in a bed of straw we shrink together
And the bleak winds shall whistle round our heads,
Wilt thou then talk thus to me? Wilt thou then
Hush my cares thus and shelter me with love?

BELVIDERA.
Oh I will love thee, even in madness love thee:
Though my distracted senses should forsake me,
I'd find some intervals when my poor heart
Should 'suage itself and be let loose to thine.
Though the bare earth be all our resting place,
Its roots our food, some cleft our habitation,
I'll make this arm a pillow for thy head,
As thou sighing ly'st and swelled with sorrow,
Creep to thy bosom, pour the balm of love
Into thy soul, and kiss thee to thy rest,
Then praise our God, and watch thee till the morning.

JAFFEIR.
Hear this, you heavens, and wonder how you made her!
Reign, reign, ye monarchs that divide the world.
Busy rebellion ne'er will let you know
Tranquility and happiness like mine.
Like gaudy ships, th'obsequious billows fall
And rise again to lift you in your pride;
They wait but for a storm and then devour you.
I, in my private bark, already wrecked,
Like a poor merchant driven on unknown land,
That had by chance packed up his choicest treasure
In one dear casket and saved only that,
Since I must wander further on the shore,
Thus hug my little but my precious store,
Resolved to scorn and trust my fate no more.

Exeunt.

Act II, [scene i. Aquilina's house.]

Enter Pierre and Aquilina.

AQUILINA.
By all thy wrongs, thou art dearer to my arms
Than all the wealth of Venice. Prithee stay,
And let us love tonight.

PIERRE.
No. There's fool,
There's fool about thee. When a woman sells
Her flesh to fools, her beauty's lost to me.
They leave a taint, a sully where they've passed;
There's such a baneful quality about 'em
Even spoils complexions with their own nauseousness;
They infect all they touch. I cannot think
Of tasting anything a fool has palled.

AQUILINA.
I loathe and scorn that fool thou mean'st, as much
Or more than thou canst, but the beast has gold
That makes him necessary, power too,
To qualify my character and poise me
Equal with peevish virtue that beholds
My liberty with envy: in their hearts
Are loose as I am, but an ugly power
Sits in their faces and frights pleasures from 'em.

PIERRE.
Much good may't do you, madam, with your senator.

AQUILINA.
My senator! Why, canst thou think that wretch
E'er filled thy Aquilina's arms with pleasure!
Think'st thou, because I sometimes give him leave
To foil himself at what he is unfit for;
Because I force myself to endure and suffer him,
Think'st thou I love him? No, by all the joys
Thou ever gav'st me, his presence is my penance;
The worst thing an old man can be's a lover,
A mere *memento mori* to poor woman.
I never lay by his decrepit side,
But all that night I pondered on my grave.

PIERRE.
Would he were well sent thither.

AQUILINA.
That's my wish too,
For then, my Pierre, I might have cause with pleasure
To play the hypocrite. Oh! how I could weep
Over the dying dotard and kiss him too
In hopes to smother him quite. Then, when the time
Was come to pay my sorrows at his funeral,
For he has already made me heir to treasures
Would make me out-act a real widow's whining,
How could I frame my face to fit my mourning!
With wringing hands attend him to his grave;
Fall swooning on his hearse; take mad possession
Even of the dismal vault where he lay buried;
There like the Ephesian matron[15] dwell, till thou,
My lovely soldier, comest to my deliverance;
Then throwing up my veil, with open arms
And laughing eyes run to new dawning joy.

PIERRE.
No more! I have friends to meet me here tonight
And must be private. As you prize my friendship,
Keep up your coxcomb. Let him not pry nor listen
Nor fisk[16] about the house as I have seen him
Like a tame, mumping* squirrel with a bell on;
Curs will be abroad to bite him, if you do.

AQUILINA.
What friends to meet? may I not be your council?

PIERRE.
How! A woman ask questions out of bed?
Go to your senator, ask him what passes
Amongst his brethren, he'll hide nothing from you,
But pump me not for politics. No more!
Give order that whoever in my name
Comes here receive admittance. So good night.

AQUILINA.
Must we ne'er meet again! Embrace no more!
Is love so soon and utterly forgotten!

PIERRE.
As you henceforward treat your fool, I'll think on't. [*Exit.*]

AQUILINA.
Cursed be all fools and doubly cursed myself,
The worst of fools. I die if he forsakes me.
And now to keep him, Heaven or Hell instruct me.

Exit.

---

15 Ephesian matron] In the *Satyricon* of Petronius Arbiter, an Ephesian matron mourned her husband's death until seduced in his very mausoleum by a handsome soldier.

16 fisk] to jump about

Scene [ii.] The Rialto.

Enter Jaffeir.

JAFFEIR.
I am here, and thus, the shades of night around me,
I look as if all hell were in my heart
And I in hell. Nay, surely 'tis so with me,
For every step I tread, methinks some fiend
Knocks at my breast and bids it not be quiet.
I've heard how desperate wretches, like myself,
Have wandered out at this dead time of night
To meet the Foe of mankind in his walk.
Sure I am so curst that, though of Heav'n forsaken,
No minister of darkness cares to tempt me.
Hell! Hell! why sleepest thou?

Enter Pierre.

PIERRE.
Sure I have stayed too long:
The clock has struck, and I may lose my proselyte.
—Speak, who goes there?

JAFFEIR.
A dog that comes to howl
At yonder moon. What's he that asks the question?

PIERRE.
A friend to dogs, for they are honest creatures
And ne'er betray their masters, never fawn
On any that they love not. Well met, friend.
Jaffeir!

JAFFEIR.
The same. Oh Pierre! Thou art come in season,
I was just going to pray.

PIERRE.
Ah that's mechanic,
Priests make a trade on't and yet starve by it too.
No praying, it spoils business, and time's precious.
Where's Belvidera?

JAFFEIR.
For a day or two
I've lodged her privately, till I see farther
What Fortune will do with me. Prithee friend,
If thou wouldst have me fit to hear good counsel,
Speak not of Belvidera—

PIERRE.
Speak not of her?

JAFFEIR.
Oh no!

PIERRE.
Nor name her? May be I wish her well.

JAFFEIR.
Who well?

PIERRE.
Thy wife, thy lovely Belvidera,
I hope a man may wish his friend's wife well
And no harm done!

JAFFEIR.
Y'are merry, Pierre!

PIERRE.
I am so.
Thou shalt smile too, and Belvidera smile,
We'll all rejoice. Here's something to buy pins;
Marriage is chargeable.

JAFFEIR.
I but half wished
To see the Devil, and he's here already.
Well!
What must this buy, rebellion, murder, treason?
Tell me which way I must be damned for this.

PIERRE.
When last we parted, we had no qualms like these
But entertained each other's thoughts like men
Whose souls were well acquainted. Is the world
Reformed since our last meeting? What new miracles
Have happened? Has Priuli's heart relented?
Can he be honest?

JAFFEIR.
Kind Heav'n! Let heavy curses
Gall his old age; cramps, aches, rack his bones;
And bitterest disquiet wring his heart.
Oh let him live till life become his burden!
Let him groan under't long, linger an age
In the worst agonies and pangs of death,
And find its ease but late.

PIERRE.
Nay, couldst thou not
As well, my friend, have stretched the curse to all
The Senate round, as to one single villain?

JAFFEIR.
But curses stick not. Could I kill with cursing,
By Heav'n I know not thirty heads in Venice
Should not be blasted. Senators should rot

Like dogs on dunghills, but their wives and daughters
Die of their own diseases. Oh for a curse
To kill with!

PIERRE.
Daggers, daggers are much better!

JAFFEIR.
Hah!

PIERRE.
Daggers.

JAFFEIR.
But where are they?

PIERRE.
Oh, a thousand
May be disposed in honest hands in Venice.

JAFFEIR.
Thou talk'st in clouds.

PIERRE.
But yet a heart half wronged
As thine has been would find the meaning, Jaffeir.

JAFFEIR.
A thousand daggers, all in honest hands,
And have not I a friend will stick one here?

PIERRE.
Yes, if I thought thou wert not to be cherished
To a nobler purpose, I'd be that friend.
But thou hast better friends, friends whom thy wrongs
Have made thy friends friends worthy to be called so.
I'll trust thee with a secret: there are spirits
This hour at work. But as thou art a man,
Whom I have picked and chosen from the world,
Swear that thou wilt be true to what I utter,
And when I have told thee that which only gods
And men like gods are privy to, then swear
No chance or change shall wrest it from thy bosom.

JAFFEIR.
When thou wouldst bind me, is there need of oaths?
(Greensickness girls lose maidenheads with such counters.)
For thou art so near my heart that thou mayst see
Its bottom, sound its strength and firmness to thee:
Is coward, fool, or villain in my face?
If I seem none of these, I dare believe
Thou wouldst not use me in a little cause,
For I am fit for honor's toughest task
Nor ever yet found fooling was my province;
And for a villainous, inglorious enterprise,
I know thy heart so well, I dare lay mine
Before thee, set it to what point thou wilt.

PIERRE.
Nay, it's a cause thou wilt be fond of, Jaffeir.
For it is founded on the noblest basis:
Our liberties, our natural inheritance.
There's no religion, no hypocrisy in't;
We'll do the business and ne'er fast and pray for't,
Openly act a deed the world shall gaze
With wonder at and envy when it is done.

JAFFEIR.
For liberty!

PIERRE.
For liberty my friend.
Thou shalt be freed from base Priuli's tyranny,
And thy sequestered fortunes healed again.
I shall be freed from opprobrious wrongs
That press me now and bend my spirit downward.
All Venice free and every growing merit
Succeed to its just right. Fools shall be pulled
From wisdom's seat; those baleful unclean birds,
Those lazy owls,* who (perched near Fortune's top)
Sit only watchful with their heavy wings
To cuff down new-fledged virtues that would rise
To nobler heights and make the grove harmonious.

JAFFEIR.
What can I do?

PIERRE.
Canst thou not kill a senator?

JAFFEIR.
Were there one wise or honest, I could kill him
For herding with that nest of fools and knaves.
By all my wrongs, thou talk'st as if revenge
Were to be had, and that brave* story warms me.

PIERRE.
Swear then!

JAFFEIR.
I do, by all those glittering stars
And yond great ruling planet of the night!
By all good Pow'rs above and ill below!
By love and friendship, dearer than my life!
No pow'r or death shall make me false to thee.

PIERRE.
Here we embrace, and I'll unlock my heart.
A council's held hard by, where the destruction

Of this great empire's hatching. There I'll lead thee!
But be a man, for thou art to mix with men
Fit to disturb the peace of all the world
And rule it when it's wildest—

JAFFEIR.
I give thee thanks
For this kind warning. Yes, I will be a man
And charge thee, Pierre, whene'er thou seest my fears
Betray me less, to rip this heart of mine
Out of my breast and show it for a coward's.
Come, let's be gone, for from this hour I chase
All little thoughts, all tender, human follies
Out of my bosom. Vengeance shall have room.
Revenge!

PIERRE.
And liberty!

JAFFEIR.
Revenge! Revenge!

Exeunt.

Scene [iii.] Aquilina's house, the Greek Courtesan.

Enter Renault.

RENAULT.
Why was my choice ambition, the worst[d] ground
A wretch can build on? It's indeed at distance
A good prospect, tempting to the view;
The height delights us, and the mountain top
Looks beautiful because it's nigh to heav'n,
But we ne'er think how sandy's the foundation,
What storm will batter and what tempest shake us!
—Who's there?

Enter Spinosa.

SPINOSA.
Renault, good morrow! for by this time
I think the scale of night has turned the balance
And weighs up morning. Has the clock struck twelve?

RENAULT.
Yes, clocks will go as they are set. But man,
Irregular man's ne'er constant, never certain.
I've spent at least three precious hours of darkness
In waiting dull attendance; 'tis the curse
Of diligent virtue to be mixed, like mine,
With giddy tempers, souls but half resolved.

SPINOSA.
Hell seize that soul amongst us it can frighten.

RENAULT.
What's then the cause that I am here alone?
Why are we not together?

Enter Eliot.

Oh sir, welcome!
You are an Englishman: when treason's hatching
One might have thought you'd not have been behindhand.
In what whore's lap have you been lolling?
Give but an Englishman his whore and ease,
Beef and sea-coal fire,[17] he's yours forever.

ELIOT.
Frenchman, you are saucy.

RENAULT.
How!

Enter Bedamore the Ambassador, Theodore, Brainveil, Durand, Brabe, Revellido, Mezzana, Ternon, Retrosi, Conspirators.

BEDAMORE.
At difference? Fie,
Is this a time for quarrels?* Thieves and rogues
Fall out and brawl. Should men of your high calling,
Men separated by the choice of Providence
From the gross heap of mankind and set here
In this great assembly as in one great jewel
T'adorn the bravest purpose it e'er smiled on,
Should you like boys wrangle for trifles?

RENAULT.
Boys!

BEDAMORE.
Renault, thy hand!

RENAULT.
I thought I'd given my heart
Long since to every man that mingles here
But grieve to find it trusted with such tempers
That can't forgive my froward age its weakness.

BEDAMORE.
Eliot, thou once hadst virtue. I have seen

---

17 sea-coal fire] In the seventeenth century, mineral coal mined in the north of England (mostly in the Newcastle area) was transported to London along the west coast by ship.

Thy stubborn temper bend with godlike goodness
Not half thus courted: 'tis thy nation's glory
To hug the foe that offers brave* alliance.
Once more embrace, my friends—we'll all embrace—
United thus, we are the mighty engine
Must twist this rooted empire from its basis!
Totters it not already?

ELIOT.
Would it were tumbling.

BEDAMORE.
Nay it shall down; this night we seal its ruin.

Enter Pierre.

Oh Pierre! thou art welcome!
Come to my breast, for by its hopes thou look'st
Lovelily dreadful, and the fate of Venice
Seems on thy sword already. Oh my Mars!
The poets that first feigned a God of War
Sure prophesied of thee.

PIERRE.
Friends! was not Brutus
(I mean that Brutus who in open senate
Stabbed the first Caesar that usurped the world)
A gallant man?

RENAULT.
Yes, and Catiline too,
Though story wrong his fame: for he conspired
To prop the reeling glory of his country;
His cause was good.

BEDAMORE.
And ours as much above it
As Renault thou art superior to Cethegus[18]
Or Pierre to Cassius.

PIERRE.
Then to what we aim at
When do we start? Or must we talk forever?

BEDAMORE.
No Pierre, the deed's near birth: Fate seems to have set
The business up and given it to our care.
I hope there's not a heart nor hand amongst us
But is firm and ready.

ALL.
All! We'll die with Bedamore.

BEDAMORE.
Oh men,
Matchless as will your glory be hereafter.
The game is for a matchless prize, if won;
If lost, disgraceful ruin.

RENAULT.
What can lose it?
The public stock's a beggar; one Venetian
Trusts not another. Look into their stores
Of general safety: empty magazines,[19]
A tattered fleet, a murmuring unpaid army,
Bankrupt nobility, a harassed commonalty,
A factious, giddy, and divided Senate
Is all the strength of Venice. Let's destroy it.
Let's fill their magazines with arms to awe them,
Man out their fleet, and make their trade maintain it;
Let loose the murmuring army on their masters
To pay themselves with plunder; lop their nobles
To the base roots whence most of 'em first sprung;
Enslave the rout, whom smarting will make humble;
Turn out their droning Senate; and possess
That seat of empire which our souls were framed for.

PIERRE.
Ten thousand men are armèd at your nod,
Commanded all by leaders fit to guide
A battle for the freedom of the world.
This wretched state has starved them in its service,
And by your bounty quickened,* they're resolved
To serve your glory and revenge their own!
They've all their different quarters in this city,
Watch for th'alarm, and grumble 'tis so tardy.

BEDAMORE.
I doubt not, friend, but thy unwearied diligence
Has still* kept waking, and it shall have ease.
After this night it is resolved we meet
No more till Venice own us for her lords.

PIERRE.
How lovely the Adriatic whore,
Dressed in her flames, will shine! Devouring flames!
Such as shall burn her to the watery bottom
And hiss in her foundation.

[18] Cethegus] a member of the Catiline conspiracy

[19] magazines] buildings where ammunition is stored

BEDAMORE.

Now if any
Amongst us that owns this glorious cause
Have friends or interest he'd wish to save,
Let it be told. The general doom is sealed,
But I'd forgo the hopes of a world's empire
Rather than wound the bowels of my friend.

PIERRE.

I must confess you there have touched my weakness:
I have a friend, hear it, such a friend
My heart was ne'er shut to him. Nay, I'll tell you,
He knows the very business of this hour,
But he rejoices in the cause and loves it.
We've changed a vow to live and die together,
And he's at hand to ratify it here.

RENAULT.

How! All betrayed?

PIERRE.

No—I've dealt nobly with you;
I've brought my all into the public stock:
I had but one friend, and him I'll share amongst you!
Receive and cherish him, or if, when seen
And searched, you find him worthless, as my tongue
Has lodged this secret in his faithful breast,
To ease your fears I wear a dagger here
Shall rip it out again and give you rest.
—Come forth, thou only good I e'er could boast of.

Enter Jaffeir with a dagger.

BEDAMORE.

His presence bears the show of manly virtue.

JAFFEIR.

I know you'll wonder all that, thus uncalled,
I dare approach this place of fatal counsels.
But I am amongst you, and by Heaven it glads me,
To see so many virtues thus united
To restore justice and dethrone oppression.
Command this sword, if you would have it quiet,
Into this breast. But if you think it worthy
To cut the throats of reverend rogues in robes,
Send me into the cursed assembled Senate;
It shrinks not, though I meet a father there.
Would you behold this city flaming? Here's
A hand shall bear a lighted torch at noon
To the Arsenal[20] and set its gates on fire.

RENAULT.

You talk this well, sir.

JAFFEIR.

Nay, by Heav'n I'll do this.
Come, come, I read distrust in all your faces.
You fear me a villain, and indeed it's odd
To hear a stranger talk thus at first meeting
Of matters that have been so well debated.
But I come ripe with wrongs as you with counsels.
I hate this Senate, am a foe to Venice,
A friend to none but men resolved like me
To push on mischief. Oh did you but know me,
I need not talk thus!

BEDAMORE.

Pierre! I must embrace him.
My heart beats to this man as if it knew him.

RENAULT.

I never loved these huggers.

JAFFEIR.

Still I see
The cause delights me not.[21] Your friends survey me
As I were dangerous, but I come armed
Against all doubts* and to your trust will give
A pledge worth more than all the world can pay for.
—My Belvidera! Ho! my Belvidera!

BEDAMORE.

What wonder next?

JAFFEIR.

Let me entreat you,
As I have henceforth hopes to call ye friends,
That all but the ambassador, this
Grave guide of councils, with my friend that owns me,
Withdraw a while to spare a woman's blushes.

Exeunt all but Bedamore, Renault, Jaffeir, Pierre.

BEDAMORE.

Pierre, whither will this ceremony lead us?

JAFFEIR.

My Belvidera! Belvidera!

Enter Belvidera.

---

[20] Arsenal] the state-run shipyard in Venice

[21] delights me not] takes no delight in me

BELVIDERA.
Who?
Who calls so loud at this late peaceful hour?
That voice was wont to come in gentler whispers
And fill my ears with the soft of breath of love.
Thou hourly image of my thoughts, where art thou?
JAFFEIR.
Indeed, 'tis late.
BELVIDERA.
Oh! I have slept, and dreamt,
And dreamt again. Where hast thou been, thou loiterer?
Though my eyes closed, my arms have still* been opened,
Stretched every way betwixt my broken slumbers
To search if thou wert come to crown my rest.
There's no repose without thee. Oh the day
Too soon will break and wake us to our sorrow.
Come, come to bed and bid thy cares good night.
JAFFEIR.
Oh Belvidera! we must change the scene
In which the past delights of life were tasted.
The poor sleep little: we must learn to watch
Our labors late, and early every morning,
Midst winter frosts, then clad and fed with sparing,
Rise to our toils and drudge away the day.
BELVIDERA.
Alas! where am I? Whither is't you lead me?
Methinks I read distraction in your face!
Something less gentle that the fate you tell me.
You shake and tremble too! Your blood runs cold!
Heavens guard my love and bless his heart with patience.
JAFFEIR.
That I have patience, let our fate bear witness,
Who has ordained it so that thou and I
(Thou the divinest good man e'er possessed,
And I the wretched'st of the race of man)
This very hour, without one tear, must part.
BELVIDERA.
Part! Must we part? Oh! am I then forsaken?
Will my love cast me off? Have my misfortunes
Offended him so highly that he'll leave me?
Why drag you from me? Whither are you going?
My dear! my life! my love! [*Falling to the ground.*]
JAFFEIR.
Oh friends!
BELVIDERA.
Speak to me.
JAFFEIR.
Take her from my heart,
She'll gain such hold else I shall ne'er get loose.
I charge thee take her, but with tender'st care
Relieve her troubles and assuage her sorrows.
RENAULT.
Rise, madam, and command amongst your servants!
JAFFEIR.
To you, sirs, and your honors, I bequeath her,
And with her this when I prove unworthy—
(*Gives a dagger.*)
You know the rest: then strike it to her heart
And tell her, he, who three whole happy years
Lay in her arms and each kind night repeated
The passionate vows of still increasing love,
Sent that reward for all her truth and sufferings.
BELVIDERA.
Nay, take my life, since he has sold it cheaply,
Or send me to some distant clime your slave,
But let it be far off, lest my complainings
Should reach his guilty ears and shake his peace.
JAFFEIR.
No Belvidera, I've contrived thy honor.
Trust to my faith, and be but Fortune kind
To me, as I'll preserve that faith unbroken
When next we meet, I'll lift thee to a height
Shall gather all the gazing world about thee
To wonder what strange virtue placed thee there.
But if we ne'er meet more—
BELVIDERA.
Oh thou unkind one,
Never meet more! Have I deserved this from you?
Look on me, tell me, tell me, speak, thou dear deceiver:
Why am I separated from thy love?
If I am false, accuse me, but if true,
Don't, prithee don't in poverty forsake me,
But pity the sad heart that's torn with parting.
Yet hear me! yet recall me—

Exeunt Renault, Bedamore, and Belvidera.

JAFFEIR.
Oh my eyes!
Look not that way but turn your selves a while
Into my heart and be weaned altogether.
—My friend, where art thou?
PIERRE.
Here, my honor's brother.
JAFFEIR.
Is Belvidera gone?
PIERRE.
Renault has led her
Back to her own apartment, but by Heav'n!
Thou must not see her more till our work's over.
JAFFEIR.
No?
PIERRE.
Not for your life.
JAFFEIR.
Oh Pierre, wert thou but she,
How I could pull thee down into my heart,
Gaze on thee till my eye-strings cracked with love,
Till all my sinews with its fire extended
Fixed me upon the rack of ardent longing;
Then swelling, sighing, raging to be blest,
Come like a panting turtle* to thy breast,
On thy soft bosom, hovering, bill and play,
Confess the cause why last I fled away,
Own 'twas a fault, but swear to give it o'er,
And never follow false ambition more.

Exeunt.

Act III. [Aquilina's house.]

Enter Aquilina and her Maid.

AQUILINA.
Tell him I am gone to bed; tell him I am not at home; tell him I've better company with me, or anything; tell him in short I will not see him, the eternal troublesome, vexatious fool. He's worse company than an ignorant physician. I'll not be disturbed at these unseasonable hours.
MAID.
But madam! He's here already, just entered the doors.
AQUILINA.
Turn him out again, you unnecessary, useless, giddy-brained ass! If he will not be gone, set the house afire and burn us both. I had rather meet a toad in my dish than that old hideous animal in my chamber tonight.

Enter Antonio.

ANTONIO.
Nacky, Nacky, Nacky—how dost do Nacky? Hurry durry. I am come, little Nacky. Past eleven o'clock, a late hour, time in all conscience to go to bed, Nacky—Nacky did I say? Aye, Nacky, Aquilina, lina, lina, quilina, quilina, quilina, Aquilina, Naquilina, Naquilina, Acky, Acky, Nacky, Nacky, Queen Nacky. Come let's to bed, you fubbs,* you pug[22] you, you little puss—puree tuzzey—I am a Senator.
AQUILINA.
You are a fool, I am sure.
ANTONIO.
May be so too, sweetheart. Never the worse senator for all that. Come Nacky, Nacky, let's have a game at rump, Nacky.
AQUILINA.
You would do well, signor, to be troublesome here no longer but leave me to myself, be sober, and go home, sir.
ANTONIO.
Home, Madonna!
AQUILINA.
Aye, home, sir. Who am I?
ANTONIO.
Madonna, as I take it you are my—you are—thou art my little Nicky Nacky—that's all!
AQUILINA.
I find you are resolved to be troublesome, and so to make short of the matter in few words, I hate you, detest you, loathe you; I am weary of you, sick of you. Hang you, you are an old, silly, impertinent, impotent, solicitous coxcomb, crazy in your head and lazy in your body, love to be meddling with everything, and if you had not money, you are good for nothing.
ANTONIO.
Good for nothing! Hurry durry, I'll try that

22 pug] a small animal

presently. Sixty-one years old [23] and good for nothing? That's brave.* (*To the Maid.*) Come, come, come, Mistress Fiddle-Faddle, turn you out for a season. Go turn out I say, it is our will and pleasure to be private some moments—out, out, when you are bid to— (*Puts her out and locks the door.*) Good for nothing, you say.

AQUILINA.

Why, what are you good for?

ANTONIO.

In the first place, madam, I am old, and consequently very wise, very wise, Madonna, d'ye mark that? In the second place, take notice, if you please, that I am a senator and, when I think fit, can make speeches, Madonna. Hurry durry, I can make a speech in the Senate House now and then would make your hair stand on end, Madonna.

AQUILINA.

What care I for your speeches in the Senate House? If you would be silent here, I should thank you.

ANTONIO.

Why, I can make speeches to thee too, my lovely Madonna; for example, "My cruel fair one, (*Takes out a purse of gold, and at every pause shakes it.*) since it is my fate that you should with your servant angry prove, though late at night—I hope 'tis not too late with this to gain reception for my love."—There's for thee, my little Nicky Nacky—take it, here take it—I say take it, or I'll throw it at your head—how now, rebel!

AQUILINA.

Truly, my illustrious senator, I must confess your Honor is at present most profoundly eloquent indeed.

ANTONIO.

Very well. Come, now let's sit down and think upon't a little—come sit I say—sit down by me a little, my Nicky Nacky, hah— (*Sits down.*) hurry durry—good for nothing—

AQUILINA.

No sir, if you please, I can know my distance and stand.

ANTONIO.

Stand? how, Nacky up and I down! Nay then let me exclaim with the poet:

Show me a case more pitiful who can:
A standing woman and a falling man.

Hurry durry—not sit down—"see this ye Gods"—You won't sit down?

AQUILINA.

No sir.

ANTONIO.

Then look you now, suppose me a bull, a Basan-bull,[24] the bull of bulls, or any bull. Thus up I get and with my brows thus bent—I broo, I say I broo, I broo, I broo. You won't sit down will you?—I broo— (*Bellows like a Bull, and drives her about.*])

AQUILINA.

Well sir, I must endure this. (*She sits down.*) Now your Honor has been a bull, pray what beast will your Worship please to be next?

ANTONIO.

Now I'll be a senator again and thy lover, little Nicky Nacky! (*He sits by her.*) Ah toad, toad, toad, toad! Spit in my face a little, Nacky—spit in my face, prithee, spit in my face, never so little: spit but a little bit—spit, spit, spit, spit, when you are bid I say; do, prithee spit—now, now, now, spit. What, you won't spit, will you? Then I'll be a dog.

AQUILINA.

A dog, my lord?

ANTONIO.

Aye, a dog—and I'll give thee this t'other purse to let me be a dog—and to use me like a dog a little. Hurry durry—I will—here 'tis. (*Gives the purse.*)

AQUILINA.

Well, with all my heart. But let me beseech your Dogship to play your tricks over as fast as you can, that you may come to stinking the sooner and be turned out of doors as you deserve.

ANTONIO.

Aye, aye—no matter for that— (*He gets under the table.*) That shan't move me. Now, bough waugh waugh, bough waugh— (*Barks like a dog.*)

---

[23] Sixty-one years old] this was also the age of the earl of Shaftesbury.

[24] Basan-bull] See Psalms 22:12-13; "Many bulls have compassed me; strong bulls of Bashan have beset me round."

AQUILINA.

Hold, hold, hold, sir, I beseech you. What is't you do? If curs bite they must be kicked, sir. Do you see, kicked thus.

ANTONIO.

Aye with all my heart. Do kick, kick on, now I am under the table, kick again—kick harder—harder yet, bough waugh waugh, waugh, bough—'Odd,* I'll have a snap at thy shins—bough waugh wough, waugh, bough.—'Odd, she kicks bravely.*

AQUILINA.

Nay then, I'll go another way to work with you and I think here's an instrument fit for the purpose. (*Fetches a whip and bell.*) What, bite your mistress, sirrah! Out, out of doors, you dog, to kennel and be hanged—bite your mistress by the legs, you rogue. (*She whips him.*)

ANTONIO.

Nay prithee Nacky, now thou art too loving. Hurry durry, 'Odd, I'll be a dog no longer.

AQUILINA.

Nay, none of your fawning and grinning, but be gone, or here's the discipline. What, bite your mistress by the legs, you mongrel? Out of doors—hout, hout, to kennel, sirrah! Go!

ANTONIO.

This is very barbarous usage, Nacky, very barbarous. Look you, I will not go—I will not stir from the door, that I resolve—hurry durry, what, shut me out?

She whips him out.

AQUILINA.

Aye, and if you come here any more tonight I'll have my footmen lug you, you cur. What, bite your poor Mistress Nacky, sirrah!

Enter Maid.

MAID.

Heavens, madam! What's the matter?

He howls at the door like a dog.

AQUILINA.

Call my footmen hither presently.*

Enter two footmen.

MAID.

They are here already, madam, the house is all alarmed with a strange noise that nobody knows what to make of.

AQUILINA.

Go all of you and turn that troublesome beast in the next room out of my house. If I ever see him within these walls again without my leave for his admittance, you sneaking rogues, I'll have you poisoned all, poisoned, like rats. Every corner of the house shall stink of one of you. Go, and learn hereafter to know my pleasure.—So now for my Pierre:
Thus when godlike lover was displeased,
We sacrifice our fool, and he's appeased.

Exeunt.

Scene ii. [Another room in Aquilina's house.]

Enter Belvidera.

BELVIDERA.

I'm sacrificed! I am sold! betrayed to shame!
Inevitable ruin has enclosed me!
No sooner was I to my bed repaired,
To weigh and (weeping) ponder my condition,
But the old, hoary wretch, to whose false care
My peace and honor was entrusted, came
(Like Tarquin) ghastly with infernal lust.
Oh thou Roman Lucrece![25]
Thou couldst find friends to vindicate thy wrong;
I never had but one, and he's proved false:
He that should guard my virtue has betrayed it,
Left me! undone me! Oh that I could hate him!
Where shall I go! Oh whither, whither wander?

Enter Jaffeir.

JAFFEIR.

Can Belvidera want* a resting place

[25] Tarquin ... Lucrece] Sextus Tarquinius, son of the tyrannical last king of Rome, raped the chaste matron Lucretia, who begged husband and father to revenge her and committed suicide. Their vengeance led to the expulsion of the Tarquins from Rome and the establishment of republican government (see Lee, *Lucius Junius Brutus*, above).

When these poor arms are open to receive her?
Oh 'tis in vain to struggle with desires
Strong as my love to thee, for every moment
I am from thy sight, the heart within my bosom
Moans like a tender infant in its cradle
Whose nurse had left it. Come, and with the songs
Of gentle love persuade it to its peace.

BELVIDERA.
I fear the stubborn wanderer will not own me,
'Tis grown a rebel to be ruled no longer,
Scorns the indulgent bosom that first lulled it,
And like a disobedient child, disdains
The soft authority of Belvidera.

JAFFEIR.
There was a time—

BELVIDERA.
Yes, yes, there was a time
When Belvidera's tears, her cries, and sorrows
Were not despised; when if she chanced to sigh
Or look but sad, there was indeed a time
When Jaffeir would have ta'en her in his arms,
Eased her declining head upon his breast,
And never left her till he found the cause.
But let her now weep seas,
Cry till she rend the earth, sigh till she burst
Her heart asunder, still* he bears it all,
Deaf as the wind, and as the rocks unshaken.

JAFFEIR.
Have I been deaf? Am I that rock unmoved
Against whose root tears beat and sighs are sent
In vain? Have I beheld thy sorrows calmly?
Witness against me, heavens, have I done this?
Then bear me in a whirlwind back again,
And let that angry dear one ne'er forgive me!
Oh thou too rashly censur'st of my love!
Couldst thou but think how I have spent this night,
Dark and alone, no pillow to my head,
Rest in my eyes, nor quiet in my heart,
Thou wouldst not, Belvidera, sure thou wouldst not
Talk to me thus but, like a pitying angel
Spreading thy wings, come settle on my breast
And hatch warm comfort there ere sorrows freeze it.

BELVIDERA.
Why then, poor mourner, in what baleful corner
Hast thou been talking with that witch, the Night?
On what cold stone hast thou been stretched along,
Gathering the grumbling winds about thy head
To mix with theirs the accents of thy woes?
Oh now I find the cause my love forsakes me!
I am no longer fit to bear a share
In his concernments: my weak female virtue
Must not be trusted; 'tis too frail and tender.

JAFFEIR.
Oh Porcia! Porcia! What a soul was thine!

BELVIDERA.
That Porcia was a woman, and when Brutus,
Big with the fate of Rome (Heav'n guard thy safety!)
Concealed from her the labors of his mind,
She let him see her blood was great as his,
Flowed from a spring as noble and a heart
Fit to partake his troubles as his love.[26]
Fetch, fetch that dagger back, the dreadful dower
Thou gav'st last night in parting with me; strike it
Here to my heart; and as the blood flows from it,
Judge if it run not pure as Cato's daughter's.

JAFFEIR.
Thou art too good, and I indeed unworthy,
Unworthy so much virtue. Teach me how
I may deserve such matchless love as thine,
And see with what attention I'll obey thee.

BELVIDERA.
Do not despise me; that's the all I ask.

JAFFEIR.
Despise thee! Hear me—

BELVIDERA.
Oh thy charming tongue
Is but too well acquainted with my weakness,
Knows, let it name but love, my melting heart
Dissolves within my breast, till with closed eyes
I reel into thy arms, and all's forgotten.

26 Porcia … love] Portia was the daughter of Cato Uticensis and wife of Marcus Junius Brutus. She cut her thigh to prove she could keep the secret of the conspiracy against Julius Caesar.

JAFFEIR.
What shall I do?
BELVIDERA.
Tell me! Be just, and tell me
Why dwells that busy cloud upon thy face?
Why am I made a stranger? Why that sigh,
And I not know the cause? Why when the world
Is wrapped in rest, why chooses then my love
To wander up and down in horrid darkness,
Loathing his bed and these desiring arms?
Why are these eyes bloodshot with tedious watching?
Why starts he now and looks as if he wished
His fate were finished? Tell me, ease my fears,
Lest when we next time meet, I want* the power
To search into the sickness of thy mind
But talk as wildly then as thou look'st now.
JAFFEIR.
Oh Belvidera!
BELVIDERA.
Why was I last night delivered to a villain?
JAFFEIR.
Hah, a villain!
BELVIDERA.
Yes! To a villain! Why at such an hour
Meets that assembly all made up of wretches
That look as Hell had drawn 'em into league?
Why, I in this hand and in that a dagger,
Was I delivered with such dreadful ceremonies?
"To you, sirs, and to your honor I bequeath her,
And with her this. Whene'er I prove unworthy,
You know the rest, then strike it to her heart."
Oh! Why's that "rest" concealed from me? Must I
Be made the hostage of a hellish trust?
For such I know I am, that's all my value!
But by the love and loyalty I owe thee,
I'll free thee from the bondage of these slaves:
Straight to the Senate, tell 'em all I know,
All that I think, all that my fears inform me!
JAFFEIR.
Is this the Roman virtue! This the blood
That boasts its purity with Cato's daughter!
Would she have e'er betrayed her Brutus?
BELVIDERA.
No:
For Brutus trusted her. Wert thou so kind,
What would not Belvidera suffer for thee?
JAFFEIR.
I shall undo myself and tell thee all.
BELVIDERA.
Look not upon me as I am a woman
But as a bone,* thy wife, thy friend, who long
Has had admission to thy heart and there
Studied the virtues of thy gallant nature:
Thy constancy, thy courage, and thy truth
Have been my daily lesson. I have learnt them,
Am bold as thou, can suffer or despise
The worst of fates for thee and with thee share them.
JAFFEIR.
Oh you divinest Powers! Look down and hear
My prayers! Instruct me to reward this virtue!
Yet think a little, ere thou tempt me further:
Think I have a tale to tell will shake thy nature,
Melt all this boasted constancy thou talkst of
Into vile tears and despicable sorrows.
Then if thou shouldst betray me!
BELVIDERA.
Shall I swear?
JAFFEIR.
No, do not swear. I would not violate
Thy tender nature with so rude a bond.
But as thou hop'st to see me live my days
And love thee long, lock this within thy breast:
I've bound myself by all the strictest sacraments,
Divine and human—
BELVIDERA.
Speak!
JAFFEIR.
To kill thy father—
BELVIDERA.
My father!
JAFFEIR.
Nay, the throats of the whole Senate
Shall bleed, my Belvidera. He amongst us
That spares his father, brother, or his friend
Is damned. How rich and beauteous will the face
Of Ruin look, when these wide streets run blood:
I and the glorious partners of my fortune
Shouting and striding o'er the prostrate dead,
Still to new waste, whilst thou, far off in safety
Smiling, shalt see the wonders of our daring
And, when night comes, with praise and love receive me.

BELVIDERA.
Oh!
JAFFEIR.
Have a care, and shrink not even in thought!
For if thou dost—
BELVIDERA.
I know it, thou wilt kill me.
Do, strike thy sword into this bosom, lay me
Dead on the earth, and then thou wilt be safe.
Murder my father! Though his cruel nature
Has persecuted me to my undoing,
Driven me to basest wants,* can I behold him
With smiles of vengeance, butchered in his age?
The sacred fountain of my life destroyed?
And canst thou shed the blood that gave me being?
Nay, be a traitor too and sell thy country?
Can thy great heart descend so vilely low,
Mix with hired slaves, bravoes, and common stabbers,
Nose-slitters, alley-lurking villains! join
With such a crew, and take a ruffian's wages
To cut the throats of wretches as they sleep?
JAFFEIR.
Thou wrong'st me, Belvidera! I've engaged
With men of souls, fit to reform the ills
Of all mankind. There's not a heart amongst them
But's as stout as death, yet honest as the nature
Of man first made ere fraud and vice were fashions.
BELVIDERA.
What's he, to whose curst hands last night thou gav'st me?
Was that well done? Oh! I could tell a story
Would rouse thy lion heart out of its den
And make it rage with terrifying fury.
JAFFEIR.
Speak on I charge thee!
BELVIDERA.
Oh my love! If e'er
Thy Belvidera's peace deserved thy care,
Remove me from this place. Last night, last night!
JAFFEIR.
Distract me not, but give me all the truth.
BELVIDERA.
No sooner wert thou gone and I alone,
Left in the pow'r of that old son of mischief;
No sooner was I lain on my sad bed,
But that vile wretch approached me, loose, unbuttoned,
Ready for violation. Then my heart
Throbbed with its fears. Oh how I wept and sighed,
And shrunk and trembled, wished in vain for him
That should protect me. Thou, alas, wert gone!
JAFFEIR.
Patience, sweet Heav'n, till I make vengeance sure.
BELVIDERA.
He drew the hideous dagger forth thou gav'st him,
And with upbraiding smiles he said, "Behold it,
This is the pledge of a false husband's love."
And in my arms then pressed and would have clasped me,
But with my cries I scared his coward heart
Till he withdrew and muttered vows to Hell.
These are thy friends! With these thy life, thy honor,
Thy love, all's staked, and all will go to ruin.
JAFFEIR.
No more. I charge thee keep this secret close,
Clear up thy sorrows, look as if thy wrongs
Were all forgot, and treat him like a friend,
As no complaint were made. No more, retire,
Retire, my life, and doubt not of my honor:
I'll heal its failings and deserve thy love.
BELVIDERA.
Oh, should I part with thee, I fear thou wilt
In anger leave me and return no more.
JAFFEIR.
Return no more! I would not live without thee
Another night to purchase the creation.
BELVIDERA.
When shall we meet again?
JAFFEIR.
Anon at twelve!
I'll steal myself to thy expecting arms,
Come like a traveled dove and bring thee peace.
BELVIDERA.
Indeed?
JAFFEIR.
By all our loves!
BELVIDERA.
'Tis hard to part,
But sure no falsehood e'er looked so fairly.
Farewell—remember, twelve. (*Exit.*)

JAFFEIR.
Let Heav'n forget me
When I remember not thy truth, thy love.
How curst is my condition, tossed and jostled
From every corner, Fortune's common fool,
The jest of rogues, an instrumental ass
For villains to lay loads of shame upon
And drive about just for their ease and scorn.

Enter Pierre.

PIERRE.
Jaffeir!
JAFFEIR.
Who calls!
PIERRE.
A friend, that could have wished
T'have found thee otherwise employed. What, hunt
A wife on the dull foil![27] Sure a staunch husband
Of all hounds is the dullest. Wilt thou never,
Never be weaned from caudles and confections?
What feminine tale hast thou been listening to
Of unaired shirts, catarrhs and toothache got
By thin-soled shoes? Damnation! that a fellow
Chosen to be a sharer in the destruction
Of a whole people should sneak thus in corners
To ease his fulsome lusts and fool his mind.
JAFFEIR.
May not a man then trifle out an hour
With a kind* woman and not wrong his calling?
PIERRE.
Not in a cause like ours.
JAFFEIR.
Then, friend, our cause
Is in a damned condition, for I'll tell thee,
That cankerworm called lechery has touched it,
'Tis tainted vilely. Wouldst thou think it, Renault
(That mortified, old, withered winter rogue)
Loves simple fornication like a priest:
I found him out for watering at my wife;
He visited her last night like a kind guardian.
Faith, she has some temptations, that's the truth on't.
PIERRE.
He durst not wrong his trust!
JAFFEIR.
'Twas something late, though,
To take the freedom of a lady's chamber.
PIERRE.
Was she in bed?
JAFFEIR.
Yes faith, in virgin sheets
White as her bosom, Pierre, dished neatly up,
Might tempt a weaker appetite to taste.
Oh how the old fox stunk, I warrant thee,
When the rank fit was on him.
PIERRE.
Patience guide me!
He used no violence?
JAFFEIR.
No, no! Out on't, violence!
Played with her neck, brushed her with his gray beard,
Struggled and toused, tickled her till she squeaked a little,
Maybe, or so—but not a jot of violence—
PIERRE.
Damn him.
JAFFEIR.
Aye, so say I. But hush, no more on't.
All hitherto is well, and I believe
Myself no monster[28] yet, though no man knows
What fate he's born to! Sure 'tis near the hour
We all should meet for our concluding orders.
Will the Ambassador be here in person?
PIERRE.
No: he has sent commission to that villain,
Renault, to give the executing charge.
I'd have thee be a man if possible
And keep thy temper, for a brave* revenge
Ne'er comes too late.
JAFFEIR.
Fear not, I am cool as patience:
Had he completed my dishonor, rather
Than hazard the success our hopes are ripe for,
I'd bear it all with mortifying virtue.

---

[27] dull foil] "Foil" means track of a hunted animal (Ghosh) and "dull" an unimportant animal.

[28] monster] cuckold

PIERRE.
He's yonder coming this way through the hall;
His thoughts seem full.
JAFFEIR.
Prithee, retire and leave me
With him alone. I'll put him to some trial,
See how his rotten part will bear the touching.
PIERRE.
Be careful then. (*Exit.*)
JAFFEIR.
Nay never doubt, but trust me.
—What, be a devil! Take a damning oath
For shedding native blood! Can there be a sin
In merciful repentance?—Oh this villain.

Enter Renault.

RENAULT.
Perverse! and peevish! What a slave is man!
To let his itching flesh thus get the better of him!
Dispatch the tool her husband, that were well.
—Who's there?
JAFFEIR.
A man.
RENAULT.
My friend, my near ally!
The hostage of your faith, my beauteous charge,
Is very well.
JAFFEIR.
Sir, are you sure of that?
Stands she in perfect health? Beats her pulse even?
Neither too hot nor cold?
RENAULT.
What means that question?
JAFFEIR.
Oh, women have fantastic constitutions,
Inconstant as their wishes, always wavering,
And ne'er fixed. Was it not boldly done
Even at the first sight to trust the thing I loved
(A tempting treasure too!) with youth so fierce
And vigorous as thine? But thou art honest.
RENAULT.
Who dares accuse me?
JAFFEIR.
Curst be him that doubts
Thy virtue. I have tried it and declare,
Were I to choose a guardian of my honor,
I'd put it into thy keeping: for I know thee.
RENAULT.
Know me!
JAFFEIR.
Aye, know thee: there's no falsehood in thee;
Thou look'st just as thou art. Let us embrace.
Now wouldst thou cut my throat or I cut thine?
RENAULT.
You dare not do't.
JAFFEIR.
You lie, sir.
RENAULT.
How!
JAFFEIR.
No more.
'Tis a base world and must reform, that's all.

Enter Spinosa, Theodore, Eliot, Revellido, Durand, Brainveil, and the rest of the conspirators.]

RENAULT.
Spinosa! Theodore!
SPINOSA.
The same.
RENAULT.
You are welcome!
SPINOSA.
You are trembling, sir.
RENAULT.
'Tis a cold night indeed, I am aged, full of decay and natural infirmities. We shall be warm, my friend, I hope tomorrow.

Pierre reenters, [talks aside to Jaffeir].

PIERRE.
'Twas not well done, thou shouldst have stroked him and not galled him.
JAFFEIR.
Damn him, let him chew on't.
—Heav'n! where am I? Beset with cursèd fiends
That wait to damn me. What a devil's man
When he forgets his nature? Hush my heart.
RENAULT.
My friends, 'tis late. Are we assembled all? Where's Theodore?
THEODORE.
At hand.

RENAULT.
Spinosa.
SPINOSA.
Here.
RENAULT.
Brainveil.
BRAINVEIL.
I am ready.
RENAULT.
Durand and Brabe.
DURAND.
Command us, we are both prepared!
RENAULT.
Mezzana, Revellido, Ternon, Retrosi:
Oh you are men I find
Fit to behold your fate, and meet her summons,
Tomorrow's rising sun must see you all
Decked in your honors!—Are the soldiers ready?
ALL.
All, all.
RENAULT.
You, Durand, with your thousand must possess
St. Marks. You, Captain, know your charge already:
'Tis to secure the ducal palace. You,
Brabe, with a hundred more must gain the Secque.
With the like number Brainveil to the
Procuralle.[29]
Be all this done with the least tumult possible,
Till in each place you post sufficient guards:
Then sheath your swords in every breast you meet.
JAFFEIR. [*Aside.*]
Oh reverend cruelty, damned bloody villain!
RENAULT.
During this execution, Durand, you
Must in the midst keep your battalia fast,
And Theodore be sure to plant the canon
That may command the streets, whilst Revellido,
Mezzana, Ternon, and Retrosi guard you.
This done, we'll give the general alarm,
Apply petards, and force the Ars'nal gates;
Then fire the city round in several places,
Or with our canon (if it dare resist)
Batter't to ruin. But above all I charge you:
Shed blood enough, spare neither sex nor age,
Name nor condition. If there live a senator
After tomorrow, though the dullest rogue
That e'er said nothing, we have lost our ends.
If possible, let's kill the very name
Of senator and bury it in blood.
JAFFEIR. [*Aside.*]
Merciless, horrid slave! Aye, blood enough!
Shed blood enough, old Renault: how thou
charm'st me!
RENAULT.
But one thing more, and then farewell till Fate
Join us again or separate us ever:
First, let's embrace, Heav'n knows who next shall
thus
Wing ye together. But let's all remember
We wear no common[30] cause upon our swords.
Let each man think that on his single virtue
Depends the good and fame of all the rest,
Eternal honor or perpetual infamy.
Let's remember, through what dreadful hazards
Propitious Fortune hitherto has led us,
How often on the brink of some discovery*
Have we stood tottering and yet still kept our ground
So well, the busiest searchers ne'er could follow
Those subtle tracks which puzzled all suspicion.
—You droop, sir.
JAFFEIR.
No. With a most profound attention
I've heard it all and wonder at thy virtue.
REANULT.
Though there be yet few hours 'twixt them and ruin,
Are not the Senate lulled in full security,
Quiet and satisfied, as fools are always!
Never did so profound repose forerun
Calamity so great. Nay, our good fortune
Has blinded the most piercing of mankind,
Strengthened the fearfull'st, charmed the most
suspectful,
Confounded the most subtle: for we live,
We live my friends, and quickly shall our life
Prove fatal to these tyrants. Let's consider

29 St. Marks ... Procuralle] St. Marks, the central piazza in Venice; the Secque, the Mint; the Procuralle, the residence of the Procurators, most important men in Venice after the Doge

30 common] vulgar

That we destroy oppression, avarice,
A people nursed up equally with vices
And loathsome lusts, which Nature most abhors
And such as without shame she cannot suffer.

JAFFEIR. [*Aside.*]
Oh Belvidera, take me to thy arms
And show me where's my peace, for I've lost it.
(*Exit.*)

RENAULT.
Without the least remorse then let's resolve
With fire and sword t'exterminate these tyrants,
And when we shall behold those curst tribunals
Stained by the tears and sufferings of the innocent,
Burning with flames rather from Heav'n than ours,
The raging, furious, and unpitying soldier
Pulling his reeking dagger from the bosoms
Of gasping wretches, death in every quarter,
With all that sad Disorder can produce
To make a spectacle of horror, then,
Then let's call to mind, my dearest friends,
That there's nothing pure upon the earth,
That the most valued things have most alloys,
And that, in change of all those vile enormities
Under whose weight this wretched country labors,
The means are only in our hands to crown them.

PIERRE.
And may those Powers above that are propitious
To gallant minds record this cause and bless it.

RENAULT.
Thus happy, thus secure of all we wish for,
Should there, my friends, be found amongst us one
False to this glorious enterprise, what fate,
What vengeance were enough for such a villain?

ELIOT.
Death here without repentance, hell hereafter.

RENAULT.
Let that be my lot: If as here I stand
Lifted by fate amongst her darling sons,
Though I had one only brother, dear by all
The strictest ties of Nature; though one hour
Had given us birth, one fortune fed our wants,*
One only love, and that but of each other,
Still* filled our minds; could I have such a friend
Joined in this cause and had but ground to fear
Meant foul play, may this right hand drop from me
If I'd not hazard all my future peace
And stab him to the heart before you.
Who would not do less? Wouldst not thou Pierre the same?

PIERRE.
You have singled me, sir, out for this hard question,
As if 'twere started only for my sake!
Am I the thing you fear? Here, here's my bosom,
Search it with all your swords! Am I a traitor?

REANULT.
No. But I fear your late commended friend
Is little less. Come sirs, 'tis now no time
To trifle with our safety. Where's this Jaffeir?

SPINOSA.
He left the room just now in strange disorder.

REANULT.
Nay, there is danger in him. I observed him
During the time I took for explanation:
He was transported from most deep attention
To a confusion which he could not smother.
His looks grew full of sadness and surprise,
All which betrayed a wavering spirit in him,
That labored with reluctancy and sorrow.
What's requisite for safety must be done
With speedy execution; he remains
Yet in our power. I for my own part wear
A dagger.

PIERRE.
Well.

RENAULT.
And I could wish it—

PIERRE.
Where?

RENAULT.
Buried in his heart.

PIERRE.
Away! we're yet all friends.
No more of this, 'twill breed ill blood amongst us.

SPINOSA.
Let us all draw our swords and search the house,
Pull him from the dark hole where he sits brooding
O'er his cold fears, and each man kill his share of him.

PIERRE.
Who talks of killing? Who's he'll shed the blood
That's dear to me? Is't you? or you? or you, sir?

What, not one speak? How you stand gaping all
On your grave oracle, your wooden god there,
Yet not a word? (*To Renault.*) Then, sir, I'll tell you a secret:
Suspicion's but at best a coward's virtue!

RENAULT.
A coward— (*Handles his sword.*)

PIERRE.
Put, put up thy sword, old man,
Thy hand shakes at it. Come, let's heal this breach,
I am too hot. We may yet live friends.

SPINOSA.
Till we are safe, our friendship cannot be so.

PIERRE.
Again! Who's that?

SPINOSA.
'Twas I.

THEODORE.
And I.

REVELLIDO.
And I.

ELIOT.
And all.

RENAULT.
Who are on my side?

SPINOSA.
Every honest sword.
Let's die like men, and not be sold like slaves.

PIERRE.
One such word more, by Heav'n I'll to the Senate
And hang ye all like dogs in clusters.
Why peep your coward swords half out their shells?
Why do you not all brandish them like mine?
You fear to die and yet dare talk of killing?

RENAULT.
Go to the Senate and betray us, hasten,
Secure thy wretched life; we fear to die
Less than thou dar'st be honest.

PIERRE.
That's rank falsehood,
Fear'st not thou death? Fie, there's a knavish itch
In that salt* blood, an utter foe to smarting.
Had Jaffeir's wife proved kind,* he had still been true.
Faugh—how that stinks!
Thou die! Thou kill my friend! or thou, or thou,
Or thou, with that lean, withered, wretched face!
Away! Disperse all to your several charges
And meet tomorrow where your honor calls you.
I'll bring that man whose blood you so much thirst for,
And you shall see him venture for you fairly.
Hence, hence, I say.

Exit Renault angrily.

SPINOSA.
I fear we have been to blame and done too much.

THEODORE.
'Twas too far urged against the man you loved.

REVILLIDO.
Here, take our swords and crush 'em with your feet.

SPINOSA.
Forgive us, gallant friend.

PIERRE.
Nay, now y'have found
The way to melt and cast me as you will.
I'll fetch this friend and give him to your mercy.
Nay, he shall die if you will take him from me;
For your repose I'll quit my heart's jewel
But would not have him torn away by villains
And spiteful villainy.

SPINOSA.
No. May you both
Forever live and fill the world with fame!

PIERRE.
Now you are too kind. Whence rose all this discord?
Oh what a dangerous precipice have we 'scaped!
How near a fall was all we had long been building!
What an eternal blot had stained our glories,
If one the bravest and the best of men
Had fallen a sacrifice to rash suspicion,
Butchered by those whose cause he came to cherish!
Oh could you know him all as I have known him,
How good he is, how just, how true, how brave,
You would not leave this place till you had seen him,
Humbled your selves before him, kissed his feet,
And gained remission for the worst of follies.
Come, but tomorrow all your doubts shall end
And to your loves me better recommend,
That I've preserved your fame and saved my friend.

Exeunt omnes.

Act IV, [scene i.]

Enter Jaffeir and Belvidera.

JAFFEIR.
Where dost thou lead me? Every step I move,
Methinks I tread upon some mangled limb
Of a racked friend. Oh my dear charming ruin!
Where are we wand'ring?

BELVIDERA.
To eternal honor,
To do a deed shall chronicle thy name
Among the glorious legends of those few
That have saved sinking nations. Thy renown
Shall be the future song of all the virgins,
Who by thy piety have been preserved
From horrid violation; every street
Shall be adorned with statues to thy honor
And at thy feet this great inscription written,
"Remember him that propped the fall of Venice."

JAFFEIR.
Rather, remember him, who after all
The sacred bond of oaths and holier friendship
In fond* compassion to a woman's tears
Forgot his manhood, virtue, truth, and honor,
To sacrifice the bosom that relieved him.
Why wilt thou damn me?

BELVIDERA.
Oh inconstant man!
How will you promise, how will you deceive!
Do, return back, replace me in my bondage,
Tell all thy friends how dangerously thou lov'st me,
And let thy dagger do its bloody office.
Oh that kind dagger, Jaffeir, how 'twill look
Stuck through my heart, drenched in my blood to th'hilts!
Whilst these poor dying eyes shall with their tears
No more torment thee; then thou wilt be free.
Or if thou think'st it nobler, let me live
Till I am a victim to the hateful lust
Of that infernal devil, that old fiend
That's damned himself and would undo mankind.
Last night, my love!

JAFFEIR.
Name, name it not again.
It shows a beastly image to my fancy
Will wake me into madness. Oh the villain!
That durst approach such purity as thine
On terms so vile. Destruction, swift destruction
Fall on my coward head and make my name
The common scorn of fools if I forgive him.
If I forgive him? if I not revenge
With utmost rage and most unstaying fury
Thy sufferings, thou dear darling of my life, love.

BELVIDERA.
Delay no longer then, but to the Senate
And tell the dismal'st story e'er was uttered,
Tell 'em what bloodshed, rapines, desolations
Have been prepared, how near's the fatal hour!
Save thy poor country, save the reverend blood
Of all its nobles, which tomorrow's dawn
Must else see shed. Save the poor, tender lives
Of those little infants which the swords
Of murtherers are whetting for this moment.
Think thou already hear'st their dying screams;
Think that thou seest their sad distracted mothers
Kneeling before thy feet and begging pity
With torn disheveled hair and streaming eyes,
Their naked, mangled breasts besmeared with blood
And even the milk with which their fondled babes
Softly they hushed dropping in anguish from 'em.
Think thou seest this, and then consult thy heart.

JAFFEIR.
Oh!

BELVIDERA.
Think too, if thou lose this present minute,
What miseries the next day bring upon thee.
Imagine all the horrors of that night:
Murther and rapine, waste and desolation
Confusedly ranging. Think what then may prove
My lot! The ravisher may then come safe
And midst the terror of the public ruin
Do a damned deed, perhaps too lay a train
May catch thy life. Then where will be revenge,
The dear revenge that's due to such a wrong?

JAFFEIR.
By all Heaven's powers, prophetic truth dwells in thee,
For every word thou speak'st strikes through my heart
Like a new light and shows it how't has wandered.
Just what th'hast made me, take me, Belvidera,
And lead me to the place where I'm to say
This bitter lesson, where I must betray

My truth, my virtue, constancy, and friends.
Must I betray my friends? Ah take me quickly,
Secure me well before that thought's renewed.
If I relapse once more, all's lost forever.

BELVIDERA.
Hast thou a friend more dear than Belvidera?

JAFFEIR.
No, th'art my soul itself, wealth, friendship, honor;
All present joys and earnest of all future
Are summed in thee. Methinks when in thy arms
Thus leaning on thy breast, one minute's more
Than a long thousand years of vulgar hours.
Why was such happiness not given me pure?
Why dashed with cruel wrongs and bitter wantings?
Come, lead me forward now like a tame lamb
To sacrifice: thus in his fatal garlands,
Decked fine and pleased, the wanton skips and plays,
    Trots by the enticing, flattering priestess' side
    And, much transported with his little pride,
    Forgets his dear companions of the plain,
    Till by her, bound, he's on the altar lain
Yet then too hardly bleats, such pleasure's in the pain.

Enter officer and six guards.

OFFICER.
Stand, who goes there?

BELVIDERA.
Friends.

JAFFEIR.
Friends, Belvidera! hide me from my friends.
By Heaven, I'd rather see the face of Hell
Than meet the man I love.

OFFICER.
But what friends are you?

BELVIDERA.
Friends to the Senate and the state of Venice.

OFFICER.
My orders are to seize on all I find
At this late hour and bring 'em to the Council,
Who now are sitting.

JAFFEIR.
Sir, you shall be obeyed.
Hold, brutes, stand off, none of your paws upon me.
—Now the lot's cast, and Fate do what thou wilt.

Exeunt guarded.

Scene [ii]. The Senate House.

Where appear sitting, the Duke of Venice, Priuli, Antonio, and eight other senators.

DUKE.
Antony, Priuli, Senators of Venice,
Speak. Why are we assembled here this night?
What have you to inform us of concerns
The state of Venice' honor or its safety?

PRIULI.
Could words express the story I have to tell you,
Fathers, these tears were useless, these sad tears
That fall from my old eyes. But there is cause
We all should weep, tear off these purple robes,
And wrap our selves in sackcloth, sitting down
On the sad earth and cry aloud to Heaven.
Heaven knows if yet there be an hour to come
Ere Venice be no more!

ALL SENATORS.
How!

PRIULI.
Nay, we stand
Upon the very brink of gaping ruin:
Within this city's formed a dark conspiracy
To massacre us all, our wives, and children,
Kindred and friends, our palaces and temples
To lay in ashes. Nay, the hour, too, fixed;
The swords, for aught I know, drawn even this moment
And the wild waste begun. From unknown hands
I had this warning. But if we are men,
Let's not be tamely butchered but do something
That may inform the world in after ages,
Our virtue was not ruined though we were.

[VOICE.] (*Without.*)
Room, room, make room for some prisoners.

SENATOR.
Let's raise the city.

Enter officer and guard.

PRIULI.
Speak there, what disturbance?

OFFICER.
Two prisoners have the guard seized in the streets,
Who say they come to inform this reverend Senate
About the present danger.

Enter Jaffeir and Belvidera guarded.

ALL.

Give 'em entrance—

[DUKE.]

Well, who are you?

JAFFEIR.

A villain.

ANTONIO.

Short and pithy.
The man speaks well.

JAFFEIR.

Would every man that hears me
Would deal so honestly and own his title.

DUKE.

'Tis rumored that a plot has been contrived
Against this state, that you have a share in't too.
If you are a villain, to redeem your honor,
Unfold the truth and be restored with mercy.

JAFFEIR.

Think not that I to save my life come hither,
I know its value better, but in pity
To all those wretches whose unhappy dooms
Are fixed and sealed. You see me here before you
The sworn and covenanted foe of Venice.
But use me as my dealings may deserve,
And I may prove a friend.

DUKE.

The slave capitulates,
Give him the tortures.

JAFFEIR.

That you dare not do,
Your fears won't let you nor the longing itch
To hear a story which you dread the truth of:
Truth which[e] the fear of smart shall ne'er get from me.
Cowards are scared with theatenings; boys are whipped
Into confessions; but a steady mind
Acts of itself, ne'er asks the body counsel.
"Give him the tortures"? Name but such a thing
Again, by Heaven I'll shut these lips forever.
Not all your racks, your engines, or your wheels
Shall force a groan away that you may guess at.

ANTONIO.

A bloody minded fellow I'll warrant, a damned bloody minded fellow.

DUKE.

Name your conditions.

JAFFEIR.

For my self full pardon,
Besides the lives of two and twenty friends
(*Delivers a list.*)
Whose names are here enrolled. Nay, let their crimes
Be ne'er so monstrous, I must have the oaths
And sacred promise of this reverend Council,
That in a full assembly of the Senate
The thing I ask be ratified. Swear this,
And I'll unfold the secrets of your danger.

ALL.

We'll swear.

DUKE.

Propose the oath.

JAFFEIR.

By all the hopes
Ye have of peace and happiness hereafter,
Swear—

ALL.

We all swear.

JAFFEIR.

To grant me what I've asked,
Ye swear.

ALL.

We swear.

JAFFEIR.

And as ye keep the oath,
May you and your posterity be blest
Or curst forever.

ALL.

Else be curst forever.

JAFFEIR.

Then here's the list, and with't the full disclose
(*Delivers another paper.*)
Of all that threatens you.—Now Fate, thou hast caught me.

ANTONIO.

Why, what a dreadful catalogue of cutthroats is here! I'll warrant you not one of these fellows but has a face like a lion. I dare not so much as read their names over.

DUKE.

Give orders that all diligent search be made
To seize these men. Their characters* are public.

The paper intimates their rendezvous
To be at the house of a famed Grecian courtesan
Called Aquilina: see that place secured.

ANTONIO. [*Aside.*]
What, my Nicky Nacky, hurry durry, Nicky Nacky in the plot? I'll make a speech.—Most noble Senators,
What headlong apprehension drives you on,
Right noble, wise, and truly solid Senators,
To violate the laws and right of nations?
The lady is a lady of renown.
'Tis true, she holds a house of fair reception,
And though I say't myself, as many more
Can say as well as I.

SENATOR.
My lord, long speeches
Are frivolous here when dangers are so near us.
We all well know your interest in that lady,
The world talks loud on't.

ANTONIO.
Verily I have done,
I say no more.

DUKE.
But since he has declared
Himself concerned, pray Captain, take great caution
To treat the fair one as becomes her character,
And let her bedchamber be searched with decency.
You, Jaffeir, must with patience bear till morning
To be our prisoner.

JAFFEIR.
Would the chains of death
Had bound me fast e'er I had known this minute.
I've done a deed will make my story hereafter
Quoted in competition with all ill ones.
The history of my wickedness shall run
Down through the low traditions of the vulgar
And boys be taught[f] to tell the tale of Jaffeir.

DUKE.
Captain, withdraw your prisoner.

JAFFEIR.
Sir, if possible,
Lead me where my own thoughts themselves may lose me,
Where I may doze out what I've left of life,
Forget myself and this day's guilt and falsehood.
Cruel remembrance, how shall I appease thee!
(*Exit guarded.*)

[VOICE.] (*Without.*)
More traitors, room, room, make room there.

DUKE.
How's this? Guards,
Where are our guards? Shut up the gates, the treason's
Already at our doors.

Enter Officer.

OFFICER.
My lords, more traitors,
Seized in the very act of consultation,
Furnished with arms and instruments of mischief.
Bring in the prisoners.

Enter Pierre, Renault, Theodore, Elliot, Revellido and other conspirators, in fetters, guarded.

PIERRE.
You, my lords and fathers
(As you are pleased to call your selves) of Venice,
If you sit here to guide the course of justice,
Why these disgraceful chains upon the limbs
That have so often labored in your service?
Are these the wreaths of triumphs ye bestow
On those that bring you conquests home and honors?

DUKE.
Go on, you shall be heard, sir.

ANTONIO.
And be hanged too, I hope.

PIERRE.
Are these the trophies I've deserved for fighting
Your battles with confederated powers,
When winds and seas conspired to overthrow you
And brought the fleets of Spain to your own harbors?
When you, great Duke, shrunk trembling in your palace
And saw your wife, th'Adriatic, ploughed
Like a lewd whore by bolder prows than yours,
Stepped not I forth and taught your loose Venetians
The task of honor and the way to greatness,
Raised you from your capitulating fears
To stipulate the terms of sued for peace,
And this my recompense? If I am a traitor,
Produce my charge, or show the wretch that's base enough
And brave enough to tell me I am a traitor.

DUKE.
Know you one Jaffeir?

All the conspirators murmur.

PIERRE.
Yes, and know his virtue.
His justice, truth, his general worth, and sufferings
From a hard father taught me first to love him.

DUKE.
See him brought forth.

Enter Jaffeir guarded.

PIERRE.
My friend too bound? Nay then,
Our fate has conquered us, and we must fall.
Why droops the man whose welfare's so much mine
They're but one thing? These reverend tyrants, Jaffeir,
Call us all traitors. Art thou one, my brother?

JAFFEIR.
To thee I am the falsest, veriest* slave
That e'er betrayed a generous trusting friend
And gave up honor to be sure of ruin:
All our fair hopes which morning was to have crowned
Has this curst tongue o'erthrown.

PIERRE.
So, then all's over:
Venice has lost her freedom, I my life.
No more, farewell.

DUKE.
Say, will you make confession
Of your vile deeds and trust the Senate's mercy?

PIERRE.
Curst be your Senate, curst your constitution.
The curse of growing factions and division
Still* vex your councils, shake your public safety,
And make the robes of government you wear
Hateful to you as these base chains to me.

DUKE.
Pardon or death?

PIERRE.
Death, honorable death.

REANULT.
Death's the best thing we ask or you can give.

ALL CONSPIRATORS.
No shameful bonds, but honorable death.

DUKE.
Break up the Council. Captain, guard your prisoners.
Jaffeir, y'are free, but these must wait for judgment.

Exeunt all the Senators [and Belvidera].

PIERRE.
Come, where's my dungeon? Lead me to my straw:
It will not be the first time I've lodged hard
To do your Senate service.

JAFFEIR.
Hold one moment.

PIERRE.
Who's he disputes the judgment of the Senate?
Presumptuous rebel—on— (*Strikes Jaffeir.*)

JAFFEIR.
By Heaven you stir not.
I must be heard, I must have leave to speak:
Thou hast disgraced me, Pierre, by a vile blow.
Had not a dagger done thee nobler justice?
But use me as thou wilt, thou canst not wrong me,
For I am fallen beneath the basest injuries.
Yet look upon me with an eye of mercy,
With pity and with charity behold me;
Shut not thy heart against a friend's repentance,
But as there dwells a godlike nature in thee,
Listen with mildness to my supplications.

PIERRE.
What whining monk art thou? What holy cheat
That wouldst encroach upon my credulous ears
And cant'st thus vilely? Hence. I know thee not.
Dissemble and be nasty. Leave me, hypocrite.

JAFFEIR.
Not know me, Pierre?

PIERRE.
No, know thee not. What art thou?

JAFFEIR.
Jaffeir, thy friend, thy once loved, valued friend,
Though now deservedly scorned and used most hardly.

PIERRE.
Thou Jaffeir! Thou my once loved, valued friend!
By Heavens thou ly'st: the man so called, my friend,
Was generous, honest, faithful, just, and valiant,
Noble in mind, and in his person lovely,
Dear to my eyes and tender to my heart,
But thou a wretched, base, false, worthless coward,

Poor even in soul, and loathsome in thy aspect.
All eyes must shun thee, and all hearts detest thee.
Prithee avoid, nor longer cling thus round me
Like something baneful that my nature's chilled at.

JAFFEIR.
I have not wronged thee, by these tears I have not,
But still am honest, true, and, hope too, valiant,
My mind still full of thee, therefore still noble.
Let not thy eyes then shun me nor thy heart
Detest me utterly. Oh look upon me,
Look back and see my sad, sincere submission!
How my heart swells as even 'twould burst my bosom,
Fond of its gaol and laboring to be at thee!
What shall I do? What say to make thee hear me?

PIERRE.
Hast thou not wronged me? Dar'st thou call thyself
Jaffeir, that once loved, valued friend of mine,
And swear thou hast not wronged me? Whence these chains?
Whence the vile death, which I may meet this moment?
Whence this dishonor, but from thee, thou false one?

JAFFEIR.
All's true, yet grant one thing, and I've done asking.

PIERRE.
What's that?

JAFFEIR.
To take thy life on such conditions
The Council have proposed. Thou and thy friends
May yet live long and to be better treated.

PIERRE.
Life! Ask my life! Confess! Record my self
A villain for the privilege to breathe
And carry up and down this cursèd city
A discontented and repining spirit,
Burdensome to itself a few years longer,
To lose, it may be, at last in a lewd quarrel*
For some new friend, treacherous and false as thou art!
No, this vile world and I have long been jangling
And cannot part on better terms than now
When only men like thee are fit to live in't.

JAFFEIR.
By all that's just—

PIERRE.
Swear by some other powers,
For thou has broke that sacred oath too lately.

JAFFEIR.
Then by that hell I merit, I'll not leave thee
Till to thyself, at least, thou'rt reconciled,
However thy resentments deal with me.

PIERRE.
Not leave me!

JAFFEIR.
No, thou shalt not force me from thee.
Use me reproachfully and like a slave,
Tread on me, buffet me, heap wrongs on wrongs
On my poor head: I'll bear it all with patience,
Shall weary out thy most unfriendly cruelty,
Lie at thy feet and kiss 'em though they spurn me,
Till, wounded by my sufferings, thou relent
And raise me to thy arms with dear forgiveness.

PIERRE.
Art thou not—

JAFFEIR.
What?

PIERRE.
A traitor?

JAFFEIR.
Yes.

PIERRE.
A villain?

JAFFEIR.
Granted.

PIERRE.
A coward, a most scandalous coward,
Spiritless, void of honor, one who has sold
Thy everlasting fame for shameless life?

JAFFEIR.
All, all, and more, much more: my faults are numberless.

PIERRE.
And wouldst thou have me live on terms like thine?
Base as thou art false—

JAFFEIR.
No, 'tis to me that's granted;
The safety of thy life was all I aimed at
In recompense for faith and trust so broken.

PIERRE.
I scorn it more because preserved by thee,

And as when first my foolish heart took pity
On thy misfortunes, sought thee in thy miseries,
Relieved thy wants,* and raised thee from thy state
Of wretchedness in which thy fate had plunged thee
To rank thee in my list of noble friends,
All I received in surety for thy truth
Were unregarded oaths. And this, this dagger,
Given with a worthless pledge, thou since hast stol'n;
So I restore it back to thee again,
Swearing by all those powers which thou hast violated
Never from this curst hour to hold communion,
Friendship, or interest with thee, though our years
Were to exceed those limited the world.
Take it—farewell—for now I owe thee nothing.

JAFFEIR.
Say thou wilt live then.

PIERRE.
For my life, dispose it
Just as thou wilt, because 'tis what I'm tired with.

JAFFEIR.
Oh, Pierre!

PIERRE.
No more.

JAFFEIR.
My eyes won't lose the sight of thee
But languish after thine and ache with gazing.

PIERRE.
Leave me—Nay, then thus, thus, I throw thee from me.
And curses, great as is thy falsehood, catch thee.
[*Exit.*]

JAFFEIR.
Amen.—He's gone, my father, friend, preserver,
And here's the portion he has left me, (*Holds the dagger up.*)
This dagger, well remembered. With this dagger
I gave a solemn vow of dire importance,
Parted with this and Belvidera together.
Have a care, mem'ry, drive that thought no farther—
No, I'll esteem it as a friend's last legacy,
Treasure it up in this wretched bosom,
Where it may grow acquainted with my heart,
That when they meet, they start not from each other.
So, now for thinking: a blow, called traitor, villain,
Coward, dishonorable coward, faugh!
Oh for a long, sound sleep and so forget it!
Down, busy devil—

Enter Belvidera.

BELVIDERA.
Whither shall I fly?
Where hide me and my miseries together?
Where's now the Roman constancy I boasted?
Sunk into trembling fears and desperation!
Not daring now to look up to that dear face
Which used to smile even on my faults, but down
Bending these miserable eyes to earth,
Must move in penance and implore much mercy.

JAFFEIR.
Mercy! Kind Heaven has surely endless stores
Hoarded for thee of blessings yet untasted.
Let wretches loaded hard with guilt as I am
Bow with[g] the weight and groan beneath the burden,
Creep with a remnant of that strength they've left
Before the footstool of that Heaven they've injured.
Oh Belvidera! I'm the wretchedest creature
E'er crawled on earth. Now if thou hast virtue, help me,
Take me into thy arms and speak the words of peace
To my divided soul that wars within me
And raises every sense to my confusion.
By Heav'n, I am tottering on the very brink
Of peace, and thou art all the hold I've left.

BELVIDERA.
Alas! I know thy sorrows are most mighty;
I know th'hast cause to mourn: to mourn, my Jaffeir,
With endless cries and never ceasing wailings.
Th'hast lost—

JAFFEIR.
Oh I have lost what can't be counted.
My friend too, Belvidera, that dear friend,
Who, next to thee, was all my health rejoiced in,
Has used me like a slave, shamefully used me.
'Twould break thy pitying heart to hear the story.
What shall I do? Resentment, indignation,
Love, pity, fear, and mem'ry how I've wronged him
Distract my quiet with the very thought on't
And tear my heart to pieces in my bosom.

BELVIDERA.
What has he done?

JAFFEIR.
Thou'dst hate me, should I tell thee.
BELVIDERA.
Why?
JAFFEIR.
Oh he has used me—yet by Heaven I bear it—
He has used me, Belvidera—but first swear
That, when I've told thee, thou'lt not loath me utterly,
Though vilest blots and stains appear upon me,
But still at least with charitable goodness
Be near me in the pangs of my affliction,
Not scorn me, Belvidera, as he has done.
BELVIDERA.
Have I then e'er been false that now I am doubted?
Speak, what's the cause I am grown into distrust,
Why thought unfit to hear my love's complainings?
JAFFEIR.
Oh!
BELVIDERA.
Tell me.
JAFFEIR.
Bear my failings, for they are many,
Oh my dear angel! In that friend I've lost
All my soul's peace, for every thought of him
Strikes my sense hard and deads it in my brains.
Wouldst thou believe it?
BELVIDERA.
Speak.
JAFFEIR.
Before we parted,
Ere yet his guards had led him to his prison,
Full of severest sorrows for his suff'rings,
With eyes o'erflowing and a bleeding heart,
Humbling myself almost beneath my nature,
As at his feet I kneeled and sued for mercy,
Forgetting all our friendship, all the dearness
In which we've lived so many years together,
With a reproachful hand, he dashed a blow;
He struck me, Belvidera, by Heaven, he struck me,
Buffeted, called me traitor, villain, coward.
Am I a coward? Am I a villain? Tell me:
Th'art the best judge and mad'st me, if I am so.
Damnation. Coward!
BELVIDERA.
Oh! forgive him, Jaffeir.
And if his sufferings wound thy heart already,
What will they do tomorrow?
JAFFEIR.
Hah!
BELVIDERA.
Tomorrow,
When thou shalt see him stretched in all the agonies
Of a tormenting and a shameful death,
His bleeding bowels and his broken limbs
Insulted o'er by a vile, butchering villain.
What will thy heart do then? Oh sure 'twill stream
Like my eyes now.
JAFFEIR.
What means thy dreadful story?
Death, and tomorrow? broken limbs and bowels?
Insulted o'er by a vile, butchering villain?
By all my fears I shall start out to madness
With barely guessing if the truth's hid longer.
BELVIDERA.
The faithless senators, 'tis they've decreed it:
They say according to our friends' request
They shall have death and not ignoble bondage,
Declare their promised mercy all as forfeited,
False to their oaths, and deaf to intercession:
Warrants are passed for public death tomorrow.
JAFFEIR.
Death! Doomed to die! Condemned unheard! Unpleaded!
BELVIDERA.
Nay, cruelest racks and torments are preparing
To force confessions from their dying pangs.
Oh do not look so terribly upon me:
How your lips shake and all your face disordered!
What means my love?
JAFFEIR.
Leave me, I charge thee leave me—strong temptations
Wake in my heart.
BELVIDERA.
For what?
JAFFEIR.
No more, but leave me.
BELVIDERA.
Why?
JAFFEIR.
Oh! by Heaven I love thee with that fondness

I would not have thee stay a moment longer
Near these curst hands: Are they not cold upon thee?
BELVIDERA.
No, everlasting comfort's in thy arms;

[Jaffeir] pulls the dagger half out of his bosom and puts it back again.

To lean thus on thy breast is softer ease
Than downy pillows decked with leaves of roses.
JAFFEIR.
Alas thou thinkest not of the thorns 'tis filled with.
Fly ere they gall[h] thee. There's a lurking serpent
Ready to leap and sting thee to thy heart:
Art thou not terrified?
BELVIDERA.
No.
JAFFEIR.
Call to mind
What thou hast done and whither thou hast brought me.
BELVIDERA.
Hah!
JAFFEIR.
Where's my friend? my friend, thou smiling mischief?
Nay, shrink not, now 'tis too late, thou shouldst have fled
When thy guilt first had cause, for dire Revenge
Is up and raging for my friend. He groans,
Hark how he groans, his screams are in my ears
Already. See, they've fixed him on the wheel,
And now they tear him— Murther! Perjured Senate!
Murther! Oh hark thee, traitress, thou hast done this.
Thanks to thy tears and false persuading love—
(*Fumbling for his dagger.*)
How her eyes speak! Oh thou bewitching creature!
Madness cannot hurt thee. Come, thou little trembler,
Creep even into my heart and there lie safe;
'Tis thy own citadel— Hah! yet stand off,
Heaven must have justice, and my broken vows
Will sink me else beneath its reaching mercy.
I'll wink and then 'tis done—
BELVIDERA.
What means the lord
Of me, my life and love? What's in thy bosom
Thou grasp'st at so? Nay, why am I thus treated?

[He] draws the dagger, offers to stab her.*

What wilt thou do? Ah, do not kill me, Jaffeir,
Pity these panting breasts and trembling limbs,
That used to clasp thee when thy looks were milder,
That yet hang heavy on my unpurged soul,
And plunge it not into eternal darkness.
JAFFEIR.
No Belvidera, when we parted last
I gave this dagger with thee as in trust
To be thy portion if I e'er proved false.
On such condition was my truth believed,
But now 'tis forfeited and must be paid for.
(*Offers* to stab her, again.*
BELVIDERA. (*Kneeling.*)
Oh, mercy!
JAFFEIR.
Nay, no struggling.
BELVIDERA.
Now then kill me,
(*Leaps upon his neck and kisses him.*)
While thus I cling about thy cruel neck,
Kiss thy revengeful lips and die in joys
Greater than any I can guess hereafter.
JAFFEIR.
I am, I am a coward: witness't, heaven,
Witness it, earth, and every being witness.
'Tis but one blow yet— By immortal love,
I cannot longer bear a thought to harm thee,
(*Throws away the dagger and embraces her.*)
The seal of Providence is sure upon thee,
And thou wert born for yet unheard of wonders.
Oh thou wert either born to save or damn me!
By all the power that's given thee o'er my soul,
By thy resistless tears and conquering smiles,
By the victorious love that still* waits on thee,
Fly to thy cruel father, save my friend,
Or all our future quiet's lost forever:
Fall at his feet, cling round his reverend knees,
Speak to him with thy eyes, and with thy tears
Melt the[i] hard heart and wake dead nature in him,
Crush him in th'arms, and torture him with thy softness,
Nor, till thy prayers are granted, set him free
But conquer him, as thou hast vanquished me.

Exeunt.

Act V[, scene i. Priuli's house.]

Enter Priuli solus.

PRIULI.
Why, cruel Heaven, have my unhappy days
Been lengthened to this sad one? Oh! dishonor
And deathless infamy is fall'n upon me.
Was it my fault? Am I a traitor? No.
But then, my only child, my daughter, wedded:
There my best blood runs foul, and a disease
Incurable has seized upon my memory
To make it rot and stink to after ages.
Curst be the fatal minute when I got her,
Or would that I'd been anything but man
And raised an issue which would ne'er have wronged me.
The miserablest creatures (man excepted)
Are not the less esteemed though their posterity
Degenerate from the virtues of their fathers;
The vilest beasts are happy in their offsprings,
While only man gets traitors, whores, and villains.
Curst be the names, and some swift blow from Fate
Lay his head deep, where mine may be forgotten.

Enter Belvidera in a long mourning veil.

BELVIDERA.
He's there, my father, my inhuman father,
That for three years has left an only child
Exposed to all the outrages of Fate
And cruel Ruin—Oh!—

PRIULI.
What child of sorrow
Art thou that com'st thus wrapped in weeds of sadness
And mov'st as if thy steps were towards a grave?

BELVIDERA.
A wretch, who from the very top of happiness
Am fallen into the lowest depths of misery
And want* your pitying hand to raise me up again.

PRIULI.
Indeed thou talk'st as thou hadst tasted sorrows.
Would I could help thee.

BELVIDERA.
'Tis greatly in your power,
The world, too, speaks you charitable, and I,
Who ne'er asked alms before, in that dear hope
Am come a-begging to you, sir.

PRIULI.
For what?

BELVIDERA.
Oh, well regard me: Is this voice a strange one?
Consider too, when beggars once pretend*
A case like mine, no little will content 'em.

PRIULI.
What wouldst thou beg for?

BELVIDERA.
Pity and forgiveness.
(*Throws up her veil.*)
By the kind, tender names of child and father,
Hear my complaints and take me to your love.

PRIULI.
My daughter?

BELVIDERA.
Yes, your daughter, by a mother
Virtuous and noble, faithful to your honor,
Obedient to your will, kind to your wishes,
Dear to your arms. By all the joys she gave you,
When in her blooming years she was your treasure,
Look kindly on me, in my face behold
The lineaments of hers y'have kissed so often
Pleading the cause of your poor, cast-off child.

PRIULI.
Thou art my daughter.

BELVIDERA.
Yes—and y'have oft told me,
With smiles of love and chaste, paternal kisses,
I'd much resemblance of my mother.

PRIULI.
Oh!
Hadst thou inherited her matchless virtues,
I'd been too blessed.

BELVIDERA.
Nay, do not call to memory
My disobedience, but let pity enter
Into your heart and quite deface the impression,
For could you think how mine's perplexed, what sadness,
Fears, and despairs distract the peace within me,
Oh, you would take me in your dear, dear arms,
Hover with strong compassion o'er your young one
To shelter me with a protecting wing

From the black, gathered storm that's just, just breaking.

PRIULI.
Don't talk thus.

BELVIDERA.
Yes, I must, and you must hear too.
I have a husband.

PRIULI.
Damn him.

BELVIDERA.
Oh, do not curse him!
He would not speak so hard a word towards you
On any terms, howe'er he deal with me.

PRIULI.
Hah! What means my child?

BELVIDERA.
Oh there's but this short moment
'Twixt me and fate, yet send me not with curses
Down to my grave, afford me one kind blessing
Before we part: just take me in your arms
And recommend me with a prayer to Heaven
That I may die in peace, and when I'm dead—

PRIULI.
How my soul's catcht!

BELVIDERA.
Lay me, I beg you, lay me
By the dear ashes of my tender mother.
She would have pitied me, had Fate yet spared her.

PRIULI.
By Heaven, my aching heart forebodes much mischief.
—Tell me thy story, for I'm still thy father.

BELVIDERA.
No, I'm contented.

PRIULI.
Speak.

BELVIDERA.
No matter.

PRIULI.
Tell me.
By you, blest Heaven, my heart runs o'er with fondness.

BELVIDERA.
Oh!

PRIULI.
Utter't

BELVIDERA.
Oh my husband, my dear husband
Carries a dagger in his once kind bosom
To pierce the heart of your poor Belvidera.

PRIULI.
Kill thee?

BELVIDERA.
Yes, kill me. When he passed his faith
And covenant against your state and senate,
He gave me up as hostage for his truth,
With me a dagger and a dire commission:
Whene'er he failed, to plunge it through this bosom.
I learned the danger, chose the hour of love
T'attempt his heart and bring it back to honor.
Great love prevailed and blessed me with success:
He came, confessed, betrayed his dearest friends
For promised mercy. Now they're doomed to suffer,
Galled with remembrance of what then was sworn.
If they are lost, he vows t'appease the gods
With this poor life and make my blood th'atonement.

PRIULI.
Heavens!

BELVIDERA.
Think you saw what passed at our last parting;
Think you beheld him like a raging lion,
Pacing the earth and tearing up his steps,
Fate in his eyes, and roaring with the pain
Of burning fury; think you saw his one hand
Fixed on my throat, while the extended other
Grasped a keen threat'ning dagger. Oh 'twas thus
We last embraced, when, trembling with revenge,
He dragged me to the ground and at my bosom
Presented horrid death, cried out, "My friends,
Where are my friends?" swore, wept, raged, threatened, loved,
For he yet loved, and that dear love preserved me
To this last trial of a father's pity.
I fear not death but cannot bear a thought
That that dear hand should do th'unfriendly office.
If I was ever then your care, now hear me:
Fly to the Senate, save the promised lives
Of his dear friends, ere mine be made the sacrifice.

PRIULI.
Oh, my heart's comfort!

BELVIDERA.
Will you not, my father?
Weep not but answer me.

PRIULI.
By Heaven, I will.
Not one of 'em but what shall be immortal.
Canst thou forgive me all my follies past?
I'll henceforth be indeed a father, never,
Never more thus expose but cherish thee
Dear as the vital warmth that feeds my life,
Dear as these eyes that weep in fondness o'er thee.
Peace to thy heart. Farewell.

BELVIDERA.
Go, and remember,
'Tis Belvidera's life her father pleads for.

Exeunt severally.

[Scene ii. Aquilina's house.]

Enter Antonio.

ANTONIO.
Hum, hum, hah: "Seignor Priuli, my Lord Priuli, my lord, my lord, my lord—" Now, we lords love to call one another by our titles. "My lord, my lord, my lord—" Pox on him, I am a lord as well as he, and so let him fiddle. I'll warrant him, he's gone to the Senate House, and I'll be there too, soon enough for somebody. 'Odd,* here's a tickling speech about the plot; I'll prove there's a plot with a vengeance— Would I had it without book. Let me see: "Most Reverend Senators, that there is plot, surely by this time no man that hath eyes or understanding in his head will presume to doubt, 'tis as plain as the light in the cucumber—" No, hold there, cucumber does not come in yet—"'tis as plain as the light in the sun or as the man in the moon even at noonday. It is indeed a pumpkin-plot,[31] which, just as it was mellow, we have gathered. And now we have gathered it, prepared and dressed it, shall we throw it like a pickled cucumber* out at the window? No. That it is not only a bloody, horrid, execrable, damnable, and audacious plot, but it is, as I may so say, a saucy plot. And we all know, most Reverend Fathers, that what is sauce for a goose is sauce for a gander; therefore, I say, as those blood-thirsty ganders of the conspiracy would have destroyed us geese of the Senate, let us make haste to destroy them. So I humbly move for hanging." Hah, hurry durry, I think this will do, though I was something out, at first, about the sun and the cucumber.

Enter Aquilina.

AQUILINA.
Good morrow, Senator.

ANTONIO.
Nacky, my dear Nacky, 'morrow, Nacky, 'Odd, I am very brisk, very merry, very pert, very jovial—haaaaa—kiss me, Nacky. How dost thou do, my little tory rory* strumpet, kiss me, I say, hussy, kiss me.

AQUILINA.
"Kiss me, Nacky." Hang you, Sir Coxcomb, hang you, sir.

ANTONIO.
Hayty tayty, is it so indeed, with all my heart, faith— (*Sings.*) "Hey then up go we," faith, "hey then up go we, dum dum derum dump."

AQUILINA.
Signor.

ANTONIO.
Madonna.

AQUILINA.
Do you intend to die in your bed?

ANTONIO.
About threescore years hence, much may be done, my dear.

AQUILINA.
You'll be hanged, Signor.

ANTONIO.
Hanged, sweetheart? Prithee be quiet, hanged quotha, that's a merry conceit, with all my heart, why thou jok'st, Nacky, thou art given to joking, I'll swear; well I protest, Nacky, nay, I must protest, and will protest that I love joking dearly, man. And

---

[31] cucumber ... pumpkin-plot] Otway hits at both scientific experiment by the Royal Society and at details of the Popish Plot: actual experiments were being conducted to discover the relationship between sunlight and vegetables; one of the putative conspirators in the Plot was said to have hidden important papers in a pumpkin.

I love thee for joking, and I'll kiss thee for joking, and touse thee for joking, and 'Odd, I have a devilish mind to take thee aside about that business for joking too, 'Odd I have, and "Hey then up go we, dum dum derum dump."

AQUILINA.
See you this, sir? (*Draws a dagger.*)

ANTONIO.
Oh Laud, a dagger! Oh Laud! it is naturally my aversion, I cannot endure the sight on't, hide it, for Heaven's sake, I cannot look that way till it be gone—hide it, hide it, oh, oh, hide it!

AQUILINA.
Yes, in your heart I'll hide it.

ANTONIO.
My heart, what, hide a dagger in my heart's blood!

AQUILINA.
Yes, in thy heart, thy throat, thou pampered devil.
Thou hast helped to spoil my peace, and I'll have vengeance
On thy curst life for all the bloody Senate,
The perjured, faithless Senate: Where's my lord,
My happiness, my love, my god, my hero?
Doomed by thy accursèd tongue, amongst the rest,
T'a shameful rack? By all the rage that's in me,
I'll be whole years in murthering thee.

ANTONIO.
Why, Nacky, wherefore so passionate? What have I done? What's the matter, my dear Nacky? Am not I thy love, thy happiness, thy lord, thy hero, thy senator, and everything in the world, Nacky?

AQUILINA.
Thou! Think'st thou, thou art fit to meet my joys,
To bear the eager clasps of my embraces?
Give me my Pierre, or—

ANTONIO.
Why, he's to be hanged, little Nacky, trussed up for treason, and so forth, child.*

AQUILINA.
Thou ly'st, stop down thy throat that hellish sentence,
Or 'tis thy last. Swear that my love shall live,
Or thou art dead.

ANTONIO.
Ahhhh.

AQUILINA.
Swear to recall his doom,
Swear at my feet and tremble at my fury.

ANTONIO.
I do.—Now if she would but kick a little bit, one kick now. Ahhhh.

AQUILINA.
Swear, or—

ANTONIO.
I do, by these dear fragrant foots and little toes, sweet as, eeee my Nacky Nacky Nacky.

AQUILINA.
How!

ANTONIO.
Nothing but untie thy shoestring a little, faith and troth, that's all, that's all, as I hope to live, Nacky, that's all.

AQUILINA.
Nay, then—

ANTONIO.
Hold, hold, thy love, thy lord, thy hero shall be preserved and safe.

AQUILINA.
Or may this poniard rust in thy heart.

ANTONIO.
With all my soul.

AQUILINA.
Farewell— (*Exit.*)

ANTONIO.
Adieu. Why what a bloody-minded, inveterate, termagant, strumpet have I been plagued with! Ohhh yet more! Nay then I die,* I die—I am dead already. (*Stretches himself out.*)

Enter Jaffeir.

JAFFEIR.
Final destruction seize on all the world:
Bend down, ye heavens, and shutting round this earth,
Crush the vile globe into its first confusion,
Scorch it with elemental flames to one curst cinder,
And all us little creepers in't, called men,
Burn, burn to nothing. But let Venice burn
Hotter than all the rest; here kindle hell
Ne'er to extinguish, and let souls hereafter
Groan here in all those pains which mine feels now.

Enter Belvidera, meeting him.

BELVIDERA.
My life—
JAFFEIR. (*Turning from her.*)
My plague—
BELVIDERA.
Nay then I see my ruin,
If I must die!
JAFFEIR.
No, Death's this day too busy:
Thy father's ill-timed mercy came too late.
I thank thee for thy labors, though, and him too,
But all my poor, betrayed, unhappy friends
Have summons to prepare for Fate's black hour.
And yet I live.
BELVIDERA.
Then be the next my doom.
I see thou hast passed my sentence in thy heart,
And I'll no longer weep or plead against it,
But with the humblest, most obedient patience
Meet thy dear hands and kiss 'em when they wound me.
Indeed I am willing, but I beg thee do it
With some remorse, and when thou giv'st the blow,
View me with eyes of a relenting love
And show me pity, for 'twill sweeten justice.
JAFFEIR.
Show pity to thee?
BELVIDERA.
Yes, and when thy hands,
Charged with my fate, come trembling to the deed,
As thou hast done a thousand thousand dear times
To this poor breast, when kinder* rage has brought thee;
When our stinged hearts have leaped to meet each other
And melting kisses sealed our lips together;
When joys have left me gasping in thy arms,
So let my death come now, and I'll not shrink from't.
JAFFEIR.
Nay, Belvidera, do not fear my cruelty
Nor let the thoughts of death perplex thy fancy,
But answer me to what I shall demand
With a firm temper and unshaken spirit.
BELVIDERA.
I will when I've done weeping—
JAFFEIR.
Fie, no more on't.
How long is't since the miserable day
We wedded first?
BELVIDERA.
Ohhh.
JAFFEIR.
Nay, keep in thy tears,
Lest they unman me too.
BELVIDERA.
Heaven knows I cannot;
The words you utter sound so very sadly
These streams will follow—
JAFFEIR.
Come, I'll kiss 'em dry then.
BELVIDERA.
But, was't a miserable day?
JAFFEIR.
A curst one.
BELVIDERA.
I thought it otherwise, and you've oft sworn
In the transporting hours of warmest love,
When sure you spoke the truth, you've sworn you blessed it.
JAFFEIR.
'Twas a rash oath.
BELVIDERA.
Then why am I not curst too?
JAFFEIR.
No Belvidera, by th'eternal truth,
I dote with too much fondness.
BELVIDERA.
Still so kind?
Still then do you love me?
JAFFEIR.
Nature, in her workings,
Inclines not with more ardor to creation
Than I do now towards thee; man ne'er was blessed,
Since the first pair first met, as I have been.
BELVIDERA.
Then sure you will not curse me.
JAFFEIR.
No, I'll bless thee.
I came on purpose, Belvidera, to bless thee.

'Tis now, I think, three years we've lived together.
BELVIDERA.
And may no fatal minute ever part us
Till, reverend grown for age and love, we go
Down to one grave, as our last bed, together,
There sleep in peace till an eternal morning.
JAFFEIR. (*Sighing.*)
When will that be?
BELVIDERA.
I hope long ages hence.
JAFFEIR.
Have I not hitherto (I beg thee tell me
Thy very fears) used thee with tenderest love?
Did e'er my soul rise up in wrath against thee?
Did I e'er frown when Belvidera smiled
Or, by the least unfriendly word, betray
A bating passion? Have I ever wronged thee?
BELVIDERA.
No.
JAFFEIR.
Has my heart, or have my eyes e'er wandered
To any other woman?
BELVIDERA.
Never, never—
I were the worst of false ones should I accuse thee.
I own I've been too happy, blessed above
My sex's charter.
JAFFEIR.
Did I not say I came
To bless thee?
BELVIDERA.
Yes.
JAFFEIR.
Then hear me, bounteous Heaven,
Pour down your blessings on this beauteous head,
Where everlasting sweets are always springing.
With a continual giving hand, let peace,
Honor, and safety always hover round her;
Feed her with plenty; let her eyes ne'er see
A sight of sorrow, nor her heart know mourning;
Crown all her days with joy, her nights with rest
Harmless as her own thoughts, and prop her virtue
To bear the loss of one that too much loved
And comfort her with patience in our parting.
BELVIDERA.
How, parting, parting!
JAFFEIR.
Yes, forever parting:
I have sworn, Belvidera, by yon Heaven,
That best can tell how much I lose to leave thee,
We part this hour forever.
BELVIDERA.
Oh, call back
Your cruel blessings, stay with me, and curse me!
JAFFEIR.
No, 'tis resolved.
BELVIDERA.
Then hear me too, just Heaven,
Pour down your curses on this wretched head
With never-ceasing vengeance; let despair,
Danger, or infamy, nay all surround me;
Starve me with wantings;* let my eyes ne'er see
A sight of comfort, nor my heart know peace,
But dash my days with sorrow, nights with horrors
Wild as my own thoughts now, and let loose fury
To make me mad enough for what I lose,
If I must lose him. If I must? I will not.
Oh turn and hear me!
JAFFEIR.
Now hold, heart, or never.
BELVIDERA.
By all the tender days we have lived together,
By all our charming nights and joys that crowned 'em,
Pity my sad condition, speak, but speak.
JAFFEIR.
Ohhh.
BELVIDERA.
By these arms that now cling round thy neck,
By this dear kiss and by ten thousand more,
By these poor streaming eyes—
JAFFEIR.
Murther! unhold me.
By th'immortal destiny that doomed me
(*Draws his dagger.*)
To this curst minute, I'll not live one longer.
Resolve to let me go or see me fall—
BELVIDERA.
Hold, sir, be patient.
Passing-bell tolls.*
JAFFEIR.
Hark, the dismal bell

Tolls out for death. I must attend its call too,
For my poor friend, my dying Pierre, expects me:
He sent a message to require I'd see him
Before he died and take his last forgiveness.
Farewell forever.

BELVIDERA.
Leave thy dagger with me.
Bequeath me something. Not one kiss at parting?
—Oh my poor heart, when wilt thou break?

JAFFEIR. (*Going out, looks back at her.*)
Yet stay:
We have a child, as yet a tender infant.
Be a kind mother to him when I am gone,
Breed him in virtue and the paths of honor,
But let him never know his father's story;
I charge thee guard him from the wrongs my fate
May do his future fortune or his name.
Now—nearer yet—

Approaching each other.

Oh that my arms were riveted
Thus round thee ever!—But my friends, my oath!
—This and no more. (*Kisses her.*)

BELVIDERA.
Another, sure another
For that poor little one you've ta'en care of,
I'll giv't him truly.

JAFFEIR.
So, now farewell.

BELVIDERA.
Forever?

JAFFEIR.
Heaven knows, forever. All good angels guard thee. [*Exit.*]

BELVIDERA.
All ill ones sure had charge of me this moment!
Curst be my days and doubly curst my nights,
Which I must now mourn out in widowed tears;
Blasted be every herb and fruit and tree;
Curst be the rain that falls upon the earth;
And may the general curse reach man and beast.
Oh give me daggers, fire, or water.
How I could bleed, how burn, how drown the waves
Huzzing and booming round my sinking head
Till I descended to the peaceful bottom!
Oh there's all quiet, here all rage and fury;
The air's too thin and pierces my weak brain.
I long for thick substantial sleep. Hell, hell,
Burst from the center, rage, and roar aloud,
If thou art half so hot, so mad as I am.

Enter Priuli and servants.

Who's there?

PRIULI.
Run, seize and bring her safely home,

They seize her.

Guard her as you would life. Alas poor creature!

BELVIDERA.
What? to my husband then conduct me quickly.
Are all things ready? Shall we die most gloriously?
Say not a word of this to my old father:
Murmuring streams, soft shades, and springing flowers,
Lutes, laurels, seas of milk, and ships of amber.

Exeunt.

[Scene iii.] Scene opening discovers* a scaffold and a wheel prepared for the executing of Pierre.

Enter officers, Pierre and guards, a friar, executioner and a great rabble.

OFFICER.
Room, room there—stand all by, make room for the prisoner.

PIERRE.
My friend not come yet?

FRIAR.
Why are you so obstinate?

PIERRE.
Why are you so troublesome, that a poor wretch
Cannot die in peace?
But you, like ravens, will be croaking round him—

FRIAR.
Yet, Heaven—

PIERRE.
I tell thee Heaven and I are friends;
I ne'er broke peace with't yet by cruel murthers,
Rapine, or perjury or vile deceiving,
But lived in moral justice towards all men
Nor am a foe to the most strong believers,
Howe'er my own shortsighted faith confine me.

FRIAR.
But an all-seeing Judge—
PIERRE.
You say my conscience
Must be mine accuser. I have searched that conscience
And find no records there of crimes that scare me.
FRIAR.
'Tis strange you should want* faith.
PIERRE.
You want to lead
My reason blindfold, like a hampered lion,
Checked of its nobler vigor then, when baited,
Down to obedient tameness, make it couch
And show strange tricks which you call signs of faith.
So silly* souls are gulled and you get money.
Away, no more.—Captain, I would hereafter
This fellow write no lies of my conversion
Because he has crept upon my troubled hours.

Enter Jaffeir.

JAFFEIR.
Hold. Eyes, be dry; heart, strengthen me to bear
This hideous sight and humble me to take
The last forgiveness of a dying friend,
Betrayed by my vile falsehood to his ruin.
Oh Pierre!
PIERRE.
Yet nearer.
JAFFEIR.
Crawling on my knees
And prostrate on the earth, let me approach thee.
How shall I look up to thy injured face,
That always used to smile with friendship on me?
It darts an air of so much manly virtue
That I, methinks, look little in thy sight
And stripes are fitter for me than embraces.
PIERRE.
Dear to my arms, though thou hast undone my fame,
I cannot forget to love thee. Prithee Jaffeir,
Forgive that filthy blow my passion dealt thee.
I am now preparing for the land of peace
And fain would have the charitable wishes
Of all good men like thee to bless my journey.
JAFFEIR.
Good! I am the vilest creature, worse than e'er
Suffered the shameful fate thou art going to taste of.
Why was I sent for to be used thus kindly?
Call, call me villain, as I am, describe
The foul complexion of my hateful deeds,
Lead me to the rack, and stretch me in thy stead:
I've crimes enough to give it its full load
And do it credit. Thou wilt but spoil the use on't,
And honest men hereafter bear its figure
About 'em as a charm from treacherous friendship.
OFFICER.
The time grows short, your friends are dead already.
JAFFEIR.
Dead!
PIERRE.
Yes, dead, Jaffeir, they've all died like men too,
Worthy their character.
JAFFEIR.
And what must I do?
PIERRE.
Oh, Jaffeir!
JAFFEIR.
Speak aloud thy burthened soul
And tell thy troubles to thy tortured friend.
PIERRE.
Friend! Couldst thou yet be a friend, a generous friend,
I might hope comfort from thy noble sorrows.
Heaven knows I want* a friend.
JAFFEIR.
And I a kind one,
That would not thus scorn my repenting virtue
Or think, when he is to die, my thoughts are idle.
PIERRE.
No! live, I charge thee, Jaffeir.
JAFFEIR.
Yes, I will live,
But it shall be to see thy fall revenged
At such a rate as Venice long shall groan for.
PIERRE.
Wilt thou?
JAFFEIR.
I will, by Heav'n.
PIERRE.
Then still thou'rt noble,
And I forgive thee, oh—yet—shall I trust thee?

JAFFEIR.
No: I've been false already.
PIERRE.
Dost thou love me?
JAFFEIR.
Rip up my heart and satisfy thy doubtings.
PIERRE.
Curse on this weakness. (*Weeps.*)
JAFFEIR.
Tears! Amazement! Tears!
I never saw thee melted thus before
And know there's something lab'ring in thy bosom
That must have vent. Though I'm a villain, tell me.
PIERRE.
Seest thou that engine? (*Pointing to the wheel.*)
JAFFEIR.
Why?
PIERRE.
Is't fit a soldier who has lived with honor,
Fought nation's quarrels,* and been crowned with conquest,
Be exposed a common carcass on a wheel?
JAFFEIR.
Hah!
PIERRE.
Speak! is't fitting?
JAFFEIR.
Fitting?
PIERRE.
Yes, is't fitting?
JAFFEIR.
What's to be done?
PIERRE.
I'd have thee undertake
Something that's noble to preserve my memory
From the disgrace that's ready to attaint it.
OFFICER.
The day grows late, sir.
PIERRE.
I'll make haste!—Oh Jaffeir,
Though thou'st betrayed me, do me some way justice.
JAFFEIR.
No more of that. Thy wishes shall be satisfied:
I have a wife, and she shall bleed, my child too
Yield up his little throat, and all t'appease thee—

Going away Pierre holds him.

PIERRE.
No—this—no more! (*Whispers Jaffeir.*)
JAFFEIR.
Hah! is't then so?
PIERRE.
Most certainly.
JAFFEIR.
I'll do't.
PIERRE.
Remember.
OFFICER.
Sir.
PIERRE.
Come, now I am ready.

He and Jaffeir ascend the scaffold.

Captain, you should be a gentleman of honor,
Keep off the rabble, that I may have room
To entertain my fate and die with decency.
Come!

Takes off his gown. Executioner prepares to bind him.

FRIAR.
Son!
PIERRE.
Hence, tempter.
OFFICER.
Stand off, priest.
PIERRE.
I thank you, sir. (*To Jaffeir.*)
You'll think on't.
JAFFEIR.
'Twon't grow stale before tomorrow.
PIERRE. (*Executioner having bound him.*)
Now, Jaffeir! Now I am going. Now—

JAFFEIR.
Have at thee,
Thou honest heart, then—here— (*Stabs him.*)
And this is well too. (*Then stabs himself.*)
FRIAR.
Damnable deed!
PIERRE.
Now thou hast indeed been faithful.
This was done nobly—we have deceived the Senate.

JAFFEIR.
Bravely.
PIERRE.
Ha ha ha—oh oh— (*Dies.*)
JAFFEIR.
Now ye curst rulers,
Thus of the blood y'have shed I make libation
And sprinkle't mingling: may it rest upon you
And all your race. Be henceforth peace a stranger
Within your walls; let plagues and famine waste
Your generations— Oh poor Belvidera!
Sir, I have a wife, bear this in safety to her,
A token that with my dying breath I blessed her
And the dear little infant left behind me.
I am sick—I am quiet— (*Dies.*)
OFFICER.
Bear this news to the Senate
And guard their bodies till there's farther order.
—Heaven grant I die so well.

Scene shuts upon them.

[Scene iv. Priuli's house.]

Soft Music. Enter Belvidera distracted, led by two of her women, Priuli, and servants.

PRIULI.
Strengthen her heart with patience, pitying Heav'n.
BELVIDERA.
Come, come, come, come, come. Nay, come to bed!
Prithee my love. The winds! hark how they whistle!
And the rain beats. Oh how the weather shrinks me!
You are angry now, who cares? Pish, no indeed.
Choose then, I say you shall not go, you shall not;
Whip your ill nature; get you gone then! Oh,

Jaffeir's ghost rises.

Are you returned? See father, here he's come again,
Am I to blame to love him! Oh thou dear one.

Ghost sinks.

Why do you fly me? Are you angry still then?
Jaffeir! where art thou? Father, why do you do thus?
Stand off, don't hide him from me. He's here somewhere.
Stand off I say! What, gone? Remember't, tyrant!
I may revenge my self for this trick one day.

Enter Officer and others.

I'll do't—I'll do't. Renault's a nasty fellow.
Hang him, hang him, hang him.
PRIULI.
News, what news?

Officer whispers Priuli.

OFFICER.
Most sad, sir.
Jaffeir upon the scaffold, to prevent
A shameful death, stabbed Pierre and next himself.
Both fell together.
PRIULI.
Daughter.

The ghosts of Jaffeir and Pierre rise together both bloody.

BELVIDERA.
Hah, look there!
My husband bloody, and his friend too! Murther!
Who has done this? Speak to me, thou sad vision,

Ghosts sink.

On these poor trembling knees I beg it.—
Vanished—
Here they went down. Oh I'll dig, dig the den up.
You shan't delude me thus. Hoa, Jaffeir, Jaffeir.
Peep up and give me but a look. I have him!
I've got him, Father. Oh now how I'll smuggle him!
My love! my dear! my blessing! Help me, help me!
They have hold on me and drag me to the bottom.
Nay—now they pull so hard—farewell— (*Dies.*)
MAID.
She's dead.
Breathless and dead.
PRIULI.
Then guard me from the sight on't.
Lead me into some place that's fit for mourning,
Where the free air, light, and the cheerful sun
May never enter. Hang it round with black,
Set up one taper that may last a day,
As long as I've to live, and there all leave me.
Sparing no tears when you this tale relate,
But bid all cruel fathers dread my fate.

Curtain falls, exeunt omnes.

[Epilogue]

EPILOGUE

The text is done, and now for application,
And, when that's ended, pass your approbation.
Though the conspiracy's prevented here,
Methinks I see another hatching there,
And there's a certain faction fain would sway,[32]
If they had strength enough, and damn this play,
But this the author bade me boldly say:
If any take his plainness in ill part,
He's glad on't from the bottom of his heart;
Poets in honor of the truth should write
With the same spirits brave men for it fight,
And though against him causeless hatreds rise
And daily where he goes of late he spies
The scowls of sullen and revengeful eyes,
'Tis what he knows with much contempt to bear
And serves a cause too good to let him fear.
He fears no poison from an incensed drab,
No ruffian's five-foot-sword, nor rascal's stab,
Nor any other snares of mischief laid:
Not a Rose Alley cudgel ambuscade,[33]
From any private cause where malice reigns,
Or general pique all blockheads have to brains.
Nothing shall daunt his pen when truth does call,
No, not the picture-mangler at Guildhall.[34]
The rebel tribe, of which that vermin's one,
Have now set forward and their course begun.
And while that prince's figure they deface,
As they before had massacred his name,
Durst their base fears but look him in the face,
They'd use his person as they've used his fame;
A face, in which such lineaments they read
Of that great martyr's[35] whose rich blood they shed
That their rebellious hate they still retain
And in his son would murther him again.
With indignation then, let each brave heart
Rouse and unite to take his injured part,
Till royal love and goodness call him home[36]
And songs of triumph meet him as he come;
Till Heaven his honor and our peace restore,
And villains never wrong his virtue more.

FINIS.

[32] certain faction] Whigs, supporters of the bill to exclude the duke of York from the succession

[33] Rose Alley cudgel ambuscade] refers to an assault on John Dryden on the evening of 18 December 1679; neither the motive nor the assailants are known, though some contemporaries—and some modern scholars—suspect Whigs.

[34] picture-mangler] A marginal note reads, "The rascal that cut the Duke of York's picture." The incident took place at Guildhall, City office building, in January 1682, shortly before the play's first performance.

[35] great martyr] Charles I

[36] call him home] To avoid the provocation of his presence in England during the Exclusion Crisis, Charles II sent James, duke of York, out of the country repeatedly between 1679 and 1682; he was currently in Scotland.

Textual Notes

[a] Copytext is the first edition, a 1682 quarto (Q1). Also consulted were the second edition, a 1696 quarto (Q2); the third edition, a 1704 quarto (Q3); the first collected edition in 1712 (C); and modern editions of 1932 (Ghosh) and of 1969 (Kelsall).

[b] make] Q3, C, Ghosh, Kelsall; may Q1-2

[c] make … tell] Q3, C, Ghosh, Kelsall; makes … tells Q 1-2

[d] worst] Q3, C, Ghosh; first Q1-2, Kelsall

[e] which] Q3, C, Ghosh, Kelsall; with Q1-2

[f] taught] Q3, C, Ghosh, Kelsall; thought Q1-2

[g] with] Q3, C, Ghosh, Kelsall; *om.* Q1-2

[h] gall] C, Ghosh, Kelsall; call Q1-3

[i] the] Ghosh, Kelsall; thy Q1-2; his Q3, C

[j] to] Ghosh, Kelsall; *om.* Q1-3, C

Oroonoko[a]

by Thomas Southerne (1660-1746)

edited by Joyce Green MacDonald

Thomas Southerne's *Oroonoko* (1695) is a dramatization of Aphra Behn's 1688 novella of the same name. Just as his play capitalized on the popularity of Behn's prose, so too did later playwrights return to Southerne's comic drama: John Hawkesworth, Francis Gentleman, John Ferriar and anonymous others all produced their own adaptations of Southerne's work. In one form or another, *Oroonoko* appeared on London stages throughout the first three-quarters of the eighteenth century.

And yet the *Oroonoko*s other playwrights modeled on Southerne's work markedly differed from it, just as his play altered Behn's powerful story of a pair of enslaved African lovers' rebellion and death in a New World jungle. Southerne paired the serious matter he borrowed from Behn with a comic plot of his own invention, in which the impecunious Welldon sisters have journeyed out from London to find rich husbands in colonial Suriname. Hawkesworth, Gentleman and the rest eliminated the Welldon sisters' plot from their adaptations of Southerne, while retaining and heightening the sentimental pathos with which he presents the doom of Oroonoko and his pregnant bride Imoinda. Southerne's adapters also retain the striking alteration he makes—without comment—in Behn: where Behn's tragic heroine is a black-skinned beauty, Southerne's is white.

Oroonoko is Southerne's second adaptation of Behn (the first was 1694's *The Fatal Marriage*). Besides Behn, his work also looks backward to the pathos of such Restoration heroic tragedies as Otway's *Venice Preserv'd.* The tone of the play's declamatory speeches about the plight of its tragic lovers and much of its language for describing Oroonoko's blackness hearken back even farther, to Shakespeare's *Othello*; Shakespearean echoes can be heard throughout the serious drama of the Restoration.

But if *Oroonoko* is thus grounded in traditional dramatic elements, it was also felt by its first audiences to be a strikingly contemporary play. Premiering near the beginnings of the development of a mercantile colonialism supported by slavery, Southerne's *Oroonoko* and its revisions increasingly came to be regarded as important documents in the eighteenth-century abolitionist movement. The play's attention to the roles of women in slavery and in slave societies perhaps offered additional interest to women in the Restoration audience. Not only were women to become notably active in English abolition, but the play also offers the comic pleasure of watching the Welldon sisters learning to negotiate the hazards of an unscrupulous sexual marketplace. As the celebrated actress Mrs. Verbruggen, who played Charlotte Welldon in the original production, declared in the epilogue:

> Men show their valor and women their discretion;
> To lands of monsters, and fierce beasts they go:
> We, to those islands, where rich husbands grow.

The clever Charlotte and the sensual Lucy can be seen as female versions of the familiar Restoration rake-hero, and as such, their success proclaims the ability of the exceptional character to recognize the essential hypocrisy and corruption of the social order, and yet to achieve romantic, social, and fiscal satisfaction within its constraints.

[Epistle]

from Epistle Dedicatory

To his Grace, William, duke of Devonshire[1]

... I stand engaged to Mrs. Behn[2] for the occasion of a most passionate distress in my last play,[3] and in a conscience that I had not made her a sufficient acknowledgement, I have run further into her debt for *Oroonoko*, with a design to oblige me to be honest; and that everyone may find me out for ingratitude when I don't say all that's fit for me upon that subject. She had a great command of the stage, and I have often wondered that she would bury her favorite hero in a *novel*, when she might have revived him in the *scene*. She thought either that no actor could represent him, or she could not bear him represented. And I believe the last, when I remember what I have heard from a friend of hers, that she always told his story more feelingly than she writ it. Whatever happened to him in *Suriname*, he has mended his condition in *England*. He was born here under your Grace's influence, and that has carried his fortune farther into the world than all the poetical stars that I could have solicited for his success.

DRAMATIS PERSONAE

MEN

Oroonoko.
Aboan.
Lieutenant Governor of Suriname.
Blanford.
Stanmore.
Jack Stanmore.
Captain Driver.
Daniel, son to Widow Lackitt.
Hottman.
Planters, Indians, Negroes, Men, Women, and Children.

WOMEN

Imoinda.
Widow Lackitt.
Charlotte Welldon, in man's clothes.
Lucy Welldon, her sister.

THE SCENE: SURINAME,[4] A COLONY IN THE WEST INDIES AT THE TIME OF THE ACTION OF THE TRAGEDY IN POSSESSION OF THE ENGLISH.

Oroonoko.

Quo fata trahunt, virtus secura sequetur. Lucan.[5]
Virtus recludens immeritis mori
Coelum, negata tentat iter via. Hor. *Od.* 2. lib. 3.[6]

Act I, scene i. [The Welldons' house.]

Enter Welldon following Lucia.

LUCIA.
What will this come to? What can it end in? You have persuaded me to leave dear England and dearer London, the place of the world most worth living in, to follow you a-husband-hunting into America. I thought husbands grew in these plantations.

WELLDON.
Why so they do, as thick as oranges, ripening one under another. Week after week they drop into some woman's mouth. 'Tis but a little patience, spreading your apron in expectation, and one of 'em will fall into your lap at last.

LUCIA.
Aye, so you say indeed.

---

1 William, duke of Devonshire] William Cavendish (1641-1707), first duke of Devonshire, was a prominent Whig politician and opponent of James, duke of York, from the Exclusion Crisis through the Glorious Revolution.

2 Mrs. Behn] Aphra Behn (c. 1640-1689), author of the novella *Oroonoko* (1688), the source of this play, lived for almost a year in Suriname.

3 last play] *The Fatal Marriage* (1694) part of which was adapted from *The History of the Nun; or, The Fair Vow Breaker* (1689).

4 Suriname] Actually on the northern coast of South America; an English colony was founded there in 1651 and ceded to the Dutch in 1667.

5 *Quo* ... Lucan.] Lucan, *Pharsalia* ii.287: "Virtue will follow fearless wherever destiny summons her" (Loeb).

6 *Virtus* ... 3] Horace, *Odes* 3.2: "True worth, opening Heaven wide for those deserving not to die, essays its course by a path denied to others" (Loeb).

WELLDON.

But you have left dear London, you say. Pray what have you left in London that was very dear to you that had not left you before?

LUCIA.

Speak for yourself, sister.

WELLDON.

Nay, I'll keep you in countenance. The young fellows, you know, the dearest part of the Town* and without whom London had been a wilderness to you and me, had forsaken us a great while.

LUCIA.

Forsaken us! I don't know that they ever had us.

WELLDON.

Forsaken us the worst way, child;* that is, did not think us worth having. They neglected us, no longer designed upon us, they were tired of us. Women in London are like the rich silks: they are out of fashion a great while before they wear out.

LUCIA.

The Devil take the fashion, I say.

WELLDON.

You may tumble 'em over and over at their first coming up and never disparage their price, but they fall upon wearing immediately lower and lower in their value, till they come to the broker at last.

LUCIA.

Aye, aye, that's the merchant they deal with. The men would have us at their own scandalous rates. Their plenty makes 'em wanton, and in a little time, I suppose, they won't know what they would have of the women themselves.

WELLDON.

Oh yes, they know what they would have. They would have a woman give the Town a pattern of her person and beauty and not stay in it so long to have the whole piece worn out. They would have the good face only discovered and not the folly that commonly goes along with it. They say there is a vast stock of beauty in the Nation, but a great part of it lies in unprofitable hands. Therefore, for the good of the public they would have a draught made once a quarter, send the decaying beauties for breeders into the country to make room for new faces to appear, to countenance the pleasures of the Town.

LUCIA.

'Tis very hard. The men must be young as long as they live, and poor women be thought decaying and unfit for the Town at one or two and twenty. I'm sure we were not seven years in London.

WELLDON.

Not half the time taken notice of, sister. The two or three last years we could make nothing of it, even in a vizard-mask: not in a vizard-mask, that has cheated many a man into an old acquaintance. Our faces began to be as familiar to the men of intrigue as their duns, and as much avoided. We durst not appear in public places and were almost grudged a gallery in the churches.[7] Even there they had their jests upon us and cried, "She's in the right on't, good gentlewoman; since no man considers her body, she does very well indeed to take care of her soul."

LUCIA.

Such unmannerly fellows there will always be.

WELLDON.

Then, you may remember, we were reduced to the last necessity, the necessity of making silly visits to our civil acquaintance to bring us into tolerable company. Nay, the young Inns of Court* beaus of but one term's standing in the fashion, who knew nobody but as they were shown 'em by the orange-women,* had nicknames for us. How often have they laughed out, "There goes my landlady. Is not she come to let lodgings yet?"[8]

LUCIA.

Young coxcombs that knew no better.

WELLDON.

And that we must have come to. For your part, what trade could you set up in? You would never arrive at the trust and credit of a guinea-bawd;[9] you would have too much business of your own, ever to mind other peoples'.

---

7 gallery in the churches] Like a playhouse box, a gallery, or side balcony, in a London church was regarded as a place for fashionable self-display.

8 landlady...lodgings] "landlady" could mean mistress (*OED*); to "let lodgings" implies setting up as a common prostitute.

9 guinea-bawd] A guinea was a common fee or tip for services rendered, in this instance by the madam of a brothel.

LUCIA.

That is true indeed.

WELLDON.

Then, as a certain sign that there was nothing more to be hoped for, the maids at the chocolate houses found us out and laughed at us. Our *billets-doux* lay there neglected for waste-paper; we were cried down so low we could not pass upon the City* and became so notorious in our galloping way, from one end of the Town to the other, that at last we could hardly compass a competent change of petticoats to disguise us to the hackney coachmen. And then it was near walking afoot indeed.

LUCIA.

Nay, that I began to be afraid of.

WELLDON.

To prevent which, with what youth and beauty was left, some experience, and the small remainder of fifteen hundred pounds apiece, which amounted to bare two hundred between us both, I persuaded you to bring your person for a venture to the Indies. Everything has succeeded in our voyage: I pass for your brother; one of the richest planters here happening to die just as we landed, I have claimed kindred with him. So, without making his will, he has left us the credit of his relation to trade upon. We pass for his cousins, coming here to Suriname chiefly upon his invitation. We live in reputation, have the best acquaintance of the place, and we shall see our account in't, I warrant you.

LUCIA.

I must rely upon you.

Enter Widow Lackitt.

WIDOW.

Mr. Welldon, your servant. Your servant, Mrs. Lucy. I am an ill visitor, but 'tis not too late, I hope, to bid you welcome to this side of the world. (*Salutes* Lucy.*)

WELLDON.

Gad so, I beg your pardon, Widow. I should have done the civilities of my house before, but as you say, 'tis not too late, I hope. (*Going to kiss her.*)

WIDOW.

What! You think now this was a civil way of begging a kiss, and by my troth, if it were, I see no harm in't; 'tis a pitiful favor indeed that is not worth asking for, though I have known a woman speak plainer before now and not understood neither.

WELLDON.

Not under my roof. Have at you, Widow.

WIDOW.

Why, that's well said, spoke like a younger brother that deserves to have a widow.

He kisses her.

You're a younger brother, I know, by your kissing.

WELLDON.

How so, pray?

WIDOW.

Why, you kiss as if you expect to be paid for't. You have birdlime upon your lips. You stick so close, there's no getting rid of you.

WELLDON.

I am akin to a younger brother.

WIDOW.

So much the better. We widows are commonly the better for younger brothers.

LUCIA. (*Aside.*)

Better, or worse, most of you. But you won't be much better for him, I can tell you.

WELLDON.

I was a younger brother, but an uncle of my mother's has maliciously left me an estate and, I'm afraid, spoiled my fortune.

WIDOW.

No, no, an estate will never spoil your fortune. I have a good estate myself, thank Heaven, and a kind husband that left it behind him.

WELLDON.

Thank Heaven, that took him away from it, Widow, and left you behind him.

WIDOW.

Nay, Heaven's will must be done; he's in a better place.

WELLDON.

A better place for you, no doubt on't. Now you may look about you. Choose for yourself, Mrs. Lackitt, that's your business, for I know you design to marry again.

WIDOW.

Oh dear! Not I, I protest and swear; I don't design

it. But I won't swear neither; one does not know what may happen to tempt one.

WELLDON.

Why, a lusty young fellow may happen to tempt you.

WIDOW.

Nay, I'll do nothing rashly; I'll resolve against nothing. The Devil, they say, is very busy upon these occasions, especially with the widows. But if I am to be tempted, it must be with a young man, I promise you.—Mrs. Lucy, your brother is a very pleasant gentleman. I came about business to him, but he turns everything into merriment.

WELLDON.

Business, Mrs. Lackitt. Then I know you would have me to yourself. Pray leave us together, sister.

Exit Lucy.

(*Aside.*) What am I drawing upon myself here?

WIDOW.

You have taken a very pretty house here, everything so neat about you already. I hear you are laying out for a plantation.

WELLDON.

Why yes, truly, I like the country and would buy a plantation if I could, reasonably.

WIDOW.

Oh! by all means, reasonably.

WELLDON.

If I could have one to my mind, I would think of settling among you.

WIDOW.

Oh! you can't do better. Indeed we can't pretend to have so good company for you as you had in England, but we shall make very much of you. For my own part, I assure you, I shall think myself very happy to be more particularly known to you.

WELLDON.

Dear Mrs. Lackitt, you do me too much honor.

WIDOW.

Then as to a plantation, Mr. Welldon, you know I have several to dispose of. Mr. Lackitt, I thank him, has left me, though I say it, the richest widow upon the place; therefore, I may afford to use you better than other people can. You shall have one upon any reasonable terms.

WELLDON.

That's a fair offer indeed.

WIDOW.

You shall find me as easy as anybody you can have to do with, I assure you. Pray try me, I would have you try me, Mr. Welldon. Well, I like that name of yours exceedingly, Mr. Welldon.

WELLDON.

My name!

WIDOW.

Oh, exceedingly! If anything could persuade me to alter my own name, I verily believe nothing in the world would do it so soon as to be called Mrs. Welldon.

WELLDON.

Why, indeed, Welldon does sound something better than Lackitt.

WIDOW.

Oh! a great deal better. Not that there is so much in a name neither. But I don't know, there is something: I should like mightily to be called Mrs. Welldon.

WELLDON.

I'm glad you like my name.

WIDOW.

Of all things. But then there's the misfortune: one can't change one's name without changing one's condition.

WELLDON.

You'll hardly think it worth that, I believe.

WIDOW.

Think it worth what, sir? Changing my condition? Indeed sir, I think it worth everything. But alas! Mr. Welldon, I have been a widow but six weeks;[b] 'tis too soon to think of changing one's condition yet, indeed it is. Pray don't desire it of me. Not but that you may persuade me to anything, sooner than any person in the world.

WELLDON.

Who, I, Mrs. Lackitt?

WIDOW.

Indeed you may, Mr. Welldon, sooner than any man living. Lord, there's a great deal in saving a decency; I never minded it before. Well, I'm glad you spoke first to excuse my modesty. But what, modesty means nothing and is the virtue of a girl that does not know what she would be at; a widow should be wiser. Now I will own to you, but I won't confess neither, I have had a great respect for you a great while. I beg your pardon, sir, and I must declare to you, indeed I must, if you desire to dispose of all I have in the world in an honorable way, which I don't pretend to be any way deserving your consideration, my fortune and person, if you won't understand me without telling you so, are both at your service. Gad so! another time—

Stanmore enters to them.

STANMORE.
So, Mrs. Lackitt, your widowhood is waning apace. I see which way 'tis going. Welldon, you're a happy man. The women and their favors come home to you.

WIDOW.
A fiddle of favor, Mr. Stanmore. I am a lone woman, you know it, left in a great deal of business, and business must be followed or lost. I have several stocks and plantations upon my hands, and other things to dispose of, which Mr. Welldon may have occasion for.

WELLDON.
We were just upon the brink of a bargain as you came in.

STANMORE.
Let me drive it on for you.

WELLDON.
So you must, I believe, you or somebody for me.

STANMORE.
I'll stand by you. I understand more of this business than you can pretend to.

WELLDON.
I don't pretend to't; 'tis quite out of my way indeed.

STANMORE.
If the widow gets you to herself, she will certainly be too hard for you. I know her of old. She has no conscience in a corner, a very Jew in a bargain, and would circumcise you to get more of you.

WELLDON.
Is this true, Widow?

WIDOW.
Speak as you find, Mr. Welldon. I have offered you very fair. Think upon't, and let me hear of you. The sooner the better, Mr. Welldon. (*Exit.*)

STANMORE.
I assure you, my friend, she'll cheat you if she can.

WELLDON.
I don't know that, but I can cheat her, if I will.

STANMORE.
Cheat her? How?

WELLDON.
I can marry her. And then I'm sure I have it in my power to cheat her.

STANMORE.
Can you marry her?

WELLDON.
Yes, faith, so she says. Her pretty person and fortune (which, one with the other, you know, are not contemptible) are both at my service.

STANMORE.
Contemptible! very considerable, egad; very desirable. Why, she's worth ten thousand pounds, man, a clear estate: no charge upon it but a boobily son. He indeed was to have half, but his father begot him and she breeds him up not to know or have more than she has a mind to. And she has a mind to something else, it seems.

WELLDON. (*Musing.*)
There's a great deal to be made of this.

STANMORE.
A handsome fortune may be made on't, and I advise you to't, by all means.

WELLDON.
To marry her! an old, wanton witch! I hate her.

STANMORE.
No matter for that. Let her go to the devil for you. She'll cheat her son of a good estate for you. That's a perquisite of a widow's portion always.

WELLDON.
I have a design and will follow her at least till I have a pennyworth of the plantation.*

STANMORE.
I speak as a friend, when I advise you to marry her. For 'tis directly against the interest of my own family. My cousin Jack has belabored her a good while that way.

WELLDON.
What! Honest Jack! I'll not hinder him. I'll give

over the thoughts of her.

STANMORE.

He'll make nothing on't; she does not care for him. I'm glad you have her in your power.

WELLDON.

I may be able to serve him.

STANMORE.

Here's a ship come into the river; I was in hopes it had been from England.

WELLDON.

From England!

STANMORE.

No, I was disappointed. I long to see this handsome cousin of yours; the picture you gave me of her has charmed me.

WELLDON.

You'll see whether it has flattered her or no, in a little time. If she recovered of that illness that was the reason of her staying behind us, I know she will come with the first opportunity. We shall see her, or hear of her death.

STANMORE.

We'll hope the best. The ships from England are expected every day.

WELLDON.

What ship is this?

STANMORE.

A rover, a buccaneer, a trader in slaves: that's the commodity we deal in, you know. If you have a curiosity to see our manner of marketing, I'll wait upon you.

WELLDON.

We'll take my sister with us.

Exeunt.

Scene ii. An open place.

Enter Lieutenant Governor and Blanford.

LIEUTENANT GOVERNOR.

There's no resisting your fortune, Blanford; you draw all the prizes.

BLANFORD.

I draw for our Lord Governor, you know; his fortune favors me.

LIEUTENANT GOVERNOR.

I grudge him nothing this time, but if fortune had favored me in the last sale, the fair slave[10] had been mine, Clemene had been mine.

BLANFORD.

Are you still in love with her?

LIEUTENANT GOVERNOR.

Every day more in love with her.

Enter Captain Driver, teased and pulled about by Widow Lackitt and several planters. Enter at another door Welldon, Lucia, Stanmore.

WIDOW.

Here have I six slaves in my lot, and not a man among 'em; all women and children.[11] What can I do with 'em, Captain? Pray consider, I am a woman myself and can't get my own slaves, as some of my neighbors do.

FIRST PLANTER.

I have all men in mine. Pray Captain, let the men and women be mingled together for procreation's sake and the good of the plantation.*

SECOND PLANTER.

Aye, aye, a man and a woman, Captain, for the good of the plantation.

CAPTAIN.

Let 'em mingle together and be damned, what care I? Would you have me pimp for the good of the plantation?

FIRST PLANTER.

I am a constant customer, Captain.

WIDOW.

I am always ready money to you, Captain.

FIRST PLANTER.

For that matter, Mistress, my money is as ready as yours.

WIDOW.

Pray hear me, Captain.

CAPTAIN.

Look you, I have done my part by you; I have brought the number of slaves you bargained for.

---

10 fair slave] perhaps "white-skinned" as well as the commoner meaning, "beautiful"

11 all women and children] A lot was a previously-contracted-for number of slaves. In her novel Behn writes that whatever the gender mix in your lot, you are obliged to take it as it is.

If your lots have not pleased you, you must draw again among yourselves.

THIRD PLANTER.

I am contented with my lot.

FOURTH PLANTER.

I am very well satisfied.

THIRD PLANTER.

We'll have no drawing again.

CAPTAIN.

Do you hear, Mistress? You may hold your tongue. For my part, I expect my money.

WIDOW.

Captain, nobody questions or scruples the payment. But I won't hold my tongue; 'tis too much to pray and pay too. One may speak for one's own, I hope.

CAPTAIN.

Well, what would you say?

WIDOW.

I say no more than I can make out.

CAPTAIN.

Out with it, then.

WIDOW.

I say, things have not been so fair carried as they might have been. How do I know how you have juggled together in my absence? You drew the lots before I came, I'm sure.

CAPTAIN.

That's your own fault, Mistress; you might have come sooner.

WIDOW.

Then here's a prince, as they say, among the slaves, and you set him down to go as a common man.

CAPTAIN.

Have you a mind to try what a man he is? You'll find him no more than a common man at your business.

WIDOW.

Sir, you're a scurvy fellow to talk at this rate to me. If my husband were alive, Gadsbodikins, you would not use me so.

CAPTAIN.

Right, Mistress, I would not use you at all.

WIDOW.

Not use me! Your betters every inch of you, I would have you to know, would be glad to use me, sirrah. Marry* come up here, who are you, I trow? You begin to think yourself a captain, forsooth, because we call you so. You forget yourself as fast as you can, but I remember you. I know you for a pitiful paltry fellow, as you are, an upstart to prosperity, one that is but just come acquainted with cleanliness and that never saw five shillings of your own without deserving to be hanged for 'em.

LIEUTENANT GOVERNOR.

She has given you a broadside, Captain. You'll stand up to her.

CAPTAIN.

Hang her, stinkpot, I'll come no nearer.

WIDOW.

By this good light, it would make a woman do a thing she never designed—marry again, though she were sure to repent it, to be revenged of such a—

JACK STANMORE.

What's the matter, Mrs. Lackitt? Can I serve you?

WIDOW.

No, no, you can't serve me. You are for serving yourself, I'm sure. Pray go about your business, I have none for you. You know I have told you so. Lord! how can you be so troublesome? nay, so unconscionable, to think that every rich widow must throw herself away upon a young fellow that has nothing?

STANMORE.

Jack, you are answered, I suppose.

JACK STANMORE.

I'll have another pluck at her.

WIDOW.

Mr. Welldon, I am a little out of order, but pray bring your sister to dine with me. Gad's my life, I'm out of all patience with that pitiful fellow. My flesh rises at him. I can't stay in the place where he is. (*Exit.*)

BLANFORD.

Captain, you have used the widow very familiarly.

CAPTAIN.

This is my way; I have no design and therefore am not over-civil. If she had ever a handsome daughter to wheedle her out of, or if I could make anything of her booby son—

WELLDON. (*Aside.*)

I may improve that hint and make something of him.

LIEUTENANT GOVERNOR.
She's very rich.

CAPTAIN.
I'm rich myself. She has nothing that I want; I have no leaks to stop. Old women are fortune-menders. I have made a good voyage and would reap the fruits of my labor. We plow the deep, my masters, but our harvest is on shore. I'm for a young woman.

STANMORE.
Look about, Captain, there's one ripe and ready for the sickle.

CAPTAIN.
A woman indeed! I will be acquainted with her. Who is she?

WELLDON.
My sister, sir.

CAPTAIN.
Would I were akin to her. If she were my sister, she should never go out of the family. What say you, mistress? You expect I should marry you, I suppose.

LUCIA. (*Turning away.*)
I shan't be disappointed, if you don't.

WELLDON.
She won't break her heart, sir.

CAPTAIN. (*Following her.*)
But I mean—

WELLDON.
And I mean (*Going between him and Lucia*) that you must not think of her without marrying.

CAPTAIN.
I mean so too.

WELLDON.
Why, then, your meaning's out.

CAPTAIN.
You're very short.[12]

WELLDON.
I will grow and be taller for you.

CAPTAIN.
I shall grow angry and swear.

WELLDON.
You'll catch no fish then.[13]

CAPTAIN.
I don't well know whether he designs to affront me or no.

STANMORE.
No, no, he's a little familiar, 'tis his way.

CAPTAIN.
Say you so? Nay, I can be as familiar as he, if that be it. Well sir, look upon me full. What say you? How do you like me for a brother-in-law?

WELLDON.
Why yes, faith, you'll do my business (*Turning him about.*), if we can agree about my sister's.

CAPTAIN.
I don't know whether your sister will like me or not. I can't say much to her. But I have money enough, and if you are her brother, as you seem to be akin to her, I know that will recommend me to you.

WELLDON.
This is your* market for slaves. My sister is a free woman and must not be disposed of in public. You shall be welcome to my house, if you please. And upon better acquaintance, if my sister likes you, and I like your offers—

CAPTAIN.
Very well, sir, I'll come and see her.

LIEUTENANT GOVERNOR.
Where are the slaves, Captain? They are long a-coming.

BLANFORD.
And who is this prince that's fallen to my lot for the Lord Governor? Let me know something of him, that I may treat him accordingly. Who is he?

CAPTAIN.
He's the devil of a fellow, I can tell you. A prince every inch of him. You have paid dear enough for him for all the good he'll do you. I was forced to clap him in irons and did not think the ship safe, neither. You are in hostility with the Indians, they say; they threaten you daily. You had best have an eye upon him.

12 short] abrupt, but also perhaps a punning reference to the stature of Susannah Verbruggen, the actress who first played Charlotte Welldon (Jordan and Love)

13 no fish then] "If you swear, you'll catch no fish": proverbial.

BLANFORD.
But who is he?

LIEUTENANT GOVERNOR.
And how do you know him to be a prince?

CAPTAIN.
He is son and heir to the great King of Angola, a mischievous monarch in those parts, who, by his good will, would never let any of his neighbors be in quiet. This son was his general, a plaguy fighting fellow. I have formerly had dealings with him for slaves, which he took prisoners, and have got pretty roundly by him. But the wars being at an end and nothing more to be got by the trade of that country, I made bold to bring the prince along with me.

LIEUTENANT GOVERNOR.
How could you do that?

BLANFORD.
What? steal a prince out of his own country? Impossible!

CAPTAIN.
'Twas hard indeed, but I did it. You must know, this Oroonoko—

BLANFORD.
Is that his name?

CAPTAIN.
Aye, Oroonoko.

LIEUTENANT GOVERNOR.
Oroonoko.

CAPTAIN.
—is naturally inquisitive about the men and manners of the white nations. Because I could give him some account of the other parts of the world, I grew very much into his favor. In return of so great an honor, you know I could do no less upon my coming away than invite him on board me. Never having been in a ship, he appointed his time, and I prepared my entertainment. He came the next evening as privately as he could with about some twenty along with him. The punch went round, and as many of his attendants as would be dangerous I sent dead drunk on shore; the rest we secured. And so you have the Prince Oroonoko.

FIRST PLANTER.
Gad-a-mercy, Captain, there you were with him, i'faith.

SECOND PLANTER.
Such men as you are fit to be employed in public affairs. The plantation* will thrive by you.

THIRD PLANTER.
Industry should be encouraged.

CAPTAIN.
There's nothing done without it, boys. I have made my fortune this way.

BLANFORD.
Unheard-of villainy!

STANMORE.
Barbarous treachery!

BLANFORD.
They applaud him for't.

LIEUTENANT GOVERNOR.
But Captain, methinks you have taken a great deal of pains for this Prince Oroonoko. Why did you part with him at the common rate of slaves?

CAPTAIN.
Why, Lieutenant Governor, I'll tell you. I did design to carry him to England to have showed him there,[14] but I found him troublesome upon my hands, and I'm glad I'm rid of him.—Oh ho, here they come.

Black slaves—men, women, and children—pass across the stage by two and two; Aboan and others of Oroonoko's attendants two and two; Oroonoko last of all in chains.

LUCIA.
Are all these wretches slaves?

STANMORE.
All sold, they and their posterity all slaves.

LUCIA.
Oh miserable fortune!

BLANFORD.
Most of 'em know no better: they were born so and only change their masters. But a prince, born only to command, betrayed and sold! My heart drops blood for him.

CAPTAIN.
Now Governor, here he comes, pray observe him.

---

14 showed him there] Possibly in the manner of a public curiosity, as American Indians were displayed in England in the sixteenth and seventeenth centuries; cf. Shakespeare's *The Tempest.*

OROONOKO.

So sir, you have kept your word with me.

CAPTAIN.

I am a better Christian, I thank you, than to keep it with a heathen.

OROONOKO.

You are a Christian, be a Christian still:
If you have any god that teaches you
To break your word, I need not curse you more;
Let him cheat you, as you are false to me.
You faithful followers of my better fortune!
We have been fellow soldiers in the field;
Now we are fellow slaves. This last farewell.
(*Embracing his friends.*)
Be sure of one thing that will comfort us:
Whatever world we next are thrown upon
Cannot be worse than this.

All slaves go off but Oroonoko.

CAPTAIN.

You see what a bloody pagan he is, Governor, but I took care that none of his followers should be in the same lot with him for fear they should undertake some desperate action to the danger of the colony.

OROONOKO.

Live still in fear, it is the villain's curse
And will revenge my chains. Fear even me,
Who have no pow'r to hurt thee. Nature abhors
And drives thee out from the society
And commerce of mankind for breach of faith.
Men live and prosper but in mutual trust,
A confidence of one another's truth.
That thou hast violated. I have done.
I know my fortune, and submit to it.

LIEUTENANT GOVERNOR.

Sir, I am sorry for your fortune and would help it, if I could.

BLANFORD.

Take off his chains. (*Applying to him.*) You know your condition, but you are fallen into honorable hands. You are the Lord Governor's slave, who will use you nobly. In his absence it shall be my care to serve you.

OROONOKO.

I hear you, but I can believe no more.

LIEUTENANT GOVERNOR.

Captain, I'm afraid the world won't speak so honorably of this action of yours, as you would have 'em.

CAPTAIN.

I have the money. Let the world speak and be damned, I care not.

OROONOKO. (*To Blanford.*)

I would forget myself. Be satisfied
I am above the rank of common slaves.
Let that content you. The Christian there, that knows me,
For his own sake will not discover* more.

CAPTAIN.

I have other matters to mind. You have him, and much good may do you with your prince. (*Exit.*)

The Planters pulling and staring at Oroonoko.

BLANFORD.

What would you have there? You stare as if you never saw a man before. Stand further off. (*Turns them away.*)

OROONOKO.

Let 'em stare on.
I am unfortunate, but not ashamed
Of being so. No, let the guilty blush,
The white man that betray'd me. Honest black
Disdains to change its color. I am ready.
Where must I go? Dispose me as you please.
I am not well acquainted with my fortune,
But must learn to know it better. So
I know you say: Degrees make all things easy.[c]

BLANFORD.

All things shall be easy.

OROONOKO.

Tear off this pomp, and let me know myself.
The slavish habit best becomes me now.
Hard fare and whips and chains may overpow'r
The frailer flesh and bow my body down,
But there's another, nobler part of me,
Out of your reach, which you can never tame.

BLANFORD.

You shall find nothing of this wretchedness
You apprehend. We are not monsters all.
You seem unwilling to disclose yourself;
Therefore, for fear the mentioning your name

Should give you new disquiets, I presume
To call you Caesar.[15]

OROONOKO.
I am myself, but call me what you please.

STANMORE.
A very good name, Caesar.

LIEUTENANT GOVERNOR.
And very fit for his great character.

OROONOKO.
Was Caesar then a slave?

LIEUTENANT GOVERNOR.
I think he was; to pirates too.[16] He was a great conqueror, but unfortunate in his friends.

OROONOKO.
His friends were Christians?

BLANFORD.
No.

OROONOKO.
No! that's strange.

LIEUTENANT GOVERNOR.
And murdered by 'em.

OROONOKO.
I would be Caesar there. Yet I will live.

BLANFORD.
Live to be happier.

OROONOKO.
Do what you will with me.

BLANFORD.
I'll wait upon you, attend, and serve you.

Exit with Oroonoko.

LUCIA.
Well, if the captain had brought this prince's country along with him and would make me queen of it, I would not have him, after doing so base a thing.

WELLDON.
He's a man to thrive in the world, sister. He'll make you the better jointure.

LUCIA.
Hang him, nothing can prosper with him.

STANMORE.
Inquire into the great estates, and you will find most of 'em depend upon the same title of honesty. The men who raise 'em first are much of the captain's principles.

WELLDON.
Ay, ay, as you say. Let him be damned for the good of his family.—Come sister, we are invited to dinner.

LIEUTENANT GOVERNOR.
Stanmore, you dine with me.

Exeunt omnes.

Act II, scene i. Widow Lackitt's house.

Widow Lackitt, Welldon.

WELLDON.
This is so great a favor, I don't know how to receive it.

WIDOW.
Oh dear sir! you know how to receive and how to return a favor as well as anybody, I don't doubt it. 'Tis not the first you have had from our sex, I suppose.

WELLDON.
But this is so unexpected.

WIDOW.
Lord, how can you say so, Mr. Welldon? I won't believe you. Don't I know you handsome gentlemen expect everything that a woman can do for you? And by my troth, you're in the right on't. I think one can't do too much for a handsome gentleman, and so you shall find it.

WELLDON.
I shall never have such an offer again, that's certain. (*Pretending a concern.*) What shall I do? I am mightily divided.

WIDOW.
Divided! Oh dear, I hope not so, sir. If I marry, truly I expect to have you to myself.

WELLDON.
There's no danger of that, Mrs. Lackitt. I am divided in my thoughts. My father upon his deathbed obliged me to see my sister disposed of,

[15] Caesar] It was standard procedure to give slaves European names, particularly Roman.

[16] to pirates too] According to legend, Julius Caesar was captured by Mediterranean pirates but later escaped, captured his former captors, and crucified them (Novak and Rodes).

before I married myself. 'Tis that sticks upon me. They say, indeed, promises are to be broken or kept, and I know 'tis a foolish thing to be tied to a promise, but I can't help it. I don't know how to get rid of it.

WIDOW.
Is that all?

WELLDON.
All in all to me. The commands of a dying father, you know, ought to be obeyed.

WIDOW.
And so they may.

WELLDON.
Impossible, to do me any good.

WIDOW.
They shan't be your hindrance. You would have a husband for your sister, you say. He must be very well to pass too in the world, I suppose?

WELLDON.
I would not throw her away.

WIDOW.
Then marry her out of hand to the sea captain you were speaking of.

WELLDON.
I was thinking of him, but 'tis to no purpose. She hates him.

WIDOW.
Does she hate him? Nay, 'tis no matter, an impudent rascal as he is, I would not advise her to marry him.

WELLDON.
Can you think of nobody else?

WIDOW.
Let me see.

WELLDON.
Aye, pray do. I should be loath to part with my good fortune in you for so small a matter as a sister. But you find how it is with me.

WIDOW.
Well remembered, i'faith. Well, if I thought you would like of it, I have a husband for her. What do you think of my son?

WELLDON.
You don't think of it yourself.

WIDOW.
I protest but I do. I am in earnest, if you are. He shall marry her within this half hour, if you'll give your consent to it.

WELLDON.
I give my consent! I'll answer for my sister. She shall have him. You may be sure I shall be glad to get over the difficulty.

WIDOW.
No more to be said then, that difficulty is over. But I vow and swear you frightened me, Mr. Welldon. If I had not had a son now for your sister, what must I have done, do you think? Were not you an ill-natured thing to boggle at a promise? I could break twenty for you.

WELLDON.
I am the more obliged to you. But this son will save all.

WIDOW.
He's in the house; I'll go and bring him myself. (*Going.*) You would do well to break the business to your sister. She's within, I'll send her to you.

WELLDON.
Pray do.

WIDOW. (*Going again, comes back.*)
But do you hear? Perhaps she may stand upon her maidenly behavior and blush and play the fool and delay. But don't be answered so. What! she is not a girl at these years. Show your authority and tell her roundly, she must be married immediately. I'll manage my son, I warrant you. (*Goes out in haste.*)

WELLDON.
The widow's in haste, I see. I thought I had laid a rub in the road about my sister. But she has stepped over that. She's making way for herself as fast as she can, but little thinks where she is going. I could tell her she is going to play the fool, but people don't love to hear of their faults. Besides, that is not my business at present.

Enter Lucia.

So, sister, I have a husband for you.

LUCIA.
With all my heart. I don't know what confinement marriage may be to the men, but I'm sure the women have no liberty without it. I am for anything that will deliver me from the care of a reputation, which I begin to find impossible to preserve.

WELLDON.
I'll ease you of that care. You must be married immediately.

LUCIA.
The sooner the better, for I am quite tired of setting up for a husband. The widow's foolish son is the man, I suppose.

WELLDON.
I considered your constitution, sister, and, finding you would have occasion for a fool, I have provided accordingly.

LUCIA.
I don't know what occasion I may have for a fool when I'm married. But I find none but fools have occasion to marry.

WELLDON.
Since he is to be a fool, then, I thought it better for you to have one of his mother's making than your own. 'Twill save you the trouble.

LUCIA.
I thank you; you take a great deal of pains for me. But pray tell me, what are you doing for yourself all this while?

WELLDON.
You were never true to your own secrets, and therefore I won't trust you with mine. Only remember this: I am your elder sister and consequently, laying my breeches aside, have as much occasion for a husband as you can have. I have a man in my eye, be satisfied.

Enter Widow Lackitt with her son Daniel.

WIDOW.
Come Daniel, hold up thy head, child. Look like a man. You must not take it as you have done. Gad's my life! there's nothing to be done with twirling your hat, man.

DANIEL.
Why Mother, what's to be done, then?

WIDOW.
Why, look me in the face and mind what I say to you.

DANIEL.
Marry,* who's the fool, then? what shall I get by minding what you say to me?

WIDOW. (*Going between Lucia and Daniel.*)
Mrs. Lucy, the boy is bashful, don't discourage him. Pray come a little forward and let him salute* you.

LUCIA. (*To Welldon.*)
A fine husband I am to have, truly.

WIDOW.
Come Daniel, you must be acquainted with this gentlewoman.

DANIEL.
Nay, I'm not proud, that is not my fault. I am perfectly acquainted when I know the company, but this gentlewoman is a stranger to me.

WIDOW.
She is your mistress. I have spoke a good word for you. Make her a bow and go kiss her.

DANIEL.
Kiss her! Have a care what you say; I warrant she scorns your words. Such fine folk are not used to be stopped and kissed. Do you think I don't know that, Mother?

WIDOW.
Try her, try her, man.

Daniel bows, she thrusts him forward.

Why, that's well done; go nearer her.

DANIEL.
Is the devil in the woman? (*To his mother.*) Why, so I can go nearer her, if you would let a body alone. (*To Lucia.*) Cry you mercy, forsooth. My mother is always shaming one before company. She would have me as unmannerly as herself and offer to kiss you.

WELLDON.
Why, won't you kiss her?

DANIEL.
Why, pray, may I?

WELLDON.
Kiss her, kiss her, man.

DANIEL.
Marry,* and I will. (*Kisses her.*) Gadsooks! she kisses rarely! An* please you, mistress, and seeing my mother will have it so, I don't much care if I kiss you again, forsooth. (*Kisses her again.*)

LUCIA.
Well, how do you like me now?

DANIEL.
Like you! marry,* I don't know. You have bewitched me, I think. I was never so in my born days before.

WIDOW.
You must marry this fine woman, Daniel.

DANIEL.
Hey day! Marry her! I was never married in all my life. What must I do with her then, Mother?

WIDOW.
You must live with her, eat and drink with her, go to bed with her, and sleep with her.

DANIEL.
Nay, marry,* if I must go to bed with her, I shall never sleep, that's certain. She'll break me of my rest, quite and clean, I tell you beforehand. As for eating and drinking with her, why I have a good stomach and can play my part in any company. But how do you think I can go to bed to a woman I don't know?

WELLDON.
You shall know her better.

DANIEL.
Say you so, sir?

WELLDON.
Kiss her again.

DANIEL. (*Kisses Lucy.*)
Nay, kissing I find will make us presently* acquainted. We'll steal into a corner to practice a little, and then I shall be able to do anything.

WELLDON.
The young man mends apace.

WIDOW.
Pray don't balk him.

DANIEL.
Mother, Mother, if you'll stay in the room by me and promise not to leave me, I don't care for once if I venture to go to bed with her.

WIDOW.
There's a good child. Go in and put on thy best clothes; pluck up a spirit. I'll stay in the room by thee. She won't hurt thee, I warrant thee.

DANIEL.
Nay, as to that matter, I'm not afraid of her. I'll give her as good as she brings. I have a Rowland for her Oliver,* and so you may tell her. (*Exit.*)

WIDOW.
Mrs. Lucy, we shan't stay for you. You are in a readiness, I suppose.

WELLDON.
She's always ready to do what I would have her, I must say that for my sister.

WIDOW.
'Twill be her own another day. Mr. Welldon, we'll marry 'em out of hand, and then—

WELLDON.
And then, Mrs. Lackitt, look to yourself.

Exeunt.

Scene ii.

Oroonoko and Blanford.

OROONOKO.
You grant I have good reason to suspect
All the professions you can make to me.

BLANFORD.
Indeed you have.

OROONOKO.
The dog that sold me did profess as much
As you can do. But yet I know not why—
Whether it is because I'm fall'n so low
And have no more to fear—that is not it,
I am a slave no longer than I please.
'Tis something nobler. Being just myself,
I am inclining to think others so.
'Tis that prevails upon me to believe you.

BLANFORD.
You may believe me.

OROONOKO.
I do believe you.
From what I know of you, you are no fool.
Fools only are the knaves, and live by tricks;
Wise men may thrive without 'em and be honest.

BLANFORD. (*Aside.*)
They won't all take your counsel.

OROONOKO.
You know my story, and you say you are
A friend to my misfortunes; that's a name
Will teach you what you owe yourself and me.

BLANFORD.
I'll study to deserve to be your friend.
When once our noble governor arrives,

With him you will not need my interest.
He is too generous not to feel your wrongs.
But be assured I will employ my pow'r
And find the means to send you home again.

OROONOKO.
I thank you, sir. My honest, wretched friends!
(*Sighing.*)
Their chains are heavy. They have hardly found
So kind a master. May I ask you, sir,
What is become of 'em? Perhaps I should not.
You will forgive a stranger.

BLANFORD.
I'll inquire
And use my best endeavors where they are
To have 'em gently used.

OROONOKO.
Once more I thank you.
You offer every cordial that can keep
My hopes alive to wait a better day.
What friendly care can do, you have applied.
But oh! I have a grief admits no cure.

BLANFORD.
You do not know, sir—

OROONOKO.
Can you raise the dead?
Pursue and overtake the wings of time?
And bring about again the hours, the days,
The years that made me happy?

BLANFORD.
That is not to be done.

OROONOKO.
No, there is nothing to be done for me. (*Kneeling and kissing the earth.*)
Thou god adored! Thou ever-glorious sun!
If she be yet on earth, send me a beam
Of thy all-seeing power to light me to her.
Or if thy sister-goddess has preferred
Her beauty to the skies to be a star,
Oh tell me where she shines, that I may stand
Whole nights and gaze upon her.

BLANFORD.
I am rude and interrupt you.

OROONOKO.
I am troublesome.
But pray give me your pardon. My swoll'n heart
Bursts out its passage, and I must complain.
Oh! Can you think of nothing dearer to me?
Dearer than liberty, my country, friends,
Much dearer than my life? That I have lost.
The tend'rest, best beloved, and loving wife.

BLANFORD.
Alas! I pity you.

OROONOKO.
Do, pity me.
Pity's akin to love, and every thought
Of that soft kind is welcome to my soul.
I would be pitied here.

BLANFORD.
I dare not ask more than you please to tell me,
But if you think it convenient to let me know
Your story, I dare promise you to bear
A part in your distress, if not assist you.

OROONOKO.
Thou honest-hearted man! I wanted such,
Just such a friend as thou art, that would sit
Still as the night and let me talk whole days
Of my Imoinda. Oh! I'll tell thee all
From first to last, and pray observe me well.

BLANFORD.
I will most heedfully.

OROONOKO.
There was a stranger in my father's court,
Valued and honored much. He was a white,
The first I ever saw of your complexion.
He changed his gods for ours and so grew great;
Of many virtues, and so famed in arms
He still* commanded all my father's wars.
I was bred under him. One fatal day,
The armies joining, he before me stepped,
Receiving in his breast a poisoned dart
Leveled at me; he died within my arms.
I've tired you already.

BLANFORD.
Pray go on.

OROONOKO.
He left an only daughter, whom he brought
An infant to Angola. When I came
Back to the court, a happy conqueror,
Humanity obliged me to condole
With this sad virgin for a father's loss,
Lost for my safety. I presented her
With all the slaves of battle to atone

Her father's ghost. But when I saw her face
And heard her speak, I offered up myself
To be the sacrifice. She bowed and blushed;
I wondered and adored. The sacred pow'r
That had subdued me then inspired my tongue,
Inclined her heart, and all our talk was love.

BLANFORD.

Then you were happy.

OROONOKO.

Oh! I was too happy.
I married her. And though my country's custom
Indulged the privilege of many wives,
I swore myself never to know but her.
She grew with child, and I grew happier still.
Oh my Imoinda! But it could not last.
Her fatal beauty reached my father's ears;
He sent for her to court, where, cursèd court!
No woman comes but for his amorous use.
He raging to possess her, she was forced
To own herself my wife. The furious king
Started at incest, but grown desperate,
Not daring to enjoy what he desired,
In mad revenge, which I could never learn,
He poisoned her, or sent her far, far off,
Far from my hopes ever to see her more.

BLANFORD.

Most barbarous of fathers! the sad tale
Has struck me dumb with wonder.

OROONOKO.

I have done.
I'll trouble you no farther; now and then
A sigh will have its way; that shall be all.

Enter Stanmore.

STANMORE.

Blanford, the Lieutenant Governor is gone to your plantation. He desires you would bring the royal slave with you. The sight of his fair mistress, he says, is an entertainment for a Prince; he would have his opinion of her.

OROONOKO.

Is he a lover?

BLANFORD.

So he says himself. He flatters a beautiful slave that I have and calls her mistress.

OROONOKO.

Must he then flatter her to call her mistress?
I pity the proud man who thinks himself
Above being in love. What though she be a slave,
She may deserve him.

BLANFORD.

You shall judge of that when you see her, sir.

OROONOKO.

I go with you.

Exeunt.

Scene iii. A plantation.

Lieutenant Governor following Imoinda.

LIEUTENANT GOVERNOR.

I have disturbed you, I confess my fault,
My fair Clemene, but begin again
And I will listen to your mournful song,
Sweet as the soft complaining nightingales,
While every note calls out my trembling soul
And leaves me silent as the midnight groves,
Only to shelter you. Sing, sing again,
And let me wonder at the many ways
You have to ravish me.

IMOINDA.

Oh! I can weep
Enough for you and me, if that will please you.

LIEUTENANT GOVERNOR.

You must not weep. I come to dry your tears
And raise you from your sorrow. Look upon me.
Look with the eyes of kind indulging love,
That I may have full cause for what I say:
I come to offer you your liberty
And be myself the slave. You turn away (*Following her.*),
But everything becomes you. I may take
This pretty hand. I know your modesty
Would draw it back, but you would take it ill
If I should let it go, I know you would.
You shall be gently forced to please yourself;
That you will thank me for.

She struggles and gets her hand from him, then he offers to kiss her.

Nay, if you struggle with me, I must take—

IMOINDA.
You may, my life, that I can part with freely. (*Exit.*)

Enter Blanford, Stanmore, Oroonoko to him.

BLANFORD.
So, Governor, we don't disturb you, I hope. Your mistress has left you; you were making love.* She's thankful for the honor, I suppose.

LIEUTENANT GOVERNOR.
Quite insensible to all I say
And do. When I speak to her, she sighs or weeps,
But never answers me as I would have her.

STANMORE.
There's something nearer than her slavery that touches her.

BLANFORD.
What do her fellow slaves say of her? Can't they find the cause?

LIEUTENANT GOVERNOR.
Some of 'em, who pretend to be wiser than the rest, and hate her, I suppose, for being used better than they are, will needs have it that she's with child.

BLANFORD.
Poor wretch! if it be so, I pity her.
She has lost a husband that perhaps was dear
To her, and then you cannot blame her.

OROONOKO. (*Sighing.*)
If it be so, indeed you cannot blame her.

LIEUTENANT GOVERNOR.
No, no, it is not so. If it be so,
I still must love her, and desiring still,
I must enjoy her.

BLANFORD.
Try what you can do with fair means, and welcome.

LIEUTENANT GOVERNOR.
I'll give you ten slaves for her.

BLANFORD.
You know she is our Lord Governor's. But if I could dispose of her, I would not now, especially to you.

LIEUTENANT GOVERNOR.
Why not to me?

BLANFORD.
I mean against her will. You are in love with her.
And we all know what your desires would have:
Love stops at nothing but possession.
Were she within your pow'r, you do not know
How soon you would be tempted to forget
The nature of the deed and, maybe, act
A violence you after would repent.

OROONOKO.
'Tis godlike in you to protect the weak.

LIEUTENANT GOVERNOR.
Fie, fie, I would not force her. Though she be
A slave, her mind is free and should consent.

OROONOKO.
Such honor will engage her to consent.
And then, if you're in love, she's worth the having.
Shall we not see this wonder?

LIEUTENANT GOVERNOR.
Have a care:
You have a heart, and she has conquering eyes.

OROONOKO.
I have a heart, but if it could be false
To my first vows, ever to love again,
These honest hands should tear it from my breast
And throw the traitor from me. Oh! Imoinda!
Living or dead, I can be only thine.

BLANFORD. (*To Lieutenant Governor and Stanmore.*)
Imoinda was his wife. She's either dead,
Or living, dead to him, forced from his arms
By an inhuman father. Another time
I'll tell you all.

STANMORE.
Hark! the slaves have done their work,
And now begins their evening's merriment.

BLANFORD.
The men are all in love with fair Clemene
As much as you are, and the women hate her
From an instinct of natural jealousy.
They sing and dance and try their little tricks
To entertain her and divert her sadness.
Maybe she is among 'em. Shall we see?

Exeunt.

[Scene iv.]

The scene drawn shows the slaves—men, women, and children—upon the ground. Some rise and dance, others sing the following songs.

A song.[17]

I.

A lass there lives upon the green,
Could I her picture draw,
A brighter nymph was never seen,
That looks and reigns a little queen
And keeps the swains in awe.

II.

Her eyes are Cupid's darts and wings,
Her eyebrows are his bow,
Her silken hair the silver strings,
Which sure and swift destruction brings
To all the vale below.

III.

If Pastorella's dawning light
Can warm and wound us so,
Her noon will shine so piercing bright
Each glancing beam will kill outright
And every swain subdue.

A song.[18]

I.

Bright Cynthia's pow'r divinely great,
What heart is not obeying?
A thousand Cupids on her wait,
And in her eyes are playing.

II.

She seems the Queen of Love to reign,
For she alone dispenses
Such sweets as best can entertain
The gust of all the senses.

III.

Her face a charming prospect brings;
Her breath gives balmy blisses;
I hear an angel, when she sings,
And taste of heaven in kisses.

IV.

Four senses thus she feasts with joy
From Nature's richest treasure;
Let me the other sense employ
And I shall die with pleasure.

During the entertainment, the [lieutenant] governor, Blanford, Stanmore, Oroonoko enter as spectators; that ended, Captain Driver, Jack Stanmore, and several planters enter with their swords drawn. A bell rings.

CAPTAIN.
Where are you, Governor? Make what haste you can to save yourself and the whole colony. I bid 'em ring the bell.

LIEUTENANT GOVERNOR.
What's the matter?

JACK STANMORE.
The Indians are come down upon us. They have plundered some of the plantations already, and are marching this way as fast as they can.

LIEUTENANT GOVERNOR.
What can we do against 'em?

BLANFORD.
We shall be able to make a stand, till more planters come in to us.

JACK STANMORE.
There are a great many more without, if you would show yourself, and put us in order.

LIEUTENANT GOVERNOR.
There's no danger of the white slaves,[19] they'll not stir. Blanford and Stanmore come you along with me. Some of you stay here to look after the black slaves.

All go out but the captain and six planters, who all at once seize Oroonoko.

17 song] written by Sir Henry Sheeres (d. 1710), a minor poet, set to music by Ralph (or Raphael) Courtevill[e] (d. ca. 1735), organist at St. James' Westminster, sung by a boy who may have been Jemmy Bowen (b. c. 1685), one of the most popular child singers in the theatre of his day, and sung to Letitia Cross (d. 1737), an ingenue actress

18 song] written by a Mr. Cheek, probably Thomas Cheek, who wrote a song for Southerne's *The Wives' Excuse*, set by Courtevill[e], sung by Richard Leveridge (c. 1670-1758), a composer of theatrical music

19 white slaves] Lower-class whites (criminals, prisoners of war like the Irish) were indentured for periods of servitude in the colonies, but they were virtual slaves and were often worked to death; Imoinda is, after all, a white slave. Cf. the intended enslavement, in the West Indies, of the steward in Shadwell's *A True Widow* (included in this anthology).

FIRST PLANTER.
Aye, aye, let us alone.
CAPTAIN.
In the first place we secure you, sir, as an enemy to the government.
OROONOKO.
Are you there, sir? You are my constant friend.
FIRST PLANTER.
You will be able to do a great deal of mischief.
CAPTAIN.
But we shall prevent you. Bring the irons hither. He has the malice of a slave in him and would be glad to be cutting his masters' throats. I know him. Chain his hands and feet that he may not run over to 'em. If they have him, they shall carry him on their backs, that I can tell 'em.

As they are chaining him, Blanford enters, runs to them.

BLANFORD.
What are you doing there?
CAPTAIN.
Securing the main chance.* This is a bosom enemy.
BLANFORD.
Away, you brutes. I'll answer with my life for his behavior; so tell the governor.
CAPTAIN, PLANTERS.
Well, sir, so we will.

Exeunt Captain and planters.

OROONOKO.
Give me a sword, and I'll deserve your trust.

A party of Indians enter, hurrying Imoinda among the slaves; another party of Indians sustains them retreating, followed at a distance by the [lieutenant] governor with the planters. Blanford, Oroonoko join them.

BLANFORD.
Hell and the Devil! They drive away our slaves before our faces. Governor, can you stand tamely by and suffer this? Clemene, sir, your mistress is among 'em.
LIEUTENANT GOVERNOR.
We throw ourselves away in the attempt to rescue 'em.
OROONOKO.
A lover cannot fall more glorious
Than in the cause of love. He that deserves
His mistress' favor wonnot stay behind.
I'll lead you on: Be bold, and follow me.

Oroonoko at the head of the planters falls upon the Indians with a great shout and beats them off. Imoinda enters.

IMOINDA.
I'm tossed about by my tempestuous fate
And nowhere must have rest. Indians or English!
Whoever has me, I am still a slave.
No matter whose I am, since I am no more
My royal master's, since I'm his no more.
Oh! I was happy! nay, I will be happy
In the dear thought that I am still his wife,
Though far divided from him. (*Draws off to a corner of the stage.*)

After a shout, enter the [lieutenant] governor with Oroonoko, Blanford, Stanmore, and the planters.

LIEUTENANT GOVERNOR.
Thou glorious man! thou something greater sure
Than Caesar ever was! That single arm
Has saved us all. Accept our general thanks.

All bow to Oroonoko.

And what we can do more to recompense
Such noble services, you shall command.
Clemene too shall thank you. She is safe. (*Brings Clemene forward, looking down on the ground.*)
Look up and bless your brave deliverer.
OROONOKO.
Bless me indeed!
BLANFORD.
You start!
OROONOKO.
Oh! all you gods
Who govern this great world and bring about
Things strange and unexpected, can it be?
LIEUTENANT GOVERNOR.
What is't you stare at so?
OROONOKO.
Answer me some of you, you who have power
And have your senses free. Or are you all
Struck through with wonder, too? (*Looking still fixed on her.*)

BLANFORD.
What would you know?
OROONOKO.
My soul steals from my body through my eyes.
All that is left of life I'll gaze away
And die upon the pleasure.
LIEUTENANT GOVERNOR.
This is strange!
OROONOKO.
If you but mock me with her image here,
If she be not Imoinda—

She looks upon him and falls into a swoon; he runs to her.

Hah! She faints!
Nay, then it must be she: it is Imoinda!
My heart confesses her and leaps for joy
To welcome her to her own empire here.
I feel her all, in every part of me.
Oh! let me press her in my eager arms,
Wake her to life, and with this kindling kiss
Give back that soul she only lent[d] to me. (*Kisses her.*)
LIEUTENANT GOVERNOR.
I am amazed!
BLANFORD.
I am as much as you.
OROONOKO.
Imoinda! Oh! thy Oroonoko calls.
IMOINDA. (*Coming to life.*)
My Oroonoko! Oh! I can't believe
What any man can say. But if I am
To be deceived, there's something in that name,
That voice, that face— (*Staring on him.*)
Oh! If I know myself,
I cannot be mistaken. (*Runs, and embraces Oroonoko.*)
OROONOKO.
Never here
You cannot be mistaken. I am yours,
Your Oroonoko, all that you would have,
Your tender, loving husband.
IMOINDA.
All indeed
That I would have: my husband! Then I am
Alive and waking to the joys I feel.
They were so great, I could not think 'em true.
But I believe all that you say to me,
For truth itself and everlasting love
Grows in this breast, and pleasure in these arms.
OROONOKO.
Take, take me all. Inquire into my heart
(You know the way to every secret there),
My heart, that sacred treasury of love,
And if in absence I have misemployed
A mite from the rich store, if I have spent
A wish, a sigh, but what I sent to you,
May I be cursed to wish and sigh in vain,
And you not pity me.
IMOINDA.
Oh! I believe
And know you by myself. If these sad eyes,
Since last we parted, have beheld the face
Of any comfort or once wished to see
The light of any other heaven but you,
May I be struck this moment blind and lose
Your blessèd sight, never to find you more.
OROONOKO.
Imoinda! Oh! This separation
Has made you dearer, if it can be so,
Than you were ever to me. You appear
Like a kind star to my benighted steps
To guide me on my way to happiness:
I cannot miss it now.—Governor, friend,
You think me mad, but let me bless you all
Who, any way, have been the instruments
Of finding her again. Imoinda's found!
And everything that I would have in her.
(*Embracing her in the most passionate fondness.*)
STANMORE.
Where's your mistress now, Governor?
LIEUTENANT GOVERNOR.
Why, where most men's mistresses are forced to be sometimes, with her husband it seems. (*Aside.*) But I won't lose her so.
STANMORE.
He has fought lustily for her and deserves her, I'll say that for him.
BLANFORD.
Sir, we congratulate your happiness. I do, most heartily.
LIEUTENANT GOVERNOR.
And all of us. But how it comes to pass—

OROONOKO.
That will require more precious time than I
Can spare you now. I have a thousand things
To ask of her, and she as many more
To know of me. But you have made me happier,
I confess, acknowledge it, much happier,
Than I have words or pow'r to tell you.—Captain,
You, ev'n you, who most have wronged me, I
Forgive. I won't say you have betrayed me now:
I'll think you but the minister of Fate
To bring me to my loved Imoinda here.

IMOINDA.
How, how shall I receive you? how be worthy
Of such endearments, all this tenderness?
These are the transports of prosperity,
When Fortune smiles upon us.

OROONOKO.
Let the fools
Who follow Fortune live upon her smiles.
All our prosperity is placed in love.
We have enough of that to make us happy.
This little spot of earth you stand upon
Is more to me than the extended plains
Of my great father's kingdom. Here I reign
In full delights, in joys to pow'r unknown:
Your love my empire, and your heart my throne.

Exeunt.

Act III, scene i.

Aboan with several slaves and Hottman.

HOTTMAN.
What! to be slaves to cowards! Slaves to rogues
Who can't defend themselves!

ABOAN. (*Aside to his gang.*)
Who is this fellow? He talks as if he were acquainted with our design. Is he one of us?

SLAVE.
Not yet. But he will be glad to make one, I believe.

ABOAN.
He makes a mighty noise.

HOTTMAN.
Go, sneak in corners, whisper out your griefs
For fear your masters hear you. Cringe and crouch
Under the bloody whip, like beaten curs
That lick their wounds and know no other cure.
All, wretches all! you feel their cruelty
As much as I can feel, but dare not groan.
For my part, while I have a life and tongue,
I'll curse the authors of my slavery.

ABOAN.
Have you been long a slave?

HOTTMAN.
Yes, many years.

ABOAN.
And do you only curse?

HOTTMAN.
Curse? only curse?
I cannot conjure to raise the spirits of other men;
I am but one. Oh! for a soul of fire,
To warm and animate our common cause,
And make a body of us. Then I would
Do something more than curse.

ABOAN.
That body set on foot, you would be one,
A limb, to lend it motion.

HOTTMAN.
I would be
The heart of it: the head, the hand, and heart.
Would I could see the day.

ABOAN.
You will do all yourself?

HOTTMAN.
I would do more than I shall speak; but I
May find a time.

ABOAN.
The time may come to you;
Be ready for't.—Methinks he talks too much.
I'll know him more, before I trust him farther.

SLAVE.
If he dares half what he says, he'll be of use to us.

Enter Blanford to them.

BLANFORD.
If there be anyone among you here
That did belong to Oroonoko, speak;
I come to him.

ABOAN.
I did belong to him.
Aboan, my name.

BLANFORD.
You are the man I want;
Pray, come with me.

Exeunt.

Scene ii.

Oroonoko and Imoinda.

OROONOKO.
I do not blame my father for his love
(Though that had been enough to ruin me).
'Twas Nature's fault, that made you like the sun,
The reasonable worship of mankind:
He could not help his adoration.
Age had not locked his senses up so close
But he had eyes that opened to his soul
And took your beauties in. He felt your pow'r,
And therefore I forgive his loving you.
But when I think on his barbarity,
That could expose you to so many wrongs,
Driving you out to wretched slavery
Only for being mine, then I confess
I wish I could forget the name of son,
That I might curse the tyrant.
IMOINDA.
I will bless him,
For I have found you here. Heav'n only knows
What is reserved for us. But if we guess
The future by the past, our Fortune must
Be wonderful, above the common size
Of good or ill; it must be in extremes:
Extremely happy or extremely wretched.
OROONOKO.
'Tis in our pow'r to make it happy now.
IMOINDA.
But not to keep it so.

Enter Blanford and Aboan.

BLANFORD.
My royal lord!
I have a present for you.
OROONOKO.
Aboan!
ABOAN.
Your lowest slave.
OROONOKO.
My tried and valued friend.
—This worthy man always prevents* my wants.
I only wished, and he has brought thee to me.
Thou art surprised. Carry thy duty there—

Aboan goes to Imoinda and falls at her feet.

While I acknowledge mine: (*To Blanford.*) How shall I thank you?
BLANFORD.
Believe me honest to your interest,
And I am more than paid. I have secured
That all your followers shall be gently used.
This gentleman, your chiefest favorite,
Shall wait upon your person while you stay
Among us.
OROONOKO.
I owe everything to you.
BLANFORD.
You must not think you are in slavery.
OROONOKO.
I do not find I am.
BLANFORD.
Kind Heaven has miraculously sent
Those comforts that may teach you to expect
Its farther care in your deliverance.
OROONOKO.
I sometimes think myself, Heav'n is concerned
For my deliverance.
BLANFORD.
It will be soon:
You may expect it. Pray, in the meantime,
Appear as cheerful as you can among us.
You have some enemies that represent
You dangerous and would be glad to find
A reason, in your discontent, to fear:
They watch your looks. But there are honest men
Who are your friends. You are secure in them.
OROONOKO.
I thank you for your caution.
BLANFORD.
I will leave you,
And be assured, I wish your liberty. (*Exit.*)
ABOAN.
He speaks you very fair.
OROONOKO.
He means me fair.
ABOAN.
If he should not, my lord—
OROONOKO.
If he should not?
I'll not suspect his truth. But if I did,
What shall I get by doubting?

ABOAN.
You secure,
Not to be disappointed. But besides,
There's this advantage in suspecting him:
When you put off the hopes of other men,
You will rely upon your godlike self,
And then you may be sure of liberty.

OROONOKO.
Be sure of liberty! what dost thou mean,
Advising to rely upon myself?
I think I may be sure on't. We must wait.
(*Turning to Imoinda.*)
'Tis worth a little patience.

ABOAN.
Oh my lord!

OROONOKO.
What dost thou drive at?

ABOAN.
Sir, another time
You would have found it sooner. But I see
Love has your heart and takes up all your thoughts.

OROONOKO.
And canst thou blame me?

ABOAN.
Sir, I must not blame you.
But as our fortune stands, there is a passion
(Your pardon, royal mistress, I must speak)
That would become you better than your love:
A brave* resentment, which, inspired by you,
Might kindle and diffuse a generous rage
Among the slaves to rouse and shake our chains
And struggle to be free.

OROONOKO.
How can we help ourselves?

ABOAN.
I knew you when you would have found a way.
How help ourselves! The very Indians teach us.
We need but to attempt our liberty,
And we may carry it. We have hands sufficient,
Double the number of our masters' force,
Ready to be employed. What hinders us
To set 'em then at work? We want* but you
To head our enterprise and bid us strike.

OROONOKO.
What would you do?

ABOAN.
Cut our oppressors' throats.

OROONOKO.
And you would have me join in your design
Of murder?

ABOAN.
It deserves a better name.
But be it what it will, 'tis justified
By self-defense and natural liberty.

OROONOKO.
I'll hear no more on't.

ABOAN.
I am sorry for't.

OROONOKO.
Nor shall you think of it.

ABOAN.
Not think of it!

OROONOKO.
No, I command you not.

ABOAN.
Remember, sir,
You are a slave yourself, and to command
Is now another's right. Not think of it!
Since the first moment they put on my chains,
I've thought of nothing but the weight of 'em
And how to throw them off. Can yours sit easy?

OROONOKO.
I have a sense of my condition
As painful and as quick* as yours can be.
I feel for my Imoinda and myself,
Imoinda much the tenderest part of me.
But though I languish for my liberty,
I would not buy it at the Christian price
Of black ingratitude. They shannot say
That we deserved our fortune by our crimes.
Murder the innocent!

ABOAN.
The innocent!

OROONOKO.
These men are so whom you would rise against.
If we are slaves, they did not make us slaves,
But bought us in an honest way of trade,
As we have done before 'em, bought and sold
Many a wretch and never thought it wrong.
They paid our price for us, and we are now
Their property, a part of their estate,
To manage as they please. Mistake me not,
I do not tamely say that we should bear

All they could lay upon us. But we find
The load so light, so little to be felt
(Considering they have us in their power
And may inflict what grievances they please),
We ought not to complain.

ABOAN.

My royal lord!
You do not know the heavy grievances,
The toils, the labors, weary drudgeries
Which they impose: burdens more fit for beasts,
For senseless beasts, to bear than thinking men.
Then if you saw the bloody cruelties
They execute on every slight offense,
Nay, sometimes in their proud, insulting sport,
How worse than dogs they lash their fellow creatures,
Your heart would bleed for 'em. Oh, could you know
How many wretches lift their hands and eyes
To you for their relief.

OROONOKO.

I pity 'em
And wish I could with honesty do more.

ABOAN.

You must do more, and may, with honesty.
Oh royal sir, remember who you are,
A prince, born for the good of other men,
Whose godlike office is to draw the sword
Against oppression and set free mankind.
And this, I'm sure, you think oppression now.
What, though you have not felt these miseries,
Never believe you are obliged to them;
They have their selfish reasons, maybe, now
For using of you well, but there will come
A time when you must have your share of 'em.

OROONOKO.

You see how little cause I have to think so:
Favored in my own person, in my friends,
Indulged in all that can concern my care,
In my Imoinda's soft society. (*Embracing her.*)

ABOAN.

And therefore would you lie contented down
In the forgetfulness and arms of love
To get young princes for 'em?

OROONOKO.

Say'st thou! Hah!

ABOAN.

Princes, the heirs of empire, and the last
Of your illustrious lineage, to be born
To pamper up their pride and be their slaves?

OROONOKO.

Imoinda! Save me, save me from that thought.

IMOINDA.

There is no safety from it. I have long
Suffered it with a mother's laboring pains
And can no longer. Kill me, kill me now,
While I am blest and happy in your love,
Rather than let me live to see you hate me,
As you must hate me, me, the only cause,
The fountain of these flowing miseries.
Dry up this spring of life, this pois'nous spring,
That swells so fast to overwhelm us all.

OROONOKO.

Shall the dear babe, the eldest of my hopes,
Whom I begot a prince, be born a slave?
The treasure of this temple was designed
T'enrich a kingdom's fortune. Shall it here
Be seized upon by vile, unhallowed hands
To be employed in uses most profane?

ABOAN.

In most unworthy uses. Think of that,
And while you may, prevent it. Oh my lord!
Rely on nothing that they say to you.
They speak you fair, I know, and bid you wait.
But think what 'tis to wait on promises,
And promises of men who know no tie
Upon their words against their interest.
And where's their interest in freeing you?

IMOINDA.

Oh! Where indeed, to lose so many slaves?

ABOAN.

Nay, grant this man you think so much your friend
Be honest and intends all that he says.
He is but one, and in a government
Where, he confesses, you have enemies
That watch your looks. What looks can you put on
To please these men, who are before resolved
To read 'em their own way? Alas, my lord!
If they incline to think you dangerous,
They have their knavish arts to make you so.
And then who knows how far their cruelty
May carry their revenge?

IMOINDA.

To everything

That does belong to you: your friends, and me.
I shall be torn from you, forced away,
Helpless and miserable. Shall I live
To see that day again?

OROONOKO.
That day shall never come.

ABOAN.
I know you are persuaded to believe
The Governor's arrival will prevent
These mischiefs and bestow your liberty.
But who is sure of that? I rather fear
More mischiefs from his coming. He is young,
Luxurious, passionate, and amorous.
Such a complexion, and made bold by power
To countenance all he is prone to do,
Will know no bounds, no law against his lusts.
If, in a fit of his intemperance,
With a strong hand he should resolve to seize
And force my royal mistress from your arms,
How can you help yourself?

OROONOKO.
Hah! Thou hast roused
The lion in his den; he stalks abroad,
And the wide forest trembles at his roar.
I find the danger now: my spirits start
At the alarm and from all quarters come
To man my heart, the citadel of love.
—Is there a power on earth to force you from me?
And shall I not resist it? not strike first
To keep, to save you? to prevent that curse?
This is your cause, and shall it not prevail?
Oh! You were born all ways to conquer me.
—Now I am fashioned to thy purpose. Speak,
What combination, what conspiracy,
Wouldst thou engage me in? I'll undertake
All thou wouldst have me now for liberty,
For the great cause of Love and Liberty.

ABOAN.
Now, my great master, you appear yourself.
And since we have you joined in our design,
It cannot fail us. I have mustered up
The choicest slaves, men who are sensible
Of their condition and seem most resolved.
They have their several parties.

OROONOKO.
Summon 'em,
Assemble 'em. I will come forth and show
Myself among 'em. If they are resolved,
I'll lead their foremost resolutions.

ABOAN.
I have provided those will follow you.

OROONOKO.
With this reserve in our proceeding still:*
The means that lead us to our liberty
Must not be bloody.

ABOAN.
You command in all.
We shall expect you, sir.

OROONOKO.
You shannot long.

Exeunt Oroonoko and Imoinda at one door, Aboan at another.

Scene iii.

Welldon coming in before Mrs. Lackitt.

WIDOW.
These unmannerly Indians were something unseasonable to disturb us just in the nick, Mr. Welldon, but I have the parson within call still to do us the good turn.

WELLDON.
We had best stay a little, I think, to see things settled again, had not we? Marriage is a serious thing, you know.

WIDOW.
What do you talk of a serious thing, Mr. Welldon? I think you have found me sufficiently serious. I have married my son to your sister to pleasure you, and now I come to claim your promise to me, you tell me marriage is a serious thing.

WELLDON.
Why, is it not?

WIDOW.
Fiddle faddle, I know what it is. 'Tis not the first time I have been married, I hope. But I shall begin to think you don't design to do fairly by me, so I shall.

WELLDON.
Why indeed, Mrs. Lackitt, I am afraid I can't do as fairly as I would by you. 'Tis what you must know, first or last, and I should be the worst man

in the world to conceal it any longer. Therefore, I must own to you that I am married already.

WIDOW.

Married! You don't say so, I hope! How have you the conscience to tell me such a thing to my face! Have you abused me then, fooled and cheated me? What do you take me for, Mr. Welldon? do you think I am to be served at this rate? But you shan't find me the silly* creature you think me. I would have you to know, I understand better things than to ruin my son without a valuable consideration. If I can't have you, I can keep my money. Your sister shan't have the catch of him she expected. I won't part with a shilling to 'em.

WELLDON.

You made the match yourself, you know: you can't blame me.

WIDOW.

Yes, yes, I can and do blame you. You might have told me before you were married.

WELLDON.

I would not have told you now, but you followed me so close I was forced to't. Indeed, I am married in England, but 'tis as if I were not, for I have been parted from my wife a great while, and to do reason on both sides, we hate one another heartily. Now I did design and will marry you still, if you'll have a little patience.

WIDOW.

A likely business, truly.

WELLDON.

I have a friend in England that I will write to, to poison my wife, and then I can marry you with a good conscience if you love me as you say you do. You'll consent to that, I'm sure.

WIDOW.

And will he do it, do you think?

WELLDON.

At the first word, or he is not the man I take him to be.

WIDOW.

Well, you are a dear devil, Mr. Welldon. And would you poison your wife for me?

WELLDON.

I would do anything for you.

WIDOW.

Well, I am mightily obliged to you. But 'twill be a great while before you can have an answer of your letter.

WELLDON.

'Twill be a great while indeed.

WIDOW.

In the meantime, Mr. Welldon—

WELLDON.

Why in the meantime— Here's company. We'll settle that within. I'll follow you.

Exit Widow. Enter Stanmore.

STANMORE.

So sir, you carry your business swimmingly. You have stolen a wedding, I hear.

WELLDON.

Aye, my sister is married. And I am very near being run away with myself.

STANMORE.

The widow will have you, then.

WELLDON.

You come very seasonably to my rescue. Jack Stanmore is to be had, I hope.

STANMORE.

At half an hour's warning.

WELLDON.

I must advise with you.

Exeunt.

Scene iv.

Oroonoko with Aboan, Hottman, slaves.

OROONOKO.

Impossible! nothing's impossible.
We know our strength only by being tried.
If you object the mountains, rivers, woods
Unpassable that lie before our march,
Woods we can set on fire; we swim by nature.
What can oppose us, then, but we may tame?
All things submit to virtuous industry.
That we can carry with us, that is ours.

SLAVE.

Great sir, we have attended all you said
With silent joy and admiration,
And, were we only men, would follow such,

So great a leader, through the untried world.
But oh! consider we have other names,
Husbands and fathers, and have things more dear
To us than life—our children and our wives,
Unfit for such an expedition.
What must become of them?

OROONOKO.
We wonnot wrong
The virtue of our women to believe
There is a wife among 'em would refuse
To share her husband's fortune. What is hard,
We must make easy to 'em in our love.
While we live, and have our limbs, we can
Take care for them.
Therefore I still propose
To lead our march down to the sea, and plant
A colony where, in our native innocence,
We shall live free and be able to defend
Ourselves till stress of weather or some accident
Provide a ship for us.

ABOAN.
An accident!
The luckiest accident presents itself:
The very ship that brought and made us slaves
Swims in the river still. I see no cause
But we may seize on that.

OROONOKO.
It shall be so.
There is a justice in it pleases me.
(*To the slaves.*) Do you agree to it?

OMNES.
We follow you.

OROONOKO. (*To Hottman.*)
You do not relish it.

HOTTMAN.
I am afraid
You'll find it difficult and dangerous.

ABOAN.
Are you the man to find the danger first?
You should have giv'n example. Dangerous!
I thought you had not understood the word:
You, who would be the head, the hand, and heart.
Sir, I remember you, you can talk well;
I wonnot doubt but you'll maintain your word.

OROONOKO. (*To Aboan.*)
This fellow is not right, I'll try him further.
—The danger will be certain to us all,
And death most certain in miscarrying.
We must expect no mercy, if we fail.
Therefore our way must be not to expect.
We'll put it out of expectation
By death upon the place or liberty.
There is no mean, but Death or Liberty.
There's no man here, I hope, but comes prepared
For all that can befall him. Death is all:
In most conditions of humanity
To be desired, but to be shunned in none,
The remedy of many, wish of some,
And certain end of all.
If there be one among us who can fear
The face of Death appearing like a friend,
As in this cause of honor Death must be,
How will he tremble when he sees Him dressed
In the wild fury of our enemies,
In all the terrors of their cruelty?
For now if we should fall into their hands,
Could they invent a thousand murd'ring ways
By racking torments, we should feel 'em all.

HOTTMAN.
What will become of us?

OROONOKO. (*To Aboan concerning Hottman.*)
Observe him now.
—I could die altogether like a man,
As you, and you, and all of us may do.
But who can promise for his bravery
Upon the rack? where fainting, weary life,
Hunted through every limb, is forced to feel
An agonizing death of all its parts?
Who can bear this? resolve to be impaled?
His skin flayed off and roasted yet alive?
The quivering flesh torn from his broken bones
By burning pincers? Who can bear these pains?

HOTTMAN. (*Discovering* all the confusion of fear.*)
They are not to be borne.

OROONOKO.
You see him now, this man of mighty words!

ABOAN.
How his eyes roll!

OROONOKO.
He cannot hide his fear.
I tried him this way and have found him out.

ABOAN.
I could not have believed it. Such a blaze,
And not a spark of fire!

OROONOKO.
His violence
Made me suspect him first. Now I'm convinced.
ABOAN.
What shall we do with him?
OROONOKO.
He is not fit—
ABOAN.
Fit! hang him, he is only fit to be
Just what he is: to live and die a slave,
The base companion of his servile fears.
OROONOKO.
We are not safe with him.
ABOAN.
Do you think so?
OROONOKO.
He'll certainly betray us.
ABOAN.
That he shan't.
I can take care of that. I have a way
To take him off his evidence.
OROONOKO.
What way?
ABOAN.
I'll stop his mouth before you, stab him here,
And then let him inform. (*Going to stab Hottman, Oroonoko holds him.*)
OROONOKO.
Thou art not mad?
ABOAN.
I would secure ourselves.
OROONOKO.
It cannot be this way, nay, cannot be.
His murder would alarm all the rest,
Make 'em suspect us of barbarity
And, maybe, fall away from our design.
We'll not set out in blood.—We have, my friends,
This night to furnish what we can provide
For our security and just defense.
If there be one among us we suspect
Of baseness or vile fear, it will become
Our common care to have our eyes on him.
I wonnot name the man.
ABOAN. (*To Hottman.*)
You guess at him.
OROONOKO.
Tomorrow, early as the breaking day,
We rendezvous behind the citron grove.
That ship secured, we may transport ourselves
To our respective homes. My father's kingdom
Shall open her wide arms to take you in
And nurse you for her own, adopt you all,
All, who will follow me.
OMNES.
All, all follow you.
OROONOKO.
There I can give you all your liberty,
Bestow its blessings, and secure 'em yours.
There you shall live with honor, as becomes
My fellow-sufferers and worthy friends.
This if we do succeed. But if we fall
In our attempt, 'tis nobler still to die
Than drag the galling yoke of slavery.

Exeunt omnes.

Act IV, scene i.

Welldon and Jack Stanmore.

WELLDON.
You see, honest Jack, I have been industrious for you. You must take some pains now to serve yourself.

JACK STANMORE.
Gad, Mr. Welldon, I have taken a great deal of pains. And if the Widow speaks honestly, faith and troth, she'll tell you what a pains-taker I am.

WELLDON.
Fie, fie, not me. I am her husband, you know; she won't tell me what pains you have taken with her. Besides, she takes you for me.

JACK STANMORE.
That's true; I'd forgot you had married her. But if you knew all—

WELLDON.
'Tis no matter for my knowing all. If she does—

JACK STANMORE.
Aye, aye, she does know, and more than ever she knew since she was a woman, for the time, I will be bold to say. For I have done—

WELLDON.
The devil take you, you'll never have done.

JACK STANMORE.
As old as she is, she has a wrinkle behind more than she had, I believe—for I have taught her what

she never knew in her life before.[20]

WELLDON.

What care I what wrinkles she has, or what you have taught her? If you'll let me advise you, you may; if not, you may prate on and ruin the whole design.

JACK STANMORE.

Well, well, I have done.

WELLDON.

Nobody but your cousin and you and I know anything of this matter. I have married Mrs. Lackitt and put you to bed to her, which she knows nothing of, to serve you. In two or three days, I'll bring it about so to resign up my claim, with her consent, quietly to you.

JACK STANMORE.

But how will you do it?

WELLDON.

That must be my business. In the meantime, if you should make any noise, 'twill come to her ears and be impossible to reconcile her.

JACK STANMORE.

Nay, as for that, I know the way to reconcile her, I warrant you.

WELLDON.

But how will you get her money? I am married to her.

JACK STANMORE.

That I don't know indeed.

WELLDON.

You must leave it to me. You find all the pains I shall put you to will be to be silent. You can hold your tongue for two or three days?

JACK STANMORE.

Truly, not well in a matter of this nature. I should be very unwilling to lose the reputation of this night's work, and the pleasure of telling.

WELLDON.

You must mortify that vanity a little. You will have time enough to brag and lie of your manhood, when you have her in a bare-faced condition to disprove you.

JACK STANMORE.

Well, I'll try what I can do. The hopes of her money must do it.

WELLDON.

You'll come at night again? 'tis your own business.

JACK STANMORE.

But you have the credit on't.

WELLDON.

'Twill be your own another day, as the widow says. Send your cousin to me; I want his advice.

JACK STANMORE.

I want to be recruited, I'm sure. A good breakfast, and to bed: she has rocked my cradle sufficiently. (*Exit.*)

WELLDON.

She would have a husband, and if all be as he says, she has no reason to complain. But there's no relying on what the men say on these occasions. They have the benefit of their bragging, by recommending their abilities to other women. Theirs is a trading estate that lives upon credit and increases by removing it out of one bank into another. Now, poor women have not these opportunities; we must keep our stocks dead by us at home to be ready for a purchase when it comes—a husband, let him be never so dear, and be glad of him. Or, venture our fortunes abroad on such rotten security that the principal and interest—nay, very often our persons—are in danger. If the women would agree (which they never will) to call home their effects,[21] how many proper gentlemen would sneak into another way of living, for want* of being responsible in this? Then husbands would be cheaper.—Here comes the widow, she'll tell truth. She'll not bear false witness against her own interest, I know.

Enter Widow Lackitt.

WELLDON.

Now, Mrs. Lackitt.

WIDOW.

Well, well, Lackitt, or what you will now, now I am married to you. I am very well pleased with what I have done, I assure you.

[20] wrinkle behind...before] A new wrinkle is a new bit of knowledge or a new trick, here obviously in a sexual sense.

[21] call home their effects] take themselves out of circulation

WELLDON.
And with what I have done too, I hope.
WIDOW.
Ah! Mr. Welldon! I say nothing, but you're a dear man, and I did not think it had been in you.
WELLDON.
I have more in me than you imagine.
WIDOW.
No, no, you can't have more than I imagine. 'Tis impossible to have more. You have enough for any woman in an honest way, that I will say for you.
WELLDON.
Then I find you are satisfied.
WIDOW.
Satisfied! no, indeed, I'm not to be satisfied, with you or without you. To be satisfied is to have enough of you. Now, 'tis a folly to lie: I shall never think I can have enough of you. I shall be very fond of you. Would you have me fond of you? What do you do to me, to make me love you so well?
WELLDON.
Can't you tell what?
WIDOW.
Go, there's no speaking to you. You bring all the blood of one's body into one's face, so you do. Why do you talk so?
WELLDON.
Why, how do I talk?
WIDOW.
You know how. But a little color becomes me, I believe. How do I look today?
WELLDON.
Oh! most lovingly, most amiably!
WIDOW.
Nay, this can't be long a secret, I find; I shall discover* it by my countenance.
WELLDON.
The women will find you out, you look so cheerfully.
WIDOW.
But do I? Do I really look so cheerfully, so amiably? There's no such paint in the world as the natural glowing of a complexion. Let 'em find me out, if they please, poor creatures, I pity 'em. They envy me, I'm sure, and would be glad to mend their looks upon the same occasion. The young, jill-flirting* girls, forsooth, believe nobody must have a husband but themselves, but I would have 'em to know there are other things to be taken care of besides their greensickness.
WELLDON.
Aye, sure, or the physicians would have but little practice.
WIDOW.
Mr. Welldon, what must I call you? I must have some pretty fond name or other for you. What shall I call you?
WELLDON.
I thought you liked my own name.
WIDOW.
Yes, yes, I like it, but I must have a nickname for you. Most women have nicknames for their husbands—
WELLDON.
Cuckold.
WIDOW.
No, no—but 'tis very pretty before company; it looks negligent, and is the fashion, you know.
WELLDON.
To be negligent of their husbands, it is indeed.
WIDOW.
Nay then, I won't be in the fashion, for I can never be negligent of dear Mr. Welldon. And to convince you, here's something to encourage you not to be negligent of me.
(*Gives him a purse and a little casket.*) Five hundred pounds in gold in this, and jewels to the value of five hundred pounds more in this.
WELLDON. (*Opens the casket.*)
Aye, marry,* this will encourage me indeed.
WIDOW.
There are comforts in marrying an elderly woman, Mr. Welldon. Now, a young woman would have fancied she had paid you with her person, or had done you the favor.
WELLDON.
What do you talk of young women? You are as young as any of 'em in everything but their folly and ignorance.
WIDOW.
And do you think me so? But I have no reason to

suspect you. Was not I seen at your house this morning, do you think?

WELLDON.

You may venture again. You'll come at night, I suppose.

WIDOW.

Oh dear! at night? so soon?

WELLDON.

Nay, if you think it so soon.

WIDOW.

Oh! no, it is not for that, Mr. Welldon, but—

WELLDON.

You won't come then.

WIDOW.

Won't! I don't say I won't. That is not a word for a wife. If you command me—

WELLDON.

To please yourself.

WIDOW.

I will come to please you.

WELLDON.

To please yourself, own it.

WIDOW.

Well, well, to please myself, then. You're the strangest man in the world, nothing can 'scape you. You'll to the bottom of everything.

Enter Daniel, Lucia following.

DANIEL. [*To Lucia.*]

What would you have? what do you follow me for?

LUCIA.

Why mayn't I follow you? I must follow you now all the world over.

DANIEL.

Hold you, hold you there. Not so far by a mile or two; I have enough of your company already, by'r Lady, and something to spare. You may go home to your brother, an* you will; I have no farther to do with you.

WIDOW.

Why, Daniel, child, thou art not out of thy wits sure, art thou?

DANIEL.

Nay, marry,* I don't know. But I am very near it, I believe; I am altered for the worse mightily since you saw me. And she has been the cause of it there.

WIDOW.

How so, child?

DANIEL.

I told you before what would come on't, of putting me to bed to a strange woman. But you would not be said nay.

WIDOW.

She is your wife now, child, you must love her.

DANIEL.

Why, so I did, at first.

WIDOW.

But you must love her always.

DANIEL.

Always! I loved her as long as I could, Mother, and as long as loving was good, I believe, for I find now I don't care a fig for her.

LUCIA.

Why, you lubberly, slovenly, misbegotten blockhead—

WIDOW.

Nay, Mistress Lucy, say anything else and spare not. But as to his begetting, that touches me. He is as honestly begotten, though I say it, that he is the worse again.

LUCIA.

I see all good nature is thrown away upon you.

WIDOW.

It was so with his father before him. He takes after him.

LUCIA.

And therefore will I use you, as you deserve, you Tony.[22]

WIDOW.

Indeed, he deserves bad enough, but don't call him out of his name; his name is Daniel, you know.

DANIEL.

She may call me hermaphrodite, if she will, for I hardly know whether I'm a boy or a girl.

WELLDON.

A boy, I warrant thee, as long as thou livest.

DANIEL.

Let her call me what she pleases, Mother. 'Tis not her tongue that I am afraid of.

LUCIA.

I will make such a beast of thee, such a cuckold!

---

22 Tony] stock name for a fool

WIDOW.
Oh pray, no, I hope. Do nothing rashly, Mrs. Lucy.

LUCIA.
Such a cuckold will I make of thee!

DANIEL.
I had rather be a cuckold than what you would make of me in a week, I'm sure. I have no more manhood left in me already than there is, saving the mark, in one of my mother's old under-petticoats here.

WIDOW.
Sirrah, Sirrah, meddle with your wife's petticoats, and let your mother's alone, you ungracious bird, you. (*Beats him.*)

DANIEL.
Why, is the devil in the woman? What have I said now? Do you know, if you were asked, I trow? But you are all of a bundle. Even hang together; he that unties you makes a rod for his own tail, and so he will find it that has anything to do with you.

WIDOW.
Aye, rogue enough, you shall find it. I have a rod for your tail still.

DANIEL.
No wife, and I care not.

WIDOW.
I'll swinge you into better manners, you booby.

(Beats him off, exit.)

WELLDON.
You have consummated our project upon him.

LUCIA.
Nay, if I have a limb of the fortune, I care not who has the whole body of the fool.

WELLDON.
That you shall, and a large one, I promise you.

LUCIA.
Have you heard the news? they talk of an English ship in the river.

WELLDON.
I have heard on't, and am preparing to receive it, as fast as I can.

LUCIA.
There's something the matter too with the slaves, some disturbance or other; I don't know what 'tis.

WELLDON.
So much the better still: we fish in troubled waters; we shall have fewer eyes upon us. Pray, go you home and be ready to assist me in your part of the design.

LUCIA.
I can't fail in mine. (*Exit.*)

WELLDON.
The widow has furnished me, I thank her, to carry it on. Now I have got a wife, 'tis high time to think of getting a husband. I carry my fortune about me, a thousand pounds in gold and jewels. Let me see. 'Twill be a considerable trust, and I think, I shall lay it out to advantage.

Enter Stanmore.

STANMORE.
So, Welldon, Jack has told me his success and his hopes of marrying the widow by your means.

WELLDON.
I have strained a point, Stanmore, upon your account, to be serviceable to your family.

STANMORE.
I take it upon my account, and am very much obliged to you. But here we are all in an uproar.

WELLDON.
So they say. What's the matter?

STANMORE.
A mutiny among the slaves. Oroonoko is at the head of 'em, our Governor is gone out with his rascally militia against 'em. What it may come to nobody knows.

WELLDON.
For my part, I shall do as well as the rest. But I'm concerned for my sister and cousin, whom I expect in the ship from England.

STANMORE.
There's no danger of 'em.

WELLDON.
I have a thousand pounds here, in gold and jewels, for my cousin's use that I would more particularly take care of. 'Tis too great a sum to venture at home, and I would not have her wronged of it. Therefore, to secure it I think my best way will be to put it into your keeping.

STANMORE.
You have a very good opinion of my honesty. (*Takes the purse and casket.*)

WELLDON.
I have indeed. If anything should happen to me in this bustle, as nobody is secure of accidents, I know you will take my cousin into your protection and care.

STANMORE.
You may be sure on't.

WELLDON.
If you hear she is dead, as she may be, then I desire you to accept of the thousand pound as a legacy and token of my friendship; my sister is provided for.

STANMORE.
Why, you amaze me. But you are never the nearer dying, I hope, for making your will?

WELLDON.
Not a jot, but I love to be beforehand with Fortune. If she comes safe—this is not a place for a single woman, you know—pray see her married as soon as you can.

STANMORE.
If she be as handsome as her picture, I can promise her a husband.

WELLDON.
If you like her when you see her, I wish nothing so much as to have you marry her yourself.

STANMORE.
From what I have heard of her, and my engagements to you, it must be her fault if I don't. I hope to have her from your own hand.

WELLDON.
And I hope to give her to you, for all this.

STANMORE.
Aye, aye, hang these melancholy reflections. Your generosity has engaged all my services.

WELLDON.
I always thought you worth making a friend.

STANMORE.
You shan't find your good opinion thrown away upon me. I am in your debt, and shall think so as long as I live.

Exeunt.

Scene ii.

Enter on one side of the stage Oroonoko, Aboan, with the slaves, Imoinda with a bow and quiver, some women leading, others carrying their children upon their backs.

OROONOKO.
The women, with their children, fall behind.
Imoinda, you must not expose yourself.
Retire, my love. I almost fear for you.

IMOINDA.
I fear no danger. Life, or death, I will
Enjoy with you.

OROONOKO.
My person is your guard.

ABOAN.
Now, sir, blame yourself. If you had not
Prevented my cutting his throat,
That coward there had not discovered* us.
He comes now to upbraid you.

Enter on the other side [the lieutenant] governor, talking to Hottman, with his rabble.

LIEUTENANT GOVERNOR.
This is the very thing I would have wished.
(*To Hottman.*) Your honest service to the government
Shall be rewarded with your liberty.

ABOAN.
His honest service! Call it what it is,
His villainy, the service of his fear.
If he pretends to honest services,
Let him stand out and meet me like a man.
(*Advancing.*)

OROONOKO.
Hold, you.—And you who come against us, hold.
I charge you in a general good to all,
And wish I could command you, to prevent
The bloody havoc of the murdering sword.
I would not urge destruction uncompelled,
But if you follow Fate, you find it here.
The bounds are set, the limits of our lives;
Between us lies the gaping gulf of Death
To swallow all. Who first advances—

Enter the captain with his crew.

CAPTAIN.
Here, here, here they are, Governor. What! seize upon my ship! Come boys, fall on!

Advancing first, Oroonoko kills him.

OROONOKO.
Thou art fall'n indeed. Thy own blood be upon thee.

LIEUTENANT GOVERNOR.
Rest it there. He did deserve his death.
Take him away. (*The body removed.*)
You see, sir, you and those mistaken men
Must be our witnesses, we do not come
As enemies and thirsting for your blood.
If we desired your ruin, the revenge
Of our companion's death had pushed it on.
But that we overlook, in a regard
To common safety and the public good.

OROONOKO.
Regard that public good. Draw off your men
And leave us to our fortune. We're resolved.

LIEUTENANT GOVERNOR.
Resolved on what? your resolutions
Are broken, overturned, prevented, lost:
What fortune now can you raise out of 'em?
Nay, grant we should draw off, what can you do?
Where can you move? What more can you resolve,
Unless it be to throw yourselves away?
Famine must eat you up if you go on.
You see, our numbers could with ease compel
What we request. And what do we request?
Only to save yourselves.

The women with their children gathering about the men.

OROONOKO.
I'll hear no more.

WOMEN.
Hear him, hear him.—He takes no care of us.

LIEUTENANT GOVERNOR.
To those poor wretches who have been seduced
And led away, to all and every one,
We offer a full pardon.

OROONOKO.
Then fall on. (*Preparing to engage.*)

LIEUTENANT GOVERNOR.
Lay hold upon't, before it be too late,
Pardon and mercy.

The women clinging about the men, they leave Oroonoko and fall upon their faces crying out for pardon.

SLAVES.
Pardon, mercy, pardon.

OROONOKO.
Let 'em go all.—Now, Governor, I see,
I own the folly of my enterprise,
The rashness of this action, and must blush
Quite through this veil of night a whitely shame
To think I could design to make those free
Who were by nature slaves, wretches designed
To be their masters' dogs and lick their feet.
Whip, whip 'em to the knowledge of your gods,
Your Christian gods, who suffer you to be
Unjust, dishonest, cowardly, and base,
And give 'em your excuse for being so.
I would not live on the same earth with creatures
That only have the faces of their kind.
Why should they look like men, who are not so?
When they put off their noble natures for
The groveling qualities of downcast beasts,
I wish they had their tails.

ABOAN.
Then we should know 'em.

OROONOKO. (*To Imoinda, Aboan.*)
We were too few before for victory.
We're still enough to die.

Blanford enters.

LIEUTENANT GOVERNOR.
Live, royal sir,
Live and be happy long on your own terms:
Only consent to yield, and you shall have
What terms you can propose, for you and yours.

OROONOKO.
Consent to yield! shall I betray myself?

LIEUTENANT GOVERNOR.
Alas! We cannot fear that your small force—
The force of two, with a weak woman's arm—
Should conquer us. I speak in the regard
And honor of your worth, in my desire
And forwardness to serve so great a man.
I would not have it lie upon my thoughts
That I was the occasion of the fall
Of such a prince, whose courage carried on
In a more noble cause would well deserve
The empire of the world.

OROONOKO.
You can speak fair.

LIEUTENANT GOVERNOR.
Your undertaking, though it would have brought

So great a loss to us, we must all say
Was generous and noble and shall be
Regarded only as the fire of youth,
That will break out sometimes in gallant souls;
We'll think it but the natural impulse,
A rash impatience of liberty:
No otherwise.

OROONOKO.
Think it what you will.
I was not born to render an account
Of what I do to any but myself.

Blanford comes forward.

BLANFORD. (*To the Lieutenant Governor.*)
I'm glad you have proceeded by fair means.
I came to be a mediator.

LIEUTENANT GOVERNOR.
Try
What you can work upon him.

OROONOKO.
Are you come
Against me too?

BLANFORD.
Is this to come against you? (*Offering his sword to Oroonoko.*)
Unarmed to put myself into your hands?
I come, I hope, to serve you.

OROONOKO.
You have served me;
I thank you for't. And I am pleased to think
You were my friend, while I had need of one.
But now 'tis past. This farewell, and be gone.
(*Embraces him.*)

BLANFORD.
It is not past, and I must serve you still.
I would make up these breaches, which the sword
Will widen more, and close us all in love.

OROONOKO.
I know what I have done, and I should be
A child to think they ever can forgive.
Forgive! Were there but that, I would not live
To be forgiven. Is there a power on earth
That I can ever need forgiveness from?

BLANFORD.
You shannot need it.

OROONOKO.
No, I wonnot need it.

BLANFORD.
You see he offers you your own conditions
For you and yours.

OROONOKO.
I must capitulate?
Precariously compound, on stinted terms,
To save my life?

BLANFORD.
Sir, he imposes none.
You make 'em for your own security.
If your great heart cannot descend to treat
In adverse fortune with an enemy,
Yet sure, your honor's safe, you may accept
Offers of peace and safety from a friend.

LIEUTENANT GOVERNOR. (*To Blanford.*)
He will rely on what you say to him.
Offer him what you can, I will confirm
And make all good. Be you my pledge of trust.

BLANFORD.
I'll answer with my life for all he says.

LIEUTENANT GOVERNOR. (*Aside.*)
Aye, do, and pay the forfeit if you please.

BLANFORD.
Consider, sir, can you consent to throw
That blessing ([*Points to] Imoinda.*) from you, you so hardly found
And so much valued once?

OROONOKO.
Imoinda! Oh!
'Tis she that holds me on this argument
Of tedious life. I could resolve it soon,
Were this curst being only in debate,
But my Imoinda struggles in my soul;
She makes a coward of me. I confess
I am afraid to part with her in death
And more afraid of life to lose her here.

BLANFORD.
This way you must lose her. Think upon
The weakness of her sex, made yet more weak
With her condition, requiring rest
And soft indulging ease to nurse your hopes
And make you a glad father.

OROONOKO.
There I feel
A father's fondness, and a husband's love.
They seize upon my heart, strain all its strings

To pull me to 'em from my stern resolve.
Husband and father! All the melting art
Of eloquence lives in those soft'ning names.
Methinks I see the babe with infant hands
Pleading for life and begging to be born.
Shall I forbid his birth? deny him light,
The heavenly comforts of all-cheering light,
And make the womb the dungeon of his death,
His bleeding mother his sad monument?
These are the calls of Nature, that call loud;
They will be heard and conquer in their cause.
He must not be a man who can resist 'em.
No, my Imoinda! I will venture all
To save thee and that little innocent.
The world may be a better friend to him
Than I have found it. Now I yield myself. (*Gives up his sword.*)
The conflict's past, and we are in your hands.

Several men get about Oroonoko and Aboan and seize them.

LIEUTENANT GOVERNOR.
So you shall find you are. Dispose of them
As I commanded you.
BLANFORD.
Good Heaven forbid!
You cannot mean—
LIEUTENANT GOVERNOR. (*To Blanford, who goes to Oroonoko.*)
This is not your concern.
(*To Imoinda.*) I must take care of you.
IMOINDA.
I'm at the end
Of all my care. Here I will die with him.
(*Holding Oroonoko.*)
OROONOKO.
You shall not force her from me. (*He holds her.*)
LIEUTENANT GOVERNOR.
Then I must
Try other means and conquer force by force.
Break, cut off his hold, bring her away.
IMOINDA.
I do not ask to live, kill me but here.
OROONOKO.
Oh bloody dogs! Inhuman murderers!

Imoinda forced out of one door by the [lieutenant] governor and others. Oroonoko and Aboan hurried out of another.

Exeunt omnes.

Act V, scene i.

Enter Stanmore, Lucia, Charlotte.

STANMORE.
'Tis strange we cannot hear of him. Can nobody give an account of him?
LUCIA.
Nay, I begin to despair; I give him for gone.
STANMORE.
Not so, I hope.
LUCIA.
There are so many disturbances in this devilish country! Would we had never seen it.
STANMORE.
This is but a cold welcome for you, madam, after so troublesome a voyage.
CHARLOTTE.
A cold welcome, indeed, sir, without my cousin Welldon. He was the best friend I had in the world.
STANMORE.
He was a very good friend of yours indeed, madam.
LUCIA.
They have made him away, murdered him for his money, I believe. He took a considerable sum out with him, I know; that has been his ruin.
STANMORE.
That has done him no injury, to my knowledge. For this morning he put into my custody what you speak of, I suppose a thousand pounds, for the use of this lady.
CHARLOTTE.
I was always obliged to him, and he has shown his care of me in placing my little affairs in such honorable hands.
STANMORE.
He gave me a particular charge of you, madam, very particular—so particular that you will be surprised when I tell you.
CHARLOTTE.
What, pray sir?

STANMORE.
I am engaged to get you a husband. I promised that before I saw you, and now I have seen you, you must give me leave to offer you myself.

LUCIA.
Nay cousin, never be coy upon the matter. To my knowledge my brother always designed you for this gentleman.

STANMORE.
You hear madam, he has given me his interest, and 'tis the favor I would have begged of him. Lord! you are so like him—

CHARLOTTE.
That you are obliged to say you like me for his sake.

STANMORE.
I should be glad to love you for your own.

CHARLOTTE.
If I should consent to the fine things you can say to me, how would you look, at last, to find 'em thrown away upon an old acquaintance?

STANMORE.
An old acquaintance!

CHARLOTTE.
Lord, how easily are you men to be imposed upon! I am no cousin newly arrived from England, not I, but the very Welldon you wot of.

STANMORE.
Welldon!

CHARLOTTE.
Not murdered, nor made away, as my sister would have you believe, but am in very good health—your old friend in breeches that was, and now your humble servant in petticoats.

STANMORE.
I'm glad we have you again. But what service can you do me in petticoats, pray?

CHARLOTTE.
Can't you tell what?

STANMORE.
Not I, by my troth. I have found my friend and lost my mistress, it seems, which I did not expect from your petticoats.

CHARLOTTE.
Come, come, you have had a friend of your mistress long enough, 'tis high time now to have a mistress of your friend.

STANMORE.
What do you say?

CHARLOTTE.
I am a woman, sir.

STANMORE.
A woman!

CHARLOTTE.
As arrant a woman as you would have had me. But now, I assure you.

STANMORE.
And at my service?

CHARLOTTE.
If you have any for me in petticoats.

STANMORE.
Yes, yes, I shall find you employment.

CHARLOTTE.
You wonder at my proceeding, I believe.

STANMORE.
'Tis a little extraordinary, indeed.

CHARLOTTE.
I have taken some pains to come into your favor.

STANMORE.
You might have had it cheaper a great deal.

CHARLOTTE.
I might have married you in the person of my English cousin, but could not consent to cheat you, even in the thing I had a mind to.

STANMORE.
'Twas done as you do everything.

CHARLOTTE.
I need not tell you I made that little plot and carried it on only for this opportunity. I was resolved to see whether you liked me as a woman or not. If I had found you indifferent, I would have endeavored to have been so, too. But you say you like me, and therefore I have ventured to discover* the truth.

STANMORE.
Like you! I like you so well that I'm afraid you won't think marriage a proof on't. Shall I give you any other?

CHARLOTTE.
No, no, I'm inclined to believe you, and that shall convince me. At more leisure I'll satisfy you how I came to be in man's clothes—for no ill, I assure you, though I have happened to play the rogue in

'em. They have assisted me in marrying my sister and have gone a great way in befriending your cousin Jack with the widow. Can you forgive me for pimping for your family?

Enter Jack Stanmore.

STANMORE.
So, Jack, what news with you?

JACK STANMORE.
I am the forepart of the widow, you know. She's coming after with the body of the family, the young squire in her hand—my son-in-law that is to be, with the help of Mr. Welldon.

CHARLOTTE.
Say you so, sir? (*Clapping Jack upon the back.*)

Enter Widow Lackitt with her son Daniel.

WIDOW.
So, Mrs. Lucy, I have brought him about again, I have chastised him, I have made him as supple as a glove for your wearing, to pull on or throw off at your pleasure.—Will you ever rebel again? Will you, sirrah? But come, come, down on your marrowbones and ask her forgiveness. (*Daniel kneels.*) Say after me, "Pray, forsooth, wife."

DANIEL.
Pray, forsooth, wife.

LUCIA.
Well, well, this is a day of good nature, and so I take you into favor. But first take the Oath of Allegiance. (*He kisses her hand and rises.*) If ever you do so again—

DANIEL.
Nay, marry,* if I do, I shall have the worst on't.

LUCIA.
Here's a stranger, forsooth, would be glad to be known to you, a sister of mine. Pray salute* her.

WIDOW. (*Starts at Charlotte.*)
Your sister! Mrs. Lucy! What do you mean? This is your brother, Mr. Welldon! Do you think I do not know Mr. Welldon?

LUCIA.
Have a care what you say. This gentleman's about marrying her; you may spoil all.

WIDOW.
Fiddle faddle, what! You would put a trick upon me.

CHARLOTTE.
No, faith, Widow, the trick is over, it has taken sufficiently. And now I will teach you the trick, to prevent your being cheated another time.

WIDOW.
How! Cheated, Mr. Welldon!

CHARLOTTE.
Why, aye, you will always take things by the wrong handle. I see you will have me Mr. Welldon. I grant you, I was Mr. Welldon a little while to please you, or so. But Mr. Stanmore here has persuaded me into a woman again.

WIDOW.
A woman! Pray let me speak with you. (*Drawing her aside.*) You are not in earnest, I hope? A woman!

CHARLOTTE.
Really a woman.

WIDOW.
Gads my life! I could not be cheated in everything. I know a man from a woman at these years, or the Devil's in't. Pray, did not you marry me?

CHARLOTTE.
You would have it so.

WIDOW.
And did not I give you a thousand pounds this morning?

CHARLOTTE.
Yes, indeed; 'twas more than I deserved. But you had your pennyworth for your penny, I suppose. You seemed to be pleased with your bargain.

WIDOW.
A rare bargain I have made on't, truly. I have laid out my money to fine purpose upon a woman.

CHARLOTTE.
You would have a husband, and I provided for you as well as I could.

WIDOW.
Yes, yes, you have provided for me.

CHARLOTTE.
And you have paid me very well for't, I thank you.

WIDOW.
'Tis very well. I may be with child, too, for aught I know, and may go look for the father.

CHARLOTTE.
Nay, if you think so, 'tis time to look about you

indeed. Even make up the matter as well as you can, I advise you as a friend, and let us live neighborly and lovingly together.

WIDOW.
I have nothing else for it, that I know now.

CHARLOTTE.
For my part, Mrs. Lackitt, your thousand pounds will engage me not to laugh at you. Then my sister is married to your son; he is to have half your estate, I know, and indeed they may live upon it very comfortably to themselves, and very creditably to you.

WIDOW.
Nay, I can blame nobody but myself.

CHARLOTTE.
You have enough for a husband still, and that you may bestow upon honest Jack Stanmore.

WIDOW.
Is he the man, then?

CHARLOTTE.
He is the man you are obliged to.

JACK STANMORE.
Yes, faith, Widow, I am the man. I have done fairly by you, you find; you know what you have to trust to beforehand.

WIDOW.
Well, well, I see you will have me, even marry me, and make an end of the business.

STANMORE.
Why, that's well said. Now we are all agreed, and all provided for.

A servant enters to Stanmore.

SERVANT.
Sir, Mr. Blanford desires you to come to him and bring as many of your friends as you can with you.

STANMORE.
I come to him.—You'll all go along with me. Come, young gentleman, marriage is the fashion, you see, you must like it now.

DANIEL.
If I don't, how shall I help myself?

LUCIA.
Nay, you may hang yourself in the noose if you please, but you'll never get out on't with struggling.

DANIEL.
Come then, let's even jog on in the old road.
Cuckold or worse, I must now be contented:
I'm not the first has married, and repented.

Exeunt.

Scene ii.

Enter [Lieutenant] Governor with Blanford and planters.

BLANFORD.
Have you no reverence of future fame?
No awe upon your actions from the tongues,
The censuring tongues of men that will be free?
If you confess humanity, believe
There is a God, or Devil, to reward
Our doings here, do not provoke your fate.
The hand of Heaven is armed against these crimes
With hotter thunderbolts prepared to shoot
And nail you to the earth: a sad example,
A monument of faithless infamy.

Enter Stanmore, Jack Stanmore, Charlotte, Lucy, Widow, and Daniel.

So, Stanmore, you I know, the women too
Will join with me. (*To the women.*) 'Tis
Oroonoko's cause,
A lover's cause, a wretched woman's cause,
That will become your intercession.

FIRST PLANTER.
Never mind 'em, Governor, he ought to be made an example for the good of the plantation.*

SECOND PLANTER.
Aye, aye, 'twill frighten the Negroes from attempting the like again.

FIRST PLANTER.
What, rise against their lords and masters! At this rate, no man is safe from his own slaves.

SECOND PLANTER.
No, no more he is. Therefore, one and all, Governor, we declare for hanging.

ALL PLANTERS.
Aye, aye, hang him, hang him.

WIDOW.
What! Hang him! Oh! forbid it, Governor!

CHARLOTTE, LUCIA.
We all petition for him.

JACK STANMORE.
They are for a holiday. Guilty or not,

Is not the business; hanging is their sport.

BLANFORD.

We are not sure so wretched to have these,
The rabble, judge for us, the changing crowd,
The arbitrary guard of Fortune's power,
Who wait to catch the sentence of her frowns
And hurry all to ruin she condemns.

STANMORE.

So far from farther wrong that 'tis a shame
He should be where he is. Good Governor,
Order his liberty. He yielded up
Himself, his all, at your discretion.

BLANFORD.

Discretion! no, he yielded on your word,
And I am made the cautionary pledge,
The gage and hostage of your keeping it.
Remember, sir, he yielded on your word,
Your word! which honest men will think should be
The last resort of truth and trust on earth.
There's no appeal beyond it but to Heaven.
An oath is a recognizance to Heaven,
Binding us over in the courts above
To plead to the indictment of our crimes,
That those who 'scape this world should suffer there.
But in the common intercourse of men
(Where the dread majesty is not invoked,
His honor not immediately concerned,
Nor made a party in our interests)
Our word is all to be relied upon.

WIDOW.

Come, come, you'll be as good as your word, we know.

STANMORE.

He's out of all power of doing any harm now, if he were disposed to it.

CHARLOTTE.

But he is not dispos'd to it.

BLANFORD.

To keep him where he is will make him soon
Find out some desperate way to liberty.
He'll hang himself or dash out his mad brains.

CHARLOTTE.

Pray try him by gentle means; we'll all be sureties for him.

OMNES.

All, all.

LUCIA.

We will all answer for him now.

LIEUTENANT GOVERNOR.

Well, you will have it so, do what you please,
Just what you will with him. I give you leave.
(*Exit.*)

BLANFORD.

We thank you, sir. This way, pray come with me.

Exeunt.

[Scene iii.]

The scene drawn shows Oroonoko upon his back, his legs and arms stretched out and chained to the ground. Enter Blanford, Stanmore, etc.

BLANFORD.

Oh miserable sight! Help, everyone,
Assist me all to free him from his chains.

They help him up and bring him forward, looking down.

Most injured prince! how shall we clear ourselves?
We cannot hope you will vouchsafe to hear
Or credit what we say in the defense
And cause of our suspected innocence.

STANMORE.

We are not guilty of your injuries,
No way consenting to 'em, but abhor,
Abominate, and loathe this cruelty.

BLANFORD.

It is our curse, but make it not our crime.
A heavy curse upon us, that we must
Share anything in common, even the light,
The elements, and seasons, with such men,
Whose principles, like the famed dragons' teeth,[23]
Scattered and sown, would shoot a harvest up
Of fighting mischiefs to confound themselves
And ruin all about 'em.

---

[23] dragons' teeth] The Greek hero Cadmus followed the Delphic oracle and went to a spring where he was told to make sacrifice. His companions were all killed by the dragon guarding the spring, and after killing the dragon, Cadmus obeyed the word of the goddess Athena by sowing the dragons' teeth into the ground. A tribe of armed men sprouted from them. Cadmus killed all except five survivors, and with these five founded the city of Thebes.

STANMORE.
Profligates!
Whose bold Titanian[24] impiety
Would once again pollute their Mother Earth,
Force her to teem with her old monstrous brood
Of giants, and forget the race* of men.

BLANFORD.
We are not so: believe us innocent.
We come prepared with all our services
To offer a redress of your base wrongs.
Which way shall we employ 'em?

STANMORE.
Tell us, sir,
If there is anything that can atone.
But nothing can that may be some amends—

OROONOKO.
If you would have me think you are not all
Confederates, all accessory to
The base injustice of your governor;
If you would have me live, as you appear
Concerned for me, if you would have me live
To thank and bless you, there is yet a way
To tie me ever to your honest love:
Bring my Imoinda to me. Give me her
To charm my sorrows and, if possible,
I'll sit down with my wrongs, never to rise
Against my fate or think of vengeance more.

BLANFORD.
Be satisfied you may depend upon us.
We'll bring her safe to you, and suddenly.

CHARLOTTE.
We wonnot leave you in so good a work.

WIDOW.
No, no, we'll go with you.

BLANFORD.
In the meantime
Endeavor to forget, sir, and forgive
And hope a better fortune.

Exeunt [all but Oroonoko].

OROONOKO.
Forget! forgive! I must indeed forget,
When I forgive. But while I am a man,
In flesh that bears the living mark of shame,
The print of his dishonorable chains,
My memory still rousing up my wrongs,
I never can forgive this governor,
This villain, the disgrace of trust and place,
Unjust[e] contempt of delegated power.
What shall I do? If I declare myself,
I know him, he will sneak behind his guard
Of followers and brave me in his fears.
Else, lionlike, with my devouring rage
I would rush on him, fasten on his throat,
Tear wide a passage to his treacherous heart,
And that way lay him open to the world.
(*Pausing.*)
If I should turn his Christian arts on him,
Promise him, speak him fair, flatter and creep
With fawning steps to get within his faith,
I could betray him then, as he has me.
But am I sure by that to right myself?
Lying's a certain mark of cowardice.
And when the tongue forgets its honesty,
The heart and hand may drop their functions too,
And nothing worthy be resolved or done.
The man must go together, bad or good:
In one part frail, he soon grows weak in all.
Honor should be concerned in honor's cause,
That is not to be cured by contraries,
As bodies are, whose health is often drawn
From rankest poisons. Let me but find out
An honest remedy. I have the hand,
A minist'ring hand, that will apply it home.

Exit.

Scene iv. The [lieutenant] governor's house.

Enter Lieutenant Governor.

LIEUTENANT GOVERNOR.
I would not have her tell me she consents.
In favor of the sex's modesty
That still* should be presumed, because there is
A greater impudence in owning it
Than in allowing all that we can do.
This truth I know, and yet against myself
(So unaccountable are lovers' ways)
I talk and lose the opportunities
Which love and she expect I should employ.
Ev'n she expects, for when a man has said
All that is fit to save the decency,

24 Titanian] of or similar to the Titans (q.v.)

The women know the rest is to be done.
I wonnot disappoint her. (*Going.*)

Enter to him Blanford, the Stanmores, Daniel, Mrs. Lackitt, Charlotte, and Lucy.

WIDOW.
Oh Governor! I'm glad we have lit upon you.

LIEUTENANT GOVERNOR.
Why! what's the matter?

CHARLOTTE.
Nay, nothing extraordinary. But one good action draws on another. You have given the prince his freedom; now we come a-begging for his wife. You won't refuse us.

LIEUTENANT GOVERNOR.
Refuse you? No, no, what have I to do to refuse you?

WIDOW.
You won't refuse to send her to him, she means.

LIEUTENANT GOVERNOR.
I send her to him!

WIDOW.
We have promised him to bring her.

LIEUTENANT GOVERNOR.
You do very well, 'tis kindly done of you. Even carry her to him, with all my heart.

LUCIA.
You must tell us where she is.

LIEUTENANT GOVERNOR.
I tell you! Why, don't you know?

BLANFORD.
Your servants say she's in the house.

LIEUTENANT GOVERNOR.
No, no. I brought her home at first indeed, but I thought it would not look well to keep her here. I removed her in the hurry, only to take care of her. What! she belongs to you; I have nothing to do with her.

CHARLOTTE.
But where is she now, sir?

LIEUTENANT GOVERNOR.
Why faith, I can't say certainly. You'll hear of her at Parham House,[25] I suppose—there, or thereabouts. I think I sent her there.

[25] Parham House] the mansion of the governor of Suriname

BLANFORD. (*Aside.*)
I'll have an eye on him.

Exit all but the [lieutenant] governor.

LIEUTENANT GOVERNOR.
I have lied myself into a little time
And must employ it. They'll be here again,
But I must be before 'em. (*Going out, he meets Imoinda and seizes her.*)
Are you come?
I'll court no longer for a happiness
That is in mine own keeping. You may still*
Refuse to grant, so I have power to take.
The man that asks deserves to be denied.

She disengages one hand and draws his sword from his side upon him. [Lieutenant] Governor starts and retires. Blanford enters behind him.

IMOINDA.
He does, indeed, that asks unworthily.

BLANFORD.
You hear her, sir, that asks unworthily.

LIEUTENANT GOVERNOR.
You are no judge.

BLANFORD.
I am of my own slave.

LIEUTENANT GOVERNOR.
Be gone and leave us.

BLANFORD.
When you let her go.

LIEUTENANT GOVERNOR.
To fasten upon you.

BLANFORD.
I must defend myself.

IMOINDA.
Help! Murder, help!

Imoinda retreats towards the door, favored by Blanford. When they are closed, she throws down the sword and runs out. [Lieutenant] Governor takes up the sword; he and Blanford fight, close, and fall, Blanford upon him. Servants enter and part them.

LIEUTENANT GOVERNOR.
She shannot 'scape me so.
I've gone too far not to go farther. Curse
On my delay, but yet she is and shall
Be in my power.

BLANFORD.
Nay then, it is the war
Of honesty. I know you and will save
You from yourself.
LIEUTENANT GOVERNOR.
All come along with me.

Exeunt.

Scene [v].

Oroonoko enters.

OROONOKO.
To honor bound! and yet a slave to love!
I am distracted by their rival powers,
And both will be obey'd. Oh great Revenge!
Thou raiser and restorer of fall'n Fame!
Let me not be unworthy of thy aid
For stopping in thy course: I still am thine,
But can't forget I am Imoinda's too.
She calls me from my wrongs to rescue her.
No man condemn me, who has never felt
A woman's power or tried the force of love:
All tempers yield and soften in those fires.
Our honors, interests, resolving down,
Run in the gentle current of our joys,
But not to sink and drown our memory.
We mount again to action, like the sun
That rises from the bosom of the sea
To run his glorious race of light anew
And carry on the world. Love, love will be
My first ambition, and my fame the next.
Aboan enters bloody.
My eyes are turned against me and combine
With my sworn enemies to represent
This spectacle of horror.[f] Aboan!
My ever-faithful friend!
ABOAN.
I have no name
That can distinguish me from the vile earth
To which I'm going: a poor, abject worm
That crawled awhile upon a bustling world
And now am trampled to my dust again.
OROONOKO.
I see thee gashed and mangled.
ABOAN.
Spare my shame
To tell how they have used me, but believe
The hangman's hand would have been merciful.
Do not you scorn me, sir, to think I can
Intend to live under this infamy.
I do not come for pity, to complain.
I've spent an honorable life with you,
The earliest servant of your rising fame,
And would attend it with my latest care.
My life was yours, and so shall be my death.
You must not live—
Bending and sinking, I have dragged my steps
Thus far to tell you that you cannot live,
To warn you of those ignominious wrongs—
Whips, rods, and all the instruments of death—
Which I have felt and are prepared for you.
This was the duty that I had to pay.
'Tis done, and now I beg to be discharged.
OROONOKO.
What shall I do for thee?
ABOAN.
My body tires
And wonnot bear me off to liberty.
I shall again be taken, made a slave.
A sword, a dagger yet would rescue me.
I have not strength to go to find out Death;
You must direct him to me.
OROONOKO. (*Gives him a dagger.*)
Here he is,
The only present I can make thee now.
And next the honorable means of life,
I would bestow the honest means of death.
ABOAN.
I cannot stay to thank you. If there is
A being after this, I shall be yours
In the next world, your faithful slave again.
This is to try. (*Stabs himself.*) I had a living sense
Of all your royal favors, but this last
Strikes through my heart. I will not say farewell,
For you must follow me. (*Dies.*)
OROONOKO.
In life and death,
The guardian of my honor! Follow thee!
I should have gone before thee: then perhaps
Thy fate had been prevented. All his care
Was to preserve me from the barbarous rage
That wronged him only for being mine.

Why, why, you gods? Why am I so accurst
That it must be a reason of your wrath,
A guilt, a crime sufficient to the fate
Of anyone, but to belong to me?
My friend has found it, and my wife will soon.
My wife! the very* fear's too much for life;
I can't support it. Where? Imoinda! Oh!

[He] going out, she meets him, running into his arms.

Thou bosom softness! Down of all my cares!
I could recline my thoughts upon this breast
To a forgetfulness of all my griefs
And yet be happy. But it wonnot be.
Thou art disordered, pale, and out of breath!
If Fate pursues thee, find a shelter here.
What is it thou wouldst tell me?

IMOINDA.
'Tis in vain
To call him villain.

OROONOKO.
Call him Governor:
Is it not so?

IMOINDA.
There's not another sure.

OROONOKO.
Villain's the common name of mankind here,
But his most properly. What? what of him?
I fear to be resolved, and must inquire.
He had thee in his power.

IMOINDA.
I blush to think it.

OROONOKO.
Blush! to think what?

IMOINDA.
That I was in his power.

OROONOKO.
He could not use it?

IMOINDA.
What can't such men do?

OROONOKO.
But did he? durst he?

IMOINDA.
What he could, he dared.

OROONOKO.
His own gods damn him, then, for ours have none,
No punishment for such unheard-of crimes.

IMOINDA.
This monster, cunning in his flatteries,
When he had wearied all his useless arts,
Leapt out, fierce as a beast of prey, to seize me.
I trembled, feared.

OROONOKO.
I fear and tremble now.
What could preserve thee? what deliver thee?

IMOINDA.
That worthy man you used to call your friend—

OROONOKO.
Blanford.

IMOINDA.
—Came in and saved me from his rage.

OROONOKO.
He was a friend indeed to rescue thee!
And for his sake, I'll think it possible
A Christian may yet be an honest man.

IMOINDA.
Oh! did you know what I have struggled through
To save me yours, sure you would promise me
Never to see me forced from you again.

OROONOKO.
To promise thee! Oh! do I need to promise?
But there is now no farther use of words.
Death is security for all our fears. (*Shows Aboan's body on the floor.*)
And yet I cannot trust him.

IMOINDA.
Aboan!

OROONOKO.
Mangled and torn, resolved to give me time
To fit myself for what I must expect,
Groaned out a warning to me, and expired.

IMOINDA.
For what you must expect?

OROONOKO.
Would that were all.

IMOINDA.
What! to be butchered thus—

OROONOKO.
Just as thou seest.

IMOINDA.
By barbarous hands to fall at last their prey!

OROONOKO.
I have run the race with honor. Shall I now

Lag and be overtaken at the goal?
IMOINDA.
No.
OROONOKO. (*Tenderly.*)
I must look back to thee.
IMOINDA.
You shannot need.
I'm always present to your purpose. Say
Which way would you dispose me?
OROONOKO.
Have a care.
Thou'rt on a precipice and dost not see
Whither that question leads thee. Oh! too soon
Thou dost inquire what the assembled gods
Have not determined and will latest doom.
Yet this I know of fate, this is most certain:
I cannot, as I would, dispose of thee,
And as I ought, I dare not. Oh Imoinda!
IMOINDA.
Alas! that sigh! why do you tremble so?
Nay then, 'tis bad indeed, if you can weep.
OROONOKO.
My heart runs over; if my gushing eyes
Betray a weakness which they never knew,
Believe thou, only thou, couldst cause these tears.
The gods themselves conspire with faithless men
To our destruction.
IMOINDA.
Heaven and earth our foes!
OROONOKO.
It is not always granted to the great
To be most happy. If the angry pow'rs
Repent their favors, let 'em take 'em back.
The hopes of empire, which they gave my youth
By making me a prince, I here resign.
Let 'em quench in me all those glorious fires
Which kindled at their beams: that lust of fame,
That fever of ambition, restless still
And burning with the sacred thirst of sway,
Which they inspired to qualify my fate
And make me fit to govern under them,
Let 'em extinguish. I submit myself
To their high pleasure and devoted bow
Yet lower to continue still a slave,
Hopeless of liberty, and, if I could
Live after it, would give up honor, too,
To satisfy their vengeance, to avert
This only curse, the curse of losing thee.
IMOINDA.
If Heav'n could be appeased, these cruel men
Are not to be entreated or believed.
Oh! think on that and be no more deceived.
OROONOKO.
What can we do?
IMOINDA.
Can I do anything?
OROONOKO.
But we were born to suffer.
IMOINDA.
Suffer both,
Both die, and so prevent* 'em.
OROONOKO.
By thy death!
Oh! Let me hunt my traveled thoughts again,
Range the wide waste of desolate despair,
Start any hope—alas! I lose myself,
'Tis pathless, dark and barren all to me.
Thou art my only guide, my light of life,
And thou art leaving me. Send out thy beams
Upon the wing; let 'em fly all around,
Discover every way. Is there a dawn,
A glimmering of comfort? The great god
That rises on the world must shine on us.
IMOINDA.
And see us set before him.
OROONOKO.
Thou bespeakst,
And go'st[g] before me.
IMOINDA.
So I would, in love:
In the dear unsuspected part of life,
In death for love. Alas! what hopes for me?
I was preserved but to acquit myself,
To beg to die with you.
OROONOKO.
And canst thou ask it?
I never durst inquire into myself
About thy fate, and thou resolv'st it all.
IMOINDA.
Alas, my lord! my fate's resolved in yours.
OROONOKO.
Oh! Keep thee there. Let not thy virtue shrink

From my support, and I will gather strength
Fast as I can to tell thee—

IMOINDA.
I must die.
I know 'tis fit, and I can die with you.

OROONOKO.
Oh! Thou hast banished hence a thousand fears
Which sickened at my heart and quite unmanned me.

IMOINDA.
Your fear's for me. I know you feared my strength
And could not overcome your tenderness
To pass this sentence on me. And indeed,
There you were kind, as I have always found you,
As you have ever been. For though I am
Resigned and ready to obey my doom,
Methinks it should not be pronounced by you.

OROONOKO.
Oh! That was all the labor of my grief.
My heart and tongue forsook me in the strife:
I never could pronounce it.

IMOINDA.
I have for you,
For both of us.

OROONOKO.
Alas for me! my death
I could regard as the last scene of life
And act it through with joy to have it done.
But then to part with thee—

IMOINDA.
'Tis hard to part.
But parting thus, as the most happy must,
Parting in death, makes it the easier.
You might have thrown me off, forsaken me
And my misfortunes: that had been a death
Indeed of terror to have trembled at.

OROONOKO.
Forsaken! thrown thee off!

IMOINDA.
But 'tis a pleasure
More than life can give, that with unconquered
Passion to the last you struggle still
And fain would hold me to you.

OROONOKO.
Ever, ever,
And let those stars, which are my enemies,
Witness against me in the other world
If I would leave this mansion of my bliss
To be the brightest ruler of their skies. (*Embracing her.*)
Oh! That we could incorporate, be one,
One body, as we have been long one mind,
That blended so, we might together mix
And, losing thus our beings to the world,
Be only found to one another's joys.

IMOINDA.
Is this the way to part?

OROONOKO.
Which is the way?

IMOINDA.
The god of love is blind, and cannot find it.
But quick, make haste, our enemies have eyes
To find us out and show us the worst way
Of parting: think on them.

OROONOKO.
Why dost thou wake me?

IMOINDA.
Oh! No more of love.
For if I listen to you, I shall quite
Forget my dangers and desire to live.
I can't live yours. (*Takes up the dagger.*)

OROONOKO.
There all the stings of death
Are shot into my heart—what shall I do?

IMOINDA.
This dagger will instruct you. (*Gives it him.*)

OROONOKO.
Hah! This dagger!
Like Fate, it points me to the horrid deed.

IMOINDA.
Strike, strike it home and bravely save us both.
There is no other safety.

OROONOKO.
It must be.
But first a dying kiss— (*Kisses her.*) This last embrace— (*Embracing her.*)
And now—

IMOINDA.
I'm ready.

OROONOKO.
Oh! where shall I strike?
Is there a smallest grain of that loved body
That is not dearer to me than my eyes,

My bosomed heart, and all the lifeblood[h] there?
Bid me cut off these limbs, hew off these hands,
Dig out these eyes, though I would keep them last
To gaze upon thee. But to murder thee!
The joy and charm of every ravished sense,
My wife! Forbid it, Nature.

IMOINDA.
'Tis your wife
Who on her knees conjures you. Oh! in time
Prevent those mischiefs that are falling on us.
You may be hurried to a shameful death,
And I too dragged to the vile Governor.
Then I may cry aloud. When you are gone,
Where shall I find a friend again to save me?

OROONOKO.
It will be so. Thou unexampled virtue!
Thy resolution has recovered mine.
And now, prepare thee.

IMOINDA.
Thus with open arms
I welcome you and death.

He drops his dagger as he looks on her, and throws himself on the ground.

OROONOKO.
I cannot bear it.
Oh, let me dash against this rock of fate,
Dig up this earth, tear, tear her bowels out
To make a grave deep as the center down
To swallow wide and bury us together.
It wonnot be. Oh! Then some pitying god
(If there be one a friend to innocence)
Find yet a way to lay her beauties down
Gently in death and save me from her blood.

IMOINDA.
Oh rise, 'tis more than death to see you thus.
I'll ease your love and do the deed myself.

She takes up the dagger; he rises in haste to take it from her.

OROONOKO.
Oh! hold, I charge thee, hold!

IMOINDA.
Though I must own
It would be nobler for us both from you.

OROONOKO.
Oh! for a whirlwind's wing to hurry us
To yonder cliff which frowns upon the flood,
That in embraces locked we might plunge in,
And perish thus in one another's arms.

IMOINDA.
Alas! what shout is that?

OROONOKO.
I see 'em coming.
They shannot overtake us. This last kiss.
And now, farewell.

IMOINDA.
Farewell, farewell forever.

OROONOKO.
I'll turn my face away and do it so.
Now, are you ready?

IMOINDA.
Now. But do not grudge me
The pleasure in my death of a last look.
Pray look upon me—now I'm satisfied.

OROONOKO.
So Fate must be by this.

Going to stab her, he stops short. She lays her hands on his in order to give the blow.

IMOINDA.
Nay, then, I must assist you.
And since it is the common cause of both,
'Tis just that both should be employed in it.
(*Stabs herself.*)
Thus, thus 'tis finished, and I bless my fate
That where I lived, I die, in these loved arms.
(*Dies.*)

OROONOKO.
She's gone. And now all's at an end with me.
Soft, lay her down. Oh, we will part no more.
(*Throws himself by her.*)
But let me pay the tribute of my grief,
A few sad tears to thy loved memory,
And then I follow. (*Weeps over her.*) But I stay too long. (*A noise again.*)
The noise comes nearer. Hold, before I go,
There's something would be done. It shall be so.
And then, Imoinda, I'll come all to thee. (*Rises.*)

Blanford and his party enter before the [lieutenant] governor and his party, swords drawn on both sides.

LIEUTENANT GOVERNOR.
You strive in vain to save him, he shall die.
BLANFORD.
Not while we can defend him with our lives.
LIEUTENANT GOVERNOR.
Where is he?
OROONOKO.
Here's the wretch whom you would have.
Put up your swords and let civil broils
Engage you in the cursèd cause of one
Who cannot live and now entreats to die.
This object will convince you.
BLANFORD.
'Tis his wife!

They gather about the body.

Alas! there was no other remedy.
LIEUTENANT GOVERNOR.
Who did the bloody deed?
OROONOKO.
The deed was mine.
Bloody I know it is, and I expect
Your laws should tell me so. Thus self-condemned,
I do resign myself into your hands,
The hands of justice. But I hold the sword
For you—and for myself. (*Stabs the [lieutenant] governor and himself, then throws himself by Imoinda's body.*)
STANMORE.
He has killed the governor and stabbed himself.
OROONOKO.
'Tis as it should be now. I have sent his ghost
To be a witness of that happiness
In the next world which he denied us here. (*Dies.*)
BLANFORD.
I hope there is a place of happiness
In the next world for such exalted virtue.
Pagan or unbeliever, yet he lived
To all he knew. And if he went astray,
There's mercy still above to set him right.
But Christians guided by the heavenly ray
Have no excuse if we mistake our way.

[Exeunt.]

FINIS.

Textual Notes

[a] Copytext is the 1696 first quarto (Q1). Other quartos have no substantive variants. Also consulted were two separate editions (a 1712 octavo [O] and a 1736 sexto [S]) and two *Collected Works* (one in 1713 [C1] and one in 1721 [C2]) that appeared during Southerne's lifetime. Consulted too were modern editions of 1976 (Novak and Rodes) and of 1988 (Jordan and Love).

[b] weeks] C1, C2, S, Novak and Rodes, Jordan and Love; months Qq, O

[c] Let … easy] Southerne's verse is not always printed as regular; here and elsewhere it is modified to be more so. Other passages printed as verse do not scan and are printed here as prose.

[d] lent] following a suggestion in Jordan and Love; sent Q1 and all subsequent editions.

[e] Unjust] And just Q1 and all subsequent editions

[f] horror] S, perhaps following the lead of a 1731 Dublin edition; honor Q1 and all other editions with authority

[g] go'st] Novak and Rodes; goes Qq; goest O, C1-2, S, Jordan and Love

[h] lifeblood] C1-2, S, Novak and Rodes, Jordan and Love; live-blood Qq, O

The Relapse; or, Virtue in Danger, Being the Sequel of The Fool in Fashion[a]

by John Vanbrugh (1664-1726)

edited by James E. Gill

The world of *The Relapse* was the politically and economically uncertain world of England in the 1690s—a world in which there were two contending kings of England and hence a world of divided and contending loyalties, of intriguing "double dealers," and of financial crisis brought on by debased coinage and war debt. The great families and important noblemen of the realm often followed their own interests and advancement rather than any single royal leader or national policy. Some toasted "the king across the water" (James II), some pursued liberal, quasi-republican ideals, and some were loyal to William III's pro-Dutch policies, but many served themselves. *The Relapse* also belonged to a world of attempted reform and answering skepticism. In this tense atmosphere John Vanbrugh, one of nineteen children born to a Dutch immigrant, struggled to make his way, first as a soldier and as a spy (perhaps), then as a playwright and theatrical manager, and finally as an architect who built two of the really impressive edifices of the day—Castle Howard and Blenheim Palace.

The play's occasion was the production of the young actor Colley Cibber's popular comedy *Love's Last Shift*, a comedy which, according to the droll Congreve, "had something like wit," and which has been described as containing four acts of bawdy and one act of reform, the conversion of Loveless to true love. Vanbrugh "continues" Cibber's play by lifting characters and some plot details and by transforming them into an original, intelligent comical satire, which exposes the instability and vanity of human desires. Loveless's conversion is portrayed as shallow, and he suffers the relapse of the title.

The Relapse's opening scenes poise the satiety and ennui of marriage against pernicious luxury and the prodigal's poverty, and thereafter the play exposes the callous treacheries of the characters in search of pleasure and money; it questions marital and familial stability; and it probes the desire for social position, the doubts and anxieties of sexual restlessness, the desire for vengeance, and even the retreat to moral rectitude. The play, having travelled back and forth from country to city and from fall to recuperation, ends with a satiric paean to fickleness in love and a dance featuring not the right couples of social comedy but the wrong couples of satire.

The Relapse seems to have been an instant success and quickly became part of the repertory, along with *Love's Last Shift*, of the Drury Lane company and its successor, where Cibber continued to play Sir Novelty Fashion and Lord Foppington until the 1730s.

DRAMATIS PERSONAE

MEN

Sir Novelty Fashion, newly created Lord Foppington.
Young Fashion, his brother.
Loveless, husband to Amanda.
Worthy, a gentleman of the Town.*
Sir Tunbelly Clumsey, a country gentleman.
Sir John Friendly, his neighbor.
Coupler, a matchmaker.
Bull, chaplain to Sir Tunbelly.
Syringe,[1] a surgeon.
Lory, servant to Young Fashion.
[La Vérole, servant to Lord Foppington.]
[Foretop,] a perriwigmaker.
[Mendlegs, a hosier.]
Shoemaker.
Tailor.
[Clerk.]
[Constable.]

WOMEN

Amanda, wife to Loveless.
Berinthia, her cousin, a young widow.
[Abigail, her maid.]
Miss Hoyden, a great fortune, daughter to Sir Tunbelly.
Nurse, her governess.
[Mrs. Callicoe, a sempstress.]

The Relapse.

Act I, scene i. [A room in Amanda's country house.][2]

Enter Loveless reading.

LOVELESS.
How true is that philosophy which says
Our heaven is seated in our minds!
Through all the roving pleasures of my youth
(Where nights and days seemed all comsumed in joy,
Where the false face of luxury*
Displayed such charms
As might have shaken the most holy hermit
And made him totter at his altar),
I never knew one moment's peace like this.
Here, in this little soft retreat,
My thoughts unbent from all the cares of life,
Content with Fortune,
Eased from the grating duties of dependence,[3]
From envy free, ambition under foot,
The raging flame of wild destructive lust
Reduced to a warm pleasing fire of lawful love,
My life glides on, and all is well within.

Enter Amanda.

LOVELESS. (*Meeting her kindly.*)
How does the happy cause of my content,
My dear Amanda?
You find me musing on my happy state
And full of grateful thoughts to Heaven and you.

AMANDA.
Those grateful offerings Heaven can't receive
With more delight than I do:
Would I could share with it as well
The dispensations of its bliss,
That I might search its choicest favors out
And shower 'em on your head forever.

LOVELESS.
The largest boons that Heaven thinks fit to grant
To things it has decreed shall crawl on earth
Are in the gift of women formed like you.
Perhaps, when time shall be no more,
When the aspiring soul shall take its flight
And drop this pond'rous lump of clay behind it,
It may have appetites we know not of,
And pleasures as refined as its desires—
But till that day of knowledge shall instruct me,
The utmmost blessing that my thought can reach

(Taking her in his arms.)

Is folded in my arms and rooted in my heart.

---

[1] Syringe] at this time not a needle for administering injections but a device for giving clysters or enemas.

[2] Amanda's country house] estate to which the couple has retired after their reconciliation at the end of *Love's Last Shift*. Loveless, having returned penniless to England after abandoning Amanda and spending several years abroad, now has Amanda's money and property at his disposal.

[3] dependence] the state of being a kept man

AMANDA.
There let it grow forever.
LOVELESS.
Well said, Amanda—let it be forever—
Would Heaven grant that—
AMANDA.
'Twere all the heaven I'd ask.
But we are clad in black mortality,
And the dark curtain of eternal night
At last must drop between us.[b]
LOVELESS.
It must:
That mournful separation we must see.
A bitter pill it is to all, but doubles
Its ungrateful taste when lovers swallow it.
AMANDA.
Perhaps that pain may only be my lot;
You possibly may be exempted from it:
Men find out softer ways to quench their fires.
LOVELESS.
Can you then doubt my constancy, Amanda?
You'll find 'tis built upon a steady basis—
The rock of reason now supports my love,
On which it stands so fixed,
The rudest hurricane of wild desire
Would, like the breath of a soft slumbering babe,
Pass by and never shake it.
AMANDA.
Yet still 'tis safer to avoid the storm;
The strongest vessels, if they put to sea,
May possibly be lost.
Would I could keep you here, in this calm port,
Forever.
Forgive the weakness of a woman:
I am uneasy at your going to stay so long in Town;*
I know its false insinuating pleasures;
I know the force of its delusions;
I know the strength of its attacks;
I know the weak defence of nature;
I know you are a man—and I—a wife.
LOVELESS.
You know then all that needs to give you rest,
For wife's the strongest claim that you can urge.
When you would plead your title to my heart,
On this you may depend; therefore, be calm,
Banish your fears, for they are traitors to your peace;
Beware of 'em, they are insinuating busy things
That gossip to and fro and do a world of mischief
Where they come:
But you shall soon be mistress of 'em all;
I'll aid you with such arms for their destruction,
They never shall erect their heads again.
You know the business is indispensible
That obliges me to go to London,
And you have no reason, that I know of,
To believe I'm glad of the occasion.
For my honest conscience is my witness,
I have found a due succession of such charms
In my retirement here with you,
I have never thrown one roving thought that way.
But since, against my will, I'm dragged once more
To that uneasy theater of noise,
I am resolved to make such use on't
As shall convince you 'tis an old cast* mistress
Who has been so lavish of her favors,
She's now grown bankrupt of her charms
And has not one allurement left to move me.
AMANDA.
Her bow, I do believe, is grown so weak,
Her arrows (at this distance) cannot hurt you,
But in approaching 'em, you give 'em strength.
The dart that has not far to fly will put
The best armor to a dangerous trial.
LOVELESS.
That trial past, and y'are at ease forever.
When you have seen the helmet proved,
You'll apprehend no more for him that wears it.
Therefore, to put a lasting period to your fears,
I am resolved, this once, to launch into temptation.
I'll give you an essay of all my virtues:
My former boon companions of the bottle
Shall fairly try what charms are left in wine;
I'll take my place amongst 'em,
They shall hem me in,
Sing praises to their god and drink his glory,
Turn wild enthusiasts* for his sake
And beasts to do him honor,
Whilst I, a stubborn atheist,
Sullenly look on
Without one reverend glass to his divinity.

That for my temperance.
Then for my constancy—

AMANDA.
Ay, there take heed;

LOVELESS.
Indeed the danger's small.

AMANDA.
And yet my fears are great.

LOVELESS.
Why are you so timorous?

AMANDA.
Because you are so bold.

LOVELESS.
My courage should disperse your apprehensions.

AMANDA.
My apprehensions should alarm your courage.

LOVELESS.
Fie, fie, Amanda! It is not kind thus to distrust me.

AMANDA.
And yet my fears are founded on my love.

LOVELESS.
Your love then is not founded as it ought,
For if you can believe 'tis possible
I should again relapse to my past follies,
I must appear to you a thing
Of such an undigested composition
That but to think of me with inclination
Would be a weakness in your taste
Your virtue scarce could answer.

AMANDA.
'Twould be a weakness in my tongue
My prudence could not answer
If I should press you farther with my fears;
I'll therefore trouble you no longer with 'em.

LOVELESS.
Nor shall they trouble you much longer.
A little time shall show you they were groundless:
This winter shall be the fiery trial of my virtue,
Which, when it once has passed,
You'll be convinced 'twas of no false allay;[4]
There all your cares will end.

AMANDA.
Pray Heaven they may.

Exeunt hand in hand.

[4] allay] obsolete form of *alloy* necessary for the tag rhyme

Scene [ii]. [By the stairs* to the Thames below] Whitehall.*

Enter Young Fashion, Lory, and waterman.[5]

FASHION.
Come, pay the waterman, and take the portmanteau.

LORY.
Faith, sir, I think the waterman had as good take the portmanteau and pay himself.

FASHION.
Why, sure there's something left in't!

LORY.
But a solitary old waistcoat, upon honor, sir.

FASHION.
Why, what's become of the blue coat, sirrah?

LORY.
Sir, 'twas eaten at Gravesend;[6] the reckoning came to thirty shillings, and your privy purse was worth but two half crowns.

FASHION.
'Tis very well.

WATERMAN.
Pray, master, will you please to dispatch me?

FASHION.
Aye, here, a—canst thou change me a guinea?

LORY. (*Aside.*)
Good!

WATERMAN.
Change a guinea, master! Ha! ha! your honor's pleased to compliment.

FASHION.
Egad, I don't know how I shall pay thee then, for I have nothing but gold about me.

LORY. (*Aside.*)
Hum, hum.

FASHION.
What dost thou expect, friend?

WATERMAN.
Why, master, so far against wind and tide is richly worth half a piece.

[5] waterman] rower of a small boat transporting customers across the river

[6] Gravesend] port city east of London on the Thames

FASHION.

Why, faith, I think thou art a good conscionable fellow. Egad, I begin to have so good an opinion of thy honesty, I care not if I leave my portmanteau with thee, till I send thee thy money.

WATERMAN.

Hah! God bless your honor; I should be as willing to trust you, master, but that you are, as a man may say, a stranger to me, and these are nimble times; there are a great many sharpers stirring. (*Taking up the portmanteau.*) Well, master, when your worship sends the money, your portmanteau shall be forthcoming: my name's Tug; my wife keeps a brandy shop in Drab Alley at Wapping.[7]

FASHION.

Very well. I'll send for't tomorrow.

Exit waterman.

LORY.

So. Now sir, I hope you'll own yourself a happy man, you have outlived all your cares.

FASHION.

How so, sir?

LORY.

Why, you have nothing left to take care of.

FASHION.

Yes, sirrah, I have myself and you to take care of still.

LORY.

Sir, if you could but prevail with somebody else to do that for you, I fancy we might both fare the better for't.

FASHION.

Why, if thou canst tell me where to apply myself, I have at present so little money and so much humility about me, I don't know but I may follow a fool's advice.

LORY.

Why then, sir, your fool advises you to lay aside all animosity and apply to Sir Novelty, your elder brother.

FASHION.

Damn my elder brother.

LORY.

With all my heart, but get him to redeem your annuity, however.

FASHION.

My annuity? 'Sdeath,* he's such a dog, he would not give his powder puff to redeem my soul.

LORY.

Look you, sir, you must wheedle him or you must starve.

FASHION.

Look you, sir, I will neither wheedle him nor starve.

LORY.

Why, what will you do then?

FASHION.

I'll go into the army.

LORY.

You can't take the oaths; you are a Jacobite.[8]

FASHION.

Thou mayst as well say I can't take orders because I'm an atheist.

LORY.

Sir, I ask your pardon. I find I did not know the strength of your conscience so well as I did the weakness of your purse.

FASHION.

Methinks, sir, a person of your experience should have known that the strength of the conscience proceeds from the weakness of the purse.

LORY.

Sir, I am very glad to find you have a conscience able to take care of us, let it proceed from what it will. But I desire you'll please to consider that the army alone will be but a scanty maintenance for a person of your generosity, at least as rents[9] now are paid. I shall see you stand in damnable need of some auxiliary guineas for your *menus plaisirs.*[10] I will therefore turn fool once more for your service, and advise you to go directly to your brother.

7 Wapping] a shore-side suburb of London

8 oaths ... Jacobite] As an adherent of James II in exile, Young Fashion was a non-juror, one who could not take the oath of loyalty to William III.

9 rents] incomes, in this instance army pay

10 *menus plaisirs*] little pleasures (Fr.)

FASHION.
Art thou then so impregnable a blockhead to believe he'll help with a farthing?
LORY.
Not if you treat him *de haut en bas*[11] as you use to do.
FASHION.
Why, how wouldst have me treat him?
LORY.
Like a trout, tickle* him.
FASHION.
I can't flatter.
LORY.
Can you starve?
FASHION.
Yes.
LORY.
I can't. (*Going.*) Good bye t'ye, sir.
FASHION.
Stay, thou wilt distract me. What wouldst thou have me say to him?
LORY.
Say nothing to him. Apply yourself to his favorites: speak to his periwig, his cravat, his feather, his snuff box, and when you are well with them, desire him to lend you a thousand pounds. I'll engage you prosper.
FASHION.
'Sdeath* and Furies! Why was that coxcomb thrust into the world before me? Oh Fortune, Fortune, thou art a bitch, by gad.

Exeunt.

Scene [iii]. A dressing room
[in Lord Foppington's Town* house].

*Enter Lord Foppington in his nightgown.**

FOPPINGTON.
Page!—

Enter Page.

PAGE.
Sir.
FOPPINGTON.
Sir! Pray sir, do me the favor to teach your tongue the title the King has thought fit to honor me with.[12]
PAGE.
I ask your lordship's pardon, my lord.
FOPPINGTON.
Oh, you can pronounce the word, then? I thought it would have choked you. D'ye hear?
PAGE.
My lord.
FOPPINGTON.
Call La Vérole.* I would dress.

Exit Page.

Well, 'tis an unspeakable pleasure to be a man of quality,* strike me dumb! My lord—your lordship—my Lord Foppington. *Ah, c'est quelque chose de beau, que le diable m'emporte.*[13] Why, the ladies were ready to puke at me whilst I had nothing but Navelty[14] to recommend me to 'em. Sure whilst I was but a knight, I was a very nauseous fellow. Well, 'tis ten thousand pawnd well given, stap my vitals.

Enter La Vérole.

LA VÉROLE.
Me lord, de shoemaker, de tailor, de hosier, de sempstress, de barber, be all ready if your lordship please to be dress.
FOPPINGTON.
'Tis well, admit 'em.
LA VÉROLE.
Hey, messieurs, entrez.

Enter tailor, etc.

FOPPINGTON.
So, gentlemen, I hope you have all taken pains to show yourselves masters in your professions.

---

[11] *de haut en bas*] condescendingly, haughtily (Fr.)

[12] title … fit] Formerly Sir Novelty Fashion in Cibber's play, Lord Foppington, it is later noted, has purchased his barony. The sale of honors might have fallen off historically since the time of James I, but it was still an important trope in literature.

[13] *Ah … 'emporte*] Ah! it's beautiful, devil take me! (Fr.)

[14] Navelty] Foppington's drawl allegedly is a court affectation; it represents the phonetic drift from close to open o.

TAILOR.
I think I may presume to say, sir—

LA VÉROLE.
"My lord," you clawn, you.

TAILOR.
Why, is he made a lord? My lord, I ask your lordship's pardon, my lord. I hope, my lord, your lordship will please to own I have brought your lordship as accomplished a suit of clothes as ever peer of England trod the stage in, my lord. Will your lordship please to try 'em now?

FOPPINGTON.
Aye, but let my people dispose the glasses* so, that I may see myself before and behind, for I love to see myself all raund.

Whilst he puts on his clothes, enter Young Fashion and Lory.

FASHION.
Hey-dey, what the devil have we here? Sure my gentleman's grown a favorite at Court,* he has got so many people at his levee.

LORY.
Sir, these people come in order to make him a favorite at Court; they are to establish him with the ladies.

FASHION.
Good God, to what an ebb of taste are women fallen that it would be in the power of a laced coat to recommend a gallant to 'em.

LORY.
Sir, tailors and periwigmakers are now become the bawds of the Nation; 'tis they debauch all the women.

FASHION.
Thou say'st true, for there's that fop now has not by nature wherewithal to move a cook-maid, and by that time these fellows have done with him, egad he shall melt down a countess.—But now for my reception: I'll engage it shall be as cold a one as a courtier's to his friend who comes to put him in mind of his promise.

FOPPINGTON. (*To his tailor.*)
Death and eternal tartures, sir, I say the packet's too high by a foot.

TAILOR.
My lord, if it had been an inch lower, it would not have held your lordship's pocket handkerchief.

FOPPINGTON.
Rat* my pocket handkerchief! Have not I a page to carry it? You may make him a packet up to his chin a-purpose for it, but I will not have mine come so near my face.

TAILOR.
'Tis not for me to dispute your lordship's fancy.

FASHION. (*To Lory.*)
His lordship! Lory, did you observe that?

LORY.
Yes sir, I always thought 'twould end there. Now I hope you'll have a little more respect for him.

FASHION.
Respect! Damn him for a coxcomb. Now has he ruined his estate to buy a title that he may be a fool of the first rate. But let's accost him.—Brother, I'm your humble servant.

FOPPINGTON.
Oh Lard, Tam, I did not expect you in England. Brother, I am glad to see you. (*Turning to his tailor.*) Look you sir, I shall never be reconciled to this nauseous packet. Therefore, pray get me another suit with all manner of expedition, for this is my eternal aversion. Mrs. Callicoe, are you not of my mind?

MRS. CALLICOE.
Oh, directly,[15] my lord, it can never be too low.

FOPPINGTON.
You are positively right on't, for the packet becomes no part of the body but the knee.

MRS. CALLICOE.
I hope your lordship is pleased with the steenkirk?*

FOPPINGTON.
In love with it, stap my vitals. Bring your bill, you shall be paid tomarrow.

MRS. CALLICOE.
I humbly thank your honor. (*Exit.*)

FOPPINGTON.
Hark thee, shoemaker, these shoes a'n't ugly, but they don't fit me.

SHOEMAKER.
My lord, methinks they fit you very well.

[15] directly] precisely (*OED*)

FOPPINGTON.
They hurt me just below the instep.

SHOEMAKER. (*Feeling his foot.*)
My lord, they don't hurt you there.

FOPPINGTON.
I tell thee they pinch me execrably.

SHOEMAKER.
My lord, if they pinch you, I'll be bound to be hanged, that's all.

FOPPINGTON.
Why, wilt thou undertake to persuade me I cannot feel?

SHOEMAKER.
Your lordship may please to feel what you think fit, but that shoe does not hurt you. I think I understand my trade.

FOPPINGTON.
Now by all that's great and powerful, thou art an incomprehensible coxcomb, but thou makest good shoes, and so I'll bear with thee.

SHOEMAKER.
My lord, I have worked for half the people of quality* in town these twenty years, and 'twere very hard I should not know when a shoe hurts and when it don't.

FOPPINGTON.
Well, prithee be gone about thy business.

Exit Shoemaker.

(*To the hosier.*) Mr. Mendlegs, a word with you. The calves of the stockings are thickened a little too much; they make my legs look like a chairman's.*

MENDLEGS.
My lord, methinks[c] they look mighty well.

FOPPINGTON.
Aye, but you are not so good a judge of these things as I am; I have studied 'em all my life. Therefore, pray let the next be the thickness of a crown piece less. (*Aside.*) If the Town* takes notice my legs are fallen away, 'twill be attributed to the violence of some new intrigue.

Exit hosier.

(*To the periwigmaker.*) Come, Mr. Foretop, let me see what you have done, and then the fatigue of the marning will be over.

FORETOP.
My lord, I have done what I defy any prince in Europe t'outdo; I have made you a periwig so long and so full of hair, it will serve you for hat and cloak in all weathers.

FOPPINGTON.
Then thou hast made me thy friend to eternity. Come, comb it out.

FASHION.
Well Lory, what dost think on't? A very friendly reception from a brother after three years' absence.

LORY.
Why sir, it's your own fault. We seldom care for those that don't love what we love. If you would creep into his heart, you must enter into his pleasures. Here have you stood ever since you came in and have not commended any one thing that belongs to him.

FASHION.
Nor never shall, whilst they belong to a coxcomb.

LORY.
Then sir, you must be content to pick a hungry bone.

FASHION.
No sir, I'll crack it and get to the marrow before I have done.

FOPPINGTON.
Gad's curse! Mr. Foretop, you don't intend to put this upon me for a full periwig?

FORETOP.
Not a full one, my lord? I don't know what your lordship may be pleased to call a full one, but I have crammed twenty ounces of hair into it.

FOPPINGTON.
What it may be by weight, sir, I shall not dispute, but by tale* there are not nine hairs of a side.

FORETOP.
Oh Lord, Oh Lord, Oh Lord! Why, as Gad shall judge me, your honor's side face is reduced to the tip of your nose.

FOPPINGTON.
My side face may be in eclipse for aught I know, but I'm sure my full face is like the full moon.

FORETOP.
Heavens bless my eyesight. (*Rubbing his eyes.*) Sure I look through the wrong end of the perspective,*

for by my faith, an't* please your honor, the broadest place I see in your face does not seem to me to be two inches in diameter.

FOPPINGTON.
If it did, it would be just two inches too broad. Far a periwig to a man should be like a mask to a woman nothing should be seen but his eyes.

FORETOP.
My lord, I have done. If you please to have more hair in your wig, I'll put it in.

FOPPINGTON.
Passitively, yes.

FORETOP.
Shall I take it back now, my lord?

FOPPINGTON.
Noh. I'll wear it today, though it show such a manstrous pair of cheeks. Stap my vitals, I shall be taken for a trumpeter.

Exit Foretop.

FASHION.
Now your people of business are gone, Brother, I hope I may obtain a quarter of an hour's audience of you.

FOPPINGTON.
Faith Tam, I must beg you'll excuse me at this time, for I must away to the House of Lards immediately. My Lady Teaser's case[16] is to come on today, and I would not be absent for the salvation of mankind.—Hey, page, is the coach at the door?

[Enter Page.]

PAGE.
Yes, my lord.

FOPPINGTON.
You'll excuse me, Brother. (*Going.*)

FASHION.
Shall you be back at dinner?

FOPPINGTON.
As Gad shall jidge me, I can't tell, for 'tis passible I may dine with some of aur House at Lacket's.[17]

[16] My Lady Teaser's case] perhaps a scandalous case of divorce, which among the nobility were tried in the House of Lords

[17] Lackets] Lockets*

FASHION.
Shall I meet you there? For I must needs talk with you.

FOPPINGTON.
That I'm afraid mayn't be so praper, for the lards I commonly eat with are people of nice* conversation, and you know, Tam, your education has been a little at large. But if you'll stay here, you'll find a family* dinner.—Hey fellow! What is there for dinner? There's beef, I suppose my brother will eat beef.—Dear Tam, I'm glad to see thee in England, stap my vitals. (*Exit with his equipage.*)

FASHION.
Hell and Furies, is this to be borne?

LORY.
Faith sir, I could amost have given him a knock o'th'pate, myself.

FASHION.
'Tis enough. I will now show thee the excess of my passion by being very calm. Come Lory, lay your loggerhead to mine, and in cool blood let us contrive his destruction.

LORY.
Here comes a head, sir, would contrive it better than us both, if he would but join in the confederacy.

Enter Coupler.

FASHION.
By this light, old Coupler alive still! Why, how now, matchmaker, art thou here still to plague the world with matrimony? You old bawd, how have you the impudence to be hobbling out of your grave twenty years after you are rotten?

COUPLER.
When you begin to rot, sirrah, you'll go off like a pippin; one winter will send you to the devil. What mischief brings you home again? Hah, you young, lascivious rogue, you. Let me put my hand in your bosom, sirrah.[d]

FASHION.
Stand off, old Sodom![18]

[18] Sodom] a pun on a kind of apple and the biblical city destroyed for its vice, especially homosexuality

COUPLER.

Nay, prithee now, don't be so coy.

FASHION.

Keep your hands to yourself, you old dog you, or I'll wring your nose off.

COUPLER.

Hast thou been a year in Italy and brought home a fool at last? By my conscience, the young fellows of this age profit no more by their going abroad than they do by their going to church. Sirrah, sirrah, if you are not hanged before you come to my years, you'll know a cock from a hen. But come, I'm still a friend to thy person, though I have contempt of thy understanding, and therefore, I would willingly know thy condition, that I may see whether thou stand'st in need of my assistance, for widows swarm, my boy, the Town's infected with 'em.

FASHION.

I stand in need of anybody's assistance that will help me to cut my elder brother's throat without the risk of being hanged for him.

COUPLER.

Egad, sirrah, I could help thee to do him almost as good a turn without the danger of being burned in the hand[19] for't.

FASHION.

Sayest thou so, old Satan? Show me but that, and my soul is thine.

COUPLER.

Pox o'thy soul, give me thy warm body, sirrah. I shall have a substantial title to't when I tell thee my project.

FASHION.

Out with it then, dear dad, and take possession as soon as thou wilt.

COUPLER.

Sayst thou so, my Hephestion?[20] Why then, thus lies the scene.—But hold, who's that? If we are heard, we are undone.

FASHION.

What, have you forgot Lory?

COUPLER.

Who? Trusty Lory, is it thee?

LORY.

At your service, sir.

COUPLER.

Give me thy hand, old boy. Egad, I did not know thee again. But I remember thy honesty, though I did not thy face; I think thou hadst like to have been hanged once or twice for thy master.

LORY.

Sir, I was very near once having that honor.

COUPLER.

Well, live and hope, don't be discouraged. Eat with him and drink with him and do what he bids thee, and it may be thy reward at last as well as another's.—Well sir, you must know I have done you the kindness to make up a match for your brother.

FASHION.

Sir, I am very much beholden[e] to you, truly.

COUPLER.

You may be, sirrah, before the wedding day yet. The lady is a great heiress: fifteen hundred pound a year and a great bag of money.[21] The match is concluded, the writings are drawn, and the pipkin's to be cracked[22] in a fortnight. Now, you must know, stripling (with respect to your mother), your brother's the son of a whore.

FASHION.

Good.

COUPLER.

He has given me a bond of a thousand pounds for helping him to this fortune and has promised me as much more in ready money upon the day of marriage, which I understand by a friend he ne'er designs to pay me. If, therefore, you will be a generous young dog and secure me five thousand pounds, I'll be a covetous old rogue and help you to the lady.

19 burned in the hand] Branding the thumb or hand was usual for felons who escaped the gallows.

20 Hephestion] the military comrade—and lover—of Alexander the Great

21 heiress … money] heir to an estate worth fifteen hundred pounds a year in revenue, who would also bring to the marriage a good deal of ready money

22 pipkin … cracked] a small earthenware pot will be broken—part of a folk wedding ceremony, symbolic of the breaking of the maidenhead as well

FASHION.

Egad, if thou canst bring this about, I'll have thy statue cast in brass. But don't you dote, you old pander you, when you talk at this rate?

COUPLER.

That your youthful parts* shall judge of. This plump partridge that I tell you of lives in the country, fifty miles off, with her honored parents, in a lonely old house which nobody comes near. She never goes abroad nor sees company at home. To prevent all misfortunes she has her breeding within doors: the parson of the parish teaches her to play upon the bass viol, the clerk to sing, her nurse to dress, and her father to dance. In short, nobody can give you admittance there but I, nor can I do it any other way than by making you pass for your brother.

FASHION.

And how the devil wilt thou do that?

COUPLER.

Without the Devil's aid, I warrant thee. Thy brother's face not one of the family ever saw. The whole business has been managed by me, and all the letters go through my hands. The last that was writ to Sir Tunbelly Clumsey (for that's the old gentleman's name) was to tell him, his lordship would be down in a fortnight to consummate. Now you shall go away immediately, pretend you writ that letter only to have the romantic pleasure of surprising your mistress, fall desperately in love as soon as you see her, make that your plea for marrying her immediately, and when the fatigue of the wedding night's over, you shall send me a swingeing purse of gold, you dog you.

FASHION.

Egad, old dad, I'll put my hand in thy bosom now—

COUPLER.

Ah, you young, hot, lusty thief, let me muzzle you. (*Kissing.*) Sirrah, let me muzzle you.

FASHION. (*Aside.*)

Psha, the old lecher!

COUPLER.

Well, I warrant thou hast not a farthing of money in thy pocket now; no, one may see it in thy face.

FASHION.

Not a sou, by Jupiter.

COUPLER.

Must I advance then? Well sirrah, be at my lodgings in half an hour, and I'll see what may be done. We'll sign and seal and eat a pullet, and when I have given thee some farther instructions, thou shalt hoist sail and be gone. (*Kissing.*) T'other buss, and so adieu.

FASHION.

Um, psha!

COUPLER.

Ah, you young, warm dog you! What a delicious night will the bride have on't! (*Exit.*)

FASHION.

So Lory. Providence, thou seest at last, takes care of men of merit. We are in a fair way to be great people.

LORY.

Aye sir, if the Devil don't step between the cup and the lip as he uses to do.

FASHION.

Why faith, he has played me many a damned trick to spoil my fortune, and egad, I'm almost afraid he's at work about it again now. But if I should tell thee how, thou'dst wonder at me.

LORY.

Indeed sir, I should not.

FASHION.

How dost know?

LORY.

Because, sir, I have wondered at you so often, I can wonder at you no more.

FASHION.

No? What wouldst thou say if a qualm of conscience should spoil my design?

LORY.

I would eat my words and wonder more than ever.

FASHION.

Why faith, Lory, though I am a young rakehell and have played many a roguish trick, this is so full-grown a cheat I find I must take pains to come up to't. I have scruples.

LORY.

They are strong symptoms of death. If you find they increase, pray sir, make your will.

FASHION.

No, my conscience shan't starve me neither. But

thus far I will hearken to it before I execute this project. I'll try my brother to the bottom: I'll speak to him with the temper of a philosospher; my reasons, though they press him home, shall yet be clothed with so much modesty not one of all the truths they urge shall be so naked to offend his sight. If he has yet so much humanity about him as to assist me, though with a moderate aid, I'll drop my project at his feet and show him I can do for him much more than what I ask he'd do for me. This one conclusive trial of him I resolve to make.

Succeed or no, still victory's my lot;
If I subdue his heart, 'tis well; if not,
I shall subdue my conscience to my plot.

Exeunt.

Act II, scene i. [Loveless's lodgings in London.]

Enter Loveless and Amanda.

LOVELESS.
How do you like these lodgings, my dear? For my part, I am so well pleased with 'em, I shall hardly remove whilst we stay in town, if you are satisfied.

AMANDA.
I am satisfied with everything that pleases you, else I had not come to town at all.

LOVELESS.
Oh, a little of the noise and bustle of the world sweetens the pleasures of retreat. We shall find the charms of our retirement doubled when we return to it.

AMANDA.
That pleasing prospect will be my chiefest entertainment whilst (much against my will) I am obliged to stand surrounded with these empty pleasures, which 'tis so much the fashion to be fond of.

LOVELESS.
I own most of 'em are indeed but empty, nay, so empty that one would wonder by what magic power they act when they induce us to be vicious for their sakes. Yet some there are we may speak kindlier of. There are delights, of which a private life is destitute, which may divert an honest man and be a harmless entertainment to a virtuous woman. The conversation* of the Town* is one, and truly, with some small allowances, the plays, I think, may be esteemed another.

AMANDA.
The plays, I must confess, have some small charms and would have more, would they restrain that loose, obscene encouragement to vice, which shocks, if not the virtue of some women, at least the modesty of all.

LOVELESS.
But till that reformation can be made, I would not leave the wholesome corn for some intruding tares that grow amongst it. Doubtless, the moral of a well-wrought scene is of prevailing force. Last night there happened one that moved me strangely.

AMANDA.
Pray what was that?

LOVELESS.
Why 'twas about—but 'tis not worth repeating.

AMANDA.
Yes, pray let me know it.

LOVELESS.
No, I think 'tis as well let alone.

AMANDA.
Nay, now you make me have mind to know.

LOVELESS.
'Twas a foolish thing. You'd perhaps grow jealous should I tell you, though without cause, Heaven knows.

AMANDA.
I shall begin to think I have cause if you persist in making it a secret.

LOVELESS.
I'll then convince you have none by making it no longer so. Know then, I happened in the play to find my very character, only with the addition of a *Relapse*, which struck me so, I put a sudden stop to a most harmless entertainment, which till then diverted me between the acts. 'Twas to admire the workmanship of Nature in the face of a young lady that sate some distance from me: she was so exquisitely handsome.

AMANDA.
So exquisitely handsome?

LOVELESS.
Why do you repeat my words, my dear?

AMANDA.
Because you seemed to speak 'em with such pleasure I thought I might oblige you with their echo.

LOVELESS.
Then you are alarmed, Amanda?

AMANDA.
It is my duty to be so when you are in danger.

LOVELESS.
You are too quick in apprehending for me; all will be well when you have heard me out. I do confess I gazed upon her; nay, eagerly I gazed upon her.

AMANDA.
Eagerly? That's with desire.

LOVELESS.
No, I desired her not. I viewed her with a world of admiration but not one glance of love.

AMANDA.
Take heed of trusting to such nice* distinctions.

LOVELESS.
I did take heed. For observing in the play that he who seemed to represent me there was by an accident like this unwarily surprised into a net in which he lay a poor entangled slave and brought a train of mischiefs on his head, I snatched my eyes away. They pleaded hard for leave to look again, but I grew absolute, and they obeyed.

AMANDA.
Were they the only things that were inquisitive? Had I been in your place, my tongue, I fancy, had been curious too; I should have asked her name and where she lived (yet still without design). Who was she, pray?

LOVELESS.
Indeed I cannot tell.

AMANDA.
You will not tell.

LOVELESS.
By all that's sacred, then, I did not ask.

AMANDA.
Nor do you know what company was with her?

LOVELESS.
I do not.

AMANDA.
Then I am calm again.

LOVELESS.
Why were you disturbed?

AMANDA.
Had I then no cause?

LOVELESS.
None, certainly.

AMANDA.
I thought I had.

LOVELESS.
But you thought wrong, Amanda. For turn the case, and let it be your story. Should you come home and tell me you had seen a handsome man, should I grow jealous because you had eyes?

AMANDA.
But should I tell you he were exquisitely so, that I had gazed on him with admiration, that I looked with eager eyes upon him, should you not think 'twere possible I might go one step farther and inquire his name?

LOVELESS. (*Aside.*)
She has reason on her side. I have talked too much, but I must turn it off another way.—Will you then make no difference, Amanda, between the language of our sex and yours? There is a modesty restrains your tongues, which makes you speak by halves when you commend, but roving flattery gives a loose to ours, which makes us still speak double what we think. You should not, therefore, in so strict a sense take what I said to her advantage.

AMANDA.
Those flights of flattery, sir, are to our faces only. When women once are out of hearing, you are as modest in your commendations as we are. But I shan't put you to the trouble of farther excuses; if you please, this business shall rest here. Only give me leave to wish both for your peace and mine that you may never meet this miracle of beauty more.

LOVELESS.
I am content.

Enter Servant.

SERVANT.
Madam, there's a young lady at the door in a chair* desires to know whether you ladyship sees company. I think her name is Berinthia.

AMANDA.
Oh dear, 'tis a relation I have not seen these five years.—Pray her to walk in.

Exit Servant.

—Here's another beauty for you. She was young when I saw her last, but I hear she's grown extremely handsome.

LOVELESS.
Don't you be jealous now, for I shall gaze upon her too—

Enter Berinthia.

(*Aside.*) Hah! By heavens, the very woman!

BERINTHIA.(*Saluting* Amanda.*)
Dear Amanda, I did not expect to meet with you in town.

AMANDA.
Sweet cousin, I'm overjoyed to see you.—Mr. Loveless, here's a relation and a friend of mine I desire you'll be better acquainted with.

LOVELESS. (*Saluting Berinthia.*)
If my wife never desires a harder thing, madam, her request will be easily granted.

BERINTHIA.
I think, madam, I ought to wish you joy.

AMANDA.
Joy! Upon what?

BERINTHIA.
Upon your marriage. You were a widow[23] when I saw you last.

LOVELESS.
You ought rather, madam, to wish me joy upon that, since I am the only gainer.

BERINTHIA.
If she has got so good a husband as the world reports, she has gained enough to expect the compliments of her friends upon it.

LOVELESS.
Aye,[f] the world is so favorable to me to allow I deserve that title; I hope 'tis so just to my wife to own I derive it from her.

BERINTHIA.
Sir, it is so just to you both to own you are (and deserve to be) the happiest pair that live in it.

LOVELESS.
I'm afraid we shall lose that character, madam, whenever you happen to change your condition.

Enter Servant.

SERVANT.
Sir, my Lord Foppington presents his humble service to you and desires to know how you do. He but just now heard you were in town. He's at the next door, and if it be not inconvenient, he'll come and wait upon you.

LOVELESS.
Lord Foppington! I know him not.

BERINTHIA.
Not his dignity, perhaps, but you do his person. 'Tis Sir Novelty; he has bought a barony in order to marry a great fortune. His patent has not been passed eight-and-forty hours, and he has already sent how-do-ye's to all the Town to make 'em acquainted with his title.

LOVELESS.
Give my service to his lordship, and let him know I am proud of the honor he intends me.

Exit [servant].

Sure this addition of quality* must have so improved his coxcomb he can't but be very good company for a quarter of an hour.

AMANDA.
Now it moves my pity more than my mirth to see a man whom Nature has made no fool to be so very industrious to pass for an ass.

LOVELESS.
No, there you are wrong, Amanda; you should never bestow your pity upon those who take pains for your contempt. Pity those whom Nature abuses, but never those who abuse Nature.

BERINTHIA.
Besides, the Town would be robbed of one of its chief diversions if it should become a crime to laugh at a fool.

AMANDA.
I could never yet perceive the Town inclined to

23 widow] In Cibber's play Amanda dresses as a widow until the last act, when she disguises herself and seduces Loveless.

part with any of its diversions for the sake of their being crimes, but I have seen it very fond of some I think had very little else to recommend 'em.

BERINTHIA.

I doubt,* Amanda, you are grown its enemy, you speak with so much warmth against it.

AMANDA.

I must confess I am not much its friend.

BERINTHIA.

Then give me leave to make you mine by not engaging in its quarrel.

AMANDA.

You have many stronger claims than that, Berinthia, whenever you think fit to plead your title.

LOVELESS.

You have done well to engage a second, my dear, for here comes one will be apt to call you to an account for your country principles.

Enter Lord Foppington.

FOPPINGTON.

Sir, I am your most humble servant.

LOVELESS.

I wish you joy, my lord.

FOPPINGTON.

O Lard, sir.—Madam, your ladyship's welcome to tawn.

AMANDA.

I wish your lordship joy.

FOPPINGTON.

Oh heavens, madam—

LOVELESS.

My lord, this young lady is a relation of my wife's.

FOPPINGTON. (*Saluting* [Berinthia].*)*

The beautifullest race* of people upon earth, rat* me! Dear Loveless, I'm overjoyed to see you have braught your family to tawn again; I am, stap my vitals! (*Aside.*) Far I design to lie with your wife.—Far Gad's sake, madam, haw has your ladyship been able to subsist thus long under the fatigue of a country life?

AMANDA.

My life has been very far from that, my lord; it has been a very quiet one.

FOPPINGTON.

Why, that's the fatigue I speak of, madam. For 'tis impossible to be quiet without thinking: now thinking is to me the greatest fatigue in the world.

AMANDA.

Does not your lordship love reading, then?

FOPPINGTON.

Oh passionately, madam. But I never think of what I read.

BERINTHIA.

Why, can your lordship read without thinking?

FOPPINGTON.

Oh Lard!—can your ladyship pray without devotion, madam?

AMANDA.

Well, I must own I think books the best entertainment in the world.

FOPPINGTON.

I am so much of you ladyship's mind, madam, that I have a private gallery (where I walk sometimes) is furnished with nothing but books and looking glasses.* Madam, I have gilded 'em and ranged 'em so prettily, before Gad, it is the most entertaining thing in the world to walk and look upon 'em.

AMANDA.

Nay, I love a neat library, too, but 'tis, I think, the inside of the book should recommend it most to us.

FOPPINGTON.

That, I must confess, I am nat altogether so fand of. Far to mind the inside of a book is to entertain one's self with the forced product of another man's brain. Naw I think a man of quality* and breeding may be much better diverted with the natural sprauts of his own. But to say the truth, madam, let a man love reading never so well, when once he comes to know this Tawn, he finds so many better ways of passing the four-and-twenty hours that 'twere ten thousand pities he should consume his time in that. Far example, madam, my life: my life, madam, is a perpetual stream of pleasure that glides through such a variety of entertainments I believe the wisest of our ancestors never had the least conception of any of 'em. I rise, madam, about ten-a-clock. I don't rise sooner, because 'tis the worst thing in the world for the complexion. Nat that I pretend to be a beau, but a man must endeavor to look wholesome, lest he make so nauseous a figure in the side-bax the ladies should be compelled to turn their eyes upon the play. So at ten a-clack, I say, I rise. Naw, if I find 'tis a good day, I resalve to take a turn in the Park* and see the fine women, so huddle on my clothes and get dressed by one. If it be nasty weather, I take a turn in the chocolate hause,[24] where, as you walk, madam, you have the prettiest prospect in the world; you have looking glasses* all round you— But I'm afraid I tire the company.

BERINTHIA.
Not at all. Pray go on.

FOPPINGTON.
Why then, ladies, from thence I go to dinner at Lacket's, where you are so nicely* and delicately served that, stap my vitals, they shall compose you a dish no bigger than a saucer shall come to fifty shillings. Between eating my dinner (and washing my mauth, ladies) I spend my time till I go to the play, where till nine a-clack I entertain myself with looking upon the company and usually dispose of one hour more in leading[25] 'em aut. So there's twelve of the four-and-twenty pretty well over. The other twelve, madam, are disposed of in two articles: in the first four I toast myself drunk, and in t'other eight I sleep myself sober again. Thus, ladies, you see my life is an eternal raund O of delights.

LOVELESS.
'Tis a heavenly one, indeed.

AMANDA.
But I thought, my lord, you beaux spent a great deal of your time in intrigues: you have given us no account of them yet.

FOPPINGTON. (*Aside.*)
Soh, she would inquire into my amours—That's jealousy—She begins to be in love with me.— Why, madam—as to time for my intrigues, I usually make detachments of it from my other pleasures according to the exigency. Far your ladyship may please to take notice that those who intrigue with women of quality* have rarely occasion far above half an hour at a time, people of that rank being under those decorums they can seldom give you a langer view than will just serve to shoot 'em flying. So that the course of my other pleasures is not very much interrupted by my amours.

LOVELESS.
But your lordship is now become a pillar of the state; you must attend the weighty affairs of the Nation.

FOPPINGTON.
Sir—as to weighty affairs, I leave them to weighty heads. I never intend mine shall be a burden to my body.

LOVELESS.
Oh but you'll find the House[26] will expect your attendance.

FOPPINGTON.
Sir, you'll find the House will compound for my appearance.

LOVELESS.
But your friends will take it ill if you don't attend their particular causes.

FOPPINGTON.
Not, sir, if I come in time enough to give 'em my particular vote.

BERINTHIA.
But pray, my lord, how do you dispose of yourself on Sundays? For that, methinks, is a day should hang wretchedly upon your hands.

FOPPINGTON.
Why faith, madam—Sunday—is a vile day, I must confess. I intend to move for leave to bring in a bill that the players may work upon it, as well as the hackney coaches. Though this I must say for the government, it leaves us the churches to entertain us. But then again, they begin so abominable early a man must rise by candlelight to get dressed by the psalm.[27]

BERINTHIA.
Pray, which church does your lordship most oblige with your presence?

---

24 chocolate hause] Chocolate was a fashionable imported item of consumption; houses which dispensed it were as popular as coffee houses for social gathering, gossip, and politics.

25 leading] formally escorting especially the ladies

26 House] of Lords

27 psalm] part of the service, a fashionably late time to arrive at church

FOPPINGTON.
Oh, St. James's,[28] madam—there's much the best company.

AMANDA.
Is there good preaching, too?

FOPPINGTON.
Why faith, madam—I can't tell. A man must have very little to do there that can give an account of the sermon.

BERINTHIA.
You can give us an account of the ladies at least?

FOPPINGTON.
Or I deserve to be excommunicated. There is my Lady Tattle, my Lady Prate, my Lady Titter, my Lady Leer, my Lady Giggle, and my Lady Grin. These sit in the front of the boxes and all church-time are the prettiest company in the world, stap my vitals. (*To Amanda*) Mayn't we hope for the honor to see your ladyship added to our society, madam?

AMANDA.
Alas, my lord, I am the worst company in the world at church: I'm apt to mind the prayers or the sermon or—

FOPPINGTON.
One is indeed strangely apt at church to mind what one should not do. But I hope, madam, at one time or other, I shall have the honor to lead your ladyship to your coach there. (*Aside.*) Methinks she seems strangely pleased with everything I say to her. 'Tis a vast pleasure to receive encouragement from a woman before her husband's face. I have a good mind to pursue my conquest and speak the thing plainly to her at once. Egad, I'll do't, and that in so cavalier a manner she shall be surprised at it.—Ladies, I'll take my leave; I'm afraid I begin to grow troublesome with the length of my visit.

AMANDA.
Your lordhip's too entertaining to grow troublesome anywhere.

FOPPINGTON. (*Aside.*)
That now was as much as if she had said—pray lie with me. I'll let her see I'm quick of apprehension.—Oh Lard, madam, I had like to have forgot a secret I must needs tell your ladyship.—Ned, you must not be so jealous now as to listen.

LOVELESS.
Not I, my lord, I am too fashionable a husband to pry into the secrets of my wife.

FOPPINGTON. (*To Amanda, squeezing her hand.*)
I am in love with you to desperation, strike me speechless!

AMANDA. (*Giving him a box o'th'ear.*)
Then thus I return your passion.—An impudent fool!

FOPPINGTON.
Gad's curse, madam, I'm a peer of the realm!

LOVELESS.
Hey, what the devil, do you affront my wife, sir? Nay then—

They draw and fight. The women run shrieking for help.

AMANDA.
Ah! What has my folly done? Help! Murder! Help! Part 'em, for Heaven's sake.

FOPPINGTON. (*Falling back and leaning upon his sword.*)
Ah—quite through the body—stap my vitals!

Enter servants.

LOVELESS. (*Running to him.*)
I hope I han't killed the fool, however.—Bear him up! Where's your wound?

FOPPINGTON.
Just through the guts.

LOVELESS.
Call a surgeon there.—Unbutton him quickly.

FOPPINGTON.
Ay, pray make haste.

[Exit servant.]

LOVELESS.
This mischief you may thank yourself for.

FOPPINGTON.
I may so—love's the devil indeed, Ned.

Enter Syringe and Servant.

[28] St. James's] new, fashionable church in Piccadilly

SERVANT.
Here's Mr. Syringe, sir, was just going by the door.

FOPPINGTON.
He's the welcomest man alive.

SYRINGE.
Stand by, stand by, stand by! Pray gentelmen, stand by. Lord have mercy upon us! did you never see a man run through the body before? Pray, stand by!

FOPPINGTON.
Ah, Mr. Syringe—I'm a dead man!

SYRINGE.
A dead man and I by! I should laugh to see that, egad!

LOVELESS.
Prithee don't stand prating, but look upon his wound.

SYRINGE.
Why, what if I won't look upon his wound this hour, sir?

LOVELESS.
Why, then he'll bleed to death, sir.

SYRINGE.
Why, then I'll fetch him to life again, sir.

LOVELESS.
'Slife,* he's run through the guts, I tell thee.

SYRINGE.
Would he were run through the heart: I should get the more credit by his cure. Now I hope you're satisfied? Come now, let me come at him; now let me come at him. (*Viewing his wound.*) Oons,* what a gash is here! Why sir, a man may drive a coach and six horses into your body.

FOPPINGTON.
Ho—

SYRINGE.
Why, what the devil, have you run the gentleman through with a scythe? (*Aside.*) A little prick between the skin and the ribs, that's all.

LOVELESS.
Let me see his wound.

SYRINGE.
Then you shall dress it, sir, for if anybody looks upon it, I won't.

LOVELESS.
Why, thou art the veriest coxcomb I ever saw.

SYRINGE.
Sir, I am not master of my trade for nothing.

FOPPINGTON.
Surgeon!

SYRINGE.
Well, sir.

FOPPINGTON.
Is there any hopes?

SYRINGE.
Hopes? I can't tell. What are you willing to give for your cure?

FOPPINGTON.
Five hundred paunds, with pleasure.

SYRINGE.
Why, then perhaps there may be hopes. But we must avoid farther delay.—Here, help the gentleman into a chair* and carry him to my house presently,* that's the properest place (*Aside.*)—to bubble* him out of his money.—Come, a chair, a chair quickly—there, in with him.

They put him into a chair.

FOPPINGTON.
Dear Loveless—adieu! If I die—I forgive thee, and if I live—I hope thou'lt do as much by me. I'm very sorry you and I should quarrel,* but I hope here's an end on't, for if you are satisfied—I am.

LOVELESS.
I shall hardly think it worth my prosecuting any farther, so you may be at rest, sir.

FOPPINGTON.
Thou art a generous* fellow, strike me dumb. (*Aside.*) But thou hast an impertinent wife, stap my vitals.

SYRINGE.
So, carry him off, carry him off. We shall have him prate himself into a fever by and by. Carry him off.

Exit with Lord Foppington.

AMANDA.
Now on my knees, my dear, let me ask your pardon for my indiscretion; my own I never shall obtain.

LOVELESS.
Oh, there's no harm done: you served him well.

AMANDA.
He did indeed deserve it. But I tremble to think

how dear my indiscreet resentment might have cost you.

LOVELESS.
Oh no matter, never trouble yourself about that.

BERINTHIA.
For Heaven's sake, what was't he did to you?

AMANDA.
Oh, nothing: he only squeezed me kindly* by the hand and frankly offered a coxcomb's heart. I know I was to blame to resent it as I did, since nothing but a quarrel* could ensue. But the fool so surpised me with his insolence, I was not mistress of my fingers.

BERINTHIA.
Now I dare swear, he thinks you had 'em at great command, they obeyed you so readily.

Enter Worthy.

WORTHY.
Save you, save you, good people: I'm glad to find you all alive; I met a wounded peer carrying off. For Heaven's sake, what was the matter?

LOVELESS.
Oh, a trifle! He would have lain with my wife before my face, so she obliged him with a box o'th'ear, and I run him through the body: that was all.

WORTHY.
Bagatelle on all sides. But pray, madam, how long has this noble lord been an humble servant of yours?

AMANDA.
This is the first I have heard on't. So I suppose 'tis his quality* more than his love has brought him into this adventure. He thinks his title an authentic passport to every woman's heart below the degree of a peeress.

WORTHY.
He's coxcomb enough to think anything. But I would not have you brought into trouble for him. I hope there's no danger of his life?

LOVELESS.
None at all. He's fallen into the hands of a roguish surgeon I perceive designs to frighten a little money out of him. But I saw his wound, 'tis nothing; he may go to the play tonight if he pleases.

WORTHY.
I am glad you have corrected him without farther mischief. And now, sir, if these ladies have no farther service for you, you'll oblige me if you can go to the place I spoke to you of t'other day.

LOVELESS.
With all my heart. (*Aside.*) Though I could wish, methinks, to stay and gaze a little longer on that creature. Good gods, how beautiful she is! But what have I to do with beauty? I have already had my portion and must not covet more.—Come sir, when you please.

WORTHY.
Ladies, your servant.

AMANDA.
Mr. Loveless, pray one word with you before you go.

LOVELESS. (*To Worthy.*)
I'll overtake you, sir.

Exit Worthy.

—What would my dear?

AMANDA.
Only a woman's foolish question: How do you like my cousin here?

LOVELESS.
Jealous already, Amanda?

AMANDA.
Not at all, I ask you for another reason.

LOVELESS. (*Aside.*)
Whate'er her reason be, I must not tell her true.—Why, I confess she's handsome. But you must not think I slight your kinswoman if I own to you, of all the women who may claim that character, she is the last would triumph in my heart.

AMANDA.
I'm satisfied.

LOVELESS.
Now tell me why you asked?

AMANDA.
At night I will. Adieu.

LOVELESS. (*Kissing her.*)
I'm yours. (*Exit.*)

[AMANDA.] (*Aside.*)
I'm glad to find he does not like her, for I have a great mind to persuade her to come and live with

me.—Now, dear Berinthia, let me inquire a little into your affairs, for I do assure you, I am enough your friend to interest myself in everything that concerns you.

BERINTHIA.

You formerly have given me such proofs on't I should be very much to blame to doubt it. I am sorry I have no secrets to trust you with, that I might convince you how entire a confidence I durst repose in you.

AMANDA.

Why, is it possible that one so young and beautiful as you should live and have no secrets?

BERINTHIA.

What secrets do you mean?

AMANDA.

Lovers.

BERINTHIA.

Oh, twenty! but not one secret one amongst 'em. Lovers in this age have too much honor to do anything underhand; they do all above board.

AMANDA.

That now, methinks, would make me hate a man.

BERINTHIA.

But the women of the Town are of another mind: for by this means a lady may (with the expense of a few coquette glances) lead twenty fools about in a string for two or three years together. Whereas if she should allow 'em greater favors and oblige 'em to secrecy, she would not keep one of 'em a fortnight.

AMANDA.

There's something indeed in that to satisfy the vanity of a woman, but I can't comprehend how the men find their account in it.

BERINTHIA.

Their entertainment, I must confess, is a riddle to me. For there's very few of 'em ever get farther than a bow and an ogle. I have half a score for my share, who follow me all over the Town and at the play, the park, and the church do (with their eyes) say the violentest things to me. But I never hear any more of 'em.

AMANDA.

What can be the reason of that?

BERINTHIA.

One reason is, they don't know how to go farther. They have had so little practice they don't understand the trade. But besides their ignorance, you must know there is not one of my half score lovers but follows half a score of mistresses. Now, their affections, being divided amongst so many, are not strong enough for any one to make 'em pursue her to the purpose. Like a young puppy in a warren, they have a flirt to all and catch none.

AMANDA.

Yet they seem to have a torrent of love to dispose of.

BERINTHIA.

They have so. But 'tis like the rivers of a modern philosopher[29] (whose works, though a woman, I have read), it sets out with a violent stream, splits in a thousand branches, and is all lost in the sands.

AMANDA.

But do you think this river of love runs all its course without doing any mischief? Do you think it overflows nothing?

BERINTHIA.

Oh yes. 'Tis true it never breaks into anybody's ground that has the least fence about it, but it overflows all the commons that lie in its way. And this is the utmost achievement of those dreadful champions in the field of love—the beaux.

AMANDA.

But prithee, Berinthia, instruct me a little farther, for I'm so great a novice I am almost ashamed on't. My husband's leaving me whilst I was young and fond* threw me into that depth of discontent that ever since I have led so private and recluse a life my ignorance is scarce conceivable. I therefore fain would be instructed. Not (Heaven knows) that what you call intrigues have any charms for me; my love and principles are too well fixed. The practick[30] part of all unlawful love is—

BERINTHIA.

Oh, 'tis abominable! But for the speculative, that, we must all confess, is entertaining. The conversation of all the virtuous women in the Town turns upon that and new clothes.

---

29 modern philosopher] Zimansky identifies as the natural historian, Thomas Burnet.

30 practick] practical as opposed to theoretical or Berinthia's "speculative" below

AMANDA.

Pray be so just then to me to believe 'tis with a world of innocency I would inquire whether you think those women we call women of reputation do really 'scape all other men, as they do those shadows of 'em, the beaux.

BERINTHIA.

Oh no, Amanda: there are a sort of men make dreadful work amongst 'em, men that may be called the beaux' antipathy, for they agree in nothing but walking upon two legs. These have brains; the beau has none. These are in love with their mistress; the beau with himself. They take care of her reputation; he's industrious to destroy it. They are decent; he's a fop. They are sound; he's rotten.[31] They are men; he's an ass.[g]

AMANDA.

If this be their character, I fancy we had here e'en now a pattern of 'em both.

BERINTHIA.

His lordship and Mr. Worthy?

AMANDA.

The same.

BERINTHIA.

As for the lord, he's eminently so, and for the other, I can assure you, there's not a man in town who has a better interest with the women that are worth having an interest with. But 'tis all private: he's like a backstair minister at Court, who whilst the reputed favorites are sauntering in the bed-chamber, is ruling the roost in the closet.*[32]

AMANDA.

He answers then the opinion I had ever of him. Heavens, what a difference there is between a man like him and that vain nauseous fop, Sir Novelty. (*Taking her hand.*) I must acquaint you with a secret, Cousin. 'Tis not that fool alone has talked to me of love. Worthy has been tampering too. 'Tis true, he has done't in vain: not all his charms or art have power to shake me. My love, my duty, and my virtue are such faithful guards I need not fear my heart should e'er betray me. But what I wonder at is this: I find I did not start at this proposal, as when it came from one whom I contemned. I therefore mention his attempt that I may learn from you whence it proceeds. That vice (which cannot change its nature) should so far change at least its shape as that the self-same crime proposed from one shall seem a monster gaping at your ruin, when from another it shall look so kind as though it were your friend and never meant to harm you. Whence, think you, can this difference proceed? For 'tis not love, Heaven knows.

BERINTHIA.

Oh no, I would not for the world believe it were. But possibly, should there a dreadful sentence pass upon you to undergo the rage of both their passions, the pain you'd apprehend from one might seem so trivial to the other the danger would not quite so much alarm you.

AMANDA.

Fie, fie, Berinthia! you would indeed alarm me could you incline me to a thought that all the merit of mankind combined could shake that tender love I bear my husband. No! he sits triumphant in my heart, and nothing can dethrone him.

BERINTHIA.

But should he abdicate again, do you think you should preserve the vacant throne ten tedious winters more in hopes of his return?

AMANDA.

Indeed, I think I should. Though I confess, after those obligations he has to me, should he abandon me once more, my heart would grow extremely urgent with me to root him thence and cast him out forever.

BERINTHIA.

Were I that thing they call a slighted wife, somebody should run the risk of being that thing they call—a husband.

AMANDA.

Oh fie, Berinthia! No revenge should ever be taken against a husband. But to wrong his bed is a vengeance, which of all vengeance—

BERINTHIA.

Is the sweetest. Ha! ha! ha! Don't I talk madly?

31 sound ... rotten] healthy, diseased—particularly with venereal disease

32 backstair ... closet] a minister who has private access to the monarch, as opposed to those who pride themselves on access to his or her more public levee

AMANDA.

Madly, indeed.

BERINTHIA.

Yet I'm very innocent.

AMANDA.

That I dare swear you are. I know how to make allowances for your humor.* You were always very entertaining company, but I find, since marriage and widowhood have shown you the world a little, you are very much improved.

BERINTHIA. (*Aside.*)

Alack-a-day, there has gone more than that to improve me, if she knew all.

AMANDA.

For Heaven's sake, Berinthia, tell me what way I shall take to persuade you to come and live with me?

BERINTHIA.

Why, one way in the world there is—and but one.

AMANDA.

Pray which is that?

BERINTHIA.

It is, to assure me—I shall be very welcome.

AMANDA.

If that be all, you shall e'en lie here tonight.

BERINTHIA.

Tonight?

AMANDA.

Yes, tonight.

BERINTHIA.

Why, the people where I lodge will think me mad.

AMANDA.

Let 'em think what they please.

BERINTHIA.

Say you so, Amanda? Why, then they shall think what they please, for I'm a young widow, and I care not what anybody thinks. Ah, Amanda, it's a delicious thing to be a young widow!

AMANDA.

You'll hardly make me think so.

BERINTHIA.

Phu! because you are in love with your husband. But that is not every woman's case.

AMANDA.

I hope 'twas yours, at least.

BERINTHIA.

Mine, say ye? Now have I a great mind to tell you a lie, but I should do it so awkwardly you'd find me out.

AMANDA.

Then e'en speak the truth.

BERINTHIA.

Shall I?—Then after all I did love him, Amanda—as a nun does penance.

AMANDA.

Why did not you refuse to marry him, then?

BERINTHIA.

Because my mother would have whipped me.

AMANDA.

How did you live together?

BERINTHIA.

Like man and wife, asunder. He loved the country, I the Town. He hawks and hounds, I coaches and equipage. He eating and drinking, I carding and playing. He the sound of horn, I the squeek of a fiddle. We were dull company at table, worse a-bed. Whenever we met, we gave one another the spleen and never agreed but once, which was about lying alone.[h]

AMANDA.

But tell me one thing, truly and sincerely.

BERINTHIA.

What's that?

AMANDA.

Notwithstanding all these jars, did not his death at last—extremely trouble you?

BERINTHIA.

Oh yes. Not that my present pangs were so very violent, but the after-pains were intolerable. I was forced to wear a beastly widow's band a twelvemonth for't.

AMANDA.

Women, I find, have different inclinations.

BERINTHIA.

Women, I find, keep different company. When your husband ran away from you, if you had fallen into some of my acquaintance, 'twould have saved you many a tear. But you go and live with a grandmother, a bishop, and an old nurse—which was enough to make any woman break her heart for her husband. Pray Amanda, if ever you are a widow again, keep yourself so, as I do.

AMANDA.

Why, do you then resolve you'll never marry?

BERINTHIA.
Oh no, I resolve I will.
AMANDA.
How so?
BERINTHIA.
That I never may.
AMANDA.
You banter me.
BERINTHIA.
Indeed I don't. But I consider I'm a woman and form my resolutions accordingly.
AMANDA.
Well, my opinion is, form what resolution you will, matrimony will be the end on't.
BERINTHIA.
Faith, it won't.
AMANDA.
How do you know?
BERINTHIA.
I'm sure on't.
AMANDA.
Why, do you think 'tis impossible for you to fall in love?
BERINTHIA.
No.
AMANDA.
Nay, but to grow so passionately fond that nothing but the man you love can give you rest.
BERINTHIA.
Well, what then?
AMANDA.
Why, then you'll marry him.
BERINTHIA.
How do you know that?
AMANDA.
Why, what can you do else?
BERINTHIA.
Nothing—but sit and cry.
AMANDA.
Psha!
BERINTHIA.
Ah, poor Amanda! you have led a country life, but if you'll consult the widows of this Town, they'll tell you you should never take a lease of a house you can hire for a quarter's warning.

Exeunt.

Act III, [scene i. A room in Lord Foppington's Town house.]

Enter Lord Foppington and servant.

FOPPINGTON.
Hey fellow, let the coach come to the door.
SERVANT.
Will your lordship venture so soon to expose yourself to the weather?
FOPPINGTON.
Sir, I will venture as soon as I can to expose myself to the ladies; though give me my cloak, however, for in that side-box, what between the air that comes in at the door on one side, and the intolerable warmth of the masks* on t'other, a man gets so many heats and colds 'twould destroy the canstitution of a harse.
SERVANT. (*Putting on his cloak.*)
I wish your lordship would please to keep house a little longer; I'm afraid your honor does not well consider your wound.
FOPPINGTON.
My wound? I would not be in eclipse another day, though I had as many wounds in my guts as I have had in my heart.

[Exit Servant.] Enter Young Fashion.

FASHION.
Brother, your servant. How do you find yourself today?
FOPPINGTON.
So well, that I have ardered my coach to the door: so there's no great danger of death this baut, Tam.
FASHION.
I'm very glad of it.
FOPPINGTON. (*Aside.*)
That I believe's a lie.—Prithee, Tam, tell me one thing: Did nat your heart cut* a caper up to your mauth when you heard I was run through the bady?
FASHION.
Why do you think it should?
FOPPINGTON.
Because I remember mine did so when I heard my father was shat through the head.
FASHION.
It then did very ill.

FOPPINGTON.
Prithee, why so?

FASHION.
Because he used you very well.

FOPPINGTON.
Well, naw strike me dumb! he starved me. He has let me want* a thausand women for want* of a thausand paund.

FASHION.
Then he hindered you from making a great many ill bargains, for I think no woman is worth money that will take money.

FOPPINGTON.
If I were a younger brother, I should think so too.

FASHION.
Why, is it possible you can value a woman that's to be bought?

FOPPINGTON.
Prithee, why not as well as a padnag?[33]

FASHION.
Because a woman has a heart to dispose of; a horse has none.

FOPPINGTON.
Look you, Tam, of all things that belang to a woman, I have an aversion to her heart, far when once a woman has given you her heart—you can never get rid of the rest of her body.

FASHION.
This is strange doctrine, but pray, in your amours, how is it with your own heart?

FOPPINGTON.
Why, my heart in my amours—is like my heart aut of my amours: *à la glace*.[34] My bady, Tam, is a watch, and my heart is the pendulum to it: whilst the finger runs raund to every hour in the circle, that still beats the same time.

FASHION.
Then you are seldom much in love?

FOPPINGTON.
Never, stap my vitals.

FASHION.
Why then did you make all this bustle about Amanda?

FOPPINGTON.
Because she was a woman of an insolent virtue, and I thought myself piqued[i] in honor to debauch her.

FASHION.
Very well. (*Aside.*) Here's a rare fellow for you to have the spending of five thousand pounds a year! But now for my business with him.—Brother, though I know to talk to you of business (especially of money) is a theme not quite so entertaining to you as that of the ladies, my necessities are such I hope you'll have patience to hear me.

FOPPINGTON.
The greatness of your necessities, Tam, is the worst argument in the world for your being patiently heard. I do believe you are going to make me a very good speech, but strike me dumb, it has the worst beginning of any speech I have heard this twelvemonth.

FASHION.
I'm very sorry you think so.

FOPPINGTON.
I do believe thau art. But come, let's know thy affair quickly, far 'tis a new play, and I shall be so rumpled and squeezed with pressing through the crawd to get to my servant the women will think I have lain all night in my clothes.

FASHION.
Why then (that I may not be the author of so great a misfortune), my case in a word is this: The necessary expenses of my travels have so much exceeded the wretched income of my annuity that I have been forced to mortgage it for five hundred pounds, which is spent; so that unless you are so kind to assist me in redeeming it, I know of no remedy but to go take a purse.[35]

FOPPINGTON.
Why faith, Tam—to give you my sense of the thing, I do think taking a purse the best remedy in the world: for if you succeed, you are relieved that way; if you are taken—you are relieved t'other.[36]

---

33 padnag] an ambling jade (*OED*); a broken-down, vicious, or worthless horse

34 *à la glace*] iced (Fr.)

35 take a purse] commit highway robbery

36 you are relieved t'other] by the gallows

FASHION.
I'm glad to see you are in so pleasant a humor. I hope I shall find the effects on't.

FOPPINGTON.
Why, do you then really think it a reasonable thing I should give you five hundred paunds?

FASHION.
I do not ask it as a due, Brother; I am willing to receive it as a favor.

FOPPINGTON.
Thau art willing to receive it anyhaw, strike me speechless! But these are damned times to give money in: taxes are so great, repairs so exorbitant, tenants such rogues, and periwigs so dear* that, the devil take me, I am reduced to that extremity in my cash I have been forced to retrench in that one article of sweet pawder till I have braught it dawn to five guineas a manth. Naw judge, Tam, whether I can spare you five hundred paunds.

FASHION.
If you can't, I must starve, that's all. (*Aside.*) Damn him!

FOPPINGTON.
All I can say is, you should have been a better husband.*

FASHION.
Oons,* if you can't live upon five thousand a year, how do you think I should do't upon two hundred?

FOPPINGTON.
Don't be in a passion, Tam, far passion is the most unbecoming thing in the world—to the face. Look you, I don't love to say anything to you to make you melancholy, but upon this occasion I must take leave to put you in mind that a running horse does require more attendance than a coach-horse. Nature has made some difference 'twixt you and I.

FASHION.
Yes, she has made you older. (*Aside.*) Pox take her!

FOPPINGTON.
That is nat all, Tam.

FASHION.
Why, what is there else?

FOPPINGTON. (*Looking first upon himself, then upon his brother.*)
Ask the ladies.

FASHION.
Why, thou essence bottle! thou musk cat![37] dost thou then think thou hast any advantage over me but what Fortune has given thee?

FOPPINGTON.
I do—stap my vitals!

FASHION.
Now, by all that's great and powerful, thou art the prince of coxcombs!

FOPPINGTON.
Sir—I am praud of being at the head of so prevailing a party.

FASHION.
Will nothing then provoke thee? Draw, coward!

FOPPINGTON.
Look you, Tam, you know I have always taken you for a mighty dull fellow, and here is one of the foolishest plats broke out that I have seen in a long time. Your paverty makes your life so burdensome to you, you would provoke me to a quarrel,* in hopes either to slip through my lungs into my estate or to get yourself run through the guts to put an end to your pain. But I will disappoint you in both your designs, far with the temper of a philasapher and the discretion of a statesman—I will go to the play with my sword in my scabbard. (*Exit.*)

FASHION.
Soh! Farewell, snuff-box! And now, conscience, I defy thee.—Lory!

Enter Lory.

LORY.
Sir.

FASHION.
Here's rare news, Lory: his lordship has given me a pill has purged off all my scruples.

LORY.
Then my heart's at ease again. For I have been in a lamentable fright, sir, ever since your conscience had the impudence to intrude into your company.

FASHION.
Be at peace, it will come there no more: my

---

37 essence ... cat] perfume bottle, civet cat (yielder of musky scent)

brother has given it a wring by the nose, and I have kicked it down stairs. So run away to the inn, get the horses ready quickly, and bring 'em to old Coupler's without a moment's delay.

LORY.
Then sir, are you going straight about the fortune?

FASHION.
I am. Away! Fly, Lory!

LORY.
The happiest day I ever saw. I'm upon the wing already.

Exeunt several ways.

Scene [ii]. A garden [adjoining Loveless's lodgings].

Enter Loveless and servant.

LOVELESS.
Is my wife within?

SERVANT.
No, sir, she has been gone out this half hour.

LOVELESS.
'Tis well; leave me.

[Exit Servant.]

Sure Fate has yet some business to be done
Before Amanda's heart and mine must rest.
Else why amongst those legions of her sex
Which throng the world
Should she pick out for her companion
The only one on earth
Whom Nature has endowed for her undoing?
Undoing, was't I said? Who shall undo her?
Is not her empire fixed? Am I not hers?
Did she not rescue me, a grov'ling slave,
When chained and bound by that black tyrant, Vice,
I labored in his vilest drudgery?
Did she not ransom me and set me free?
Nay, more: When by my follies sunk
To a poor, tattered, despicable beggar,
Did she not lift me up to envied fortune?
Give me herself and all that she possessed
Without a thought of more return
Than what a poor, repenting heart might make her?
Han't she done this? And if she has,
Am I not strongly bound to love her for it?
To love her! Why, do I not love her then?
By earth and heaven I do.
Nay, I have demonstration that I do:
For I would sacrifice my life to serve her.
Yet hold—if laying down my life
Be demonstration of my love,
What is't I feel in favor of Berinthia?
For should she be in danger, methinks I could
Incline to risk it for her service too,
And yet I do not love her.
How then subsists my proof?—
Oh, I have found it out!
What I would do for one
Is demonstration of my love,
And if I'd do as much for t'other,
It[k] there is demonstration of my friendship—
Aye—it must be so. I find I'm very much her friend.
—Yet let me ask myself one puzzling question more:
Whence springs this mighty friendship all at once?
For our acquaintaince is of later date.
Now friendship's said to be a plant of tedious growth:
Its root composed of tender fibers, nice* in their taste,
Cautious in spreading, checked with the least
Corruption in the soil long ere it take
And longer still ere it appear to do so.
Whilst mine is in a moment shot so high
And fixed so fast it seems
Beyond the power of storms to shake it.
I doubt* it thrives too fast.[l] (*Musing.*)

Enter Berinthia.

Hah! she here! Nay, then take heed my heart,
For there are dangers towards.

BERINTHIA.
What makes you look so thoughtful, sir? I hope you are not ill.

LOVELESS.
I was debating, madam, whether I was so or not, and that was it which made me look so thoughtful.

BERINTHIA.
Is it then so hard a matter to decide? I thought all people had been acquainted with their own bodies, though few people know their own minds.

LOVELESS.
What if the distemper I suspect be in the mind?

BERINTHIA.
Why, then I'll undertake to prescribe you a cure.

LOVELESS.
Alas! you undertake you know not what.

BERINTHIA.
So far at least then allow me to be a physician.

LOVELESS.
Nay, I'll allow you so yet farther, for I have reason to believe, should I put myself into your hands, you would increase my distemper.

BERINTHIA.
Perhaps I might have reasons from the College not to be too quick in your cure,[38] but 'tis possible I might find ways to give you often ease, sir.

LOVELESS.
Were I but sure of that, I'd quickly lay my case before you.

BERINTHIA.
Whether you are sure of it or no, what risk do you run in trying?

LOVELESS.
Oh! a very great one.

BERINTHIA.
How?

LOVELESS.
You might betray my distemper to my wife.

BERINTHIA.
And so lose all my practice.

LOVELESS.
Will you then keep my secret?

BERINTHIA.
I will, if it don't burst me.

LOVELESS.
Swear.

BERINTHIA.
I do.

LOVELESS.
By what?

BERINTHIA.
By Woman.

LOVELESS.
That's swearing by my deity. Do it by your own, or I shan't believe you.

BERINTHIA.
By Man, then.

LOVELESS.
I'm satisfied.
Now hear my symptoms and give me your advice.
The first were these:
When 'twas my chance to see you at the play,
A random glance you threw at first alarmed me;
I could not turn my eyes from whence the danger came.
I gazed upon you till you shot again,
And then my fears came on me.
My heart began to pant, my limbs to tremble,
My blood grew thin, my pulse beat quick, my eyes
Grew hot and dim, and all the frame of nature
Shook with apprehension.
'Tis true, some small recruits of resolution
My manhood brought to my assistance,
And by their help I made a stand a while
But found at last your arrows flew so thick
They could not fail to pierce me, so left the field
And fled for shelter to Amanda's arms.
What think you of these symptoms, pray?

BERINTHIA.
Feverish, every one of 'em.
But what relief, pray, did your wife afford you?

LOVELESS.
Why, instantly, she let me blood,[39]
Which for the present much assuaged my flame.
But when I saw you, out it burst again,
And raged with greater fury than before.
Nay, since you now appear, 'tis so increased
That in a moment, if you do not help me,
I shall, whilst you look on, consume to ashes.[m]
(*Taking hold of her hand.*)

BERINTHIA. (*Breaking from him.*)
Oh Lard, let me go! 'Tis the plague, and we shall all be infected.

LOVELESS. (*Catching her in his arms and kissing her.*)
Then we'll die together, my charming angel!

---

[38] College ... cure] College of Physicians, who would forego extra fees in the event of a rapid cure

[39] let me blood] Draining blood (bloodletting) was state-of-the-art therapy for many maladies.

BERINTHIA.
Oh Ged—the Devil's in you!—Lord, let me go, here's somebody coming.

Enter servant.

SERVANT.
Sir, my lady's come home and desires to speak with you. She's in her chamber.

LOVELESS.
Tell her I'm coming.

Exit servant.

—But before I go, one glass of nectar more to drink her health.

BERINTHIA.
Stand off, or I shall hate you, by heavens!

LOVELESS. (*Kissing her.*)
In matters of love, a woman's oath is no more to be minded than a man's.

BERINTHIA.
Um—

Enter Worthy.

WORTHY. [*Aside.*]
Hah! What's here? My old mistress, and so close, i'faith! I would not spoil her sport for the universe. (*He retires.*)

BERINTHIA.
Oh Ged!—Now do I pray to Heaven—

Exit Loveless running.

with all my heart and soul, that the Devil in hell may take me—if ever—I was better pleased in my life! This man has bewitched me, that's certain. (*Sighing.*) Well, I am condemned, but thanks to Heaven, I feel myself each moment more and more prepared for my execution. Nay to that degree, I don't perceive I have the least fear of dying. No, I find, let the executioner be but a man, and there's nothing will suffer with more resolution than a woman. Well, I never had but one intrigue yet—but I confess I long to have another. Pray Heaven it end as the first did though, that we may both grow weary at a time, for 'tis a melancholy thing for lovers to outlive one another.[n]

Enter Worthy.

WORTHY. (*Aside.*)
This discovery's a lucky one; I hope to make a happy use on't. That gentlewoman there is no fool, so I shall be able to make her understand her interest.—Your servant, madam; I need not ask how you do, you have got so good a color.

BERINTHIA.
No better than I used to have, I suppose?

WORTHY.
A little more blood in your cheeks.

BERINTHIA.
The weather's hot.

WORTHY.
If it were not, a woman may have color.

BERINTHIA.
What do you mean by that?

WORTHY.
Nothing.

BERINTHIA.
Why do you smile then?

WORTHY.
Because the weather's hot.

BERINTHIA.
You'll never leave roguing, I see that.

WORTHY.
You'll never leave— (*Putting his finger to his nose.*[40]) I see that.

BERINTHIA.
Well, I can't imagine what you drive at. Pray tell me what you mean?

WORTHY.
Do you tell me; it's the same thing.

BERINTHIA.
I can't.

WORTHY.
Guess!

BERINTHIA.
I shall guess wrong.

WORTHY.
Indeed you won't.

BERINTHIA.
Psha! either tell or let it alone.

40 nose] The upper is often taken as the sign of the nether nose (penis).

WORTHY.

Nay, rather than let it alone, I will tell. But first I must put you in mind that, after what has passed 'twixt you and I, very few things ought to be secrets between us.

BERINTHIA.

Why, what secrets do we hide? I know of none.

WORTHY.

Yes, there are two: one I have hid from you, and t'other you would hide from me. You are fond of Loveless, which I have discovered, and I am fond of his wife—

BERINTHIA.

Which I have discovered.

WORTHY.

Very well, now I confess your discovery to be true, what do you say to mine?

BERINTHIA.

Why, I confess—I would swear 'twere false, if I thought you were fool enough to believe me.

WORTHY.

Now am I almost in love with you again. Nay, I don't know but I might be quite so, had I made one short campaign with Amanda. Therefore, if you find 'twould tickle your vanity to bring me down once more to your lure, e'en help me quickly to dispatch her business, that I may have nothing else to do but to apply myself to yours.

BERINTHIA.

Do you then think, sir, I am old enough to be a bawd?

WORTHY.

No, but I think you are wise enough to—

BERINTHIA.

To do what?

WORTHY.

To hoodwink Amanda with a gallant, that she mayn't see who is her husband's mistress.

BERINTHIA. (*Aside.*)

He has reason: the hint's a good one.

WORTHY.

Well madam, what think you on't?

BERINTHIA.

I think you are so much a deeper politician in these affairs than I am, that I ought to have a very great regard for your advice.

WORTHY.

Then give me leave to put you in mind: that the most easy, safe, and pleasant situation for your own amour is the house in which you now are, provided you keep Amanda from any sort of suspicion; that the way to do that is to engage her in an intrigue of her own, making yourself her confidante; and the way to bring her to intrigue is to make her jealous of her husband in a wrong place—which the more you foment, the less you'll be suspected. This is my scheme, in short, which if you follow as you should do, my dear Berinthia, we may all four pass the winter[41] very pleasantly.

BERINTHIA.

Well, I could be glad to have nobody's sins to answer for but my own. But where there is a necessity—

WORTHY.

Right as you say, where there is a necessity, a Christian is bound to help his neighbor. So, good Berinthia, lose no time, but let us begin the dance as fast as we can.

BERINTHIA.

Not till the fiddles are in tune, pray, sir. Your lady's strings will be very apt to fly, I can tell you that, if they are wound up too hastily. But if you'll have patience to screw 'em to their pitch by degrees, I don't doubt but she may endure to be played upon.

WORTHY.

Aye, and will make admirable music too, or I'm mistaken. But have you had no private closet* discourse with her yet about males and females and so forth, which may give you hopes in her constitution, for I know her morals are the devil against us?

BERINTHIA.

I have had so much discourse with her that I believe, were she once cured of her fondness for her husband, the fortress of her virtue would not be so impregnable as she fancies.

WORTHY.

What! she runs, I warrant you, into that common

41 winter] It was fashionable for the aristocracy, from nobility to gentry, to pass the winter in the Town and the summer in the country (away from the plague and other diseases).

mistake of fond* wives, who conclude themselves virtuous because they can refuse a man they don't like, when they have got one they do.

BERINTHIA.
True, and therefore I think 'tis a presumptuous thing in a woman to assume the name of virtuous till she has heartily hated her husband and been soundly in love with somebody else. Whom, if she has withstood—then—much good may it do her.

WORTHY.
Well, so much for her virtue. Now, one word of her inclinations, and every one to their post. What opinion do you find she has of me?

BERINTHIA.
What you could wish: she thinks you handsome and discreet.

WORTHY.
Good, that's thinking half-seas over. One tide more brings us into port.

BERINTHIA.
Perhaps it may, though still remember, there's a difficult bar to pass.[42]

WORTHY.
I know there is, but I don't question I shall get well over it by the help of such a pilot.

BERINTHIA.
You may depend upon your pilot—she'll do the best she can; so weigh anchor and be gone as soon as you please.

WORTHY.
I'm under sail already. Adieu! (*Exit.*)

BERINTHIA.
Bon voyage! So, here's fine work! What a business have I undertaken! I'm a very pretty gentlewoman, truly. But there was no avoiding it: he'd have ruined me if I had refused him. Besides, faith, I begin to fancy there may be as much pleasure in carrying on another body's intrigue as one's own. This at least is certain, it exercises almost all the entertaining faculties of a woman. For there's employment for hypocrisy, invention, deceit, flattery, mischief, and lying.

Enter Amanda, her woman following her.

WOMAN.
If you please, madam, only to say whether you'll have me buy 'em or not.

AMANDA.
Yes, no, go fiddle! I care not what you do. Prithee leave me.

WOMAN.
I have done. (*Exit.*)

BERINTHIA.
What in the name of Jove's the matter with you?

AMANDA.
The matter, Berinthia! I'm almost mad, I'm plagued to death.

BERINTHIA.
Who is it that plagues you?

AMANDA.
Who do you think should plague a wife but her husband?

BERINTHIA.
Oh ho, is it come to that? We shall have you wish yourself a widow by and by.

AMANDA.
Would I were anything but what I am! A base, ungrateful man, after what I have done for him, to use me thus!

BERINTHIA.
What, he has been ogling now, I'll warrant you?

AMANDA.
Yes, he has been ogling.

BERINTHIA.
And so you are jealous? Is that all?

AMANDA.
That all! Is jealousy then nothing?

BERINTHIA.
It should be nothing, if I were in your case.

AMANDA.
Why, what would you do?

BERINTHIA.
I'd cure myself.

AMANDA.
How?

BERINTHIA.
Let blood in the fond* vein: care as little for my husband as he did for me.

---

42 half-seas over . . . pass] Half the journey is accomplished . . . all one has to do is pass the sand bar at the harbor's mouth at high tide.

AMANDA.
That would not stop his course.

BERINTHIA.
Nor nothing else, when the wind's in the warm corner.[43] Look you, Amanda, you may build castles in the air and fume and fret and grow thin and lean and pale and ugly, if you please. But I tell you, no man worth having is true to his wife or can be true to his wife or ever was or ever will be so.

AMANDA.
Do you then really think he's false to me? For I did but suspect him.

BERINTHIA.
Think so? I know he's so.

AMANDA.
Is it possible? Pray tell me what you know.

BERINTHIA.
Don't press me then to name names, for that I have sworn I won't do.

AMANDA.
Well, I won't, but let me know all you can without perjury.

BERINTHIA.
I'll let you know enough to prevent any wise woman's dying of the pip, and I hope you'll pluck up your spirits and show upon occasion you can be as good a wife as the best of 'em.

AMANDA.
Well, what a woman can do I'll endeavor.

BERINTHIA.
Oh, a woman can do a great deal, if once she sets her mind to it. Therefore, pray don't stand trifling any longer and teasing yourself with this and that and your love and your virtue and I know not what. But resolve to hold up your head, get a tip-toe, and look over 'em all, for to my certain knowledge your husband is a-pickering[44] elsewhere.

AMANDA.
You are sure on't?

BERINTHIA.
Positively. He fell in love at the play.

AMANDA.
Right, the very same. Do you know the ugly thing?

BERINTHIA.
Yes, I know her well enough, but she's no such an ugly thing neither.

AMANDA.
Is she very handsome?

BERINTHIA.
Truly I think so.

AMANDA.
Hey ho!

BERINTHIA.
What do you sigh for now?

AMANDA.
Oh, my heart!

BERINTHIA. (*Aside.*)
Only the pangs of nature; she's in labor of her love. Heaven send her a quick delivery, I'm sure she has a good midwife.

AMANDA.
I'm very ill, I must go to my chamber. Dear Berinthia, don't leave me a moment.

BERINTHIA.
No, don't fear. (*Aside.*) I'll see you safe brought to bed, I'll warrant you.

Exeunt, Amanda leaning upon Berinthia.

Scene [iii. The gate of] a country house.

Enter Young Fashion and Lory.

FASHION.
So here's our inheritance, Lory, if we can but get into possession. But methinks the seat of our family looks like Noah's ark, as if the chief part on't were designed for the fowls of the air and the beasts of the field.

LORY.
Pray sir, don't let your head run upon the orders of building[45] here; get but the heiress, let the Devil take the house.

FASHION.
Get but the house, let the Devil take the heiress, I

43 when the wind's in the warm corner] when a comfortable situation is troubled (Tilley)

44 a-pickering] reconnoitering, maneuvering

45 orders of building] the Classical forms of architecture, called orders, as in Doric, Ionic, and Corinthian columns

say, at least if she be as old Coupler describes her. But come, we have no time to squander. Knock at the door.

Lory knocks two or three times.

What the devil, have they got no ears in this house? Knock harder.

LORY.
Egad, sir, this will prove some enchanted castle; we shall have the giant come out by and by with his club and beat our brains out.(*Knocks again.*)

FASHION.
Hush, they come.

[SERVANT.] (*From within.*)
Who is there?

LORY.
Open the door and see. Is that your country breeding?

[SERVANT.] (*Within.*)
Aye, but two words to a bargain.—Tummas, is the blunderbuss primed?

FASHION.
Oons,* give 'em good words, Lory; we shall be shot here a fortune-catching.

LORY.
Egad, sir, I think y'are in the right on't.—Ho! Mr. What-d'ye-call'um.

Servant appears at the window with a blunderbuss.

SERVANT.
Weall, naw what's yare business?

FASHION.
Nothing, sir, but to wait upon Sir Tunbelly, with your leave.

SERVANT.
To weat upon Sir Tunbelly? Why, you'll find that's just as Sir Tunbelly pleases.

FASHION.
But will you do me the favor, sir, to know whether Sir Tunbelly pleases or not?

SERVANT.
Why, look you, do you see, with good words much may be done.—Ralph, go thy weas, and ask Sir Tunbelly if he pleases to be waited upon. And dost hear? Call to Nurse that she may lock up Miss Hoyden before the geat's open.

FASHION.
D'ye hear that, Lory?

LORY.
Aye sir, I'm afraid we shall find a difficult job on't. Pray Heaven that old rogue Coupler han't sent us to fetch milk out of the gunroom.

FASHION.
I'll warrant thee all will go well. See, the door opens.

Enter Sir Tunbelly, with his servants armed with guns, clubs, pitchforks, scythes, etc.

LORY. (*Running behind his master.*)
Oh Lord! O Lord! O Lord! We are both dead men!

FASHION.
Take heed, fool! Thy fear will ruin us.

LORY.
My fear, sir! 'Sdeath,* sir, I fear nothing. (*Aside*) Would I were well up to the chin in a horsepond!

SIR TUNBELLY.
Who is it here has any business with me?

FASHION.
Sir, 'tis I, if your name be Sir Tunbelly Clumsey.

SIR TUNBELLY.
Sir, my name is Sir Tunbelly Clumsey whether you have any business with me or not. So you see I am not ashamed of my name—nor my face neither.

FASHION.
Sir, you have no cause that I know of.

SIR TUNBELLY.
Sir, if you have no cause neither, I desire to know who you are, for till I know your name, I shall not ask you to come into my house, and when I know your name, 'tis six to four I don't ask you neither.

FASHION. (*Giving him a letter.*)
Sir, I hope you'll find this letter an authentic passport.

SIR TUNBELLY.
Cod's my life! I ask your lordship's pardon ten thousand times. (*To his servants.*) Here, run in a-doors quickly. Get a Scotch-coal fire in the great parlor; set all the Turkey-work chairs[46] in their places; get the great brass candlesticks out, and be sure stick the sockets full of laurel. Run!—My lord,

46 Turkey-work chairs] chairs covered with Turkish tapestry

I ask your lordship's pardon. (*To other servants*) And do you hear, run away to Nurse, bid her let Miss Hoyden loose again, and if it was not shifting day,[47] let her put on a clean tucker quick.

Exeunt servants confusedly.

—I hope your honor will excuse the disorder of my family;* we are not used to receive men of your lordship's great quality* every day. Pray where are your coaches and servants, my lord?

FASHION.

Sir, that I might give you and your fair daughter a proof how impatient I am to be nearer akin to you, I left my equipage to folow me and came away post[48] with only one servant.

SIR TUNBELLY.

Your lordship does me too much honor. It was exposing your person to too much fatigue and danger, I protest it was. But my daughter shall endeavor to make you what amends she can, and though I say it that should not say it—Hoyden has charms.

FASHION.

Sir, I am not a stranger to them, though I am to her. Common fame has done her justice.

SIR TUNBELLY.

My lord, I am common fame's very grateful humble servant. My lord—my girl's young, Hoyden is young, my lord. But this I must say for her, what she wants* in art, she has by nature; what she wants in experience, she has in breeding; and what's wanting in her age, is made good in her constitution. So pray, my lord, walk in; pray, my lord, walk in.

FASHION.

Sir, I wait upon you.

Exeunt.

Scene [iv. A room in Sir Tunbelly's house.]

Miss Hoyden sola.

[HOYDEN].

Sure never nobody was used as I am. I know well enough what other girls do, for all they think to make a fool of me. It's well I have a husband a-coming, or, i'cod, I'd marry the baker, I would so. Nobody can knock at the gate but presently* I must be locked up, and here's the young greyhound bitch can run loose about the house all day long, she can; 'tis very well.

NURSE. (*Without, opening the door.*)

Miss Hoyden, Miss, Miss, Miss! Miss Hoyden!

Enter nurse.

HOYDEN.

Well, what do you make such a noise for, hah? What do you din a body's ears for? Can't one be at quiet for you?

NURSE.

What do I din your ears for? Here's one come will din your ears[49] for you.

HOYDEN.

What care I who's come. I care not a fig who comes nor who goes, as long as I must locked up like the ale cellar.

NURSE.

That, Miss, is for fear you should be drank before you are ripe.

HOYDEN.

Oh, don't trouble your head about that; I'm as ripe as you, though not so mellow.

NURSE.

Very well! Now have I a good mind to lock you up again and not let you see my lord tonight.

HOYDEN.

My lord? Why, is my husband come?

NURSE.

Yes, marry is he, and a goodly person too.

HOYDEN. (*Hugging nurse.*)

Oh my dear nurse, forgive me this once and I'll never misuse you again. No, if I do, you shall give me three thumps on the back and a great pinch by the cheek.

NURSE.

Ah the poor thing, see how it melts; it's as full of good nature as an egg's full of meat.

HOYDEN.

But my dear nurse, don't lie now. Is he come, by your troth?

[47] shifting day] when one changes linen

[48] post] both in a hurry and on horseback

[49] ears] ear was slang for female genitalia

NURSE.
Yes, by my truly, is he.

HOYDEN.
Oh Lord! I'll go put on my laced smock, though I am whipped till the blood run down my heels for't. (*Exit running.*)

NURSE.
Eh! The Lord succor thee, how thou art delighted!

Exit after her.

[Scene v. Another room in Sir Tunbelly's house.]

Enter Sir Tunbelly and Young Fashion, a servant with wine.

SIR TUNBELLY.
My Lord, I am proud of the honor to see your lordship within my doors, and I humbly crave leave to bid you welcome in a cup of sack* wine.

FASHION.
Sir, to your daughter's health. (*Drinks.*)

SIR TUNBELLY.
Ah poor girl, she'll be scared out of her wits on her wedding night, for honestly speaking, she does not know a man from a woman but by his beard and his britches.

FASHION.
Sir, I don't doubt but she has a virtuous education, which with the rest of her merit makes me long to see her mine. I wish you should dispense with the canonical hour* and let it be this very night.

SIR TUNBELLY.
Oh not so soon neither, that's shooting my girl before you bid her stand. No, give her fair warning; we'll sign and seal tonight, if you please, and this day seven-night—let the jade look to her quarters.

FASHION.
This day sennight? Why, what do you take me for, a ghost, sir? 'Slife,* sir, I'm made of flesh and blood and bones and sinews and can no more live a week without your daughter—(*Aside.*) than I can a month with her.

SIR TUNBELLY.
Oh, I'll warrant you, my hero, young men are hot, I know, but they don't boil over at that rate neither; besides, my wench's wedding gown is not come home yet.

FASHION.
Oh, no matter, sir, I'll take her in her shift. (*Aside.*) A pox of this old fellow; he'll delay the business 'till my damned star[50] finds me out and discovers me.—Pray, sir, let it be done without ceremony, 'twill save money.

SIR TUNBELLY.
Money?—Save money when Hoyden's to be married? Udswoons,* I'll give my wench a wedding dinner though I go to grass with the King of Assyria[51] for't, and such a dinner it shall be as is not to be cooked in the poaching of an egg. Therefore, my noble lord, have a little patience; we'll go and look over our deeds and settlements immediately, and as for your bride, though you may be sharp[52] before she's quite ready, I'll engage for my girl she stays your stomach at last.

Exeunt.

Act IV, scene i. [Another room in Sir Tunbelly's house.]

Enter Miss Hoyden and nurse.

NURSE.
Well miss, how do you like your husband that is to be?

HOYDEN.
Oh Lord, Nurse, I'm so overjoyed I can scarce contain myself.

NURSE.
Oh, but you must have a care of being too fond, for men nowadays hate a woman that loves 'em.

HOYDEN.
Love him! Why, do you think I love him, Nurse? Ecod, I would not care if he were hanged so I were but once married to him. No, that which pleases me is to think what work I'll make when I get to London, for when I am a wife and a lady both, Nurse, ecod, I'll flaunt it with the best of 'em.

---

50 damned star] ill or evil planetary influence

51 King of Assyria] Nebuchadnezzar, ruler of Babylon, not Assyria, went mad and "did eat grass as oxen" (Daniel 4:33).

52 sharp] hungry

NURSE.
Look, look, if his honor not be coming again to you; now if I were sure you would behave yourself handsomely and not disgrace me that have brought you up, I'd leave you alone together.

HOYDEN.
That's my best nurse, do as you would be done by. Trust us together this once, and if I don't show my breeding from the head to the foot of me, may I be twice married and die a maid.

NURSE.
Well, this once I'll venture you, but if you disparage[53] me—

HOYDEN.
Never fear. I'll show him my parts,* I'll warrant him.

Exit Nurse.

These old women are so wise when they get a poor girl in their clutches, but ere it be long, I shall know what's what as well as the best of 'em.

Enter Young Fashion.

FASHION.
Your servant, madam. I'm glad to find you alone, for I have something of importance to speak to you about.

HOYDEN.
Sir—my lord, I meant—you may speak to me about what you please, I shall give you a civil answer.

FASHION.
You give me so obliging a one, it encourages me to tell you in a few words what I think both for your interest and mine. Your father, I suppose you know, has resolved to make me happy in being your husband, and I hope I may depend upon your consent to perform what he desires.

HOYDEN.
Sir, I never disobey my father in anything but eating of green gooseberries.

FASHION.
So good a daughter must needs make an admirable wife; I am therefore impatient till you are mine and hope you will so far consider the violence of my love that you won't have the cruelty to defer my happiness so long as your father designs it.

HOYDEN.
Pray, my lord, how long is that?

FASHION.
Madam, a thousand year—a whole week.

HOYDEN.
A week! Why, I shall be an old woman by that time.

FASHION.
And I an old man, which you'll find a greater misfortune than t'other.

HOYDEN.
Why, I thought 'twas to be tomorrow morning, as soon as I was up; I'm sure Nurse told me so.

FASHION.
And it shall be tomorrow morning still, if you'll consent?

HOYDEN.
If I'll consent? Why, I thought I was to obey you as my husband.

FASHION.
That's when we are married; till then, I am to obey you.

HOYDEN.
Why then, if we are to take it by turns, it's the same thing. I'll obey you now, and when we are married you shall obey me.

FASHION.
With all my heart, but I doubt* we must get Nurse on our side or we shall hardly prevail with the chaplain.

HOYDEN.
No more we shan't indeed, for he loves her better than he loves his pulpit and would always be a-preaching to her, by his good will.

FASHION.
Why then, my dear little bedfellow, if you'll call her hither, we'll try to persuade her presently.*

HOYDEN.
Oh Lord, I can tell you a way how to persuade her to anything.

FASHION.
How's that?

[53] disparage] bring discredit on

HOYDEN.

Why, tell her she's a wholesome, comely woman—and give her half a crown.

FASHION.

Nay, if that will do, she shall have half a score of 'em.

HOYDEN.

Oh jiminy,* for half that she'd marry you herself. I'll run and call her. (*Exit.*)

FASHION.

So, matters go swimmingly. This is a rare girl, i'faith; I shall have a fine time on't with her at London. I'm much mistaken if she don't prove a March hare all year round. What a scamp'ring chase will she make on't when she finds the whole kennel of beaux at her tail! Hey to the park and the play and the church and the devil! She'll show 'em sport, I'll warrant 'em. But no matter: she brings an estate will afford me a separate maintenance.[54]

Enter Miss Hoyden and Nurse.

How do you do, good Mistress Nurse. I desired your young lady would give me leave to see you, that I might thank you for your extraordinary care and conduct of her education. Pray accept of this small acknowledgement for it at present, and depend upon my farther kindness when I shall be that happy thing her husband. [*Gives a purse.*]

NURSE. (*Aside.*)

Gold, by makings![55]—Your honor's goodness is too great. Alas, all I can boast of is, I gave her pure good milk, and so your honor would have said, an* you had seen how the poor thing sucked it. Eh, God's blessing on the sweet face on't, how it used to hang at this poor teat, and suck and squeeze and kick and sprawl it would, till the belly on't was so full it would drop off like a leech.

HOYDEN. (*To Nurse, taking her angrily aside.*)

Pray one word with you. Prithee, Nurse, don't stand ripping up old stories to make one ashamed before one's love. Do you think such a fine proper gentleman as he cares for a fiddlecome[56] tale of a draggle-tailed girl? If you have a mind to make him have a good opinion of a woman, don't tell him what one did then, tell him what one can do now.—I hope your honor will excuse my mismanners to whisper before you; it was only to give some orders about the family.*

FASHION.

Oh, everything, madam, is to give way to business; besides, good housewifery is a very commendable quality in a young lady.

HOYDEN.

Pray, sir, are the young ladies good housewives at London town? Do they darn their own linen?

FASHION.

Oh no, they study how to spend money, not to save it.

HOYDEN.

I'cod, I don't know but that may be better sport than t'other, hah, Nurse?

FASHION.

Well, then you shall have your choice when you come there.

HOYDEN.

Shall I? Then by my troth I'll get there as fast as I can.—His honor desires you'll be so kind as to let us be married tomorrow.

NURSE.

Tomorrow, my dear madam?

FASHION.

Yes, tomorrow, sweet Nurse, privately. Young folks you know are impatient, and Sir Tunbelly would make us stay a week for a wedding dinner. Now all things being signed and sealed and agreed, I fancy there could be no great harm in practicing a scene or two of matrimony in private, if it were only to give us better assurance when we come to play it in public.

NURSE.

Nay, I must confess stolen pleasures are sweet. But if you should be married now, what will you do when Sir Tunbelly calls for you to be wed?

54 separate maintenance] an arrangement whereby husband and wife agreed to live apart and receive support for separate living

55 by makings] a variant of "by mackins," an emphatic but otherwise meaningless phrase (Zimansky)

56 fiddlecome] silly, absurd

HOYDEN.
Why then we'll be married again.
NURSE.
What, twice, my child?
HOYDEN.
I'cod, I don't care how often I'm married, not I.
FASHION.
Pray, Nurse, don't you be against your young lady's good, for by this means she'll have the pleasure of two wedding days.
HOYDEN. (*To Nurse softly.*)
And of two wedding nights, too, Nurse.
NURSE.
Well, I'm such a tender-hearted fool, I find I can refuse nothing; so you shall e'en follow your own inventions.
HOYDEN.
Shall I? (*Aside.*) Oh Lord, I could leap over the moon.
FASHION.
Dear Nurse, this goodness of yours shan't go unrewarded, but now you must employ your power with Mr. Bull the chaplain that he may do us his friendly office too, and then we shall all be happy. Do you think you can prevail with him?
NURSE.
Prevail with him? Or he shall never prevail with me, I can tell him that.
HOYDEN.
My lord, she has had him upon the hip this seven year.
FASHION.
I'm glad to hear it; however, to strengthen your interest with him, you may let him know I have several fat livings in my gift and that the first that falls shall be in your disposal.
NURSE.
Nay, then I'll make him marry more folks than one, I'll promise him.
HOYDEN.
Faith do, Nurse. Make him marry you too; I'm sure he'll do't for a fat living, for he loves eating more than he loves his Bible, and I have often heard him say, a fat living was the best meat in the world.
NURSE.
Aye, and I'll make him commend the sauce too, or I'll bring his gown to a cassock,[57] I will so.
FASHION.
Well, Nurse, whilst you go and settle matters with him, then your lady and I will go take a walk in the garden.
NURSE.
I'll do your honor's business in the catching up of a garter. (*Exit.*)
FASHION. (*Giving her his hand.*)
Come, madam, dare you venture yourself alone with me?
HOYDEN.
Oh dear, yes sir; I don't think you'll do anything to me I need be afraid on.

Exeunt.

[Scene ii. Loveless's lodgings.]

Enter Amanda and Berinthia.

Song.

"I smile at love and all its arts,"
The charming Cynthia cried;
"Take heed, for Love has piercing darts,"
A wounded swain replied.
"Once free and blest as you are now,
I trifled with his charms;
I pointed at his little bow
And sported with his arms.
Till, urged too far, 'Revenge!' he cries;
A fatal shaft he drew.
It took its passage through your eyes,
And to my heart it flew.

II

"To tear it thence, I tried in vain,
To strive I quickly found
Was only to increase the pain
And to enlarge the wound.
Ah, much too well I fear you know
What pain I'm to endure,
Since what your eyes alone could do,
Your heart alone can cure.

[57] bring his gown to a cassock] tear off the gown which a clergyman wore over his cassock: to expose

And that (grant Heaven I may mistake)
I doubt* is doomed to bear
A burden for another's sake
Who ill rewards its care."

AMANDA.
Well, now Berinthia, I'm at leisure to hear what 'twas you had to say to me.

BERINTHIA.
What I had to say was only to echo the sighs and groans of a dying lover.

AMANDA.
Phu, will you never learn to talk in earnest of anything?

BERINTHIA.
Why, this shall be in earnest, if you please. For my part, I only tell you matter of fact. You may take it which way you like best, but if you'll follow the women of the Town, you'll take it both ways, for when a man offers himself to one of them, first she takes him in jest, and then she takes him in earnest.

AMANDA.
I'm sure there's so much jest and earnest in what you say to me I scarce know how to take it, but I think you have bewitched me, for I don't find it possible to be angry with you, say what you will.

BERINTHIA.
I'm very glad to hear it, for I have no mind to quarrel with you, for more reasons than I'll brag of. But quarrel or not, smile or frown, I must tell you what I have suffered upon your account.

AMANDA.
Upon my account?

BERINTHIA.
Yes, upon yours. I have been forced to sit still and hear you commended for two hours together, without one compliment to myself. Now don't you think a woman had a blessed time of that?

AMANDA.
Alas, I should have been unconcerned at it; I never knew where the pleasure lay of being praised by the men. But pray, who was this that commended me so?

BERINTHIA.
One you have a mortal aversion to, Mr. Worthy. He used you like a text: he took you all to pieces but spoke so learnedly upon every point one might see the spirit of the church was in him; if you are a woman, you'd have been in an ectasy to have heard how feelingly he handled your hair, your eyes, your nose, your mouth, your teeth, your tongue, your chin, your neck, and so forth. Thus he preached for an hour, but when he came to use and application, he observed that all these without a gallant were nothing. Now consider of what has been said, and Heaven give you grace to put it in practice.

AMANDA.
Alas Berinthia, did I incline to a gallant (which you know I do not), do you think a man so nice* as he could have the least concern for such a plain unpolished thing as I am? It is impossible!

BERINTHIA.
Now have you a great mind to put me upon commending you.

AMANDA.
Indeed that was not my design.

BERINTHIA.
Nay, if it were, it's all one, for I won't do't; I'll leave that to your looking glass.* But to show you I have some good nature left, I'll commend him, and maybe that will do as well.

AMANDA.
You have a great mind to persuade me I am in love with him.

BERINTHIA.
I have a great mind to persuade you, you don't know what you are in love with.

AMANDA.
I am sure I am not in love with him nor never shall be; so let that pass. But you were saying something you would commend him for.

BERINTHIA.
Oh, you'd be glad to hear a good character* of him, however.

AMANDA.
Psha!

BERINTHIA.
Psha! Well, 'tis a foolish undertaking for women in these kind of matters to pretend to deceive one another. Have not I been bred a woman as well as you?

AMANDA.
What then?

BERINTHIA.
Why then, I understand my trade so well that whenever I am told of a man I like, I cry, psha. But that I may spare you the pains of putting me a second time in mind to commend him, I'll proceed and give you this account of him: that though 'tis possible he may have had women with as good faces as your ladyship's (no discredit to it neither), yet you must know your cautious behavior, with that reserve in your humor,* has given him his death's wound; he mortally hates a coquette; he says 'tis impossible to love where we cannot esteem and that no woman can be esteemed by a man who has sense if she makes herself cheap in the eye of a fool; that pride to a woman is as necessary as humility to a divine; and that far-fetched and dear-bought is meat for gentlemen as well as for ladies—in short, that every woman who has beauty may set a price on herself and that by underselling the market they ruin the trade. This is his doctrine. How do you like it?

AMANDA.
So well that, since I never intend to have a gallant for myself, if I were to recommend one to a friend, he should be the man.

Enter Worthy.

Bless me, he's here! Pray Heaven he did not hear me.

BERINTHIA.
If he did, it won't hurt your reputation; your thoughts are as safe in his heart as in your own.

WORTHY.
I venture in at an unseasonable time of night, ladies; I hope if I'm troublesome, you'll use the same freedom in turning me out again.

AMANDA.
I believe it can't be late, for Mr. Loveless is not come home yet, and he usually keeps good hours.

WORTHY.
Madam, I'm afraid he'll transgress a little tonight, for he told me about half an hour ago he was going to sup with some company he doubted* would keep him out till three or four o'clock in the morning and desired I would let my servant acquaint you with it, that you might not expect him. But my fellow's a blunderhead, so lest he should make some mistake, I thought it my duty to deliver the message myself.

AMANDA.
I'm very sorry he should give you that trouble, sir. But—

BERINTHIA.
But since he has, will you give me leave, madam, to keep him to play at ombre with us?

AMANDA.
Cousin, you know you command my house.

WORTHY. (*To Berinthia.*)
And, madam, you know you command me, though I'm a very wretched gamester.

BERINTHIA.
Oh, you play well enough to lose your money, and that's all the ladies require. So, without any more ceremony, let us go into the next room and call for the cards.

AMANDA.
With all my heart.

Exit Worthy leading Amanda.

BERINTHIA.
Well, how this business will end, Heaven knows, but she seems to me to be in as fair a way—as a boy is to be a rogue when he's put as clerk to an attorney.

Exit.

Scene [iii.] Berinthia's chamber.

Enter Loveless cautiously in the dark.

LOVELESS.
So, thus far all's well. I'm got into her bedchamber, and I think nobody has perceived me steal into the house; my wife don't expect me home till four o'clock, so if Berinthia comes to bed by eleven, I shall have a chase of five hours. Let me see, where shall I hide myself? Under her bed? No, we shall have her maid searching there for something or other. Her closet's* a better place, and I have a master key will open it; I'll e'en in there and attack her just when she comes to her prayers; that's the most likely to prove her critical minute, for then

the Devil will be there to assist me. (*He opens the closet, goes in, and shuts the door after him.*)

Enter Berinthia with a candle in her hand.

BERINTHIA.
Well, sure I am the best-natured woman in the world. I that love cards so well (there is but one thing upon earth I love better) have pretended letters to write, to give my friends—a *tête-à-tête.* However, I'm innocent, for piquet is the game I set 'em to; at her own peril be it if she ventures to play with him at any other. But now what shall I do with myself? I don't know how in the world to pass my time; would Loveless were here to *badiner*[58] a little. Well, he's a charming fellow; I don't wonder his wife's so fond of him. What if I should sit down and think of him till I fall asleep and dream of the Lord knows what? Oh, but then if I should dream we were married, I should be frightened out of my wits. (*Seeing a book.*) What's this book? I think I had best go read. Oh, *splénétique*![59] It's a sermon. Well, I'll go into my closet and read *The Plotting Sisters.*[60] (*She opens the closet, sees Loveless, and shrieks out.*) Oh Lord, a ghost, a ghost, a ghost, a ghost!

Enter Loveless running to her.

LOVELESS.
Peace, my dear, it's no ghost; take it in your arms, you'll find 'tis worth a hundred of 'em.

BERINTHIA.
Run in again; here's somebody coming.

[Loveless enters the closet.] Enter her Maid.

MAID.
Lord, madam, what's the matter?

BERINTHIA.
Oh heavens! I'm almost frighted out of my wits. I thought verily I had seen a ghost, and 'twas nothing but the white curtain with a black hood pinned up against it. You may be gone again. I am the fearfull'st fool.

58 *badiner*] to banter, trifle (Fr.)

59 *splénétique*] causing spleen, depressing (Fr.)

60 *The Plotting Sisters*] Durfey's *A Fond Husband* (see below)

Exit Maid. Re-enter Loveless.

LOVELESS.
Is the coast clear?

BERINTHIA.
The coast clear! I suppose you are clear,[61] you'd never play such a trick as this else.

LOVELESS.
I am very well pleased with my trick thus far and shall be so till I have played it out, if it ben't your fault. Where's my wife?

BERINTHIA.
At cards.

LOVELESS.
With whom?

BERINTHIA.
With Worthy.

LOVELESS.
Then we are safe enough.

BERINTHIA.
Are you so? Some husbands would be of another mind if he were at cards with their wives.

LOVELESS.
And they'd be in the right on't, too. But I dare trust mine. Besides, I know he's in love in another place, and he's not one of those who court half a dozen at a time.

BERINTHIA.
Nay, the truth on't is, you'd pity him if you saw how uneasy he is at being engaged with us. But 'twas my malice. I fancied he was to meet his mistress somewhere else, so did it to have the pleasure of seeing him fret.

LOVELESS.
What says Amanda to my staying abroad so late?

BERINTHIA.
Why, she's as much out of humor as he; I believe they wish one another at the devil.

LOVELESS.
Then I'm afraid they'll quarrel at play and soon throw up the cards. (*Offering to pull her into the closet.*) Therefore, my dear charming angel, let us make good use of our time.

BERINTHIA.
Heavens, what do you mean?

61 clear] drunk

LOVELESS.
Pray, what do you think I mean?
BERINTHIA.
I don't know.
LOVELESS.
I'll show you.
BERINTHIA.
You may as well tell me.
LOVELESS.
No, that would make you blush worse than t'other.
BERINTHIA.
Why, do you intend to make me blush?
LOVELESS.
Faith, I can't tell that, but if I do, it shall be in the dark. (*Pulling her.*)
BERINTHIA.
Oh heavens! I would not be in the dark with you for all the world.
LOVELESS.
I'll try that. (*Puts out the candles.*)
BERINTHIA.
Oh Lord! Are you mad? What shall I do for light?
LOVELESS.
You'll do as well without it.
BERINTHIA.
Why, one can't find a chair to sit down.
LOVELESS.
Come into the closet, madam; there's moonshine upon the couch.
BERINTHIA.
Nay, never pull, for I will not go.
LOVELESS. (*Carrying her.*)
Then you must be carried.
BERINTHIA. (*Very softly.*)
Help, help, I'm ravished, ruined, undone! Oh Lord, I shall never be able to bear it.

[Exeunt.]

Scene [iv]. Sir Tunbelly's house.

Enter Miss Hoyden, Nurse, Young Fashion, and Bull.

FASHION.
This quick dispatch of yours, Mr. Bull, I take so kindly it shall give you a claim on my favor as long as I live, I do assure you.
HOYDEN.
And to mine, too, I promise you.
BULL.
I most humbly thank your honors, and I hope, since it has been my lot to join you in the holy bands of wedlock, you will so well cultivate the soil which I have craved a blessing on that your children may swarm about you like bees about a honeycomb.
HOYDEN.
I'cod with all my heart, the more the merrier, I say. Hah, Nurse?

Enter Lory taking his master hastily aside.

LORY.
One word with you, for Heaven's sake.
FASHION.
What the devil's the matter?
LORY.
Sir, your fortune's ruined, and I don't think your life's worth a quarter of an hour's purchase. Yonder's your brother arrived with two coaches and six horses, twenty footmen and pages, a coat worth fourscore pound, and a periwig down to his knees. So judge what will become of your lady's heart.
FASHION.
Death and Furies, 'tis impossible!
LORY.
Fiends and specters, sir, 'tis true.
FASHION.
Is he in the house yet?
LORY.
No, they are capitulating with him at the gate; the porter tells him, he's come to run away with Miss Hoyden, and has cocked the blundrbuss at him; your brother swears, Gad damme, they are a parcel of clawns and he has a good mind to break off the match, but they have given the word for Sir Tunbelly, so I doubt* all will come out presently.* Pray, sir, resolve what you'll do this moment, for egad, they'll maul you.
FASHION.
Stay a little.—My dear, here's a troublesome business my man tells me of, but don't be frightened, we shall be too hard for the rogue. Here's an impudent fellow at the gate (not

knowing I was come hither incognito) has taken my name upon him in hopes to run away with you.

HOYDEN.
Oh, the brazen-faced varlet! It's well we are married, or maybe we might never a been so.

FASHION. (*Aside.*)
Egad, like enough!—Prithee dear doctor, run to Sir Tunbelly and stop him from going to the gate before I speak with him.

BULL.
I fly, my good lord. (*Exit.*)

NURSE.
An't* please your honor, my lady and I had best lock ourselves up till the danger be over.

FASHION.
Aye, by all means.

HOYDEN.
Not so fast! I won't be locked up any more. I'm married.

FASHION.
Yes, pray my dear, do, till we have seized this rascal.

HOYDEN.
Nay, if you pray me, I'll do anything.

Exeunt Hoyden and Nurse.

FASHION.
Oh, here's Sir Tunbelly coming.—Hark you, sirrah, things are better than you imagine; the wedding's over.

LORY.
The devil it is, sir.

FASHION.
Not a word, all's safe. But Sir Tunbelly don't know it, nor must not yet, so I am resolved to brazen the business out and have the pleasure of turning the imposter upon his lordship,[62] which I believe may be easily done.

Enter Sir Tunbelly, Bull, and servants armed.

Did you ever hear, sir, of so impudent an undertaking?

SIR TUNBELLY.
Never, by the mass! But we'll tickle* him, I warrant him.

FASHION.
They tell me, sir, he has a great many people with him disguised like servants.

SIR TUNBELLY.
Aye, aye, rogues enough, but I'll soon raise the posse upon 'em.

FASHION.
Sir, if you'll take my advice, we'll go a shorter way to work. I find whoever this spark is, he knows nothing of my being privately here; so if you pretend to receive him civilly, he'll enter without suspicion, and as soon as he is within the gate, we'll whip up the drawbridge upon his back, let fly the blunderbuss to disperse his crew, and so commit him to gaol.

SIR TUNBELLY.
Egad, your lordship is an ingenious person and a very great general. But shall we kill any of 'em or not?

FASHION.
No, no, fire over their heads only to fright 'em; I'll warrant the regiment scours[63] when the colonel's a prisoner.

SIR TUNBELLY.
Then come along, my boys, and let your courage be great—for your danger is but small.

Exeunt.

Scene [v]. The gate.

Enter Lord Foppington and followers.

FOPPINGTON.
A pax of these bumkinly people, will they open the gate, or do they desire I should grow at their moat-side like a willow? (*To the Porter.*) Hey, fellow, prithee do me the favor, in as few words as thou canst find to express thyself, to tell me whether thy master will admit me or not, that I may turn about my coach and be gone.

PORTER.
Here's my master himself now at hand; he's of age, he'll give you his answer.

---

62 turning the imposter upon his lordship] making his lordship seem to be the imposter

63 scours] scurries, flees

Enter Sir Tunbelly and servants.

SIR TUNBELLY.
My most noble lord, I crave your pardon for making your honor wait so long, but my orders to my servants have been to admit nobody without my knowledge for fear of some attempt upon my daughter, the times being full of plots and roguery.[64]

FOPPINGTON.
Much caution, I must confess, is a sign of great wisdom. But stap my vitals, I have got a cold enough to destroy a porter—he, hem—

SIR TUNBELLY.
I am very sorry for't indeed, my lord, but if your lordship please to walk in, we'll help you to some brown-sugar candy. My lord, I'll show you the way.

FOPPINGTON.
Sir, I follow you with pleasure.

Exeunt [Sir Tunbelly and Lord Foppington]. As Lord Foppington's servants go to follow him him in, [Sir Tunbelly's servants] clap the door against La Vérole.

SERVANTS. (*Within.*)
Nay, hold you me there, sir!

LA VÉROLE.
Jernie die, qu'est-ce que veut dire ça?*[65]

SIR TUNBELLY. (*Within.*)
Fire, Porter.

PORTER. (*Fires.*)
Have among ye, my masters!

LA VÉROLE.
Ah, je suis mort![66]

The servants all run off.

PORTER.
Not one soldier left, by the mass!

[Exit.]

Scene [vi]. Changes to the hall.

Enter Sir Tunbelly, Bull, and servants [including a clerk and a constable], with Lord Foppington disarmed.

SIR TUNBELLY.
Come, bring him along, bring him along!

FOPPINGTON.
What the pax do you mean, gentlmen? Is it Fair time, that you are all drunk before dinner?

SIR TUNBELLY.
Drunk, sirrah! Here's an impudent rogue for you. Drunk or sober, bully, I'm a Justice of the Peace and know how to deal with strollers.

FOPPINGTON.
Strollers!

SIR TUNBELLY.
Aye, strollers. Come, give an account of yourself: What's your name? where do you live? do you pay scot and lot? are you a Williamite or a Jacobite?[67] Come!

FOPPINGTON.
And why dost thou ask me so many impertinent questions?

SIR TUNBELLY.
Because I'll make you answer 'em before I have done with you, you rascal, you.

FOPPINGTON.
Before Gad, all the answer I can make thee to 'em is that thou art a very extraordinary old fellow, stap my vitals.

SIR TUNBELLY.
Nay, if you are for joking with deputy lieutenants, we'st[68] know how to deal with you. Here, draw a warrant for him immediately.

FOPPINGTON.
A warrant! What the devil is't thou wouldst be at, old gentleman?

SIR TUNBELLY.
I would be at you, sirrah, if my hands were not tied as a magistrate, and with these two double fists beat your teeth down your throat, you dog you!

---

64 the times being full of plots and roguery] There were ongoing plots to restore James II to the throne.

65 *qu'est-ce que veut dire ça?*] What's that he says? (Fr.)

66 *Ah, je suis mort!*] Oh, I am dead! (Fr.)

67 Williamite or a Jacobite] a follower of William III or of James II (see General Introduction)

68 we'st] obviously a dialectal variant of *we*

FOPPINGTON.

And why wouldst thou spoil my face at that rate?

SIR TUNBELLY.

For your design to rob me of my daughter, villain.

FOPPINGTON.

Rab thee of thy daughter!—[*Aside.*] Now do I begin to believe I am abed and asleep and that all this is but a dream. If it be, 'twill be an agreeable surprise enough to waken by and by, and instead of the impertinent company of a nasty country justice, find myself, perhaps, in the arms of a woman of quality.*—Prithee, old father, wilt thou give me leave to ask thee one question?

SIR TUNBELLY.

I can't tell whether I will or not till I know what it is.

FOPPINGTON.

Why, then it is whether thou didst not write to my Lord Foppington to come down and marry thy daughter?

SIR TUNBELLY.

Yes, marry,* did I, and my Lord Foppington is come down and shall marry my daughter before she's a day older.

FOPPINGTON.

Now give me thy hand, dear Dad, I thought we should understand one another at last.

SIR TUNBELLY.

This fellow's mad. Here, bind him hand and foot.

They bind him.

FOPPINGTON.

Nay, prithee knight, leave fooling; thy jest begins to grow dull.

SIR TUNBELLY.

Bind him, I say, he's mad. Bread and water, a dark room, and a whip may bring him to his senses again.

FOPPINGTON. (*Aside.*)

Egad, if I don't waken quickly, by all I can see this is like to prove one of the most impertinent dreams that ever I dreamt in my life.

Enter Miss Hoyden and Nurse.

HOYDEN. (*Going up to him.*)

Is this he that would have run away with me? Faugh, how he stinks of sweets! Pray father, let him be dragged through the horse pond.

FOPPINGTON. (*Aside.*)

This must be my wife by her natural inclination to her husband.

HOYDEN.

Pray father, what do you intend to do with him, hang him?

SIR TUNBELLY.

That at least, child.

NURSE.

Aye, and it's e'en too good for him too.

FOPPINGTON. (*Aside.*)

Madame la gouvernante, I presume. Hitherto this appears to me to be one of the most extraordinary families that ever man of quality* matched into.

SIR TUNBELLY.

What's become of my lord, daughter?

HOYDEN.

He's just coming, sir.

FOPPINGTON. (*Aside.*)

My lord—What does he mean by that now?

Enter Young Fashion and Lory.

(*Seeing him.*) Stap my vitals, Tam, now the dream's out.

FASHION.

Is this the fellow, sir, that designed to trick me of your daughter?

SIR TUNBELLY.

This is he, my lord. How do you like him? Is not he a pretty fellow to get a fortune?

FASHION.

I find by his dress he thought your daughter might be taken with a beau.

HOYDEN.

Oh jiminy!* Is this a beau? Let me see him again. Hah, I find a beau's no such an ugly thing neither.

FASHION. [*Aside.*]

Egad, she'll be in love with him presently;* I'll e'en have him sent way to gaol. (*To Lord Foppington.*) Sir, though your understanding shows you are a person of no extraordinary modesty, I suppose you han't confidence enough to expect much favor from me?

FOPPINGTON.
Strike me dumb, Tam, thou art a very impudent fellow.

NURSE.
Look if the varlet has not the 'frontery to call his lordship plain Thomas.

BULL.
The business is, he would feign himself mad to avoid going to gaol.

FOPPINGTON. (*Aside.*)
That must be the chaplain, by his unfolding of mysteries.

SIR TUNBELLY.
Come, is the warrant writ?

CLERK.
Yes, sir.

SIR TUNBELLY.
Give me the pen; I'll sign it. So, now constable, away with him.

FOPPINGTON.
Hold one moment. Pray, gentlemen.—My Lord Foppington, shall I beg one word with your lordship?

NURSE.
Oh ho, it's my lord with him now; see how afflictions will humble folks.

HOYDEN.
Pray my lord, don't let him whisper too close, lest he bite your ear off.

FOPPINGTON.
I am not altogether so hungry as your ladyship is pleased to imagine.—Look you, Tam, I am sensible I have not been so kind to you as I ought, but I hope you'll forget what's past and accept of the five thousand pounds I offer; thou mayst live in extreme splendor with it, stap my vitals.

FASHION.
It's a much easier matter to prevent a disease than to cure it. A quarter of that sum would have secured your mistress; twice as much won't redeem her. (*Leaving him.*)

SIR TUNBELLY.
Well, what says he?

FASHION.
Only the rascal offered me a bribe to let him go.

SIR TUNBELLY.
Aye, he shall go with a pox to him. Lead on, Constable.

FOPPINGTON.
One word more, and I have done.

SIR TUNBELLY.
Before Gad, thou art an impudent fellow to trouble the court at this rate after thou art condemned, but speak once and for all.

FOPPINGTON.
Why then once for all: I have at last luckily called to mind that there is a gentleman of this country, who I believe cannot live far from this place, if he were here would satisfy you I am Navelty, Baron of Foppington, with five thousand pounds a year, and that fellow there, a rascal not worth a groat.

SIR TUNBELLY.
Very well. Now who is this honest gentleman you are so well acquainted with? (*To Young Fashion.*) Come sir, we shall hamper him.

FOPPINGTON.
'Tis Sir John Friendly.

SIR TUNBELLY.
So: he lives within half a mile and came down into the country but last night; this bold-faced fellow thought he had been at London still and so quoted him. Now we shall display him in his colors; I'll send for Sir John immediately. Here, fellow, away presently* and desire my neighbor he'll do me the favor to step over upon an extraordinary occasion—and in the meanwhile you had best secure this sharper in the gate house.

CONSTABLE.
An't* please your worship, he may chance to give us the slip thence. If I were worthy to advise, I think the dog kennel's a surer place.

SIR TUNBELLY.
With all my heart, anywhere.

FOPPINGTON.
Nay, for Heaven's sake, sir, do me the favor to put me in a clean room, that I mayn't daub my clothes.

SIR TUNBELLY.
Oh, when you have married my daughter, her estate will afford you new ones. Away with him.

FOPPINGTON.
A dirty country justice is a barbarous magistrate, stap my vitals!

Exit constable with Lord Foppington.

FASHION. (*Aside.*)
Egad, I must prevent this knight's coming, or the house will grow soon too hot to hold me.—Sir, I fancy 'tis not worth while to trouble Sir John upon this impertinent fellow's desire; I'll send and call the messenger back.

SIR TUNBELLY.
Nay, with all my heart, for to be sure he thought he was far enough off, or the rogue would never have named him.

Enter servant.

SERVANT.
Sir, I met Sir John just lighting at the gate; he's come to wait upon you.

SIR TUNBELLY.
Nay, then it happens as one could wish.

FASHION. (*Aside.*)
The devil it does! [*To Lory, apart.*] Lory, you see how things are: here will be a discovery presently,* and we shall have our brains beat out, for my older brother will be sure to swear he don't know me. Therefore, run into the stable, take the two first horses you can light on; I'll slip out at the back door, and we'll away immediately.

LORY.
What, and leave your lady, sir?

FASHION.
There's no danger in that; as long as I have taken possession, I shall know how to treat with 'em well enough, if once I am out of their reach. Away, I'll steal after thee.

Exit Lory; his master follows him out at one door as Sir John enters at t'other.

Enter Sir John.

SIR TUNBELLY.
Sir John, you are the wecomest man alive; I had just sent a messenger to desire you'd step over upon a very extraordinary occasion. We are all in arms here.

SIR JOHN.
How so?

SIR TUNBELLY.
Why you must know, a finical sort of tawdry fellow here (I don't know who the devil he is, not I), hearing, I suppose, that the match was concluded between my Lord Foppington and my girl Hoyden, comes impudently to the gate with a whole pack of rogues in liveries and would have passed upon me for his lordship. But what does I? I comes up to him boldly at the head of his guards, takes him by the throat, strikes up his heels, binds him hand and foot, dispatches a warrant, and commits him prisoner to the dog kennel.

SIR JOHN.
So, but how do you know but this was my lord? For I was told he set out from London the day before me with a very fine retinue and intended to come directly hither.

SIR TUNBELLY.
Why now, to show you how many lies people raise in that damned town, he came two nights ago post, with only one servant, and is now in the house with me. But you don't know the cream of the jest yet: this same rogue (that lies yonder neck and heels among the hounds), thinking you were out of the country, quotes you for his acquaintance and said, if you were here, you'd justify him to be Lord Foppington and I know not what.

SIR JOHN.
Pray will you let me see him?

SIR TUNBELLY.
Aye, that you shall presently.—Here, fetch the prisoner.

Exit servant.

SIR JOHN.
I wish there ben't some mistake in this business. Where's my lord? I know him very well.

SIR TUNBELLY.
He was here just now.—See for him, doctor, tell him Sir John is here to wait upon him.

Exit Bull.

SIR JOHN.
I hope, Sir Tunbelly, the young lady is not married yet.
SIR TUNBELLY.
No, things won't be ready this week. But why do you say you hope she is not married ?
SIR JOHN.
Some foolish fancies only; perhaps I'm mistaken.
Re-enter Bull.
BULL.
Sir, his lordship is just rid out to take the air.
SIR TUNBELLY.
To take the air! Is that his London breeding to go take the air when gentlemen come to visit him?
SIR JOHN.
'Tis possible he might want it; he might not be well, some sudden qualm perhaps.

Enter Constable, etc., with Lord Foppington.

FOPPINGTON.
Stap my vitals, I'll have satisfaction.
SIR JOHN. (*Running to him.*)
My dear Lord Foppington!
FOPPINGTON.
Dear Friendly, thou art come in the critical minute, strike me dumb.
SIR JOHN.
Why, I little thought I should have found you in fetters.
FOPPINGTON.
Why, truly, the world must do me the justice to confess I do use to appear a little more *dégagé*.[69] But this old gentleman, not liking the freedom of my air, has been pleased to skewer down my arms like a rabbit.
SIR TUNBELLY.
Is it then possible that this should be the true Lord Foppington at last?
FOPPINGTON.
Why, what do you see in his face to make you doubt of it? Sir, without presuming to have any extraordinary opinion of my figure, give me leave to tell you, if you had seen as many lords as I have done, you would not think it impossible a person of a worse *taille*[70] than mine might be a modern man of quality.*
SIR TUNBELLY.
Unbind him, slaves.—My lord, I'm struck dumb; I can only beg pardon by signs, but if a sacrifice will appease you, you shall have it.—Here, pursue this tartar, bring him back. Away, I say!—A dog, oons!* I'll cut off his ears and his tail, I'll draw out all his teeth, pull his skin over his head, and—and what shall I do more?
SIR JOHN.
He does indeed deserve to be made an example of.
FOPPINGTON.
He does deserve to be *chartré*,°[71] stap my vitals.
SIR TUNBELLY.
May I then hope I have your honor's pardon?
FOPPINGTON.
Sir, we courtiers do nothing without a bribe; that fair young lady might do miracles.
SIR TUNBELLY.
Hoyden, come hither, Hoyden.
FOPPINGTON.
Hoyden is her name, sir?
SIR TUNBELLY.
Yes, my lord.
FOPPINGTON.
The prettiest name for a song I ever heard.
SIR TUNBELLY.
My lord, here's my girl, she's yours: she has a wholesome body and a virtuous mind; she's a woman complete both in flesh and in spirit; she has a bag of milled crowns, as scarce as they are, and fifteen hundred a year stitched fast to her tail.[72] So go thy ways, Hoyden.

---

69 *dégagé*] nonchalant, at ease (Fr.)

70 *taille*] figure, bearing (Fr.)

71 *chartré*] jailed, perhaps from *mis en chartre* (Fr.); modern editors who emend to *châtré* (castrated) do so in anticipation of Foppington's later threat to "qualify" Fashion for a "seraglio."

72 milled crowns … tail] Hoyden brings with her into a marriage both ready money—coins which retain their full value because they have not been clipped* or debased—and her father's estate, worth fifteen hundred pounds revenue per year, which etate will pass to her husband upon her father's death: thus it is entailed (with a sexual pun).

FOPPINGTON.

Sir, I do receive her like a gentleman.

SIR TUNBELLY.

Then I'm a happy man, I bless Heaven, and if your lordship will give me leave, I will, like a good Christian at Christmas, be very drunk by way of thanksgiving. Come, my noble peer, I believe dinner's ready; if your honor pleases to follow me, I'll lead you on to the attack of a venison pasty. (*Exit.*)

FOPPINGTON.

Sir, I wait upon you.—Will your ladyship do me the favor of your little finger, madam?

HOYDEN.

My lord, I'll follow you presently; I have a little business with my nurse.

FOPPINGTON.

Your ladyship's most humble servant. Come Sir John, the ladies have *des affaires.*[73]

Exeunt Lord Foppington and Sir John.

HOYDEN.

So, Nurse, we are finely brought to bed. What shall we do now?

NURSE. (*Crying.*)

Ah, dear miss, we are all undone. Mr. Bull, you were used to help a woman to a remedy.

BULL.

Alack-a-day, but it's past my skill now; I can do nothing.

NURSE.

Who would have thought that ever your invention should have been drained so dry?

HOYDEN.

Well, I have often thought old folks fools, and now I am sure they are so. I have found a way myself to secure us all.

NURSE.

Dear lady, what's that?

HOYDEN.

Why, if you two will be sure to hold your tongues and not say a word of what's past, I'll e'en marry this lord too.

NURSE.

What! Two husbands, my dear?

HOYDEN.

Why you have had three, good Nurse; you may hold your tongue.

NURSE.

Aye, but not all together, sweet child.

HOYDEN.

Psha, if you had, you'd ne'er a-thought much on't.

NURSE.

Oh, but 'tis a sin, sweeting.

BULL.

Nay, that's my business to speak to, Nurse. I do confess, to take two husbands for the satisfaction of the flesh is to commit the sin of exorbitancy, but to do it for the peace of the spirit is no more than to be drunk by way of physic; besides, to prevent a parent's wrath is to avoid the sin of disobedience, for when the parent's angry, the child is froward. So that upon the whole matter, I do think, though miss should marry again, she may be saved.

HOYDEN.

I'cod, and I will marry again, then, and so there's an end of the story.

Exeunt.

Act V, scene [i]. London.

Enter Coupler, Young Fashion, and Lory.

COUPLER.

Well, and so Sir John coming in—

FASHION.

And so Sir John coming in, I thought it might be manners in me to go out, which I did, and getting on horseback as fast as I could, rid away as if the Devil had been at the rear of me. What has happened since, Heaven knows.

COUPLER.

Egad, sirrah, I know as well as Heaven.

FASHION.

What do you know?

COUPLER.

That you are a cuckold.

FASHION.

The devil I am! By who?

COUPLER.

By your brother.

73 *des affaires*] their own concerns (Fr.)

FASHION.

My brother! Which way?

COUPLER.

The old way: he has lain with your wife.

FASHION.

Hell and Furies, what dost thou mean?

COUPLER.

I mean plainly; I speak no parable.

FASHION.

Plainly! Thou dost not speak common sense; I cannot understand one word thou say'st.

COUPLER.

You will do soon, youngster. In short, you left your wife a widow, and she married again.

FASHION.

It's a lie.

COUPLER.

I'cod, if I were a young fellow, I'd break your head, sirrah.

FASHION.

Dear dad, don't be angry, for I'm as mad as Tom of Bedlam.[74]

COUPLER.

When I had fitted you with a wife, you should have kept her.

FASHION.

But is it possible the young strumpet could play me such a trick?

COUPLER.

A young strumpet, sir, can play twenty tricks.

FASHION.

But prithee instruct me a little farther: Whence comes thy intelligence?

COUPLER.

From your brother, in this letter. There, you may read it.

FASHION. (*Reads, pulling off his hat.*[75])

"Dear Coupler, I have only time to tell thee in three lines, or thereabouts, that here has been the devil. That rascal Tam, having stole the letter thou hadst formerly writ for me to bring to Sir Tunbelly, formed a damnable design upon my mistress and was in a fair way of success when I arrived. But after having suffered some indignities (in which I have all daubed my embroidered coat), I put him to flight. I sent out a party of horse after him in hopes to have made him my prisoner, which if I had done, I would have qualified him for the seraglio,[76] stap my vitals!

"The danger I have thus narrowly 'scaped has made me fortify myself against further attempts by entering immediately into an association with the young lady by which we engage to stand by one another as long as we both shall live.

"In short, the papers are sealed and the contract is signed, so the business of the lawyers is *achevé*, but I defer the divine part of the thing till I arrive at London, not being willing to consummate in any other bed but my own.

"Postscript. 'Tis passible I may be in tawn as soon as this letter, far I find the lady is so violently in love with me I have determined to make her happy with all the dispatch that is practicable without disardering my coach harses." So here's rare work, i'faith!

LORY.

Egad, Miss Hoyden has laid about her bravely.

COUPLER.

I think my country girl has played her part as well as if she had been born and bred in St. James's parish.

FASHION.

That rogue the chaplain—

LORY.

And then that jade the nurse, sir.

FASHION.

And then that drunken sot Lory, sir, that could not keep himself sober to be a witness to the marriage.

LORY.

Sir, with respect, I know very few drunken sots that do keep themselves sober.

FASHION.

Hold your prating, sirrah, or I'll break your head.—Dear Coupler, what's to be done?

74 Tom of Bedlam] legendary wandering madman pursued by the devil: see Edgar's ruse in Shakespeare's *King Lear*.

75 *pulling off his hat*] in mock deference to Lord Foppington's dignity?

76 qualified … seraglio] Women in seraglios (harems) were guarded by eunuchs.

COUPLER.
Nothing's to be done till the bride and bridegroom come to town.

FASHION.
Bride and bridegroom! Death and Furies! I can't bear that thou shouldst call 'em so.

COUPLER.
Why, what shall I call 'em, dog and cat?

FASHION.
Not for the world, that sounds more like man and wife than t'other.

COUPLER.
Well, if you'll hear of 'em in no language, we'll leave 'em for the nurse and the chaplain.

FASHION.
The devil and the witch.[77]

COUPLER.
When they come to town—

LORY.
We shall have stormy weather.

COUPLER.
Will you hold your tongues, gentlemen, or not?

LORY.
Mum.

COUPLER.
I say, when they come, we must find what stuff they are made of, whether the churchman be chiefly composed of the flesh or the spirit. I presume the former, for as chaplains now go, 'tis probable he eats three pound of beef to the reading of one chapter. This gives him carnal desires: he wants money, preferment, wine, a whore; therefore, we must invite him to supper, give him fat capons, sack* and sugar, a purse of gold, and a plump sister.[78] Let this be done, and I'll warrant thee, my boy, he speaks truth like an oracle.

FASHION.
Thou art a profound statesman, I allow it, but how shall we gain the nurse?

COUPLER.
Oh, never fear the nurse if once you have got the priest, for the devil always rides the hag. Well, there's nothing more to be said of the matter at this time that I know of. So let us go and enquire if there's any news of our people yet; perhaps they may be come. But let me tell you one thing by the way, sirrah, I doubt you have been an idle fellow; if thou hadst behaved thyself as thou shouldst have done, the girl would never have left thee.

Exeunt.

Scene [ii]. Berinthia's apartment.

Enter her maid, passing the stage, followed by Worthy.

WORTHY.
Hem, Mrs. Abigail, is your mistress to be spoken with?

ABIGAIL.
By you, sir, I believe she may.

WORTHY.
Why 'tis by me I would have her spoken with.

ABIGAIL.
I'll acquaint her, sir. (*Exit.*)

WORTHY.
One lift more I must persuade her to give me, and then I'm mounted. Well, a young bawd and a handsome one for my money, 'tis they do the execution; I'll never go to an old one but when I have occasion for a witch. Lewdness looks heavenly to a woman when an angel appears in its cause, but when a hag is advocate, she thinks it comes from the Devil. An old woman has something so terrible in her looks that, whilst she is persuading your mistress to forget she has a soul, she stares hell and damnation full in her face.

Enter Berinthia.

BERINTHIA.
Well, sir, what news bring you?

WORTHY.
No news, madam, there's a woman going to cuckhold her husband.

BERINTHIA.
Amanda?

77 the devil and the witch] proverbially contending lovers; also a metaphor for thunder and lightning (cf. Lory's "stormy weather")

78 sister] member of the congregation, as in "bretheren and sisters."

WORTHY.
I hope so.
BERINTHIA.
Speed her well.
WORTHY.
Aye, but there must more than a Godspeed, or your charity won't be worth a farthing.
BERINTHIA.
Why, han't I done enough already?
WORTHY.
Not quite.
BERINTHIA.
What's the matter?
WORTHY.
The lady has a scruple still, which you must remove.
BERINTHIA.
What's that?
WORTHY.
Her virtue—she says.
BERINTHIA.
And do you believe her?
WORTHY.
No, but I believe it's what she takes for her virtue; it's some relics of lawful love. She is not yet fully satisfied her husband has got another mistress, which unless I can convince her of, I have opened the trenches in vain, for the breach must be wider before I dare storm the town.
BERINTHIA.
And so I'm to be your engineer?*
WORTHY.
I'm sure you know best how to manage the battery.
BERINTHIA.
What do you think of springing a mine? I have a thought just now come into my head, how to blow her up at once.
WORTHY.
That would be a thought, indeed.
BERINTHIA.
Faith, I'll do't, and thus the execution of it shall be: we are invited to my Lord Foppington's tonight to supper; he's come to town with his bride and makes a ball, with an entertainment of music. Now you must know, my undoer here, Loveless, says he must needs meet me about some private business (I don't know what 'tis) before we go to the company. To which end he has told his wife one lie, and I have told her another. But to make her amends, I'll go immediately and tell her a solemn truth.
WORTHY.
What's that?
BERINTHIA.
Why, I'll tell her that to my certain knowldege her husband has a rendezvous with his mistress this afternoon and that, if she'll give me her word she'll be satisfied with the discovery without making any violent inquiry after the woman, I'll direct her to a place where she shall see 'em meet. Now friend, this I fancy may help you to a critical minute. For home she must go again to dress. You (with your good breeding) come to wait upon us to the ball, find her alone, her spirit enflamed against her husband for his treason and her flesh in heat from some contemplations upon the treachery, her blood on fire, her conscience in ice; a lover to draw, and the devil to drive—ah, poor Amanda.
WORTHY. (*Kneeling.*)
Thou angel of light, let me fall down and adore thee.
BERINTHIA.
Thou minister of darkness, get up again, for I hate to see the Devil at his devotions.
WORTHY.
Well, my incomparable Berinthia, how I shall requite you—
BERINTHIA.
Oh, ne'er trouble yourself about that: virtue is its own reward. There's a pleasure in doing good which sufficiently pays itself. Adieu.
WORTHY.
Farewell, thou best of women.

Exeunt several ways. Enter Amanda, meeting Berinthia [on her way out].

AMANDA.
Who was that went from you?
BERINTHIA.
A friend of yours.
AMANDA.
What does he want?

BERINTHIA.

Something you might spare him and be ne'er the poorer.

AMANDA.

I can spare him nothing but my friendship; my love already's all disposed of. Though, I confess, to one ungrateful to my bounty.

BERINTHIA.

Why, there's the mystery: you have been so bountiful you have cloyed him. Fond wives do by their husbands as barren wives do by their lapdogs, cram 'em with sweatmeats till they spoil their stomachs.

AMANDA.

Alas! Had you but seen how passionately fond he has been since our last reconciliation, you would have thought it were impossible he ever should have breathed an hour without me.

BERINTHIA.

Aye, but there you thought wrong again, Amanda: you should consider that in matters of love men's eyes are always bigger than their bellies. They have violent appetites, 'tis true, but they have soon dined.

AMANDA.

Well, there's nothing upon earth astonishes me more than men's inconstancy.

BERENTHIA.

Now, there's nothing upon earth astonishes me less, when I consider what they and we are composed of. For Nature has made them children and us babies.* Now Amanda, how we used our babies you may remember. We were mad to have 'em as soon as we saw 'em, kissed 'em to pieces as soon as we got 'em, then pulled off their clothes, saw 'em naked, and so threw 'em away.

AMANDA.

But do you think all men are of this temper?

BERINTHIA.

All but one.

AMANDA.

Who is that?

BERINTHIA.

Worthy.

AMANDA.

Why, he's weary of his wife, too, you see.

BERINTHIA.

Aye, that's no proof.

AMANDA.

What can be a greater?

BERINTHIA.

Being weary of his mistress.

AMANDA.

Don't you think 'twere possible he might give you that, too?

BERINTHIA.

Perhaps he might if he were my gallant, not if he were yours.

AMANDA.

Why do you think he should be more constant to me than he would to you? I'm sure I'm not so handsome.

BERINTHIA.

Kissing goes by favor;[79] he likes you best.

AMANDA.

Suppose he does? That's no demonstration he would be constant to me.

BERINTHIA.

No, that I'll grant you. But there are other reasons to expect it. For you must know after all, Amanda, the inconstancy we commonly see in men of brains does not so much proceed from the uncertainty of their temper as from the misfortunes of their love. A man sees perhaps a hundred women he likes well enough for an intrigue, and away, but possibly, through the whole course of his life, does not find above one who is exactly what he could wish her; now her, 'tis a thousand to one, he never gets. Either she is not to be had at all (though that seldom happens, you'll say) or he wants* those opportunities that are necessary to gain her. Either she likes somebody else much better than him, or uses him like a dog because he likes nobody so well as her. Still* something or other fate claps in the way between them and the woman they are capable of being fond of, and this makes them wander about from mistress to mistress, like a pilgrim from town to town, who every night must have a fresh lodging and's in haste to be gone in the morning.

---

[79] Kissing goes by favor] We love as we are individually inclined.

AMANDA.
'Tis possible there may be something in what you say. But what do you infer from it as to the man we were talking of?

BERINTHIA.
Why, I infer that, you being the woman in the world the most to his humor, 'tis not likely he would quit you for one that is less.

AMANDA.
That is not to be depended upon, for you see Mr. Loveless does so.

BERINTHIA.
What does Mr. Loveless do?

AMANDA.
Why, he runs after something for variety I'm sure he does not like so well as he does me.

BERINTHIA.
That's more than you know, madam.

AMANDA.
No, I'm sure on't. I am not very vain, Berinthia, and yet I'd lay my life, if I could look into his heart, he thinks I deserve to be preferred to a thousand of her.

BERINTHIA.
Don't be too positive in that neither; a million to one but she has the same opinion of you. What would you give to see her?

AMANDA.
Hang her, dirty trull! though I really believe she's so ugly she'd cure me of my jealousy.

BERINTHIA.
All the men of sense about town say she's handsome.

AMANDA.
They are as often out in those things as any people.

BERINTHIA.
Then I'll give you farther proof: all the women about town say she's a fool. Now I hope you are convinced?

AMANDA.
Whate'er she be, I'm satisfied he does not like her well enough to bestow anything more than a little outward gallantry upon her.

BERINTHIA.
Outward gallantry? (*Aside.*) I can't bear this.—Don't you think she's a woman to be fobbed off so. Come, I'm too much your friend to suffer you should be thus grossly imposed upon by a man who does not deserve the least part about you unless he knew how to set a greater value upon it. Therefore in one word, to my certain knowledge he is to meet her now, within a quarter of an hour, somewhere about that Babylon of wickedness, Whitehall.* And if you'll give me your word that you'll be content with seeing her masked in his hand without pulling her head-clothes off, I'll step immediately to the person from whom I have my intelligence and send you word whereabouts you may stand to see 'em meet. My friend and I'll watch 'em from another place and dodge[80] 'em to their private lodging. But don't you offer to follow 'em, lest you do it awkwardly and spoil all. I'll come home to you again as soon as I have earthed 'em and give you an account in what corner of the house the scene of their lewdness lies.

AMANDA.
If you can do this, Berinthia, he's a villain.

BERINTHIA.
I can't help that; men will be so.

AMANDA.
Well! I'll follow your directions, for I shall never rest till I know the worst of this matter.

BERINTHIA.
Pray, go immediately and get yourself ready then. Put on some of your woman's clothes, a great scarf and a mask, and you shall presently receive orders. (*Calls within.*) Here, who's there? Get me a chair* quickly.

SERVANT [*Without.*]
There are chairs at the door, madam.

BERINTHIA.
'Tis well, I'm coming.

AMANDA.
But pray, Berinthia, before you go, tell me how I may know this filthy thing if she should be so forward (as I suppose she will) to come to the rendezvous first, for methinks I would fain view her a little.

BERINTHIA.
Why, she's about my height and very well shaped.

---

80 dodge] surreptitiously follow

AMANDA.
I thought she had been a little crooked.

BERINTHIA.
Oh no, she's as straight as I am. But we lose time; come away.

Exeunt.

[Act V, scene iii. Young Fashion's lodgings.]

Enter Young Fashion, meeting Lory.

FASHION.
Well, will the doctor come?

LORY.
Sir, I sent a porter to him as you ordered me. He found him with a pipe of tobacco and a great tankard of ale, which he said he would dispatch while I could tell three, and be here.

FASHION.
He does not suspect 'twas I that sent for him?

LORY.
Not a jot, sir; he divines as little for himself as for other folks.

FASHION.
Will he bring Nurse with him?

LORY.
Yes.

FASHION.
That's well. Where's Coupler?

LORY.
He's half way up the stairs taking breath; he must play his bellows a little before he can get to the top.

Enter Coupler.

FASHION.
Oh, here he is.—Well, old phthisic,[81] the doctor's coming.

COUPLER.
Would the pox had the doctor—I'm quite out of wind. (*To Lory.*) Set me a chair, sirrah. Ah— (*Sits down. To Young Fashion.*) Why the plague canst not thou lodge upon the ground floor?

FASHION.
Because I love to lie as near heaven as I can.

[81] phthisic] asthmatic or consumptive

COUPLER.
Prithee let heaven alone. Ne'er affect tending that way; thy center's downward.

FASHION.
That's impossible. I have too much ill luck in this world to be damned in the next.

COUPLER.
Thou art out in thy logic. Thy major is true but thy minor[82] is false, for thou art the luckiest fellow in the universe.

FASHION.
Make that out.

COUPLER.
I'll do it. Last night the Devil ran away with the parson of Fatgoose living.

FASHION.
If he had run away with the parish too, what's that to me?

COUPLER.
I'll tell thee what it's to thee. This living is worth five hundred pound a year,[83] and the presentation of it is thine if thou canst prove thyself a lawful husband to Miss Hoyden.

FASHION.
Say'st thou so, my protector? Then i'cad, I shall have a brace of evidences* here presently.*

COUPLER.
The nurse and the doctor?

FASHION.
The same; the Devil himself won't have interest enough to make 'em withstand it.

COUPLER.
That we shall see presently; here they come.

Enter Nurse and Bull; they start back, seeing Young Fashion.

NURSE.
Ah goodness, Roger, we are betrayed.

[82] major ... minor] premises, terms in logic; the argument goes: All those with bad luck here go to heaven. I have bad luck here. Ergo: I'll go to heaven.

[83] five hundred pound a year] a very good living indeed since an annual income of as little as one hundred pounds might elevate one into the ranks of the lesser gentry

FASHION. (*Laying hold on 'em.*)

Nay, nay, ne'er flinch for the matter, for I have you safe. Come, to your trials immediately; I have no time to give you copies of your indictment. There sits your judge—

NURSE, BULL. (*Kneeling.*)

Pray sir, have compassion on us.

NURSE.

I hope, sir, my years will move your pity; I am an aged woman.

COUPLER.

That is a moving argument indeed.

BULL.

I hope, sir, my character will be considered; I am Heaven's ambassador.

COUPLER. (*To Bull.*)

Are not you a rogue of sanctity?

BULL.

Sir (with respect to my function) I do wear a gown.

COUPLER.

Did not you marry this vigorous young fellow to a plump, young, buxom wench?

NURSE. (*To Bull.*)

Don't confess, Roger, unless you are hard put to it, indeed.

COUPLER.

Come, out with't.—Now is he chewing the cud of his roguery and grinding a lie between his teeth.

BULL.

Sir—I cannot positively say—I say, sir—positively I cannot say—

COUPLER.

Come, no equivocations, no Roman turns[84] upon us. Consider thou standest upon Protestant ground, which will slip from under thee like a Tyburn* cart, for in this country we have always ten hangmen for one Jesuit.

BULL. (*To Young Fashion.*)

Pray sir, then will you but permit me to speak one word in private with Nurse?

FASHION.

Thou art always for doing something in private with Nurse.

84 Roman turns] Equivocation was associated with Roman Catholics, especially Jesuits, since Elizabethan times.

COUPLER.

But pray, let his betters be served before him for once. I would do something in private with her myself.—Lory, take care of this reverend gownman in the next room a little. Retire, priest.

Exit Lory with Bull.

Now, virgin, I must put the matter home to you a little: Do you think it might not be possible to make you speak truth?

NURSE.

Alas! Sir, I don't know what you mean by truth.

COOUPLER.

Nay, 'tis possible thou mayst be a stranger to it.

FASHION.

Come Nurse, you and I were better friends when we saw one another last, and I still believe you are a very good woman in the bottom. I did deceive you and your young lady, 'tis true, but I always designed to make a very good husband to her and to be a very good friend to you. And 'tis possible in the end, she might have found herself happier and you richer than ever my brother will make you.

NURSE.

Brother! Why, is your worship then his lordship's brother?

FASHION.

I am, which you should have known if I durst have stayed to have told you, but I was forced to take horse a little in haste, you know.

NURSE.

You were indeed, sir; poor young man, how he was bound to scour for't. Now won't your worship be angry if I confess the truth to you; when I found you were a cheat (with respect be it spoken), I verily believed Miss had got some pitiful skip-jack[85] varlet or other for her husband, or I had ne'er let her think of marrying again.

COUPLER.

But where was your conscience all this while, woman? Did not that stare in your face with huge saucer eyes and a great horn upon the forehead? Did not you think you should be damned for such a sin? Hah?

85 skip-jack] foolish, pert

FASHION.

Well said, divinity, press[p] that home upon her.

NURSE.

Why, in good truly, sir, I had some fearful thoughts on't and could never be brought to consent till Mr. Bull said it was a peccadillo and he'd secure my soul for a tithe pig.

FASHION.

There was a rogue for you.

COUPLER.

And he shall thrive accordingly; he shall have a good living. Come, honest Nurse, I see you have butter in your compound: you can melt. Some compassion you can have of this handsome young fellow.

NURSE.

I have indeed, sir.

FASHION.

Why then, I'll tell you what you shall do for me. You know what a warm living here is fallen and that it must be in the disposal of him who has the disposal of Miss. Now if you and the doctor will agree to prove my marriage, I'll present him to it upon condition he makes you his bride.

NURSE.

Naw the blessing of the Lord follow your good worship both by night and by day. Let him be fetched in by the ears; I'll soon bring his nose to the grindstone.

COUPLER. (*Aside.*)

Well said, old white-leather.[86]—Hey, bring in the prisoner there.

Enter Lory with Bull.

COUPLER.

Come, advance, holy man. Here's your duck does not think fit to retire with you into the chancel at this time but has a proposal to make to you in the face of the congregation. Come Nurse, speak for yourself; you are of age.

NURSE.

Roger, are not you a wicked man, Roger, to set your strength against a weak woman and persuade her it was no sin to conceal Miss's nuptials? My conscience flies in my face for it, thou priest of Baal, and I find by woeful experience thy absolution is not worth an old cassock. Therefore, I am resolved to confess the truth to the whole world, though I die a beggar for it. But his worship overflows with his mercy and his bounty; he is not only pleased to forgive us our sins but designs thou sha't squat thee down in Fatgoose living and, which is more than all, has prevailed with me to become the wife of thy bosom.

FASHION.

All this I intend for you, doctor. What you are to do for me, I need not tell you.

BULL.

Your worship's goodness is unspeakable. Yet there is one thing seems a point of conscience, and conscience is a tender babe. If I should bind myself, for the sake of this living, to marry Nurse and maintain her afterwards, I doubt it might be looked on as a kind of simony.

COUPLER. (*Rising up.*)

If it were sacrilege, the living's worth it. Therefore, no more words, good doctor. But with the parish (*Giving Nurse to him.*)—here—take the parsonage house. 'Tis true, 'tis a little out of repair; some dilapidations there are to be made good. The windows are broke, the wainscot warped, the ceilings are peeled, and the walls are cracked, but a little glazing, painting, whitewash, and plaster will make it last thy time.

BULL.

Well sir, if it must be so, I shan't contend; what Providence orders, I submit to.

NURSE.

And so do I, with all humility.

COUPLER.

Why, that now was spoke like good people. Come my turtle doves, let us go help this poor pigeon to his wandering mate again, and after institution and induction[87] you shall all go a-cooing together.

Exeunt.

86 white-leather] a bleached leather, indicating Nurse's complexion

87 institution and induction] The installation of a clergyman in a parish is parallelled to marriage and consummation.

[Act V, scene iv. Loveless's lodgings.]

Enter Amanda in a scarf, etc., as just returned, her woman following her.

AMANDA.
Prithee, what care I who has been here?

WOMAN.
Madam, 'twas my Lady Bridle and my Lady Tiptoe.

AMANDA.
My Lady Fiddle and my Lady Faddle. What dost stand troubling me with the visits of a parcel of impertinent women? When they are well seamed with the smallpox they won't be so fond of showing their faces. There are more coquettes about this Town—

WOMAN.
Madam, I suppose they only came to return your ladyship's visit, according to the custom of the world.

AMANDA.
Would the world were on fire and you in the middle on't.
Be gone; leave me.

Exit Woman.

—At last I am convinced.
My eyes are testimonies of his falsehood.
The base, ungrateful, perjured villain—
Good gods—what slippery stuff are men composed of?
Sure the account of their creation's false
And 'twas the woman's rib that they were formed of.
But why am I thus angry?
This poor relapse should only move my scorn.
'Tis true, the roving flights of his unfinished youth
Had strong excuses¶ from the plea of nature;
Reason had thrown the reins loose on his neck
And slipped him to unlimited desire.
If therefore he went wrong, he had a claim
To my forgiveness, and I did him right.
But since the years of manhood rein him in,
And reason well digested into thought
Has pointed out the course he ought to run,
If now he strays,
'Twould be as weak and mean in me to pardon
As it has been in him t'offend. But hold:
'Tis an ill cause indeed, where nothing's to be said for't.
My beauty possibly is in the wane;
Perhaps sixteen has greater charms for him.
Yes, there's the secret. But let him know,
My quiver's not entirely emptied yet:
I still have darts, and I can shoot 'em too;
They're not so blunt but they can enter still—
The want's* not in my power but in my will.
Virtue's his friend, or through another's heart
I yet could find the way to make his smart.

Going off, she meets Worthy.

Hah! He here?
Protect me, Heaven, for this looks ominous.

WORTHY.
You seem disordered, madam. I hope there's no misfortune happened to you?

AMANDA.
None that will long disorder me, I hope.

WORTHY.
What e'er it be disturbs you, I would to Heaven 'twere in my power to bear the pain till I were able to remove the cause.

AMANDA.
I hope e'ere long it will remove itself.
At least, I have given it warning to be gone.

WORTHY.
Would I durst ask where 'tis the thorn torments you?
Forgive me if I grow inquisitive.
'Tis only with desire to give you ease.

AMANDA.
Alas! 'Tis in a tender part.
It can't be drawn without a world of pain.
Yet out it must,
For it begins to fester in my heart.

WORTHY.
If 'tis the sting of unrequited love,
Remove it instantly.
I have a balm will quickly heal the wound.

AMANDA.
You'll find the undertaking difficult.
The surgeon who already has attempted it
Has much tormented me.

WORTHY.
I'll aid him with a gentler hand,
If you will give me leave.
AMANDA.
How soft soe'er the hand may be,
There still is terror in the operation.
WORTHY.
Some few preparatives would make it easy,
Could I persuade you to apply 'em.
Make home reflections, madam, on your slighted love,
Weigh well the strength and beauty of your charms,
Rouse up that spirit women ought to bear,
And slight your god if he neglects his angel.
With arms of ice receive his cold embraces,
And keep your fire for those who come in flames.
Behold a burning lover at your feet,
His fever raging in his veins.
See how he trembles, how he pants;
See how he glows, how he consumes.
Extend the arms of mercy to his aid.
His zeal may give him title to your pity,
Although his merit cannot claim your love.
AMANDA.
Of all my feeble sex, sure I must be the weakest,
Should I again presume to think on love.
(*Sighing.*) Alas! my heart has been too roughly treated.
WORTHY.
'Twill find the greater bliss in softer usage.
AMANDA.
But where's that usage to be found?
WORTHY.
'Tis here,
Within this faithful breast; which, if you doubt,
I'll rip it up before your eyes,
Lay all its secrets open to your view,
And then you'll see 'twas sound.
AMANDA.
With just such honest words as these
The worst of men deceived me.
WORTHY.
He therefore merits
All revenge can do; his fault is such,
The extent and stretch of vengeance cannot reach it.
Oh, make me but your instrument of justice;
You'll find me execute it with such zeal
As shall convince you I abhor the crime.
AMANDA.
The rigor of an executioner
Has more the face of cruelty than justice,
And he who puts the cord about the wretch's neck
Is seldom known to exceed him in his morals.
WORTHY.
What proof then can I give you of my truth?
AMANDA.
There is on earth but one.
WORTHY.
And is that in my power?
AMANDA.
It is.
And one that would so thoroughly convince me,
I should be apt to rate your heart so high
I possibly might purchase't with a part of mine.
WORTHY.
Then, Heav'n, thou art my friend, and I am blest,
For if 'tis in my power, my will, I'm sure
Will reach it—no matter what the terms may be—
When such a recompense is offererd.
Oh, tell me quickly what this proof must be.
What is it will convince you of my love?
AMANDA.
I shall believe you love me as you ought
If from this moment you forbear to ask
Whatever is unfit for me to grant.
—You pause upon it, sir.—I doubt on such hard terms
A woman's heart is scarcely worth the having.
WORTHY.
A heart like yours on any terms is worth it.
'Twas not on that I paused. But I was thinking (*Drawing nearer to her.*)
Whether some things there may not be
Which women cannot grant without a blush
And yet which men may take without offense.
(*Taking her hand.*) Your hand, I fancy, may be of the number:
Oh, pardon me if I commit a rape
Upon it (*Kissing it eagerly.*) and thus devour it with my kisses.
AMANDA.
Oh heavens! Let me go.

WORTHY.
Never, whilst I have strength to hold you here.
(*Forcing her to sit down on a couch.*)
My life, my soul, my goddess, oh, forgive me!
AMANDA.
Oh, whither am I going? Help, Heaven, or I am lost.
WORTHY.
Stand neuter, gods, this once I do invoke you.
AMANDA.
Then save me, virtue, and the glory's thine.
WORTHY.
Nay, never strive.
AMANDA.
I will, and conquer too.
My forces rally bravely to my aid, (*Breaking from him.*)
And thus I gain the day.
WORTHY.
Then mine as bravely double their attack,
(*Seizing her again.*) And thus I wrest it from you.
Nay, struggle not,
For all's in vain: or death or victory,
I am determined.
AMANDA.
And so am I. (*Rushing from him.*)
Now keep your distance, or we part forever.
WORTHY. (*Offering again.*)
For Heaven's sake—
AMANDA. (*Going.*)
Nay then, farewell.
WORTHY. (*Kneeling and holding her by her clothes.*)
Oh stay, and see the magic force of love:
Behold this raging lion at your feet,
Struck dead with fear, and tame as charms can make him.
What must I do to be forgiven by you?
AMANDA.
Repent, and never more offend.
WORTHY.
Repentence for past crimes is just and easy,
But sin no more's a task too hard for mortals.
AMANDA.
Yet those who hope for heaven
Must use their best endeavors to perform it.
WORTHY.
Endeavors we may use, but flesh and blood
Are got in t'other scale,
And they are ponderous things.
AMANDA.
Whate'er they are,
There is a weight in resolution
Sufficient for their balance. The soul, I do confess,
Is usually so careless of its charge,
So soft, and so indulgent to desire
It leaves the reins in the wild hand of nature,
Who, like a Phaeton,[88] drives the fiery chariot
And sets the world on flame.
Yet still* the sovereignty is in the mind
Whene'er it pleases to exert its force.
Perhaps you may not think it worth your while
To take such mighty pains for my esteem,
But that I leave to you.
You see the price I set upon my heart;
Perhaps 'tis dear,* but spite of all your art,
You'll find on cheaper terms we ne'er shall part.
(*Exit.*)
WORTHY.
Sure there's divinity about her,
And sh'as dispensed some portion on't to me.
For what but now was the wild flame of love,
Or (to dissect that specious term)
The vile, the gross desires of flesh and blood,
Is in a moment turned to adoration.
The coarser appetite of nature's gone,
And 'tis, methinks, the food of angels I require.
How long this influence may last, Heaven knows,
But in this moment of my purity
I could on her own terms accept her heart.
Yes, lovely woman, I can accept it,
For now 'tis doubly worth my care.
Your charms are much increased since thus adorned.
When truth's extorted from us, then we own
The robe of virtue is a graceful habit.
Could women but our secret counsels scan,
Could they but reach the deep reserves of man,
They'd wear it on, that that of love might last,
For when they throw off one, we soon the other cast.

---

88 Phaeton] son of Helios, the sun god, who won his father's permission to drive the chariot of the sun and lost control

Their sympathy is such—
The fate of one, the other scarce can fly;
They live together and together die.

Exit.

[Scene v. Lord Foppington's Town house.]

Enter Hoyden and Nurse.

HOYDEN.
But is it sure and certain, say you, he's my lord's own brother?

NURSE.
As sure as he's your lawful husband.

HOYDEN.
I'cod, if I had known that in time, I don't know but I might have kept him. For between you and I, Nurse, he'd have made a husband worth two of this I have. But which do you think you should fancy most, Nurse?

NURSE.
Why truly, in my poor fancy, madam, your first husband is the prettier gentleman.

HOYDEN.
I don't like my lord's shapes, Nurse.

NURSE.
Why, in good truly, as a body may say, he is but a slam.[89]

HOYDEN.
What do you think now he puts me in mind of? Don't you remember a long, loose, shambling sort of a horse my father called Washy?

NURSE.
As like as two twin brothers.

HOYDEN.
I'cod, I have thought so a hundred times; faith, I'm tired of him.

NURSE.
Indeed, madam, I think you had e'en as good stand to your first bargain.

HOYDEN.
Oh but Nurse, we han't considered the main thing yet. If I leave my lord, I must leave my lady too, and when I rattle about the streets in my coach, they'll only say, there goes Mistress—Mistress—Mistress what? What's this man's name I have married, Nurse?

NURSE.
Squire Fashion.

HOYDEN.
Squire Fashion is it? Well squire, that's better than nothing. Do you think one could not get him made a knight, Nurse?

NURSE.
I don't know but one might, madam, when the King's in a good humor.

HOYDEN.
I'cod, that would do rarely. For then he'd be as good a man as my father, you know.

NURSE.
By'r Lady, and that's as good as the best of 'em.

HOYDEN.
So 'tis, faith, for then I shall be my lady and your ladyship at every word, and that's all I have to care for. Hah, Nurse, but hark you me; one thing more, and then I have done. I'm afraid, if I change my husband again, I shan't have so much money to throw about, Nurse.

NURSE.
Oh, enough's as good as a feast. Besides, madam, one don't know but as much may fall to your share with the younger brother as with the elder. For though these lords have a power of wealth indeed, yet as I have heard say, they give it all to their sluts and their trulls, who joggle it about in their coaches, with a murrain to 'em, whilst poor madam sits sighing and wishing and knotting and crying and has not a spare half-crown to buy her a *Practice of Piety*.[90]

HOYDEN.
Oh but for that, don't deceive yourself, Nurse. For this I must say for my lord, and a—(*Snapping her fingers.*) for him. He's as free as an open house at Christmas. For this very morning he told me I should have two hundred a year to buy pins. Now Nurse, if he gives me two hundred a year to buy pins, what do you think he'll give me to buy fine petticoats?

---

89 a slam] an ill-shaped person (*OED* gives this as the only instance of the word.)

90 *Practice of Piety*] an extremely popular devotional manual by Lewis Bayley, appearing in over 100 editions

NURSE.
Ah my dearest, he deceives thee foully, and he's no better than a rogue for his pains. These Londoners have got a gibberish with 'em would confound a Gypsy. That which they call pin money is to buy their wives everything in the varsal[91] world, down to their very shoe ties; nay, I have heard folks say that some ladies, if they will have gallants, as they call 'um, are forced to find them out of their pin money too.

HOYDEN.
Has he served me so, say ye? Then I'll be his wife no longer, so that's fixed. Look, here he comes, with all the fine folk at's heels. I'cod, Nurse, these London ladies will laugh till they crack again to see me slip my collar and run away from my husband. But d'ye hear? Pray take care of one thing: when the busniess comes to break out, be sure you get between me and my father, for you know his tricks; he'll knock me down.

NURSE.
I'll mind him, never fear, madam.

Enter Lord Foppington, Loveless, Worthy, Amanda, and Berinthia.

FOPPINGTON.
Ladies and gentlemen, you are all welcome.—Loveless, that's my wife: prithee do me the favor to salute* her, and dost hear—(*Aside to him.*) if thau hast a mind to try thy fartune to be revenged of me, I won't take it ill, stap my vitals.

LOVELESS.
You need not fear, sir; I'm too fond of my own wife to have the least inclination to yours.

All salute Hoyden.

FOPPINGTON. (*Aside.*)
I'd give you a thausand paund he would make love to her, that he may see she has sense enough to prefer me to him, though his own wife has not. (*Viewing him.*) He's a very beastly fellow, in my opinion.

HOYDEN. (*Aside.*)
What a power of fine men there are in this London! He that kissed me first is a goodly gentleman, I promise you. Sure those wives have a rare time on't that live here always!

Enter Sir Tunbelly, with musicians, dancers, etc.

SIR TUNBELLY.
Come, come in, good people, come in; come, tune your fiddles, tune your fiddles.—(*To the hautboys.*) Bagpipes, make ready there. Come, strike up. (*Sings.*)

For this is Hoyden's wedding day,
And therefore we keep holiday,
    And come to be merry.

Hah, there's my wench, i'faith! Touch and take, I'll warrant her; she'll breed like a tame rabbit.

HOYDEN. (*Aside.*)
I'cod, I think my father's gotten drunk before supper.

SIR TUNBELLY. (*To Loveless and Worthy.*)
Gentlemen, you are welcome. (*Saluting Amanda and Berinthia.*) Ladies, by your leave.—Hah, they bill like turtles.* Udsookers,* they set my old blood afire; I shall cuckold somebody before morning.

FOPPINGTON. (*To Sir Tunbelly.*)
Sir, you being master of the entertainment, will you desire the company to sit?

SIR TUNBELLY.
Oons,* sir, I'm the happiest man on this side the Ganges.

FOPPINGTON. (*Aside.*)
This is a mighty unaccountable old fellow.—I said, sir, it would be convenient to ask the company to sit.

SIR TUNBELLY.
Sit? With all my heart! Come, take your places, ladies, take your places, gentlemen. Come, sit down, sit down; a pox of ceremony, take your places.

They sit, and the masque begins.

Dialogue between Cupid and Hymen.

1

CUPID.
Thou bane to my empire, thou spring of contest,
Thou source of all discord, thou period to rest,
Instruct me, what wenches in bondage can see
That the aim of their life is still pointed to thee.

[91] varsal] universal

2

HYMEN.

Instruct me, thou little impertinent god,
From whence all thy subjects have taken the mode
To grow fond of a change, to whatever it be,
And I'll tell thee why those would be bound who are free.

CHORUS.

For change, we're for change, to whatever it be,
We are neither contented with freedom nor thee.
Constancy's an empty sound.
Heaven and earth and all go round,
All the works of nature move,
And the joys of life and love
Are in variety.

3

CUPID.

Were love the reward of a painstaking life,
Had a husband the art to be fond of his wife,
Were virtue so plenty, a wife could afford
These very hard times to be true to her lord,
Some specious account might be given of those
Who are tied by the tail to be led by the nose.

4

But since 'tis the fate of a man and his wife
To consume all their days in contention and strife;
Since whatever the bounty of Heaven may create her,
He's morally sure he shall heartily hate her;
I think 'twere much wiser to ramble at large,
And the volleys of love on the herd to discharge.

5

HYMEN.

Some color of reason thy counsel might bear,
Could a man have no more than his wife to his share,
Or were I a monarch, so cruelly just,
To oblige a poor wife to be true to her trust,
But I have not pretended, for many years past,
By marrying of people, to make 'em grow chaste.

6

I therefore advise thee to let me go on,
Thou'lt find I'm the strength and support of thy throne,
For hadst thou but eyes thou wouldst quickly perceive it,
How smoothly thy dart
Slips into the heart
Of a woman that's wed,
Whilst the shivering maid
Stands trembling and wishing, but dare not receive it.

CHORUS.

For change, *etc.*

The masque ended, enter Young Fashion, Coupler, and Bull.

SIR TUNBELLY.

So, very fine, very fine, i'faith, this is something like a wedding; now if supper were but ready, I'd say a short grace, and if I had such a bedfellow as Hoyden tonight—I'd say as short prayers. (*Seeing Young Fashion.*) How now, what have we got here? A ghost? Nay, it must be so, for his flesh and blood could never have dared to appear before me. (*To him.*) Ah, rogue—

FOPPINGTON.

Stap my vitals, Tam again.

SIR TUNBELLY.

My lord, will you cut his throat? Or shall I?

FOPPINGTON.

Leave him to me, sir, if you please.—Prithee, Tam, be so ingenuous now as to tell me what thy business is here?

FASHION.

'Tis with your bride.

FOPPINGTON.

Thau art the impudent'st fellow that Nature has yet spawned into the warld, strike me speechless.

FASHION.

Why, you know my modesty would have starved me; I sent it a-begging to you, and you would not give a groat.

FOPPINGTON.

And dost thau expect by an excess of assurance to extart a maintenance from me?

FASHION. (*Taking Hoyden by the hand.*)

I do intend to extort your mistress from you, and that I hope will prove one.

FOPPINGTON.

I ever thaught Newgate or Bedlam would be his fartune, and naw his fate's decided. Prithee, Loveless, dost know of a mad-doctor hard by?

FASHION.
There's one at your elbow will cure you presently.*—Prithee doctor, take him in hand quickly.
FOPPINGTON.
Shall I beg the favor of you, sir, to pull your fingers out of my wife's hand.
FASHION.
His wife! Look you there, now I hope you are all satisfied he's mad.
FOPPINGTON.
Naw it is nat passible far me to penetrate what species of fally it is thau art driving at.
SIR TUNBELLY.
Here, here, here! Let me beat out his brains, and that will decide all.
FOPPINGTON.
No, pray sir hold, we'll destray him presently accarding to law.
FASHION. (*To Bull.*)
Nay then, advance, doctor. Come, you are a man of conscience; answer boldly to the questions I shall ask: Did not you marry me to this young lady, before ever that gentleman there saw her face?
BULL.
Since the truth must out, I did.
FASHION.
Nurse, sweet Nurse, were not you a witness to it?
NURSE.
Since my conscience bids me speak—I was.
FASHION. (*To Hoyden.*)
Madam, am not I your lawful husband?
HOYDEN.
Truly I can't tell, but you married me first.
FASHION.
Now I hope you are all satisfied?
SIR TUNBELLY. (*Offering to strike him, is held by Loveless and Worthy.*)
Oons* and thunder, you lie.
FOPPINGTON.
Pray sir, be calm, the battle is in disarder but requires more canduct than courage to rally our forces. Pray dactar, one word with you. (*To Bull, aside.*) Look you, sir, though I will not presume to calculate your notions of damnation fram the description you give us of hell, yet since there is at least a passibility you may have a pitchfark thrust in your backside, methinks it should not be worth your while to risk your soul in the next world for the sake of a beggarly yaunger brather who is not able to make your bady happy in this.
BULL.
Alas, my lord, I have no worldly ends; I speak the truth, Heaven knows.
FOPPINGTON.
Nay, prithee never engage Heaven in the matter, far, by all I can see, 'tis like to prove a business for the Devil.
FASHION.
Come, pray sir, all above-board, no corrupting of evidences,* if you please. This young lady is my lawful wife, and I'll justify it in all the courts of England; so your lordship (who always had a passion for variety) may go seek a new mistress if you think fit.
FOPPINGTON.
I am struck dumb with his impudence and cannot passitively tell whether ever I shall speak again or nat.
SIR TUNBELLY.
Then let me come and examine the business a little; I'll jerk the truth out of 'em presently.* Here, give me my dog-whip.
FASHION.
Look you, old gentleman, 'tis in vain to make a noise; if you grow mutinous, I have some friends within call have swords by their sides above four foot long. Therefore, be calm, hear the evidence patiently, and when the jury have given their verdict, pass sentence according to law: here's honest Coupler shall be foreman and ask as many questions as he pleases.
COUPLER.
All I have to ask is whether Nurse persists in her evidence? The parson, I dare swear, will never flinch from his.
NURSE. (*To Sir Tunbelly, kneeling.*)
I hope in heaven your worship will pardon me; I have served you long and faithfully, but in this thing I was overreached; your worship, however, was deceived as well as I, and if the wedding dinner had been ready, you had put madam to bed to him with your own hands.

SIR TUNBELLY.
But how durst you do this without acquainting of me?
NURSE.
Alas! If your worship had seen how the poor thing begged and prayed and clung and twined about me like ivy to an old wall, you would say I, who had suckled it and swaddled it and nursed it both wet and dry, must have had a heart of adamant to refuse it.
SIR TUNBELLY.
Very well.
FASHION.
Foreman, I expect your verdict.
COUPLER.
Ladies and gentlemen, what's your opinions?
ALL.
A clear case, a clear case.
COUPLER.
Then, my young folks, I wish you joy.
SIR TUNBELLY. (*To Young Fashion.*)
Come hither, stripling. If it be true, then, that thou hast married my daughter, prithee tell me who thou art.
FASHION.
Sir, the best of my condition is, I am your son-in-law, and the worst of it is, I am brother to that noble peer there.
SIR TUNBELLY.
Art thou brother to that noble peer? Why then that noble peer and thee and thy wife and the nurse and the priest—may all go and be damned together. (*Exit.*)
FOPPINGTON. (*Aside.*)
Now for my part, I think the wisest thing a man can do with an aching heart is to put on a serene countenance, for a philosophical air is the most becoming thing in the world to the face of a person of quality;* I will therefore bear my disgrace like a great man and let the people see I am above an affront.—Dear Tam, since things are thus fallen aut, prithee give me leave to wish thee jay. I do it *de bon coeur*,[92] strike me dumb; you have married a woman beautiful in her person, charming in her airs, prudent in her canduct, canstant in her inclinations, and of a nice* marality, split my windpipe.
FASHION.
Your lordship may keep up your spirits with your grimace if you please; I shall support mine with this lady and two thousand pound a year. (*Taking Hoyden.*) Come, madam.
We once again, you see, are man and wife,
And now perhaps the bargain's struck for life;
If I mistake and we should part again,
At least you see you may have choice of men.
Nay, should the war[93] at length such havoc make
That lovers should grow scarce, yet for your sake
Kind Heaven always will preserve a beau—

(Pointing to Lord Foppington)

You'll find his lordship ready to come to.
FOPPINGTON.
Her ladyship shall stap my vitals, if I do.

[Exeunt.]

Epilogue
Spoken by Lord Foppington.

Gentlemen and Ladies,
These people have regaled you here today
(In my opnion) with a saucy play,
In which the author does presume to show
That coxcomb, *ab origine*—was beau.
Truly, I think the thing of so much weight
That, if some sharp chatisement ben't his fate,
Gad's curse! it may in time destroy the state.
I hold no one its friend, I must confess,
Who would discauntenance your men of dress.
Far, give me leave t'abserve, good clothes are things
Have ever been of great support to kings.
All treasons come from slovens; it is nat
Within the reach of gentle* beaux to plat:
They have no gall, no spleen, no teeth, no stings—
Of all Gad's creatures, the most harmless things.

[92] *de bon coeur*] cheerfully (Fr.)

[93] the war] England and Holland were at war with France from 1689 to 1697.

[Epilogue]

Through all recard, no prince was ever slain
By one who had a feather in his brain.
They're men of too refined an education
To squabble with a court—for a vile dirty nation.
I'm very very pasitive you never saw
A through[94] republican a finished beau.
Nor, truly, shall you very often see
A Jacobite much better dressed than he.
In shart, through all the courts that I have been in,
Your men of mischief—still are in faul linen.
Did ever one yet dance the Tyburn jig
With a free air ar a well-pawdered wig?
Did ever highwayman yet bid you stand
With a sweet bawdy snuff box[95] in his hand?
Ar do you ever find they ask your purse
As men of breeding do?—Ladies, Gad's curse!
This author is a dag, and 'tis not fit
You should allow him ev'n one grain of wit;
To which, that his pretence may ne'er be named,
My humble motion is—he may be damned.

FINIS.

94 through] thorough-going (Harris)

95 bawdy snuff box] Snuff boxes could apparently have bawdy decorations or images within.

Textual Notes

a Copytext is the first quarto edition in 1697 (Q1). Also consulted: a quarto edition in 1698 (Q2), a quarto edition of 1708 (Q3), a collected edition in 1719 (C), and modern editions in 1970 (Zimansky) and in 1971 (Harris).

b But … us] Q1 printed as prose. Sometimes hereafter speeches which read as poetry are printed as prose. Printing them as poetry—even when it produces hemstiches and hypermetric lines—seems authorized by other passages containing these features and clearly printed as poetry. I have scanned them without further comment as best I can.

c methinks] my thinks Q1, Q2, Q3, C, Zimansky, Harris

d When … sirrah] Q1 prints as verse.

e beholden] Q2, Q3, C; beholding Q1, Zimansky, Harris

f Aye,] Ay, Q2, Q3; I Q1; If C, Zimansky, Harris. Zimansky claims his copy of Q1 has space for a dropped letter after the I; ours does not, and I is common for Ay throughout the period.

g These have brains … ass] Q1 prints as verse.

h Like man … alone] Q1 prints as verse.

i piqued] C, Zimansky, Harris; pickt Q1; prickt Q2, Q3

j in] Zimansky; *om.* Q1, Q2, Q3, C, Harris

k It] C, Zimansky, Harris; If Q1, Q2, Q3

l How then subsists … fast] Q1 prints as a hopeless jumble of verse and prose.

m I'm satisfied … ashes] Q1 has another hopeless jumble of verse and prose

n Oh Ged— … one another] Q1 prints as verse.

o *chartré*] Chartre Q1, Q2, Q3 C; *châtré* Zimansky, Harris (following some other modern editors). See also explanatory note.

p press] Zimansky, Harris; pass Q1, Q2, Q3, C

q excuses] Zimansky (emending for the meter); excuse Q1, Q2, Q3, C, Harris

The Way of the World[a]

by William Congreve (1670-1729)

edited by Richard Kroll

Though William Congreve was to remain active into the eighteenth century, *The Way of the World*, performed in 1700 and considered in subsequent theater history to be a jewel of great comedy, marked the end of a brief but brilliant stage career. The commonly held view that *The Way of the World* was a flop is mistaken, though that may reflect the notorious difficulty—for critics and audiences alike—of disentangling the complex web of social relations in the play. The central action of the play, however, can be understood by the following question: How can Mirabell successfully court Millamant, a vastly rich heiress, yet secure her entire fortune of 12,000 pounds, which depends on her marrying with her aunt and guardian Lady Wishfort's consent?

Though performed in 1700, this play is often thought of as one of the last true Restoration comedies, bearing close affinities in theme and style to some of the great comedies of the 1670s. It is important to see how this play both follows and differs from plays like Etherege's *The Man of Mode* (1676). Both plays bring witty rakes into proximate union with heiresses. Yet Congreve was writing in a new social atmosphere that seems to have emerged after 1688. This change of opinion is epitomized, both in theater histories and in Congreve's own references in the play itself, by Jeremy Collier's misleadingly titled *A Short View of the Immorality and Profaneness of the English Stage, Together with the Sense of Antiquity upon this Argument* (1698). In this tract, which follows a long line of seventeenth-century attacks on the stage (and which Congreve also places satirically as reading matter in Lady Wishfort's closet*), Collier vents his fury against what he sees as the excesses of the comedies of the 1670s, in particular plays like Wycherley's *The Country Wife* (1675). At one level Congreve rebuffs Collier by writing a play which, in its broad outline and in its language, echoes those of his distinguished forerunners, but at another level, Congreve massages the plot in such a way as to avoid any further attacks like Collier's. It is true that Dorimant (Etherege's hero) and Mirabell (Congreve's) are cousins, but there are important differences. Whereas we are allowed to witness the messy consequences of Dorimant's various affairs in *The Man of Mode*, the entire plot of *The Way of the World* hinges on the fact that Mirabell is a reformed rake, having arranged that his former lover marry Fainall, while at the same time arranging for her future security by holding her money in trust, so that Fainall cannot do what he attempts, which is to seize her assets for his own purposes.

Finally, the play echoes its era by being a play very much about the difficulties and dangers of women in the sexual marketplace, seen from their own perspective. Millamant is a splendid creation who lives with the consciousness that she will grow older and perhaps as desperate as Lady Wishfort, who will not commit Mrs. Fainall's mistake, and who cannot allow herself to be governed by vengeful jealousies like Mrs. Marwood. All round her are warnings of the dangers in her situation, in which she must delay marriage so that she can choose well, while marriage itself remains inescapable. The inevitability of marriage for a woman, with the hope that some of its otherwise draconian consequences can be mitigated by negotiation, is the moral framework for the proviso scene, in which Mirabell and Millamant debate the circumstances of their intended union. Some critics have pointed out that this scene—the most famous one in Restoration comedy after the china scene in *The Country Wife*—shows Congreve's approval of the Glorious Revolution because Mirabell's and

[I]

Millamant's compact echoes the terms of Locke's second *Treatise of Government*, which had been published five years before. For Congreve, apparently, the "way of the world" involves the need to forge workable political compromises.

DRAMATIS PERSONAE

MEN

Fainall, in love with Mrs.* Marwood.
Mirabell, in love with Mrs.* Millamant.
Witwoud,
Petulant, followers of Mrs. Millamant.
Sir Wilfull Witwoud, half–brother to Witwoud and nephew to Lady Wishfort.
Waitwell, servant to Mirabell.

WOMEN

Lady Wishfort, enemy to Mirabell for having falsely pretended love to her.
Mrs.* Millamant, a fine lady, niece to Lady Wishfort and loves Mirabell.
Mrs.* Marwood, friend to Mr. Fainall, and likes Mirabell.
Mrs. Fainall, daughter to Lady Wishfort and wife to Fainall, formerly friend to Mirabell.
Foible, woman* to Lady Wishfort.
Mincing, woman* to Mrs. Millamant.
Dancers, footmen, and attendants.

SCENE: LONDON. THE TIME EQUAL TO THAT OF THE PRESENT ACTION.

The Way of the World.

Audire est Operae pretium, procedere recte
Qui moechis non voltis … Hor. Sat. 2.l.1
… Metuat, doti deprensa. … Ibid.[1]

[1] *Audire … Ibid.*] Horace, *Satire* 1.2.37 ff, 131. Congreve expects his audience to remember the rest of the opening sentence: "*ut omni parte laborent, / utque illis multo corrupta dolore voluptas / atque haec rara cadat dura inter saepe pericla*": "It is worth your while, ye who would have disaster wait on adulterers, to hear how on every side they fare ill, and how for them pleasure is marred by much pain, and, rare as it is, comes oft amid cruel perils" (Loeb); "She fears being deprived of her dowry" (ed.).

Act I. A chocolate house.

Mirabell and Fainall rising from cards, Betty waiting.

MIRABELL.
You are a fortunate man, Mr. Fainall.

FAINALL.
Have we done?

MIRABELL.
What you please. I'll play on to entertain you.

FAINALL.
No, I'll give you your revenge another time, when you are not so indifferent; you are thinking of something else now, and play too negligently. The coldness of a losing gamester lessens the pleasure of the winner. I'd no more play with a man that slighted his ill fortune, than I'd make love* to a woman who undervalued the loss of her reputation.

MIRABELL.
You have a taste extremely delicate and are for refining on your pleasures.

FAINALL.
Prithee, why so reserved? Something has put you out of humor.

MIRABELL.
Not at all. I happen to be grave today, and you are gay. That's all.

FAINALL.
Confess, Millamant and you quarrelled last night after I left you. My fair cousin has some humors* that would tempt the patience of a Stoic. What, some coxcomb came in and was well received by her while you were by.

MIRABELL.
Witwoud and Petulant. And what was worse, her aunt, your wife's mother, my evil genius,* or to sum up all in her own name, my old Lady Wishfort came in.

FAINALL.
Oh there it is then. She has a lasting passion for you, and with reason. What, then my wife was there?

MIRABELL.
Yes, and Mrs.* Marwood and three or four more, whom I never saw before. Seeing me, they all put on their grave faces, whispered one another, then

complained aloud of the vapors, and after fell into a profound silence.

FAINALL.

They had a mind to be rid of you.

MIRABELL.

For which reason I resolved not to stir. At last the good old lady broke through her painful taciturnity with an invective against long visits. I would not have understood her, but Millamant joining in the argument, I rose and with a constrained smile told her I thought nothing was so easy as to know when a visit began to be troublesome; she reddened and I withdrew, without expecting her reply.

FAINALL.

You were to blame to resent what she spoke only in compliance with her aunt.

MIRABELL.

She is more mistress of herself than to be under the necessity of such a resignation.

FAINALL.

What? Though half her fortune depends upon her marrying with my lady's approbation?

MIRABELL.

I was then in such a humor that I should have been better pleased if she had been less discreet.

FAINALL.

Now I remember, I wonder not that they were weary of you. Last night was one of their cabal nights; they have 'em three times a week and meet by turns at one another's apartments, where they come together like the coroner's inquest, to sit upon the murdered reputations of the week. You and I are excluded, and it was once proposed that all the male sex should be excepted, but somebody moved that to avoid scandal there might be one man of the community, upon which motion Witwoud and Petulant were enrolled members.

MIRABELL.

And who may have been the foundress of this sect? My Lady Wishfort, I warrant, who publishes her detestation of mankind and, full of the vigor of fifty-five, declares for a friend and ratafia, and let posterity shift for itself, she'll breed no more.

FAINALL.

The discovery of your sham addresses to her, to conceal your love to her niece, has provoked this separation. Had you dissembled better, things might have continued in the state of nature.

MIRABELL.

I did as much as man could with any reasonable conscience: I proceeded to the very last act of flattery with her and was guilty of a song in her commendation. Nay, I got a friend to put her into a lampoon and complement her with the imputation of an affair with a young fellow, which I carried so far that I told her the malicious Town took notice that she was grown fat of a sudden and, when she lay in of a dropsy, persuaded her she was reported to be in labor. The devil's in't if an old woman is to be flattered further, unless a man should endeavor downright personally to debauch her, and that my virtue forbade me. But for the discovery* of that amour, I am indebted to your friend, or your wife's friend, Mrs. Marwood.

FAINALL.

What should provoke her to be your enemy, without she has made you advances which you have slighted? Women do not easily forgive omissions of that nature.

MIRABELL.

She was always civil to me, till of late. I confess I am not one of those coxcombs who are apt to interpret a woman's good manners to her prejudice and think that she who does not refuse 'em everything can refuse 'em nothing.

FAINALL.

You are a gallant man, Mirabell, and though you may have cruelty enough not to satisfy a lady's longing, you have too much generosity not to be tender of her honor. Yet you speak with an indifference which seems to be affected and confesses you are conscious of a negligence.

MIRABELL.

You pursue the argument with a distrust that seems to be unaffected and confesses you are conscious of a concern for which the lady is more indebted to you than your wife.

FAINALL.

Fie, fie, friend, if you grow censorious, I must leave you; I'll look upon the gamesters in the next room.

MIRABELL.

Who are they?

FAINALL.

Petulant and Witwoud. [*To Betty.*] Bring me some chocolate. (*Exit.*)

MIRABELL.

Betty, what says your clock?

BETTY.

Turned of the last canonical hour, sir.* (*Exit.*)

MIRABELL.

How pertinently the jade answers me! (*Looking on his watch.*) Hah? Almost one o'clock!

Enter a servant.

Oh, you are come. Well, is the grand affair over? You have been something tedious.

SERVANT.

Sir, there's such coupling at Pancras[2] that they stand behind one another as 'twere in a country dance. Ours was the last couple to lead up, and no hopes appearing of despatch; besides, the parson growing hoarse, we were afraid his lungs would have failed before it came to our turn, so we drove round to Duke's Place,[3] and there they were riveted in a trice.

MIRABELL.

So, so, you are sure they are married.

SERVANT.

Married and bedded, sir, I am witness.

MIRABELL.

Have you the certificate?

SERVANT.

Here it is, sir.

MIRABELL.

Has the tailor brought Waitwell's clothes home and the new liveries?

SERVANT.

Yes sir.

MIRABELL.

That's well. Do you go home again, d'ye hear, and adjourn the consummation till farther order. Bid Waitwell shake his ears and Dame Partlet[4] rustle up her feathers and meet me at one o'clock by Rosamond's Pond* that I may see her before she returns to her lady. And as you tender your ears, be secret.

Exit servant. Reenter Fainall [and Betty].

FAINALL.

Joy of your success, Mirabell; you look pleased.

MIRABELL.

Aye, I have been engaged in a matter of some sort of mirth, which is not ripe for discovery.* I am glad this is not a cabal night. I wonder, Fainall, that you who are married, and of consequence should be discreet, will suffer your wife to be of such a party.

FAINALL.

Faith, I am not jealous. Besides, most who are engaged are women and relations, and for the men, they are of a kind too contemptible to give scandal.

MIRABELL.

I am of another opinion. The greater the coxcomb, always the more the scandal: for a woman who is not a fool can have but one reason for associating with a man that is.

FAINALL.

Are you jealous as often as you see Witwoud entertained by Millamant?

MIRABELL.

Of her understanding I am, if not of her person.

FAINALL.

You do her wrong, for to give her her due, she has wit.

MIRABELL.

She has beauty enough to make any man think so and complaisance enough not to contradict him who shall tell her so.

FAINALL.

For a passionate lover, methinks you are a man somewhat too discerning in the failings of your mistress.

MIRABELL.

And for a discerning man, somewhat too passionate a lover, for I like her with all her faults,

2 Pancras] At the time, St. Pancras was outside City jurisdiction and so marriages could be performed for a fee on demand.

3 Dukes' Place] St. James's church, Duke's Place, Aldgate, notorious for irregular marriages

4 Dame Partlet] wife of Chanticleer in Chaucer's fable (the *Nun's Priest's Tale*)

nay, like her for her faults. Her follies are so natural or so artful that they become her, and those affectations which in another woman would be odious serve but to make her more agreeable. I'll tell thee, Fainall, she once used me with that insolence, that in revenge I took her to pieces, sifted her and separated her failings; I studied 'em and got 'em by rote. The catalogue was so large, that I was not without hopes one day or other to hate her heartily: to which end I so used myself to think of 'em, that at length, contrary to my design and expectation, they gave me every hour less and less disturbance, till in a few days it became habitual to me to remember 'em without being displeased. They are now grown as familiar to me as my own frailties, and in all probability in a little time longer I shall like 'em as well.

FAINALL.
Marry her, marry her. Be half as well acquainted with her charms as you are with her defects, and my life on't, you are your own man again.

MIRABELL.
Say you so?

FAINALL.
Aye, aye, I have experience: I have a wife, and so forth.

Enter messenger.

MESSENGER.
Is one Squire Witwoud here?

BETTY.
Yes, what's your business?

MESSENGER.
I have a letter for him, from his brother Sir Wilfull, which I am charged to deliver into his own hands.

BETTY.
He's in the next room, friend—that way.

Exit messenger.

MIRABELL.
What, is the chief of that noble family in Town, Sir Wilfull Witwoud?

FAINALL.
He is expected today. Do you know him?

MIRABELL.
I have seen him. He promises to be an extraordinary person. I think you have the honor to be related to him.

FAINALL.
Yes, he is half-brother to this Witwoud by a former wife, who was sister to my Lady Wishfort, my wife's mother. If you marry Millamant, you must call cousins too.

MIRABELL.
I had rather be his relation than his acquaintance.

FAINALL.
He comes to Town in order to equip himself for travel.

MIRABELL.
For travel? Why the man that I mean is above forty.

FAINALL.
No matter for that; 'tis for the honor of England that all Europe should know that we have blockheads of all ages.

MIRABELL.
I wonder there is not an act of Parliament to save the credit of the Nation and prohibit the exportation of fools.

FAINALL.
By no means, 'tis better as 'tis; 'tis better to trade with a little loss than to be quite eaten up with being overstocked.

MIRABELL.
Pray, are the follies of this knight-errant, and those of the squire his brother, anything related?

FAINALL.
Not at all. Witwoud grows by the knight, like a medlar grafted on a crab. One will melt in your mouth, and t'other set your teeth on edge; one is all pulp, and the other all core.

MIRABELL.
So one will be rotten before he be ripe, and the other will be rotten without ever being ripe at all.

FAINALL.
Sir Wilfull is an odd mixture of bashfulness and obstinacy. But when he's drunk, he's as loving as the monster in *The Tempest*[5] and after much the same manner. To give t'other his due, he has

[5] *Tempest*] an allusion to Caliban in Dryden's and Davenant's version of Shakespeare's play

something of good nature and does not always want* wit.

MIRABELL.

Not always, but as often as his memory fails him and his commonplace of comparisons. He is a fool with a good memory and some few scraps of other folks' wit. He is one whose conversation can never be approved, yet it is now and then to be endured. He has indeed one good quality: he is not exceptious, for he so passionately affects the reputation of understanding raillery that he will construe an affront into a jest and call downright rudeness and ill language satire and fire.

FAINALL.

If you have a mind to finish his picture, you have an opportunity to do it at full length. Behold the original.

Enter Witwoud.

WITWOUD.

Afford me your compassion, my dears, pity me, Fainall, Mirabell, pity me.

MIRABELL.

I do from my soul.

FAINALL.

Why, what's the matter?

WITWOUD.

No letters for me, Betty?

BETTY.

Did not the messenger bring you one but now, sir?

WITWOUD.

Aye, but no other?

BETTY.

No sir.

WITWOUD.

That's hard, that's very hard. A messenger, a mule, a beast of burden, he has brought me a letter from the fool my brother as heavy as a panegyric in a funeral sermon or a copy of commendatory verses from one poet to another. And what's worse, 'tis as sure a forerunner of the author as an epistle dedicatory.

MIRABELL.

A fool, and your brother, Witwoud!

WITWOUD.

Aye, aye, my half-brother. My half-brother he is, no nearer, upon honor.

MIRABELL.

Then 'tis possible he may be but half a fool.

WITWOUD.

Good, good Mirabell, *le drôle*! Good, good, hang him, don't let's talk of him.—Fainall, how does your lady? Gad, I say anything in the world to get this fellow out of my head. I beg pardon that I should ask a man of pleasure and the Town a question at once so foreign and domestic. But I talk like an old maid at a marriage, I don't know what I say, but she's the best woman in the world.

FAINALL.

'Tis well you don't know what you say, or else your commendation would go near to make me either vain or jealous.

WITWOUD.

No man in Town lives well with a wife but Fainall.—Your judgment, Mirabell?

MIRABELL.

You had better step and ask his wife if you would be credibly informed.

WITWOUD.

Mirabell.

MIRABELL.

Aye.

WITWOUD.

My dear, I ask ten thousand pardons—Gad I have forgot what I was going to say to you.

MIRABELL.

I thank you heartily, heartily.

WITWOUD.

No, but prithee excuse me—my memory is such a memory.

MIRABELL.

Have a care of such apologies, Witwoud, for I never knew a fool but he affected to complain either of the spleen or his memory.

FAINALL.

What have you done with Petulant?

WITWOUD.

He's reckoning his money—my money it was. I have no luck today.

FAINALL.

You may allow him to win of you at play, for you are sure to be too hard for him at repartee. Since you monopolize the wit that is between you, the fortune must be his of course.

MIRABELL.

I don't find that Petulant confesses the superiority of wit to be your talent, Witwoud.

WITWOUD.

Come, come, you are malicious now and would breed debates. Petulant's my friend and a very honest fellow and a very pretty fellow and has a smattering, faith and troth, a pretty deal of an odd sort of a small wit. Nay, I'll do him justice. I'm his friend, I won't wrong him neither. And if he had but any judgment in the world, he would not be altogether contemptible. Come, come, don't detract from the merits of my friend.

FAINALL.

You don't take your friend to be over-nicely* bred.

WITWOUD.

No, no, hang him, the rogue has no manners at all, that I must own. No more breeding than a bum-baily,[6] that I grant you. 'Tis pity, faith, the fellow has fire and life.

MIRABELL.

What, courage?

WITWOUD.

Hum, faith I don't know as to that—I can't say as to that— Yes faith, in a controversy he'll contradict anybody.

MIRABELL.

Though 'twere a man whom he feared or a woman whom he loved?

WITWOUD.

Well, well, he does not always think before he speaks. We have all our failings. You're too hard upon him, you are faith. Let me excuse him. I can defend most of his faults except one or two; one he has, that's the truth on't, if he were my brother, I could not acquit him, that indeed I could wish were otherwise.

MIRABELL.

Aye marry,* what's that, Witwoud?

WITWOUD.

Oh pardon me—expose the infirmities of my friend—no, my dear, excuse me there.

[6] bum-baily] the lowest kind of bailiff, involved in enforcing arrests

FAINALL.

What, I warrant he's unsincere, or 'tis some such trifle.

WITWOUD.

No, no, what if he be? 'Tis no matter for that, his wit will excuse that: a wit should no more be sincere than a woman constant; one argues a decay of parts,* as t'other of beauty.

MIRABELL.

Maybe you think him too positive?

WITWOUD.

No, no, his being positive is an incentive to argument and keeps up conversation.

FAINALL.

Too illiterate!

WITWOUD.

That! That's his happiness. His want* of learning gives him more opportunities to show his natural parts.*

MIRABELL.

He wants* words?

WITWOUD.

Aye, but I like him for that now, for his want* of words gives me the pleasure very often to explain his meaning.

FAINALL.

He's impudent?

WITWOUD.

No, that's not it.

MIRABELL.

Vain?

WITWOUD.

No.

MIRABELL.

What! He speaks unseasonable truths sometimes, because he has not wit enough to invent an evasion.

WITWOUD.

Truths! Ha, ha, ha! No, no, since you will have it—I mean he never speaks truth at all, that's all. He will lie like a chambermaid or a woman of quality's* porter. Now that is a fault.

Enter coachman.

COACHMAN.

Is Master Petulant here, mistress?

BETTY.
Yes.

COACHMAN.
Three gentlewomen in the coach would speak with him.

FAINALL.
Oh brave* Petulant, three!

BETTY.
I'll tell him.

COACHMAN.
You must bring two dishes of chocolate and a glass of cinnamon-water.

Exeunt Coachman [and Betty].

WITWOUD.
That should be for two fasting strumpets and a bawd troubled with wind. Now you may know what the three are.

MIRABELL.
You are very free with your friend's acquaintance.

WITWOUD.
Aye, aye, friendship without freedom is as dull as love without enjoyment or wine without toasting. But to tell you a secret, these are trulls that he allows coach-hire, and something more by the week, to call on him once a day at public places.

MIRABELL.
How!

WITWOUD.
You shall see that he won't go to 'em because there's no more company here to take notice of him. Why, this is nothing to what he used to do. Before he found out this way, I have known him call for himself.

FAINALL.
Call for himself? What dost thou mean?

WITWOUD.
Mean? Why he would slip you out of this chocolate house, just when you had been talking to him. As soon as your back was turned, whip he was gone, then trip to his lodging, clap on a hood and scarf and mask, slap into a hackney-coach, and drive hither to the door again in a trice, where he would send in for himself, that I mean, call for himself, wait for himself, nay and what's more, not finding himself, sometimes leave a letter for himself.

MIRABELL.
I confess this is something extraordinary. I believe he waits for himself now, he is so long a-coming. Oh, I ask his pardon.

Enter Petulant.

BETTY.
Sir, the coach stays.

PETULANT.
Well, well, I come. 'Sbud,* a man had as good be a professed midwife as a professed whoremaster, at this rate: to be knocked up and raised at all hours and in all places. Pox on 'em, I won't come, d'ye hear, tell 'em I won't come. Let 'em snivel and cry their hearts out.

[Exit Betty.]

FAINALL.
You are very cruel, Petulant.

PETULANT.
All's one, let it pass. I have a humor to be cruel.

MIRABELL.
I hope they are not persons of condition that you use at this rate.

PETULANT.
Condition! Condition's a dried fig, if I am not in humor. By this hand, if they were your—a—a—your* what-d'ye-call-'ems themselves, they must wait or rub off, if I want* appetite.

MIRABELL.
What-d'ye-call-'ems! What are they, Witwoud?

WITWOUD.
Empresses, my dear, by your what-d'ye-call-'ems he means sultana queens.

PETULANT.
Aye, Roxolanas.[7]

MIRABELL.
Cry you mercy.

FAINALL.
Witwoud says they are—

PETULANT.
What does he say th'are?

WITWOUD.
I? Fine ladies, I say.

---

7 Roxolanas] ironically named after the Sultana in Davenant's *Siege of Rhodes*

PETULANT.

Pass on Witwoud.—Harkee by this light, his relations: two coheiresses, his cousins, and an old aunt that loves caterwauling better than a conventicle.

WITWOUD.

Ha, ha, ha, I had a mind to see how the rogue would come off. Ha, ha, ha, Gad, I can't be angry with him if he said they were my mother and my sisters.

MIRABELL.

No!

WITWOUD.

No, the rogue's wit and readiness of invention charm me. Dear Petulant.

[Exit Betty.]

BETTY.

They are gone, sir, in great anger.

PETULANT.

Enough, let 'em trundle. Anger helps complexion, saves paint.

FAINALL.

This continence is all dissembled; this is in order to have something to brag of the next time he makes court to Millamant and swear he has abandoned the whole sex for her sake.

MIRABELL.

Have you not left off your impudent pretensions there yet? I shall cut your throat sometime or other, Petulant, about that business.

PETULANT.

Aye, aye, let that pass, there are other throats to be cut—

MIRABELL.

Meaning mine, sir?

PETULANT.

Not I—I mean nobody—I know nothing—but there are uncles and nephews in the world—and they may be rivals—what then? All's one for that—

MIRABELL.

How! Harkee Petulant, come hither. Explain, or I shall call your interpreter.

PETULANT.

Explain? I know nothing. Why you have an uncle, have you not, lately come to Town and lodges by my Lady Wishfort's?

MIRABELL.

True.

PETULANT.

Why that's enough. You and he are not friends, and if he should marry and have a child, you may be disinherited, hah?

MIRABELL.

Where hast thou stumbled upon all this truth?

PETULANT.

All's one for that. Why, then say I know something.

MIRABELL.

Come, thou art an honest fellow, Petulant, and shalt make love* to my mistress, thou sha't, faith. What hast thou heard of my uncle?

PETULANT.

I? Nothing I. If throats are to be cut, let swords clash. Snug's the word, I shrug and am silent.

MIRABELL.

Oh raillery, raillery. Come, I know thou art in the women's secrets. What, you're a cabalist. I know you stayed at Millamant's last night after I went. Was there any mention made of my uncle or me? Tell me. If thou hadst but good nature equal to thy wit, Petulant, Tony Witwoud, who is now thy competitor in fame, would show as dim by thee as a dead whiting's eye by a pearl of orient; he would no more be seen by thee than Mercury is by the sun. Come, I'm sure thou wouldst tell me.

PETULANT.

If I do, will you grant me common sense, then, for the future?

MIRABELL.

Faith, I'll do what I can for thee, and I'll pray that Heaven may grant it thee in the meantime.

PETULANT.

Well, harkee.

FAINALL.

Petulant and you both will find Mirabell as warm a rival as a lover.

WITWOUD.

Pshaw, pshaw, that she laughs at Petulant is plain. And for my part, but that it is almost a fashion to admire her, I should— Harkee, to tell you a secret, but let it go no further, between friends, I shall never break my heart for her.

FAINALL.

How!

WITWOUD.
She's handsome, but she's sort of an uncertain woman.

FAINALL.
I thought you had died for her.

WITWOUD.
Umh—no—

FAINALL.
She has wit.

WITWOUD.
'Tis what she will hardly allow anybody else. Now demme, I should hate that if she were as handsome as Cleopatra. Mirabell is not so sure of her as he thinks for.

FAINALL.
Why do you think so?

WITWOUD.
We stayed pretty late there last night and heard something of an uncle to Mirabell who is lately come to Town and is between him and the best part of his estate. Mirabell and he are at some distance, as my Lady Wishfort has been told, and you know she hates Mirabell worse than a Quaker hates a parrot or than a fishmonger hates a hard frost. Whether this uncle has seen Mrs.* Millamant or not I cannot say, but there were items of such a treaty being in embryo, and if it should come to life, poor Mirabell would be in some sort unfortunately fobbed, i'faith.

FAINALL.
'Tis impossible Millamant should hearken to it.

WITWOUD.
Faith my dear, I can't tell; she's a woman and a kind of humorist.

MIRABELL.
And this is the sum of what you could collect last night?

PETULANT.
The quintessence. Maybe Witwoud knows more: he stayed longer. Besides, they never mind him; they say anything before him.

MIRABELL.
I thought you had been the greatest favorite.

PETULANT.
Aye, tête-a-tête, but not in public, because I make remarks.

MIRABELL.
Do you?

PETULANT.
Aye, aye, pox I'm malicious, man. Now he's soft you know, they are not in awe of him. The fellow's well bred, he's what you call a—what-d'ye-call-'em, a fine gentleman, but he's silly withal.

MIRABELL.
I thank you, I know as much as my curiosity requires.—Fainall, are you for the Mall?*

FAINALL.
Aye, I'll take a turn before dinner.

WITWOUD.
Aye, we'll all walk in the Park.* The ladies talked of being there.

MIRABELL.
I thought you were obliged to watch for your brother Sir Wilfull's arrival.

WITWOUD.
No, no, he comes to his aunt's, my Lady Wishfort. Pox on him, I shall be troubled with him too. What shall I do with the fool?

PETULANT.
Beg him for his estate, that I may beg you afterwards and so have but one trouble with you both.

WITWOUD.
Oh rare Petulant, thou art as quick as a fire in a frosty morning; thou shalt to the Mall with us, and we'll be very severe.

PETULANT.
Enough, I'm in a humor to be severe.

MIRABELL.
Are you? Pray then walk by yourselves. Let us not be accessory to your putting the ladies out of countenance with your senseless ribaldry, which you roar out aloud as often as they pass by you, and when you have made a handsome woman blush, then you think you have been severe.

PETULANT.
What, what? Then let 'em either show their innocence by not understanding what they hear or else show their discretion by not hearing what they would not be thought to understand.

MIRABELL.
But hast not thou then sense enough to know that thou ought'st to be most ashamed thyself when thou hast put another out of countenance.

PETULANT.

Not I, by this hand, I always take blushing either for a sign of guilt or ill breeding.

MIRABELL.

I confess you ought to think so. You are in the right, that you may plead the error of your judgment in defence of your practice.
Where modesty's ill manners, 'tis but fit
That impudence and malice pass for wit.

Exeunt.

Act II. St. James's Park.*

Enter Mrs. Fainall and Mrs. * *Marwood.*

MRS. FAINALL.

Aye, aye, dear Marwood, if we will be happy, we must find the means in ourselves and among ourselves. Men are ever in extremes, either doting or averse. While they are lovers, if they have fire and sense, their jealousies are insupportable. And when they cease to love (we ought to think at least), they loathe; they look upon us with horror and distaste; they meet us like the ghosts of what we were and as such fly from us.

MRS. MARWOOD.

True, 'tis an unhappy circumstance of life that love should ever die before us and that the man so often should outlive the lover. But say what you will, 'tis better to be left than never to have been loved. To pass our youth in dull indifference, to refuse the sweets of life because they once must leave us, is as preposterous as to wish to have been born old because we one day must be old. For my part, my youth may wear and waste, but it shall never rust in my possession.

MRS. FAINALL.

Then it seems you dissemble an aversion to mankind only in compliance with my mother's humor.

MRS. MARWOOD.

Certainly. To be free, I have no taste of those insipid dry discourses with which our sex of force must entertain themselves apart from men. We may affect endearments to each other, profess eternal friendships, and seem to dote like lovers, but 'tis not in our natures long to persevere. Love will resume his empire in our breasts, and every heart, or soon or late, receive and readmit him as its lawful tyrant.

MRS. FAINALL.

Bless me, how have I been deceived! Why you profess a libertine.

MRS. MARWOOD.

You see my friendship by my freedom. Come, be as sincere, acknowledge that your sentiments agree with mine.

MRS. FAINALL.

Never.

MRS. MARWOOD.

You hate mankind.

MRS. FAINALL.

Heartily, inveterately.

MRS. MARWOOD.

Your husband?

MRS. FAINALL.

Most transcendently, aye, though I say it, meritoriously.

MRS. MARWOOD.

Give me your hand upon it.

MRS. FAINALL.

There.

MRS. MARWOOD.

I join with you. What I have said has been to try you.

MRS. FAINALL.

Is it possible? Dost thou hate those vipers, men?

MRS. MARWOOD.

I have done hating 'em and am now come to despise 'em; the next thing I have to do is eternally to forget 'em.

MRS. FAINALL.

There spoke the spirit of an Amazon, a Penthesilea.[8]

MRS. MARWOOD.

And yet I am thinking sometimes to carry my aversion further.

MRS. FAINALL.

How?

MRS. MARWOOD.

Faith, by marrying. If I could but find one that loved me very well and would be thoroughly

---

[8] Penthesilea] a queen of the Amazons

sensible of ill usage, I think I should do myself the violence of undergoing the ceremony.

MRS. FAINALL.
You would not make him a cuckold?

MRS. MARWOOD.
No, but I'd make him believe I did, and that's as bad.

MRS. FAINALL.
Why, had you as good do it?

MRS. MARWOOD.
Oh if he should ever discover it, he would then know the worst and be out of his pain, but I would have him ever to continue upon the rack of fear and jealousy.

MRS. FAINALL.
Ingenious mischief! Would thou wert married to Mirabell.

MRS. MARWOOD.
Would I were.

MRS. FAINALL.
You change color.

MRS. MARWOOD.
Because I hate him.

MRS. FAINALL.
So do I, but I can hear him named. But what reason have you to hate him in particular?

MRS. MARWOOD.
I never loved him. He is and always was insufferably proud.

MRS. FAINALL.
By the reason you gave for your aversion, one would think it dissembled, for you have laid a fault to his charge of which his enemies must acquit him.

MRS. MARWOOD.
Oh, then it seems you are one of his favorable enemies. Methinks you look a little pale, and now you flush again.

MRS. FAINALL.
Do I? I think I am a little sick o'the sudden.

MRS. MARWOOD.
What ails you?

MRS. FAINALL.
My husband. Don't you see him? He turned short upon me unawares and has almost overcome me.

Enter Fainall and Mirabell.

MRS. MARWOOD.
Ha, ha, ha, he comes opportunely for you.

MRS. FAINALL.
For you, for he has brought Mirabell with him.

FAINALL.
My dear.

MRS. FAINALL.
My soul.

FAINALL.
You don't look well today, child.*

MRS. FAINALL.
D'ye think so?

MIRABELL.
He is the only man that does, madam.

MRS. FAINALL.
The only man that would tell me so at least, and the only man from whom I could hear it without mortification.

FAINALL.
Oh my dear, I am satsified of your tenderness; I know you cannot resent anything from me, especially what is an effect of my concern.

MRS. FAINALL.
Mr. Mirabell, my mother interrupted you in a pleasant relation last night. I would fain hear it out.

MIRABELL.
The persons concerned in that affair have yet a tolerable reputation. I am afraid Mr. Fainall will be censorious.

MRS. FAINALL.
He has a humor* more prevailing than his curiosity and will willingly dispense with the hearing of one scandalous story to avoid giving an occasion to make another by being seen to walk with his wife. This way, Mr. Mirabell, and I dare promise you will oblige us both.

Exeunt Mrs. Fainall and Mirabell.

FAINALL.
Excellent creature! Well, sure if I should live to be rid of my wife, I should be a miserable man.

MRS. MARWOOD.
Aye!

FAINALL.
For having only that one hope, the accomplishment of it of consequence must put an end to all my

hopes. And what a wretch is he who must survive his hopes! Nothing remains when that day comes but to sit down and weep like Alexander[9] when he wanted other worlds to conquer.

MRS. MARWOOD.

Will you not follow 'em?

FAINALL.

Faith, I think not.

MRS. MARWOOD.

Pray let us; I have a reason.

FAINALL.

You are not jealous?

MRS. MARWOOD.

Of whom?

FAINALL.

Of Mirabell.

MRS. MARWOOD.

If I am, is it inconsistent with my love to you that I am tender of your honor?

FAINALL.

You would intimate, then, as if there were a fellow-feeling between my wife and him.

MRS. MARWOOD.

I think she does not hate him to that degree she would be thought.

FAINALL.

But he, I fear, is too insensible.

MRS. MARWOOD.

It may be you are deceived.

FAINALL.

It may be so. I do now begin to apprehend it.

MRS. MARWOOD.

What?

FAINALL.

That I have been deceived madam, and you are false.

MRS. MARWOOD.

That I am false! What mean you?

FAINALL.

To let you know I see through all your little arts. Come, you both love him, and both have equally dissembled your aversion. Your mutual jealousies of one another have made you clash till you have both struck fire. I have seen the warm confession reddening on your cheeks and sparkling from your eyes.

MRS. MARWOOD.

You do me wrong.

FAINALL.

I do not. 'Twas for my ease to oversee and wilfully neglect the gross advances made him by my wife, that by permitting her to be engaged, I might continue unsuspected in my pleasures and take you oftener to my arms in full security. But could you think because the nodding husband would not wake, that e'er the watchful lover slept?

MRS. MARWOOD.

And wherewithal can you reproach me?

FAINALL.

With infidelity, with loving of another, with love of Mirabell.

MRS. MARWOOD.

'Tis false. I challenge you to show an instance that can confirm your groundless accusation. I hate him.

FAINALL.

And wherefore do you hate him? He is insensible, and your resentment follows his neglect. An instance? The injuries you have done him are a proof: your interposing in his love. What cause had you to make discoveries* of his pretended passion? To undeceive the credulous aunt and be the officious obstacle of his match with Millamant.

MRS. MARWOOD.

My obligations to my lady urged me. I had professed a friendship to her and could not see her easy nature so abused by that dissembler.

FAINALL.

What, was it conscience then? Professed a friendship! Oh the pious friendships of the female sex!

MRS. MARWOOD.

More tender, more sincere, and more enduring than all the vain and empty vows of men, whether professing love to us or mutual faith to one another.

FAINALL.

Ha, ha, ha, you are my wife's friend too.

MRS. MARWOOD.

Shame and ingratitude! Do you reproach me? You, you upbraid me! Have I been false to her through strict fidelity to you and sacrificed my friendship

[9] Alexander] the Great.

to keep my love inviolate, and have you the baseness to charge me with the guilt, unmindful of the merit? To you it should be meritorious that I have been vicious. And do you reflect that guilt upon me which should lie buried in your bosom?

FAINALL.
You misinterpret my reproof. I meant but to remind you of the slight account you once could make of strictest ties when set in competition with your love to me.

MRS. MARWOOD.
'Tis false, you urged it with deliberate malice. 'Twas spoke in scorn, and I never will forgive it.

FAINALL.
Your guilt, not your resentment, begets your rage. If yet you loved, you could forgive a jealousy, but you are stung to find you are discovered.

MRS. MARWOOD.
It shall be all discovered.* You too shall be discovered,* be sure you shall. I can but be exposed. If I do it myself, I shall prevent* your baseness.

FAINALL.
Why, what will you do?

MRS. MARWOOD.
Disclose it to your wife, own what has passed between us.

FAINALL.
Frenzy!

MRS. MARWOOD.
By all my wrongs, I'll do't, I'll publish to the world the injuries you have done me both in my fame and fortune. With both I trusted you, you bankrupt in honor as indigent of wealth.

FAINALL.
Your fame I have preserved. Your fortune has been bestowed as the prodigality of your love would have it, in pleasures which we both have shared. Yet had not you been false, I had ere this repaid it. 'Tis true, had you permitted Mirabell with Millamant to have stolen their marriage, my lady had been incensed beyond all means of reconcilement: Millamant had forfeited the moiety of her fortune, which then would have descended to my wife. And wherefore did I marry but to make lawful prize of a rich widow's wealth and squander it on love and you?

MRS. MARWOOD.
Deceit and frivolous pretence.

FAINALL.
Death, am I not married? What's pretence? Am I not imprisoned, fettered? Have I not a wife? Nay a wife that was a widow, a young widow, a handsome widow, and would be again a widow but that I have a heart of proof and something of a constitution to bustle through the ways of wedlock and this world. Will you yet be reconciled to truth and me?

MRS. MARWOOD.
Impossible. Truth and you are inconsistent. I hate you, and shall forever.

FAINALL.
For loving you?

MRS. MARWOOD.
I loathe the name of love after such usage, and next to the guilt with which you would asperse me, I scorn you most. Farewell.

FAINALL.
Nay, we must not part thus.

MRS. MARWOOD.
Let me go.

FAINALL.
Come, I'm sorry.

MRS. MARWOOD.
I care not. Let me go. Break my hands, do, I'd leave 'em to get loose.

FAINALL.
I would not hurt you for the world. Have I no other hold to keep you here?

MRS. MARWOOD.
Well, I have deserved it all.

FAINALL.
You know I love you.

MRS. MARWOOD.
Poor dissembling! Oh that— Well, it is not yet—

FAINALL.
What? What is it not? What is it not yet? It is not yet too late?

MRS. MARWOOD.
No, it is not yet too late, I have that comfort.

FAINALL.
It is to love another.

MRS. MARWOOD.
But not to loathe, detest, abhor mankind, myself, and the whole treacherous world.

FAINALL.

Nay, this is extravagance. Come, I ask your pardon. No tears. I was to blame. I could not love you and be easy in my doubts.* Pray forbear. I believe you. I'm convinced I've done you wrong and any way, every way will make amends. I'll hate my wife yet more. Damn her, I'll part with her, rob her of all she's worth, and will retire somewhere, anywhere to another world. I'll marry thee. Be pacified.—'Sdeath,* they come. Hide your face, your tears. You have a mask, wear it a moment. This way, this way, be persuaded.

Exeunt. Enter Mirabell and Mrs. Fainall.

MRS. FAINALL.

They are here yet.

MIRABELL.

They are turning into the other walk.

MRS. FAINALL.

While I only hated my husband, I could bear to see him, but since I have despised him, he's too offensive.

MIRABELL.

Oh, you should hate with prudence.

MRS. FAINALL.

Yes, for I have loved with indiscretion.

MIRABELL.

You should have just so much disgust for your husband as may be sufficient to make you relish your lover.

MRS. FAINALL.

You have been the cause that I have loved without bounds, and would you set limits to that aversion of which you have been the occasion? Why did you make me marry this man?

MIRABELL.

Why do we daily commit disagreeable and dangerous actions? To save that idol reputation. If the familiarities of our loves had produced that consequence of which you were apprehensive, where could you have fixed a father's name with credit but on a husband? I knew Fainall to be a man lavish of his morals, an interested and professing friend, a false and designing lover, yet one whose wit and outward fair behavior have gained a reputation with the Town, enough to make that woman stand excused who has suffered herself to be won by his addresses. A better man ought not to have been sacrificed to the occasion; a worse had not answered to the purpose. When you are weary of him, you know your remedy.

MRS. FAINALL.

I ought to stand in some degree of credit with you, Mirabell.

MIRABELL.

In justice to you I have made you privy to my whole design and put it in your power to ruin or advance my fortune.

MRS. FAINALL.

Whom have you instructed to represent your pretended uncle?

MIRABELL.

Waitwell, my servant.

MRS. FAINALL.

He is an humble servant to Foible my mother's woman* and may win her to your interest.

MIRABELL.

Care is taken for that: she is won and worn by this time. They were married this morning.

MRS. FAINALL.

Who?

MIRABELL.

Waitwell and Foible. I would not tempt my servant to betray me by trusting him too far. If your mother, in hopes to ruin me, should consent to marry my pretended uncle, he might, like Mosca in *The Fox*,[10] stand upon terms; so I made him sure beforehand.

MRS. FAINALL.

So, if my poor mother is caught in a contract, you will discover* the imposture betimes and release her by producing a certificate of her gallant's former marriage.

MIRABELL.

Yes, upon condition she consent to my marriage with her niece and surrender the moiety of her fortune in her possession.

---

[10] Mosca in *The Fox*] the tricky servant who betrays his master, the title character in Ben Jonson's Jacobean comedy, *Volpone*

MRS. FAINALL.
She talked last night of endeavoring at a match between Millamant and your uncle.

MIRABELL.
That was by Foible's direction and my instruction, that she might seem to carry it more privately.

MRS. FAINALL.
Well, I have an opinion of your success, for I believe my lady will do anything to get a husband, and when she has this, which you have provided for her, I suppose she will submit to anything to get rid of him.

MIRABELL.
Yes, I think the good lady would marry anything that resembled a man, though 'twere no more than what a butler could pinch out of a napkin.

MRS. FAINALL.
Female frailty! We must all come to it if we live to be old and feel the craving of a false appetite when the true is decayed.

MIRABELL.
An old woman's appetite is depraved like that of a girl: 'tis the green sickness of a second childhood and, like the faint offer of a latter spring, serves but to usher in the fall and withers in an affected bloom.

MRS. FAINALL.
Here's your mistress.

Enter Mrs. Millamant, Witwoud, and Mincing.*

MIRABELL.
Here she comes i'faith full sail, with her fan spread and her streamers out and a shoal of fools for tenders. Hah, no, I cry her mercy.

MRS. FAINALL.
I see but one poor empty sculler, and he tows her woman* after him.

MIRABELL.
You seem to be unattended, madam. You used to have the beau monde throng after you, and a flock of gay fine perrukes hovering round you.

WITWOUD.
Like moths about a candle. I had like to have lost my comparison for want of breath.

MILLAMANT.
Oh I have denied myself airs today. I have walked as fast through the crowd—

WITWOUD.
As a favorite in disgrace, and with as few followers.

MILLAMANT.
Dear Mr. Witwoud, truce with your similitudes, for I am as sick of 'em—

WITWOUD.
As a physician of a good air. I cannot help it madam, though 'tis against myself.

MILLAMANT.
Yet again! Mincing, stand between me and his wit.

WITWOUD.
Do Mrs.* Mincing, like a screen before a great fire. I confess I do blaze today, I am too bright.

MRS. FAINALL.
But dear Millamant, why were you so long?

MILLAMANT.
Long! Lord, have I not made violent haste? I have asked every living thing I met for you; I have enquired after you as after a new fashion.

WITWOUD.
Madam, truce with your similitudes. No, you met her husband and did not ask him for her.

MIRABELL.
By your leave, Witwoud, that were like enquiring after an old fashion, to ask a husband for his wife.

WITWOUD.
Hum, a hit, a hit, a palpable hit, I confess it.

MRS. FAINALL.
You were dressed before I came abroad.

MILLAMANT.
Aye, that's true. Oh, but then I had—Mincing, what had I? Why was I so long?

MINCING.
Oh mem, your la'ship stayed to peruse a packet of letters.

MILLAMANT.
Oh aye, letters—I had letters—I am persecuted with letters—I hate letters—nobody knows how to write letters, and yet one has 'em, one does not know why. They serve one to pin up one's hair.

WITWOUD.
Is that the way? Pray madam, do you pin up your hair with all your letters? I find I must keep copies.

MILLAMANT.
Only with those in verse, Mr. Witwoud. I never

pin up my hair with prose. I fancy one's hair would not curl if it were pinned up with prose.[b] I think I tried once, Mincing.

MINCING.

Oh mem, I shall never forget it.

MILLAMANT.

Aye, poor Mincing tiffed[11] and tiffed all the morning.

MINCING.

'Till I had the cremp in my fingers, I'll vow mem. And all to no purpose. But when your la'ship pins it up with poetry, it sits so pleasant the next day as anything, and is so pure and so crips.

WITWOUD.

Indeed, so crips?

MINCING.

You are such a critic, Mr. Witwoud.

MILLAMANT.

Mirabell, did not you take exceptions last night? Oh aye, and went away. Now I think on't, I'm angry—No, now I think on't, I'm pleased. For I believe I gave you some pain.

MIRABELL.

Does that please you?

MILLAMANT.

Infinitely. I love to give pain.

MIRABELL.

You would affect a cruelty which is not in your nature; your true vanity is in the power of pleasing.

MILLAMANT.

Oh I ask your pardon for that. One's cruelty is one's power, and when one parts with one's cruelty, one parts with one's power, and when one has parted with that, I fancy one's old and ugly.

MIRABELL.

Aye, aye, suffer your cruelty to ruin the object of your power, to destroy your lover. And then how vain, how lost a thing you'll be! Nay, 'tis true: you are no longer handsome when you've lost your lover; your beauty dies upon the instant, for beauty is the lover's gift. 'Tis he bestows your charms; your glass* is all a cheat. The ugly and the old, whom the looking glass mortifies, yet after commendation can be flattered by it and discover beauties in it, for that reflects our praises rather than your face.

MILLAMANT.

Oh the vanity of these men! Fainall, d'ye hear him? If they did not commend us, we were not handsome! Now you must know they could not commend one if one was not handsome. Beauty the lover's gift! Lord, what is a lover, that it can give? Why, one makes lovers as fast as one pleases, and they live as long as one pleases, and they die as soon as one pleases, and then if one pleases, one makes more.

WITWOUD.

Very pretty. Why, you make no more of making of lovers, madam, than of making so many card-matches.[12]

MILLAMANT.

One no more owes one's beauty to a lover than one's wit to an echo. They can but reflect what we look and say: vain empty things if we are silent or unseen, and want* a being.

MIRABELL.

Yet to those two vain empty things, you owe two the greatest pleasures of your life.

MILLAMANT.

How so?

MIRABELL.

To your lover you owe the pleasure of hearing yourselves praised, and to an echo the pleasure of hearing yourselves talk.

WITWOUD.

But I know a lady that loves talking so incessantly she won't give an echo fair play; she has that everlasting rotation of tongue, that an echo must wait till she dies before it can catch her last words.

MILLAMANT.

Oh fiction. Fainall, let us leave these men.

MIRABELL. (*Aside to Mrs. Fainall.*)

Draw off Witwoud.

MRS. FAINALL.

Immediately.—I have a word or two for Mr. Witwoud.

MIRABELL.

I would beg a little private audience too.

Exeunt Witwoud and Mrs. Fainall.

11 tiffed] arranged, decked out

12 card-matches] matches made of cardboard

You had the tyranny to deny me last night, though you knew I came to impart a secret to you that concerned my love.

MILLAMANT.

You saw I was engaged.

MIRABELL.

Unkind. You had the leisure to entertain a herd of fools, things who visit you from their excessive idleness, bestowing on your easiness that time which is the encumbrance of their lives. How can you find delight in such society? It is impossible they should admire you; they are not capable, or if they were, it should be to you as a mortification, for sure to please a fool is some degree of folly.

MILLAMANT.

I please myself. Besides, sometimes to converse with fools is for my health.

MIRABELL.

Your health? Is there a worse disease than the conversation of fools?

MILLAMANT.

Yes, the vapors; fools are physic for it, next to asafoetida.

MIRABELL.

You are not in a course of fools?

MILLAMANT.

Mirabell, if you persist in this offensive freedom, you'll displease me. I think I must resolve after all not to have you. We shan't agree.

MIRABELL.

Not in our physic it may be.

MILLAMANT.

And yet our distemper in all likelihood will be the same, for we shall be sick of one another. I shan't endure to be reprimanded nor instructed. 'Tis so dull to act always by advice and so tedious to be told of one's faults. I can't bear it. Well, I won't have you Mirabell—I'm resolved—I think—you may go—ha, ha, ha. What would you give that you could help loving me?

MIRABELL.

I would give something that you did not know I could not help it.

MILLAMANT.

Come, don't look grave then. Well, what do you say to me?

MIRABELL.

I say that a man may as soon make a friend by his wit or a fortune by his honesty as win a woman with plain dealing and sincerity.

MILLAMANT.

Sententious Mirabell! Prithee don't look with that violent and inflexible wise face, like Solomon at the dividing of the child in an old tapestry-hanging.[13]

MIRABELL.

You are merry, madam, but I would persuade you for one moment to be serious.

MILLAMANT.

What, with that face? No, if you keep your countenance, 'tis impossible I should hold mine. Well, after all, there is something very moving in a love-sick face. Ha, ha, ha! Well I won't laugh, don't be peevish. Heigho! Now I'll be melancholy, as melancholy as a watch-light.[14] Well Mirabell, if ever you will win me, woo me now. Nay, if you are so tedious, fare you well.—I see they are walking away.

MIRABELL.

Can you not find in the variety of your disposition one moment—

MILLAMANT.

To hear you tell me that Foible's married and your plot like to speed? No.

MIRABELL.

But how you came to know it—

MILLAMANT.

Unless by the help of the devil, you can't imagine. Unless she should tell me herself. Which of the two it may have been, I will leave you to consider, and when you have done thinking of that, think of me. (*Exit.*)

MIRABELL.

I have something more— Gone. Think of you! To think of a whirlwind, though 'twere in a whirlwind, were a case of more steady contemplation, a very tranquility of mind and mansion.

---

13 Solomon ... tapestry-hanging] a portrayal of Solomon's clever decision concerning the parentage of a child; see 1 Kings 3:16-28.

14 watch-light] night-light, hence dim, dark

A fellow that lives in a windmill has not a more whimsical dwelling than the heart of a man that is lodged in a woman. There is no point of the compass to which they cannot turn and by which they are not turned and by one as well as another, for motion not method is their occupation. To know this and yet continue to be in love is to be made wise from the dictates of reason and yet persevere to play the fool by the force of instinct.—Oh, here come my pair of turtles.*

Enter Waitwell and Foible.

What, billing so sweetly! Is not Valentine's Day over with you yet? Sirrah Waitwell, why sure you think you were married for your own recreation and not for my conveniency.

WAITWELL.

Your pardon, sir. With submission, we have indeed been solacing in lawful delights, but still with an eye to business, sir. I have instructed her as well as I could. If she can take your directions as readily as my instructions, sir, your affairs are in a prosperous way.

MIRABELL.

Give you joy, Mrs. Foible.

FOIBLE.

Oh las sir, I am so ashamed. I'm afraid my lady has been in a thousand inquietudes for me. But I protest, sir, I made as much haste as I could.

WAITWELL.

That she did indeed, sir. It was my fault that she did not make more.

MIRABELL.

That I believe.

FOIBLE.

But I told my lady as you instructed me, sir: that I had a prospect of seeing Sir Rowland, your uncle, and that I would put her ladyship's picture in my pocket to show him, which I'll be sure to say has made him so enamored of her beauty that he burns with impatience to lie at her ladyship's feet and worship the original.

MIRABELL.

Excellent Foible! Matrimony has made you eloquent in love.

WAITWELL.

I think she has profited, sir. I think so.

FOIBLE.

You have seen madam Millamant, sir?

MIRABELL.

Yes.

FOIBLE.

I told her, sir, because I did not know that you might find an opportunity. She had so much company last night.

MIRABELL. (*Gives money.*)

Your diligence will merit more. In the meantime—

FOIBLE.

Oh dear sir, your humble servant.

WAITWELL.

Spouse.

MIRABELL.

Stand off sir, not a penny.—Go on and prosper, Foible. The lease shall be made good and the farm stocked, if we succeed.

FOIBLE.

I don't question your generosity, sir, and you need not doubt of success. If you have no more commands, sir, I'll be gone. I'm sure my lady is at her toilet* and can't dress till I come. (*Looking out.*) Oh dear, I'm sure that was Mrs. Marwood that went by in a mask. If she has seen me with you, I'm sure she'll tell my lady. I'll make haste home and prevent* her. Your servant, sir. B'w'y, Waitwell. (*Exit.*)

WAITWELL.

Sir Rowland, if you please.—The jade's so pert upon her preferment, she forgets herself.

MIRABELL.

Come sir, will you endeavor to forget yourself and transform into Sir Rowland?

WAITWELL.

Why sir, it will be impossible I should remember myself: married, knighted, and attended all in one day! 'Tis enough to make any man forget himself. The difficulty will be how to recover my acquaintance and familiarity with my former self and fall from my transformation to a reformation into Waitwell. Nay, I shan't be quite the same Waitwell neither. For now I remember me, I am married and can't be my own man again.

Aye, there's the grief; that's the sad change of life:
To lose my title and yet keep my wife.

Exeunt.

[III]

Act III. A room in Lady Wishfort's house.

Lady Wishfort at her toilet, * *Peg waiting.*

LADY WISHFORT.
Merciful, no news of Foible yet?

PEG.
No madam.

LADY WISHFORT.
I have no more patience. If I have not fretted myself till I am pale again, there's no veracity in me. Fetch me the red. The red, do you hear, sweetheart? An arrant ash color, as I'm a person. Look you how this wench stirs! Why dost thou not fetch me a little red? Didst thou not hear me, Mopus?[15]

PEG.
The red ratafia does your ladyship mean or the cherry brandy?

LADY WISHFORT.
Ratafia, fool? No, fool. Not the ratafia, fool. Grant me patience! I mean the Spanish paper,[16] idiot. Complexion darling. Paint, paint, paint, dost thou understand that, changeling, dangling thy hands like bobbins before thee. Why dost thou not stir, puppet? Thou wooden thing upon wires.

PEG.
Lord madam, your ladyship is so impatient. I cannot come at the paint, madam; Mrs. Foible has locked it up and carried the key with her.

LADY WISHFORT.
A pox take you both. Fetch me the cherry brandy then.

Exit Peg.

I'm as pale and as faint, I look like Mrs. Qualmsick the curate's wife that's always breeding.—Wench, come, come, wench. What art thou doing? Sipping? Tasting? Save thee, dost thou not know the bottle?

Enter Peg with a bottle and china cup.

PEG.
Madam, I was looking for a cup.

LADY WISHFORT.
A cup, save thee, and what a cup hast thou brought! Dost thou take me for a fairy, to drink out of an acorn? Why didst thou not bring thy thimble? Hast thou ne'er a brass thimble clinking in thy pocket with a bit of nutmeg?[17] I warrant thee. Come, fill, fill. So. Again.

One knocks.

See who that is. Set down the bottle first. Here, here, under the table. What, wouldst thou go with the bottle in thy hand like a tapster? As I'm a person, this wench has lived in an inn upon the road before she came to me, like Maritornes the Asturian in *Don Quixote.* No Foible yet?

PEG.
No madam, Mrs. Marwood.

LADY WISHFORT.
Oh Marwood, let her come in. Come in, good Marwood.

Enter Mrs. Marwood.

MRS. MARWOOD.
I'm surprised to find your Ladyship in deshabille at this time of day.

LADY WISHFORT.
Foible's a lost thing, has been abroad since morning and never heard of since.

MRS. MARWOOD.
I saw her but now as I came masked through the Park,* in conference with Mirabell.

LADY WISHFORT.
With Mirabell! You call my blood into my face with mentioning that traitor. She durst not have the confidence. I sent her to negotiate an affair, in which if I'm detected I'm undone. If that wheedling villain has wrought upon Foible to detect me, I'm ruined. Oh my dear friend, I'm a wretch of wretches if I'm detected.

MRS. MARWOOD.
Oh madam, you cannot suspect Mrs. Foible's integrity.

LADY WISHFORT.
Oh, he carries poison in his tongue that would corrupt integrity itself. If she has given him an

---

15 Mopus] a stupid person

16 Spanish paper] either a kind of rouge or a method of applying it

17 thimble … nutmeg] used as good-luck charms

opportunity, she has as good put her integrity into his hands. Ah dear Marwood, what's integrity to an opportunity? Hark! I hear her.—Go, you thing, and send her in.

Exit Peg.

Dear friend, retire into my closet* that I may examine her with more freedom. You'll pardon me, dear friend, I can make bold with you. There are books over the chimney—Quarles and Prynne, and the *Short View of the Stage*, with Bunyan's works—to entertain you.[18]

Exit Marwood. Enter Foible.

Oh Foible, where hast thou been? What hast thou been doing?

FOIBLE.
Madam, I have seen the party.

LADY WISHFORT.
But what hast thou done?

FOIBLE.
Nay, 'tis your ladyship has done, and are to do; I have only promised. But a man so enamored, so transported! Well, here it is, all that is left, all that is not kissed away.[c] Well, if worshipping of pictures be a sin, poor Sir Rowland, I say.

LADY WISHFORT.
The miniature has been counted like. But hast thou not betrayed me, Foible? Hast thou not detected me to that faithless Mirabell? What hadst thou to do with him in the Park? Answer me, has he got nothing out of thee?

FOIBLE. [*Aside.*]
So, the devil has been beforehand with me. What shall I say?—Alas madam, could I help it if I met that confident thing? Was I in fault? If you had heard how he used me, and all upon your ladyship's account, I'm sure you would not suspect my fidelity. Nay, if that had been the worst, I could have borne, but he had a fling at your Ladyship too, and then I could not hold. But i'faith, I gave him his own.

LADY WISHFORT.
Me? What did the filthy fellow say?

FOIBLE.
Oh madam, 'tis a shame to say what he said, with his taunts and his fleers, tossing up his nose. "Humph," says he, "what, you are a-hatching some plot," says he, "you are so early abroad, or catering," says he, "ferreting for some disbanded officer, I warrant. Half pay is but thin subsistence," says he, "well, what pension does your lady propose? Let me see," says he, "what, she must come down pretty deep now she's superannuated," says he, "and"—

LADY WISHFORT.
'Odds* my life, I'll have him, I'll have him murdered. I'll have him poisoned. Where does he eat? I'll marry a drawer to have him poisoned in his wine. I'll send for Robin from Locket's* immediately.

FOIBLE.
Poison him? Poisoning's too good for him. Starve him, madam, starve him: marry Sir Rowland and get him disinherited. Oh you would bless yourself to hear what he said.

LADY WISHFORT.
A villain. Superannuated!

FOIBLE.
"Humph," says he, "I hear you are laying designs against me too," says he, "and Mrs.* Millamant is to marry my uncle." (He does not suspect a word of your ladyship.) "But," says he, "I'll fit you for that, I warrant you," says he, "I'll hamper you for that," says he, "you and your old frippery too," says he, "I'll handle you"—

LADY WISHFORT.
Audacious villain! Handle me, would he durst. Frippery? Old frippery! Was there ever such a foul-mouthed fellow? I'll be married tomorrow; I'll be contracted tonight.

FOIBLE.
The sooner the better, madam.

LADY WISHFORT.
Will Sir Rowland be here, say'st thou? When, Foible?

FOIBLE.
Incontinently, madam. No new sheriff's wife expects

[18] Quarles … Bunyan] Francis Quarles and John Bunyan wrote devotional works; William Prynne and Jeremy Collier, author of the *Short View*, wrote tracts against the stage.

the return of her husband after knighthood with that impatience in which Sir Rowland burns for the dear hour of kissing your ladyship's hands after dinner.

LADY WISHFORT.

Frippery? Superannuated frippery! I'll frippery the villain; I'll reduce him to frippery and rags. A tatterdemalion! I hope to see him hung with tatters, like a Long Lane penthouse[19] or a gibbet-thief. A slander-mouthed railer. I warrant the spendthrift prodigal's in debt as much as the million lottery[20] or the whole Court upon a birthday.* I'll spoil his credit with his tailor. Yes, he shall have my niece with her fortune, he shall.

FOIBLE.

He! I hope to see him lodge in Ludgate[21] first and angle into Blackfriars[22] for brass farthings with an old mitten.

LADY WISHFORT.

Aye, dear Foible. Thank thee for that, dear Foible. He has put me out of all patience. I shall never recompose my features to receive Sir Rowland with any economy of face. This wretch has fretted me that I am absolutely decayed. Look Foible.

FOIBLE.

Your ladyship has frowned a little too rashly, indeed, madam. There are some cracks discernible in the white varnish.

LADY WISHFORT.

Let me see the glass.* Cracks, say'st thou? Why, I'm arrantly flayed; I look like an old peeled wall. Thou must repair me, Foible, before Sir Rowland comes, or I shall never keep up to my picture.

FOIBLE.

I warrant you, madam, a little art once made your picture like you, and now a little of the same art must make you like your picture. Your picture must sit for you, madam.

LADY WISHFORT.

But art thou sure Sir Rowland will not fail to come? Or will a* not fail when he does come? Will he be importunate, Foible, and push? For if he should not be importunate, I shall never break decorums. I shall die with confusion if I am forced to advance. Oh no, I can never advance; I shall swoon if he should expect advances. No, I hope Sir Rowland is better bred than to put a lady to the necessity of breaking her forms. I won't be too coy neither. I won't give him despair. But a little disdain is not amiss; a little scorn is alluring.

FOIBLE.

A little scorn becomes your ladyship.

LADY WISHFORT.

Yes, but tenderness becomes me best, a sort of a-dyingness. You see that picture has a sort of a—hah, Foible? A swimmingness in the eyes. Yes, I'll look so. My niece affects it, but she wants* features. Is Sir Rowland handsome? Let my toilet* be removed. I'll dress above. I'll receive Sir Rowland here. Is he handsome? Don't answer me. I won't know; I'll be surprised. I'll be taken by surprise.

FOIBLE.

By storm, madam. Sir Rowland's a brisk man.

LADY WISHFORT.

Is he? Oh then he'll importune, if he's a brisk man. I shall save decorums if Sir Rowland importunes. I have a mortal terror at the apprehension of offending against decorums. Nothing but importunity can surmount decorums.[d] Oh I'm glad he's a brisk man. Let my things be removed, good Foible. (*Exit.*)

Enter Mrs. Fainall.

MRS. FAINALL.

Oh Foible, I have been in a fright lest I should come too late. That devil Marwood saw you in the Park with Mirabell, and I'm afraid will discover* it to my lady.

FOIBLE.

Discover what, madam?

MRS. FAINALL.

Nay, nay, put not on that strange face. I am privy to the whole design and know what Waitwell, to whom thou wert this morning married, is to

---

[19] Long Lane penthouse] Long Lane is where the rag trade flourished.

[20] million lottery] possibly referring to the government lottery of 1694, which attempted to raise 1,000,000 pounds

[21] Ludgate] prison near the west gate of the City of London

[22] Blackfriars] residential district of the City on the Thames

personate Mirabell's uncle, and as such winning my lady, to involve her in those difficulties from which Mirabell only must release her by his making his conditions to have my cousin and her fortune left to her own disposal.

FOIBLE.

Oh dear madam, I beg your pardon. It was not my confidence in your ladyship that was deficient, but I thought the former good correspondence between your ladyship and Mr. Mirabell might have hindered his communicating this secret.

MRS. FAINALL.

Dear Foible, forget that.

FOIBLE.

Oh dear madam, Mr. Mirabell is such a sweet winning gentleman—but your ladyship is the pattern of generosity, sweet lady, to be so good! Mr. Mirabell cannot choose but be grateful. I find your ladyship has his heart still. Now madam, I can safely tell your ladyship our success. Mrs. Marwood had told my lady, but I warrant, I managed myself. I turned it all for the better. I told my lady that Mr. Mirabell railed at her. I laid horrid things to his charge, I'll vow, and my lady is so incensed that she'll be contracted to Sir Rowland tonight, she says. I warrant, I worked her up, that he may have her for asking for, as they say of a Welsh maidenhead.

MRS. FAINALL.

Oh rare Foible!

FOIBLE.

Madam, I beg your ladyship to acquaint Mr. Mirabell of his success. I would be seen as little as possible to speak to him; besides, I believe Madam Marwood watches me. She has a month's mind,* but I know Mr. Mirabell can't abide her.

Enter Footman.

John, remove my lady's toilet.*—Madam, your servant. My lady is so impatient, I fear she'll come for me if I stay.

MRS. FAINALL.

I'll go with you up the back stairs, lest I should meet her.

Exeunt. Enter Mrs. Marwood.

MRS. MARWOOD.

Indeed Mrs. Engine,* is it thus with you? Are you become a go-between of this importance? Yes, I shall watch you. Why, this wench is the passe-partout, a very master-key to everybody's strongbox. My friend Fainall, have you carried it so swimmingly? I thought there was something in it, but it seems it's over with you. Your loathing is not from a want* of appetite, then, but from a surfeit. Else you could never be so cool to fall from a principal to be an assistant, to procure for him! A pattern of generosity, that I confess. Well, Mr. Fainall, you have met with your match. Oh man, man! Woman, woman! The devil's an ass. If I were a painter, I would draw him like an idiot, a driveler, with a bib and bells. Man should have his head and horns,* and woman the rest of him. Poor simple fiend! Madam Marwood has a month's mind, but he can't abide her. 'Twere better for him you had not been his confessor in that affair without you had kept his counsel closer. I shall not prove another pattern of generosity and stalk for him till he takes his stand to aim at a fortune.[e] He has not obliged me to that with those excesses of himself. And now I'll have none of him.—Here comes the good lady, panting ripe, with a heart full of hope and a head full of care, like any chemist* upon the day of projection.

Enter Lady Wishfort.

LADY WISHFORT.

Oh dear Marwood, what shall I say for this rude forgetfulness? But my dear friend is all goodness.

MRS. MARWOOD.

No apologies, dear madam. I have been very well entertained.

LADY WISHFORT.

As I'm a person, I am in a very chaos to think I should so forget myself. But I have such an olio of affairs, really I know not what to do. (*Calls.*) Foible. —I expect my nephew Sir Wilfull every moment too.—Why Foible.—He means to travel for improvement.

MRS. MARWOOD.

Methinks Sir Wilfull should rather think of marrying than travelling at his years. I hear he is turned of forty.

LADY WISHFORT.
Oh he's in less danger of being spoiled by his travels. I am against my nephew's marrying too young. It will be time enough when he comes back and has acquired discretion to choose for himself.

MRS. MARWOOD.
Methinks Mrs. Millamant and he would make a very fit match. He may travel afterwards. 'Tis a thing very usual with young gentlemen.

LADY WISHFORT.
I promise you I have thought on't. And since 'tis your judgment, I'll think on't again. I assure you I will; I value your judgment extremely. On my word I'll propose it.

Enter Foible.

Come, come Foible, I had forgot my nephew will be here before dinner. I must make haste.

FOIBLE.
Mr. Witwoud and Mr. Petulant are come to dine with your ladyship.

LADY WISHFORT.
Oh dear, I can't appear till I'm dressed. Dear Marwood, shall I be free with you again and beg you to entertain 'em? I'll make all imaginable haste. Dear friend excuse me.

Exeunt Lady Wishfort and Foible. Enter Mrs. Millamant and Mincing.

MILLAMANT.
Sure never anything was so unbred as that odious man.—Marwood, your servant.

MRS. MARWOOD.
You have a color. What's the matter?

MILLAMANT.
That horrid fellow Petulant has provoked me into a flame. I have broke my fan.—Mincing, lend me yours.—Is not all the powder out of my hair?

MRS. MARWOOD.
No. What has he done?

MILLAMANT.
Nay, he has done nothing; he has only talked. Nay, he has said nothing neither, but he has contradicted everything that has been said. For my part, I thought Witwoud and he would have quarrelled.*

MINCING.
I vow mem, I thought once they would have fit.

MILLAMANT.
Well, 'tis a lamentable thing, I'll swear, that one has not the liberty of choosing one's acquaintance as one does one's clothes.

MRS. MARWOOD.
If we had the liberty, we should be as weary of one set of acquaintance, though never so good, as we are of one suit, though never so fine. A fool and a doily stuff[23] would now and then find days of grace and be worn for variety.

MILLAMANT.
I could consent to wear 'em if they would wear alike, but fools never wear out. They are such Drap-du-Berry[24] things without one could give 'em to one's chambermaid after a day or two.

MRS. MARWOOD.
'Twere better so indeed. Or what think you of the playhouse? A fine, gay, glossy fool should be given there, like a new masking habit after the masquerade is over and we have done with the disguise. For a fool's visit is always a disguise and never admitted by a woman of wit but to blind her affair with a lover of sense. If you would but appear bare-faced now and own Mirabell, you might as easily put off Petulant and Witwoud as your hood and scarf. And indeed 'tis time, for the Town has found it: the secret is grown too big for the pretence. 'Tis like Mrs. Primly's great belly: she may lace it down before, but it burnishes on her hips. Indeed Millamant, you can no more conceal it than my Lady Strammel can her face, that goodly face, which, in defiance of her Rhenish-wine tea,[25] will not be comprehended in a mask.

MILLAMANT.
I'll take my death, Marwood, you are more censorious than a decayed beauty or a discarded toast.—Mincing, tell the men they may come up. My aunt is not dressing.

Exit Mincing.

23 doily stuff] light, cheap woollen material

24 Drap-du-Berry] woollen cloth from Berry, France

25 Rhenish-wine-tea] Rhine wines were thought to be slimming.

Their folly is less provoking than your malice; the Town has found it. What has it found? That Mirabell loves me is no more a secret than it is a secret that you discovered* it to my aunt or than the reason why you discovered it is a secret.

MRS. MARWOOD.

You are nettled.

MILLAMANT.

You're mistaken. Ridiculous!

MRS. MARWOOD.

Indeed my dear, you'll tear another fan if you don't mitigate those violent airs.

MILLAMANT.

Oh silly! Ha, ha, ha. I could laugh immoderately. Poor Mirabell! His constancy to me has quite destroyed his complaisance for all the world beside. I swear, I never enjoined it him to be so coy. If I had the vanity to think he would obey me, I would command him to show more gallantry. 'Tis hardly well bred to be so particular on one hand and so insensible on the other. But I despair to prevail and so let him follow his own way. Ha, ha, ha. Pardon me, dear creature, I must laugh, ha, ha, ha, though I grant you 'tis a little barbarous, ha, ha, ha.

MRS. MARWOOD.

What pity 'tis, so much fine raillery, and delivered with so significant gesture, should be so unhappily directed to miscarry.

MILLAMANT.

Hah? Dear creature, I ask your pardon. I swear, I did not mind you.

MRS. MARWOOD.

Mr. Mirabell and you both may think it a thing impossible, when I shall tell him, by telling you—

MILLAMANT.

Oh dear, what? For it is the same thing, if I hear it—ha, ha, ha.

MRS. MARWOOD.

That I detest him, hate him, madam.

MILLAMANT.

Oh madam, why so do I. And yet the creature loves me, ha, ha, ha. How can one forbear laughing to think of it. I am a sibyl if I am not amazed to think what he can see in me. I'll take my death, I think you are handsomer. And within a year or two as young. If you could but stay for me, I should overtake you. But that cannot be. Well, that thought makes me melancholy. Now I'll be sad.

MRS. MARWOOD.

Your merry note may be changed sooner than you think.

MILLAMANT.

D'ye say so? Then I'm resolved I'll have a song to keep up my spirits.

Enter Mincing.

MINCING.

The gentlemen stay but to comb, madam, and will wait on you.

MILLAMANT.

Desire Mrs. ____* that is in the next room to sing the song I would have learned yesterday.—You shall hear it, madam. Not that there's any great matter in it. But 'tis agreeable to my humor.

Song.[26]

I.

Love's but the frailty of the mind
When 'tis not with ambition joined,
A sickly flame, which if not fed expires,
And feeding, wastes in self-consuming fires.

II.

'Tis not to wound a wanton boy
Or am'rous youth that gives the joy,
But 'tis the glory to have pierced a swain,
For whom inferior beauties sighed in vain.

III.

Then I alone the conquest prize
When I insult a rival's eyes;
If there's delight in love, 'tis when I see
The heart which others bleed for, bleed for me.

Enter Petulant and Witwoud.

MILLAMANT.

Is your animosity composed, gentlemen?

WITWOUD.

Raillery, raillery, madam. We have no animosity. We hit off a little wit now and then, but no animosity. The falling out of wits is like the falling out of lovers. We agree in the main,[27] like treble and bass. Hah, Petulant?

---

26 Song] composed by John Eccles and sung by a "Mrs. Hodgson"

27 main] the middle or tenor part

PETULANT.

Aye in the main, but when I have a humor to contradict—

WITWOUD.

Aye, when he has a humor to contradict, then I contradict too. What, I know my cue. Then we contradict one another like two battledores, for contradictions beget one another like Jews.

PETULANT.

If he says black's black—if I have a humor to say 'tis blue—let that pass—all's one for that. If I have a humor to prove it, it must be granted.

WITWOUD.

Not positively must, but it may, it may.

PETULANT.

Yes, it positively must, upon proof positive.

WITWOUD.

Aye, upon proof positive it must, but upon proof presumptive it only may. That's a logical distinction now, madam.

MRS. MARWOOD.

I perceive your debates are of importance and very learnedly handled.

PETULANT.

Importance is one thing, and learning's another, but a debate's a debate, that I assert.

WITWOUD.

Petulant's an enemy to learning; he relies altogether on his parts.*

PETULANT.

No, I'm no enemy to learning; it hurts not me.

MRS. MARWOOD.

That's a sign indeed it's no enemy to you.

PETULANT.

No, no, it's no enemy to anybody but them that have it.

MILLAMANT.

Well, an illiterate man's my aversion. I wonder at the impudence of any illiterate man to offer to make love.*

WITWOUD.

That I confess I wonder at too.

MILLAMANT.

Ah! To marry an ignorant that can hardly read or write!

PETULANT.

Why should a man be ever the further from being married though he can't read any more than he is from being hanged? The ordinary's[28] paid for setting the psalm, and the parish priest for reading the ceremony. And for the rest which is to follow in both cases, a man may do it without book. So all's one for that.

MILLAMANT.

D'ye hear that creature? Lord, here's company. I'll be gone.

Exeunt Millamant and Mincing.

WITWOUD.

In the name of Bartlemew and his fair,[29] what have we here?

MRS. MARWOOD.

'Tis your brother, I fancy. Don't you know him?

WITWOUD.

Not I—yes, I think it is he—I've almost forgotten him; I have not seen him since the Revolution.[30]

Enter Sir Wilfull Witwoud in a country riding habit, and servant to Lady Wishfort.

SERVANT.

Sir, my lady's dressing. Here's company, if you please to walk in, in the mean time.

SIR WILFULL.

Dressing! What, it's but morning here I warrant with you in London; we should count it towards afternoon in our parts, down in Shropshire. Why then belike my aunt han't dined yet, hah friend?

SERVANT.

Your aunt, sir?

SIR WILFULL.

My aunt sir, yes my aunt sir, and your lady sir. Your lady is my aunt, sir. Why, what, dost thou not

[28] being hanged … ordinary] Prisoners who could read (usually a psalm chosen by the ordinary or prison chaplain) were saved from being hanged "by benefit of clergy."

[29] Bartlemew] Bartholemew Fair occurred at Smithfield on August 24 (St. Bartholemew's Day); it was the site of many curiosities.

[30] Revolution] the Revolution of 1688, or "Glorious" Revolution

know me, friend? Why then send somebody here that does. How long hast thou lived with thy lady, fellow, hah?

SERVANT.

A week, sir, longer than anybody in the house, except my lady's woman.*

SIR WILFULL.

Why then belike thou dost not know thy lady if thou see'st her, hah friend?

SERVANT.

Why truly sir, I cannot safely swear to her face in a morning before she is dressed. 'Tis like I may give a shrewd guess at her by this time.

SIR WILFULL.

Well prithee try what thou canst do. If thou canst not guess, enquire her out, dost hear fellow? And tell her, her nephew Sir Wilfull Witwoud is in the house.

SERVANT.

I shall, sir.

SIR WILFULL.

Hold ye, hear me friend. A word with you in your ear. Prithee who are these gallants?

SERVANT.

Really sir, I can't tell; here come so many here, 'tis hard to know 'em all. (*Exit.*)

SIR WILFULL.

'Oons,* this fellow knows less than a starling; I don't think a* knows his own name.

MRS. MARWOOD.

Mr. Witwoud, your brother is not behindhand in forgetfulness. I fancy he has forgot you too.

WITWOUD.

I hope so. The devil take him that remembers first, I say.

SIR WILFULL.

Save you gentlemen and lady.

MRS. MARWOOD.

For shame Mr. Witwoud. Why won't you speak to him?—And you, sir.

WITWOUD.

Petulant, speak.

PETULANT.

And you, sir.

SIR WILFULL.

No offence, I hope. (*Salutes* Marwood.*)

MRS. MARWOOD.

No sure, sir.

WITWOUD.

This is a vile dog, I see that already. No offence! Ha, ha, ha, to him, to him, Petulant. Smoke him.

PETULANT. (*Surveying him round.*)

It seems as if you had come a journey, sir, hem, hem.

SIR WILFULL.

Very likely, sir, that it may seem so.

PETULANT.

No offence, I hope, sir.

WITWOUD.

Smoke the boots, the boots, Petulant, the boots, ha, ha, ha.

SIR WILFULL.

Maybe not, sir; thereafter as 'tis meant, sir.

PETULANT.

Sir, I presume upon the information of your boots.

SIR WILFULL.

Why 'tis like you may, sir. If you are not satisfied with the information of my boots, sir, if you will step to the stable, you may enquire further of my horse, sir.

PETULANT.

Your horse, sir! Your horse is an ass, sir!

SIR WILFULL.

Do you speak by way of offence, sir?

MRS. MARWOOD.

The gentleman's merry, that's all, sir.—S'life,* we shall have a quarrel betwixt an horse and an ass before they find one another out.—You must not take anything amiss from your friends, sir. You are among your friends here, though it may be you don't know it. If I am not mistaken, you are Sir Wilfull Witwoud.

SIR WILFULL.

Right lady, I am Sir Wilfull Witwoud, so I write myself—no offence to anybody, I hope—and nephew to the Lady Wishfort of this mansion.

MRS. MARWOOD.

Don't you know this gentleman, sir?

SIR WILFULL.

Hum! What, sure 'tis not—yea by'r lady, but 'tis—'sheart* I know not whether 'tis or no—yea but 'tis, by the Wrekin.[31] Brother Anthony! What, Tony

31 Wrekin] an important hill in Shropshire

i'faith! What, dost thou not know me? By'r lady, nor I thee, thou art so becravatted and beperriwigged. 'Sheart, why dost not speak? Art thou o'erjoyed?

WITWOUD.

'Odso* brother, is it you? Your servant, brother.

SIR WILFULL.

Your servant! Why yours, sir. Your servant again. 'Sheart, and your friend and servant to that—and a—(*Puff.*) and a flap-dragon[32] for your service, sir. And a hare's foot and a hare's scut for your service, sir, an* you be so cold and so courtly!

WITWOUD.

No offence, I hope, brother.

SIR WILFULL.

'Sheart, sir, but there is, and much offence. A pox, is this your Inns o'Court* breeding not to know your friends and your relations, your elders and your betters.

WITWOUD.

Why, brother Wilfull of Salop, you may be as short as a Shrewsbury cake,[33] if you please. But I tell you, 'tis not modish to know relations in Town. You think you're in the country, where great lubberly brothers slabber and kiss one another when they meet, like a call of serjeants.[34] 'Tis not the fashion here, 'tis not indeed, dear brother.

SIR WILFULL.

The fashion's a fool, and you're a fop, dear brother. 'Sheart, I've suspected this. By'r lady, I conjectured you were a fop since you began to change the style of your letters and write in a scrap of paper gilt round the edges no broader than a subpoena. I might expect this, when you left off "honored brother" and "hoping you are in good health," and so forth, to begin with a "Rat* me, knight, I am so sick of last night's debauch," 'Od's* heart, and then tell a familiar tale of a cock and a bull and a whore and a bottle and so conclude. You could write news before you were out of your time,[35] when you lived with honest Pimple Nose the attorney of Furnival's Inn.[36] You could entreat to be remembered then to your friends round the Wrekin. We could have gazettes then, and *Dawks's Letter*,[37] and the weekly bill,* till of late days.

PETULANT.

'Slife,* Witwoud, were you ever an attorney's clerk? Of the family of the Furnivals? Ha, ha, ha.

WITWOUD.

Aye, aye, but that was for a while. Not long, not long. Pshaw, I was not in my own power then. An orphan, and this fellow was my guardian. Aye, aye, I was glad to consent to that man to come to London. He had the disposal of me then. If I had not agreed to that, I might have been bound prentice to a felt-maker in Shrewsbury. This fellow would have bound me to a maker of felts.

SIR WILFULL.

'Sheart, and better than to be bound to a maker of fops, where, I suppose, you have served your time, and now you may set up for yourself.

MRS. MARWOOD.

You intend to travel, sir, as I'm informed.

SIR WILFULL.

Belike I may, madam. I may chance to sail upon the salt seas, if my mind hold.

PETULANT.

And the wind serve.

SIR WILFULL.

Serve or not serve, I shan't ask licence of you, sir, nor the weathercock your companion. I direct my discourse to the lady, sir.—'Tis like my aunt may have told you, madam. Yes, I have settled my concerns, I may say now, and am minded to see foreign parts. If and how that the peace[38] holds, whereby, that is, taxes abate.

MRS. MARWOOD.

I thought you had designed for France at all adventures.

SIR WILFULL.

I can't tell that. 'Tis like I may, and 'tis like I may

---

32 flap-dragon] raisin snatched from burning brandy and popped into the mouth, hence insignificant thing

33 Shrewsbury cake] a flat cake associated with the chief market town in Shropshire.

34 call of serjeants] a group called to the bar at the same time

35 out of your time] while you were still indentured to a lawyer

36 Furnival's Inn] associated with the major Inns of Court*

37 *Dawks's Letter*] a contemporary newspaper

38 peace] the Peace of Ryswick (1697), creating a lull in William III's wars with France

not. I am somewhat dainty in making a resolution, because when I make it, I keep it. I don't stand shilly-shally, then. If I say't, I'll do't. But I have thoughts to tarry a small matter in Town, to learn somewhat of your lingo first before I cross the seas. I'd gladly have a spice of your French, as they say, whereby to hold discourse in foreign countries.

MRS. MARWOOD.
Here is an academy in Town for that use.

SIR WILFULL.
There is? 'Tis like there may.

MRS. MARWOOD.
No doubt you will return very much improved.

WITWOUD.
Yes, refined, like a Dutch skipper from a whale-fishing.

Enter Lady Wishfort and Fainall.

LADY WISHFORT.
Nephew, you are welcome.

SIR WILFULL.
Aunt, your servant.

FAINALL.
Sir Wilfull, your most faithful servant.

SIR WILFULL.
Cousin Fainall, give me your hand.

LADY WISHFORT.
Cousin Witwoud, your servant. Mr. Petulant, your servant. Nephew, you are welcome again. Will you drink anything after your journey, Nephew, before you eat? Dinner's almost ready.

SIR WILFULL.
I'm very well, I thank you, Aunt. However, I thank you for your courteous offer. 'Sheart, I was afraid you would have been in the fashion too and have remembered to have forgot your relations. Here's your cousin Tony. Belike I mayn't call him brother for fear of offence.

LADY WISHFORT.
Oh, he's a railer, Nephew. My cousin's a wit. And your wits always rally their best friends to choose. When you have been abroad, Nephew, you'll understand raillery better.

Fainall and Mrs. Marwood talk apart.

SIR WILFULL.
Why then, let him hold his tongue in the meantime and rail when that day comes.

Enter Mincing.

MINCING.
Mem, I come to acquaint your la'ship that dinner is impatient.

SIR WILFULL.
Impatient? Why then belike it won't stay till I pull off my boots. Sweetheart, can you help me to a pair of slippers? My man's with his horses, I warrant.

LADY WISHFORT.
Fie, fie, Nephew, you would not pull off your boots here. Go down into the hall. Dinner shall stay for you.—My nephew's a little unbred; you'll pardon him, madam. Gentlemen will you walk? Marwood—

MRS. MARWOOD.
I'll follow you, madam, before Sir Wilfull is ready.

[Exeunt all but] Mrs. Marwood and Fainall.

FAINALL.
Why then, Foible's a bawd, an arrant, rank, match-making bawd. And I it seems am a husband, a rank husband, and my wife a very arrant, rank wife—all in the way of the world. 'Sdeath,* to be an anticipated cuckold, a cuckold in embryo! Sure I was born with budding antlers like a young satyr or a citizen's child.[39] 'Sdeath, to be outwitted, to be out-jilted, out-matrimonied. If I had kept my speed like a stag, 'twere somewhat, but to crawl after with my horns* like a snail and outstripped by my wife, 'tis scurvy wedlock.

MRS. MARWOOD.
Then shake it off. You have often wished for an opportunity to part, and now you have it. But first, prevent their plot. The half of Millamant's fortune is too considerable to be parted with to a foe, to Mirabell.

FAINALL.
Damn him, that had been mine, had you not made that fond* discovery*. That had been forfeited, had they been married. My wife had added luster to my

[39] citizen's child] Citizens or burghers were conventionally cuckolded by fine gentlemen or courtiers.

horns by that increase of fortune: I could have worn 'em tipped with gold, though my forehead had been furnished like a deputy-lieutenant's hall.

MRS. MARWOOD.

They may prove a cap of maintenance[40] to you still, if you can away with your wife. And she's no worse than when you had her. I dare swear she had given up her game before she was married.

FAINALL.

Hum! That may be. She might throw up her cards, but I'll be hanged if she did not put Pam[41] in her pocket.[f]

MRS. MARWOOD.

You married her to keep* you, and if you can contrive to have her keep* you better than you expected, why should you not keep her longer than you intended?

FAINALL.

The means, the means?

MRS. MARWOOD.

Discover* to my lady your wife's conduct. Threaten to part with her. My lady loves her and will come to any composition to save her reputation. Take the opportunity of breaking it just upon the discovery* of this imposture. My lady will be enraged beyond bounds and sacrifice niece and fortune and all at that conjuncture. And let me alone to keep her warm. If she should flag in her part, I will not fail to prompt her.

FAINALL.

Faith, this has an appearance.

MRS. MARWOOD.

I'm sorry I hinted to my lady to endeavor a match between Millamant and Sir Wilfull. That may be an obstacle.

FAINALL.

Oh for that matter, leave me to manage him. I'll disable him for that; he will drink like a Dane. After dinner, I'll set his hand in.

MRS. MARWOOD.

Well, how do you stand affected towards your lady?

FAINALL.

Why faith, I'm thinking of it. Let me see. I am married already, so that's over. My wife has played the jade with me. Well, that's over too. I never loved her, or if I had, why, that would have been over too by this time. Jealous of her I cannot be, for I am certain; so there's an end of jealousy. Weary of her I am and shall be. No, there's no end of that; no, no, that were too much to hope. Thus far concerning my repose. Now for my reputation. As to my own, I married not for it, so that's out of the question. And as to my part in my wife's, why, she had parted with hers before. So, bringing none to me, she can take none from me. 'Tis against all rule of play that I should lose to one who has not wherewithal to stake.

MRS. MARWOOD.

Besides, you forget, marriage is honorable.

FAINALL.

Hum! Faith, and that's well thought on. Marriage is honorable, as you say, and if so, wherefore should cuckoldom be a discredit, being derived from so honorable a root?

MRS. MARWOOD.

Nay, I know not. If the root be honorable, why not the branches?

FAINALL.

So, so, why this point's clear. Well, how do we proceed?

MRS. MARWOOD.

I will contrive a letter which shall be delivered to my lady at the time when the rascal who is to act Sir Rowland is with her. It shall come as from an unknown hand, for the less I appear to know of the truth, the better I can play the incendiary. Besides, I would not have Foible provoked if I could help it, because, you know, she knows some passages. Nay, I expect all will come out, but let the mine be sprung first, and then I care not if I'm discovered.

FAINALL.

If the worst come to the worst, I'll turn my wife to grass. I have already a deed of settlement of the best part of her estate, which I wheedled out of her, and that you shall partake at least.

MRS. MARWOOD.

I hope you are convinced that I hate Mirabell. Now you'll be no more jealous.

---

40 cap of maintenance] cap with two points like horns behind, and a feature in some families' coats of arms

41 Pam] The Jack of Clubs was highest trumps in the game of loo.

FAINALL.

Jealous, no, by this kiss. Let husbands be jealous, but let the lover still* believe. Or if he doubt, let it be only to endear his pleasure and prepare the joy that follows when he proves his mistress true. But let husbands' doubts convert to endless jealousy, or if they have belief, let it corrupt to superstition and blind credulity. I am single and will herd no more with 'em. True, I wear the badge, but I'll disown the order. And since I take my leave of 'em, I care not if I leave 'em a common motto, to their common crest:

All husbands must or pain or shame endure;
The wise too jealous are, fools too secure.

Exeunt.

Act IV. [Scene continues.]

Enter Lady Wishfort and Foible.

LADY WISHFORT.

Is Sir Rowland coming, say'st thou, Foible? And are things in order?

FOIBLE.

Yes, madam. I have put wax lights in the sconces and placed the footmen in a row in the hall in their best liveries, with the coachman and postilion to fill up the equipage.

LADY WISHFORT.

Have you pullvilled the coachman and postilion that they may not stink of the stable when Sir Rowland comes by?

FOIBLE.

Yes, madam.

LADY WISHFORT.

And are the dancers and the music ready, that he may be entertained in all points with correspondence to his passion?

FOIBLE.

All is ready, madam.

LADY WISHFORT.

And—well—and how do I look, Foible?

FOIBLE.

Most killing well, madam.

LADY WISHFORT.

Well, and how shall I receive him? In what figure shall I give his heart the first impression? There is a great deal in the first impression. Shall I sit? No I won't sit. I'll walk. Aye, I'll walk from the door upon his entrance, and then turn full upon him. No, that will be too sudden. I'll lie—aye, I'll lie down. I'll receive him in my little dressing room: there's a couch. Yes, yes, I'll give the first impression on a couch. I won't lie neither but loll and lean upon one elbow with one foot a little dangling off, jogging in a thoughtful way. Yes. And then as soon as he appears, start, aye, start and be surprised, and rise to meet him in a pretty disorder. Yes. Oh, nothing is more alluring than a levee from a couch in some confusion. It shows the foot to advantage and furnishes with blushes and recomposing airs beyond comparison. Hark! There's a coach.

FOIBLE.

'Tis he, madam.

LADY WISHFORT.

Oh dear, has my nephew made his addresses to Millamant? I ordered him.

FOIBLE.

Sir Wilfull is set into drinking, madam, in the parlor.

LADY WISHFORT.

'Od's* my life, I'll send him to her. Call her down, Foible, bring her hither. I'll send him as I go. When they are together, then come to me, Foible, that I may not be too long alone with Sir Rowland. (*Exit.*)

Enter Mrs. Millamant and Mrs. Fainall.

FOIBLE.

Madam, I stayed here to tell your ladyship that Mr. Mirabell has waited this half hour for an opportunity to talk with you, though my lady's orders were to leave you and Sir Wilfull together. Shall I tell Mr. Mirabell that you are at leisure?

MILLAMANT.

No. What would the dear man have? I am thoughtful and would amuse myself. Bid him come another time. (*Repeating and walking about.*)

"There never yet was woman made
Nor shall but to be cursed."[42]

That's hard!

42 "There ... cursed"] the opening lines of a lyric by Sir John Suckling (1609-42)

MRS. FAINALL.
You are very fond of Sir John Suckling today, Millamant, and the poets.

MILLAMANT.
He? Aye, and filthy verses. So I am.

FOIBLE.
Sir Wilfull is coming, madam. Shall I send Mr. Mirabell away?

MILLAMANT.
Aye, if you please, Foible, send him away, or send him hither. Just as you will, dear Foible. I think I'll see him. Shall I? Aye, let the wretch come. (*Repeating.*)

"Thyrsis a youth of the inspired train"—[43]

Dear Fainall, entertain Sir Wilfull. Thou hast philosophy to undergo a fool; thou art married and hast patience. I would confer with my own thoughts.

MRS. FAINALL.
I am obliged to you that you would make me your proxy in this affair, but I have business of my own.

Enter Sir Wilfull.

Oh Sir Wilfull, you are come at the critical instant. There's your mistress up to the ears in love and contemplation. Pursue your point, now or never.

SIR WILFULL. (*This while Millamant walks about repeating to herself.*)
Yes, my aunt would have it so. I would gladly have been encouraged with a bottle or two, because I'm somewhat wary at first before I am acquainted. But I hope after a time I shall break my mind, that is, upon further acquaintance. So for the present, cousin, I'll take my leave. If so be you'll be so kind to make my excuse, I'll return to my company.

MRS. FAINALL.
Oh fie, Sir Wilfull! What, you must not be daunted.

SIR WILFULL.
Daunted? No, that's not it; it is not so much for that, for if so be that I set on't, I'll do't. But only for the present. 'Tis sufficient till further acquaintance. That's all. Your servant.

MRS. FAINALL.
Nay, I'll swear you shall never lose so favorable an opportunity, if I can help it. I'll leave you together and lock the door. (*Exit.*)

SIR WILFULL.
Nay, nay, cousin, I have forgot my gloves. What d'ye do? 'Sheart,* a* has locked the door indeed, I think. Nay, cousin Fainall, open the door. Pshaw, what a vixen trick is this? Nay, now a* has seen me too.—Cousin, I made bold to pass through as it were. I think this door's enchanted.

MILLAMANT. (*Repeating.*)
"I prithee spare me gentle boy,
Press me no more for that slight toy."[44]

SIR WILFULL.
Anon? Cousin, your servant.

MILLAMANT.
"That foolish trifle of a heart."—Sir Wilfull!

SIR WILFULL.
Yes, your servant. No offence I hope, cousin.

MILLAMANT. (*Repeating.*)
"I swear it will not do its part,
Though thou dost thine, employ'st thy power and art."

Natural, easy Suckling!

SIR WILFULL.
Anon? Suckling! No such suckling neither, cousin, nor stripling. I thank heaven, I'm no minor.

MILLAMANT.
Ah rustic! Ruder than Gothic.

SIR WILFULL.
Well, well, I shall understand your lingo one of these days, cousin. In the meanwhile, I must answer in plain English.

MILLAMANT.
Have you any business with me, Sir Wilfull?

SIR WILFULL.
Not at present, cousin. Yes, I made bold to see, to come and know if that how you were disposed to fetch a walk this evening. If so be that I might not be troublesome, I would have sought a walk with you.

MILLAMANT.
A walk? What then?

---

43 "Thyrsis ... train"] opening line of "The Story of Phoebus and Daphne, Applied," by Edmund Waller (1606-87)

44 "I ... toy"] Millmant continues to quote Suckling.

SIR WILFULL.
Nay, nothing. Only for the walk's sake, that's all.

MILLAMANT.
I nauseate walking. 'Tis a country diversion. I loathe the country and everything that relates to it.

SIR WILFULL.
Indeed! Hah! Look ye, look ye, you do? Nay, 'tis like you may. Here are choice of pastimes here in Town, as plays and the like; that must be confessed indeed.

MILLAMANT.
Ah *l'etourdi*![45] I hate the Town too.

SIR WILFULL.
Dear heart, that's much. Hah! That you should hate 'em both! Hah! 'Tis like you may. There are some can't relish the Town, and others can't away with the country. 'Tis like you may be one of those, cousin.

MILLAMANT.
Ha, ha, ha. Yes, 'tis like I may. You have nothing further to say to me?

SIR WILFULL.
Not at present, cousin. 'Tis like when I have an opportunity to be more private, I may break my mind in some measure. I conjecture you partly guess. However that's as time shall try, but spare to speak and spare to speed, as they say.

MILLAMANT.
If it is of no great importance, Sir Wilfull, you will oblige me to leave me. I have just now a little business.

SIR WILFULL.
Enough, enough, cousin. Yes, yes, all a case. When you're disposed, when you're disposed. Now's as well as another time, and another time as well as now. All's one for that. Yes, yes, if your concerns call you, there's no haste. It will keep cold as they say. Cousin, your servant. I think this door's locked.

MILLAMANT.
You may go this way, sir.

SIR WILFULL.
Your servant, then. With your leave, I'll return to my company. (*Exit.*)

MILLAMANT.
Aye, aye, ha, ha, ha.
"Like Phoebus sung the no less am'rous boy"—

Enter Mirabell.

MIRABELL.
"Like Daphne she as lovely and as coy."[46]
Do you lock your self up from me to make my search more curious?* Or is this pretty artifice contrived to signify that here the chase must end and my pursuit be crowned, for you can fly no further.

MILLAMANT.
Vanity! No. I'll fly and be followed to the last moment, though I am upon the very verge of matrimony. I expect you should solicit me as much as if I were wavering at the grate of a monastery with one foot over the threshold. I'll be solicited to the very last, nay and afterwards.

MIRABELL.
What, after the last?

MILLAMANT.
Oh, I should think I was poor and had nothing to bestow if I were reduced to an inglorious ease and freed from the agreeable fatigues of solicitation.

MIRABELL.
But do not you know that, when favors are conferred upon instant and tedious solicitation, that they diminish in their value, and that both the giver loses the grace and the receiver lessens his pleasure?

MILLAMANT.
It may be in things of common application, but never sure in love. Oh, I hate a lover that can dare to think he draws a moment's air independent on the bounty of his mistress. There is not so impudent thing in nature as the saucy look of an assured man, confident of success. The pedantic arrogance of a very* husband has not so pragmatical an air. Ah! I'll never marry unless I am first made sure of my will and pleasure.

MIRABELL.
Would you have 'em both before marriage? Or will

---

45 *l'etourdi*] scatterbrain

46 Like Phoebus ... coy] a couplet from Waller's "Story of Phoebus and Daphne"

you be contented with the first now and stay for the other till after grace?[47]

MILLAMANT.

Ah, don't be impertinent.—My dear liberty, shall I leave thee? My faithful solitude, my darling contemplation, must I bid you then adieu? Ayy, adieu my morning thoughts, agreeable wakings, indolent slumbers, all ye *douceurs*, ye *sommeils du matin*,[48] adieu. I can't do't. 'Tis more than impossible. Positively, Mirabell, I'll lie a bed in a morning as long as I please.

MIRABELL.

Then I'll get up in a morning as early as I please.

MILLAMANT.

Ah! Idle creature, get up when you will. And d'ye hear, I won't be called names after I'm married. Positively, I won't be called names.

MIRABELL.

Names?

MILLAMANT.

Aye, as wife, spouse, my dear, joy, jewel, love, sweetheart and the rest of that nauseous cant in which men and their wives are so fulsomely familiar. I shall never bear that. Good Mirabell, don't let us be familiar or fond nor kiss before folks, like my Lady Fadler[49] and Sir Francis, nor go to Hyde Park* together the first Sunday in a new chariot* to provoke eyes and whispers and then never to be seen there together again, as if we were proud of one another the first week and ashamed of one another forever after. Let us never visit together nor go to a play together, but let us be very strange and well bred. Let us be as strange as if we had been married a great while and as well bred as if we were not married at all.

MIRABELL.

Have you any more conditions to offer? Hitherto your demands are pretty reasonable.

MILLAMANT.

Trifles: as liberty to pay and receive visits to and from whom I please; to write and receive letters without interrogatories or wry faces on your part; to wear what I please and choose conversation* with regard only to my own taste; to have no obligation upon me to converse with wits that I don't like because they are your acquaintance or to be intimate with fools because they may be your relations. Come to dinner when I please. Dine in my dressing room when I'm out of humor without giving a reason. To have my closet* inviolate. To be sole empress of my tea table, which you must never presume to approach without first asking leave. And lastly, wherever I am, you shall always knock at the door before you come in. These articles subscribed, if I continue to endure you a little longer, I may by degrees dwindle into a wife.

MIRABELL.

Your bill of fare is something advanced in this latter account. Well, have I liberty to offer conditions, that when you are dwindled into a wife, I may not be beyond measure enlarged into a husband?

MILLAMANT.

You have free leave. Propose your utmost. Speak and spare not.

MIRABELL.

I thank you. Imprimis, then, I covenant that your acquaintance be general; that you admit no sworn confidante or intimate of your own sex; no she friend to screen her affairs under your countenance and tempt you to make trial of a mutual secrecy. No decoy-duck to wheedle you a fop, scrambling to the play in a mask, then bring you home in a pretended fright, when you think you shall be found out, and rail at me for missing the play and disappointing the frolic which you had, to pick me up and prove my constancy.

MILLAMANT.

Detestable imprimis! I go to the play in a mask!

MIRABELL.

Item, I article that you continue to like your own face as long as I shall and, while it passes current with me, that you endeavor not to new coin it. To which end, together with all vizards for the day, I prohibit all masks for the night made of oiled skins and I know not what: hog's bones, hare's gall, pig water, and the marrow of a roasted cat. In short, I forbid all commerce with the gentlewoman in what-d'ye-call-it court. Item, I shut my doors

[47] grace] the prayer concluding the marriage ceremony

[48] *douceurs ... matin*] sweetnesses ... morning slumbers

[49] Fadler] To "faddle" is to fondle.

against all bawds with baskets and pennyworths of muslin, china, fans, atlases,[50] etcetera. Item, when you shall be breeding—

MILLAMANT.
Ah! Name it not.

MIRABELL.
Which may be presumed, with a blessing on our endeavors—

MILLAMANT.
Odious endeavors!

MIRABELL.
I denounce against all strait-lacing, squeezing for a shape, till you mold my boy's head like a sugarloaf and, instead of a man-child, make me the father to a crooked billet. Lastly, to the dominion of the tea table I submit. But with proviso that you exceed not in your province but restrain yourself to native and simple tea-table drinks, as tea, chocolate, and coffee. As likewise to genuine and authorized tea-table talk, such as mending of fashions, spoiling reputations, railing at absent friends, and so forth, but that on no account you encroach upon the men's prerogative and presume to drink healths or toast fellows. For prevention of which, I banish all foreign forces, all auxiliaries to the tea table, as orange-brandy, all aniseed, cinnamon, citron, and Barbados-Waters, together with ratafia and the most noble spirit of clary.[51] But for cowslip-wine, poppy-water, and all dormatives,[52] those I allow. These provisos admitted, in other things I may prove a tractable and complying husband.

MILLAMANT.
Oh horrid provisos! Filthy strong waters! I toast fellows, odious men! I hate your odious provisos.

MIRABELL.
Then we're agreed. Shall I kiss your hand upon the contract? And here comes one to be a witness to the sealing of the deed.

Enter Mrs. Fainall.

MILLAMANT.
Fainall, what shall I do? Shall I have him? I think I must have him.

MRS. FAINALL.
Aye, aye, take him, take him. What should you do?

MILLAMANT.
Well then. I'll take my death: I'm in a horrid fright. Fainall, I shall never say it. Well—I think—I'll endure you.

MRS. FAINALL.
Fie, fie, have him, have him, and tell him so in plain terms, for I am sure you have a mind to him.

MILLAMANT.
Are you? I think I have—and the horrid man looks as if he thought so too.—Well, you ridiculous thing you, I'll have you. I won't be kissed, nor I won't be thanked. Here, kiss my hand though. So, hold your tongue now, and don't say a word.

MRS. FAINALL.
Mirabell, there's a necessity for your obedience. You have neither time to talk nor stay. My mother is coming and, in my conscience, if she should see you, would fall into fits and maybe not recover time enough to return to Sir Rowland, who as Foible tells me is in a fair way to succeed. Therefore, spare your extasies for another occasion and slip down the back stairs, where Foible waits to consult you.

MILLAMANT.
Aye, go, go. In the meantime, I suppose you have said something to please me.

MIRABELL.
I am all obedience. (*Exit.*)

MRS. FAINALL.
Yonder Sir Wilfull's drunk and so noisy that my mother has been forced to leave Sir Rowland to appease him, but he answers her only with singing and drinking. What they have done by this time, I know not. But Petulant and he were upon quarrelling* as I came by.

MILLAMANT.
Well, if Mirabell should not make a good husband, I am a lost thing, for I find I love him violently.

MRS. FAINALL.
So it seems, when you mind not what's said to you. If you doubt him, you had best take up with Sir Wilfull.

---

[50] atlas] silk-satin manufactured in the orient

[51] orange-brandy ... clary] strong fortified drinks

[52] dormatives] sleeping-draughts

MILLAMANT.
How can you name that superannuated lubber? Faugh!

Enter Witwoud from drinking.

MRS. FAINALL.
So, is the fray made up, that you have left 'em?

WITWOUD.
Left 'em? I could stay no longer. I have laughed like ten christenings—I am tipsy with laughing. If I had stayed any longer I should have burst; I must have been let out and pieced in the sides like an unsized camlet. Yes, yes, the fray is composed. My lady came in like a nolle prosequi and stopped their proceedings.

MILLAMANT.
What was the dispute?

WITWOUD.
That's the jest. There was no dispute. They could neither of 'em speak for rage and so fell a-sputtering at one another like two roasting apples.

Enter Petulant drunk.

Now Petulant, all's over, all's well. Gad, my head begins to whim it about. Why dost thou not speak? Thou art both as drunk and as mute as a fish.

PETULANT.
Look you, Mrs.* Millamant, if you can love me, dear nymph, say it, and that's the conclusion. Pass on or pass off. That's all.

WITWOUD.
Thou hast uttered volumes, folios, in less than *decimo sexto*,[53] my dear Lacedaemonian. Sirrah Petulant, thou art an epitomizer of words.

PETULANT.
Witwoud, you are an annihilator of sense.

WITWOUD.
Thou art a retailer of phrases and dost deal in remnants of remnants, like a maker of pincushions. Thou art in truth (metaphorically speaking) a speaker of shorthand.

PETULANT.
Thou art (without a figure) just one half of an ass, and Baldwin[54] yonder, thy half-brother, is the rest. A gemini of asses split would make just four of you.

WITWOUD.
Thou dost bite, my dear mustard seed. Kiss me for that.

PETULANT.
Stand off. I'll kiss no more males. I have kissed your twin yonder in a humor of reconciliation till he (*Hiccup.*) rises upon my stomach like a radish.

MILLAMANT.
Eh! Filthy creature. What was the quarrel?

PETULANT.
There was no quarrel. There might have been a quarrel.

WITWOUD.
If there had been words enow between 'em to have expressed provocation, they had gone together by the ears like a pair of castanets.

PETULANT.
You were the quarrel.

WITWOUD.
Me?

PETULANT.
If I had a humor to quarrel, I can make less matters conclude premises. If you are not handsome, what then, if I have a humor to prove it? If I shall have my reward, say so; if not, fight for your face the next time yourself. I'll go sleep.

WITWOUD.
Do, wrap thyself up like a wood louse and dream revenge. And hear me, if thou canst learn to write by tomorrow morning, pen me a challenge. I'll carry it for thee.

PETULANT.
Carry your mistress's monkey a spider. Go flay dogs and read romances. I'll go to bed to my maid. (*Exit.*)

MRS. FAINALL.
He's horridly drunk. How came you all in this pickle?

WITWOUD.
A plot, a plot to get rid of the knight. Your husband's advice, but he sneaked off.

---

53 *decimo sexto*] a very small book, about 1/8 the size of a folio (a large book)

54 Baldwin] an ass in the beast epic, *Reynard the Fox*.

Enter Lady Wishfort and Sir Wilfull drunk.

LADY WISHFORT.

Out upon't, out upon't, at years of discretion and comport yourself at this rantipole[55] rate.

SIR WILFULL.

No offence, Aunt.

LADY WISHFORT.

Offence? As I'm a person, I'm ashamed of you. Faugh! How you stink of wine! D'ye think my niece will ever endure such a borachio?[56] You're an absolute borachio.

SIR WILFULL.

Borachio?

LADY WISHFORT.

At a time when you should commence an amour and put your best foot foremost.

SIR WILFULL.

'Sheart,* an* you grudge me your liquor, make a bill. Give me more drink and take my purse. (*Sings.*)

Prithee fill me the glass
Till it laugh in my face,
With ale that is potent and mellow;
He that whines for a lass
Is an ignorant ass,
For a bumper has not its fellow.

But if you would have me marry my cousin, say the word, and I'll do't. Wilfull will do't, that's the word. Wilfull will do't, that's my crest. My motto I have forgot.

LADY WISHFORT.

My nephew's a little overtaken, cousin. But 'tis with drinking your health. O'my word, you are obliged to him.

SIR WILFULL.

In vino veritas, Aunt.—If I drunk your health today, cousin, I am a borachio. But if you have a mind to be married, say the word and send for the piper: Wilfull will do't. If not, dust it away, and let's have t'other round.—Tony, 'Odd's* heart, where's Tony? Tony's an honest fellow, but he spits after a bumper, and that's a fault. (*Sings.*)

We'll drink and we'll never have done, boys,
Put the glass then around with the sun, boys.
Let Apollo's example invite us;
For he's drunk every night,
And that makes him so bright,
That he's able next morning to light us.

The sun's a good pimple,[57] an honest soaker: he has a cellar at your antipodes. If I travel, Aunt, I touch at your* antipodes. Your antipodes are a good rascally sort of topsy-turvy fellows. If I had a bumper, I'd stand upon my head and drink a health to 'em.—A match or no match, cousin with the hard name.—Aunt, Wilfull will do't. If she has her maidenhead, let her look to't. If she has not, let her keep her own counsel in the meantime and cry out at the nine months' end.

MILLAMANT.

Your pardon madam, I can stay no longer. Sir Wilfull grows very powerful. Egh! How he smells! I shall be overcome if I stay.—Come, cousin.

Exeunt Millamant and Mrs. Fainall.

LADY WISHFORT.

Smells! He would poison a tallow chandler and his family. Beastly creature, I know not what to do with him. Travel, quotha. Aye travel, travel. Get thee gone, get thee but far enough, to the Saracens or the Tartars or the Turks, for thou art not fit to live in a Christian commonwealth, thou beastly pagan.

SIR WILFULL.

Turks, no. No Turks, Aunt. Your* Turks are infidels and believe not in the grape. Your* Mahometan, your Mussulman is a dry stinkard. No offence, Aunt. My map says that your* Turk is not so honest a man as your* Christian. I cannot find by the map that your* mufti is orthodox, whereby it is a plain case, that orthodox is a hard word, Aunt, and (*Hiccup.*) Greek for claret. (*Sings.*)

To drink is a Christian diversion,
Unknown to the Turk and the Persian:
Let Mahometan fools
Live by heathenish rules,
And be damned over teacups and coffee.

---

55 rantipole] unmannerly

56 borachio] drunkard

57 pimple] boon companion

But let British lads sing,
Crown a health to the King,
And a fig for your sultan and sophy.
Ah, Tony!

Enter Foible and whispers Lady Wishfort.

LADY WISHFORT.
Sir Rowland impatient? Good lack! What shall I do with this beastly tumbrel?—Go lie down and sleep, you sot, or, as I'm a person, I'll have you bastinadoed with broomsticks.—Call up the wenches.

Exit Foible.

SIR WILFULL.
Ahey! Wenches, where are the wenches?

LADY WISHFORT.
Dear cousin Witwoud, get him away and you will bind me to you inviolably. I have an affair of moment that invades me with some precipitation. You will oblige me to all futurity.

WITWOUD.
Come, knight.—Pox on him, I don't know what to say to him.—Will you go to a cock-match?

SIR WILFULL.
With a wench, Tony? Is she a shake-bag,[58] sirrah? Let me bite your cheek for that.

WITWOUD.
Horrible! He has a breath like a bagpipe.—Aye, aye, come, will you march, my Salopian?

SIR WILFULL.
Lead on, little Tony. I'll follow thee, my Anthony, my Tantony. Sirrah, thou shalt be my Tantony, and I'll be thy pig.[59]
And a fig for your sultan and sophy. (*Exit singing with Witwoud.*)

LADY WISHFORT.
This will never do. It will never make a match at least before he has been abroad.

Enter Waitwell, disguised as Sir Rowland.

Dear Sir Rowland, I am confounded with confusion at the retrospection of my own rudeness. I have more pardons to ask than the Pope distributes in the year of jubilee. But I hope where there is likely to be so near an alliance, we may unbend the severity of decorum and dispense with a little ceremony.

WAITWELL.
My impatience, madam, is the effect of my transport, and till I have possession of your adorable person, I am tantalized on a rack and do but hang, madam, on the tenter of expectation.

LADY WISHFORT.
You have excess of gallantry, Sir Rowland, and press things to a conclusion with the most prevailing vehemence. But a day or two for decency of marriage—

WAITWELL.
For decency of funeral, madam. The delay will break my heart, or if that should fail, I shall be poisoned. My nephew will get an inkling of my designs and poison me, and I would willingly starve him before I die. I would gladly go out of the world with that satisfaction. That would be some comfort to me, if I could but live so long as to be revenged on that unnatural viper.

LADY WISHFORT.
Is he so unnatural, say you? Truly, I would contribute much both to the saving of your life and the accomplishment of your revenge. Not that I respect myself, though he has been a perfidious wretch to me.

WAITWELL.
Perfidious to you!

LADY WISHFORT.
Oh Sir Rowland, the hours that he has died away at my feet, the tears that he has shed, the oaths that he has sworn, the palpitations that he has felt. The trances and the tremblings, the ardors and the extacies, the keelings and the risings, the heart-heavings and the hand-grippings, the pangs and the pathetic regards of his protesting eyes! Oh no memory can register.

WAITWELL.
What, my rival? Is the rebel my rival? A* dies.

LADY WISHFORT.
No, don't kill him at once, Sir Rowland; starve him gradually inch by inch.

---

58 shake-bag] a large fowl

59 Anthony … pig] St. Anthony was often shown accompanied by a pig.

WAITWELL.

I'll do't. In three weeks he shall be barefoot, in a month out at knees with begging an alms. He shall starve upward and upward, till he has nothing living but his head and then go out in a stink like a candle's end upon a save-all.

LADY WISHFORT.

Well Sir Rowland, you have the way. You are no novice in the labyrinth of love: you have the clue. But as I am a person, Sir Rowland, you must not attribute my yielding to any sinister appetite or indigestion of widowhood nor impute my complacency to any lethargy of continence. I hope you do not think me prone to any iteration of nuptials.

WAITWELL.

Far be it from me—

LADY WISHFORT.

If you do, I protest I must recede—or think that I have made a prostitution of decorums, but in the vehemence of compassion and to save the life of a person of so much importance.

WAITWELL.

I esteem it so.

LADY WISHFORT.

Or else you wrong my condescension—

WAITWELL.

I do not, I do not—

LADY WISHFORT.

Indeed you do.

WAITWELL.

I do not, fair shrine of virtue.

LADY WISHFORT.

If you think the least scruple of carnality was an ingredient—

WAITWELL.

Dear madam, no. You are all camphor[60] and frankincense, all chastity and odor.

LADY WISHFORT.

Or that—

Enter Foible.

FOIBLE.

Madam, the dancers are ready, and there's one with a letter, who must deliver it into your own hands.

LADY WISHFORT.

Sir Rowland, will you give me leave? Think favorably, judge candidly, and conclude you have found a person who would suffer racks in honor's cause, dear Sir Rowland, and will wait on you incessantly. (*Exit.*)

WAITWELL.

Fie, fie! What a slavery have I undergone. Spouse, hast thou any cordial? I want spirits.

FOIBLE.

What a washy rogue art thou to pant thus for a quarter of an hour's lying and swearing to a fine lady.

WAITWELL.

Oh, she is the antidote to desire. Spouse, thou wilt fare the worse for't. I shall have no appetite to iteration of nuptials this eight and forty hours. By this hand I had rather be a chairman* in the dog days than act Sir Rowland till this time tomorrow.

Enter Lady Wishfort with a letter.

LADY WISHFORT.

Call in the dancers.—Sir Rowland, we'll sit if you please, and see the entertainment.

Dance.

Now with your permission, Sir Rowland, I will peruse my letter. I would open it in your presence, because I would not make you uneasy. If it should make you uneasy, I would burn it. Speak if it does. But you may see by the superscription it is like a woman's hand.

FOIBLE. [*Aside.*]

By Heaven! Mrs.* Marwood's. I know it. My heart aches. (*To Waitwell.*) Get it from her.

WAITWELL.

A woman's hand? No madam, that's no woman's hand. I see that already. That's somebody whose throat must be cut.

LADY WISHFORT.

Nay Sir Rowland, since you give me a proof of your passion by your jealousy, I'll promise you I'll make you a return by a frank communication. You shall see it. We'll open it together. Look you here. (*Reads.*) "Madam, though unknown to you"—Look you there, 'tis from nobody that I know. "I have that honor for your character, that I think myself obliged to let you know you are abused. He

60 camphor] thought to modify sexual desire

who pretends to be Sir Rowland is a cheat and a rascal"— Oh heavens! What's this?

FOIBLE. [*Aside.*]

Unfortunate, all's ruined.

WAITWELL.

How, how, let me see, let me see. (*Reading.*) "A rascal, and disguised and suborned for that imposture"— Oh villainy, oh villainy! "by the contrivance of"—

LADY WISHFORT.

I shall faint, I shall die, I shall die, oh!

FOIBLE. (*To Waitwell.*)

Say 'tis your nephew's hand. Quickly, his plot, swear, swear it.

WAITWELL.

Here's a villain! Madam, don't you perceive it, don't you see it?

LADY WISHFORT.

Too well, too well. I have seen too much.

WAITWELL.

I told you at first I knew the hand. A woman's hand? The rascal writes a sort of a large hand, your Roman[61] hand. I saw there was a throat to be cut presently. If he were my son as he is my nephew, I'd pistol him.

FOIBLE.

Oh treachery! But are you sure, Sir Rowland, it is his writing?

WAITWELL.

Sure? Am I here? Do I live? Do I love this pearl of India? I have twenty letters in my pocket from him in the same character.

LADY WISHFORT.

How!

FOIBLE.

Oh what luck it is, Sir Rowland, that you were present at this juncture! This was the business that brought Mr. Mirabell disguised to Madam Millamant this afternoon. I thought something was contriving when he stole by me and would have hid his face.

LADY WISHFORT.

How, how! I heard the villain was in the house indeed, and now I remember, my niece went away abruptly when Sir Wilfull was to have made his addresses.

FOIBLE.

Then, then madam, Mr. Mirabell waited for her in her chamber, but I would not tell your ladyship to discompose you when you were to receive Sir Rowland.

WAITWELL.

Enough, his date is short.

FOIBLE.

No, good Sir Rowland, don't incur the law.

WAITWELL.

Law? I care not for law. I can but die, and 'tis in a good cause. My lady shall be satisfied of my truth and innocence, though it cost me my life.

LADY WISHFORT.

No, dear Sir Rowland, don't fight. If you should be killed, I must never show my face—or hanged. Oh consider my reputation, Sir Rowland. No, you shan't fight. I'll go in and examine my niece. I'll make her confess. I conjure you, Sir Rowland, by all your love not to fight.

WAITWELL.

I am charmed madam, I obey. But some proof you must let me give you. I'll go for a black box, which contains the writings of my whole estate, and deliver that into your hands.

LADY WISHFORT.

Aye, dear Sir Rowland, that will be some comfort. Bring the black box.

WAITWELL.

And may I presume to bring a contract to be signed this night? May I hope so far?

LADY WISHFORT.

Bring what you will but come alive, pray come alive. Oh this is a happy discovery.

WAITWELL.

Dead or alive, I'll come, and married we will be in spite of treachery, aye, and get an heir that shall defeat the last remaining glimpse of hope in my abandoned nephew. Come, my buxom widow.
Ere long you shall substantial proof receive
That I'm an errant knight—

FOIBLE.

Or arrant knave.

Exeunt.

[61] Roman] round and bold

Act V. Scene continues.

Lady Wishfort and Foible.

LADY WISHFORT.

Out of my house, out of my house, thou viper, thou serpent that I have fostered, thou bosom traitress that I raised from nothing. Be gone, be gone, be gone, go, go, that I took from washing of old gauze and weaving of dead hair, with a bleak, blue nose, over a chafing dish of starved embers and dining behind a traverse rag in a shop no bigger than a bird cage. Go, go, starve again, do, do.

FOIBLE.

Dear madam, I'll beg pardon on my knees.

LADY WISHFORT.

Away, out, out, go set up for yourself again. Do, drive a trade, do, with your threepenny-worth of small ware, flaunting upon a packthread, under a brandy-seller's bulk,[62] or against a dead wall by a ballad-monger. Go hang out an old frisoneer-gorget,[63] with a yard of yellow colberteen[64] again, do, an old gnawed mask, two rows of pins and a child's fiddle, a glass necklace with the beads broken, and a quilted nightcap with one ear. Go, go, drive a trade: these were your commodities, you treacherous trull, this was your merchandise you dealt in when I took you into my house, placed you next myself, and made you governante of my whole family. You have forgot this, have you? Now you have feathered your nest.

FOIBLE.

No, no, dear madam. Do but hear me, have but a moment's patience. I'll confess all. Mr. Mirabell seduced me. I am not the first that he has wheedled with his dissembling tongue. Your ladyship's own wisdom has been deluded by him. Then how should I, a poor ignorant, defend myself? Oh madam, if you knew but what he promised me and how he assured me your Ladyship should come to no damage, or else the wealth of the Indies should not have bribed me to conspire against so good, so sweet, so kind a lady as you have been to me.

LADY WISHFORT.

No damage? What, to betray me, to marry me to a cast* serving man, to make me a receptacle and hospital for a decayed pimp? No damage? Oh thou frontless impudence, more than a big-bellied actress.

FOIBLE.

Pray, do but hear me, madam: he could not marry your ladyship, madam. No indeed, his marriage was to have been void in law, for he was married to me first to secure your ladyship. He could not have bedded your ladyship, for if he had consummated with your ladyship, he must have run the risk of the law and been put upon his clergy.[65] Yes indeed, I enquired of the law in that case before I would meddle or make.

LADY WISHFORT.

What, then I have been your property, have I? I have been convenient to you it seems. While you were catering for Mirabell, I have been broker for you? What, have you made a passive bawd of me? This exceeds all precedent. I am brought to fine uses, to become a botcher of second-hand marriages between Abigails and Andrews! I'll couple you. Yes, I'll baste you together, you and your Philander. I'll Duke's Place you, as I'm a person. Your turtle* is in custody already; you shall coo in the same cage, if there be constable or warrant in the parish. (*Exit.*)

FOIBLE.

Oh that ever I was born. Oh that I was ever married. A bride, aye I shall be a Bridewell bride. Oh!

Enter Mrs. Fainall.

MRS. FAINALL.

Poor Foible, what's the matter?

FOIBLE.

Oh madam, my lady's gone for a constable. I shall be had to a justice and put to Bridewell to beat hemp. Poor Waitwell's gone to prison already.

---

[62] bulk] stall

[63] frisoneer-gorget] woolen covering for the neck

[64] colberteen] cheap lace

[65] risk … clergy] of being potentially hanged for bigamy, from which he could escape through benefit of clergy

MRS. FAINALL.
Have a good heart, Foible, Mirabell's gone to give security for him. This is all Marwood's and my husband's doing.

FOIBLE.
Yes, yes, I know it madam. She was in my lady's closet* and overheard all that you said to me before dinner. She sent the letter to my lady, and that missing effect, Mr. Fainall laid this plot to arrest Waitwell, when he pretended to go for the papers, and in the meantime, Mrs. Marwood declared all to my lady.

MRS. FAINALL.
Was there no mention made of me in the letter? My mother does not suspect my being in the confederacy? I fancy Marwood has not told her, though she has told my husband.

FOIBLE.
Yes madam, but my lady did not see that part: we stifled the letter before she read so far. Has that mischievous devil told Mr. Fainall of your ladyship then?

MRS. FAINALL.
Aye, all's out: my affair with Mirabell, everything discovered.* This is the last day of our living together, that's my comfort.

FOIBLE.
Indeed madam, and so 'tis a comfort if you knew all. He has been even with your ladyship, which I could have told you long enough since, but I love to keep peace and quietness by my goodwill. I had rather bring friends together than set 'em at distance. But Mrs. Marwood and he are nearer related than ever their parents thought for.

MRS. FAINALL.
Say'st thou so, Foible? Canst thou prove this?

FOIBLE.
I can take my oath of it, madam. So can Mrs. Mincing. We have had many a fair word from Madam Marwood to conceal something that passed in our chamber one evening when you were at Hyde Park* and we were thought to have gone a-walking. But we went up unawares, though we were sworn to secrecy too. Madam Marwood took a book and swore us upon it, but it was but a book of verses and poems. So long as it was not a Bible oath, we may break it with a safe conscience.

MRS. FAINALL.
This discovery* is the most opportune thing I could wish.—Now Mincing?

Enter Mincing.

MINCING.
My lady would speak with Mrs. Foible, mem. Mr. Mirabell is with her. He has set your spouse at liberty, Mrs. Foible, and would have you hide yourself in my lady's closet,* till my old lady's anger is abated. Oh, my old lady is in a perilous passion at something Mr. Fainall has said. He swears, and my old Lady cries. There's a fearful hurricane, I vow. He says, mem, how that he'll have my lady's fortune made over to him or he'll be divorced.

MRS. FAINALL.
Does your lady and Mirabell know that?

MINCING.
Yes mem, they have sent me to see if Sir Wilfull be sober and to bring him to them. My lady is resolved to have him, I think, rather than lose such a vast sum as six thousand pound.—Oh come, Mrs. Foible, I hear my old lady.

MRS. FAINALL.
Foible, you must tell Mincing that she must prepare to vouch when I call her.

FOIBLE.
Yes, yes madam.

MINCING.
Oh yes, mem, I'll vouch anything for your ladyship's service, be what it will.

Exeunt Mincing and Foible. Enter Lady Wishfort and Marwood.

LADY WISHFORT.
Oh my dear friend, how can I enumerate the benefits that I have received from your goodness? To you I owe the timely discovery* of the false vows of Mirabell, to you the detection of the impostor Sir Rowland. And now you are become an intercessor with my son-in-law to save the honor of my house and compound for the frailties of my daughter. Well friend, you are enough to reconcile me to the bad world, or else I would retire to deserts and solitudes and feed harmless sheep by groves and purling streams. Dear

Marwood, let us leave the world and retire by ourselves and be shepherdesses.

MRS. MARWOOD.

Let us first despatch the affair in hand, madam. We shall have leisure to think of retirement afterwards. Here is one who is concerned in the treaty.

LADY WISHFORT.

Oh daughter, daughter, is it possible thou shouldst be my child, bone of my bone and flesh of my flesh, and as I may say, another me, and yet transgress the most minute particle of severe virtue? Is it possible you should lean aside to iniquity who have been cast in the direct mold of virtue? I have not only been a mold but a pattern for you and a model for you after you were brought into the world.

MRS. FAINALL.

I don't understand your ladyship.

LADY WISHFORT.

Not understand? Why, have you not been naught?* Have you not been sophisticated?* Not understand? Here I am ruined to compound for your caprices and your cuckoldoms. I must pawn my plate* and my jewels and ruin my niece, and all little enough—

MRS. FAINALL.

I am wronged and abused, and so are you. 'Tis a false accusation, as false as hell, as false as your friend there, aye, or your friend's friend, my false husband.

MRS. MARWOOD.

My friend, Mrs. Fainall? Your husband my friend? What do you mean?

MRS. FAINALL.

I know what I mean, madam, and so do you, and so shall the world at a time convenient.

MRS. MARWOOD.

I am sorry to see you so passionate, madam. More temper would look more like innocence. But I have done.—I am sorry my zeal to serve your ladyship and family should admit of misconstruction or make me liable to affronts. You will pardon me, madam, if I meddle no more with an affair in which I am not personally concerned.

LADY WISHFORT.

Oh dear friend, I am so ashamed that you should meet with such returns.—You ought to ask pardon on your knees, ungrateful creature: she deserves more from you than all your life can accomplish.—Oh don't leave me destitute in this perplexity. No, stick to me, my good genius.*

MRS. FAINALL.

I tell you, madam, you're abused. Stick to you? Aye, like a leech, to suck your best blood. She'll drop off when she's full. Madam, you shan't pawn a bodkin nor part with a brass counter in composition for me. I defy 'em all. Let 'em prove their aspersions. I know my own innocence and dare stand a trial.[g] (*Exit.*)

LADY WISHFORT.

Why, if she should be innocent, if she should be wronged after all, hah? I don't know what to think, and I promise you, her education has been unexceptionable. I may say it, for I chiefly made it my own care to initiate her very infancy in the rudiments of virtue and to impress upon her tender years a young odium and aversion to the very sight of men. Aye friend, she would ha' shrieked if she had but seen a man till she was in her teens. As I am a person, 'tis true. She was never suffered to play with a male child, though but in coats;[66] nay, her very babies* were of the feminine gender. Oh, she never looked a man in the face but her own father or the chaplain, and him we made a shift to put upon her for a woman by the help of his long garments and his sleek face till she was going in her fifteen.

MRS. MARWOOD.

'Twas much she should be deceived so long.

LADY WISHFORT.

I warrant you, or she would never have borne to have been catechised by him and have heard his long lectures against singing and dancing and such debaucheries and going to filthy plays and profane music-meetings, where the lewd trebles squeak nothing but bawdy and the basses roar blasphemy. Oh, she would have swooned at the sight or name of an obscene playbook. And can I think after all this that my daughter can be naught?* What, a

66 male … coats] Young males were dressed in (petti)coats, not breeches.

whore? And thought it excommunication to set her foot within the door of a playhouse. Oh my dear friend, I can't believe it. No, no, as she says, let him prove it, let him prove it.

MRS. MARWOOD.

Prove it, madam? What, and have your name prostituted in a public court, yours and your daughter's reputation worried at the bar by a pack of bawling lawyers? To be ushered in by an oyez of scandal and have your case opened by an old fumbling lecher in a coif like a man midwife to bring your daughter's infamy to light, to be a theme for legal punsters and quibblers by the statute and become a jest, against a rule of court, where there is no precedent for a jest in any record, not even in Domesday Book. To discompose the gravity of the bench and provoke naughty interrogatories in more naughty law-Latin, while the good judge, tickled with the proceeding, simpers under a gray beard and fidges off and on his cushion as if he had swallowed cantharides, or sat upon cow-itch.[67]

LADY WISHFORT.

Oh, 'tis very hard.

MRS. MARWOOD.

And then to have my young revellers of the Temple* take notes like prentices at a conventicle and, after, talk it all over again in commons or before drawers in an eating house.

LADY WISHFORT.

Worse and worse.

MRS. MARWOOD.

Nay, this is nothing; if it would end here, 'twere well. But it must after this be consigned by the shorthand writers to the public press and from thence be transferred to the hands, nay, into the throats and lungs of hawkers with voices more licentious than the loud flounder-man's or the woman that cries "gray peas."[h] And this you must hear till you are stunned; nay, you must hear nothing else for some days.

LADY WISHFORT.

Oh, 'tis insupportable. No, no, dear friend, make it up, make it up. Aye, aye, I'll compound. I'll give up all, myself and my all, my niece and her all—anything, everything for composition.

MRS. MARWOOD.

Nay madam, I advise nothing. I only lay before you as a friend the inconveniencies which perhaps you have overseen. Here comes Mr. Fainall. If he will be satisfied to huddle up all in silence, I shall be glad. You must think I would rather congratulate than condole with you.

Enter Fainall.

LADY WISHFORT.

Aye, aye, I do not doubt it, dear Marwood. No, no, I do not doubt it.

FAINALL.

Well madam, I have suffered myself to be overcome by the importunity of this lady your friend and am content you shall enjoy your own proper estate during life, on condition you oblige yourself never to marry, under such penalty as I think convenient.

LADY WISHFORT.

Never to marry?

FAINALL.

No more Sir Rowlands. The next imposture may not be so timely detected.

MRS. MARWOOD.

That condition, I dare answer, my lady will consent to without difficulty. She has already but too much experienced the perfidiousness of men. Besides, madam, when we retire to our pastoral solitude, we shall bid adieu to all other thoughts.

LADY WISHFORT.

Aye, that's true, but in case of necessity, as of health or some such emergency—

FAINALL.

Oh, if you are prescribed marriage, you shall be considered. I will only reserve to myself the power to choose for you. If your physic be wholesome, it matters not who is your apothecary. Next, my wife shall settle on me the remainder of her fortune not made over already and for her maintenance depend entirely on my discretion.

LADY WISHFORT.

This is most inhumanly savage, exceeding the barbarity of a Muscovite husband.

---

67 cow-itch] stinging plant

FAINALL.

I learned it from his Czarish majesty's retinue[68] in a winter evening's conference over brandy and pepper, amongst other secrets of matrimony and policy as they are at present practiced in the northern hemisphere. But this must be agreed unto and that positively. Lastly, I will be endowed in right of my wife with that six thousand pound which is the moiety of Mrs.* Millamant's fortune in your possession and which she has forfeited (as will appear by the last will and testament of your deceased husband, Sir Jonathan Wishfort) by her disobedience in contracting herself against your consent or knowledge and by refusing the offered match with Sir Wilfull Witwoud, which you like a careful aunt had provided for her.

LADY WISHFORT.

My nephew was *non compos*[69] and could not make his addresses.

FAINALL.

I come to make demands. I'll hear no objections.

LADY WISHFORT.

You will grant me time to consider.

FAINALL.

Yes, while the instrument is drawing, to which you must set your hand till more sufficient deeds can be perfected, which I will take care shall be done with all possible speed. In the meanwhile, I will go for the said instrument, and till my return you may balance this matter in your own discretion. (*Exit.*)

LADY WISHFORT.

This insolence is beyond all precedent, all parallel. Must I be subject to this merciless villain?

MRS. MARWOOD.

'Tis severe indeed, madam, that you should smart for your daughter's wantonness.

LADY WISHFORT.

'Twas against my consent that she married this barbarian, but she would have him, though her year[70] was not out. Ah! Her first husband, my son Languish, would not have carried it thus. Well, that was my choice; this is hers. She is matched now, with a witness. I shall be mad, dear friend. Is there no comfort for me? Must I live to be confiscated at this rebel-rate? Here come two more of my Egyptian plagues[71] too.

Enter Millamant and Sir Wilfull.

SIR WILFULL.

Aunt, your servant.

LADY WISHFORT.

Out caterpillar, call not me aunt. I know thee not.

WILFULL.

I confess I have been a little in disguise* as they say. S'heart!* And I am sorry for't. What would you have? I hope I committed no offence, Aunt, and if I did, I am willing to make satisfaction. And what can a man say fairer? If I have broke anything, I'll pay for't, an* it cost a pound. And so let that content for what's past, and make no more words. For what's to come, to pleasure you I'm willing to marry my cousin. So pray, let's all be friends. She and I are agreed on the matter before a witness.

LADY WISHFORT.

How's this, dear niece? Have I any comfort? Can this be true?

MILLAMANT.

I am content to be a sacrifice to your repose, madam, and to convince you that I had no hand in the plot, as you were misinformed, I have laid my commands on Mirabell to come in person and be a witness that I give my hand to this flower of knighthood. And for the contract that passed between Mirabell and me, I have obliged him to make a resignation of it in your ladyship's presence. He is without and waits your leave for admittance.

LADY WISHFORT.

Well, I'll swear I am something revived at this testimony of your obedience, but I cannot admit that traitor. I fear I cannot fortify myself to support his appearance. He is as terrible to me as a Gorgon; if I see him, I fear I shall turn to stone, petrify incessantly.[72]

68 Czarish … retinue] Peter the Great had visited London in the mid 1690s.

69 *non compos*] not in his right mind

70 her year] conventional period of mourning after the death of an husband

71 Egyptian plagues] those visited on Egypt by Moses (Exodus 7-11)

72 incessantly] immediately

MILLAMANT.
If you disoblige him, he may resent your refusal and insist upon the contract still. Then, 'tis the last time he will be offensive to you.
LADY WISHFORT.
Are you sure it will be the last time? If I were sure of that—shall I never see him again?
MILLAMANT.
Sir Wilfull, you and he are to travel together, are you not?
SIR WILFULL.
'Sheart,* the gentleman's a civil gentleman. Aunt, let him come in. Why, we are sworn brothers and fellow travelers. We are to be Pylades and Orestes,[73] he and I; he is to be my interpreter in foreign parts. He has been overseas once already and, with proviso that I marry my cousin, will cross 'em once again only to bear me company. 'Sheart, I'll call him in. An* I set on't once, he shall come in, and see who'll hinder him. (*Exit.*)
MRS. MARWOOD. [*Aside.*]
This is precious fooling, if it would pass, but I'll know the bottom of it.
LADY WISHFORT.
Oh dear Marwood, you are not going?
MRS. MARWOOD.
Not far madam; I'll return immediately. (*Exit.*)

Reenter Sir Wilfull and Mirabell.

SIR WILFULL.
Look up man, I'll stand by you; 'sbud,* an* she do frown, she can't kill you. Besides, hearkee, she dare not frown desperately, because her face is none of her own. 'Sheart, an she should, her forehead would wrinkle like the coat of a cream cheese, but mum for that, fellow traveler.
MIRABELL.
If a deep sense of the many injuries I have offered to so good a lady, with a sincere remorse and a hearty contrition, can but obtain the least glance of compassion, I am too happy. Ah madam, there was a time—but let it be forgotten. I confess I have deservedly forfeited the high place I once held of sighing at your feet. Nay, kill me not by turning from me in disdain. I come not to plead for favor, nay not for pardon; I am a suppliant only for your pity. I am going where I never shall behold you more—
SIR WILFULL.
How, fellow traveler! You shall go by yourself, then.
MIRABELL.
Let me be pitied first and afterwards forgotten. I ask no more.
SIR WILFULL.
By'r lady, a very reasonable request and will cost you nothing, Aunt. Come, come, forgive and forget, Aunt. Why, you must an* you are a Christian.
MIRABELL.
Consider madam, in reality you could not receive much prejudice. It was an innocent device; though I confess it had a face of guiltiness, it was at most an artifice which love contrived, and errors which love produces have ever been accounted venial. At least think it is punishment enough that I have lost what in my heart I hold most dear; that to your cruel indignation I have offered up this beauty and with her my peace and quiet, nay, all my hopes of future comfort.
SIR WILFULL.
An* he does not move me, would I might never be o'the quorum.[74] An* it were not as good a deed as to drink to give her to him again, I would I might never take shipping. Aunt, if you don't forgive quickly, I shall melt, I can tell you that. My contract went no further than a little mouth glue, and that's hardly dry. One doleful sigh more from my fellow traveller and 'tis dissolved.
LADY WISHFORT.
Well Nephew, upon your account—ah, he has a false insinuating tongue.—Well sir, I will stifle my just resentment at my nephew's request. I will endeavor what I can to forget but on proviso that you resign the contract with my niece immediately.
MIRABELL.
It is in writing and with papers of concern, but I have sent my servant for it, and will deliver it to you with all acknowledgments for your transcendant goodness.

---

73 Pylades and Orestes] classical emblem of friendship

74 o'the quorum] a justice of the peace or county magistrate

LADY WISHFORT. (*Apart.*)

Oh, he has witchcraft in his eyes and tongue. When I did not see him, I could have bribed a villain to his assassination, but his appearance rakes the embers which have so long lain smothered in my breast.

Enter Fainall and Mrs. Marwood.

FAINALL.

Your date of deliberation, madam, is expired. Here is the instrument. Are you prepared to sign?

LADY WISHFORT.

If I were prepared, I am not empowered. My niece exerts a lawful claim, having matched herself by my direction to Sir Wilfull.

FAINALL.

That sham is too gross to pass on me, though 'tis imposed on you, madam.

MILLAMANT.

Sir, I have given my consent.

MIRABELL.

And sir, I have resigned my pretensions.

SIR WILFULL.

And sir, I assert my right and will maintain it in defiance of you, sir, and of your instrument. S'heart,* an* you talk of an instrument, sir, I have an old fox by my thigh shall hack your instrument of ram vellum to shreds, sir. It shall not be sufficient for a mittimus or a tailor's measure.[75] Therefore, withdraw your instrument, sir, or by'r lady, I shall draw mine.

LADY WISHFORT.

Hold, Nephew, hold.

MILLAMANT.

Good Sir Wilfull, respite your valor.

FAINALL.

Indeed? Are you provided of a guard, with your single beefeater there? But I'm prepared for you and insist on my first proposal. You shall submit your own estate to my management and absolutely make over my wife's to my sole use, as pursuant to the purport and tenor of this other covenant.— I suppose, madam, your consent is not requisite in this case, nor, Mr. Mirabell, your resignation, nor, Sir Wilfull, your right. You may draw your fox if you please, sir, and make a Bear Garden* flourish somewhere else, for here it will not avail. This, my Lady Wishfort, must be subscribed, or your darling daughter's turned adrift like a leaky hulk to sink or swim as she and the current of this lewd Town can agree.

LADY WISHFORT.

Is there no means, no remedy, to stop my ruin? Ungrateful wretch! Dost thou not owe thy being, thy subsistence to my daughter's fortune?

FAINALL.

I'll answer you when I have the rest of it in my possession.

MIRABELL.

But that you would not accept of a remedy from my hands— I own I have not deserved you should owe any obligation to me, or else perhaps I could advise—

LADY WISHFORT.

Oh what? What? To save me and my child from ruin, from want,* I'll forgive all that's past. Nay, I'll consent to anything to come, to be delivered from this tyranny.

MIRABELL.

Aye madam, but that is too late: my reward is intercepted. You have disposed of her who only could have made me a compensation for all my services. But be it as it may, I am resolved I'll serve you. You shall not be wronged in this savage manner.

LADY WISHFORT.

How! Dear Mr. Mirabell, can you be so generous at last? But it is not possible. Hearkee, I'll break my nephew's match: you shall have my niece yet and all her fortune, if you can but save me from this imminent danger.

MIRABELL.

Will you? I take you at your word. I ask no more. I must have leave for two criminals to appear.

LADY WISHFORT.

Aye, aye, anybody, anybody.

MIRABELL.

Foible is one, and a penitent.

Enter Mrs. Fainall, Foible, and Mincing. Mirabell and Lady Wishfort go to Mrs. Fainall and Foible.

[75] tailor's measure] tape measure, often made from a strip of parchment

MRS. MARWOOD. (*To Fainall.*)

Oh my shame! These corrupt things are bought and brought hither to expose me.

FAINALL.

If it must all come out, why, let 'em know it. 'Tis but the way of the world. That shall not urge me to relinquish or abate one tittle of my terms. No, I will insist the more.

FOIBLE.

Yes indeed madam, I'll take my Bible oath of it.

MINCING.

And so will I, mem.

LADY WISHFORT.

Oh Marwood, Marwood, art thou false? My friend deceive me? Hast thou been a wicked accomplice with that profligate man?

MRS. MARWOOD.

Have you so much ingratitude and injustice to give credit against your friend to the aspersions of two such mercenary trulls?

MINCING.

Mercenary, mem? I scorn your words. 'Tis true we found you and Mr. Fainall in the blue garret. By the same token, you swore us to secrecy upon Messalina's poems. Mercenary? No, if we would have been mercenary, we should have held our tongues. You would have bribed us sufficiently.

FAINALL.

Go, you are an insignificant thing. Well, what are you the better for this? Is this Mr. Mirabell's expedient? I'll be put off no longer. You thing that was a wife shall smart for this. I will not leave thee wherewithal to hide thy shame; your body shall be naked as your reputation.

MRS. FAINALL.

I despise you and defy your malice. You have aspersed me wrongfully. I have proved your falsehood. Go you and your treacherous—I will not name it—but starve together, perish.

FAINALL.

Not while you are worth a groat, indeed, my dear.—Madam, I'll be fooled no longer.

LADY WISHFORT.

Ah Mr. Mirabell, this is small comfort, the detection of this affair.

MIRABELL.

Oh in good time. Your leave for the other offender and penitent to appear, madam.

Enter Waitwell with a box of writings.

LADY WISHFORT.

Oh Sir Rowland— Well, rascal?

WAITWELL.

What your ladyship pleases. I have brought the black box at last, madam.

MIRABELL.

Give it me.—Madam, you remember your promise?

LADY WISHFORT.

Aye, dear sir!

MIRABELL.

Where are the gentlemen?

WAITWELL.

At hand, sir, rubbing their eyes, just risen from sleep.

FAINALL.

S'death,* what's this to me? I'll not wait your private concerns.

Enter Petulant and Witwoud.

PETULANT.

How now? What's the matter? Whose hand's out?

WITWOUD.

Hey day! What, are you all got together like players at the end of the last act?

MIRABELL.

You may remember, gentlemen, I once requested your hands as witnesses to a certain parchment.

WITWOUD.

Aye, I do, my hand I remember. Petulant set his mark.

MIRABELL.

You wrong him; his name is fairly written, as shall appear. (*Undoing the box.*) You do not remember, gentlemen, anything of what that parchment contained?

WITWOUD.

No.

PETULANT.

Not I. I writ. I read nothing.

MIRABELL.

Very well, now you shall know.—Madam, your promise.

LADY WISHFORT.

Aye, aye, sir, upon my honor.

MIRABELL.

Mr. Fainall, it is now time that you should know that your lady, while she was at her own disposal and before you had by your insinuations wheedled her out of a pretended settlement of the greatest part of her fortune—

FAINALL.

Sir! Pretended?

MIRABELL.

Yes sir. I say that this lady, while a widow, having, it seems, received some cautions respecting your inconstancy and tyranny of temper, which from her own partial opinion and fondness of you she could never have suspected, she did, I say, by the wholesome advice of friends and of sages learned in the laws of this land, deliver this same as her act and deed to me in trust and to the uses within mentioned. (*Holding out the parchment.*) You may read if you please, though perhaps what is inscribed on the back may serve your occasions.

FAINALL.

Very likely sir. What's here? Damnation! (*Reads.*) "A deed of conveyance of the whole estate real of Arabella Languish, widow, in trust to Edward Mirabell." Confusion!

MIRABELL.

Even so, sir, 'tis the way of the world, sir, of the widows of the world. I suppose this deed may bear an elder date than what you have obtained from your lady.

FAINALL.

Perfidious fiend! Then thus I'll be revenged—(*Offers* to run at Mrs. Fainall.*)

SIR WILFULL.

Hold sir. Now you may make your Bear Garden flourish somewhere else, sir.

FAINALL.

Mirabell, you shall hear of this, sir, be sure you shall.—Let me pass, oaf. (*Exit.*)

MRS. FAINALL.

Madam, you seem to stifle your resentment. You had better give it vent.

MRS. MARWOOD.

Yes, it shall have vent—and to your confusion, or I'll perish in the attempt. (*Exit.*)

LADY WISHFORT.

Oh daughter, daughter, 'tis plain thou hast inherited thy mother's prudence.

MRS. FAINALL.

Thank Mr. Mirabell, a cautious friend, to whose advice all is owing.

LADY WISHFORT.

Well Mr. Mirabell, you have kept your promise, and I must perform mine. First, I pardon for your sake Sir Rowland there and Foible. The next thing is to break the matter to my nephew. And how to do that—

MIRABELL.

For that, madam, give yourself no trouble. Let me have your consent. Sir Wilfull is my friend; he has had compassion upon lovers and generously engaged a volunteer in this action for our service and now designs to prosecute his travels.

SIR WILFULL.

S'heart,* Aunt, I have no mind to marry. My cousin's a fine lady, and the gentleman loves her and she loves him, and they deserve one another. My resolution is to see foreign parts. I have set on't, and when I'm set on't, I must do't. And if these two gentlemen would travel too, I think they may be spared.

PETULANT.

For my part, I say little. I think things are best off or on.

WITWOUD.

Egad, I understand nothing of the matter. I'm in a maze yet, like a dog in a dancing school.

LADY WISHFORT.

Well sir, take her, and with her all the joy I can give you.

MILLAMANT.

Why does not the man take me? Would you have me give myself to you over again?

MIRABELL. (*Kisses her hand.*)

Aye, and over and over again, for I would have you as often as possibly I can. Well, Heaven grant I love you not too well; that's all my fear.

SIR WILFULL.

S'heart, you'll have him time enough to toy after

you're married, or if you will, toy now. Let us have a dance in the meantime, that we who are not lovers may have some other employment besides looking on.

MIRABELL.

With all my heart, dear Sir Wilfull. What shall we do for music?

FOIBLE.

Oh sir, some that were provided for Sir Rowland's entertainment are yet within call.

A dance.

LADY WISHFORT.

As I am a person, I can hold out no longer. I have wasted my spirits so today already, that I am ready to sink under the fatigue, and I cannot but have some fears upon me yet that my son Fainall will pursue some desperate course.

MIRABELL.

Madam, disquiet not yourself on that account. To my knowledge his circumstances are such he must of force comply. For my part, I will contribute all that in me lies to a reunion. (*To Mrs. Fainall.*) In the meantime, madam, let me before these witnesses restore to you this deed of trust. It may be a means, well managed, to make you live easily together.

From hence let those be warned who mean to wed,
Lest mutual falsehood stain the bridal bed,
For each deceiver to his cost may find
That marriage frauds too oft are paid in kind.

Exeunt omnes.

FINIS.

Textual Notes

[a] Copytext is the first edition, a 1700 quarto (Q1). Also consulted, the second quarto of 1706 (Q2) and editions of the collected works in 1710 (W1) and 1719 (W2); the definitive modern edition of 1967 (Davis). The omitting of certain phrases, marked below, indicate a tidying up of indecorums as the Revolutionary reform movement wore on.

[b] I fancy ... prose] Q1, Davis; *om.* Q2, Ww

[c] Well ... away] Q1, Davis; *om.* Q2, Ww

[d] Nothing ... decorums] Q1, Davis; *om.* Q2, Ww

[e] and ... fortune] Q1, Davis; *om.* Q2, Ww

[f] She ... pocket] Q1, Davis; *om.* Q2, Ww

[g] a trial] Q2, W1, W2, Davis; by a trial Q1

[h] or ... peas] Q1, Davis; *om.* Q2, Ww

Love at a Loss; or, Most Votes Carry It[a]

by Catharine Trotter (1679—1749)

edited by Roxanne M. Kent-Drury

Catharine Trotter's career as a playwright began in 1696 when she was only seventeen and ended in 1708, when she married Patrick Cockburn, a Scottish clergyman. She was best known by contemporaries as a writer of moral tragedies and philosophical essays, for which she earned the respect and friendship of such important figures as playwrights William Wycherley and William Congreve and philosophers John Locke and Gottfried Wilhelm Leibnitz. Her social comedy *Love at a Loss; or, Most Votes Carry It* premiered at Drury Lane Theater on 23 November 1700, the only performance listed in *The London Stage.* Trotter later updated the play as *The Honourable Deceivers; or, All Right at the Last,* though no copy of the later version survives.

Although it was not a successful play when performed, *Love at a Loss* is important today for its uncharacteristic exploration of social comedy's familiar marriage plot from the perspective of the play's female characters. Like most contemporary social comedy, *Love at a Loss* examines the interactions of betrothed couples as they encounter and resolve impediments to marriage. Trotter does use several conventional plot devices, such as intercepted letters, overheard conversations, and the intervention of witty servants to resolve conflicts. Many of the central characters are also stock types and were played by actors Drury Lane audiences expected to see in those roles. Beaumine was acted by Robert Wilks, who usually played fine gentlemen. Cleon, a "vain and affected fellow," was played by the famous actor Colley Cibber, who often portrayed fops. The role of Bonsot, the play's most foolish character, may have been written for William Pinkethman, who was notorious for his clowning and impromptu adlibbing to the audience. Anne Oldfield, who as one of the theater's most famous actresses later portrayed sophisticated heroines opposite Wilks, was only beginning her career when cast as Lucilia.

Despite its reliance on stock characters and plot devices, however, *Love at a Loss* avoids the usual trajectory of social comedy, which tacitly approves both trickster men who marry for land and money and the women who marry them over the objections of their obstructing guardians. Although they are mentioned, marriage settlements are of secondary importance to issues of affection and choice, and the only obstructing guardian is the one Beaumine fabricates to postpone his marriage to Lesbia. Instead, the play analyzes the institution of marriage itself and the infrequency of happy marriage, especially for women. Even though Miranda loves Constant, she puts off their marriage and flirts with Beaumine because she equates marriage to subjection and tyranny. The libertine Beaumine avoids marrying his Lesbia, whom he has seduced, because marriage to him involves loss of freedom and novelty. Although the play ends predictably with a series of marriages, Lesbia's lack of agency is demonstrated when her future partner is chosen, not by her, but by a vote of the other characters. Lesbia complacently accepts the result because honor demands that she fulfill her contractual obligations to Beaumine, even though she loves Grandfoy and faces the probability of an unhappy marriage to a philanderer who has already tired of the relationship. The result is a play that upsets the conventional endings of social comedy, thereby offering a critique of the institutional basis of marriage and its restrictive effects on women. In this sense, it contrasts sharply with many of the social comedies written by Trotter's contemporaries.

[I.i]

DRAMATIS PERSONAE

MEN

Beaumine, a gay, roving spark.
Phillabell, in love with Lucilia.
Constant, contracted to Miranda.
Grandfoy, in love with Lesbia.
Cleon, a vain, affected fellow.
Bonsot, a good-natured, officious fool.

WOMEN

Lesbia, contracted to Beaumine.
Miranda, a gay coquette.
[Her woman.*]
Lucilia, in love with Phillabell.
Lysetta, her governess.
[Young woman, servant of Lucilia's, niece to Lysetta.]
Servants.

Love at a Loss; or, Most Votes Carry It.

Act I, scene i. [Lucilia's lodging.]

Enter Lucilia and Lysetta.

LUCILIA.

Does the fool think to threaten me into love? Hearts must be won a softer way.

LYSETTA.

Aye madam, but our fear often does the men's business as well as our inclinations. More women have sacrificed their virtue to reputation than ever love has ruined, and if they can but make us kind,* what need they care why we are so?

LUCILIA.

Cleon seems indeed to be of that opinion.

LYSETTA.

Every man is that would be master of his pleasure.

LUCILIA.

Phillabell has told me a thousand times he should not think me his unless my inclination gave me to him.

LYSETTA.

Because he finds that his best friend. If he would refuse you from any other, it does not much recommend his love.

LUCILIA.

That's your notion, but ever since I have begun to know myself, your maxims are not oracles with me. You shall no more debauch my reason.

LYSETTA.

Why madam, what false maxims did I ever give you?

LUCILIA.

Should you not have warned me of the deceit and treachery of men? Instead of that, what did you entertain me with but tales of happy or unhappy lovers? All to insinuate the violence of Cleon's passion. How did you represent him to my vanity, adoring, dying for me. I thought it a fine thing to be courted in rhymes and ecstasies, though even in that distinguishing age he never pleased me, which you knew, and therefore to move my pity, made my credulous ignorance believe that if I would not give him some hopes, he must infallibly die for me. The poor innocent thought she was obliged in conscience to save a man's life!

LYSETTA.

Lord madam, what ado is here about nothing! Where was the harm of writing a few kind letters to a man? Is there ever a lady in Paris that has not done more for half a dozen before she can resolve to marry one? And a wise husband would no more repine at that than he would that his clothes does not come directly to him from the weavers. All the little gallantries do but fashion her for his wearing.

LUCILIA.

Phillabell loves too nicely* not to grudge the least kind thought for any other man, and should this Cleon expose your letters (for so I must call 'em, since I was but the scribe of what you dictated), I'm utterly undone, my reputation ruined, and what is worse, Phillabell lost forever.

LYSETTA.

That would be a base balk to a young lady just upon the point of yielding to her wishes. Tomorrow is to be the happy day.

LUCILIA.

Was to be, but Cleon's resolute to hinder it. Can you invent a way to countermine him? You have been cunning to undo me. Employ your art for once to save me.

LYSETTA.

Madam, whatever the event has been, my aim was never to undo, but serve you. If I had known that you could never have loved Cleon or foreseen your passion for Phillabell, I had not engaged you so far, but since 'tis past recalling, we should only think of preventing future mischiefs. But all my counsels will be suspected.

LUCILIA.

Indeed I believe you wish me well. Prithee advise me.

LYSETTA.

You must by no means undeceive Cleon till you are married. Persuade him that you love him still and only marry Phillabell in obedience to your father. Give him some hopes of making him happy afterwards.

LUCILIA.

Well, and what will this do?

LYSETTA.

Do? Is there any man that would not rather have another man's wife than make her his own? 'Twill do all that you would have it, make him as eager for the match as you are yourself, instead of preventing it, as his letter threatens.

LUCILIA.

But can I endure he should imagine I would wrong Phillabell so basely?

LYSETTA.

What are you the worse for his imaginations? Besides, you can easily dispossess him of 'em when you have once secured your husband.

LUCILIA.

Methinks 'tis so dishonorable a deceit I can't relish it.

LYSETTA.

Nay, if you scruple the cheat, you may keep your word with him.

LUCILIA.

Prithee be serious.

LYSETTA.

Well madam, this is certain: unless you give him hopes false or true, he will not fail to expose all your letters to Phillabell. I need not make you apprehend the consequence.

LUCILIA.

'Tis such a fatal one, I would not at any rate[1] prevent it. But you know he's not allowed to visit me. 'Tis impossible for me to see him today in private, and to write a letter after the manner proposed, you would be putting it more in his power to ruin me than I have ever done before.

LYSETTA.

Aye, but at the same time you give him the power, you show him that 'tis against his own interest to use it. And when you are once believed (which his vanity will help you in) and have gained a little time, twenty wiles may be thought of to get the letters out of his hands.

LUCILIA.

My case is desperate, and therefore the remedy must be so. Once more I will be governed by you. He sends me word he shall be in the walks this evening. You shall carry the letter thither to him.

Enter Lesbia.

LESBIA.

'Tis seasonable to wish you joy today, Lucilia; tomorrow Phillabell will give it you, and then my wishes would be needless.

LUCILIA.

He is indeed a man to make a woman happy.

LESBIA.

Ha, ha, ha! Are you practising the decent gravities of a bride against tomorrow? Prithee, away with that sullen look, or I shall think you are angry with this impertinent day for stepping between you and the wedding one.

LUCILIA.

You are not so much in haste I find. But my dear, what if you should marry Beaumine tomorrow? 'Twould be friendly to keep me in countenance.

LESBIA.

No, no, I won't lose the pleasure of making observations upon you.

LUCILIA.

But tell me seriously why you delay your marriage so long.

LESBIA.

Faugh, I came to divert myself with talking of your wedding, and you would make me dull with the thoughts of my own.

LUCILIA.

Believe me, Lesbia, if I did not love you, I would

[1] not at any rate] the negative is an intensifier: at any cost whatsoever

not urge you farther, but I am vexed to hear some malicious reflections that are whispered of you and must ask you why you give the occasion.

LESBIA.
Some fitter time I'll tell you.

LUCILIA.
Lysetta, we would be private.

Exit Lysetta.

Now be free with me.

LESBIA.
Well, if I must lay aside my mirth awhile to tell you a sad tale: you have often heard me speak of one Grandfoy, whom I loved before I knew Beaumine.

LUCILIA.
You have told me he was false.

LESBIA.
I thought him so, but he has since convinced me that I wronged him, though my suspicions were, you know, well grounded. He's still the man which he appeared at first, all truth and goodness, and loves me more than I can now deserve.

LUCILIA.
I shall think you deserve a great deal of him, an* if you decline so considerable a match as Beaumine for his sake.

LESBIA.
When you know my story, I fear you'll say he ought to despise me.

LUCILIA.
That's impossible, but pray, my dear, go on.

LESBIA.
Just in the height of my resentment against Grandfoy, Beaumine first saw and loved me. He addressed to my mother, who easily gave her consent, his fortune being very considerable. To be short, her commands were sacred to me, and I believed it would be some revenge upon Grandfoy, which was the chief motive of my resolving to marry Beaumine. He proposed to have it secret whilst his mother lived, because she designed him for another. No priest would marry us without her consent.[2] He told me then it was the tie of hearts that made a marriage, but fearing mine should change, to make me sure, he writ a contract, which we both signed with our blood. And to confirm it, he led me to the holy altar, where he vowed to take me for his wife—I don't know how to tell you the rest.

LUCILIA.
You e'en took him for a husband,[3] is it not so?

LESBIA.
He often importuned me to live with him as such and at my refusal lost all the natural gaiety of his temper and much avoided seeing me. My mother dying, he came to condole with me. I saw myself unguarded, and willing to engage him in my interests, I flattered him with all the artful tenderness I could affect. This made him press me more eagerly than ever. Agreeable as he is, I never loved him much, and yet I don't know how he found the yielding minute. Betwixt you and I, Lucilia, is not there one of which we are not master?

LUCILIA.
I will believe so for your sake, though I think it would be always in my power to refuse a man anything that is not fit for him to ask. But how did Beaumine behave himself afterwards?

LESBIA.
Very fond at first, but now grows careless and sometimes insolent. Still* he let me hope that he would marry me after his mother's death, which satisfied till Grandfoy assured me she died just after mine, though he conceals it from me.

LUCILIA.
That does not look as if he meant you fairly, but your contract will oblige him to do you justice.

LESBIA.
If it could, I would not marry him against his inclination.

LUCILIA.
What do you resolve on then?

---

[2] No … consent] Beaumine may have been underage (21) and therefore, according to the canons of 1604, could not marry legally without parental consent.

[3] You … husband] They were solemnly betrothed, pre-contracted. At this time, such promises were binding and, even though absent church ceremony with a priest, sufficient to constitute an actual marriage under the law if the marriage was subsequently consummated.

LESBIA.

I must first know certainly what he intends.

LUCILIA.

His intentions seem so indifferent to you, that I must believe yours are more for Grandfoy.

LESBIA.

Indeed he shows so generous an affection for me, it claims all my gratitude. And since I find my suspicions of him were unjust, did not my honor oppose it, I confess I could love him more than ever.

LUCILIA.

Does he know of your affair with Beaumine?

LESBIA.

He does and made me promise that, if upon the trial I found Beaumine unfaithful, I would be governed by him. To confirm my word I gave him a ring, which was Beaumine's first gift to me. You have seen me wear it.

LUCILIA.

Did not Beaumine miss it?

LESBIA.

I told him I had lost it, which he easily believed, not having ever heard that I loved another, and I have taken care as far as art would go to persuade him that I love him, for that I thought both my interest and duty.

LUCILIA.

I wish you may not find yourself abused. The world is much mistaken in him if he has any thoughts of marriage but to rail or make his jest of it.

LESBIA.

A man of this age must no more speak well of it than of religion, and yet perhaps there are as few marriage haters as atheists.

LUCILIA.

What then can put the men upon professing it? One would think it can be neither much for their honor or interest.

LESBIA.

At first to gain the reputation of wit by affecting a singularity in their notions. And since that by imitation or humor* they are become the common topics of raillery, many take up with it for want* of resolution to bear with their being the ridicule of their companions.

LUCILIA.

And is this your opinion of Beaumine?

LESBIA.

I believe there's more humor* and affectation than any serious reflection in it and have less reason to fear his love of liberty than some other chains.

LUCILIA.

Why, are you jealous of him?

LESBIA.

Only of his rambling temper; he takes care to give me no particular aim.

LUCILIA.

He seems indeed to make love* to every woman and mean it to none.

LESBIA.

Miranda and he were mightily pleased with one another t'other day. She happened to come in when he was with me. She gave him leave to visit her and talks of him perpetually ever since. He does not seem to think much of her, or I should apprehend her a dangerous rival, she's so much of his own humor.*

LUCILIA.

But she's engaged to another too.

LESBIA.

Aye, and says she loves him.

LUCILIA.

'Tis strange she should; there can't be two more opposite tempers than Constant's and hers.

LESBIA.

And what pleasure she takes in teasing and tormenting his gravity.

LUCILIA.

And in pleasing every man else.

LESBIA.

Well, coquette as she is, I should not be pleased to have Beaumine pursue the acquaintance.

LUCILIA.

Then he has not made her a visit yet.

LESBIA.

He does not own it to me.

LUCILIA.

I shall see her today, and if I hear anything of him, you shall be sure to know it, for if he is not sincere, the sooner you are undeceived, the better. My dear, will you go to my closet* with me? I have a letter to write in haste. 'Twill be quickly done; you'll excuse me for a minute.

LESBIA.
I expect to see Grandfoy immediately and must take my leave of you.
LUCILIA.
May all you undertake succeed to your own wishes.
LESBIA.
I scarce know what I wish, only all happiness to you.

Exeunt severally.

Scene [ii]. Phillabell's lodgings.

Enter Beaumine and a servant.

BEAUMINE.
Is your master busy?
SERVANT.
He'll be at leisure to see you, sir, I am sure.
BEAUMINE.
Tell him I'm here.

Exit servant.

Egad, I pity this poor fellow. He might have been a fit companion for us men of spirit and pleasure but for this damned, dull matrimony.

Enter Phillabell.

PHILLABELL.
Beaumine! What sudden dearth of wine or kind women has reduced thee to thinking?
BEAUMINE.
Only a sense of my friend's misfortune. I came to condole with you. Faith Phillabell, I am heartily sorry for thee.
PHILLABELL.
For me! Why, what's the matter? I know no cause you have. I was never so satisfied, so easy, so full of joy, as in this minute.
BEAUMINE.
Why, is your marriage broke off?
PHILLABELL.
Broke! Heaven forbid! You would have reason to condole with me then indeed.
BEAUMINE.
And are you certainly to be married tomorrow?
PHILLABELL.
I hope so.
BEAUMINE.
Strange! But he's mad, poor man.
PHILLABELL.
Why, did you hear anything to the contrary?
BEAUMINE.
No, and therefore am amazed to hear such agreeable words—satisfied, easy, full of joy—out of the mouth of a condemned man, if thou art in thy senses.
PHILLABELL.
Oh, a satire upon marriage. Is that your intent?
BEAUMINE.
Faith, I would willingly reclaim thee if thou art not too far gone to hear reason.
PHILLABELL.
I could never find any reason why a man should be uneasy in the possession of a woman that he loves only because he enjoys her without breaking human or divine laws.
BEAUMINE.
What are laws but chains to our wills, our inclinations? Destroyers of liberty, the dear prerogative of Nature.
PHILLABELL.
But libertinism is not a privilege to be very fond of, and that's all we are denied.
BEAUMINE.
'Tis better to be lost with pleasure than preserved in pain.
PHILLABELL.
The pain of being always my Lucilia's won't much employ my philosophy to support it.
BEAUMINE.
And are you sure you will be always of this mind? Do you imagine she will be always young, always handsome, and that you shall always love her?
PHILLABELL.
I am sure she will always have wit, good humor, and virtue and, by consequence, that I shall always love her.
BEAUMINE.
But what if all that you call good humor should prove affectation, nothing else, and virtue but the art of well dissembling?
PHILLABELL.
To dissemble well is virtue, or what we can't distinguish from it.
BEAUMINE.
Aye, aye, but the disguise is always laid aside when

there's no farther need of it. When you are entered into bonds, 'twon't be worth her pains; the fear of losing a lover only can make 'em careful to please. If you but saw the fond, endearing Lesbia, what arts she uses to engage me, how well she thinks 'em all returned by one kind word or look, and then the tender niceness of her passion: she lost a ring the other day which I had given her. Never was anything so moving as her complaints; I told her she should have one twice the value, but that would not appease her. She said 'twas the first present I had made her, and she feared the loss, a sad presage that she should lose my heart. Nothing could comfort her but my repeated vows of never changing. Are there such tender sentiments in marriage? You'll find a cold civility the best part of their entertainment after a month's enjoyment.

PHILLABELL.

I should expect no better if I had chose an unthinking coquette or one whose broken fortune might make her snatch at the first hope of repairing it, but Lucilia is reserved and prudent. Her fortune equals mine, she has refused many considerable matches, and I have reason to think myself the only man that has found the way to her heart. I know she hates Cleon and treats with scorn or coldness the rest that languish for her. In fine, I have all the security for a lasting love and happiness that reason can desire or give.

BEAUMINE.

Lasting! Why, thou hast named the very bane of love and happiness. What that's old can charm to ecstasy? Or not be dull with being oft repeated?

PHILLABELL.

And what that's new can be relied upon? Or how can you enjoy a happiness that you are always in danger of losing?

BEAUMINE.

Relied on? Oh most firmly, Phil. (*Sings.*) "They still* are constant whilst possessed and can do more for no man——"[4] And faith, fickle as they are, they must be plaguey quick to make me complain of losing them. But if any of 'em should run out of my arms to another's (for then she is sure to have the start of me), I have always one in hand that supplies the vacancy.

PHILLABELL.

Nay, that's the way indeed not to be much grieved at their loss, for betwixt two, you can't be very fond of either.

BEAUMINE.

You're mistaken man; it makes me very fond of both. If they knew nature, a woman would never fear losing a man so much as when the coyness* or jealousy of one has vexed him. He flies to another that with kindness* restores his good humor, and when her over-fondness has cloyed him, he returns to the first for fresh appetite, for by one of these extremes the women always lose us. They are either so capricious, they grow troublesome, or so tender, they grow dull. But tempered thus, they give the relish to each other.

PHILLABELL.

If you could convince the women of this doctrine, you might both have your ends by it. But whilst they are of another opinion, whatever advantage it may be to them you'll hardly find your account in it. He that pursues two hares will catch neither.

BEAUMINE.

Still he has the greater pleasure in the chase, to observe their different crossings, windings, and little arts. Sometimes their very fear, you know, makes 'em run full into the hound's mouth. But if you do not give over too soon, there's none of them but may be wearied out. Then seize the panting quarry, and she's yours.

PHILLABELL.

Well, give me the woman that resigns herself upon deliberation and solid reason that, as it makes the gift more valuable, so more secure.

BEAUMINE.

That is, more insipid.

PHILLABELL.

There's no disputing tastes. The very trouble of continual fresh pursuits would make variety disgustful to me.

BEAUMINE.

Which gives me the highest relish. But I need not endeavor to convince thee; thy wife will do it

---

4 "They … man—"] unidentified, as are most of the song snatches

effectually, since thou art resolved to purchase wisdom at the dearest rate, experience. What a lamentable figure thou'lt make, preaching it to others, as a fellow at the gallows does honesty when 'tis too late to make use of it himself. But I'll leave you to prepare for your solid blessing. Will you meet me in the walk this evening?

PHILLABELL.
If I have nothing else to do, perhaps I may.

BEAUMINE.
Egad, I beg thy pardon. I forgot thou'rt a man of business.[5] Honest matrimony. Adieu.

PHILLABELL.
Well, well, laugh on. I am contented you should have your jest, so I secure my happiness,
With a chaste wife, like my Lucilia, true.

BEAUMINE.
I, with a mistress, ever gay and new.

Exeunt severally.

Act II, scene [i]. Lesbia's lodgings.

Enter Lesbia and Grandfoy.

GRANDFOY.
I would not appear in your defense till you have tried Beaumine to the utmost, that he may have no pretence against you.

LESBIA.
I never gave him any yet, nor can he find an excuse now for deferring our marriage, since the only obstacle he pretended is removed by his mother's death.

GRANDFOY.
But I advise you not to take notice of your knowing it nor show any distrust of him. If he has the least honor, the confidence you seem to have in him will be a stronger[b] engagement.

LESBIA.
But should he still refuse me?

GRANDFOY.
You promise then to be disposed by me; I wear the pledge of your fidelity.

LESBIA.
Won't it be a bold venture to put myself in the power of a man I have injured?

GRANDFOY.
Unless in your unjust suspicions of me, you only have been injured. Your misfortune with Beaumine has a thousand excuses on your part, as unhappy as it makes me. Oh Lesbia, that I should ever think it reasonable to wish you another's! To force a man to deprive me of all I value!

LESBIA.
'Tis scarce reasonable indeed to value me now so much as to care whose I am.

GRANDFOY.
I have such an opinion of your sincerity and virtue that even now, would you consent to be mine, I should receive you as the greatest earthly blessing, but that you have refused me unless Beaumine, by a declared infidelity, entirely release you.

LESBIA.
Imagine with what difficulty I do it whilst I receive such proofs of love from you, whom I have had too much kindness for ever to be indifferent to or equally to value any other.

GRANDFOY.
Curse on that fate that forced me from you so abruptly to make me lose that kindness by seeming false then when I loved you most, and ever must, though now your heart's another's.

LESBIA.
I fear, Grandfoy, you are still but too dear to it.

GRANDFOY.
Yet you refuse the offer I have made to marry you.

LESBIA.
'Tis the only return I can make to so generous an offer. If my own honor did not oblige me to it, I owe it to your love and good opinion, for 'tis the only way I can deserve 'em.

GRANDFOY.
How little does Beaumine deserve this treasure that values it so lightly! I must approve the virtue that undoes me. And to preserve it as free from suspicion as it is of guilt, I'll leave you, since you expect Beaumine. For your sake I would not have him know me, unless he force me to revenge your wrongs.

LESBIA.
You are in all things noble.

GRANDFOY.
If you are for the walks this evening, I shall see you

[5] man of business] like a cit*

again. Cleon sent this morning to desire I would meet him there. He has something to ask my advice in, I suppose some love adventure, for that's his only business.

LESBIA.

His only discourse indeed, but the great talkers of intrigues, as of religion, have usually the least of either. And indeed, whatever a man studiously affects to seem, 'tis a shrewd sign he's conscious of not being it in reality.

GRANDFOY.

But the reality of intrigues are generally private and only to be known by talking of 'em, which, believe me, is the chief part of the pleasure of many of our sex.

LESBIA.

I fancy only to those that are allowed no other part, but they who are truly well received among us, if not in gratitude to those who have obliged 'em, will be cautious to secure their designs upon others. Love is not to be raised like valor, by emulation.

GRANDFOY.

I don't know what it may do towards kindling a flame, but I am sure 'twill increase it. Many a woman from a little liking to a man has become passionately in love, only upon finding another was pleased with him.

LESBIA.

Then she must know it by her rival's indiscretion and not his vanity, for that only shows his weakness, but the other the force of his merit. But indeed, if Cleon should rely upon that, his mistress would scarce find any occasion of jealousy. His vanity appears too grossly; the good-natured fool his brother is the more supportable.

GRANDFOY.

Poor Bonsot. He always means well but unluckily makes more mischief by officiously endeavoring to prevent it and pretending to know everybody's business.

LESBIA.

Then his bulls[6] are diverting enough, they fall so naturally from him.

GRANDFOY.

As near relations, I must bear with and would hide their follies. But we shall forget ourselves, till we give Beaumine occasion of jealousy, which, though sometimes our sex find their ends in, 'tis always a dangerous expedient for yours, for what you gain in inclination, you lose in our esteem.
Fear of a rival will enflame desire,
But distrust of her soon quench the fire.

LESBIA.

That way leads to the back door. You'll be secure from meeting him.

Exit Grandfoy.

Few men would use as Grandfoy does such a confidence as I have had in him. But sure never any woman made the experiment before me. If the lover can but be kept ignorant, no matter what he discover when secured a husband—I must own those women have more courage than I. Cheating in all other cases may be only playing the knave, but any deceit in marriage must be egregiously playing the fool, when the very injury we do gives the power of revenging it.

Enter Beaumine.

BEAUMINE. [*Aside.*]

Aye, at home you're as sure of finding an old mistress as a creditor that expects you to pay him an old debt, in good humor too, I warrant.—I was afraid, madam, you had not come home yet.

LESBIA.

How could you imagine that, when I had hopes of seeing you?

BEAUMINE. [*Aside.*]

Ay, I thought so; well, this is the devil.—Faith Lesbia, I do what I can to be very fond of you, but you will take pains to hinder it. I cannot help it.

LESBIA.

I don't know that I have done anything to displease you.

BEAUMINE.

Why, there's it. You should do something to displease me:
Love is an active, restless fire
That without agitation must expire.

6 bulls] verbal blunders

LESBIA.
I thought a constant fuel of lasting worth and kindness would preserve it.

BEAUMINE.
It may keep it in, but 'twill burn very dimly without blowing, Lesbia.

LESBIA.
I wish I knew the art of doing it.

BEAUMINE.
Why, you should go abroad when you're sure I shall come to see you; look angry or cold upon me without telling me why when I would caress you; and when I expect you should be fond of me, make me suspect you are thinking of another. In short, vex, perplex, and disquiet me, that supplying me always with something to employ my thoughts on, they may have no leisure to wander.

LESBIA.
I rather take care by the regularity of my conduct to show you what you may always expect from me. For though these arts may be agreeable in a mistress, you would scarce be pleased with 'em in a wife.

BEAUMINE.
Nay, thou hast thought of a way now to put a man out of his humor with a vengeance by[c] the worst contrivance to raise an appetite you could have found out. You have all of a wife but the name. The want* of that flatters me with an imagined liberty, and you must bring it in to spoil a man's fancy.

LESBIA.
I like your raillery, Beaumine, since I don't doubt but your serious thoughts are to make me that in earnest, which the name of serves you for a jest.

BEAUMINE.
Aye, aye, there will be a time for serious thoughts, respect, and reverence, which wives should have, and that, you know, is paid to antiquity, Lesbia, but love and raptures, for the young and free.

LESBIA.
Thus I can never be satisfied or angry with this man. Is it impossible for you ever to answer seriously and directly, Beaumine?

BEAUMINE.
Why truly, if you would have my thoughts, I would counsel you against the most unaccountable extravagance you are designing.

LESBIA.
What's that?

BEAUMINE.
You have now a great deal of my love; 'tis certain marriage won't add one jot to it, and very possible it may extremely lessen it. Now would anyone in their senses that were in possession of a good estate, without any prospect of bettering it, put it to the chance of a die whether they should keep it or lose it? I am thy own, and keep me as thou hast me. (*Sings.*) "Thus ever frolic, ever gay."[7]

LESBIA.
Thou art the most agreeable, tormenting devil. But prithee, tell me what I am to expect.

BEAUMINE.
Expect! Why, that the old woman will die, and that—

LESBIA.
But will the old woman ever die, Beaumine?

BEAUMINE.
Humph! pugh, what's age and death to us, my love? They are melancholy thoughts. We've life and youth and liberty, my Lesbia. (*Sings.*) "And live a thousand years a day."

LESBIA. [*Aside.*]
Thus may this gay humor fool me on forever. I must try him farther.—Well, thou art the maddest fellow. Sure there is not your peer in France, unless Miranda. 'Tis pity Fate has not joined you. What did you think of her?

BEAUMINE.
I thought very well of her whilst I saw her but have not thought at all of her since. She's a very* coquette, pleased with every man and pleases all whilst with 'em, but no sooner out of sight than she forgets and is as easily forgot.

LESBIA.
She has not forgot you so soon, I assure you. But have not you refreshed her memory?

BEAUMINE.
Not I, upon honor.

---

7 "Ever frolic, ever gay"] probably from a drinking song; cf. Sir Fopling's song in Etherege's *Man of Mode* (IV.ii) praising champagne as that which "Makes us frolic and gay, and drowns all our sorrow."

LESBIA.
I'm glad of it.

BEAUMINE.
Why? You would not have been jealous.

LESBIA.
No, but I think 'twill be better you should not visit her at all, for I know she likes you.

BEAUMINE.
Not visit her because she likes me! Now hang me if I can find that out to be a good reason.

LESBIA.
It might be dangerous to fan a fire that's yet but kindled.

BEAUMINE.
Nay, I have no design to see her, but what whim of yours is this? She likes anything for her diversion.

LESBIA.
But talks of you in heroics.

BEAUMINE.
A new humor.

LESBIA.
And is very importunate to know if there's any amour betwixt you and me.

BEAUMINE.
Curiosity, I hope, did not satisfy her.

LESBIA.
She seemed so much concerned I could not deny her positively but betwixt raillery and earnest left her in doubt, which made her so uneasy she said she would soon see me again and hoped I would be more sincere with her.

BEAUMINE.
By no means, I charge you. Women of her humor* are always prying into the intrigues of their companions by gaining their confidence or raising their jealousy to make 'em the jest of the next company. Never trust any of your own sex, especially such a giddy thing as Miranda.

LESBIA.
Since you desire it, you may be sure I'll be cautious, though I know she was serious.

BEAUMINE.
I suppose you can't think you have any reason to fear her.

LESBIA.
If I had distrusted you, I would not have told you of such an agreeable rival, and I expect, in return of the confidence I have in you, you should avoid a woman that I believe loves you.

BEAUMINE.
Egad, a very nice* piece of honor. I must have no mind to a handsome woman because you have let me know she has a mind to me. Well, as far as flesh and blood can reach it, I'll act this romantic lover.

LESBIA.
Then you won't visit Miranda.

BEAUMINE.
No, since you would not have me, not that I think there's any danger in it, but I'm very indifferent in the matter. If she happen to fall in my way and mischief should ensue—remember you were my tempter.

LESBIA.
I dare trust you.

BEAUMINE.
Well then, to put my virtue to the proof. (*Going.*)

LESBIA.
Where are you going?

BEAUMINE.
To Miranda.

LESBIA.
Pshaw, you're always fooling, but I have business.

BEAUMINE.
So have I, but what's yours about?

LESBIA.
Our marriage.

BEAUMINE.
And mine is love. I cannot think of two things at once so directly opposite. So first for that of greatest moment. (*Going.*)

LESBIA.
But will you tell me—

BEAUMINE.
How Miranda receives me, what favors she refuses, what she grants. All, all.

LESBIA.
But Beaumine.

BEAUMINE.
But Miranda.

LESBIA.
Pugh, that's a jest.

BEAUMINE.
Then you don't believe I'm going to her.

LESBIA.

No, I'm sure you won't.

BEAUMINE. [*Aside.*]

Now the De—il take her for not being jealous, that I might have a right to deceive her, for I'm afraid I cannot forbear. But 'tis no matter; there's no truth in these cases, and since

We all are false alike in love, 'tis clear,
He that dissembles best is most sincere. (*Exit.*)

LESBIA.

Thou maggoty, barbarous, good-humored, ill-natured toad. He is gone as fleet as winds, but I as fast shall fly,

Since, whilst a stale, tried lover I pursue,
If he escape me, I secure a new.

Exit.

Scene [ii]. Miranda's lodgings.

Enter Lucilia and Miranda.

LUCILIA.

Nay I protest you're to blame, Miranda, to use a man thus that dotes upon you.

MIRANDA.

If he does not like the humor,* what makes him dote on me? We're both pleased with one another, only have different ways of showing it. He's fond of my gaiety, I laugh at his gravity. He whines, I sing. He takes care to show his fidelity, I to make him jealous. That's his way, this is mine. We take several roads, but I fear both lead to the same dreadful end. We shall e'en meet at last in matrimony, though I am for going the farthest way about.

LUCILIA.

Since you are resolved to go through the journey, 'tis the wisest way to make it as short as possible for fear you should spend too much of your stock of love or be robbed of it by another upon the road and not have enough to subsist on when your travels are over.

MIRANDA.

I'm not so extravagant in my expenses of it, and for robbers there's more danger of them in our place of rest. For though matrimony is too strong an edifice to be demolished, its guards and enclosures are weak and easily broke through. And love is a treasure not to be confined; it slips like water from the hand that would restrain it. If you would secure it, leave it loose and free.

LUCILIA.

But 'tis impossible you can love Constant and not have a mind to marry him.

MIRANDA.

Indeed I don't love him so well but that I had rather torment him than he should torment me, rather have variety of diversions lie heavy upon my hands than the affairs of my family. I like the squeaking of a fiddle better than the squalling of brats, and an obsequious humble servant better than a surly lord and master.

LUCILIA.

I fancy 'tis some other humble servant you like better; this Beaumine you were talking of runs mightily in your head.

MIRANDA.

In my head! In my heart, in my sleep. I dream of him, sigh for him, die for him. Oh 'tis the easiest, gayest, wildest, most engaging, everything that suits my humor.* I long for him again. If he likes me well enough to visit me, I shall grow so fond of him.

LUCILIA.

Why, you can't love 'em both.

MIRANDA.

I'll swear, I do extremely. I love Constant best at a distance, Beaumine when he's with me: to think of one, laugh with t'other. He diverts me, t'other improves me. One will make the better husband, t'other the more agreeable gallant.

LUCILIA.

Well, wildly as you talk, I don't doubt but you'll make a very good wife.

MIRANDA.

I don't doubt but he'll make me so, take a full revenge of my tyranny when he has got the power in his hands; therefore, I resolve to reign as long as I can.

Enter Constant.

But here comes my sovereign elect.—I thought, sir, you had business with my uncle and therefore left you without hopes of this happiness so soon.

CONSTANT.

I thought, madam, you had business, that you ran from me so abruptly when I was talking to you of what concerns me nearest, but it seems 'twas only to be rid of me. I'm sorry my company is so displeasing.

MIRANDA.

'Tis a strange lover that won't give his mistress leave to think of him; I came but to sigh for you in secret.

CONSTANT.

Sigh in secret, when we may smile together? Oh Miranda, sure you but abuse my doting heart and make my love your sport.

MIRANDA.

Why, what's love or anything else good for, unless to divert us?

CONSTANT.

I might have thought, indeed, your sprightly temper could not long brook my heavy, sullen nature, but tell me freely I am troublesome, and as I never asked your uncle his consent till you permitted me, so will I not now use his authority but leave you free to choose a humor* that may suit you better.

MIRANDA.

Don't disturb yourself about that. I shall quickly be as sullen as you when we're married, no doubt.

CONSTANT.

That would but hinder our resemblance then, for sure that happy day that calls you mine will quite dissolve the earthly part of me, refine this mass, and make me spirit all.

MIRANDA.

Leave you the ghost of your departed love
And me to mourn in tears my wretched fate:
That yours expired too soon, mine lived too late.
There's rapture for your rapture, Constant.

CONSTANT.

Well dear tormenter, don't weary out my love then ere you use it, but cherish it whilst young and vigorous, and it will be immortal.

MIRANDA.

Then I must keep it in its native air, for they say marriage is a very cold climate.

LUCILIA.

I believe indeed it kills the hottest hasty plants but preserves and often produces such solid fruits as are most fit for constant nourishment and bears sweets of its own growth too, Miranda.

MIRANDA.

Well seriously Lucilia, I have been trying this month to compose my face for the wedding day, for I fancy if one has not a most reverend countenance, one will never be thought in earnest at so unreasonable a thing as taking for better, for worse. It looks so like a jest or stark madness.

CONSTANT.

Keep your mad countenance, then, and do it in jest.

MIRANDA.

Aye, but that surly one of yours, Constant, has such a husbandly air 'twill spoil the jest. I never look upon it but I'm afraid I'm married already.

CONSTANT.

I'll endeavor to put on a more agreeable one, turn merry-andrew, anything to please you.

MIRANDA.

Then 'tis resolved we will be kings no more?

CONSTANT.

Oh when, my life? My joy, now I am gay as thou art.

MIRANDA.

Nay that has undone all again. Those laughing eyes bring to my thoughts that charming fellow that danced and sung himself into my heart; I must have some time to drive him out again, and then Constant—

CONSTANT.

Who? What is it you talk of?

MIRANDA.

Oh such a grace, such an air, such a humor;* if you knew him, you must be fond of him for love of me. He's just my counterpart.

CONSTANT. [*Aside.*]

I know she rallies, yet it tortures me.

MIRANDA.

What, in the dumps! Nay, don't be jealous.

CONSTANT.

No, no, but 'tis intolerable cruelty to make your sport of what my life depends on.

MIRANDA.

'Tis in concern for your life I would delay this marriage, for if in the height of my passion the tempter should come in my way, he makes an attack, duty opposes, inclination assists him, prohibition strengthens it, nature prevails, runs away with me, you pursue and cut his throat, I break my heart. You can do no less than stab yourself to complete the tragedy and prevent this mischief.

CONSTANT.

We'll take care to avoid the tempter.

MIRANDA.

That can't be done without having him always in my thoughts. No, no, Constant, you have a better way of curing a woman's love: being perpetually with her. And since you have found it so effectual an experiment, I'm resolved to try it upon my new inclination till he has said all the fine things he can, showed all his humors,* played over all his tricks, left nothing farther for imagination to work on, but grown as dull to me as a book I have just read.

CONSTANT.

Or as I am to you now.

MIRANDA.

Then you'll be new again, like one that has been long out of print, and I am always fond of the second edition, revised, corrected, and amended. But be sure you take care never to let me peruse it through. Reserve something for my curiosity, Constant, for you know the best books, when we have studied 'em perfectly, are thrown aside or only kept for show, and any trifling novel that we never met with before entertains us better.

CONSTANT.

Thou art never to be thoroughly known; the more I study thee, the more I am perplexed: find something clear enough to engage my search, but still too doubtful to determine on. Would you provoke me first to break a contract you repent? Or is't to try my constancy you thus torment me? Are you not satisfied? What fool but I could have endured so much? But madam, I'm not made to bear forever.

MIRANDA.

What, is it nangry[8] now? And what would it do? Can it break its cage? Flutter about, tire itself, and hurt its wings? And to what purpose?

CONSTANT.

I am thy slave, Miranda, but 'tis the more ungenerous to use a creature in thy power so inhumanly. I dote upon thee, dote on that very humor* that distracts me. Be serious once to free me from the fear of losing thee, and ever after I would have thee gay as nature formed thee.

MIRANDA.

Forever after, I am sure, be dull enough and therefore now indulge my natural gaiety. But let me see what time of the moon is it; about the full, I may be disposed.

CONSTANT.

Still in raillery. I beg thee. I conjure thee.

MIRANDA.

Well, I am good-natured, and since you are so impatient—

CONSTANT.

Oh speak.

MIRANDA.

I am resolved—

CONSTANT.

When, when, my charmer?

MIRANDA.

As soon as possible to engage my charmer, grow weary of him as fast as I can, return to you with new pleasure, then here's my hand on't.

CONSTANT.

Oh torture, torture. 'Tis too much, Miranda. You may find, fond of my prison as I am, I'm not so strongly chained as you imagine.

MIRANDA.

Alas, and will you leave me?

CONSTANT.

Well madam, you shall no more insult. (*Exit.*)

MIRANDA.

Not these two hours, I'll engage.

LUCILIA.

Nay, he can never return after this.

MIRANDA.

Only half a dozen times a day he makes and breaks these noble resolutions.

LUCILIA.

I'm sure you deserve to lose his love, and for my part, I'm amazed it has subsisted so long with such ill usage.

---

8 nangry] Rendered babytalk often adds an *n* to the beginning of a word (as in *nown**).

MIRANDA.

Oh! The men's love is not so easily starved as surfeited; 'twill live upon the lightest airy hope, though soon destroyed with fondness. We lose lovers by overcare than neglect, Lucilia.

LUCILIA.

You would make 'em very ungenerous creatures, but I believe gratitude is as strong a tie to them as to us.

MIRANDA.

Just as strong indeed, and if you would speak your heart as freely as I do, you would own we take most pains to appear agreeable to a new acquaintance, put on our best looks, show all our wit, all our good humor, everything that may engage, whilst a lover we have well enough secured not to fear losing is received and entertained as negligently as a cousin-german.

LUCILIA.

On the contrary, if I would use any arts, it should be to please a man who by proofs of a lasting affection had engaged mine, and I could never think it returned with sufficient tenderness.

MIRANDA.

Think! But I speak of what we do without thinking, the natural effect of such a composition as mankind are of. Vanity is inconstancy.

Enter Beaumine.

LUCILIA. (*Aside.*)

Of which behold the very abstract! Lesbia must know this.

MIRANDA.

This wild creature here! And who the deuce expected him.

LUCILIA.

There was no need of expectation to make the blessing dear.

MIRANDA.

Psha, because I jested. Would he were hanged for coming.

LUCILIA.

Nay, now I shall believe you love him in earnest.

MIRANDA. (*Aside.*)

I'll swear, so shall I too. I was never so confounded in my life.—Love him, aye, I love him well enough—anywhere else—but methinks here—I don't know—I wish he had not come.

LUCILIA.

Well, I'll leave you, for I believe he wishes so too, finding me here. [*Exit.*]

BEAUMINE. [*Aside.*]

A very odd reception. Maybe she does not know me again, but I'm sure Lucilia does, and this goes to Lesbia immediately. But no matter: I know how to make peace with her when I have settled my new conquest.

MIRANDA. (*Aside.*)

Wish she had not seen him here? What can that mean? Is she my rival too?

BEAUMINE.

I fear I am unwelcome, madam, though I had not ventured without your permission.

MIRANDA.

Pardon me, sir, I was persuading the lady to stay, the more to oblige you in return of this favor.

BEAUMINE.

The lady knew better how to oblige me.

MIRANDA.

I don't doubt but she knows much better how to please you.

BEAUMINE.

She has only put me in the way of being pleased. But that depends upon the fair Miranda, which if she design, she need only be herself again; indeed, that gravity is no more becoming than natural to you.

MIRANDA.

Why d'ye think I affect it?

BEAUMINE.

That I can't tell: whether you are displeased with seeing me or mightily pleased and have no mind to show it, those eyes must better inform me.

MIRANDA.

Whatever they say, I find you can make a favorable interpretation of it.

BEAUMINE.

I confess, madam, I love to be easy and to give everything the most advantageous sense it will bear. If it ben't the way to the truth, I am sure it is to happiness.

MIRANDA.

Giving yourself false hopes is the sure way to meet with disappointments.

BEAUMINE.

Not at all. Vanity gives a man confidence, and that's successful with the fair as well as the great.

MIRANDA.

Why, do you believe any woman ever loved a man because he had the vanity to fancy she did?

BEAUMINE.

At least it gives him a chance for being beloved, which he can never have without the courage to attempt. For example, madam, had I modestly said to myself, "Beaumine, thou'rt a very disagreeable fellow. Miranda can never like thee; 'tis in vain to hope it," I had certainly not come near you; you had thought of me no more; or I had lost the advantage of your thoughts, however favorable.

MIRANDA.

And you have the impudence to tell me you believe I shall like you.

BEAUMINE.

And does not every man that tells you he likes you mean the same thing? But I beg your pardon, madam, I confess 'twas very indecent, so unmodish a thing as speaking truth to a lady.

MIRANDA.

Which is so far from offending me, you could not have obliged me more than by telling me your thoughts to give me the pleasure of disappointing you. And to show you how vain, how mistaken you are, how little an opinion I have of you, I must tell you when you came in, I was thinking you the most fickle, inconstant, falsest thing in nature.

BEAUMINE.

Now cannot I help thinking you would not have troubled your head whether I was false or not, if you had not been concerned in it.

MIRANDA.

And do you imagine I can like a man I have such an opinion of?

BEAUMINE.

We are naturally fond of our own resemblance, and by that rule, to gain Miranda's good graces, I can't be too false or too *volage*.[9] (*Sings.*)

When present we'll love, when absent agree,
I think not of Iris, nor Iris of me.[10]

MIRANDA.

Nay, now you have vanquished. There's no resisting that, the very image of my own heart. I can make the exchange without missing it. But not a word of sighing, dying, fidelity, constancy, or any of that dull form, for 'twill immediately be sensible of being out of its element and return upon the wing.

BEAUMINE.

And upon peril of losing mine, let me never hear you have the least remembrance of me when I am from you; not a word of me in heroics to Lesbia.

MIRANDA.

For fear of spoiling your amour with her.

BEAUMINE.

What, jealous? That's against the very end of our agreement. But I don't care if we do clear accounts to this day and begin upon a new score of roving.

MIRANDA.

In which we'll strive to outdo one another in extravagance. But first, how far you are engaged with Lesbia?

BEAUMINE.

That you may be judge yourself, whether she can have any concern in me: know, she told me you had a penchant for my person.

MIRANDA.

By which I conclude she was jealous.

BEAUMINE.

And do you think then she would have ventured to let me know of so dangerous a rival?

MIRANDA.

'Twas in raillery no doubt.

BEAUMINE.

Aye indeed, she did rally enough upon it, that the gay, the free Miranda should be caught at last. Therefore, not only for fear I should suspect you of constancy, but if you would not be subject of her mirth, speak of me for the future with more caution.

MIRANDA.

And Lesbia's jest, I suppose, has occasioned me this favor.

---

9 *volage*] flighty or fickle (Fr.)

10 When … me] from Mercury's song to Phaedra in Dryden's *Amphitryon* IV.490-91

BEAUMINE.

Why really, madam, I might protest and lie and swear I could neither eat nor rest since I saw you. But if you'd have the truth, I have always found, among all other attractions, kindness* only has resistless charms, and by the means you've gained, secure your conquest.

MIRANDA.

A way by which most of your sex are lost. But why may not you be as particular as I am? This plain dealing of yours has charmed me beyond all things, and sure 'tis as much out of the road for a woman's affection to be engaged by sincerity as a man's to be secured by kindness.*

BEAUMINE.

Aye indeed, you are seldom to be satisfied unless we engage for as much more love than we have as we are willing to release you from paying. But I am no dissembler, madam, and must confess my love for you is none of those violent passions that will of course abate. 'Tis in so moderate a degree that even your fondness could not lessen it.

MIRANDA.

And mine so indifferent your sincerity can't disturb me. So without scruple, confess what interest Lucilia has in you.

BEAUMINE.

Really madam, she's at present very indifferent to me, but I believe I shall shortly have a violent passion for her. She's going to ruin an honest friend of mine, and I shall hate her heartily for it.

MIRANDA.

How will she ruin him?

BEAUMINE.

Marry him. How can a woman ruin a man else?

MIRANDA.

Oh mischievous! But to show you that I know she is not indifferent to you, she said herself you would wish she had not been here at your coming.

BEAUMINE. (*Aside.*)

And thereby hangs a tale.—Faith madam, she was in the right on't. I had much rather have had you alone; she knew my thoughts and complied with 'em. I thank her, the first favor she ever did me or I ever wished from her. So now, I hope all past accounts are cleared.

MIRANDA.

And for the future. Beaumine,
(Sings.)
We'll neither believe what either can say,
So neither believing, can neither betray.[11]

BEAUMINE.

And at this rate our loves must be eternal; there's no danger of quarrels or satiety.

MIRANDA.

Aye, if all lovers had followed our example, we had not heard so many complaints of faithless nymphs and perjured swains.

BEAUMINE.

But they must be perpetually dangling at one another's elbows and, the little time they are parted, inquiring after every action or step they take for fear they should go astray.

MIRANDA.

So tire one another when together and torment themselves asunder. And no wonder: they soon break a knot that with drawing too straight sits uneasy upon them and is the weaker itself. It bursts upon the least irregular motion.

BEAUMINE.

Well madam, that we may profit by others' follies, I believe it's time to part before we are weary of one another.

MIRANDA.

For now we have told all our thoughts, we are in great danger of growing dull. Next time we meet, ten to one, but we shall be quite of another mind and so new again. In order to it, I'll give you a song made by a heroic lover of mine. Perhaps it may infect you with sighing, whining, dying love.—Who's there? Desire the gentlewoman in the next room to walk in.

[Enter gentlewoman.]

You'll oblige us, madam, with the song I gave you last to learn. *Song.*
Well Beaumine, how does that affect you?

---

[11] We'll ... betray] from the same song in *Amphitryon* (IV.486-87)

BEAUMINE.
I melt, I languish, am all transport now, (*Sings a line of the song.*) "What shall I say to work upon thy soul!"

MIRANDA.
Oh most apish! How ridiculous a man appears when he would cross nature! He may as well expect to be finely shaped by putting on another man's clothes because they fit well upon him they were made for, as to please by affecting the most agreeable humor* in another. It hangs as awkwardly upon him and is as easily perceived not to be his own.

BEAUMINE.
Then I must e'en stay from you till I am so much forgot my own will be new again.

MIRANDA.
Which need not be long, I assure you: out of sight, out of mind.

BEAUMINE.
A pleasant way of inviting me to return soon.
Thus whilst the artful sex in words deny,
The secret sense and their kind* looks comply.
(*Exit.*)

MIRANDA.
Thus we gain lovers and secure our fame:
We promise nothing, and they nought can claim;
They fancy pleasures, when we speak of pain,
And hopes enough, their passion to maintain.

Exit.

Act III, scene i. The Public Walks.

Enter Lesbia and Lucilia.

LESBIA.
By his manner of speaking I could not imagine he would visit her; this is a new way to deceive by speaking truth.

LUCILIA.
A sure one: 'tis so little expected from a lover.

LESBIA.
I'll never forgive it him. What pretence can he have to excuse this?

LUCILIA.
If he get off now, 'twill be a masterpiece of his art indeed.

LESBIA.
Impossible. I wish we may see Grandfoy here tonight; he said he was to meet Cleon in the walks, and I would willingly have his advice how to behave myself now, before I see Beaumine.

LUCILIA.
I'm mistaken if that is not Beaumine coming this way with Phillabell.

LESBIA.
The very same, and gay as innocence itself.

LUCILIA.
There's no avoiding 'em now. They're so near, they see us.

LESBIA.
Well, I won't disappoint you, for I know you would be so peevish all this evening; if you should not speak to him now, there would be no enduring you, though he was with you so lately.

LUCILIA.
You're mistaken. Though I never think I see him too often, I could have spared it now. Since Cleon is to be here, their meeting might prove of ill consequence, considering that coxcomb's design I told you of. 'Tis not yet the time he appointed me to send my answer, but we'll go off soon and oblige them to go with us, if we can.

Enter Beaumine and Phillabell.

BEAUMINE.
So the friends are together, and all's out. Well, I must take the old way of complaining first when we know ourselves in fault.

PHILLABELL.
I'm pleased at this unexpected good fortune. Madam, the sight of you gives me soft pleasures that compose my soul transported, now my happiness approaches, with my impatience of one day's delay and joy to think it is but one.

BEAUMINE.
Indeed Lesbia, I did not imagine you had so much indiscretion, but women can no more forbear talking of their amours than an ill poet of his verses, though they equally expose their folly by what they design to gratify their vanity with and usually prove as tiresome to their hearers, unless such as have ill nature enough to divert themselves with everything that's ridiculous in another.

LESBIA.

I don't know what you aim at, but I think indeed women deserve to be laughed at that boast of any kind thoughts for such faithless things as men are.

BEAUMINE.

You'll guess what I mean when I tell you I have seen Miranda and know all you said to her.

LESBIA.

You'll know what I mean when I tell you I heard that before and guess what you said to her.

BEAUMINE.

Really madam, so you may. You gave me cause enough to suspect you had let her know of our engagement, and I resolved to see her to find out how far you had discovered.* I was never so out of countenance in my life.

LESBIA.

'Twould have been a wonder to have seen that indeed, for I'll swear you have an extraordinary assurance.

BEAUMINE.

To be so laughed at, to hear you so ridiculed for being overreached by a creature that professes abusing everybody; you would have been ashamed to have seen yourself so described, so mimicked, so—I did not know what to say for myself or you.

LESBIA.

She abused you if she told you I said anything positive.

BEAUMINE.

Positive! but such signs, such things— Oh Lesbia, Lesbia, that you could be caught by such a shallow artifice.

LESBIA.

I'm sorry, sir—

BEAUMINE.

Well, you know I love you and can easily forgive you anything, but I hope you'll be more cautious hereafter.

LESBIA.

I think, Beaumine, 'tis time our engagement were made known to everybody.

BEAUMINE.

Aye, Aye,
We'll write each other's name on every bark;
The winds shall bear our vows to distant climes,
And Echo every tender word rebound.

LESBIA.

Good romantic sir, will you condescend for once to answer directly a little intelligible sense?

BEAUMINE.

Oh! That were to wrong my love! A lover and speak sense! To answer in cross purposes, in broken murmurs, and disjointed words expresses passion.

LESBIA.

Do you think I'll be always put off with this trifling, Beaumine?

BEAUMINE.

Oh! Mighty things have been produced from trifles. The cackling of geese* once saved the capitol. Men's promises have gained many a fair one, and women's favors lost 'em many lovers. Trifles, trifles all, but great effects.

LESBIA.

Is not that to tell me I have lost you by what you think a trifle?

BEAUMINE.

No, to show you I don't think your favors a trifle and have no mind you should lose me, I would have 'em still* favors, the more to engage me and not turn all to duty.

LESBIA.

Had you talked thus to me at first, Beaumine—

BEAUMINE.

You had lost a great deal of pleasure, Lesbia, and laughed at me for a fool.

LESBIA.

Which is something better than a knave.

BEAUMINE.

Good words, good words, madam. Knaves are precise, protesting, plotting, thinking creatures, but you'll find this mad, maggoty fellow a very honest fellow at last.

LESBIA.

At last.

BEAUMINE.

Well, if you'll have me marry you just now, I'll run and fetch a priest immediately. (*Going.*)

LESBIA.

I think you're mad in earnest. Why Beaumine!

BEAUMINE.

Oh gad, I forgot. The canonical hour* is over. (Sings.) "But if I ever play the fool, dear Cloris, I am thine."

(*Turning to Phillabell [and Lucilia].*) Well, what can you have to say to one another all this while? You are agreed upon the premises, are convinced of that mutual affection, and to answer for the future can only serve to call the sincerity of the present in question.

LUCILIA.
Why so, sir? I think 'tis rather a proof of the present, a sign we find it so great we believe it will always last.

BEAUMINE.
Aye madam, but if I hear a man swear to a thing done out of his sight, though it may happen to be true, I shall think he has a large conscience and scarce believe him in what he might know. And indeed, we may as well swear to anything done in Japan; as for our future inclinations, they are no less out of our knowledge or power.

PHILLABELL.
I think a man that knows himself not to be of a wavering temper, if he has well considered the merit of his choice, may venture to promise for his constancy without prejudice to his honor.

BEAUMINE.
But to what end should he promise? Will it secure his inclination one minute the longer? Oh, but it secures the woman he would engage.—Madam, my friend's a very honest fellow; I believe he thinks what he says, but 'tis your fault if you take his word for what he cannot know. We had rather you should rely upon the power of your charms, and if the ladies will force us to add perjury to our natural levity, the sin must lie at their door.

LESBIA.
'Tis a folly indeed to rely upon their word for future inclinations, since few of 'em can answer for their future actions.

BEAUMINE.
Really madam, our actions are generally guided by our inclinations; this is not an age of much mortification. But are not you for walking, ladies?

LUCILIA.
I'm a little tired. What think you of going off, Lesbia?

LESBIA.
I'll wait upon you, madam.

PHILLABELL.
We'll attend to your coach, ladies.

LUCILIA.
Maybe you would not leave the walks so soon.

PHILLABELL.
Well, come back and take another turn or two. Tomorrow early as the day I'll visit you and hope your wishes, my fair bride, will meet me.

LUCILIA.
You never yet could come too early for 'em.

BEAUMINE.
What a deal of tenderness are they going tomorrow to destroy! (*Sings.*)
Would you, would you love the nymph forever,
Never, never, never, never, never let her be your wife.

Exeunt.

[Scene ii. The same.]

Enter Grandfoy, Cleon, and Bonsot.

CLEON.
Let me expire. My false nymph, going off with her lover! Before my face! In the very place where I sent her word I would be tonight! The inexpressible confidence of a faithless woman!

BONSOT.
Nay Brother, don't be angry. I dare say she meant no affront to you, only to make him believe she don't care for you.

CLEON.
Then she's the greater jilt, Brother.

BONSOT.
Humph, pugh, Lord, you will think the worst of everything! Do but look how loath she is to leave you; she stands still all the while she goes.

GRANDFOY.
That's an extraordinary art indeed.

CLEON.
I don't doubt her affection. But the fellow's rich, if she consulted her honor or happiness. Is such a *grossier*[12] as Phillabell to be preferred to me? I protest, I almost pity her.

GRANDFOY.
Aye, aye, e'en let the weakness of her choice be her punishment. 'Tis below your resentment.

[12] *grossier*] coarse, crude fellow (Fr.)

CLEON.

Nay, 'tis not that I value the creature, but then to disappoint my rival will be a good revenge for his presuming to hope where I had once made my pretensions; therefore, he shall see all her letters. I can't but think how sillily the fellow will look. Ha, ha, ha.

GRANDFOY.

But you don't consider what a kindness you'll do your rival in preventing his marriage with such an undistinguishing coquette; I fancy they'll better revenge you upon one another.

CLEON.

Egad, thou art in the right, Coz.

BONSOT.

Aye faith, that's well said. I hate mischief. And then you know, Brother, 'twould vex you more if she should refuse you after you had shown so much concern for her.

CLEON.

Impertinent suppositions! To show you the impossibility of it, I'm now positively resolved to pursue my design.

BONSOT.

Hey, why, I meant, in case, d'ye see— Pugh, Brother, you are so hasty. I would have said, psha, do not be so ill-natured. But I mean, that if, suppose, he should be very fond of the honor of being your rival—aye, d'ye mind that now? and so force her willingly to marry him.

CLEON.

Then would I, after they are married, expose her letters to the whole Tawn; that will be an immoderate pleasure, rat[13] me.

BONSOT.

That might breed quarrels now between a man and his wife.

CLEON.

She'll be the more sensible of the ill judgment of her choice.

BONSOT.

Faugh.

GRANDFOY.

Oh but that is not *en cavalier*,* 'twill be looked upon as vanity.

BONSOT.

Aye this will do—but now I think on't better, I don't believe he'll be angry. Being a very humble sort of a man, he's likely to be proud that you should be vain of his wife's letters.

CLEON.

Vain! No, no, the Town know well enough, if I would boast, there are ladies of more wit and better judgment than Lucilia that have afforded me *de quoi.*[14]

BONSOT.

Aye Brother, the lady, you know, that never worked in her life and made you a cravat all with her own hands.

GRANDFOY.

What, she drew the picture of his cravat?

CLEON.

Oh no, she really made the very lace I have on. Now you know women of a great deal of wit never work, but as love once raised a blacksmith to a painter,[15] so it made her descend from her nicer* speculations to this mechanic employment, that I might wear the product of her fingers.

GRANDFOY.

Oh wonderful effect of passion, I confess.

Beaumine and Phillabell enter unseen.

CLEON.

Aye, if you consider the elegancy of the work.

GRANDFOY.

Oh extremely elegant.

CLEON.

That's a very fine ring. I never saw thee wear it before. Some lady's favor* undeniably. Come, confess, confess.

---

13 Tawn … rat] Town,* rot; Cibber's characters often speak with open o's, represented by a's (cf. *The Relapse* above).

14 *de quoi*] of what [shall go unspoken] (Fr.); a euphemism for sexual favors

15 blacksmith … painter] Quentin Massys (c. 1465-1530), Flemish landscape and portrait painter, who worked as a blacksmith but became an artist after he fell in love with an artist's daughter

GRANDFOY.
Why, yes faith, 'twas a lady's favor.

CLEON.
She must be of quality* by the value of the present.

GRANDFOY.
'Twas given her by another lover, his first present too.

CLEON.
Oh most obliging! But how did he bear it?

[Beaumine] sees the ring.

BONSOT.
Aye, if he should hear of it now, what a deal of mischief might come on't.

GRANDFOY.
I laughed heartily at the pains he took and the presents he made, that she might be the less afflicted at the loss.

CLEON.
Kind cully! So, she pretended she had lost it?

GRANDFOY.
Aye, the jest is— (*Seeing Beaumine.*) Prithee Cleon, turn this way.

CLEON.
This is the place I appointed to send the answer of my letter.

GRANDFOY.
Damn your letter, prithee come.

Exit Cleon and Grandfoy in confusion.

BONSOT.
Hey day, what vagary's this? He's afraid of somebody, I think.

BEAUMINE.
Hah! This confirms me. Damned jilt.

BONSOT.
And this gentleman seems angry. I have a good mind to stay and hear what he says that I may prevent their quarrelling* together whilst they're asunder.

PHILLABELL.
How now, Beaumine! What's the matter?

BEAUMINE.
Did you know him that turned off just now?

PHILLABELL.
Very well. 'Tis my coxcombly rival, Cleon. Don't you know him?

BEAUMINE.
Pox of your rival. T'other, he with the ring I'd know.

BONSOT.
Aye, 'tis so.

PHILLABELL.
But why so fretful?

BEAUMINE.
Plague! Do you know him? Can't you answer?

PHILLABELL.
Why, I do not know him, but what if I did?

BEAUMINE.
Oh dissembling witch!

PHILLABELL.
What's this passion for? Who has offended you?

BONSOT.
I hope, sir, you are not angry with the gentleman you inquire after; he's a relation of mine, sir, and a very honest gentleman. I dare say, if he offends anybody willfully, it must be without his knowledge.

BEAUMINE.
Then you may give him the knowledge, sir, that he willfully wears a ring I may make bold to take from him, sir.

BONSOT.
Oh Lord, sir, as for that, if you have a mind for the ring, I'll engage 'twill be at your service. My cousin's a generous person that does not value such a trifle nor the person he had it from, in comparison of your friendship, I dare say, sir.

BEAUMINE.
Why, do you know the person he had it from, sir?

BONSOT.
Aye sir, anybody may know her: a mere common creature. She's kept* indeed by a coxcomb, a soft-headed cully.

BEAUMINE.
You know him too, sir, I suppose.

BONSOT.
A fellow not worth knowing—but the wench is very fond of my cousin, and a man does not know how to deny a woman.

BEAUMINE.
Very well, sir—

BONSOT.
I tell you the plain truth to show you that you need

not quarrel* with my cousin about the ring, for he does not care this ____* for it, nor the lady neither. You may have them both, if you please, sir.

BEAUMINE.
You are very impertinently civil, sir.

BONSOT.
Oh Lord, sir, nay I must say that for myself. I am a very civil, good-natured fellow. I can't abide to see people when they are at quiet and in good humor quarrelling with one another.

PHILLABELL.
That's a strange sight indeed, sir.

BONSOT.
Aye sir, I hope you'll persuade your friend not to be in a passion for nothing, about something of a ring and a lady, a jilt not worth his concern, sir.

BEAUMINE.
That I am very well convinced of, sir. Your cousin and the lady and the ring may go to the Devil for me, as they please, sir.

BONSOT.
Oh sir, your very humble servant. That's all I desire, that they may have leave to go to the Devil in quiet, sir, I have no more to say, sir. I'll be sure to tell him how civil a person you are, and I don't doubt he'll have the same complaisance for you, begin your journey when you will. He's none of the hottest choleric fellows; whenever he's in a heat against any, 'tis in cold blood. Your very humble servant, sir. I'm extremely obliged to you indeed, sir. (*Exit.*)

PHILLABELL.
What a soft officious fool this is! But prithee, what concern have you in the ring you talked of?

BEAUMINE.
By Heaven, the very same I gave to Lesbia.

PHILLABELL.
Ha, ha, ha, ha, ha! Why, thou can'st not be jealous, what of Lesbia! The fear of losing thee, you know, will keep her faithful.

BEAUMINE.
Who could have suspected?

PHILLABELL.
Oh never think it: she that valued not the loss but as a sad presage thy dearer heart would follow. Ha, ha, ha!

BEAUMINE.
Prithee leave thy fooling.

PHILLABELL.
Were she a wife, indeed. But Lesbia, she whom nothing could console but thy repeated vows of never changing. Ha, ha, ha!

BEAUMINE.
Lesbia false! Where shall we look for truth?

PHILLABELL.
Not in a woman that has sacrificed her honor, but such a one as my Lucilia. Oh what a treasure! This makes me more impatient to be master of it; 'tis an age till tomorrow. Would she this night were mine.

BEAUMINE.
Why, truly when a man is to be hanged, a night's reprieve gives him but so much time to torment himself with the apprehension. Oh I could curse the whole jilting, hypocritical sex.

PHILLABELL.
They are all Lesbias, but thou mayst rail. Thy malice cannot reach Lucilia, the abstract of all goodness, so true, so innocent. I had much ado to persuade her t'other day that any woman could be false to her husband or even pretend to love where she did not.

BEAUMINE.
And you believe her? Is there any of 'em that cannot talk of sincerity?

PHILLABELL.
Oh! 'Tis stamped on all her actions. Then she's so reserved, she hated Cleon for his impudence. He has made her blush a thousand times with the liberty of his discourse and actions.—Is not that her governess?

BEAUMINE.
I think so.

Enter Lysetta with a letter, which, going to hide as she sees Phillabell, she lets fall accidentally.

LYSETTA.
This is the place, but I see Phillabell here! Then I must not stay for Cleon. (*Exit.*)

BEAUMINE.
She's in mighty haste. What have we here? A billet-doux!

PHILLABELL.
I believe 'tis Lysetta's. You had best call after her.

BEAUMINE.

The direction gives me a curiosity to open it. (*Reads it to himself.*) Nay now, Phillabell, I'm made a convert to marriage.

PHILLABELL.

What can have wrought such a miracle!

BEAUMINE.

Why a proof of thy Lucilia's virtue and sincerity. Do you know her hand?

PHILLABELL.

Perfectly.

BEAUMINE.

Is this like it?

PHILLABELL.

The same, to Cleon. Some severe repulse I suppose.

BEAUMINE.

Aye really, 'tis pity to use the poor man so severely.

PHILLABELL.

She never thinks she can use him ill, or me well enough. (*Reads.*) "You are ignorant what force the first engagements have, and you as little know my heart, when you imagine it capable of loving anything—but you." Am I awake! "If I marry Phillabell, 'tis to obey a cruel father, who will sacrifice me to his interest—" The rest is yet more baseness. It can't be Lucilia's.

BEAUMINE.

No, no, Lucilia's! You know she hates the impudent fellow, for making her blush so often.

PHILLABELL.

I can scarce credit my own eyes.

BEAUMINE.

Oh! Why should you against so much sincerity? 'Tis stamped on all her actions—I dare swear 'tis in this—she can't think it possible for a woman to be false to her husband or pretend to love where she does not. There's a treasure! 'Tis an age till tomorrow; shan't we have a wedding tonight, Phil?

PHILLABELL.

I'll not believe it.

BEAUMINE.

Never, never: were she a woman that had sacrificed her honor, indeed. But one so reserved as thy Lucilia. Ha, ha, ha! Prithee let's have the wedding tonight, Phil. Come, hang delays.

PHILLABELL.

Torment me. Am I thus paid for all my doting love and generous trust?

BEAUMINE.

The sure reward of trusting. What should hinder people from being false, when they are certain not to be suspected?

PHILLABELL.

'Tis a base principle.

BEAUMINE.

A woman's principle.

PHILLABELL.

Nay, I can join with thee now in railing.

BEAUMINE.

Let's bid defiance together to the whole ensnaring, damned, lying sex.

PHILLABELL.

Agreed, and yet there was such pleasure in believing, I could almost wish I had not been undeceived; had she but truth, she were an angel.

BEAUMINE.

Maybe so, for I am sure she could not be a woman. Betwixt you and I, what a couple of coxcombs we are to dote upon what we despise! I see you love this Lucilia still, and to confess the truth (now neither of us can laugh at t'other) I find Lesbia's infidelity strikes deeper at my heart than I thought any of her sex could reach. She has in gaining and losing spoiled more of my good humor than the whole kind could be worth in exchange.

BEAUMINE.

Oh! A mere liking only. She is young and airy.[d]

PHILLABELL.

And new.

BEAUMINE.

Aye, if you could add kind.* I do not know but those two monosyllables might have more force to make me bear Lesbia's inconstancy than all Seneca's morals.[16] But there is an old mistress of mine that still rivals them all, the faithful bottle. Shall we try it?

PHILLABELL.

I care not if I do, for I fear I shall never forget Lucilia but when I forget myself.

---

16 Seneca's morals] L. Annæus Seneca (d. 65 CE), stoic philosopher and dramatist famous for his moralizing

BEAUMINE.

Come along then, this is a mistress we can both enjoy without being jealous of one another.

Love's niggard spirit must the bliss engross;
Companions would the happiness destroy.
But wine does all its charming pleasure lose,
Unless we generously share the joy.

Exeunt.

[Scene iii. The same.]

Enter Lucilia and Lysetta.

LYSETTA.

Aye, this is the unlucky place.

LUCILIA.

There's no hopes of finding it. I am undone. I shall be exposed to the whole town; nay, for ought I know, Phillabell himself may have found it.

LYSETTA.

This comes of a woman's taking pains to do good, laboring out of her own vocation.—Oh! Madam, there's Cleon coming this way. Now you may e'en carry your message yourself, that it may be sure not to fail.

LUCILIA.

'Twill be the likelier to fail. I cannot speak such things as you made me write, or if I should, 'twould be with so much constraint, he must perceive it false. You know I can't dissemble.

LYSETTA.

I know you have practiced it as little as any woman, but trust nature, madam, trust nature and consider, a young husband will do you a great deal of good. Your sincerity? e'en have none at all. 'Tis not a virtue for this designing world. Nay on my conscience, I don't know why it should not be thought as much a vice to prostitute our minds to every fool as our bodies. Truth is the chastity of the soul and should not be exposed to any man that would put it to the proof.—Here he is. Have a care of your metaphorical chastity, or you may be forced to keep the real one for Philabell. And if that does not frighten you—

LUCILIA.

Peace, fool.

Enter Cleon.

CLEON.

I hope I have not missed the letter, for I cannot positively determine whether I shall condescend to hinder her marriage or not till I know how she expresses herself. Here in person! This is excess of civility indeed. I always thought her well bred.—This unexpected favor, madam—

LUCILIA.

And undesigned, sir, I assure you.

LYSETTA.

Oh sir, the most unfortunate accident. My lady sent me with a letter to you, but meeting with one here I was afraid should see me, I dropped it in my surprise. My lady, in a fright, came hither to look for it, but in vain. 'Twas gone, and nobody knows what mischief may be done with it.

CLEON.

Was the subject of it dangerous?

LUCILIA.

Indeed it was.

LYSETTA.

It complained of your injustice in suspecting my lady's love, because she was forced to marry another, and said such kind things of hereafter.

CLEON.

Was there a superscription?

LYSETTA.

Aye, aye, your name was upon it.

CLEON.

Oh very well. That will be an excuse for what it contains to those that know me.

LUCILIA. [*Aside.*]

Ridiculous vanity! There need not much pains, I find, to persuade this thing he is beloved.

CLEON.

So madam, you marry Phillabell to express your aversion very emphatically! But how do you show your affection for me?

LUCILIA.

By not marrying you.

CLEON.

That is a favor I confess, but methinks not very particular. I've a world of rivals in it.

LUCILIA.

Oh that can't be avoided, but you are the only person I particularly resolve never to marry.

CLEON.
As a proof of your fondness.

LYSETTA.
Aye sir, my lady fears she should have such a world of rivals, she could never be easy with you.

CLEON.
Oh Lard, madam, there's no danger. But really I think, when a man is singularly eminent, he should never marry, for he injures the person he bestows himself upon, by exposing her to the envy of your sex, and the rest by giving 'em despair. It was worth the care of the government in this scarcity of persons of merit to forbid monopolizing 'em.

LUCILIA.
Indeed I would not injure my sex so much as to monopolize such an extraordinary person as Cleon. (*Aside.*) This fool can't be flattered too grossly.

CLEON.
Well madam, since you are pleased to prefer me to Phillabell in your esteem, I won't disturb his imaginary felicity. But I was thinking it might not be amiss to show some of your obliging letters to my friends, that it might justify to the world (who might judge you by your choice in a husband) the niceness* of your wit and judgment.

LUCILIA.
Oh by no means, sir. They'll conclude you would not have done it but by my consent and take it as an effect of my vanity.

CLEON.
You are in the right, madam. There may be cause to suspect it, and vanity is of all follies the most odious.

LUCILIA. [*Aside.*]
And yet he thinks himself agreeable!—Nay really I think vanity a very harmless thing; it does nobody any hurt. Those it deceives are the better for it, having no other quality to make 'em satisfied with 'emselves. The rest of the world know, that like all other artificial lights, 'tis only to supply the defect of the natural, and as they burn the brighter in the darkest nights, so it appears most where there's least merit.

CLEON.
Justly observed, madam. Vanity is a very charitable flatterer. I have known it encourage an unbred, ill-dressed fellow to make love* to a lady that everybody knew I was well with.

LUCILIA.
That might make him despair of pleasing her indeed, but I hope the lady judged better of your merits.

CLEON.
Yes faith, madam, she judged him blockhead enough for that dull animal a husband, avoided me to secure her virtue, and carried him out of town to show she was ashamed of him. And if that did not mortify his vanity—

LUCILIA.
And secure him from jealousy, it showed her discretion as great as her judgment.

CLEON.
No, strike me dead, it had been wiser to have stayed and given him a cause of jealousy. The only excuse a woman can have for marrying a man she does not love is to secure her pleasure with the man she does. 'Tis a way among the women of condition to contrive for their interest before they marry, and their inclination after. But the rustic had infected her with his stupid society. 'Twas only want* of modish conversation, a finished good breeding.

LUCILIA.
Well, to show you I am better bred and not to be spoiled by the stupid conversation of a husband, I'll always have it with the ceremony of a new and the coldness of an old acquaintance, never have the same diversions, and seldom the same bed.

CLEON.
Very courtly, upon honor. Then for your lover, madam, he must make one in all your avowed pleasures for a blind to the secret stolen ones, be always with you at cards, hand you to your coach from the play, be very free together in public to appear more innocent. Then he must be very intimate with your husband to make him the more secure of you—and the Town the more suspicious.

LUCILIA.
I don't doubt but with your instructions to prove as modish a mistress as a wife. I promise never to avoid you to secure my virtue.

CLEON.
Then I have no obstacle to fear, for all the women

I have addressed to would never see me again, knowing the only way to conquer was to fly. I shall certainly attack, madam, and then you will not find your virtue in danger—but no virtue at all, I am positive.

LUCILIA.

Indeed, I positively believe there will be no virtue at all in the case. I shall not once struggle with my inclinations to resist you.

CLEON.

Ah, ah, it would be in vain, but a little for decorum.—The poor thing is strangely fond.—Well madam, that I may be happy hereafter, I will be secret now and, if you please, appear at your wedding more gay than the bridegroom.

LUCILIA.

You'll be a welcome guest. But I dare stay no longer. Live upon hopes.—Substantial food enough for thee:
Vain, empty things, more solid could not bear;
Who're nothing else themselves must live on air.
(*Exit.*)

CLEON.

Well I profess this is a very generous age. These married men are at the expense of what we don't care to do, and we in return do for them what they never could do.
In mutual charities we pass our lives:
They keep* our mistresses, we please their wives!

Act IV, scene [i]. Miranda's lodgings.

*Enter Miranda and her woman.**

MIRANDA.

Oh aye, I'm within to her. Desire her to walk up.

Exit woman.

This is a very quick return of my visit. How fond Lesbia and I grow of late; there are not such dear friends and constant companions in the world as women that are jealous of one another.

Enter Lesbia.

Oh my dear, this is so obliging.

LESBIA.

I could not deny myself the satisfaction any longer, and I hope you'll take it kindly, for there's nobody I desire more to be believed a friend to than Miranda.

MIRANDA.

And nobody, I assure you, desires more to be yours. But how can I think you mine when you are not free with me? You always speak with so much reserve.

LESBIA.

Indeed, if I had any secret to impart, I should do it freely, but since Beaumine has been to visit you, no doubt he has convinced you, you had no reason to think there was anything between us. You may engage with him as you think fit, without any injury to me.

MIRANDA.

I engage with him! Lord, I but jested. Sure you did not think me serious. I had a curiosity indeed to know your amour, but did you imagine I could have any design upon such a vain, pert, unaccountable creature?

LESBIA. (*Aside.*)

This is certainly affected. I'll be hanged if the traitor has not cautioned her too against trusting me.—You gave him much better epithets once, Miranda, but instead of thinking him that charming fellow, I find now you extremely dislike him.

MIRANDA.

No extremes indeed; he's perfectly indifferent to me.

LESBIA.

'Tis true, that's all he deserves to be. I see nothing extraordinary in him.

MIRANDA.

You thought much better of him once too, Lesbia. (*Aside.*) Now have I a shrewd suspicion this faithless swain has made us distrust one another that he might the better deceive us both. Well, if it is so, I'm resolved to torment her and be revenged of him.—Well my dear, since you assure me you have no concern in him, I'll confess my weakness that 'twas with all the difficulty imaginable I constrained myself for your sake not to make a return to such tender, engaging things as I thought him uncapable of saying.

LESBIA. [*Aside.*]

Oh villain!—No doubt he can say what he pleases, madam.

MIRANDA.

Oh, but in a manner so persuading— And yet, till you confirmed it, I would not believe him, though he vowed he had no love for you and told me all you said to him of me.

LESBIA. [*Aside.*]

Traitor!—As a friend, Miranda, I advise you not to rely too much upon what he tells you, for to my knowledge, you are not the only person he makes addresses to.

MIRANDA.

Nor is he the only I'll receive addresses from. (*Sings.*) "He's fickle and false, and there we agree."[17] We shall have the more adventures to entertain one another with, so be diverting always, always new, and I'll engage to secure him the more by not endeavoring to confine him.

LESBIA.

Secure him! Sure you forget you're engaged to Constant.

MIRANDA.

No, but I'm in hopes very soon to torment him out of his love or his senses, that I may have my liberty.

LESBIA.

Faugh, now I find you jest indeed.

MIRANDA.

The D—'s in me, I think, I'm so possessed with this giddy humor. It gives a tincture to my most weighty affairs. But if I could look languishing, and sigh, "Oh the dear charming man! There are no joys, no life without him!" 'twould not half express my heart now I have found he's not insensible. And then you know his fortune's very considerable; I can't see how I can do better.

LESBIA.

Whether you are in earnest or no, Miranda, I must tell you seriously it won't be for your reputation to receive from a man of his wild character.

MIRANDA.

Really! I'll swear I should not have thought so, having met him at your lodgings.

LESBIA.

I intend to get rid of him as soon as I can.

MIRANDA.

Oh! If everybody throws him off, I'm resolved to receive him, for by being so scandalously general, he'll be forced to be particular, and 'tis many a pious man's case, who would never have been honest if he had not lost his credit, never virtuous if his appetites had not decayed. 'Tis the best thing you can do for his reformation and my happiness.

LESBIA.

Well, well, madam, however you flatter yourself, I don't doubt but you'll find yourself as unhappy with him as he has made others. So, your servant madam. I shan't trouble you more with my counsel, but you'll repent—

MIRANDA.

What? Nay Lesbia, I can't let you go now. 'Tis so obliging to be moved at this rate for your friend's good. Come, come, had not you better confess what this concern enough discovers.* If you would be sincere with me, I could tell you a secret worth two of yours and would give you more satisfaction than all your own art or resentment ever can.

LESBIA.

Perhaps I could tell you something, too, that would undeceive you, but I have no great encouragement from the use you made of what I hinted before for your advantage, repeating it to Beaumine, and ridiculing me for it.

MIRANDA.

The lying toad! May I never have a secret of my own worth keeping or of another's worth telling if I said one word of it. But 'twas a wonder I did not, for if I discover anything of myself that can make a jest, out it comes at all adventures. But when I am thoroughly trusted, though with a jest, I can keep it without bursting and faithfully will, I promise you.

LESBIA.

Then I will own to you, Beaumine and I are so solemnly engaged that if he has made you any proposal, he's the most perfidious man on earth.

MIRANDA.

Nay, then 'tis past jesting, and I must tell you, what I said was only to try you. All his discourse to me was a mere gallantry and with his usual gaiety and humor. Yet by the care I find he has taken to

[17] He's … agree] Mercury's song to Phaedra, *Amphitryon* IV.484 (slightly modified)

hinder us from confiding in one another, I apprehend he may have some farther design.

LESBIA.

Then if you've none upon him, you may assist me in one I have of consequence.

MIRANDA.

With all my heart, for whatever little inclinations I may have, they only amuse me for the present but the more endear Constant to my serious thought, whose plain dealing and true affection I find nowhere equaled and will get the better of my fickleness at last.

LESBIA.

But that I desire you to disguise from Beaumine and to pretend you are dissatisfied with your uncle's choice, which will encourage him to declare himself if he has any serious designs, and you carry it on handsomely.

MIRANDA.

Let me alone for that. I have acted an indifference for Constant long enough to be perfect in't.

Enter Miranda's woman.

WOMAN.

A gentleman, madam, that calls himself Bonsot, inquires if you are here.

MIRANDA.

Oh, by all means let him come.

[Exit woman.]

That creature can never be unentertaining; if we can furnish no occasion for his good nature to do mischief in, the elegancy of his bulls must divert us.

Enter Bonsot.

BONSOT.

Since you command me to do myself this honor, I hope, madam, you'll forgive my intruding without your leave, where I have no business, being 'tis a concern of consequence brings me.

MIRANDA.

Then it seems, sir, you have business here.

BONSOT.

Aye, with this lady, madam. I was to wait on you at your lodgings and was told you were at Miranda's, so having something to say to you, I came to let you know it because I can't inform you of it there.[e]

MIRANDA.

Pray use your liberty, sir.

BONSOT.

Your very humble servant. Why look you, madam, my brother sending me, I came of my own accord to desire you will tell your friend Lucilia that he don't know but he's very certain Phillabell found the last letter she writ to him. For I saw him just in the place where it was lost, mightily concerned at a paper he had in his hand. I knew by his voice he was in a passion, but he was not within hearing.

LESBIA.

I thought you heard his voice.

BONSOT.

Aye madam, but I could not tell what he said, for though I was pretty near, 'twas at a good distance.

LESBIA.

Well sir, I'll be sure to tell her what you don't know, but are very certain of.

BONSOT.

That will be very kind, madam, but if I could meet with him, I warrant I'd appease him.

Enter woman.

WOMAN.

A gentleman below, madam, desires to wait on you.

MIRANDA.

Who is it?

WOMAN.

The young brisk gentleman that I told your ladyship would make a rare gallant for you when you are married, but he looks sullen enough now for a husband.

MIRANDA.

Beaumine, on my life. Let him come up.

Exit woman.

Now if you'll step into that closet,* you may be witness of the whole scene.

LESBIA.

With all my heart. This is lucky, but should not Bonsot retire too?

MIRANDA.

No, he may stay if he'll be sure not to discover* your being here.

BONSOT.

You need not fear me, madam. I never discover a secret, unless it should happen to be something I don't know.

MIRANDA.

In! In! He's coming!

Enter Beaumine.

BEAUMINE.

I was told, madam, Lesbia was here.

MIRANDA.

She's just gone.

BEAUMINE.

Do you know whither, madam?

BONSOT.

No sir, I can assure you she does not know.

MIRANDA.

Now, do you think to make me jealous, or is it to make yourself new? It is indeed extremely new but no very taking way of addressing to a woman by showing a concern for another.

BEAUMINE.

Faith madam, the concern I have for her at present need disturb nobody but myself, for I do hate her heartily.

MIRANDA.

Which would not disturb you, if you had not rather love her heartily.

BONSOT.

Nay, why so madam? I don't believe the gentleman had rather love her, but a man may love a woman that he hates, whether he will or not, and then 'tis not his fault.

MIRANDA.

So you have mended the matter.

BEAUMINE.

A man can't bear to be imposed upon.

MIRANDA.

And now, can a woman impose upon a man when they have no interest in one another, as you would have me believe?

BEAUMINE.

Damn her, I shall be an extravagant lover indeed to lose a new mistress for grief that I have lost an old one.

BONSOT.

There you are too hard again, madam. Mayn't a woman impose upon a man, merely out of a jilting nature, though she have no interest at all in it? Especially if she finds him fond and credulous.

BEAUMINE.

I have a rare advocate.—Well madam, in anger as well as in wine there is truth. I confess, Lesbia once had such an interest in me as would have cost the best part of my possessions to satisfy. But thanks to the virtue of her sex, she has forfeited.

MIRANDA.

What, a debt upon your estate?

BEAUMINE.

Upon my liberty, the most unreasonable of debts. But I'm released and—seized again by another. But there's no more bond and judgments against me. I shall only be your prisoner at large; you may call me in when you please, Miranda.

MIRANDA.

How can I trust you when Lesbia, that had so fast confined, could not secure you? Come Beaumine, honestly own you broke loose from her to give yourself to me. 'Twill be far the better compliment, and more generous to her than to wrong her every way.

BONSOT.

Really, the gentleman seems to me a very honest gentleman, that would not wrong any lady unless it were in a just cause. I warrant if he had not been in love with you or somebody else, he would never have forsaken her, but when a greater merit claims his heart, d'ye see, a man has right on his side to do wrong to the less worthy.

MIRANDA.

Most solidly and eloquently argued.

BEAUMINE.

'Tis such a well-meaning blunderer.—I'm extremely obliged to you, sir.

BONSOT.

Not at all, sir, I always endeavor to make a right understanding between any persons that I am acquainted with, though they are absolute strangers to me.

BEAUMINE.

Ha, ha, ha! Very charitably done indeed, sir.—But

madam, on my honor I have not injured Lesbia. Hah, I feel my liberty: "Lighter by what I've lost, I tread on air." Have a care of yourself, Miranda: she has left a plaguy deal of love upon my hands, and if you should be forced to bear it all—

MIRANDA.
I dare undertake it, like Æsop's choice of the bread: though the heaviest burden at first, being our constant subsistence, 'twill waste every day, and soon be light enough.[18]

BEAUMINE.
Then you must resolve to have no other subsistence.

MIRANDA.
Oh such a dry diet! a little variety to make it relish the better. But if you are for devouring it so fast, let's e'en make but one meal on't: marry, and there's an end. What think you of that, Beaumine?

BEAUMINE.
Think? Aye faith, we must e'en do it without thinking, or we shall never have the courage.

MIRANDA.
Nay, but I'm serious.

BEAUMINE.
What, before we're married? Time enough after. This is a time for gaiety and joy. Hah, my fair bride, here let me plight my vows on this soft hand.

Constant enters here unseen.

CONSTANT.
So close!

BEAUMINE.
But now I think on't, there's a matrimonial rival in the case. He'll certainly forbid the banns.

MIRANDA.
Ah, name him not. I am so sick of his fulsome, whining stuff.

BEAUMINE.
I'm afraid there's more love than you'll confess, by what I have heard of the matter.

MIRANDA.
They talk of putting us together indeed, but sure you're more a man of this age than to think love a consequence of marriage.

BONSOT.
Aye pox, love is never any part of the concern in marriage. Some indeed marry only for love, but then—

BEAUMINE.
Aye madam, 'tis sometimes the cause of it. Love has many extravagant effects.

MIRANDA.
His love may be the cause of it, for it makes him so indefatigable a tormentor that, if you have not courage enough to free me, I must marry him at last, for that's a sure way to be rid of him.

CONSTANT.
Fortune has found you out a quicker way. My passion now no longer shall torment you, nor I be more the subject of your mirth.

MIRANDA. [*Aside.*]
What must I say now! If I undeceive him, it will discover* Lesbia's secret; besides, I lose the dear pleasure of teasing him.

BONSOT.
What can I contrive now!

CONSTANT.
Is there excuse for this ungenerous usage? Had I by violent means or indirect pursued you— But how oft, Miranda, with bleeding heart and gushing eyes have I sworn rather to place you in another's arms than fetter you in mine against your will? Why then, if I were so uneasy to you, could you not rid yourself with honor of me? Why this unfair proceeding?

BONSOT.
Nay sir, I must needs say, the whole fault was partly mine, of their being so good friends, for when they first met, this lady was jealous of another, and he was in an anger. They seemed to have very little kind thoughts for one another, but you must know, I, sir—

CONSTANT.
Have very well reconciled 'em since, I see sir—so far engaged anger and jealousy between 'em. Oh faithless woman! What pretence.

[18] Æsop's … enough] In this popular story, Aesop goes on a journey with fellow slaves, who make fun of him for choosing to carry a heavy load of bread. He proves wisest, however, because his load becomes lighter each time they stop to eat.

MIRANDA.
Well, who can tell when to believe these lovers? 'Twas but yesterday he swore I was too great a good to be engrossed. Nature designed me an universal blessing. And now I must make nobody happy but himself.

CONSTANT.
Miranda, you're a woman.—Sir, this is no proper place for our dispute. (*Going.*)

BEAUMINE.
Now must I fight with him for having taken his mistress from him and with her relations for not taking her.

BONSOT.
Oh madam—pray sir, hear me, for you must know, I was with them all the time they were alone, though somebody, that shall be nameless, would have had me go, but I assured her, I could keep a secret.

CONSTANT.
You would have obliged her more in giving her a privater opportunity, no doubt. (*Aside.*) Oh torture!

BONSOT.
Pugh, that was as I told you, a person that must be nameless.

CONSTANT.
Sir, I am not in a humor to be fooled with. (*Going.*)

BONSOT.
Fooled, sir!

MIRANDA.
This is carrying the jest a little too far, though. Constant—

CONSTANT.
Madam.

MIRANDA.
I would fain know upon what terms we part, before you go.

CONSTANT.
Terms of never meeting. I know no other can be made between us. (*Going.*)

MIRANDA.
But one thing more: I am considering which of us must wear the willow.* Can you resolve me?

CONSTANT.
Am I your jest?

MIRANDA.
Well, but in earnest now, stay but a minute.

CONSTANT.
What to be more abused? I have been fooled enough.

As he is going, Lesbia comes out of the closet and stops him.

LESBIA.
Stay to be disabused.

CONSTANT.
I know enough.

BEAUMINE.
Lesbia here! Then I am afraid, 'tis I have been fooled.

BONSOT.
Lord, that she should discover* herself! But do what she will, I'm resolved not to betray my trust.

LESBIA.
Nay, you shall stay and know the truth.

BEAUMINE.
I know, madam, that you are a very virtuous, generous person.

LESBIA.
Thou the basest of men, but I have not leisure to upbraid thee till I have justified my friend.

BONSOT.
So, more mischief forwards. I must not betray my trust.

LESBIA.
I dare affirm she had not now a thought of wronging you, for 'twas at my request, to try Beaumine's truth, she gave him this obliging reception. Bonsot can witness—

BONSOT.
I scorn to betray my trust, madam.—As for me, sir, I can't say Lesbia was here before, but I can affirm this to my knowledge, that Miranda had no design of quarrelling with you. But you not being here, d'ye see, and this gentleman a very engaging person, she could not be so hard-hearted, you must think, to put him quite in despair.

CONSTANT.
Do you insult me, sir?

BONSOT.
Sir—

MIRANDA.
He does not know his humor.*

BONSOT.
Why should you be so peevish, sir? What if she had sent him away in despair, and he had gone and hanged himself?

CONSTANT.
Then you might have hanged with him for company, sir.

BONSOT.
Oh, oh, oh, to do you service, sir.

LESBIA.
An officious coxcomb not worth your anger, but what I have asserted—

CONSTANT.
You'll pardon me if I believe herself. She has not offered to deny but justifies her infidelity.

LESBIA.
That was, I suppose, her too scrupulous care to conceal what I entrusted her with. But I saw there could be no other proof of her innocence but my appearing, which must convince you 'twas a plot between us. What else could I be hid for? You need not conceal it now, Bonsot.

BONSOT.
Nay, nay, don't think to draw me in so. I know better things. (*To Beaumine.*) This is all to make a difference betwixt you and Miranda. Now I see the drift on't. But don't mind her.

CONSTANT.
Your witness is not well enough instructed.

BONSOT. (*To Constant.*)
Oh, as to that I know all, and if you will have it, Lesbia did hide herself indeed. Not that there was any plot against Beaumine, but Miranda having a desire to be alone with him— Not that she designed to injure you, sir, intending you should know all— (*To Beaumine.*) Not that she would have betrayed you, sir, but for fear he should discover it— (*To Constant.*) Though there was no harm, but you might have been jealous, and made a fighting business on't— (*To Beaumine.*) So you might have been killed, sir— (*To Constant.*) And your life in danger, sir— (*To Beaumine.*) But the lady having a great value for you, sir— (*To Constant.*) And fearing to lose you, sir— And as I was saying— Ay pox, I'd fain have you both satisfied.

CONSTANT.
What impertinence is this?

BEAUMINE.
Is it not my turn to complain now, madam? Well, there is no confiding in you women. Your vanity or jealousy is sure to betray us. But if ever I trust two that know one another with the same secret again— You are the strangest incontinent creatures.

MIRANDA.
And have you the impudence to complain of us that you were endeavoring to deceive!

BEAUMINE.
Why, have you not both deceived me?

MIRANDA.
Hang me, if I could not be fond of him again for this humor.—But you, I hope, Constant, are now convinced.

CONSTANT.
Yes madam, though I took pains to cheat myself, now every act of your disdain and coldness upbraids the folly of my blinded passion that would believe they rise from any cause but strong aversion.

MIRANDA.
One would think a woman of my fortune need not be so desperate at these years to bestow herself upon one that is her aversion.

CONSTANT.
You knew my credulous nature fit to work on, and now I should deserve to be so used, be made the tool you meant me for, if I again believed. But no, Miranda, I've broke my chain, and here I throw it from me. Thus, from my injured heart, I'll throw you too forever. (*Going.*)

MIRANDA.
Oh come back, I beg you.

CONSTANT.
Never.

MIRANDA.
Then he is lost indeed, and I am wretched.

BONSOT.
But sir, pray consider, as the lady was saying, she's a young lady, and a rich lady, and might have anybody she pleases. I would marry her with all my heart, myself, though I'm resolved never to marry, so what need can she have—

CONSTANT.
None of me, sir, so pray give me leave.

BONSOT.
Nor of any man for a tool, sir, for this I can say, she had no design to have a gallant, for as soon as the gentleman talked of love to her, she proposed marriage.

CONSTANT.
She was very forward it seems. I must be gone, sir.

As Constant offers to go, Bonsot still stops him.*

BONSOT.
Forward, sir? Oh, I suppose that. Nay hear me, sir.

CONSTANT.
Provoking coxcomb.

LESBIA.
This is barbarous. For shame, Constant, you won't leave her thus in tears.

CONSTANT.
Tears? Come madam, you need not hide your mirth. I can laugh with you now. (*He takes her handkerchief from her face.*) Hah! She weeps indeed! Oh let those precious drops fall on this bosom, soften this stubborn heart, that would contend against thy virtue and its own persuasion.

BONSOT.
Aye, I knew I should reconcile 'em at last.

MIRANDA.
Why, will you believe? These tears may be dissembled.

CONSTANT.
No, thou art truth itself, and my proud heart wanted* but this excuse for its submission. Can you forgive me?

MIRANDA.
Indeed you were unkind, though you had reason, for, I confess, I have not used you well.

CONSTANT.
Do you confess it? 'Tis too large atonement. Oh that in this soft minute I could hear my charmer speak me happy. Tell me, Miranda, when will you be mine?

MIRANDA.
Indeed the apprehension of losing you was so dreadful to me, that now, methinks, I can't be secure of you too soon.

CONSTANT.
Shall it be tomorrow then?

MIRANDA.
You dispose of me.

CONSTANT.
Tomorrow then, Miranda, makes us one. Oh my transported soul leaps at the thought as if it would break forth to speak its joy! It will not stay but flies to meet with thine through this loved bosom and take an earnest of our coming bliss. Tomorrow, my Miranda, oh my love!

LESBIA.
I wish you would take an earnest large enough to subsist on a day or two longer. I shall be at a loss else how to divide myself betwixt you and Lucilia.

BEAUMINE.
You may engage yourself here, if you please, madam, for I believe Lucilia will have no great occasion for you tomorrow unless it be to condole with her.

LESBIA.
Condole with her! For what?

[BEAUMINE.]
Only for being disappointed of a good-natured cuckold, madam, that's all.

BONSOT.
That is pity!

LESBIA.
Scandalous! You are such an enemy to virtue. None that profess it can 'scape your censure. What is't you mean by these accusations?

BEAUMINE.
Why, I mean that a very civil letter which she designed for her gallant fell by chance into Phillabell's hands at the very same time that the ring you had given yours happened into the sight of your humble servant.

LESBIA.
I suppose you both wanted* an excuse[19] for your constancy and so fell upon this invention.

BONSOT.
No indeed, madam, 'tis not his invention. The thing is true, only 'tis a mistake. A ring there was, but you know sir, I told you 'twas given by a wench, a very jilt.

BEAUMINE.
I believe you, sir, indeed.

[19] wanted an excuse for] lacked the means to escape

CONSTANT.

As you have been an instrument in this division, I hope, Miranda, it will be your care to reconcile these lovers. I must leave you to give some orders for tomorrow's happy business. [*Exit.*]

MIRANDA.

Come, what say you to it? Will you accept of me for arbitrator? I'll be a very impartial judge.

BEAUMINE.

Lesbia, I have still some regard for your honor and would be loath to publish your baseness.

MIRANDA.

Will you, Beaumine, do her justice, if she is innocent and can clear herself?

BEAUMINE.

Aye, aye, if the sky fall, madam.

LESBIA.

I don't doubt my justification, but that must be deferred.

BEAUMINE. [*Aside.*]

Venus forbid! Upon the assurance that was impossible, I was just going to make her the promise.

LESBIA.

Methinks, Beaumine, it would become you at this time to answer Miranda's question in a more serious manner.

BONSOT.

Seriously then, be it known, Lesbia, there is a law that excludes anyone from witnessing in their own cause.[20]

BONSOT.

That's a very silly law though, for does not one know their own cause best and are most concerned to clear themselves, right or wrong?

BEAUMINE.

Therefore, sir—

LESBIA.

But if I should bring proofs?

BEAUMINE.

Aye, aye, there are proofs that the earth moves, and that it does not move. Everything can be proved, but where we are concerned, the strongest argument is always on the side our inclinations are for. So, first make me sensible you were innocent.

LESBIA.

Are you resolved then?

BEAUMINE.

Never resolve anything. I did resolve to believe you faithful; you resolved to deceive me. Both have been disappointed. Little said's soon amended. Words are but wind. All promises are either broke or kept. Proverbs flow against you.

LESBIA.

Intolerable trifler, Beaumine, I shall find a way to force a juster answer from you.

BEAUMINE. (*Sings.*)

"Women's rage like shallow waters."[21]

BONSOT.

Egad, I love to see people merry. Come madam, never spoil company. You see this gentleman's pleased; here's nobody out of humor now but you.

LESBIA.

Here nobody has cause but I.

BONSOT.

Pugh, not a whit. I'll engage Beaumine will never give you any farther trouble.

LESBIA.

Prithee Bonsot, I'm not in a humor now to be pleased with your good-natured impertinence.

BONSOT.

Ay, ay, this is always my reward for taking pains to do good. When people are in a peevish mood, presently* I'm impertinent.

MIRANDA.

Come, come. A truce with your anger till a better opportunity of clearing the debate.

LESBIA. (*Aside.*)

I had almost forgot Lucilia. She must know of the letter he talks of.—Adieu, my dear, 'tis late and time to leave you. (*Exit.*)

BONSOT.

I must follow her, for I never leave people till I have argued or teased 'em out of their anger.—And sir, if you don't find her as fond of you as ever she

---

20 witnessing ... cause] Not strictly accurate: defendants could testify, but could not be compelled to do so after the Interregnum.

21 "Women's rage like shallow waters."] from Thomas Durfey's *Don Quixote* (2.III.i.99-100)

was in her life next time you meet, say I'm an officious, impertinent, insignificant fellow. (*Exit.*)

BEAUMINE.

That will be an extraordinary obligation indeed, sir.

MIRANDA.

Well, Beaumine, you must consider too it grows late, and that I must begin to think of the virtues of a wife's discretion and obedience.

BEAUMINE.

Ah! That's a virtue I must have too, but mightily against my will when you command me to leave you. This has been a very tragical day to lovers: Phillabell his* mistress false; Lesbia lost a believing coxcomb, I my hopes of the most agreeable woman in France; and she I'm afraid will find herself in a greater distress than any of us, for faith, Miranda, whatever the inexperienced may fancy of marriage,

As those who furrowed fields at distance view
May think 'em smooth and flowery as they shew,
But he that enters, curses what they praise,
Finds 'em deceitful, toilsome, rugged ways.

Act V, scene i. The Walks.

Enter Bonsot with Grandfoy.

BONSOT.

Cousin, I say, trouble yourself no more about this matter. Beaumine is thoroughly satisfied, for you must know, I told him the person you had the ring from was a common jilt, a wench you had no value for, and he presently* believed me.

GRANDFOY.

Thy folly's so ridiculous it mocks my anger. Would thou couldst at once be sensible how unluckily thou ever toil'st against thy own designs, thy good nature then would surely silence thee. To be always meddling where you have nothing to do in things you know nothing of!

BONSOT.

Aye, aye, I know nothing. I don't know that he was in such a passion with you. If I had not hindered him, he'd have cut your throat before now, without giving you time to say your prayers.

GRANDFOY.

Better he had than she had been abused, the woman in the world whose honors I am most concerned to vindicate and most to him.

BONSOT.

Why, her honor's ne'er the worse for what I said of her. But to please you now, I'll go to him again and tell him I was mistaken, that the lady never had a kindness for any man but you—

GRANDFOY.

That will mend the matter indeed.

BONSOT. (*Going.*)

Well, then you shall see how I'll manage it.

GRANDFOY.

Prithee Bonsot be quiet. All the kindness I ask of thee is never to intend me any.

BONSOT.

But would not you have me do justice to a lady you say I have wronged?

GRANDFOY.

No, no, I am just going to Beaumine, where I have appointed him to meet me, and shall find a way to do her justice myself.

BONSOT.

Oh ho, then I'll go with you.

GRANDFOY.

Indeed you shan't, sir.

BONSOT.

Try me but once, if I don't make all well again—

GRANDFOY.

Pray, hold your tongue, sir.

BONSOT.

Well, I will hold my tongue, then, if you'll let me go, for I know you'll begin a quarrel* now and put Beaumine out of his good humor, and then he'll never let you go to the devil in quiet, cousin.—Oh there's my brother's rival. I must talk with him. Stay for me but a little while now.

Enter Phillabell.

GRANDFOY.

Little enough, I promise you—a lucky deliverance. (*Exit.*)

BONSOT.

Sir, your humble servant. Happening to see you take up a letter in the walks, I imagine it might be one my brother expected there because he did not receive it.

PHILLABELL.
If he would know what it contained, no doubt the lady that sent it will inform him.

BONSOT.
Aye sir, but that is not the thing now. I can tell you more, because you have reason to take it ill, to show you have no reason, sir.

PHILLABELL.
No reason, sir?

BONSOT.
Not a dram, sir, upon my word, for you must know all the kind* things in it were only to pacify my brother for fear he should show you the rest of her fond letters, not but she really designed to marry you.

PHILLABELL.
I don't question it, upon my word, sir.

BONSOT.
Aye sir, to be sure she was in earnest with you. She admitted you to the house, when he could only see her by stealth.

PHILLABELL.
Confound 'em.

BONSOT.
And then, you have a much better estate than he, sir.

PHILLABELL.
I believe she was sincere with that, sir.

BONSOT.
So I hope, sir, I have satisfied you, and since you know she designed you her sober choice and only to play the fool a little with him, you won't be angry if he shows you her letters, and I may have leave to wish you joy, sir.

PHILLABELL.
Joy sir! Thou busy trifler, hence and don't provoke my rage. What devil sent thee, when I am going to Lucilia, whom I would meet as calmly as if I were not injured?

BONSOT.
Injured? Why don't I tell you, sir, I'm certain she designs to marry you.

PHILLABELL.
Thy folly gives thee a privilege to abuse men safely; there's no way to resent it but by flying from impertinence. (*Exit.*)

BONSOT.
Psha, psha. As I was saying, sir— Faugh, why so fast sir— That men should be such enemies to truth they don't care to hear it, though for their good! Everybody runs away from me when I would tell it 'em as if I were a monster. Oh yonder's Beaumine. I'll go satisfy him, and then to see what humor Lesbia's in, and then to my cousin, and my brother's. I'll go to 'em all round. I do take a deal of pains, and do a world of good—to no purpose. (*Exit.*)

[Scene ii. Lucilia's lodgings.]

Enter Lucilia and Lysetta.

LUCILIA.
This comes of taking your pernicious counsels. They have always been fatal to me.

LYSETTA.
I'm sure I meant well, though it falls out so unluckily. Who could dream of such an accident?

LUCILIA.
Dream! For aught I know the fool hired you to betray the letter to Phillabell.

LYSETTA.
Nay madam, I know you can't suspect my fidelity to you.

LUCILIA.
How dare you talk to me? Get you out of my sight.

LYSETTA.
Dear madam, have patience. If you'll be advised, all may be well yet.

LUCILIA.
You're very free of your wise counsels indeed, but I'll hear no more of 'em.

LYSETTA.
Nay good madam, be pacified. I know I have been the cause of this misfortune, and therefore I would fain do you some service that may recompense it.

LUCILIA.
What recompense? What service can you pretend to do me? Has he not seen the letter under my own hand?

LYSETTA.
If you can but deny it confidently enough, I don't doubt your coming off, for all that.

LUCILIA.

Deny it! What, when he has the proof in his possession? What could that signify, unless to show him I had joined impudence to infidelity?

LYSETTA.

Nay, it must be managed artfully. You must seem angry with him as if you suspected a forgery. You know I can counterfeit that hand. Insinuate that to him cunningly. Do you observe me, madam?

LUCILIA.

Well, what does all this tend to?

LYSETTA.

'Tis a nice* business and will require no little artifice, but let all your care be very slyly to give him a suspicion of me.

LUCILIA.

Do you think he'll be imposed upon so? It can but make him doubt at most.

LYSETTA.

Aye, but I have a further plot. We may be thankful for this time to be prepared for him before he comes, instead of repining at the accident. How lucky it was that Lesbia should hear of it and that you were not at home when Phillabell came last night before she had given you notice of it.

LUCILIA.

I shall be little the better for it, I'm afraid.

LYSETTA.

Look you, madam, take my advice. He's a lover and by consequence credulous. That will make him believe you enough to have a mind to examine me, and being jealous, he'll probably doubt you enough to do it immediately, that we mayn't have time to lay our heads together. 'Tis very likely he'll come directly from you to look for me; then let me alone for the rest of the project. I engage to return him to you the most satisfied, humble thing, begging pardon, calling himself a jealous pated coxcomb and you the most innocent injured—

Enter a young woman, servant of Lucilia's, niece to Lysetta.

YOUNG WOMAN.

Madam, here's Phillabell coming up.

LYSETTA.

Dear madam, will you follow my directions?

LUCILIA.

Well, well, be gone, I hear him.

LYSETTA.

Niece, come with me hussy. I have business with you. Quick. Quick.

Exit Lysetta and niece.

LUCILIA.

I hate deceit, but sure 'tis of all others the most innocent to cheat a man to a belief of truth. How my heart trembles.

Enter Phillabell.

You seem disturbed. Can there be any cause of sadness on this day?

PHILLABELL.

Why, madam, not on this?

LUCILIA.

Does Phillabell ask why! He who so often swore this day would pay the sum of all his wishes!

PHILLABELL.

Alas there's nothing man so much deceives himself in as the means to his own happiness. I thought to make you mine the certain way, but unless your heart could be secured, all other ties is wretched slavery.

LUCILIA.

That you need not doubt, for whom I've laid aside my virgin modesty to confess I loved you.

PHILLABELL.

You have told me so indeed, but are you sure th'obedience of a daughter has not swayed you against your inclination?

LUCILIA.

Heaven can witness that you are much less my father's choice than mine.

PHILLABELL.

Have a care, madam, what you call Heaven to attest, and deal with me sincerely, for I am come as one that truly loves you, to offer you my service in whatever way can best conduce to make you happy.

LUCILIA.

Your service! Can anything in nature make me happy but your love?

PHILLABELL.

I would not have you made a sacrifice, and if you fear t'offend your father in refusing me, confess it generously.* I'll take it upon me, seem to fall off, and whatever his resentment may proceed to, I promise you to bear it all, rather than expose you to it.

LUCILIA.

I don't know what you mean. This is strange language to me.

PHILLABELL.

Does this speak plain enough? (*Gives her a letter, and whilst she reads, says [aside.]*) So unmoved! She must be practiced sure in falsehood.

LUCILIA.

What's the design of all this?

PHILLABELL.

You best know that, madam.

LUCILIA.

I know it! What, to disguise your own inconstancy must you tax me with such baseness?

PHILLABELL.

Why, you won't pretend to deny your own handwriting, I hope.

LUCILIA.

My writing! Who dares say I writ it?

PHILLABELL.

Oh woman! woman!

LUCILIA.

This is a masterpiece of villainy indeed!

PHILLABELL. [*Aside.*]

I was not prepared for this turn, I confess, but who can reach the depths of woman's artifice?

LUCILIA.

'Twill be enough to wrong my love by your infidelity without this forgery to injure my reputation. This from a man whom I despised all others for!

PHILLABELL.

I forge it! I have not the art of counterfeiting so well as you, madam, but I may learn in time of so perfect a mistress.

LUCILIA.

You have found a much better for your purpose, I assure you.

PHILLABELL.

That would be a prodigy indeed.

LUCILIA.

There's few can exceed my sweet governess, who I don't doubt was employed in this contrivance.

PHILLABELL.

Employed by whom? For what?

LUCILIA.

To sacrifice my honor for your base ends.

PHILLABELL.

Oh madam, you need not distrust her. 'Twas not she betrayed you. Fortune was my only friend in this matter.

LUCILIA.

Indeed, I shall hardly take your word for it. Perhaps you imagine I don't know her skill in counterfeiting my hand, though she might have told you I did.

PHILLABELL. [*Aside.*]

Is it possible there can be a deceit in this? If my reason would be as soon convinced as my fond heart, I could not think her false one minute. Lysetta counterfeit her hand? To what end? And yet I can see nothing of that confusion or disorder in her looks which guilt would naturally have upon so unexpected a discovery.* What can resolve me in this hell of doubts?

LUCILIA. (*Aside.*)

So there's some hopes. It begins to work.—I see you are surprised to find your accomplice so soon suspected.

PHILLABELL.

Madam, I thought you had known me too well to believe me capable of such a villainy. If you are innocent, we are both abused.

LUCILIA.

I thought too my virtue had been better known, and I will clear it. If my false governess dare deny it, there may be ways to force the truth from you and her.

PHILLABELL.

There may be ways too, madam, to make her own whatever you please.

LUCILIA.

You may prevent that if you please, but I suppose you'll be loath to lose so good a pretence for denying my innocence, if I should make it appear.

PHILLABELL.

Oh could you look into my heart, Lucilia, it would tell you that with the forfeiture of half my reason I would believe you're wronged, so much I wish it. But though I should be easily convinced, yet for your sake, that there may be no room left for malice, I'll tax your governess before you see her with this forgery, as if I knew it hers. That perhaps may induce her to confess it.

LUCILIA.

You may do as you think fit.

PHILLABELL.

Till then believe I suffer more than you. What different effects does passionate love produce:
Fearful to lose, we quickly jealous grow,
And wishing to be loved, soon think we're so. (*Exit.*)

LUCILIA.

Now, if Lysetta play her part as well, who can condemn this harmless artifice? The main points, that I love Phillabell and despise Cleon, are truths. Where then would be the virtue or wisdom to let him know some disagreeable circumstances which would make us both really uneasy, though there were only an imaginary reason for it? But happy are those who have ruled their lives with so much prudence that every action may appear barefaced, for to be forced to the least disguise is some violence to an honest nature, and though 'tis not disused to injure others, 'tis a corruption, at least a blemish, to do injury to itself. Yet would the men dissemble no otherwise with us, we could easily forgive 'em, but they with baser arts,
All their past faults with impudence reveal,
And only those which they intend conceal.

Exit.

Scene [iii]. The Walks.

Enter Beaumine and Grandfoy.

GRANDFOY.

Thus sir, lest my sword should fail to do her justice, I have endeavored to convince you how little Lesbia has deserved such unhandsome usage from you and am ready to confirm the truth of what I have said with the hazard of my life. We need go no farther, sir. This place is private and convenient—

BEAUMINE.

To give me satisfaction, sir, for you have done me such an injury.

GRANDFOY.

I thought, sir, what I have told you with so much frankness and Lesbia's letters, which you saw, refusing the offer I had made to marry her and mentioning on what account the ring was given me were proofs that we never injured you.

BEAUMINE.

Why, that's the mischief on't. You have convinced me she has been so honorable that I must be married, the greatest misfortune you could have drawn me into that I know of, indeed, sir.

GRANDFOY.

Then it seems you don't love her, sir.

BEAUMINE.

Because I have no mind to marry her? Then no man ever did love, for no man ever had or can have a mind absolutely to marry any woman.

GRANDFOY.

Why, has not many a man married merely* for love?

BEAUMINE.

Aye sir, and many a man has taken a house he liked, with a considerable fine upon it, because he knew it would not be let otherwise, but I'll be hanged if any man had not rather have it without.

GRANDFOY.

And be the more unwilling to pay it after he has been long in possession.

BEAUMINE.

But rather than forfeit his word or his house, for I find there's love as well as honor in the case.

GRANDFOY.

Well sir, if you resolve to do her justice upon any motive, 'tis all that Lesbia can require of you. But since we both have a claim to her, nothing but our swords can decide it.

BEAUMINE.

Oh yes, sir, she can do it much better, for though it's true, women are seldom favorable to merit, we must own they are better judges than the most judicious sword in Europe; the advantage is, the person she rejects will be in a better condition than may be his chance if we fall to cutting of throats. For him she chooses, I can't promise it, indeed.

GRANDFOY.

You talk very little like a lover. I wish her choice were placed where 'twould be welcomer, but I prefer Lesbia's satisfaction to my own and therefore am content to submit to her sentence.

BEAUMINE.
Wisely resolved, sir. A man of honor should not decline fighting upon any reasonable occasion but where it can answer the end. If it be for revenge, stabbing a man is a very substantial one, but for a mistress, how the devil does my sword know her inclinations? If it happen to dispatch the man she likes, I am sure to be hated the more for it; if a man she dislikes, there was no danger in him. So it can never be to any purpose. Come sir, let us try other means. Capitulate with the lady:
Women by force of arms can ne'er be won,
Unless the guards within betray the town.
Sound a parley, ye fair, and surrender.

Exit singing with Grandfoy.

Scene [iv]. Lesbia's Lodgings.

Enter Lesbia and Lucilia [and Bonsot].

LUCILIA.
You see how dear* this foolish gallantry had like to have cost me, if your timely notice had not put me upon my guard.

LESBIA.
This comes of being so hasty to run into an amour. Before the heart engages, we must retreat and know not how to do it with honor, but when love leads us on, however dangerous the consequences are, it makes 'em easy to us.

LUCILIA.
But 'tis indeed a strange folly to hazard our reputation only for the vanity of securing a conquest. The prize is so little worth in respect of the venture.

LESBIA.
What think you of the contrary fault, affecting an indifference for those we really love?

LUCILIA.
That's as much a greater folly, as our own happiness is of more consequence to us than other people's opinion.

LESBIA.
How blind we are to our own faults! Now don't you see that what you have been condemning you are at this instant guilty of: flying Phillabell when you most wish to meet him and seeming angry with him when you know he's in the right?

LUCILIA.[f]
But 'twould not be wise to know it, as our affairs stand, and I have ordered Lysetta to tell Phillabell I am at your lodgings. If he comes here I can't avoid him and so give him an opportunity of reconciling himself without seeming to desire it.

BONSOT.
I'll engage, madam, he'll come. I'm sure I said enough in your defense to satisfy any reasonable man.

LESBIA.
No doubt a little harmless artifice is sometimes necessary, and for a young beginner, you have performed pretty well, but Lysetta's part was managed with wonderful dexterity.

LUCILIA.
The design indeed was cunningly laid and happily effected.

LESBIA.
Hold. Is not that Phillabell's voice below?

Enter Phillabell and Lysetta.

LUCILIA.
I think it is. Now for my last deceit.—Madam, I'll take my leave of you.

LESBIA.
Nay, now indeed you shan't.

PHILLABELL.
Be so just to hear what I have to say before you condemn me, madam.

LUCILIA.
I have heard you say too much.

BONSOT.
Now what can she be angry at?

PHILLABELL.
But hear Lysetta, madam.—Come, you must speak the truth.

LYSETTA.
I beg your pardon, madam, I did not think any harm would come on't, but truly I did write some letters in your name to Cleon. Indeed I did not intend to do you any injury by it.

LUCILIA.
No injury! What else could induce you to it? Who set you on?

LYSETTA.
Nobody set me on, but Cleon took care to pay me

so well for deceiving him, that I thought it worth my pains.

LUCILIA.

It seems, Phillabel, you have great power with her to make her confess all this.

BONSOT.

What, is she jealous of her?—Oh, madam, there's nothing in that but money too. He has only given her money enough, take my word for it.

LUCILIA.

So I imagine, sir.

BONSOT.

Psha, you think 'twas upon some slippery account now, but 'twas only to make her own this cheat. I can answer for him.

PHILLABELL.

Prithee give me leave to vindicate myself, Bonsot.

BONSOT.

With all my heart, sir, now I have satisfied her as to the main point.

LESBIA.

Aye, like all other universal friends, commendingg everyone alike, their praises always injure.

PHILLABELL.

I took her in the very fact, madam: my good genius* led me thither just as she was writing and so intent upon her treachery, I came into the chamber unperceived, heard her admiring with her niece her skill in counterfeiting your hand so perfectly. When I had heard enough, I snatched the paper, which was to the same effect of that I showed you. It having miscarried, she was writing it again, which left her no room to deny her guilt, nor me to doubt your innocence.

LUCILIA.

'Twas happy, since it proves a means of putting an end to this cheat and gives us power to punish the author of it, which she shall find severely.

PHILLABELL.

But first, Lucilia, let us think of our own happiness that no new chance may cross it.

LUCILIA.

'Tis not enough that you believe me innocent. Since Cleon and perhaps, by his vanity, many others suspect me of infidelity, I must not let you share in my dishonor.

BONSOT.

Why madam, 'twill make your part the less.

LYSETTA.

If I might hope for pardon of my fault by making some kind of reparation, I would tell Cleon how I have all this while abused him.

BONSOT.

And let me alone to appease him. I'll tell him 'tis all but a sham, to a certain purpose.

LUCILIA.

I hope he knows his brother well enough to esteem what he says as it deserves.

LESBIA.

Upon those terms I must become her intercessor.

PHILLABELL.

And I have reason to join with you.

LUCILIA.

You have too much power with me to be refused anything you desire.

PHILLABELL.

Then you are mine again. At your feet receive my thanks, and let this hand give me possession.

As he kneels, Beaumine, Grandfoy, and Cleon enter.

BONSOT.

See now how good friends I have made you, and here comes my cousin and Beaumine together. I thought I had made up matters between them too.

BEAUMINE.

So this is the way on't. When the women have played us false, we must submit and beg pardon for having the impudence to see it.

PHILLABELL.

Oh Beaumine, my Lucilia's innocent.

BEAUMINE.

Aye, aye, so they are all, if they have but cunning enough.

PHILLABELL.

Thou'rt a mere* infidel.

BEAUMINE.

No faith, Phillabell, no offense to thee. I'm e'en as credulous a coxcomb as thyself. Prithee don't laugh at me. There are two evils you know that go by destiny.

PHILLABELL.

Of which I should least expect marriage to be thine, indeed.

GRANDFOY.

My cousin Cleon, madam, met us as we were coming hither and would needs have me bring him to wait on you.

LESBIA.

Being your relation, he must be welcome to me, but I'm sorry it happens at a time when things are in such a posture that I cannot be so easy, so much at liberty as I should to be entertained by so extraordinary a person.

CLEON. (*Aside.*)

That is, she would be alone with me.—Oh madam, I shall find a happier opportunity, but since I cannot enjoy it now, I'm extremely pleased to meet such good company here.—I have a great respect for these lovers, and wish you joy with all my heart, upon my word, sir.

PHILLABELL.

Oh I thank you, sir, but must desire another favor of you: you received some letters in this lady's name, which I expect you should return.

CLEON.

In that lady's name, sir? Then it seems she is not ashamed of her name, that she has told you where to find it. I protest, I resolved to conceal 'em, but if you have a mind to have 'em published, madam, I can put 'em in the press. They will be a very extraordinary epithalamium.

LUCILIA.

Sir, you have been deceived. Those letters never expressed my thoughts.

CLEON.

Very probable. Women's words seldom express their thoughts. I did not doubt but you had more kindness* for me than they expressed.

LYSETTA.

Ah sir, my lady never thought one word of what was writ. 'Twas all of my contrivance. I confess, sir, I was loath to let you despair.

BONSOT.

Hark you, Brother, this is only a plot to make you part with your mistress the more easily, but don't you seem to know it, and yet don't be angry neither.

CLEON.

But seem as good-natured a fool as you. Brother, you had the best contrivance last night in the walks to keep me from despair.—But not one word of your lady's thoughts?

LUCILIA.

I'll be sworn I spoke truth, but abusing a man is complimenting him when vanity's the interpreter.

LYSETTA.

Well sir, since the deceit is discovered,* I suppose you won't think my letters worth keeping.

CLEON.

Her letters— *Madame la Gouvernante*,[22] when you grant me the favor, I desire it may be in the same shape you made me the promise in last night.

LYSETTA.

Aye, aye, sir. This shape is only put on, that we may keep it with the more security.

CLEON.

Oh, I apprehend.

PHILLABELL.

I hope, sir, you believe Lucilia had no hand in deceiving you?

CLEON.

Pasitively, I assure you, sir.

PHILLABELL.

And be so ungenerous to refuse the letters.

CLEON.

Sir, I happen to have 'em all about me; I had some thoughts you might have a curiosity to know how well she could write before you married her. They're at your service, sir, if you please to peruse 'em. (*Gives the letters.*)

PHILLABELL.

I have not the curiosity indeed, sir.—Here Lysetta. (*Gives 'em her.*)

CLEON. [*Aside.*]

The best bred husband in the world, rat me.

BONSOT.

I told you I should satisfy him, sir. Now you must know he thinks the letters were Lucilia's, for all this.

PHILLABELL.

Does he so, sir? I shall find a way then to convince him they are not.

22 *Gouvernante*] governess (Fr.)

BONSOT.

Hey, why are you angry at that? Nay, rather than you should quarrel,* I'll tell him myself that she only ordered Lysetta to write 'em.

PHILLABELL.

What you say is of so little consequence, I care not what you tell him.

BONSOT.

Aye, aye. This is always my reward, but for all that, I shall never give over—

PHILLABELL.

Being impertinent, I dare engage for thee. 'Tis the happiest, though the most incurable distemper a man can have, and both for the same reason: he can never be made sensible of it.

BEAUMINE.

Among the many interposers in affairs they have nothing to do with, who, when they laugh at this officious meddler, will consider him as their own picture?

LUCILIA. [*Aside.*]

Well, I am happily come off, but through such dangers, such anxieties, as might warn all our sex against those little gallantries with which they only think to amuse themselves but, though innocent, too often gain 'em such a character* of lightness as their future conduct never can efface. Nay, though I have succeeded better, I find within all is not as it should be: a secret check, that so entire a confidence as Phillabell has in me is not returned with that plain, open, artless dealing it deserves. That will be the lasting punishment of my childish fault.

LESBIA.

Grandfoy tells me, Beaumine, you will both submit to my choice between you.

BEAUMINE.

So we agreed, madam. I'm impatient to know which blessing I must lose, you or my liberty.

Enter Constant and Miranda.

LESBIA.

Miranda! And married I'll engage, by that affected gravity.

LUCILIA.

Miranda married at last!

LESBIA.

I hope, sir, I may give you joy?

MIRANDA.

Aye, you may give him joy, for 'tis the first day of his reign.

CONSTANT.

Of my happiness indeed, but 'twould be ungrateful to use it to the prejudice of your power, from whom I have received it.

MIRANDA.

I begin to be terribly afraid I shall certainly love you, and you have loved me so fast, you must be near the end of the race before I am set out.

CONSTANT.

Oh! 'Tis an endless race; endeavor but to overtake me.

BEAUMINE.

This is a dreadful omen to me, madam; there was so much sympathy between us, I'm afraid it reaches to our destinies too.

MIRANDA.

Do the planets incline to conjunction then? I could not forbear coming to inquire how your affairs went?

BEAUMINE.

Very ill indeed, madam: there is but a woman's inclinations betwixt me and ruin, which would certainly give her to that gentleman, if I were as fond of marrying her as he is. But your sex's darling, contradiction, I fear will carry it.

MIRANDA.

What, Lesbia in profound meditation?

LESBIA.

Advise me, Miranda: I'm a little puzzled in this affair.

MIRANDA.

Divided betwixt love and honor?

BONSOT.

Now, I advise you, madam, in this case—

LESBIA.

What, without knowing it?

BONSOT.

Let it be what it will, I am never of honor's side. It's good for nothing but to make people uneasy, and I would have everybody please themselves, whether they can or no.

LESBIA.

You must teach 'em the art then.—But prithee should I, out of a foolish scruple, tie myself to Beaumine when we are weary of one another—

MIRANDA.

Or lay the yoke upon a fresh lover that will hold out longer—

LESBIA.

And bear it easier? How shall I resolve? I think they had best throw dice for me.

MIRANDA.

E'en put it to the vote.

LESBIA.

With all my heart.

MIRANDA.

What say you, gentlemen? Lesbia is so unwilling to disoblige either of you, she's resolved to be his that has most voices for him.

BEAUMINE.

What she pleases.

GRANDFOY.

I shall never dispute her will.

CLEON.

This is extremely new. But I don't know why it should not be brought into a custom to marry as well as to divorce by vote,[23] unless indeed, that getting rid of our wives will be more for the general good.

MIRANDA.

Well sir, which are you for?

CLEON.

Since there is so good a relief, for him that will soonest be weary of her.

GRANDFOY.

That I grant is on Beaumine's side.

MIRANDA.

What say you, Constant?

CONSTANT.

I am for him that loves her best.

GRANDFOY.

That favors me.

BONSOT.

I am for him that won't quarrel with her.

BEAUMINE.

That's likely to be me, for I shall be least with her.

LUCILIA.

I am for him that can plead most right in her.

BEAUMINE.

Ah the devil! That's me again.

PHILLABELL.

I am for him that she loves best.

MIRANDA.

And I for him that she loves least.

BEAUMINE.

That's undone me; 'twas pure malice, Miranda.

LESBIA.

The odds are on Beaumine's side: whether I declare I love him least or best, there's a vote for him; his right is indisputable; he says he shan't quarrel with me; and he's weary of me already. So there can be but two against him.

BEAUMINE.

You'll find hereafter there were more: my late suspicion of you gave me such disquiets as showed me how dear you are to me, and the proofs of your innocence confirm my love with my esteem.

LESBIA.

Which to preserve, and for all our quiets, I propose that for the future Grandfoy be a stranger to us.

BONSOT.

Oh! That's cruel. Sir, my cousin has a great kindness for you and your lady. I'll engage he'll do her no harm.

BEAUMINE.

Oh, no sir.

GRANDFOY.

I must submit but may have still, I hope, some pretence to your friendship.

BEAUMINE.

You have deserved it, sir, and are welcome to share with us this day's diversions.

CONSTANT.

I have ordered some music. With your leave, madam, we'll employ 'em.

A dance.

PHILLABELL.

'Tis time now to think upon the ceremony that yet remains to make us master of our wishes.

23 marry … vote] Since only Parliament had the authority to dissolve marriages at this time, divorces were, in a sense, subject to a vote.

BEAUMINE.
Which performed, I resolve to show those married men whom I have laughed out of their fondness or civility for their wives that I have learned by their weakness how to avoid giving 'em a revenge and will so shamelessly boast of loving mine that 'twill put raillery out of countenance and, by preserving my complaisance for her, show I know how to value myself.
For treating them with rudeness or neglect
Does most dishonor on ourselves reflect;
If that respect which their own merit drew
We think by their becoming ours less due,
And as in choosing we their worth approve,
We tax our judgment when we cease to love.

[Exeunt.]

FINIS.

Textual Notes

[a] Copytext is the corrected state of the first edition, a 1701 quarto (Qc). Also consulted were the uncorrected state (Qu), and a modern edition of 1988 (Kendall).
[b] stronger] stranger Qc, Qu, Kendall
[c] by] but Qc, Qu, Kendall
[d] exchange. BEAUMINE. Oh! … airy.] Qc, Qu; exchange. Oh! … airy. Kendall [Obviously a speech by Phillabell inquiring about Miranda has been omitted.]
[e] there] here, Qc, Qu, Kendall
[f] LUCILIA.] Kendall; LES. Qc, Qu
[g] commending] commanding Qc, Qu, Kendall

The Fair Penitent[a]

by Nicholas Rowe (1674-1718)

edited by Jean I. Marsden

The Fair Penitent is the third of Nicholas Rowe's tragedies and the first of the acclaimed "she-tragedies" on which his reputation as a dramatist rests. The play was first performed at Lincoln's Inn Fields in March of 1703, and, despite a disappointing premiere, soon became one of the most enduringly popular plays of the century. The title role was played by (and created for) Elizabeth Barry, the greatest tragic actress of her generation.

In *The Fair Penitent*, Rowe combines harmonious blank verse with innovations in the subject matter of serious drama. He rejects the emphasis on the affairs of kings and princes common to most earlier tragedies, and focuses instead on the lives of characters with whom his audience could more readily identify. As he famously states in his prologue, his tragedy presents "a melancholy tale of private woes" where viewers could "meet with sorrows like [their] own." Rowe does not break radically with tradition; his characters are well-to-do upper class citizens, but the focus of the tragedy remains within the domestic rather than the political sphere. Rowe's interest in private rather than public woes and the concerns of family rather than empire foreshadows the development later in the eighteenth century of domestic tragedies such as George Lillo's *The London Merchant.*

Although Rowe was not the first playwright to write she-tragedy (see also Banks, *The Unhappy Favorite*), he became the most famed practitioner of the genre and the playwright whose name became almost synonymous with the term (he even coined the phrase). Popular in the 1680s and 1690s, she-tragedies emphasize the suffering of a sympathetic female figure, often a woman who, like Rowe's heroine Calista, has committed a sexual sin. In *The Fair Penitent*, Rowe reinvigorates a form which by the early eighteenth century had become hackneyed and formulaic, using as his source an older tragedy, Philip Massinger's *The Fatal Dowry* (ca. 1630). In contrast to Massinger's play in which the female figure is distinctly unsympathetic and appears infrequently, Rowe makes Calista the play's central focus. The lack of pathos displayed by the title character distinguishes Rowe's play from many contemporary she-tragedies. Seduced and abandoned by the man she loves and forced into a marriage with another, she repents of her sin but nonetheless rebels against her fate. In fact, Calista's strong will and refusal to indulge in self-incrimination angered some contemporary playgoers, and Rowe's enemies complained that he made a "whore" his heroine. In particular they claimed that the play's title was misleading as Calista never, to their minds, truly repented. One such critic was Samuel Johnson, who, although he praised *The Fair Penitent* as "one of the most pleasing tragedies on the stage," nonetheless objected that Calista felt "pain from detection rather than from guilt, and expresses more shame than sorrow, and more rage than shame" (*Lives of the Poets*).

Despite such complaints, *The Fair Penitent* was exceeded in popularity only by the tragedies of Shakespeare and a handful of tragedies by Otway, Southerne, and Rowe himself. Calista became a stock role for all great actresses of the eighteenth century. The play also introduced the figure of Lothario, a character so vivid that his name has survived into modern usage as synonymous with the charming seducer.

PROLOGUE

Long has the fate of kings and empires been
The common bus'ness of the tragic scene,
As if misfortune made the throne her seat,
And none could be unhappy but the great.
Dearly, 'tis true, each buys the crown he wears,
And many are the mighty monarch's cares:
By foreign foes and home-bred factions pressed,
Few are the joys he knows, and short his hours of rest.
Stories like these with wonder we may hear,
But far remote, and in a higher sphere:
We ne'er can pity what we ne'er can share.
Like distant battles of the Pole and Swede,[1]
Which frugal citizens o'er coffee read,
Careless for who shall fail or who succeed.
Therefore an humbler theme our author chose,
A melancholy tale of private woes:
No princes here lost royalty bemoan,
But you shall meet with sorrows like your own;
Here see imperious Love his vassals treat
As hardly as Ambition does the great;
See how succeeding passions rage by turns,
How fierce the youth with joy and rapture burns,
And how to death, for beauty lost, he mourns.
Let no nice* taste the poet's art arraign,
If some frail vicious characters he feign:
Who writes should still let Nature be his care,
Mix shades with lights, and not paint all things fair,
But show you men and women as they are.
With deference to the fair he bade me say,
Few to perfection ever found the way;
Many in many parts are known t'excel,
But 'twere too hard for one to act all well.
Whom justly life should through each scene commend,
The maid, the wife, the mistress, and the friend:
This age, 'tis true, has one great instance seen,
And Heav'n in justice made that one a queen.[2]

[1] Pole and Swede] In 1702-3, Charles XII of Sweden conducted a military campaign in Poland, deposing one Polish king and installing another.

[2] queen] Queen Anne (1701-14)

DRAMATIS PERSONAE

MEN

Sciolto, a nobleman of Genoa, father to Calista.
Altamont, a young lord, in love with Calista and designed her husband by Sciolto.
Horatio, his friend.
Lothario, a young lord, enemy to Altamont.
Rossano, his friend.
Servants to Sciolto.

WOMEN

Calista, daughter to Sciolto.
Lavinia, sister to Altamont and wife to Horatio.
Lucilla, confidant to Calista.

SCENE: SCIOLTO'S PALACE AND GARDEN, WITH SOME PART OF THE STREET NEAR IT, IN GENOA.

The Fair Penitent.

Quin morere, ut merita es, ferroque averte dolorem.
Virg. *Aen.* Lib. 4.[3]

Act I, scene i. A garden belonging to Sciolto's palace.

Enter Altamont and Horatio.

ALTAMONT.

Let this auspicious day be ever sacred,
No mourning, no misfortunes happen on it;
Let it be marked for triumphs and rejoicings;
Let happy lovers ever make it holy,
Choose it to bless their hopes and crown their wishes,
This happy day that gives me my Calista.

HORATIO.

Yes, Altamont, today thy better stars
Are joined to shed their kindest influence on thee:
Sciolto's noble hand, that raised thee first,
Half dead and drooping o'er thy father's grave,
Completes its bounty and restores thy name
To that high rank and luster which it boasted
Before ungrateful Genoa had forgot
The merit of thy godlike father's arms;

[3] *Quin* … 4] Virgil, *Aeneid* IV.547: "Rather with steel thy guilty breast invade, / And take the fortune thou thyself hast made" (Dryden IV.789-90). Dido contemplates leaving Carthage with Aeneas or committing suicide.

Before that country, which he long had served
In watchful councils and in winter camps,
Had cast off his white age to want and wretchedness
And made their court to faction by his ruin.

ALTAMONT.
Oh great Sciolto! oh my more than father!
Let me not live, but at thy very name
My eager heart springs up and leaps with joy.
When I forget the vast, vast debt I owe thee—
Forget! (but 'tis impossible)—then let me
Forget the use and privilege of reason,
Be driven from the commerce of mankind
To wander in the desert among brutes,
To bear the various fury of the seasons,
The night's unwholesome dew and noonday's heat,
To be the scorn of earth and curse of Heav'n.

HORATIO.
So open, so unbounded was his goodness,
It reached ev'n me because I was thy friend.
When that great man I loved, thy noble father,
Bequeathed thy gentle sister to my arms,
His last dear pledge and legacy of friendship,
That happy tie made me Sciolto's son.
He called us his, and with a parent's fondness
Indulged us in his wealth, blest us with plenty,
Healed all our cares, and sweetened love itself.

ALTAMONT.
By Heav'n, he found my fortunes so abandoned
That nothing but a miracle could raise 'em:
My father's bounty and the state's ingratitude
Had stripped him bare, nor left him ev'n a grave;
Undone myself and sinking with his ruin,
I had no wealth to bring, nothing to succor him
But fruitless tears.

HORATIO.
Yet what thou couldst thou didst
And didst it like a son: when his hard creditors,
Urged and assisted by Lothario's father
(Foe to thy house and rival of their greatness),
By sentence of the cruel law forbid
His venerable corpse to rest in earth,
Thou gav'st thyself a ransom for his bones,
With piety uncommon didst give up
Thy hopeful youth to slaves who ne'er knew mercy,
Sour, unrelenting, money-loving villains,
Who laugh at human nature and forgiveness
And are, like fiends, the factors for destruction.
Heav'n, who beheld the pious act, approved it
And bade Sciolto's bounty be its proxy
To bless thy filial virtue with abundance.

ALTAMONT.
But see he comes, the author of my happiness,
The man who saved my life from deadly sorrow,
Who bids my days be blest with peace and plenty
And satisfies my soul with love and beauty.

Enter Sciolto, he runs to Altamont and embraces him.

SCIOLTO.
Joy to thee, Altamont! Joy to myself!
Joy to this happy morn that makes thee mine,
That kindly grants what Nature had denied me
And makes me father of a son like thee.

ALTAMONT.
My Father! oh, let me unlade my breast,
Pour out the fullness of my soul before you,
Show ev'ry tender, ev'ry grateful thought
This wondrous goodness stirs. But 'tis impossible,
And utterance all is vile,* since I can only
Swear you reign here, but never tell how much.

SCIOLTO.
It is enough, I know thee: thou art honest;
Goodness innate and worth hereditary
Are in thy mind; thy noble father's virtues
Spring freshly forth and blossom in thy youth.

ALTAMONT.
Thus Heav'n from nothing raised his fair creation
And then with wondrous joy beheld its beauty,
Well pleased to see the excellence he gave.

SCIOLTO.
Oh noble youth! I swear since first I knew thee,
Ev'n from that day of sorrows when I saw thee
Adorned and lovely in thy filial tears,
The mourner and redeemer of thy father,
I set thee down and sealed thee for my own:
Thou art my son, ev'n near me as Calista.
—Horatio and Lavinia too are mine. (*Embraces Horatio.*)
All are my children and shall share my heart.
But wherefore waste we thus this happy day?
The laughing minutes summon thee to joy
And with new pleasures court thee as they pass;
Thy waiting bride ev'n chides thee for delaying,

And swears thou com'st not with a bridegroom's haste.

ALTAMONT.

Oh! could I hope there was one thought of Altamont,
One kind remembrance in Calista's breast,
The winds with all their wings would be too slow
To bear me to her feet. For oh! my father,
Amidst this stream of joy that bears me on,
Blest as I am and honored in your friendship,
There is one pain that hangs upon my heart.

SCIOLTO.

What means my son?

ALTAMONT.

When, at your intercession,
Last night Calista yielded to my happiness,
Just ere we parted, as I sealed my vows
With rapture on her lips, I found her cold
As a dead lover's statue on his tomb;
A rising storm of passion shook her breast,
Her eyes a piteous show'r of tears let fall,
And then she sighed as if her heart were breaking.
With all the tend'rest eloquence of love
I begged to be a sharer in her grief,
But she, with looks averse and eyes that froze me,
Sadly replied, her sorrows were her own
Nor in a father's pow'r to dispose of.

SCIOLTO.

Away! It is the cozenage of their sex,
One of the common arts they practice on us,
To sigh and weep then when their hearts beat high
With expectation of the coming joy.
Thou hast in camps and fighting fields been bred,
Unknowing in the subtleties of women:
The virgin bride, who swoons with deadly fear
To see the end of all her wishes near,
When, blushing from the light and public eyes,
To the kind covert of the night she flies,
With equal fires to meet the bridegroom moves,
Melts in his arms, and with a loose[4] she loves.

Exeunt.

[Scene ii. The same.]

Enter Lothario and Rossano.

LOTHARIO.

The father and the husband!

ROSSANO.

Let them pass,
They saw us not.

LOTHARIO.

I care not if they did,
Ere long I mean to meet 'em face to face
And gall 'em with my triumph o'er Calista.

ROSSANO.

You loved her once.

LOTHARIO.

I liked her, would have married her,
But that it pleased her father to refuse me,
To make this honorable fool her husband.
For which, if I forget him, may the shame
I mean to brand his name with stick on mine.

ROSSANO.

She, gentle soul, was kinder than her father.

LOTHARIO.

She was, and oft in private gave me hearing,
Till by long list'ning to the soothing tale
At length her easy heart was wholly mine.

ROSSANO.

I have heard you oft describe her haughty, insolent,
And fierce with high disdain; it moves my wonder
That virtue thus defended should be yielded
A prey to loose desires.

LOTHARIO.

Hear then, I'll tell thee.
Once in a lone and secret hour of night,
When ev'ry eye was closed and the pale moon
And stars alone shone conscious of the theft,
Hot with the Tuscan grape[5] and high in blood,
Haply I stole unheeded to her chamber.

ROSSANO.

That minute sure was lucky.

LOTHARIO.

Oh 'twas great.
I found the fond,* believing, lovesick maid,
Loose, unattired, warm, tender, full of wishes;
Fierceness and pride, the guardians of her honor,
Were charmed to rest, and love alone was waking.
Within her rising bosom all was calm

---

4 with a loose] with abandon, without restraint

5 Tuscan grape] wine from Tuscany in central Italy

As peaceful seas that know no storms and only
Are gently lifted up and down by tides.
I snatched the glorious, golden opportunity
And with prevailing, youthful ardor pressed her,
Till with short sighs and murmuring reluctance
The yielding fair one gave me perfect happiness.
Ev'n all the livelong night we passed in bliss,
In ecstasies too fierce to last forever.
At length the morn and cold indifference came;
When fully sated with the luscious banquet,
I hastily took leave and left the nymph
To think on what was past and sigh alone.

ROSSANO.
You saw her soon again.

LOTHARIO.
Too soon I saw her,
For oh! that meeting was not like the former:
I found my heart no more beat high with transport,
No more I sighed and languished for enjoyment,
'Twas past, and reason took her turn to reign,
While ev'ry weakness fell before her throne.

ROSSANO.
What of the lady?

LOTHARIO.
With uneasy fondness
She hung upon me, wept and sighed and swore
She was undone, talked of a priest and marriage,
Of flying with me from her father's pow'r,
Called ev'ry saint and blessèd angel down
To witness for her that she was my wife.
I started at that name.

ROSSANO.
What answer made you?

LOTHARIO.
None, but pretending sudden pain and illness
Escaped the persecution; two nights since,
By message urged and frequent importunity,
Again I saw her. Straight with tears and sighs,
With swelling breasts, with swooning, with distraction,
With all the subtleties and pow'rful arts
Of wilful woman lab'ring for her purpose,
Again she told the same dull, nauseous tale.
Unmoved, I begged her spare th'ungrateful subject
Since I resolved, that love and peace of mind
Might flourish long inviolate betwixt us,
Never to load it with the marriage chain;
That I would still retain her in my heart
My ever gentle mistress and my friend.
But for those other names of wife and husband,
They only meant ill-nature, cares, and quarrels.

ROSSANO.
How bore she this reply?

LOTHARIO.
Ev'n as the earth
When (winds pent up, or eating fires beneath
Shaking the mass) she labors with destruction.
At first her rage was dumb and wanted* words,
But when the storm found way, 'twas wild and loud.
Mad as the priestess of the Delphic god,[6]
Enthusiastic* passion swelled her breast,
Enlarged her voice, and ruffled all her form;
Proud, and disdainful of the love I proffered,
She called me "Villain! Monster! Base! Betrayer!"[b]
At last, in very bitterness of soul,
With deadly imprecations on herself,
She vowed severely ne'er to see me more,
Then bid me fly that minute. I obeyed
And, bowing, left her to grow cool at leisure.

ROSSANO.
She has relented since, else why this message
To meet the keeper of her secrets here
This morning?

LOTHARIO.
See the person whom you named.

Enter Lucilla.

Well, my ambassadress, what must we treat of?
Come you to menace war and proud defiance,
Or does the peaceful olive grace your message?
Is your fair mistress calmer? does she soften?
And must we love again? Perhaps she means
To treat in juncture with her new ally
And make her husband party to th'agreement.

LUCILLA.
Is this well done, my lord? Have you put off
All sense of human nature? Keep a little,
A little pity to distinguish manhood,
Lest other men, though cruel, should disclaim you
And judge you to be numbered with the brutes.

---

6 priestess … god] The priestess of Apollo's temple at Delphi often spoke incoherently or in riddles.

LOTHARIO.
I see thou'st learnt to rail.
LUCILLA.
I've learnt to weep:
That lesson my sad mistress often gives me;
By day she seeks some melancholy shade
To hide her sorrows from the prying world;
At night she watches all the long, long hours
And listens to the winds and beating rain
With sighs as loud and tears that fall as fast.
Then ever and anon she wrings her hands
And cries, "False! false Lothario!"
LOTHARIO.
Oh, no more!
I swear thou'lt spoil thy pretty face with crying,
And thou hast beauty that may make thy fortune:
Some keeping* cardinal shall dote upon thee
And barter his church treasure for thy freshness.
LUCILLA.
What! shall I sell my innocence and youth,
For wealth or titles, to perfidious man!
To man! who makes his mirth of our undoing!
The base, professed betrayer of our sex.
Let me grow old in all misfortunes else,
Rather than know the sorrows of Calista.
LOTHARIO.
Does she send thee to chide in her behalf?
I swear thou dost it with so good a grace
That I could almost love thee for thy frowning.
LUCILLA.
Read there, my lord, there, in her own sad lines,
(*Giving a letter.*)
Which best can tell the story of her woes,
That grief of heart which your unkindness gives her.
LOTHARIO. (*Reads.*)
"Your cruelty—obedience to my father—give my hand to Altamont."
(*Aside.*) By Heav'n! 'tis well, such ever be the gifts
With which I greet the man whom my soul hates.
But to go on!
"—Wish—heart—honor—too faithless—weakness—tomorrow—last trouble—lost Calista."
Women, I see, can change as well as men:
She writes me here, forsaken as I am,
That I should bind my brows with mournful willow,*
For she has given her hand to Altamont.
Yet tell the fair inconstant—
LUCILLA.
How, my lord?
LOTHARIO.
Nay, no more angry words. Say to Calista,
The humblest of her slaves shall wait her pleasure,
If she can leave her happy husband's arms
To think upon so lost a thing as I am.
LUCILLA.
Alas! for pity, come with gentler looks,
Wound not her heart with this unmanly triumph
And, though you love her not, yet swear you do.
So shall dissembling once be virtuous in you.
LOTHARIO.
Hah! who comes here?
LUCILLA.
The bridegroom's friend, Horatio.
He must not see us here. Tomorrow early
Be at the garden gate.
LOTHARIO.
Bear to my love
My kindest thoughts and swear I will not fail her.

Lothario, putting up the letter hastily, drops it as he goes out.

Exeunt Lothario and Rossano one way, Lucilla another.

[Scene iii. Continues.]

Enter Horatio.

HORATIO.
Sure 'tis the very error of my eyes:
Waking I dream, or I beheld Lothario;
He seemed conferring with Calista's woman;*
At my approach they started and retired.
What business could he have here, and with her?
I know he bears the noble Altamont
Professed and deadly hate—What paper's this?
(*Taking up the letter.*)
Hah! To Lothario! 'Sdeath!* Calista's name!
(*Opening it.*)
Confusion and misfortune! (*Reads.*)
"Your cruelty has at length determined me, and I have resolved this morning to yield a perfect obedience to my father and to give my hand to

Altamont, in spite of my weakness for the false Lothario. I could almost wish I had that heart—and that honor to bestow with it—which you have robbed me of."

Damnation! to the rest— (*Reads again.*)

"But oh! I fear could I retrieve 'em, I should again be undone by the too faithless, yet too lovely Lothario. This is the last weakness of my pen, and tomorrow shall be the last in which I will indulge my eyes. Lucilla shall conduct you if you are kind enough to let me see you; it shall be the last trouble you shall meet with from,
The Lost Calista."

The lost indeed! for thou art gone as far
As there can be perdition, fire, and sulfur:
Hell is the sole avenger of such crimes.
Oh that the ruin were but all thy own!
Thou wilt ev'n make thy father curse his age;
At sight of this black scroll the gentle Altamont
(For oh! I know his heart is set upon thee)
Shall droop and hang his discontented head,
Like merit scorned by insolent authority,
And never grace the public with his virtues.—
Perhaps ev'n now he gazes fondly on her
And, thinking soul and body both alike,
Blesses the perfect workmanship of Heav'n,
Then sighing to his ev'ry care, speaks peace
And bids his heart be satisfied with happiness.
Oh wretched husband! while she hangs about thee
With idle blandishments and plays the fond one,
Ev'n then her hot imagination wanders,
Contriving riot and loose scapes[7] of love,
And, while she clasps thee close, makes thee a monster.[8]
What if I give this paper to her father?
It follows that his justice dooms her dead
And breaks his heart with sorrow: hard return
For all the good his hand has heaped on us.
Hold, let me take a moment's thought.

Enter Lavinia.

LAVINIA.

My lord!
Trust me, it joys my heart that I have found you.
Enquiring wherefore you had left the company
Before my brother's nuptial rites were ended,
They told me you had felt some sudden illness.
Where are you sick? Is it your head? your heart?
Tell me, my love, and ease my anxious thoughts,
That I may take you gently in my arms,
Sooth you to rest, and soften all your pains.

HORATIO.

It were unjust, no, let me spare my friend,
Lock up the fatal secret in my breast,
Nor tell him that which will undo his quiet.

LAVINIA.

What means my lord?

HORATIO.

Hah! saidst thou my Lavinia?

LAVINIA.

Alas! you know not what you make me suffer.
Why are you pale? Why did you start and tremble?
Whence is that sigh? And wherefore are your eyes
Severely raised to Heav'n? The sick man thus,
Acknowledging the summons of his fate,
Lifts up his feeble hands and eyes for mercy
And with confusion thinks upon his audit.

HORATIO.

Oh no! thou hast mistook my sickness quite,
These pangs are of the soul. Would I had met
Sharpest convulsions, spotted pestilences,
Or any other deadly foe to life,
Rather than heave beneath this load of thought.

LAVINIA.

Alas, what is it? Wherefore turn you from me?
Why did you falsely call me your Lavinia
And swear I was Horatio's better half,
Since now you mourn unkindly by yourself
And rob me of my partnership of sadness?
Witness you holy Pow'rs, who know my truth,
There cannot be a chance in life so miserable,
Nothing so very hard but I could bear it
Much rather than my love should treat me coldly
And use me like a stranger to his heart.

HORATIO.

Seek not to know what I would hide from all,
But most from thee. I never knew a pleasure,
Aught that was joyful, fortunate, or good,
But straight I ran to bless thee with the tidings
And laid up all my happiness with thee.
But wherefore, wherefore should I give thee pain?

[7] scapes] scenes

[8] monster] man with horns, cuckold

Then spare me, I conjure thee, ask no further,
Allow my melancholy thoughts this privilege
And let 'em brood in secret o'er their sorrows.

LAVINIA.
It is enough, chide not, and all is well.
Forgive me if I saw you sad, Horatio,
And asked to weep out part of your misfortunes;
I wonnot press to know what you forbid me.
Yet, my loved lord, yet you must grant me this:
Forget your cares for this one happy day;
Devote this day to mirth and to your Altamont;
For his dear sake let peace be in your looks.
Ev'n now the jocund bridegroom wants* your wishes;
He thinks the priest has but half blest his marriage
Till his friend hails him with the sound of joy.

HORATIO.
Oh never! never! never! Thou art innocent:
Simplicity from ill, pure native truth,
And candor of the mind adorn thee ever.
But there are such, such false ones in the world,
'Twould fill thy gentle soul with wild amazement
To hear their story told.

LAVINIA.
False ones, my lord?

HORATIO.
Fatally fair they are, and in their smiles
The graces, little loves, and young desires inhabit,
But all that gaze upon 'em are undone,
For they are false, luxurious in their appetites,
And all the heav'n they hope for is variety:
One lover to another still* succeeds,
Another, and another after that,
And the last fool is welcome as the former
Till, having loved his hour out, he gives place
And mingles with the herd that went before him.

LAVINIA.
Can there be such? and have they peace of mind?
Have they in all the series of their changing
One happy hour? If women are such things,
How was I formed so different from my sex?
My little heart is satisfied with you:
You take up all her room, as in a cottage
Which harbors some benighted princely stranger,
Where the good man, proud of his hospitality,
Yields all his homely dwelling to his guest
And hardly keeps a corner for himself.

HORATIO.
Oh were they all like thee, men would adore 'em
And all the bus'ness of their lives be loving;
The nuptial band should be the pledge of peace,
And all domestic cares and quarrels cease;
The world should learn to love by virtuous rules,
And marriage be no more the jest of fools.

Exeunt.

Act II, scene i. A hall.

Enter Calista and Lucilla.

CALISTA.
Be dumb forever, silent as the grave,
Nor let thy fond, officious love disturb
My solemn sadness with the sound of joy.
If thou wilt soothe me, tell some dismal tale
Of pining discontent and black despair.
For oh! I've gone around through all my thoughts,
But all are indignation, love, or shame,
And my dear peace of mind is lost forever.

LUCILLA.
Why do you follow still that wand'ring fire
That has misled your weary steps and leaves you
Benighted in a wilderness of woe?
That false Lothario! Turn from the deceiver,
Turn and behold where gentle Altamont,
Kind as the softest virgin of our sex
And faithful as the simple village swain
That never knew the courtly vice of changing
Sighs at your feet and woos you to be happy.

CALISTA.
Away, I think not of him. My sad soul
Has formed a dismal melancholy scene,
Such a retreat as I would wish to find:
An unfrequented vale, o'ergrown with trees
Mossy and old within whose lonesome shade
Ravens and birds ill-omened only dwell;
No sound to break the silence, but a brook
That bubbling winds among the weeds; no mark
Of any human shape that had been there,
Unless a skeleton of some poor wretch
Who had long since, like me, by love undone,
Sought that sad place out to despair and die in.

LUCILLA.
Alas for pity!

CALISTA.
There I fain would hide me
From the base world, from malice, and from shame,
For 'tis the solemn counsel of my soul
Never to live with public loss of honor:
'Tis fixed to die, rather than bear the insolence
Of each affected she that tells my story
And blesses her good stars that she is virtuous.
To be a tale for fools! Scorned by the women
And pitied by the men! oh insupportable!

LUCILLA.
Can you perceive the manifest destruction,
The gaping gulf that opens just before you,
And yet rush on, though conscious of the danger?
Oh hear me, hear your ever faithful creature:
By all the good I wish, by all the ill
My trembling heart forebodes, let me entreat you
Never to see this faithless man again.
Let me forbid his coming.

CALISTA.
On thy life
I charge thee, no! My genius* drives me on.
I must, I will behold him once again.
Perhaps it is the crisis of my fate,
And this one interview shall end my cares.
My lab'ring heart, that swells with indignation,
Heaves to discharge the burden; that once done,
The busy thing shall rest within its cell
And never beat again.

LUCILLA.
Trust not to that:
Rage is the shortest passion of our souls;
Like narrow brooks that rise with sudden show'rs,
It swells in haste and falls again as soon;
Still* as it ebbs, the softer thoughts flow in,
And the deceiver Love supplies its place.

CALISTA.
I have been wronged enough to arm my temper
Against the smooth delusion. But alas!
(Chide not my weakness, gentle maid, but pity me)
A woman's softness hangs about me still.
Then let me blush and tell thee all my folly.
I swear I could not see the dear betrayer
Kneel at my feet and sigh to be forgiven,
But my relenting heart would pardon all
And quite forget 'twas he that had undone me.

LUCILLA.
Ye sacred Powers, whose gracious providence
Is watchful for our good, guard me from men,
From their deceitful tongues, their vows and flatteries;
Still* let me pass neglected by their eyes,
Let my bloom wither and my form decay,
That none may think it worth his while to ruin me,
And fatal love may never be my bane.

CALISTA.
Hah, Altamont! Calista now be wary
And guard thy soul's accesses with dissembling,
Nor let this hostile husband's eyes explore
The warring passions and tumultuous thoughts
That rage within thee and deform thy reason.

Enter Altamont.

ALTAMONT.
Be gone, my cares, I give you to the winds,
Far to be borne, far from the happy Altamont,
For from this sacred era of my love
A better order of succeeding days
Come smiling forward, white[9] and lucky all.
Calista is the mistress of the year:
She crowns the seasons with auspicious beauty
And bids ev'n all my hours be good and joyful.

CALISTA. [*Aside.*]
If I was ever mistress of such happiness,
Oh! wherefore did I play th'unthrifty fool
And, wasting all on others, leave myself
Without one thought of joy to give me comfort?

ALTAMONT.
Oh mighty love! Shall that fair face profane
This thy great festival with frowns and sadness!
I swear it shannot be, for I will woo thee
With sighs so moving, with so warm a transport,
That thou shalt catch the gentle flame from me
And kindle into joy.

CALISTA.
I tell thee, Altamont,
Such hearts as ours were never paired above:
Ill-suited to each other; joined, not matched.
Some sullen influence,* a foe to both,
Has wrought this fatal marriage to undo us.
Mark but the frame and temper of our minds,

[9] white] fortunate, happy

How very much we differ. Ev'n this day,
That fills thee with such ecstasy and transport,
To me brings nothing that should make me bless it
Or think it better than the day before
Or any other in the course of time
That dully took its turn and was forgotten.

ALTAMONT.

If to behold thee as my pledge of happiness,
To know none fair, none excellent beside thee;
If still* to love thee with unwearied constancy
Through ev'ry season, ev'ry change of life,
Through wrinkled age, through sickness and misfortune,
Be worth the least return of grateful love,
Oh then let my Calista bless this day,
And set it down for happy.

CALISTA.

'Tis the day
In which my father gave my hand to Altamont;
As such I will remember it forever.

Enter Sciolto, Horatio, and Lavinia.

SCIOLTO.

Let mirth go on, let pleasure know no pause,
But fill up ev'ry minute of this day.
'Tis yours, my children, sacred to your loves.
The glorious sun himself for you looks gay;
He shines for Altamont and for Calista.
Let there be music, let the master touch
The sprightly string and softly-breathing flute
Till harmony rouse ev'ry gentle passion,
Teach the cold maid to lose her fears in love
And the fierce youth to languish at her feet.
Begin, ev'n age itself is cheered with music,
It wakes a glad remembrance of our youth,
Calls back past joys, and warms us into transport.

Here an entertainment of music and dancing.

Song.[10]

I

Ah stay! ah turn! ah whither would you fly,
Too charming, too relentless maid?
I follow not to conquer but to die,
You of the fearful are afraid.

II

In vain I call, for she like fleeting air,
When pressed by some tempestuous wind,
Flies swifter from the voice of my despair
Nor casts one pitying look behind.

SCIOLTO.

Take care my gates be open, bid all welcome;
All who rejoice with me today are friends.
Let each indulge his genius, each be glad,
Jocund and free, and swell the feast with mirth.
The sprightly bowl shall cheerfully go round,
None shall be grave, nor too severely wise;
Losses and disappointments, cares and poverty,
The rich man's insolence and great man's scorn,
In wine shall be forgotten all. Tomorrow
Will be too soon to think and to be wretched.
Oh! grant, ye Powers, that I may see these happy,
(*Pointing to Altamont and Calista.*)
Completely blest, and I have life enough
And leave the rest indifferently to Fate.

Exeunt. Manet Horatio.

HORATIO.

What if, while all are here intent on revelling,
I privately went forth and sought Lothario?
This letter may be forged: perhaps the wantonness
Of his vain youth, to stain a lady's fame;
Perhaps his malice, to disturb my friend.
Oh no! my heart forebodes it must be true.
Methought ev'n now I marked the starts of guilt
That shook her soul, though damned dissimulation
Screened her dark thoughts and set to public view
A specious face of innocence and beauty.
Oh false appearance! What is all our sovereignty,
Our boasted pow'r? When they oppose their arts,
Still* they prevail, and we are found their fools.
With such smooth looks and many a gentle word
The first fair she[11] beguiled her easy lord;
Too blind with love and beauty to beware,
He fell unthinking in the fatal snare
Nor could believe that such a heav'nly face
Had bargained with the Devil, to damn her wretched race.

Exit.

---

10 Song] written by William Congreve

11 she] Eve

Scene ii. The street near Sciolto's palace.

Enter Lothario and Rossano.

LOTHARIO.
To tell thee then the purport of my thoughts:
The loss of this fond* paper would not give me
A moment of disquiet, were it not
My instrument of vengeance on this Altamont;
Therefore, I mean to wait some opportunity
Of speaking with the maid we saw this morning.

ROSSANO.
I wish you, sir, to think upon the danger
Of being seen: today their friends are round 'em,
And any eye that lights by chance on you
Shall put your life and safety to the hazard.

They confer aside. Enter Horatio.

HORATIO.
Still I must doubt* some mystery of mischief,
Some artifice beneath: Lothario's father,
I knew him well, he was sagacious, cunning,
Fluent in words, and bold in peaceful councils,
But of a cold, unactive hand in war,
Yet with these coward's virtues he undid
My unsuspecting, valiant, honest friend.
This son, if fame mistakes not, is more hot,
More open, and unartful. (*Seeing him.*) Hah! he's here!

LOTHARIO.
Damnation! He again! This second time
Today he has crossed me like my evil genius.*

HORATIO.
I sought you, sir.

LOTHARIO.
'Tis well then I am found.

HORATIO.
'Tis well you are: The man who wrongs my friend
To the earth's utmost verge I would pursue;
No place, though e'er so holy, should protect him;
No shape that artful fear e'er formed should hide him,
Till he fair answer made and did me justice.

LOTHARIO.
Hah! dost thou know me? that I am Lothario?
As great a name as this proud city boasts of.
Who is this mighty man, then, this Horatio,
That I should basely hide me from his anger,
Lest he should chide me for his friend's displeasure?

HORATIO.
The brave, 'tis true, do never shun the light;
Just are their thoughts, and open are their tempers;
Freely without disguise they love and hate;
Still* are they found in the fair face of day,
And Heav'n and men are judges of their actions.

LOTHARIO.
Such let 'em be of mine: there's not a purpose
Which my soul ever framed or my hand acted
But I could well have bid the world look on
And what I once durst do have dared to justify.

HORATIO.
Where was this open boldness, this free spirit,
When but this very morning I surprised thee
In base, dishonest privacy, consulting
And bribing a poor mercenary wretch
To sell her lady's secrets, stain her honor,
And with a forged contrivance blast her virtue?
At sight of me thou fled'st!

LOTHARIO.
Hah! Fled from thee?

HORATIO.
Thou fled'st, and guilt was on thee like a thief,
A pilferer descried in some dark corner
Who there had lodged with mischievous intent
To rob and ravage at the hour of rest
And do a midnight murder on the sleepers.

LOTHARIO.
Slave! Villain!*— (*Offers* to draw, Rossano holds him.*)

ROSSANO.
Hold, my lord! think where you are,
Think how unsafe and hurtful to your honor
It were to urge a quarrel* in this place
And shock the peaceful city with a broil.

LOTHARIO.
Then since thou dost provoke my vengeance, know
I would not for this city's wealth, for all
Which the sea wafts to our Ligurian shore,
But that the joys I reaped with that fond wanton,
The wife of Altamont, should be as public
As is the noonday sun, air, earth, or water
Or any common benefit of nature.
Think'st thou I meant the shame should be concealed?

Oh no! by Hell and Vengeance, all I wanted*
Was some fit messenger to bear the news
To the dull, doting husband. Now I have found him,
And thou art he.

HORATIO.
I hold thee base enough
To break through law and spurn at sacred order
And do a brutal injury like this,
Yet mark me well, young lord, I think Calista
Too nice,* too noble, and too great of soul
To be the prey of such a thing as thou art.
'Twas base and poor, unworthy of a man,
To forge a scroll so villainous and loose
And mark it with a noble lady's name.
These are the mean, dishonest arts of cowards,
Strangers to manhood and to glorious dangers,
Who, bred at home in idleness and riot,
Ransack for mistresses th'unwholesome stews
And never know the worth of virtuous love.

LOTHARIO.
Think'st thou I forged the letter? Think so still,*
Till the broad shame comes staring in thy face
And boys shall hoot the cuckold as he passes.

HORATIO.
Away, no woman could descend so low:
A skipping, dancing, worthless tribe you are,
Fit only for yourselves. You herd together,
And when the circling glass warms your vain hearts,
You talk of beauties that you never saw
And fancy raptures that you never knew.
Legends of saints, who never yet had being,
Or being, ne'er were saints,[12] are not so false
As the fond tales which you recount of love.

LOTHARIO.
But that I do not hold it worth my leisure,
I could produce such damning proof—

HORATIO.
'Tis false!
You blast the fair with lies because they scorn you,
Hate you like age, like ugliness and impotence.
Rather than make you blest they would die virgins
And stop the propagation of mankind.

LOTHARIO.
It is the curse of fools to be secure,
And that be thine and Altamont's. Dream on,
Nor think upon my vengeance till thou feel'st it.

HORATIO.
Hold sir, another word, and then farewell:
Though I think greatly of Calista's virtue
And hold it far beyond thy pow'r to hurt,
Yet as she shares the honor of my Altamont,
That treasure of a soldier, bought with blood
And kept at life's expense, I must not have
(Mark me, young sir) her very name profaned.
Learn to restrain the license of your speech;
'Tis held you are too lavish. When you are met
Among your set of fools, talk of your dress,
Of dice, of whores, of horses, and yourselves:
'Tis safer and becomes your understandings.

LOTHARIO.
What if we pass beyond this solemn order
And, in defiance of the stern Horatio,
Indulge our gayer thoughts, let laughter loose,
And use his sacred friendship for our mirth?

HORATIO.
'Tis well! Sir, you are pleasant—

LOTHARIO.
By the joys
Which yet my soul has uncontrolled pursued,
I would not turn aside from my least pleasure,
Though all thy force were armed to bar my way,
But like the birds, great Nature's happy commoners[13]
That haunt in woods, in meads, and flow'ry gardens,
Rifle the sweets and taste the choicest fruits
Yet scorn to ask the lordly owner's leave.

HORATIO.
What liberty has vain presumptuous youth,
That thou shouldst dare provoke me unchastised?
But henceforth, boy, I warn thee shun my walks.
If in the bounds of yon forbidden place
Again thou'rt found, expect a punishment
Such as great souls, impatient of an injury,
Exact from those who wrong 'em much, ev'n death

[12] Legends … ne'er were saints] A veiled attack on Catholicism: radical European Protestants during the Reformation called the existence of saints into question, seeing them as another example of Catholic "idolotry."

[13] commoners] those who have community rights such as the right to use common land

Or something worse: an injured husband's vengeance
Shall print a thousand wounds, tear thy fine form,
And scatter thee to all the winds of heav'n.

LOTHARIO.
Is then my way in Genoa prescribed
By a dependant on the wretched Altamont,
A talking sir that brawls for him in taverns
And vouches for his valor's reputation—

HORATIO.
Away, thy speech is fouler than thy manners.

LOTHARIO.
Or if there be a name more vile, his parasite,
A beggar's parasite?

HORATIO.
Now learn humanity,
(*Offers* to strike him, Rossano interposes.*)
Since brutes and boys are only taught with blows.

LOTHARIO.
Damnation!

They draw.

ROSSANO.
Hold, this goes no further here—
Horatio—'tis too much—already, see,
The crowd are gath'ring to us.

LOTHARIO.
Oh Rossano!
Or give me way, or thou'rt no more my friend.

ROSSANO.
Sciolto's servants too have ta'en th'alarm:[c]
You'll be oppressed by numbers. Be advised,
Or I must force you hence. Take't on my word,
You shall have justice done you on Horatio.
Put up, my lord.

LOTHARIO.
This wonnot brook delay:
West of the town a mile, among the rocks,
Two hours ere noon tomorrow I expect thee,
Thy single hand to mine.

HORATIO.
I'll meet thee there.

LOTHARIO.
Tomorrow, oh my better stars! tomorrow,
Exert your influence, shine strongly for me.
'Tis not a common conquest I would gain,
Since love, as well as arms, must grace my triumph.

Exeunt Lothario and Rossano.

HORATIO.
Two hours ere noon tomorrow! hah! ere that
He sees Calista! oh unthinking fool—
What if I urged her with the crime and danger?
If any spark from Heav'n remain unquenched
Within her breast, my breath perhaps may wake it.
Could I but prosper there, I would not doubt
My combat with that loud vainglorious boaster.
Were you, ye fair, but cautious whom ye trust,
Did you but think how seldom fools are just,
So many of your sex would not in vain
Of broken vows and faithless men complain.
Of all the various wretches love has made,
How few have been by men of sense betrayed!
Convinced by reason, they your pow'r confess,
Pleased to be happy, as you're pleased to bless,
And conscious of your worth, can never love you less.

Exit.

Act III, scene i. An apartment in Sciolto's palace.

Enter Sciolto and Calista.

SCIOLTO.
Now by my life, my honor, 'tis too much.
Have I not marked thee wayward as thou art,
Perverse, and sullen all this day of joy?
When ev'ry heart was cheered and mirth went round,
Sorrow, displeasure, and repining anguish
Sate on thy brow like some malignant planet,
Foe to the harvest and the healthy year,
Who scowls adverse and low'rs upon the world,
When all the other stars, with gentle aspect,
Propitious shine and meaning good to man.

CALISTA.
Is then the task of duty half performed?
Has not your daughter giv'n herself to Altamont,
Yielded the native freedom of her will
To an imperious husband's lordly rule,
To gratify a father's stern command?

SCIOLTO.
Dost thou complain?

CALISTA.
For pity do not frown then,
If in despite of all my vowed obedience,

A sigh breaks out or a tear falls by chance.
For oh! that sorrow which has drawn your anger
Is the sad native of Calista's breast
And, once possessed, will never quit its dwelling
Till life, the prop of[d] all, shall leave the building
To tumble down and molder into ruin.

SCIOLTO.
Now by the sacred dust of that dear saint
That was thy mother, by her wondrous goodness,
Her soft, her tender, most complying sweetness,
I swear some sullen thought that shuns the light
Lurks underneath that sadness in thy visage.
But mark me well, though by yon heaven I love thee
As much, I think, as a fond parent can,
Yet shouldst thou (which the Pow'rs above forbid)
E'er stain the honor of thy name with infamy,
I cast thee off as one whose impious hands
Had rent asunder nature's nearest ties,
Which once divided never join again.
Today I have made a noble youth thy husband.
Consider well his worth, reward his love,
Be willing to be happy and thou art so. (*Exit.*)

CALISTA.
How hard is the condition of our sex!
Through ev'ry state of life the slaves of man.
In all the dear delightful days of youth
A rigid father dictates to our wills
And deals out pleasure with a scanty hand.
To his, the tyrant husband's reign succeeds:
Proud with opinion of superior reason,
He holds domestic bus'ness and devotion
All we are capable to know, and shuts us,
Like cloistered idiots, from the world's acquaintance
And all the joys of freedom. Wherefore are we
Born with high souls but to assert ourselves,
Shake off this vile obedience they exact,
And claim an equal empire o'er the world?

Enter Horatio.

HORATIO.
She's here! yet oh! my tongue is at a loss.
Teach me, some Pow'r, that happy art of speech
To dress my purpose up in gracious words
Such as may softly steal upon her soul
And never waken the tempestuous passions.
By Heaven she weeps!—Forgive me, fair Calista,
If I presume on privilege of friendship
To join my grief to yours and mourn the evils
That hurt your peace and quench those eyes in tears.

CALISTA.
To steal unlooked for on my private sorrow
Speaks not the man of honor nor the friend
But rather means the spy.

HORATIO.
Unkindly said!
For oh! as sure as you accuse me falsely,
I come to prove myself Calista's friend.

CALISTA.
You are my husband's friend, the friend of Altamont.

HORATIO.
Are you not one? Are you not joined by Heav'n,
Each interwoven with the other's fate?
Are you not mixed like streams of meeting rivers,
Whose blended waters are no more distinguished
But roll into the sea one common flood?
Then, who can give his friendship but to one?
Who can be Altamont's, and not Calista's?

CALISTA.
Force, and the wills of our imperious rulers,
May bind two bodies in one wretched chain,
But minds will still look back to their own choice.
So the poor captive in a foreign realm
Stands on the shore and sends his wishes back
To the dear native land from whence he came.

HORATIO.
When souls that should agree to will the same,
To have one common object for their wishes,
Look different ways, regardless of each other,
Think what a train of wretchedness ensues:
Love shall be banished from the genial[14] bed,
The nights shall all be lonely and unquiet,
And ev'ry day shall be a day of cares.

CALISTA.
Then all the boasted office of thy friendship
Was but to tell Calista what a wretch she is.
Alas! what needed that?

HORATIO.
Oh! rather say,
I came to tell her how she might be happy,
To soothe the secret anguish of her soul,

[14] genial] of or relating to marriage and generation

To comfort that fair mourner, that forlorn one,
And teach her steps to know the paths of peace.

CALISTA.
Say thou to whom this paradise is known,
Where lies the blissful region? Mark my way to it,
For oh! 'tis sure I long to be at rest.

HORATIO.
Then—to be good is to be happy. Angels
Are happier than mankind, because they are better.
Guilt is the source of sorrow: 'tis the fiend,
The avenging fiend, that follows us behind
With whips and stings. The blest know none of this
But rest in everlasting peace of mind
And find the height of all their heav'n is goodness.

CALISTA.
And what bold parasite's officious tongue
Shall dare to tax Calista's name with guilt?

HORATIO.
None should. But 'tis a busy, talking world,
That with licentious breath blows, like the wind,
As freely on the palace as the cottage.

CALISTA.
What mystic riddle lurks beneath thy words
Which thou wouldst seem unwilling to express,
As if it meant dishonor to my virtue?
Away with this ambiguous, shuffling phrase
And let thy oracle be understood.

HORATIO.
Lothario!

CALISTA.
Hah! what wouldst thou mean by him?

HORATIO.
Lothario and Calista—thus they join
Two names which Heav'n decreed should never meet.
Hence have the talkers of this populous city
A shameful tale to tell for public sport
Of an unhappy beauty, a false fair one,
Who plighted to a noble youth her faith,
When she had giv'n her honor to a wretch.

CALISTA.
Death! and confusion! Have I lived to this?
Thus to be treated with unmanly insolence!
To be the sport of a loose ruffian's tongue!
Thus to be used! thus! like the vilest creature
That ever was a slave to vice and infamy.

HORATIO.
By honor and fair truth, you wrong me much,
For on my soul nothing but strong necessity
Could urge my tongue to this ungrateful office.
I came with strong reluctance, as if death
Had stood across my way, to save your honor,
Yours and Sciolto's, yours and Altamont's,
Like one who ventures through a burning pile[15]
To save his tender wife, with all her brood
Of little fondlings, from the dreadful ruin.

CALISTA.
Is this! Is this the famous friend of Altamont,
For noble worth and deeds of arms renowned?
Is this! this tale-bearing, officious fellow,
That watches for intelligence from eyes,
This wretched Argus of a jealous husband,
That fills his easy ears with monstrous tales
And makes him toss and rave and wreak at length
Bloody revenge on his defenseless wife,
Who guiltless dies because her fool ran mad?

HORATIO.
Alas! this rage is vain, for if your fame
Or peace be worth your care, you must be calm
And listen to the means are left to save 'em.
'Tis now the lucky minute of your fate:
By me your[e] genius* speaks, by me it warns you
Never to see that curst Lothario more—
Unless you mean to be despised, be shunned
By all your virtuous maids and noble matrons,
Unless you have devoted this rare beauty
To infamy, diseases, prostitution—

CALISTA.
Dishonor blast thee, base, unmannered slave!
That dar'st forget my birth and sacred sex
And shock me with that rude unhallowed sound.

HORATIO.
Here kneel, and in the awful* face of Heav'n
Breathe out a solemn vow never to see
Nor think, if possible, on him that ruined thee,
Or by my Altamont's dear life I swear,
This paper—nay you must not fly (*Holding her.*)—this paper,
This guilty paper shall divulge your shame.

---

15 pile] a large building or group of buildings

CALISTA.
What mean'st thou by that paper? What contrivance
Hast thou been forging to deceive my father,
To turn his heart against his wretched daughter,
That Altamont and thou may share his wealth?
A wrong like this will make me ev'n forget
The weakness of my sex.—Oh for a sword,
To urge my vengeance on the villain's[f] hand
That forged the scroll.

HORATIO.
Behold, can this be forged?
See where Calista's name—
(*Showing the letter near.*)

CALISTA.
To atoms thus, (*Tearing it.*)
Thus let me tear the vile, detested falsehood,
The wicked, lying evidence of shame.

HORATIO.
Confusion!

CALISTA.
Henceforth, thou officious fool,
Meddle no more nor dare ev'n on thy life
To breathe an accent that may touch my virtue:
I am myself the guardian of my honor
And wonnot bear so insolent a monitor.

Enter Altamont.

ALTAMONT.
Where is my life, my love, my charming bride,
Joy of my heart, and pleasure of my eyes,
The wish, the care, and bus'ness of my youth?
Oh! let me find her, snatch her to my breast,
And tell her she delays my bliss too long,
Till my soft soul ev'n sickens with desire.
Disordered! and in tears! Horatio too!
My friend is in amaze! What can it mean?
Tell me, Calista, who has done thee wrong,
That my swift sword may find out the offender
And do thee ample justice.

CALISTA.
Turn to him!

ALTAMONT.
Horatio!

CALISTA.
To that insolent.

ALTAMONT.
My friend!
Could he do this? He, who was half myself!
One faith has ever bound us, and one reason
Guided our wills. Have I have not found him just,
Honest as truth itself? And could he break
The sanctity of friendship? Could he wound
The heart of Altamont in his Calista?

CALISTA.
I thought what justice I should find from thee!
Go fawn upon him, listen to his tale,
Applaud his malice, that would blast my fame
And treat me like a common prostitute.
Thou art perhaps confederate in his mischief
And wilt believe the legend, if he tells it.

ALTAMONT.
Oh impious! What presumptuous wretch shall dare
To offer* at an injury like that?
Priesthood, nor age, nor cowardice itself
Shall save him from the fury of my vengeance.

CALISTA.
The man who dared to do it was Horatio!
Thy darling friend! 'Twas Altamont's Horatio!
But mark me well: while thy divided heart
Dotes on a villain that has wronged me thus,
No force shall drag me to thy hated bed,
Nor can my cruel father's pow'r do more
Than shut me in a cloister. There, well pleased,
Religious hardships will I learn to bear:
To fast and freeze at midnight hours of pray'r,
Nor think it hard, within a lonely cell,
With melancholy, speechless saints to dwell,
But bless the day I to that refuge ran,
Free from the marriage chain—and from that
tyrant, man. (*Exit.*)

ALTAMONT.
She's gone, and as she went, ten thousand fires
Shot from her angry eyes, as if she meant
Too well to keep the cruel vow she made.
Now as thou art a man, Horatio, tell me,
What means this wild confusion in thy looks,
As if thou wert at variance with thyself,
Madness and reason combating within thee,
And thou wert doubtful which should get the better?

HORATIO.
I would be dumb forever, but thy fate

Has otherwise decreed it: thou hast seen
That idol of thy soul, that fair Calista;
Thou hast beheld her tears.

ALTAMONT.
I have seen her weep;
I have seen that lovely one, that dear Calista,
Complaining in the bitterness of sorrow
That thou! my friend! Horatio! thou hadst wronged her.

HORATIO.
That I have wronged her! Had her eyes been fed
From that rich stream which warms her heart and numbered
For ev'ry falling tear a drop of blood,
It had not been too much, for she has ruined thee,
Ev'n thee, my Altamont! She has undone thee.

ALTAMONT.
Dost thou join ruin with Calista's name?
What is so fair, so exquisitely good?
Is she not more than painting can express
Or youthful poets' fancy when they love?
Does she not come, like wisdom or good fortune,
Replete with blessings, giving wealth and honor?
The dowry which she brings is peace and pleasure,
And everlasting joys are in her arms.

HORATIO.
It had been better thou hadst lived a beggar
And fed on scraps at great men's surly doors
Than to have matched with one so false, so fatal—

ALTAMONT.
It is too much for friendship to allow thee.
Because I tamely bore the wrong thou didst her,
Thou dost avow the barb'rous, brutal part
And urge the injury ev'n to my face.

HORATIO.
I see she has got possession of thy heart.
She has charmed thee, like a Siren, to her bed
With looks of love and with enchanting sounds.
Too late the rocks and quicksands will appear:
When thou art wrecked upon the faithless shore,
Then vainly wish thou hadst not left thy friend
To follow her delusion.

ALTAMONT.
If thy friendship
Do churlishly deny my love a room,
It is not worth my keeping: I disclaim it.

HORATIO.
Canst thou so soon forget what I've been to thee?
I shared the task of nature with thy father
And formed with care thy unexperienced youth
To virtue and to arms.
Thy noble father, oh thou light young man!
Would he have used me thus? One fortune fed us,
For his was ever mine, mine his, and both
Together flourished and together fell.
He called me friend, like thee. Would he have left me
Thus? for a woman? nay, a vile one too?

ALTAMONT.
Thou canst not, dar'st not mean it. Speak again,
Say, who is vile? but dare not name Calista.

HORATIO.
I had not spoke at first, unless compelled
And forced to clear myself, but since thus urged,
I must avow I do not know a viler.

ALTAMONT.
Thou wert my father's friend, he loved thee well;
A kind of venerable mark of him
Hangs round thee and protects thee from my vengeance:
I cannot, dare not lift my sword against thee,
But henceforth never let me see thee more.
(*Going out.*)

HORATIO.
I love thee still, ungrateful as thou art,
And must, and will preserve thee from dishonor,
Ev'n in despite of thee. (*Holds him.*)

ALTAMONT.
Let go my arm.

HORATIO.
If honor be thy care, if thou wouldst live
Without the name of credulous, wittol husband,
Avoid thy bride, shun her detested bed:
The joys it yields are dashed with poison—

ALTAMONT.
Off!
To urge me but a minute more is fatal.

HORATIO.
She is polluted! stained!

ALTAMONT.
Madness and raving!
But hence!

HORATIO.
Dishonored by the man you hate—

ALTAMONT.
I prithee loose me yet, for thy own sake,
If life be worth the keeping—
HORATIO.
By Lothario.
ALTAMONT.
Perdition take thee, villain,* for the falsehood.
(*Strikes him.*)
Now nothing but thy life can make atonement.
HORATIO.
A blow! Thou hast used me well— (*Draws.*)
ALTAMONT.
This to thy heart—
HORATIO.
Yet hold!—By Heav'n, his father's in his face.
Spite of my wrongs my heart runs o'er with tenderness,
And I could rather die myself than hurt him.
ALTAMONT.
Defend thyself, for by my much wronged love,
I swear the poor evasion shall not save thee.
HORATIO.
Yet hold! thou know'st I dare—think how we've lived—

They fight; Altamont presses on Horatio, who retires.

Nay! then 'tis brutal* violence! And thus,
Thus Nature bids me guard the life she gave.

They fight. Lavinia enters and runs between their swords.

LAVINIA.
My brother! My Horatio! is it possible?
Oh! turn your cruel swords upon Lavinia.
If you must quench your impious rage in blood,
Behold, my heart shall give you all her store
To save those dearer streams that flow from yours.
ALTAMONT.
'Tis well thou hast found a safeguard; none but this,
No pow'r on earth could save thee from my fury.
LAVINIA.
Oh fatal, deadly sound!
HORATIO.
Safety from thee!
Away, vain boy! Hast thou forgot the reverence
Due to my arm, thy first, thy great example,
Which pointed out thy way to noble daring
And showed thee what it was to be a man?
LAVINIA.
What busy, meddling fiend, what foe to goodness,
Could kindle such a discord? Oh! lay by
Those most ungentle looks and angry weapons,
Unless you mean my griefs and killing fears
Should stretch me out at your relentless feet
A wretched corse, the victim of your fury.
HORATIO.
Ask'st thou what made us foes? 'Twas base ingratitude,
'Twas such a sin to friendship as Heaven's mercy,
That strives with man's untoward, monstrous wickedness,
Unwearied with forgiving, scarce could pardon.
He, who was all to me—child! brother! friend!—
With barb'rous, bloody malice sought my life.
ALTAMONT.
Thou art my sister, and I would not make thee
The lonely mourner of a widowed bed;
Therefore, thy husband's life is safe, but warn him
No more to know this hospitable roof:
He has but ill repaid Sciolto's bounty.
We must not meet, 'tis dangerous—farewell.

He is going; Lavinia holds him.

LAVINIA.
Stay Altamont, my brother stay, if ever
Nature, or what is nearer much than nature,
The kind consent of our agreeing minds,
Have made us dear to one another, stay,
And speak one gentle word to your Horatio.
Behold, his anger melts, he longs to love you,
To call you friend, then press you hard with all
The tender, speechless joy of reconcilement.
ALTAMONT.
It cannot, shannot be! You must not hold me.
LAVINIA.
Look kindly then!
ALTAMONT.
Each minute that I stay
Is a new injury to fair Calista.—
From thy false friendship to her arms I'll fly.
There, if in any pause of love I rest,
Breathless with bliss, upon her panting breast,

In broken, melting accents I will swear
Henceforth to trust my heart with none but her,
Then own the joys which on her charms attend
Have more than paid me for my faithless friend.
(*Breaks from Lavinia and exits.*)

HORATIO.
Oh raise thee, my Lavinia, from the earth.
It is too much, this tide of flowing grief,
This wondrous waste of tears, too much to give
To an ungrateful friend and cruel brother.

LAVINIA.
Is there not cause for weeping? Oh Horatio!
A brother and a husband were my treasure:
'Twas all the little wealth that poor Lavinia
Saved from the shipwreck of her father's fortunes.
One half is lost already; if thou leav'st me,
If thou shouldst prove unkind to me, as Altamont,
Whom shall I find to pity my distress,
To have compassion on a helpless wanderer
And give her where to lay her wretched head?

HORATIO.
Why dost thou wound me with thy soft complainings?
Though Altamont be false and use me hardly,
Yet think not I impute his crimes to thee.
Talk not of being forsaken, for I'll keep thee
Next to my heart, my certain pledge of happiness.
Heav'n formed thee gentle, fair, and full of goodness
And made thee all my portion here on earth;
It gave thee to me as a large amends
For fortune, friends, and all the world beside.

LAVINIA.
Then you will love me still,* cherish me ever,
And hide me from misfortune in your bosom?
Here end my cares, nor will I lose one thought
How we shall live or purchase food and raiment.
The holy Pow'r, who clothes the senseless earth
With woods, with fruits, with flow'rs and verdant grass,
Whose bounteous hand feeds the whole brute creation,
Knows all our wants and has enough to give us.

HORATIO.
From Genoa, from falsehood and inconstancy,
To some more honest distant clime we'll go,
Nor will I be beholding to my country
For ought but thee, the partner of my flight.

LAVINIA.
Yes, I will follow thee, forsake for thee
My country, brother, friends, ev'n all I have;
Though mine's a little all, yet were it more,
And better far, it should be left for thee,
And all that I would keep should be Horatio.
So when the merchant sees his vessel lost,
Though richly freighted from a foreign coast,
Gladly for life the treasure he would give
And only wishes to escape, and live.
Gold and his gains no more employ his mind
But, driving o'er the billows with the wind,
Cleaves to one faithful plank, and leaves the rest behind.

Exeunt.

Act IV, scene i. A garden.

Enter Altamont.

ALTAMONT.
With what unequal tempers are we formed!
One day the soul, supine with ease and fullness,
Revels secure and fondly* tells herself
The hour of evil can return no more;
The next, the spirits, palled and sick of riot,
Turn all to discord, and we hate our beings,
Curse the past joy, and think it folly all
And bitterness and anguish. Oh! last night!
What has ungrateful beauty paid me back
For all that mass of friendship which I squandered?
Coldness, aversion, tears, and sullen sorrow
Dashed all my bliss and damped my bridal bed.
Soon as the morning dawned, she vanished from me,
Relentless to the gentle call of love.
I have lost a friend, and I have gained—a wife!
Turn not to thought, my brain, but let me find
Some unfrequented shade; there lay me down
And let forgetful dullness steal upon me
To soften and assuage this pain of thinking.
(*Exit.*)

Enter Lothario and Calista.

LOTHARIO.
Weep not, my fair, but let the God of Love
Laugh in thy eyes and revel in thy heart,
Kindle again his torch and hold it high

To light us to new joys, nor let a thought
Of discord or disquiet past molest thee,
But to a long oblivion give thy cares
And let us melt the present hour in bliss.

CALISTA.
Seek not to soothe me with thy false endearments,
To charm me with thy softness, 'tis in vain:
Thou canst no more betray, nor I be ruined.
The hours of folly and of fond* delight
Are wasted all and fled; those that remain
Are doomed to weeping, anguish, and repentance.
I come to charge thee with a long account
Of all the sorrows I have known already
And all I have to come: thou hast undone me.

LOTHARIO.
Unjust Calista! Dost thou call it ruin
To love as we have done: to melt, to languish,
To wish for somewhat exquisitely happy,
And then be blest ev'n to that wish's height?
To die with joy, and straight to live again,
Speechless to gaze, and with tumultuous transport—

CALISTA.
Oh! let me hear no more, I cannot bear it:
'Tis deadly to remembrance. Let that night,
That guilty night, be blotted from the year;
Let not the voice of mirth or music know it;
Let it be dark and desolate, no stars
To glitter o'er it; let it wish for light
Yet want* it still* and vainly wait the dawn,
For 'twas the night that gave me up to shame,
To sorrow, to perfidious, false Lothario.

LOTHARIO.
Hear this, ye Pow'rs, mark how the fair deceiver
Sadly complains of violated truth.
She calls me false, ev'n she, the faithless she,
Whom day and night, whom heav'n and earth have heard
Sighing to vow and tenderly protest
Ten thousand times she would be only mine.
And yet, behold, she has giv'n herself away,
Fled from my arms, and wedded to another,
Ev'n to the man whom most I hate on earth.

CALISTA.
Art thou so base to upbraid me with a crime
Which nothing but thy cruelty could cause?
If indignation, raging in my soul,
For thy unmanly insolence and scorn
Urged me to do a deed of desperation
And wound myself to be revenged on thee,
Think whom I should devote to death and hell,
Whom curse as my undoer but Lothario.
Hadst thou been just, not all Sciolto's pow'r,
Not all the vows and pray'rs of sighing Altamont,
Could have prevailed or won me to forsake thee.

LOTHARIO.
How have I failed in justice or in love?
Burns not my flame as brightly as at first?
Ev'n now my heart beats high, I languish for thee,
My transports are as fierce, as strong my wishes,
As if thou hadst never blest me with thy beauty.

CALISTA.
How didst thou dare to think that I would live
A slave to base desires and brutal* pleasures,
To be a wretched wanton for thy leisure
To toy and waste an hour of idle time with?
My soul disdains thee for so mean a thought.

LOTHARIO.
The driving storm of passion will have way,
And I must yield before it. Wert thou calm,
Love, the poor criminal whom thou hast doomed,
Has yet a thousand tender things to plead
To charm thy rage and mitigate his fate.

Enter behind them Altamont.

ALTAMONT.
I have lost my peace.—Hah! do I live and wake!

CALISTA.
Hadst thou been true, how happy had I been?
Nor Altamont but thou hadst been my lord.
But wherefore named I happiness with thee?
It is for thee, for thee, that I am curst;
For thee, my secret soul each hour arraigns me,
Calls me to answer for my virtue stained,
My honor lost to thee; for thee, it haunts me,
With stern Sciolto vowing vengeance on me,
With Altamont complaining for his wrongs—

ALTAMONT.
Behold him here— (*Coming forward.*)

CALISTA. (*Starting.*)
Ah!—

ALTAMONT.
The wretch whom thou hast made!

Curses and sorrows hast thou heaped upon him,
And vengeance is the only good is left. (*Drawing.*)

LOTHARIO.

Thou hast ta'en me somewhat unawares, 'tis true,
But love and war take turns like day and night,
And little preparation serves my turn,
Equal to both and armed for either field.
We've long been foes, this moment ends our quarrel.*
Earth, Heav'n, and fair Calista judge the combat.

CALISTA.

Distraction! Fury! Sorrow! Shame! and Death!

ALTAMONT.

Thou hast talked too much, thy breath is poison to me:
It taints the ambient air. This for my father,
This for Sciolto, and this last for Altamont.

They fight; Lothario is wounded once or twice and then falls.

LOTHARIO.

Oh Altamont! thy genius* is the stronger,
Thou hast prevailed! My fierce, ambitious soul
Declining droops, and all her fires grow pale,
Yet let not this advantage swell thy pride:
I conquered in my turn, in love I triumphed.
Those joys are lodged beyond the reach of fate;
That sweet revenge comes smiling to my thoughts,
Adorns my fall, and cheers my heart in dying. (*Dies.*)

CALISTA.

And what remains for me? Beset with shame,
Encompassed round with wretchedness, there is
But this one way to break the toil and 'scape.

She catches up Lothario's sword and offers to kill herself; Altamont runs to her and wrests it from her.*

ALTAMONT.

What means thy frantic rage?

CALISTA.

Off! let me go.

ALTAMONT.

Oh! thou hast more than murdered me, yet still,
Still art thou here! and my soul starts with horror
At thought of any danger that may reach thee.

CALISTA.

Think'st thou I mean to live? to be forgiven?
Oh! thou hast known but little of Calista.
If thou hadst never heard my shame, if only
The midnight moon and silent stars had seen it,
I would not bear to be reproached by them,
But dig down deep to find a grave beneath
And hide me from their beams.

SCIOLTO. (*Within.*)

What ho! my son!

ALTAMONT.

It is Sciolto calls.—Come near and find me,
The wretched'st thing of all my kind on earth.

CALISTA.

Is it the voice of thunder or my father?
Madness! Confusion! let the storm come on,
Let the tumultuous roar drive all upon me.
Dash my devoted bark, ye surges, break it;
'Tis for my ruin that the tempest rises.
When I am lost, sunk to the bottom low,
Peace shall return and all be calm again.

Enter Sciolto.

SCIOLTO.

Ev'n now Rossano leaped the garden walls—
Hah! Death has been among you—oh my fears!
Last night thou hadst a diff'rence with thy friend;
The cause thou gav'st me for it was a damned one.
Didst thou not wrong the man who told thee truth?
Answer me quick—

ALTAMONT.

Oh! press me not to speak,
Ev'n now my heart is breaking, and the mention
Will lay me dead before you. See that body
And guess my shame! my ruin! oh Calista!

SCIOLTO.

It is enough! but I am slow to execute,
And justice lingers in my lazy hand.
Thus let me wipe dishonor from my name
And cut thee from the earth, thou stain to goodness—

Offers to kill Calista, Altamont holds him.*

ALTAMONT.

Stay thee, Sciolto, thou rash father, stay,
Or turn the point on me and through my breast
Cut out the bloody passage to Calista.
So shall my love be perfect while for her
I die, for whom alone I wished to live.

CALISTA.
No, Altamont! my heart, that scorned thy love,
Shall never be indebted to thy pity.
Thus torn, defaced, and wretched as I seem,
Still I have something of Sciolto's virtue.
Yes! yes my father, I applaud thy justice.
Strike home, and I will bless thee for the blow.
Be merciful and free me from my pain.
'Tis sharp, 'tis terrible, and I could curse
The cheerful day, men, earth, and heav'n and thee,
Ev'n thee, thou venerable, good old man,
For being author of a wretch like me.

ALTAMONT.
Listen not to the wildness of her raving,
Remember nature! Should thy daughter's murder
Defile that hand—so just, so great in arms—
Her blood would rest upon thee to posterity,
Pollute thy name, and sully all thy wars.

CALISTA.
Have I not wronged his gentle[16] nature much?
And yet behold him pleading for my life.
Lost as thou art to virtue, oh Calista!
I think thou canst not bear to be outdone.
Then haste to die, and be obliged no more.

SCIOLTO.
Thy pious care has giv'n me time to think
And saved me from a crime. Then rest my sword:
To honor have I kept thee ever sacred,
Nor will I stain thee with a rash revenge.
But mark me well, I will have justice done.
Hope not to bear away thy crimes unpunished.
I will see justice executed on thee,
Ev'n to a Roman strictness. And thou, Nature,
Or whatsoe'er thou art that plead'st within me,
Be still, thy tender strugglings are in vain.

CALISTA.
Then am I doomed to live and bear your triumph?
To groan beneath your scorn and fierce upbraidings,
Daily to be reproached, and have my misery
At morn, at noon and night told over to me,
Lest my remembrance might grow pitiful
And grant a moment's interval of peace:
Is this, is this the mercy of a father?
I only beg to die, and he denies me.

SCIOLTO.
Hence from my sight, thy father cannot bear thee.
Fly with thy infamy to some dark cell,
Where on the confines of eternal night
Mourning, misfortune, cares, and anguish dwell;
Where ugly shame hides her opprobrious head,
And death and hell detested rule maintain,
There howl out the remainder of thy life
And wish thy name may be no more remembered.

CALISTA.
Yes, I will fly to some such dismal place
And be more curst than you can wish I were.
This fatal form that drew on my undoing
Fasting and tears and hardship shall destroy,
Nor light, nor food, nor comfort will I know,
Nor aught that may continue hated life.
Then when you see me meager, wan, and changed,
Stretched at my length and dying in my cave
On that cold earth I mean shall be my grave,
Perhaps you may relent and sighing say,
At length her tears have washed her stains away,
At length 'tis time her punishment should cease:
Die, thou poor suff'ring wretch, and be at peace.
(*Exit.*)

SCIOLTO.
Who of my servants wait there?

Enter two or three servants.

On your lives
Take care my doors be guarded well, that none
Pass out or enter but by my appointment.

Exeunt servants.

ALTAMONT.
There is a fatal fury in your visage;
It blazes fierce and menaces destruction.
My father, I am sick of many sorrows,
Ev'n now my easy heart is breaking with 'em,
Yet above all, one fear distracts me most:
I tremble at the vengeance which you meditate
On the poor, faithless, lovely, dear Calista.

SCIOLTO.
Hast thou not read what brave Virginius did?
With his own hand he slew his only daughter

16 gentle] the adjective contains both the older sense of *descended from a noble family* and the new bourgeois sense of *tender, non-aggressive*

To save her from the fierce Decemvir's lust.[17]
He slew her yet unspotted to prevent
The shame which she might know. Then what should I do?
But thou hast tied my hand—I wonnot kill her.
Yet by the ruin she has brought upon us,
The common infamy that brands us both,
She shannot 'scape.

ALTAMONT.
You mean that she shall die then?

SCIOLTO.
Ask me not what, nor how I have resolved,
For all within is anarchy and uproar.
Oh Altamont! what a vast scheme of joy
Has this one day destroyed! Well did I hope
This daughter would have blest my latter days,
That I should live to see you the world's wonder,
So happy, great, and good, that none were like you.
While I, from busy life and care set free,
Had spent the ev'ning of my age at home
Among a little prattling race* of yours:
There, like an old man, talked awhile and then
Lain down and slept in peace. Instead of this,
Sorrow and shame must bring me to my grave.
Oh damn her! damn her!

Enter a Servant.

SERVANT.
Arm yourself, my lord.
Rossano, who but now escaped the garden,
Has gathered in the street a band of rioters
Who threaten you and all your friends with ruin,
Unless Lothario be returned in safety.

SCIOLTO.
By Heav'n, their fury rises to my wish,
Nor shall misfortune know my house alone,
But thou, Lothario, and thy race,* shall pay me
For all the sorrows which my age is curst with.
I think my name as great, my friends as potent,
As any in the state; all shall be summoned.
I know that all will join their hands to ours
And vindicate thy vengeance. Raise the body
And bear it in; his friends shall buy him dearly:
I will have blood for ransom. When our force
Is full and armed, we shall expect thy sword
To join with us and sacrifice to justice. (*Exit.*)

The body of Lothario is carried off by servants. Manet Altamont.

ALTAMONT.
There is a stupid* weight upon my senses,
A dismal sullen stillness that succeeds
The storm of rage and grief like silent death
After the tumult and the noise of life.
Would it were death, as sure 'tis wondrous like it,
For I am sick of living, my soul's palled,
She kindles not with anger or revenge.
Love was th'informing, active fire within;
Now that is quenched, the mass forgets to move
And longs to mingle with its kindred earth.

A tumultuous noise, with clashing of swords, as at a little distance. Enter Lavinia with two servants, their swords drawn.

LAVINIA.
Fly, swiftly fly to my Horatio's aid,
Nor lose your vain, officious cares on me.
Bring me my lord, my husband, to my arms:
He is Lavinia's life. Bring him me safe,
And I shall be at ease, be well and happy.

Exeunt servants.

ALTAMONT.
Art thou Lavinia? Oh! what barb'rous hand
Could wrong thy poor, defenseless innocence
And leave such marks of more than savage fury?

LAVINIA.
My brother! Oh, my heart is full of fears,
Perhaps ev'n now my dear Horatio bleeds.
Not far from hence, as passing to the port,
By a mad multitude we were surrounded,
Who ran upon us with uplifted swords
And cried aloud for vengeance and Lothario.
My lord with ready boldness stood the shock
To shelter me from danger, but in vain,
Had not a party from Sciolto's palace
Rushed out and snatched me from amidst the fray.

[17] Virginius … lust] Virginius stabbed his daughter Virginia rather than allow Appius to rape her. Appius was one of the Decemvirs, ten men acting as the ruling authority in Rome, c. 450 BCE.

ALTAMONT.
What of my friend?
LAVINIA. (*Looking out.*)
Hah! by my joys 'tis he,
He lives, he comes to bless me, he is safe!

Enter Horatio with two or three servants, their swords drawn.

SERVANT.
'Twere at the utmost hazard of your life
To venture forth again till we are stronger;
Their number trebles ours.
HORATIO.
No matter, let it.
Death is not half so shocking as that traitor.
My honest soul is mad with indignation
To think her plainness could be so abused
As to mistake that wretch and call him friend.
I cannot bear the sight.
ALTAMONT.
Open, thou earth,
Gape wide and take me down to thy dark bosom,
To hide me from Horatio.
HORATIO.
Oh Lavinia,
Believe not but I joy to see thee safe.
Would our ill fortune had not drove us hither.
I could ev'n wish we rather had been wrecked
On any other shore than saved on this.
LAVINIA.
Oh let us bless the mercy that preserved us,
That gracious Pow'r that saved us for each other,
And to adorn the sacrifice of praise
Offer forgiveness too. Be thou like Heav'n
And put away th'offences of thy friend
Far, far from thy remembrance.
ALTAMONT.
I have marked him
To see if one forgiving glance stole hither,
If any spark of friendship were alive,
That would by sympathy at meeting glow
And strive to kindle up the flame anew.
'Tis lost, 'tis gone, his soul is quite estranged
And knows me for its counterpart no more.
HORATIO. [*To Lavinia.*]
Thou know'st thy rule, thy empire in Horatio,
Nor canst thou ask in vain, command in vain,
Where nature, reason, nay where love is judge.
But when you urge my temper to comply
With what it most abhors, I cannot do it.
LAVINIA.
Where didst thou get this sullen, gloomy hate?
It was not in thy nature to be thus.
Come, put it off and let thy heart be cheerful,
Be gay again, and know the joys of friendship,
The trust, security, and mutual tenderness,
The double joys, where each is glad for both:
Friendship, the wealth, the last retreat and strength
Secure against ill fortune and the world.
HORATIO.
I am not apt to take a light offence
But patient of the failings of my friends
And willing to forgive. But when an injury
Stabs to the heart and rouses my resentment
(Perhaps it is the fault of my rude nature),
I own I cannot easily forget[h] it.
ALTAMONT.
Thou hast forgot me.
HORATIO.
No.
ALTAMONT.
Why are thy eyes
Impatient of me then, scornful, and fierce?
HORATIO.
Because they speak the meaning of my heart,
Because they are honest and disdain a villain.*
ALTAMONT.
I have wronged thee much, Horatio.
HORATIO.
True, thou hast.
When I forget it, may I be a wretch,
Vile as thyself, a false perfidious fellow,
An infamous, believing, British husband.[18]
ALTAMONT.
I've wronged thee much, and Heav'n has well
avenged it.
I have not, since we parted, been at peace
Or known one joy sincere. Our broken friendship

[18] British husband] overly fond or lenient; British women were believed to have more liberties than women in other European countries such as Italy

Pursued me to the last retreat of love,
Stood glaring like a ghost, and made me cold with horror.
Misfortunes on misfortunes press upon me,
Swell o'er my head, like waves, and dash me down.
Sorrow, remorse, and shame have torn my soul;
They hang like winter on my youthful hopes
And blast the spring and promise of my year.

LAVINIA.
So flow'rs are gathered to adorn a grave,
To lose their freshness amongst bones and rottenness
And have their odors stifled in the dust.
Canst thou hear this, thou cruel, hard Horatio?
Canst thou behold thy Altamont undone?
That gentle, that dear youth! canst thou behold him,
His poor heart broken, death in his pale visage,
And groaning out his woes, yet stand unmoved?

HORATIO.
The brave and wise I pity in misfortune,
But when ingratitude and folly suffers,
'Tis weakness to be touched.

ALTAMONT.
I wonnot ask thee
To pity or forgive me, but confess
This scorn, this insolence of hate is just;
'Tis constancy of mind and manly in thee.
But oh! had I been wronged by thee, Horatio,
There is a yielding softness in my heart
Could ne'er have stood it out, but I had ran,
With streaming eyes and open arms, upon thee,
And pressed thee close, close!

HORATIO.
I must hear no more,
The weakness is contagious, I shall catch it,
And be a tame, fond* wretch.

LAVINIA.
Where wouldst thou go?
Wouldst thou part thus? You shannot, 'tis impossible,
For I will bar thy passage, kneeling thus.
Perhaps thy cruel hand may spurn me off,
But I will throw my body in thy way,
And thou shalt trample o'er my faithful bosom,
Tread on me, wound me, kill me ere thou pass.

ALTAMONT.
Urge not in vain thy pious suit, Lavinia,
I have enough to rid me of my pain.
Calista, thou hadst reached my heart before;
To make all sure, my friend repeats the blow.
But in the grave our cares shall be forgotten,
There love and friendship cease. (*Falls.*)

Lavinia runs to him and endeavors to raise him.

LAVINIA.
Speak to me, Altamont.
He faints! he dies!—Now turn and see thy triumph.
—My brother! But our cares shall end together;
Here will I lay me down by thy dear side,
Bemoan thy too hard fate, then share it with thee
And never see my cruel lord again.

Horatio runs to Altamont and raises him in his arms.

HORATIO.
It is too much to bear! Look up, my Altamont!
My stubborn, unrelenting heart has killed him.
Look up and bless me, tell me that thou liv'st.
Oh! I have urged thy gentleness too far.

Altamont revives.

Do thou and my Lavinia both forgive me;
A flood of tenderness comes o'er my soul.
I cannot speak—I love! forgive! and pity thee.

ALTAMONT.
I thought that nothing could have stayed my soul,
That long ere this her flight had reached the stars,
But thy known voice has lured her back again.
Methinks I fain would set all right with thee,
Make up this most unlucky breach, and then,
With thine and Heav'n's forgiveness on my soul,
Shrink to my grave and be at ease forever.

HORATIO.
By Heav'n my heart bleeds for thee. Ev'n this moment
I feel thy pangs of disappointed love.
Is it not pity that this youth should fail,
That all this wondrous goodness should be lost,
And the world never know it? oh my Altamont!
Give me thy sorrows, let me bear 'em for thee
And shelter thee from ruin.

LAVINIA.
Oh my brother!
Think not but we will share in all thy woes,
We'll sit all day and tell sad tales of love,

And when we light upon some faithless woman,
Some beauty, like Calista, false and fair,
We'll fix our grief and our complaining there;
We'll curse the nymph that drew the ruin on
And mourn the youth that was like thee undone.

Exeunt.

Act V, scene i. A room hung with black: on one side, Lothario's body on a bier; on the other, a table with a skull and other bones, a book, and a lamp on it.

Calista is discovered on a couch in black, her hair hanging loose and disordered. After music and a song, she rises and comes forward.*

Song.

I

Hear, you midnight phantoms, hear:
You, who pale and wan appear
And fill the wretch, who wakes, with fear;
You, who wander, scream, and groan
Round the mansions once your own;
You, whom still your crimes upbraid;
You, who rest not with the dead;
From the coverts where you stray,
Where you lurk and shun the day,
From the charnel and the tomb,
Hither haste ye, hither come.

II

Chide Calista for delay;
Tell her, 'tis for her you stay;
Bid her die, and come away.
See the sexton with his spade,
See the grave already made.
Listen, fair one, to thy knell:
This music is thy passing bell.

CALISTA.
'Tis well! these solemn sounds, this pomp of horror,
Are fit to feed the frenzy in my soul.
Here's room for meditation, ev'n to madness,
Till the mind burst with thinking. This dull flame
Sleeps in the socket. Sure the book was left
To tell me something—for instruction then—
He teaches holy sorrow and contrition
And penitence—Is it become an art then?
A trick that lazy, dull, luxurious gownsmen
Can teach us to do over? I'll no more on't!
(*Throwing away the book.*)
I have more real anguish in my heart
Than all their pedant discipline e'er knew.
What charnel has been rifled for these bones?
Fie! this is pageantry—they look uncouthly,
But what of that, if he or she that owned 'em,
Safe from disquiet, sit and smile to see
The farce their miserable relics play?
But here's a sight is terrible indeed:
Is this that haughty, gallant, gay Lothario,
That dear perfidious—Ah!—how pale he looks!
How grim with clotted blood, and those dead eyes!
Ascend ye ghosts, fantastic forms of night,
In all your diff'rent, dreadful shapes ascend
And match the present horror if you can.

Enter Sciolto.

SCIOLTO.
This dead of night, this silent hour of darkness,
Nature for rest ordained and soft repose,
And yet distraction and tumultuous jars
Keep all our frighted citizens awake.
The Senate, weak, divided, and irresolute,
Want* pow'r to succor the afflicted state;
Vainly in words and long debates they're wise,
While the fierce factions scorn their peaceful orders
And drown the voice of law in noise and anarchy.
Amidst the general wreck, see where she stands,
(*Pointing to Calista.*)
Like Helen in the night when Troy was sacked,
Spectatress of the mischief which she made.[19]

CALISTA.
It is Sciolto! be thyself, my soul,
Be strong to bear his fatal indignation,
That he may see thou art not lost so far
But somewhat still of his great spirit lives
In the forlorn Calista.

SCIOLTO.
Thou wert once
My daughter.

---

[19] Helen … made] See Virgil, *Aeneid* II.567-574, for the famous description of Helen of Troy on the night Troy was sacked.

CALISTA.

Happy were it I had died
And never lost that name.

SCIOLTO.

That's something yet.
Thou wert the very darling of my age:
I thought the day too short to gaze upon thee,
That all the blessings I could gather for thee,
By cares on earth and by my pray'rs to Heav'n,
Were little for my fondness to bestow.
Why didst thou turn to folly, then, and curse me?

CALISTA.

Because my soul was rudely drawn from yours,
A poor imperfect copy of my father,
Where goodness and the strength of manly virtue
Was thinly planted, and the idle void
Filled up with light belief and easy fondness.
It was because I loved, and was a woman.

SCIOLTO.

Hadst thou been honest,* thou hadst been a cherubim,
But of that joy, as of a gem long lost,
Beyond redemption gone, think we no more.
Hast thou e'er dared to meditate on death?

CALISTA.

I have, as on the end of shame and sorrow.

SCIOLTO.

Hah! answer me! say, hast thou coolly thought?
'Tis not the Stoic's lessons got by rote,
The pomp of words, and pedant dissertations
That can sustain thee in that hour of terror:
Books have taught cowards to talk nobly of it,
But when the trial comes, they start and stand aghast.
Hast thou considered what may happen after it?
How thy account may stand, and what to answer?

CALISTA.

I have turned my eyes inward upon myself,
Where foul offence and shame have laid all waste;
Therefore, my soul abhors the wretched dwelling
And longs to find some better place of rest.

SCIOLTO.

'Tis justly thought and worthy of that spirit
That dwelt in ancient Latian[20] breasts when Rome
Was mistress of the world. I would go on
And tell thee all my purpose, but it sticks
Here at my heart and cannot find a way.

CALISTA.

Then spare the telling, if it be a pain,
And write the meaning with your poniard here.

SCIOLTO.

Oh! truly guessed—seest thou this trembling hand—(*Holding up a dagger.*)
Thrice justice urged—and thrice the slack'ning sinews
Forgot their office and confessed the father.
At length the stubborn virtue has prevailed:
It must, it must be so—Oh! take it then, (*Giving the dagger.*)
And know the rest untaught.

CALISTA.

I understand you:
It is but thus, and both are satisfied.

She offers to kill herself, Sciolto catches hold of her arm.*

SCIOLTO.

A moment, give me yet a moment's space.
The stern, the rigid judge has been obeyed;
Now nature and the father claim their turns.
I have held the balance with an iron hand
And put off ev'ry tender, human thought
To doom my child to death. But spare my eyes
The most unnatural sight, lest their strings crack
And my old brain split and grow mad with horror.

CALISTA.

Hah! Is it possible? And is there yet
Some little, dear remain of love and tenderness
For poor, undone Calista in your heart?

SCIOLTO.

Oh! when I think what pleasure I took in thee,
What joys thou gav'st me in thy prattling infancy,
Thy sprightly wit and early blooming beauty,
How I have stood and fed my eyes upon thee,
Then lifted up my hands and, wond'ring, blest thee.
By my strong grief, my heart ev'n melts within me;
I could curse Nature and that tyrant, Honor,
For making me thy father and thy judge.
Thou art my daughter still.

CALISTA.

For that kind word,

[20] Latian] synecdoche for *Roman*, from *Latium*, original kingdom assumed by Aeneas

Thus let me fall, thus humbly to the earth,
Weep on your feet and bless you for this goodness.
Oh! 'tis too much for this offending wretch,
This parricide, that murders with her crimes,
Shortens her father's age and cuts him off
Ere little more than half his years be numbered.

SCIOLTO.

Would it were otherwise! but thou must die.

CALISTA.

That I must die! it is my only comfort:
Death is the privilege of human nature,
And life without it were not worth our taking;
Thither the poor, the pris'ner, and the mourner
Fly for relief and lay their burdens down.
Come then, and take me now to thy cold arms,
Thou meager shade; here let me breathe my last,
Charmed with my father's pity and forgiveness
More than if angels tuned their golden viols
And sung a requiem to my parting soul.

SCIOLTO.

I am summoned hence, ere this my friends expect me.
There is I know not what of sad presage
That tells me I shall never see thee more;
If it be so, this is our last farewell
And these the parting pangs which nature feels
When anguish rends the heartstrings—Oh! my daughter. (*Exit.*)

CALISTA.

Now think thou, curst Calista, now behold
The desolation, horror, blood, and ruin
Thy crimes and fatal folly spread around,
That loudly cry for vengeance on thy head.
Yet Heav'n, who knows our weak, imperfect natures—
How blind with passions and how prone to evil—
Makes not too strict enquiry for offences
But is atoned by penitence and pray'r.
Cheap recompense! here 'twould not be received:
Nothing but blood can make the expiation
And cleanse the soul from inbred, deep pollution.
And see, another injured wretch is come
To call for justice from my tardy hand.

Enter Altamont.

ALTAMONT.

Hail to you horrors! hail thou house of death!
And thou the lovely mistress of these shades,
Whose beauty gilds the more than midnight darkness
And makes it grateful as the dawn of day.
Oh! take me in a fellow-mourner with thee;
I'll number groan for groan, and tear for tear,
And when the fountain[i] of thy eyes are dry,
Mine shall supply the stream and weep for both.

CALISTA.

I know thee well, thou art the injured Altamont,
Thou com'st to urge me with the wrongs I ha'done thee.
But know I stand upon the brink of life
And in a moment mean to set me free
From shame and thy upbraiding.

ALTAMONT.

Falsely, falsely
Dost thou accuse me. When did I complain
Or murmur at my fate? For thee I have
Forgot the temper of Italian husbands,[21]
And fondness has prevailed upon revenge.
I bore my load of infamy with patience,
As holy men do punishments from Heav'n,
Nor thought it hard, because it came from thee.
Oh! then forbid me not to mourn thy loss,
To wish some better fate had ruled our loves,
And that Calista had been mine, and true.

CALISTA.

Oh! Altamont, 'tis hard for souls like mine,
Haughty and fierce, to yield they have done amiss.
But oh! behold my proud, disdainful heart
Bends to thy gentler virtue. Yes, I own,
Such is thy truth, thy tenderness and love,
Such are the graces that adorn thy youth,
That were I not abandoned to destruction,
With thee I might have lived for ages blest
And died in peace within thy faithful arms.

ALTAMONT.

Then happiness is still within our reach.
Here let remembrance lose our past misfortunes,
Tear all records that hold the fatal story;
Here let our joys begin, from hence go on
In long successive order.

---

21 temper of Italian husbands] who were proverbially hot-blooded and passionately jealous to the point of violence

CALISTA.
What! in death?
ALTAMONT.
Then art thou fixed to die? But be it so,
We'll go together; my advent'rous love
Shall follow thee to those uncertain beings:
Whether our lifeless shades are doomed to wander
In gloomy groves with discontented ghosts
Or whether through the upper air we fleet
And tread the fields of light, still* I'll pursue thee
Till Fate ordains that we shall part no more.
CALISTA.
Oh no! Heav'n has some better lot in store
To crown thee with: live, and be happy long;
Live for some maid that shall deserve thy goodness,
Some kind, unpracticed heart, that never yet
Has listened to the false ones of thy sex,
Nor known the arts of ours. She shall reward thee,
Meet thee with virtues equal to thy own,
Charm thee with sweetness, beauty, and with truth,
Be blest in thee alone, and thou in her.

Enter Horatio.

HORATIO.
Now mourn indeed, ye miserable pair,
For now the measure of your woes is full.
ALTAMONT.
What dost thou mean, Horatio?
HORATIO.
Oh! 'tis dreadful:
The great, the good Sciolto dies this moment.
CALISTA.
My father!
ALTAMONT.
That's a deadly stroke indeed.
HORATIO.
Not long ago he privately went forth,
Attended but by few, and those unbidden.
I heard which way he took and straight pursued him,
But found him compassed by Lothario's faction,
Almost alone, amidst a crowd of foes.
Too late we brought him aid and drove them back;
Ere that his frantic valor had provoked
The death he seemed to wish for from their swords.
CALISTA.
And dost thou bear me yet, thou patient earth?
Dost thou not labor with my murd'rous weight?
And you, ye glitt'ring, heav'nly host of stars,
Hide your fair heads in clouds, or I shall blast you,
For I am all contagion, death, and ruin,
And Nature sickens at me. Rest, thou world,
This parricide shall be thy plague no more:
Thus, thus I set thee free. (*Stabs herself.*)
HORATIO.
Oh! fatal rashness.
ALTAMONT.
Thou dost instruct me well: to lengthen life
Is but to trifle now.

Altamont offers to kill himself; Horatio prevents him and wrests his sword from him.*

HORATIO.
Hah! what means
The frantic Altamont? Some foe to man
Has breathed on ev'ry breast contagious fury
And epidemic madness.

Enter Sciolto, pale and bloody, supported by servants.

CALISTA.
Oh my heart!
Well mayst thou fail, for see the spring that fed
Thy vital stream is wasted and runs low.
My father! will you now at last forgive me,
If after all my crimes and all your suff'rings,
I call you once again by that dear name?
Will you forget my shame and those wide wounds,
Lift up your hand and bless me ere I go
Down to my dark abode?
SCIOLTO.
Alas! my daughter?
Thou hast rashly ventured in a stormy sea,
Where life, fame, virtue, all were wrecked and lost.
But sure thou hast born thy part in all the anguish
And smarted with the pain. Then rest in peace,
Let silence and oblivion hide thy name
And save thee from the malice of posterity,
And mayst thou find with Heav'n the same forgiveness
As with thy father here. Die, and be happy.
CALISTA.
Celestial sounds! Peace dawns upon my soul,
And ev'ry pain grows less.—Oh! gentle Altamont,

Think not too hardly of me when I'm gone,
But pity me. Had I but early known
Thy wondrous worth, thou excellent young man,
We had been happier both. Now 'tis too late,
And yet my eyes take pleasure to behold thee:
Thou art their last dear object.—Mercy, Heav'n!
(*Dies.*)

ALTAMONT.

Cold! dead and cold! and yet thou art not changed,
But lovely still! Hadst thou a thousand faults,
What heart so hard, what virtue so severe,
But at that beauty must of force relented,
Melted to pity, love, and to forgiveness?

SCIOLTO.

Oh! turn thee from the fatal object. Altamont,
Come near, and let me bless thee e'er I die.
To thee, and brave* Horatio, I bequeath
My fortunes. Lay me by thy noble father
And love my memory as thou hast done his,
For thou hast been my son.—Oh! gracious Heav'n!
Thou that hast endless blessings still* in store
For virtue and for filial piety,
Let grief, disgrace, and want be far away,
But multiply thy mercies on his head;
Let honor, greatness, goodness still* be with him
And peace in all his ways— (*Dies.*)

ALTAMONT.

Take, take it all,
To thee, Horatio, I resign the gift,
While I pursue my father and my love
And find my only portion in the grave.

HORATIO.

The storm of grief bears hard upon his youth
And bends him like a drooping flower to earth.
Raise him and bear him in.

Altamont is carried off.

By such examples are we taught to prove
The sorrows that attend unlawful love:
Death or some worse misfortunes soon divide
The injured bridegroom from his guilty bride.
If you would have the nuptial union last,
Let virtue be the bond that ties it fast.

Exeunt omnes.

FINIS.

Textual Notes

[a] Copytext is the first edition in 1703 (Q). Also consulted: the second edition in 1714 (D1), the third edition in 1718 (D2), the fourth edition in 1730 (D3), the first collected edition in 1747 (W), and modern editions in 1929 (Sutherland), in 1931 (Macmillan and Jones) and 1969 (Goldstein).

[b] Base! Betrayer!] Q, Dd, Sutherland; base betrayer! W, Macmillan and Jones, Goldstein.

[c] th'alarm] Dd, W; the alarm Q, Sutherland, Macmillan and Jones, Goldstein

[d] of] Dd, W, Sutherland, Macmillan and Jones, Goldstein; *om.* Q

[e] your] Dd, W, Sutherland, Macmillan and Jones, Goldstein; our Q.

[f] villain's] Dd, W; villainous Q, Sutherland, Macmillan and Jones, Goldstein

[g] me] D2, D3, W, Sutherland; *om.* Q, D1, Macmillan and Jones, Goldstein

[h] forget] Q, D1, Sutherland, Macmillan and Jones, Goldstein; forgive D2, D3, W.

[i] fountain] Q1, Dd, Macmillan and Jones; fountains W, Sutherland, Goldstein

The Beaux' Stratagem[a]

by George Farquhar (1677?-1707)

edited by Helen M. Burke

George Farquhar was the son of a Protestant clergyman from the north of Ireland, and as such, he was born into the Anglo-Irish colonial ruling class. Nevertheless, as a refugee of war—his family was burnt out of their estate in the 1689–91 wars—and as a penniless Anglo-Irishman living in London, Farquhar was always somewhat of an outsider in the English society of his day, and this outsider's perspective informs all his comedies, including his last work, *The Beaux' Stratagem.*

First performed on March 8, 1707, at the Queen's Theatre in the Haymarket, the play seems, on the surface, to endorse the entrepreneurial and militaristic values of the mercantile class that was then energetically supporting the long-drawn-out War of Spanish Succession. In what could be read as an allegory of the wished-for outcome of this war, the play's two heroes, Archer and Aimwell, defeat a plot by a French count and an Irish priest, and in the process, find wealth and happiness. The militaristic connotations of the beaux's names also underline the connection between their "stratagem" and the ongoing war effort.

Anticipating Gay's *The Beggar's Opera* (1728), however, *The Beaux' Stratagem* also focuses on the activities of a gang of common house-breakers and highwaymen, and by showing the overlap between their robbery plot and the beaux's plot, the play offers a subtle critique of the expansionist ethos of the new Great Britain. Fine gentlemen, like Archer and Aimwell, it suggests, are, in many ways, indistinguishable from "gentlemen of the pad" (highwaymen); money and power are the dominant values in both groups.

A similar instability marks the sexual politics of this play. Again the play pays lip service to emerging middle-class values when it ensures that Mrs. Sullen never breaks her marriage vows and when it shows Aimwell reforming under the influence of Dorinda's goodness. However, in presenting a graphic image of the horrors of a bad marriage, and in advocating divorce on the grounds of irreconcilable differences, *The Beaux' Stratagem* also advances notions that were far in advance of eighteenth-century bourgeois morality and contemporary English marital law.

It was undoubtedly this play's ability to appeal to all sides of the political, social, and sexual spectrum that explains its lasting success. During the entire eighteenth century, it was performed on the London stage every season but one, and it was equally a favorite in Dublin and in provincial theaters.

[I.i]

DRAMATIS PERSONAE

MEN

Aimwell and Archer, two gentlemen of broken fortunes, the first as master, and the second as servant.

Count Bellair, a French officer, prisoner at Litchfield.[1]

Sullen, a country blockhead, brutal to his wife.

Freeman, a gentleman from London.

Foigard,[2] a priest, chaplain to the French officers.

Gibbet, a highwayman.

Hounslow and Bagshot,[3] his companions.

Bonniface, landlord of the inn.

Scrub, servant to Mr. Sullen.

WOMEN

Lady Bountiful, an old, civil country gentlewoman, that cures all her neighbors of all distempers, foolishly fond of her son, Sullen.

Dorinda, Lady Bountiful's daughter.

Mrs. Sullen, her daughter-in-law.

Gipsey, maid to the ladies.

Cherry, the landlord's daughter in the inn.

SCENE: LITCHFIELD.

The Beaux' Stratagem.

Act I, scene i. An inn.

Enter Bonniface running.

BONNIFACE.
Chamberlain![4] Maid! Cherry! daughter Cherry! all asleep? all dead?

Enter Cherry running.

CHERRY.
Here, here! Why d'ye bawl so, father? D'ye think we have no ears?

BONNIFACE.
You deserve to have none, you young minx! The company of the Warrington[5] coach has stood in the hall this hour and nobody to show them to their chambers.

CHERRY.
And let 'em wait farther![b] There's neither redcoat in the coach, nor footman behind it.

BONNIFACE.
But they threaten to go to another inn tonight.

CHERRY.
That they dare not, for fear the coachman should overturn them tomorrow.—Coming! coming!—Here's the London coach arrived!

Enter several people with trunks, bandboxes, and other luggage, and cross the stage.

BONNIFACE.
Welcome, ladies!

CHERRY.
Very welcome, gentlemen!—Chamberlain, show the Lion and the Rose.[6] (*Exit with the company.*)

Enter Aimwell in riding habit, Archer as footman carrying a portmanteau.

BONNIFACE.
This way, this way, gentlemen!

AIMWELL.
Set down the things. Go to the stable, and see my horses well rubbed.

ARCHER.
I shall, sir. (*Exit.*)

AIMWELL.
You're my landlord, I suppose?

BONNIFACE.
Yes sir, I'm old Will Bonniface, pretty well known upon this road, as the saying is.

AIMWELL.
Oh Mr. Bonniface, your servant!

BONNIFACE.
Oh sir! What will your honor please to drink, as the saying is?

---

1 Litchfield] modern Lichfield, a town in Staffordshire in central England

2 Foigard] garbled French for, ironically, guardian of the faith

3 Hounslow and Bagshot] named after two London heaths that were favorite haunts of highwaymen

4 Chamberlain] the servant in charge of the bedchambers

5 Warrington] a town about sixty miles from Litchfield

6 Lion … Rose] names of bedrooms in the inn

AIMWELL.

I have heard your town of Litchfield much famed for ale. I think I'll taste that.

BONNIFACE.

Sir, I have now in my cellar ten tun of the best ale in Staffordshire; 'tis smooth as oil, sweet as milk, clear as amber, and strong as brandy and will be just fourteen year old the fifth day of next March old style.[7]

AIMWELL.

You're very exact, I find, in the age of your ale.

BONNIFACE.

As punctual, sir, as I am in the age of my children. I'll show you such ale!—Here, tapster, broach number 1706,[8] as the saying is.—Sir, you shall taste my *Anno Domini.* I have lived in Litchfield, man and boy, above eight and fifty years and, I believe, have not consumed eight and fifty ounces of meat.

AIMWELL.

At a meal, you mean, if one may guess your sense by your bulk.

BONNIFACE.

Not in my life, sir; I have fed purely upon ale. I have eat my ale, drank my ale, and I always sleep upon ale.

Enter tapster with a bottle and glass.

Now, sir, you shall see! (*Filling it out.*) Your worship's health. Hah! delicious, delicious—fancy it burgundy, only fancy it, and 'tis worth ten shillings a quart!

AIMWELL. (*Drinks.*)

'Tis confounded strong!

BONNIFACE.

Strong! It must be so, or how should we be strong that drink it?

AIMWELL.

And have you lived so long upon this ale, landlord?

BONNIFACE.

Eight and fifty years, upon my credit, sir, but it killed my wife, poor woman, as the saying is.

AIMWELL.

How came that to pass?

BONNIFACE.

I don't know how, sir. She would not let the ale take its natural course, sir; she was for qualifying it every now and then with a dram, as the saying is, and an honest gentleman that came this way from Ireland made her a present of a dozen bottles of usquebaugh[9]—but the poor woman was never well after. But howe'er, I was obliged to the gentleman, you know.

AIMWELL.

Why, was it the usquebaugh that killed her?

BONNIFACE.

My Lady Bountiful said so. She, good lady, did what could be done: she cured her of three tympanies, but the fourth carried her off. But she's happy, and I'm contented, as the saying is.

AIMWELL.

Who's that Lady Bountiful, you mentioned?

BONNIFACE.

'Od's* my life, sir, we'll drink her health! (*Drinks.*) My Lady Bountiful is one of the best of women. Her last husband, Sir Charles Bountiful, left her worth a thousand pound a year, and I believe she lays out one half on't in charitable uses for the good of her neighbors. She cures rheumatisms, ruptures, and broken shins in men; greensickness, obstructions, and fits of the mother* in women; the king's evil, chincough,[10] and chilblains in children. In short, she has cured more people in and about Litchfield within ten years than the doctors have killed in twenty, and that's a bold word.

AIMWELL.

Has the lady been any other way useful in her generation?

BONNIFACE.

Yes, sir. She has a daughter by Sir Charles, the finest woman in all our country, and the greatest fortune.

---

[7] old style] Until 1752, England used the Julian calendar which was eleven days behind the calendar used in many other parts of western Europe.

[8] 1706] The code number given to this ale (1706) suggests that it was brewed the previous year, not fourteen years earlier.

[9] usquebaugh] whiskey; *uisce beatha,* literally "the water of life" (Irish)

[10] chincough] whooping-cough

She has a son, too, by her first husband, Squire Sullen, who married a fine lady from London t'other day; if you please, sir, we'll drink his health.

AIMWELL.
What sort of a man is he?

BONNIFACE.
Why sir, the man's well enough: says little, thinks less, and does—nothing at all, faith! But he's a man of a great estate, and values nobody.

AIMWELL.
A sportsman, I suppose?

BONNIFACE.
Yes sir, he's a man of pleasure. He plays at whist and smokes his pipe eight and forty hours together sometimes.

AIMWELL.
And married, you say?

BONNIFACE.
Aye, and to a curious woman, sir. But he's a —he wants* it, here, sir. (*Pointing to his forehead.*)

AIMWELL.
He has it there, you mean.[11]

BONNIFACE.
That's none of my business. He's my landlord, and so a man, you know, would not—but, icod,[12] he's no better than—sir, my humble service to you. (*Drinks.*) Though I value not a farthing what he can do to me, I pay him his rent at quarter day,[13] I have a good running trade, I have but one daughter, and I can give her—but no matter for that.

AIMWELL.
You're very happy, Mr. Bonniface. Pray what other company have you in town?

BONNIFACE.
A power of fine ladies, and then we have the French officers.[14]

AIMWELL.
Oh, that's right, you have a good many of those gentlemen. Pray how do you like their company?

BONNIFACE.
So well, as the saying is, that I could wish we had as many more of 'em. They're full of money and pay double for every thing they have. They know, sir, that we paid good round taxes for the taking of 'em, and so they are willing to reimburse us a little. One of 'em lodges in my house.

Enter Archer.

ARCHER.
Landlord, there are some French gentlemen below that ask for you.

BONNIFACE.
I'll wait on 'em. (*[Aside] to Archer.*) Does your master stay long in town, as the saying is?

ARCHER.
I can't tell, as the saying is.

BONNIFACE.
Come from London?

ARCHER.
No.

BONNIFACE.
Going to London, mayhap?

ARCHER.
No.

BONNIFACE.
An odd fellow this!—I beg your worship's pardon. I'll wait on you in half a minute. (*Exit.*)

AIMWELL.
The coast's clear, I see.—Now, my dear Archer, welcome to Litchfield!

ARCHER.
I thank thee, my dear brother in iniquity.

AIMWELL.
Iniquity! prithee leave canting! You need not change your style with your dress.

ARCHER.
Don't mistake me, Aimwell, for 'tis still* my maxim that there is no scandal like rags nor any crime so shameful as poverty.

AIMWELL.
The world confesses it every day in its practice, though men won't own it for their opinion. Who did that worthy lord, my brother, single out of the side box to sup with him t'other night?

11 has it there] wears the horns of a cuckold

12 icod] rural variant of egad, a mild oath

13 quarter day] one of four fixed days of the year for paying rent

14 French officers] officers captured during the ongoing War of Spanish Succession and quartered on parole in various parts of England

ARCHER.

Jack Handicraft, a handsome, well dressed, mannerly, sharping[15] rogue, who keeps the best company in town.

AIMWELL.

Right, and pray who married my Lady Manslaughter t'other day, the great fortune?

ARCHER.

Why, Nick Marrabone,* a professed pickpocket, and a good bowler, but he makes a handsome figure and rides in his coach that he formerly used to ride behind.

AIMWELL.

But did you observe poor Jack Generous* in the Park* last week?

ARCHER.

Yes, with his autumnal periwig shading his melancholy face, his coat older than anything but its fashion, with one hand idle in his pocket and with the other picking his useless teeth. And though the Mall* was crowded with company, yet was poor Jack as single and solitary as a lion in a desert.

AIMWELL.

And as much avoided for no crime upon earth but the want* of money.

ARCHER.

And that's enough. Men must not be poor; idleness is the root of all evil. The world's wide enough; let 'em bustle. Fortune has taken the weak under her protection, but men of sense are left to their industry.

AIMWELL.

Upon which topic we proceed and, I think, luckily hitherto. Would not any man swear now that I am a man of quality* and you my servant, when if our intrinsic value were known—

ARCHER.

Come, come, we are the men of intrinsic value, who can strike our fortunes out of ourselves, whose worth is independent of accidents in life or revolutions in government. We have heads to get money and hearts to spend it.

AIMWELL.

As to our hearts, I grant ye, they are as willing tits[16] as any within twenty degrees, but I can have no great opinion of our heads from the service they have done us hitherto, unless it be that they have brought us from London hither to Litchfield, made me a lord, and you my servant.

ARCHER.

That's more than you could expect already. But what money have we left?

AIMWELL.

But two hundred pound.

ARCHER.

And our horses, clothes, rings, etcetera— Why, we have very good fortunes now for moderate people, and let me tell you, besides, that this two hundred pound, with the experience that we are now masters of, is a better estate than the ten thousand[c] we have spent. Our friends, indeed, began to suspect that our pockets were low, but we came off with flying colors, showed no signs of want* either in word or deed.

AIMWELL.

Aye, and our going to Brussels was a good pretence enough for our sudden disappearing, and, I warrant you, our friends imagine that we are gone a-volunteering.

ARCHER.

Why faith, if this prospect fails, it must e'en come to that. I am for venturing one of the hundreds, if you will, upon this knight-errantry, but in case it should fail, we'll reserve the t'other to carry us to some counter scarp, where we may die as we lived—in a blaze.

AIMWELL.

With all my heart. And we have lived justly, Archer: we can't say that we have spent our fortunes but that we have enjoyed 'em.

ARCHER.

Right! So much pleasure for so much money! We have had our pennyworths, and had I millions, I would go to the same market again. Oh London, London! Well, we have had our share, and let us be thankful. Past pleasures, for aught I know, are best, such as we are sure of; those to come may disappoint us.

AIMWELL.

It has often grieved the heart of me to see how some inhuman wretches murder their kind fortunes—those that by sacrificing all to one appetite shall

15 sharping] cheating

16 tits] serviceable horses

starve all the rest. You shall have some that live only in their palates and, in their sense of tasting, shall drown the other four. Others are only epicures in appearances, such who shall starve their nights to make a figure a-days and famish their own to feed the eyes of others. A contrary sort confine their pleasures to the dark and contract their spacious acres to the circuit of a muff-string.[17]

ARCHER.

Right, but they find the Indies in the spot where they consume 'em, and I think your kind keepers* have much the best on't, for they indulge the most senses by one expense. There's the seeing, hearing, and feeling amply gratified, and some philosophers will tell you that from such a commerce, there arises a sixth sense that gives infinitely more pleasure than the other five put together.

AIMWELL.

And to pass to the other extremity, of all keepers, I think those the worst that keep their money.

ARCHER.

Those are the most miserable wights in being: they destroy the rights of Nature, and disappoint the blessings of Providence. Give me a man that keeps his five senses keen and bright as his sword, that has 'em always drawn out in their just order and strength with his reason as commander at the head of 'em, that detaches 'em by turns upon whatever party of pleasure agreeably offers* and commands 'em to retreat upon the least appearance of disadvantage or danger. For my part I can stick to my bottle, while my wine, my company, and my reason holds good. I can be charmed with Sappho's singing without falling in love with her face; I love hunting, but would not, like Actaeon, be eaten up by my own dogs; I love a fine house, but let another keep it; and just so I love a fine woman.

AIMWELL.

In that last particular you have the better of me.

ARCHER.

Aye, you're such an amorous puppy that I'm afraid you'll spoil our sport: you can't counterfeit the passion without feeling it.

[17] muff-string] string attaching a hand-covering to a woman's neck

AIMWELL.

Though the whining part be out-of-doors[18] in Town,* 'tis still in force with the country ladies. And let my tell you, Frank, the fool in that passion shall outdo the knave at any time.

ARCHER.

Well, I won't dispute it now; you command for the day, and so I submit. At Nottingham, you know, I am to be master.

AIMWELL.

And at Lincoln, I again.

ARCHER.

Then at Norwich I mount, which, I think, shall be our last stage, for if we fail there, we'll embark for Holland, bid adieu to Venus, and welcome Mars.

AIMWELL.

A match!

Enter Bonniface.

Mum!

BONNIFACE.

What will your worship please to have for supper?

AIMWELL.

What have you got?

BONNIFACE.

Sir, we have a delicate piece of beef in the pot and a pig at the fire.

AIMWELL.

Good supper-meat, I must confess. I can't eat beef, landlord.

ARCHER.

And I hate pig.

AIMWELL.

Hold your prating, sirrah! Do you know who you are?

BONNIFACE.

Please to bespeak something else; I have everything in the house.

AIMWELL.

Have you any veal?

BONNIFACE.

Veal! Sir, we had a delicate loin of veal on Wednesday last.

AIMWELL.

Have you got any fish or wildfowl?

[18] out-of-doors] unfashionable

BONNIFACE.

As for fish, truly, sir, we are an inland town and indifferently provided with fish, that's the truth on't, and then for wildfowl—we have a delicate couple of rabbits.

AIMWELL.

Get me the rabbits fricasseed.

BONNIFACE.

Fricasseed! Lard, sir, they'll eat much better smothered with onions.

ARCHER.

Pshaw! Damn your onions!

AIMWELL.

Again, sirrah!—Well landlord, what you please. But hold, I have a small charge of money, and your house is so full of strangers that I believe it may be safer in your custody than mine, for when this fellow of mine gets drunk, he minds nothing.—Here sirrah, reach me the strongbox.

ARCHER.

Yes, sir. (*Aside.*) This will give us a reputation. (*Brings the box.*)

AIMWELL.

Here, landlord. The locks are sealed down both for your security and mine. It holds somewhat above two hundred pound; if you doubt it, I'll count it to you after supper. But be sure you lay it where I may have it at a minute's warning, for my affairs are a little dubious at present: perhaps I may be gone in half an hour, perhaps I may be your guest till the best part of that be spent. And pray order your ostler to keep my horses always saddled. But one thing above the rest I must beg, that you would let this fellow have none of your *Anno Domini*, as you call it, for he's the most insufferable sot.—Here sirrah, light me to my chamber. (*Exit, lighted by Archer.*)

BONNIFACE.

Cherry! daughter Cherry!

Enter Cherry.

CHERRY.

D'ye call, father?

BONNIFACE.

Aye, child. You must lay by this box for the gentleman: 'tis full of money.

CHERRY.

Money! all that money! Why sure, father, the gentleman comes to be chosen parliament-man.[19] Who is he?

BONNIFACE.

I don't know what to make of him. He talks of keeping his horses ready saddled and of going perhaps at a minute's warning or of staying perhaps till the best part of this be spent.

CHERRY.

Aye, ten to one, father, he's a highwayman.

BONNIFACE.

A highwayman! Upon my life, girl, you have hit it, and this box is some new-purchased booty. Now could we find him out, the money were ours.

CHERRY.

He don't belong to our gang.

BONNIFACE.

What horses have they?

CHERRY.

The master rides upon a black.

BONNIFACE.

A black! Ten to one the man upon the black mare! And since he don't belong to our fraternity, we may betray him with a safe conscience. I don't think it lawful to harbor any rogues but my own. Look'ye, child, as the saying is, we must go cunningly to work; proofs we must have. The gentleman's servant loves drink—I'll ply him that way—and ten to one loves a wench—you must work him t'other way.

CHERRY.

Father, would you have me give my secret for his?

BONNIFACE.

Consider, child, there's two hundred pound to boot. (*Ringing without.*) Coming! coming!—Child, mind your business. [*Exit.*]

CHERRY.

What a rogue is my father! My father! I deny it—my mother was a good, generous, free-hearted woman, and I can't tell how far her good nature might have extended for the good of her children. This landlord of mine, for I think I can call him no more, would betray his guest and debauch his daughter into the bargain—by a footman too!

---

19 parliament-man] Candidates for parliamentary election commonly used bribes to ensure their seats.

Enter Archer.

ARCHER.
What footman, pray mistress, is so happy as to be the subject of your contemplation?

CHERRY.
Whoever he is, friend, he'll be but little the better for't.

ARCHER.
I hope so, for I'm sure you did not think of me.

CHERRY.
Suppose I had?

ARCHER.
Why then, you're but even with me, for the minute I came in, I was a-considering in what manner I should make love* to you.

CHERRY.
Love to me, friend!

ARCHER.
Yes, child.*

CHERRY.
Child? Manners! If you kept a little more distance, friend, it would become you much better.

ARCHER.
Distance! Good night, saucebox! (*Going.*)

CHERRY.
A pretty fellow! I like his pride.—Sir, pray sir, you see, sir, (*Archer returns.*) I have the credit to be entrusted with your master's fortune here, which sets me a degree above his footman. I hope, sir, you an't affronted.

ARCHER.
Let me look you full in the face, and I'll tell you whether you can affront me or no.—S'death,* child, you have a pair of delicate eyes, and you don't know what to do with 'em!

CHERRY.
Why sir, don't I see everybody?

ARCHER.
Aye, but if some women had 'em, they would kill everybody. Prithee instruct me, I would fain make love to you, but I don't know what to say.

CHERRY.
Why, did you never make love to anybody before?

ARCHER.
Never to a person of your figure, I can assure you, madam. My addresses have been always confined to people within my own sphere; I never aspired so high before. (*Sings*)

A Song.

But you look so bright,
And are dressed so tight,
That a man would swear you're right,
As arm was e'er laid over.
Such an air
You freely wear
To ensnare
As makes each guest a lover.

Since then, my dear, I'm your guest,
Prithee give me of the best
Of what is ready dressed:
Since then, my dear, etc.[d]

CHERRY. (*Aside.*)
What can I think of this man?—Will you give me that song, sir?

ARCHER.
Aye my dear, take it while 'tis warm. (*Kisses her.*) Death and fire! her lips are honeycombs.

CHERRY.
And I wish there had been bees too, to have stung you for your impudence.

ARCHER.
There's a swarm of Cupids, my little Venus, that has done the business much better.

CHERRY. (*Aside.*)
This fellow is misbegotten as well as I.—What's your name, sir?

ARCHER. (*Aside.*)
Name! Egad, I have forgot it!—Oh! Martin.

CHERRY.
Where were you born?

ARCHER.
In St. Martin's parish.

CHERRY.
What was your father?

ARCHER.
St. Martin's Parish.[20]

---

[20] Parish] an orphan raised by the parish

CHERRY.
Then, friend, good night!

ARCHER.
I hope not.

CHERRY.
You may depend upon't.

ARCHER.
Upon what?

CHERRY.
That you're very impudent.

ARCHER.
That you're very handsome.

CHERRY.
That you're a footman.

ARCHER.
That you're an angel.

CHERRY.
I shall be rude.

ARCHER.
So shall I.

CHERRY.
Let go my hand.

ARCHER.
Give me a kiss. (*Kisses her.*)

[BONIFACE.] (*Calls without.*)
Cherry! Cherry!

CHERRY.
I'm-m^e—my father calls. You plaguy devil, how durst you stop my breath so? Offer* to follow me one step, if you dare! [*Exit.*]

ARCHER.
A fair challenge, by this light! This is a pretty fair opening of an adventure, but we are knight-errants, and so Fortune be our guide.

Exit.

Act II, scene [i]. A gallery in Lady Bountiful's house.

Mrs. Sullen and Dorinda meeting.

DORINDA.
Morrow, my dear sister. Are you for church this morning?

MRS. SULLEN.
Anywhere to pray, for Heaven alone can help me. But I think, Dorinda, there's no form of prayer in the liturgy against bad husbands.

DORINDA.
But there's a form of law in Doctors Commons,* and I swear, sister Sullen, rather than see you thus continually discontented, I would advise you to apply to that. For besides the part that I bear in your vexatious broils, as being sister to the husband and friend to the wife, your example gives me such an impression of matrimony that I shall be apt to condemn my person to a long vacation all its life. But supposing, madam, that you brought it to a case of separation, what can you urge against your husband? My brother is, first, the most constant man alive.

MRS. SULLEN.
The most constant husband, I grant ye.

DORINDA.
He never sleeps from you.

MRS. SULLEN.
No, he always sleeps with me.

DORINDA.
He allows you a maintenance suitable to your quality.*

MRS. SULLEN.
A maintenance! Do you take me, madam, for an hospital child,[21] that I must sit down and bless my benefactors for meat, drink and clothes? As I take it, madam, I brought your brother ten thousand pounds, out of which I might expect some pretty things called pleasures.

DORINDA.
You share in all the pleasures that the country affords.

MRS. SULLEN.
Country pleasures! Racks and torments! Dost think, child,* that my limbs were made for leaping of ditches and clambering over stiles? or that my parents, wisely foreseeing my future happiness in country pleasures, had early instructed me in the rural accomplishments of drinking fat[22] ale, playing at whist, and smoking tobacco with my husband? or of spreading of plasters, brewing of diet-drinks, and stilling rosemary-water with the good old gentlewoman, my mother-in-law?

---

[21] hospital child] one in a charitable institution

[22] fat] full-bodied

DORINDA.

I'm sorry, madam, that it is not more in our power to divert you; I could wish, indeed, that our entertainments were a little more polite or your taste a little less refined. But pray madam, how came the poets and philosophers, that labored so much in hunting after pleasure, to place it at last in a country life?

MRS. SULLEN.

Because they wanted* money, child, to find out the pleasures of the Town. Did you ever see a poet or philosopher worth ten thousand pound? If you can show me such a man, I'll lay you fifty pound you'll find him somewhere within the weekly bills.* Not that I disapprove rural pleasures, as the poets have painted them! In their landscape, every Phyllis has her Corydon,[23] every murmuring stream and every flowery mead gives fresh alarms to love. Besides, you'll find that their couples were never married.—But yonder I see my Corydon, and a sweet swain it is, Heaven knows!—Come Dorinda, don't be angry, he's my husband and your brother, and between both is he not a sad brute?

DORINDA.

I have nothing to say to your part of him. You're the best judge.

MRS. SULLEN.

Oh sister, sister! if ever you marry, beware of a sullen, silent sot, one that's always musing but never thinks! There's some diversion in a talking blockhead, and since a woman must wear chains, I would have the pleasure of hearing 'em rattle a little. Now you shall see, but take this by the way: He came home this morning at his usual hour of four, wakened me out of a sweet dream of something else by tumbling over the tea table, which he broke all to pieces; after his man and he had rolled about the room like sick passengers in a storm, he comes flounce into bed, dead as a salmon into a fishmonger's basket, his feet cold as ice, his breath hot as a furnace, and his hands and his face as greasy as his flannel nightcap—oh, matrimony! He tosses up the clothes with a barbarous swing over his shoulders, disorders the whole economy of my bed, leaves me half naked, and my whole night's comfort is the tuneable serenade of that wakeful nightingale, his nose! Oh, the pleasure of counting the melancholy clock by a snoring husband! But now, sister, you shall see how handsomely, being a well-bred man, he will beg my pardon.

Enter Sullen.

SULLEN.

My head aches consumedly.

MRS. SULLEN.

Will you be pleased, my dear, to drink tea with us this morning? It may do your head good.

SULLEN.

No.

DORINDA.

Coffee, brother?

SULLEN.

Pshaw!

MRS. SULLEN.

Will you please to dress and go to church with me? The air may help you.

SULLEN.

Scrub![24]

Enter Scrub.

SCRUB.

Sir!

SULLEN.

What day o'th'week is this?

SCRUB.

Sunday, an't* please your worship.

SULLEN.

Sunday! Bring me a dram, and d'ye hear, set out the venison pasty and a tankard of strong beer upon the hall table. I'll go to breakfast. (*Going.*)

DORINDA.

Stay, stay, brother, you shan't get off so; you were very naught* last night and must make your wife reparation. Come, come, brother, won't you ask pardon?

---

23 Phyllis ... Corydon] typical names for a nymph and her swain in pastoral poetry

24 Scrub] His name refers to his household function but also to his stunted growth; this role was originally played by Norris, an actor who was short in stature.

SULLEN.
For what?

DORINDA.
For being drunk last night.

SULLEN.
I can afford it, can't I?

MRS. SULLEN.
But I can't, sir.

SULLEN.
Then you may let it alone.

MRS. SULLEN.
But I must tell you, sir, that this is not to be borne.

SULLEN.
I'm glad on't.

MRS. SULLEN.
What is the reason, sir, that you use me thus inhumanely?

SULLEN.
Scrub?

SCRUB.
Sir!

SULLEN.
Get things ready to shave my head. (*Exit [with Scrub].*)

MRS. SULLEN.
Have a care of coming near his temples, Scrub, for fear you meet something there that may turn the edge of your razor.—Inveterate stupidity! Did you ever know so hard, so obstinate a spleen as his! Oh, sister, sister! I shall never ha' good of the beast till I get him to Town: London, dear London, is the place for managing and breaking a husband.

DORINDA.
And has not a husband the same opportunities there for humbling a wife?

MRS. SULLEN.
No, no, child,* 'tis a standing maxim in conjugal discipline that when a man would enslave his wife, he hurries her into the country, and when a lady would be arbitrary with her husband, she wheedles her booby up to Town. A man dare not play the tyrant in London because there are so many examples to encourage the subject to rebel. Oh, Dorinda! Dorinda! a fine woman may do anything in London; o'my conscience, she may raise an army of forty thousand men!

DORINDA.
I fancy, sister, you have a mind to be trying your power that way here in Litchfield: you have drawn the French count to your colors already.

MRS. SULLEN.
The French are a people that can't live without their gallantries.

DORINDA.
And some English that I know, sister, are not averse to such amusements.

MRS. SULLEN.
Well sister, since the truth must out, it may do as well now as hereafter. I think one way to rouse my lethargic, sottish husband is to give him a rival. Security begets negligence in all people, and men must be alarmed to make 'em alert in their duty. Women are like pictures of no value in the hands of a fool till he hears men of sense bid high for the purchase.

DORINDA.
This might do, sister, if my brother's understanding were to be convinced into a passion for you. But I fancy there's a natural aversion of his side, and I fancy, sister, that you don't come much behind him, if you dealt fairly.

MRS. SULLEN.
I own it: we are united contradictions, fire and water. But I could be contented, with a great many other wives, to humor the censorious mob and give the world an appearance of living well with my husband, could I bring him but to dissemble a little kindness to keep me in countenance.[25]

DORINDA.
But how do you know, sister, but that instead of rousing your husband by this artifice to a counterfeit kindness, he should awake in a real fury?

MRS. SULLEN.
Let him! If I can't entice him to the one, I would provoke him to the other.

DORINDA.
But how must I behave myself between ye?

MRS. SULLEN.
You must assist me.

---

25 in countenance] so I could save face

DORINDA.
What, against my own brother!

MRS. SULLEN.
He's but half a brother, and I'm your entire friend. If I go a step beyond the bounds of honor, leave me; till then I expect you should go along with me in everything. While I trust my honor in your hands, you may trust your brother's in mine.—The count is to dine here today.

DORINDA.
'Tis a strange thing, sister, that I can't like that man.

MRS. SULLEN.
You like nothing; your time is not come. Love and death have their fatalities and strike home one time or other. You'll pay for all one day, I warrant ye.—But come, my lady's tea is ready, and 'tis almost church time.

Exeunt.

Scene [ii]. The inn.

Enter Aimwell dressed, and Archer.

AIMWELL.
And was she the daughter of the house?

ARCHER.
The landlord is so blind as to think so, but I dare swear she has better blood in her veins.

AIMWELL.
Why dost think so?

ARCHER.
Because the baggage has a pert je ne sais quoi; she reads plays, keeps a monkey, and is troubled with vapors.

AIMWELL.
By which discoveries I guess that you know more of her.

ARCHER.
Not yet, faith! The lady gives herself airs; forsooth, nothing under a gentleman!

AIMWELL.
Let me take her in hand.

ARCHER.
Say one word more o'that, and I'll declare myself, spoil your sport there, and everywhere else. Look'ye, Aimwell, every man in his own sphere!

AIMWELL.
Right, and therefore, you must pimp for your master.

ARCHER.
In the usual forms, good sir, after I have served myself.—But to our business. You are so well dressed, Tom, and make so handsome a figure, that I fancy you may do execution in a country church; the exterior part strikes first, and you're in the right to make that impression favorable.

AIMWELL.
There's something in that which may turn to advantage. The appearance of a stranger in a country church draws as many gazers as a blazing star; no sooner he comes into the cathedral but a train of whispers runs buzzing round the congregation in a moment: "Who is he? Whence comes he? Do you know him?" Then I, sir, tips me the verger with half a crown; he pockets the simony and inducts me into the best pew in the church; I pull out my snuffbox, turn my self round, bow to the bishop, or the dean if he be the commanding officer; single out a beauty, rivet both my eyes to hers, set my nose a-bleeding by the strength of imagination, and show the whole church my concern by my endeavoring to hide it. After the sermon, the whole town gives me to her for a lover, and by persuading the lady that I am a-dying for her, the tables are turned, and she in good earnest falls in love with me.

ARCHER.
There's nothing in this, Tom, without a precedent, but instead of riveting your eyes to a beauty, try to fix 'em upon a fortune; that's our business at present.

AIMWELL.
Pshaw! no woman can be a beauty without a fortune. Let me alone, for I am a marksman.

ARCHER.
Tom!

AIMWELL.
Aye.

ARCHER.
When were you at church before, pray?

AIMWELL.
Um—I was there at the coronation.[26]

[26] coronation] of Queen Anne in 1702

ARCHER.
And how can you expect a blessing by going to church now?

AIMWELL.
Blessing! nay, Frank, I ask but for a wife. (*Exit.*)

ARCHER.
Truly the man is not very unreasonable in his demands. (*Exit at the opposite door.*)

Enter Bonniface and Cherry.

BONNIFACE.
Well, daughter, as the saying is, have you brought Martin to confess?

CHERRY.
Pray father, don't put me upon getting anything out of a man; I'm but young, you know, father, and I don't understand wheedling.

BONNIFACE.
Young! why, you jade, as the saying is, can any woman wheedle that is not young? Your mother was useless at five and twenty. Not wheedle! would you make your mother a whore and me a cuckold, as the saying is? I tell you his silence confesses it, and his master spends his money so freely and is so much a gentleman every manner of way that he must be a highwayman.

Enter Gibbet in a cloak.

GIBBET.
Landlord, landlord, is the coast clear?

BONNIFACE.
Oh, Mr. Gibbet, what's the news?

GIBBET.
No matter, ask no questions, all fair and honourable.—Here, my dear Cherry. (*Gives her a bag.*) Two hundred sterling pounds, as good as any that ever hanged or saved a rogue; lay 'em by with the rest, and here—three wedding or mourning rings,[27] 'tis much the same you know. Here, two silver-hilted swords; I took those from fellows that never show any part of their swords but the hilts. Here is a diamond necklace which the lady hid in the privatest place in the coach, but I found it out. This gold watch I took from a pawnbroker's wife; it was left in her hands by a person of quality;* there's the arms upon the case.

CHERRY.
But who had you the money from?

GIBBET.
Ah! poor woman! I pitied her—from a poor lady just eloped from her husband. She had made up her cargo and was bound for Ireland as hard as she could drive; she told me of her husband's barbarous usage, and so I left her half a crown. But I had almost forgot, my dear Cherry, I have a present for you.

CHERRY.
What is't?

GIBBET.
A pot of ceruse, my child, that I took out of a lady's under-pocket.

CHERRY.
What, Mr. Gibbet, do you think that I paint?

GIBBET.
Why you jade, your betters do! I'm sure the lady that I took it from had a coronet upon her handkerchief. Here, take my cloak and go, secure the premises.

CHERRY.
I will secure 'em. (*Exit.*)

BONNIFACE.
But hark ye, where's Hounslow and Bagshot?

GIBBET.
They'll be here tonight.

BONNIFACE.
D'ye know of any other gentlemen o'the pad on this road?

GIBBET.
No.

BONNIFACE.
I fancy that I have two that lodge in the house just now.

GIBBET.
The devil! How d'ye smoke 'em?

BONNIFACE.
Why, the one is gone to church.

GIBBET.
That's suspicious, I must confess.

BONNIFACE.
And the other is now in his master's chamber; he pretends to be servant to the other. We'll call him out and pump him a little.

27 mourning rings] worn by friends of the deceased

GIBBET.
With all my heart.

BONNIFACE.
Mr. Martin! Mr. Martin!

Enter Archer combing a periwig and singing.

GIBBET.
The roads are consumed deep; I'm as dirty as old Brentford at Christmas.[28]—A good pretty fellow that.—Whose servant are you, friend?

ARCHER.
My master's.

GIBBET.
Really?

ARCHER.
Really.

GIBBET.
That's much.—The fellow has been at the bar by his evasions!—But pray sir, what is your master's name?

ARCHER. (*Sings and combs the periwig.*)
Tall, all dall! This is the most obstinate curl—

GIBBET.
I ask you his name?

ARCHER.
Name, sir?—*Tall, all dall!*—I never asked him his name in my life. *Tall, all dall!*

BONNIFACE. [*Aside to Gibbet.*]
What think you now?

GIBBET. [*Aside to Bonniface.*]
Plain, plain: he talks now as if he were before a judge.—But pray friend, which way does your master travel?

ARCHER.
A-horseback.

GIBBET. [*Aside to Bonniface.*]
Very well again, an old offender, right!—But, I mean does he go upwards or downwards?

ARCHER.
Downwards, I fear, sir.—*Tall, all!*

GIBBET.
I'm afraid my fate will be a contrary way.[29]

BONNIFACE.
Ha, ha, ha! Mr. Martin, you're very arch! This gentleman is only travelling towards Chester, and would be glad of your company, that's all.—Come Captain, you'll stay tonight, I suppose? I'll show you a chamber. Come, Captain.

GIBBET.
Farewell, friend. (*Exit [with Bonniface].*)

ARCHER.
Captain, your servant.—Captain! a pretty fellow! S'death,* I wonder that the officers of the army don't conspire to beat all scoundrels in red but their own!

Enter Cherry.

CHERRY. (*Aside.*)
Gone, and Martin here! I hope he did not listen: I would have the merit of the discovery all my own, because I would oblige him to love me.—Mr. Martin, who was that man with my father?

ARCHER.
Some recruiting sergeant or whipped-out[30] trooper, I suppose.

CHERRY. [*Aside.*]
All's safe, I find.

ARCHER.
Come my dear, have you conned over the catechise[31] I taught you last night?

CHERRY.
Come, question me.

ARCHER.
What is Love?

CHERRY.
Love is I know not what, it comes I know not how, and goes I know not when.

ARCHER.
Very well, an apt scholar! (*Chucks her under the chin.*) Where does Love enter?

CHERRY.
Into the eyes.

ARCHER.
And where go out?

[28] Brentford at Christmas] a town that was notoriously muddy in winter

[29] contrary way] Gibbet fears he is going to hung up on the gallows (the fate of convicted highwaymen).

[30] whipped-out] flogged out of the army

[31] catechise] Mock-catechisms like the one that follows had become popular as exercises of libertine wit in the early eighteenth century.

CHERRY.
I won't tell ye.

ARCHER.
What are objects[f] of that passion?

CHERRY.
Youth, beauty, and clean linen.

ARCHER.
The reason?

CHERRY.
The two first are fashionable in Nature, and the third at Court.

ARCHER.
That's my dear! What are the signs and tokens of that passion?

CHERRY.
A stealing look, a stammering tongue, words improbable, designs impossible, and actions impracticable.

ARCHER.
That's my good child!* Kiss me.—What must a lover do to obtain his mistress?

CHERRY.
He must adore the person that disdains him, he must bribe the chambermaid that betrays him, and court the footman that laughs at him. He must, he must—

ARCHER.
Nay child, I must whip you if you don't mind your lesson. He must treat his—

CHERRY.
Oh, aye! He must treat his enemies with respect, his friends with indifference, and all the world with contempt; he must suffer much and fear more; he must desire much and hope little; in short, he must embrace his ruin and throw himself away.

ARCHER.
Had ever man so hopeful a pupil as mine? Come my dear, why is Love called a riddle?

CHERRY.
Because being blind, he leads those that see, and though a child, he governs a man.

ARCHER.
Mighty well!—And why is Love pictured blind?

CHERRY.
Because the painters out of the weakness or privilege of their art chose to hide those eyes that they could not draw.

ARCHER.
That's my dear little scholar! Kiss me again.—And why should Love, that's a child, govern a man?

CHERRY.
Because that a child is the end of Love.

ARCHER.
And so ends Love's catechism.—And now, my dear, we'll go in and make my master's bed.

CHERRY.
Hold, hold, Mr. Martin! You have taken a great deal of pains to instruct me, and what d'ye think I have learnt by it?

ARCHER.
What?

CHERRY.
That your discourse and your habit are contradictions, and it would be nonsense in me to believe you a footman any longer.

ARCHER.
'Oons,* what a witch it is!

CHERRY.
Depend upon this, sir, nothing in this garb shall ever tempt me, for though I was born to servitude, I hate it. Own your condition, swear you love me, and then—

ARCHER.
And then we shall go make the bed?

CHERRY.
Yes.

ARCHER.
You must know, then, that I am born a gentleman. My education was liberal, but I went to London a younger brother, fell into the hands of sharpers who stripped me of my money. My friends disowned me, and now my necessity brings me to what you see.

CHERRY.
Then take my hand—promise to marry me before you sleep, and I'll make you master of two thousand pound.

ARCHER.
How!

CHERRY.
Two thousand pound that I have this minute in my own custody; so throw off your livery this instant, and I'll go find a parson.

ARCHER.
What said you? A parson!

CHERRY.
What! Do you scruple?
ARCHER.
Scruple! No, no, but—two thousand pound, you say?
CHERRY.
And better.
ARCHER. [*Aside.*]
S'death, what shall I do?—But hark ye, child, what need you make me master of yourself and money, when you may have the same pleasure out of me and still keep your fortune in your hands?
CHERRY.
Then you won't marry me?
ARCHER.
I would marry you, but—
CHERRY.
Oh, sweet sir, I'm your humble servant! You're fairly caught! Would you persuade me that any gentleman who could bear the scandal of wearing livery would refuse two thousand pound, let the condition be what it would? No, no, sir! But I hope you'll pardon the freedom I have taken, since it was only to inform myself of the respect that I ought to pay you. (*Going.*)
ARCHER.
Fairly bit,* by Jupiter!—Hold! hold! And have you actually two thousand pound?
CHERRY.
Sir, I have my secrets as well as you—when you please to be more open, I shall be more free. And be assured that I have discoveries* that will match yours, be what they will. In the meanwhile, be satisfied that no discovery I make shall ever hurt you, but beware of my father! [*Exit.*]
ARCHER.
So! We're like to have as many adventures in our inn as Don Quixote had in his. Let me see—two thousand pound! If the wench would promise to die when the money were spent, egad, one would marry her, but the fortune may go off in a year or two, and the wife may live—Lord knows how long! Then, an innkeeper's daughter! Aye, that's the devil—there my pride brings me off.

For whatsoe'er the sages charge on pride,
The angels fall, and twenty faults beside,
On earth I'm sure, 'mong us of mortal calling,
Pride saves man oft, and woman too, from falling.

Exit.

Act III, scene [i.
The gallery in Lady Bountiful's house].

Enter Mrs. Sullen, Dorinda.

MRS. SULLEN.
Ha, ha, ha! My dear sister, let me embrace thee! Now we are friends indeed, for I shall have a secret of yours as a pledge for mine—now you'll be good for something. I shall have you conversable in the subjects of the sex.
DORINDA.
But do you think that I am so weak as to fall in love with a fellow at first sight?
MRS. SULLEN.
Pshaw! Now you spoil all! Why should not we be as free in our friendships as the men? I warrant you the gentleman has got to his confidant already, has avowed his passion, toasted your health, called you ten thousand angels, has run over your lips, eyes, neck, shape, air, and everything, in a description that warms their mirth to a second enjoyment.
DORINDA.
Your hand, sister, I an't well.
MRS. SULLEN.
So—she's breeding already!—Come child,* up with it—hem a little—so—now tell me, don't you like the gentleman that we saw at church just now?
DORINDA.
The man's well enough.
MRS. SULLEN.
Well enough! Is he not a demigod, a Narcissus, a star, the man i'the moon?
DORINDA.
Oh sister, I'm extremely ill!
MRS. SULLEN.
Shall I send to your mother, child, for a little of her cephalic plaster to put to the soles of your feet, or shall I send to the gentleman for something for you?—Come, unlace your stays, unbosom yourself.—The man is perfectly a pretty fellow; I saw him when he first came into church.

DORINDA.
I saw him too, sister, and with an air that shone, methought, like rays about his person.

MRS. SULLEN.
Well said! Up with it!

DORINDA.
No forward coquet behavior, no airs to set him off, no studied looks nor artful posture—but nature did it all—

MRS. SULLEN.
Better and better!—One touch more—come!—

DORINDA.
But then his looks!—Did you observe his eyes?

MRS. SULLEN.
Yes, yes, I did—his eyes, well, what of his eyes?

DORINDA.
Sprightly, but not wandering; they seemed to view, but never gazed on anything but me—and then his looks so humble were and yet so noble, that they aimed to tell me that he could with pride die at my feet, though he scorned slavery anywhere else.

MRS. SULLEN.
The physic works purely!—How d'ye find yourself, now, my dear?

DORINDA.
Hem! much better, my dear.—Oh, here comes our Mercury!

Enter Scrub.

Well Scrub, what news of the gentleman?

SCRUB.
Madam, I have brought you a packet of news.

DORINDA.
Open it quickly, come!

SCRUB.
In the first place, I inquired who the gentleman was; they told me he was a stranger. Secondly, I asked what the gentleman was; they answered and said, that they never saw him before. Thirdly, I inquired what countryman he was; they replied 'twas more than they knew. Fourthly, I demanded whence he came; their answer was, they could not tell. And fifthly, I asked whither he went, and they replied they knew nothing of the matter—and this is all I could learn.

MRS. SULLEN.
But what do people say? Can't they guess?

SCRUB.
Why, some think he's a spy, some guess he's a mountebank, some say one thing, some another—but for my part, I believe he's a Jesuit.

DORINDA.
A Jesuit! Why a Jesuit?

SCRUB.
Because he keeps his horses always ready saddled, and his footman talks French.[32]

MRS. SULLEN.
His footman!

SCRUB.
Aye, he and the count's footman were jabbering French like two intriguing ducks in a mill pond, and I believe they talked of me, for they laughed consumedly.

DORINDA.
What sort of livery has the footman?

SCRUB.
Livery! Lord, madam, I took him for a captain, he's so bedizened with lace, and then he has tops to his shoes up to his mid leg, a silver headed cane dangling at his knuckles; he carries his hands in his pockets just so— (*Walks in the French air.*) and has a long fine periwig tied up in a bag. Lord, madam, he's clear another sort of man than I!

MRS. SULLEN.
That may easily be.—But what shall we do now, sister?

DORINDA.
I have it! This fellow has a world of simplicity and some cunning; the first hides the latter by abundance.—Scrub!

SCRUB.
Madam!

DORINDA.
We have a great mind to know who the gentleman is, only for our satisfaction.

SCRUB.
Yes madam, it would be a satisfaction, no doubt.

DORINDA.
You must go and get acquainted with his footman

---

32 Jesuit … French] Jesuits were commonly thought to be in the secret service of the French government; they were known to be conspirators against the English.

and invite him hither to drink a bottle of your ale, because you're butler today.

SCRUB.

Yes, madam. I am butler every Sunday.

MRS. SULLEN.

Oh brave!* Sister, o'my conscience, you understand the mathematics already—'tis the best plot in the world! Your mother, you know, will be gone to church, my spouse will be got to the alehouse with his scoundrels, and the house will be our own—so we drop in by accident and ask the fellow some questions ourselves. In the country, you know, any stranger is company, and we're glad to take up with the butler in a country dance, and happy if he'll do us the favor.

SCRUB.

Oh madam, you wrong me! I never refused your ladyship the favor in my life.

Enter Gipsey.

GIPSEY.

Ladies, dinner's upon table.

DORINDA.

Scrub, we'll excuse your waiting. Go where we ordered you.

SCRUB.

I shall.

Exeunt.

Scene [ii]. The inn.

Enter Aimwell and Archer.

ARCHER.

Well Tom, I find you're a marksman.

AIMWELL.

A marksman! who so blind could be as not discern a swan among the ravens.

ARCHER.

Well, but hark ye, Aimwell—

AIMWELL.

Aimwell! Call me Oroondates, Cesario, Amadis[33]—all that romance can in a lover paint, and then I'll answer. Oh Archer, I read her thousands in her looks! She looked like Ceres in her harvest: corn, wine and oil, milk and honey, gardens, groves, and purling streams played on her plenteous face.

ARCHER.

Her face! her pocket, you mean: the corn, wine and oil lies there. In short, she has ten thousand pound; that's the English on't.

AIMWELL.

Her eyes—

ARCHER.

Are demi-cannons, to be sure, so I won't stand their battery. (*Going.*)

AIMWELL.

Pray excuse me, my passion must have vent.

ARCHER.

Passion! what a plague! D'ye think these romantic airs will do our business? Were my temper as extravagant as yours, my adventures have something more romantic by half.

AIMWELL.

Your adventures!

ARCHER.

Yes,

The nymph that with her twice ten hundred pounds,
With brazen engine* hot and coif clear starched,
Can fire the guest in warming of the bed—

There's a touch of sublime Milton for you, and the subject but an innkeeper's daughter! I can play with a girl as an angler does with his fish; he keeps it at the end of his line, runs it up the stream and down the stream, till at last he brings it to hand, tickles the trout,* and so whips it into his basket.

Enter Bonniface.

BONNIFACE.

Mr. Martin, as the saying is, yonder's an honest fellow below, my Lady Bountiful's butler, who begs the honor that you would go home with him and see his cellar.

ARCHER.

Do my *baisemains*[34] to the gentleman, and tell him I will do myself the honor to wait on him immediately.

---

33 Oroondates ... Amadis] names of heroes in well-known romances

34 Do my *baisemains*] Pay my respects.

Exit Bonniface.

AIMWELL.
What do I hear?
Soft Orpheus play, and fair Toftida[35] sing?

ARCHER.
Pshaw! damn your raptures! I tell you here's a pump going to be put into the vessel, and the ship will get into harbor, my life on't! You say there's another lady very handsome there?

AIMWELL.
Yes, faith.

ARCHER.
I'm in love with her already.

AIMWELL.
Can't you give me a bill[36] upon Cherry in the meantime?

ARCHER.
No, no, friend, all her corn, wine and oil is engrossed to my market. And once more I warn you to keep your anchorage clear of mine, for if you fall foul of me, by this light, you shall go to the bottom. What! Make prize of my little frigate while I am upon the cruise for you! (*Exit.*)

Enter Bonniface.

AIMWELL.
Well, well, I won't.—Landlord, have you any tolerable company in the house? I don't care for dining alone.

BONNIFACE.
Yes sir, there's a captain below, as the saying is, that arrived about an hour ago.

AIMWELL.
Gentlemen of his coat are welcome everywhere. Will you make him a compliment from me, and tell him I should be glad of his company?

BONNIFACE.
Who shall I tell him, sir, would—

AIMWELL. [*Aside.*]
Hah! that stroke was well thrown in.—I'm only a traveler like himself and would be glad of his company, that's all.

BONNIFACE.
I obey your commands, as the saying is. (*Exit.*)

Enter Archer.

ARCHER.
S'Death!* I had forgot! What title will you give yourself?

AIMWELL.
My brother's, to be sure; he would never give me anything else, so I'll make bold with his honor this bout—you know the rest of your cue.

ARCHER.
Aye, aye. (*Exit.*)

Enter Gibbet.

GIBBET.
Sir, I'm yours.

AIMWELL.
'Tis more than I deserve, sir, for I don't know you.

GIBBET.
I don't wonder at that, sir, for you never saw me before— (*Aside.*) I hope.

AIMWELL.
And pray sir, how came I by the honor of seeing you now?

GIBBET.
Sir, I scorn to intrude upon any gentleman, but my landlord—

AIMWELL.
Oh, sir, I ask your pardon! You're the captain he told me of?

GIBBET.
At your service, sir.

AIMWELL.
What regiment, may I be so bold?

GIBBET.
A marching regiment, sir, an old corps.

AIMWELL. (*Aside.*)
Very old, if your coat be regimental.—You have served abroad, sir?

GIBBET.
Yes sir, in the plantations;[37] 'twas my lot to be sent into the worst service. I would have quitted it, indeed, but a man of honor, you know—besides,

---

[35] Toftida] Katherine Tofts was a well-known contemporary soprano.

[36] bill] of lading

[37] plantations] the colonies; criminals were frequently transported to the plantations overseas.

'twas for the good of my country that I should be abroad—anything for the good of one's country—I'm a Roman for that.

AIMWELL. (*Aside.*)

One of the first,[38] I'll lay my life.—You found the West Indies very hot, sir?

GIBBET.

Aye sir, too hot for me.

AIMWELL.

Pray sir, han't I seen your face at Will's coffee-house?

GIBBET.

Yes sir, and at White's, too.[39]

AIMWELL.

And where is your company now, Captain?

GIBBET.

They an't come yet.

AIMWELL.

Why, d'ye expect 'em here?

GIBBET.

They'll be here tonight, sir.

AIMWELL.

Which way do they march?

GIBBET.

Across the country.—The devil's in't, if I han't said enough to encourage him to declare, but I'm afraid he's not right; I must tack about.

AIMWELL.

Is your company to quarter in Litchfield?

GIBBET.

In this house, sir.

AIMWELL.

What! all?

GIBBET.

My company's but thin. Ha, ha, ha! We are but three! Ha, ha, ha!

AIMWELL.

You're merry, sir.

GIBBET.

Aye sir, you must excuse me, sir; I understand the world, especially the art of travelling. I don't care, sir, for answering questions directly upon the road—for I generally ride with a charge[40] about me.

AIMWELL. (*Aside.*)

Three or four, I believe!

GIBBET.

I am credibly informed that there are highwaymen upon this quarter. Not, sir, that I could suspect a gentleman of your figure—but truly, sir, I have got such a way of evasion upon the road that I don't care for speaking truth to any man.

AIMWELL.

Your caution may be necessary.—Then I presume you're no captain?

GIBBET.

Not I, sir. Captain is a good travelling name, and so I take it; it stops a great many foolish inquiries that are generally made about gentlemen that travel. It gives a man an air of something, and makes the drawers obedient—and thus far I am a captain, and no farther.

AIMWELL.

And pray sir, what is your true profession?

GIBBET.

Oh sir, you must excuse me: upon my word, sir, I don't think it safe to tell you.

AIMWELL.

Ha, ha, ha! upon my word, I commend you.

Enter Bonniface.

Well, Mr. Bonniface, what's the news?

BONNIFACE.

There's another gentleman below, as the saying is, that hearing you were but two, would be glad to make the third man, if you would give him leave.

AIMWELL.

What is he?

BONNIFACE.

A clergyman, as the saying is.

[38] Roman … first] Gibbet implies that he has the Roman virtue of patriotism; besides continuing to suggest that he is old, Aimwell perhaps suggests that he is more like the rabble who settled early Rome.

[39] Will's … White's] the former was a resort of literary men; the latter was a chocolate house popular with gamblers.

[40] charge] sum of money, but also, as Aimwell takes it, either multiple loads of powder for his pistols or criminal charges—or both

AIMWELL.
A clergyman! Is he really a clergyman? or is it only his travelling name, as my friend the captain has it.

BONNIFACE.
Oh sir, he's a priest and a chaplain to the French officers in town.

AIMWELL.
Is he a Frenchman?

BONNIFACE.
Yes sir, born at Brussels.

GIBBET.
A Frenchman and a priest! I won't be seen in his company, sir; I have a value for my reputation, sir.

AIMWELL.
Nay but Captain, since we are by ourselves.—Can he speak English, landlord?

BONNIFACE.
Very well, sir. You may know him, as the saying is, to be a foreigner by his accent, and that's all.

AIMWELL.
Then he has been in England before?

BONNIFACE.
Never, sir, but he's a master of languages, as the saying is. He talks Latin; it does me good to hear him talk Latin.

AIMWELL.
Then you understand Latin, Mr. Bonniface?

BONNIFACE.
Not I, sir, as the saying is, but he talks it so very fast that I'm sure it must be good.

AIMWELL.
Pray, desire him to walk up.

BONNIFACE.
Here he is, as the saying is.

Enter Foigard.

FOIGARD.
Save you, gentlemens, both.

AIMWELL. [*Aside.*]
A Frenchman!—Sir, your most humble servant.

FOIGARD.
Och, dear joy,* I am your most faithful shervant, and yours alsho.[41]

GIBBET.
Doctor, you talk very good English, but you have a mighty twang of the foreigner.

FOIGARD.
My English is very vel for the vords, but we foreigners, you know, cannot bring our tongues about the pronunciation so soon.

AIMWELL. (*Aside.*)
A foreigner! a downright Teague,* by this light!— Were you born in France, Doctor?

FOIGARD.
I was educated in France, but I was borned at Brussels. I am a subject of the King of Spain, joy.

GIBBET.
What King of Spain, sir? speak!

FOIGARD.
Upon my shoul, joy, I cannot tell you as yet.[42]

AIMWELL.
Nay Captain, that was too hard upon the doctor: he's a stranger.

FOIGARD.
Oh, let him alone, dear joy! I am of a nation that is not easily put out of countenance.

AIMWELL.
Come, gentlemen, I'll end the dispute.—Here landlord, is dinner ready?

BONNIFACE.
Upon the table, as the saying is.

AIMWELL.
Gentlemen—pray—that door—

FOIGARD.
No, no, fait! the captain must lead.

AIMWELL.
No Doctor, the church is our guide.

GIBBET.
Aye, aye, so it is.—

Exit foremost, they follow.

41 Och … alsho] Foigard is speaking the exaggerated form of Hiberno-English that was characteristically attributed to Irish characters on the eighteenth-century English stage.

42 King of Spain … as yet] The War of Spanish Succession, which was to determine the heir to the Spanish throne, was still in progress.

Scene [iii]. A gallery in Lady Bountiful's house.

Enter Archer and Scrub singing and hugging one another, Scrub with a tankard in his hand, Gipsey listening at a distance.

SCRUB.
Tall, all dall.—Come my dear boy, let's have that song once more.

ARCHER.
No, no, we shall disturb the family.—But will you be sure to keep the secret?

SCRUB.
Pho! upon my honor, as I'm a gentleman!

ARCHER.
'Tis enough. You must know, then, that my master is the Lord Viscount Aimwell. He fought a duel t'other day in London, wounded his man so dangerously that he thinks fit to withdraw till he hears whether the gentleman's wounds be mortal or not. He never was in this part of England before, so he chose to retire to this place, that's all.

GIPSEY. [*Aside.*]
And that's enough for me. (*Exit.*)

SCRUB.
And where were you when your master fought?

ARCHER.
We never know of our masters' quarrels.*

SCRUB.
No! If our masters in the country here receive a challenge, the first thing they do is tell their wives; the wife tells the servants, the servants alarm the tenants, and in half an hour you shall have the whole county in arms.

ARCHER.
To hinder two men from doing what they have no mind for.—But if you should chance to talk now of my business?

SCRUB.
Talk! aye sir, had I not learned the knack of holding my tongue, I had never lived so long in a great family.

ARCHER.
Aye, aye, to be sure, there are secrets in all families.

SCRUB.
Secrets, aye! But I'll say no more. Come, sit down, we'll make an end of our tankard. Here—

ARCHER.
With all my heart! Who knows but you and I may come to be better acquainted, eh? Here's your ladies' healths! You have three, I think, and to be sure there must be secrets among 'em.

SCRUB.
Secrets! Aye, friend. I wish I had a friend—

ARCHER.
Am not I your friend? Come, you and I will be sworn brothers.

SCRUB.
Shall we?

ARCHER.
From this minute. Give me a kiss.—And now, brother Scrub—

SCRUB.
And now, brother Martin, I will tell you a secret that will make your hair stand on end: you must know that I am consumedly in love.

ARCHER.
That's a terrible secret, that's the truth on't.

SCRUB.
That jade, Gipsey, that was with us just now in the cellar, is the arrantest whore that ever wore a petticoat, and I'm dying for love of her.

ARCHER.
Ha, ha, ha! Are you in love with her person or her virtue, brother Scrub?

SCRUB.
I should like virtue best because it is more durable than beauty, for virtue holds good with some women long and many a day after they have lost it.

ARCHER.
In the country, I grant ye, where no woman's virtue is lost till a bastard be found.

SCRUB.
Aye, could I bring her to a bastard, I should have her all to myself, but I dare not put it upon that lay for fear of being sent for a soldier. Pray brother, how do you gentlemen in London like that same Pressing Act?[43]

---

[43] Pressing Act] By a 1703-1704 law, men could be impressed into military service for various causes, among them petty offenses.

ARCHER.

Very ill, brother Scrub—'tis the worst that ever was made for us. Formerly I remember the good days when we could dun our masters for our wages, and if they refused to pay us, we could have a warrant to carry 'em before a justice. But now if we talk of eating, they have a warrant for us, and carry us before three justices.

SCRUB.

And to be sure we go if we talk of eating, for the justices won't give their own servants a bad example. Now this is my misfortune: I dare not speak in the house while that jade Gipsey dings about like a fury.—Once I had the better end of the staff.

ARCHER.

And how comes the change now?

SCRUB.

Why, the mother of all this mischief is a priest.

ARCHER.

A priest!

SCRUB.

Aye, the damned son of a whore of Babylon* that came over hither to say grace to the French officers and eat up our provisions. There's not a day goes over his head without dinner or supper in this house.

ARCHER.

How came he so familiar in the family?

SCRUB.

Because he speaks English as if he had lived here all his life and tells lies as if he had been a traveler from his cradle.

ARCHER.

And this priest, I'm afraid, has converted the affections of your Gipsey.

SCRUB.

Converted! aye, and perverted, my dear friend, for I'm afraid he has made her a whore and a papist. But this is not all. There's the French count and Mrs. Sullen. They're in the confederacy and for some private ends of their own, to be sure.

ARCHER.

A very hopeful family, yours, brother Scrub! I suppose the maiden lady has her lover too?

SCRUB.

Not that I know; she's the best on 'em, that's the truth on't. But they take care to prevent my curiosity by giving me so much business that I'm a perfect slave. What d'ye think is my place in this family?

ARCHER.

Butler, I suppose.

SCRUB.

Ah, Lord help you! I'll tell you. Of a Monday, I drive the coach; of a Tuesday, I drive the plough; on Wednesday, I follow the hounds; a-Thursday, I dun the tenants; on Friday, I go to market; on Saturday, I draw warrants;[44] and a-Sunday, I draw beer.

ARCHER.

Ha, ha, ha! If variety be a pleasure in life, you have enough on't, my dear brother.—But what ladies are those?

SCRUB.

Ours, ours: that upon the right hand is Mrs. Sullen, and the other is Mrs.* Dorinda. Don't mind 'em; sit still, man—

Enter Mrs. Sullen and Dorinda.

MRS. SULLEN.

I have heard my brother talk of my Lord Aimwell, but they say that his brother is the finer gentleman.

DORINDA.

That's impossible, sister.

MRS. SULLEN.

He's vastly rich, but very close, they say.

DORINDA.

No matter for that: if I can creep into his heart, I'll open his breast, I warrant him. I have heard say that people may be guessed at by the behavior of their servants. I could wish we might talk to that fellow.

MRS. SULLEN.

So do I, for I think he's a very pretty fellow. Come this way. I'll throw out a lure for him presently.*

They walk a turn towards the opposite side of the stage.

ARCHER. [*Aside.*]

Corn, wine, and oil, indeed—but, I think, the wife has the greatest plenty of flesh and blood; she should be my choice.

---

44 warrants] for arrests: Squire Sullen is a Justice of the Peace.

Mrs. Sullen drops her glove, Archer runs, takes it up, and gives it to her.

Aha,[g] say you so.—Madam, your ladyship's glove.

MRS. SULLEN.

Oh sir, I thank you! [*To Dorinda.*] What a handsome bow the fellow has!

DORINDA.

Bow! Why I have known several footmen come down from London, set up here for dancing masters, and carry off the best fortunes in the country.

ARCHER. (*Aside.*)

That project, for ought I know, had been better than ours.—Brother Scrub, why don't you introduce me?

SCRUB.

Ladies, this is the strange gentleman's servant that you see at church today. I understood he came from London, and so I invited him to the cellar that he might show me the newest flourish in whetting my knives.

DORINDA.

And I hope you have made much of him?

ARCHER.

Oh yes, madam, but the strength of your ladyship's liquor is a little too potent for the constitution of your humble servant.

MRS. SULLEN.

What! then you don't usually drink ale?

ARCHER.

No madam, my constant drink is tea or a little wine and water; 'tis prescribed me by the physician for a remedy against the spleen.

SCRUB.

Oh la! Oh la! a footman have the spleen!

MRS. SULLEN.

I thought that distemper had been only proper to people of quality.*

ARCHER.

Madam, like all other fashions, it wears out, and so descends to their servants,[45] though in a great many of us, I believe, it proceeds from some melancholy particles in the blood occasioned by the stagnation of wages.

DORINDA. [*Aside.*]

How affectedly the fellow talks!—How long, pray, have you served your present master?

ARCHER.

Not long: my life has been mostly spent in the service of the ladies.

MRS. SULLEN.

And pray, which service do you like best?

ARCHER.

Madam, the ladies pay best. The honor of serving them is sufficient wages; there is a charm in their looks that delivers a pleasure with their commands and gives our duty the wings of inclination.

MRS. SULLEN. [*Aside.*]

That flight was above the pitch of a livery.—And, sir, would not you be satisfied to serve a lady again?

ARCHER.

As a groom of the chamber, madam, but not as a footman.

MRS. SULLEN.

I suppose you served as footman before?

ARCHER.

For that reason I would not serve in that post again, for my memory is too weak for the load of messages that the ladies lay upon their servants in London. My Lady Howd'ye, the last mistress I served, called me up one morning and told me: "Martin, go to my Lady Allnight with my humble service; tell her I was to wait on her ladyship yesterday and left word with Mrs.* Rebecca that the preliminaries of the affair she knows of are stopped till we know the concurrence of the person that I know of, for which there are circumstances wanting* which we shall accommodate at the old place, but that, in the meantime, there is a person about her ladyship that, from several hints and surmises, was accessory at a certain time to the disappointments that naturally attend things, that to her knowledge are of more importance—"

MRS. SULLEN, DORINDA.

Ha, ha, ha! Where are you going, sir?

ARCHER.

Why I han't half done! The whole howd'ye was about half an hour long; so I happened to misplace

[45] fashions ... servants] Rich people commonly gave their outmoded clothes to their servants.

two syllables and was turned off and rendered incapable—

DORINDA. [*Aside to Mrs. Sullen.*]

The pleasantest fellow, sister, I ever saw!—But friend, if your master be married, I presume you still serve a lady?

ARCHER.

No, madam, I take care never to come into a married family: the commands of the master and mistress are always so contrary that 'tis impossible to please both.

DORINDA. (*Aside.*)

There's a main point gained: my lord is not married, I find.

MRS. SULLEN.

But I wonder, friend, that in so many good services, you had not a better provision made for you.

ARCHER.

I don't know how, madam. I had a lieutenancy offered me three or four times, but that is not bread, madam. I live much better as I do.

SCRUB.

Madam, he sings rarely. I was thought to do pretty well here in the country till he came, but alack a day, I'm nothing to my brother Martin.

DORINDA.

Does he? Pray sir, will you oblige us with a song?

ARCHER.

Are you for passion, or humor?

SCRUB.

Oh la! He has the purest ballad about a trifle—

MRS. SULLEN.

A trifle! pray sir, let's have it!

ARCHER.

I'm ashamed to offer you a trifle, madam. But since you command me— (*Sings to the tune of Sir Simon the King.*[46])

A trifling song you shall hear,
Begun with a trifle and ended;
All trifling people draw near,
And I shall be nobly attended.

Were it not for trifles, a few,
That lately have come into play,
The men would want* something to do,
And the women want something to say.

What makes men trifle in dressing?
Because the ladies (they know)
Admire, by often possessing,
That eminent trifle, a beau.

When the lover his moments has trifled
The trifle of trifles to gain,
No sooner the virgin is rifled
But a trifle shall part 'em again.

What mortal man would be able
At White's half an hour to sit?
Or who could bear a tea table
Without talking of trifles for wit?

The Court is from trifles secure,
Gold keys are no trifles, we see;
White rods[47] are no trifles, I'm sure,
Whatever their bearers may be.

But if you will go to the place
Where trifles abundantly breed,
The levee will show you his grace
Makes promises trifles indeed.

A coach with six footmen behind
I count neither trifle nor sin,
But ye gods! how oft do we find
A scandalous trifle within?

A flask of champagne, people think it
A trifle or something as bad,
But if you'll contrive how to drink it,
You'll find it no trifle, egad!

A parson's a trifle at sea,
A widow's a trifle in sorrow,
A peace is a trifle today,
Who knows what may happen tomorrow?

[46] Sir Simon the King] a popular tune, first printed in the seventeenth century

[47] Gold keys … White rods] symbols of high offices

A black coat a trifle may cloak,
Or to hide it, the red[48] may endeavor:
But if once the army is broke,[49]
We shall have more trifles than ever.

The stage is a trifle, they say,
The reason, pray carry along,
Because at every new play,
The house they with trifles so throng.

But with people's malice to trifle,
And to set us all on a foot:
The author of this is a trifle,
And his song is a trifle to boot.[h]

MRS. SULLEN.
Very well, sir, we're obliged to you. (*Offering him money.*) Something for a pair of gloves.

ARCHER.
I humbly beg leave to be excused. My master, madam, pays me, nor dare I take money from any other hand without injuring his honor and disobeying his commands. (*Exit.*)

DORINDA.
This is surprising! Did you ever see so pretty a well-bred fellow?

MRS. SULLEN.
The devil take him for wearing that livery!

DORINDA.
I fancy, sister, he may be some gentleman, a friend of my lord's, that his lordship has pitched upon for his courage, fidelity, and discretion to bear him company in this dress and who, ten to one, was his second too.

MRS. SULLEN.
It is so, it must be so, and it shall be so: for I like him.

DORINDA.
What! better than the count?

MRS. SULLEN.
The count happened to be the most agreeable man upon the place, and so I chose him to serve me in my design upon my husband. But I should like this fellow better in a design upon myself.

DORINDA.
But now, sister, for an interview with this lord and this gentleman: How shall we bring that about?

MRS. SULLEN.
Patience! you country ladies give no quarter, if once you be entered.[50] Would you prevent* their desires and give the fellows no wishing-time? Look ye, Dorinda, if my Lord Aimwell loves you or deserves you, he'll find a way to see you, and there we must leave it. My business comes now upon the tapis. Have you prepared your brother?

DORINDA.
Yes, yes.

MRS. SULLEN.
And how did he relish it?

DORINDA.
He said little, mumbled something to himself, promised to be guided by me. But here he comes—

Enter Sullen.

SULLEN.
What singing was that I heard just now?

MRS. SULLEN.
The singing in your head, my dear. You complained of it all day.

SULLEN.
You're impertinent.

MRS. SULLEN.
I was ever so, since I became one flesh with you.

SULLEN.
One flesh! rather two carcasses joined unnaturally together.[51]

MRS. SULLEN.
Or rather a living soul coupled to a dead body.

DORINDA.
So, this is fine encouragement for me!

SULLEN.
Yes, my wife shows you what you must do.

---

48 black … red] the former worn by clergymen, the latter by soldiers

49 broke] discharged at the end of a war

50 entered] engaged in action

51 one flesh … together] the play on the biblical description of marriage ("and they shall be one flesh" [Gen. 2:24]), plus a number of the ideas in Mrs. Sullen's subsequent speech on marriage and divorce, are borrowed from John Milton's *The Doctrine and Discipline of Divorce.*

MRS. SULLEN.
And my husband shows you what you must suffer.

SULLEN.
S'death,* why can't you be silent?

MRS. SULLEN.
S'death, why can't you talk?

SULLEN.
Do you talk to any purpose?

MRS. SULLEN.
Do you think to any purpose?

SULLEN.
Sister, hark ye. (*Whispers [to Dorinda, then says aloud].*) I shan't be home till it be late. (*Exit.*)

MRS. SULLEN.
What did he whisper to ye?

DORINDA.
That he would go round the back way, come into the closet,* and listen as I directed him. But let me beg you once more, dear sister, to drop this project, for as I told you before, instead of awaking him to kindness, you may provoke him to a rage, and then who knows how far his brutality may carry him?

MRS. SULLEN.
I'm provided to receive him, I warrant you. But here comes the count—vanish!

Exit Dorinda;[i] *enter Count Bellair.*

Don't you wonder, Monsieur le Count, that I was not at church this afternoon?

COUNT BELLAIR.
I more wonder, madam, that you go dere at all or how you dare lift those eyes to Heaven that are guilty of so much killing.

MRS. SULLEN.
If Heaven, sir, has given to my eyes with the power of killing the virtue of making a cure, I hope the one may atone for the other.

COUNT BELLAIR.
Oh largely, madam, would your ladyship be as ready to apply the remedy as to give the wound. Consider, madam, I am doubly a prisoner: first to the arms of your general, then to your more conquering eyes. My first chains are easy—there a ransom may redeem me—but from your fetters, I never shall get free.

MRS. SULLEN.
Alas sir, why should you complain to me of your captivity, who am in chains myself? You know, sir, that I am bound, nay, most be-tied[j] up, in that particular that might give you ease. I am like you, a prisoner of war—of war indeed! I have given my parole of honor. Would you break yours to gain your liberty?

COUNT BELLAIR.
Most certainly I would, were I a prisoner among the Turks. Dis is your case: you're a slave, madam, slave to the worst of Turks, a husband.

MRS. SULLEN.
There lies my foible, I confess. No fortifications, no courage, conduct, nor vigilancy can pretend to defend a place where the cruelty of the governor forces the garrison to mutiny.

COUNT BELLAIR.
And where de besieger is resolved to die before de place. Here I will fix. (*Kneels.*) With tears, vows, and prayers assault your heart, and never rise till you surrender. Or if I must storm—Love and St. Michael! And so I begin the attack—

MRS. SULLEN.
Stand-off! (*Aside.*) Sure, he hears me not! And I could almost wish he—did not—the fellow makes love very prettily.—But sir, why should you put such a value upon my person, when you see it despised by one that knows it so much better?

COUNT BELLAIR.
He knows it not, though he possesses it. If he but knew the value of the jewel he is master of, he would always wear it next his heart and sleep with it in his arms.

MRS. SULLEN.
But since he throws me unregarded from him—

COUNT BELLAIR.
And one that knows your value well comes by and takes you up, is it not justice? (*Goes to lay hold on her.*)

Enter Sullen with his sword drawn.

SULLEN.
Hold, villain, hold!

MRS. SULLEN. (*Presenting a pistol.*)
Do you hold!

SULLEN.
What! murder your husband to defend your bully?[52]

MRS. SULLEN.
Bully! for shame, Mr. Sullen! Bullies wear long swords, the gentleman has none; he's a prisoner, you know. I was aware of your outrage and prepared this to receive your violence and, if occasion were, to preserve myself against the force of this other gentleman.

COUNT BELLAIR.
Oh madam, your eyes be bettre firearms than your pistol; they nevre miss.

SULLEN.
What! court my wife to my face!

MRS. SULLEN.
Pray Mr. Sullen, put up. Suspend your fury for a minute.

SULLEN.
To give you time to invent an excuse!

MRS. SULLEN.
I need none.

SULLEN.
No, for I heard every syllable of your discourse.

COUNT BELLAIR.
Aye! and begar,* I tink de dialogue was vera pretty.

MRS. SULLEN.
Then I suppose, sir, you heard something of your own barbarity?

SULLEN.
Barbarity! 'oons,* what does the woman call barbarity? Do I ever meddle with you?

MRS. SULLEN.
No.

SULLEN.
As for you, sir, I shall take another time.

COUNT BELLAIR.
Ah, begar, and so must I.

SULLEN.
Look ye, madam, don't think that my anger proceeds from any concern I have for your honor but for my own, and if you can contrive any way of being a whore without making me a cuckold, do it and welcome.

MRS. SULLEN.
Sir, I thank you kindly; you would allow me the sin but rob me of the pleasure. No, no, I'm resolved never to venture upon the crime without the satisfaction of seeing you punished for't.

SULLEN.
Then will you grant me this, my dear? Let anybody else do you the favor but that Frenchman, for I mortally hate his whole generation. (*Exit.*)

COUNT BELLAIR.
Ah sir, that be ungrateful, for begar, I love some of yours. (*Approaching her.*) Madam—

MRS. SULLEN.
No, sir.

COUNT BELLAIR.
No, sir! Garzoon,[53] madam, I am not your husband!

MRS. SULLEN.
'Tis time to undeceive you, sir. I believed your addresses to me were no more than an amusement, and I hope you will think the same of my complaisance. And to convince you that you ought, you must know that I brought you hither only to make you instrumental in setting me right with my husband, for he was planted to listen by my appointment.

COUNT BELLAIR.
By your appointment?

MRS. SULLEN.
Certainly.

COUNT BELLAIR.
And so, madam, while I was telling twenty stories to part you from your husband, begar, I was bringing you together all the while.

MRS. SULLEN.
I ask your pardon, sir, but I hope this will give you a taste of the virtue of the English ladies.

COUNT BELLAIR.
Begar, madam, your virtue be vera great, but garzoon, your honeste be vera little.

Enter Dorinda.

MRS. SULLEN.
Nay, now you're angry, sir.

---

[52] bully] here sweetheart; Mrs. Sullen takes it in the sense of ruffian as well.

[53] Garzoon] a pseudo-French version of "God's wounds"

COUNT BELLAIR.

Angry!—"Fair Dorinda." (*Sings "Dorinda," the opera tune, and addresses to Dorinda.*) Madam, when your ladyship want a fool, send for me. "Fair Dorinda, Revenge," etc.[54] (*Exit.*)

MRS. SULLEN.

There goes the true humor of his nation: resentment with good manners and the height of anger in a song.—Well sister, you must be judge, for you have heard the trial.

DORINDA.

And I bring in my brother guilty.

MRS. SULLEN.

But I must bear the punishment. 'Tis hard, sister.

DORINDA.

I own it—but you must have patience.

MRS. SULLEN.

Patience! the cant of custom! Providence sends no evil without a remedy: should I lie groaning under a yoke I can shake off, I were accessory to my ruin, and my patience were no better than self-murder.[55]

DORINDA.

But how can you shake off the yoke? Your divisions don't come within the reach of the law for divorce.

MRS. SULLEN.

Law! what law can search into the remote abyss of nature? What evidence can prove the unaccountable disaffections of wedlock? Can a jury sum up the endless aversions that are rooted in our souls, or can a bench give judgment upon antipathies?

DORINDA.

They never pretended, sister; they never meddle but in case of uncleanness.[56]

MRS. SULLEN.

Uncleanness! Oh sister, casual violation is a transient injury and may possibly be repaired, but can radical hatreds be ever reconciled? No, no, sister. Nature is the first lawgiver, and when she has set tempers opposite, not all the golden links of wedlock nor iron manacles of law can keep 'em fast.

Wedlock we own ordained by Heaven's decree,
But such as Heaven ordained it first to be,
Concurring tempers in the man and wife
As mutual helps to draw the load of life.
View all the works of Providence above,
The stars with harmony and concord move;
View all the works of Providence below,
The fire, the water, earth, and air, we know,
All in one plant agree to make it grow.
Must man, the chiefest work of art divine,
Be doomed in endless discord to repine?
No, we should injure Heaven by that surmise:
Omnipotence is just, were man but wise.

[Exeunt.]

Act IV, scene [i]. Continues.

Enter Mrs. Sullen.

MRS. SULLEN.

Were I born an humble Turk, where women have no soul nor property, there I must sit contented. But in England, a country whose women are its glory, must women be abused? Where women rule, must women be enslaved? nay, cheated into slavery, mocked by a promise of comfortable society into a wilderness of solitude! I dare not keep the thought about me.—Oh, here comes something to divert me—

Enter a Country Woman.

WOMAN.

I come, an't* please your ladyships—you're my Lady Bountiful, an't ye?

MRS. SULLEN.

Well good woman, go on.

WOMAN.

I come seventeen long mail to have a cure for my husband's sore leg.

MRS. SULLEN.

Your husband! What, woman, cure your husband!

WOMAN.

Aye, poor man, for his sore leg won't let him stir from home.

[54] "Fair Dorinda" ... etc.] The count sings snatches of two songs, "Fair Dorinda" and "Revenge, Revenge," from the opera *Camilla* (1706).

[55] cant ... self-murder] There are frequent echoes of Milton's *Doctrine and Discipline of Divorce* in this and the next two speeches by Mrs. Sullen.

[56] uncleanness] adultery

MRS. SULLEN.
There, I confess, you have given me a reason. Well good woman, I'll tell you what you must do. You must lay your husband's leg upon a table, and with a chopping-knife you must lay it open as broad as you can; then you must take out the bone and beat the flesh soundly with a rolling pin; then take salt, pepper, cloves, mace, and ginger, some sweet herbs, and season it very well; then roll it up like brawn and put it into the oven for two hours.

WOMAN.
Heavens reward your ladyship! I have two little babies too that are piteous bad with the graips,[57] an't* please ye.

MRS. SULLEN.
Put a little pepper and salt in their bellies, good woman.

Enter Lady Bountiful.

I beg your ladyship's pardon for taking your business out of your hands; I have been a-tampering here a little with one of your patients.

LADY BOUNTIFUL.
Come good woman, don't mind this mad creature. I am the person that you want, I suppose. What would you have, woman?

MRS. SULLEN.
She wants something for her husband's sore leg.

LADY BOUNTIFUL.
What's the matter with his leg, goody?

WOMAN.
It come first, as one might say, with a sort of dizziness in his foot, then he had a kind of a laziness in his joints, and then his leg broke out, and then it swelled, and then it closed again, and then it broke out again, and then it festered, and then it grew better, and then it grew worse again.

MRS. SULLEN.
Ha, ha, ha!

LADY BOUNTIFUL.
How can you be merry with the misfortunes of other people?

MRS. SULLEN.
Because my own make me sad, madam.

LADY BOUNTIFUL.
The worst reason in the world, daughter; your own misfortunes should teach you to pity others.

MRS. SULLEN.
But the woman's misfortunes and mine are nothing alike; her husband is sick, and mine, alas, is in health.

LADY BOUNTIFUL.
What! would you wish your husband sick?

MRS. SULLEN.
Not of a sore leg, of all things.

LADY BOUNTIFUL.
Well good woman, go to the pantry, get your bellyful of victuals, then I'll give you a receipt* of diet-drink for your husband. But d'ye hear, goody, you must not let your husband move too much.

WOMAN.
No, no, madam, the poor man's inclinable enough to lie still. (*Exit.*)

LADY BOUNTIFUL.
Well, daughter Sullen, though you laugh, I have done miracles about the country here with my receipts.

MRS. SULLEN.
Miracles, indeed, if they have cured anybody. But I believe, madam, the patient's faith goes farther toward the miracle than your prescription.

LADY BOUNTIFUL.
Fancy helps in some cases. But there's your husband who has as little fancy as anybody; I brought him from death's door.

MRS. SULLEN.
I suppose, madam, you made him drink plentifully of ass's milk.

Enter Dorinda, runs to Mrs. Sullen.

DORINDA.
News, dear sister! News! News!

Enter Archer running.

ARCHER.
Where, where is my Lady Bountiful? Pray, which is the old lady of you three?

LADY BOUNTIFUL.
I am.

ARCHER.
Oh madam, the fame of your ladyship's charity,

57 graips] gripes or colic

goodness, benevolence, skill, and ability have drawn me hither to implore your ladyship's help in behalf of my unfortunate master, who is this moment breathing his last.

LADY BOUNTIFUL.
Your master! where is he?

ARCHER.
At your gate, madam. Drawn by the appearance of your handsome house to view it nearer and walking up the avenue within five paces of the courtyard, he was taken ill of a sudden with a sort of I know not what, but down he fell, and there he lies.

LADY BOUNTIFUL.
Here Scrub! Gipsey! all run, get my easy chair* downstairs, put the gentleman in it, and bring him in quickly, quickly!

ARCHER.
Heaven will reward your ladyship for this charitable act.

LADY BOUNTIFUL.
Is your master used to these fits?

ARCHER.
Oh yes, madam, frequently: I have known him have five or six of a night.

LADY BOUNTIFUL.
What's his name?

ARCHER.
Lord madam, he's a-dying! A minute's care or neglect may save or destroy his life!

LADY BOUNTIFUL.
Ah, poor gentleman! come friend, show me the way. I'll see him brought in myself. (*Exit with Archer.*)

DORINDA.
Oh sister, my heart flutters about strangely! I can hardly forbear running to his assistance.

MRS. SULLEN.
And I'll lay my life he deserves your assistance more than he wants* it! Did not I tell you that my lord would find a way to come at you? Love's his distemper, and you must be the physician: put on all your charms, summon all your fire into your eyes, plant the whole artillery of your looks against his breast, and down with him.

DORINDA.
Oh sister, I'm but a young gunner! I shall be afraid to shoot for fear the piece should recoil and hurt myself.

MRS. SULLEN.
Never fear! you shall see me shoot before you, if you will.

DORINDA.
No, no, dear sister. You have missed your mark so unfortunately that I shan't care for being instructed by you.

Enter Aimwell in a chair, carried by Archer and Scrub, Lady Bountiful, Gipsey; Aimwell counterfeiting a swoon.*

LADY BOUNTIFUL.
Here, here, let's see the hartshorn-drops.—Gipsey, a glass of fair[58] water! His fit's very strong. Bless me, how his hands are clinched!

ARCHER.
For shame, ladies, what d'ye do? Why don't you help us? (*To Dorinda.*) Pray madam, take his hand and open it if you can, whilst I hold his head.

DORINDA.
Poor gentleman! (*Taking his hand.*) Oh! he has got my hand within his and squeezes it unmercifully—

LADY BOUNTIFUL.
'Tis the violence of his convulsion, child.

ARCHER.
Oh madam, he's perfectly possessed in these cases: he'll bite if you don't have a care.

DORINDA.
Oh, my hand! my hand!

LADY BOUNTIFUL.
What's the matter with the foolish girl? I have got this hand open, you see, with a great deal of ease.

ARCHER.
Aye, but madam, your daughter's hand is somewhat warmer than your ladyship's, and the heat of it draws the force of the spirits that way.

MRS. SULLEN.
I find, friend, you're very learned in these sorts of fits.

ARCHER.
'Tis no wonder, madam, for I'm often troubled with them myself. I find myself extremely ill at this minute. (*Looking hard at Mrs. Sullen.*)

---

58 fair] pure

MRS. SULLEN. (*Aside.*)
I fancy I could find a way to cure you.

LADY BOUNTIFUL.
His fit holds him very long.

ARCHER.
Longer than usual, madam.—Pray young lady, open his breast and give him air.

LADY BOUNTIFUL.
Where did his illness take him first, pray?

ARCHER.
Today at church, madam.

LADY BOUNTIFUL.
In what manner was he taken?

ARCHER.
Very strangely, my lady. He was of a sudden touched with something in his eyes, which at the first he only felt, but could not tell whether 'twas pain or pleasure.

LADY BOUNTIFUL.
Wind, nothing but wind.

ARCHER.
By soft degrees it grew and mounted to his brain; there his fancy caught it; there formed it so beautiful and dressed it up in such gay, pleasing colors that his transported appetite seized the fair idea and straight conveyed it to his heart. That hospitable seat of life sent all its sanguine spirits forth to meet, and opened all its sluicy gates to take the stranger in.

LADY BOUNTIFUL.
Your master should never go without a bottle to smell to—oh—he recovers! The lavender water, some feathers to burn under his nose, Hungary-water[59] to rub his temples. Oh, he comes to himself! Hem a little, sir, hem.—Gipsey, bring the cordial-water.

Aimwell seems to awake in amaze.

DORINDA.
How d'ye, sir?

AIMWELL.
Where am I? (*Rising.*)

Sure I have passed the gulph of silent death,
And now I land on the Elysian shore.
Behold the goddess of those happy plains:
Fair Proserpine, let me adore thy bright divinity.

Kneels to Dorinda and kisses her hand.

MRS. SULLEN.
So, so, so! I knew where the fit would end!

AIMWELL.
Eurydice, perhaps—
How could thy Orpheus keep his word
And not look back upon thee?
No treasure but thyself could sure have bribed him
To look one minute off thee.

LADY BOUNTIFUL.
Delirious, poor gentleman!

ARCHER.
Very delirious, madam, very delirious!

AIMWELL.
Martin's voice, I think.

ARCHER.
Yes my lord. How does your lordship?

LADY BOUNTIFUL.
Lord! did you mind that, girls?

AIMWELL.
Where am I?

ARCHER.
In very good hands, sir. You were taken just now with one of your old fits under the trees just by this good lady's house; her ladyship had you taken in and has miraculously brought you to yourself, as you see.

AIMWELL.
I am so confounded with shame, madam, that I can now only beg pardon—and refer my acknowledgements for your ladyship's care till an opportunity offers of making some amends. I dare be no longer troublesome.—Martin, give two guineas to the servants. (*Going.*)

DORINDA.
Sir, you may catch cold by going so soon into the air. You don't look, sir, as if you were perfectly recovered.

Here Archer talks to Lady Bountiful in dumb show.

AIMWELL.
That I shall never be, madam. My present illness is so rooted that I must expect to carry it to my grave.

59 Hungary-water] a concoction of wine and rosemary flowers

MRS. SULLEN.

Don't despair, sir. I have known several in your distemper shake it off with a fortnight's physic.

LADY BOUNTIFUL.

Come, sir, your servant has been telling me that you're apt to relapse if you go into the air. Your good manners shan't get the better of ours: you shall sit down again, sir. Come sir, we don't mind ceremonies in the country. Here sir, my service t'ye. You shall taste my water; 'tis a cordial, I can assure you, and of my own making—drink it off, sir.

Aimwell drinks.

And how d'ye find yourself now, sir?

AIMWELL.

Somewhat better—though very faint still.

LADY BOUNTIFUL.

Aye, aye, people are always faint after these fits.—Come girls, you shall show the gentleman the house.—'Tis but an old family building, sir, but you had better walk about and cool by degrees than venture immediately into the air. You'll find some tolerable pictures.—Dorinda, show the gentleman the way. I must go to the poor woman below. (*Exit.*)

DORINDA.

This way, sir.

AIMWELL.

Ladies, shall I beg leave for my servant to wait on you, for he understands pictures very well?

MRS. SULLEN.

Sir, we understand originals[60] as well as he does pictures, so he may come along.

Exit Dorinda, Mrs. Sullen, Aimwell, Archer; Aimwell leads Dorinda. Enter Foigard and Scrub, meeting.

FOIGARD.

Save you, master Scrub.

SCRUB.

Sir, I won't be saved your way: I hate a priest, I abhor the French, and I defy the devil. Sir, I'm a bold Briton, and will spill the last drop of my blood to keep out popery and slavery.

FOIGARD.

Master Scrub, you would put me down in politics, and so I would be speaking with Mrs.* Shipsey.

SCRUB.

Good Mr. Priest, you can't speak with her. She's sick, sir, she's gone abroad, sir, she's—dead two months ago, sir.

Enter Gipsey.

GIPSEY.

How now, impudence! How dare you talk so saucily to the doctor?—Pray sir, don't take it ill, for the common people of England are not so civil to strangers as—

SCRUB.

You lie! You lie! 'Tis the common people that are civilest to strangers.

GIPSEY.

Sirrah, I have a good mind to—get you out, I say.

SCRUB.

I won't.

GIPSEY.

You won't, sauce-box!—Pray Doctor, what is the captain's name that came to your inn last night?

SCRUB. [*Aside.*]

The captain! Ah the devil, there she hampers me again! The captain has me on one side, and the priest on t'other, so between the gown and the sword, I have a fine time on't. But *Cedunt arma togae.*[61] (*Going.*)

GIPSEY.

What sirrah, won't you march?

SCRUB.

No my dear, I won't march—but I'll walk—[*Aside.*] and I'll make bold to listen a little too.

Goes behind the side-scene and listens.

GIPSEY.

Indeed Doctor, the count has been barbarously treated, that's the truth on't.

FOIGARD.

Ah, Mrs. Gipsey, upon my shoul, now, gra,[62] his complainings would mollify the marrow in your bones and move the bowels of your commiseration; he veeps, and he dances, and he fistles, and he swears, and he laughs, and he stamps, and he

---

60 originals] both paintings (not copies) and odd persons

61 *Cedunt arma togae*] Arms yield to the gown (Cicero).

62 gra] abbreviated form of "a ghra": "loved one" (Irish)

sings: in conclusion, joy, he's afflicted, *a la françois*,[63] and a stranger would not know whider to cry or to laugh with him.

GIPSEY.

What would you have me do, Doctor?

FOIGARD.

Noting, joy, but only hide the count in Mrs. Sullen's closet* when it is dark.

GIPSEY.

Nothing! Is that nothing? It would be both a sin and a shame, Doctor.

FOIGARD.

Here is twenty louis d'ors, joy, for your shame, and I will give you an absolution for the shin.

GIPSEY.

But won't that money look like a bribe?

FOIGARD.

Dat is according as you shall tauk it: if you receive the money beforehand, 'twill be *logicè*[64] a bribe, but if you stay till afterwards, 'twill be only a gratification.

GIPSEY.

Well Doctor, I'll take it *logicè*. But what must I do with my conscience, sir?

FOIGARD.

Leave dat wid me, joy; I am your priest, gra, and your conscience is under my hands.

GIPSEY.

But should I put the count into the closet—

FOIGARD.

Vel, is dere any shin for a man's being in a closhet? One may go to prayers in a closhet.

GIPSEY.

But if the lady should come into her chamber and go to bed?

FOIGARD.

Vel, and is dere any shin in going to bed, joy?

GIPSEY.

Aye, but if the parties should meet, Doctor?

FOIGARD.

Vel den the parties must be responsible. Do you be after putting the count in the closet and leave the shins wid themselves. I will come with the count to instruct you in your chamber.

GIPSEY.

Well Doctor, your religion is so pure! Methinks I'm so easy after an absolution and can sin afresh with so much security, that I'm resolved to die a martyr to't.—Here's the key of the garden door; come in the back way when 'tis late—I'll be ready to receive you. But don't so much as whisper; only take hold of my hand, I'll lead you, and do you lead the count, and follow me.

Exeunt. Enter Scrub.

SCRUB.

What witchcraft now have these two imps of the devil been a hatching here? There's twenty louis d'ors; I heard that and saw the purse. But I must give room to my betters. [*Exit.*]

Enter Aimwell, leading Dorinda and making love in dumb show; Mrs. Sullen and Archer.*

MRS. SULLEN. (*To Archer.*)

Pray sir, how d'ye like that piece?

ARCHER.

Oh, 'tis Leda!—You find, madam, how Jupiter comes disguised to make love—

MRS. SULLEN.

But what think you there of Alexander's battles?

ARCHER.

We want* only a Le Brun, madam, to draw greater battles and a greater general of our own. The Danube, madam, would make a greater figure in a picture than the Granicus, and we have our Ramillies to match their Arbela.[65]

MRS. SULLEN.

Pray sir, what head is that in the corner there.

---

[63] *a la françois*] *a la française*: in the French manner

[64] *logicè*] logically (It.); Foigard's moral hairsplitting represents the specious casuistry supposedly practiced by the Jesuits.

[65] Le Brun … Arbela] a French court painter who did a series of paintings on the battles of Alexander the Great, including Alexander's victories at Granicus and Arbela. Archer is suggesting that the recent victories of the Duke of Marlborough (the "greater general of our own") at Blenheim (1707) on the Danube and at Ramillies (1706) would make at least as good, if not a better, subject for painting.

ARCHER.
Oh madam, 'tis poor Ovid in his exile.

MRS. SULLEN.
What was he banished for?

ARCHER.
His ambitious love, madam. (*Bowing.*) His misfortune touches me.

MRS. SULLEN.
Was he successful in his amours?

ARCHER.
There he has left us in the dark. He was too much a gentleman to tell.

MRS. SULLEN.
If he were secret, I pity him.

ARCHER.
And if he were successful, I envy him.

MRS. SULLEN.
How d'ye like that Venus over the chimney?

ARCHER.
Venus! I protest, madam, I took it for your picture, but now I look again, 'tis not handsome enough.

MRS. SULLEN.
Oh, what a charm is flattery! If you would see my picture, there it is, over that cabinet. How d'ye like it?

ARCHER.
I must admire anything, madam, that has the least resemblance of you. But methinks, madam— (*He looks at the picture and Mrs. Sullen three or four times, by turns.*) Pray madam, who drew it?

MRS. SULLEN.
A famous hand, sir.

Here Aimwell and Dorinda go off.

ARCHER.
A famous hand, madam! Your eyes, indeed, are featured there, but where's the sparkling moisture, shining fluid in which they swim? The picture indeed has your dimples, but where's the swarm of killing Cupids that should ambush there? The lips too are figured out, but where's the carnation dew, the pouting ripeness that tempts the taste in the original?

MRS. SULLEN. [*Aside.*]
Had it been my lot to have matched with such a man!

ARCHER.
Your breasts, too! presumptuous man! What, paint Heaven! Apropos, madam, in the very next picture is Salmoneus, that was struck dead with lightning for offering to imitate Jove's thunder; I hope you served the painter so, madam?

MRS. SULLEN.
Had my eyes the power of thunder, they should employ their lightning better.

ARCHER.
There's the finest bed in that room, madam. I suppose 'tis your ladyship's bedchamber?

MRS. SULLEN.
And what then, sir?

ARCHER.
I think the quilt is the richest that ever I saw. I can't at this distance, madam, distinguish the figures of the embroidery. Will you give me leave, madam?

MRS. SULLEN. [*Aside.*]
The devil take his impudence! Sure if I gave him an opportunity, he durst not offer* it? I have a great mind to try. (*Going; returns.*) S'death,* what am I doing? And alone too!—Sister! sister! (*Runs out.*)

ARCHER.
I'll follow her close—

For where a Frenchman durst attempt to storm,
A Briton sure may well the work perform. (*Going.*)

Enter Scrub.

SCRUB.
Martin! brother Martin!

ARCHER.
Oh brother Scrub, I beg your pardon; I was not a-going. Here's a guinea my master ordered you.

SCRUB.
A guinea! Hi, hi, hi! a guinea! eh? by this light, it is a guinea! But I suppose you expect one and twenty shillings in change?

ARCHER.
Not at all! I have another for Gipsey.

SCRUB.
A guinea for her! Faggot and fire for the witch! Sir, give me that guinea, and I'll discover* a plot.

ARCHER.
A plot!

SCRUB.

Aye sir, a plot, and a horrid plot! First, it must be a plot because there's a woman in't; secondly, it must be a plot because there's a priest in't; thirdly, it must be a plot because there's French gold in't; and fourthly it must be a plot because I don't know what to make on't.

ARCHER.

Nor anybody else, I'm afraid, brother Scrub.

SCRUB.

Truly, I'm afraid so too, for where there's a priest and a woman, there's always a mystery and a riddle. This I know, that here has been the doctor with a temptation in one hand and an absolution in the other, and Gipsey has sold herself to the Devil. I saw the price paid down, my eyes shall take their oath on't.

ARCHER.

And is all this bustle about Gipsey?

SCRUB.

That's not all; I could hear but a word here and there, but I remember they mentioned a count, a closet, a back door, and a key.

ARCHER.

The count! Did you hear nothing of Mrs. Sullen?

SCRUB.

I did hear some word that sounded that way, but whether it was Sullen or Dorinda, I could not distiguish.

ARCHER.

You have told this matter to nobody, brother?

SCRUB.

Told! No sir, I thank you for that! I'm resolved never to speak one word, pro nor con, till we have a peace.

ARCHER.

You're i'th right, brother Scrub. Here's a treaty afoot between the count and the lady; the priest and the chambermaid are the plenipotentiaries. It shall go hard but I find a way to be included in the treaty. Where's the doctor now?

SCRUB.

He and Gipsey are this moment devouring my lady's marmalade in the closet.

AIMWELL. (*From without.*)

Martin! Martin!

ARCHER.

I come, sir! I come!

SCRUB.

But you forget the other guinea, brother Martin.

ARCHER.

Here, I give it with all my heart.

SCRUB.

And I take it with all my soul.

Exit Archer.

I'cod, I'll spoil your plotting, Mrs. Gipsey, and if you should set the captain upon me, these two guineas will buy me off. (*Exit.*)

Enter Mrs. Sullen and Dorinda, meeting.

MRS. SULLEN.

Well, sister.

DORINDA.

And well, sister.

MRS. SULLEN.

What's become of my lord?

DORINDA.

What's become of his servant?

MRS. SULLEN.

Servant! He's a prettier fellow and a finer gentleman by fifty degrees than his master.

DORINDA.

O'my conscience, I fancy you could beg that fellow at the gallows-foot![66]

MRS. SULLEN.

O'my conscience, I could, provided I could put a friend of yours in his room.

DORINDA.

You desired me, sister, to leave you, when you transgressed the bounds of honor.

MRS. SULLEN.

Thou dear censorious country girl! What dost mean? You can't think of the man without the bedfellow, I find.

DORINDA.

I don't find anything unnatural in that thought; while the mind is conversant with flesh and blood, it must conform to the humors* of the company.

66 beg … gallows-foot] Under an old law, a condemned criminal could be reprieved from the gallows if a respectable woman offered to marry him.

MRS. SULLEN.

How a little love and good company improves a woman! Why child,* you begin to live—you never spoke before.

DORINDA.

Because I was never spoke to. My lord has told me that I have more wit and beauty than any of my sex and, truly, I begin to think the man is sincere!

MRS. SULLEN.

You're in the right, Dorinda. Pride is the life of a woman, and flattery is our daily bread, and she's a fool that won't believe a man there, as much as she that believes him in anything else. But I'll lay you a guinea that I had finer things said to me than you had.

DORINDA.

Done! What did your fellow say to ye?

MRS. SULLEN.

My fellow took the picture of Venus for mine.

DORINDA.

But my lover took me for Venus herself.

MRS. SULLEN.

Common cant! Had my spark called me a Venus directly, I should have believed him a footman in good earnest.

DORINDA.

But my lover was upon his knees to me.

MRS. SULLEN.

And mine was upon his tiptoes to me.

DORINDA.

Mine vowed to die for me.

MRS. SULLEN.

Mine swore to die* with me.

DORINDA.

Mine spoke the softest moving things.

MRS. SULLEN.

Mine had his moving things too.

DORINDA.

Mine kissed my hand ten thousand times.

MRS. SULLEN.

Mine has all that pleasure to come.

DORINDA.

Mine offered marriage.

MRS. SULLEN.

O Lard! D'ye call that a moving thing?

DORINDA.

The sharpest arrow in his quiver, my dear sister! Why, my ten thousand pounds may lie brooding here this seven years and hatch nothing at last but some ill- natured clown* like yours! Whereas if I marry my Lord Aimwell, there will be title, place and precedence, the Park,* the play, and the Drawing Room,* splendor, equipage, noise, and flambeaux: "Hey, my Lady Aimwell's servants there!—Lights, lights to the stairs!*—My Lady Aimwell's coach put forward!—Stand by, make room for her ladyship!" Are not these things moving? What! melancholy of a sudden?

MRS. SULLEN.

Happy, happy sister! Your angel has been watchful for your happiness, whilst mine has slept regardless of his charge. Long smiling years of circling joys for you, but not one hour for me! (*Weeps.*)

DORINDA.

Come my dear, we'll talk of something else.

MRS. SULLEN.

Oh Dorinda, I own myself a woman, full of my sex, a gentle, generous soul, easy and yielding to soft desires, a spacious heart, where Love and all his train might lodge. And must the fair apartment of my breast be made a stable for a brute to lie in?

DORINDA.

Meaning your husband, I suppose.

MRS. SULLEN.

Husband! No, even husband is too soft a name for him.—But come, I expect my brother here tonight or tomorrow. He was abroad when my father married me; perhaps he'll find a way to make me easy.

DORINDA.

Will you promise not to make yourself easy in the meantime with my lord's friend?

MRS. SULLEN.

You mistake me, sister. It happens with us, as among the men. The greatest talkers are the greatest cowards, and there's a reason for it: those spirits evaporate in prattle which might do more mischief if they took another course. Though to confess the truth, I do love that fellow, and if I met him dressed as he should be, and I undressed as I should be— Look ye, sister, I have no supernatural gifts; I can't swear I could resist the temptation, though I can safely promise to avoid it, and that's as much as the best of us can do.

Exeunt Mrs. Sullen and Dorinda.

[Scene ii. The inn.]

Enter Aimwell and Archer laughing.

ARCHER.
And the awkward kindness of the good motherly old gentlewoman—

AIMWELL.
And the coming easiness of the young one—s'death,* tis pity to deceive her!

ARCHER.
Nay, if you adhere to those principles, stop where you are.

AIMWELL.
I can't stop, for I love her to distraction.

ARCHER.
S'death, if you love her a hair's breadth beyond discretion you must go no farther.

AIMWELL.
Well, well, any thing to deliver us from sauntering away our idle evenings at White's, Tom's,[67] or Will's, and be stinted to bear looking at our old acquaintance, the cards, because our impotent pockets can't afford us a guinea for the mercenary drabs.

ARCHER.
Or be obliged to some purse-proud coxcomb for a scandalous bottle, where we must not pretend to our share of the discourse, because we can't pay our club o'th'reckoning. Damn it, I had rather sponge upon Morris,[68] and sup upon a dish of bohea scored behind the door!

AIMWELL.
And there expose our want* of sense by talking criticisms, as we should our want of money by railing at the government.

ARCHER.
Or be obliged to sneak into the side box and between both houses steal two acts of a play,[69] and because we han't money to see the other three, we come away discontented and damn the whole five.

AIMWELL.
And ten thousand such rascally tricks—had we outlived our fortunes among our acquaintance. But now—

ARCHER.
Aye, now is the time to prevent all this. Strike while the iron is hot.—This priest is the luckiest part of our adventure: he shall marry you, and pimp for me.

AIMWELL.
But I should not like a woman that can be so fond of a Frenchman.

ARCHER.
Alas, sir! Necessity has no law. The lady may be in distress; perhaps she has a confounded husband, and her revenge may carry her farther than her love. Egad, I have so good an opinion of her, and of myself, that I begin to fancy strange things, and we must say this for the honor of our women, and indeed of ourselves, that they do stick to their men, as they do to their Magna Charta. If the plot lies as I suspect, I must put on the gentleman.—But here comes the doctor. I shall be ready. (*Exit.*)

Enter Foigard.

FOIGARD.
Sauve you, noble friend.

AIMWELL.
Oh sir, your servant! Pray Doctor, may I crave your name?

FOIGARD.
Fat naam is upon me? My name is Foigard, joy.

AIMWELL.
Foigard, a very good name for a clergyman! Pray Doctor Foigard, were you ever in Ireland?

FOIGARD.
Ireland! No, joy. Fat sort of plaace is dat saam Ireland? Dey say de people are catched dere when dey are young.

AIMWELL.
And some of 'em when they're old—as, for example: (*Takes Foigard by the shoulder.*) Sir, I arrest you as a traitor against the government; you're a subject of England, and this morning showed me a commission by which you served as chaplain in

[67] Tom's] another London coffee-house

[68] Morris] owner of another coffee-shop in London

[69] both houses … play] Payment was not demanded if a patron only stayed for one act of a play; by moving between the two playhouses, it was possible to see two acts without paying anything.

the French army. This is death by our law, and your reverence must hang for't.[70]

FOIGARD.

Upon my shoul, noble friend, dis is strange news you tell me! Fader Foigard, a subject of England! De son of a burgomaster of Brussels a subject of England! Ubooboo—[71]

AIMWELL.

The son of a bogtrotter[72] in Ireland! Sir, your tongue will condemn you before any bench in the kingdom.

FOIGARD.

And is my tongue all your evidence, joy?

AIMWELL.

That's enough.

FOIGARD.

No, no, joy, for I vill never spake English no more.

AIMWELL.

Sir, I have other evidence.—Here Martin, you know this fellow.

Enter Archer.

ARCHER. (*In a brogue.*)

Saave you, my dear cussen, how does your health?

FOIGARD. (*Aside.*)

Ah! Upon my shoul dere is my countryman, and his brogue will hang mine.—*Mynheer, Ick wet neat watt hey zacht. Ick universton ewe neat, sacramant.*[73]

AIMWELL.

Altering your language won't do, sir. This fellow knows your person and will swear to your face.

FOIGARD.

Faace! fey, is dere a brogue upon my faash, too?

ARCHER.

Upon my soulvation dere ish, joy! But cussen Mackshane, vil you not put a remembrance upon me?

[70] traitor ... hang for't] The Irish were subjects of the Crown at this time; therefore, by serving in the army of the enemy (the French), Foigard was committing treason. Many dispossessed Irish Catholics did serve in the French army in support of the Jacobite cause.

[71] Ubooboo] an anglicization of the Irish "ababu," an exclamation of displeasure

[72] bogtrotter] pejorative term for an Irishman

[73] *Mynheer ... sacramant*] fractured Flemish: "Sir, I don't know what he says. I don't understand you, by the sacrament!"

FOIGARD. (*Aside.*)

Mackshane! By St. Paatrick, dat is naame,[k] shure enough.

AIMWELL. [*Aside to Archer.*]

I fancy Archer, you have it.

FOIGARD.

The Devil hang you, joy! By fat acquaintance are you my cussen?

ARCHER.

Oh, de Devil hang yourshelf, joy! You know we were little boys togeder upon de school, and your foster moder's son was married upon my nurse's chister, joy, and so we are Irish cussens.[74]

FOIGARD.

De Devil taak the relation! Vel, joy, and fat school was it?

ARCHER.

I tinks it vas—aay—'twas Tipperary.

FOIGARD.

No, no, joy: it vas Kilkenny.

AIMWELL.

That's enough for us—self-confession! Come sir, we must deliver you into the hands of the next magistrate.

ARCHER.

He sends you to gaol; you're tried next assizes, and away you go swing into purgatory.

FOIGARD.

And is it so wid you, cussen?

ARCHER.

It vil be sho wid you, cussen, if you don't immediately confess the secret between you and Mrs. Gipsey.—Look ye, sir, the gallows or the secret, take your choice.

FOIGARD.

The gallows! Upon my shoul I hate that saam gallow, for it is a diseash dat is fatal to our family. Vel den, dere is nothing, shentlemens, but Mrs. Shullen would spaak wid the count in her chamber at midnight, and dere is no haarm, joy, for I am to conduct the count to the plash myshelf.

[74] Irish cussens] Gaelic Irish families traditionally fostered out their children into other families, creating a complex kinship web that was often the subject of ridicule by English commentators.

ARCHER.

As I guessed.—Have you communicated the matter to the count?

FOIGARD.

I have not sheen him since.

ARCHER.

Right again.—Why then, Doctor, you shall conduct me to the lady instead of the count.

FOIGARD.

Fat, my cussin to the lady! Upon my shoul, gra, dat is too much upon the brogue.

ARCHER.

Come, come, Doctor. Consider we have got a rope about your neck, and if you offer* to squeak, we'll stop your windpipe, most certainly; we shall have another job for you in a day or two, I hope.

AIMWELL.

Here's company coming this way. Let's into my chamber and there concert our affair farther.

ARCHER.

Come, my dear cussen, come along.

Exeunt. Enter Bonniface, Hounslow and Bagshot at one door, Gibbet at the opposite.

GIBBET.

Well, gentlemen, 'tis a fine night for our enterprise.

HOUNSLOW.

Dark as hell.

BAGSHOT.

And blows like the devil. Our landlord here has showed us the window where we must break in and tells us the plate* stands in the wainscot cupboard in the parlor.

BONNIFACE.

Aye, aye, Mr. Bagshot, as the saving is—knives and forks, and cups and cans, and tumblers and tankards. There's one tankard, as the saying is, that's near upon as big as me; it was a present to the squire from his godmother and smells of nutmeg and toast like an East India ship.

HOUNSLOW.

Then you say we must divide at the stair-head?

BONNIFACE.

Yes, Mr. Hounslow, as the saying is. At one end of that gallery lies my Lady Bountiful and her daughter, and at the other Mrs. Sullen. As for the squire—

GIBBET.

He's safe enough; I have fairly entered him, and he's more than half-seas-over* already. But such a parcel of scoundrels are got about him now that, egad, I was ashamed to be seen in their company!

BONNIFACE.

'Tis now twelve, as the saying is. Gentlemen, you must set out at one.

GIBBET.

Hounslow, do you and Bagshot see our arms fixed, and I'll come to you presently.*

HOUNSLOW, BAGSHOT.

We will. (*Exeunt.*)

GIBBET.

Well, my dear Bonny, you assure me that Scrub is a coward.

BONNIFACE.

A chicken, as the saying is. You'll have no creature to deal with but the ladies.

GIBBET.

And I can assure you, friend, there's a great deal of address and good manners in robbing a lady; I am the most a gentleman that way that ever traveled the road. But my dear Bonny, this prize will be a galleon, a Vigo business;[75] I warrant you we shall bring off three or four thousand pound.

BONNIFACE.

In plate, jewels, and money, as the saying is, you may.

GIBBET.

Why then, Tyburn, I defy thee! I'll get up to Town, sell off my horse and arms, buy myself some pretty employment in the Household,[76] and be as snug and as honest as any courtier of 'um all.

BONNIFACE.

And what think you then of my daughter Cherry for a wife?

GIBBET.

Look ye, my dear Bonny, Cherry is the goddess I adore, as the song goes, but it is a maxim that man and wife should never have it in their power to hang one another, for if they should, the Lord have mercy on 'um both.

Exeunt.

75 Vigo business] The English captured Spanish treasure-ships in Vigo harbor in Spain in 1702.

76 Household] dwelling of the Royals

Act V, scene [i]. Scene continues.

Knocking without. Enter Bonniface.

BONNIFACE.
Coming! coming!—A coach and six foaming horses at this time o'night! Some great man, as the saying is, for he scorns to travel with other people.

Enter Sir Charles Freeman.

SIR CHARLES.
What fellow! a public house, and abed when other people sleep!

BONNIFACE.
Sir, I an't abed, as the saying is.

SIR CHARLES.
Is Mr. Sullen's family abed, think ye?

BONNIFACE.
All but the squire himself, sir, as the saying is. He's in the house.

SIR CHARLES.
What company has he?

BONNIFACE.
Why sir, there's the constable, Mr. Gage the exciseman, the hunchbacked barber, and two or three other gentlemen.

SIR CHARLES. [*Aside.*]
I find my sister's letters gave me the true picture of her spouse.

Enter Sullen drunk.

BONNIFACE.
Sir, here's the squire.

SULLEN.
The puppies left me asleep.—Sir!

SIR CHARLES.
Well sir.

SULLEN.
Sir, I'm an unfortunate man: I have three thousand pound a year, and I can't get a man to drink a cup of ale with me.

SIR CHARLES.
That's very hard.

SULLEN.
Aye sir. And unless you have pity upon me and smoke one pipe with me, I must e'en go home to my wife, and I had rather go to the devil by half.

SIR CHARLES.
But I presume, sir, you won't see your wife tonight; she'll be gone to bed. You don't use to lie with your wife in that pickle?

SULLEN.
What! not lie with my wife! Why sir, do you take me for an atheist or a rake?

SIR CHARLES.
If you hate her, sir, I think you had better lie from her.

SULLEN.
I think so too, friend. But I'm a justice of peace and must do nothing against the law.

SIR CHARLES.
Law! As I take it, Mr. Justice, nobody observes law for law's sake, only for the good of those for whom it was made.

SULLEN.
But if the law orders me to send you to gaol, you must lie there, my friend.

SIR CHARLES.
Not unless I commit a crime to deserve it.

SULLEN.
A crime! 'Oons,* an't I married?

SIR CHARLES.
Nay sir, if you call marriage a crime, you must disown it for a law.

SULLEN.
Eh! I must be acquainted with you, sir. But sir, I should be very glad to know the truth of this matter.

SIR CHARLES.
Truth, sir, is a profound sea, and few there be that dare wade deep enough to find out the bottom on't. Besides sir, I'm afraid the line of your understanding mayn't be long enough.

SULLEN.
Look ye, sir, I have nothing to say to your sea of truth, but if a good parcel of land can entitle a man to a little truth, I have as much as any he in the country.

BONNIFACE.
I never heard your worship, as the saying is, talk so much before.

SULLEN.
Because I never met with a man that I liked before—

BONNIFACE.
Pray sir, as the saying is, let me ask you one question: Are not man and wife one flesh?
SIR CHARLES.
You and your wife, Mr. Guts, may be one flesh, because ye are nothing else—but rational creatures have minds that must be united.
SULLEN.
Minds!
SIR CHARLES.
Aye, minds, sir. Don't you think that the mind takes place of[77] the body?
SULLEN.
In some people.
SIR CHARLES.
Then the interest of the master must be consulted before that of his servant.
SULLEN.
Sir, you shall dine with me tomorrow. 'Oons, I always thought that we were naturally one.
SIR CHARLES.
Sir, I know that my two hands are naturally one, because they love one another, kiss one another, help one another in all the actions of life, but I could not say so much, if they were always at cuffs.
SULLEN.
Then 'tis plain that we are two.
SIR CHARLES.
Why don't you part with her, sir?
SULLEN.
Will you take her, sir?
SIR CHARLES.
With all my heart.
SULLEN.
You shall have her tomorrow morning and a venison pasty into the bargain.
SIR CHARLES.
You'll let me have her fortune too?
SULLEN.
Fortune! why sir, I have no quarrel at her fortune. I only hate the woman, sir, and none but the woman shall go.
SIR CHARLES.
But her fortune, sir—

SULLEN.
Can you play at whist, sir?
SIR CHARLES.
No, truly, sir.
SULLEN.
Nor at all-fours?[78]
SIR CHARLES.
Neither!
SULLEN. (*Aside.*)
'Oons! where was this man bred?—Burn me, sir, I can't go home; 'tis but two o'clock.
SIR CHARLES.
For half an hour, sir, if you please, but you must consider 'tis late.
SULLEN.
Late! that's the reason I can't go to bed. Come, sir!

Exeunt. Enter Cherry, runs across the stage and knocks at Aimwell's chamber door. Enter Aimwell in his nightcap and gown.

AIMWELL.
What's the matter? You tremble, child,* you're frighted.
CHERRY.
No wonder, sir—but in short, sir, this very minute a gang of rogues are gone to rob my Lady Bountiful's house.
AIMWELL.
How!
CHERRY.
I dogged 'em to the very door and left 'em breaking in.
AIMWELL.
Have you alarmed anybody else with the news?
CHERRY.
No, no, sir. I wanted to have discovered* the whole plot and twenty other things to your man Martin, but I have searched the whole house and can't find him. Where is he?
AIMWELL.
No matter, child. Will you guide me immediately to the house?
CHERRY.
With all my heart, sir. My Lady Bountiful is my godmother, and I love Mrs. Dorinda so well—

77 place of] precedence over

78 all-fours] card game, played by two

AIMWELL.

Dorinda! The name inspires me! The glory and the danger shall be all my own.—Come, my life, let me but get my sword.

Exeunt.

Scene [ii]. A bedchamber in Lady Bountiful's house.

Enter Mrs. Sullen, Dorinda undressed;[79] *a table and lights.*

DORINDA.

'Tis very late, sister. No news of your spouse yet?

MRS. SULLEN.

No, I'm condemned to be alone till towards four, and then perhaps I may be executed with his company.

DORINDA.

Well my dear, I'll leave you to your rest; you'll go directly to bed, I suppose.

MRS. SULLEN.

I don't know what to do. Heigh-ho!

DORINDA.

That's a desiring sigh, sister.

MRS. SULLEN.

This is a languishing hour, sister.

DORINDA.

And might prove a critical minute, if the pretty fellow were here.

MRS. SULLEN.

Here! what, in my bedchamber, at two o'clock o'th'morning, I undressed, the family asleep, my hated husband abroad, and my lovely fellow at my feet? Oh gad, sister!

DORINDA.

Thoughts are free, sister, and them I allow you. So my dear, good night. [*Exit.*]

MRS. SULLEN.

A good rest to my dear Dorinda.—Thoughts free! Are they so? Why then, suppose him here, dressed like a youthful, gay and burning bridegroom, (*Here Archer steals out of the closet.*) with tongue enchanting, eyes bewitching, knees imploring—(*Turns a little o' one side and sees Archer in the posture she describes.*) Ah! (*Shrieks, and runs to the other side of the stage.*) Have my thoughts raised a spirit?—What are you, sir, a man or a devil?

ARCHER. (*Rising.*)

A man! a man, madam!

MRS. SULLEN.

How shall I be sure of it?

ARCHER.

Madam, I'll give you demonstration this minute. (*Takes her hand.*)

MRS. SULLEN.

What, sir! Do you intend to be rude?

ARCHER.

Yes madam, if you please.

MRS. SULLEN.

In the name of wonder, whence came ye?

ARCHER.

From the skies, madam: I'm a Jupiter in love, and you shall be my Alcmene.

MRS. SULLEN.

How came you in?

ARCHER.

I flew in at the window, madam; your cousin Cupid lent me his wings, and your sister Venus opened the casement.

MRS. SULLEN.

I'm struck dumb with admiration!*

ARCHER. (*Looks passionately at her.*)

And I with wonder.

MRS. SULLEN.

What will become of me?

ARCHER.

How beautiful she looks! The teeming jolly spring smiles in her blooming face, and when she was conceived, her mother smelt to roses, looked on lilies—

Lilies unfold their white, their fragrant charms,
When the warm sun thus darts into their arms.
(*Runs to her.*)

MRS. SULLEN. (*Shrieks.*)

Ah!

ARCHER.

'Oons,* madam, what d'ye mean? You'll raise the house.

MRS. SULLEN.

Sir, I'll wake the dead before I bear this. What! approach me with the freedoms of a keeper!* I'm glad on't; your impudence has cured me.

79 *undressed*] in night attire

ARCHER.
If this be impudence, (*Kneels.*) I leave to your partial self; no panting pilgrim after a tedious, painful voyage, e'er bowed before his saint with more devotion.

MRS. SULLEN. (*Aside*)
Now, now, I'm ruined if he kneels!—Rise thou prostrate engineer;* not all thy undermining skill shall reach my heart. Rise, and know, I am a woman without my sex: I can love to all the tenderness of wishes, sighs, and tears—but go no farther. Still, to convince you that I'm more than woman, I can speak my frailty, confess my weakness even for you—but—

ARCHER. (*Going to lay hold on her.*)
For me!

MRS. SULLEN.
Hold, sir, build not upon that, for my most mortal hatred follows if you disobey what I command you now: Leave me this minute. (*Aside.*) If he denies, I'm lost.

ARCHER.
Then you'll promise—

MRS. SULLEN.
Anything another time.

ARCHER.
When shall I come?

MRS. SULLEN.
Tomorrow, when you will.

ARCHER.
Your lips must seal the promise.

MRS. SULLEN.
Pshaw!

ARCHER.
They must, they must! (*Kisses her.*) Raptures and paradise! And why not now, my angel? The time, the place, silence and secrecy, all conspire—and the now conscious stars have preordained this moment for my happiness. (*Takes her in his arms.*)

MRS. SULLEN.
You will not! cannot, sure!

ARCHER.
If the sun rides fast and disappoints not mortals of tomorrow's dawn, this night shall crown my joys.

MRS. SULLEN.
My sex's pride assist me!

ARCHER.
My sex's strength help me!

MRS. SULLEN.
You shall kill me first.

ARCHER.
I'll die* with you. (*Carrying her off.*)

MRS. SULLEN.
Thieves! Thieves! Murder!

Enter Scrub in his breeches and one shoe.

SCRUB.
Thieves! Thieves! Murder! Popery!

ARCHER.
Hah! the very* timorous stag will kill in rutting time. (*Draws and offers* to stab Scrub.*)

SCRUB. (*Kneeling.*)
Oh, pray, sir, spare all I have and take my life.

MRS. SULLEN. (*Holding Archer's hand.*)
What does the fellow mean?

SCRUB.
Oh madam, down upon your knees, your marrowbones—he's one of 'um!

ARCHER.
Of whom?

SCRUB.
One of the rogues—I beg your pardon, sir, one of the honest gentlemen that just now are broke into the house.

ARCHER.
How!

MRS. SULLEN.
I hope you did not come to rob me?

ARCHER.
Indeed I did, madam, but I would have taken nothing but what you might ha' spared. But your crying "Thieves" has waked this dreaming fool, and so he takes 'em for granted.

SCRUB.
Granted! 'tis granted, sir, take all we have.

MRS. SULLEN.
The fellow looks as if he were broke out of Bedlam.

SCRUB.
'Oons madam, they're broke into the house with fire and sword! I saw them, heard them, they'll be here this minute.

ARCHER.
What, thieves?

SCRUB.
Under favor, sir, I think so.
MRS. SULLEN.
What shall we do, sir?
ARCHER.
Madam, I wish your ladyship a good night.
MRS. SULLEN.
Will you leave me?
ARCHER.
Leave you! Lord madam, did not you command me to be gone just now upon pain of your immortal hatred?
MRS. SULLEN.
Nay, but pray sir— (*Takes hold of him.*)
ARCHER.
Ha, ha, ha! now comes my turn to be ravished. You see now, madam, you must use men one way or other. But take this by the way, good madam, that none but a fool will give you the benefit of his courage, unless you'll take his love along with it.—How are they armed, friend?
SCRUB.
With sword and pistol, sir.
ARCHER.
Hush! I see a dark lantern coming through the gallery.—Madam, be assured I will protect you or lose my life.
MRS. SULLEN.
Your life! No, sir, they can rob me of nothing that I value half so much; therefore, now sir, let me entreat you to be gone.
ARCHER.
No madam, I'll consult my own safety for the sake of yours; I'll work by stratagem. Have you courage enough to stand the appearance of 'em?
MRS. SULLEN.
Yes, yes, since I have 'scaped your hands, I can face anything.
ARCHER.
Come hither, brother Scrub. Don't you know me?
SCRUB.
Eh! My dear brother, let me kiss thee. (*Kisses Archer.*)
ARCHER.
This way—here— (*Archer and Scrub hide behind the bed.*)

Enter Gibbet with a dark lantern in one hand and a pistol in t'other.

GIBBET.
Aye, aye, this is the chamber, and the lady alone.
MRS. SULLEN.
Who are you, sir? What would you have? D'ye come to rob me?
GIBBET.
Rob you! Alack a day, madam, I'm only a younger brother, madam. And so, madam, if you make a noise, I'll shoot you through the head, but don't be afraid, madam. (*Laying his lantern and pistol upon the table.*) These rings, madam. Don't be concerned, madam, I have a profound respect for you, madam. Your keys, madam. (*Searching her pockets.*) Don't be frighted, madam, I'm the most of a gentleman. This necklace, madam. I never was rude to a lady. I have a veneration—for this necklace—

Here Archer having come round and seized the pistol takes Gibbet by the collar, trips up his heels, and claps the pistol to his breast.

ARCHER.
Hold, profane villain, and take the reward of thy sacrilege!
GIBBET.
Oh! Pray sir, don't kill me: I an't prepared.
ARCHER.
How many is there of 'em, Scrub?
SCRUB.
Five and forty, sir.
ARCHER.
Then I must kill the villain to have him out of the way.
GIBBET.
Hold, hold, sir! We are but three, upon my honor!
ARCHER.
Scrub, will you undertake to secure him?
SCRUB.
Not I, sir! Kill him, kill him!
ARCHER.
Run to Gipsey's chamber. There you'll find the doctor; bring him hither presently.*

Exit Scrub running.

Come rogue, if you have a short prayer, say it.

GIBBET.
Sir, I have no prayer at all; the government has provided a chaplain to say prayers for us on these occasions.

MRS. SULLEN.
Pray sir, don't kill him. You fright me as much as him.

ARCHER.
The dog shall die, madam, for being the occasion of my disappointment.—Sirrah, this moment is your last.

GIBBET.
Sir, I'll give you two hundred pound to spare my life.

ARCHER.
Have you no more, rascal?

GIBBET.
Yes sir, I can command four hundred, but I must reserve two of 'em to save my life at the sessions.

Enter Scrub and Foigard.

ARCHER.
Here Doctor, I suppose Scrub and you between you may manage him. Lay hold of him, Doctor.

Foigard lays hold of Gibbet.

GIBBET.
What! Turned over to the priest already!—Look ye, Doctor, you come before your time: I'ant condemned yet, I thank ye.

FOIGARD.
Come, my dear joy, I vill secure your body and your shoul too; I vill make you a good Catholic and give you an absolution.

GIBBET.
Absolution! Can you procure me a pardon, Doctor?

FOIGARD.
No, joy.

GIBBET.
Then you and your absolution may go to the devil.

ARCHER.
Convey him into the cellar; there bind him. Take the pistol, and if he offers* to resist, shoot him through the head and come back to us with all the speed you can.

SCRUB.
Aye, aye. Come Doctor, do you hold him fast, and I'll guard him.

[Exeunt Scrub and Foigard with Gibbet.]

MRS. SULLEN.
But how came the doctor?

ARCHER.
In short, madam— (*Shrieking without.*) S'death,* the rogues are at work with the other ladies! I'm vexed I parted with the pistol, but I must fly to their assistance. Will you stay here, madam, or venture yourself with me?

MRS. SULLEN.
Oh, with you, dear sir, with you.

Takes him by the arm and exeunt.

Scene [iii]. Another apartment in the same house.

Enter [Bagshot] dragging in Lady Bountiful, and [Hounslow] hauling in Dorinda; the rogues with swords drawn.

HOUNSLOW.
Come, come, your jewels, mistress!

BAGSHOT.
Your keys, your keys, old gentlewoman!

Enter Aimwell and Cherry.

AIMWELL.
Turn this way, villains! I durst engage an army in such a cause. (*He engages 'em both.*)

DORINDA.
Oh madam, had I but a sword to help the brave man!

LADY BOUNTIFUL.
There's three or four hanging up in the hall, but they won't draw. I'll go fetch one, however. (*Exit.*)

Enter Archer and Mrs. Sullen.

ARCHER.
Hold, hold, my lord! every man his bird, pray.

They engage man to man; the rogues are thrown and disarmed.

CHERRY. [*Aside.*]
What! the rogues taken! Then they'll impeach my father; I must give him timely notice. (*Runs out.*)

ARCHER.
Shall we kill the rogues?

AIMWELL.
No, no, we'll bind them.

ARCHER.
Aye, aye. (*To Mrs. Sullen who stands by him.*) Here madam, lend me your garter.

MRS. SULLEN. [*Aside.*]
The devil's in this fellow! He fights, loves, and banters, all in a breath.—Here's a cord that the rogues brought with 'em, I suppose.

ARCHER.
Right, right, the rogue's destiny, a rope to hang himself.—Come my lord, this is but a scandalous sort of an office, (*Binding the rogues together.*) if our adventures should end in this sort of hangman-work. But I hope there is something in prospect that—

Enter Scrub.

Well, Scrub, have you secured your Tartar?

SCRUB.
Yes sir, I left the priest and him disputing about religion.

AIMWELL.
And pray, carry these gentlemen to reap the benefit of the controversy.

Delivers the prisoners to Scrub, who leads 'em out.

MRS. SULLEN.
Pray sister, how came my lord here?

DORINDA.
And pray, how came the gentleman here?

MRS. SULLEN.
I'll tell you the greatest piece of villainy—

They talk in dumb show.

AIMWELL.
I fancy, Archer, you have been more successful in your adventures than the house-breakers.

ARCHER.
No matter for my adventure, yours is the principal. Press her this minute to marry you, now while she's hurried between the palpitation of her fear and the joy of her deliverance, now while the tide of her spirits are at high-flood. Throw yourself at her feet, speak some romantic nonsense or other, address her like Alexander[80] in the height of his victory, confound her senses, bear down her reason, and away with her. The priest is now in the cellar and dare not refuse to do the work.

Enter Lady Bountiful.

AIMWELL.
But how shall I get off without being observed?

ARCHER.
You a lover, and not find a way to get off! Let me see—

AIMWELL.
You bleed, Archer!

ARCHER.
S'death,* I'm glad on't: this wound will do the business. I'll amuse the old lady and Mrs. Sullen about dressing my wound, while you carry off Dorinda.

LADY BOUNTIFUL.
Gentlemen, could we understand how you would be gratified for the services—

ARCHER.
Come, come, my lady, this is no time for compliments. I'm wounded, madam.

LADY BOUNTIFUL, MRS. SULLEN.
How! wounded!

DORINDA.
I hope, sir, you have received no hurt?

AIMWELL.
None but what you may cure. (*Makes love* in dumb show.*)

LADY BOUNTIFUL.
Let me see your arm, sir. I must have some powder-sugar to stop the blood. Oh me! an ugly gash, upon my word! Sir, you must go into bed.

ARCHER.
Aye my lady, a bed would do very well. (*To Mrs. Sullen.*) Madam, will you do me the favor to conduct me to a chamber?

LADY BOUNTIFUL.
Do, do, daughter, while I get the lint and the probe and the plaster ready.

---

80 address … Alexander] In Nathaniel Lee's still popular play, *The Rival Queens* (1677), Alexander the Great uses his rhetorical skills to woo Statira.

Runs out one way; Aimwell carries off Dorinda another.

ARCHER.
Come madam, why don't you obey your mother's commands?

MRS. SULLEN.
How can you, after what is past, have the confidence to ask me?

ARCHER.
And if you go to that, how can you, after what is past, have the confidence to deny me? Was not this blood shed in your defense and my life exposed for your protection? Look ye, madam, I'm none of your romantic fools that fight giants and monsters for nothing; my valor is downright Swiss;[81] I'm a soldier of fortune and must be paid.

MRS. SULLEN.
'Tis ungenerous in you, sir, to upbraid me with your services.

ARCHER.
'Tis ungenerous in you, madam, not to reward 'em.

MRS. SULLEN.
How! at the expense of my honor?

ARCHER.
Honor! Can honor consist with ingratitude? If you would deal like a woman of honor, do like a man of honor. D'ye think I would deny you in such a case?

Enter a servant.

SERVANT.
Madam, my lady ordered me to tell you that your brother is below at the gate. [*Exit.*]

MRS. SULLEN.
My brother! Heavens be praised!—Sir, he shall thank you for your services. He has it in his power.

ARCHER.
Who is your brother, madam?

MRS. SULLEN.
Sir Charles Freeman. You'll excuse me, sir; I must go and receive him. [*Exit.*]

ARCHER.
Sir Charles Freeman! S'death and hell! my old acquaintance! Now unless Aimwell has made good use of his time, all our fair machine goes souse into the sea like the Eddystone.[82]

Exit.

Scene [iv]. The gallery in the same house.

Enter Aimwell and Dorinda.

DORINDA.
Well, well, my lord, you have conquered. Your late generous action will, I hope, plead for my easy yielding, though I must own your lordship had a friend in the fort before.

AIMWELL.
The sweets of Hybla[83] dwell upon her tongue!

Enter Foigard with a book.

Here, Doctor—

FOIGARD.
Are you prepared boat?

DORINDA.
I'm ready. But first, my lord, one word: I have a frightful example of a hasty marriage in my own family; when I reflect upon't, it shocks me. Pray my lord, consider a little—

AIMWELL.
Consider! Do you doubt my honor or my love?

DORINDA.
Neither: I do believe you equally just as brave. And were your whole sex drawn out for me to choose, I should not cast a look upon the multitude if you were absent. But my lord, I'm a woman: colors, concealments may hide a thousand faults in me; therefore, know me better first. I hardly dare affirm I know myself in anything except my love.

AIMWELL. (*Aside.*)
Such goodness who could injure? I find myself unequal to the task of villain; she has gained my soul and made it honest like her own. I cannot, cannot hurt her.—Doctor, retire.

Exit Foigard.

Madam, behold your lover and your proselyte and judge of my passion by my conversion: I'm all a

---

81 Swiss] The Swiss were renowned for being mercenary soldiers.

82 Eddystone] lighthouse destroyed by a great storm in 1703

83 Hybla] mountain in Sicily known for its honey

lie, nor dare I give a fiction to your arms; I'm all counterfeit except my passion.

DORINDA.

Forbid it, Heaven! A counterfeit!

AIMWELL.

I am no lord, but a poor needy man come with a mean, a scandalous design to prey upon your fortune. But the beauties of your mind and person have so won me from myself, that like a trusty servant, I prefer the interest of my mistress to my own.

DORINDA.

Sure I have had the dream of some poor mariner, a sleepy image of a welcome port, and wake involved in storms!—Pray sir, who are you?

AIMWELL.

Brother to the man whose title I usurped, but stranger to his honor or his fortune.

DORINDA.

Matchless honesty! Once I was proud, sir, of your wealth and title but now am prouder that you want* it. Now I can show my love was justly leveled and had no aim but love.—Doctor, come in.

Enter Foigard at one door, Gipsey at another, who whispers Dorinda.

[*To Foigard.*] Your pardon, sir, we shannot want you now.[1] [*To Aimwell.*] Sir, you must excuse me, I'll wait on you presently.* (*Exit with Gipsey.*)

FOIGARD.

Upon my shoul, now, dis is foolish! (*Exit.*)

AIMWELL.

Gone! and bid the priest depart! It has an ominous look.

Enter Archer.

ARCHER.

Courage, Tom! Shall I wish you joy?

AIMWELL.

No.

ARCHER.

'Oons* man, what ha' you been doing?

AIMWELL.

Oh Archer, my honesty, I fear, has ruined me.

ARCHER.

How?

AIMWELL.

I have discovered* myself.

ARCHER.

Discovered! and without my consent? What! have I embarked my small remains in the same bottom with yours, and you dispose of all without my partnership?

AIMWELL.

Oh Archer, I own my fault!

ARCHER.

After conviction, 'tis then too late for pardon. You may remember, Mr. Aimwell, that you proposed this folly. As you begun, so end it. Henceforth I'll hunt my fortune single. So farewell!

AIMWELL.

Stay, my dear Archer, but a minute!

ARCHER.

Stay! What, to be despised, exposed and laughed at? No, I would sooner change conditions with the worst of the rogues we just now bound, than bear one scornful smile from the proud knight that once I treated as my equal.

AIMWELL.

What knight?

ARCHER.

Sir Charles Freeman, brother to the lady that I had almost—but no matter for that. 'Tis a cursed night's work, and so I leave you to make your best on't. (*Going.*)

AIMWELL.

Freeman! One word, Archer. Still I have hopes; methought she received my confession with pleasure.

ARCHER.

S'death! who doubts it?

AIMWELL.

She consented after to the match, and still I dare believe she will be just.

ARCHER.

To herself, I warrant her, as you should have been.

AIMWELL.

By all my hopes, she comes, and smiling comes!

Enter Dorinda, mighty gay.

DORINDA.

Come my dear lord, I fly with impatience to your

arms. The minutes of my absence was a tedious year. Where's this tedious priest?

Enter Foigard.

ARCHER.
'Oons, a brave* girl!

DORINDA.
I suppose, my lord, this gentleman is privy to our affairs?

ARCHER.
Yes, yes, madam. I'm to be your father.

DORINDA.
Come priest, do your office.

ARCHER.
Make haste, make haste! Couple 'em any way. (*Takes Aimwell's hand.*) Come madam, I'm to give you—

DORINDA.
My mind's altered. I won't.

ARCHER.
Eh?

AIMWELL.
I'm confounded.

FOIGARD.
Upon my shoul, and sho is myshelf.

ARCHER.
What's the matter now, madam?

DORINDA.
Look ye, sir, one generous* action deserves another: this gentleman's honor obliged him to hide nothing from me; my justice engages me to conceal nothing from him. In short, sir, you are the person that you thought you counterfeited: you are the true Lord Viscount Aimwell, and I wish your lordship joy.—Now priest, you may be gone. If my lord is pleased now with the match, let his lordship marry me in the face of the world.

AIMWELL, ARCHER.
What does she mean?

DORINDA.
Here's a witness for my truth.

Enter Sir Charles and Mrs. Sullen.

SIR CHARLES.
My dear Lord Aimwell, I wish you joy.

AIMWELL.
Of what?

SIR CHARLES.
Of your honor and estate: your brother died the day before I left London, and all your friends have writ after you to Brussels; among the rest I did myself the honor.

ARCHER.
Hark ye, Sir Knight, don't you banter now?

SIR CHARLES.
'Tis truth upon my honor.

AIMWELL.
Thanks to the pregnant stars that formed this accident!

ARCHER.
Thanks to the womb of time that brought it forth! Away with it!

AIMWELL.
Thanks to my guardian angel that led me to the prize. (*Taking Dorinda's hand.*)

ARCHER.
And double thanks to the noble Sir Charles Freeman. My lord, I wish you joy.—My lady, I wish you joy.—Egad, Sir Freeman, you're the honestest fellow living.—S'death, I'm grown strange airy upon this matter!—My lord, how d'ye? A word, my lord: don't you remember something of a previous agreement that entitles me to the moiety of this lady's fortune, which, I think, will amount to five thousand pound?

AIMWELL.
Not a penny, Archer! You would ha' cut my throat just now because I would not deceive this lady.

ARCHER.
Aye, and I'll cut your throat again, if you should deceive her now.

AIMWELL.
That's what I expected, and to end the dispute: the lady's fortune is ten thousand pound; we'll divide stakes. Take the ten thousand pound, or the lady.

DORINDA.
How! Is your lordship so indifferent?

ARCHER.
No, no, no, madam, his lordship knows very well that I'll take the money. I leave you to his lordship, and so we're both provided for.

Enter Count Bellair.

COUNT BELLAIR.
Mesdames and Messieurs, I am your servant trice humble! I hear you be rob here.

AIMWELL.
The ladies have been in some danger, sir.

COUNT BELLAIR.
And begar,* our inn be rob too!

AIMWELL.
Our inn! By whom?

COUNT BELLAIR.
By the landlord, begar! Garzoon, he has rob himself and run away!

ARCHER.
Robbed himself!

COUNT BELLAIR.
Aye, begar, and me too of a hundre pound.

ARCHER.
A hundred pound?

COUNT BELLAIR.
Yes, that I owed him.

AIMWELL.
Our money's gone, Frank.

ARCHER.
Rot the money! My wench is gone.—*Savez-vous quelque chose de Mademoiselle Cherry?*[84]

Enter a fellow with a strongbox and a letter.

FELLOW.
Is there one Martin, here?

ARCHER.
Aye, aye, who wants him?

FELLOW.
I have a box here and letter for him.

ARCHER. (*Taking the box.*)
Ha, ha, ha! what's here? Legerdemain! By this light, my lord, our money again! But this unfolds the riddle. (*Opening the letter, reads.*) Hum, hum, hum. Oh, 'tis for the public good and must be communicated to the company. "Mr. Martin, My father being afraid of an impeachment by the rogues that are taken tonight is gone off, but if you can procure him a pardon, he will make great discoveries* that may be useful to the country. Could I have met you instead of your master tonight, I would have delivered myself into your hands with a sum that much exceeds that in your strongbox, which I have sent you, with an assurance to my dear Martin, that I shall ever be his most faithful friend till death. Cherry Bonniface." There's a billet-doux for you! As for the father, I think he ought to be encouraged, and for the daughter—pray my lord, persuade your bride to take her into her service instead of Gipsey.

AIMWELL.
I can assure you, madam, your deliverance was owing to her discovery.*

DORINDA.
Your command, my lord, will do without the obligation. I'll take care of her.

SIR CHARLES.
This good company meets opportunely in favor of a design I have in behalf of my unfortunate sister. I intend to part her from her husband.—Gentlemen, will you assist me?

ARCHER.
Assist you! S'death, who would not!

COUNT BELLAIR.
Assist! Garzoon, we all assest!

Enter Sullen.

SULLEN.
What's all this? They tell me, Spouse, that you had like to have been robbed.

MRS. SULLEN.
Truly, Spouse, I was pretty near it, had not these two gentlemen interposed.

SULLEN.
How came these gentlemen here?

MRS. SULLEN.
That's his way of returning thanks, you must know.

COUNT BELLAIR.
Garzoon, the question be apropos for all dat!

SIR CHARLES.
You promised last night, sir, that you would deliver your lady to me this morning.

SULLEN.
Humph!

ARCHER.
Humph! What do you mean by humph? Sir, you shall deliver her. In short, sir, we have saved you

84 *Savez-vous … Cherry?*] "Do you know anything about Miss Cherry?" (Fr.).

and your family, and if you are not civil, we'll unbind the rogues, join with 'um, and set fire to your house.—What does the man mean? not part with his wife!

COUNT BELLAIR.
Aye garzoon, de man no understand common justice.

MRS. SULLEN.
Hold gentlemen, all things here must move by consent. Compulsion would spoil us. Let my dear and I talk the matter over, and you shall judge it between us.

SULLEN.
Let me know first who are to be our judges.—Pray sir, who are you?

SIR CHARLES.
I am Sir Charles Freeman, come to take away your wife.

SULLEN.
And you, good sir?

AIMWELL.
Thomas[m] Viscount Aimwell, come to take away your sister.

SULLEN.
And you pray, sir?

ARCHER.
Francis Archer, Esquire, come—

SULLEN.
To take away my mother, I hope. Gentlemen, you're heartily welcome. I never met with three more obliging people since I was born.—And now, my dear, if you please, you shall have the first word.

ARCHER.
And the last for five pound.

MRS. SULLEN.
Spouse.

SULLEN.
Rib.*

MRS. SULLEN.
How long have we been married?

SULLEN.
By the almanac, fourteen months—but by my account, fourteen years.

MRS. SULLEN.
'Tis thereabout by my reckoning.

COUNT BELLAIR.
Garzoon, their account will agree.

MRS. SULLEN.
Pray Spouse, what did you marry for?

SULLEN.
To get an heir to my estate.

SIR CHARLES.
And have you succeeded?

SULLEN.
No.

ARCHER.
The condition fails of his side.—Pray madam, what did you marry for?

MRS. SULLEN.
To support the weakness of my sex by the strength of his, and to enjoy the pleasures of an agreeable society.

SIR CHARLES.
Are your expectations answered?

MRS. SULLEN.
No.

COUNT BELLAIR.
A clear case! a clear case!

SIR CHARLES.
What are the bars to your mutual contentment?

MRS. SULLEN.
In the first place I can't drink ale with him.

SULLEN.
Nor can I drink tea with her.

MRS. SULLEN.
I can't hunt with you.

SULLEN.
Nor can I dance with you.

MRS. SULLEN.
I hate cocking[85] and racing.

SULLEN.
And I abhor ombre and piquet.

MRS. SULLEN.
Your silence is intolerable.

SULLEN.
Your prating is worse.

MRS. SULLEN.
Have we not been a perpetual offence to each other—a gnawing vulture at the heart?

---

85 cocking] cock-fighting

SULLEN.
A frightful goblin to the sight?

MRS. SULLEN.
A porcupine to the feeling?

SULLEN.
Perpetual wormwood to the taste?

MRS. SULLEN.
Is there on earth a thing we could agree in?

SULLEN.
Yes: to part.

MRS. SULLEN.
With all my heart.

SULLEN.
Your hand.

MRS. SULLEN.
Here.

SULLEN.
These hands joined us, these shall part us. Away!

MRS. SULLEN.
North.

SULLEN.
South.

MRS. SULLEN.
East.

SULLEN.
West—far as the poles asunder.

COUNT BELLAIR.
Begar, the ceremony be vera pretty.

SIR CHARLES.
Now Mr. Sullen, there wants* only my sister's fortune to make us easy.

SULLEN.
Sir Charles, you love your sister, and I love her fortune; every one to his fancy.

ARCHER.
Then you won't refund?

SULLEN.
Not a stiver.

ARCHER.
Then I find, madam, you must e'en go to your prison again.

COUNT BELLAIR.
What is the portion?

SIR CHARLES.
Ten thousand pound, sir.

COUNT BELLAIR.
Garzoon, I'll pay it, and she shall go home with me.

ARCHER.
Ha, ha, ha! French all over! Do you know, sir, what ten thousand pound English is?

COUNT BELLAIR.
No begar, not *justement.*[86]

ARCHER.
Why sir, 'tis a hundred thousand livres.

COUNT BELLAIR.
A hundre tousand livres! Ah garzoon! me canno do't. Your beauties and their fortunes are both too much for me.

ARCHER.
Then I will. This night's adventure has proved strangely lucky to us all, for Captain Gibbet in his walk had made bold, Mr. Sullen, with your study and escritoire, and had taken out all the writings of your estate, all the articles of marriage with this[n] lady, bills, bonds, leases, receipts to an infinite value. I took 'em from him, and I deliver them to Sir Charles. (*Gives him a parcel of papers and parchments.*)

SULLEN.
How, my writings! my head aches consumedly.—Well gentlemen, you shall have her fortune, but I can't talk. If you have a mind, Sir Charles, to be merry and celebrate my sister's wedding and my divorce,[87] you may command my house. But my head aches consumedly.—Scrub, bring me a dram.

ARCHER. (*To Mrs. Sullen.*)
Madam, there's a country dance to the trifle that I sung today; your hand, and we'll lead it up.

Here a dance.

ARCHER.
'Twould be hard to guess which of these parties is the better pleased, the couple joined or the couple parted: the one rejoicing in hopes of an untasted happiness, and the other in their deliverance from an experienced misery.

---

86 *justement*] exactly (Fr.)

87 divorce] Divorces were legal only by act of Parliament; however, in the comic world of the play, the Sullens have, in effect, been granted an annulment.

Both happy in the several states we find,
Those parted by consent, and those conjoined.
Consent, if mutual, saves the lawyer's fee,
Consent is law enough to set you free.

[Exeunt.]

FINIS.

Textual Notes

[a] The copytext is the first edition, a 1707 quarto (Q1). Other editions consulted include a 1708 collection of Farquhar's comedies (C), a 1728 edition of his works (W) and the modern editions of 1930 (Stonehill); of 1939, revised 1969 (Nettleton, Case, and Stone—NCS); of 1977 (Fifer); and of 1988 (Kenny).

[b] wait farther] Q1, Stonehill, NCS, Fifer, Kenny; wait, father C, W

[c] besides, that … than the ten thousand we have spent] W, Stonehill, NCSS, Fifer; besides thousand, that … than the ten we have spent Q1, Kenny (who notes no textual problem); besides, that … than the ten we have spent (C)

[d] Song … etc.] W, Stonehill, NCS, Fifer, Kenny; only the first two lines of the song are in Q1, C

[e] I'm-m] NCS; I'mm Q1, Stonehill, Fifer, Kenny; I'm C, W

[f] are objects] Q1, Kenny; are the objects C, W, Stonehill, NCS, Fifer

[g] Aha] Fifer; Ah, a Q1, Stonehill, NCS, Kenny; Ay, ay C, W

[h] A trifling … boot] W (after the epilogue), Stonehill, NCS, Fifer, Kenny; only the first two lines are in Q1, C.

[i] *Exit Dorinda*] The remainder of this act was printed in italics in the 1728 *Works* (W), with a note that said that "the entire part of the Count was cut out by the Author, after the first Night's Representation; and where he should enter in the last scene of the fifth Act, it is added to the part of Foigard."

[j] most be-tied] Q1, Stonehill, NCS (all without the hyphen); must be tied C, W, Fifer, Kenny

[k] dat is naame] Q1, C, Stonehill, Fifer, Kenny; dat is my name W, NCS

[l] shannot want you now. … Sir,] W, NCS, Fifer; shannot; won't you now, Sir? Q1, C, Stonehill; shannot want you now, Sir? Kenny

[m] Thomas] NCS, Fifer (Aimwell is called Tom in Act II, scene ii); Charles Q1, C, W, Stonehill, Kenny

[n] this] Fifer (citing a 1710 octavo); his Q1, C, W, Stonehill, NCS; your Kenny (citing a 1711 octavo)

A Bold Stroke for a Wife[a]

by Susanna Centlivre (1669?-1723)
edited by Nancy Copeland

Susanna Centlivre was one of the most important comic playwrights of the first part of the eighteenth century. She was also the most successful female dramatist between 1660 and 1800, in terms of the number of her plays that were produced and the number of years some of them, including *A Bold Stroke for a Wife*, remained in the repertoire. *A Bold Stroke* typifies her comic style in its combination of an intricate love intrigue, humours comedy (in the characterization of the guardians), and the outrageous situations and physical comedy of farce. In its emphasis on action and situation rather than wit, its mild satire, and the honest, straightforward relationship of its lovers, it exemplifies the kind of play that Shirley Strum Kenny terms "humane comedy."

First performed on 3 February 1718 at Lincoln's Inn Fields, *A Bold Stroke* was well suited to the resources of the company, which featured established comic performers such as William Bullock (Tradelove) and George Pack (Prim). Fainwell was a vehicle for Christopher Bullock, son of William, who was also co-manager of the theater during this season, while his wife, Jane, played Anne Lovely. Some of the play's features recall the harlequinades that were a mainstay of the company's repertoire. Such entertainments, not yet called pantomimes, are particularly evoked by the play's fairy-tale plot; by the centrality of transformation; and by some of the more extravagant farce, notably the scene in act three in which Fainwell convinces Periwinkle that he can make himself invisible by sinking through the stage's trapdoor.

The play portrays the mercantile culture of early-Georgian London, most explicitly in the scene inside Jonathan's Coffee-house (IV.i), but also through its characters. The guardians represent a range of propertied urban types, and Fainwell's plotting is well suited to his capitalist milieu. Like a tradesman who suits his manner to his customers, Fainwell adopts characters that flatter the prejudices of each of the guardians to get the better of them in a bargain for Anne Lovely, a bargain which is confirmed by a written contract. Anne's position within these transactions is that of a commodity, coveted by Fainwell and traded by her guardians. Her largely passive role is characteristic of the developing position of the genteel middle-class woman within capitalism, and she struggles against the Prims to exercise her right to be an idle consumer of luxury goods. The guardians too, despite their differences, all participate in the pervasive commercial culture, either as producers or consumers.

Centlivre was unequivocally Whig in her politics, and *A Bold Stroke* is permeated by Whig principles. The play constructs an implicit, Whiggish argument that the propertied interests represented by the guardians, both "trading" and "landed," should cooperate with one another and unite behind the army through supporting Colonel Fainwell, one of Centlivre's many soldier heroes. The concept of liberty, fundamental to Whig ideology, connects Centlivre's political views to her feminism: Anne Lovely, for example, speaks of the "tyranny" of her guardians in the language of political liberty.

The play was successful from its first production and became one of Centlivre's most-performed plays. Thanks to the opportunities Fainwell offers to the virtuoso comic actor, the play continued to be frequently performed throughout the eighteenth century and well into the nineteenth.

[I.i]

DRAMATIS PERSONAE

MEN

Sir Philip Modelove, an old beau.
Periwinkle, a kind of a silly virtuoso.[1]
Tradelove, a changebroker.[2]
Obadiah Prim, a Quaker.
Colonel Fainwell, in love with Mrs.* Lovely.
Freeman, his friend, a merchant.
Simon Pure, a Quaking preacher.
Mr. Sackbut,[3] a tavern-keeper.

WOMEN

Mrs. Lovely, a fortune of thirty thousand pound.
Mrs. Prim, wife to Prim the hosier.[4]
Betty, servant to Mrs. Lovely.
Footmen, drawers, etc.

A Bold Stroke for a Wife.

Omnia vincit amor.[5]

Act I, scene i. A tavern.

Colonel Fainwell and Freeman over a bottle.

FREEMAN.
Come, Colonel, His Majesty's health. You are as melancholy as if you were in love; I wish some of the beauties at Bath[6] ha'n't snapped your heart.

COLONEL.
Why, faith, Freeman, there is something in't; I have seen a lady at Bath who has kindled such a flame in me that all the waters there can't quench.

FREEMAN.
Women, like some poisonous animals, carry their antidote about 'em. Is she not to be had, Colonel?

COLONEL.
That's a difficult question to answer; however, I resolve to try. Perhaps you may be able to serve me; you merchants know one another. The lady told me herself she was under the charge of four persons.

FREEMAN.
Odso! 'Tis Mrs. Anne Lovely.

COLONEL.
The same. Do you know her?

FREEMAN.
Know her! Aye—Faith, Colonel, your condition is more desperate than you imagine; why she is the talk and pity of the whole Town; and it is the opinion of the learned that she must die a maid.

COLONEL.
Say you so? That's somewhat odd, in this charitable city. She's a woman, I hope.

FREEMAN.
For aught I know; but it had been as well for her had nature made her any other part of the creation. The man which keeps this house served her father; he is a very honest fellow and may be of use to you; we'll send for him to take a glass with us; he'll give you the whole history, and 'tis worth your hearing.

COLONEL.
But may one trust him?

FREEMAN.
With your life; I have obligations enough upon him to make him do anything; I serve him with wine. (*Knocks.*)

COLONEL.
Nay, I know him pretty well myself; I once used to frequent a club that was kept here.

Enter drawer.

DRAWER.
Gentlemen, d'you call?

FREEMAN.
Aye, send up your master.

DRAWER.
Yes, sir. (*Exit.*)

[1] virtuoso] a collector of antiquities and natural curiosities

[2] changebroker] an exchange broker, a middleman in the exchange of bills of credit

[3] Sackbut] a compound: sack,* white wine imported from Spain or the Canary Islands; butt, a wine cask

[4] hosier] a dealer in stockings and knitted underclothes

[5] *Omnia ... amor.*] Virgil, *Eclogues* X: Love conquers all (Lat.).

[6] Bath] In the eighteenth century Bath, with its medicinal springs and baths, became a fashionable summer resort for the titled and the wealthy.

COLONEL.

Do you know any of this lady's guardians, Freeman?

FREEMAN.

Yes, I know two of them very well.

COLONEL.

What are they?

Enter Sackbut.

FREEMAN.

Here comes one will give you an account of them all.—Mr. Sackbut, we sent for you to take a glass with us. 'Tis a maxim among the friends of the bottle, that as long as the master is in company one may be sure of good wine.

SACKBUT.

Sir, you shall be sure to have as good wine as you send in.—Colonel, your most humble servant; you are welcome to town.

COLONEL.

I thank you, Mr. Sackbut.

SACKBUT.

I am as glad to see you as I should a hundred tun of French claret custom-free. My service to you, sir. (*Drinks.*) You don't look so merry as you used to do. Are you not well, Colonel?

FREEMAN.

He has got a woman in his head, landlord, can you help him?

SACKBUT.

If 'tis in my power, I shan't scruple to serve my friend.

COLONEL.

'Tis one perquisite of your calling.

SACKBUT.

Aye, at t'other end of the Town,[7] where you officers use, women are good forcers of trade; a well-customed house, a handsome bar-keeper, with clean, obliging drawers, soon gets the master an estate; but our citizens* seldom do anything but cheat within the walls. But as to the lady, Colonel: Point you at particulars, or have you a good champagne[8] stomach? Are you in full pay or reduced, Colonel?

COLONEL.

Reduced, reduced, landlord.

FREEMAN.

To the miserable condition of a lover!

SACKBUT.

Pish! That's preferable to half pay; a woman's resolution may break before the peace;[9] push her home, Colonel, there's no parleying with that sex.

COLONEL.

Were the lady her own mistress, I have some reasons to believe I should soon command in chief.

FREEMAN.

You know Mrs. Lovely, Mr. Sackbut.

SACKBUT.

Know her! Aye, poor Nancy;[10] I have carried her to school many a frosty morning. Alas! If she's the woman, I pity you, Colonel. Her father, my old master, was the most whimsical, out-of-the-way tempered man I ever heard of, as you will guess by his last will and testament. This was his only child: I have heard him wish her dead a thousand times.

COLONEL.

Why so?

SACKBUT.

He hated posterity, you must know, and wished the world were to expire with himself. He used to swear if she had been a boy, he would have qualified him for the opera.[11]

FREEMAN.

'Tis a very unnatural resolution in a father.

SACKBUT.

He died worth thirty thousand pounds, which he left to this daughter, provided she married with the

---

7 t'other ... Town] the West End, the fashionable part of London, which Sackbut contrasts with the City.* Women in West End establishments would draw in customers with the prospect of sex, to the profit of the tavern owners; city cheaters were not, according to Sackbut, so enterprising.

8 champagne] probably in two senses: an open field and a military campaign

9 the peace] the Peace of Utrecht (1713) led to officers being reduced to half pay; it was unpopular with many Whigs, including Centlivre.

10 Nancy] diminutive of Anne

11 qualified ... opera] castrated him, as were the *castrati* who sang male soprano roles in Italian opera

consent of her guardians. But that she might be sure never to do so, he left her in the care of four men as opposite to each other as light and darkness. Each has his quarterly rule, and three months in a year she is obliged to be subject to each of their humours, and they are pretty different, I assure you. She is just come from Bath.

COLONEL.

'Twas there I saw her.

SACKBUT.

Aye, sir, the last quarter was her beau-guardian's. She appears in all public places during his reign.

COLONEL.

She visted a lady who boarded in the same house with me. I liked her person,* and found an opportunity to tell her so. She replied, she had no objection to mine; but if I could not reconcile contradictions, I must not think of her, for that she was condemned to the caprice of four persons who never yet agreed in any one thing, and she was obliged to please them all.

SACKBUT.

'Tis most true, sir; I'll give you a short description of the men and leave you to judge of the poor lady's condition. One is a kind of a virtuoso, a silly, half-witted fellow, but positive and surly; fond of nothing but what is antique and foreign, and wears his clothes of the fashion of the last century; dotes upon travelers and believes Sir John Mandeville[12] more than the Bible.

COLONEL.

That must be a rare old fellow!

SACKBUT.

Another is a changebroker; a fellow that will out-lie the devil for the advantage of stock and cheat his father that got him in a bargain. He is a great stickler for trade and hates everything that wears a sword.

FREEMAN.

He is a great admirer of the Dutch management[13] and swears they understand trade better than any nation under the sun.

SACKBUT.

The third is an old beau that has May in his fancy and dress, but December in his face and his heels; he admires nothing but new fashions, and those must be French; loves operas, balls, masquerades, and is always the most tawdry of the whole company on a birthday.*

COLONEL.

These are pretty opposite to one another, truly! And the fourth, what is he, landlord?

SACKBUT.

A very rigid Quaker, whose quarter begun this day. I saw Mrs. Lovely go in not above two hours ago. Sir Philip set her down. What think you now, Colonel, is not the poor lady to be pitied?

COLONEL.

Aye, and rescued too, landlord.

FREEMAN.

In my opinion, that's impossible.

COLONEL.

There is nothing impossible to a lover. What would not a man attempt for a fine woman and thirty thousand pounds? Besides, my honor is at stake; I promised to deliver her—and she bade me win her and take her.

SACKBUT.

That's fair, faith.

FREEMAN.

If it depended upon knight-errantry, I should not doubt your setting free the damsel; but to have avarice, impertinence, hypocrisy, and pride at once to deal with, requires more cunning than generally attends a man of honor.

COLONEL.

My fancy tells me I shall come off with glory; I resolve to try, however.—Do you know all the guardians, Mr. Sackbut?

SACKBUT.

Very well, sir, they all use my house.

COLONEL.

And will you assist me, if occasion be?

SACKBUT.

In everything I can, Colonel.

12 Sir John Mandeville] (fl. 1356) the ostensible author of a collection of travelers' tales, who by the eighteenth century was regarded as a great liar

13 Dutch management] The Dutch provided the English with models for advanced trade and financial practices, including the national debt and the stock market.

FREEMAN.
I'll answer for him; and whatever I can serve you in, you may depend on. I know Mr. Periwinkle and Mr. Tradelove; the latter has a very great opinion of my interest abroad. I happened to have a letter from a correspondent two hours before the news arrived of the French king's death;[14] I communicated it to him; upon which he bought up all the stock he could, and what with that and some wagers he laid, he told me, he had got to the tune of five hundred pounds; so that I am much in his good graces.

COLONEL.
I don't know but you may be of service to me, Freeman.

FREEMAN.
If I can, command me, Colonel.

COLONEL.
Is it not possible to find a suit of clothes ready-made at some of these sale shops,[15] fit to rig out a beau, think you, Mr. Sackbut?

SACKBUT.
Oh, hang 'em. No, Colonel, they keep nothing ready-made that a gentleman would be seen in. But I can fit you with a suit of clothes, if you'd make a figure—velvet and gold brocade—they were pawned to me by a French Count, who had been stripped at play and wanted money to carry him home; he promised to send for them, but I have heard nothing from him.

FREEMAN.
He has not fed upon frogs long enough yet to recover his loss! Ha, ha.

COLONEL.
Ha, ha. Well, those clothes will do, Mr. Sackbut—though we must have three or four fellows in tawdry liveries; those can be procured, I hope.

FREEMAN.
Egad, I have a brother come from the West Indies that can match you; and, for expedition sake, you shall have his servants; there's a black, a tawny-moor,[16] and a Frenchman; they don't speak one word of English, so can make no mistake.

COLONEL.
Excellent. Egad, I shall look like an Indian prince. First I'll attack my beau-guardian. Where lives he?

SACKBUT.
Faith, somewhere about St. James's;* though to say in what street, I cannot; but any chairman* will tell you where Sir Philip Modelove lives.

FREEMAN.
Oh! You'll find him in the Park* at eleven every day; at least I never passed through at that hour without seeing him there. But what do you intend?

COLONEL.
To address him in his own way, and find what he designs to do with the lady.

FREEMAN.
And what then?

COLONEL.
Nay, that I can't tell, but I shall take my measures accordingly.

SACKBUT.
Well, 'tis a mad undertaking, in my mind; but here's to your success, Colonel. (*Drinks.*)

COLONEL.
'Tis something out of the way, I confess; but Fortune may chance to smile, and I succeed. Come, landlord, let me see those clothes. Freeman, I shall expect you'll leave word with Mr. Sackbut where one may find you upon occasion; and send my equipage of India immediately, do you hear?

FREEMAN.
Immediately. (*Exit.*)

COLONEL.
Bold was the man who ventured first to sea,
But the first vent'ring lovers bolder were:
The path of love's a dark and dangerous way,
Without a landmark, or one friendly star,
And he that runs the risk, deserves the fair. (*Exit.*)

[14] French king's death] Louis XIV died September 1, 1715; this prevented France from carrying out plans to support the Jacobite rebellion in England and was therefore good for trade.

[15] sale shops] shops specializing in inferior, ready-made clothing

[16] tawny-moor] brown-skinned foreigner, originally referring to North Africans

Scene ii. Prim's House.

Enter Mrs. Lovely and her maid Betty.

BETTY.

Bless me, madam! Why do you fret and tease yourself so? This is giving them the advantage with a witness.

MRS. LOVELY.

Must I be condemned all my life to the preposterous humours of other people and pointed at by every boy in Town? Oh! I could tear my flesh and curse the hour I was born. Is it not monstrously ridiculous that they should desire to impose their Quaking dress[17] upon me at these years? When I was a child, no matter what they made me wear; but now—

BETTY.

I would resolve against it, madam; I'd see 'em hanged before I'd put on the pinched[18] cap again.

MRS. LOVELY.

Then I must never expect one moment's ease; she has rung such a peal in my ears already that I shan't have the right use of them this month. What can I do?

BETTY.

What can you not do, if you will but give your mind to it? Marry, madam.

MRS. LOVELY.

What! and have my fortune go to build churches and hospitals?

BETTY.

Why, let it go. If the Colonel loves you, as he pretends, he'll marry you without a fortune, madam; and I assure you, a colonel's lady is no despicable thing; a colonel's post will maintain you like a gentlewoman, madam.

MRS. LOVELY.

So you would advise me to give up my own fortune and throw myself upon the colonel's.

BETTY.

I would advise you to make yourself easy, madam.

MRS. LOVELY.

That's not the way, I am sure. No, no, girl, there are certain ingredients to be mingled with matrimony without which I may as well change for the worse as for the better. When the woman has fortune enough to make the man happy, if he has either honor or good manners, he'll make her easy. Love makes but a slovenly figure in that house where poverty keeps the door.

BETTY.

And so you resolve to die a maid, do you, madam?

MRS. LOVELY.

Or have it in my power to make the man I love master of my fortune.

BETTY.

Then you don't like the colonel so well as I thought you did, madam, or you would not take such a resolution.

MRS. LOVELY.

It is because I do like him, Betty, that I take such a resolution.

BETTY.

Why, do you expect, madam, the colonel can work miracles? Is it possible for him to marry you with the consent of all your guardians?

MRS. LOVELY.

Or he must not marry me at all, and so I told him; and he did not seem displeased with the news. He promised to set me free, and I, on that condition, promised to make him master of that freedom.

BETTY.

Well! I have read of enchanted castles, ladies delivered from the chains of magic, giants killed, and monsters overcome; so that I shall be the less surprised if the colonel should conjure you out of the power of your guardians. If he does, I am sure he deserves your fortune.

MRS. LOVELY.

And shall have it, girl, if it were ten times as much. For I'll ingenuously confess to thee, that I do like the colonel above all men I ever saw. There's something so *jantée*[19] in a soldier, a kind of a je ne sais quoi air that makes 'em more agreeable than the rest of mankind. They command regard, as who should say, "We are your defenders, we preserve your beauties from the insults of rude, unpolished foes," and ought to be preferred before

17 Quaking dress] the very plain, old-fashioned, and concealing style of dress worn by Quaker women

18 pinched] pleated

19 *jantée*] dashing (Fr.)

those lazy, indolent mortals, who, by dropping into their father's estate, set up their coaches and think to rattle themselves into our affections.

BETTY.

Nay, madam, I confess that the army has engrossed all the prettiest fellows. A laced coat and feather have irresistible charms.

MRS. LOVELY.

But the colonel has all the beauties of the mind, as well as person. Oh all ye powers that favor happy lovers, grant he may be mine! Thou God of Love, if thou be'st ought but name, assist my Fainwell.
Point all thy darts to aid my love's design,
And make his plots as prevalent as thine.

Act II, scene i. The park.

Enter Colonel finely dressed, three footmen after him.

COLONEL.

So, now if I can but meet this beau. Egad, methinks I cut a smart figure, and have as much of the tawdry air as any Italian count or French marquis of 'em all. Sure I shall know this knight again.—Hah! Yonder he sits, making love* to a mask,* i'faith. I'll walk up the Mall,* and come down by him. (*Exit.*)

Scene draws and discovers Sir Philip upon a bench with a woman, masked.*

SIR PHILIP.

Well, but, my dear, are you really constant to your keeper*?

WOMAN.

Yes, really, sir.—Hey day! Who comes yonder? He cuts a mighty figure.

SIR PHILIP.

Hah! A stranger, by his equipage keeping so close at his heels. He has the appearance of a man of quality.* Positively French by his dancing air.

WOMAN.

He crosses, as if he meant to sit down here.

SIR PHILIP.

He has a mind to make love to thee, child.

Enter Colonel and seats himself upon the bench by Sir Philip.

WOMAN.

It will be to no purpose if he does.

SIR PHILIP.

Are you resolved to be cruel then?

COLONEL.

You must be very cruel, indeed, if you can deny anything to so fine a gentleman, madam. (*Takes out his watch.*)

WOMAN.

I never mind the outside of a man.

COLONEL.

And I'm afraid thou art no judge of the inside.

SIR PHILIP.

I am, positively, of your mind, sir. For creatures of her function seldom penetrate beyond the pocket.

WOMAN. (*Aside.*)

Creatures of your composition have, indeed, generally more in their pockets than in their heads.

SIR PHILIP.

Pray what says your watch? Mine is down. (*Pulling out his watch.*)

COLONEL.

I want* thirty-six minutes of twelve, sir. (*Puts up his watch and takes out his snuffbox.*)

SIR PHILIP.

May I presume, sir?

COLONEL.

Sir, you honor me. (*Presenting the box.*)

SIR PHILIP. [*Aside.*]

He speaks good English, though he must be a foreigner.—This snuff is extremely good and the box prodigious fine; the work is French, I presume, sir.

COLONEL.

I bought it in Paris, sir. I do think the workmanship pretty neat.

SIR PHILIP.

Neat, 'tis exquisitely fine, sir; pray, sir, if I may take the liberty of inquiring—what country is so happy to claim the birth of the finest gentleman in the universe? France, I presume.

COLONEL.

Then you don't think me an Englishman?

SIR PHILIP.

No, upon my soul don't I.

COLONEL.
I am sorry for't.

SIR PHILIP.
Impossible you should wish to be an Englishman. Pardon me, sir, this island could not produce a person of such alertness.

COLONEL.
As this mirror shows you, sir. (*Puts up a pocket-glass to Sir Philip's face.*)

WOMAN. [*Aside.*]
Coxcombs, I'm sick to hear 'em praise one another; one seldom gets anything by such animals, not even a dinner, unless one can dine upon soup and celery. (*Exit.*)

SIR PHILIP.
Oh Ged, sir!—Will you leave us, madam? Ha, ha.

COLONEL.
She fears 'twill be only losing time to stay here, ha, ha. I know not how to distinguish you, sir, but your mien and address speak you Right Honorable.[20]

SIR PHILIP.
Thus great souls judge of others by themselves. I am only adorned with knighthood, that's all, I assure you, sir; my name is Sir Philip Modelove.

COLONEL.
Of French extraction?

SIR PHILIP.
My father was French.

COLONEL.
One may plainly perceive it—there is a certain gaiety peculiar to my nation (for I will own myself a Frenchman), which distinguishes us everywhere. A person of your figure would be a vast addition to a coronet.

SIR PHILIP.
I must own, I had the offer of a barony about five years ago,[21] but I abhorred the fatigue which must have attended it. I could never yet bring myself to join with either party.

COLONEL.
You are perfectly in the right, Sir Philip. A fine person should not embark himself in the slovenly concern of politics; dress and pleasure are objects proper for the soul of a fine gentleman.

SIR PHILIP.
And love—

COLONEL.
Oh! That's included under the article of pleasure.

SIR PHILIP.
Parbleu, il est un homme d'esprit.[22]—I must embrace you. (*Rises and embraces.*) Your sentiments are so agreeable to mine that we appear to have but one soul, for our ideas and conceptions are the same.

COLONEL. (*Aside.*)
I should be sorry for that.—You do me too much honor, Sir Philip.

SIR PHILIP.
Your vivacity and *jantée* mien assured me at first sight there was nothing of this foggy island in your composition. May I crave your name, sir?

COLONEL.
My name is La Fainwell, sir, at your service.

SIR PHILIP.
The La Fainwells are French, I know; though the name is become very numerous in Great Britain of late years. I was sure you was French the moment I laid my eyes upon you; I could not come into the supposition of your being an Englishman; this island produces few such ornaments.

COLONEL.
Pardon me, Sir Philip, this island has two things superior to all nations under the sun.

SIR PHILIP.
Aye! What are they?

COLONEL.
The ladies and the laws.

SIR PHILIP.
The laws indeed do claim a preference of other nations, but by my soul there are fine women everywhere. I must own I have felt their power in all countries.

COLONEL.
There are some finished beauties, I confess, in France, Italy, Germany, nay, even in Holland; *mais*

[20] Right Honorable] i.e. a member of the nobility

[21] offer … ago] a reference to Queen Anne's creation of twelve new Tory peers in 1712 to ensure that the Treaty of Utrecht would pass the House of Lords

[22] *Parbleu … d'esprit*] Good Lord, he is a man of wit. (Fr.)

sont bien rares.[23] But *les belles Anglaises*![24] Oh, Sir Philip, where find we such women! such symmetry of shape! such elegancy of dress! such regularity of features! such sweetness of temper! such commanding eyes! and such bewitching smiles?

SIR PHILIP.

Ah! *Parbleu, vous êtes attrapé.*[25]

COLONEL.

Non, je vous assure, chevalier[26]—but I declare there is no amusement so agreeable to my *goût*,[27] as the conversation* of a fine woman. I could never be prevailed upon to enter into what the vulgar calls the pleasure of the bottle.

SIR PHILIP.

My own taste, *positivement.* A ball or a masquerade is certainly preferable to all the productions of the vineyard.

COLONEL.

Infinitely! I hope the people of quality in England will support that branch of pleasure which was imported with their peace[28] and since naturalized by the ingenious Mr. Heidegger.[29]

SIR PHILIP.

The ladies assure me it will become part of the constitution, upon which I subscribed an hundred guineas. It will be of great service to the public, at least to the Company of Surgeons[30] and the City in general.

COLONEL.

Ha, ha, it may help to ennoble the blood of the City.[31] Are you married, Sir Philip?

SIR PHILIP.

No, nor do I believe I ever shall enter into that honorable state; I have an absolute tender for the whole sex.

COLONEL. (*Aside.*)

That's more than they have for you I dare swear.

SIR PHILIP.

And I have the honor to be very well with the ladies, I can assure you, sir, and I won't affront a million of fine women to make one happy.

COLONEL.

Nay, marriage is really reducing a man's taste to a kind of half-pleasure, but then it carries the blessing of peace along with it; one goes to sleep without fear and wakes without pain.

SIR PHILIP.

There is something of that in't; a wife is a very good dish for an English stomach, but gross feeding for nicer* palates, ha, ha, ha!

COLONEL.

I find I was very much mistaken—I imagined you had been married to that young lady which I saw in the chariot* with you this morning in Gracechurch Street.[32]

SIR PHILIP.

Who, Nancy Lovely? I am a piece of a guardian to that lady, you must know; her father, I thank him, joined me with three of the most preposterous old fellows—that upon my soul I'm in pain for the poor girl—she must certainly lead apes,[33] as the saying is, ha, ha.

COLONEL.

That's pity. Sir Philip, if the lady would give me leave, I would endeavor to avert that curse.

SIR PHILIP.

As to the lady, she'd gladly be rid of us at any rate, I believe; but here's the mischief, he who marries

---

23 *mais … rares*] but they are very rare (Fr.)

24 *les … Anglaises*] the English beauties (Fr.)

25 *Parbleu … attrapé.*] Good Lord, you are caught. (Fr.)

26 *Non … chevalier*] No, I assure you, knight. (Fr.)

27 *goût*] taste (Fr.)

28 branch … peace] The French ambassador to England, the Duc D'Aumont, held some of the earliest masked balls in London in 1713, after the Peace of Utrecht.

29 Mr. Heidegger] John James ("Count") Heidegger (1659?-1749), the manager of the Haymarket Theater, who began presenting public masquerades there in 1717

30 Company of Surgeons] the doctors' guild, the members of which will be paid for cures for venereal disease

31 ennoble … City] Masquerades were condemned for promoting immorality and the indiscriminate mingling of classes (thanks to the leveling anonymity of masquerade costume which fostered sexual liasions across class boundaries).

32 Gracechurch Street] in the City, running from London Bridge and the Monument to Cornhill; nearby was the oldest Quaker meeting-house in London.

33 lead apes] proverbial: old maids lead apes in hell as punishment for not marrying while they could.

Miss Lovely, must have the consent of us all four, or not a penny of her portion. For my part, I shall never approve of any but a man of figure, and the rest are not only averse to cleanliness, but have each a peculiar taste to gratify. For my part, I declare, I would prefer you to all men I ever saw—

COLONEL.

And I her to all women—

SIR PHILIP.

I assure you, Mr. Fainwell, I am for marrying her, for I hate the trouble of a guardian, especially among such wretches; but resolve never to agree to the choice of any one of them, and I fancy they'll be even with me, for they never came into any proposal of mine yet.

COLONEL.

I wish I had your leave to try them, Sir Philip.

SIR PHILIP.

With all my soul, sir, I can refuse a person of your appearance nothing.

COLONEL.

Sir, I am infinitely obliged to you.

SIR PHILIP.

But do you really like matrimony?

COLONEL.

I believe I could with that lady, sir.

SIR PHILIP.

The only point in which we differ—but you are master of so many qualifications that I can excuse one fault, for I must think it a fault in a fine gentleman; and that you are such, I'll give it under my hand.

COLONEL.

I wish you'd give me your consent to marry Mrs. Lovely under your hand, Sir Philip.

SIR PHILIP.

I'll do't, if you'll step into St. James's Coffee-house,[34] where we may have pen and ink. Though I can't forsee what advantage my consent will be to you without you could find a way to get the rest of the guardians'. But I'll introduce you, however; she is now at a Quaker's, where I carried her this morning, when you saw us in Gracechurch Street. I assure you she has an odd *ragoût* of guardians, as you will find when you hear the characters,* which I'll endeavor to give you as we go along.— Hey! Pierre, Jacques, Renault—where are you all, scoundrels? Order the chariot to St. James's Coffee-house.

COLONEL.

Le noir, le brun, le blanc—mortbleu, où sont ces coquins-là? Allons, monsieur le chevalier.[35]

SIR PHILIP.

Ah! *Pardonnez moi, monsieur.*

COLONEL.

Not one step, upon my soul, Sir Philip.

SIR PHILIP.

The best-bred man in Europe, positively.

Exeunt.

Scene ii. Obadiah Prim's house.

Enter Mrs. Lovely followed by Mrs. Prim.

MRS. PRIM.

Then thou[36] wilt not obey me; and thou dost really think those fal-lals becometh thee?

MRS. LOVELY.

I do, indeed.

MRS. PRIM.

Now will I be judged by all sober people, if I don't look more like a modest woman than thou dost, Anne.

MRS. LOVELY.

More like a hypocrite, you mean, Mrs. Prim.

MRS. PRIM.

Ah! Anne, Anne, that wicked Philip Modelove will undo thee. Satan so fills thy heart with pride during the three months of his guardianship, that thou becomest a stumbling block to the upright.

MRS. LOVELY.

Pray, who are they? Are the pinched cap and formal

---

34 St. James's Coffee-house] on St. James's Street, a Whig establishment, patronized by Steele and Addison

35 *Le noir … chevalier.*] The black, the brown, the white—zounds, where are these rascals? Let us go, sir knight. (Fr.)

36 thou] the use of "thee" and "thou" was one of the Quaker "public testimonies" of conversion; it was intended to reproduce biblical language and to eliminate one of the designations of rank, since inferiors were expected to use "you" to their superiors.

hood the emblems of sanctity? Does your virtue consist in your dress, Mrs. Prim?

MRS. PRIM.

It doth not consist in cut hair, spotted face,[37] and bare necks. Oh, the wickedness of this generation! The primitive women[38] knew not the abomination of hooped petticoats.

MRS. LOVELY.

No, nor the abomination of cant neither. Don't tell me, Mrs. Prim, don't. I know you have as much pride, vanity, self-conceit, and ambition among you, couched under that formal habit and sanctified countenance, as the proudest of us all; but the world begins to see your prudery.

MRS. PRIM.

Prudery! What! Do they invent new words[39] as well as new fashions? Ah! Poor, fantastic age, I pity thee. Poor deluded Anne, which dost thou think most resemblest the saint and which the sinner, thy dress or mine? Thy naked bosom allureth the eye of the bystander, encourageth the frailty of human nature, and corrupteth the soul with evil longings.

MRS. LOVELY.

And pray who corrupted your son Tobias with evil longings? Your maid Tabitha wore a handkerchief,[40] and yet he made the Saint* a sinner.

MRS. PRIM.

Well, well, spit thy malice. I confess Satan did buffet my son Tobias and my servant Tabitha; the evil spirit was at that time too strong and they both became subject to its workings—not from any outward provocation—but from an inward call; he was not tainted with the rottenness of the fashions, nor did his eyes take in the drunkenness of beauty.

MRS. LOVELY.

No! That's plainly to be seen.

MRS. PRIM.

Tabitha is one of the faithful, he fell not with a stranger.

MRS. LOVELY.

So! Then you hold wenching no crime, provided it be within the pale of your own tribe. You are an excellent casuist, truly.

Enter Obadiah Prim.

OBADIAH PRIM.

Not stripped of thy vanity yet, Anne? Why dost not thou make her put it off, Sarah?

MRS. PRIM.

She will not do it.

OBADIAH PRIM.

Verily, thy naked breasts troubleth my outward man; I pray thee hide 'em, Anne; put on a handkerchief, Anne Lovely.

MRS. LOVELY.

I hate handkerchiefs when 'tis not cold weather, Mr. Prim.

MRS. PRIM.

I have seen thee wear a handkerchief; nay, and a mask to boot, in the middle of July.

MRS. LOVELY.

Aye, to keep the sun from scorching me.

OBADIAH PRIM.

If thou couldst not bear the sunbeams, how dost thou think man should bear thy beams? Those breasts inflame desire; let them be hid, I say.

MRS. LOVELY.

Let me be quiet, I say. Must I be tormented thus forever? Sure no woman's condition ever equalled mine; foppery, folly, avarice, and hypocrisy are by turns my constant companions, and I must vary shapes as often as a player. I cannot think my father meant this tyranny! No; you usurp an authority which he never intended you should take.

OBADIAH PRIM.

Hark thee, dost thou call good counsel tyranny? Do I, or my wife, tyrannize when we desire thee in all love to put off thy tempting attire and veil thy provokers to sin?

[37] cut hair, spotted face] hair trimmed to frame the face, rather than being pulled straight back; face fashionably decorated with patches made of silk or velvet

[38] primitive women] women of the earliest Christian church

[39] Prudery … new words] prudishness; originally a French word; the first recorded English usage occurs in *The Tatler,* No. 126 (1709).

[40] handkerchief] scarf draped around the neck to conceal a low neckline

MRS. LOVELY.
Deliver me, good Heaven! Or I shall go distracted. (*Walks about.*)

MRS. PRIM.
So! Now thy pinners are tossed and thy breasts pulled up; verily they were seen enough before; fie upon the filthy tailor who made them stays.

MRS. LOVELY.
I wish I were in my grave! Kill me rather than treat me thus.

OBADIAH PRIM.
Kill thee! Ha, ha; thou think'st thou art acting some lewd play sure; kill thee! Art thou prepared for death, Anne Lovely? No, no, thou wouldst rather have a husband, Anne. Thou wantest a gilt coach with six lazy fellows behind to flaunt it in the Ring* of vanity among the princes and rulers of the land, who pamper themselves with the fatness thereof; but I will take care that none shall squander away thy father's estate; thou shalt marry none such, Anne.

MRS. LOVELY.
Would you marry me to one of your own canting sect?[b]

OBADIAH PRIM.
Yea, verily, none else shall ever get my consent, I do assure thee, Anne.

MRS. LOVELY.
And I do assure thee, Obadiah, that I will as soon turn papist and die in a convent.

MRS. PRIM.
Oh wickedness!

MRS. LOVELY.
Oh stupidity!

OBADIAH PRIM.
Oh blindness of heart!

MRS. LOVELY. [*Aside to Prim.*]
Thou blinder of the world, don't provoke me, lest I betray your sanctity and leave your wife to judge of your purity. What were the emotions of your spirit when you squeezed Mary by the hand last night in the pantry, when she told you, you bussed so filthily? Ah! You had no aversion to naked bosoms when you begged her to show you a little, little, little bit of her delicious bubby. Don't you remember those words, Mr. Prim?

MRS. PRIM.
What does she say, Obadiah?

OBADIAH PRIM.
She talketh unintelligibly, Sarah. (*Aside.*) Which way did she hear this? This should not have reached the ears of the wicked ones; verily, it troubleth me.

Enter servant.

SERVANT.
Philip Modelove, whom they call Sir Philip,[41] is below, and such another with him; shall I send them up?

OBADIAH PRIM.
Yea. (*Exit [servant].*)

Enter Sir Philip and Colonel.

SIR PHILIP.
How dost thou do, Friend Prim. Odso! My she-Friend here too! What, you are documenting[42] Miss Nancy, reading her a lecture upon the pinched coif, I warrant ye.

MRS. PRIM.
I am sure thou never readest her any lecture that was good.—My flesh riseth so at these wicked ones that prudence adviseth me to withdraw from their sight. (*Exit.*)

COLONEL. (*Aside.*)
Oh! That I could find means to speak to her! How charming she appears! I wish I could get this letter into her hand.

SIR PHILIP.
Well, Miss Cocky,[43] I hope thou hast got the better of them.

MRS. LOVELY.
The difficulties of my life are not to be surmounted, Sir Philip. (*Aside.*) I hate the impertinence of him as much as the stupidity of the other.

OBADIAH PRIM.
Verily, Philip, thou wilt spoil this maiden.

41 Philip ... Sir Philip] the refusal to use honorific titles was another Quaker public testimony.

42 documenting] admonishing in an authoritative or imperious manner

43 Miss Cocky] a term of endearment

SIR PHILIP.

I find we still differ in opinion; but that we may none of us spoil her, prithee, Prim, let us consent to marry her. I have sent for our brother guardians to meet me here about that very thing.—Madam, will you give me leave to recommend a husband to you? Here's a gentleman which, in my mind, you can have no objection to. (*Presents the Colonel to her; she looks another way.*)

MRS. LOVELY. (*Aside.*)

Heaven deliver me from the formal and the fantastic fool.

COLONEL.

A fine woman, a fine horse, and fine equipage are the finest things in the universe. And if I am so happy to possess you, madam, I shall become the envy of mankind, as much as you outshine your whole sex. (*As he takes her hand to kiss it, he endeavors to put a letter into it; she lets it drop; Prim takes it up.*)

MRS. LOVELY. (*Turning from him.*)

I have no ambition to appear conspicuously ridiculous, sir.

COLONEL.

So fall[c] the hopes of Fainwell.

MRS. LOVELY. (*Aside.*)

Hah! Fainwell! 'Tis he! What have I done? Prim has the letter and all will be discovered.

OBADIAH PRIM.

Friend, I know not thy name, so cannot call thee by it, but thou seest thy letter is unwelcome to the maiden; she will not read it.

MRS. LOVELY.

Nor shall you. (*Snatches the letter.*) I'll tear it in a thousand pieces and scatter it, as I will the hopes of all those that any of you shall recommend to me. (*Tears the letter.*)

SIR PHILIP.

Hah! Right woman, faith!

COLONEL. (*Aside.*)

Excellent woman.

OBADIAH PRIM.

Friend, thy garb favoreth too much of the vanity of the age for my approbation; nothing that resembleth Philip Modelove shall I love, mark that; therefore, Friend Philip, bring no more of thy own apes under my roof.

SIR PHILIP.

I am so entirely a stranger to the monsters of thy breed that I shall bring none of them, I am sure.

COLONEL. (*Aside.*)

I am likely to have a pretty task by that time I have gone through them all; but she's a city worth taking and egad I'll carry on the siege. If I can but blow up the outworks, I fancy I am pretty secure of the town.

Enter servant.

SERVANT. (*To Sir Philip.*)

Toby Periwinkle and Thomas Tradelove demandeth to see thee.

SIR PHILIP.

Bid them come up.

MRS. LOVELY.

Deliver me from such an inundation of noise and nonsense. [*Aside.*] Oh Fainwell! Whatever thy contrivance is, prosper it Heaven; but oh, I fear thou never canst redeem me. (*Exit.*)

SIR PHILIP.

Sic transit gloria mundi.

Enter Mr. Periwinkle and Tradelove.

(*Aside to the Colonel.*) These are my brother guardians, Mr. Fainwell; prithee observe the creatures.

TRADELOVE.

Well, Sir Philip, I obey your summons.

PERIWINKLE.

Pray, what have you to offer for the good of Mrs. Lovely, Sir Philip?

SIR PHILIP.

First, I desire to know what you intend to do with that lady. Must she be sent to the Indies for a venture,[44] or live to be an old maid and then entered amongst your curiosities and shown for a monster,[45] Mr. Periwinkle?

---

44 sent … venture] sent to the colonies in one of Tradelove's enterprises, here perhaps securing a marriage to a wealthy planter

45 live … monster] old maids were considered unnatural in the sense that their reproductive capacities were not turned to account; as a virtuoso, Periwinkle collects such oddities ("curiosities").

COLONEL. (*Aside.*)

Humph, curiosities! That must be the virtuoso.

PERIWINKLE.

Why, what would you do with her?

SIR PHILIP.

I would recommend this gentleman to her for a husband, sir—a person whom I have picked out from the whole race of mankind.

OBADIAH PRIM.

I would advise thee to shuffle him again with the rest of mankind, for I like him not.

COLONEL.

Pray, sir, without offence to your formality, what may be your objections?

OBADIAH PRIM.

Thy person; thy manners; thy dress; thy acquaintance; thy everything, Friend.

SIR PHILIP.

You are most particulary obliging, Friend, ha, ha.

TRADELOVE.

What business do you follow, pray, sir?

COLONEL. (*Aside.*)

Humph, by that question he must be the broker.—Business, sir! The business of a gentleman.

TRADELOVE.

That is as much to say, you dress fine, feed high, lie with every woman you like, and pay your surgeon's bills[46] better than your tailor's or your butcher's.

COLONEL.

The Court is much obliged to you, sir, for your character* of a gentleman.

TRADELOVE.

The Court, sir! What would the Court do without us citizens?

SIR PHILIP.

Without your wives and daughters, you mean, Mr. Tradelove?

PERIWINKLE.

Have you ever traveled, sir?

COLONEL. [*Aside.*]

That question must not be answered now.—In books I have, sir.

PERIWINKLE.

In books? That's fine traveling indeed!—Sir Philip, when you present a person I like, he shall have my consent to marry Mrs. Lovely—till when, your servant. (*Exit.*)

COLONEL. (*Aside.*)

I'll make you like me before I have done with you, or I am mistaken.

TRADELOVE.

And when you can convince me that a beau is more useful to my country than a merchant, you shall have mine—till then, you must excuse me. (*Exit.*)

COLONEL. (*Aside.*)

So much for trade. I'll fit* you too.

SIR PHILIP.

In my opinion, this is very inhumane treatment as to the lady, Mr. Prim.

OBADIAH PRIM.

Thy opinion and mine happens to differ as much as our occupations, Friend; business requireth my presence and folly thine, and so I must bid thee farewell. (*Exit.*)

SIR PHILIP.

Here's breeding for you, Mr. Fainwell! Gad take me, I'd give half my estate to see these rascals bit.*

COLONEL. (*Aside.*)

I hope to bite you all, if my plots hit.

Act III, scene i. The tavern.

Sackbut and the Colonel in an Egyptian dress.[47]

SACKBUT.

A lucky beginning, Colonel—you have got the old beau's consent.

COLONEL.

Aye, he's a reasonable creature, but the other three will require some pains. Shall I pass upon him, think you? Egad, in my mind, I look as antique as if I had been preserved in the ark.

SACKBUT.

Pass upon him! Aye, aye, as roundly as white wine

---

46 pay … bills] payment for cures for venereal disease

47 *an Egyptian dress*] probably the conventional theatrical costume for Middle-Eastern characters: a long robe, baggy breeches, and a turban

dashed with sack* does for mountain[48] and sherry, if you have but assurance enough.

COLONEL.

I have no apprehension from that quarter; assurance is the cockade of a soldier.

SACKBUT.

Aye, but the assurance of a soldier differs much from that of a traveler. Can you lie with a good grace?

COLONEL.

As heartily, when my mistress is the prize, as I would meet the foe when my country called and king commanded; so don't you fear that part; if he don't know me again, I'm safe. I hope he'll come.

SACKBUT.

I wish all my debts would come as sure. I told him you had been a great traveler, had many valuable curiosities, and was a person of a most singular taste; he seemed transported and begged me to keep you till he came.

COLONEL.

Aye, aye, he need not fear my running away. Let's have a bottle of sack, landlord, our ancestors drank sack.

SACKBUT.

You shall have it.

COLONEL.

And whereabouts is the trap door you mentioned?

SACKBUT.

There's the conveyance, sir. (*Exit.*)

COLONEL.

Now if I should cheat all these roguish guardians and carry off my mistress in triumph, it would be what the French call a *grand coup d'éclat.*[49] Odso! Here comes Periwinkle. Ah! Deuce take this beard; pray Jupiter it does not give me the slip and spoil all.

Enter Sackbut with wine and Periwinkle following.

SACKBUT.

Sir, this gentleman, hearing you have been a great traveler and a person of fine speculation,[50] begs leave to take a glass with you; he is a man of curious taste himself.

COLONEL.

The gentleman has it in his face and garb: sir, you are welcome.

PERIWINKLE.

Sir, I honor a traveler and men of your inquiring disposition. The oddness of your habit pleases me extremely; 'tis very antique, and for that I like it.

COLONEL.

It is very antique, sir. This habit once belonged to the famous Claudius Ptolemeus,[51] who lived in the year a hundred and thirty five.

SACKBUT. (*Aside.*)

If he keeps up to the sample, he shall lie with the devil for a bean-stack and win it every straw.[52]

PERIWINKLE.

A hundred and thirty-five! Why, that's prodigious now. Well, certainly 'tis the finest thing in the world to be a traveler.

COLONEL.

For my part, I value none of the modern fashions of[53] a fig-leaf.

PERIWINKLE.

No more do I, sir; I had rather be the jest of a fool, than his favorite. I am laughed at here for my singularity. This coat, you must know, sir, was formerly worn by that ingenious and very learned person, John Tradescant.[54]

COLONEL.

John Tradescant! Let me embrace you, sir. John Tradescant was my uncle, by mother-side; and I thank you for the honor you do his memory; he was a very curious man indeed.

PERIWINKLE.

Your uncle, sir! Nay then, 'tis no wonder that your taste is so refined; why, you have it in your blood.

48 mountain] a variety of Malaga white wine made from grapes grown in the mountains

49 *grand ... d'éclat*] great, dazzling feat (Fr.)

50 speculation] profound, conjectural reasoning

51 Claudius Ptolemeus] famous Greek astronomer, mathematician, and geographer of Alexandria, also known as Ptolemy

52 lie ... straw] In a lying contest with the devil for a stack of recently harvested beans, the Colonel would win it down to the last straw.

53 of] at

54 John Tradsescant] (1608-1662) traveler, naturalist, and gardener; his collection of natural curiosities was famous and became the basis of the Ashmolean Museum.

My humble service to you, sir, to the immortal memory of John Tradescant, your never-to-be-forgotten uncle. (*Drinks.*)

COLONEL.

Give me a glass, landlord.

PERIWINKLE.

I find you are primitive even in your wine; canary was the drink of our wise forefathers; 'tis balsamic and saves the charge of apothecaries' cordials. Oh! that I had lived in your uncle's days! Or rather, that he were now alive. Oh! How proud he'd be of such a nephew!

SACKBUT. (*Aside.*)

Oh pox! That would have spoiled the jest.

PERIWINKLE.

A person of your curiosity must have collected many rarities.

COLONEL.

I have some, sir, which are not yet come ashore, as an Egyptian's idol.

PERIWINKLE.

Pray, what might that be?

COLONEL.

It is, sir, a kind of an ape, which they formerly worshipped in that country; I took it from the breast of a female mummy.

PERIWINKLE.

Ha, ha! Our women retain part of their idolatry to this day, for many an ape lies on a lady's breast, ha, ha—

SACKBUT. (*Aside.*)

A smart old thief.

COLONEL.

Two tusks of an hippopotamus, two pair of Chinese nutcrackers, and one Egyptian mummy.

PERIWINKLE.

Pray, sir, have you never a crocodile?

COLONEL.

Humph! The boatswain brought one with design to show it, but touching at Rotterdam and hearing it was no rarity in England, he sold it to a Dutch poet.

SACKBUT.

The devil's in that nation, it rivals us in everything.

PERIWINKLE.

I should have been very glad to have seen a living crocodile.

COLONEL.

My genius led me to things more worthy of my regard. Sir, I have seen the utmost limits of this globular world; I have seen the sun rise and set; know in what degree of heat he is at noon to the breadth of a hair and what quantity of combustibles he burns in a day, how much of it turns to ashes and how much to cinders.

PERIWINKLE.

To cinders? You amaze me, sir; I never heard that the sun consumed anything. Descartes[55] tells us—

COLONEL.

Descartes, with the rest of his brethren both ancient and modern, knew nothing of the matter. I tell you, sir, that nature admits an annual decay, though imperceptible to vulgar eyes. Sometimes his rays destroy below, sometimes above. You have heard of blazing comets, I suppose?

PERIWINKLE.

Yes, yes, I remember to have seen one and our astrologers tell us of another which shall happen very quickly.[56]

COLONEL.

Those comets are little islands bordering on the sun, which at certain times are set on fire by that luminous body's moving over them perpendicular, which will one day occasion a general conflagration.

SACKBUT. (*Aside.*)

One need not scruple the colonel's capacity, faith.

PERIWINKLE.

This is marvellous strange! These cinders are what I never read of in any of our learned dissertations.

COLONEL. (*Aside.*)

I don't know how the devil you should.

SACKBUT. (*Aside.*)

He has it at his fingers' ends; one would swear he had learned to lie at school, he does it so cleverly.

PERIWINKLE.

Well, you travelers see strange things! Pray, sir, have you any of those cinders?

---

55 Descartes] René Descartes (1596-1650) wrote about sun spots in his unfinished scientific work, *The World*.

56 astrologers … quickly] "astrologers" for "astronomers"; in 1705 Edmund Halley predicted the return of the comet he had observed in 1682.

COLONEL.
I have, among my other curiosities.

PERIWINKLE.
Oh, what have I lost for want of traveling! Pray, what have you else?

COLONEL.
Several things worth your attention. I have a muff made of the feathers of those geese* that saved the Roman Capitol.

PERIWINKLE.
Is't possible?

SACKBUT. (*Aside.*)
Yes, if you are such a goose to believe him.

COLONEL.
I have an Indian leaf, which open will cover an acre of land, yet folds up into so little a compass,* you may put it into your snuffbox.

SACKBUT. (*Aside.*)
Humph! That's a thunderer.

PERIWINKLE.
Amazing!

COLONEL.
Ah! Mine is but a little one; I have seen some of them that would cover one of the Caribbean islands.

PERIWINKLE.
Well, if I don't travel before I die, I shan't rest in my grave. Pray, what do the Indians with them?

COLONEL.
Sir, they use them in their wars for tents, the old women for riding hoods, the young for fans and umbrellas.

SACKBUT. (*Aside.*)
He has a fruitful invention.

PERIWINKLE.
I admire our East India Company[57] imports none of them; they would certainly find their account in them.

COLONEL. (*Aside.*)
Right, if they could find the leaves.—Look ye, sir, do you see this little vial?

PERIWINKLE.
Pray you, what is it?

COLONEL.
This is called *poluflosboio.*[58]

PERIWINKLE.
Poluflosboio! It has a rumbling sound.

COLONEL.
Right, sir, it proceeds from a rumbling nature. This water was part of those waves which bore Cleopatra's vessel when she sailed to meet Anthony.

PERIWINKLE.
Well, of all that ever traveled, none had a taste like you.

COLONEL.
But here's the wonder of the world. This, sir, is called, *zona*[59] or *moros musphonon,*[60] the virtues of this is inestimable.

PERIWINKLE.
Moros musphonon! What in the name of wisdom can that be? To me it seems a plain belt.

COLONEL.
This girdle has carried me all the world over.

PERIWINKLE.
You have carried it, you mean.

COLONEL.
I mean as I say, sir. Whenever I am girded with this, I am invisible; and by turning this little screw can be in the court of the Great Mogul, the Grand Seignior,[61] and King George in as little time as your cook can poach an egg.

PERIWINKLE.
You must pardon me, sir, I can't believe it.

COLONEL.
If my landlord pleases, he shall try the experiment immediately.

SACKBUT.
I thank you kindly, sir, but I have no inclination to ride post to the Devil.

---

57 East India Company] joint-stock trading company with the monopoly on trade with India and Asia

58 *poluflosboio*] [*poluphloisboio*] loud-roaring (as of the sea—Greek)

59 *zona*] Latin form of the Greek word *zone*, a sash wrapped about the waist, usually having magical properties, often called in earlier periods a girdle

60 *moros musphonon*] fanciful Greek: "mousetrap for a fool" (Stathas)

61 Grand Seignior] the Sultan of Turkey

COLONEL.
No, no, you shan't stir a foot; I'll only make you invisible.

SACKBUT.
But if you could not make me visible again?

PERIWINKLE.
Come try it upon me, sir, I am not afraid of the Devil nor all his tricks. 'Zbud,* I'll stand 'em all.

COLONEL.
There, sir, put it on. Come, landlord, you and I must face the east. (*They turn about.*) Is it on, sir?

PERIWINKLE.
'Tis on. (*They turn about again.*)

SACKBUT.
Heaven protect me! Where is he?

PERIWINKLE.
Why here, just where I was.

SACKBUT.
Where, where, in the name of virtue? Ah, poor Mr. Periwinkle! Egad, look to't, you had best, sir, and let him be seen again, or I shall have you burnt for a wizard.

COLONEL.
Have patience, good landlord.

PERIWINKLE.
But really, don't you see me now?

SACKBUT.
No more than I see my grandmother that died forty years ago.

PERIWINKLE.
Are you sure you don't lie? Methinks I stand just where I did and see you as plain as I did before.

SACKBUT.
Ah! I wish I could see you once again.

COLONEL.
Take off the girdle, sir. (*He takes it off.*)

SACKBUT.
Ah, sir, I am glad to see you with all my heart. (*Embraces him.*)

PERIWINKLE.
This is very odd; certainly, there must be some trick in't.—Pray, sir, will you do me the favor to put it on yourself?

COLONEL.
With all my heart.

PERIWINKLE.
But first I'll secure the door.

COLONEL.
You know how to turn the screw, Mr. Sackbut.

SACKBUT.
Yes, yes.—Come, Mr. Periwinkle, we must turn full east.

They turn; the Colonel sinks down a trapdoor.

COLONEL.
'Tis done; now turn.

They turn.

PERIWINKLE.
Hah! Mercy upon me! My flesh creeps upon my bones.—This must be a conjurer, Mr. Sackbut.

SACKBUT.
He is the Devil, I think.

PERIWINKLE.
Oh! Mr. Sackbut, why do you name the Devil when perhaps he may be at your elbow.

SACKBUT.
At my elbow! Marry, Heaven forbid.

COLONEL.
(*Below.*) Are you satisfied, sir?

PERIWINKLE.
Yes, sir, yes.—How hollow his voice sounds!

SACKBUT.
Yours seemed just the same. Faith, I wish this girdle were mine, I'd sell wine no more. Hark ye, Mr. Periwinkle (*takes him aside till the Colonel rises again*), if he would sell this girdle, you might travel with great expedition.

COLONEL.
But it is not to be parted with for money.

PERIWINKLE.
I am sorry for't, sir, because I think it the greatest curiosity I ever heard of.

COLONEL.
By the advice of a learned physiognomist in Grand Cairo, who consulted the lines in my face, I returned to England, where he told me I should find a rarity in the keeping of four men, which I was born to possess for the benefit of mankind, and the first of the four that gave me his consent, I should present him with this girdle. Till I have found this jewel, I shall not part with the girdle.

PERIWINKLE.
What can that rarity be? Did he not name it to you?

COLONEL.
Yes, sir; he called it a chaste, beautiful, unaffected woman.

PERIWINKLE.
Pish! Women are no rarities. I never had any great taste that way. I married, indeed, to please a father and I got a girl to please my wife; but she and the child (thank Heaven) died together. Women are the very gewgaws of the creation; playthings for boys, which, when they write man, they ought to throw aside.

SACKBUT. (*Aside.*)
A fine lecture to be read to a circle of ladies!

PERIWINKLE.
What woman is there, dressed in all the pride and foppery of the times, can boast of such a foretop[62] as the cockatoo?

COLONEL.
(*Aside.*) I must humor him.—Such a skin as the lizard?

PERIWINKLE.
Such a shining breast as the hummingbird?

COLONEL.
Such a shape as the antelope?

PERIWINKLE.
Or, in all the artful mixture of their various dresses, have they half the beauty of one box of butterflies?

COLONEL.
No, that must be allowed. For my part, if it were not for the benefit of mankind, I'd have nothing to do with them, for they are as indifferent to me as a sparrow or a flesh fly.

PERIWINKLE.
Pray, sir, what benefit is the world to reap from this lady?

COLONEL.
Why, sir, she is to bear me a son, who shall restore the art of embalming and the old Roman manner of burying their dead, and, for the benefit of posterity, he is to discover the longitude,[63] so long sought for in vain.

[62] foretop] a nautical term, applied to hair arranged on the forehead; by analogy, the cockatoo's crest

[63] discover the longitude] In 1714 Parliament had passed a bill offering a prize of £20,000 for the first person to develop an accurate way of finding the longitude at sea.

PERIWINKLE.
Od! These are very valuable things, Mr. Sackbut.

SACKBUT. (*Aside.*)
He hits it off admirably and t'other swallows it like sack* and sugar.—Certainly this lady must be your ward, Mr. Periwinkle, by her being under the care of four persons.

PERIWINKLE.
By the description it should. (*Aside.*) Egad, if I could get that girdle, I'd ride with the sun and make the tour of the whole world in four-and-twenty hours.—And are you to give that girdle to the first of the four guardians that shall give his consent to marry that lady, say you, sir?

COLONEL.
I am so ordered, when I can find him.

PERIWINKLE.
I fancy I know the very woman—her name is Anne Lovely.

COLONEL.
Excellent! He said, indeed, that the first letter of her name was *L.*

PERIWINKLE.
Did he really? Well, that's prodigiously amazing, that a person in Grand Cairo should know anything of my ward.

COLONEL.
Your ward?

PERIWINKLE.
To be plain with you, sir, I am one of those four guardians.

COLONEL.
Are you indeed, sir? I am transported to find the man who is to possess[d] this *moros musphonon* is a person of so curious a taste. Here is a writing drawn up by that famous Egyptian, which, if you will please to sign, you must turn your face full north, and the girdle is yours.

PERIWINKLE.
If I live till this boy is born, I'll be embalmed and sent to the Royal Society[64] when I die.

COLONEL.
That you shall most certainly.

[64] Royal Society] scientific society founded by Royal Charter in 1662; by 1718 it was the butt of many a joke.

Enter drawer.

DRAWER.
Here's Mr. Staytape the tailor, inquires for you, Colonel.

SACKBUT.
Who do you speak to, you son of a whore?

PERIWINKLE. (*Aside.*)
Hah! Colonel!

COLONEL. (*Aside.*)
Confound the blundering dog!

DRAWER.
Why, to Colonel—

SACKBUT.
Get you out, you rascal. (*Kicks him out and exit after him.*)

DRAWER. [*As he exits.*]
What the devil is the matter?

COLONEL.(*Aside.*)
This dog has ruined all my scheme, I see by Periwinkle's looks.

PERIWINKLE.
How finely I should have been choused.—Colonel, you'll pardon me that I did not give you your title before; it was pure ignorance, faith it was. Pray—hem, hem—pray, Colonel, what post had this learned Egyptian in your regiment?

COLONEL. (*Aside.*)
A pox of your sneer.—I don't understand you, sir.

PERIWINKLE.
No? That's strange! I understand you, Colonel. An Egyptian of Grand Cairo! Ha, ha, ha. I am sorry such a well-invented tale should do you no more service. We old fellows can see as far into a millstone* as him that picks it. I am not to be tricked out of my trust, mark that.

COLONEL. (*Aside.*)
The devil! I must carry it off; I wish I were fairly out.—Look ye, sir, you may make what jest you please, but the stars will be obeyed, sir, and, depend upon it, I shall have the lady and you none of the girdle. (*Aside.*) Now for Freeman's part of the plot. (*Exit.*)

PERIWINKLE.
The stars! Ha, ha. No star has favored you, it seems. The girdle! Ha, ha, ha, none of your legerdemain tricks can pass upon me. Why, what a pack of trumpery has this rogue picked up? His *pagod*,[65] *poluflosboios*, his *zonas*, *moros musphonons*, and the devil knows what. But I'll take care—Hah! Gone? Aye, 'twas time to sneak off.—Soho! the house! (*Enter Sackbut.*) Where is this trickster? Send for a constable, I'll have this rascal before the Lord Mayor; I'll Grand Cairo him, with a pox to him. I believe you had a hand in putting this imposture upon me, Sackbut.

SACKBUT.
Who, I, Mr. Periwinkle? I scorn it; I perceived he was a cheat and left the room on purpose to send for a constable to apprehend him, and endeavored to stop him when he went out, but the rogue made but one step from the stairs to the door, called a coach, leapt into it, and drove away like the devil, as Mr. Freeman can witness, who is at the bar and desires to speak with you; he is this minute come to town.

PERIWINKLE.
Send him in. (*Exit Sackbut.*) What a scheme this rogue had laid! How I should have been laughed at, had it succeeded! (*Enter Freeman booted and spurred.*) Mr. Freeman, your dress commands your welcome to town. What will you drink? I had like to have been imposed upon here by the veriest rascal—

FREEMAN.
I am sorry to hear it. The dog flew for't—he had not 'scaped me if I had been aware of him; Sackbut struck at him, but missed his blow, or he had done his business for him.

PERIWINKLE.
I believe you never heard of such a contrivance, Mr. Freeman, as this fellow had found out.

FREEMAN.
Mr. Sackbut has told me the whole story, Mr. Periwinkle, but now I have something to tell you of much more importance to yourself. I happened to lie one night at Coventry, and knowing your uncle, Sir Toby Periwinkle, I paid him a visit and to my great surprise found him dying.

PERIWINKLE.
Dying!

FREEMAN.
Dying, in all appearance; the servants weeping, the

---

[65] *pagod*] an Eastern idol

room in darkness; the apothecary, shaking his head, told me the doctors had given him over, and then there is small hopes, you know.

PERIWINKLE.
I hope he has made his will. He always told me he would make me his heir.

FREEMAN.
I have heard you say as much and therefore resolved to give you notice. I should think it would not be amiss if you went down tomorrow morning.

PERIWINKLE.
It is a long journey, and the roads very bad.

FREEMAN.
But he has a great estate, and the land very good. Think upon that.

PERIWINKLE.
Why, that's true, as you say; I'll think upon it. In the meantime, I give you many thanks for your civility, Mr. Freeman, and should be glad of your company to dine with me.

FREEMAN.
I am obliged to be at Jonathan's Coffee-house[66] at two, and it is now half-an-hour after one; if I dispatch my business, I'll wait on you; I know your hour.

PERIWINKLE.
You shall be very welcome, Mr. Freeman; and so, your humble servant. (*Exit.*)

Re-enter Colonel and Sackbut.

FREEMAN.
Ha, ha, ha! I have done your business, Colonel; he has swallowed the bait.

COLONEL.
I overheard all, though I am a little in the dark. I am to personate a highwayman, I suppose. That's a project I am not fond of; for though I may fright him out of his consent, he may fright me out of my life[67] when he discovers me, as he certainly must in the end.

FREEMAN.
No, no, I have a plot for you without danger, but first we must manage Tradelove. Has the tailor brought your clothes?

SACKBUT.
Yes, pox take the thief.

COLONEL.
Pox take your drawer for a jolt-headed rogue.

FREEMAN.
Well, well, no matter, I warrant we have him yet. But now you must put on the Dutch merchant.

COLONEL.
The deuce of this trading-plot. I wish he had been an old soldier, that I might have attacked him in my own way, heard him fight over all the battles of the Civil War—but for trade, by Jupiter, I shall never do it.

SACKBUT.
Never fear, Colonel, Mr. Freeman will instruct you.

FREEMAN.
You'll see what others do, the coffee-house will instruct you.

COLONEL.
I must venture, however. But I have a farther plot in my head upon Tradelove, which you must assist me in, Freeman; you are in credit with him, I heard you say.

FREEMAN.
I am, and will scruple nothing to serve you, Colonel.

COLONEL.
Come along then. Now for the Dutchman. Honest Ptolemy, by your leave,
Now must bob wig[68] and business come in play,
And a fair thirty-thousand-pounder leads the way.

Act IV, scene i. Jonathan's Coffee-house in Exchange Alley.

Crowd of people with rolls of paper and parchment[69] *in their hands; a bar, and coffee-boys waiting. Enter Tradelove and stockjobbers with rolls of paper and parchment.*

[66] Jonathan's Coffee-house] in Exchange Alley near the Royal Exchange; center for speculators; the forerunner of the Stock Exchange

[67] fright … life] because highway robbery was punishable by death

[68] bob wig] a simple, undress wig

[69] *rolls … parchment*] for recording stock transactions

FIRST STOCKJOBBER.
South Sea at seven-eighths![70] Who buys?

SECOND STOCKJOBBER.
South Sea bonds due at Michaelmas,[71] 1718. Class lottery tickets.[72]

THIRD STOCKJOBBER.
East India bonds?

FOURTH STOCKJOBBER.
What, all sellers and no buyers? Gentlemen, I'll buy a thousand pound for Tuesday next at three-fourths.

COFFEE-BOY.
Fresh coffee, gentlemen, fresh coffee?

TRADELOVE.
Hark ye, Gabriel, you'll pay the difference of that stock we transacted for t'other day.

GABRIEL.
Aye, Mr. Tradelove, here's a note for the money upon the Sword Blade Company.[73] (*Gives him a note.*)

COFFEE-BOY.
Bohea tea, gentlemen?

Enter a Man.

MAN.
Is Mr. Smuggle here?

FIRST COFFEE-BOY.
Mr. Smuggle's not here, sir, you'll find him at the books.

SECOND STOCKJOBBER.
Ho! Here come[e] two sparks from the other end of the town. What news bring they?

Enter Two Gentlemen.

TRADELOVE.
I would fain bite* that spark in the brown coat: he comes very often into the Alley, but never employs a broker.

Enter Colonel and Freeman.

SECOND STOCKJOBBER.
Who does anything in the Civil List lottery?[74] Or cacao? Zounds, where are all the Jews[75] this afternoon? Are you a bull or a bear today, Abraham?

THIRD STOCKJOBBER.
A bull, faith, but I have a good put for next week.

TRADELOVE.
Mr. Freeman, your servant! Who is that gentleman?

FREEMAN.
A Dutch merchant, just come to England. But hark ye, Mr. Tradelove, I have a piece of news will get you as much as the French king's death did, if you are expeditious.

TRADELOVE.
Say you so, sir! Pray, what is it?

FREEMAN. (*Showing him a letter.*)
Read there, I received it just now from one that belongs to the Emperor's[76] minister.

TRADELOVE. (*Reads.*)
"Sir, As I have many obligations to you, I cannot miss any opportunity to show my gratitude; this moment my lord has received a private express that the Spaniards have raised their siege from before Cagliari;[77] if this prove any advantage to you, it will answer both the ends and wishes of, sir, your most obliged humble servant, Henricus

---

70 South Sea at seven-eighths] stock in the South Sea Company, a chartered joint-stock trading company, with the monopoly on English trade with South America and the Pacific; founded in 1711, mainly to fund the national debt. Stock prices were conventionally quoted in eighths; only the final fraction is quoted.

71 Michaelmas] Feast of St. Michael, 29 September; one of the four quarter days of the business year, on which financial transactions were completed

72 Class lottery tickets] one of the lotteries run by the government to fund the national debt; tickets were divided into classes with different prizes for each.

73 Sword Blade Company] the major stock brokerage firm of the time and banker for the South Sea Company

74 Civil ... lottery] a government lottery (1713) to discharge the debts of the royal household

75 Jews] many jobbers and brokers were Jews, but prejudice reinforced the association between Jews and the market

76 Emperor's] Charles VI, Emperor of Austria

77 siege ... Cagliari] Cagliari is the capital of Sardinia, at this time part of the Austrian empire; Spain had invaded Sardinia in August 1717, provoking a crisis in the Mediterranean.

Dusseldorp. Postscript, In two or three hours the news will be public." (*Aside to Freeman.*) May one depend upon this, Mr. Freeman?

FREEMAN.
You may. I never knew this person send me a false piece of news in my life.

TRADELOVE.
Sir, I am much obliged to you. Egad, 'tis rare news.—Who sells South Sea[78] for next week?

STOCKJOBBERS. (*All together.*)
I sell; I, I, I, I, I sell.

FIRST STOCKJOBBER.
I'll sell five thousand pounds for next week at five-eighths.

SECOND STOCKJOBBER.
I'll sell ten thousand at five-eighths for the same time.

TRADELOVE.
Nay, nay, hold, hold, not all together, gentlemen, I'll be no bull, I'll buy no more than I can take. Will you sell ten thousand pound at a half for any day next week, except Saturday?

FIRST STOCKJOBBER.
I'll sell it you, Mr. Tradelove.

Freeman whispers to one of the gentlemen.

GENTLEMAN. (*Aloud.*)
The Spaniards raised the siege of Cagliari! I don't believe one word of it.

SECOND GENTLEMAN.
Raised the siege! As much as you have raised the Monument.[79]

FREEMAN.
'Tis raised, I assure you, sir.

SECOND GENTLEMAN.
What will you lay on't?

FREEMAN.
What you please.

FIRST GENTLEMAN.
Why, I have a brother upon the spot in the Emperor's service; I am certain if there were any such thing, I should have had a letter.

A STOCKJOBBER.
How's this? The siege of Cagliari raised; I wish it may be true, 'twill make business stir and stocks rise.

FIRST STOCKJOBBER.
Tradelove's a cunning fat bear; if this news proves true, I shall repent I sold him the five thousand pounds.[80]—Pray, sir, what assurance have you that the siege is raised?

FREEMAN.
There is come an express to the Emperor's minister.

SECOND STOCKJOBBER.
I'll know that presently. (*Exit.*)

FIRST GENTLEMAN.
Let it come where it will, I'll hold you fifty pounds 'tis false.

FREEMAN.
'Tis done.

SECOND GENTLEMAN.
I'll lay you a brace of hundreds upon the same.

FREEMAN.
I'll take you.

FOURTH STOCKJOBBER.
Egad, I'll hold twenty pieces 'tis not raised, sir.

FREEMAN.
Done with you too.

TRADELOVE.
I'll lay any man a brace of thousands the siege is raised.

FREEMAN. (*Aside to Tradelove.*)
The Dutch merchant is your man to take in.

TRADELOVE.
Does not he know the news?

FREEMAN. (*To Tradelove.*)
Not a syllable; if he did, he would bet a hundred thousand pound as soon as one penny; he's plaguy rich, and a mighty man at wagers.

TRADELOVE.
Say you so.—Egad, I'll bite* him if possible.—Are you from Holland, sir?

COLONEL.
Ya, mynheer.

78 South Sea] The South Sea Company traded with the Spanish empire, whose military fortunes would affect stock prices.

79 Monument] a column designed by Christopher Wren commemorating the Great Fire of 1666

80 five thousand pounds] ten thousand according to the first stockjobber's revised offer to Tradelove

TRADELOVE.
Had you the news before you came away?
COLONEL.
Wat believe you, mynheer?
TRADELOVE.
What do I believe? Why, I believe that the Spaniards have actually raised the siege of Cagliari.
COLONEL.
Wat duyvels niews is dat? 'Tis niet waer, mynheer,—'tis no true, sir.
TRADELOVE.
'Tis so true, mynheer, that I'll lay you two thousand pounds upon it.—You are sure the letter may be depended upon, Mr. Freeman?
FREEMAN. (*Aside to Tradelove.*)
Do you think I would venture my money if I were not sure of the truth of it?
COLONEL.
Two duysend pond, mynheer, 'tis gedaen—dis gentleman sal hold de gelt.[f] (*Gives Freeman money.*)
TRADELOVE.
With all my heart—this binds the wager. You have certainly lost, mynheer, the siege is raised indeed.
COLONEL.
Ik gelove't niet, Mynheer Freeman, ik sal ye dubbled houden, if you please.
FREEMAN.
I am let into the secret, therefore won't win your money.
TRADELOVE.
Ha, ha, ha! I have snapped the Dutchman, faith, ha, ha! This is no ill day's work.—Pray, may I crave your name, mynheer?
COLONEL.
Myn naem, mynheer! Myn naem is Jan Van Timtamtirelireletta Heer Van Fainwell.
TRADELOVE.
Zounds, 'tis a damned long name, I shall never remember it: Mynheer Van Tim, Tim, Tim— What the devil is it?
FREEMAN.
Oh! Never heed, I know the gentleman and will pass my word for twice the sum.
TRADELOVE.
That's enough.
COLONEL. (*Aside.*)
You'll hear of me sooner than you'll wish, old gentleman, I fancy.—You'll come to Sackbut's, Freeman? (*Exit.*)
FREEMAN. (*Aside to the Colonel.*)
Immediately.
FIRST MAN.
Humphrey Hump here?
SECOND COFFEE-BOY.
Mr. Humphrey Hump is not here; you'll find him upon the Dutch walk.[81]
TRADELOVE.
Mr. Freeman, I give you many thanks for your kindness.
FREEMAN. (*Aside.*)
I fear you'll repent when you know all.
TRADELOVE.
Will you dine with me?
FREEMAN.
I am engaged at Sackbut's; adieu. (*Exit.*)
TRADELOVE.
Sir, your humble servant. Now I'll see what I can do upon Change* with my news. (*Exit.*)

Scene ii. The tavern.

Enter Freeman and Colonel.

FREEMAN.
Ha, ha, ha! The old fellow swallowed the bait as greedily as a gudgeon.
COLONEL.
I have him, faith, ha, ha, ha. His two thousand pound's secure—if he would keep his money, he must part with the lady, ha, ha. What came of your two friends? They performed their part very well; you should have brought 'em to take a glass with us.
FREEMAN.
No matter, we'll drink a bottle together another time. I did not care to bring them hither; there's no necessity to trust them with the main secret, you know, Colonel.
COLONEL.
Nay, that's right, Freeman.

[81] Dutch walk] meeting place for Dutch merchants in the courtyard of the Royal Exchange

Enter Sackbut.

SACKBUT.

Joy, joy, Colonel, the luckiest accident in the world!

COLONEL.

What say'st thou?

SACKBUT.

This letter does your business.

COLONEL. (*Reads.*)

"To Obadiah Prim, hosier, near the building called the Monument, in London."

FREEMAN.

A letter to Prim; how came you by it?

SACKBUT.

Looking over the letters our post-woman brought, as I always do, to see what letters are directed to my house (for she can't read, you must know), I spied this to Prim, so paid for't[82] among the rest; I have given the old jade a pint of wine on purpose to delay time, till you see if the letter will be of any service; then I'll seal it up again and tell her I took it by mistake; I have read it and fancy you'll like the project—read, read, Colonel.

COLONEL. (*Reads.*)

"Friend Prim, There is arrived from Pennsylvania one Simon Pure, a leader of the faithful, who hath sojourned with us eleven days and hath been of great comfort to the brethren. He intendeth for the quarterly meeting in London; I have recommended him to thy house; I pray thee intreat him kindly and let thy wife cherish him, for he's of weakly constitution. He will depart from us the third day;[83] which is all from thy Friend in the faith, Aminidab Holdfast." Ha, ha! Excellent! I understand you, landlord, I am to personate this Simon Pure, am I not?

SACKBUT.

Don't you like the hint?

COLONEL.

Admirably well!

FREEMAN.

'Tis the best contrivance in the world, if the right Simon gets not there before you.

COLONEL.

No, no, the Quakers never ride post; he can't be here before tomorrow at soonest. Do you send and buy me a Quaker's dress, Mr. Sackbut; and suppose, Freeman, you should wait at the Bristol coach, that if you see any such person, you might contrive to give me notice.

FREEMAN.

I will.—The country dress and boots, are they ready?

SACKBUT.

Yes, yes, everything, sir.

FREEMAN.

Bring 'em in then. (*Exit Sackbut.*) Thou must dispatch Periwinkle first. Remember his uncle, Sir Toby Periwinkle, is an old bachelor of seventy-five; that he has seven hundred a year, most in abbey land;[84] that he was once in love with your mother, and shrewdly suspected by some to be your father; that you have been thirty years his steward, and ten years his gentleman—remember to improve these hints.

COLONEL.

Never fear, let me alone for that—but what's the steward's name?

FREEMAN.

His name is Pillage.

COLONEL.

Enough. (*Enter Sackbut with clothes.*) Now for the country put.[85] (*Dresses.*)

FREEMAN.

Egad, landlord, thou deservest to have the first night's lodging with the lady for thy fidelity. What say you, Colonel, shall we settle a club here, you'll make one?

COLONEL.

Make one? I'll bring a set of honest officers that will spend their money as freely to their King's health as they would their blood in his service.

82 paid for't] Postage at the time was paid by the recipient.

83 third day] Tuesday; Quakers designated the days of the week in this way to avoid the conventional designations derived from the names of the pagan gods.

84 abbey land] part of the estate of an abbey before the dissolution of the monasteries at the Reformation

85 country put] bumpkin

SACKBUT.
I thank you, Colonel. (*Bell rings.*) Here, here. (*Exit Sackbut.*)

COLONEL.
So now for my boots. (*Puts on boots.*) Shall I find you here, Freeman, when I come back?

FREEMAN.
Yes, or I'll leave word with Sackbut where he may send for me. Have you the writings? the will, and everything?

COLONEL.
All, all!

Enter Sackbut.

SACKBUT.
Zounds! Mr. Freeman! Yonder is Tradelove in the damnedest passion in the world. He swears you are in the house—he says you told him you was to dine here.

FREEMAN.
I did so. Ha, ha, ha! He has found himself bit* already.

COLONEL.
The devil! He must not see me in this dress.

SACKBUT.
I told him I expected you here, but you were not come yet.

FREEMAN.
Very well.—Make you haste out, Colonel, and let me alone to deal with him. Where is he?

SACKBUT.
In the King's Head.

COLONEL.
You remember what I told you?

FREEMAN.
Aye, aye, very well.—Landlord, let him know I am come in.—And now, Mr. Pillage, success attend you.

Exit Sackbut.

COLONEL.
Mr. Proteus, rather.
From changing shape and imitating Jove,
I draw the happy omens of my love.
I'm not the first young brother of the blade
Who made his fortune in a masquerade. (*Exit Colonel.*)

Enter Tradelove.

FREEMAN.
Zounds! Mr. Tradelove, we're bit it seems.

TRADELOVE.
Bit do you call it, Mr. Freeman, I am ruined. Pox on your news.

FREEMAN.
Pox on the rascal that sent it me.

TRADELOVE.
Sent it you! Why Gabriel Skinflint has been at the minister's and spoke with him, and he has assured him 'tis every syllable false; he received no such express.

FREEMAN.
I know it. I this minute parted with my friend, who protested he never sent me any such letter. Some roguish stockjobber has done it on purpose to make me lose my money, that's certain. I wish I knew who he was, I'd make him repent it—I have lost three hundred pounds by it.

TRADELOVE.
What signifies your three hundred pounds to what I have lost? There's two thousand pounds to that Dutchman with the cursed long name, besides the stock I bought. The devil! I could tear my flesh. I must never show my face upon Change more, for, by my soul, I can't pay it.

FREEMAN.
I am heartily sorry for't! What can I serve you in? Shall I speak to the Dutch merchant and try to get you time for the payment?

TRADELOVE.
Time! Odsheart!* I shall never be able to look up again.

FREEMAN.
I am very much concerned that I was the occasion and wish I could be an instrument of retrieving your misfortune; for my own, I value it not.—Odso! A thought comes into my head, that well improved, may be of service.

TRADELOVE.
Ah! There's no thought can be of any service to me, without paying the money or running away.

FREEMAN.
How do you know? What do you think of my proposing Mrs. Lovely to him? He is a single man,

and I heard him say he had a mind to marry an English woman. Nay, more than that, he said somebody told him, you had a pretty ward. He wished you had bet her instead of your money.

TRADELOVE.
Aye, but he'd be hanged before he'd take her instead of the money: the Dutch are too covetous for that. Besides, he did not know that there were three more of us, I suppose.

FREEMAN.
So much the better; you may venture to give him your consent, if he'll but forgive you the wager. It is not your business to tell him that your consent will signify nothing.

TRADELOVE.
That's right, as you say, but will he do it, think you?

FREEMAN.
I can't tell that, but I'll try what I can do with him. He has promised me to meet me here an hour hence; I'll feel his pulse and let you know. If I find it feasible, I'll send for you; if not, you are at liberty to take what measures you please.

TRADELOVE.
You must extol her beauty, double her portion, and tell him I have the entire disposal of her and that she can't marry without my consent and that I am a covetous rogue and will never part with her without a valuable consideration.

FREEMAN.
Aye, aye, let me alone for a lie at a pinch.

TRADELOVE.
Egad, if you can bring this to bear, Mr. Freeman, I'll make you whole again; I'll pay the three hundred pounds you lost, with all my soul.

FREEMAN.
Well, I'll use my best endeavors. Where will you be?

TRADELOVE.
At home. Pray Heaven you prosper. If I were but the sole trustee now, I should not fear it. Who the devil would be a guardian,
If when cash runs low, our coffers t'enlarge,
We can't, like other stocks, transfer our charge?
(*Exit.*)

FREEMAN.
Ha, ha, ha! He has it. (*Exit.*)

Scene iii. Periwinkle's house.

Enter Periwinkle on one side and footman on the other.

FOOTMAN.
A gentleman from Coventry inquires for you, sir.

PERIWINKLE.
From my uncle, I warrant you, bring him up. [*Exit footman.*] This will save me the trouble, as well as the expenses of a journey.

Enter Colonel.

COLONEL.
Is your name Periwinkle, sir?

PERIWINKLE.
It is, sir.

COLONEL.
I am sorry for the message I bring. My old master, whom I served these forty years, claims the sorrow due from a faithful servant to an indulgent master. (*Weeps.*)

PERIWINKLE.
By this I understand, sir, my uncle, Sir Toby Periwinkle, is dead.

COLONEL.
He is, sir, and he has left you heir to seven hundred a year in as good abbey land as ever paid Peter's pence to Rome. I wish you long to enjoy it, but my tears will flow when I think of my benefactor. (*Weeps.*) Ah! He was a good man—he has not left many of his fellows—the poor laments him sorely.

PERIWINKLE.
I pray, sir, what office bore you?

COLONEL.
I was his steward, sir.

PERIWINKLE.
I have heard him mention you with much respect; your name is—

COLONEL.
Pillage, sir.

PERIWINKLE.
Aye, Pillage! I do remember he called you Pillage. Pray, Mr. Pillage, when did my uncle die?

COLONEL.
Monday last, at four in the morning. About two he signed this will and gave it into my hands and strictly charged me to leave Coventry the moment

he expired and deliver it to you with what speed I could. I have obeyed him, sir, and there is the will. (*Gives it to Periwinkle.*)

PERIWINKLE.

'Tis very well, I'll lodge it in the Commons.*

COLONEL.

There are two things which he forgot to insert, but charged me to tell you that he desired you'd perform them as readily as if you had found them written in the will, which is to remove his corpse and bury him by his father in St. Paul, Covent Garden,* and to give all his servants mourning.

PERIWINKLE. (*Aside.*)

That will be a considerable charge; a pox of all modern fashions.—Well! It shall be done, Mr. Pillage; I will agree with one of death's fashion-mongers, called an undertaker, to go down and bring up the body.

COLONEL.

I hope, sir, I shall have the honor to serve you in the same station I did your worthy uncle; I have not many years to stay behind him and would gladly spend them in the family where I was brought up. (*Weeps.*) He was a kind and tender master to me.

PERIWINKLE.

Pray don't grieve, Mr. Pillage; you shall hold your place and everything else which you held under my uncle. You make me weep to see you so concerned. (*Weeps.*) He lived to a good old age—and we are all mortal.

COLONEL.

We are so, sir, and therefore I must beg you to sign this lease. You'll find Sir Toby has ta'en particular notice of it in his will. I could not get it time enough from the lawyer, or he had signed it before he died. (*Gives him a paper.*)

PERIWINKLE.

A lease for what?

COLONEL.

I rented a hundred a year of Sir Toby upon lease, which lease expires at Lady Day next, and I desire to renew it for twenty years—that's all, sir.

PERIWINKLE.

Let me see. (*Looks over the lease.*)

COLONEL. (*Aside.*)

Matters go swimmingly, if nothing intervene.

PERIWINKLE.

Very well. Let's see what he says in his will about it. (*Lays the lease upon the table and looks on the will.*)

COLONEL. (*Aside.*)

He's very wary, yet I fancy I shall be too cunning for him.

PERIWINKLE.

Ho, here it is. "—The farm lying—now in possession of Samuel Pillage—suffer him to renew his lease—at the same rent."—Very well, Mr. Pillage, I see my uncle does mention it, and I'll perform his will. Give me the lease. (*Colonel gives it him; he looks upon it and lays it upon the table.*) Pray you step to the door and call for a pen and ink, Mr. Pillage.

COLONEL.

I have pen and ink in my pocket, sir. (*Pulls out an inkhorn.*) I never go without that.

PERIWINKLE.

I think it belongs to your profession. (*He looks upon the pen while the Colonel changes the lease and lays down the contract.*) I doubt this is but a sorry pen, though it may serve to write my name. (*Writes.*)

COLONEL. (*Aside.*)

Little does he think what he signs.

PERIWINKLE.

There is your lease, Mr. Pillage. (*Gives him the paper.*) Now I must desire you to make what haste you can down to Coventry and take care of everything, and I'll send down the undertaker for the body; do you attend it up, and whatever charge you are at, I will repay you.

COLONEL. (*Aside.*)

You have paid me already, I thank you, sir.

PERIWINKLE.

Will you dine with me?

COLONEL.

I would rather not; there are some of my neighbors which I met as I came along, who leaves the Town this afternoon, they told me, and I should be glad of their company down.

PERIWINKLE.

Well, well, I won't detain you.

COLONEL. (*Aside.*)

I don't care how soon I am out.

PERIWINKLE.
I will give orders about mourning.

COLONEL. [*Aside.*]
You will have cause to mourn, when you know your estate imaginary only.
You'll find your hopes and cares alike are vain,
In spite of all the caution you have ta'en,
Fortune rewards the faithful lover's pain. (*Exit.*)

PERIWINKLE.
Seven hundred a year! I wish he had died seventeen years ago. What a valuable collection of rarities might I have had by this time? I might have traveled over all the known parts of the globe and made my own closet* rival the Vatican at Rome. Odso,* I have a good mind to begin my travels now—let me see—I am but sixty! My father, grandfather, and great-grandfather reached ninety-odd; I have almost forty years good. Let me consider! What will seven hundred a year amount to—in—aye! in thirty years, I'll say but thirty—thirty times seven, is seven times thirty—that is—just twenty-one thousand pound—'tis a great deal of money—I may very well reserve sixteen hundred of it for a collection of such rarities as will make my name famous to posterity. I would not die like other mortals, forgotten in a year or two, as my uncle will be. No.
With nature's curious works I'll raise my fame,
That men, till doomsday, may repeat my name.
(*Exit.*)

Scene iv. A tavern.

Freeman and Tradelove over a bottle.

TRADELOVE.
Come, Mr. Freeman, here's Mynheer Jan Van Tim, Tam, Tam—I shall never think of that Dutchman's name.

FREEMAN.
Mynheer Jan Van Timtamtirelireletta Heer Van Fainwell.

TRADELOVE.
Aye, Heer Van Fainwell, I never heard such a confounded name in life—here's his health, I say. (*Drinks.*)

FREEMAN.
With all my heart.

TRADELOVE.
Faith, I never expected to have found so generous a thing in a Dutchman.

FREEMAN.
Oh, he has nothing of the Hollander in his temper—except an antipathy to monarchy.[86] As soon as I told him your circumstances, he replied he would not be the ruin of any man for the world and immediately made this proposal himself. Let him take what time he will for the payment, said he, or if he'll give me his ward, I'll forgive him the debt.

TRADELOVE.
Well, Mr. Freeman, I can but thank you. Egad, you have made a man of me again, and if ever I lay a wager more, may I rot in a gaol.

FREEMAN.
I assure you, Mr. Tradelove, I was very much concerned because I was the occasion—though very innocently, I protest.

TRADELOVE.
I dare swear you was, Mr. Freeman.

Enter a fiddler.

FIDDLER.
Please to have a lesson of music or a song, gentlemen?

FREEMAN.
A song, aye, with all our hearts. Have you ever a merry one?

FIDDLER.
Yes, sir, my wife and I can give you a merry dialogue.

Here is the song.

TRADELOVE.
'Tis very pretty, faith.

FREEMAN.
There's something for you to drink, friend; go, lose no time.

FIDDLER.
I thank you, sir. (*Exit.*)

Enter drawer and Colonel, dressed for the Dutch merchant.

86 antipathy to monarchy] Holland was a republic.

COLONEL.
Hah, Mynheer Tradelove, Ik ben sorry voor your troubles, maer Ik sal you easie maeken, Ik wil de gelt niet hebben.
TRADELOVE.
I shall forever acknowledge the obligation, sir.
FREEMAN.
But you understand upon what condition, Mr. Tradelove: Mrs. Lovely.
COLONEL.
Ya, de juffrow sal al te regt setten, mynheer.
TRADELOVE.
With all my heart, mynheer, you shall have my consent to marry her freely.
FREEMAN.
Well then, as I am a party concerned between you, Mynheer Jan Van Timtamtirelireletta Heer Van Fainwell shall give you a discharge of your wager under his own hand, and you shall give him your consent to marry Mrs. Lovely under yours; that is the way to avoid all manner of disputes hereafter.
COLONEL.
Ya, waeragtig.
TRADELOVE.
Aye, aye, so it is, Mr. Freeman, I'll give it under mine this minute. (*Sits down to write.*)
COLONEL.
And so sal Ik. (*Sits down to write.*)
FREEMAN.
So, ho, the house. (*Enter drawer.*) Bid your master come up. [*Exit drawer.*] (*Aside.*) I'll see there be witnesses enough to the bargain.

Enter Sackbut.

SACKBUT.
Do you call, gentlemen?
FREEMAN.
Aye, Mr. Sackbut, we shall want your hand here.
TRADELOVE.
There, mynheer, there's my consent as amply as you can desire, but you must insert your own name, for I know not how to spell it; I have left a blank for it. (*Gives the Colonel a paper.*)
COLONEL.
Ya, Ik sal dat well doen.
FREEMAN.
Now, Mr. Sackbut, you and I will witness it. (*They write.*)
COLONEL.
Daer, Mynheer Tradelove, is your discharge. (*Gives him a paper.*)
TRADELOVE.
Be pleased to witness this receipt too, gentlemen.

Freeman and Sackbut put their hands.

FREEMAN.
Aye, aye, that we will.
COLONEL.
Well, mynheer, ye most meer doen, ye most myn voorspraek to de juffrow syn.
FREEMAN.
He means you must recommend him to the lady.
TRADELOVE.
That I will, and to the rest of my brother guardians.
COLONEL.
Wat, voor den duyvel, heb you meer guardians?
TRADELOVE.
Only three, mynheer.
COLONEL.
Wat donder heb ye myn betrocken, mynheer? Had Ik that gewoeten, Ik soude eaven met you geweest syn.
SACKBUT.
But Mr. Tradelove is the principal, and he can do a great deal with the rest, sir.
FREEMAN.
And he shall use his interest I promise you, mynheer.
TRADELOVE.
I will say all that ever I can think on to recommend you, mynheer, and if you please, I'll introduce you to the lady.
COLONEL.
Well, dat is waer. Maer ye must first spreken of myn to de juffrow and to de oudere gentlemen.
FREEMAN.
Aye, that's the best way, and then I and the Heer Van Fainwell will meet you there.
TRADELOVE.
I will go this moment, upon honor. Your most

obedient humble servant.—My speaking will do you little good, mynheer, ha, ha. We have bit* you, faith, ha, ha. My debt's discharged, and for the man, He's my consent—to get her if he can. (*Exit.*)

COLONEL.

Ha, ha, ha, this was a masterpiece of contrivance, Freeman.

FREEMAN.

He hugs himself with his supposed good fortune and little thinks the luck's of our side, but come, pursue the fickle goddess while she's in the mood. Now for the Quaker.

COLONEL.

That's the hardest task.
Of all the counterfeits performed by man,
A soldier makes the simplest Puritan. (*Exit.*)

Act V, scene i. Prim's house.

Enter Mrs. Prim and Mrs. Lovely in Quaker's dress, meeting.

MRS. PRIM.

So, now I like thee, Anne. Art thou not better without thy monstrous hoop coat[87]and patches! If Heaven should make thee so many black spots upon thy face, would it not fright thee, Anne?

MRS. LOVELY.

If it should turn your inside outward and show all the spots of your hypocrisy, 'twould fright me worse.

MRS. PRIM.

My hypocrisy! I scorn thy words, Anne. I lay no baits.

MRS. LOVELY.

If you did, you'd catch no fish.

MRS. PRIM.

Well, well, make thy jests, but I'd have thee to know, Anne, that I could have catched as many fish (as thou call'st them) in my time, as ever thou didst with all thy fool-traps about thee. If admirers be thy aim, thou wilt have more of them in this dress than thy other. The men, take my word for't, are most desirous to see what we are most careful to conceal.

MRS. LOVELY.

Is that the reason for your formality, Mrs. Prim? Truth will out. I ever thought, indeed, there was more design than godliness in the pinched cap.

MRS. PRIM.

Go, thou art corrupted with reading lewd plays and filthy romances, good for nothing but to lead youth into the high road of fornication. Ah! I wish thou art not already too familiar with the wicked ones.

MRS. LOVELY.

Too familiar with the wicked ones! Pray, no more of those freedoms, madam. I am familiar with none so wicked as yourself. How dare you talk thus to me! You, you, you unworthy woman you. (*Bursts into tears.*)

Enter Tradelove.

TRADELOVE.

What, in tears, Nancy? What have you done to her, Mrs. Prim, to make her weep?

MRS. LOVELY.

Done to me! I admire I keep my senses among you. But I will rid myself of your tyranny, if there be either law or justice to be had; I'll force you to give me up my liberty.

MRS. PRIM.

Thou hast more need to weep for thy sins, Anne—yea, for thy manifold sins.

MRS. LOVELY.

Don't think that I'll be still the fool which you have made me. No, I'll wear what I please, go when and where I please, and keep what company I think fit and not what you shall direct—I will.

TRADELOVE.

For my part, I do think all this very reasonable, Mrs. Lovely—'tis fit you should have your liberty, and for that very purpose I am come.

Enter Mr. Periwinkle and Obadiah Prim, with a letter in his hand.

PERIWINKLE.

I have bought some black stockings of your husband, Mrs. Prim, but he tells me the glover's trade belongs to you; therefore, I pray you look me out five or six dozen of mourning gloves, such as are given at funerals, and send them to my house.

87 hoop coat] hooped petticoat

OBADIAH PRIM.
My friend Periwinkle has got a good windfall today—seven hundred a year.

MRS. PRIM.
I wish thee joy of it, neighbor.

TRADELOVE.
What, is Sir Toby dead then?

PERIWINKLE.
He is!—You'll take care, Mrs. Prim?

MRS. PRIM.
Yea, I will, neighbor.

OBADIAH PRIM.
This letter recommendeth a speaker,[88] 'tis from Aminidab Holdfast of Bristol. Peradventure, he will be here this night; therefore, Sarah, do thou take care for his reception. (*Gives her the letter.*)

MRS. PRIM.
I will obey thee. (*Exit.*)

OBADIAH PRIM.
What art thou in the dumps for, Anne?

TRADELOVE.
We must marry her, Mr. Prim.

OBADIAH PRIM.
Why truly, if we could find a husband worth having, I should be as glad to see her married as thou wouldst, neighbor.

PERIWINKLE.
Well said, there are but few worth having.

TRADELOVE.
I can recommend you a man now, that I think you can none of you have an objection to!

Enter Sir Philip Modelove.

PERIWINKLE.
You recommend! Nay, whenever she marries, I'll recommend the husband.

SIR PHILIP.
What, must it be a whale or a rhinoceros, Mr. Periwinkle? Ha, ha, ha!—Mr. Tradelove, I have a bill* upon you (*Gives him a paper.*) and have been seeking for you all over the Town.

TRADELOVE.
I'll accept it, Sir Philip, and pay it when due.

PERIWINKLE.
He shall be none of the fops at your end of the Town, with full perukes and empty skulls, nor yet none of your trading gentry, who puzzle the heralds to find arms for their coaches. No, he shall be a man famous for travels, solidity, and curiosity, one who has searched into the profundity of nature. When Heaven shall direct such a one, he shall have my consent, because it may turn to the benefit of mankind.

MRS. LOVELY.
The benefit of mankind! What, would you anatomize me?

SIR PHILIP.
Aye, aye, madam, he would dissect you.

TRADELOVE.
Or pore over you through a microscope to see how your blood circulates from the crown of your head to the sole of your foot, ha, ha! But I have a husband for you, a man that knows how to improve your fortune, one that trades to the four corners of the globe.

MRS. LOVELY.
And would send me for a venture perhaps.

TRADELOVE.
One that will dress you in all the pride of Europe, Asia, Africa, and America—a Dutch merchant, my girl!

SIR PHILIP.
A Dutchman! Ha, ha, there's a husband for a fine lady — Ya, juffrow, will you met myn slapen? Ha, ha! He'll learn you to talk the language of the hogs, madam, ha, ha.

TRADELOVE.
He'll learn you that one merchant is of more service to a nation than fifty coxcombs. The Dutch know the trading interest to be of more benefit to the state than the landed.

SIR PHILIP.
But what is either interest to a lady?

TRADELOVE.
'Tis the merchant makes the belle. How would the ladies sparkle in the box without the merchant? The Indian diamonds! The French brocade! The Italian fan! The Flanders* lace! The fine Dutch holland! How would they vent their scandal over their tea tables? And where would you beaus have champagne to toast your mistresses, were it not for the merchant?

[88] speaker] minister

OBADIAH PRIM.

Verily, neighbor Tradelove, thou dost waste thy breath about nothing. All that thou hast said tendeth only to debauch youth and fill their heads with the pride and luxury of this world. The merchant is a very great friend to Satan and sendeth as many to his dominions as the pope.

PERIWINKLE.

Right, I say knowledge makes the man.

OBADIAH PRIM.

Yea, but not thy kind of knowledge—it is the knowledge of Truth. Search thou for the light within and not for baubles, Friend.

MRS. LOVELY.

Ah, study your country's good, Mr. Periwinkle, and not her insects. Rid you of your homebred monsters before you fetch any from abroad. I dare swear you have maggots enough in your own brain to stock all the virtuosos in Europe with butterflies.

SIR PHILIP.

By my soul, Miss Nancy's a wit.

OBADIAH PRIM.

That is more than she can say by thee, Friend. Look ye, it is in vain to talk; when I meet a man worthy of her, she shall have my leave to marry him.

MRS. LOVELY.

Provided he be one of the faithful. (*Aside.*) Was there ever such a swarm of caterpillars to blast the hopes of a woman!—Know this, that you contend in vain: I'll have no husband of your choosing, nor shall you lord it over me long. I'll try the power of an English senate. Orphans have been redressed and wills set aside, and none did ever deserve their pity more.—Oh Fainwell! Where are thy promises to free me from these vermin? Alas! The task was more difficult than he imagined!

A harder task than what the poets tell
Of yore, the fair Andromeda befell;
She but one monster feared, I've four to fear,
And see no Perseus, no deliv'rer near. (*Exit.*)

Enter servant and whispers to Prim.

SERVANT.

One Simon Pure inquireth for thee.

PERIWINKLE.

The woman is mad. (*Exit.*)

SIR PHILIP.

So are you all, in my opinion. (*Exit.*)

OBADIAH PRIM.

Friend Tradelove, business requireth my presence.

TRADELOVE.

Oh, I shan't trouble you.—Pox take him for an unmannerly dog.—However, I have kept my word with my Dutchman, and will introduce him too for all you. (*Exit.*)

Enter Colonel in a Quaker's habit.

OBADIAH PRIM.

Friend Pure, thou art welcome. How is it with Friend Holdfast and all Friends in Bristol? Timothy Littlewit, John Slenderbrain, and Christopher Keepfaith?

COLONEL. (*Aside.*)

A goodly company!—They are all in health, I thank thee for them.

OBADIAH PRIM.

Friend Holdfast writes me word that thou camest lately from Pennsylvania. How do all Friends there?

COLONEL. (*Aside.*)

What the devil shall I say? I know just as much of Pennsylvania as I do of Bristol.

OBADIAH PRIM.

Do they thrive?

COLONEL.

Yea, Friend, the blessing of their good works fall upon them.

Enter Mrs. Prim and Mrs. Lovely.

OBADIAH PRIM.

Sarah, know our Friend Pure.

MRS. PRIM.

Thou art welcome.

He salutes her.*

COLONEL. (*Aside.*)

Here comes the sum of all my wishes. How charming she appears, even in that disguise.

OBADIAH PRIM.

Why dost thou consider the maiden so intentively,[89] Friend?

89 intentively] earnestly, intently

COLONEL.

I will tell thee. About four days ago I saw a vision—this very maiden, but in vain attire, standing on a precipice—and heard a voice, which called me by my name and bade me put forth my hand and save her from the pit. I did so, and methought the damsel grew to my side.

MRS. PRIM.

What can that portend?

OBADIAH PRIM.

The damsel's conversion, I am persuaded.

MRS. LOVELY. (*Aside.*)

That's false, I'm sure.

OBADIAH PRIM.

Wilt thou use the means, Friend Pure?

COLONEL.

Means! What means? Is she not thy daughter and already one of the faithful?

MRS. PRIM.

No, alas! She's one of the ungodly.

OBADIAH PRIM.

Pray thee mind what this good man will say unto thee; he will teach thee the way that thou shouldst walk, Anne.

MRS. LOVELY.

I know my way without his instructions. I hoped to have been quiet, when once I had put on your odious formality here.

COLONEL.

Then thou wearest it out of compulsion, not choice, Friend?

MRS. LOVELY.

Thou art in the right of it, Friend.

MRS. PRIM.

Art not thou ashamed to mimic the good man? Ah! Thou art a stubborn girl.

COLONEL.

Mind her not; she hurteth not me. If thou wilt leave her alone with me, I will discuss some few points with her that may, perchance, soften her stubborness and melt her into compliance.

OBADIAH PRIM.

Content, I pray thee put it home to her. Come, Sarah, let us leave the good man with her.

MRS. LOVELY. (*Catching hold of Prim; he breaks loose and exits [with Mrs. Prim].*)

What do you mean—to leave me with this old enthusiastical[90] canter? Don't think, because I complied with your formality, to impose your ridiculous doctrine upon me.

COLONEL.

I pray thee, young woman, moderate thy passion.

MRS. LOVELY.

I pray thee, walk after thy leader; you will but lose your labor upon me.—These wretches will certainly make me mad.

COLONEL.

I am of another opinion; the spirit telleth me that I shall convert thee, Anne.

MRS. LOVELY.

'Tis a lying spirit; don't believe it.

COLONEL.

Say'st thou so? Why then thou shalt convert me, my angel. (*Catching her in his arms.*)

MRS. LOVELY. (*Shrieks.*)

Ah! Monster, hold off, or I'll tear thy eyes out.

COLONEL.

Hush! For Heaven's sake—dost thou know me? I am Fainwell.

MRS. LOVELY.

Fainwell! (*Enter old Prim. [Mrs. Lovely says] aside.*) Oh I'm undone, Prim here. I wish with all my soul I had been dumb.

OBADIAH PRIM.

What is the matter? Why didst thou shriek out, Anne?

MRS. LOVELY.

Shriek out! I'll shriek and shriek again, cry murder, thieves, or anything to drown the noise of that eternal babbler, if you leave me with him any longer.

OBADIAH PRIM.

Was that all? Fie, fie, Anne.

COLONEL.

No matter, I'll bring down her stomach, I'll warrant thee—leave us, I pray thee.

OBADIAH PRIM.

Fare thee well. (*Exit.*)

COLONEL. (*Embraces her.*)

My charming, lovely woman.

---

90 enthusiastical] having the quality of religious fanaticism

MRS. LOVELY.
What means thou by this disguise, Fainwell?
COLONEL.
To set thee free, if thou wilt perform thy promise.
MRS. LOVELY.
Make me mistress of my fortune and make thy own conditions.
COLONEL.
This night shall answer all thy wishes. See here, I have the consent of three of thy guardians already and doubt not but Prim shall make the fourth.

Prim listening.

OBADIAH PRIM. (*Aside.*)
I would gladly hear what argument the good man useth to bend her.
MRS. LOVELY.
Thy words give me new life, methinks.
OBADIAH PRIM.
What do I hear?
MRS. LOVELY.
Thou best of men, Heaven meant to bless me sure, when first I saw thee.
OBADIAH PRIM.
He hath mollified her. Oh wonderful conversion!
COLONEL.
Hah! Prim listening.—No more, my love, we are observed; seem to be edified and give 'em hopes that thou wilt turn Quaker, and leave the rest to me. (*Aloud.*) I am glad to find that thou art touched with what I said unto thee, Anne; another time I will explain the other article to thee; in the meanwhile, be thou dutiful to our Friend Prim.
MRS. LOVELY.
I shall obey thee in everything.

Enter old Prim.

OBADIAH PRIM.
Oh what a prodigious change is here! Thou hast wrought a miracle, Friend! Anne, how dost thou like the doctrine he hath preached?
MRS. LOVELY.
So well, that I could talk to him forever, methinks. I am ashamed of my former folly and ask your pardon, Mr. Prim.
COLONEL.
Enough, enough that thou art sorry; he is no pope, Anne.
OBADIAH PRIM.
Verily, thou dost rejoice me exceedingly, Friend. Will it please thee to walk into the next room and refresh thyself? Come, take the maiden by the hand.
COLONEL.
We will follow thee.

Enter servant.

SERVANT.
There is another Simon Pure inquireth for thee, master.
COLONEL. (*Aside.*)
The devil there is.
OBADIAH PRIM.
Another Simon Pure? I do not know him. Is he any relation of thine?
COLONEL.
No, Friend, I know him not. (*Aside.*) Pox take him, I wish he were in Pennsylvania again, with all my blood.
MRS. LOVELY. (*Aside.*)
What shall I do?
OBADIAH PRIM.
Bring him up.
COLONEL. [*Aside.*]
Humph! Then one of us must go down, that's certain. Now Impudence assist me.

Enter Simon Pure.

OBADIAH PRIM.
What is thy will with me, Friend?
SIMON PURE.
Didst thou not receive a letter from Aminidab Holdfast of Bristol concerning one Simon Pure?
OBADIAH PRIM.
Yea, and Simon Pure is already here, Friend.
COLONEL. (*Aside.*)
And Simon Pure will stay here, Friend, if possible.
SIMON PURE.
That's an untruth, for I am he.
COLONEL.
Take thou heed, Friend, what thou dost say; I do affirm that I am Simon Pure.

SIMON PURE.

Thy name may be Pure, Friend, but not that Pure.

COLONEL.

Yea, that Pure which my good Friend Aminidab Holdfast wrote to my Friend Prim about, the same Simon Pure that came from Pennsylvania and sojourned in Bristol eleven days. Thou wouldst not take my name from me, wouldst thou? (*Aside.*) Till I have done with it.

SIMON PURE.

Thy name! I am astonished.

COLONEL.

At what? at thy own assurance? (*Going up to him; Simon Pure starts back.*)

SIMON PURE.

Avaunt, Sathan, approach me not; I defy thee and all thy works.[91]

MRS. LOVELY. (*Aside.*)

Oh, he'll outcant him. Undone, undone forever.

COLONEL.

Hark thee, Friend, thy sham will not take. Don't exert thy voice; thou art too well acquainted with Sathan to start at him, thou wicked reprobate. What can thy design be here?

Enter servant and gives Prim a letter.

OBADIAH PRIM.

One of these must be a counterfeit, but which I cannot say.

COLONEL. (*Aside.*)

What can that letter be?

SIMON PURE.

Thou must be the Devil, Friend, that's certain, for no human power can stock so great a falsehood.

OBADIAH PRIM.

This letter sayeth that thou art better acquainted with that Prince of Darkness than any here. Read that, I pray thee, Simon. (*Gives it the Colonel.*)

COLONEL. [*Aside.*]

'Tis Freeman's hand. (*Reads.*) "There is a design formed to rob your house this night and cut your throat, and for that purpose there is a man disguised like a Quaker, who is to pass for one Simon Pure; the gang whereof I am one, though now resolved to rob no more, has been at Bristol; one of them came up in the coach with the Quaker, whose name he hath taken, and from what he gathered from him, formed that design, and did not doubt but he should impose so far upon you as to make you turn out the real Simon Pure and keep him with you. Make the right use of this. Adieu." (*Aside.*) Excellent well!

OBADIAH PRIM. (*To Simon Pure.*)

Dost thou hear this?

SIMON PURE.

Yea, but it moveth me not; that, doubtless, is the impostor. (*Pointing at the Colonel.*)

COLONEL.

Ah! Thou wicked one—now I consider thy face I remember thou didst come up in the leathern convenience[92] with me—thou hadst a black bob wig on, and a brown camblet[93] coat with brass buttons. Canst thou deny it, hah?

SIMON PURE.

Yea, I can, and with a safe conscience too, Friend.

OBADIAH PRIM.

Verily, Friend, thou art the most impudent villain I ever saw.

MRS. LOVELY. (*Aside.*)

Nay then, I'll have a fling at him too.—I remember the face of this fellow at Bath. Aye, this is he that picked my Lady Raffle's pocket upon the Grove.[94] Don't you remember that the mob pumped[95] you, Friend? This is the most notorious rogue.

SIMON PURE.

What doth provoke thee to seek my life? Thou wilt not hang me, wilt thou, wrongfully?

OBADIAH PRIM.

She will do thee no hurt, nor thou shalt do me none; therefore, get thee about thy business, Friend, and leave thy wicked course of life, or thou may'st not come off so favorably everywhere.

---

[91] *Sathan* ... works] formulaic rejection of Satan, using an archaic spelling

[92] leathern convenience] Quaker for coach

[93] camblet] a light cloth of mixed silk and wool

[94] the Grove] the Orange Grove, a public walk planted with trees named for a column honoring William of Orange

[95] pumped] put under a stream of water from a pump, for punishment

COLONEL.

Go, Friend, I would advise thee, and tempt thy fate no more.

SIMON PURE.

Yea, I will go, but it shall be to thy confusion; for I shall clear myself. I will return with some proofs that shall convince thee, Obadiah, that thou art highly imposed upon. (*Exit.*)

COLONEL. (*Aside.*)

Then here will be no staying for me, that's certain. What the devil shall I do?

OBADIAH PRIM.

What monstrous works of iniquity are there in this world, Simon!

COLONEL.

Yea, the age is full of vice. (*Aside.*) 'Sdeath,* I am so confounded, I know not what to say.

OBADIAH PRIM.

Thou art disordered, Friend—art thou not well?

COLONEL.

My spirit is greatly troubled, and something telleth me, that though I have wrought a good work in converting this maiden, this tender maiden, yet my labor will be in vain; for the evil spirit fighteth against her, and I see, yea I see with the eyes of my inward man, that Sathan will rebuffet her again, whenever I withdraw myself from her, and she will, yea this very damsel will return again to that abomination from whence I have retrieved her, as if it were, yea, as if it were out of the jaws of the Fiend—hum—

OBADIAH PRIM.

Good lack! Thinkest thou so?

MRS. LOVELY. (*Aside.*)

I must second him.—What meaneth this struggling within me? I feel the spirit resisting the vanities of this world, but the flesh is rebellious, yea the flesh—I greatly fear the flesh and the weakness thereof—hum—

OBADIAH PRIM.

The maid is inspired.

COLONEL.

Behold, her light begins to shine forth. (*Aside.*) Excellent woman!

MRS. LOVELY.

This good man hath spoken comfort unto me, yea comfort, I say; because the words which he hath breathed into my outward ears are gone through and fixed in mine heart, yea verily in mine heart, I say—and I feel the spirit doth love him exceedingly, hum—

COLONEL. (*Aside.*)

She acts it to the life.

OBADIAH PRIM.

Prodigious! The damsel is filled with the spirit, Sarah!

Enter Mrs. Prim.

MRS. PRIM.

I am greatly rejoiced to see such a change in our beloved Anne. I came to tell thee that supper stayeth for thee.

COLONEL.

I am not disposed for thy food—my spirit longeth for more delicious meat; fain would I redeem this maiden from the tribe of sinners and break those cords asunder wherewith she is bound—hum—

MRS. LOVELY.

Something whispers in my ears, methinks, that I must be subject to the will of this good man and from him only must hope for consolation—hum—it also telleth me that I am a chosen vessel to raise up seed to the faithful and that thou must consent that we two be one flesh according to the Word—hum—

OBADIAH PRIM.

What a Revelation is here? This is certainly part of thy vision, Friend, this is the maiden's growing to thy side. Ah! With what willingness should I give thee my consent, could I give thee her fortune too, but thou wilt never get the consent of the wicked ones.

COLONEL. (*Aside.*)

I wish I was as sure of yours.

OBADIAH PRIM.

My soul rejoiceth, yea, it rejoiceth, I say, to find the spirit within thee; for lo, it moveth thee with natural agitation—yea, with natural agitation, I say again, and stirreth up the seeds of thy virgin inclination towards this good man—yea, it stirreth, as one may say—yea verily, I say it stirreth up thy inclination—yea, as one would stir a pudding.

MRS. LOVELY.
I see, I see! The spirit guiding of thy hand, good Obadiah Prim, and now behold thou art signing thy consent, and now I see myself within thy arms, my Friend and Brother, yea, I am become bone of thy bone and flesh of thy flesh. (*Embraces him.*) Hum—

COLONEL. (*Aside.*)
Admirably performed.—And I will take thee in all spiritual love for an helpmeet, yea, for the wife of my bosom—and now, methinks—I feel a longing—yea, a longing, I say, for the consummation of thy love, hum—yea, I do long exceedingly.

MRS. LOVELY.
And verily, verily my spirit feeleth the same longing.

MRS. PRIM.
The spirit hath greatly moved them both. Friend Prim, thou must consent; there is no resisting of the spirit.

OBADIAH PRIM.
Yea, the light within showeth me that I shall fight a good fight—and wrestle through those reprobate fiends, thy other guardians—yea, I perceive the spirit will hedge thee into the flock of the righteous—Thou art a chosen Lamb—yea, a chosen Lamb, and I will not push thee back—no, I will not, I say—no, thou shalt leap-a, and frisk-a, and skip-a, and bound, and bound, I say—yea, bound within the fold of the righteous—yea, even within thy fold, my Brother. Fetch me the pen and ink, Sarah—and my hand shall confess its obedience to the spirit. [*Exit Mrs. Prim.*]

COLONEL. [*Aside.*]
I wish it were over.

Enter Mrs. Prim with pen and ink.

MRS. LOVELY. (*Aside.*)
I tremble lest this quaking rogue should return and spoil all.

OBADIAH PRIM.
Here, Friend, do thou write what the spirit prompteth, and I will sign it.

Colonel sits down [and writes].

MRS. PRIM.
Verily, Anne, it greatly rejoiceth me, to see thee reformed from that original wickedness wherein I found thee.

MRS. LOVELY.
I do believe thou art, and I thank thee.

COLONEL. (*Reads.*)
"This is to certify all whom it may concern, that I do freely give up all my right and title in Anne Lovely to Simon Pure, and my full consent that she shall become his wife according to the form of marriage. Witness my hand."

OBADIAH PRIM.
That is enough—give me the pen. (*Signs it.*)

Enter Betty running to Mrs. Lovely.

BETTY.
Oh! Madam, madam, here's the Quaking man again; he has brought a coachman and two or three more.

MRS. LOVELY. (*Aside to Colonel.*)
Ruined past redemption.

COLONEL. [*Aside to her.*]
No, no, one minute sooner had spoiled all, but now—(*Going up to Prim hastily.*) Here is company coming, Friend, give me the paper.

OBADIAH PRIM.
Here it is, Simon, and I wish thee happy with the maiden.

MRS. LOVELY.
'Tis done, and now, devil do thy worst.

Enter Simon Pure and coachman, etc.

SIMON PURE.
Look thee, Friend, I have brought these people to satisfy thee that I am not that impostor which thou didst take me for; this is the man which did drive the leathern conveniency that brought me from Bristol, and this is—

COLONEL.
Look ye, Friend, to save the Court the trouble of examining witnesses, I plead guilty, ha, ha!

OBADIAH PRIM.
How's this? Is not thy name Pure, then?

COLONEL.
No really, sir, I only made bold with this gentleman's name, but I here give it up safe and sound; it has done the business which I had

occasion for, and now I intend to wear my own, which shall be at his service upon the same occasion at any time, ha, ha, ha!

SIMON PURE.
Oh! The wickedness of this age.

COACHMAN.
Then you have no farther need of us, sir. (*Exit.*)

COLONEL.
No, honest man, you may go about your business.

OBADIAH PRIM.
I am struck dumb with thy impudence, Anne; thou hast deceived me and perchance undone thyself.

MRS. PRIM.
Thou art a dissembling baggage, and shame will overtake thee. (*Exit.*)

SIMON PURE.
I am grieved to see thy wife so much troubled; I will follow and console her. (*Exit.*)

Enter servant.

SERVANT.
Thy brother guardians inquireth for thee; there is another man with them.

MRS. LOVELY. (*To the Colonel.*)
Who can that other man be?

COLONEL.
'Tis one Freeman, a friend of mine, whom I ordered to bring the rest of thy guardians here.

Enter Sir Philip, Tradelove, Periwinkle, and Freeman.

FREEMAN. (*To the Colonel.*)
Is all safe? Did my letter do you service?

COLONEL. (*Aside [to Freeman].*)
All! All's safe; ample service.

SIR PHILIP.
Miss Nancy, how dost do, child?

MRS. LOVELY.
Don't call me miss, Friend Philip, my name is Anne, thou knowest.

SIR PHILIP.
What, is the girl metamorphosed?

MRS. LOVELY.
I wish thou wert so metamorphosed. Ah! Philip, throw off that gaudy attire and wear the clothes becoming of thy age.

OBADIAH PRIM. (*Aside.*)
I am ashamed to see these men.

SIR PHILIP.
My age! The woman is possessed.

COLONEL.
No, thou art possessed rather, friend.

TRADELOVE.
Hark ye, Mrs. Lovely, one word with you. (*Takes hold of her hand.*)

COLONEL.
This maiden is my wife, thanks to Friend Prim, and thou hast no business with her. (*Takes her from him.*)

TRADELOVE.
His wife! Hark ye, Mr. Freeman—

PERIWINKLE.
Why, you have made a very fine piece of work of it, Mr. Prim.

SIR PHILIP.
Married to a Quaker! Thou art a fine fellow to be left guardian to an orphan, truly—there's a husband for a young lady!

COLONEL.
When I have put on my beau clothes, Sir Philip, you'll like me better.

SIR PHILIP.
Thou wilt make a very scurvy beau, Friend.

COLONEL.
I believe I can prove it under your hand that you thought me a very fine gentleman in the park today, about thirty-six minutes after eleven; will you take a pinch, Sir Philip—out of the finest snuffbox you ever saw. (*Offers him snuff.*)

SIR PHILIP.
Ha, ha, ha! I am overjoyed, faith I am, if thou be'st that gentleman. I own I did give my consent to the gentleman I brought here today, but if this is he I can't be positive.

OBADIAH PRIM.
Canst thou not. Now I think thou art a fine fellow to be left guardian to an orphan. Thou shallow-brained shuttlecock, he may be a pickpocket for aught thou dost know.

PERIWINKLE.
You would have been two rare fellows to have been trusted with the sole management of her fortune, would ye not, think ye? But Mr. Tradelove and myself shall take care of her portion.

TRADELOVE.

Aye, aye, so we will. Did not you tell me the Dutch merchant desired me to meet him here, Mr. Freeman?

FREEMAN.

I did so, and I am sure he will be here, if you have a little patience.

COLONEL.

What, is Mr. Tradelove impatient? Nay then, ik ben gereet veor you, heb ye Jan Van Timtamtirelireletta Heer Van Fainwell vergeeten?

TRADELOVE.

Oh! Pox of the name! What, have you tricked me too, Mr. Freeman?

COLONEL.

Tricked, Mr. Tradelove! Did I not give you two thousand pound for your consent fairly? And now do you tell a gentleman that he has tricked you?

PERIWINKLE.

So, so, you are a pretty guardian, faith, sell your charge. What, did you look upon her as part of your stock?

OBADIAH PRIM.

Ha, ha, ha! I am glad thy knavery is found out however. I confess the maiden overreached me, and no sinister end at all.

PERIWINKLE.

Aye, aye, one thing or another overreached you all, but I'll take care he shall never finger a penny of her money, I warrant you. Overreached, quoth'a? Why I might have been overreached too, if I had had no more wit. I don't know but this very fellow may be him that was directed to me from Grand Cairo today. Ha, ha, ha.

COLONEL.

The very same, sir.

PERIWINKLE.

Are you so, sir, but your trick would not pass upon me.

COLONEL.

No, as you say, at that time it did not, that was not my lucky hour, but hark ye, sir, I must let you into one secret—you may keep honest John Tradescant's coat on, for your uncle, Sir Toby Periwinkle, is not dead—so the charge of mourning will be saved, ha, ha! Don't you remember Mr. Pillage, your uncle's steward, ha, ha, ha?

PERIWINKLE.

Not dead! I begin to fear I am tricked too.

COLONEL.

Don't you remember the signing of a lease, Mr. Periwinkle?

PERIWINKLE.

Well, and what signifies that lease, if my uncle is not dead? Hah! I am sure it was a lease I signed.

COLONEL.

Aye, but it was a lease for life, sir, and of this beautiful tenement, I thank you. (*Taking hold of Mrs. Lovely.*)

OMNES.

Ha, ha, ha, neighbor's fare![96]

FREEMAN.

So then, I find you are all tricked, ha, ha!

PERIWINKLE.

I am certain I read as plain a lease as ever I read in my life.

COLONEL.

You read a lease I grant you, but you signed this contract. (*Showing a paper.*)

PERIWINKLE.

How durst you put this trick upon me, Mr. Freeman, did not you tell me my uncle was dying?

FREEMAN.

And would tell you twice as much to serve my friend, ha, ha.

SIR PHILIP.

What, the learned, famous Mr. Periwinkle choused too? Ha, ha, ha! I shall die with laughing, ha, ha, ha.

OBADIAH PRIM.

It had been well if her father had left her to wiser heads than thine and mine, Friend, ha, ha.

TRADELOVE.

Well, since you have outwitted us all, pray you, what and who are you, sir?

SIR PHILIP.

Sir, the gentleman is a fine gentleman. I am glad you have got a person, madam, who understands dress and good breeding. I was resolved she should have a husband of my choosing.

OBADIAH PRIM.

I am sorry the maiden is fallen into such hands.

[96] neighbor's fare] same fate or luck

TRADELOVE.

A beau! Nay then, she is finely helped up.

MRS. LOVELY.

Why, beaus are great encouragers of trade, sir, ha, ha!

COLONEL.

Look ye, gentlemen, I am the person who can give the best account of myself, and I must beg Sir Philip's pardon, when I tell him that I have as much aversion to what he calls dress and breeding as I have to the enemies of my religion. I have had the honor to serve his Majesty and headed a regiment of the bravest fellows that ever pushed bayonet in the throat of a Frenchman, and notwithstanding the fortune this lady brings me, whenever my country wants my aid, this sword and arm are at her service.

And now, my fair, if you'll but deign to smile,
I meet a recompense for all my toil:
Love and religion ne'er admit restraint,
Force makes many a sinner, not one saint;
Still free as air the active mind does rove,
And searches proper objects for its love,
But that once fixed, 'tis past the power of art
To chase the dear ideas from the heart:
'Tis liberty of choice that sweetens life,
Makes the glad husband and the happy wife.

[Exeunt.]

FINIS.

Textual Notes

[a] The copytext is the 1718 duodecimo, which exists in two states, with a copy in the British Library containing three press variants. This issue is designated D1a, the others D1b. When all three copies of the first edition agree, they are referred to as D1. There was another duocecimo edition (D2) in 1724, of doubtful authority. Also consulted are modern editions by Stathis (1968) and Rogers (1994).

[b] sect] Sex D1, D2

[c] fall] D2; falls D1

[d] possess] D2; profess D1

[e] come] D2; comes D1

[f] gelt] D2; Celt D1

The Conscious Lovers[a]

by Richard Steele (1672-1729)

edited by Lisa A. Freeman

Students of the eighteenth century are, perhaps, better acquainted with Richard Steele as one of the editors and authors of influential periodicals such as *The Spectator*, *The Guardian*, and *The Tatler*. Yet Steele played an active role in the London theater world both as a shareholder in the patent of Drury Lane Theatre and as the author of four plays, the last of which was his masterwork, *The Conscious Lovers*.

The Conscious Lovers was first performed on November 7, 1722, at Drury Lane and was an immediate sensation, with an initial run of eighteen consecutive nights followed by eight additional performances over the course of the 1722–1723 season. This success qualified *The Conscious Lovers* as a smash hit on the London stage, and it remained a part of the repertory throughout the eighteenth century, reaching its height of popularity in the 1730s, 1740s, and 1750s. Yet the success of *The Conscious Lovers* was not without controversy. Indeed, Steele's incorporation of what he termed in his preface "a joy too exquisite for laughter" in the dramatic resolution of the forced marriage plot of the play, as well as his insistence on the primacy of filial obligation against the expression of individual passion, elicited charges that he had created a bastard breed of comedy and that he had violated all rules of probability.

Such controversy notwithstanding, *The Conscious Lovers* is generally regarded as an exemplary text in the genre called sentimental comedy. Also known as *la comédie larmoyante*, or the comedy of tears, this genre was influenced by emerging theories of sentiment and sensibility which emphasized the goodness both of human nature and of Providence. Reacting against the bawdy humor of the Restoration comedies, moreover, sentimental comedies were aimed at producing what Steele termed "innocent performance," featuring displays of moral and emotional pathos and examples of virtue rewarded. Significantly, the rise of sentiment and sensibility has been associated with the emergence of the middling classes in eighteenth-century England and with the growing influence of bourgeois moral values. In Steele's satirical portrait of the aristocratic pedant Cimberton and in the exchange between the aristocrat Sir John Bevil and the merchant Mr. Sealand, we can begin to trace one of the main projects of sentimental comedies, that of representing the middling classes as the new polite and moral gentry of their day. One might argue, in this respect, that the comedy of manners is transformed here into the comedy of good manners.

Dramatis Personae

MEN

Sir John Bevil.
Mr. Sealand.
Bevil Junior, in love with Indiana.
Myrtle, in love with Lucinda.
Cimberton, a coxcomb.
Humphrey, an old servant to Sir John.
Tom, servant to Bevil Junior.
Daniel, a country boy, servant to Indiana.

WOMEN

Mrs. Sealand, second wife to Sealand.
Isabella, sister to Sealand.
Indiana, Sealand's daughter by his first wife.
Lucinda, Sealand's daughter by his second wife.
Phillis, maid to Lucinda.

SCENE: LONDON.

The Conscious Lovers.

Illud Genus Narrationis, quod in Personis positum est, debet habere Sermonis Festivitatem, Animorum Dissimilitudinem, Gravitatem, Lenitatem, Spem, Metum, Suspicionem, Desiderium, Dissimulationem, Misericordiam, Rerum Varietates, Fortunae Commutationem, Insperatum Incommodum, Subitam Letitiam, Jucundum Exitum Rerum.

Cic. Rhetor. ad Herenn. Lib. I.[1]

Act I, scene i. Sir John Bevil's house.

Enter Sir John Bevil and Humphrey.

SIR JOHN BEVIL.
Have you ordered that I should not be interrupted while I am dressing?

HUMPHREY.
Yes sir. I believed you had something of moment to say to me.

SIR JOHN BEVIL.
Let me see, Humphrey: I think it is now full forty years since I first took thee to be about myself.

HUMPHREY.
I thank you, sir. It has been an easy forty years, and I have passed 'em without much sickness, care, or labor.

SIR JOHN BEVIL.
Thou hast a brave* constitution; you are a year or two older than I am, sirrah.

HUMPHREY.
You have ever been of that mind, sir.

SIR JOHN BEVIL.
You knave, you know it; I took thee for thy gravity and sobriety in my wild years.

HUMPHREY.
Ah sir! Our manners were formed from our different fortunes, not our different age. Wealth gave a loose to your youth, and poverty put a restraint upon mine.

SIR JOHN BEVIL.
Well Humphrey, you know I have been a kind master to you; I have used you, for the ingenuous nature I observed in you from the beginning, more like an humble friend than a servant.

HUMPHREY.
I humbly beg you'll be so tender of me as to explain your commands, sir, without any farther preparation.

SIR JOHN BEVIL.
I'll tell thee then. In the first place, this wedding of my son's, in all probability—shut the door—will never be at all.

HUMPHREY.
How sir! Not be at all? For what reason is it carried on in appearance?

SIR JOHN BEVIL.
Honest Humphrey, have patience, and I'll tell thee all in order. I have myself, in some part of my life, lived, indeed, with freedom, but, I hope, without reproach. Now, I thought liberty would be as little injurious to my son; therefore, as soon as he grew towards man, I indulged him in living after his own manner. I knew not how, otherwise, to judge of his inclination. For what can be concluded from a behavior under restraint and fear? But what

---

1 *Illud* ... Lib I] *Rhetorica ad Herennium* (no longer attributed to Cicero) I.viii: A narrative based on the persons should present a lively style and diverse traits of character, such as austerity and gentleness, hope and fear, distrust and desire, hypocrisy and compassion, and the vicissitudes of life, such as reversal of fortune, unexpected disaster, sudden joys and a happy outcome.

charms me above all expression is that my son has never in the least action, the most distant hint or word, valued himself upon that great estate of his mother's, which, according to our marriage settlement, he has had ever since he came to age.

HUMPHREY.

No sir, on the contrary, he seems afraid of appearing to enjoy it before you or any belonging to you. He is as dependent and resigned to your will, as if he had not a farthing but what must come from your immediate bounty. You have ever acted like a good and generous father, and he like an obedient and grateful son.

SIR JOHN BEVIL.

Nay, his carriage is so easy to all with whom he converses that he is never assuming, never prefers himself to others, nor ever is guilty of that rough sincerity which a man is not called to, and certainly disobliges most of his acquaintance. To be short, Humphrey, his reputation was so fair in the world that old Sealand, the great India[2] merchant, has offered his only daughter, and sole heiress to that vast estate of his, as a wife for him. You may be sure I made no difficulties, the match was agreed on, and this very day named for the wedding.

HUMPHREY.

What hinders the proceeding?

SIR JOHN BEVIL.

Don't interrupt me. You know, I was last Thursday at the masquerade; my son, you may remember, soon found us out. He knew his grandfather's habit, which I then wore, and though it was the mode in the last age, yet the maskers, you know, followed us as if we had been the most monstrous figures in that whole assembly.

HUMPHREY.

I remember indeed a young man of quality* in the habit of a clown* that was particularly troublesome.

SIR JOHN BEVIL.

Right. He was too much what he seemed to be. You remember how impertinently he followed and teased us and would know who we were.

[2] India] not necessarily the Asian subcontinent but possibly the Indies, East or West

HUMPHREY. (*Aside.*)

I know he has a mind to come into that particular.

SIR JOHN BEVIL.

Aye, he followed us, till the gentleman who led the lady in the Indian mantle presented the gay creature to the rustic and bid him, like Cymon in the fable,[3] grow polite by falling in love and let that worthy old gentleman alone, meaning me. The clown was not reformed, but rudely persisted and offered* to force off my mask; with that the gentleman, throwing off his own, appeared to be my son, and in his concern for me, tore off that of the nobleman. At this they seized each other, the company called the guards, and in the surprise, the lady swooned away. Upon which my son quitted his adversary and had now no care but of the lady, when raising her in his arms, "Art thou gone," cried he, "forever—forbid it Heaven!" She revives at his known voice, and with the most familiar though modest gesture hangs in safety over his shoulder weeping, but wept as in the arms of one before whom she could give herself a loose, were she not under observation. While she hides her face in his neck, he carefully conveys her from the company.

HUMPHREY.

I have observed this accident has dwelt upon you very strongly.

SIR JOHN BEVIL.

Her uncommon air, her noble modesty, the dignity of her person, and the occasion itself, drew the whole assembly together, and I soon heard it buzzed about, she was the adopted daughter of a famous sea-officer, who had served in France. Now this unexpected and public discovery* of my son's so deep concern for her—

HUMPHREY.

Was what I suppose alarmed Mr. Sealand, in behalf of his daughter, to break off the match.

[3] Cymon in the fable] In Boccaccio's fable of Cymon and Iphigenia (translated in John Dryden's *Fables*), Cymon was a fair youth, who, because of his dull, brutish mind was exiled to the country by his father; there he encountered and fell in love with Iphigenia and was inspired by his love to cultivate his mind and acquire the civilities of life.

SIR JOHN BEVIL.

You are right. He came to me yesterday and said he thought himself disengaged from the bargain, being credibly informed my son was already married, or worse, to the lady at the masquerade. I palliated matters and insisted on our agreement, but we parted with little less than a direct breach between us.

HUMPHREY.

Well sir, and what notice have you taken of all this to my young master?

SIR JOHN BEVIL.

That's what I wanted to debate with you. I have said nothing to him yet. But look you, Humphrey, if there is so much in this amour of his that he denies upon my summons to marry, I have cause enough to be offended, and then by my insisting upon his marrying today, I shall know how far he is engaged to this lady in masquerade and from thence only shall be able to take my measures. In the meantime I would have you find out how far that rogue his man is let into his secret. He, I know, will play tricks as much to cross me as to serve his master.

HUMPHREY.

Why do you think so of him, sir? I believe he is no worse than I was for you, at your son's age.

SIR JOHN BEVIL.

I see it in the rascal's looks. But I have dwelt on these things too long; I'll go to my son immediately, and while I'm gone, your part is to convince his rogue Tom that I am in earnest. I'll leave him to you. (*Exit.*)

HUMPHREY.

Well, though this father and son live as well together as possible, yet their fear of giving each other pain is attended with constant mutual uneasiness. I'm sure I have enough to do to be honest and yet keep well with them both. But they know I love 'em, and that makes the task less painful however.—Oh, here's the prince of poor coxcombs, the representative of all the better fed than taught. Ho! ho! Tom, whither so gay and so airy this morning?

Enter Tom, singing.

TOM.

Sir, we servants of single gentlemen are another kind of people than you domestic ordinary drudges that do business. We are raised above you. The pleasures of board-wages,[4] tavern-dinners, and many a clear gain; vails,[5] alas, you never heard or dreamt of.

HUMPHREY.

Thou hast follies and vices enough for a man of ten thousand a year, though 'tis but as t'other day that I sent for you to Town* to put you into Mr. Sealand's family,* that you might learn a little before I put you to my young master, who is too gentle for training such a rude thing as you were into proper obedience. You then pulled off your hat to everyone you met in the street, like a bashful, great, awkward cub as you were. But your great oaken cudgel when you were a booby became you much better than that dangling stick at your button[6] now you are a fop. That's fit for nothing, except it hangs there to be ready for your master's hand when you are impertinent.

TOM.

Uncle Humphrey, you know my master scorns to strike his servants. You talk as if the world was now just as it was when my old master and you were in your youth, when you went to dinner because it was so much o'clock, when the great blow was given in the hall at the pantry-door and all the family* came out of their holes in such strange dresses and formal faces as you see in the pictures in our long gallery in the country.

HUMPHREY.

Why, you wild rogue!

TOM.

You could not fall to your dinner till a formal fellow in a black gown said something over the meat, as if the cook had not made it ready enough.

HUMPHREY.

Sirrah, who do you prate after? Despising men of sacred characters! I hope you never heard my good young master talk so like a profligate?

---

4 board-wages] allowances paid to cover food expenses

5 vails] gratuities

6 stick … button] cane suspended from a large button on a coat

TOM.

Sir, I say you put upon me, when I first came to Town, about being orderly and the doctrine of wearing shams[7] to make linen last clean a fortnight, keeping my clothes fresh, and wearing a frock within doors.

HUMPHREY.

Sirrah, I gave you those lessons, because I supposed at that time your master and you might have dined at home everyday and cost you nothing; then you might have made a good family servant. But the gang you have frequented since at chocolate houses and taverns in a continual round of noise and extravagance—

TOM.

I don't know what you heavy inmates call noise and extravagance, but we gentlemen, who are well fed and cut a figure, sir, think it a fine life and that we must be very pretty fellows who are kept only to be looked at.

HUMPHREY.

Very well, sir, I hope the fashion of being lewd and extravagant, despising of decency and order, is almost at an end, since it is arrived at persons of your quality.

TOM.

Master Humphrey, ha, ha, you were an unhappy lad to be sent up to Town in such queer days as you were. Why now sir, the lackeys are the men of pleasure of the age; the top-gamesters and many a laced coat about Town have had their education in our parti-colored regiment.[8] We are false lovers, have a taste of music, poetry, billets-doux, dress, politics; ruin damsels; and when we are weary of this lewd town and have a mind to take up,[9] whip into our masters wigs and linen and marry fortunes.

HUMPHREY.

Hey-day!

TOM.

Nay sir, our order is carried up to the highest dignities and distinctions: step but into the Painted Chamber,[10] and by our titles you'd take us all for men of quality.* Then again, come down to the Court of Requests,[11] and you see us all laying our broken heads together[12] for the good of the Nation. And though we never carry a question *nemine contradicente*,[13] yet this I can say with a safe conscience—and I wish every gentleman of our cloth could lay his hand upon his heart and say the same—that I never took so much as a single mug of beer for my vote in all my life.

HUMPHREY.

Sirrah, there is no enduring your extravagance; I'll hear you prate no longer. I wanted to see you to inquire how things go with your master, as far as you understand them. I suppose he knows he is to be married today.

TOM.

Aye sir, he knows it and is dressed as gay as the sun, but between you and I, my dear, he has a very heavy heart under all that gaiety. As soon as he was dressed, I retired, but overheard him sigh in the most heavy manner. He walked thoughtfully to and fro in the room, then went into his closet;* when he came out, he gave me this for his mistress, whose maid you know—

HUMPHREY.

Is passionately fond of your fine person.

TOM.

The poor fool is so tender and loves to hear me talk of the world and the plays, operas, and ridottos, for the winter; the parks and Belsize,[14] for our summer diversions; and "Lard!" says she, "you are so wild—but you have a world of humor."

HUMPHREY.

Coxcomb! Well, but why don't you run with your master's letter to Mrs.* Lucinda, as he ordered you?

---

7 shams] false fronts

8 parti-colored regiment] servants in livery

9 to take up] to settle down

10 Painted Chamber] a chamber in the old Palace of Westminster in which Parliament met in early times; in the eighteenth century servants would wait for Members here and address each other by the names of their masters

11 Court of Requests] the building where the House of Lords met

12 laying … together] coming to blows

13 *Nemine Contradicente*] unanimously (literally, no man speaking against—Lat.)

14 Belsize] suburban field outside London used for summer entertainments

TOM.

Because Mrs. Lucinda is not so easily come at as you think for.

HUMPHREY.

Not easily come at? Why sirrah, are not her father and my old master agreed that she and Mr. Bevil are to be one flesh before tomorrow morning?

TOM.

It's no matter for that; her mother, it seems, Mrs. Sealand, has not agreed to it. And you must know, Mr. Humphrey, that in that family the gray mare is the better horse.

HUMPHREY.

What dost thou mean?

TOM.

In one word, Mrs. Sealand pretends to have a will of her own and has provided a relation of hers, a stiff, starched philosopher and a wise fool, for her daughter; for which reason, for these ten days past, she has suffered no message nor letter from my master to come near her.

HUMPHREY.

And where had you this intelligence?

TOM.

From a foolish, fond soul that can keep nothing from me. One that will deliver this letter too, if she is rightly managed.

HUMPHREY.

What! Her pretty handmaid, Mrs.* Phillis?

TOM.

Even she, sir; this is the very hour, you know, she usually comes hither under a pretence of a visit to your housekeeper forsooth, but in reality to have a glance at—

HUMPHREY.

Your sweet face, I warrant you.

TOM.

Nothing else in nature. You must know, I love to fret and play with the little wanton—

HUMPHREY.

Play with the little wanton! What will this world come to!

TOM.

I met her, this morning, in a new manteau and petticoat,[15] not a bit the worse for her lady's wearing, and she has always new thoughts and new airs with new clothes. Then she never fails to steal some glance or gesture from every visitant at their house and is indeed the whole Town of coquettes at second hand.—But here she comes; in one motion she speaks and describes herself better than all the words in the world can.

HUMPHREY.

Then I hope, dear sir, when your own affair is over, you will be so good as to mind your master's with her.

TOM.

Dear Humphrey, you know my master is my friend, and those are people I never forget.

HUMPHREY.

Sauciness itself! But I'll leave you to do your best for him. (*Exit.*)

Enter Phillis.

PHILLIS.

Oh Mr. Thomas, is Mrs. Sugar-key at home? Lard, one is almost ashamed to pass along the streets. The Town is quite empty, and nobody of fashion left in it, and the ordinary people do so stare to see anything dressed like a woman of condition, as it were on the same floor with them, pass by. Alas! Alas! It is a sad thing to walk. Oh Fortune! Fortune!

TOM.

What! A sad thing to walk? Why, Madam Phillis, do you wish your self lame?

PHILLIS.

No Mr. Tom, but I wish I were generally carried in a coach or chair* and of a fortune neither to stand nor go, but to totter or slide, to be short-sighted or stare, to fleer in the face, to look distant, to observe, to overlook, yet all become me. And if I was rich, I could twire* and loll as well as the best of them. Oh Tom! Tom! Is it not a pity that you should be so great a coxcomb and I so great a coquette, and yet be such poor devils as we are?

TOM.

Mrs.* Phillis, I am your humble servant for that—

PHILLIS.

Yes Mr. Thomas, I know how much you are my humble servant and know what you said to Mrs.* Judy upon seeing her in one of her lady's cast

[15] manteau and petticoat] a loose gown, the skirt of which split in a triangle to reveal the underskirt

manteaus, that any one would have thought her the lady and that she had ordered the other to wear it till it sat easy, for now only it was becoming: to my lady it was only a covering, to Mrs. Judy it was a habit. This you said, after somebody or other. Oh Tom! Tom! Thou art as false and as base as the best gentleman of them all. But you wretch, talk to me no more on the old odious subject. Don't, I say.

TOM. (*In a submissive tone, retiring.*)

I know not how to resist your commands, madam.

PHILLIS.

Commands about parting are grown mighty easy to you of late.

TOM. (*Aside.*)

Oh, I have her: I have nettled and put her into the right temper to be wrought upon and set a prating. —Why truly, to be plain with you, Mrs. Phillis, I can take little comfort of late in frequenting your house.

PHILLIS.

Pray Mr. Thomas, what is it all of a sudden offends your nicety at our house?

TOM.

I don't care to speak particulars, but I dislike the whole.

PHILLIS.

I thank you, sir, I am a part of that whole.

TOM.

Mistake me not, good Phillis.

PHILLIS.

Good Phillis! Saucy enough. But however—

TOM.

I say, it is that thou art a part, which gives me pain for the disposition of the whole. You must know, madam, to be serious, I am a man, at the bottom, of prodigious nice* honor. You are too much exposed to company at your house. To be plain, I don't like so many that would be your mistress's lovers whispering to you.

PHILLIS.

Don't think to put that upon me. You say this, because I wrung you to the heart when I touched your guilty conscience about Judy.

TOM.

Ah Phillis! Phillis! If you but knew my heart!

PHILLIS.

I know too much on't.

TOM.

Nay then, poor Crispo's fate and mine are one.[16] Therefore give me leave to say, or sing at least, as he does upon the same occasion—

Sings "Se vedette," etc.[17]

PHILLIS.

What, do you think I'm to be fobbed off with a song? I don't question but you have sung the same to Mrs. Judy too.

TOM.

Don't disparage your charms, good Phillis, with jealousy of so worthless an object; besides, she is a poor hussy, and if you doubt the sincerity of my love, you will allow me true to my interest. You are a fortune, Phillis—

PHILLIS.

What would the fop be at now?—In good time indeed, you shall be setting up for a fortune!

TOM.

Dear Mrs. Phillis, you have such a spirit that we shall never be dull in marriage when we come together. But I tell you, you are a fortune, and you have an estate in my hands. *He pulls out a purse; she eyes it.*

PHILLIS.

What pretence have I to what is in your hands, Mr. Tom?

TOM.

As thus: there are hours, you know, when a lady is neither pleased or displeased, neither sick or well, when she lolls or loiters, when she's without

---

16 Crispo's fate] Crispo was the hero of *Crispus*, a recently performed Italian Opera by Paolo Rolli and Giovanni Bononcini; at one point Crispo is falsely accused of making advances on his mother-in-law, the wife of the emperor, and is condemned to death. Crispo was played on the London stage by the famous castrato Senesino.

17 "Se vedette"] Crispo sings this aria just after he has been condemned, trans. in the English edition of 1721: "If you see / My Thoughts, / Ye just Gods, defend / The Innocence of my Heart. / No one hears me, / And you are silent: / Wicked Malice / Condemns me, and / Deceives my Father."

desires, from having more of everything than she knows what to do with.

PHILLIS.

Well, what then?

TOM.

When she has not life enough to keep her bright eyes quite open to look at her own dear image in the glass.*

PHILLIS.

Explain thyself, and don't be so fond of thy own prating.

TOM.

There are also prosperous and good-natured moments, as when a knot or a patch is happily fixed, when the complexion particularly flourishes.

PHILLIS.

Well, what then? I have not patience!

TOM.

Why then, or on the like occasions, we servants, who have skill to know how to time business, see when such a pretty folded thing as this (*Shows the letter.*) may be presented, laid, or dropped, as best suits the present humor. And madam, because it is a long, wearisome journey to run through all the several stages of a lady's temper, my master, who is the most reasonable man in the world, presents you this to bear your charges on the road. (*Gives her the purse.*)

PHILLIS.

Now you think me a corrupt hussy.

TOM.

Oh fie, I only think you'll take the letter.

PHILLIS.

Nay, I know you do, but I know my own innocence; I take it for my mistress's sake.

TOM.

I know it, my pretty one, I know it.

PHILLIS.

Yes, I say I do it because I would not have my mistress deluded by one who gives no proof of his passion. But I'll talk more of this, as you see me on my way home.—No Tom, I assure thee, I take this trash of thy master's, not for the value of the thing, but as it convinces me he has a true respect for my mistress. I remember a verse to the purpose.

They may be false who languish and complain,
But they who part with money never feign.

Exeunt.

Scene ii. Bevil Junior's lodgings.

Bevil Junior, reading.

BEVIL JUNIOR.

These moral writers practice virtue after death. This charming Vision of Mirza![18] Such an author consulted in a morning sets the spirit for the vicissitudes of the day better than the glass* does a man's person. But what a day have I to go through! To put on an easy look with an aching heart. If this lady my father urges me to marry should not refuse me, my dilemma is insupportable. But why should I fear it? Is not she in equal distress with me? Has not the letter I have sent her this morning confessed my inclination to another? Nay, have I not moral assurances of her engagements too, to my friend Myrtle. It's impossible but she must give in to it. For sure, to be denied is a favor any man may pretend to. It must be so. Well then, with the assurance of being rejected, I think I may confidently say to my father, I am ready to marry her. Then let me resolve upon what I am not very good at, though it is an honest dissimulation.

Enter Tom.

TOM.

Sir John Bevil, sir, is in the next room.

BEVIL JUNIOR.

Dunce! Why did not you bring him in?

TOM.

I told him, sir, you were in your closet.*

BEVIL JUNIOR.

I thought you had known, sir, it was my duty to see my father anywhere. (*Going himself to the door.*)

TOM. (*Aside.*)

The devil's in my master! He has always more wit than I have.

Bevil Junior introducing Sir John.

---

18 after death ... Vision of Mirza] an allegorical anecdote, presented by Addison (d. 1719) in *Spectator #159* as an oriental tale in which the protagonist, Mirzah, contemplates the vanity of human wishes and is treated to a vision both of human folly and the eternal reward that awaits those who strive to be worthy

BEVIL JUNIOR.

Sir, you are the most gallant, the most complaisant of all parents. Sure 'tis not a compliment to say these lodgings are yours. Why would you not walk in, sir?

SIR JOHN BEVIL.

I was loath to interrupt you unseasonably on your wedding day.

BEVIL JUNIOR.

One to whom I am beholden for my birthday might have used less ceremony.

SIR JOHN BEVIL.

Well son, I have intelligence you have writ to your mistress this morning. It would please my curiosity to know the contents of a wedding-day letter, for courtship must then be over.

BEVIL JUNIOR.

I assure you, sir, there was no insolence in it upon the prospect of such a vast fortune's being added to our family, but much acknowledgment of the lady's greater desert.

SIR JOHN BEVIL.

But dear Jack, are you in earnest in all this? And will you really marry her?

BEVIL JUNIOR.

Did I ever disobey any command of yours, sir? Nay, any inclination that I saw you bent upon?

SIR JOHN BEVIL.

Why, I can't say you have, son, but methinks in this whole business you have not been so warm as I could have wished you. You have visited her, it's true, but you have not been particular. Everyone knows you can say and do as handsome things as any man, but you have done nothing but lived in the general, been complaisant only.

BEVIL JUNIOR.

As I am ever prepared to marry if you bid me, so I am ready to let it alone if you will have me.

Humphrey enters unobserved.

SIR JOHN BEVIL.

Look you there now! Why what am I to think of this so absolute and so indifferent a resignation?

BEVIL JUNIOR.

Think? That I am still* your son, sir.—Sir—you have been married, and I have not. And you have, sir, found the inconvenience there is when a man weds with too much love in his head. I have been told, sir, that at the time you married, you made a mighty bustle on the occasion. There was challenging and fighting, scaling walls, locking up the lady, and the gallant under an arrest for fear of killing all his rivals. Now sir, I suppose you having found the ill consequences of these strong passions and prejudices, in preference of one woman to another, in case of a man's becoming a widower—

SIR JOHN BEVIL.

How is this!

BEVIL JUNIOR.

I say, sir, experience has made you wiser in your care of me. For sir, since you lost my dear mother, your time has been so heavy, so lonely, and so tasteless, that you are so good as to guard me against the like unhappiness by marrying me prudentially by way of bargain and sale. For as you well judge, a woman that is espoused for a fortune is yet a better bargain if she dies, for then a man still enjoys what he did marry, the money, and is disencumbered of what he did not marry, the woman.

SIR JOHN BEVIL.

But pray sir, do you think Lucinda then a woman of such little merit?

BEVIL JUNIOR.

Pardon me, sir, I don't carry it so far neither; I am rather afraid I shall like her too well: she has, for one of her fortune, a great many needless and superfluous good qualities.

SIR JOHN BEVIL.

I am afraid, son, there's something I don't see yet, something that's smothered under all this raillery.

BEVIL JUNIOR.

Not in the least, sir. If the lady is dressed and ready, you see I am. I suppose the lawyers are ready too.

HUMPHREY. (*Aside.*)

This may grow warm, if I don't interpose.—Sir, Mr. Sealand is at the coffee house and has sent to speak with you.

SIR JOHN BEVIL.

Oh! That's well! Then I warrant the lawyers are ready.—Son, you'll be in the way, you say—

BEVIL JUNIOR.

If you please, sir, I'll take a chair* and go to Mr.

Sealand's, where the young lady and I will wait your leisure.

SIR JOHN BEVIL.
By no means. The old fellow will be so vain, if he sees—

BEVIL JUNIOR.
Aye, but the young lady, sir, will think me so indifferent—

HUMPHREY. (*Aside to Bevil Junior.*)
Aye, there you are right. Press your readiness to go to the bride. He won't let you.

BEVIL JUNIOR. (*Aside to Humphrey.*)
Are you sure of that?

HUMPHREY. (*Aside.*)
How he likes being prevented.

SIR JOHN BEVIL. (*Looking on his watch.*)
No, no. You are an hour or two too early.

BEVIL JUNIOR.
You'll allow me, sir, to think it too late to visit a beautiful, virtuous young woman, in the pride and bloom of life, ready to give herself to my arms, and to place her happiness or misery for the future in being agreeable or displeasing to me, is a—Call a chair.

SIR JOHN BEVIL.
No, no, no, dear Jack, this Sealand is a moody old fellow. There's no dealing with some people, but by managing with indifference. We must leave to him the conduct of this day. It is the last of his commanding his daughter.

BEVIL JUNIOR.
Sir, he can't take it ill that I am impatient to be hers.

SIR JOHN BEVIL.
Pray let me govern in this matter. You can't tell how humoursome old fellows are. There's no offering reason to some of 'em, especially when they are rich. (*Aside.*) If my son should see him before I've brought old Sealand into better temper, the match would be impracticable.

HUMPHREY. (*Aside to Sir John.*)
Pray sir, let me beg you to let Mr. Bevil go. See, whether he will or not. (*To Bevil Junior.*) Pray sir, command yourself; since you see my master is positive, it is better you should not go.

BEVIL JUNIOR.
My father commands me as to the object of my affections, but I hope he will not as to the warmth and height of them.

SIR JOHN BEVIL.
So! I must even leave things as I found them. And in the meantime, at least, keep old Sealand out of his sight.—Well son, I'll go myself and take orders in your affair. You'll be in the way, I suppose, if I send to you. I'll leave your old friend with you.—Humphrey, don't let him stir, d'ye hear?—Your servant, your servant. (*Exit.*)

HUMPHREY.
I have a sad time on't, sir, between you and my master. I see you are unwilling, and I know his violent inclinations for the match.—I must betray neither and yet deceive you both for your common good.—Heaven grant a good end of this matter. But there is a lady, sir, that gives your father much trouble and sorrow—you'll pardon me.

BEVIL JUNIOR.
Humphrey, I know thou art a friend to both, and in that confidence, I dare tell thee—that lady—is a woman of honor and virtue. You may assure yourself, I never will marry without my father's consent. But give me leave to say too, this declaration does not come up to a promise that I will take whomsoever he pleases.

HUMPHREY.
Come sir, I wholly understand you. You would engage my services to free you from this woman whom my master intends you, to make way in time for the woman you have really a mind to.

BEVIL JUNIOR.
Honest Humphrey, you have always been an useful friend to my father and myself. I beg you continue your good offices and don't let us come to the necessity of a dispute, for if we should dispute, I must either part with more than life or lose the best of fathers.

HUMPHREY.
My dear master, were I but worthy to know this secret that so near concerns you, my life, my all should be engaged to serve you. This, sir, I dare promise: that I am sure I will and can be secret. Your trust, at worst, but leaves you where you were, and if I cannot serve you, I will at once be plain and tell you so.

BEVIL JUNIOR.
That's all I ask. Thou hast made it now my interest to trust thee. Be patient, then, and hear the story of my heart.

HUMPHREY.
I am all attention, sir.

BEVIL JUNIOR.
You may remember, Humphrey, that in my last travels my father grew uneasy at my making so long a stay at Toulon.

HUMPHREY.
I remember it; he was apprehensive some woman had laid hold of you.

BEVIL JUNIOR.
His fears were just, for there I first saw this lady. She is of English birth: her father's name was Danvers, a younger brother of an ancient family and originally an eminent merchant of Bristol, who upon repeated misfortunes was reduced to go privately to the Indies. In this retreat Providence again grew favorable to his industry and in six years time restored him to his former fortunes. On this he sent directions over that his wife and little family should follow him to the Indies. His wife, impatient to obey such welcome orders, would not wait the leisure of a convoy but took the first occasion of a single ship, and with her husband's sister only and this daughter, then scarce seven years old, undertook the fatal voyage. For here, poor creature, she lost her liberty and life. She and her family, with all they had, were unfortunately taken by a privateer from Toulon. Being thus made a prisoner, though as such not ill treated, yet the fright, the shock, and cruel disappointment seized with such violence upon her unhealthy frame, she sickened, pined, and died at sea.

HUMPHREY.
Poor soul! Oh, the helpless infant!

BEVIL JUNIOR.
Her sister yet survived and had the care of her. The captain too proved to have humanity and became a father to her, for having himself married an English woman, and being childless, he brought home into Toulon this her little countrywoman, presenting her, with all her dead mother's moveables of value, to his wife to be educated as his own adopted daughter.

HUMPHREY.
Fortune here seemed, again, to smile on her.

BEVIL JUNIOR.
Only to make her frowns more terrible. For in his height of fortune, this captain too, her benefactor, unfortunately was killed at sea, and dying intestate, his estate fell wholly to an advocate his brother, who coming soon to take possession, there found, among his other riches, this blooming virgin at his mercy.

HUMPHREY.
He durst not, sure, abuse his power!

BEVIL JUNIOR.
No wonder if his pampered blood was fired at the sight of her—in short, he loved. But when all arts and gentle means had failed to move, he offered too his menaces in vain, denouncing vengeance on her cruelty, demanding her to account for all her maintenance from her childhood, seized on her little fortune as his own inheritance, and was dragging her by violence to prison when Providence at the instant interposed and sent me, by miracle, to relieve her.

HUMPHREY.
'Twas Providence indeed. But pray sir, after all this trouble, how came this lady at last to England?

BEVIL JUNIOR.
The disappointed advocate, finding she had so unexpected a support, on cooler thoughts, descended to a composition, which I, without her knowledge, secretly discharged.

HUMPHREY.
That generous concealment made the obligation double.

BEVIL JUNIOR.
Having thus obtained her liberty, I prevailed, not without some difficulty, to see her safe to England, where no sooner arrived, but my father, jealous of my being imprudently engaged, immediately proposed this other, fatal match that hangs upon my quiet.

HUMPHREY.
I find, sir, you are irrecoverably fixed upon this lady.

BEVIL JUNIOR.
As my vital life dwells in my heart. And yet you see what I do to please my father: walk in this

pageantry of dress, this splendid covering of sorrow. But, Humphrey, you have your lesson.

HUMPHREY.
Now sir, I have but one material question.

BEVIL JUNIOR.
Ask it freely.

HUMPHREY.
Is it, then, your own passion for this secret lady or hers for you that gives you this aversion to the match your father has proposed you?

BEVIL JUNIOR.
I shall appear, Humphrey, more romantic in my answer than in all the rest of my story. For though I dote on her to death and have no little reason to believe she has the same thoughts for me, yet in all my acquaintance and utmost privacies with her, I never once directly told her that I loved.

HUMPHREY.
How was it possible to avoid it?

BEVIL JUNIOR.
My tender obligations to my father have laid so inviolable a restraint upon my conduct that, till I have his consent to speak, I am determined on that subject to be dumb forever.

HUMPHREY.
Well sir, to your praise be it spoken, you are certainly the most unfashionable lover in Great Britain.

Enter Tom.

TOM.
Sir, Mr. Myrtle's at the next door and, if you are at leisure, will be glad to wait on you.

BEVIL JUNIOR.
Whenever he pleases—hold, Tom! Did you receive no answer to my letter?

TOM.
Sir, I was desired to call again, for I was told her mother would not let her be out of her sight. But about an hour hence, Mrs. Phillis[b] said I should certainly have one.

BEVIL JUNIOR.
Very well.

Exit Tom.[c]

HUMPHREY.
Sir, I will take another opportunity. In the meantime, I only think it proper to tell you that from a secret I know, you may appear to your father as forward as you please to marry Lucinda, without the least hazard of its coming to a conclusion—sir, your most obedient servant.

BEVIL JUNIOR.
Honest Humphrey, continue but my friend in this exigence and you shall always find me yours.

Exit Humphrey.

I long to hear how my letter has succeeded with Lucinda, but I think it cannot fail. For at worst, were it possible she could take it ill, her resentment of my indifference may as probably occasion a delay as her taking it right.—Poor Myrtle, what terrors must he be in all this while? Since he knows she is offered to me and refused to him, there is no conversing or taking any measures with him for his own service. But I ought to bear with my friend and use him as one in adversity:
All his disquiets by my own I prove,
The greatest grief's perplexity in love.

Exit.

Act II, scene i. The scene continues.

Enter Bevil Junior and Tom.

TOM.
Sir, Mr. Myrtle.

BEVIL JUNIOR.
Very well, do you step again and wait for an answer to my letter.

[Exit Tom.] Enter Myrtle.

BEVIL JUNIOR.
Well Charles, why so much care in thy countenance? Is there anything in this world deserves it? You, who used to be so gay, so open, so vacant!

MYRTLE.
I think we have of late changed complexions. You, who used to be much the graver man, are now all air in your behavior. But the cause of my concern may, for aught I know, be the same object that gives you all this satisfaction. In a word, I am told that you are this very day, and your dress confirms me in it, to be married to Lucinda.

BEVIL JUNIOR.

You are not misinformed. Nay, put not on the terrors of a rival till you hear me out. I shall disoblige the best of fathers, if I don't seem ready to marry Lucinda. And you know I have ever told you, you might make use of my secret resolution never to marry her for your own service, as you please. But I am now driven to the extremity of immediately refusing or complying, unless you help me to escape the match.

MYRTLE.

Escape? Sir, neither her merit or her fortune are below your acceptance. Escaping, do you call it!

BEVIL JUNIOR.

Dear sir, do you wish I should desire the match?

MYRTLE.

No, but such is my humorous* and sickly state of mind, since it has been able to relish nothing but Lucinda, that though I must owe my happiness to your aversion to this marriage, I can't bear to hear her spoken of with levity or unconcern.

BEVIL JUNIOR.

Pardon me, sir, I shall transgress that way no more. She has understanding, beauty, shape, complexion, wit—

MYRTLE.

Nay dear Bevil, don't speak of her as if you loved her, neither.

BEVIL JUNIOR.

Why then, to give you ease at once, though I allow Lucinda to have good sense, wit, beauty, and virtue, I know another in whom these qualities appear to me more amiable than in her.

MYRTLE.

There you spoke like a reasonable and good-natured friend. When you acknowledge her merit and own your prepossession for another at once, you gratify my fondness and cure my jealousy.

BEVIL JUNIOR.

But all this while you take no notice, you have no apprehension of another man that has twice the fortune of either of us.

MYRTLE.

Cimberton! Hang him, a formal, philosophical, pedantic coxcomb! For the sot,* with all these crude notions of diverse things, under the direction of great vanity and very little judgment, shows his strongest bias is avarice, which is so predominant in him that he will examine the limbs of his mistress with the caution of a jockey and pays no more compliment to her personal charms than if she were a mere breeding animal.

BEVIL JUNIOR.

Are you sure that is not affected? I have known some women sooner set on fire by that sort of negligence than by—

MYRTLE.

No, no, hang him, the rogue has no art; it is pure simple insolence and stupidity.

BEVIL JUNIOR.

Yet with all this, I don't take him for a fool.

MYRTLE.

I own the man is not a natural;* he has a very quick sense, though very slow understanding. He says indeed many things that want* only the circumstances of time and place to be very just and agreeable.

BEVIL JUNIOR.

Well, you may be sure of me, if you can dissapoint him, but my intelligence says the mother has actually sent for the conveyancer to draw articles for his marriage with Lucinda, though those for mine with her are, by her father's order, ready for signing. But it seems she has not thought fit to consult either him or his daughter in the matter.

MYRTLE.

Pshaw! A poor, troublesome woman. Neither Lucinda nor her father will ever be brought to comply with it. Besides, I am sure Cimberton can make no settlement upon her without the concurrence of his great uncle Sir Geoffry in the West.

BEVIL JUNIOR.

Well sir, and I can tell you, that's the very point that is now laid before her counsel: to know whether a firm settlement can be made without his uncle's actual joining in it. Now pray consider, sir, when my affair with Lucinda comes, as it soon must, to an open rupture, how are you sure that Cimberton's fortune may not then tempt her father too to hear his proposals?

MYRTLE.

There you are right indeed. That must be provided against. Do you know who are her counsel?

BEVIL JUNIOR.

Yes, for your service I have found out that too: they are Serjeant[19] Bramble and old Target. By the way, they are neither of 'em known in the family; now I was thinking why you might not put a couple of false counsel upon her to delay and confound matters a little. Besides, it may probably let you into the bottom of her whole design against you.

MYRTLE.

As how, pray?

BEVIL JUNIOR.

Why, can't you slip on a black wig and a gown and be old Bramble yourself?

MYRTLE.

Hah! I don't dislike it. But what shall I do for a brother in the case?

BEVIL JUNIOR.

What think you of my fellow, Tom? The rogue's intelligent and is a good mimic; all his part will be but to stutter heartily, for that's old Target's case. Nay, it would be an immoral thing to mock him, were it not that his impertinence is the occasion of its breaking out to that degree. The conduct of the scene will chiefly lie upon you.

MYRTLE.

I like it of all things. If you'll send Tom to my chambers, I will give him full instructions. This will certainly give me occasion to raise difficulties, to puzzle, or confound her project for a while at least.

BEVIL JUNIOR.

I'll warrant you success. So far we are right then. And now, Charles, your apprehension of my marrying her is all you have to get over.

MYRTLE.

Dear Bevil! Though I know you are my friend, yet when I abstract myself from my own interest in the thing, I know no objection she can make to you or you to her and therefore hope—

BEVIL JUNIOR.

Dear Myrtle, I am as much obliged to you for the cause of your suspicion as I am offended at the effect. But be assured, I am taking measures for your certain security and that all things with regard to me will end in your entire satisfaction.

[19] Serjeant] serjeant-at-law (q.v.)

MYRTLE.

Well, I'll promise you to be as easy and as confident as I can, though I cannot but remember that I have more than life at stake on your fidelity. (*Going.*)

BEVIL JUNIOR.

Then depend upon it, you have no chance against you.

MYRTLE.

Nay no ceremony, you know I must be going. (*Exit.*)

BEVIL JUNIOR.

Well! This is another instance of the perplexities which arise too in faithful friendship. We must often in this life go on in our good offices, even under the displeasure of those to whom we do them, in compassion to their weaknesses and mistakes.—But all this while poor Indiana is tortured with the doubt of me! She has no support or comfort but in my fidelity yet sees me daily pressed to marriage with another! How painful in such a crisis must be every hour she thinks on me? I'll let her see at least my conduct to her is not changed. I'll take this opportunity to visit her, for though the religious vow I have made to my father restrains me from ever marrying without his approbation, yet that confines me not from seeing a virtuous woman that is the pure delight of my eyes and the guiltless joy of my heart. But the best condition of human life is but a gentler misery.
To hope for perfect happiness is vain,
And love has ever its alloys of pain.

Exit.

[Scene ii. Indiana's lodgings.]

Enter Isabella and Indiana.

ISABELLA.

Yes, I say 'tis artifice, dear child; I say to thee again and again, 'tis all skill and management.

INDIANA.

Will you persuade me there can be an ill design in supporting me in the condition of a woman of quality?* Attended, dressed, and lodged like one in my appearance abroad and my furniture at home, every way in the most sumptuous manner, and he that does it has an artifice, a design in it?

ISABELLA.

Yes, yes.

INDIANA.

And all this without so much as explaining to me that all about me comes from him!

ISABELLA.

Aye, aye, the more for that. That keeps the title to all you have the more in him.

INDIANA.

The more in him! He scorns the thought—

ISABELLA.

Then he—he—he—

INDIANA.

Well, be not so eager. If he is an ill man, let us look into his stratagems. Here is another of them. (*Showing a letter.*) Here's two hundred and fifty pound in bank notes, with these words, "To pay for the set of dressing-plate,[20] which will be brought home tomorrow." Why dear aunt, now here's another piece of skill for you, which I own I cannot comprehend. And it is with a bleeding heart I hear you say anything to the disadvantage of Mr. Bevil. When he is present, I look upon him as one to whom I owe my life and the support of it. Then again, as the man who loves me with sincerity and honor. When his eyes are cast another way and I dare survey him, my heart is painfully divided between shame and love. Oh, could I tell you—

ISABELLA.

Ah, you need not. I imagine all this for you.

INDIANA.

This is my state of mind in his presence, and when he is absent, you are ever dinning my ears with notions of the arts of men: that his hidden bounty, his respectful conduct, his careful provision for me, after his preserving me from utmost misery, are certain signs he means nothing but to make I know not what of me.

ISABELLA.

Oh! You have a sweet opinion of him, truly.

INDIANA.

I have when I am with him ten thousand things besides my sex's natural decency and shame to suppress my heart that yearns to thank, to praise, to say it loves him. I say, thus it is with me while I see him, and in his absence I am entertained with nothing but your endeavors to tear this amiable image from my heart and in its stead to place a base dissembler, an artful invader of my happiness, my innocence, my honor.

ISABELLA.

Ah poor soul! Has not his plot taken? Don't you die for him? Has not the way he has taken been the most proper with you? Oh ho! He has sense and has judged the thing right.

INDIANA.

Go on then, since nothing can answer you; say what you will of him. Heigh ho!

ISABELLA.

Heigh ho, indeed! It is better to say so, as you are now, than as many others are. There are among the destroyers of women the gentle,* the generous,* the mild, the affable, the humble, who all, soon after their success in their designs, turn to the contrary of those characters. I will own to you, Mr. Bevil carries his hypocrisy the best of any man living, but still he is a man, and therefore a hypocrite. They have usurped an exemption from shame for any baseness, any cruelty towards us. They embrace without love; they make vows without conscience of obligation; they are partners, nay, seducers to the crime wherein they pretend to be less guilty.

INDIANA. (*Aside.*)

That's truly observed.—But what's all this to Bevil?

ISABELLA.

This it is to Bevil and all mankind: trust not those who will think the worse of you for your confidence in them. Serpents who lie in wait for doves. Won't you be on your guard against those who would betray you? Won't you doubt those who would condemn you for believing 'em? Take it from me, fair and natural dealing is to invite injuries; 'tis bleating to escape wolves who would devour you! Such is the world. (*Aside.*) And such (since behavior of one man to myself) have I believed all the rest of the sex.

INDIANA.

I will not doubt* the truth of Bevil; I will not doubt it. He has not spoke it by an organ that is given to lying. His eyes are all that have ever told

[20] dressing-plate] silver-covered articles for the toilet*

me that he was mine. I know his virtue, I know his filial piety, and ought to trust his management with a father to whom he has uncommon obligations. What have I to be concerned for? My lesson is very short. If he takes me forever, my purpose of life is only to please him. If he leaves me, which Heaven avert, I know he'll do it nobly, and I shall have nothing to do but to learn to die after worse than death has happened to me.

ISABELLA.

Aye, do, persist in your credulity! Flatter yourself that a man of his figure and fortune will make himself the jest of the Town* and marry a handsome beggar for love.

INDIANA.

The Town! I must tell you, madam, the fools that laugh at Mr. Bevil will but make themselves more ridiculous; his actions are the result of thinking, and he has sense enough to make even virtue fashionable.

ISABELLA.

Oh my conscience, he has turned her head. Come, come, if he were the honest* fool you take him for, why has he kept you here these three weeks without sending you to Bristol in search of your father, your family, and your relations?

INDIANA.

I am convinced he still designs it and that nothing keeps him here but the necessity of not coming to a breach with his father in regard to the match he has proposed him. Beside, has he not writ to Bristol? And has not he advice that my father has not been heard of there almost these twenty years?

ISABELLA.

All sham, mere evasion; he is afraid if he should carry you thither, your honest relations may take you out of his hands and so blow up all his wicked hopes at once.

INDIANA.

Wicked hopes! Did I ever give him any such?

ISABELLA.

Has he ever given you any honest* ones? Can you say, in your conscience, he has ever once offered to marry you?

INDIANA.

No! But by his behavior I am convinced he will offer it the moment 'tis in his power or consistent with his honor to make such a promise good to me.

ISABELLA.

His honor!

INDIANA.

I will rely upon it, therefore desire you will not make my life uneasy by these ungrateful jealousies of one to whom I am and wish to be obliged. For from his integrity alone, I have resolved to hope for happiness.

ISABELLA.

Nay, I have done my duty; if you won't see, at your peril be it—

INDIANA.

Let it be. This is his hour of visiting me.

ISABELLA. (*Apart.*)

Oh, to be sure, keep up your form, don't see him in a bedchamber. This is pure prudence, when she is liable, wherever he meets her, to be conveyed where'er he pleases.

INDIANA.

All the rest of my life is but waiting till he comes. I live only when I'm with him. (*Exit.*)

ISABELLA.

Well, go thy ways, thou willful innocent! I once had almost as much love for a man who poorly left me to marry an estate. And I am now, against my will, what they call an old maid. But I will not let the peevishness of that condition grow upon me, only keep up the suspicion of it to prevent this creature's being any other than a virgin, except upon proper terms. (*Exit.*)

Re-enter Indiana, speaking to a servant.

INDIANA.

Desire Mr. Bevil to walk in.—Design! Impossible! A base designing mind could never think of what he hourly puts in practice. And yet, since the late rumor of his marriage, he seems more reserved than formerly. He sends in too, before he sees me, to know if I am at leisure. Such new respect may cover coldness in the heart. It certainly makes me thoughtful. I'll know the worst at once; I'll lay such fair occasions in his way that it shall be impossible to avoid an explanation. For these doubts are insupportable!—But see! he comes, and clears them all.

[II.ii]

Enter Bevil Junior

BEVIL JUNIOR.

Madam, your most obedient. I am afraid I broke in upon your rest last night. 'Twas very late before we parted, but 'twas your own fault. I never saw you in such agreeable humor.

INDIANA.

I am extremely glad we were both pleased, for I thought I never saw you better company.

BEVIL JUNIOR.

Me, madam! You rally; I said very little.

INDIANA.

But I am afraid you heard me say a great deal, and when a woman is in the talking vein, the most agreeable thing a man can do, you know, is to have patience to hear her.

BEVIL JUNIOR.

Then it's pity, madam, you should ever be silent, that we might be always agreeable to one another.

INDIANA.

If I had your talent or power to make my actions speak for me, I might indeed be silent and yet pretend to something more than the agreeable.

BEVIL JUNIOR.

If I might be vain of anything in my power, madam, 'tis that my understanding from all your sex has marked you out as the most deserving object of my esteem.

INDIANA.

Should I think I deserve this, 'twere enough to make my vanity forfeit the very esteem you offer me.

BEVIL JUNIOR.

How so, madam?

INDIANA.

Because esteem is the result of reason, and to deserve it from good sense, the height of human glory. Nay, I had rather a man of honor should pay me that than all the homage of a sincere and humble love.

BEVIL JUNIOR.

You certainly distinguish right, madam; love often kindles from external merit only—

INDIANA.

But esteem arises from a higher source, the merit of the soul—

BEVIL JUNIOR.

True. And great souls only can deserve it. (*Bowing respectfully.*)

INDIANA.

Now, I think, they are greater still that can so charitably part with it.

BEVIL JUNIOR.

Now madam, you make me vain, since the utmost pride and pleasure of my life is that I esteem you—as I ought.

INDIANA. (*Aside.*)

As he ought! Still more perplexing! He neither saves nor kills my hope.

BEVIL JUNIOR.

But madam, we grow grave methinks. Let's find some other subject.—Pray how did you like the opera last night?

INDIANA.

First give me leave to thank you for my tickets.

BEVIL JUNIOR.

Oh your servant, madam. But pray tell me, you now, who are never partial to the fashion, I fancy must be the properest judge of a mighty dispute among the ladies, that is, whether *Crispo* or *Griselda*[21] is the more agreeable entertainment.

INDIANA.

With submission now, I cannot be a proper judge of this question.

BEVIL JUNIOR.

How so, madam?

INDIANA.

Because I find I have a partiality for one of them.

BEVIL JUNIOR.

Pray which is that?

INDIANA.

I do not know. There's something in that rural cottage of Griselda, her forlorn condition, her poverty, her solitude, her resignation, her innocent slumbers, and that lulling "Dolce Sogno"[22] that's sung over her; it had an effect upon me that—in

21 *Griselda*] the patient wife portrayed in another recent popular Italian Opera by Bononcini and Rolli, based on a story by both Boccaccio and Chaucer recounting her trials at the hands of a cruel husband

22 "Dolce Sogno"] "Sweet Dream" (It.)

short I never was so well deceived at any of them.

BEVIL JUNIOR.

Oh! Now then, I can account for the dispute: *Griselda*, it seems, is the distress of an injured innocent woman; *Crispo* that only of a man in the same condition. Therefore the men are mostly concerned for *Crispo*, and, by a natural indulgence, both sexes for *Griselda*.

INDIANA.

So that judgment, you think, ought to be for one, though fancy and complaisance have got ground for the other. Well! I believe you will never give me leave to dispute with you on any subject, for I own *Crispo* has its charms for me too. Though in the main, all the pleasure the best opera gives us is but mere sensation. Methinks it's pity the mind can't have a little more share in the entertainment. The music's certainly fine, but in my thoughts there's none of your* composers come up to old Shakespeare and Otway.

BEVIL JUNIOR.

How, madam! Why if a woman of your sense were to say this in the Drawing Room*—

Enter a servant.

SERVANT.

Sir, here's Signior Carbonelli says he waits your commands in the next room.

BEVIL JUNIOR.

Apropos! You were saying yesterday, madam, you had a mind to hear him. Will you give him leave to entertain you now?

INDIANA.

By all means.—Desire the gentleman to walk in. *Exit servant.*

BEVIL JUNIOR.

I fancy you will find something in this hand that is uncommon.

INDIANA.

You are always finding ways, Mr. Bevil, to make life seem less tedious to me.

Enter music master.

When the Gentleman pleases.

After a sonata is played, Bevil waits on the master to the door, etc.

BEVIL JUNIOR.

You smile, madam, to see me so complaisant to one whom I pay for his visit. Now, I own I think it is not enough barely to pay those whose talents are superior to our own—I mean such talents as would become our condition, if we had them. Methinks we ought to do something more than barely gratify them for what they do at our command only because their fortune is below us.

INDIANA.

You say I smile. I assure you it was a smile of approbation, for indeed I cannot but think it the distinguishing part of a gentleman to make his superiority of fortune as easy to his inferiors as he can. (*Aside.*) Now once more to try him.—I was saying just now, I believed you would never let me dispute with you, and I dare say it will always be so. However I must have your opinion upon a subject which created a debate between my aunt and me just before you came hither. She would needs have it that no man ever does any extra-ordinary kindness or service for a woman but for his own sake.

BEVIL JUNIOR.

Well, madam! Indeed I can't but be of her mind.

INDIANA.

What, though he should maintain and support her without demanding anything of her on her part?

BEVIL JUNIOR.

Why madam, is making an expense in the service of a valuable woman, for such I must suppose her, though she should never do him any favor, nay, though she should never know who did her such service, such a mighty heroic business?

INDIANA.

Certainly! I should think he must be a man of an uncommon mold.

BEVIL JUNIOR.

Dear madam, why so? 'Tis but, at best, a better taste in expense. To bestow upon one whom he may think one of the ornaments of the whole creation, to be conscious that from his superfluity an innocent, a virtuous spirit is supported above the temptations and sorrows of life! That he sees satisfaction, health, and gladness in her countenance while he enjoys the happiness of seeing her, as that I will suppose too, or he must be too abstracted, too insensible. I say, if he is allowed to delight in that prospect, alas, what mighty matter is there in all this?

INDIANA.

No mighty matter in so disinterested a friendship!

BEVIL JUNIOR.

Disinterested! I can't think him so. Your hero, madam, is no more than what every gentleman ought to be, and I believe very many are. He is only one who takes more delight in reflections than in sensations. He is more pleased with thinking than eating. That's the utmost you can say of him. Why madam, a greater expense than all this men lay out upon an unnecessary stable of horses.

INDIANA.

Can you be sincere in what you say?

BEVIL JUNIOR.

You may depend upon it. If you know any such man, he does not love dogs inordinately.

INDIANA.

No, that he does not.

BEVIL JUNIOR.

Nor cards, nor dice.

INDIANA.

No.

BEVIL JUNIOR.

Nor bottle companions.

INDIANA.

No.

BEVIL JUNIOR.

Nor loose women.

INDIANA.

No, I'm sure he does not.

BEVIL JUNIOR.

Take my word then, if your admired hero is not liable to any of these kind of demands, there's no such preeminence in this as you imagine. Nay, this way of expense you speak of is what exalts and raises him that has a taste for it. And at the same time, his delight is incapable of satiety, disgust, or penitence.

INDIANA.

But still I insist his having no private interest in the action makes it prodigious, almost incredible.

BEVIL JUNIOR.

Dear madam, I never knew you more mistaken. Why, who can be more an usurer than he who lays out his money in such valuable purchases? If pleasure be worth purchasing, how great a pleasure is it to him, who has a true taste of life, to ease an aching heart, to see the human countenance lighted up into smiles of joy on the receipt of a bit of ore which is superfluous and otherwise useless in a man's own pocket? What could a man do better with his cash? This is the effect of an humane disposition, where there is only a general tie of nature and common necessity. What then must it be when we serve an object of merit, of admiration!

INDIANA.

Well! The more you argue against it, the more I shall admire the generosity.

BEVIL JUNIOR.

Nay, nay. Then madam, 'tis time to fly after a declaration that my opinion strengthens my adversary's argument. I had best hasten to my appointment with Mr. Myrtle and be gone while we are friends and—before things are brought to an extremity— (*Exit carelessly.*)

Enter Isabella.

ISABELLA.

Well madam, what think you of him now pray?

INDIANA.

I protest I begin to fear he is wholly disinterested in what he does for me. On my heart, he has no other view but the mere pleasure of doing it and has neither good or bad designs upon me.

ISABELLA.

Ah dear niece! Don't be in fear of both! I'll warrant you, you will know time enough that he is not indifferent.

INDIANA.

You please me when you tell me so. For if he has any wishes towards me, I know he will not pursue them but with honor.

ISABELLA.

I wish I were as confident of one as t'other. I saw the respectful downcast of his eye when you caught him gazing at you during the music. He, I warrant, was surprised, as if he had been taken stealing your watch. Oh, the undissembled guilty look.

INDIANA.

But did you observe any such thing, really? I thought he looked most charmingly graceful! How engaging is modesty in a man when one knows there is a great mind within. So tender a confusion! And yet, in other respects, so much himself, so collected, so dauntless, so determined!

ISABELLA.

Ah niece! There is a sort of bashfulness, which is the best engine* to carry on a shameless purpose. Some men's modesty serves their wickedness, as hypocrisy gains the respect due to piety. But I will own to you, there is one hopeful symptom, if there could be such a thing as a disinterested lover. But it's all a perplexity, till—till—till—

INDIANA.

Till what?

ISABELLA.

Till I know whether Mr. Myrtle and Mr. Bevil are really friends or foes. And that I will be convinced of before I sleep, for you shall not be deceived.

INDIANA.

I'm sure I never shall, if your fears can guard me. In the meantime, I'll wrap myself up in the integrity of my own heart, nor dare to doubt of his.

As conscious honor all his actions steers,
So conscious innocence dispels my fears.

Exeunt.

Act III. Sealand's house.

Enter Tom meeting Phillis.

TOM.

Well Phillis, what, with a face as if you had never seen me before. (*Aside.*) What a work have I to do now? She has seen some new visitant at their house whose airs she has caught and is resolved to practice them upon me. Numberless are the changes she'll dance through before she'll answer this plain question, videlicet, have you delivered my master's letter to your lady? Nay, I know her too well to ask an account of it in an ordinary way; I'll be in my airs as well as she.—Well madam, as unhappy as you are at present pleased to make me, I would not, in the general, be any other than what I am. I would not be a bit wiser, a bit richer, a bit taller, a bit shorter than I am at this instant. (*Looking steadfastly at her.*)

PHILLIS.

Did ever anybody doubt, Master Thomas, but that you were extremely satisfied with your sweet self?

TOM.

I am indeed. The thing I have least reason to be satisfied with is my fortune, and I am glad of my poverty. Perhaps if I were rich, I should overlook the finest woman in the world that wants* nothing but riches to be thought so.

PHILLIS. (*Aside.*)

How prettily was that said? But, I'll have a great deal more before I'll say one word.

TOM.

I should, perhaps, have been stupidly above her had I not been her equal and, by not being her equal, never had opportunity of being her slave. I am my master's servant for hire; I am my mistress's from choice, would she but approve my passion.

PHILLIS.

I think it's the first time I ever heard you speak of it with any sense of the anguish, if you really do suffer any.

TOM.

Ah Phillis, can you doubt after what you have seen?

PHILLIS.

I know not what I have seen, nor what I have heard. But since I'm at leisure, you may tell me when you fell in love with me, how you fell in love with me, and what you have suffered or are ready to suffer for me.

TOM. (*Aside.*)

Oh the unmerciful jade! When I'm in haste about my master's letter. But I must go through it.—Ah, too well I remember when and how and on what occasion I was first surprised. It was on the first of April, one thousand seven hundred and fifteen, I came into Mr. Sealand's service. I was then a hobbledehoy and you a pretty little tight girl, a favorite handmaid of the housekeeper. At that time, we neither of us knew what was in us. I remember I was ordered to get out of the window, one pair of stairs,[23] to rub the sashes clean. The person employed on the innerside was your charming self, whom I had never seen before.

---

[23] one pair of stairs] one flight up

PHILLIS.

I think I remember the silly accident. What made ye, you oaf, ready to fall down into the street?

TOM.

You know not, I warrant you. You could not guess what surprised me. You took no delight when you immediately grew wanton in your conquest and put your lips close and breathed upon the glass, and when my lips approached, a dirty cloth you rubbed against my face and hid your beauteous form. When I again drew near, you spit and rubbed and smiled at my undoing.

PHILLIS.

What silly thoughts you men have!

TOM.

We were Pyramus and Thisbe, but ten times harder was my fate. Pyramus could peep only through a wall; I saw her, saw my Thisbe in all her beauty but as much kept from her as if a hundred walls between, for there was more, there was her will against me. Would she but yet relent! Oh Phillis! Phillis! Shorten my torment and declare you pity me.

PHILLIS.

I believe it's very sufferable; the pain is not so exquisite but that you may bear it a little longer.

TOM.

Oh my charming Phillis, if all depended on my fair one's will, I could with glory suffer. But dearest creature, consider our miserable state.

PHILLIS.

How! Miserable!

TOM.

We are miserable to be in love and under the command of others than those we love. With that generous passion in the heart, to be sent to and fro on errands, called, checked, and rated for the meanest trifles. Oh Phillis! You don't know how many china cups and glasses my passion for you has made me break. You have broke my fortune as well as my heart.

PHILLIS.

Well Mr. Thomas, I cannot but own to you that I believe your master writes and you speak the best of any men of the world. Never was woman so well pleased with a letter, as my young lady was with his, and this is an answer to it. (*Gives him a letter.*)

TOM.

This was well done, my dearest. Consider we must strike out some pretty livelihood for ourselves by closing their affairs. It will be nothing for them to give us a little being of our own, some small tenement out of their large possessions. Whatever they give us, 'twill be more than what they keep for themselves. One acre, with Phillis, would be worth a whole county without her.

PHILLIS.

Oh, could I but believe you!

TOM.

If not the utterance, believe the touch of my lips. (*Kisses her.*)

PHILLIS.

There's no contradicting you. How closely you argue, Tom!

TOM.

And will closer, in due time. But I must hasten with this letter, to hasten towards the possession of you. Then Phillis, consider how I must be revenged, look to it, of all your skittishness, shy looks, and at best but coy compliances.

PHILLIS.

Oh Tom, you grow wanton and sensual, as my lady calls it. I must not endure it. Oh! Faugh! You are a man, an odious filthy male creature; you should behave, if you had a right sense or were a man of sense like Mr. Cimberton, with distance and indifference or, let me see some other becoming hard word, with seeming in- in- inadvertency, and not rush on one as if you were seizing a prey. But hush—the ladies are coming. Good[d] Tom, don't kiss me above once and be gone. Lard, we have been fooling and toying and not considered the main business of our masters and mistresses.

TOM.

Why, their business is to be fooling and toying as soon as the parchments are ready.

PHILLIS.

Well remembered—parchments—my lady, to my knowledge, is preparing writings between her coxcomb cousin Cimberton and my mistress, though my master has an eye to the parchments already prepared between your master Mr. Bevil and my mistress, and I believe my mistress herself has signed and sealed, in her heart, to Mr. Myrtle.—Did I not bid you kiss me but once and be gone? But I know you won't be satisfied.

TOM.

No, you smooth creature, how should I! (*Kissing her hand.*)

PHILLIS.

Well, since you are so humble, or so cool, as to ravish my hand only, I'll take my leave of you like a great lady and you a man of quality.* (*They salute* formally.*)

TOM.

Pox of all this state. (*Offers to kiss her more closely.*)

PHILLIS.

No, prithee, Tom, mind your business. We must follow that interest which will take, but endeavor at that which will be most for us and we like most.—Oh here's my young mistress!

Tom taps her neck behind and kisses his fingers.

Go, ye lickerish fool.

Exit Tom. Enter Lucinda.

LUCINDA.

Who was that you was hurrying away?

PHILLIS.

One that I had no mind to part with.

LUCINDA.

Why did you turn him away then?

PHILLIS.

For your ladyship's service, to carry your ladyship's letter to his master. I could hardly get the rogue away.

LUCINDA.

Why, has he so little love for his master?

PHILLIS.

No, but he has so much love for his mistress.

LUCINDA.

But I thought I heard him kiss you. Why do you suffer that?

PHILLIS.

Why madam, we vulgar take it to be a sign of love. We servants, we poor people that have nothing but our persons to bestow or treat for are forced to deal and bargain by way of sample. And therefore, as we have no parchments or wax necessary in our agreements, we squeeze with our hands and seal with our lips to ratify vows and promises.

LUCINDA.

But can't you trust one another without such earnest down?

PHILLIS.

We don't think it safe, any more than you gentry, to come together without deeds executed.

LUCINDA.

Thou art a pert, merry hussy.

PHILLIS.

I wish, madam, your lover and you were as happy as Tom and your servant are.

LUCINDA.

You grow impertinent.

PHILLIS.

I have done, madam, and I won't ask you what you intend to do with Mr. Myrtle, what your father will do with Mr. Bevil, nor what you all, especially my lady, mean by admitting Mr. Cimberton as particularly here as if he were married to you already. Nay, you are married actually as far as people of quality* are.

LUCINDA.

How's that?

PHILLIS.

You have different beds in the same house.

LUCINDA.

Pshaw! I have a very great value for Mr. Bevil, but have absolutely put an end to his pretensions in the letter I gave you for him. But my father, in his heart, still has a mind to him, were it not for this woman they talk of, and I am apt to imagine he is married to her, or never designs to marry at all.

PHILLIS.

Then Mr. Myrtle—

LUCINDA.

He had my parents' leave to apply to me and by that has won me and my affections. Who is to have this body of mine without 'em, it seems, is nothing to me. My mother says it's indecent for me to let my thoughts stray about the person of my husband. Nay, she says a maid rigidly virtuous, though she may have been where her lover was a thousand times, should not have made observations enough to know him from another man when she sees him in a third place.

PHILLIS.

That is more than the severity of a nun, for not to see, when one may, is hardly possible; not to see when one can't, is very easy. At this rate, madam, there are a great many whom you have not seen who—

LUCINDA.

Mamma says the first time you see your husband should be at that instant he is made so, when your father, with the help of the minister, gives you to him. Then you are to see him, then you are to observe and take notice of him, because then you are to obey him.

PHILLIS.

But does not my lady remember you are to love as well as obey?

LUCINDA.

To love is a passion, 'tis a desire, and we must have no desires. Oh! I cannot endure the reflection! With what insensibility on my part, with what more than patience, have I been exposed and offered to some awkward booby or other in every county of Great Britain?

PHILLIS.

Indeed madam, I wonder I never heard you speak of it before with this indignation.

LUCINDA.

Every corner of the land has presented me with a wealthy coxcomb. As fast as one treaty has gone off, another has come on, till my name and person have been the tittle-tattle of the whole Town. What is this world come to! No shame left! To be bartered for like the beasts of the fields, and that in such an instance as coming together to an entire familiarity and union of soul and body. Oh! And this without being so much as well-wishers to each other, but for increase of fortune.

PHILLIS.

But madam, all these vexations will end very soon in one for all. Mr. Cimberton is your mother's kinsman, and three hundred years an older gentleman than any lover you ever had, for which reason, with that of his prodigious large estate, she is resolved on him and has sent to consult the lawyers accordingly. Nay, has, whether you know it or no, been in treaty with Sir Geoffry, who, to join in the settlement, has accepted of a sum to do it and is every moment expected in Town for that purpose.

LUCINDA.

How do you get all this intelligence?

PHILLIS.

By an art I have, I thank my stars, beyond all the waiting maids in Great Britain, the art of list'ning, madam, for your ladyship's service.

LUCINDA.

I shall soon know as much as you do. Leave me, leave me, Phillis, be gone. Here, here, I'll turn you out. My mother says I must not converse with my servants, though I must converse with no one else.

Exit Phillis.

How unhappy are we who are born to great fortunes! No one looks at us with indifference or acts toward us on the foot of plain dealing. Yet by all I have been heretofore offered to or treated for, I have been used with the most agreeable of all abuses, flattery. But now, by this phlegmatic fool, I am used as nothing or a mere thing. He, forsooth, is too wise, too learned to have any regard to desires, and I know not what the learned oaf calls sentiments of love and passion.—Here he comes with my mother. It's much if he looks at me or, if he does, takes no more notice of me than of any other moveable in the room.

Enter Mrs. Sealand and Mr. Cimberton.

MRS. SEALAND.

How do I admire this noble, this learned taste of yours, and the worthy regard you have to our own ancient and honorable house in consulting a means to keep the blood as pure and as regularly descended as may be.

CIMBERTON.

Why really madam, the young women of this age are treated with discourses of such a tendency, and their imaginations so bewildered in flesh and blood, that a man of reason can't talk to be understood. They have no ideas of happiness, but what are more gross than the gratification of hunger and thirst.

LUCINDA. (*Aside.*)

With how much reflection he is a coxcomb?

CIMBERTON.

And in truth, madam, I have considered it as a most brutal custom that persons of the first character in the world should go as ordinarily, and with as little shame, to bed, as to dinner with one another. They proceed to the propagation of the species as openly as to the preservation of the individual.

LUCINDA. (*Aside.*)

She that willingly goes to bed to thee must have no shame, I'm sure.

MRS. SEALAND.

Oh Cousin Cimberton! Cousin Cimberton! How abstracted, how refined is your sense of things! But indeed, it is too true, there is nothing so ordinary as to say in the best governed families, "My master and lady are gone to bed." One does not know but it might have been said of one's self. (*Hiding her face with her fan.*)

CIMBERTON.

Lycurgus, madam, instituted otherwise. Among the Lacedaemonians, the whole female world was pregnant, but none but the mothers themselves knew by whom. Their meetings were secret, and the amorous congress always by stealth, and no such professed doings between the sexes as are tolerated among us under the audacious word, marriage.

MRS. SEALAND.

Oh, had I lived in those days and been a matron of Sparta, one might with less indecency have had ten children according to that modest institution than one under the confusion of our modern, barefaced manner.

LUCINDA. (*Aside.*)

And yet, poor woman, she has gone through the whole ceremony, and here I stand a melancholy proof of it.

MRS. SEALAND.

We will talk then of business. That girl walking about the room there is to be your wife. She has, I confess, no ideas, no sentiments, that speak her born of a thinking mother.

CIMBERTON.

I have observed her; her lively look, free air, and disengaged countenance speak her very—

LUCINDA.

Very what?

CIMBERTON.

If you please, madam, to set her a little that way.

MRS. SEALAND.

Lucinda, say nothing to him; you are not a match for him. When you are married, you may speak to such a husband when you're spoken to. But I am disposing of you above yourself every way.

CIMBERTON.

Madam, you cannot but observe the inconveniences I expose myself to in hopes that your ladyship will be the consort of my better part. As for the young woman, she is rather an impediment than a help to a man of letters and speculation.[24] Madam, there is no reflection, no philosophy, can at all times subdue the sensitive[25] life, but the animal shall sometimes carry away the man. Hah! Ay, the vermilion of her lips.

LUCINDA.

Pray, don't talk of me thus.

CIMBERTON.

The pretty enough—pant of her bosom.

LUCINDA.

Sir! Madam, don't you hear him?

CIMBERTON.

Her forward chest.

LUCINDA.

Intolerable!

CIMBERTON.

High health.

LUCINDA.

The grave, easy impudence of him!

CIMBERTON.

Proud heart.

LUCINDA.

Stupid coxcomb!

CIMBERTON.

I say, madam, her impatience while we are looking at her throws out all attractions—her arms—her neck—what a spring in her step!

LUCINDA.

Don't you run me over thus, you strange unaccountable!

---

24 speculation] intellectual interests

25 sensitive] based upon the five senses

CIMBERTON.
What an elasticity in her veins and arteries!
LUCINDA.
I have no veins, no arteries.
MRS. SEALAND.
Oh child, hear him, he talks finely, he's a scholar, he knows what you have.
CIMBERTON.
The speaking invitation of her shape, the gathering of herself up, and the indignation you see in the pretty little thing—now, I am considering her, on this occasion, but as one that is to be pregnant.
LUCINDA. (*Aside.*)
The familiar, learned, unseasonable puppy!*
CIMBERTON.
And pregnant undoubtedly she will be yearly. I fear I shan't for many years have discretion enough to give her one fallow season.
LUCINDA.
Monster! There's no bearing it. The hideous sot!* There's no enduring it, to be thus surveyed like a steed at sale.
CIMBERTON.
At sale! She's very illiterate. But she's very well limbed too. Turn her in.[26] I see what she is.

Exit Lucinda in a rage.

MRS. SEALAND.
Go, you creature, I am ashamed of you.
CIMBERTON.
No harm done. You know, madam, the better sort of people, as I observed to you, treat by their lawyers of weddings (*Adjusting himself at the glass.**) and the woman in the bargain, like the mansion house in the sale of the estate, is thrown in, and what that is, whether good or bad, is not at all considered.
MRS. SEALAND.
I grant it, and therefore make no demand for her youth and beauty and every other accomplishment, as the common world think 'em, because she is not polite.
CIMBERTON.
Madam, I know your exalted understanding, abstracted as it is from vulgar prejudices, will not be offended when I declare to you I marry to have an heir to my estate and not to beget a colony or a plantation.* This young woman's beauty and constitution will demand provision[27] for a tenth child at least.
MRS. SEALAND. (*Aside.*)
With all that wit and learning, how considerate! What an economist!—Sir, I cannot make her any other than she is or say she is much better than the other young women of this age or fit for much besides being a mother, but I have given directions for the marriage settlements, and Sir Geoffrey Cimberton's counsel is to meet ours here at this hour concerning his joining in the deed, which when executed, makes you capable of settling what is due to Lucinda's fortune. Herself, as I told you, I say nothing of.
CIMBERTON.
No, no, no, indeed, madam, it is not usual, and I must depend upon my own reflection and philosophy not to overstock my family.
MRS. SEALAND.
I cannot help her, Cousin Cimberton, but she is, for aught I see, as well as the daughter of anybody else.
CIMBERTON.
That is very true, madam.

Enter a servant, who whispers Mrs. Sealand.

MRS. SEALAND.
The lawyers are come, and now we are to hear what they have resolved as to the point whether it's necessary that Sir Geoffry should join in the settlement, as being what they call in the remainder. But good cousin, you must have patience with 'em. These lawyers, I am told, are of a different kind. One is what they call a chamber-counsel,[28] the other a pleader. The conveyancer is slow, from an imperfection in his speech, and therefore shunned the bar, but

[26] Turn her in] keep her from leaving (equestrian phrase)

[27] provision] a clause in a marriage contract providing for a monetary settlement to be made in anticipation of future offspring

[28] chamber-counsel] a lawyer who offers opinions in private not in court

extremely passionate and impatient of contradiction. The other is as warm as he, but has a tongue so voluble and head so conceited, he will suffer nobody to speak but himself.

CIMBERTON.

You mean old Serjeant Target and Counsellor Bramble? I have heard of 'em.

MRS. SEALAND.

The same.—Show in the gentlemen.

Exit servant. Re-enter servant, introducing Myrtle and Tom, disguised as Bramble and Target.

MRS. SEALAND.

Gentlemen, this is the party concerned, Mr. Cimberton, and I hope you have considered of the matter.

TOM.

Yes madam, we have agreed that it must be by indent—dent—dent—dent—

MYRTLE.

Yes madam, Mr. Serjeant and myself have agreed, as he is pleased to inform you, that it must be an indenture[29] tripartite, and tripartite let it be, for Sir Geoffry must needs be a party. Old Cimberton, in the year 1619, says in that ancient roll in Mr. Serjeant's hands, "as recourse thereto being had, will more at large appear—"

TOM.

Yes and by the deeds in your hands it appears, that—

MYRTLE.

Mr. Serjeant, I beg of you to make no inferences upon what is in our custody, but speak to the titles in your own deeds. I shall not show that deed till my client is in Town.

CIMBERTON.

You know best your own methods.

MRS. SEALAND.

The single question is whether the entail is such that my cousin Sir Geoffry is necessary in this affair?

MYRTLE.

Yes, as to the lordship of Tretriplet, but not as to the messuage of Grimgribber.

[29] indenture] a deed or sealed agreement between two or more parties

TOM.

I say that Gr—gr— that Gr—gr—Grimgribber, Grimgribber is in us. That is to say the remainder thereof, as well as that of Tr—tr—Triplet.

MYRTLE.

You go upon the deed of Sir Ralph, made in the middle of the last century, precedent to that in which old Cimberton made over the remainder and made it pass to the heirs general, by which your client comes in, and I question whether the remainder even of Tretriplet is in him. But we are willing to wave that and give him a valuable consideration. But we shall not purchase what is in us for ever, as Grimgribber is, at the rate as we guard against the contingent of Mr. Cimberton having no son. Then we know Sir Geoffry is the first of the collateral male line in this family. Yet—

TOM.

Sir, Gr—gr—ber is—

MYRTLE.

I apprehend you very well, and your argument might be of force, and we would be inclined to hear that in all its parts. But sir, I see very plainly what you are going into. I tell you, it is as probable a contingent that Sir Geoffry may die before Mr. Cimberton, as that he may outlive him.

TOM.

Sir, we are not ripe for that yet, but I must say—

MYRTLE.

Sir, I allow you the whole extent of that argument, but that will go no farther than as to the claimants under old Cimberton. I am of opinion that according to the instruction of Sir Ralph, he could not dock the entail and then create a new estate for the heirs general.

TOM.

Sir, I have not patience to be told that, when Gr—gr—ber—

MYRTLE.

I will allow it you, Mr. Serjeant, but there must be the word "heirs forever" to make such an estate as you pretend.

CIMBERTON.

I must be impartial, though you are counsel for my side of the question. Were it not that you are so good as to allow him what he has not said, I should think it very hard you should answer him without hearing him. But gentlemen, I believe you have both considered this matter and are firm in your different opinions. 'Twere better therefore you proceeded according to the particular sense of each of you and gave your thoughts distinctly in writing. And do you see, sirs, pray let me have a copy of what you say, in English.

MYRTLE.

Why, what is all we have been saying? In English! Oh, but I forgot myself, you're a wit. But however, to please you, sir, you shall have it in as plain terms as the law will admit of.

CIMBERTON.

But I would have it, sir, without delay.

MYRTLE.

That, sir, the law will not admit of. The courts are sitting at Westminster,[30] and I am this moment obliged to be at every one of them, and 'twould be wrong if I should not be in the hall to attend one of 'em at least; the rest would take it ill else. Therefore, I must leave what I have said to Mr. Serjeant's consideration, and I will digest his arguments on my part, and you shall hear from me again, sir. (*Exit.*)

TOM.

Agreed, agreed.

CIMBERTON.

Mr. Bramble is very quick. He parted a little abruptly.

TOM.

He could not bear my argument; I pinched him to the quick about that Gr—gr—ber.

MRS. SEALAND.

I saw that, for he durst not so much as hear you. I shall send to you, Mr. Serjeant, as soon as Sir Geoffry comes to Town, and then I hope all may be adjusted.

TOM.

I shall be at my chambers at my usual hours. (*Exit.*)

CIMBERTON.

Madam, if you please, I'll now attend you to the tea table, where I shall hear from your ladyship reason and good sense, after all this law and gibberish.

MRS. SEALAND.

'Tis a wonderful[31] thing, sir, that men of professions do not study to talk the substance of what they have to say in the language of the rest of the world. Sure they'd find their account in it.

CIMBERTON.

They might perhaps, madam, with people of your good sense but with the generality 'twould never do. The vulgar would have no respect for truth and knowledge if they were exposed to naked view.
Truth is too simple, of all art* bereaved:
Since the world will—why, let it be deceived.

Exeunt.

Act IV, scene i. Bevil Junior's lodgings.

Bevil Junior with a letter in his hand, followed by Tom.

TOM.

Upon my life, sir, I know nothing of the matter. I never opened my lips to Mr. Myrtle about anything of your honor's letter to Madam Lucinda.

BEVIL JUNIOR. (*Aside.*)

What's the fool in such a fright for?—I don't suppose you did. What I would know is whether Mr. Myrtle showed any suspicion or asked you any questions to lead you to say casually that you had carried any such letter for me this morning.

TOM.

Why sir, if he did ask me any questions, how could I help it?

BEVIL JUNIOR.

I don't say you could, oaf! I am not questioning you but him. What did he say to you?

TOM.

Why sir, when I came to his chambers to be dressed for the lawyer's part your honor was pleased to put me upon, he asked me if I had been at Mr. Sealand's this morning. So I told him, sir, I often went thither, because, sir, if I had not said that, he might have thought there was something more in my going now than at another time.

BEVIL JUNIOR.

Very well! (*Aside.*) The fellow's caution, I find, has

[30] Westminster] Westminster Hall*

[31] wonderful] odd, perplexing

given him this jealousy.—Did he ask you no other questions?

TOM.

Yes sir, now I remember, as we came away in the hackney coach from Mr. Sealand's, "Tom," says he, "as I came in to your master this morning, he bad you go for an answer to a letter he had sent. Pray did you bring him any?" says he. "Ah!" says I, "Sir, your honor is pleased to joke with me; you have a mind to know whether I can keep a secret or no."

BEVIL JUNIOR.

And so, by showing him you could, you told him you had one?

TOM. (*Confused.*)

Sir—

BEVIL JUNIOR. (*Aside.*)

What mean* actions does jealousy make a man stoop to? How poorly has he used art* with a servant to make him betray his master.—Well! And when did he give you this letter for me?

TOM.

Sir, he writ it before he pulled off his lawyer's gown at his own chambers.

BEVIL JUNIOR.

Very well, and what did he say when you brought him my answer to it?

TOM.

He looked a little out of humor, sir, and said it was very well.

BEVIL JUNIOR.

I knew he would be grave upon't. Wait without.

TOM.

Humh! 'Gad, I don't like this; I am afraid we are all in the wrong box here. (*Exit.*)

BEVIL JUNIOR.

I put on a serenity while my fellow was present. But I have never been more thoroughly disturbed. This hot man! To write me a challenge on supposed artificial dealing, when I professed myself his friend! I can live contented without glory, but I cannot suffer shame. What's to be done? But first, let me consider Lucinda's letter again. (*Reads.*) "Sir, I hope it is consistent with the laws a woman ought to impose upon herself to acknowledge that your manner of declining a treaty of marriage in our family and desiring the refusal may come from hence has something more engaging in it than the courtship of him, who, I fear, will fall to my lot, except your friend exerts himself for our common safety and happiness. I have reasons for desiring Mr. Myrtle may not know of this letter till hereafter and am your most obliged humble servant, Lucinda Sealand." Well, but the postscript. (*Reads.*) "I won't, upon second thoughts, hide anything from you. But my reason for concealing this is that Mr. Myrtle has a jealousy in his temper which gives me some terrors. But my esteem for him inclines me to hope that only an ill effect, which sometimes accompanies a tender love, and what may be cured by a careful and unblameable conduct." Thus has this lady made me her friend and confidant and put herself, in a kind, under my protection. I cannot tell him immediately the purport of her letter, except I could cure him of the violent and untractable passion of jealousy and so serve him and her by disobeying her in the article of secrecy more than I should by complying with her directions. But then this dueling, which custom has imposed upon every man who would live with reputation and honor in the world: How must I preserve myself from imputations there? He'll, forsooth, call it or think it fear, if I explain without fighting. But his letter, I'll read it again. (*Reads.*) "Sir, you have used me basely in corresponding and carrying on a treaty where you told me you were indifferent. I have changed my sword since I saw you, which advertisement[32] I thought proper to send you against the next meeting between you and the injured, Charles Myrtle."

Enter Tom.

TOM.

Mr. Myrtle, sir. Would your honor please to see him?

BEVIL JUNIOR.

Why you stupid creature! Let Mr. Myrtle wait at my lodgings! Show him up.

Exit Tom.

Well! I am resolved upon my carriage to him. He is in love and in every circumstance of life a little distrustful, which I must allow for. But here he is.

32 advertisement] warning

Enter Tom introducing Myrtle.

Sir, I am extremely obliged to you for this honor.—But sir, you, with your very discerning face, leave the room.

Exit Tom.

Well Mr. Myrtle, your commands with me?

MYRTLE.

The time, the place, our long acquaintance, and many other circumstances which affect me on this occasion oblige me without farther ceremony or conference to desire you would not only, as you already have, acknowledge the receipt of my letter but also comply with the request in it. I must have farther notice taken of my message than these half lines, "I have yours, I shall be at home."

BEVIL JUNIOR.

Sir, I own I have received a letter from you in a very unusual style. But as I design everything in this matter shall be your own action, your own seeking, I shall understand nothing but what you are pleased to confirm face to face, and I have already forgot the contents of your epistle.

MYRTLE.

This cool manner is very agreeable to the abuse you have already made of my simplicity and frankness, and I see your moderation tends to your own advantage and not mine, to your own safety, not consideration of your friend.

BEVIL JUNIOR.

My own safety, Mr. Myrtle!

MYRTLE.

Your own safety, Mr. Bevil.

BEVIL JUNIOR.

Look you, Mr. Myrtle, there's no disguising that I understand what you would be at. But sir, you know I have often dared to disapprove of the decisions a tyrant custom has introduced to the breach of all laws, both divine and human.

MYRTLE.

Mr. Bevil, Mr. Bevil, it would be a good first principle in those who have so tender a conscience that way to have as much abhorrence of doing injuries as—

BEVIL JUNIOR.

As what?

MYRTLE.

As fear of answering for 'em.

BEVIL JUNIOR.

As fear of answering for 'em! But that apprehension is just or blameable according to the object of that fear. I have often told you in confidence of heart, I abhorred the daring to offend the Author of life and rushing into His presence, I say, by the very same act to commit the crime against Him and immediately to urge on to His tribunal.

MYRTLE.

Mr. Bevil, I must tell you this coolness, this gravity, this show of conscience, shall never cheat me of my mistress. You have, indeed, the best excuse for life, the hopes of possessing Lucinda. But consider, sir, I have as much reason to be weary of it, if I am to lose her, and my first attempt to recover her shall be to let her see the dauntless man who is to be her guardian and protector.

BEVIL JUNIOR.

Sir, show me but the least glimpse of argument that I am authorized by my own hand to vindicate any lawless insult of this nature, and I will show thee, to chastise thee hardly deserves the name of courage—slight, inconsiderate man! There is, Mr. Myrtle, no such terror in quick anger, and you shall, you know not why, be cool, as you have, you know not why, been warm.

MYRTLE.

Is the woman one loves so little an occasion of anger? You perhaps, who know not what it is to love, who have your ready, your commodious, your foreign trinket for your loose hours and from your fortune, your specious outward carriage, and other lucky circumstances as easy a way to the possession of a woman of honor. You know nothing of what it is to be alarmed, to be distracted with anxiety and terror of losing more than life. Your marriage, happy man, goes on like common business, and in the interim, you have your rambling captive, your Indian princess, for your soft moments of dalliance, your convenient, your ready Indiana.

BEVIL JUNIOR.

You have touched me beyond the patience of a man, and I'm excusable, in the guard of innocence or from the infirmity of human nature which can bear no more, to accept your invitation and observe your letter. Sir, I'll attend you.

Enter Tom.

TOM.

Did you call, sir? I thought you did; I heard you speak aloud.

BEVIL JUNIOR.

Yes, go call a coach.

TOM.

Sir—Master—Mr. Myrtle—Friends—Gentlemen—what d'ye mean? I am but a servant, or—

BEVIL JUNIOR.

Call a coach.

Exit Tom. A long pause, walking sullenly by each other.

(*Aside.*) Shall I, though provoked to the uttermost, recover myself at the entrance of a third person, and that my servant too, and not have respect enough to all I have ever been receiving from infancy, the obligation to the best of fathers, to an unhappy virgin too, whose life depends on mine. (*Shutting the door.*) —I have, thank Heaven, had time to recollect myself and shall not, for fear of what such a rash man as you think of me, keep longer unexplained the false appearances under which your infirmity of temper makes you suffer, when, perhaps, too much regard to a false point of honor makes me prolong that suffering.

MYRTLE.

I am sure Mr. Bevil cannot doubt* but I had rather have satisfaction from his innocence than his sword.

BEVIL JUNIOR.

Why then would you ask it first that way?

MYRTLE.

Consider, you kept your temper yourself no longer than till I spoke to the disadvantage of her you loved.

BEVIL JUNIOR.

True. But let me tell you, I have saved you from the most exquisite distress, even though you had succeeded in the dispute. I know you so well that I am sure to have found this letter about a man you had killed would have been worse than death to yourself. Read it. (*Aside.*) When he is thoroughly mortified and shame has got the better of jealousy, when he has seen himself thoroughly, he will deserve to be assisted towards obtaining Lucinda.

MYRTLE. (*Aside.*)

With what a superiority has he turned the injury on me as the aggressor! I begin to fear I have been too far transported. "A treaty in our family!" Is not that saying too much? I shall relapse. But I find, on the postscript, "something like jealousy." With what face can I see my benefactor? My advocate? Whom I have treated like a betrayer.—Oh Bevil, with what words shall I—

BEVIL JUNIOR.

There needs none; to convince is much more than to conquer.

MYRTLE.

But can you—

BEVIL JUNIOR.

You have o'erpaid the inquietude you gave me in the change I see in you towards me. Alas! What machines are we! Thy face is altered to that of another man, to that of my companion, my friend.

MYRTLE.

That I could be such a precipitant wretch!

BEVIL JUNIOR.

Pray, no more.

MYRTLE.

Let me reflect how many friends have died by the hands of friends for want of temper, and you must give me leave to say again and again how much I am beholden to that superior spirit you have subdued me with. What had become of one of us, or perhaps both, had you been as weak as I was and as incapable of reason?

BEVIL JUNIOR.

I congratulate to us both the escape from ourselves and hope the memory of it will make us dearer friends than ever.

MYRTLE.

Dear Bevil, your friendly conduct has convinced me that there is nothing manly but what is conducted by reason and agreeable to the practice of virtue and justice. And yet how many have been sacrificed to that idol, the unreasonable opinion of men! Nay, they are so ridiculous in it that they often use their swords against each other with dissembled anger and real fear.

Betrayed by honor and compelled by shame,
They hazard being to preserve a name,
Nor dare inquire into the dread mistake
Till plunged in sad eternity they wake.

Exeunt.

Scene [ii]. St. James's Park.*

Enter Sir John Bevil and Mr. Sealand.

SIR JOHN BEVIL.
Give me leave however, Mr. Sealand, as we are upon a treaty for uniting our families, to mention only the business of an ancient house: genealogy and descent are to be of some consideration in an affair of this sort—

MR. SEALAND.
Genealogy and descent! Sir, there has been in our family a very large one. There was Galfrid the father of Edward, the father of Ptolomey, the father of Crassus, the father of Earl Richard, the father of Henry the Marquis, the father of Duke John—

SIR JOHN BEVIL.
What, do you rave, Mr. Sealand? All these great names in your family?

MR. SEALAND.
These? Yes sir, I have heard my father name 'em all and more.

SIR JOHN BEVIL.
Aye sir? And did he say they were all in your family?

MR. SEALAND.
Yes sir, he kept 'em all. He was the greatest cocker in England. He said Duke John won him many battles and never lost one.

SIR JOHN BEVIL.
Oh sir, your servant, you are laughing at my laying any stress upon descent. But I must tell you, sir, I never knew anyone but he that wanted* that advantage turn it into ridicule.

MR. SEALAND.
And I never knew anyone who had many better advantages put that into his account. But Sir John, value yourself as you please upon your ancient house, I am to talk freely of everything you are pleased to put into your bill of rates[33] on this occasion. Yet sir, I have made no objections to your son's family. 'Tis his morals that I doubt.

SIR JOHN BEVIL.
Sir, I can't help saying that what might injure a citizen's* credit may be no stain to a gentleman's honor.

MR. SEALAND.
Sir John, the honor of a gentleman is liable to be tainted by as small a matter as the credit of a trader. We are talking of a marriage, and in such a case the father of a young woman will not think it an addition to the honor or credit of her lover—that he is a keeper*—

SIR JOHN BEVIL.
Mr. Sealand, don't take upon you to spoil my son's marriage with any woman else.

MR. SEALAND.
Sir John, let him apply to any woman else and have as many mistresses as he pleases—

SIR JOHN BEVIL.
My son, sir, is a discreet and sober gentleman—

MR. SEALAND.
Sir, I never saw a man that wenched soberly and discreetly that ever left it off. The decency observed in the practice hides even from the sinner the iniquity of it. They pursue it not that their appetites hurry 'em away but, I warrant you, because 'tis their opinion they may do it

SIR JOHN BEVIL.
Were what you suspect a truth, do you design to keep your daughter a virgin till you find a man unblemished that way?

MR. SEALAND.
Sir, as much a cit* as you take me for, I know the Town* and the world. And give me leave to say that we merchants are a species of gentry that have grown into the world this last century and are as honorable, and almost as useful, as you landed folks that have always thought yourselves so much above us. For your trading, forsooth, is extended no farther than a load of hay or a fat ox. You are pleasant people, indeed, because you are generally bred up to be lazy; therefore, I warrant you, industry is dishonorable.

SIR JOHN BEVIL.
Be not offended, sir; let us go back to our point.

MR. SEALAND.
Oh, not at all offended, but I don't love to leave

[33] bill of rates] charges, in this case used to indicate considerations for calculating marriage contract settlements

any part of the account unclosed. Look you, Sir John, comparisons are odious, and more particularly so on occasions of this kind, when we are projecting races* that are to be made out of both sides of the comparisons.

SIR JOHN BEVIL.

But my son, sir, is, in the eye of the world, a gentleman of merit.

MR. SEALAND.

I own to you, I think him so. But Sir John, I am a man exercised and experienced in chances and disasters. I lost in my earlier years a very fine wife and with her a poor little infant; this makes me, perhaps, over-cautious to preserve the second bounty of Providence to me and be as careful as I can of this child. You'll pardon me, my poor girl, sir, is as valuable to me as your boasted son to you.

SIR JOHN BEVIL.

Why, that's one very good reason, Mr. Sealand, why I wish my son had her.

MR. SEALAND.

There is nothing but this strange lady here, this incognita, that can be objected to him. Here and there a man falls in love with an artful creature and gives up all the motives of life to that one passion.

SIR JOHN BEVIL.

A man of my son's understanding cannot be supposed to be one of them.

MR. SEALAND.

Very wise men have been so enslaved, and when a man marries with one of them upon his hands, whether moved from the demand of the world or slighter reasons, such a husband soils[34] with his wife for a month perhaps, then good b'w'y'[35] madam, the show's over. Ah! John Dryden points out such a husband to a hair, where he says,

And while abroad so prodigal the dolt is,
Poor spouse at home as ragged as a colt is.[36]

Now in plain terms, sir, I shall not care to have my poor girl turned a-grazing, and that must be the case when—

SIR JOHN BEVIL.

But pray consider, sir, my son—

MR. SEALAND.

Look you, sir, I'll make the matter short. This unknown lady, as I told you, is all the objection I have to him. But one way or other he is or has been certainly engaged to her. I am therefore resolved this very afternoon to visit her. Now from her behavior or appearance I shall soon be let into what I may fear or hope for.

SIR JOHN BEVIL.

Sir, I am very confident there can be nothing inquired into relating to my son that will not, upon being understood, turn to his advantage.

MR. SEALAND.

I hope that as sincerely as you believe it. Sir John Bevil, when I am satisfied in this great point, if your son's conduct answers the character you give him, I shall wish your alliance more than that of any gentleman in Great Britain, and so your servant. (*Exit.*)

SIR JOHN BEVIL.

He is gone in a way but barely civil, but his great wealth and the merit of his only child, the heiress of it, are not to be lost for a little peevishness.

Enter Humphrey.

Oh Humphrey, you are come in a seasonable minute. I want to talk to thee and to tell thee that my head and heart are on the rack about my son.

HUMPHREY.

Sir, you may trust his discretion, I am sure you may.

SIR JOHN BEVIL.

Why, I do believe I may, and yet I'm in a thousand fears when I lay this vast wealth before me. When I consider his prepossessions, either generous to a folly in an honorable love or abandoned past redemption in a vicious one, and, from the one or the other, his insensibility to the fairest prospect towards doubling our estate, a father who knows how useful wealth is and how necessary even to those who despise it, I say a father, Humphrey, a father cannot bear it.

HUMPHREY.

Be not transported, sir; you will grow incapable of taking any resolution in your perplexity.

[34] soils] cohabits

[35] b'w'y'] goodbye, from "God be with ye"

[36] And ... is] from Dryden's epilogue to Sir John Vanbrugh's adaptation of John Fletcher's *The Pilgrim* (1700), slightly misquoted

SIR JOHN BEVIL.

Yet as angry as I am with him, I would not have him surprised in anything. This mercantile, rough man may go grossly into the examination of this matter and talk to the gentlewoman so as to—

HUMPHREY.

No, I hope, not in an abrupt manner.

SIR JOHN BEVIL.

No, I hope not! Why, dost thou know anything of her or of him or of anything of it or all of it?

HUMPHREY.

My dear master, I know so much that I told him this very day you had reason to be secretly out of humor about her.

SIR JOHN BEVIL.

Did you go so far? Well, what said he to that?

HUMPHREY.

His words were, looking upon me steadfastly: "Humphrey," says he, "that woman is a woman of honor."

SIR JOHN BEVIL.

How! Do you think he is married to her or designs to marry her?

HUMPHREY.

I can say nothing to the latter. But he says he can marry no one without your consent while you are living.

SIR JOHN BEVIL.

If he said so much, I know he scorns to break his word with me.

HUMPHREY.

I am sure of that.

SIR JOHN BEVIL.

You are sure of that. Well, that's some comfort. Then I have nothing to do but to see the bottom of this matter during this present ruffle. Oh Humphrey—

HUMPHREY.

You are not ill, I hope, sir.

SIR JOHN BEVIL.

Yes, a man is very ill that's in a very ill humor. To be a father is to be in care for one whom you oftener disoblige than please by that very care. Oh! That sons could know the duty to a father before they themselves are fathers. But perhaps, you'll say now that I am one of the happiest fathers in the world. But I assure you that of the very happiest is not a condition to be envied.

HUMPHREY.

Sir, your pain arises not from the thing itself but your particular sense of it. You are overfond, nay, give me leave to say, you are unjustly apprehensive from your fondness. My Master Bevil never disobliged you, and he will, I know he will, do everything you ought to expect.

SIR JOHN BEVIL.

He won't take all this money with this girl. For aught I know, he will, forsooth, have so much moderation as to think he ought not to force his liking for any consideration.

HUMPHREY.

He is to marry her, not you; he is to live with her, not you, sir.

SIR JOHN BEVIL.

I know not what to think. But I know nothing can be more miserable than to be in this doubt. Follow me; I must come to some resolution.

Exeunt.

Scene [iii]. Bevil Junior's lodgings.

Enter Tom and Phillis.

TOM.

Well madam, if you must speak with Mr. Myrtle, you shall; he is now with my master in the library.

PHILLIS.

But you must leave me alone with him, for he can't make me a present nor I so handsomely take anything from him before you; it would not be decent.

TOM.

It will be very decent, indeed, for me to retire and leave my mistress with another man.

PHILLIS.

He is a gentleman and will treat one properly—

TOM.

I believe so. But however, I won't be far off and therefore will venture to trust you. I'll call him to you. (*Exit.*)

PHILLIS.

What a deal of pother and sputter here is between my mistress and Mr. Myrtle from mere punctilio?

I could any hour of the day get her to her lover and would do it. But she, forsooth, will allow no plot to get him. But if he can come to her, I know she would be glad of it. I must therefore do her an acceptable violence and surprise her into his arms. I am sure I go by the best rule imaginable: if she were my maid, I should think her the best servant in the world for doing so by me.

Enter Myrtle and Tom.

Oh sir, you and Mr. Bevil are fine gentlemen to let a lady remain under such difficulties as my poor mistress and no attempt to set her at liberty or release her from the danger of being instantly married to Cimberton.

MYRTLE.

Tom has been telling. But what is to be done?

PHILLIS.

What is to be done—when a man can't come at his mistress! Why, can't you fire our house or the next house to us, to make us run out and you take us?

MYRTLE.

How, Mrs. Phillis—

PHILLIS.

Aye, let me see that rogue deny to fire a house, make a riot, or any other little thing, when there were no other way to come at me.

TOM.

I am obliged to you, madam.

PHILLIS.

Why, don't we hear everyday of people's hanging themselves for love, and won't they venture the hazard of being hanged for love? Oh! Were I a man—

MYRTLE.

What manly thing would you have me undertake, according to your ladyship's notion of a man?

PHILLIS.

Only be at once what, one time or other, you may be and wish to be or must be.

MYRTLE.

Dear girl, talk plainly to me and consider, I in my condition can't be in very good humor. You say, to be at once what I must be.

PHILLIS.

Aye, aye. I mean no more than to be an old man; I saw you do it very well at the masquerade. In a word, old Sir Geoffry Cimberton is every hour expected in Town to join in the deeds and settlements for marrying Mr. Cimberton. He is half blind, half lame, half deaf, half dumb; though as to his passions and desires, he is as warm and ridiculous as when in the heat of youth—

TOM.

Come to the business and don't keep the gentleman in suspense for the pleasure of being courted, as you serve me.

PHILLIS.

I saw you at the masquerade act such a one to perfection. Go and put on that very habit and come to our house as Sir Geoffry. There is not one there but myself knows his person. I was born in the parish where he is lord of the manor. I have seen him often and often at church in the country. Do not hesitate, but come thither. They will think you bring a certain security against Mr. Myrtle, and you bring Mr. Myrtle. Leave the rest to me. I leave this with you and expect. They don't, I told you, know you. They think you out of town, which you had as good be forever if you lose this opportunity. I must be gone; I know I am wanted at home.

MYRTLE.

My dear Phillis! (*Catches and kisses her, and gives her money.*)

PHILLIS.

Oh fie! My kisses are not my own; you have committed violence. But I'll carry 'em to the right owner. (*Tom kisses her.*) —Come, see me downstairs and leave the lover to think of his last game for the prize.

Exeunt Tom and Phillis.

MYRTLE.

I think I will instantly attempt this wild expedient. The extravagance of it will make me less suspected, and it will give me opportunity to assert my own right to Lucinda, without whom I cannot live. But I am so mortified at this conduct of mine towards poor Bevil. He must think meanly of me. I know not how to reassume myself and be in spirit enough for such an adventure as this. Yet I must attempt it, if it be only to be near Lucinda, under

her present perplexities. And sure—
The next delight to transport with the fair
Is to relieve her in her hours of care.

Exit.

Act V, scene i. Sealand's house.

Enter Phillis, with lights, before Myrtle, disguised like old Sir Geoffry, supported by Mrs. Sealand, Lucinda, and Cimberton.

MRS. SEALAND.
Now I have seen you thus far, Sir Geoffry, will you excuse me a moment, while I give my necessary orders for your accommodation? (*Exit.*)

MYRTLE.
I have not seen you, Cousin Cimberton, since you were ten years old, and as it is incumbent on you to keep up our name and family, I shall, upon very reasonable terms, join with you in a settlement to that purpose. Though I must tell you, Cousin, this is the first merchant that has married into our house.

LUCINDA. (*Aside.*)
Deuce on 'em! Am I a merchant because my father is?

MYRTLE.
But is he directly a trader at this time?

CIMBERTON.
There's no hiding the disgrace, sir: he trades to all parts of the world.

MYRTLE.
We never had one of our family before who descended from persons that did anything.

CIMBERTON.
Sir, since it is a girl that they have, I am, for the honor of my family, willing to take it in again and to sink her into our name and no harm done.

MYRTLE.
'Tis prudently and generously resolved. Is this the young thing?

CIMBERTON.
Yes sir.

PHILLIS. (*Aside to Lucinda.*)
Good madam, don't be out of humor, but let them run to the utmost of their extravagance. Hear them out.

MYRTLE.
Can't I see her nearer? My eyes are but weak.

PHILLIS. (*Aside to Lucinda.*)
Beside, I am sure the uncle has something worth your notice. I'll take care to get off the young one and leave you to observe what may be wrought out of the old one for your good. (*Exit.*)

CIMBERTON.
Madam, this old gentleman, your great uncle, desires to be introduced to you and to see you nearer.—Approach, sir.

MYRTLE.
By your leave, young lady. (*Puts on spectacles.*) — Cousin Cimberton! She has exactly that sort of neck and bosom for which my sister Gertrude was so much admired in the year sixty one, before the French dresses first discovered* anything in women below the chin.

LUCINDA. (*Aside.*)
What a very odd situation am I in. Though I cannot but be diverted at the extravagance of their humors,* equally unsuitable to their age.—"Chin," quotha! I don't believe my passionate lover there knows whether I have one or not. Ha! Ha!

MYRTLE.
Madam, I would not willingly offend, but I have a better glass— (*Pulls out a large one.*)

Enter Phillis to Cimberton.

PHILLIS.
Sir, my lady desires to show the apartment to you that she intends for Sir Geoffry.

CIMBERTON.
Well sir, by that time you have sufficiently gazed and sunned yourself in the beauties of my spouse there, I will wait on you again.

Exeunt Cimberton and Phillis.

MYRTLE.
Were it not, madam, that I might be troublesome, there is something of importance, though we are alone, which I would say more safe from being heard.

LUCINDA. (*Aside.*)
There is something in this old fellow, methinks, that raises my curiosity.

MYRTLE.

To be free, madam, I as heartily contemn this kinsman of mine as you do and am sorry to see so much beauty and merit devoted by your parents to so insensible a possessor.

LUCINDA. [*Aside.*]

Surprising!—I hope then, sir, you will not contribute to the wrong you are so generous as to pity, whatever may be the interest of your family.

MYRTLE.

This hand of mine shall never be employed to sign anything against your good and happiness.

LUCINDA.

I am sorry, sir, it is not in my power to make you proper acknowledgments, but there is a gentleman in the world whose gratitude will, I am sure, be worthy of the favor.

MYRTLE.

All the thanks I desire, madam, are in your power to give.

LUCINDA.

Name them, and command them.

MYRTLE.

Only, madam, that the first time you are alone with your lover, you will with open arms receive him.

LUCINDA.

As willingly as his heart could wish it.

MYRTLE.

Thus then he claims your promise! Oh Lucinda!

LUCINDA.

Oh! A cheat! A cheat! A cheat!

MYRTLE.

Hush! 'Tis I, 'tis I, your lover, Myrtle himself, madam.

LUCINDA.

Oh bless me! What a rashness and folly to surprise me so.—But hush, my mother—

Enter Mrs. Sealand, Cimberton, and Phillis.

MRS. SEALAND.

How now! What's the matter?

LUCINDA.

Oh madam! As soon as you left the room, my uncle fell into a sudden fit, and—and—so I cried out for help to support him and conduct him to his chamber.

MRS. SEALAND.

That was kindly done. Alas sir, how do you find yourself?

MYRTLE.

Never was taken in so odd a way in my life. Pray lead me. Oh! I was talking here—pray carry me—to my Cousin Cimberton's young lady—

MRS. SEALAND. (*Aside.*)

My Cousin Cimberton's young lady! How zealous he is, even in his extremity, for the match! A right Cimberton.

Cimberton and Lucinda lead him, as one in pain, etc.

CIMBERTON.

Pox! Uncle, you will pull my ear off.

LUCINDA.

Pray Uncle! You will squeeze me to death.

MRS. SEALAND.

No matter, no matter. He knows not what he does.—Come sir, shall I help you out?

MYRTLE.

By no means; I'll trouble nobody but my young cousins here.

They lead him off.

PHILLIS.

But pray, madam, does your ladyship intend that Mr. Cimberton shall really marry my young mistress at last? I don't think he likes her.

MRS. SEALAND.

That's not material. Men of his speculation are above desires. But be it as it may, now I have given old Sir Geoffry the trouble of coming up to sign and seal, with what countenance can I be off?

PHILLIS.

As well as with twenty others, madam. It is the glory and honor of a great fortune to live in continual treaties and still to break off. It looks great, madam.

MRS. SEALAND.

True, Phillis. Yet to return our blood again into the Cimberton's is an honor not to be rejected. But were not you saying that Sir John Bevil's creature Humphrey has been with Mr. Sealand?

PHILLIS.

Yes madam, I overheard them agree that Mr.

Sealand should go himself and visit this unknown lady that Mr. Bevil is so great with. And if he found nothing there to fright him, that Mr. Bevil should still marry my young mistress.

MRS. SEALAND.

How! Nay then, he shall find she is my daughter as well as his. I'll follow him this instant and take the whole family* along with me. The disputed power of disposing of my own daughter shall be at an end this very night. I'll live no longer in anxiety for a little hussy that hurts my appearance wherever I carry her and for whose sake I seem to be not[e] at all regarded, and that in the best of my days.

PHILLIS.

Indeed, madam, if she were married, your ladyship might very well be taken for Mr. Sealand's daughter.

MRS. SEALAND.

Nay, when the chit has not been with me, I have heard the men say as much. I'll no longer cut off the greatest pleasure of a woman's life—the shining in assemblies—by her forward anticipation of the respect that's due to her superior. She shall down to Cimberton Hall—she shall—she shall.

PHILLIS.

I hope, madam, I shall stay with your ladyship.

MRS. SEALAND.

Thou shalt, Phillis, and I'll place thee then more about me. But order chairs* immediately; I'll be gone this minute.

Exeunt.

Scene [ii]. Charing Cross.[37]

Enter Mr. Sealand and Humphrey.

MR. SEALAND.

I am very glad, Mr. Humphrey, that you agree with me that it is for our common good I should look thoroughly into this matter.

HUMPHREY.

I am, indeed, of that opinion, for there is no artifice, nothing concealed, in our family, which ought in justice to be known. I need not desire you, sir, to treat the lady with care and respect.

MR. SEALAND.

Master Humphrey, I shall not be rude, though I design to be a little abrupt and come into the matter at once, to see how she will bear upon a surprise.

HUMPHREY.

That's the door, sir; I wish you success.

While Humphrey speaks, Sealand consults his table-book.[38] (*Aside.*) I am less concerned what happens there, because I hear Mr. Myrtle is well-lodged as old Sir Geoffry. So I am willing to let this gentleman employ himself here to give them time at home, for I am sure 'tis necessary for the quiet of our family Lucinda were disposed of out of it, since Mr. Bevil's inclination is so much otherwise engaged. (*Exit.*)

MR. SEALAND.

I think this is the door. (*Knocks.*) I'll carry this matter with an air of authority to inquire, though I make an errand to begin discourse.

Knocks again, and enter Daniel, a foot-boy.

So young man, is your lady within?

DANIEL.

Alack sir, I am but a country boy. I dan't know whether she is or noa, but an* you'll stay a bit, I'll goa and ask the gentlewoman that's with her.

MR. SEALAND.

Why sirrah, though you are a country boy, you can see, can't you? You know whether she is at home when you see her, don't you?

DANIEL.

Nay, nay, I'm not such a country lad neither, master, to think she's at home because I see her. I have been in Town but a month, and I lost one place already for believing my own eyes.

MR. SEALAND.

Why sirrah, have you learnt to lie already?

DANIEL.

Ah Master, things that are lies in the country are not lies at London. I begin to know my business a little better than so. But an you please to walk in, I'll call a gentlewoman to you that can tell you for certain. She can make bold to ask my lady herself.

[37] Charing Cross] crossroads in Westminster (from *cering*, bend, either of the Thames or of the Roman road running west out of London); after the Restoration, the site of executions of rebels; a fashionable area of the Town*

[38] table-book] notebook

MR. SEALAND.
Oh! Then she is within, I find, though you dare not say so.

DANIEL.
Nay, nay! That's neither here, nor there. What's matter whether she is within or no, if she has not a mind to see anybody.

MR. SEALAND.
I can't tell, sirrah, whether you are arch or simple, but however, get me a direct answer and here's a shilling for you.

DANIEL.
Will you please to walk in; I'll see what I can do for you.

MR. SEALAND.
I see you will be fit for your business in time, child. But I expect to meet with nothing but extraordinaries[39] in such a house.

DANIEL.
Such a house! Sir, you han't seen it yet. Pray walk in.

MR. SEALAND.
Sir, I'll wait upon you.

Exeunt.

Scene [iii.] Indiana's house.

Enter Isabella.

ISABELLA.
What anxiety do I feel for this poor creature! What will be the end of her? Such a languishing, unreserved passion for a man that at last must certainly leave or ruin her, and perhaps both! Then the aggravation of the distress is that she does not believe he will. Not but I must own, if they are both what they would seem, they are made for one another as much as Adam and Eve were, for there is no other of their kind but themselves.

Enter Daniel.

So Daniel, what news with you?

DANIEL.
Madam, there's a gentleman below would speak with my lady.

39 extraordinaries] unusual, fantastic, irrational, or extravagant doings

ISABELLA.
Sirrah! Don't you know Mr. Bevil yet?

DANIEL.
Madam, 'tis not the gentleman who comes everyday and asks for you and won't go till he knows whether you are with her or no.

ISABELLA. (*Aside.*)
Hah! That's a particular I did not know before.—Well, be it who it will, let him come up to me.

Exit Daniel, and re-enters with Mr. Sealand. Isabella looks amazed.

MR. SEALAND.
Madam, I can't blame your being a little surprised to see a perfect stranger make a visit, and—

ISABELLA.
I am indeed surprised! (*Aside.*) I see he does not know me.

MR. SEALAND.
You are very prettily lodged here, madam. In troth, you seem to have everything in plenty. (*Aside, and looking about.*) A thousand a year, I warrant you, upon this pretty nest of rooms and the dainty one within them.

ISABELLA. (*Apart.*)
Twenty years, it seems, have less effect in the alteration of a man of thirty than of a girl of fourteen. He's almost still the same, but alas, I find by other men, as well as himself, I am not what I was. As soon as he spoke, I was convinced 'twas he. How shall I contain my surprise and satisfaction? He must not know me yet.

MR. SEALAND.
Madam, I hope I don't give you any disturbance. But there is a young lady here with whom I have a particular business to discourse, and I hope she will admit me to that favor.

ISABELLA.
Why sir, have you had any notice concerning her? I wonder who could give it you.

MR. SEALAND.
That, madam, is fit only to be communicated to herself.

ISABELLA.
Well sir, you shall see her. (*Aside.*) I find he knows nothing yet, nor shall from me. I am resolved I will

observe this interlude, this sport of nature and of fortune.—You shall see her presently, sir. For now I am as a mother and will trust her with you. (*Exit.*)

MR. SEALAND.

As a mother![40] Right, that's the old phrase for one of those commode[41] ladies who lend out beauty for hire to young gentlemen that have pressing occasions.—But here comes the precious lady herself. In troth a very sightly woman—

Enter Indiana.

INDIANA.

I am told, sir, you have some affair that requires your speaking with me.

MR. SEALAND.

Yes, madam. There came to my hands a bill* drawn by Mr. Bevil which is payable tomorrow, and he, in the intercourse of business, sent it to me, who have cash of his, and desired me to send a servant with it. But I have made bold to bring you the money myself.

INDIANA.

Sir! Was that necessary?

MR. SEALAND.

No madam, but to be free with you, the fame of your beauty and the regard which Mr. Bevil is a little too well known to have for you excited my curiosity.

INDIANA.

Too well known to have for me! Your sober appearance, sir, which my friend described, made me expect no rudeness or absurdity at least.—Who's there?—Sir, if you pay the money to a servant, 'twill be as well.

MR. SEALAND.

Pray madam, be not offended. I came hither on an innocent, nay a virtuous design, and if you will have patience to hear me, it may be as useful to you, as you are in a friendship with Mr. Bevil, as to my only daughter, whom I was this day disposing of.

INDIANA.

You make me hope, sir, I have mistaken you. I am composed again. Be free, say on— (*Aside.*) what I am afraid to hear—

MR. SEALAND.

I feared, indeed, an unwarranted passion here, but I did not think it was in abuse of so worthy an object, so accomplished a lady, as your sense and mien bespeak. But the youth of our age care not what merit and virtue they bring to shame, so they gratify—

INDIANA.

Sir, you are going into very great errors. But as you are pleased to say you see something in me that has changed at least the color of your suspicions, so has your appearance altered mine and made me earnestly attentive to what has any way concerned you to inquire into my affairs and character.

MR. SEALAND. (*Aside.*)

How sensibly, with what an air she talks!

INDIANA.

Good sir, be seated and tell me tenderly—keep all your suspicions concerning me alive that you may, in a proper and prepared way, acquaint me why the care of your daughter obliges a person of your seeming worth and fortune to be thus inquisitive about a wretched, helpless, friendless— (*Weeping.*) But I beg your pardon. Though I am an orphan, your child is not, and your concern for her, it seems, has brought you hither. I'll be composed. Pray go on, sir.

MR. SEALAND.

How could Mr. Bevil be such a monster to injure such a woman?

INDIANA.

No, sir, you wrong him. He has not injured me. My support is from his bounty.

MR. SEALAND.

Bounty! When gluttons give high prices for delicates, they are prodigious bountiful.

INDIANA.

Still, still you will persist in that error. But my own fears tell me all. You are the gentleman, I suppose, for whose happy daughter he is designed a husband by his good father, and he has, perhaps, consented to the overture. He was here this morning, dressed beyond his usual plainness, nay most sumptuously, and he is to be, perhaps, this night a bridegroom.

40 mother] procuress

41 commode] accommodating

MR. SEALAND.
I own he was intended such. But madam, on your account I have determined to defer my daughter's marriage till I am satisfied from your own mouth of what nature are the obligations you are under to him.

INDIANA.
His actions, sir, his eyes have only made me think he designed to make me the partner of his heart. The goodness and gentleness of his demeanor made me misinterpret all. 'Twas my own hope, my own passion, that deluded me. He never made one amorous advance to me. His large heart and bestowing hand have only helped the miserable. Nor know I why, but from his mere* delight in virtue, that I have been his care, the object on which to indulge and please himself with pouring favors.

MR. SEALAND.
Madam, I know not why it is, but I, as well as you, am methinks afraid of entering into the matter I came about. But 'tis the same thing, as if we had talked never so distinctly—he ne'er shall have a daughter of mine.

INDIANA.
If you say this from what you think of me, you wrong yourself and him. Let not me, miserable though I may be, do injury to my benefactor. No sir, my treatment ought rather to reconcile you to his virtues. If to bestow without prospect of return; if to delight in supporting what might, perhaps, be thought an object of desire with no other view than to be her guard against those who would not be so disinterested; if these actions, sir, can in a careful parent's eye commend him to a daughter, give yours, sir, give her to my honest, generous Bevil. What have I to do but sigh and weep, to rave, run wild, a lunatic in chains, or, hid in darkness, mutter in distracted starts and broken accents my strange, strange story!

MR. SEALAND.
Take comfort, madam.

INDIANA.
All my comfort must be to expostulate in madness, to relieve with frenzy my despair, and shrieking to demand of fate: Why, why was I born to such variety of sorrows?

MR. SEALAND.
If I have been the least occasion—

INDIANA.
No, 'twas Heaven's high will I should be such: to be plundered in my cradle! Tossed on the seas! And even there, an infant captive! To lose my mother, hear but of my father! To be adopted! Lose my adopter! Then plunged again in worse calamities!

MR. SEALAND.
An infant captive!

INDIANA.
Yet then, to find the most charming of mankind once more to set me free from what I thought the last distress; to load me with his services, his bounties, and his favors; to support my very life in a way that stole, at the same time, my very soul itself from me.

MR. SEALAND.
And has young Bevil been this worthy man?

INDIANA.
Yet, then again, this very man to take another! Without leaving me the right, the pretence of easing my fond heart with tears! For oh, I can't reproach him, though the same hand that raised me to this height now throws me down the precipice.

MR. SEALAND.
Dear lady! Oh, yet one moment's patience. My heart grows full with your affliction. But yet, there's something in your story that—

INDIANA.
My portion here is bitterness and sorrow.

MR. SEALAND.
Do not think so. Pray answer me, does Bevil know your name and family?

INDIANA.
Alas! Too well! Oh, could I be any other thing than what I am. I'll tear away all traces of my former self, my little ornaments, the remains of my first state, the hints of what I ought to have been—

In her disorder, she throws away a bracelet, which Sealand takes up and looks earnestly on.

MR. SEALAND.
Hah! What's this? My eyes are not deceived? It is, it is the same! The very bracelet which I bequeathed my wife at our last mournful parting.

INDIANA.

What said you, sir! Your wife! Whither does my fancy carry me? What means this unfelt motion at my heart? And yet again my fortune but deludes me, for if I err not, sir, your name is Sealand. But my lost father's name was—

MR. SEALAND.

Danvers! Was it not?

INDIANA.

What new amazement! That is indeed my family.

MR. SEALAND.

Know then, when my misfortunes drove me to the Indies, for reasons too tedious now to mention, I changed my name of Danvers into Sealand.

Enter Isabella.

ISABELLA.

If yet there wants* an explanation of your wonder, examine well this face—yours, sir, I well remember—gaze on, and read in me your sister Isabella!

MR. SEALAND.

My sister!

ISABELLA.

But here's a claim more tender yet: your Indiana, sir, your long lost daughter.

MR. SEALAND.

Oh, my child! My child!

INDIANA.

All-gracious Heaven! Is it possible! Do I embrace my father!

MR. SEALAND.

And do I hold thee? These passions are too strong for utterance. Rise, rise, my child, and give my tears their way.—Oh, my sister! (*Embracing her.*)

ISABELLA.

Now dearest niece, my groundless fears, my painful cares no more shall vex thee. If I have wronged thy noble lover with too hard suspicions, my just concern for thee, I hope, will plead my pardon.

MR. SEALAND.

Oh, make him then the full amends and be yourself the messenger of joy. Fly this instant! Tell him all these wondrous turns of Providence in his favor! Tell him I have now a daughter to bestow which he no longer will decline, that this day he still shall be a bridegroom, nor shall a fortune, the merit which his father seeks, be wanting.* Tell him the reward of all his virtues waits on his acceptance.

Exit Isabella.

My dearest Indiana! (*Turns, and embraces her.*)

INDIANA.

Have I then at last a father's sanction on my love! His bounteous hand to give and make my heart a present worthy of Bevil's generosity?

MR. SEALAND.

Oh my child! How are our sorrows past o'erpaid by such a meeting! Though I have lost so many years of soft, paternal dalliance with thee, yet in one day to find thee thus and thus bestow thee in such perfect happiness is ample, ample reparation! And yet, again the merit of thy lover?

INDIANA.

Oh, had I spirits left to tell you of his actions! How strongly filial duty has suppressed his love and how concealment still* has doubled all his obligations, the pride, the joy of his alliance, sir, would warm your heart, as he has conquered mine.

MR. SEALAND.

How laudable is love when born of virtue! I burn to embrace him—

INDIANA.

See, sir, my aunt already has succeeded and brought him to your wishes.

Enter Isabella, with Sir John Bevil, Bevil Junior, Mrs. Sealand, Cimberton, Myrtle [as Sir Geoffry], and Lucinda.

SIR JOHN BEVIL. (*Entering.*)

Where! Where's this scene of wonder! Mr. Sealand, I congratulate, on this occasion, our mutual happiness. Your good sister, sir, has, with the story of your daughter's fortune, filled us with surprise and joy! Now all exceptions are removed; my son has now avowed his love and turned all former jealousies and doubts to approbation, and, I am told, your goodness has consented to reward him.

MR. SEALAND.

If, sir, a fortune equal to his father's hopes can make this object worthy his acceptance.

BEVIL JUNIOR.

I hear your mention, sir, of fortune with pleasure

only, as it may prove the means to reconcile the best of fathers to my love. Let him be provident, but let me be happy.—My ever-destined, my acknowledged wife! (*Embracing Indiana.*)

INDIANA.

Wife! Oh, my ever loved! My lord! My master!

SIR JOHN BEVIL.

I congratulate myself, as well as you, that I had a son who could, under such disadvantages, discover your great merit.

MR. SEALAND.

Oh Sir John! How vain, how weak is human prudence? What care, what foresight, what imagination could contrive such blest events to make our children happy, as Providence in one short hour has laid before us?

CIMBERTON. (*To Mrs. Sealand.*)

I am afraid, madam, Mr. Sealand is a little too busy for our affair. If you please we'll take another opportunity.

MRS. SEALAND.

Let us have patience, sir.

During this, Bevil Junior presents Lucinda to Indiana.

CIMBERTON.

But we make Sir Geoffry wait, madam.

MYRTLE.

Oh sir! I am not in haste.

MR. SEALAND.

But here! Here's our general benefactor! Excellent young man that could be, at once, a lover to her beauty and a parent to her virtue.

BEVIL JUNIOR.

If you think that an obligation, sir, give me leave to overpay myself in the only instance that can now add to my felicity, by begging you to bestow this lady on Mr. Myrtle.

MR. SEALAND.

She is his without reserve. I beg he may be sent for.—Mr. Cimberton, notwithstanding you never had my consent, yet there is, since I last saw you, another objection to your marriage with my daughter.

CIMBERTON.

I hope, sir, your lady has concealed nothing from me?

MR. SEALAND.

Troth sir, nothing but what was concealed from myself: another daughter, who has an undoubted title to half my estate.

CIMBERTON.

How Mr. Sealand! Why then if half Mrs.* Lucinda's fortune is gone, you can't say that any of my estate is settled upon her. I was in treaty for the whole, but if that is not to be come at, to be sure there can be no bargain. Sir, I have nothing to do but to take my leave of your good lady, my cousin, and beg pardon for the trouble I have given this old gentleman.

MYRTLE.

That you have, Mr. Cimberton, with all my heart. *Discovers* himself.*

OMNES.

Mr. Myrtle!

MYRTLE.

And I beg pardon of the whole company that I assumed the person of Sir Geoffry only to be present at the danger of this lady's being diposed of and in her utmost exigence to assert my right to her, which if her parents will ratify, as they once favored my pretensions, no abatement of fortune shall lessen her value to me.

LUCINDA.

Generous* man!

MR. SEALAND.

If, sir, you can overlook the injury of being in treaty with one who as meanly left her as you have generously asserted your right in her, she is yours.

LUCINDA.

Mr. Myrtle, though you have ever had my heart, yet now I find I love you more, because I bring you less.

MYRTLE.

We have much more than we want,* and I am glad any event has contributed to the discovery* of our real inclinations to each other.

MRS. SEALAND. (*Aside.*)

Well! However, I'm glad the girl's disposed of any way.

BEVIL JUNIOR.

Myrtle! No longer rivals now, but brothers.

MYRTLE.

Dear Bevil! You are born to triumph over me! But

now our competition ceases, I rejoice in the preeminence of your virtue, and your alliance adds charms to Lucinda.

SIR JOHN BEVIL.

Now ladies and gentlemen, you have set the world a fair example. Your happiness is owing to your constancy and merit, and the several difficulties you have struggled with evidently show
Whate'er the generous* mind itself denies,
The secret care of Providence supplies.

Exeunt.

FINIS.

Textual Notes

[a] Copytext is the first edition corrected, a 1723 octavo (O1c). Also consulted: the uncorrected first edition (O1) and the second edition (O2), both of which were also published in 1723; modern editions of 1939 by Nettleton and Case, revised by Stone in 1969 (NCS) and of 1971 (Kenny).

[b] Phillis] Kenny; Lettice O1, O1c, O2, NCS

[c] *Exit Tom*] Kenny; *om.* O1, O1c, O2, NCS

[d] Good] O2, NCS, Kenny; God O1, O1c

[e] not] NCS, Kenny (following the 1722 Dublin edition); *om.* O1, O1c, O2

The Beggar's Opera[a]

by John Gay (1685-1732)

edited by Dianne Dugaw

John Gay's *The Beggar's Opera* was arguably the most influential English drama of the eighteenth century. Staged continuously for more than a century, the play continues to be revived in our own day. With it, Gay invented the ballad opera, in which spoken dramatic parts are interspersed with songs set to well-known popular tunes, a form that presages modern musical comedy. Within a few years of the play's opening, hundreds of imitations were staged. In our own era, *The Beggar's Opera* has been reworked by three important modern playwrights: Bertolt Brecht in the 1920s, John Latouche in the 1940s, Václav Havel and Wole Soyinka in the 1970s, and Alan Ayckbourn in the 1980s.

Orphaned at an early age, Gay went to London as a young man from Devon in the west of England and after a short stint working in trade became a well-known literary figure until his death. Gay did not receive a university education, and though in time he moved in circles of the social and artistic elite, his family background was only precariously "genteel." From the beginning his writing shows an attention to rank and socio-cultural modes and mores that probably derives from his own ambiguous class background. Hinging on burlesque reversals of high and low, *The Beggar's Opera* identifies as similar the antics of beggars and thieves, on the one hand, and nobles and chief ministers, on the other. Thus the play brings us to consider power, justice, honor, and heroism in a world divided into social categories of power, wealth, and gender.

When it premiered at Lincoln's Inn Fields on 29 January 1728, *The Beggar's Opera* was immediately seen as not only a parody of the new fashion for opera in England, especially as written by G. F. Händel,[1] whom George I brought over from Germany, but also as a satire on the Whig ministry of Robert Walpole. At a deeper level, Gay satirizes the corruption, self-interest, and profiteering of the ruling political and social order of the day as the profit-driven schemes of Georgian businessmen and courtiers were establishing the mercantile capitalism that has dominated world politics and economics from that time to this. So perceptively did *The Beggar's Opera* propose the ironies, predicaments, and moral dilemmas of the new order that its satire continues to fit our post-modern era of globalization and website investment. Moreover, Gay's critique is shaped by a comic wit that reveals in the play's rascals and tarts the all-too-human sentiments and behaviors that we all share. In addition, the songs that fill the play, for all their humor, satiric bite, and confounding ironies, are not only lively, artful, and memorable, but often beautifully poignant as well. Gay's *The Beggar's Opera* introduced to the English theater an ingenious mix of social satire, comic wit, and popular musical art that continues to amuse and accuse us nearly three hundred years later.

---

1 parody ... Händel] Although Gay certainly parodies Händelian opera, he and G. F. Händel actually traveled in the same circles, especially during the first decade of Händel's career in England. The two collaborated on an operatic masque, *Acis and Galatea,* in 1718.

[Introduction]

DRAMATIS PERSONAE

MEN

Peachum.[2]
Lockit.
Macheath.[3]
Filch.
Jemmy Twitcher,[4]
Crook-fingered Jack,
Wat Dreary,
Robin of Bagshot,[5]
Nimming[6] Ned,
Harry Padington,[7]
Matt of the Mint,[8]
Ben Budge,[9] Macheath's gang.
Beggar.
Player.
Constables, drawer, turnkey, [musicians], etc.

WOMEN

Mrs. Peachum.
Polly Peachum.
Lucy Lockit.
Diana Trapes,[10]
Mrs.* Coaxer,
Dolly Trull,
Mrs.* Vixen,
Betty Doxy,
Jenny Diver,[11]
Mrs.* Slammekin,[12]
Suky Tawdry,
Molly Brazen, women of the Town.

[2] Peachum] peach (q.v.) 'em. Gay's characters usually have names relating to underworld activities; some are self-explanatory, some require glossing, as below.

[3] Macheath] *mac* (son of); *heath* (typical setting for highway robbery)

[4] Twitcher] pickpocket

[5] Bagshot] name of heath notorious for highwaymen

[6] Nimming] stealing

[7] Padington] notorious district, housing the gallows at Tyburn* (the day of execution was referred to as Padington Fair Day)

[8] Mint] formerly a sanctuary for debtors, now a refuge for various outlaws

[9] Budge] clothes thief

[10] Trapes] slattern

[11] Diver] pickpocket

[12] Slammekin] slut

INTRODUCTION.

Beggar, player.

BEGGAR.

If poverty be a title to poetry, I am sure nobody can dispute mine. I own myself of the Company of Beggars, and I make one at their weekly festivals at St. Giles's.[13] I have a small yearly salary for my catches and am welcome to a dinner there whenever I please, which is more than most poets can say.

PLAYER.

As we live by the Muses, 'tis but gratitude in us to encourage poetical merit wherever we find it. The Muses, contrary to all other ladies, pay no distinction to dress and never partially mistake the pertness of embroidery for wit, nor the modesty of want* for dullness. Be the author who he will, we push his play as far as it will go. So (though you are in want) I wish you success heartily.

BEGGAR.

This piece I own was originally writ for the celebrating the marriage of James Chanter and Moll Lay, two most excellent ballad singers.[14] I have introduced the similes that are in all your celebrated operas: the swallow, the moth, the bee, the ship, the flower, etcetera. Besides, I have a prison scene which the ladies always reckon charmingly pathetic. As to the parts, I have observed such a nice* impartiality to our two ladies that it is impossible for either of them to take offence.[15] I hope I may be forgiven that I have not made my opera throughout

[13] St. Giles] The parish of St. Giles, Holborn, named after the patron saint of beggars and lepers, extends to the east of Charing Cross Road. The area was a crime-ridden slum in the eighteenth century.

[14] Chanter … singers] The names of these singers signify their disreputable occupation. A "chanter" was a street singer; "lay" is a word for a song that also was used as a slang term for a criminal activity such as picking pockets. Ballad singers on the streets often worked together with pick-pockets.]

[15] ladies … offence] This is a joking reference to Italian opera in London in the 1720s. Two rival prima donnas, Francesca Cuzzoni and Faustina Bordoni, quarreled publicly over parts and preference in 1726 and 1727, even coming to blows during a performance.

unnatural, like those in vogue, for I have no recitative. Excepting this, as I have consented to have neither prologue nor epilogue, it must be allowed an opera in all its forms. The piece indeed hath been heretofore frequently represented by ourselves in our great room at St. Giles's, so that I cannot too often acknowledge your charity in bringing it now on the stage.

PLAYER.

But I see 'tis time for us to withdraw; the actors are preparing to begin.—Play away the overture.

Exeunt.

The Beggar's Opera.

Act I, scene i. Peachum's house.

Peachum sitting at a table with a large book of accounts before him.

Air 1. "An old woman clothed in gray," etc.

[PEACHUM.]

Through all the employments of life
    Each neighbor abuses his brother;
Whore and rogue they call husband and wife:
    All professions be-rogue one another.
The priest calls the lawyer a cheat,
    The lawyer be-knaves the divine,
And the statesman, because he's so great,
    Thinks his trade as honest as mine.

A lawyer is an honest employment, so is mine. Like me too he acts in a double capacity, both against rogues and for 'em, for 'tis fitting that we should protect and encourage cheats, since we live by them.

Scene ii.

Peachum, Filch.

FILCH.

Sir, Black Moll hath sent word her trial comes on in the afternoon, and she hopes you will order matters so as to bring her off.

PEACHUM.

Why, she may plead her belly[16] at worst; to my knowledge she hath taken care of that security. But as the wench is very active and industrious, you may satisfy her that I'll soften the evidence.*

FILCH.

Tom Gagg, sir, is found guilty.

PEACHUM.

A lazy dog! When I took him the time before, I told him what he would come to if he did not mend his hand. This is death without reprieve. I may venture to book him. (*Writes.*) "For Tom Gagg, forty Pounds."[17] Let Betty Sly know that I'll save her from transportation, for I can get more by her staying in England.

FILCH.

Betty hath brought more goods into our lock[18] to-year than any five of the gang, and in truth, 'tis a pity to lose so good a customer.[19]

PEACHUM.

If none of the gang take her off, she may, in the common course of business, live a twelvemonth longer. I love to let women 'scape. A good sportsman always lets the hen partridges fly, because the breed of the game depends upon them. Besides, here the law allows us no reward; there is nothing to be got by the death of women—except our wives.

---

16 plead her belly] A pregnant woman could not be executed.

17 forty pounds] the standard government reward to an informer when the person reported on was convicted of theft

18 lock] "A cant word, signifying a warehouse where stolen goods are deposited" (Gay in a note later in the play).

19 customer] (1) a prostitute; and (2) an official who collects custom money or dues

FILCH.

Without dispute, she is a fine woman! 'Twas to her I was obliged for my education, and (to say a bold word) she hath trained up more young fellows to the business than the gaming table.

PEACHUM.

Truly Filch, thy observation is right. We and the surgeons are more beholden to women than all the professions besides.[20]

Air 2. "The bonny gray-eyed morn," etc.

FILCH.

'Tis woman that seduces all mankind;
By her we first were taught the wheedling arts.
Her very eyes can cheat; when most she's kind,*
She tricks us of our money with our hearts.
For her like wolves by night we roam for prey
And practice ev'ry fraud to bribe her charms.
For suits of love, like law, are won by pay,
And beauty must be feed into our arms.

PEACHUM.

But make haste to Newgate, boy, and let my friends know what I intend, for I love to make them easy one way or other.

FILCH.

When a gentleman is long kept in suspense, penitence may break his spirit ever after. Besides, certainty gives a man a good air upon his trial and makes him risk another without fear or scruple. But I'll away, for 'tis a pleasure to be the messenger of comfort to friends in affliction. [*Exit.*]

20 surgeons ... besides] Doctors received fees for treating venereal disease.

Scene iii.

Peachum.

[PEACHUM.]

But 'tis now high time to look about me for a decent execution against next sessions. I hate a lazy rogue, by whom one can get nothing till he is hanged. A register of the gang: (*Reads.*) "Crook-fingered Jack," a year and a half in the service. Let me see how much the stock owes to his industry: one, two, three, four, five gold watches and seven silver ones. A mighty clean-handed fellow! Sixteen snuffboxes, five of them of true gold. Six dozen of handkerchiefs, four silver-hilted swords, half a dozen of shirts, three tie-periwigs, and a piece of broadcloth. Considering these are only the fruits of his leisure hours, I don't know a prettier fellow, for no man alive hath a more engaging presence of mind upon the road. "Wat Dreary, alias Brown Will," an irregular dog, who hath an underhand way of disposing of his goods. I'll try him only for a sessions or two longer upon his good behavior. "Harry Padington," a poor petty-larceny rascal, without the least genius; that fellow, though he were to live these six months, will never come to the gallows with any credit. "Slippery Sam." He goes off the next sessions, for the villain hath the impudence to have views of following his trade as a tailor, which he calls an honest employment. "Matt of the Mint," listed not above a month ago, a promising sturdy fellow and diligent in his way, somewhat too bold and hasty, and may raise good contributions on the public, if he does not cut himself short by murder. "Tom Tipple," a guzzling, soaking sot, who is always too drunk to stand himself or to make others stand. A cart[21] is absolutely necessary for him. "Robin of Bagshot, alias Gorgon, alias Bluff Bob, alias Carbuncle, alias Bob Booty."[22]

21 cart] mode of conveyance to carry condemned criminals to the gallows

22 Robin ... Booty] This list of aliases would have been recognized by contemporary audiences as well-known insulting nicknames for the chief minister, Robert Walpole.

Scene iv.

Peachum, Mrs. Peachum.

MRS. PEACHUM.

What of Bob Booty, Husband? I hope nothing bad hath betided him. You know, my dear, he's a favorite customer of mine. 'Twas he made me a present of this ring.

PEACHUM.

I have set his name down in the blacklist, that's all, my dear. He spends his life among women, and as soon as his money is gone, one or other of the ladies will hang him for the reward, and there's forty pound lost to us forever.

MRS. PEACHUM.

You know, my dear, I never meddle in matters of death; I always leave those affairs to you. Women indeed are bitter bad judges in these cases, for they are so partial to the brave that they think every man handsome who is going to the camp or the gallows.

Air 3. "Cold and raw," etc.

If any wench Venus's Girdle[23] wear,
    Though she be never so ugly,
Lilies and roses will quickly appear,
    And her face look wondrous smugly.
Beneath the left ear so fit but a cord
    (A rope so charming a zone is!)
The youth in his cart hath the air of a lord,
    And we cry, "There dies an Adonis!"

But really, Husband, you should not be too hard-hearted, for you never had a finer, braver set of men than at present. We have not had a murder among them all these seven months. And truly, my dear, that is a great blessing.

PEACHUM.

What a dickens is the woman always a-whimpering about murder for? No gentleman is ever looked upon the worse for killing a man in his own defense, and if business cannot be carried on without it, what would you have a gentleman do?

MRS. PEACHUM.

If I am in the wrong, my dear, you must excuse me, for nobody can help the frailty of an over-scrupulous conscience.

PEACHUM.

Murder is as fashionable a crime as a man can be guilty of. How many fine gentlemen have we in Newgate every year, purely upon that article! If they have wherewithal to persuade the jury to bring it in manslaughter, what are they the worse for it? So, my dear, have done upon this subject. Was Captain Macheath here this morning for the banknotes he left with you last week?

MRS. PEACHUM.

Yes, my dear, and though the bank hath stopped payment, he was so cheerful and so agreeable! Sure there is not a finer gentleman upon the road[24] than the captain! If he comes from Bagshot at any reasonable hour he hath promised to make one this evening with Polly and me and Bob Booty at a party of quadrille. Pray my dear, is the Captain rich?

PEACHUM.

The Captain keeps too good company ever to grow rich. Marrabone* and the chocolate houses are his undoing. The man that proposes to get money by play should have the education of a fine gentleman and be trained up to it from his youth.

MRS. PEACHUM.

Really, I am sorry upon Polly's account the Captain hath not more discretion. What business hath he to keep company with lords and gentlemen? He should leave them to prey upon one another.

PEACHUM.

Upon Polly's account! What a plague does the woman mean, upon Polly's account?

---

23 Venus's Girdle] The belt (or zone) belonging to Venus, goddess of Love, made the wearer instantly desirable.

24 gentleman upon the road] euphemism for highwayman

MRS. PEACHUM.

Captain Macheath is very fond of the girl.

PEACHUM.

And what then?

MRS. PEACHUM.

If I have any skill in the ways of women, I am sure Polly thinks him a very pretty man.

PEACHUM.

And what then? You would not be so mad to have the wench marry him! Gamesters and highwaymen are generally very good to their whores, but they are very* devils to their wives.

MRS. PEACHUM.

But if Polly should be in love, how should we help her or how can she help herself? Poor girl, I am in the utmost concern about her.

Air 4. "Why is your faithful slave disdained?" etc.

If Love the virgin's heart invade,
How, like a moth, the simple maid
    Still* plays about the flame!
If soon she be not made a wife,
Her honor's singed, and then for life
    She's—what I dare not name.

PEACHUM.

Look ye, Wife, a handsome wench in our way of business is as profitable as at the bar of a Temple* coffee house, who looks upon it as her livelihood to grant every liberty but one. You see I would indulge the girl as far as prudently we can. In anything but marriage! After that, my dear, how shall we be safe? Are we not then in her husband's power? For a husband hath the absolute power over all a wife's secrets but her own. If the girl had the discretion of a Court lady, who can have a dozen young fellows at her ear without complying with one, I should not matter it. But Polly is tinder, and a spark will at once set her on a flame. Married! If the wench does not know her own profit, sure she knows her own pleasure better than to make herself a property! My daughter to me should be, like a Court lady to a minister of state, a key to the whole gang. Married! If the affair is not already done, I'll terrify her from it by the example of our neighbors.

MRS. PEACHUM.

Mayhap, my dear, you may injure the girl. She loves to imitate the fine ladies, and she may only allow the Captain liberties in the view of interest.

PEACHUM.

But 'tis your duty, my dear, to warn the girl against her ruin and to instruct her how to make the most of her beauty. I'll go to her this moment and sift her. In the meantime, Wife, rip out the coronets and marks[25] of these dozen of cambric handkerchiefs, for I can dispose of them this afternoon to a chap[26] in the City.* [*Exit.*]

Scene v.

Mrs. Peachum.

[MRS. PEACHUM.]

Never was a man more out of the way in an argument than my husband! Why must our Polly, forsooth, differ from her sex and love only her husband? And why must Polly's marriage, contrary to all observation, make her the less followed by other men? All men are thieves in love and like a woman the better for being another's property.

Air 5. "Of all the simple things we do," etc.

25 coronets and marks] embroidered insignia, the first for aristocratic members of the peerage

26 chap] short for chapman (q.v.)

A maid is like the golden ore,
Which hath guineas intrinsical in't,
Whose worth is never known before
It is tried and imprest in the mint.
A wife's like a guinea in gold,
Stamped with the name of her spouse:
Now here, now there, is bought or is sold,
And is current in every house.

Scene vi.

Mrs. Peachum, Filch.

MRS. PEACHUM.
Come hither, Filch. I am as fond of this child as though my mind misgave me he were my own. He hath as fine a hand at picking a pocket as a woman and is as nimble-fingered as a juggler. If an unlucky session does not cut the rope of thy life, I pronounce, Boy, thou wilt be a great man* in history. Where was your post last night, my boy?

FILCH.
I plied at the opera, madam, and considering 'twas neither dark nor rainy, so that there was no great hurry in getting chairs* and coaches, made a tolerable hand on't. These seven handkerchiefs, madam.

MRS. PEACHUM.
Colored ones, I see. They are of sure sale from our warehouse at Redriff[27] among the seamen.

FILCH.
And this snuffbox.

MRS. PEACHUM.
Set in gold! A pretty encouragement this to a young beginner.

FILCH.
I had a fair tug at a charming gold watch. Pox take the tailors for making the fobs so deep and narrow! I stuck by the way, and I was forced to make my escape under a coach. Really madam, I fear I shall be cut off in the flower of my youth, so that every now and then (since I was pumped[28]) I have thoughts of taking up and going to sea.

MRS. PEACHUM.
You should go to Hockley in the Hole[29] and to Marrabone,* child, to learn valor. These are the schools that have bred so many brave men. I thought, Boy, by this time thou hadst lost fear as well as shame. Poor lad! how little does he know as yet of the Old Bailey![30] For the first fact I'll insure thee from being hanged, and going to sea, Filch, will come time enough upon a sentence of transportation. But now, since you have nothing better to do, ev'n go to your book and learn your catechism, for really a man makes but an ill figure in the ordinary's paper[31] who cannot give a satisfactory answer to his questions. But hark you, my lad: don't tell me a lie, for you know I hate a liar. Do you know of any thing that hath past between Captain Macheath and our Polly?

FILCH.
I beg you, madam, don't ask me, for I must either tell a lie to you or to Miss Polly. For I promised her I would not tell.

MRS. PEACHUM.
But when the honor of our family is concerned—

FILCH.
I shall lead a sad life with Miss Polly if ever she come to know that I told you. Besides, I would not willingly forfeit my own honor by betraying anybody.

MRS. PEACHUM.
Yonder comes my husband and Polly. Come Filch, you shall go with me into my own room and tell me the whole story. I'll give thee a glass of a most delicious cordial[b] that I keep for my own drinking.

[Exeunt.]

---

27 Redriff] the common name for Rotherhithe, the port district of London on the south bank of the Thames about a mile down river from the Tower of London

28 pumped] Pickpockets caught in the act were often punished as first offenders by being held under a water pump.

29 Hockley in the Hole] an arena near Clerkenwell Green in north London for such rough crowd sports as bear- and bull-baiting, sword fighting, wrestling, dog- and cock-fighting, and so on.

30 Old Bailey] London's criminal court near Newgate Prison

31 ordinary's paper] the chaplain-in-ordinary of Newgate often published accounts of criminals called "Newgate biographies."

Scene vii.

Peachum, Polly.

POLLY.

I know as well as any of the fine ladies how to make the most of my self and of my man too. A woman knows how to be mercenary, though she hath never been in a court or at an assembly.[32] We have it in our natures, Papa. If I allow Captain Macheath some trifling liberties, I have this watch and other visible marks of his favor to show for it. A girl who cannot grant some things, and refuse what is most material, will make but a poor hand of her beauty and soon be thrown upon the common.

Air 6. "What shall I do to show how much I love her," etc.

Virgins are like the fair flower in its luster,
    Which in the garden enamels the ground;
Near it the bees in play flutter and cluster,
    And gaudy butterflies frolic around.
But when once plucked, 'tis no longer alluring;
    To Covent Garden* 'tis sent (as yet sweet),
There fades and shrinks and grows past all enduring,
    Rots, stinks, and dies and is trod under feet.

PEACHUM.

You know, Polly, I am not against your toying and trifling with a customer in the way of business or to get out a secret or so. But if I find out that you have played the fool and are married, you jade you, I'll cut your throat, hussy. Now you know my mind.

32 assembly] a fashionable gathering, usually with music and dancing

Scene viii.

Peachum, Polly, Mrs. Peachum.

Air 7. "Oh London is a fine town."

MRS. PEACHUM. (*In a very great Passion.*)

Our Polly is a sad slut! nor heeds what we have taught her.
I wonder any man alive will ever rear a daughter!
For she must have both hoods and gowns, and hoops to swell her pride,
With scarves and stays, and gloves and lace, and she will have men beside.
And when she's dressed with care and cost, all tempting, fine and gay,
As men should serve a cucumber,* she flings herself away.
Our Polly is a sad slut, etc.

You baggage! you hussy! you inconsiderate jade! Had you been hanged, it would not have vexed me, for that might have been your misfortune, but to do such a mad thing by choice! The wench is married,[33] Husband.

PEACHUM.

Married! The Captain is a bold man and will risk any thing for money; to be sure he believes her a fortune.—Do you think your mother and I should have lived comfortably so long together, if ever we had been married, baggage?

MRS. PEACHUM.

I knew she was always a proud slut, and now the wench hath played the fool and married, because forsooth she would do like the gentry. Can you support the expense of a husband, hussy, in gaming, drinking, and whoring? have you money enough to carry on the daily quarrels of man and wife about who shall squander most? There are not many husbands and wives who can bear the

33 married] Clandestine marriages were illegal but binding.

charges of plaguing one another in a handsome way. If you must be married, could you introduce nobody into our family but a highwayman? Why thou foolish jade, thou wilt be as ill-used and as much neglected as if thou hadst married a lord!

PEACHUM.

Let not your anger, my dear, break through the rules of decency, for the captain looks upon himself in the military capacity, as a gentleman by his profession. Besides what he hath already, I know he is in a fair way of getting or of dying, and both these ways, let me tell you, are most excellent chances for a wife.—Tell me, hussy, are you ruined or no?

MRS. PEACHUM.

With Polly's fortune, she might very well have gone off to a person of distinction.—Yes, that you might, you pouting slut!

PEACHUM.

What, is the wench dumb? Speak or I'll make you plead by squeezing out an answer from you. Are you really bound wife to him or are you only upon liking? (*Pinches her.*)

POLLY. (*Screaming.*)

Oh!

MRS. PEACHUM.

How the mother is to be pitied who hath handsome daughters! Locks, bolts, bars, and lectures of morality are nothing to them, they break through them all. They have as much pleasure in cheating a father and mother as in cheating at cards.

PEACHUM.

Why Polly, I shall soon know if you are married by Macheath's keeping from our house.

Air 8. "Grim king of the ghosts," etc.

POLLY.

Can love be controlled by advice?
    Will Cupid our mothers obey?
Though my heart were as frozen as ice,
    At his flame 'twould have melted away.

When he kissed me so closely he pressed,
    'Twas so sweet that I must have complied;
So I thought it both safest and best
    To marry for fear you should chide.

MRS. PEACHUM.

Then all the hopes of our family are gone forever and ever!

PEACHUM.

And Macheath may hang his father and mother-in-law in hope to get into their daughter's fortune.

POLLY.

I did not marry him (as 'tis the fashion) coolly and deliberately for honor and money. But I love him.

MRS. PEACHUM.

Love him! worse and worse! I thought the girl had been better bred. Oh Husband, Husband! her folly makes me mad! my head swims! I'm distracted! I can't support myself—oh! (*Faints.*)

PEACHUM.

See, wench, to what a condition you have reduced your poor mother! a glass of cordial, this instant.—How the poor woman takes it to heart!

Polly goes out and returns with it.

Ah hussy, now this is the only comfort your mother has left!

POLLY.

Give her another glass, sir; my mama drinks double the quantity whenever she is out of order. This, you see, fetches her.

MRS. PEACHUM.

The girl shows such a readiness and so much concern that I could almost find in my heart to forgive her.

Air 9. "Oh Jenny, oh Jenny, where hast thou been."

Oh Polly, you might have toyed and kissed.
By keeping men off, you keep them on.

POLLY.

But he so teased me,
And he so pleased me,
What I did, you must have done.

MRS. PEACHUM.

Not with a highwayman, you sorry slut!

PEACHUM.

A word with you, Wife. 'Tis no new thing for a wench to take man without consent of parents. You know 'tis the frailty of woman, my dear.

MRS. PEACHUM.

Yes indeed, the sex is frail. But the first time a woman is frail, she should be somewhat nice,* methinks, for then or never is the time to make her fortune. After that, she hath nothing to do but to guard herself from being found out, and she may do what she pleases.

PEACHUM.

Make your self a little easy; I have a thought shall soon set all matters again to rights.—Why so melancholy, Polly? Since what is done cannot be undone, we must all endeavor to make the best of it.

MRS. PEACHUM.

Well Polly, as far as one woman can forgive another, I forgive thee. Your father is too fond of you, hussy.

POLLY.

Then all my sorrows are at an end.

MRS. PEACHUM.

A mighty likely speech, in troth, for a wench who is just married!

Air 10. "Thomas, I cannot," etc.

POLLY.

I, like a ship in storms, was tossed
Yet afraid to put in to land,
For seized in the port the vessel's lost,
Whose treasure is contraband.

The waves are laid,
My duty's paid—
Oh joy beyond expression!
Thus, safe ashore,
I ask no more,
My all is in my possession.

PEACHUM.

I hear customers in t'other room. Go talk with 'em, Polly, but come to us again as soon as they are gone. But hark ye, child, if 'tis the gentleman who was here yesterday about the repeating-watch,[34] say you believe we can't get intelligence of it till tomorrow. For I lent it to Suky Straddle to make a figure with it tonight at a tavern in Drury Lane. If t'other gentleman calls for the silver-hilted sword, you know beetle-browed Jemmy hath it on, and he doth not come from Tunbridge till Tuesday night so that it cannot be had till then.[35]

[Exit Polly.]

Scene ix.

Peachum, Mrs. Peachum.

PEACHUM.

Dear Wife, be a little pacified. Don't let your passion run away with your senses. Polly, I grant you, hath done a rash thing.

MRS. PEACHUM.

If she had had only an intrigue with the fellow, why the very best families have excused and huddled up a frailty of that sort. 'Tis marriage, Husband, that makes it a blemish.

PEACHUM.

But money, Wife, is the true Fuller's Earth[36] for reputations: there is not a spot or a stain but what it can take out. A rich rogue nowadays is fit company for any gentleman, and the world, my

---

[34] repeating-watch] one that chimes

[35] customers … then] Victims of theft frequently advertised and offered a reward for return of their possessions. Fences such as Peachum would contact them and arrange for a recovery though perhaps, as here, not before they had been put to some use. Drury Lane was an area of London notorious for prostitutes; Tunbridge Wells was a fashionable resort about thirty-five miles southeast of London.

[36] Fuller's Earth] a clay used to clean fabrics

dear, hath not such a contempt for roguery as you imagine. I tell you, Wife, I can make this match turn to our advantage.

MRS. PEACHUM.

I am very sensible, Husband, that Captain Macheath is worth money, but I am in doubt whether he hath not two or three wives already, and then if he should die in a session or two, Polly's dower would come into dispute.

PEACHUM.

That, indeed, is a point which ought to be considered.

Air 11. "A soldier and a sailor."

A fox may steal your hens, sir,
A whore your health and pence, sir,
Your daughter rob your chest, sir;
Your wife may steal your rest, sir,
    A thief your goods and plate.*
But this is all but picking,
With rest, pence, chest and chicken;
It ever was decreed, sir,
If lawyer's hand is feed, sir,
    He steals your whole estate.

The lawyers are bitter enemies to those in our way. They don't care that anybody should get a clandestine livelihood but themselves.

Scene x.

Mrs. Peachum, Peachum, Polly.

POLLY.

'Twas only Nimming Ned. He brought in a damask window curtain, a hoop-petticoat, a pair of silver candlesticks, a periwig, and one silk stocking from the fire that happened last night.

PEACHUM.

There is not a fellow that is cleverer in his way and saves more goods out of the fire than Ned. But now, Polly, to your affair, for matters must not be left as they are. You are married then, it seems?

POLLY.

Yes sir.

PEACHUM.

And how do you propose to live, child?

POLLY.

Like other women, sir, upon the industry of my husband.

MRS. PEACHUM.

What, is the wench turned fool? A highwayman's wife, like a soldier's, hath as little of his pay as of his company.

PEACHUM.

And had not you the common views of a gentlewoman in your marriage, Polly?

POLLY.

I don't know what you mean, sir.

PEACHUM.

Of a jointure and of being a widow.

POLLY.

But I love him, sir: How then could I have thoughts of parting with him?

PEACHUM.

Parting with him! Why, that is the whole scheme and intention of all marriage articles. The comfortable estate of widowhood is the only hope that keeps up a wife's spirits. Where is the woman who would scruple to be a wife, if she had it in her power to be a widow whenever she pleased? If you have any views of this sort, Polly, I shall think the match not so very unreasonable.

POLLY.

How I dread to hear your advice! Yet I must beg you to explain yourself.

PEACHUM.

Secure what he hath got, have him peached the next sessions, and then at once you are made a rich widow.

POLLY.

What, murder the man I love! The blood runs cold at my heart with the very thought of it.

PEACHUM.

Fie Polly! What hath murder to do in the affair?

Since the thing sooner or later must happen, I dare say the captain himself would like that we should get the reward for his death sooner than a stranger. Why Polly, the captain knows that as 'tis his employment to rob, so 'tis ours to take robbers. Every man in his business. So that there is no malice in the case.

MRS. PEACHUM.

Aye Husband, now you have nicked the matter. To have him peached is the only thing could ever make me forgive her.

Air 12. "Now ponder well, ye parents dear."

POLLY.

Oh, ponder well! be not severe,
So save a wretched wife!
For on the rope that hangs my dear
Depends poor Polly's life.

MRS. PEACHUM.

But your duty to your parents, hussy, obliges you to hang him. What would many a wife give for such opportunity!

POLLY.

What is a jointure, what is widowhood to me? I know my heart. I cannot survive him.

Air 13. "Le printemps rappelle aux armes."[37]

The turtle* thus with plaintive crying,
Her lover dying,
The turtle thus with plaintive crying,
Laments her dove.

[37] Le printemps … armes] Springtime recalls one to arms (Fr.).

Down she drops quite spent with sighing,
Paired in death, as paired in love.
Thus, sir, it will happen to your poor Polly.

MRS. PEACHUM.

What is the fool in love in earnest then? I hate thee for being particular. Why, wench, thou art a shame to thy very* sex.

POLLY.

But hear me, Mother. If you ever loved—

MRS. PEACHUM.

Those cursed playbooks she reads have been her ruin.—One word more, hussy, and I shall knock your brains out, if you have any.

PEACHUM.

Keep out of the way, Polly, for fear of mischief and consider of what is proposed to you.

MRS. PEACHUM.

Away, hussy. Hang your husband and be dutiful.

[Polly starts out.]

Scene xi.

Mrs. Peachum, Peachum, Polly listening.

MRS. PEACHUM.

The thing, Husband, must and shall be done. For the sake of intelligence[38] we must take other measures and have him peached the next session without her consent. If she will not know her duty, we know ours.

PEACHUM.

But really, my dear, it grieves one's heart to take off a great man.* When I consider his personal bravery, his fine stratagem, how much we have already got by him, and how much more we may get, methinks I can't find in my heart to have a hand in his death. I wish you could have made Polly undertake it.

MRS. PEACHUM.

But in a case of necessity: our own lives are in danger.

PEACHUM.

Then, indeed, we must comply with the customs of the world and make gratitude give way to interest. He shall be taken off.

MRS. PEACHUM.

I'll undertake to manage Polly.

[38] intelligence] information Macheath possesses

PEACHUM.
And I'll prepare matters for the Old Bailey.

[Exeunt.]

Scene xii.

Polly.

[POLLY.]
Now I'm a wretch, indeed: methinks I see him already in the cart, sweeter and more lovely than the nosegay in his hand! I hear the crowd extolling his resolution and intrepidity! What volleys of sighs are sent from the windows of Holborn,[39] that so comely a youth should be brought to disgrace! I see him at the tree! The whole circle are in tears, even butchers weep! Jack Ketch[40] himself hesitates to perform his duty and would be glad to lose his fee by a reprieve. What then will become of Polly! As yet I may inform him of their design and aid him in his escape— It shall be so— But then he flies, absents himself, and I bar myself from his dear, dear conversation!* That too will distract me— If he keep out of the way, my papa and mama may in time relent, and we may be happy— If he stays, he is hanged, and then he is lost forever! He intended to lie concealed in my room till the dusk of the evening: If they are abroad, I'll this instant let him out, lest some accident should prevent him.

Exit and returns.

Scene xiii.

Polly, Macheath.

Air 14. "Pretty parrot, say—"

MACHEATH.
Pretty Polly, say,
When I was away,
Did your fancy never stray
To some newer lover?

POLLY.
Without disguise,
Heaving sighs,
Doting eyes,
My constant heart discover.*
Fondly let me loll!

MACHEATH.
Oh pretty, pretty Poll.

POLLY.
And are you as fond as ever, my dear?

MACHEATH.
Suspect my honor, my courage, suspect anything but my love. May my pistols misfire and my mare slip her shoulder while I am pursued if I ever forsake thee!

POLLY.
Nay my dear, I have no reason to doubt you, for I find in the romance you lent me, none of the great heroes were ever false in love.

Air 15. "Pray, fair one, be kind*"—

MACHEATH.
My heart was so free,
It roved like the bee,
Till Polly my passion requited;

39 nosegay … Holborn] Holborn street led from Newgate prison to Tyburn.* Spectators lined the streets to see about-to-be-executed criminals riding by in carts, with nooses around their necks, and frequently threw them nosegays.

40 Jack Ketch] generic name for the public hangman, after the notoriously inefficient original, who held the post from 1663 to 1686

I sipped each flower,
I changed ev'ry hour,
But here ev'ry flower is united.

POLLY.

Were you sentenced to transportation, sure my dear, you could not leave me behind you—could you?

MACHEATH.

Is there any power, any force that could tear me from thee? You might sooner tear a pension out of the hands of a courtier, a fee from a lawyer, a pretty woman from a looking glass, or any woman from quadrille. But to tear me from thee is impossible!

Air 16. "Over the hills and far away."

Were I laid on Greenland's coast,
And in my arms embraced my lass,
Warm amidst eternal frost,
Too soon the half-year's night would pass.

POLLY.

Were I sold on Indian soil,
Soon as the burning day was closed,
I could mock the sultry toil,
When on my charmer's breast reposed.

MACHEATH.

And I would love you all the day,

POLLY.

Every night would kiss and play,

MACHEATH.

If with me you'd fondly stray—

POLLY.

Over the hills and far away.

Yes, I would go with thee. But oh! how shall I speak it? I must be torn from thee. We must part.

MACHEATH.

How! Part!

POLLY.

We must, we must. My papa and mama are set against thy life. They now, even now are in search after thee. They are preparing evidence against thee. Thy life depends upon a moment.

Air 17. "Gin thou wert mine awn thing"—

Oh what pain it is to part!
Can I leave thee, can I leave thee?
Oh what pain it is to part!
Can thy Polly ever leave thee?
But lest death my love should thwart
And bring thee to the fatal cart,
Thus I tear thee from my bleeding heart!
Fly hence and let me leave thee.
One kiss and then—one kiss—be gone—farewell.

MACHEATH.

My hand, my heart, my dear, is so riveted to thine that I cannot unloose my hold.

POLLY.

But my papa may intercept thee and then I should lose the very glimmering of hope. A few weeks, perhaps, may reconcile us all. Shall thy Polly hear from thee?

MACHEATH.

Must I then go?

POLLY.

And will not absence change your love?

MACHEATH.

If you doubt* it, let me stay—and be hanged.

POLLY.

Oh how I fear! how I tremble! Go—but when safety will give you leave, you will be sure to see me again, for till then Polly is wretched.

Air 18. "Oh the broom," etc.

Parting, and looking back at each other with fondness; he at one door, she at the other.

MACHEATH.

The miser thus a shilling sees
Which he's obliged to pay,
With sighs resigns it by degrees
And fears 'tis gone for aye.

POLLY.

The boy thus, when his sparrow's flown,
The bird in silence eyes,
But soon as out of sight 'tis gone,
Whines, whimpers, sobs, and cries.

Act II, scene i. A tavern near Newgate.

Jemmy Twitcher, Crook-fingered Jack, Wat Dreary, Robin of Bagshot, Nimming Ned, Henry Padington, Matt of the Mint, Ben Budge, and the rest of the gang at the table with wine, brandy, and tobacco.

BEN.

But prithee Matt, what is become of thy brother Tom? I have not seen him since my return from transportation.

MATT.

Poor brother Tom had an accident this time twelvemonth, and so clever a made fellow he was that I could not save him from those flaying rascals the surgeons, and now, poor man, he is among the otamies at Surgeon's Hall.[41]

BEN.

So it seems, his time was come.

JEMMY.

But the present time is ours, and no body alive hath more. Why are the laws leveled at us? Are we more dishonest than the rest of mankind? What we win, gentlemen, is our own by the law of arms and the right of conquest.

CROOK-FINGERED JACK.

Where shall we find such another set of practical philosophers, who to a man are above the fear of death?

WAT.

Sound men, and true!

ROBIN.

Of tried courage and indefatigable industry!

NED.

Who is there here that would not die for his friend?

HARRY.

Who is there here that would betray him for his interest?

MATT.

Show me a gang of courtiers that can say as much.

BEN.

We are for a just partition of the world, for every man hath a right to enjoy life.

MATT.

We retrench the superfluities of mankind. The world is avaricious, and I hate avarice. A covetous fellow, like a jackdaw, steals what he was never made to enjoy for the sake of hiding it. These are the robbers of mankind, for money was made for the free-hearted and generous, and where is the injury of taking from another what he hath not the heart to make use of?

JEMMY.

Our several stations for the day are fixed. Good luck attend us all. Fill the glasses.

Air 19. "Fill ev'ry glass," etc.

MATT.

Fill ev'ry glass, for wine inspires us,
And fires us

41 accident ... Hall] Tom's "accident" was to be executed, and he is now a skeleton (an "otamy") on display after he was dissected by the "flaying" surgeons for an anatomy demonstration.

With courage, love, and joy.
Women and wine should life employ.
Is there aught else on earth desirous?

CHORUS.

Fill ev'ry glass, etc.

Scene ii.

To them enter Macheath.

MACHEATH.

Gentlemen, well met. My heart hath been with you this hour, but an unexpected affair hath detained me. No ceremony, I beg you.

MATT.

We were just breaking up to go upon duty. Am I to have the honor of taking the air with you, sir, this evening upon the heath? I drink a dram now and then with the stage-coachmen in the way of friendship and intelligence, and I know that about this time there will be passengers upon the Western Road,[42] who are worth speaking with.

MACHEATH.

I was to have been of that party—but—

MATT.

But what sir?

MACHEATH.

Is there any man who suspects my courage?

MATT.

We have all been witnesses of it.

MACHEATH.

My honor and truth to the gang?

MATT.

I'll be answerable for it.

MACHEATH.

In the division of our booty, have I ever shown the least marks of avarice or injustice?

MATT.

By these questions something seems to have ruffled you. Are any of us suspected?

MACHEATH.

I have a fixed confidence, gentlemen, in you all as men of honor, and as such I value and respect you. Peachum is a man that is useful to us.

[42] Western Road] the principal route from London to Cornwall. Macheath's men probably plan to rob travelers on Bagshot Heath along this route.

MATT.

Is he about to play us any foul play? I'll shoot him through the head.

MACHEATH.

I beg you, gentlemen, act with conduct and discretion. A pistol is your last resort.

MATT.

He knows nothing of this meeting.

MACHEATH.

Business cannot go on without him. He is a man who knows the world and is a necessary agent to us. We have had a slight difference, and till it is accommodated, I shall be obliged to keep out of his way. Any private dispute of mine shall be of no ill consequence to my friends. You must continue to act under his direction, for the moment we break loose from him, our gang is ruined.

MATT.

As a bawd to a whore, I grant you, he is to us of great convenience.

MACHEATH.

Make him believe I have quitted the gang, which I can never do but with life. At our private quarters I will continue to meet you. A week or so will probably reconcile us.

MATT.

Your instructions shall be observed. 'Tis now high time for us to repair to our several duties; so till the evening at our quarters in Moorfields[43] we bid you farewell.

MACHEATH.

I shall wish myself with you. Success attend you. (*Sits down melancholy at the table.*)

Air 20. "March in Rinaldo,[44] with drums and Trumpets."

[43] Moorfields] a disreputable area north of the city famous for brandy shops and rough sports and pastimes

[44] *Rinaldo*] Händel's first English opera (1711).

MATT.

Let us take the road.
Hark! I hear the sound of coaches!
The hour of attack approaches,
To your arms, brave boys, and load.
See the ball I hold!
Let the chemists* toil like asses,
Our fire their fire surpasses,
And turns all our lead to gold.

The gang, ranged in the front of the stage, load their pistols, and stick them under their girdles then go off singing the first part in chorus.

Scene iii.

Macheath.

MACHEATH.

What a fool is a fond wench! Polly is most confoundedly bit. I love the sex. And a man who loves money might as well be contented with one guinea as I with one woman. The Town* perhaps hath been as much obliged to me for recruiting it with free-hearted ladies as to any recruiting officer in the army. If it were not for us and the other gentlemen of the sword, Drury Lane would be uninhabited.

Air 21. "Would you have a young virgin," etc.

If the heart of a man is depressed with cares,
The mist is dispelled when a woman appears.
Like the notes of a fiddle, she sweetly, sweetly
Raises the spirits and charms our ears;
Roses and lilies her cheeks disclose,
But her ripe lips are more sweet than those.
Press her,
Caress her

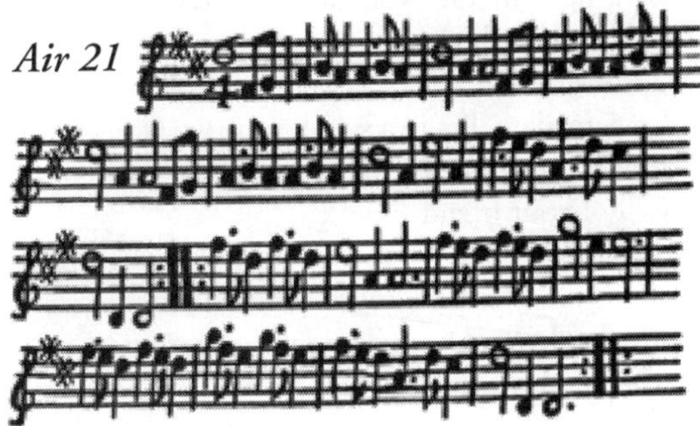

With blisses,
Her kisses
Dissolve us in pleasure and soft repose.

I must have women. There is nothing unbends the mind like them. Money is not so strong a cordial for the time.—Drawer.

Enter drawer.

Is the porter gone for all the ladies, according to my directions?

DRAWER.

I expect him back every minute. But you know, sir, you sent him as far as Hockley in the Hole for three of the ladies, for one in Vinegar Yard, and for the rest of them somewhere about Lewkner's Lane.[45] Sure some of them are below, for I hear the bar bell. As they come I will show them up.—Coming, coming. [*Exit.*]

Scene iv.

Macheath, Mrs. Coaxer, Dolly Trull, Mrs. Vixen, Betty Doxy, Jenny Diver, Mrs. Slammekin, Suky Tawdry, and Molly Brazen.

MACHEATH.

Dear Mrs.* Coaxer, you are welcome. You look charmingly today. I hope you don't want the repairs of quality,* and lay on paint.—Dolly Trull! kiss me, you slut. Are you as amorous as ever, hussy? You are always so taken up with stealing hearts that you don't allow yourself time to steal anything else. Ah Dolly, thou wilt ever be a coquette!—Mrs.* Vixen, I'm yours, I always loved a woman of wit and spirit; they make charming mistresses, but plaguy wives.—Betty Doxy! Come hither, hussy. Do you drink as hard as ever? You had better stick to good wholesome beer, for in troth, Betty, strong waters will in time ruin your constitution. You should leave those to your betters.—What! and my pretty Jenny Diver too! As prim and demure as ever! There is not any prude, though ever so high bred, hath a more sanctified look, with a more mischievous heart. Ah!

45 Vinegar ... Lane] Vinegar Yard, properly Vine Garden Yard, or Vineyard, was a small court just off Drury Lane. Lewkner's Lane (now Macklin Street) is also near Drury Lane.

thou art a dear artful hypocrite.—Mrs.* Slammekin! as careless and genteel as ever! all you fine ladies, who know your own beauty, affect an undress.—But see, here's Suky Tawdry come to contradict what I was saying. Everything she gets one way she lays out upon her back. Why Suky, you must keep* at least a dozen tallymen.—Molly Brazen!

She kisses him.

That's well done. I love a free-hearted wench. Thou hast a most agreeable assurance, girl, and art as willing as a turtle.*—But hark! I hear music. The harper is at the door. "If music be the food of love, play on."[46] Ere you seat yourselves, ladies, what think you of a dance?—Come in.

Enter harper.

Play the French tune that Mrs.* Slammekin was so fond of.

A dance à la ronde[47] in the French manner; near the end of it this song and chorus.

Air 22. Cotillion.

Youth's the season made for joys;
    Love is then our duty.
She alone who that employs
    Well deserves her beauty.
        Let's be gay,
        While we may:
    Beauty's a flower despised in decay.

[CHORUS.]

Youth's the season, etc.

Let us drink and sport today;
    Ours is not tomorrow.
Love with youth flies swift away;
    Age is naught but sorrow.
        Dance and sing;
        Time's on the wing:
    Life never knows the return of spring.

CHORUS.

Let us drink, etc.

MACHEATH.

Now pray ladies, take your places.—Here fellow. (*Pays the harper.*) Bid the drawer bring us more wine.

Exit harper.

If any of the ladies choose gin, I hope they will be so free to call for it.

JENNY.

You look as if you meant me. Wine is strong enough for me. Indeed sir, I never drink strong waters, but when I have the colic.

MACHEATH.

Just the excuse of the fine ladies! Why, a lady of quality* is never without the colic. I hope, Mrs.* Coaxer, you have had good success of late in your visits among the mercers.

COAXER.

We have so many interlopers, yet with industry one may still have a little picking. I carried a silver flowered lutestring and a piece of black paduasoy to Mr. Peachum's lock but last week.

VIXEN.

There's Molly Brazen hath the ogle of a rattlesnake. She riveted a linen draper's eye so fast upon her that he was nicked of three pieces of cambric before he could look off.

BRAZEN.

Oh dear madam! But sure nothing can come up to your handling of laces! And then you have such a sweet deluding tongue! To cheat a man is nothing, but the woman must have fine parts* indeed who cheats a woman!

VIXEN.

Lace, madam, lies in a small compass and is of easy conveyance. But you are apt, madam, to think too well of your friends.

COAXER.

If any woman hath more art than another, to be sure 'tis Jenny Diver. Though her fellow be never so agreeable, she can pick his pocket as coolly as

[46] "If ... on."] opening line of Shakespeare's *Twelfth Night*

[47] dance à la ronde] a dignified and formal dance, an expression of aristocratic taste, further identified in the text as a cotillion

if money were her only pleasure. Now that is a command of the passions uncommon in a woman!

JENNY.

I never go to the tavern with a man but in the view of business. I have other hours and other sort of men for my pleasure. But had I your address, madam—

MACHEATH.

Have done with your compliments, ladies, and drink about.—You are not so fond of me, Jenny, as you use to be.

JENNY.

'Tis not convenient, sir, to show my fondness among so many rivals. 'Tis your own choice and not the warmth of my inclination that will determine you.

Air 23. "All in a misty morning," etc.

Before the barn door crowing,
    The cock by hens attended,
His eyes around him throwing,
    Stands for a while suspended.
Then one he singles from the crew
    And cheers the happy hen
With how do you do, and how do you do,
    And how do you do again.

MACHEATH.

Ah Jenny! thou art a dear slut.

TRULL.

Pray madam, were you ever in keeping?*

TAWDRY.

I hope, madam, I ha'nt been so long upon the Town, but I have met with some good fortune as well as my neighbors.

TRULL.

Pardon me, madam, I meant no harm by the question; 'twas only in the way of conversation.

TAWDRY.

Indeed madam, if I had not been a fool, I might have lived very handsomely with my last friend. But upon his missing five guineas, he turned me off. Now I never suspected he had counted them.

SLAMMEKIN.

Who do you look upon, madam, as your best sort of keepers?*

TRULL.

That, madam, is thereafter as they be.

SLAMMEKIN.

I, madam, was once kept by a Jew, and bating their religion, to women they are a good sort of people.

TAWDRY.

Now for my part, I own I like an old fellow, for we always make them pay for what they can't do.

VIXEN.

A spruce prentice, let me tell you, ladies, is no ill thing, they bleed freely. I have sent at least two or three dozen of them in my time to the plantations.*

JENNY.

But to be sure, sir, with so much good fortune as you have had upon the road, you must be grown immensely rich.

MACHEATH.

The road, indeed, hath done me justice, but the gaming table hath been my ruin.

Air 24. "When once I lay with another man's wife," etc.

JENNY.

The gamesters and lawyers are jugglers alike:
    If they meddle, your all is in danger.
Like Gypsies, if once they can finger a souse,[48]
Your pockets they pick, and they pilfer your house
    And give your estate to a stranger.
A man of courage should never put anything to the risk but his life.[c]

She takes up his pistol. Tawdry takes up the other.

These are the tools of a man of honor. Cards and dice are only fit for cowardly cheats who prey upon their friends.

48 souse] a sou, a trifling coin

TAWDRY.

This, sir, is fitter for your hand. Besides your loss of money, 'tis a loss to the ladies. Gaming takes you off from women. How fond could I be of you! but before company, 'tis ill bred.

MACHEATH.

Wanton hussies!

JENNY.

I must and will have a kiss to give my wine a zest.

They take him about the neck and make signs to Peachum and the constables, who rush in upon him.

Scene v.

To them, Peachum and constables.

PEACHUM.

I seize you, sir, as my prisoner.

MACHEATH.

Was this well done, Jenny? Women are decoy ducks. Who can trust them? Beasts, jades, jilts, harpies, furies, whores!

PEACHUM.

Your case, Mr. Macheath, is not particular. The greatest heroes have been ruined by women. But to do them justice, I must own they are a pretty sort of creatures, if we could trust them. You must now, sir, take your leave of the ladies, and if they have a mind to make you a visit, they will be sure to find you at home.—The gentleman, ladies, lodges in Newgate. —Constables, wait upon the captain to his lodgings.

Air 25. "When first I laid siege to my Chloris," etc.

MACHEATH.

At the tree I shall suffer with pleasure,
At the tree I shall suffer with pleasure;
Let me go where I will,
In all kinds of ill,
I shall find no such furies as these are.

PEACHUM.

Ladies, I'll take care the reckoning shall be discharged.

Exit Macheath, guarded with Peachum and Constables.

Scene vi.

The women remain.

VIXEN.

Look ye, Mrs.* Jenny, though Mr. Peachum may have made a private bargain with you and Suky Tawdry for betraying the captain, as we were all assisting, we ought all to share alike.

COAXER.

I think Mr. Peachum, after so long an acquaintance, might have trusted me as well as Jenny Diver.

SLAMMEKIN.

I am sure at least three men of his hanging and in a year's time too (if he did me justice) should be set down to my account.

TRULL.

Mrs.* Slammekin, that is not fair. For you know one of them was taken in bed with me.

JENNY.

As far as a bowl of punch or a treat, I believe Mrs.* Suky will join with me. As for anything else, ladies, you cannot in conscience expect it.

SLAMMEKIN.

Dear madam—

TRULL.

I would not for the world—

SLAMMEKIN.

'Tis impossible for me—

TRULL.

As I hope to be saved, madam—

SLAMMEKIN.

Nay, then I must stay here all night—

TRULL.

Since you command me.

Exeunt with great ceremony.

Scene vii. Newgate.

Lockit, turnkeys, Macheath, constables.

LOCKIT.

Noble Captain, you are welcome. You have not been a lodger of mine this year and half. You know the custom, sir: garnish, Captain, garnish.—Hand me down those fetters there.

MACHEATH.

Those, Mr. Lockit, seem to be the heaviest of the

whole set. With your leave, I should like the further pair better.

LOCKIT.

Look ye, Captain, we know what is fittest for our prisoners. When a gentleman uses me with civility, I always do the best I can to please him.—Hand them down, I say.—We have them of all prices, from one guinea to ten, and 'tis fitting every gentleman should please himself.

MACHEATH.

I understand you, sir. (*Gives money.*) The fees here are so many and so exorbitant that few fortunes can bear the expense of getting off handsomely or of dying like a gentleman.

LOCKIT.

Those, I see, will fit the captain better. Take down the further pair.—Do but examine them, sir. Never was better work. How genteelly they are made! They will sit as easy as a glove, and the nicest* man in England might not be ashamed to wear them. (*He puts on the chains.*) If I had the best gentleman in the land in my custody I could not equip him more handsomely. And so, sir, I now leave you to your private meditations.

[Exeunt. Manet Macheath.]

Scene viii.

Macheath.

Air 26. "Courtiers, courtiers think it no harm," etc.

[MACHEATH.]

Man may escape from rope and gun.
Nay, some have outlived the doctor's pill.
Who takes a woman must be undone;
That basilisk is sure to kill.
The fly that sips treacle is lost in the sweets,
So he that tastes woman, woman, woman,
He that tastes woman ruin meets.

To what a woeful plight have I brought myself! Here must I (all day long till I am hanged) be confined to hear the reproaches of a wench who lays her ruin at my door. I am in the custody of her father, and to be sure, if he knows of the matter, I shall have a fine time on't betwixt this and my execution. But I promised the wench marriage. What signifies a promise to a woman? Does not man in marriage itself promise a hundred things that he never means to perform? Do all we can, women will believe us, for they look upon a promise as an excuse for following their own inclinations.—But here comes Lucy, and I cannot get from her. Would I were deaf!

Scene ix.

Macheath, Lucy.

LUCY.

You base man you, how can you look me in the face after what hath passed between us? See here, perfidious wretch, how I am forced to bear about the load of infamy you have laid upon me. Oh Macheath! thou hast robbed me of my quiet. To see thee tortured would give me pleasure.

Air 27. "A lovely lass to a friar came," etc.

Thus when a good housewife sees a rat
In her trap in the morning taken,
With pleasure her heart goes pit-a-pat
In revenge for her loss of bacon.
Then she throws him
To the dog or cat
To be worried, crushed, and shaken.

MACHEATH.

Have you no bowels, no tenderness, my dear Lucy, to see a husband in these circumstances?

LUCY.

A husband!

MACHEATH.

In ev'ry respect but the form, and that, my dear, may be said over us at any time. Friends should not insist upon ceremonies. From a man of honor, his word is as good as his bond.

LUCY.

'Tis the pleasure of all you fine men to insult the women you have ruined.

Air 28. "'Twas when the sea was roaring," etc.

How cruel are the traitors
 Who lie and swear in jest
To cheat unguarded creatures
 Of virtue, fame, and rest!
Whoever steals a shilling
 Through shame the guilt conceals;
In love the perjured villain
 With boasts the theft reveals.

MACHEATH.

The very first opportunity, my dear (have but patience), you shall be my wife in whatever manner you please.

LUCY.

Insinuating monster! And so you think I know nothing of the affair of Miss Polly Peachum. I could tear thy eyes out!

MACHEATH.

Sure Lucy, you can't be such a fool as to be jealous of Polly!

LUCY.

Are you not married to her, you brute you?

MACHEATH.

Married! Very good. The wench gives it out only to vex thee and to ruin me in thy good opinion. 'Tis true, I go to the house; I chat with the girl; I kiss her; I say a thousand things to her (as all gentlemen do) that mean nothing, to divert my self. And now the silly* jade hath set it about that I am married to her, to let me know what she would be at. Indeed my dear Lucy, these violent passions may be of ill consequence to a woman in your condition.

LUCY.

Come, come, Captain, for all your assurance, you know that Miss Polly hath put it out of your power to do me the justice you promised me.

MACHEATH.

A jealous woman believes everything her passion suggests. To convince you of my sincerity, if we can find the ordinary, I shall have no scruples of making you my wife. And I know the consequence of having two at a time.

LUCY.

That you are only to be hanged, and so get rid of them both.

MACHEATH.

I am ready, my dear Lucy, to give you satisfaction—if you think there is any in marriage. What can a man of honor say more?

LUCY.

So then it seems, you are not married to Miss Polly.

MACHEATH.

You know, Lucy, the girl is prodigiously conceited. No man can say a civil thing to her, but (like other fine ladies) her vanity makes her think he's her own forever and ever.

Air 29. "The sun had loosed his weary teams," etc.

The first time at the looking glass
 The mother sets her daughter,
The image strikes the smiling lass
 With self-love ever after.
Each time she looks, she, fonder grown,
 Thinks ev'ry charm grows stronger.
But alas, vain maid, all eyes but your own
 Can see you are not younger.

When women consider their own beauties, they are all alike unreasonable in their demands, for they expect their lovers should like them as long as they like themselves.

LUCY.

Yonder is my father—perhaps this way we may light upon the ordinary, who shall try if you will be as good as your word. For I long to be made an honest woman.

[Exeunt.]

Scene x.

Peachum, Lockit with an account book.

LOCKIT.

In this last affair, brother Peachum, we are agreed. You have consented to go halves in Macheath.

PEACHUM.

We shall never fall out about an execution. But as to that article, pray how stands our last year's account?

LOCKIT.

If you will run your eye over it, you'll find 'tis fair and clearly stated.

PEACHUM.

This long arrear of the government is very hard upon us! Can it be expected that we should hang our acquaintance for nothing, when our betters will hardly save theirs without being paid for it. Unless the people in employment pay better, I promise them for the future I shall let other rogues live besides their own.

LOCKIT.

Perhaps brother, they are afraid these matters may be carried too far. We are treated too by them with contempt, as if our profession was not reputable.

PEACHUM.

In one respect indeed, our employment may be reckoned dishonest, because, like great statesmen, we encourage those who betray their friends.

LOCKIT.

Such language, brother, anywhere else, might turn to your prejudice. Learn to be more guarded, I beg you.

Air 30. "How happy are we," etc.

When you censure the age,
Be cautious and sage,
Lest the courtiers offended should be:
If you mention vice or bribe,
'Tis so pat to all the tribe,
Each cries, "That was leveled at me."

PEACHUM.

Here's poor Ned Clincher's name, I see. Sure brother Lockit, there was a little unfair proceeding in Ned's case: for he told me in the condemned hold that, for value received, you had promised him a session or two longer without molestation.

LOCKIT.

Mr. Peachum, this is the first time my honor was ever called in question.

PEACHUM.

Business is at an end if once we act dishonorably.

LOCKIT.

Who accuses me?

PEACHUM.

You are warm, brother.

LOCKIT.

He that attacks my honor attacks my livelihood. And this usage—sir—is not to be borne.

PEACHUM.

Since you provoke me to speak, I must tell you too that Mrs.* Coaxer charges you with defrauding her of her information-money for the apprehending of Curl-pated Hugh. Indeed, indeed, brother, we must punctually pay our spies, or we shall have no information.[49]

LOCKIT.

Is this language to me, sirrah, who have saved you from the gallows, sirrah!

49 spies ... information] This is one of many oblique references throughout the play to the chief minister, Robert Walpole. A grievance of Walpole's critics was his intelligence budget which funded secret methods of gaining damaging evidence against those he opposed.

Collaring each other.

PEACHUM.

If I am hanged, it shall be for ridding the world of an arrant rascal.

LOCKIT.

This hand shall do the office of the halter you deserve and throttle you, you dog!

PEACHUM.

Brother, brother, we are both in the wrong. We shall be both losers in the dispute. For you know we have it in our power to hang each other. You should not be so passionate.

LOCKIT.

Nor you so provoking.

PEACHUM.

'Tis our mutual interest, 'tis for the interest of the world we should agree. If I said anything, brother, to the prejudice of your character, I ask pardon.

LOCKIT.

Brother Peachum, I can forgive as well as resent. Give me your hand. Suspicion does not become a friend.

PEACHUM.

I only meant to give you occasion to justify yourself. But I must now step home, for I expect the gentleman about this snuffbox that Filch nimmed two nights ago in the park. I appointed him at this hour. [*Exit.*]

Scene xi.

Lockit, Lucy.

LOCKIT.

Whence come you, hussy?

LUCY.

My tears might answer that question.

LOCKIT.

You have then been whimpering and fondling, like a spaniel, over the fellow that hath abused you.

LUCY.

One can't help love; one can't cure it. 'Tis not in my power to obey you and hate him.

LOCKIT.

Learn to bear your husband's death like a reasonable woman. 'Tis not the fashion nowadays so much as to affect sorrow upon these occasions. No woman would ever marry if she had not the chance of mortality for a release. Act like a woman of spirit, hussy, and thank your father for what he is doing.

Air 31. "Of a noble race* was Shenkin."

LUCY.

Is then his fate decreed, sir?
Such a man can I think of quitting?
When first we met, so moves me yet,
Oh see how my heart is splitting!

LOCKIT.

Look ye, Lucy, there is no saving him. So I think you must even do like other widows: buy yourself weeds and be cheerful.

Air 32.

You'll think ere many days ensue
This sentence not severe;
I hang your husband, child, 'tis true,
But with him hang your care.
Twang dang dillo dee.

Like a good wife, go moan over your dying husband. That, child, is your duty. Consider, girl, you can't have the man and the money too, so make yourself as easy as you can by getting all you can from him. [*Exit.*]

Scene xii.

Lucy, Macheath.

LUCY.

Though the ordinary was out of the way today, I hope, my dear, you will upon the first opportunity quiet my scruples. Oh sir! my father's hard heart is not to be softened, and I am in the utmost despair.

MACHEATH.

But if I could raise a small sum, would not twenty guineas, think you, move him? Of all the arguments in the way of business, the perquisite is the most prevailing. Your father's perquisites for the escape of prisoners must amount to a considerable sum in the year. Money well timed and properly applied will do anything.

Air 33. "London Ladies."

If you at an office solicit your due
    And would not have matters neglected,
You must quicken the clerk with the perquisite too,
    To do what his duty directed.
Or would you the frowns of a lady prevent,
    She too has this palpable failing:
The perquisite softens her into consent;
    That reason with all is prevailing.

LUCY.

What love or money can do shall be done, for all my comfort depends upon your safety.

Scene xiii.

Lucy, Macheath, Polly.

POLLY.

Where is my dear husband? Was a rope ever intended for this neck! Oh let me throw my arms about it and throttle thee with love! Why dost thou turn away from me? 'Tis thy Polly, 'tis thy wife.

MACHEATH.

Was ever such an unfortunate rascal as I am!

LUCY.

Was there ever such another villain!

POLLY.

Oh Macheath! was it for this we parted? Taken! imprisoned! Tried! Hanged! Cruel reflection! I'll stay with thee till death; no force shall tear thy dear wife from thee now. What means my love? Not one kind word! not one kind look! Think what thy Polly suffers to see thee in this condition.

Air 34. "All in the downs," etc.

Thus when the swallow, seeking prey,
    Within the sash is closely pent,
His consort, with bemoaning lay,
    Without sits pining for th'event.
Her chatt'ring lovers all around her skim;
She heeds them not (poor bird!), her soul's with him.

MACHEATH. (*Aside.*)

I must disown her.—The wench is distracted.

LUCY.

Am I then bilked of my virtue? Can I have no reparation? Sure men were born to lie and women to believe them! Oh villain! villain!

POLLY.

Am I not thy wife? Thy neglect of me, thy aversion to me too severely proves it. Look on me. Tell me, am I not thy wife?

LUCY.

Perfidious wretch!

POLLY.

Barbarous husband!

LUCY.

Hadst thou been hanged five months ago, I had been happy.

POLLY.

And I too. If you had been kind* to me till death, it would not have vexed me—and that's no very unreasonable request (though from a wife) to a man who hath not above seven or eight days to live.

LUCY.

Art thou then married to another? Hast thou two wives, monster?

MACHEATH.

If women's tongues can cease for an answer, hear me.

LUCY.

I won't. Flesh and blood can't bear my usage.

POLLY.

Shall I not claim my own? Justice bids me speak.

Air 35. "Have you heard of a frolicsome ditty," etc.

MACHEATH.

How happy could I be with either,
Were t'other dear charmer away!
But while you thus tease me together,
To neither a word will I say,
But tol de rol, etc.

POLLY.

Sure my dear, there ought to be some preference shown to a wife! At least she may claim the appearance of it.—He must be distracted with his misfortunes, or he could not use me thus!

LUCY.

Oh villain, villain! thou hast deceived me. I could even inform against thee with pleasure. Not a prude wishes more heartily to have facts against her intimate acquaintance than I now wish to have facts against thee. I would have her satisfaction, and they should all out.

Air 36. Irish trot.

POLLY.

I'm bubbled.[50]

LUCY.

I'm bubbled.

POLLY.

Oh how I am troubled!

LUCY.

Bamboozled, and bit!*

POLLY.

My distresses are doubled.

LUCY.

When you come to the tree, should the hangman refuse,
These fingers with pleasure could fasten the noose.

POLLY.

I'm bubbled, etc.

MACHEATH.

Be pacified, my dear Lucy. This is all a fetch of Polly's to make me desperate with you in case I get off. If I am hanged, she would fain have the credit of being thought my widow.—Really, Polly, this is no time for a dispute of this sort, for whenever you are talking of marriage, I am thinking of hanging.

POLLY.

And hast thou the heart to persist in disowning me?

MACHEATH.

And hast thou the heart to persist in persuading me that I am married? Why Polly, dost thou seek to aggravate my misfortunes?

---

50 bubbled] cheated; also refers to the South Sea Company stock bubble and crash of 1720, in which many, including Gay, lost money. In resolving the crisis, Walpole consolidated his ministerial power, using strong arm tactics to stabilize the government and shield the monarchy from investigation and scandal.

LUCY.

Really Miss Peachum, you but expose yourself. Besides, 'tis barbarous in you to worry a gentleman in his circumstances.

Air 37.

POLLY.

Cease your funning;
Force or cunning
Never shall my heart trepan.
All these sallies
Are but malice
To seduce my constant man.
'Tis most certain
By their flirting
Women oft have envy shown:
Pleased to ruin
Others wooing,
Never happy in their own!

POLLY.

Decency, madam, methinks might teach you to behave yourself with some reserve with the husband while his wife is present.

MACHEATH.

But seriously, Polly, this is carrying the joke a little too far.

LUCY.

If you are determined, madam, to raise a disturbance in the prison, I shall be obliged to send for the turnkey to show you the door. I am sorry, madam, you force me to be so ill-bred.

POLLY.

Give me leave to tell you, madam, these forward airs don't become you in the least, madam. And my duty, madam, obliges me to stay with my husband, madam.

Air 38. "Good morrow, Gossip Joan."

LUCY.

Why how now, Madam Flirt:
If you thus must chatter
And are for flinging dirt,
Let's try who best can spatter, Madam Flirt!

POLLY.

Why how now, saucy jade:
Sure the wench is tipsy!
(*To him.*)
How can you see me made
The scoff of such a Gypsy?
(*To her.*)
Saucy jade!

Scene xiv.

Lucy, Macheath, Polly, Peachum.

PEACHUM.

Where's my wench? Ah hussy! hussy! Come you home, you slut, and when your fellow is hanged, hang yourself to make your family some amends.

POLLY.

Dear, dear father, do not tear me from him. I must speak. I have more to say to him.—Oh! twist thy fetters about me that he may not haul me from thee!

PEACHUM.

Sure all women are alike! If ever they commit the folly, they are sure to commit another by exposing themselves.—Away, not a word more. You are my prisoner now, hussy.

Air 39. Irish howl.

POLLY. (*Holding Macheath, Peachum pulling her.*)
No power on earth can e'er divide
The knot that sacred love hath tied.
When parents draw against our mind,

The true-love's knot they faster bind.
Oh, oh ray, oh amborah—oh, oh, etc.

[Exeunt Polly and Peachum.]

Scene xv.

Lucy, Macheath.

MACHEATH.

I am naturally compassionate, wife, so that I could not use the wench as she deserved, which made you at first suspect there was something in what she said.

LUCY.

Indeed my dear, I was strangely puzzled.

MACHEATH.

If that had been the case, her father would never have brought me into this circumstance. No Lucy, I had rather die than be false to thee.

LUCY.

How happy am I, if you say this from your heart! For I love thee so, that I could sooner bear to see thee hanged than in the arms of another.

MACHEATH.

But couldst thou bear to see me hanged?

LUCY.

Oh Macheath, I can never live to see that day.

MACHEATH.

You see, Lucy, in the account of love you are in my debt, and you must now be convinced that I rather choose to die than be another's. Make me, if possible, love thee more, and let me owe my life to thee. If you refuse to assist me, Peachum and your father will immediately put me beyond all means of escape.

LUCY.

My father, I know, hath been drinking hard with the prisoners, and I fancy he is now taking his nap in his own room. If I can procure the keys, shall I go off with thee, my dear?

MACHEATH.

If we are together, 'twill be impossible to lie concealed. As soon as the search begins to be a little cool, I will send to thee. Till then my heart is thy prisoner.

LUCY.

Come then, my dear husband, owe thy life to me, and though you love me not, be grateful. But that Polly runs in my head strangely.

MACHEATH.

A moment of time may make us unhappy forever.

Air 40. "The lass of Patie's Mill," etc.

LUCY.

I like the fox shall grieve,
Whose mate hath left her side,
Whom hounds, from morn to eve,
Chase o'er the country wide.
Where can my lover hide?
Where cheat the wary[d] pack?
If Love be not his guide,
He never will come back!

[Exeunt.]

Act III, scene i. Newgate.

Lockit, Lucy.

LOCKIT.

To be sure, wench, you must have been aiding and abetting to help him to this escape.

LUCY.

Sir, here hath been Peachum and his daughter Polly, and to be sure they know the ways of Newgate as well as if they had been born and bred in the place all their lives. Why must all your suspicion light upon me?

LOCKIT.

Lucy, Lucy, I will have none of these shuffling answers.

LUCY.

Well then, if I know anything of him, I wish I may be burnt![51]

LOCKIT.

Keep your temper, Lucy, or I shall pronounce you guilty.

LUCY.

Keep yours, sir, I do wish I may be burnt, I do. And what can I say more to convince you?

LOCKIT.

Did he tip handsomely? How much did he come down with? Come hussy, don't cheat your father, and I shall not be angry with you. Perhaps you have made a better bargain with him than I could have done. How much, my good girl?

LUCY.

You know, sir, I am fond of him and would have given money to have kept him with me.

LOCKIT.

Ah Lucy! thy education might have put thee more upon thy guard, for a girl in the bar of an alehouse is always besieged.

LUCY.

Dear sir, mention not my education, for 'twas to that I owe my ruin.

Air 41. "If love's a sweet passion," etc.

When young at the bar you first taught me to score
And bid me be free of my lips and no more,
I was kissed by the parson, the squire, and the sot.
When the guest was departed, the kiss was forgot.
But his kiss was so sweet and so closely he pressed,
That I languished and pined till I granted the rest.

If you can forgive me, sir, I will make a fair confession, for to be sure, he hath been a most barbarous villain to me.

LOCKIT.

And so you have let him escape, hussy, have you?

LUCY.

When a woman loves, a kind look, a tender word can persuade her to anything. And I could ask no other bribe.

LOCKIT.

Thou wilt always be a vulgar slut, Lucy. If you would not be looked upon as a fool, you should never do anything but upon the foot of interest. Those that act otherwise are their own bubbles.*

LUCY.

But love, sir, is a misfortune that may happen to the most discreet woman, and in love we are all fools alike. Notwithstanding all he swore, I am now fully convinced that Polly Peachum is actually his wife. Did I let him escape (fool that I was!) to go to her? Polly will wheedle herself into his money, and then Peachum will hang him and cheat us both.

LOCKIT.

So I am to be ruined because, forsooth, you must be in love—a very pretty excuse!

LUCY.

I could murder that impudent, happy strumpet. I gave him his life, and that creature enjoys the sweets of it. Ungrateful Macheath!

Air 42. "South Sea Ballad."

51 burnt] Being burned to death was the punishment for women convicted of treason; alternatively, Lucy may be referring to the punishment for first offenders who, receiving the benefit of clergy, were branded on the thumb to ensure that they not use the plea again (LT).

My love is all madness and folly:
Alone I lie,
Toss, tumble, and cry,
"What a happy creature is Polly!"
Was e'er such a wretch as I:
With rage I redden like scarlet
That my dear inconstant varlet,
Stark blind to my charms,
Is lost in the arms
Of that jilt, that inveigling harlot!
Stark blind to my charms,
Is lost in the arms
Of that jilt, that inveigling harlot!
This, this my resentment alarms.

LOCKIT.

And so, after all this mischief, I must stay here to be entertained with your caterwauling, mistress puss! Out of my sight, wanton strumpet! you shall fast and mortify yourself into reason, with now and then a little handsome discipline to bring you to your senses. Go.

[Exit Lucy.]

Scene ii.

LOCKIT.

Peachum then intends to outwit me in this affair, but I'll be even with him. The dog is leaky in his liquor, so I'll ply him that way, get the secret from him, and turn this affair to my own advantage. Lions, wolves, and vultures don't live together in herds, droves, or flocks. Of all animals of prey, man is the only sociable one. Every one of us preys upon his neighbor, and yet we herd together. Peachum is my companion, my friend. According to the custom of the world, indeed, he may quote thousands of precedents for cheating me. And shall not I make use of the privilege of friendship to make him a return?

Air 43. "Packington's Pound."

Thus gamesters united in friendship are found,
Though they know that their industry all is a cheat;
They flock to their prey at the dice box's sound
And join to promote one another's deceit.
But if by mishap
They fail of a chap,
To keep in their hands they each other entrap.
Like pikes, lank with hunger, who miss of their ends,
They bite their companions and prey on their friends.

Now Peachum, you and I, like honest tradesmen, are to have a fair trial which of us two can overreach the other.—Lucy.

Enter Lucy.

Are there any of Peachum's people now in the house?

LUCY.

Filch, sir, is drinking a quartern of strong-waters in the next room with Black Moll.

LOCKIT.

Bid him come to me.

[Exit Lucy.]

Scene iii.

Lockit, Filch.

LOCKIT.

Why boy, thou lookest as if thou wert half starved, like a shotten herring.

FILCH.

One had need have the constitution of a horse to go through the business. Since the favorite child-getter was disabled by a mishap, I have picked up a little money by helping the ladies to a pregnancy against their being called down to sentence. But if a man cannot get an honest livelihood an easier way, I am sure 'tis what I can't undertake for another session.

LOCKIT.

Truly, if that great man* should tip off, 'twould be an irreparable loss. The vigor and prowess of a knight-errant never saved half the ladies in distress that he hath done. But boy, canst thou tell me where thy master is to be found?

FILCH.

At his lock, sir, at the Crooked Billet.

LOCKIT.
Very well, I have nothing more with you.

Exit Filch.

I'll go to him there, for I have many important affairs to settle with him, and in the way of those transactions, I'll artfully get into his secret so that Macheath shall not remain a day longer out of my clutches.

Scene iv. A gaming house.

Macheath in a fine, tarnished coat, Ben Budge, Matt of the Mint.

MACHEATH.
I am sorry, gentlemen, the road was so barren of money. When my friends are in difficulties, I am always glad that my fortune can be serviceable to them. (*Gives them money.*) You see, gentlemen, I am not a mere Court friend who professes everything and will do nothing.

Air 44. "Lillibullero."

The modes of the Court so common are grown,
That a true friend can hardly be met;
Friendship for interest is but a loan,
Which they let out for what they can get.
'Tis true, you find
Some friends so kind,
Who will give you good counsel themselves to defend.
In sorrowful ditty,
They promise, they pity,
But shift you for money from friend to friend.

But we, gentlemen, have still honor enough to break through the corruptions of the world. And while I can serve you, you may command me.

BEN.
It grieves my heart that so generous a man should be involved in such difficulties as oblige him to live with such ill company and herd with gamesters.

MATT.
See the partiality of mankind: one man may steal a horse better than another look over a hedge. Of all mechanics, of all servile handicraftsmen, a gamester is the vilest. But yet, as many of the quality* are of the profession, he is admitted amongst the politest company. I wonder we are not more respected.

MACHEATH.
There will be deep play tonight at Marrabone,* and consequently money may be picked up upon the road. Meet me there, and I'll give you the hint who is worth setting.

MATT.
The fellow with a brown coat with a narrow gold binding, I am told, is never without money.

MACHEATH.
What do you mean, Matt? Sure you will not think of meddling with him! He's a good, honest kind of a fellow and one of us.

BEN.
To be sure, sir, we will put ourselves under your direction.

MACHEATH.
Have an eye upon the moneylenders. A rouleau or two would prove a pretty sort of an expedition. I hate extortion.

MATT.
Those rouleaus are very pretty things. I hate your* bank bills. There is such a hazard in putting them off.

MACHEATH.
There is a certain man of distinction, who in his time hath nicked me out of a great deal of the ready. He is in my cash, Ben. I'll point him out to you this evening, and you shall draw upon him for the debt.—The company are met; I hear the dice box in the other room. So gentlemen, your servant. You'll meet me at Marrabone.

[Exeunt.]

Scene v. Peachum's lock.

A table with wine, brandy, pipes and tobacco. Peachum, Lockit.

LOCKIT.

The Coronation account,[52] brother Peachum, is of so intricate a nature, that I believe it will never be settled.

PEACHUM.

It consists indeed of a great variety of articles. It was worth to our people, in fees of different kinds, above ten installments.[53] This is part of the account, brother, that lies open before us.

LOCKIT.

"A lady's tail[54] of rich brocade"—that, I see, is disposed of.

PEACHUM.

To Mrs.* Diana Trapes, the tallywoman, and she will make a good hand on't in shoes and slippers to trick out young ladies upon their going into keeping.*

LOCKIT.

But I don't see any article of the jewels.

PEACHUM.

Those are so well known, that they must be sent abroad. You'll find them entered under the article of exportation. As for the snuffboxes, watches, swords, etcetera, I thought it best to enter them under their several heads.

LOCKIT.

"Seven and twenty women's pockets complete with the several things therein contained"—all sealed, numbered, and entered.

PEACHUM.

But brother, it is impossible for us now to enter upon this affair. We should have the whole day before us. Besides, the account of the last half year's plate* is in a book by itself, which lies at the other office.

LOCKIT.

Bring us then more liquor. Today shall be for pleasure, tomorrow for business. Ah brother, those daughters of ours are two slippery hussies. Keep a watchful eye upon Polly, and Macheath in a day or two shall be our own again.

Air 45. "Down in the North Country," etc.

LOCKIT.

What gudgeons are we men!
　　Ev'ry woman's easy prey.
Though we have felt the hook, again
　　We bite, and they betray.
The bird that hath been trapped,
　　When he hears his calling mate,
To her he flies, again he's clapped
　　Within the wiry grate.

PEACHUM.

But what signifies catching the bird, if your daughter Lucy will set open the door of the cage?

LOCKIT.

If men were answerable for the follies and frailties of their wives and daughters, no friends could keep a good correspondence together for two days. This is unkind of you, brother, for among good friends, what they say or do goes for nothing.

Enter a servant.

SERVANT.

Sir, here's Mrs.* Diana Trapes wants to speak with you.

PEACHUM.

Shall we admit her, brother Lockit?

LOCKIT.

By all means. She's a good customer and a fine-spoken woman—and a woman who drinks and talks so freely, will enliven the conversation.

PEACHUM.

Desire her to walk in.

Exit Servant.

[52] Coronation account] account of goods stolen during the lavish coronation ceremonies of George II in October 1727, three months before *The Beggar's Opera* opened

[53] installment] public installation of the Lord Mayor of the City of London

[54] tail] train

Scene vi.

Peachum, Lockit, Mrs. Trapes.*

PEACHUM.

Dear Mrs. Di, your servant. One may know by your kiss, that your gin is excellent.

TRAPES.

I was always very curious* in my liquors.

LOCKIT.

There is no perfumed breath like it. I have been long acquainted with the flavor of those lips, han't I, Mrs. Di?

TRAPES.

Fill it up. I take as large draughts of liquor, as I did of love. I hate a flincher in either.

Air 46. "A shepherd kept sheep," etc.

In the days of my youth I could bill like a dove,
fa, la, la, etc.
Like a sparrow at all times was ready for love, fa,
la, la, etc.
The life of all mortals in kissing should pass,
Lip to lip while we're young—then the lip to the
glass, fa, etc.

But now, Mr. Peachum, to our business. If you have blacks[55] of any kind brought in of late, mantuas, velvet scarves, petticoats—let it be what it will, I am your chap, for all my ladies are very fond of mourning.

PEACHUM.

Why, look ye, Mrs. Di, you deal so hard with us that we can afford to give the gentlemen who venture their lives for the goods little or nothing.

TRAPES.

The hard times oblige me to go very near in my dealing. To be sure, of late years I have been a great sufferer by the Parliament. Three thousand pounds would hardly make me amends. The act for destroying the Mint[56] was a severe cut upon our business: till then, if a customer stepped out of the way, we knew where to have her. No doubt you know Mrs.* Coaxer: there's a wench now (till today) with a good suit of clothes of mine upon her back, and I could never set eyes upon her for three months together. Since the act too against imprisonment for small sums,[57] my loss there too hath been very considerable, and it must be so, when a lady can borrow a handsome petticoat or a clean gown and I not have the least hank upon her! And o'my conscience, nowadays most ladies take a delight in cheating, when they can do it with safety.

PEACHUM.

Madam, you had a handsome gold watch of us t'other day for seven guineas. Considering we must have our profit, to a gentleman upon the road a gold watch will be scarce worth the taking.

TRAPES.

Consider, Mr. Peachum, that watch was remarkable, and not of very safe sale. If you have any black velvet scarves, they are a handsome winter wear and take with most gentlemen who deal with my customers. 'Tis I that put the ladies upon a good foot. 'Tis not youth or beauty that fixes their price. The gentlemen always pay according to their dress, from half a crown to two guineas. And yet those hussies make nothing of bilking of me. Then too, allowing for accidents (I have eleven fine customers now down under the surgeon's hands), what with fees and other expenses, there are great goings-out, and no comings-in, and not a farthing to pay for at least a month's clothing. We run great risks—great risks indeed.

PEACHUM.

As I remember, you said something just now of Mrs.* Coaxer.

TRAPES.

Yes sir, to be sure, I stripped her of a suit of my own clothes about two hours ago and have left her

55 blacks] mourning clothes

56 act … Mint] After 1722 debtors could be arrested in this former sanctuary.

57 act … sums] Parliament passed an act in 1725 against imprisonment of people for small debts.

as she should be, in her shift, with a lover of hers at my house. She called him upstairs as he was going to Marrabone in a hackney coach. And I hope, for her own sake and mine, she will persuade the captain to redeem her, for the captain is very generous to the ladies.

LOCKIT.

What captain?

TRAPES.

He thought I did not know him. An intimate acquaintance of yours, Mr. Peachum: only Captain Macheath, as fine as a lord.

PEACHUM.

Tomorrow, dear Mrs. Di, you shall set your own price upon any of the goods you like. We have at least half a dozen velvet scarves and all at your service. Will you give me leave to make you a present of this suit of nightclothes for your own wearing? But are you sure it is Captain Macheath?

TRAPES.

Though he thinks I have forgot him, nobody knows him better. I have taken a great deal of the captain's money in my time at second hand, for he always loved to have his ladies well dressed.

PEACHUM.

Mr. Lockit and I have a little business with the captain—you understand me—and we will satisfy you for Mrs. Coaxer's debt.

LOCKIT.

Depend upon it, we will deal like men of honor.

TRAPES.

I don't enquire after your affairs, so whatever happens, I wash my hands on't. It hath always been my maxim that one friend should assist another. But if you please, I'll take one of the scarves home with me. 'Tis always good to have something in hand.

[Exeunt.]

Scene vii. Newgate.

Lucy.

LUCY.

Jealousy, rage, love, and fear are at once tearing me to pieces. How I am weather-beaten and shattered with distresses!

Air 47. "One evening, having lost my way," etc.

I'm like a skiff on the ocean tossed,
Now high, now low, with each billow borne,
With her rudder broke and her anchor lost,
Deserted and all forlorn.
While thus I lie rolling and tossing all night,
That Polly lies sporting on seas of delight!
Revenge, revenge, revenge,
Shall appease my restless sprite.

I have the ratsbane ready. I run no risk, for I can lay her death upon the gin,[58] and so many die of that naturally that I shall never be called in question. But say I were to be hanged, I never could be hanged for anything that would give me greater comfort than the poisoning that slut.

Enter Filch.

FILCH.

Madam, here's our Miss Polly come to wait upon you.

LUCY.

Show her in.

[Exit Filch.]

Scene viii.

Lucy, Polly.

LUCY.

Dear madam, your servant. I hope you will pardon my passion, when I was so happy to see you last. I was so overrun with the spleen that I was perfectly out of myself. And really, when one hath the spleen, everything is to be excused by a friend.

58 gin] The cheap gin sold in great quantities to Londoners in the 1720s was often so improperly distilled as to be poisonous.

Air 48. "Now Roger, I'll tell thee, because thou'rt my son."

When a wife's in her pout
(As she's sometimes, no doubt),
The good husband as meek as a lamb,
Her vapors to still
First grants her her will,
And the quieting draught is a dram.
Poor man! And the quieting draught is a dram.

I wish all our quarrels might have so comfortable a reconciliation.

POLLY.

I have no excuse for my own behavior, madam, but my misfortunes. And really madam, I suffer too upon your account.

LUCY.

But Miss Polly, in the way of friendship, will you give me leave to propose a glass of cordial to you?

POLLY.

Strong-waters are apt to give me the headache. I hope madam, you will excuse me.

LUCY.

Not the greatest lady in the land could have better in her closet* for her own private drinking. You seem mighty low in spirits, my dear.

POLLY.

I am sorry, madam, my health will not allow me to accept of your offer. I should not have left you in the rude manner I did when we met last, madam, had not my papa hauled me away so unexpectedly. I was indeed somewhat provoked and perhaps might use some expressions that were disrespectful. But really madam, the captain treated me with so much contempt and cruelty that I deserved your pity, rather than your resentment.

LUCY.

But since his escape, no doubt all matters are made up again. Ah Polly! Polly! 'tis I am the unhappy wife, and he loves you as if you were only his mistress.

POLLY.

Sure madam, you cannot think me so happy as to be the object of your jealously. A man is always afraid of a woman who loves him too well, so that I must expect to be neglected and avoided.

LUCY.

Then our cases, my dear Polly, are exactly alike. Both of us indeed have been too fond.

Air 49. "Oh Bessy Bell."

POLLY.

A curse attends that woman's love,
Who always would be pleasing.

LUCY.

The pertness of the billing dove,
Like tickling, is but teasing.

POLLY.

What then in love can woman do?

LUCY.

If we grow fond they shun us.

POLLY.

And when we fly them, they pursue—

LUCY.

But leave us when they've won us.
Love is so very whimsical in both sexes that it is impossible to be lasting. But my heart is particular and contradicts my own observation.

POLLY.

But really, Mistress Lucy, by his last behavior I think I ought to envy you. When I was forced from him, he did not show the least tenderness. But perhaps, he hath a heart not capable of it.

Air 50. "Would fate to me Belinda give—"

Among the men coquets we find,
Who court by turns all womankind,
And we grant all their hearts desired,
When they are flattered and admired.

The coquets of both sexes are self-lovers, and that is a love no other whatever can dispossess. I fear, my dear Lucy, our husband is one of those.

LUCY.

Away with these melancholy reflections. Indeed, my dear Polly, we are both of us a cup too low. Let me prevail upon you to accept of my offer.

Air 51. "Come, sweet lass," etc.

Come, sweet lass,
Let's banish sorrow
Till tomorrow;
Come, sweet lass,
Let's take a chirping[59] glass.
Wine can clear
The vapors of despair
And make us light as air;
Then drink, and banish care.

I can't bear, child,* to see you in such low spirits. And I must persuade you to what I know will do you good. (*Aside.*) I shall now soon be even with the hypocritical strumpet.

[Exit.]

59 chirping] cheering

Scene ix.

Polly.

POLLY.

All this wheedling of Lucy cannot be for nothing. At this time too, when I know she hates me! The dissembling of a woman is always the forerunner of mischief. By pouring strong- waters down my throat, she thinks to pump some secrets out of me. I'll be upon my guard and won't taste a drop of her liquor, I'm resolved.

Scene x.

Lucy, with strong-waters, Polly.

LUCY.

Come, Miss Polly.

POLLY.

Indeed child,* you have given yourself trouble to no purpose. You must, my dear, excuse me.

LUCY.

Really Miss Polly, you are so squeamishly affected about taking a cup of strong-waters as a lady before company. I vow, Polly, I shall take it monstrously ill if you refuse me. Brandy and men (though women love them never so well) are always taken by us with some reluctance—unless 'tis in private.

POLLY.

I protest, madam, it goes against me.—What do I see! Macheath again in custody! Now every glimmering of happiness is lost. (*Drops the glass of liquor on the ground.*)

LUCY. (*Aside.*)

Since things are thus, I'm glad the wench hath escaped, for by this event 'tis plain she was not happy enough to deserve to be poisoned.

Scene xi.

Lockit, Macheath, Peachum, Lucy, Polly.

LOCKIT.

Set your heart to rest, Captain. You have neither the chance of love or money for another escape, for you are ordered to be called down upon your trial immediately.

PEACHUM.

Away, hussies! This is not a time for a man to be hampered with his wives. You see, the gentleman is in chains already.

LUCY.

Oh Husband, Husband, my heart longed to see thee, but to see thee thus distracts me!

POLLY.

Will not my dear husband look upon his Polly? Why hadst thou not flown to me for protection? with me thou hadst been safe.

Air 52. "The last time I went o'er the moor."

POLLY.

Hither, dear Husband, turn your eyes—

LUCY.

        Bestow one glance to cheer me.

POLLY.

Think with that look thy Polly dies.

LUCY.

        Oh shun me not but hear me.

POLLY.

'Tis Polly sues.

LUCY.

                'Tis Lucy speaks.

POLLY.

Is thus true love requited?

LUCY.

        My heart is bursting.

POLLY.

                        Mine too breaks.

LUCY.

        Must I—

POLLY.

                Must I be slighted?

MACHEATH.

What would you have me say, ladies? You see, this affair will soon be at an end without my disobliging either of you.

PEACHUM.

But the settling this point, Captain, might prevent a lawsuit between your two widows.

Air 53. "Tom Tinker's my true love."

MACHEATH.

Which way shall I turn me? How can I decide?
Wives, the day of our death, are as fond as a bride.
One wife is too much for most husbands to hear,
But two at a time there's no mortal can bear.
This way and that way and which way I will,
What would comfort the one, t'other wife would
    take ill.

POLLY.

But if his own misfortunes have made him insensible to mine, a father sure will be more compassionate.—Dear, dear sir, sink the material evidence and bring him off at his trial. Polly upon her knees begs it of you.

Air 54. "I am a poor shepherd undone."

When my hero in court appears
    And stands arraigned for his life,
Then think of poor Polly's tears,
        For ah! Poor Polly's his wife.

Like the sailor he holds up his hand,
Distressed on the dashing wave.
To die a dry death at land
Is as bad as a wat'ry grave.
And alas, poor Polly!
Alack and well-a-day!
Before I was in love,
Oh! every month was May.

LUCY. (*Kneeling.*)

If Peachum's heart is hardened, sure you, sir, will have more compassion on a daughter. I know the evidence is in your power. How then can you be a tyrant to me?

Air 55. "Ianthe the lovely," etc.

When he holds up his hand, arraigned for his life,
Oh think of your daughter, and think I'm his wife!
What are cannons or bombs or clashing of swords?
For death is more certain by witnesses' words.
Then nail up their lips, that dread thunder allay,
And each month of my life will hereafter be May.

LOCKIT.

Macheath's time is come, Lucy. We know our own affairs; therefore, let us have no more whimpering or whining.

Air 56. "A Cobbler there was," etc.

Ourselves, like the great, to secure a retreat,
When matters require it, must give up our gang:
And good reason why,
Or instead of the fry,
Ev'n Peachum and I,
Like poor petty rascals, might hang, hang,
Like poor petty rascals, might hang.[e]

PEACHUM.

Set your heart at rest, Polly. Your husband is to die today; therefore, if you are not already provided, 'tis high time to look about for another. There's comfort for you, you slut.

LOCKIT.

We are ready, sir, to conduct you to the Old Bailey.

Air 57. "Bonny Dundee."

MACHEATH.

The charge is prepared; the lawyers are met;
The judges all ranged (a terrible show!).
I go undismayed, for death is a debt,
A debt on demand. So, take what I owe.
Then farewell, my love, dear charmers, adieu.
Contented I die: 'tis the better for you.
Here ends all dispute the rest of our lives,
For this way at once I please all my wives.
Now gentlemen, I am ready to attend you.

[Exeunt Peachum, Lockit, Macheath.]

Scene xii.

Lucy, Polly, Filch.

POLLY.

Follow them, Filch, to the court. And when the trial is over, bring me a particular account of his behavior and of everything that happened. You'll find me here with Miss Lucy.

Exit Filch.

But why is all this music?

LUCY.

The prisoners whose trials are put off till next session are diverting themselves.

POLLY.

Sure there is nothing so charming as music! I'm fond of it to distraction! But alas, now all mirth seems an insult upon my affliction. Let us retire, my dear Lucy, and indulge our sorrows. The noisy crew, you see, are coming upon us.

Exeunt.

A dance of prisoners in chains, etc.

Scene xiii. The condemned hold.

Macheath, in a melancholy posture.

Air 58. "Happy Groves."

Oh cruel, cruel, cruel case!
Must I suffer this disgrace?

Air 59. "Of all the girls that are so smart."

Of all the friends in time of grief,
When threat'ning death looks grimmer,
Not one so sure can bring relief
As this best friend, a brimmer. (*Drinks.*)

Air 60. "Britons strike home."

(Rises.)

Since I must swing, I scorn, I scorn to wince or whine.

Air 61. "Chevy Chase."

But now again my spirits sink;
I'll raise them high with wine. (*Drinks a Glass of Wine.*)

Air 62. "To old Sir Simon the King."

But valor the stronger grows,
The stronger liquor we're drinking.
And how can we feel our woes,
When we've lost the trouble of thinking? (*Drinks.*)

Air 63. "Joy to great Caesar."

If thus—a man can die
Much bolder with brandy. (*Pours out a bumper of brandy.*)

Air 64. "There was an old woman."

So I drink off this bumper, and now I can stand the test.
And my comrades shall see that I die as brave as the best. (*Drinks.*)

Air 65. "Did you ever hear of a gallant sailor."

But can I leave my pretty hussies
Without one tear or tender sigh?

Air 66. "Why are mine eyes still flowing."

Their eyes, their lips, their busses
Recall my love. Ah must I die?

Air 67. "Green Sleeves."

Since laws were made for ev'ry degree
To curb vice in others, as well as me,
I wonder we han't better company
Upon Tyburn* tree!
But gold from law can take out the sting,
And if rich men like us were to swing,
'Twould thin the land such numbers to string
Upon Tyburn tree!

[Enter jailer.]

JAILER.
Some friends of yours, Captain, desire to be admitted. I leave you together.

[Exit.]

Scene xiv.

Macheath, Ben Budge, Matt of the Mint.

MACHEATH.
For my having broke prison, you see, gentlemen, I am ordered immediate execution. The sheriff's officers, I believe, are now at the door. That Jemmy Twitcher should peach me, I own surprised me! 'Tis a plain proof that the world is all alike and that even our gang can no more trust one another than other people. Therefore, I beg you, gentlemen, look well to yourselves, for in all probability you may live some months longer.

MATT.
We are heartily sorry, Captain, for your misfortune. But 'tis what we must all come to.

MACHEATH.
Peachum and Lockit, you know, are infamous scoundrels. Their lives are as much in your power as yours are in theirs. Remember your dying friend. 'Tis my last request: bring those villains to the gallows before you, and I am satisfied.

MATT.
We'll do't.

[Enter jailer.]

JAILER.
Miss Polly and Miss Lucy entreat a word with you.

MACHEATH.
Gentlemen, adieu.

[Exeunt Matt, Ben, jailer.]

Scene xv.

Lucy, Macheath, Polly.

MACHEATH.
My dear Lucy, my dear Polly, whatsoever hath passed between us is now at an end. If you are fond of marrying again, the best advice I can give you is to ship yourselves off for the West Indies, where you'll have a fair chance of getting a husband apiece, or by good luck, two or three, as you like best.

POLLY.
How can I support this sight!

LUCY.
There is nothing moves one so much as a great man* in distress.

Air 68. "All you that must take a leap," etc.

LUCY.
Would I might be hanged!

POLLY.
And I would so too!

LUCY.
To be hanged with you—

POLLY.
My dear, with you.

MACHEATH.
Oh leave me to thought! I fear! I doubt!
I tremble! I droop! See, my courage is out. (*Turns up the empty bottle.*)

POLLY.
No token of love?

MACHEATH.
See, my courage is out.
(*Turns up the empty pot.*)

LUCY.
No token of love?

POLLY.
Adieu.

LUCY.
Farewell.

MACHEATH.
But hark! I hear the toll of the bell.*

CHORUS.
Tol de rol lol, etc.

[Enter jailer.]

JAILER.
Four women more, Captain, with a child apiece! See, here they come.

Enter women and children.

MACHEATH.
What, four wives more! This is too much. Here, tell the sheriff's officers I am ready.

Exit Macheath guarded.

Scene xvi.

To them, enter player and beggar.

PLAYER.
But honest friend, I hope you don't intend that Macheath shall be really executed.

BEGGAR.
Most certainly, sir. To make the piece perfect I was for doing strict poetical justice: Macheath is to be hanged, and for the other personages of the drama, the audience must have supposed they were all either hanged or transported.

PLAYER.
Why then, friend, this is a downright deep tragedy. The catastrophe is manifestly wrong, for an opera must end happily.

BEGGAR.
Your objection, sir, is very just, and is easily removed. For you must allow, that in this kind of drama 'tis no matter how absurdly things are brought about.—So, you rabble there, run and cry a reprieve. Let the prisoner be brought back to his wives in triumph.

PLAYER.
All this we must do to comply with the taste of the Town.*

BEGGAR.
Through the whole piece you may observe such a similitude of manners in high and low life that it is difficult to determine whether (in the fashionable vices) the fine gentlemen imitate the gentlemen of the road, or the gentlemen of the road the fine gentlemen. Had the play remained as I at first intended, it would have carried a most excellent moral: 'twould have shown that the lower sort of people have their vices in a degree as well as the rich: And that they are punished for them.

Scene xvii.

To them, Macheath with rabble, etc.

MACHEATH.
So it seems I am not left to my choice but must have a wife at last.—Look ye, my dears, we will have no controversy now. Let us give this day to mirth, and I am sure she who thinks herself my wife will testify her joy by a dance.

ALL.
Come, a dance, a dance.

MACHEATH.
Ladies, I hope you will give me leave to present a partner to each of you. And (if I may without

offence) for this time, I take Polly for mine. (*To Polly.*) And for life, you slut, for we were really married. As for the rest— But at present keep your own secret.

A dance.

Air 69. "Lumps of pudding," etc.

Thus I stand like the Turk with his doxies around;
From all sides their glances his passion confound;
For black,* brown, and fair, his inconstancy burns,
And the different beauties subdue him by turns:
Each calls forth her charms to provoke his desires;
Though willing to all, with but one he retires.
But think of this maxim, and put off your sorrow:
The wretch of today may be happy tomorrow.

CHORUS.
But think of this maxim, etc.

[Exeunt.]

FINIS.

Textual Notes

[a] Copytext is the first edition, a 1728 octavo, which exists in two states (O1a, O1b). Also consulted were the second edition, another 1728 octavo (O2); the third edition, a 1729 quarto (Q); and modern editions of 1939, revised 1969 (Nettleton, Case, and Stone—NCS), of 1983 (Fuller), and of 1986 (Loughrey and Treadwell—LT).

[b] glass of a most delicious cordial] Q, NCS, Fuller, LT; most delicious glass of a cordial O1-2

[c] A man ... life.] O2, Q, NCS, Fuller, LT; *om.* O1

[d] wary] O2, Q, NCS; weary O1 and some copies of O2, Fuller, LT

[e] Air 15a ... hang] O1b, O2, Q, NCS, Fuller, LT; *om.* O1a

The London Merchant; or, The History of George Barnwell[a]

by George Lillo (1691-1739)

edited by Lincoln Faller

First performed at Drury Lane Theatre in June 1731, *The London Merchant* was the work of a relative unknown, in fact a jeweller by trade; it became an immediate and somewhat surprising success. Those who came to the playhouse to scoff and sneer at what they expected to be a low and vulgar entertainment, according to the oft-told story, found themselves moved instead to admiring tears. Queen Caroline requested a copy of the play within days of its premiere, and within months a "command" performance would be staged for her and George II. The play would eventually become one of the most frequently performed tragedies of the eighteenth century.

For all that, readers have had some notable difficulty appreciating it over the last two hundred years. The play's strenuous, sententious speechifying in praise of merchants and the art of merchandise, the lurid melodrama of Barnwell's seduction, of his murder of his uncle, of Millwood's apprehension—which at times can verge dangerously on farce—as well as the thinness and stiffness of its characters except Millwood and perhaps Lucy, have made it all too easy a target. Audiences in its own day were better able to value its excitements. Though somewhat of an anomaly in eighteenth-century theater, there being nothing quite like it before or after, the play does combine elements from the pathetic tradition of Otway, Southerne, and Rowe—all of whom were highly valued for their capacity to raise intense sympathy for their tragic characters—with certain qualities of heroic drama. As in tragedies of the latter kind, Barnwell faces a conflict between love and honor. In his capacity to suffer and fall, in the pain his friends feel as a result, and in their abilities, each of them, to bear up under the pressures entailed, Barnwell and his friends can seem for all their middle-class status just as important and heroic as the great.

Bourgeois is beautiful, the play seems to say. Indeed it announces a new era, characterized by a new political economy based on exchange rather than conquest, to be distinguished on a global level from the rapacious imperialism of the Spanish and, on a personal and domestic level, from Millwood's exploitation of the hapless Barnwell. Where mutuality and shared respect characterize Thorowgood's relations with both his family and the world, Barnwell and Millwood are linked only by his lust for her and her lust for money as well as revenge for the exploitation she herself has suffered. Barnwell might have married the boss's daughter, but his tragedy is that he gives up Thorowgood's world for the chaos and death of Millwood's.

Though redolent with Old Testament allusions and echoes of Shakespeare's great tragedies, *The London Merchant* offers a far more optimistic vision of human suffering and evil. Terrible as it is, Barnwell's fate opens heaven's door to him. Even Millwood might find a place there, for all her hopeless, hapless, dying agonies. People in the play are good, if given the chance, and do evil without quite wanting to or because they're overwhelmed by circumstance. However oddly conjoined to the heroicization of business and businessmen, such ideas can of course seem quite contemporary to us as heirs of progressive, bourgeois morality.

[Prologue]

From the dedication to Sir John Eyles, Baronet, Member of Parliament for and Alderman of the City of London, and Sub-Governor of the South Sea Company:

If tragic poetry be, as Mr. Dryden has somewhere said,[1] the most excellent and most useful kind of writing, the more extensively useful the moral of any tragedy is the more excellent that piece must be of its kind.

I hope I shall not be thought to insinuate that this ... is such; that depends on its fitness to answer the end of tragedy, the exciting of the passions in order to the correcting such of them as are criminal either in their nature or through their excess. ...

What I would infer is this, I think, evident truth: that tragedy is so far from losing its dignity by being accommodated to the circumstances of the generality of mankind that it is more truly august in proportion to the extent of its influence and the numbers that are properly affected by it. As it is more truly great to be the instrument of good to many who stand in need of our assistance than to a very small part of that number.

If princes, etc., were alone liable to misfortunes arising from vice or weakness in themselves or others, there would be good reason for confining the characters in tragedy to those of superior rank; but, since the contrary is evident, nothing can be more reasonable to proportion the remedy to the disease.

... I have attempted, indeed, to enlarge the province of the graver kind of poetry and should be glad to see it carried on by some abler hand. Plays founded on moral tales in private life may be of admirable use by carrying conviction to the mind with such irresistible force as to engage all the faculties and powers of the soul in the cause of virtue, by stifling vice in its first principles. They who imagine this to be too much to be attributed to tragedy must be strangers to the energy of that noble species of poetry.

[1] somewhere said] The reference, McBurney suggests, is to Dryden's quoting Aristotle to the effect that "the most perfect work of poetry is tragedy" in his *Discourse Concerning the Original and Progress of Satire* (1693); Steffenson suggests a generalized reference to claims made in Dryden's *An Essay of Dramatic Poesy* (1668).

PROLOGUE

The tragic muse, sublime, delights to show
Princes distressed and scenes of royal woe,
In awful* pomp, majestic, to relate
The fall of nations or some hero's fate
That sceptered chiefs may by example know
The strange vicissitude of things below,
What dangers on security attend,
How pride and cruelty in ruin end,
Hence Providence supreme to know, and own
Humanity adds glory to a throne.
In every former age and foreign tongue,
With native grandeur thus the goddess sung.
Upon our stage indeed, with wished success,
You've sometimes seen her in a humbler dress,
Great only in distress. When she complains
In Southerne's, Rowe's, or Otway's moving strains,
The brilliant drops that fall from each bright eye
The absent pomp with brighter gems supply.
Forgive us then, if we attempt to show
In artless strains a tale of private woe.
A London prentice ruined is our theme,
Drawn from the famed old song that bears his name.[2]
We hope your taste is not so high to scorn
A moral tale esteemed ere you were born,
Which for a century of rolling years
Has filled a thousand thousand eyes with tears.
If thoughtless youth to warn, and shame the age
From vice destructive well becomes the stage,
If this example innocence insure,
Prevent our guilt, or by reflection cure,
If Millwood's dreadful crimes and sad despair
Commend the virtue of the good and fair,
Though art be wanting* and our numbers fail,
Indulge th'attempt in justice to the tale.

[2] old song ... name] The inspiration if not exactly the source for Lillo's play is the popular "Ballad of George Barnwell," for which see McBurney, Appendix C.

DRAMATIS PERSONAE

MEN

Thorowgood.
Barnwell, uncle to George.
George Barnwell.
Trueman.
Blunt.
Officers with their attendants, keeper, and footmen.

WOMEN

Maria.
Millwood.
Lucy.

SCENE: LONDON AND AN ADJACENT VILLAGE.

The London Merchant; or, The History of George Barnwell.

Learn to be wise from others' harm
And you shall do full well.[3]

Act I, scene i. A room in Thorowgood's house.

Enter Thorowgood and Trueman.

TRUEMAN.
Sir, the packet from Genoa is arrived. (*Gives letters.*)

THOROWGOOD.
Heaven be praised, the storm that threatened our royal mistress, pure religion, liberty and laws is for a time diverted. The haughty and revengeful Spaniard, disappointed of the loan on which he depended from Genoa, must now attend the slow return of wealth from his new world to supply his empty coffers ere he can execute his purposed invasion of our happy island,[4] by which means time is gained to make such preparations on our part as may, Heaven concurring, prevent his malice or turn the meditated mischief on himself.

TRUEMAN.
He must be insensible indeed who is not affected when the safety of his country is concerned. Sir, may I know by what means? If I am too bold—

THOROWGOOD.
Your curiosity is laudable, and I gratify it with the greater pleasure because from thence you may learn how honest merchants, as such, may sometimes contribute to the safety of their country as they do at all times to its happiness; that if hereafter you should be tempted to any action that has the appearance of vice or meanness in it, upon reflecting on the dignity of our profession, you may with honest scorn reject whatever is unworthy of it.

TRUEMAN.
Should Barnwell or I, who have the benefit of your example, by our ill conduct bring any imputation on that honorable name, we must be left without excuse.

THOROWGOOD.
You compliment, young man.

Trueman bows respectfully.

Nay, I'm not offended. As the name of merchant never degrades the gentleman, so by no means does it exclude him. Only take heed not to purchase the character of complaisant at the expense of your sincerity. But to answer your question: the bank of Genoa had agreed, at excessive interest and on good security, to advance the King of Spain a sum of money sufficient to equip his vast Armado. Of which our peerless Elizabeth—more than in name the mother of her people—being well informed, sent Walsingham,[5] her wise and faithful secretary, to consult the merchants of this loyal City,* who all agreed to direct their several agents to influence, if possible, the Genoese to break their contract with the Spanish court. 'Tis done. The state and bank of Genoa, having maturely weighed and rightly judged of their true interest, prefer the friendship of the merchants of London to that of

[3] Learn … well] final lines of "Old Ballad of *The Lady's Fall*," as Lillo names it in the text, though in a version, according to Steffenson, somewhat at variance from other printed versions.

[4] storm … island] the attempted invasion by the Spanish Armada in 1588, which was partly defeated by a storm

[5] Walsingham] Sir Francis Walsingham (1530-1590) was Secretary of State to Elizabeth I. There is no historical evidence to support Thorowgood's story.

a monarch who proudly styles himself King of both Indies.

TRUEMAN.

Happy success of prudent councils! What an expense of blood and treasure is here saved! Excellent queen! Oh how unlike those princes who make the danger of foreign enemies a pretence to oppress their subjects by taxes great and grievous to be borne.

THOROWGOOD.

Not so our gracious queen, whose richest exchequer is her people's love, as their happiness is her greatest glory.

TRUEMAN.

On these terms to defend us is to make our protection a benefit worthy her who confers it and well worth our acceptance.—Sir, have you any commands for me at this time?

THOROWGOOD.

Only look carefully over the files to see whether there are any tradesmen's bills unpaid. If there are, send and discharge 'em. We must not let artificers lose their time, so useful to the public and their families, in unnecessary attendance.

Exit Trueman. Enter Maria.

THOROWGOOD.

Well, Maria, have you given orders for the entertainment? I would have it in some measure worthy the guests. Let there be plenty and of the best, that the courtiers may[b] at least commend our hospitality.

MARIA.

Sir, I have endeavored not to wrong your well known generosity by an ill-timed parsimony.

THOROWGOOD.

Nay, 'twas a needless caution. I have no cause to doubt your prudence.

MARIA.

Sir, I find myself unfit for conversation.* I should but increase the number of the company without adding to their satisfaction.

THOROWGOOD.

Nay my child, this melancholy must not be indulged.

MARIA.

Company will but increase it. I wish you would dispense with[6] my absence; solitude best suits my present temper.

THOROWGOOD.

You are not insensible that it is chiefly on your account these noble lords do me the honor so frequently to grace my board. Should you be absent, the disappointment may make them repent their condescension and think their labor lost.

MARIA.

He that shall think his time or honor lost in visiting you can set no real value on your daughter's company, whose only merit is that she is yours. The man of quality* who chooses to converse with a gentleman and merchant of your worth and character may confer honor by so doing, but he loses none.

THOROWGOOD.

Come, come, Maria, I need not tell you that a young gentleman may prefer your conversation* to mine, yet intend me no disrespect at all. For though he may lose no honor in my company, 'tis very natural for him to expect more pleasure in yours. I remember the time when the company of the greatest and wisest man in the kingdom would have been insipid and tiresome to me if it had deprived me of an opportunity of enjoying your mother's.

MARIA.

Yours no doubt was as agreeable to her, for generous minds know no pleasure in society but where 'tis mutual.

THOROWGOOD.

Thou knowest I have no heir, no child but thee; the fruits of many years' successful industry must all be thine. Now it would give me pleasure great as my love to see on whom you would bestow it. I am daily solicited by men of the greatest rank and merit for leave to address you, but I have hitherto declined it in hopes that by observation I should learn which way your inclination tends. For as I know love to be essential to happiness in the marriage state, I had rather my approbation should confirm your choice than direct it.

MARIA.

What can I say? How shall I answer as I ought this

6 dispense with] excuse

tenderness so uncommon even in the best of parents? But you are without example. Yet had you been less indulgent, I had been most wretched. That I look on the crowd of courtiers that visit here with equal esteem but equal indifference you have observed, and I must needs confess. Yet had you asserted your authority and insisted on a parent's right to be obeyed, I had submitted and to my duty sacrificed my peace.

THOROWGOOD.
From your perfect obedience in every other instance I feared as much and therefore would leave you without a bias in an affair wherein your happiness is so immediately concerned.

MARIA.
Whether from a want* of that just ambition that would become your daughter or from some other cause, I know not, but I find high birth and titles don't recommend the man who owns them to my affections.

THOROWGOOD.
I would not that they should, unless his merit recommends him more. A noble birth and fortune, though they make not a bad man good, yet they are a real advantage to a worthy one and place his virtues in the fairest light.

MARIA.
I cannot answer for my inclinations, but they shall ever be submitted to your wisdom and authority, and as you will not compel me to marry where I cannot love, love shall never make me act contrary to my duty. Sir, have I your permission to retire?

THOROWGOOD.
I'll see you to your chamber.

Exeunt.

Scene ii. A room in Millwood's house.

Millwood at her toilet, * *Lucy waiting.*

MILLWOOD.
How do I look today, Lucy?

LUCY.
Oh, killingly, madam! A little more red, and you'll be irresistible! But why this more than ordinary care of your dress and complexion? What new conquest are you aiming at?

MILLWOOD.
A conquest would be new indeed!

LUCY.
Not to you, who make 'em every day. But to me, well! 'Tis what I'm never to expect, unfortunate as I am. But your wit and beauty—

MILLWOOD.
First made me a wretch and still continue me so. Men, however generous or sincere to one another, are all selfish hypocrites in their affairs with us. We are no otherwise esteemed or regarded by them but as we contribute to their satisfaction.

LUCY.
You are certainly, madam, on the wrong side in this argument. Is not the expense all theirs? And I am sure it is our own fault if we haven't our share of the pleasure.

MILLWOOD.
We are but slaves to men.

LUCY.
Nay, 'tis they that are slaves most certainly, for we lay them under contribution.

MILLWOOD.
Slaves have no property, no, not even in themselves. All is the victor's.

LUCY.
You are strangely arbitrary in your principles, madam.

MILLWOOD.
I would have my conquests complete, like those of the Spaniards in the New World, who first plundered the natives of all the wealth they had and then condemned the wretches to the mines for life to work for more.

LUCY.
Well, I shall never approve of your scheme of government. I should think it much more politic, as well as just, to find my subjects an easier employment.

MILLWOOD.
It's a general maxim among the knowing part of mankind that a woman without virtue, like a man without honor or honesty, is capable of any action though never so vile. And yet what pains will they not take, what arts not use, to seduce us from our innocence and make us contemptible and wicked,

even in their own opinions? Then is it not just the villains to their cost should find us so? But guilt makes them suspicious and keeps them on their guard; therefore, we can take advantage only of the young and innocent part of the sex, who, having never injured women, apprehend no injury from them.

LUCY.

Aye, they must be young indeed.

MILLWOOD.

Such a one, I think, I have found. As I've passed through the City,* I have often observed him receiving and paying considerable sums of money; from thence I conclude he is employed in affairs of consequence.

LUCY.

Is he handsome?

MILLWOOD.

Aye, aye, the stripling is well made and has a good face.

LUCY.

About—

MILLWOOD.

Eighteen—

LUCY.

Innocent, handsome, and about eighteen. You'll be vastly happy. Why, if you manage well, you may keep him to yourself these two or three years.

MILLWOOD.

If I manage well, I shall have done with him much sooner. Having long had a design on him and meeting him yesterday, I made a full stop and, gazing wishfully on his face, asked him his name. He blushed and, bowing very low, answered, "George Barnwell." I begged his pardon for the freedom I had taken and told him that he was the person I had long wished to see and to whom I had an affair of importance to communicate at a proper time and place. He named a tavern; I talked of honor and reputation, and invited him to my house. He swallowed the bait, promised to come, and this is the time I expect him.

Knocking at the door.

Somebody knocks, d'ye hear? I am at home to nobody today but him.

Exit Lucy.

MILLWOOD.

Less affairs must give way to those of more consequence, and I am strangely mistaken if this does not prove of great importance to me and him too, before I have done with him. Now, after what manner shall I receive him? Let me consider. What manner of person am I to receive? He is young, innocent, and bashful; therefore, I must take care not to put him out of countenance[c] at first. But then, if I have any skill in physiognomy, he is amorous and, with a little assistance, will soon get the better of his modesty. I'll e'en trust to Nature, who does wonders in these matters. If to seem what one is not in order to be the better liked for what one really is, if to speak one thing and mean the direct contrary be art in a woman, I know nothing of Nature.

Enter Barnwell bowing very low. Lucy at a distance.

MILLWOOD.

Sir! The surprise and joy!

BARNWELL.

Madam.

MILLWOOD.

This is such a favor— (*Advancing.*)

BARNWELL.

Pardon me, madam—

MILLWOOD.

So unhoped for— (*Still advances.*)

Barnwell salutes her, and retires in confusion.*

MILLWOOD.

To see you here. Excuse the confusion.

BARNWELL.

I fear I am too bold.

MILLWOOD.

Alas, sir! I may justly apprehend you think me so. Please, sir, to sit. I am as much at a loss how to receive this honor as I ought, as I am surprised at your goodness in conferring it.

BARNWELL.

I thought you had expected me. I promised to come.

MILLWOOD.

That is the more surprising. Few men are such religious observers of their word.

BARNWELL.
All who are honest are.

MILLWOOD.
To one another. But we simple women are seldom thought of consequence enough to gain a place in your remembrance. (*Laying her hand on his, as if by accident.*)

BARNWELL. (*Aside.*)
Her disorder is so great, she don't perceive she has laid her hand on mine. Heaven! How she trembles! What can this mean!

MILLWOOD.
The interest I have in all that relates to you—the reason of which you shall know hereafter—excites my curiosity. And were I sure you would pardon my presumption, I should desire to know your real sentiments on a very particular subject.

BARNWELL.
Madam, you may command my poor thoughts on any subject. I have none that I would conceal.

MILLWOOD.
You'll think me bold.

BARNWELL.
No, indeed.

MILLWOOD.
What then are your thoughts of love?

BARNWELL.
If you mean the love of women, I have not thought of it at all. My youth and circumstances make such thoughts improper in me yet. But if you mean the general love we owe to mankind, I think no one has more of it in his temper than myself. I don't know that person in the world whose happiness I don't wish and wouldn't promote, were it in my power. In an especial manner I love my uncle, and my master, but above all my friend.

MILLWOOD.
You have a friend then, whom you love?

BARNWELL.
As he does me, sincerely.

MILLWOOD.
He is no doubt often blessed with your company and conversation.

BARNWELL.
We live in one house and both serve the same worthy merchant.

MILLWOOD.
Happy, happy youth! Whoe'er thou art, I envy thee, and so must all who see and know this youth. What have I lost by being formed a woman! I hate my sex, my self. Had I been a man, I might, perhaps, have been as happy in your friendship as he who now enjoys it. But as it is, oh!

BARNWELL. (*Aside.*)
I never observed women before, or this is sure the most beautiful of her sex.—You seem disordered, madam! May I know the cause?

MILLWOOD.
Do not ask me, I can never speak it, whatever is the cause. I wish for things impossible: I would be a servant bound to the same master, to live in one house with you.

BARNWELL. (*Aside.*)
How strange and yet how kind her words and actions are! And the effect they have on me is strange. I feel desires I never knew before. I must be gone, while I have power to go.—Madam, I humbly take my leave.

MILLWOOD.
You will not, sure, leave me so soon!

BARNWELL.
Indeed I must.

MILLWOOD.
You cannot be so cruel! I have prepared a poor supper, at which I promised myself your company.

BARNWELL.
I am sorry I must refuse the honor you designed me. But my duty to my master calls me hence. I never yet neglected his service. He is so gentle and so good a master that should I wrong him, though he might forgive me, I never should forgive myself.

MILLWOOD.
Am I refused, by the first man, the second favor I ever stooped to ask? Go then, thou proud, hard-hearted youth. But know, you are the only man that could be found who would let me sue twice for greater favors.

BARNWELL.
What shall I do! How shall I go or stay!

MILLWOOD.
Yet do not, do not leave me. I with my sex's pride would meet your scorn. But when I look upon you,

when I behold those eyes, oh! spare my tongue and let my blushes—this flood of tears to that will force their way—declare what woman's modesty should hide.

BARNWELL. [*Aside.*]

Oh heavens! She loves me, worthless as I am. Her looks, her words, her flowing tears confess it. And can I leave her then? Oh, never, never.—Madam, dry up your tears. You shall command me always. I will stay here forever, if you'd have me.

LUCY. (*Aside.*)

So! She has wheedled him out of his virtue of obedience already and will strip him of all the rest, one after another, till she has left him as few as her ladyship or myself.

MILLWOOD.

Now you are kind, indeed. But I mean not to detain you always. I would have you shake off all slavish obedience to your master, but you may serve him still.

LUCY. (*Aside.*)

Serve him still! Aye, or he'll have no opportunity of fingering his cash, and then he'll not serve your end, I'll be sworn.

Enter Blunt.

BLUNT.

Madam, supper's on the table.

MILLWOOD.

Come sir, you'll excuse all defects. My thoughts were too much employed on my guest to observe the entertainment.

Exeunt Barnwell and Millwood.

BLUNT.

What, is all this preparation, this elegant supper, variety of wines and music, for the entertainment of that young fellow!

LUCY.

So it seems.

BLUNT.

What, is our mistress turned fool at last! She's in love with him, I suppose.

LUCY.

I suppose not. But she designs to make him in love with her if she can.

BLUNT.

What will she get by that? He seems underage and can't be supposed to have much money.

LUCY.

But his master has, and that's the same thing, as she'll manage it.

BLUNT.

I don't like this fooling with a handsome young fellow. While she's endeavoring to ensnare him, she may be caught herself.

LUCY.

Nay, were she like me that would certainly be the consequence. For I confess, there is something in youth and innocence that moves me mightily.

BLUNT.

Yes, so does the smoothness and plumpness of a partridge move a mighty desire in the hawk to be the destruction of it.

LUCY.

Why, birds are their prey as men are ours; though, as you observed, we are sometimes caught ourselves. But that, I dare say, will never be the case with our mistress.

BLUNT.

I wish it may prove so, for you know we all depend upon her. Should she trifle away her time with a young fellow that there's nothing to be got by, we must all starve.

LUCY.

There's no danger of that, for I am sure she has no view in this affair but interest.

BLUNT.

Well, and what hopes are there of success in that?

LUCY.

The most promising that can be. 'Tis true, the youth has his scruples, but she'll soon teach him to answer them, by stifling his conscience. Oh, the lad is in a hopeful way, depend upon't.

Exeunt.

Scene draws and discovers Barnwell and Millwood at supper. An entertainment of music and singing, after which they come forward.*

BARNWELL.

What can I answer! All that I know is that you are fair and I am miserable.

MILLWOOD.

We are both so, and yet the fault is in ourselves.

BARNWELL.

To ease our present anguish by plunging into guilt is to buy a moment's pleasure with an age of pain.

MILLWOOD.

I should have thought the joys of love as lasting as they are great. If ours prove otherwise, 'tis your inconstancy must make them so.

BARNWELL.

The law of Heaven will not be reversed, and that requires us to govern our passions.

MILLWOOD.

To give us sense of beauty and desires and yet forbid us to taste and be happy is cruelty to nature. Have we passions only to torment us!

BARNWELL.

To hear you talk, though in the cause of vice, to gaze upon your beauty, press your hand, and see your snow-white bosom heave and fall enflames my wishes. My pulse beats high, my senses all are in a hurry, and I am on the rack of wild desire. Yet for a moment's guilty pleasure shall I lose my innocence, my peace of mind, and hopes of solid happiness?

MILLWOOD.

Chimeras all,
Come on with me and prove,
No joy's like womankind, no heaven like love.

BARNWELL.

I would not, yet must on.
Reluctant thus, the merchant quits his ease
And trusts to rocks and sands and stormy seas,
In hopes some unknown golden coast to find,
Commits himself, though doubtful, to the wind,
Longs much for joys to come, yet mourns those left behind.

Exeunt.

Act II, scene i. A room in Thorowgood's house.

Enter Barnwell.

BARNWELL.

How strange are all things round me? Like some thief who treads forbidden ground and fain would lurk unseen, fearful I enter each apartment of this well-known house. To guilty love, as if that were too little, already have I added breach of trust. A thief! Can I know myself that wretched thing and look my honest friend and injured master in the face? Though hypocrisy may awhile conceal my guilt, at length it will be known, and public shame and ruin must ensue. In the meantime, what must be my life? Ever to speak a language foreign to my heart, hourly to add to the number of my crimes in order to conceal 'em. Sure such was the condition of the Grand Apostate[7] when first he lost his purity. Like me disconsolate he wandered and while yet in heaven bore all his future hell about him.

Enter Trueman.

TRUEMAN.

Barnwell! Oh how I rejoice to see you safe! So will our master and his gentle daughter, who during your absence often inquired after you.

BARNWELL. (*Aside.*)

Would he were gone; his officious love will pry into the secrets of my soul.

TRUEMAN.

Unless you knew the pain the whole family* has felt on your account, you can't conceive how much you are beloved. But why thus cold and silent? When my heart is full of joy for your return, why do you turn away? Why thus avoid me? What have I done? How am I altered since you saw me last? Or rather, what have you done? And why are you thus changed? For I am still the same.

BARNWELL. (*Aside.*)

What have I done indeed?

TRUEMAN.

Not speak nor look upon me!

BARNWELL. (*Aside.*)

By my face he will discover all I would conceal. Methinks already I begin to hate him.

TRUEMAN.

I cannot bear this usage from a friend, one whom till now I ever found so loving, whom yet I love, though this unkindness strikes at the root of friendship and might destroy it in any breast but mine.

BARNWELL.

I am not well. (*Turning to him.*) Sleep has been a stranger to these eyes since you beheld them last.

TRUEMAN.

Heavy they look indeed, and swollen with tears; now they overflow. Rightly did my sympathizing

[7] Grand Apostate] Lucifer or Satan

heart forbode last night, when thou wast absent, something fatal to our peace.

BARNWELL.

Your friendship engages you too far. My troubles, whate'er they are, are mine alone. You have no interest in them, nor ought your concern for me give you a moment's pain.

TRUEMAN.

You speak as if you knew of friendship nothing but the name. Before I saw your grief I felt it. Since we parted last I have slept no more than you, but pensive in my chamber sat alone and spent the tedious night in wishes for your safety and return. E'en now, though ignorant of the cause, your sorrow wounds me to the heart.

BARNWELL.

'Twill not always be thus. Friendship and all engagements cease as circumstances and occasions vary, and since you once may hate me, perhaps it might be better for us both that now you loved me less.

TRUEMAN.

Sure I but dream! Without a cause would Barnwell use me thus? Ungenerous and ungrateful youth, farewell. (*Going.*) I shall endeavor to follow your advice. [*Aside.*] Yet stay: perhaps I am too rash and angry when the cause demands compassion. Some unforeseen calamity may have befallen him too great to bear.

BARNWELL.

What part am I reduced to act? 'Tis vile and base to move his temper thus, the best of friends and men.

TRUEMAN.

I am to blame; prithee forgive me, Barnwell. Try to compose your ruffled mind, and let me know the cause that thus transports you from yourself. My friendly counsel may restore your peace.

BARNWELL.

All that is possible for man to do for man, your generous friendship may effect. But here even that's in vain.

TRUEMAN.

Something dreadful is laboring in your breast. Oh, give it vent and let me share your grief. 'Twill ease your pain, should it admit no cure, and make it lighter by the part I bear.

BARNWELL.

Vain supposition! My woes increase by being observed; should the cause be known they would exceed all bounds.

TRUEMAN.

So well I know thy honest heart, guilt cannot harbor there.

BARNWELL. (*Aside.*)

Oh torture insupportable!

TRUEMAN.

Then why am I excluded? Have I a thought I would conceal from you?

BARNWELL.

If still you urge me on this hated subject, I'll never enter more beneath this roof nor see your face again.

TRUEMAN.

'Tis strange. But I have done; say but you hate me not.

BARNWELL.

Hate you! I am not that monster yet.

TRUEMAN.

Shall our friendship still continue?

BARNWELL.

It's a blessing I never was worthy of yet now must stand on terms and but upon conditions can confirm it.

TRUEMAN.

What are they?

BARNWELL.

Never hereafter, though you should wonder at my conduct, desire to know more than I am willing to reveal.

TRUEMAN.

'Tis hard, but upon any conditions I must be your friend.

BARNWELL.

Then, as much as one lost to himself can be another's, I am yours. (*Embracing.*)

TRUEMAN.

Be ever so, and may Heaven restore your peace.

BARNWELL.

Will yesterday return? We have heard the glorious sun that, till then incessant rolled, once stopped his rapid course and once went back. The dead have risen, and parched rocks poured forth a liquid stream to quench a people's thirst. The sea divided and formed walls of water while a whole nation passed in safety through its sandy bosom. Hungry lions have refused their prey, and men unhurt have walked amidst consuming flames.[8] But never yet did time, once past, return.

TRUEMAN.

Though the continued chain of time has never once been broke, nor ever will, but uninterrupted must keep on its course till, lost in eternity, it ends there where it first begun, yet as Heaven can repair whatever evils time can bring upon us, we[d] ought never to despair. But business requires our attendance: business, the youth's best preservative from ill, as idleness his worst of snares. Will you go with me?

BARNWELL.

I'll take a little time to reflect on what has passed, and follow you.

Exit Trueman.

I might have trusted Trueman and engaged him to apply to my uncle to repair the wrong I have done my master, but what of Millwood? Must I expose her too? Ungenerous and base! Then Heaven requires it not. But Heaven requires that I forsake her. What! Never see her more! Does Heaven require that? I hope I may see her, and Heaven not be offended. Presumptuous hope. Dearly already have I proved my frailty. Should I once more tempt Heaven, I may be left to fall never to rise again. Yet shall I leave her, forever leave her, and not let her know the cause? She who loves me with such a boundless passion! Can cruelty be duty? I judge of what she then must feel by what I now endure. The love of life and fear of shame, opposed by inclination strong as death or shame, like wind and tide in raging conflict met when neither can prevail, keep me in doubt. How then can I determine?

Enter Thorowgood.

THOROWGOOD.

Without a cause assigned or notice given, to absent yourself last night was a fault, young man, and I came to chide you for it, but hope I am prevented.* That modest blush, the confusion so visible in your face, speak grief and shame. When we have offended Heaven, it requires no more, and shall man, who needs himself to be forgiven, be harder to appease? If my pardon or love be of moment to your peace, look up secure of both.

BARNWELL. (*Aside.*)

This goodness has o'ercome me.—Oh sir! You know not the nature and extent of my offense, and I should abuse your mistaken bounty to receive 'em. Though I had rather die than speak my shame, though racks could not have forced the guilty secret from my breast, your kindness has.

THOROWGOOD.

Enough, enough, whate'er it be, this concern shows you're convinced, and I am satisfied. (*Aside.*) How painful is the sense of guilt to an ingenuous mind—some youthful folly, which it were prudent not to inquire into. When we consider the frail condition of humanity, it may raise our pity, not our wonder, that youth should go astray when reason, weak at the best when opposed to inclination, scarce formed and wholly unassisted by experience, faintly contends or willingly becomes the slave of sense. The state of youth is much to be deplored, and the more so because they see it not, being then to danger most exposed when they are least prepared for their defense.

BARNWELL.

It will be known, and you recall your pardon and abhor me.

THOROWGOOD.

I never will.[e] Yet be upon your guard in this gay, thoughtless season of your life. When the sense of pleasure's quick and passion high, the voluptuous appetites, raging and fierce, demand the strongest curb. Take heed of a relapse. When vice becomes habitual, the very power of leaving it is lost.

BARNWELL.

Hear me on my knees confess.

THOROWGOOD.

Not a syllable more upon this subject. It were not mercy but cruelty to hear what must give you such torment to reveal.

---

8 sun … flames] biblical allusions to the stories of Joshua, Lazarus and Jesus, Moses, Daniel, and Shadrach, Meshach and Abednego.

BARNWELL.
This generosity amazes and distracts me.

THOROWGOOD.
This remorse makes thee dearer to me than if thou hadst never offended. Whatever is your fault, of this I'm certain, 'twas harder for you to offend than me to pardon. (*Exit.*)

BARNWELL.
Villain, villain, villain! basely to wrong so excellent a man. Should I again return to folly—detested thought! But what of Millwood then? Why, I renounce her, I give her up, the struggle's over, and virtue has prevailed. Reason may convince, but gratitude compels. This unlooked for generosity has saved me from destruction. (*Going.*)

Enter a footman.

FOOTMAN.
Sir, two ladies from your uncle in the country desire to see you.

BARNWELL. (*Aside.*)
Who should they be?—Tell them I'll wait upon 'em.

Exit footman.

Methinks I dread to see 'em. Now everything alarms me. Guilt, what a coward hast thou made me.

[Exit.]

Scene ii. Another room in Thorowgood's house.

Millwood and Lucy discovered. * *Enter footman.*

FOOTMAN.
Ladies, he'll wait upon you immediately.

MILLWOOD.
'Tis very well. I thank you.

Exit footman. Enter Barnwell.

BARNWELL.
Confusion! Millwood!

MILLWOOD.
That angry look tells me that here I'm an unwelcome guest. I feared as much; the unhappy are so everywhere.

BARNWELL.
Will nothing but my utter ruin content you?

MILLWOOD.
Unkind and cruel! Lost myself, your happiness is now my only care.

BARNWELL.
How did you gain admission?

MILLWOOD.
Saying we were desired by your uncle to visit and deliver a message to you, we were received by the family* without suspicion and with much respect conducted here.

BARNWELL.
Why did you come at all?

MILLWOOD.
I never shall trouble you more. I'm come to take my leave forever. Such is the malice of my fate. I go hopeless, despairing ever to return. This hour is all I have left me. One short hour is all I have to bestow on love and you, for whom I thought the longest life too short.

BARNWELL.
Then we are met to part forever?

MILLWOOD.
It must be so. Yet think not that time or absence shall ever put a period to my grief or make me love you less. Though I must leave you, yet condemn me not.

BARNWELL.
Condemn you? No, I approve your resolution and rejoice to hear it. 'Tis just, 'tis necessary; I have well weighed and found it so.

LUCY. (*Aside.*)
I'm afraid the young man has more sense than she thought he had.

BARNWELL.
Before you came I had determined never to see you more.

MILLWOOD. (*Aside.*)
Confusion!

LUCY. (*Aside.*)
Aye! We are all out. This is a turn so unexpected that I shall make nothing of my part. They must e'en play the scene betwixt themselves.

MILLWOOD.
'Twas some relief to think, though absent, you would love me still. But to find though Fortune had been indulgent that you, more cruel and

inconstant, had resolved to cast me off, this, as I never could expect, I have not learned to bear.

BARNWELL.
I am sorry to hear you blame in me a resolution that so well becomes us both.

MILLWOOD.
I have reason for what I do, but you have none.

BARNWELL.
Can we want* a reason for parting who have so many to wish we never had met?

MILLWOOD.
Look on me, Barnwell. Am I deformed or old, that satiety so soon succeeds enjoyment? Nay, look again. Am I not she whom yesterday you thought the fairest and the kindest of her sex? Whose hand, trembling with ecstasy, you pressed and molded thus, while on my eyes you gazed with such delight as if desire increased by being fed?

BARNWELL.
No more. Let me repent my former follies, if possible, without remembering what they were.

MILLWOOD.
Why?

BARNWELL.
Such is my frailty that 'tis dangerous.

MILLWOOD.
Where is the danger, since we are to part?

BARNWELL.
The thought of that already is too painful.

MILLWOOD.
If it be painful to part, then I may hope at least you do not hate me?

BARNWELL.
No, no, I never said I did.—Oh my heart!

MILLWOOD.
Perhaps you pity me?

BARNWELL.
I do, I do, indeed I do.

MILLWOOD.
You'll think upon me?

BARNWELL.
Doubt it not while I can think at all.

MILLWOOD.
You may judge an embrace at parting too great a favor, though it would be the last? (*He draws back.*) A look shall then suffice. Farewell forever.

Exeunt Millwood and Lucy.

BARNWELL.
If to resolve to suffer be to conquer, I have conquered. Painful victory!

Re-enter Millwood and Lucy.

MILLWOOD.
One thing I had forgot: I never must return to my own house again. This I thought proper to let you know, lest your mind should change and you should seek in vain to find me there. Forgive me this second intrusion. I only came to give you this caution, and that perhaps was needless.

BARNWELL.
I hope it was, yet it is kind, and I must thank you for it.

MILLWOOD. (*To Lucy.*)
My friend, your arm.—Now I am gone forever. (*Going.*)

BARNWELL.
One thing more: sure there's no danger in my knowing where you go? If you think otherwise—

MILLWOOD.
Alas! (*Weeping.*)

LUCY. (*Aside.*)
We are right I find; that's my cue.—Ah, dear sir, she's going she knows not whither, but go she must.

BARNWELL.
Humanity obliges me to wish you well. Why will you thus expose yourself to needless troubles?

LUCY.
Nay, there's no help for it. She must quit the Town* immediately, and the kingdom as soon as possible. It was no small matter, you may be sure, that could make her resolve to leave you.

MILLWOOD.
No more, my friend. Since he for whose dear sake alone I suffer, and am content to suffer, is kind and pities me. Whene'er I wander through wilds and deserts, benighted and forlorn, that thought shall give me comfort.

BARNWELL.
For my sake! Oh tell me how? Which way am I so cursed as to bring such ruin on thee?

MILLWOOD.
No matter, I am contented with my lot.

BARNWELL.
Leave me not in this incertainty.

MILLWOOD.
I have said too much.

BARNWELL.
How, how am I the cause of your undoing?

MILLWOOD.
To know it will but increase your troubles.

BARNWELL.
My troubles can't be greater than they are.

LUCY.
Well, well, sir, if she won't satisfy you, I will.

BARNWELL.
I am bound to you beyond expression.

MILLWOOD.
Remember, sir, that I desired you not to hear it.

BARNWELL.
Begin, and ease my racking expectation.

LUCY.
Why, you must know, my lady here was an only child, but her parents, dying while she was young, left her and her fortune—no inconsiderable one, I assure you—to the care of a gentleman who has a good estate of his own.

MILLWOOD.
Aye, aye, the barbarous man is rich enough, but what are riches when compared to love?

LUCY.
For a while he performed the office of a faithful guardian, settled her in a house, hired her servants—but you have seen in what manner she lived, so I need say no more of that.

MILLWOOD.
How I shall live hereafter, Heaven knows.

LUCY.
All things went on as one could wish till, some time ago, his wife dying, he fell violently in love with his charge and would fain have married her. Now the man is neither old nor ugly but a good personable sort of a man, but I don't know how it was, she could never endure him. In short, her ill usage so provoked him that he brought in an account of his executorship, wherein he makes her debtor to him.

MILLWOOD.
A trifle in itself but more than enough to ruin me, whom, by his unjust account, he had stripped of all before.

LUCY.
Now she having neither money nor friend except me, who am as unfortunate as herself, he compelled her to pass his account and give bond for the sum he demanded, but still provided handsomely for her and continued his courtship. Till, being informed by his spies—truly I suspect some in her own family*—that you were entertained* at her house and stayed with her all night, he came this morning raving and storming like a madman, talks no more of marriage—so there's no hopes of making up matters that way—but vows her ruin unless she'll allow him the same favor that he supposes she granted you.

BARNWELL.
Must she be ruined or find her refuge in another's arms?

MILLWOOD.
He gave me but an hour to resolve in. That's happily spent with you, and now I go.

BARNWELL.
To be exposed to all the rigors of the various seasons, the summer's parching heat and winter's cold, unhoused to wander friendless through the unhospitable world in misery and want, attended with fear and danger and pursued by malice and revenge—would'st thou endure all this for me, and can I do nothing, nothing to prevent it?

LUCY.
'Tis really a pity there can be no way found out.

BARNWELL.
Oh where are all my resolutions now? Like early vapors or the morning dew chased by the sun's warm beams, they're vanished and lost as though they had never been.

LUCY.
Now I advised her, sir, to comply with the gentleman. That would not only put an end to her troubles but make her fortune at once.

BARNWELL.
Tormenting fiend, away. I had rather perish, nay, see her perish, than have her saved by him. I will myself prevent her ruin though with my own. A moment's patience; I'll return immediately. (*Exit.*)

LUCY.
'Twas well you came, or by what I can perceive, you had lost him.

MILLWOOD.
That, I must confess, was a danger I did not foresee. I was only afraid he should have come without money. You know a house of entertainment, like mine, is not kept without expense.

LUCY.
That's very true. But then you should be reasonable in your demands. 'Tis pity to discourage a young man.

MILLWOOD.
Leave that to me.

Re-enter Barnwell with a bag of money.

BARNWELL.
What am I about to do! Now you, who boast your reason all sufficient, suppose yourselves in my condition and determine for me whether it's right to let her suffer for my faults or, by this small addition to my guilt, prevent the ill effects of what is past.

LUCY. (*Aside.*)
These young sinners think everything in the ways of wickedness so strange. But I could tell him that this is nothing but what's very common, for one vice as naturally begets another as a father a son. But he'll find out that himself, if he lives long enough.

BARNWELL.
Here, take this, and with it purchase your deliverance. Return to your house and live in peace and safety.

MILLWOOD.
So I may hope to see you there again.

BARNWELL.
Answer me not, but fly, lest in the agonies of my remorse I take again what is not mine to give and abandon thee to want and misery.

MILLWOOD.
Say but you'll come.

BARNWELL.
You are my fate, my heaven or my hell. Only leave me now, dispose of me hereafter as you please.

Exeunt Millwood and Lucy.

BARNWELL.
What have I done? Were my resolutions founded on reason and sincerely made, why then has Heaven suffered me to fall? I sought not the occasion and, if my heart deceives me not, compassion and generosity were my motives. Is virtue inconsistent with itself, or are vice and virtue only empty names? Or do they depend on accidents beyond our power to produce or to prevent, wherein we have no part and yet must be determined by the event? But why should I attempt to reason? All is confusion, horror, and remorse. I find I am lost, cast down from all my late erected hopes and plunged again in guilt, yet scarce know how or why.
Such undistinguished horrors make my brain,
Like hell, the seat of darkness and of pain.

Exit.

Act III, scene i. A room in Thorowgood's house.

Enter Thorowgood and Trueman.

THOROWGOOD.
Methinks I would not have you only learn the method of merchandise and practice it hereafter merely as a means of getting wealth. 'Twill be well worth your pains to study it as a science, to see how it is founded in reason and the nature of things, how it promotes humanity as it has opened and yet keeps up an intercourse between nations far remote from one another in situation, customs, and religion, promoting arts, industry, peace, and plenty, by mutual benefits diffusing mutual love from pole to pole.

TRUEMAN.
Something of this I have considered and hope, by your assistance, to extend my thoughts much farther. I have observed those countries where trade is promoted and encouraged do not make discoveries to destroy but to improve mankind, by love and friendship to tame the fierce and polish the most savage, to teach them the advantages of honest traffic by taking from them, with their own consent, their useless superfluities and giving them in return what, from their ignorance in manual arts, their situation, or some other accident, they stand in need of.

THOROWGOOD.
'Tis justly observed. The populous East, luxuriant, abounds with glittering gems, bright pearls, aromatic spices, and health-restoring drugs. The late found western world's rich earth glows with unnumbered veins of gold and silver ore. On every

climate and on every country Heaven has bestowed some good peculiar to itself. It is the industrious merchant's business to collect the various blessings of each soil and climate and, with the product of the whole, to enrich his native country. Well! I have examined your accounts. They are not only just, as I have always found them, but regularly kept and fairly entered. I commend your diligence. Method in business is the surest guide. He who neglects it frequently stumbles and always wanders perplexed, uncertain, and in danger. Are Barnwell's accounts ready for my inspection? He does not use to be the last on these occasions.

TRUEMAN.

Upon receiving your orders he retired, I thought in some confusion. If you please, I'll go and hasten him. I hope he hasn't been guilty of any neglect.

THOROWGOOD.

I'm now going to the Exchange.[9] Let him know, at my return, I expect to find him ready.

Exeunt. Enter Maria with a book, sits and reads.

MARIA.

How forcible is truth! The weakest mind, inspired with love of that, fixed and collected in itself, with indifference beholds the united force of earth and hell opposing. Such souls are raised above the sense of pain or so supported that they regard it not. The martyr cheaply purchases his heaven: small are his sufferings, great is his reward. Not so the wretch who combats love with duty when the mind, weakened and dissolved by the soft passion, feeble and hopeless opposes its own desires. What is an hour, a day, a year of pain to a whole life of tortures such as these?

Enter Trueman.

TRUEMAN.

Oh, Barnwell! Oh, my friend, how art thou fallen?

MARIA.

Hah! Barnwell! What of him? Speak, say what of Barnwell.

TRUEMAN.

'Tis not to be concealed. I've news to tell of him that will afflict your generous father, yourself, and all who knew him.

MARIA.

Defend us, Heaven!

TRUEMAN.

I cannot speak it. See there. (*Gives a letter.*)

MARIA. (*Reads.*)

"Trueman, I know my absence will surprise my honored master and yourself, and the more when you shall understand that the reason of my withdrawing is my having embezzled part of the cash with which I was entrusted. After this, 'tis needless to inform you that I intend never to return again. Though this might have been known by examining my accounts, yet to prevent that unnecessary trouble and to cut off all fruitless expectations of my return I have left this from the lost George Barnwell."

TRUEMAN.

Lost indeed! Yet how he should be guilty of what he there charges himself withal raises my wonder equal to my grief. Never had youth a higher sense of virtue. Justly he thought, and as he thought he practiced. Never was life more regular than his: an understanding uncommon at his years, an open, generous, manliness of temper, his manners easy, unaffected, and engaging.

MARIA.

This and much more you might have said with truth. He was the delight of every eye and joy of every heart that knew him.

TRUEMAN.

Since such he was, and was my friend, can I support his loss? See, the fairest and happiest maid this wealthy City* boasts kindly condescends to weep for thy unhappy fate, poor, ruined Barnwell!

MARIA.

Trueman, do you think a soul so delicate as his, so sensible of shame, can e'er submit to live a slave to vice?

TRUEMAN.

Never, never. So well I know him, I'm sure this act of his, so contrary to his nature, must have been caused by some unavoidable necessity.

MARIA.

Is there no means yet to preserve him?

[9] Exchange] the Royal Exchange built in 1566 and so named by Queen Elizabeth, a central meeting place for business and financial transactions

TRUEMAN.

Oh! that there were. But few men recover reputation lost, a merchant never. Nor would he, I fear, though I should find him, ever be brought to look his injured master in the face.

MARIA.

I fear as much, and therefore would never have my father know it.

TRUEMAN.

That's impossible.

MARIA.

What's the sum?

TRUEMAN.

'Tis considerable. I've marked it here to show it with the letter to your father at his return.

MARIA.

If I should supply the money, could you so dispose of that and the account as to conceal this unhappy mismanagement from my father?

TRUEMAN.

Nothing more easy. But can you intend it? Will you save a helpless wretch from ruin? Oh! 'twere an act worthy such exalted virtue as Maria's. Sure Heaven, in mercy to my friend, inspired the generous thought.

MARIA.

Doubt not but I would purchase so great a happiness at a much dearer price. But how shall he be found?

TRUEMAN.

Trust to my diligence for that. In the meantime I'll conceal his absence from your father or find such excuses for it that the real cause shall never be suspected.

MARIA.

In attempting to save from shame one whom we hope may yet return to virtue, to Heaven and you, the only witnesses of this action, I appeal whether I do anything misbecoming my sex and character.

TRUEMAN.

Earth must approve the deed, and Heaven, I doubt not, will reward it.

MARIA.

If Heaven succeeds it, I am well rewarded. A virgin's fame is sullied by suspicion's lightest breath, and therefore as this must be a secret from my father and the world, for Barnwell's sake, for mine, let it be so to him.

Exeunt.

Scene ii. A room in Millwood's house.

Enter Lucy and Blunt.

LUCY.

Well! What do you think of Millwood's conduct now!

BLUNT.

I own it is surprising. I don't know which to admire most, her feigned or his real passion, though I have sometimes been afraid that her avarice would discover* her. But his youth and want* of experience make it the easier to impose on him.

LUCY.

No, it is his love. To do him justice, notwithstanding his youth, he don't want understanding. But you men are much easier imposed on in these affairs than your vanity will allow you to believe. Let me see the wisest of you all as much in love with me as Barnwell is with Millwood, and I'll engage to make as great a fool of him.

BLUNT.

And all circumstances considered, to make as much money of him, too?

LUCY.

I can't answer for that. Her artifice in making him rob his master at first, and the various stratagems by which she has obliged him to continue that course, astonish even me who know her so well.

BLUNT.

But then you are to consider that the money was his master's.

LUCY.

There was the difficulty of it. Had it been his own, it had been nothing. Were the world his, she might have it for a smile. But those golden days are done; he's ruined, and Millwood's hopes of farther profits there are at an end.

BLUNT.

That's no more than we all expected.

LUCY.

Being called by his master to make up his accounts, he was forced to quit his house and service and wisely flies to Millwood for relief and entertainment.

BLUNT.

I have not heard of this before! How did she receive him?

LUCY.

As you would expect: she wondered what he meant, was astonished at his impudence, and, with an air of modesty peculiar to herself, swore so heartily that she never saw him before that she put me out of countenance.

BLUNT.

That's much indeed! But how did Barnwell behave?

LUCY.

He grieved and, at length enraged at this barbarous treatment, was preparing to be gone, when, making toward the door, he showed a sum of money which he had brought[f] from his master's—the last he's ever like to have from thence.

BLUNT.

But then Millwood?

LUCY.

Aye, she with her usual address returned to her old arts of lying, swearing, and dissembling, hung on his neck and wept and swore 'twas meant in jest, till the amorous youth[g] melted into tears, threw the money into her lap, and swore he had rather die than think her false.

BLUNT.

Strange infatuation!

LUCY.

But what followed was stranger still. As doubts and fears, followed by reconcilement, ever increase love where the passion is sincere, so in him it caused so wild a transport of excessive fondness, such joy, such grief, such pleasure, and such anguish, that nature in him seemed sinking with the weight and the charmed soul disposed to quit his breast for hers. Just then, when every passion with lawless anarchy prevailed and reason was in the raging tempest lost, the cruel, artful Millwood prevailed upon the wretched youth to promise—what I tremble but to think on.

BLUNT.

I am amazed! What can it be?

LUCY.

You will be more so to hear it is to attempt the life of his nearest relation and best benefactor—

BLUNT.

His uncle, whom we have often heard him speak of as a gentleman of a large estate and fair character in the country, where he lives.

LUCY.

The same. She was no sooner possessed of the last, dear purchase of his ruin, but her avarice, insatiate as the grave, demanded this horrid sacrifice. Barnwell's near relation and unsuspected virtue must give too easy means to seize the good man's treasure, whose blood must seal the dreadful secret and prevent the terrors of her guilty fears.

BLUNT.

Is it possible she could persuade him to do an act like that! He is by nature honest, grateful, compassionate, and generous. And though his love and her artful persuasions have wrought him to practice what he most abhors, yet we all can witness for him with what reluctance he has still complied! So many tears he shed o'er each offense as might, if possible, sanctify theft and make a merit of a crime.

LUCY.

'Tis true, at the naming the murder of his uncle he started into rage and, breaking from her arms where she till then had held him with well-dissembled love and false endearments, called her cruel monster, devil, and told her she was born for his destruction. She thought it not for her purpose to meet his rage with rage but affected a most passionate fit of grief, railed at her fate, and cursed her wayward stars that still her wants* should force her to press him to act such deeds as she must needs abhor as well as he, but told him necessity had no law and love no bounds, that therefore he never truly loved but meant in her necessity to forsake her. Then kneeled and swore that since, by his refusal, he had given her cause to doubt his love, she never would see him more unless, to prove it true, he robbed his uncle to supply her wants and murdered him to keep it from discovery.

BLUNT.

I am astonished! What said he?

LUCY.

Speechless he stood, but in his face you might have read that various passions tore his very soul. Oft he in anguish threw his eyes towards heaven and then as often bent their beams on her, then wept and groaned and beat his troubled breast. At length, with horror not to be expressed, he cried, "Thou cursed fair! Have I not given dreadful proofs of love! What drew me from my youthful innocence to stain my then unspotted soul, but love? What caused me to rob my worthy gentle master, but cursed love? What makes me now a fugitive from his service, loathed by myself and scorned by all the world, but love? What fills my eyes with tears, my soul with torture never felt on this side death before? Why love, love, love. And why, above all, do I resolve"—for, tearing his hair, he cried, "I do resolve"—"to kill my uncle?"

BLUNT.

Was she not moved? It makes me weep to hear the sad relation.

LUCY.

Yes, with joy that she had gained her point. She gave him no time to cool but urged him to attempt it instantly. He's now gone. If he performs it and escapes, there's more money for her. If not, he'll ne'er return, and then she's fairly rid of him.

BLUNT.

'Tis time the world was rid of such a monster.

LUCY.

If we don't do our endeavors to prevent this murder, we are as bad as she.

BLUNT.

I'm afraid it is too late.

LUCY.

Perhaps not. Her barbarity to Barnwell makes me hate her. We have run too great a length with her already. I did not think her or myself so wicked as I find upon reflection we are.

BLUNT.

'Tis true we have all been too much so. But there is something so horrid in murder that all other crimes seem nothing when compared to that. I would not be involved in the guilt of that for all the world.

LUCY.

Nor I, Heaven knows. Therefore let us clear ourselves by doing all that is in our power to prevent it. I have just thought of a way that to me seems probable. Will you join with me to detect this cursed design?

BLUNT.

With all my heart.[h] He who knows of a murder intended to be committed and does not discover* it, in the eye of the law and reason, is a murderer.

LUCY.

Let us lose no time. I'll acquaint you with the particulars as we go.

Exeunt.

Scene iii. A walk at some distance from a country seat.[10]

Enter Barnwell.

BARNWELL.

A dismal gloom obscures the face of day. Either the sun has slipped behind a cloud or journeys down the west of heaven with more than common speed to avoid the sight of what I'm doomed to act. Since I set forth on this accursed design, where'er I tread, methinks, the solid earth trembles beneath my feet. Yonder limpid stream, whose hoary fall has made a natural cascade, as I passed by in doleful accents seemed to murmur, "Murder." The earth, the air, and water seemed concerned, but that's not strange. The world is punished and Nature feels a shock when Providence permits a good man's fall. Just Heaven! Then what should I be! For him that was my father's only brother and since his death has been to me a father, who took me up an infant and an orphan, reared me with tenderest care and still indulged me with most paternal fondness. Yet here I stand avowed his destined murderer. I stiffen with horror at my own impiety. 'Tis yet unperformed. What if I quit my bloody purpose and fly the place! (*Going, then stops.*) But whither, oh whither, shall I fly! My master's once friendly doors are ever shut against me, and without money Millwood will never see me more, and life is not to be endured without her. She's got such firm possession of my heart and governs there with such despotic sway. Aye, there's the cause of all my sin and sorrow. 'Tis more than love: 'tis the fever of the soul and madness of desire. In vain does nature, reason, conscience, all oppose it.

---

10 country seat] the residence of a country gentleman, a country house

The impetuous passion bears down all before it and drives me on to lust, to theft, and murder. Oh conscience! feeble guide to virtue, who only shows us when we go astray but wants* the power to stop us in our course. Hah! in yonder shady walk I see my uncle. He's alone. Now for my disguise. (*Plucks out a vizor.*) This is his hour of private meditation. Thus daily he prepares his soul for heaven whilst I—but what have I to do with heaven! Hah! No struggles, conscience—

Hence! hence remorse and every thought that's
  good;
The storm that lust began must end in blood.

Puts on the vizor and draws a pistol. Exit.

Scene iv. A close walk in a wood.

Enter Uncle.

UNCLE.

If I was superstitious I should fear some danger lurked unseen, or death were nigh. A heavy melancholy clouds my spirits. My imagination is filled with gashly[11] forms of dreary graves and bodies changed by death, when the pale, lengthened visage attracts each weeping eye and fills the musing soul at once with grief and horror, pity and aversion. I will indulge the thought. The wise man prepares himself for death by making it familiar to his mind. When strong reflections hold the mirror near, and the living in the dead behold their future selves, how does each inordinate passion and desire cease or sicken at the view! The mind scarce moves. The blood, curdling and chilled, creeps slowly through the veins. Fixed, still, and motionless we stand, so like the solemn object of our thoughts we are almost at present what we must be hereafter, till curiosity awakes the soul and sets it on inquiry.

Enter George Barnwell at a distance.

Oh Death, thou strange, mysterious power, seen everyday yet never understood but by the incommunicative dead, what art thou? The extensive mind of man—that with a thought circles the earth's vast globe, sinks to the center or ascends above the stars, that worlds exotic finds or thinks it finds—thy thick clouds attempts to pass in vain, lost and bewildered in the horrid gloom. Defeated she returns more doubtful than before, of nothing certain but of labor lost.

During this speech Barnwell sometimes presents the pistol and draws it back again.

BARNWELL.

Oh, 'tis impossible!

He throws down the pistol. His uncle starts and attempts to draw his sword.

UNCLE.

A man so near me, armed and masked!

BARNWELL.

Nay, then there's no retreat. (*Plucks a poniard from his bosom and stabs him.*)

UNCLE.

Oh! I am slain! All-gracious Heaven regard the prayer of thy dying servant. Bless with thy choicest blessings my dearest nephew. Forgive my murderer and take my fleeting soul to endless mercy.

Barnwell throws off his mask, runs to him, and, kneeling by him, raises and chafes him.

BARNWELL.

Expiring saint! Oh murdered, martyred uncle! Lift up your dying eyes and view your nephew in your murderer. Oh do not look so tenderly upon me. Let indignation lighten from your eyes and blast me ere you die. By Heaven, he weeps in pity of my woes. Tears, tears, for blood. The murdered in the agonies of death weeps for his murderer. Oh speak your pious purpose, pronounce my pardon then, and take me with you. He would, but cannot. Oh why, with such fond affection do you press my murdering hand! What! will you kiss me!

Barnwell kisses his uncle, who groans and dies.

Life, that hovered on his lips till he had sealed my pardon, in that kiss expired. He's gone forever, and oh! I follow. (*Swoons away upon his uncle's dead body.*) Do I still live to press the suffering bosom of the earth? Do I still breathe and taint with my infectious breath the wholesome air! Let Heaven

[11] gashly] ghastly

from its high throne, in justice or in mercy, now look down on that dear, murdered saint, and me the murderer. And if his vengeance spares, let pity strike and end my wretched being. Murder the worst of crimes and parricide the worst of murders, and this the worst of parricides. Cain, who stands on record from the birth of time and must to its last, final period as accursed, slew a brother favored above him. Detested Nero, by another's hand, dispatched a mother that he feared and hated. But I, with my own hand, have murdered a brother, mother, father, and a friend most loving and beloved. This execrable act of mine's without a parallel. Oh may it ever stand alone, the last of murders as it is the worst.

The rich man thus, in torment and despair,
Preferred[12] his vain but charitable prayer.
The fool, his own soul lost, would fain be wise
For others' good, but Heaven his suit denies.[13]
By laws and means well-known we stand or fall,
And one eternal rule remains for all.

[Scene closes on Barnwell and the body of his uncle.]

Act IV, scene i. A room in Thorowgood's house.

Enter Maria.

MARIA.
How falsely do they judge who censure or applaud as we're afflicted or rewarded here. I know I am unhappy yet cannot charge myself with any crime more than the common frailties of our kind that should provoke just Heaven to mark me out for sufferings so uncommon and severe. Falsely to accuse ourselves Heaven must abhor. Then it is just and right that innocence should suffer, for Heaven must be just in all its ways. Perhaps by that they are kept from moral evils much worse than penal, or more improved in virtue. Or may not the lesser ills that they sustain be made the means of greater good to others? Might all the joyless days and sleepless nights that I have passed but purchase peace for thee,
Thou dear, dear cause of all my grief and pain.
Small were the loss and infinite the gain,
Though to the grave in secret love I pine,
So life and fame and happiness were thine.

Enter Trueman.

What news of Barnwell?

TRUEMAN.
None. I have sought him with the greatest diligence, but all in vain.

MARIA.
Does my father yet suspect the cause of his absence?

TRUEMAN.
All appeared so just and fair to him, it is not possible he ever should. But his absence will no longer be concealed. Your father's wise, and though he seems to hearken to the friendly excuses I would make for Barnwell, yet I am afraid he regards 'em only as such, without suffering them to influence his judgment.

MARIA.
How does the unhappy youth defeat all our designs to serve him! Yet I can never repent what we have done. Should he return, 'twill make his reconciliation with my father easier and preserve him from future reproach from a malicious, unforgiving world.

Enter Thorowgood and Lucy.

THOROWGOOD.
This woman here has given me a sad and—bating some circumstances—too probable account of Barnwell's defection.

LUCY.
I am sorry, sir, that my frank confession of my former, unhappy course of life should cause you to suspect my truth on this occasion.

THOROWGOOD.
It is not that. Your confession has in it all the appearance of truth. (*To them.*) Among many other particulars, she informs me that Barnwell has been influenced to break his trust and wrong me at several times of considerable sums of money. Now, as I know this to be false, I would fain doubt the whole of her relation, too dreadful to be willingly believed.

12 preferred] offered

13 rich man ... denies] See Luke 16:19-31 for the story of Dives, as the rich man was called in tradition, and Lazarus.

MARIA.

Sir, your pardon. I find myself on a sudden so indisposed that I must retire. (*Aside.*) Providence opposes all attempts to save him. Poor, ruined Barnwell! Wretched, lost Maria! (*Exit.*)

THOROWGOOD.

How am I distressed on every side: pity for that unhappy youth, fear for the life of a much valued friend, and then my child, the only joy and hope of my declining life. Her melancholy increases hourly and gives me painful apprehensions of her loss.—Oh Trueman! This person informs me that your friend, at the instigation of an impious woman, is gone to rob and murder his venerable uncle.

TRUEMAN.

Oh execrable deed! I am blasted with the horror of the thought!

LUCY.

This delay may ruin all.

THOROWGOOD.

What to do or think I know not. That he ever wronged me I know is false. The rest may be so too. There's all my hope.

TRUEMAN.

Trust not to that. Rather suppose all true than lose a moment's time. Even now the horrid deed may be adoing—dreadful imagination!—or it may be done, and we are vainly debating on the means to prevent what is already past.

THOROWGOOD. [*Aside.*]

This earnestness convinces me that he knows more than he has yet discovered.*—What ho! Without there! Who waits?

Enter a servant.

Order the groom to saddle the swiftest horse and prepare to set out with speed. An affair of life and death demands his diligence.

Exit servant.

[*To Lucy.*] For you, whose behavior on this occasion I have no time to commend as it deserves, I must engage your farther assistance. Return and observe this Millwood till I come. I have your directions and will follow you as soon as possible.

Exit Lucy.

Trueman, you I am sure would not be idle on this occasion. (*Exit.*)

TRUEMAN.

He only who is a friend can judge of my distress.

Exit.

Scene ii. Millwood's house.

Enter Millwood.

MILLWOOD.

I wish I knew the event of his design. The attempt, without success, would ruin him. Well! What have I to apprehend from that? I fear too much. The mischief being only intended, his friends, in pity of his youth, turn all their rage on me. I should have thought of that before. Suppose the deed done; then, and then only I shall be secure. Or what if he returns without attempting it at all?

Enter Barnwell bloody.

But he is here, and I have done him wrong. His bloody hands show he has done the deed, but show he wants* the prudence to conceal it.

BARNWELL.

Where shall I hide me? Whither shall I fly to avoid the swift, unerring hand of justice?

MILLWOOD.

Dismiss your fears. Though thousands had pursued you to the door, yet being entered here you are safe as innocence. I have such a cavern by art so cunningly contrived that the piercing eyes of jealousy and revenge may search in vain nor find the entrance to the safe retreat. There will I hide you if any danger's near.

BARNWELL.

Oh hide me from myself, if it be possible. For while I bear my conscience in my bosom, though I were hid where man's eye never saw nor light e'er dawned, 'twere all in vain. For oh! that inmate, that impartial judge, will try, convict, and sentence me for murder and execute me with never-ending torments. Behold these hands all crimsoned o'er with my dear uncle's blood! Here's a sight to make a statue start with horror or turn a living man into a statue.

MILLWOOD.

Ridiculous! Then it seems you are afraid of your

own shadow or what's less than a shadow, your conscience.

BARNWELL.

Though to man unknown I did the accursed act, what can we hide from Heaven's all-seeing eye?

MILLWOOD.

No more of this stuff. What advantage have you made of his death? Or what advantage may yet be made of it? Did you secure the keys of his treasure? Those no doubt were about him? What gold, what jewels, or what else of value have you brought me?

BARNWELL.

Think you I added sacrilege to murder? Oh! had you seen him as his life flowed from him in a crimson flood and heard him praying for me by the double name of nephew and murderer (alas, alas! he knew not then that his nephew was his murderer), how would you have wished as I did, though you had a thousand years of life to come, to have given them all to have lengthened his one hour. But being dead, I fled the sight of what my hands had done. Nor could I, to have gained the empire of the world, have violated by theft his sacred corpse.

MILLWOOD.

Whining, preposterous, canting villain: to murder your uncle, rob him of life (nature's first, last, dear prerogative, after which there's no injury) then fear to take what he no longer wanted and bring to me your penury and guilt. Do you think I'll hazard my reputation, nay my life, to entertain* you?

BARNWELL.

Oh, Millwood! this from thee. But I have done. If you hate me, if you wish me dead, then are you happy. For oh! 'tis sure my grief will quickly end me.

MILLWOOD. (*Aside.*)

In his madness he will discover* all and involve me in his ruin. We are on a precipice from whence there's no retreat for both. Then, to preserve myself. (*Pauses.*) There is no other way, 'tis dreadful, but reflection comes too late when danger's pressing and there's no room for choice. It must be done. (*Rings a bell.*)

Enter a servant.

Fetch me an officer and seize this villain. He has confessed himself a murderer. Should I let him escape, I justly might be thought as bad as he.

Exit servant.

BARNWELL.

Oh Millwood! Sure you do not, cannot mean it. Stop the messenger, upon my knees I beg you, call him back. 'Tis fit I die indeed, but not by you. I will this instant deliver myself into the hands of justice, indeed I will, for death is all I wish. But thy ingratitude so tears my wounded soul, 'tis worse ten thousand times than death with torture.

MILLWOOD.

Call it what you will, I am willing to live, and live secure, which nothing but your death can warrant.

BARNWELL.

If there be a pitch of wickedness that seats the author beyond the reach of vengeance, you must be secure. But what remains for me but a dismal dungeon, hard-galling fetters, an awful* trial, and ignominious death, justly to fall unpitied and abhorred? After death to be suspended between heaven and earth, a dreadful spectacle, the warning and horror of a gaping crowd.[14] This I could bear, nay wish not to avoid, had it but come from any hand but thine.

Enter Blunt, officer and attendants.

MILLWOOD.

Heaven defend me! Conceal a murderer! Here sir, take this youth into your custody. I accuse him of murder and will appear to make good my charge.

They seize him.

BARNWELL.

To whom, of what, or how shall I complain? I'll not accuse her, the hand of Heaven is in it, and this the punishment of lust and parricide. Yet Heaven, that justly cuts me off, still suffers her to live, perhaps to punish others. Tremendous mercy! So fiends are cursed with immortality, to be the executioners of Heaven.

Be warned ye youths who see my sad despair,

---

14 After … crowd] Criminals were hanged publicly, their bodies left dangling on the gallows until collected by family or friends. The bodies of the most notorious criminals were kept to be hung up for public display on gibbets until they moldered away.

Avoid lewd women, false as they are fair;
By reason guided, honest joys pursue.
The fair, to honor and to virtue true,
Just to herself, will ne'er be false to you.
By my example learn to shun my fate
(How wretched is the man who's wise too late?),
Ere innocence and fame and life be lost;
Here purchase wisdom cheaply, at my cost.

Exeunt Barnwell, officer and attendants.

MILLWOOD.
Where's Lucy? Why is she absent at such a time?

BLUNT.
Would I had been so too. Lucy will soon be here and, I hope, to thy confusion, thou devil!

MILLWOOD.
Insolent! This, to me?

BLUNT.
The worst that we know of the Devil is that he first seduces to sin and then betrays to punishment. (*Exit.*)

MILLWOOD.
They disapprove of my conduct, then, and mean to take this opportunity to set up for themselves. My ruin is resolved. I see my danger but scorn both it and them. I was not born to fall by such weak instruments. (*Going.*)

Enter Thorowgood.

THOROWGOOD.
Where is this scandal of her own sex and curse of ours?

MILLWOOD.
What means this insolence? Who do you seek?

THOROWGOOD.
Millwood.

MILLWOOD.
Well, you have found her then. I am Millwood.

THOROWGOOD.
Then you are the most impious wretch that e'er the sun beheld.

MILLWOOD.
From your appearance I should have expected wisdom and moderation, but your manners belie your aspect. What is your business here? I know you not.

THOROWGOOD.
Hereafter you may know me better. I am Barnwell's master.

MILLWOOD.
Then you are master to a villain, which, I think, is not much to your credit.

THOROWGOOD.
Had he been as much above thy arts as my credit is superior to thy malice, I need not have blushed to own him.

MILLWOOD.
My arts? I don't understand you, sir! If he has done amiss, what's that to me? Was he my servant, or yours? You should have taught him better.

THOROWGOOD.
Why should I wonder to find such uncommon impudence in one arrived to such a height of wickedness? When innocence is banished, modesty soon follows. Know, sorceress, I'm not ignorant of any of the arts by which you first deceived the unwary youth. I know how, step by step, you've led him on—reluctant and unwilling—from crime to crime to this last horrid act which you contrived and, by your cursed wiles, even forced him to commit[i].

MILLWOOD. (*Aside.*)
Hah! Lucy has got the advantage and accused me first. Unless I can turn the accusation and fix it upon her and Blunt, I am lost.

THOROWGOOD.
Had I known your cruel design sooner, it had been prevented. To see you punished as the law directs is all that now remains. Poor satisfaction! For he, innocent as he is compared to you, must suffer too. But Heaven, who knows our frame and graciously distinguishes between frailty and presumption, will make a difference though man cannot, who sees not the heart but only judges by the outward action.

MILLWOOD.
I find, sir, we are both unhappy in our servants. I was surprised at such ill treatment without cause from a gentleman of your appearance and therefore too hastily returned it. For which I ask your pardon. I now perceive you have been so far imposed on as to think me engaged in a former correspondence with your servant and, some way or other, accessory to his undoing.

THOROWGOOD.

I charge you as the cause, the sole cause, of all his guilt and all his suffering, of all he now endures and must endure till a violent and shameful death shall put a dreadful period to his life and miseries together.

MILLWOOD.

'Tis very strange, but who's secure from scandal and detraction? So far from contributing to his ruin, I never spoke to him till since that fatal accident, which I lament as much as you. 'Tis true, I have a servant on whose account he has of late frequented my house. If she has abused my good opinion of her, am I to blame? Hasn't Barnwell done the same by you?

THOROWGOOD.

I hear you. Pray go on.

MILLWOOD.

I have been informed he had a violent passion for her, and she for him. But till now I always thought it innocent. I know her poor and given to expensive pleasures. Now who can tell but she may have influenced the amorous youth to commit this murder to supply her extravagances; it must be so. I now recollect a thousand circumstances that confirm it. I'll have her, and a manservant that I suspect as an accomplice, secured immediately. I hope, sir, you will lay aside your ill-grounded suspicions of me and join to punish the real contrivers of this bloody deed. (*Offers to go.*)

THOROWGOOD.

Madam, you pass not this way. I see your design, but shall protect them from your malice.

MILLWOOD.

I hope you will not use your influence and the credit of your name to screen such guilty wretches. Consider, sir, the wickedness of persuading a thoughtless youth to such a crime.

THOROWGOOD.

I do, and of betraying him when it was done.

MILLWOOD.

That which you call betraying him may convince you of my innocence. She who loves him, though she contrived the murder, would never have delivered him into the hands of justice as I—struck with horror at his crimes—have done.

THOROWGOOD. [*Aside.*]

How should an unexperienced youth escape her snares? The powerful magic of her wit and form might betray the wisest to simple dotage and fire the blood that age had froze long since. Even I, that with just prejudice came prepared, had by her artful story been deceived but that my strong conviction of her guilt makes even a doubt impossible.—Those whom subtly you would accuse, you know are your accusers and—what proves unanswerably their innocence and your guilt—they accused you before the deed was done and did all that was in their power to have prevented it.

MILLWOOD.

Sir, you are very hard to be convinced. But I have such a proof which, when produced, will silence all objections. (*Exit.*)

Enter Lucy, Trueman, Blunt, officers, etc.

LUCY.

Gentlemen, pray place yourselves some on one side of that door and some on the other. Watch her entrance, and act as your prudence shall direct you. (*To Thorowgood.*) This way and note her behavior. I have observed her; she's driven to the last extremity and is forming some desperate resolution. I guess at her design.

Enter Millwood with a pistol. Trueman secures her.

TRUEMAN.

Here thy power of doing mischief ends, deceitful, cruel, bloody woman!

MILLWOOD.

Fool, hypocrite, villain—man! Thou canst not call me that.

TRUEMAN.

To call thee woman were to wrong the sex, thou devil!

MILLWOOD.

That imaginary being is an emblem of thy cursed sex collected, a mirror wherein each particular man may see his own likeness and that of all mankind.

THOROWGOOD.

Think not by aggravating the faults of others to extenuate thy own, of which the abuse of such uncommon perfections of mind and body is not the least.

MILLWOOD.

If such I had, well may I curse your barbarous sex who robbed me of 'em ere I knew their worth then left me, too late, to count their value by their loss. Another and another spoiler came, and all my gain was poverty and reproach. My soul disdained, and yet disdains, dependence and contempt. Riches, no matter by what means obtained, I saw secured the worst of men from both. I found it therefore necessary to be rich, and to that end I summoned all my arts. You call 'em wicked, be it so; they were such as my conversation* with your sex had furnished me withal.

THOROWGOOD.

Sure none but the worst of men conversed with thee.

MILLWOOD.

Men of all degrees and all professions I have known, yet found no difference but in their several capacities. All were alike wicked to the utmost of their power. In pride, contention, avarice, cruelty, and revenge, the reverend priesthood were my unerring guides. From suburb magistrates, who live by ruined reputations as the unhospitable natives of Cornwall do by shipwrecks,[15] I learned that to charge my innocent neighbors with my crimes was to merit their protection. For to screen the guilty is the less scandalous when many are suspected, and detraction, like darkness and death, blackens all objects and levels all distinction. Such are your venal magistrates, who favor none but such as by their office they are sworn to punish. With them not to be guilty is the worst of crimes, and large fees, privately paid, is every needful virtue.

THOROWGOOD.

Your practice has sufficiently discovered* your contempt of laws both human and divine. No wonder then that you should hate the officers of both.

MILLWOOD.

I know you and I hate you all. I expect no mercy and I ask for none.[j] I followed my inclinations, and that the best of you does every day. All actions seem[k] alike natural and indifferent to man and beast who devour, or are devoured, as they meet with others weaker or stronger than themselves.

THOROWGOOD.

What pity it is, a mind so comprehensive, daring, and inquisitive, should be a stranger to religion's sweet and powerful charms.

MILLWOOD.

I am not fool enough to be an atheist, though I have known enough of men's hypocrisy to make a thousand simple women so. Whatever religion is in itself, as practiced by mankind it has caused the evils you say it was designed to cure. War, plague, and famine has not destroyed so many of the human race as this pretended piety has done, and with such barbarous cruelty, as if the only way to honor Heaven were to turn the present world into Hell.

THOROWGOOD.

Truth is truth, though from an enemy and spoke in malice. You bloody, blind, and superstitious bigots, how will you answer this?

MILLWOOD.

What are your laws, of which you make your boast, but the fool's wisdom and the coward's valor, the instrument and screen of all your villainies, by which you punish in others what you act yourselves or would have acted had you been in their circumstances. The judge who condemns the poor man for being a thief had been a thief himself had he been poor. Thus you go on deceiving and being deceived, harrassing, plaguing, and destroy-ing one another, but women are your universal prey:
Women, by whom you are, the source of joy,
With cruel arts you labor to destroy.
A thousand ways our ruin you pursue,
Yet blame in us those arts first taught by you.
Oh! may from hence each violated maid
By flatt'ring, faithless, barb'rous man betrayed,
When robbed of innocence and virgin fame,
From your destruction raise a nobler name:

15 suburb magistrates ... shipwrecks] The suburbs were the areas immediately outside the City, many of them disreputable. Magistrates lived by fees collected for administering the law, and so profited from charges and accusations. The rocky coast of Cornwall was especially dangerous to shipping, and the more so as people living there would sometimes set out false beacons so that ships might founder and their goods be retrieved as salvage.

To right their sex's wrongs devote their mind,
And future Millwoods prove to plague mankind.

[Exeunt.]

Act V, scene i. A room in a prison.

Enter Thorowgood, Blunt and Lucy.

THOROWGOOD.
I have recommended to Barnwell a reverend divine whose judgment and integrity I am well acquainted with. Nor has Millwood been neglected, but she, unhappy woman, still obstinate, refuses his assistance.

LUCY.
This pious charity to the afflicted well becomes your character. Yet pardon me, sir, if I wonder you were not at their trial.

THOROWGOOD.
I knew it was impossible to save him, and I and my family* bear so great a part in his distress that to have been present would have aggravated our sorrows without relieving his.

BLUNT.
It was mournful indeed. Barnwell's youth and modest deportment as he passed drew tears from every eye. When placed at the bar and arraigned before the reverend judges, with many tears and interrupting sobs he confessed and aggravated his offenses without accusing or once reflecting on Millwood, the shameless author of his ruin, who dauntless and unconcerned stood by his side viewing with visible pride and contempt the vast assembly, who all with sympathizing sorrow wept for the wretched youth. Millwood, when called upon to answer, loudly insisted upon her innocence and made an artful and a bold defense. But finding all in vain, the impartial jury and the learned bench concurring to find her guilty, how did she curse herself, poor Barnwell, us, her judges, all mankind! But what could that avail? She was condemned and is this day to suffer with him.

THOROWGOOD.
The time draws on. I am going to visit Barnwell, as you are Millwood.

LUCY.
We have not wronged her, yet I dread this interview. She's proud, impatient, wrathful, and unforgiving. To be the branded instruments of vengeance, to suffer in her shame and sympathize with her in all she suffers is the tribute we must pay for our former, ill-spent lives and long confederacy with her in wickedness.

THOROWGOOD.
Happy for you it ended when it did. What you have done against Millwood I know proceeded from a just abhorrence of her crimes, free from interest, malice, or revenge. Proselytes to virtue should be encouraged. Pursue your purposed reformation, and know me hereafter for your friend.

LUCY.
This is a blessing as unhoped for as unmerited, but Heaven that snatched us from impending ruin sure intends you as its instrument to secure us from apostasy.

THOROWGOOD.
With gratitude to impute your deliverance to Heaven is just. Many, less virtuously disposed than Barnwell was, have never fallen in the manner he has done. May not such owe their safety rather to Providence than to themselves? With pity and compassion let us judge him. Great were his faults, but strong was the temptation. Let his ruin learn us diffidence, humanity, and circumspection. For we who wonder at his fate, perhaps had we like him been tried, like him we had fallen too.

[Exeunt.]

Scene ii. A dungeon, a table and lamp.

Barnwell reading. Enter Thorowgood at a distance.

THOROWGOOD.
There see the bitter fruits of passion's detested reign and sensual appetite indulged: severe reflections, penitence, and tears.

BARNWELL.
My honored, injured master, whose goodness has covered me a thousand times with shame, forgive this last, unwilling disrespect. Indeed I saw you not.

THOROWGOOD.
'Tis well. I hope you were better employed in viewing of yourself. Your journey's long, your time for preparation almost spent. I sent a reverend

divine to teach you to improve it and should be glad to hear of his success.

BARNWELL.

The Word of Truth, which he recommended for my constant companion in this my sad retirement, has at length removed the doubts I labored under. From thence I've learned the infinite extent of heavenly mercy, that my offences though great are not unpardonable, and that 'tis not my interest only but my duty to believe and to rejoice in that hope. So shall Heaven receive the glory and future penitents the profit of my example.

THOROWGOOD.

Proceed.[1]

BARNWELL.

'Tis wonderful that words should charm despair, speak peace and pardon to a murderer's conscience. But truth and mercy flow in every sentence, attended with force and energy divine. How shall I describe my present state of mind? I hope in doubt, and trembling I rejoice. I feel my grief increase even as my fears give way. Joy and gratitude now supply more tears than horror and anguish of despair before.

THOROWGOOD.

These are the genuine signs of true repentance, the only preparatory, the certain way to everlasting peace. Oh the joy it gives to see a soul formed and prepared for heaven! For this the faithful minister devotes himself to meditation, abstinence, and prayer, shunning the vain delights of sensual joys, and daily dies that others may live forever. For this he turns the sacred volumes o'er and spends his life in painful search of truth. The love of riches and the lust of power he looks on with just contempt and detestation, who only counts for wealth the souls he wins and whose highest ambition is to serve mankind. If the reward of all his pains be to preserve one soul from wandering or turn one from the error of his ways, how does he then rejoice and own his little labors overpaid.

BARNWELL.

What do I owe for all your generous kindness! But though I cannot, Heaven can and will reward you.

THOROWGOOD.

To see thee thus is joy too great for words. Farewell. Heaven strengthen thee. Farewell.

BARNWELL.

Oh! Sir, there's something I would say if my sad, swelling heart would give me leave.

THOROWGOOD.

Give it vent awhile, and try.

BARNWELL.

I had a friend. 'Tis true I am unworthy, yet methinks your generous example might persuade. Could I not see him once before I go from whence there's no return?

THOROWGOOD.

He's coming, and as much thy friend as ever. (*Aside.*) But I'll not anticipate his sorrow. Too soon he'll see the sad effect of his contagious ruin. This torrent of domestic misery bears too hard upon me. I must retire to indulge a weakness I find impossible to overcome.—Much loved and much lamented youth, farewell. Heaven strengthen thee. Eternally farewell.

BARNWELL.

The best of masters and of men, farewell. While I live, let me not want* your prayers.

THOROWGOOD.

Thou shalt not. Thy peace being made with Heaven, death's already vanquished. Bear a little longer the pains that attend this transitory life, and cease from pain forever. (*Exit.*)

BARNWELL.

Perhaps I shall. I find a power within that bears my soul above the fears of death and, spite of conscious shame and guilt, gives me a taste of pleasure more than mortal.

Enter Trueman and keeper.

KEEPER.

Sir, there's the prisoner. (*Exit.*)

BARNWELL.

Trueman! My friend, whom I so wished to see, yet now he's here I dare not look upon him. (*Weeps.*)

TRUEMAN.

Oh Barnwell! Barnwell!

BARNWELL.

Mercy! Mercy, gracious Heaven! For death, but not for this was I prepared.

TRUEMAN.

What have I suffered since I saw you last? What

pain has absence given me? But oh! to see thee thus!

BARNWELL.

I know it is dreadful! I feel the anguish of thy generous soul. But I was born to murder all who love me.

Both weep.

TRUEMAN.

I came not to reproach you. I thought to bring you comfort, but I'm deceived, for I have none to give. I came to share thy sorrow, but cannot bear my own.

BARNWELL.

My sense of guilt indeed you cannot know. 'Tis what the good and innocent, like you, can ne'er conceive. But other griefs at present I have none but what I feel for you. In your sorrow I read you love me still, but yet methinks 'tis strange when I consider what I am.

TRUEMAN.

No more of that. I can remember nothing but thy virtues, thy honest, tender friendship, our former happy state and present misery. Oh had you trusted me when first the fair seducer tempted you, all might have been prevented.

BARNWELL.

Alas, thou knowest not what a wretch I've been! Breach of friendship was my first and least offence. So far was I lost to goodness, so devoted to the author of my ruin that, had she insisted on my murdering thee, I think I should have done it.

TRUEMAN.

Prithee aggravate thy faults no more.

BARNWELL.

I think I should! Thus good and generous as you are, I should have murdered you!

TRUEMAN.

We have not yet embraced and may be interrupted. Come to my arms.

BARNWELL.

Never, never will I taste such joys on earth. Never will I so soothe my just remorse. Are those honest arms and faithful bosom fit to embrace and to support a murderer? These iron fetters only shall clasp, and flinty pavement bear me (*Throwing himself on the ground.*), even these too good for such a bloody monster.

TRUEMAN.

Shall fortune sever those whom friendship joined! Thy miseries cannot lay thee so low but love will find thee.[m] Here will we offer to stern calamity, this place[n] the altar and ourselves the sacrifice. Our mutual groans shall echo to each other through the dreary vault. Our sighs shall number the moments as they pass, and mingling tears communicate such anguish as words were never made to express.

BARNWELL.

Then be it so. (*Rising.*) Since you propose an intercourse of woe, pour all your griefs into my breast and in exchange take mine. (*Embracing.*) Where's now the anguish that you promised? You've taken mine and make me no return. Sure peace and comfort dwell within these arms, and sorrow can't approach me while I'm here! This, too, is the work of Heaven which, having before spoke peace and pardon to me, now sends thee to confirm it. Oh take, take some of the joy that overflows my breast!

TRUEMAN.

I do, I do. Almighty Power, how have you made us capable to bear at once the extremes of pleasure and of pain?

Enter keeper.

KEEPER.

Sir.

TRUEMAN.

I come.

Exit keeper.

BARNWELL.

Must you leave me! Death would soon have parted us forever.

TRUEMAN.

Oh my Barnwell, there's yet another task behind. Again your heart must bleed for others' woes.

BARNWELL.

To meet and part with you I thought was all I had to do on earth! What is there more for me to do or suffer?

TRUEMAN.

I dread to tell thee, yet it must be known. Maria.

BARNWELL.
Our master's fair and virtuous daughter!

TRUEMAN.
The same.

BARNWELL.
No misfortune, I hope, has reached that lovely maid! Preserve her, Heaven, from every ill to show mankind that goodness is your care.

TRUEMAN.
Thy, thy misfortunes, my unhappy friend, have reached her. Whatever you and I have felt and more, if more be possible, she feels for you.

BARNWELL. (*Aside.*)
I know he doth abhor a lie and would not trifle with his dying friend. This is, indeed, the bitterness of death!

TRUEMAN.
You must remember, for we all observed it, for some time past a heavy melancholy weighed her down. Disconsolate she seemed, and pined and languished from a cause unknown till, hearing of your dreadful fate, the long-stifled flame blazed out. She wept, she wrung her hands and tore her hair, and in the transport of her grief discovered* her own lost state whilst she lamented yours.

BARNWELL.
Will all the pain I feel restore thy ease, lovely, unhappy maid? (*Weeping.*) Why did not you let me die and never know it?

TRUEMAN.
It was impossible. She makes no secret of her passion for you and is determined to see you ere you die. She waits for me to introduce her. (*Exit.*)

BARNWELL.
Vain, busy thoughts be still! What avails it to think on what I might have been? I now am—what I've made myself.

Enter Trueman and Maria.

TRUEMAN.
Madam, reluctant I lead you to this dismal scene. This is the seat of misery and guilt. Here awful* justice reserves her public victims. This is the entrance to shameful death.

MARIA.
To this sad place then no improper guest, the abandoned, lost Maria brings despair. And see the subject and cause of all this world of woe: silent and motionless he stands, as if his soul had quitted her abode and the lifeless form alone was left behind. Yet that so perfect that beauty and death, ever at enmity, now seem united there.

BARNWELL.
I groan but murmur not. Just Heaven, I am your own. Do with me what you please.

MARIA.
Why are your streaming eyes still fixed below? As though thou'dst give the greedy earth thy sorrows and rob me of my due. Were happiness within your power, you should bestow it where you pleased, but in your misery I must and will partake.

BARNWELL.
Oh! say not so, but fly, abhor, and leave me to my fate. Consider what you are, how vast your fortune and how bright your fame. Have pity on your youth, your beauty, and unequalled virtue, for which so many noble peers have sighed in vain. Bless with your charms some honorable lord. Adorn with your beauty and by your example improve the English court, that justly claims such merit. So shall I quickly be to you as though I had never been.

MARIA.
When I forget you, I must be so indeed. Reason, choice, virtue, all forbid it. Let women like Millwood, if there be more such women, smile in prosperity and in adversity forsake. Be it the pride of virtue to repair, or to partake, the ruin such have made.

TRUEMAN.
Lovely, ill-fated maid! Was there ever such generous distress before? How must this pierce his grateful heart and aggravate his woes?

BARNWELL.
Ere I knew guilt or shame, when Fortune smiled and when my youthful hopes were at the highest, if then to have raised my thoughts to you had been presumption in me never to have been pardoned, think how much beneath yourself you condescend to regard me now.

MARIA.
Let her blush who, professing love, invades the freedom of your sex's choice and meanly sues in

hopes of a return. Your inevitable fate hath rendered hope impossible as vain. Then why should I fear to avow a passion so just and so disinterested?

TRUEMAN.

If any should take occasion from Millwood's crimes to libel the best and fairest part of the creation, here let them see their error. The most distant hopes of such a tender passion from so bright a maid might add to the happiness of the most happy and make the greatest proud. Yet here 'tis lavished in vain. Though by the rich present the generous donor is undone, he on whom it is bestowed receives no benefit.

BARNWELL.

So the aromatic spices of the East, which all the living covet and esteem, are with unavailing kindness wasted on the dead.

MARIA.

Yes, fruitless is my love and unavailing all my sighs and tears. Can they save thee from approaching death? From such a death? Oh terrible idea! What is her misery and distress who sees the first, last object of her love, for whom alone she'd live, for whom she'd die a thousand, thousand deaths if it were possible, expiring in her arms? Yet she is happy when compared to me. Were millions of worlds mine, I'd gladly give them in exchange for her condition. The most consummate woe is light to mine. The last of curses to other miserable maids is all I ask for my relief, and that's denied me.

TRUEMAN.

Time and reflection cure all ills.

MARIA.

All but this. His dreadful catastrophe virtue herself abhors: to give a holiday to suburb slaves and passing entertain the savage herd who, elbowing each other for a sight, pursue and press upon him like his fate.[16] A mind with piety and resolution armed may smile on death. But public ignominy, everlasting shame—shame, the death of souls—to die a thousand times and yet survive even death itself in never dying infamy, is this to be endured? Can I who live in him and must, each hour of my devoted life, feel all these woes renewed, can I endure this!

TRUEMAN.

Grief has so impaired her spirits, she pants as in the agonies of death.

BARNWELL.

Preserve her, Heaven, and restore her peace. Nor let her death be added to my crimes.

Bell tolls.*

I am summoned to my fate.

Enter keeper and officers.

KEEPER.

Sir, the officers attend you. Millwood is already summoned.

BARNWELL.

Tell 'em I'm ready. And now, my friend, farewell. (*Embracing.*) Support and comfort the best you can this mourning fair. No more. Forget not to pray for me. (*Turning to Maria.*) Would you, bright excellence, permit me the honor of a chaste embrace, the last happiness this world could give were mine.

She inclines towards him; they embrace.

Exalted goodness! Oh turn your eyes from earth, and me, to heaven, where virtue like yours is ever heard. Pray for the peace of my departing soul. Early my race of wickedness began and soon I reached the summit. Ere nature has finished her work and stamped me man, just at the time that others begin to stray, my course is finished. Though short my span of life and few my days, yet count my crimes for years and I have lived whole ages. Thus justice in compassion to mankind cuts off a wretch like me, by one such example to secure thousands from future ruin. Justice and mercy are in Heaven the same. Its utmost severity is mercy to the whole, thereby to cure man's folly and presumption which else would render even infinite mercy vain and ineffectual.

---

16 to give … fate] "Passing" means more than dying. Condemned criminals were carried in carts to the place of execution, which could be miles away from the jail, in processions that typically attracted large crowds of spectators. These were often in a celebratory mood, there more for entertainment than edification.

If any youth, like you, in future times
Shall mourn my fate though he abhor my crimes,
Or tender maid, like you, my tale shall hear
And to my sorrows give a pitying tear,
To each such melting eye and throbbing heart
Would gracious Heaven this benefit impart:
Never to know my guilt nor feel my pain.
Then must you own you ought not to complain,
Since you nor weep, nor shall I die in vain.

Exeunt Barnwell and officers. Enter Blunt, and Lucy.

LUCY.
Heartbreaking sight. Oh wretched, wretched Millwood!

TRUEMAN.
You came from her, then. How is she disposed to meet her fate?

BLUNT.
Who can describe unutterable woe?

LUCY.
She goes to death encompassed with horror, loathing life and yet afraid to die. No tongue can tell her anguish and despair.

TRUEMAN.
Heaven be better to her than her fears. May she prove a warning to others, a monument of mercy in herself.

LUCY.
Oh sorrow insupportable! Break, break my heart.

TRUEMAN.
In vain
With bleeding hearts and weeping eyes we show
A human, gen'rous sense of others' woe,
Unless we mark what drew their ruin on
And, by avoiding that, prevent our own.

FINIS.

Appendix.

The fifth edition (misnamed the sixth) introduced a new final scene in 1735. This begins immediately after what had been until then Barnwell's last exit, with the officers in V.ii. Trueman must now also exit at that point, in order to re-enter at the end of the newly added dialogue and so conclude the play in conversation with Lucy and Blunt, as he does in earlier versions. Maria, with no lines at all in this new scene, would also appear to have exited with Trueman, Barnwell, and the others. As the new scene was not regularly presented on stage,[17] it has been printed here as an appendix.

Scene the last. The place of execution. The gallows and ladders[18] at the farther end of the stage.

A crowd of spectators. Blunt and Lucy.

LUCY.
Heavens! What a throng!

BLUNT.
How terrible is death when thus prepared!

LUCY.
Support them, Heaven. Thou only canst support them. All other help is vain.

OFFICER. (*Within.*)
Make way there, make way, and give the prisoners room.

LUCY.
They are here. Observe them well. How humble and composed young Barnwell seems! But Millwood looks wild, ruffled with passion, confounded and amazed.

Enter Barnwell, Millwood, officers and executioner.

BARNWELL.
See, Millwood, see, our journey's at an end. Life, like a tale that's told, is passed away. That short

17 The whole scene, for instance, is among those "lines distinguished by inverted commas" and "omitted in the representation" in *George Barnwell .... Adapted for Theatrical Representation, as Performed at the Theatres-Royal, Drury-Lane and Covent-Garden. Regulated from the Prompt-Books* in *Bell's British Theatre* (London, 1791-93). It is omitted entirely from the "10th" edition of the play (London, 1760), "as it is acted at the Theatre-Royal in Drury Lane."

18 gallows and ladders] Gallows were typically a stout bar or bars supported by equally stout posts, to which the hangman's rope could be attached. The condemned, nooses around their necks, were compelled to climb up ladders to a sufficient height before being "turned off" with a push or by having the ladders knocked out from under them.

but dark and unknown passage, death, is all the space 'tween us and endless joys or woes eternal.

MILLWOOD.

Is this the end of all my flattering hopes? Were youth and beauty given me for a curse and wisdom only to insure my ruin? They were, they were. Heaven, thou hast done thy worst. Or if thou hast in store some untried plague, somewhat that's worse than shame, despair, and death, unpitied death, confirmed despair, and soul-confounding shame—something that men and angels can't describe and only fiends who bear it can conceive—now, pour it now on this devoted[19] head that I may feel the worst thou canst inflict and bid defiance to thy utmost power.

BARNWELL.

Yet ere we pass the dreadful gulf of death, yet ere you're plunged in everlasting woe, oh bend your stubborn knees and harder heart humbly to deprecate the wrath divine. Who knows but Heaven in your dying moments may bestow that grace and mercy which your life despised.

MILLWOOD.

Why name you mercy to a wretch like me? Mercy's beyond my hope, almost beyond my wish. I can't repent nor ask to be forgiven.

BARNWELL.

Oh think what 'tis to be forever, ever miserable, nor with vain pride oppose a Power that's able to destroy you.

MILLWOOD.

That will destroy me. I feel it will. A deluge of wrath is pouring on my soul. Chains, darkness, wheels, racks, sharp-stinging scorpions, molten lead, and seas of sulpher are light to what I feel.

BARNWELL.

Oh! add not to your vast account despair, a sin more injurious to Heaven than all you've yet committed.

MILLWOOD.

Oh! I have sinned beyond the reach of mercy.

BARNWELL.

Oh say not so. 'Tis blasphemy to think it. As yon bright roof is higher than the earth, so and much more does Heaven's goodness pass our apprehension. Oh, what created being shall presume to circumscribe mercy that knows no bounds?

MILLWOOD.

This yields no hope. Though mercy may be boundless, yet 'tis free. And I was doomed before the world began to endless pains and thou to joys eternal.[20]

BARNWELL.

Oh! gracious Heaven! Extend thy pity to her. Let thy rich mercy flow in plenteous streams to chase her fears and heal her wounded soul.

MILLWOOD.

It will not be. Your prayers are lost in air or else returned perhaps with double blessing to your bosom, but me they help not.

BARNWELL.

Yet hear me, Millwood!

MILLWOOD.

Away, I will not hear thee. I tell thee, youth, I am by Heaven devoted a dreadful instance of its power to punish.

Barnwell seems to pray.

If thou wilt pray, pray for thyself not me.—How doth his fervent soul mount with his words, and both ascend to heaven! That heaven, whose gates are shut with adamantine bars against my prayers, had I the will to pray. I cannot bear it. Sure 'tis the worst of torments to behold others enjoy that bliss that we must never taste.

OFFICER.

The utmost limit of your time's expired.

MILLWOOD.

Encompassed with horror, whither must I go? I would not live, nor die. That I could cease to be! Or ne'er had been!

BARNWELL.

Since peace and comfort are denied her here, may

[19] devoted] formally consigned to evil or destruction, doomed

[20] doomed … eternal] Millwood here invokes the doctrines of foredestination and predestination, which assert that most people are damned but some few are destined to be saved even before they are born, indeed from the beginning of time.

she find mercy where she least expects it, and this be all her hell. From our example may all be taught to fly the first approach of vice, but if o'ertaken
By strong temptation, weakness, or surprise,
Lament their guilt and by repentance rise.
Th'impenitent alone die unforgiven;
To sin's like man, and to forgive like Heaven.

Enter Trueman.

[the scene then continues from "LUCY. Heartbreaking sight. ..." and omitting the first sentence of Trueman's subsequent speech]

Textual Notes

[a] The copy text is the third edition "revised," a 1731 duodecimo (D1), adopted here because it includes substantive changes with authority, including new stage directions. Also consulted were the first edition, a 1731 octavo (O1); modern editions of 1939, revised 1969, based on the fifth edition (Nettleton, Case, and Stone—NCS); of 1965 based on the first edition (McBurney); and of 1993 based on the first edition (Steffenson).

[b] courtiers may] D1, NCS, Steffenson; courtiers, though they should deny us citizens politeness, may O1, McBurney

[c] put him out of countenance] D1, NCS, Steffenson; shock him O1, McBurney

[d] we] D1, NCS, Steffenson; he who trusts heaven O1, McBurney

[e] will] D1, NCS, Steffenson; will; so heaven confirm to me the pardon of my offenses O1, McBurney

[f] brought] D1, NCS, Steffenson; stolen O1, McBurney

[g] amorous youth] D1, NCS, Steffenson; easy fool O1, McBurney

[h] heart.] D1, NCS, Steffenson; heart. How else shall I clear myself? O1, McBurney

[i] commit] D1, NCS, Steffenson; commit, and then betrayed him O1, McBurney

[j] I know ... none.] D1, NCS, Steffenson; I hate you all. I know you and expect no mercy. Nay, I ask for none. I have done nothing I am sorry for. O1, McBurney

[k] seem] D1, NCS, Steffenson; are O1, McBurney

[l] Proceed.] D1, NCS, Steffenson; Go on. How happy am I who live to see this? O1, McBurney

[m] thee.] D1, NCS, Steffenson; thee. [*Lies down by him.*] Upon this rugged couch then let us lie, for well it suits our most deplorable condition. O1, McBurney

[n] place] D1, NCS, Steffenson; earth O1, McBurney

She Stoops to Conquer; or, The Mistakes of a Night[a]

by Oliver Goldsmith (1730-74)

edited by Richard A. Barney

Oliver Goldsmith's *She Stoops to Conquer* has been one of the most beloved English comedies since it was first staged in March 1773. The events leading to its production, however, were anything but promising. Goldsmith had no abiding interest in theater per se, since this play was only the second one he ever wrote, the first being *The Good Natured Man*, which was staged with moderate success in 1768. As with that play, *She Stoops to Conquer* was the brainchild of financial necessity, because Goldsmith wrote it with the hope of a windfall to get himself out of extreme debt, a chronic condition that dogged him most of his life. Moreover, because Goldsmith's play departed from the theatrical fashions of the times, it was initially rejected for production by the managers of the two key London theaters, George Colman of Covent Garden and David Garrick of Drury Lane. Despite his misgivings, Colman later agreed to take on Goldsmith's play, but problems persisted: Colman insisted on several controversial changes to the script; at least two better actors were lost because of the play's staging so late in the season; Goldsmith wrestled with three versions of the epilogue before settling on one that served; and the play's title was decided only at the last minute. Beginning with its opening night, however, *She Stoops to Conquer* proved a blazing success, as if confirming the peculiar logic by which its characters also ultimately thrive despite—or because of—their mutually chaotic lives.

Goldsmith's play seemed risky because, as one eighteenth-century critic explained, it was "taking the field against that monster called Sentimental Comedy." Goldsmith saw his play as an attempt to revive the edgier wit of Restoration comedy in the face of what the Prologue calls the "mawkish drab" of sentimental moralizing. Diggory's clownish antics, Tony Lumpkins' rambunctious capers, and Kate Hard-castle's disguising herself as a barmaid were all "low" elements intended not only for laughs, but also for the purpose of undermining the confident gentility of many of its characters—or of the audience. Hence Charles Marlow's and George Hastings' inability to distinguish Mr. Hardcastle from an innkeeper—the initial "mistake" producing a cascade of comic misrecognitions throughout the play—is part of a larger dynamic in which the usual markers of class distinction become disoriented or fluid at best.

Ultimately, Goldsmith's play did not slay that theatrical dragon, since the genre flourished well into the nineteenth century, partly under the guise of melodrama. What is more, on its own terms, his play does not so much reject sentimental elements as it does juxtapose them with characters' other, venal propensities, usually with a twist of dramatic irony that links the "high" and "low" inextricably to each other. Such a dual perspective is fitting for Goldsmith's aim that comedy should be, as he put it, "perfectly satirical yet perfectly goodnatured." That capacious, comic vision seems to account for the play's enormous success, even during its premiere, when Goldsmith reintegrated the role of individuals who had been initially unhelpful. In a conciliatory gesture for having rejected the play earlier, Garrick ended up contributing the prologue, and Henry Woodward, a leading comic actor who had declined to play Tony Lumpkin, delivered that prologue during the first run. Since then, *She Stoops to Conquer* has been one of the most restaged and reproduced of English comedies, appearing in more than 300 editions since the 1770s.

PROLOGUE

Enter Mr. Woodward, dressed in black and holding a handkerchief to his eyes.

Excuse me, sirs, I pray—I can't yet speak—
I'm crying now—and have been all the week!
'Tis not alone this mourning suit, good masters;
I've that within[1]—for which there are no plasters!
Pray would you know the reason why I'm crying?
The comic muse, long sick, is now a-dying!
And if she goes, my tears will never stop,
For as a player, I can't squeeze out one drop.
I am undone, that's all—shall lose my bread—
I'd rather, but that's nothing—lose my head.
When the sweet maid is laid upon the bier,
Shuter and I shall be chief mourners here.
To her a mawkish drab of spurious breed
Who deals in sentimentals[2] will succeed!
Poor Ned[3] and I are dead to all intents;
We can as soon speak Greek as sentiments!
Both nervous grown, to keep our spirits up
We now and then take down a hearty cup.
What shall we do? If Comedy forsake us,
They'll turn us out, and no one else will take us![4]
But why can't I be moral?—Let me try—
My heart thus pressing—fixed my face and eye
With a sententious look that nothing means
(Faces are blocks,[5] in sentimental scenes).
Thus I begin: "All is not gold that glitters;
Pleasure seems sweet but proves a glass of bitters;
When ign'rance enters, folly is at hand;
Learning is better far than house and land;
Let not your virtue trip, who trips may stumble,
And virtue is not virtue, if she tumble."
    I give it up—morals won't do for me;
To make you laugh I must play tragedy.
One hope remains: hearing the maid was ill,
A doctor[6] comes this night to show his skill.
To cheer her heart and give your muscles motion,
He in five draughts prepared presents a potion:
A kind of magic charm—for be assured,
If you will swallow it, the maid is cured.
But desperate the Doctor and her case is,
If you reject the dose and make wry faces!
This truth he boasts, will boast it while he lives:
No pois'nous drugs are mixed in what he gives.
Should he succeed, you'll give him his degree;
If not, within he will receive no fee!
The college, you, must his pretensions back,
Pronounce him regular, or dub him quack.

DRAMATIS PERSONAE

MEN

Sir Charles Marlow.
Young Marlow, his son.
Hardcastle.
Hastings.
Tony* Lumpkin.
Diggory.
[Roger.]
[Jeremy]
Landlord, servants, etc.

WOMEN

Mrs. Hardcastle.
Miss Hardcastle.
Miss Neville.
Maid.

She Stoops to Conquer; or, The Mistakes of a Night.

Act I, scene i. A chamber in an old-fashioned house.

Enter Mrs. Hardcastle and Mr. Hardcastle.

MRS. HARDCASTLE.
I vow, Mr. Hardcastle, you're very particular. Is there a creature in the whole country but ourselves that does not take a trip to Town* now and then to rub off the rust a little? There's the two Miss Hoggs and our neighbor, Mrs. Grigsby, go to take a month's polishing every winter.

---

1 'Tis not ... within] allusion to *Hamlet* I.ii.77, 85

2 sentimentals] the currently popular dramas, whose pious moralizing is parodied in the lines below

3 Shuter ... Ned] Edward Shuter, the fine comic actor who played Mr. Hardcastle

4 They'll ... take us] slightly misquoted from Buckingham's *The Rehearsal* (1671), II.iv.67-68

5 blocks] wooden heads used as wig stands

6 A doctor] Goldsmith, who used the title after 1763 (including on the titlepage of this play)

HARDCASTLE.

Aye, and bring back vanity and affectation to last them the whole year. I wonder why London cannot keep its own fools at home. In my time, the follies of the Town crept slowly among us, but now they travel faster than a stagecoach. Its fopperies come down not only as inside passengers but in the very basket.[7]

MRS. HARDCASTLE.

Aye, *your* times were fine times, indeed; you have been telling us of *them* for many a long year. Here we live in an old rumbling[8] mansion that looks for all the world like an inn, but that we never see company. Our best visitors are old Mrs. Oddfish, the curate's wife, and little Cripplegate, the lame dancing master, and all our entertainment your old stories of Prince Eugene and the Duke of Marlborough.[9] I hate such old-fashioned trumpery.

HARDCASTLE.

And I love it. I love everything that's old: old friends, old times, old manners, old books, old wine. And I believe, Dorothy, (*Taking her hand.*) you'll own I have been pretty fond of an old wife.

MRS. HARDCASTLE.

Lord, Mr. Hardcastle, you're forever at your Dorothy's and your old wife's. You may be a Darby, but I'll be no Joan,[10] I promise you. I'm not so old as you'd make me, by more than one good year. Add twenty to twenty, and make money of that.

HARDCASTLE.

Let me see, twenty added to twenty, makes just fifty and seven.

MRS. HARDCASTLE.

It's false, Mr. Hardcastle: I was but twenty when I was brought to bed of Tony, that I had by Mr. Lumpkin, my first husband, and he's not come to years of discretion yet.

HARDCASTLE.

Nor ever will, I dare answer for him. Aye, you have taught *him* finely.

MRS. HARDCASTLE.

No matter, Tony Lumpkin has a good fortune. My son is not to live by his learning. I don't think a boy wants* much learning to spend fifteen hundred a year.

HARDCASTLE.

Learning, quotha! A mere composition of tricks and mischief.

MRS. HARDCASTLE.

Humor,* my dear, nothing but humor. Come, Mr. Hardcastle, you must allow the boy a little humor.

HARDCASTLE.

I'd sooner allow him a horsepond.[11] If burning the footmen's shoes, frighting the maids, and worrying the kittens be humor, he has it. It was but yesterday he fastened my wig to the back of my chair, and when I went to make a bow, I popped my bald head in Mrs. Frizzle's face.

MRS. HARDCASTLE.

And am I to blame? The poor boy was always too sickly to do any good. A school would be his death. When he comes to be a little stronger, who knows what a year or two's Latin may do for him?

HARDCASTLE.

Latin for him! A cat and fiddle. No, no, the alehouse and the stable are the only schools he'll ever go to.

MRS. HARDCASTLE.

Well, we must not snub the poor boy now, for I believe we shan't have him long among us. Anybody that looks in his face may see he's consumptive.

HARDCASTLE.

Aye, if growing too fat be one of the symptoms.

MRS. HARDCASTLE.

He coughs sometimes.

HARDCASTLE.

Yes, when his liquor goes the wrong way.

MRS. HARDCASTLE.

I'm actually afraid of his lungs.

---

[7] basket] the outside back seat or baggage carrier of a stagecoach

[8] rumbling] rambling; apparently an old-fashioned usage by 1773

[9] Eugene … Marlborough] leaders (q.v.) during the War of the Spanish Succession (1701-14).

[10] Darby … Joan] old married couple whose happiness is proverbial

[11] horsepond] a pond for watering horses

HARDCASTLE.
And truly so am I, for he sometimes whoops like a speaking trumpet—
Tony hallooing behind the scenes.
Oh there he goes—a very consumptive figure, truly.

Enter Tony, crossing the stage.

MRS. HARDCASTLE.
Tony, where are you going, my charmer? Won't you give papa and I a little of your company, lovey?
TONY.
I'm in haste, mother, I cannot stay.
MRS. HARDCASTLE.
You shan't venture out this raw evening, my dear: you look most shockingly.
TONY.
I can't stay, I tell you. The Three Pigeons expects me down every moment. There's some fun going forward.
HARDCASTLE.
Aye, the alehouse, the old place: I thought so.
MRS. HARDCASTLE.
A low, paltry set of fellows.
TONY.
Not so low neither. There's Dick Muggins the exciseman, Jack Slang the horse doctor, Little Aminadab that grinds the music box,[12] and Tom Twist that spins the pewter platter.
MRS. HARDCASTLE.
Pray my dear, disappoint them for one night at least.
TONY.
As for disappointing *them,* I should not so much mind, but I can't abide to disappoint *myself.*
MRS. HARDCASTLE. (*Detaining him.*)
You shan't go.
TONY.
I will, I tell you.
MRS. HARDCASTLE.
I say you shan't.

TONY.
We'll see which is strongest, you or I.

Exit, hauling her out.

HARDCASTLE.
Aye, there goes a pair that only spoil each other. But is not the whole age in a combination to drive sense and discretion out of doors? There's my pretty darling Kate; the fashions of the times have almost infected her too. By living a year or two in Town, she is as fond of gauze and French frippery as the best of them.

Enter Miss Hardcastle.

Blessings on my pretty innocence! Dressed out as usual, my Kate. Goodness! What a quantity of superfluous silk hast thou got about thee, girl! I could never teach the fools of this age that the indigent world could be clothed out of the trimmings of the vain.
MISS HARDCASTLE.
You know our agreement, sir. You allow me the morning to receive and pay visits and to dress in my own manner, and in the evening, I put on my housewife's dress to please you.
HARDCASTLE.
Well, remember I insist on the terms of our agreement. And by the bye, I believe I shall have occasion to try your obedience this very evening.
MISS HARDCASTLE.
I protest, sir, I don't comprehend your meaning.
HARDCASTLE.
Then to be plain with you, Kate, I expect the young gentleman I have chosen to be your husband from Town this very day. I have his father's letter, in which he informs me his son is set out and that he intends to follow himself shortly after.
MISS HARDCASTLE.
Indeed! I wish I had known something of this before. Bless me, how shall I behave? It's a thousand to one I shan't like him. Our meeting will be so formal and so like a thing of business that I shall find no room for friendship or esteem.
HARDCASTLE.
Depend upon it child, I'll never control your choice, but Mr. Marlow, whom I have pitched upon, is the

[12] Dick Muggins … box] A muggins is a fool; Dick is a tax collector; slang meant "humbug, nonsense"; Aminadab was a Jew, the father-in-law of Aaron in the Bible (Davis).

son of my old friend, Sir Charles Marlow, of whom you have heard me talk so often. The young gentleman has been bred a scholar and is designed for an employment in the service of his country. I am told he's a man of an excellent understanding.

MISS HARDCASTLE.
Is he?

HARDCASTLE.
Very generous.

MISS HARDCASTLE.
I believe I shall like him.

HARDCASTLE.
Young and brave.

MISS HARDCASTLE.
I'm sure I shall like him.

HARDCASTLE.
And very handsome.

MISS HARDCASTLE.
My dear papa, say no more. (*Kissing his hand.*) He's mine, I'll have him.

HARDCASTLE.
And to crown all, Kate, he's one of the most bashful and reserved young fellows in all the world.

MISS HARDCASTLE.
Eh! You have frozen me to death again. That word "reserved" has undone all the rest of his accomplishments. A reserved lover, it is said, always makes a suspicious husband.

HARDCASTLE.
On the contrary, modesty seldom resides in a breast that is not enriched with nobler virtues. It was the very feature in his character that first struck me.

MISS HARDCASTLE.
He must have more striking features to catch me, I promise you. However, if he be so young, so handsome, and so everything, as you mention, I believe he'll do still. I think I'll have him.

HARDCASTLE.
Aye Kate, but there is still an obstacle. It's more than an even wager he may not have *you.*

MISS HARDCASTLE.
My dear papa, why will you mortify one so? Well, if he refuses, instead of breaking my heart at his indifference I'll only break my glass* for its flattery, set my cap to some newer fashion, and look out for some less difficult admirer.

HARDCASTLE.
Bravely* resolved! In the meantime, I'll go prepare the servants for his reception; as we seldom see company, they want* as much training as a company of recruits the first day's muster. (*Exit.*)

MISS HARDCASTLE.
Lud,* this news of Papa's puts me all in a flutter. Young, handsome: these he put last, but I put them foremost. Sensible,[13] good-natured: I like all that. But then, reserved and sheepish: that's much against him. Yet can't he be cured of his timidity by being taught to be proud of his wife? Yes, and can't I— But I vow I'm disposing of the husband before I have secured the lover.

Enter Miss Neville.

I'm glad you're come, Neville, my dear. Tell me, Constance, how do I look this evening? Is there anything whimsical about me? Is it one of my well looking days, child?* Am I in face today?

MISS NEVILLE.
Perfectly, my dear. Yet now I look again—bless me!—sure no accident has happened among the canary birds or the goldfishes. Has your brother or the cat been meddling? Or has the last novel been too moving?

MISS HARDCASTLE.
No, nothing of all this. I have been threatened—I can scarce get it out—I have been threatened with a lover.

MISS NEVILLE.
And his name—

MISS HARDCASTLE.
Is Marlow.

MISS NEVILLE.
Indeed!

MISS HARDCASTLE.
The son of Sir Charles Marlow.

MISS NEVILLE.
As I live, the most intimate friend of Mr. Hastings, *my* admirer. They are never asunder. I believe you must have seen him when we lived in Town.

MISS HARDCASTLE.
Never.

13 Sensible] having sensibility; capable of delicate or tender feeling (*OED*)

MISS NEVILLE.
He's a very singular character, I assure you. Among women of reputation and virtue, he is the modestest man alive, but his acquaintance give him a very different character* among creatures of another stamp: you understand me.

MISS HARDCASTLE.
An odd character, indeed. I shall never be able to manage him. What shall I do? Pshaw, think no more of him but trust to occurrences for success. But how goes on your own affair, my dear? Has my mother been courting you for my brother Tony as usual?

MISS NEVILLE.
I have just come from one of our agreeable tête-à-têtes. She has been saying a hundred tender things and setting off her pretty monster as the very pink of perfection.

MISS HARDCASTLE.
And her partiality is such that she actually thinks him so. A fortune like yours is no small temptation. Besides, as she has the sole management of it, I'm not surprised to see her unwilling to let it go out of the family.

MISS NEVILLE.
A fortune like mine, which chiefly consists in jewels, is no such mighty temptation. But at any rate, if my dear Hastings be but constant, I make no doubt to be too hard for her at last. However, I let her suppose that I am in love with her son, and she never once dreams that my affections are fixed upon another.

MISS HARDCASTLE.
My good brother holds out stoutly. I could almost love him for hating you so.

MISS NEVILLE.
It is a good-natured creature at bottom and, I'm sure, would wish to see me married to anybody but himself. But my aunt's bell rings for our afternoon's walk round the improvements. Allons.[14] Courage is necessary, as our affairs are critical.

MISS HARDCASTLE.
Would it were bedtime and all were well.

Exeunt.

[14] Allons] "Let's go"; an anglicized version of the French, "Allons y"

Scene [ii]. An alehouse room.

Several shabby fellows, with punch and tobacco. Tony at the head of the table, a little higher than the rest: a mallet in his hand.

OMNES.
Hurrah, hurrah, hurrah, bravo.

FIRST FELLOW.
Now gentlemen, silence for a song. The squire is going to knock himself down for a song.

OMNES.
Aye, a song, a song.

TONY.
Then I'll sing you, gentlemen, a song I made upon this alehouse, the Three Pigeons.

Song.

Let schoolmasters puzzle their brain
    With grammar and nonsense and learning;
Good liquor, I stoutly maintain,
    Gives genus[15] a better discerning.
Let them brag of their heathenish gods,
    Their Lethes, their Styxes, and Stygians,
Their *quis*, and their *quaes*, and their *quods*,[16]
    They're all but a parcel of pigeons.
        Toroddle, toroddle, toroll.
When Methodist preachers come down,
    A-preaching that drinking is sinful,
I'll wager the rascals a crown,
    They always preach best with a skinful.
But when you come down with your pence,
    For a slice of their scurvy religion,
I'll leave it to all men of sense,
    But you my good friend are the pigeon.
        Toroddle, toroddle, toroll.
Then come, put the jorum about,
    And let us be merry and clever;
Our hearts and our liquors are stout;
    Here's the Three Jolly Pigeons forever.
Let some cry up woodcock or hare,
    Your bustards, your ducks, and your widgeons

[15] genus] a Lumpkinism for "genius" in the sense of natural capacity or quality of mind

[16] *quis ... quods*] the nominative forms of Latin relative pronouns, Latin being a sign of a learned education

But of all the birds in the air,
Here's a health to the Three Jolly Pigeons.
Toroddle, toroddle, toroll.

OMNES.
Bravo, bravo.

FIRST FELLOW.
The squire has got spunk in him.

SECOND FELLOW.
I loves to hear him sing, bekeays he never gives us nothing that's *low.*

THIRD FELLOW.
Oh damn anything that's *low*, I cannot bear it.

FOURTH FELLOW.
The genteel thing is the genteel thing at any time. If so be that a gentleman bees in a concatenation ackoardingly.[b]

THIRD FELLOW.
I like the maxum[17] of it, Master Muggins. What, though I am obligated to dance a bear, a man may be a gentleman for all that. May this be my poison if my bear ever dances but to the very genteelest of tunes. "Water Parted"[18] or the minuet in *Adriadne.*[19]

SECOND FELLOW.
What a pity it is the squire is not come to his own. It would be well for all the publicans within ten miles round of him.

TONY.
Ecod and so it would, Master Slang. I'd then show what it was to keep choice of company.

SECOND FELLOW.
Oh he takes after his own father for that. To be sure, old Squire Lumpkin was the finest gentleman I ever set my eyes on. For winding the straight horn or beating a thicket for a hare or a wench, he never had his fellow. It was a saying in the place that he kept the best horses, dogs, and girls in the whole county.

TONY.
Ecod, and when I'm of age I'll be no bastard I promise you. I have been thinking of Bett Bouncer and the miller's grey mare to begin with. But come, my boys, drink about and be merry, for you pay no reckoning.

Enter landlord.

Well Stingo, what's the matter?

LANDLORD.
There be two gentlemen in a post chaise at the door. They have lost their way upo'the forest, and they are talking something about Mr. Hardcastle.

TONY.
As sure as can be one of them must be the gentleman that's coming down to court my sister. Do they seem to be Londoners?

LANDLORD.
I believe they may. They look woundily[20] like Frenchmen.

TONY.
Then desire them to step this way, and I'll set them right in a twinkling.

Exit landlord.

Gentlemen, as they mayn't be good enough company for you, step down for a moment, and I'll be with you in the squeezing of a lemon.

Exeunt mob.

TONY.
Father-in-law[21] has been calling me whelp and hound this half year. Now if I pleased, I could be so revenged upon the old grumbletonian.* But then, I'm afraid—afraid of what! I shall soon be worth fifteen hundred a year, and let him frighten me out of *that* if he can.

Enter landlord, conducting Marlow and Hastings.

MARLOW.
What a tedious, uncomfortable day have we had of it! We were told it was but forty miles across the country, and we have come above threescore.

HASTINGS.
And all, Marlow, from that unaccountable reserve of yours, that would not let us enquire more frequently on the way.

17 maxum] maxim

18 "Water Parted"] an aria from Thomas Augustine Arne's opera *Artaxerxes* (1762)

19 minuet … *Adriadne*] The minuet forms part of the overture of Händel's opera *Arianna in Creta* (1734).

20 woundily] extremely

21 Father-in-law] stepfather

MARLOW.
I own, Hastings, I am unwilling to lay myself under an obligation to everyone I meet and often stand the chance of an unmannerly answer.

HASTINGS.
At present, however, we are not likely to receive any answer.

TONY.
No offense, gentlemen. But I'm told you have been enquiring for one Mr. Hardcastle in these[c] parts. Do you know what part of the country you are in?

HASTINGS.
Not in the least, sir, but should thank you for information.

TONY.
Nor the way you came?

HASTINGS.
No sir, but if you can inform us—

TONY.
Why gentlemen, if you know neither the road you are going, nor where you are, nor the road you came, the first thing I have to inform you is that—you have lost your way.

MARLOW.
We wanted* no ghost to tell us that.[22]

TONY.
Pray gentlemen, may I be so bold as to ask the place from whence you came?

MARLOW.
That's not necessary towards directing us where we are to go.

TONY.
No offense, but question for question is all fair, you know. Pray gentlemen, is not this same Hardcastle a cross-grained, old-fashioned, whimsical fellow, with an ugly face, a daughter, and a pretty son?

HASTINGS.
We have not seen the gentleman, but he has the family you mention.

TONY.
The daughter, a tall traipsing,[23] trolloping, talkative maypole; the son, a pretty, well-bred, agreeable youth, that everybody is fond of.

MARLOW.
Our information differs in this. The daughter is said to be well-bred and beautiful; the son, an awkward booby, reared up and spoiled at his mother's apron string.

TONY.
He-he-hem— Then gentlemen, all I have to tell you is that you won't reach Mr. Hardcastle's house this night, I believe.

HASTINGS.
Unfortunate!

TONY.
It's a damned long, dark, boggy, dirty, dangerous way.—Stingo, tell the gentlemen the way to Mr. Hardcastle's. (*Winking upon the landlord.*) Mr. Hardcastle's of Quagmire Marsh, you understand me.

LANDLORD.
Master Hardcastle's! Lock-a-daisy, my masters, you're come a deadly deal wrong! When you came to the bottom of the hill, you should have crossed down Squash Lane.

MARLOW. (*Noting it down.*)[d]
Cross down Squash Lane!

LANDLORD.
Then you were to keep straight forward till you came to four roads.

MARLOW. (*Still noting.*)[e]
Come to where four roads meet!

TONY.
Aye, but you must be sure to take only one of them.

MARLOW.
Oh sir, you're facetious.

TONY.
Then keeping to the right, you are to go sideways till you come upon Crackskull Common: there you must look sharp for the track of the wheel and go forward till you come to Farmer Murrain's[24] barn. Coming to the farmer's barn, you are to turn to the right, and then, to the left, and then to the right about again, till you find out the old mill—

22 We … that] adapted from *Hamlet* I.v.125-26

23 traipsing] going about in a slovenly manner (*OED*)

24 Murrain] a pestilence or plague affecting domestic plants or animals

MARLOW. (*Who had been noting.*)[f]
Zounds, man! we could as soon find out the longitude![25]

HASTINGS.
What's to be done, Marlow?

MARLOW.
This house promises but a poor reception, though perhaps the landlord can accommodate us.

LANDLORD.
Alack master, we have but one spare bed in the whole house.

TONY.
And to my knowledge, that's taken up by three lodgers already. (*After a pause, in which the rest seem disconcerted.*) I have hit it. Don't you think, Stingo, our landlady could accommodate the gentlemen by the fireside, with—three chairs and a bolster?

HASTINGS.
I hate sleeping by the fireside.

MARLOW.
And I detest your three chairs and a bolster.

TONY.
You do, do you?—then let me see—what if you go on a mile further, to the Buck's Head, the old Buck's Head on the hill, one of the best inns in the whole county?

HASTINGS.
Oh ho! so we have escaped an adventure for this night, however.

LANDLORD. (*Apart to Tony.*)
Sure, you ben't sending them to your father's as an inn, be you?

TONY.
Mum, you fool you. Let *them* find that out. (*To them.*) You have only to keep on straight forward, till you come to a large old house by the roadside. You'll see a pair of large horns over the door. That's the sign. Drive up the yard and call stoutly about you.

[25] we could … longitude] Since 1713, Parliament had offered a £20,000 reward for an invention that could determine the longitude at sea. After John Harrison had claimed the prize for his marine chronometer in 1761, the reward was tardily granted in 1773.

HASTINGS.
Sir, we are obliged to you. The servants can't miss the way?

TONY.
No, no, but I tell you, though, the landlord is rich and going to leave off business, so he wants to be thought a gentleman, saving your presence, he! he! he! He'll be for giving you his company, and ecod if you mind him, he'll persuade you that his mother was an alderman and his aunt a justice of peace.

LANDLORD.
A troublesome old blade to be sure, but 'a* keeps as good wines and beds as any in the whole county.[g]

MARLOW.
Well, if he supplies us with these, we shall want* no further connection. We are to turn to the right, did you say?

TONY.
No, no, straight forward. I'll just step myself and show you a piece of the way. (*To the landlord.*) Mum.

LANDLORD.
Ah, bless your heart, for a sweet, pleasant—damned mischievous son of a whore.

Exeunt.

Act II, scene i. An old-fashioned house.

Enter Hardcastle, followed by three or four awkward servants.

HARDCASTLE.
Well, I hope you're perfect in the table exercise I have been teaching you these three days. You all know your posts and your places and can show that you have been used to good company without ever stirring from home.

OMNES.
Aye, aye.

HARDCASTLE.
When company comes, you are not to pop out and stare, and then run in again, like frighted rabbits in a warren.

OMNES.
No, no.

HARDCASTLE.

You, Diggory, whom I have taken from the barn, are to make a show at the side table, and you, Roger, whom I have advanced from the plough, are to place yourself behind *my* chair. But you're not to stand so, with your hands in your pockets. Take your hands from your pockets, Roger—and from your head, you blockhead you. See how Diggory carries his hands. They're a little too stiff, indeed, but that's no great matter.

DIGGORY.

Aye, mind how I hold them. I learned to hold my hands this-aways[h] when I was upon drill for the militia. And so being upon drill—

HARDCASTLE.

You must not be so talkative, Diggory. You must be all attention to the guests. You must hear us talk, and not think of talking; you must see us drink, and not think of drinking; you must see us eat, and not think of eating.

DIGGORY.

By the laws, your worship, that's parfectly unpossible. Whenever Diggory sees yeating going forward, ecod he's always wishing for a mouthful himself.

HARDCASTLE.

Blockhead! Is not a bellyful in the kitchen as good as a bellyful in the parlor? Stay your stomach with that reflection.

DIGGORY.

Ecod, I thank your worship, I'll make a shift to stay my stomach with a slice of cold beef in the pantry.

HARDCASTLE.

Diggory, you are too talkative. Then if I happen to say a good thing or tell a good story at table, you must not all burst out a-laughing, as if you made part of the company.

DIGGORY.

Then ecod, your worship must not tell the story of Auld Grouse in the gun room: I can't help laughing at that—he! he! he!—for the soul of me. We have laughed at that these twenty years—ha! ha! ha!

HARDCASTLE.

Ha! ha! ha! The story is a good one. Well, honest Diggory, you may laugh at that—but still remember to be attentive. Suppose one of the company should call for a glass of wine, how will you behave? "A glass of wine, sir, if you please." Eh, why don't you move?

DIGGORY.

Ecod, your worship, I never have courage till I see the eatables and drinkables brought upo'the table, and then I'm as bauld as a lion.

HARDCASTLE.

What, will nobody move?

FIRST SERVANT.

I'm not to leave this pleace.

SECOND SERVANT.

I'm sure it's no pleace of mine.

THIRD SERVANT.

Nor mine, for sartain.

DIGGORY.

Wauns,[26] and I'm sure it canna be mine.

HARDCASTLE.

You numbskulls! and so while, like your betters, you are quarreling for places, the guests must be starved. Oh you dunces! I find I must begin all over again.—But don't I hear a coach drive into the yard? To your posts, you blockheads. I'll go in the meantime and give my old friend's son a hearty reception at the gate. (*Exit.*)

DIGGORY.

By the elevens,[27] my pleace is gone quite out of my head.

ROGER.

I know that my pleace is to be everywhere.

FIRST SERVANT.

Where the devil is mine?

SECOND SERVANT.

My pleace is to be nowhere at all, and so I's go about my business.

Exeunt servants, running about as if frighted, different ways. Enter servant with candles, showing in Marlow and Hastings.

SERVANT.

Welcome, gentlemen, very welcome. This way.

---

26 Wauns] (God's) wounds; a mild oath

27 By the elevens] obscure exclamation. Davis speculates: "'Heavens'? 'Apostles' (minus Judas)?"

HASTINGS.

After the disappointments of the day, welcome once more, Charles, to the comforts of a clean room and a good fire. Upon my word, a very well-looking house—antique but creditable.

MARLOW.

The usual fate of a large mansion. Having first ruined the master by good housekeeping, it at last comes to levy contributions as an inn.

HASTINGS.

As you say, we passengers are to be taxed to pay all these fineries. I have often seen a good sideboard or a marble chimney piece, though not actually put in the bill, inflame a reckoning confoundedly.

MARLOW.

Travelers, George, must pay in all places. The only difference is, that in good inns, you pay dearly for luxuries; in bad inns, you are fleeced and starved.

HASTINGS.

You have lived pretty much among them. In truth, I have been often surprised that you, who have seen so much of the world, with your natural good sense and your many opportunities could never yet acquire a requisite share of assurance.

MARLOW.

The Englishman's malady. But tell me, George, where could I have learned that assurance you talk of? My life has been chiefly spent in a college or an inn,[28] in seclusion from that lovely part of the creation that chiefly teach men confidence. I don't know that I was ever familiarly acquainted with a single modest woman—except my mother. But among females of another class, you know—

HASTINGS.

Aye, among them you are impudent enough of all conscience.

MARLOW.

They are of *us* you know.

HASTINGS.

But in the company of women of reputation I never saw such an idiot, such a trembler; you look for all the world as if you wanted an opportunity of stealing out of the room.

MARLOW.

Why man, that's because I *do* want to steal out of the room. Faith, I have often formed a resolution to break the ice and rattle away at any rate. But I don't know how, a single glance from a pair of fine eyes has totally overset my resolution. An impudent fellow may counterfeit modesty, but I'll be hanged if a modest man can ever counterfeit impudence.

HASTINGS.

If you could but say half the fine things to them that I have heard you lavish upon the barmaid of an inn or even a college bedmaker—

MARLOW.

Why George, I can't say fine things to them. They freeze, they petrify me. They may talk of a comet or a burning mountain or some such bagatelle. But to me, a modest woman, dressed out in all her finery, is the most tremendous object of the whole creation.

HASTINGS.

Ha! ha! ha! At this rate, man, how can you ever expect to marry!

MARLOW.

Never, unless as among kings and princes, my bride were to be courted by proxy. If indeed, like an Eastern bridegroom, one were to be introduced to a wife he never saw before, it might be endured. But to go through all the terrors of a formal courtship, together with the episode of aunts, grandmothers, and cousins, and at last to blurt out the broad, staring[29] question, of, "Madam, will you marry me?"—no, no, that's a strain much above me I assure you.

HASTINGS.

I pity you. But how do you intend behaving to the lady you are come down to visit at the request of your father?

MARLOW.

As I behave to all other ladies: bow very low, answer yes or no to all her demands. But for the rest, I don't think I shall venture to look in her face till I see my father's again.

HASTINGS.

I'm surprised that one who is so warm a friend can be so cool a lover.

---

28 inn] one of the Inns of Court*

29 staring] obvious, conspicuous

MARLOW.

To be explicit, my dear Hastings, my chief inducement down was to be instrumental in forwarding your happiness, not my own. Miss Neville loves you; the family don't know you; as my friend you are sure of a reception, and let honor do the rest.

HASTINGS.

My dear Marlow! But I'll suppress the emotion. Were I a wretch, meanly seeking to carry off a fortune, you should be the last man in the world I would apply to for assistance. But Miss Neville's person is all I ask, and that is mine, both from her deceased father's consent and her own inclination.

MARLOW.

Happy man! You have talents and art to captivate any woman. I'm doomed to adore the sex and yet to converse with the only part of it I despise. This stammer in my address and this awkward prepossessing[i][30] visage of mine can never permit me to soar above the reach of a milliner's prentice or one of the duchesses of Drury Lane.[31]—Pshaw! this fellow here to interrupt us.

Enter Hardcastle.

HARDCASTLE.

Gentlemen, once more you are heartily welcome. Which is Mr. Marlow? Sir, you're heartily welcome. It's not my way, you see, to receive my friends with my back to the fire. I like to give them a hearty reception in the old style at my gate. I like to see their horses and trunks taken care of.

MARLOW. (*Aside.*)

He has got our names from the servants already. (*To him.*) We approve your caution and hospitality, sir. (*To Hastings.*) I have been thinking, George, of changing our traveling dresses in the morning. I am grown confoundedly ashamed of mine.

HARDCASTLE.

I beg, Mr. Marlow, you'll use no ceremony in this house.

HASTINGS.

I fancy, Charles,[j] you're right: the first blow is half the battle. I intend opening the campaign with the white and gold.

HARDCASTLE.

Mr. Marlow—Mr. Hastings—gentlemen—pray be under no constraint in this house. This is Liberty Hall, gentlemen. You may do just as you please here.

MARLOW.

Yet, George, if we open the campaign too fiercely at first, we may want* ammunition before it is over. I think to reserve the embroidery to secure a retreat.

HARDCASTLE.

Your talking of a retreat, Mr. Marlow, puts me in mind of the Duke of Marlborough, when we went to besiege Denain.[32] He first summoned the garrison.

MARLOW.

Don't you think the *ventre d'or*[33] waistcoat will do with the plain brown?

HARDCASTLE.

He first summoned the garrison, which might consist of about five thousand men—

HASTINGS.

I think not: brown and yellow mix but very poorly.

HARDCASTLE.

I say, gentlemen, as I was telling you, he summoned the garrison, which might consist of about five thousand men—

MARLOW.

The girls like finery.

HARDCASTLE.

Which might consist of about five thousand men, well appointed with stores, ammunition, and other implements of war. "Now," says the Duke of Marlborough to George Brooks, that stood next

---

30 prepossessing] Marlow is using this word in its older sense of "creating prejudice." He may be alluding to his propensity to blush.

31 duchesses of Drury Lane] women of dubious repute, including prostitutes, who frequented the theater on Drury Lane, often claiming to be nobility

32 Marlborough ... Denain] During the War of the Spanish Succession the French defeated the Allies (England, Netherlands, and Prussia) in Denain, France in 1712. It was Lord Albemarle who led the Allies during that battle, rather than Marlborough, who was not even present because he had been dismissed in 1711.

33 *ventre d'or*] gold-fronted

to him—you must have heard of George Brooks—"I'll pawn my dukedom," says he, "but I take that garrison without spilling a drop of blood." So—

MARLOW.

What, my good friend, if you gave us a glass of punch in the meantime? It would help us to carry on the siege with vigor.

HARDCASTLE.

Punch, sir! (*Aside.*) This is the most unaccountable kind of modesty I ever met with.

MARLOW.

Yes sir, punch. A glass of warm punch after our journey will be comfortable. This is Liberty Hall, you know.

HARDCASTLE.

Here's cup,[34] sir.

MARLOW. (*Aside.*)

So this fellow, in his Liberty Hall, will only let us have just what he pleases.

HARDCASTLE. (*Taking the cup.*)

I hope you'll find it to your mind. I have prepared it with my own hands, and I believe you'll own the ingredients are tolerable. Will you be so good as to pledge me, sir? Here, Mr. Marlow, here is to our better acquaintance. (*Drinks.*)

MARLOW. (*Aside.*)

A very impudent fellow this! But he's a character, and I'll humor him a little.—Sir, my service to you. (*Drinks.*)

HASTINGS. (*Aside.*)

I see this fellow wants to give us his company and forgets that he's an innkeeper before he has learned to be a gentleman.

MARLOW.

From the excellence of your cup, my old friend, I suppose you have a good deal of business in this part of the country. Warm work now and then at elections, I suppose.

HARDCASTLE.

No sir, I have long given that work over. Since our betters have hit upon the expedient of electing each other, there's no business for us that sell ale.[35]

HASTINGS.

So then you have no turn for politics, I find.

HARDCASTLE.

Not in the least. There was a time, indeed, I fretted myself about the mistakes of government, like other people, but finding myself every day grow more angry and the government growing no better, I left it to mend itself. Since that, I no more trouble my head about Hyder Ali,[36] or Ali Kahn,[37] than about Ally Croaker.[38] Sir, my service to you.

HASTINGS.

So that with eating above stairs, and drinking below, with receiving your friends without, and amusing them within,[k] you lead a good pleasant bustling life of it.

HARDCASTLE.

I do stir about a great deal, that's certain. Half the differences of the parish are adjusted in this very parlor.

MARLOW. (*After drinking.*)

And you have an argument in your cup, old gentleman, better than any in Westminster Hall.*

HARDCASTLE.

Aye, young gentleman, that, and a little philosophy.

MARLOW. (*Aside.*)

Well, this is the first time I ever heard of an innkeeper's philosophy.

HASTINGS.

So then, like an experienced general, you attack them on every quarter. If you find their reason manageable, you attack it with your philosophy; if you find they have no reason, you attack them with this. Here's your health, my philosopher. (*Drinks.*)

HARDCASTLE.

Good, very good, thank you, ha! ha! Your Generalship puts me in mind of Prince Eugene, when he fought the Turks at the Battle of Belgrade.[39] You shall hear.

---

[34] cup] flavored, sweetened wine

[35] us ... ale] referring to the practice of electoral candidates giving free drinks to voters

[36] Hyder Ali] maharaja of Mysore in India, who defeated the English in 1767

[37] Ali Khan] the subahdar of Bengal known for his cruelty

[38] Ally Croker] a figure in a popular Irish ballad

[39] Prince Eugene ... Belgrade] Eugene led the military of Holy Roman Emperor Charles VI in assisting Venice

MARLOW.
Instead of the Battle of Belgrade, I believe it's almost time to talk about supper. What has your philosophy got in the house for supper?

HARDCASTLE.
For supper, sir! (*Aside.*) Was ever such a request to a man in his own house!

MARLOW.
Yes sir, supper sir. I begin to feel an appetite. I shall make devilish work tonight in the larder, I promise you.

HARDCASTLE. (*Aside.*)
Such a brazen dog sure never my eyes beheld. (*To him.*) Why really, sir, as for supper I can't well tell. My Dorothy and the cook maid settle these things between them. I leave these kind of things entirely to them.

MARLOW.
You do, do you?

HARDCASTLE.
Entirely. By the bye, I believe they are in actual consultation upon what's for supper this moment in the kitchen.

MARLOW.
Then I beg they'll admit *me* as one of their privy council. It's a way I have got. When I travel, I always choose to regulate my own supper. Let the cook be called. No offence I hope, sir.

HARDCASTLE.
Oh no, sir, none in the least, yet I don't know how, our Bridget, the cook maid, is not very communicative upon these occasions. Should we send for her, she might scold us all out of the house.

HASTINGS.
Let's see your list of the larder, then. I ask it as a favor. I always match my appetite to my bill of fare.

MARLOW. (*To Hardcastle, who looks at them with surprise.*)
Sir, he's very right, and it's my way too.

HARDCASTLE.
Sir, you have a right to command here.—Here, Roger, bring us the bill of fare for tonight's supper. I believe it's drawn out.—Your manner, Mr. Hastings, puts me in mind of my uncle, Colonel Wallop. It was a saying of his, that no man was sure of his supper till he had eaten it.

Enter Roger, who gives a bill of fare[l] *[and exits].*

HASTINGS. (*Aside.*)
All upon the high ropes![40] His uncle a Colonel! We shall soon hear of his mother being a justice of peace. But let's hear the bill of fare.

MARLOW. (*Perusing.*)
What's here? For the first course; for the second course; for the dessert. The devil, sir, do you think we have brought down the whole Joiners Company or the Corporation of Bedford[41] to eat up such a supper? Two or three little things, clean and comfortable, will do.

HASTINGS.
But, let's hear it.

MARLOW. (*Reading.*)
For the first course at the top, a pig's face and prune sauce.

HASTINGS.
Damn your pig's face, I say.

MARLOW.
And damn your prune sauce, say I.

HARDCASTLE.
And yet, gentlemen, to men that are hungry, a pig's face[m] with prune sauce is very good eating.

MARLOW.
At the bottom, a calf's tongue and brains.

HASTINGS.
Let your brains be knocked out, my good sir, I don't like them.

MARLOW.
Or you may clap them on a plate by themselves. I do.

HARDCASTLE. (*Aside.*)
Their impudence confounds me. (*To them.*) Gentlemen, you are my guests, make what

---

during the Turkish War of 1715-18. He took Belgrade in 1717.

40 All ... ropes!] on his high horse

41 Joiners Company ... Corporation of Bedford] The Joiners Company was a guild of woodworkers; the Corporation was either the city council or an organization of merchants. All three groups sponsored well-known banquets.

alterations you please. Is there anything else you wish to retrench or alter, gentlemen?

MARLOW.

Item: a pork pie, a boiled rabbit and sausages, a florentine,[42] a shaking pudding,[43] and a dish of tiff—taff—taffety cream![44]

HASTINGS.

Confound your made dishes,[45] I shall be as much at a loss in this house as at a green and yellow dinner at the French ambassador's table. I'm for plain eating.

HARDCASTLE.

I'm sorry, gentlemen, that I have nothing you like, but if there be anything you have a particular fancy to—

MARLOW.

Why really, sir, your bill of fare is so exquisite that any one part of it is full as good as another. Send us what you please. So much for supper. And now to see that our beds are aired and properly taken care of.

HARDCASTLE.

I entreat you'll leave all that to me. You shall not stir a step.

MARLOW.

Leave that to you! I protest, sir, you must excuse me, I always look to these things myself.

HARDCASTLE.

I must insist, sir, you'll make yourself easy on that head.

MARLOW.

You see I'm resolved on it. (*Aside.*) A very troublesome fellow this, as ever I met with.

HARDCASTLE.

Well sir, I'm resolved at least to attend you. (*Aside.*) This may be modern modesty, but I never saw anything look so like old-fashioned impudence.

Exeunt Marlow and Hardcastle.

HASTINGS.

So I find this fellow's civilities begin to grow troublesome. But who can be angry at those assiduities which are meant to please him?—Hah! what do I see? Miss Neville, by all that's happy!

Enter Miss Neville.

MISS NEVILLE.

My dear Hastings! To what unexpected good fortune, to what accident am I to ascribe this happy meeting?

HASTINGS.

Rather let me ask the same question, as I could never have hoped to meet my dearest Constance at an inn.

MISS NEVILLE.

An inn! Sure you mistake! My aunt, my guardian, lives here. What could induce you to think this house an inn?

HASTINGS.

My friend Mr. Marlow, with whom I came down, and I, have been sent here as to an inn, I assure you. A young fellow whom we accidentally met at a house hard by directed us hither.

MISS NEVILLE.

Certainly it must be one of my hopeful cousin's tricks, of whom you have heard me talk so often, ha! ha! ha! ha!

HASTINGS.

He whom your aunt intends for you? he of whom I have such just apprehensions?

MISS NEVILLE.

You have nothing to fear from him, I assure you. You'd adore him if you knew how heartily he despises me. My aunt knows it too and has undertaken to court me for him and actually begins to think she has made a conquest.

HASTINGS.

Thou dear dissembler! You must know, my Constance, I have just seized this happy opportunity of my friend's visit here to get admittance into the family. The horses that carried us down are now fatigued with their journey, but they'll soon be refreshed, and then if my dearest

---

42 florentine] a deepdish pie or tart made of meat and spices

43 shaking pudding] eggs, cream, and flour boiled with flavorings

44 taffety cream] a dish of cream made with ground spices and sugar

45 made dishes] dishes made by combining several ingredients, considered by the English as either refined eating or the stuff of excessive foreign appetites

girl will trust in her faithful Hastings, we shall soon be landed in France, where even among slaves the laws of marriage are respected.[46]

MISS NEVILLE.

I have often told you that, though ready to obey you, I yet should leave my little fortune behind with reluctance. The greatest part of it was left me by my uncle, the India Director,[47] and chiefly consists in jewels. I have been for some time persuading my aunt to let me wear them. I fancy I'm very near succeeding. The instant they are put into my possession you shall find me ready to make them and myself yours.

HASTINGS.

Perish the baubles! Your person is all I desire. In the meantime, my friend Marlow must not be let into his mistake. I know the strange reserve of his temper is such that, if abruptly informed of it, he would instantly quit the house before our plan was ripe for execution.

MISS NEVILLE.

But how shall we keep him in the deception? Miss Hardcastle is just returned from walking. What if we still continue to deceive him?—This, this way— (*They confer.*)

Enter Marlow.

MARLOW.

The assiduities of these good people tease me beyond bearing. My host seems to think it ill manners to leave me alone, and so he claps not only himself but his old-fashioned wife on my back. They talk of coming to sup with us too, and then, I suppose, we are to run the gauntlet through all the rest of the family.—What have we got here!

HASTINGS.

My dear Charles! Let me congratulate you! The most fortunate accident! Who do you think is just alighted?

MARLOW.

Cannot guess.

HASTINGS.

Our mistresses, my boy,[n] Miss Hardcastle and Miss Neville. Give me leave to introduce Miss Constance Neville to your acquaintance. Happening to dine in the neighborhood, they called, on their return to take fresh horses, here. Miss Hardcastle has just stepped into the next room and will be back in an instant. Wasn't it lucky, eh?

MARLOW. (*Aside.*)

I have just been mortified enough of all conscience, and here comes something to complete my embarrassment.

HASTINGS.

Well! but wasn't it the most fortunate thing in the world?

MARLOW.

Oh yes! Very fortunate—a most joyful encounter—but our dresses, George, you know, are in disorder. What if we should postpone the happiness till tomorrow? Tomorrow at her own house? It will be every bit as convenient—and rather more respectful—tomorrow let it be. (*Offering* to go.*)

MISS NEVILLE.

By no means, sir. Your ceremony will displease her. The disorder of your dress will show the ardor of your impatience. Besides, she knows you are in the house and will permit you to see her.

MARLOW.

Oh! the devil! how shall I support it? Hem! hem! Hastings, you must not go. You are to assist me, you know. I shall be confoundedly ridiculous. Yet, hang it! I'll take courage. Hem!

HASTINGS.

Pshaw, man! it's but the first plunge, and all's over. She's but a woman, you know.

MARLOW.

And of all women, she that I dread most to encounter!

[46] the laws of marriage] a reference to the unpopular Royal Marriage Act of 1772, which prohibited relations of the monarch from marrying at will. William Henry, Duke of Gloucester and brother to George III, had been partly responsible for provoking this law because of his marriage to Lady Waldegrave; when he attended the play's first performance, the audience enthusiastically applauded this line, perceiving it as an attack on the recent legislation.

[47] the India Director] Director of the East India Company

Enter Miss Hardcastle as returned from walking, with a bonnet, etc.

HASTINGS. (*Introducing them.*)
Miss Hardcastle, Mr. Marlow, I'm proud of bringing two persons of such merit together, that only want* to know, to esteem each other.

MISS HARDCASTLE. (*Aside.*)
Now, for meeting my modest gentleman with a demure face and quite in his own manner. (*After a pause, in which he appears very uneasy and disconcerted.*) I'm glad of your safe arrival, sir. I'm told you had some accidents by the way.

MARLOW.
Only a few madam. Yes, we had some. Yes madam, a good many accidents, but should be sorry—madam—or rather glad of any accidents—that are so agreeably concluded. Hem!

HASTINGS. (*To him.*)
You never spoke better in your whole life. Keep it up, and I'll insure you the victory.

MISS HARDCASTLE.
I'm afraid you flatter, sir. You that have seen so much of the finest company can find little entertainment in an obscure corner of the country.

MARLOW. (*Gathering courage.*)
I have lived, indeed, in the world, madam, but I have kept very little company. I have been but an observer upon life, madam, while others were enjoying it.

MISS NEVILLE.
But that, I am told, is the way to enjoy it at last.

HASTINGS. (*To him.*)
Cicero never spoke better. Once more, and you are confirmed in assurance forever.

MARLOW. (*To him.*)
Hem! Stand by me, then, and when I'm down, throw in a word or two to set me up again.

MISS HARDCASTLE.
An observer, like you, upon life, were, I fear, disagreeably employed, since you must have had much more to censure than to approve.

MARLOW.
Pardon me, madam. I was always willing to be amused. The folly of most people is rather an object of mirth than uneasiness.

HASTINGS. (*To him.*)
Bravo, bravo. Never spoke so well in your whole life.—Well! Miss Hardcastle, I see that you and Mr. Marlow are going to be very good company. I believe our being here will but embarrass the interview.

MARLOW.
Not in the least, Mr. Hastings. We like your company of all things. (*To him.*) Zounds! George, sure you won't go? How can you leave us?

HASTINGS.
Our presence will but spoil conversation, so we'll retire to the next room. (*To him.*) You don't consider, man, that we are to manage a little tête-à-tête of our own.

Exeunt [Hastings and Miss Neville].

MISS HARDCASTLE. (*After a pause.*)
But you have not been wholly an observer, I presume, sir: the ladies I should hope have employed some part of your addresses.

MARLOW. (*Relapsing into timidity.*)
Pardon me, madam, I—I—I—as yet have° studied—only—to—deserve them.

MISS HARDCASTLE.
And that some say is the very worst way to obtain them.

MARLOW.
Perhaps so, madam. But I love to converse only with the more grave and sensible part of the sex.—But I'm afraid I grow tiresome.

MISS HARDCASTLE.
Not at all, sir, there is nothing I like so much as grave conversation myself; I could hear it forever. Indeed, I have often been surprised how a man of *sentiment* could ever admire those light, airy pleasures where nothing reaches the heart.

MARLOW.
It's—a disease—of the mind, madam. In the variety of tastes there must be some who, wanting* a relish—for—um—a—um—

MISS HARDCASTLE.
I understand you, sir. There must be some who, wanting* a relish for refined pleasures, pretend to despise what they are incapable of tasting.

MARLOW.

My meaning, madam, but infinitely better expressed. And I can't help observing—a—

MISS HARDCASTLE. (*Aside.*)

Who could ever suppose this fellow impudent upon some occasions? (*To him.*) You were going to observe, sir—

MARLOW.

I was observing, madam—I protest, madam, I forget what I was going to observe.

MISS HARDCASTLE. (*Aside.*)

I vow and so do I. (*To him.*) You were observing, sir, that in this age of hypocrisy—something about hypocrisy, sir.

MARLOW.

Yes, madam. In this age of hypocrisy there are few who upon strict enquiry do not—a—a—a—

MISS HARDCASTLE.

I understand you perfectly, sir.

MARLOW. (*Aside.*)

Egad! and that's more than I do myself.

MISS HARDCASTLE.

You mean that in this hypocritical age there are few that do not condemn in public what they practice in private and think they pay every debt to virtue when they praise it.

MARLOW.

True, madam. Those who have most virtue in their mouths have least of it in their bosoms. But I'm sure I tire you, madam.

MISS HARDCASTLE.

Not in the least, sir. There's something so agreeable and spirited in your manner, such life and force—pray sir, go on.

MARLOW.

Yes, madam. I was saying—that there are some occasions—when a total want* of courage, madam, destroys all the—and puts us—upon a—a—a—

MISS HARDCASTLE.

I agree with you entirely, a want* of courage upon some occasions assumes the appearance of ignorance and betrays us when we most want to excel. I beg you'll proceed.

MARLOW.

Yes, madam. Morally speaking, madam— But I see Miss Neville expecting us in the next room. I would not intrude for the world.

MISS HARDCASTLE.

I protest, sir, I never was more agreeably entertained in all my life. Pray go on.

MARLOW.

Yes, madam. I was— But she beckons us to join her. Madam, shall I do myself the honor to attend you?

MISS HARDCASTLE.

Well then, I'll follow.

MARLOW (*aside.*)

This pretty smooth dialogue has done for me. (*Exit.*)

MISS HARDCASTLE.

Ha! ha! ha! Was there ever such a sober, sentimental interview? I'm certain he scarce looked in my face the whole time. Yet the fellow, but for his unaccountable bashfulness, is pretty well too. He has good sense, but then so buried in his fears, that it fatigues one more than ignorance. If I could teach him a little confidence, it would be doing somebody that I know of a piece of service. But who is that somebody?—that, faith, is a question I can scarce answer. (*Exit.*)

Enter Tony and Miss Neville, followed by Mrs. Hardcastle and Hastings.

TONY.

What do you follow me for, Cousin Con? I wonder you're not ashamed to be so very engaging.

MISS NEVILLE.

I hope, Cousin, one may speak to one's own relations and not be to blame.

TONY.

Aye, but I know what sort of a relation you want to make me, though, but it won't do. I tell you, Cousin Con, it won't do, so I beg you'll keep your distance, I want no nearer relationship. (*She follows coquetting him to the back scene.*)

MRS. HARDCASTLE.

Well! I vow, Mr. Hastings, you are very entertaining. There's nothing in the world I love to talk of so much as London, and the fashions, though I was never there myself.

HASTINGS.

Never there! You amaze me! From your air and manner, I concluded you had been bred all your life either at Ranelagh,[48] St. James's,* or Tower Wharf.[49]

MRS. HARDCASTLE.

Oh, sir! you're only pleased to say so. We country persons can have no manner at all. I'm in love with the Town, and that serves to raise me above some of our neighboring rustics. But who can have a manner that has never seen the Pantheon,* the Grotto Gardens, the Borough,[50] and such places where the nobility chiefly resort? All I can do is to enjoy London at second hand. I take care to know every tête-à-tête from the *Scandalous Magazine*[51] and have all the fashions, as they come out, in a letter from the two Miss Rickets of Crooked Lane. Pray, how do you like this head,[52] Mr. Hastings?

HASTINGS.

Extremely elegant and dégagé, upon my word, madam. Your friseur is a Frenchman, I suppose?

MRS. HARDCASTLE.

I protest I dressed it myself from a print in the *Ladies Memorandum Book*[53] for the last year.

HASTINGS.

Indeed. Such a head in a side box at the playhouse would draw as many gazers as my Lady Mayoress at a city ball.

MRS. HARDCASTLE.

I vow, since inoculation began,[54] there is no such thing to be seen as a plain woman; so one must dress a little particular, or one may escape in the crowd.

HASTINGS.

But that can never be your case, madam, in any dress. (*Bowing.*)

MRS. HARDCASTLE.

Yet, what signifies *my* dressing when I have such a piece of antiquity by my side as Mr. Hardcastle: all I can say will never argue down a single button from his clothes. I have often wanted him to throw off his great flaxen wig and, where he was bald, to plaster it over, like my Lord Pately, with powder.

HASTINGS.

You are right, madam, for as among the ladies, there are none ugly, so among the men, there are none old.

MRS. HARDCASTLE.

But what do you think his answer was? Why, with his usual Gothic vivacity, he said I only wanted him to throw off his wig to convert it into a tête for my own wearing.

HASTINGS.

Intolerable! At your age you may wear what you please, and it must become you.

MRS. HARDCASTLE.

Pray Mr. Hastings, what do you take to be the most fashionable age about Town?

HASTINGS.

Some time ago, forty was all the mode, but I'm told the ladies intend to bring up fifty for the ensuing winter.

MRS. HARDCASTLE.

Seriously? Then I shall be too young for the fashion.

HASTINGS.

No lady begins now to put on jewels till she's past forty. For instance, Miss there, in a polite circle, would be considered as a child, as a mere maker of samplers.

MRS. HARDCASTLE.

And yet Mrs.* Niece thinks herself as much a woman, and is as fond of jewels, as the oldest of us all.

HASTINGS.

Your niece, is she? And that young gentleman, a brother of yours, I should presume?

MRS. HARDCASTLE.

My son, sir. They are contracted to each other.

---

48 Ranelagh] highly fashionable center for the upper classes

49 Tower Wharf] a hangout of the lower classes

50 Grotto Gardens ... Borough] the former a rendezvous for the "vulgar" classes and, by 1773, the latter (in Southwark) for wealthy tradesmen

51 tête ... *Magazine*] a reference to the monthly articles in the *Town and Country Magazine* about scandals, accompanied by engravings of the heads of a well-known man and his mistress

52 this head] this hairstyle, probably shaped around an internal frame

53 *Ladies Memorandum Book*] a magazine of fashions that first appeared in January 1773

54 inoculation began] 1721 in England and typically available only for the well off

Observe their little sports. They fall in and out ten times a day, as if they were man and wife already. (*To them.*) Well Tony, child, what soft things are you saying to your cousin Constance this evening?

TONY.

I have been saying no soft things, but that it's very hard to be followed about so. Ecod! I've not a place in the house now that's left to myself but the stable.

MRS. HARDCASTLE.

Never mind him, Con, my dear. He's in another story behind your back.

MISS NEVILLE.

There's something generous in my cousin's manner. He falls out before faces to be forgiven in private.

TONY.

That's a damned, confounded—crack.[55]

MRS. HARDCASTLE.

Ah! he's a sly one. Don't you think they're like each other about the mouth, Mr. Hastings? The Blenkinsop mouth to a T. They're of a size too.—Back to back, my pretties, that Mr. Hastings may see you. Come Tony.

TONY.

You had as good not make me, I tell you. (*Measuring.*)

MISS NEVILLE.

Oh Lud!* he has almost cracked my head.

MRS. HARDCASTLE.

Oh the monster! For shame, Tony. You a man, and behave so!

TONY.

If I'm a man, let me have my fortin.[56] Ecod! I'll not be made a fool of no longer.

MRS. HARDCASTLE.

Is this, ungrateful boy, all that I'm to get for the pains I have taken in your education? I that have rocked you in your cradle and fed that pretty mouth with a spoon! Did not I work that waistcoat to make you genteel? Did not I prescribe for you every day and weep while the receipt* was operating?

TONY.

Ecod! you had reason to weep, for you have been dosing me ever since I was born. I have gone through every receipt in the *Complete Houswife*[57] ten times over, and you have thoughts of coursing me through *Quincy*[58] next spring. But ecod! I tell you, I'll not be made a fool of no longer.

MRS. HARDCASTLE.

Wasn't it all for your good, viper? Wasn't it all for your good?

TONY.

I wish you'd let me and my good alone then. Snubbing this way when I'm in spirits. If I'm to have any good, let it come of itself, not to keep dinging it, dinging it into one so.

MRS. HARDCASTLE.

That's false: I never see you when you're in spirits. No Tony, you then go to the alehouse or kennel. I'm never to be delighted with your agreeable, wild notes, unfeeling monster!

TONY.

Ecod! Mamma, your own notes are the wildest of the two.

MRS. HARDCASTLE.

Was ever the like? But I see he wants to break my heart, I see he does.

HASTINGS.

Dear madam, permit me to lecture the young gentleman a little. I'm certain I can persuade him to his duty.

MRS. HARDCASTLE.

Well! I must retire.—Come, Constance, my love.—You see, Mr. Hastings, the wretchedness of my situation. Was ever poor woman so plagued with a dear, sweet, pretty, provoking, undutiful boy!

Exeunt Mrs. Hardcastle and Miss Neville.

TONY. (*Singing.*)

"There was a young man riding by, and fain would have his will. Rang do didlo dee." Don't mind her. Let her cry. It's the comfort of her heart. I have

55 crack] a lie; an antiquated expression by the 1770s

56 fortin] fortune

57 *Complete Housewife*] a popular handbook of cooking recipes and medical treatments used in eighteenth-century households

58 *Quincy*] Dr. John Quincy's *Compleat English Dispensatory*, first published in 1718 and reissued numerous times thereafter

seen her and sister cry over a book for an hour together, and they said they liked the book the better the more it made them cry.

HASTINGS.

Then you're no friend to the ladies, I find, my pretty young gentleman?

TONY.

That's as I find 'um.

HASTINGS.

Not to her of your mother's choosing, I dare answer? And yet she appears to me a pretty, well-tempered girl.

TONY.

That's because you don't know her as well as I. Ecod! I know every inch about her, and there's not a more bitter, cantankerous toad in all Christendom.

HASTINGS. (*Aside.*)

Pretty encouragement this for a lover!

TONY.

I have seen her since the height of that. She has as many tricks as a hare in a thicket or a colt the first day's breaking.

HASTINGS.

To me she appears sensible and silent!

TONY.

Aye, before company. But when she's with her playmates, she's as loud as a hog in a gate.

HASTINGS.

But there is a meek modesty about her that charms me.

TONY.

Yes, but curb her never* so little, she kicks up, and you're flung in a ditch.

HASTINGS.

Well, but you must allow her a little beauty. Yes, you must allow her some beauty.

TONY.

Bandbox! She's all a made up thing, mun. Ah! could you but see Bet Bouncer of these parts, you might then talk of beauty. Ecod, she has two eyes as black as sloes and cheeks as broad and red as a pulpit cushion. She'd make two of she.

HASTINGS.

Well, what say you to a friend that would take this bitter bargain off your hands?

TONY.

Anon?[59]

HASTINGS.

Would you thank him that would take Miss Neville and leave you to happiness and your dear Betsy?

TONY.

Aye, but where is there such a friend, for who would take *her*?

HASTINGS.

I am he. If you but assist me, I'll engage to whip her off to France, and you shall never hear more of her.

TONY.

Assist you! Ecod I will, to the last drop of my blood. I'll clap a pair of horses to your chaise that shall trundle you off in a twinkling and may beget you a part of her fortin beside, in jewels, that you little dream of.

HASTINGS.

My dear squire, this looks like a lad of spirit.

TONY.

Come along then, and you shall see more of my spirit before you have done with me. (*Singing.*) "We are the boys that fears no noise where the thundering cannons roar."

Exeunt.

Act III, scene i.

Enter Hardcastle.

HARDCASTLE.

What could my old friend Sir Charles mean by recommending his son as the modestest young man in Town? To me he appears the most impudent piece of brass that ever spoke with a tongue. He has taken possession of the easy chair by the fireside already. He took off his boots in the parlor and desired me to see them taken care of. I'm desirous to know how his impudence affects my daughter. She will certainly be shocked at it.

Enter Miss Hardcastle, plainly dressed.

Well my Kate, I see you have changed your dress as I bid you, and yet, I believe, there was no great occasion.

---

59 Anon?] Say that again?

MISS HARDCASTLE.
I find such a pleasure, sir, in obeying your commands that I take care to observe them without ever debating their propriety.
HARDCASTLE.
And yet, Kate, I sometimes give you some cause, particularly when I recommended my *modest* gentleman to you as a lover today.
MISS HARDCASTLE.
You taught me to expect something extraordinary, and I find the original exceeds the description.
HARDCASTLE.
I was never so surprised in my life! He has quite confounded all my faculties!
MISS HARDCASTLE.
I never saw anything like it: and a man of the world too!
HARDCASTLE.
Aye, he learned it all abroad. What a fool was I to think a young man could learn modesty by traveling. He might as soon learn wit at a masquerade.
MISS HARDCASTLE.
It seems all natural to him.
HARDCASTLE.
A good deal assisted by bad company and a French dancing master.
MISS HARDCASTLE.
Sure you mistake, Papa! A French dancing master could never have taught him that timid look, that awkward address, that bashful manner—
HARDCASTLE.
Whose look? whose manner? child!
MISS HARDCASTLE.
Mr. Marlow's: his *mauvaise honte*,[60] his timidity, struck me at the first sight.
HARDCASTLE.
Then your first sight deceived you, for I think him one of the most brazen first sights that ever astonished my senses.
MISS HARDCASTLE.
Sure, sir, you rally! I never saw any one so modest.
HARDCASTLE.
And can you be serious! I never saw such a bouncing, swaggering puppy since I was born. Bully Dawson[61] was but a fool to him.
MISS HARDCASTLE.
Surprising! He met me with a respectful bow, a stammering voice, and a look fixed on the ground.
HARDCASTLE.
He met me with a loud voice, a lordly air, and a familiarity that made my blood freeze again.
MISS HARDCASTLE.
He treated me with diffidence and respect; censured the manners of the age; admired the prudence of girls that never laughed; tired me with apologies for being tiresome; then left the room with a bow, and, "Madam, I would not for the world detain you."
HARDCASTLE.
He spoke to me as if he knew me all his life before; asked twenty questions, and never waited for an answer; interrupted my best remarks with some silly pun; and when I was in my best story of the Duke of Marlborough and Prince Eugene, he asked if I had not a good hand at making punch. Yes Kate, he asked your father if he was a maker of punch!
MISS HARDCASTLE.
One of us must certainly be mistaken.
HARDCASTLE.
If he be what he has shown himself, I'm determined he shall never have my consent.
MISS HARDCASTLE.
And if he be the sullen thing I take him, he shall never have mine.
HARDCASTLE.
In one thing then we are agreed—to reject him.
MISS HARDCASTLE.
Yes. But upon conditions. For if you should find him less impudent, and I more presuming; if you find him more respectful, and I more importunate—I don't know—the fellow is well enough for a man. Certainly we don't meet many such at a horse race in the country.
HARDCASTLE.
If we should find him so—but that's impossible. The first appearance has done my business. I'm seldom deceived in that.

60 *mauvaise honte*] shamefacedness, awkward shyness

61 Bully Dawson] a notorious ruffian of the early eighteenth century

MISS HARDCASTLE.
And yet there may be many good qualities under that first appearance.

HARDCASTLE.
Aye, when a girl finds a fellow's outside to her taste, she then sets about guessing the rest of his furniture. With her, a smooth face stands for good sense and a genteel figure for every virtue.

MISS HARDCASTLE.
I hope, sir, a conversation begun with a compliment to my good sense won't end with a sneer at my understanding?

HARDCASTLE.
Pardon me, Kate. But if young Mr. Brazen can find the art of reconciling contradictions, he may please us both, perhaps.

MISS HARDCASTLE.
And as one of us must be mistaken, what if we go to make further discoveries?

HARDCASTLE.
Agreed. But depend on't, I'm in the right.

MISS HARDCASTLE.
And depend on't, I'm not much in the wrong.
Exeunt. Enter Tony running in with a casket.

TONY.
Ecod! I have got them. Here they are. My cousin Con's necklaces, bobs[62] and all. My mother shan't cheat the poor souls out of their fortune neither. Oh! my genus,* is that you?

Enter Hastings.

HASTINGS.
My dear friend, how have you managed with your mother? I hope you have amused her with pretending love for your cousin and that you are willing to be reconciled at last? Our horses will be refreshed in a short time, and we shall soon be ready to set off.

TONY.
And here's something to bear your charges by the way. (*Giving the casket.*) Your sweetheart's jewels. Keep them, and hang those, I say, that would rob you of one of them.

HASTINGS.
But how have you procured them from your mother?

62 bobs] pendants, earrings

TONY.
Ask me no questions, and I'll tell you no fibs. I procured them by the rule of thumb. If I had not a key to every drawer in mother's bureau, how could I go to the alehouse so often as I do? An honest man may rob himself of his own at any time.

HASTINGS.
Thousands do it every day. But to be plain with you, Miss Neville is endeavoring to procure them from her aunt this very instant. If she succeeds, it will be the most delicate way at least of obtaining them.

TONY.
Well, keep them, till you know how it will be. But I know how it will be well enough: she'd as soon part with the only sound tooth in her head.

HASTINGS.
But I dread the effects of her resentment when she finds she has lost them.

TONY.
Never you mind her resentment, leave *me* to manage that. I don't value her resentment the bounce of a cracker.[63]—Zounds! here they are. Morris.[64] Prance.

Exit Hastings. Enter Mrs. Hardcastle and Miss Neville.

MRS. HARDCASTLE.
Indeed, Constance, you amaze me. Such a girl as you want jewels? It will be time enough for jewels, my dear, twenty years hence, when your beauty begins to want* repairs.

MISS NEVILLE.
But what will repair beauty at forty will certainly improve it at twenty, madam.

MRS. HARDCASTLE.
Yours, my dear, can admit of none. That natural blush is beyond a thousand ornaments. Besides, child, jewels are quite out at present. Don't you see, half the ladies of our acquaintance, my Lady Killdaylight and Mrs. Crump[65] and the rest of them, carry their jewels to Town and bring nothing but paste and marcasites back.

63 bounce of a cracker] bang of a firework

64 Morris] Get going.

65 Crump] hunchback (*OED*)

MISS NEVILLE.
But who knows, madam, but somebody that shall be nameless would like me best with all my little finery about me?

MRS. HARDCASTLE.
Consult your glass,* my dear, and then see, if with such a pair of eyes, you want* any better sparklers.—What do you think, Tony, my dear, does your cousin Con want* any jewels, in your eyes, to set off her beauty?

TONY.
That's as thereafter may be.

MISS NEVILLE.
My dear aunt, if you knew how it would oblige me.

MRS. HARDCASTLE.
A parcel of old-fashioned rose- and table-cut things.[66] They would make you look like the court of King Solomon at a puppet show. Besides, I believe I can't readily come at them. They may be missing for aught I know to the contrary.

TONY. (*Apart to Mrs. Hardcastle.*)
Then why don't you tell her so at once, as she's so longing for them. Tell her they're lost. It's the only way to quiet her. Say they're lost, and call me to bear witness.

MRS. HARDCASTLE. (*Apart to Tony.*)
You know, my dear, I'm only keeping them for you. So if I say, they're gone, you'll bear me witness, will you? He! he! he!

TONY.
Never fear me. Ecod! I'll say I saw them taken out with my own eyes.

MISS NEVILLE.
I desire them but for a day, madam, just to be permitted to show them as relics, and then they may be locked up again.

MRS. HARDCASTLE.
To be plain with you, my dear Constance, if I could find them, you should have them. They're missing, I assure you. Lost, for aught I know. But we must have patience wherever they are.

MISS NEVILLE.
I'll not believe it; this is but a shallow pretense to deny me. I know they're too valuable to be so slightly kept, and as you are to answer for the loss.

MRS. HARDCASTLE.
Don't be alarmed, Constance. If they be lost, I must restore an equivalent. But my son knows they are missing and not to be found.

TONY.
That I can bear witness to. They are missing, and not to be found, I'll take my oath on't.

MRS. HARDCASTLE.
You must learn resignation, my dear, for though we lose our fortune, yet we should not lose our patience. See me, how calm I am.

MISS NEVILLE.
Aye, people are generally calm at the misfortunes of others.

MRS. HARDCASTLE.
Now, I wonder a girl of your good sense should waste a thought upon such trumpery. We shall soon find them, and in the meantime, you shall make use of my garnets till your jewels be found.

MISS NEVILLE.
I detest garnets.

MRS. HARDCASTLE.
The most becoming things in the world to set off a clear complexion. You have often seen how well they look upon me. You *shall* have them. (*Exit.*)

MISS NEVILLE.
I dislike them of all things. You shan't stir— Was ever anything so provoking to mislay my own jewels and force me to wear her trumpery?

TONY.
Don't be a fool. If she gives you the garnets, take what you can get. The jewels are your own already. I have stolen them out of her bureau, and she does not know it. Fly to your spark, he'll tell you more of the matter. Leave me to manage *her*.

MISS NEVILLE.
My dear cousin.

TONY.
Vanish. She's here and has missed them already.
[Exit Miss Neville.]
Zounds! how she fidgets and spits about like a Catherine wheel.[67]

---

66 rose- and table-cut things] two modes of cutting lesser stones, the better kind being reserved for a brilliant-cut

67 Catherine wheel] a pinwheeled firework, named after St.

Enter Mrs. Hardcastle.

MRS. HARDCASTLE.

Confusion! thieves! robbers! We are cheated, plundered, broke open, undone.

TONY.

What's the matter, what's the matter, mamma? I hope nothing has happened to any of the good family!

MRS. HARDCASTLE.

We are robbed. My bureau has been broke open, the jewels taken out, and I'm undone.

TONY.

Oh! is that all? Ha! ha! ha! By the laws, I never saw it better acted in my life. Ecod, I thought you was ruined in earnest, ha! ha! ha!

MRS. HARDCASTLE.

Why boy, I *am* ruined in earnest. My bureau has been broke open and all taken away.

TONY.

Stick to that, ha! ha! ha! Stick to that. I'll bear witness, you know, call me to bear witness.

MRS. HARDCASTLE.

I tell you, Tony, by all that's precious, the jewels are gone, and I shall be ruined forever.

TONY.

Sure I know they're gone, and I am to say so.

MRS. HARDCASTLE.

My dearest Tony, but hear me. They're gone, I say.

TONY.

By the laws, mamma, you make me for to laugh, ha! ha! I know who took them well enough, ha! ha! ha!

MRS. HARDCASTLE.

Was there ever such a blockhead that can't tell the difference between jest and earnest.—I tell you, I'm not in jest, booby.

TONY.

That's right, that's right: you must be in a bitter passion, and then nobody will suspect either of us. I'll bear witness that they are gone.

MRS. HARDCASTLE.

Was there every such a cross-grained brute that won't hear me! Can you bear witness that you're no better than a fool? Was ever poor woman so beset with fools on one hand and thieves on the other?

TONY.

I can bear witness to that.

MRS. HARDCASTLE.

Bear witness again, you blockhead you, and I'll turn you out of the room directly. My poor niece, what will become of *her*? Do you laugh, you unfeeling brute, as if you enjoyed my distress?

TONY.

I can bear witness to that.

MRS. HARDCASTLE.

Do you insult me, monster? I'll teach you to vex your mother, I will.

TONY.

I can bear witness to that.

He runs off; she follows him. Enter Miss Hardcastle and maid.

MISS HARDCASTLE.

What an unaccountable creature is that brother of mine to send them to the house as an inn, ha! ha! I don't wonder at his impudence.

MAID.

But what is more, madam, the young gentleman, as you passed by in your present dress, asked me if you were the barmaid? He mistook you for the barmaid, madam.

MISS HARDCASTLE.

Did he? Then as I live, I'm resolved to keep up the delusion. Tell me, pimple, how do you like my present dress? Don't you think I look something like Cherry[68] in *The Beaux' Stratagem*?

MAID.

It's the dress, madam, that every lady wears in the country but when she visits or receives company.

MISS HARDCASTLE.

And are you sure he does not remember my face or person?

MAID.

Certain of it.

MISS HARDCASTLE.

I vow I thought so, for though we spoke for some

Catherine of Alexandria (4th century AD), who was famously martyred on a breaking wheel

68 Cherry] the landlord's daughter in Farquhar's comedy of 1707 (see above)

time together, yet his fears were such that he never once looked up during the interview. Indeed, if he had, my bonnet would have kept him from seeing me.

MAID.
But what do you hope from keeping him in his mistake?

MISS HARDCASTLE.
In the first place, I shall be *seen*, and that is no small advantage to a girl who brings her face to market. Then I shall perhaps make an acquaintance, and that's no small victory gained over one who never addresses any but the wildest of her sex. But my chief aim is to take my gentleman off his guard and, like an invisible champion of romance, examine the giant's force before I offer* to combat.

MAID.
But are you sure you can act your part and disguise your voice so that he may mistake that, as he has already mistaken your person?

MISS HARDCASTLE.
Never fear me. I think I have got the true bar cant: Did your honor call? Attend the Lion there. Pipes and tobacco for the Angel. The Lamb[69] has been outrageous this half hour.

MAID.
It will do, madam. But he's here. (*Exit.*)

Enter Marlow.

MARLOW.
What a bawling in every part of the house. I have scarce a moment's repose. If I go the best room, there I find my host and his story. If I fly to the gallery, there we have my hostess with her curtsy down to the ground. I have at last got a moment to myself, and now for recollection. (*Walks and muses.*)

MISS HARDCASTLE.
Did you call, sir? Did your honor call?

MARLOW. (*Musing.*)
As for Miss Hardcastle, she's too grave and sentimental for me.

MISS HARDCASTLE.
Did your honor call? (*She still* places herself before him, he turning away.*)

MARLOW.
No, child.* (*Musing.*) Besides, from the glimpse I had of her, I think she squints.

MISS HARDCASTLE.
I'm sure, sir, I heard the bell ring.

MARLOW.
No, no. (*Musing.*) I have pleased my father, however, by coming down, and I'll tomorrow please myself by returning. (*Taking out his tablets and perusing.*)

MISS HARDCASTLE.
Perhaps the other gentleman called, sir.

MARLOW.
I tell you, no.

MISS HARDCASTLE.
I should be glad to know, sir. We have such a parcel of servants.

MARLOW.
No, no, I tell you. (*Looks full in her face.*) Yes, child, I think I did call. I wanted—I wanted—I vow, child, you are vastly handsome.

MISS HARDCASTLE.
Oh la, sir, you'll make one ashamed.

MARLOW.
Never saw a more sprightly, malicious eye. Yes, yes, my dear, I did call. Have you got any of your—a—what d'ye call it in the house?

MISS HARDCASTLE.
No sir, we have been out of that these ten days.

MARLOW.
One may call in this house, I find, to very little purpose. Suppose I should call for a taste, just by way of trial, of the nectar of your lips; perhaps I might be disappointed in that too.

MISS HARDCASTLE.
Nectar! nectar! that's a liquor there's no call for in these parts. French, I suppose. We keep no French wines here, sir.

MARLOW.
Of true English growth, I assure you.

MISS HARDCASTLE.
Then it's odd I should not know it. We brew all sorts of wines in this house, and I have lived here these eighteen years.

69 Lion … Angel … Lamb] Rooms at inns were often assigned fanciful names.

MARLOW.

Eighteen years! Why, one would think, child, you kept the bar before you were born. How old are you?

MISS HARDCASTLE.

Oh! sir, I must not tell my age. They say women and music should never be dated.

MARLOW.

To guess at this distance, you can't be much above forty. (*Approaching.*) Yet nearer I don't think so much. (*Approaching.*) By coming close to some women they look younger still, but when we come very close indeed— (*Attempting to kiss her.*)

MISS HARDCASTLE.

Pray sir, keep your distance. One would think you wanted to know one's age as they do horses, by mark of mouth.

MARLOW.

I protest, child, you use me extremely ill. If you keep me at this distance, how is it possible you and I can be ever acquainted?

MISS HARDCASTLE.

And who wants to be acquainted with you? I want no such acquaintance, not I. I'm sure you did not treat Miss Hardcastle that was here awhile ago in this obstropalous[70] manner. I'll warrant me, before her you looked dashed and kept bowing to the ground and talked, for all the world, as if you was before a justice of peace.

MARLOW. (*Aside.*)

Egad! She has hit it, sure enough. (*To her.*) In awe of her, child? Ha! ha! ha! A mere, awkward, squinting thing, no, no. I find you don't know me. I laughed and rallied her a little, but I was unwilling to be too severe. No, I could not be too severe, *curse me*!

MISS HARDCASTLE.

Oh! then, sir, you are a favorite, I find, among the ladies?

MARLOW.

Yes my dear, a great favorite. And yet, hang me, I don't see what they find in me to follow. At the Ladies Club[71] in Town, I'm called their agreeable Rattle. Rattle, child, is not my real name, but one I'm known by. My name is Solomons. Mr. Solomons, my dear, at your service. (*Offering* to salute* her.*)

MISS HARDCASTLE.

Hold, sir, you were introducing me to your club, not to yourself. And you're so great a favorite there, you say?

MARLOW.

Yes, my dear. There's Mrs. Mantrap, Lady Betty Blackleg,[72] the Countess of Sligo, Mrs. Longhorns,[P] old Miss Biddy Buckskin,[73] and your humble servant, keep up the spirit of the place.

MISS HARDCASTLE.

Then it's a very merry place, I suppose.

MARLOW.

Yes, as merry as cards, suppers, wine, and old women can make us.

MISS HARDCASTLE.

And their agreeable Rattle, ha! ha! ha!

MARLOW. (*Aside.*)

Egad! I don't quite like this chit. She looks knowing, methinks.—You laugh, child!

MISS HARDCASTLE.

I can't but laugh to think what time they all have for minding their work or their family.

MARLOW. (*Aside.*)

All's well, she don't laugh at me. (*To her.*) Do *you* ever work, child?

MISS HARDCASTLE.

Aye, sure. There's not a screen or a quilt in the whole house but what can bear witness to that.

MARLOW.

Odso!* Then you must show me your embroidery. I embroider and draw patterns myself a little. If you want a judge of your work, you must apply to me. (*Seizing her hand.*)

MISS HARDCASTLE. (*Struggling.*)

Aye, but the colors don't look well by candlelight. You shall see all in the morning.

70 obstropalous] illiterate variant of obstreperous (*OED*)

71 Ladies Club] a fashionable club that met in London's Albemarle Street and often invited men to visit

72 Blackleg] A turf swindler; also, a swindler in other species of gambling (*OED*)

73 Biddy Buckskin] "Biddy" was originally "Rachel" (in the Larpent ms.), an allusion to Rachel Lloyd, one of the leading women of the Albemarle club.

MARLOW.
And why not now, my angel? Such beauty fires beyond the power of resistance.—Pshaw! the father here! My old luck: I never nicked seven that I did not throw ambsace three times following. (*Exit.*)

Enter Hardcastle, who stands in surprise.

HARDCASTLE.
So, madam! So I find *this* is your *modest* lover. This is your humble admirer that kept his eyes fixed on the ground and only adored at humble distance. Kate, Kate, art thou not ashamed to deceive your father so?

MISS HARDCASTLE.
Never trust me, dear papa, but he's still the modest man I first took him for; you'll be convinced of it as well as I.

HARDCASTLE.
By the hand of my body, I believe his impudence is infectious! Didn't I see him seize your hand? Didn't I see him haul you about like a milkmaid? And now you talk of his respect and his modesty, forsooth!

MISS HARDCASTLE.
But if I shortly convince you of his modesty, that he has only the faults that will pass off with time and the virtues that will improve with age, I hope you'll forgive him.

HARDCASTLE.
The girl would actually make one run mad! I tell you I'll not be convinced. I am convinced. He has scarcely been three hours in the house, and he has already encroached on all my prerogatives. You may like his impudence and call it modesty, but my son-in-law, madam, must have very different qualifications.

MISS HARDCASTLE.
Sir, I ask but this night to convince you.

HARDCASTLE.
You shall not have half the time, for I have thoughts of turning him out this very hour.

MISS HARDCASTLE.
Give me that hour, then, and I hope to satisfy you.

HARDCASTLE.
Well, an hour let it be then. But I'll have no trifling with your father. All fair and open, do you mind me?

MISS HARDCASTLE.
I hope, sir, you have ever found that I considered your commands as my pride, for your kindness is such that my duty as yet has been inclination. (*Exeunt.*)

Act IV, scene i.

Enter Hastings and Miss Neville.

HASTINGS.
You surprise me! Sir Charles Marlow expected here this night? Where have you had your information?

MISS NEVILLE.
You may depend upon it. I just saw his letter to Mr. Hardcastle, in which he tells him he intends setting out a few hours after his son.

HASTINGS.
Then, my Constance, all must be completed before he arrives. He knows me, and should he find me here, would discover* my name, and perhaps my designs, to the rest of the family.

MISS NEVILLE.
The jewels, I hope, are safe.

HASTINGS.
Yes, yes. I have sent them to Marlow, who keeps the keys of our baggage. In the meantime, I'll go to prepare matters for our elopement. I have had the squire's promise of a fresh pair of horses and, if I should not see him again, will write him further directions. (*Exit.*)

MISS NEVILLE.
Well! success attend you. In the meantime, I'll go amuse my aunt with the old pretense of a violent passion for my cousin. (*Exit.*)

Enter Marlow, followed by a servant.

MARLOW.
I wonder what Hastings could mean by sending me so valuable a thing as a casket to keep for him, when he knows the only place I have is the seat of a post coach at an inn door.—Have you deposited the casket with the landlady, as I ordered you? Have you put it into her own hands?

SERVANT.
Yes, your honor.

MARLOW.
She said she'd keep it safe, did she?

SERVANT.
Yes, she said she'd keep it safe enough; she asked me how I came by it, and she said she had a great mind to make me give an account of myself. (*Exit.*)

MARLOW.
Ha! ha! ha! They're safe, however. What an unaccountable set of beings have we got amongst! This little barmaid, though, runs in my head most strangely and drives out the absurdities of all the rest of the family. She's mine, she must be mine, or I'm greatly mistaken.

Enter Hastings.

HASTINGS.
Bless me! I quite forgot to tell her that I intended to prepare at the bottom of the garden.—Marlow here, and in spirits too!

MARLOW.
Give me joy, George! Crown me, shadow me with laurels! Well George, after all, we modest fellows don't want* for success among the women.

HASTINGS.
Some women, you mean. But what success has your honor's modesty been crowned with now, that it grows so insolent upon us?

MARLOW.
Didn't you see the tempting, brisk, lovely little thing that runs about the house with a bunch of keys to its girdle?

HASTINGS.
Well! and what then?

MARLOW.
She's mine, you rogue you. Such fire, such motion, such eyes, such lips—but egad! she would not let me kiss them, though.

HASTINGS.
But are you so sure, so very sure of her?

MARLOW.
Why man, she talked of showing me her work above-stairs,[74] and I am to improve the pattern.

HASTINGS.
But how can *you*, Charles, go about to rob a woman of her honor?

MARLOW.
Pshaw! pshaw! we all know the honor of the barmaid of an inn. I don't intend to *rob* her; take my word for it, there's nothing in this house I shan't honestly *pay* for.

HASTINGS.
I believe the girl has virtue.

MARLOW.
And if she has, I should be the last man in the world that would attempt to corrupt it.

HASTINGS.
You have taken care, I hope, of the casket I sent you to lock up? It's in safety?

MARLOW.
Yes, yes. It's safe enough. I have taken care of it. But how could you think the seat of a post coach at an inn door a place of safety? Ah! numbskull! I have taken better precautions for you than you did for yourself. I have—

HASTINGS.
What!

MARLOW.
I have sent it to the landlady to keep for you.

HASTINGS.
To the landlady!

MARLOW.
The landlady.

HASTINGS.
You did.

MARLOW.
I did. She's to be answerable for its forthcoming, you know.

HASTINGS.
Yes, she'll bring it forth, with a witness.

MARLOW.
Wasn't I right? I believe you'll allow that I acted prudently upon this occasion?

HASTINGS. (*Aside.*)
He must not see my uneasiness.

MARLOW.
You seem a little disconcerted though, methinks. Sure nothing has happened?

HASTINGS.
No, nothing. Never was in better spirits in all my life. And so you left it with the landlady, who, no doubt, very readily undertook the charge?

MARLOW.
Rather too readily. For she not only kept the casket

74 above-stairs] upstairs

but, through her great precaution, was going to keep the messenger too. Ha! ha! ha!

HASTINGS.

He! he! he! They're safe, however.

MARLOW.

As a guinea in a miser's purse.

HASTINGS. (*Aside.*)

So now all hopes of fortune are at an end, and we must set off without it. (*To him.*) Well Charles, I'll leave you to your meditations on the pretty barmaid, and, he! he! he! may you be as successful for yourself as you have been for me. (*Exit.*)

MARLOW.

Thank ye, George! I ask no more. Ha! ha! ha!

Enter Hardcastle.

HARDCASTLE.

I no longer know my own house. It's turned all topsy-turvy. His servants have got drunk already. I'll bear it no longer, and yet, from the respect for his father, I'll be calm. (*To him.*) Mr. Marlow, your servant, I'm your very humble servant. (*Bowing low.*)

MARLOW.

Sir, your humble servant. (*Aside.*) What's to be the wonder now?

HARDCASTLE.

I believe, sir, you must be sensible, sir, that no man alive ought to be more welcome than your father's son, sir. I hope you think so?

MARLOW.

I do from my soul, sir. I don't want* much entreaty. I generally make my father's son welcome wherever he goes.

HARDCASTLE.

I believe you do, from my soul, sir. But though I say nothing to your own conduct, that of your servants is insufferable. Their manner of drinking is setting a very bad example in this house, I assure you.

MARLOW.

I protest, my very good sir, that's no fault of mine. If they don't drink as they ought, *they* are to blame. I ordered them not to spare the cellar. I did, I assure you. (*To the side scene.*) Here, let one of my servants come up. (*To him.*) My positive directions were, that as I did not drink myself, they should make up for my deficiencies below.

HARDCASTLE.

Then they had your orders for what they do! I'm satisfied!

MARLOW.

They had, I assure you.¶ You shall hear from one of themselves.

Enter [Jeremy] drunk.

You, Jeremy! Come forward, sirrah! What were my orders? Were you not told to drink freely and call for what you thought fit for the good of the house?

HARDCASTLE. (*Aside.*)

I begin to lose my patience.

JEREMY.

Please your honor, liberty and Fleet Street forever![75] Though I'm but a servant, I'm as good as another man. I'll drink for no man before supper, sir, damme! Good liquor will sit upon a good supper, but a good supper will not sit upon—(*Hiccups.*) upon my conscience, sir.

MARLOW.

You see, my old friend, the fellow is as drunk as he can possibly be. I don't know what you'd have more, unless you'd have the poor devil soused in a beer barrel.

HARDCASTLE. [*Aside.*]

Zounds! He'll drive me distracted if I contain myself any longer.—Mr. Marlow. Sir, I have submitted to your insolence for more than four hours, and I see no likelihood of its coming to an end. I'm now resolved to be master here, sir, and I desire that you and your drunken pack may leave my house directly.

---

75 liberty and Fleet Street forever!] This is an ambiguous reference to the slogans of the 1760s in support of John Wilkes, the politician, journalist, and agitator whose vituperative attacks on the government produced severe judicial retaliation and in turn his martyrdom for the cause of a free press. Goldsmith may be citing Fleet Street in its late eighteenth-century capacity as London's center for journalism, but he may also be using it here as an emblem of the metropolis–or as the area in London that had numerous taverns.

MARLOW.

Leave your house!—Sure you jest, my good friend? What, when I'm doing what I can to please you?

HARDCASTLE.

I tell you, sir, you don't please me, so I desire you'll leave my house.

MARLOW.

Sure you cannot be serious? At this time o'night, and such a night. You only mean to banter me?

HARDCASTLE.

I tell you, sir, I'm serious, and now that my passions are roused, I say this house is mine, sir, this house is mine, and I command you to leave it directly.

MARLOW.

Ha! ha! ha! A puddle in a storm. I shan't stir a step, I assure you. (*In a serious tone.*) This, your house, fellow! It's my house. This is my house. Mine, while I choose to stay. What right have you to bid me leave this house, sir? I never met with such impudence, curse me, never in my whole life before.

HARDCASTLE.

Nor I, confound me if ever I did. To come to my house, to call for what he likes, to turn me out of my own chair, to insult the family, to order his servants to get drunk, and then to tell me "This house is mine, sir." By all that's impudent, it makes me laugh. Ha! ha! ha! Pray sir, (*Bantering.*) as you take the house, what think you of taking the rest of the furniture? There's a pair of silver candlesticks, and there's a fire screen, and here's a pair of brazen-nosed bellows, perhaps you may take a fancy to them?

MARLOW.

Bring me your bill, sir, bring me your bill, and let's make no more words about it.

HARDCASTLE.

There are a set of prints too. What think you of the *Rake's Progress*[76] for your own apartment?

MARLOW.

Bring me your bill, I say, and I'll leave you and your infernal house directly.

76 *Rake's Progress*] a famous series of paintings (and later, engravings) by William Hogarth that charted the downward spiral of the life of a profligate young man in London

HARDCASTLE.

Then there's a mahogany table that you may see your own face in.

MARLOW.

My bill, I say.

HARDCASTLE.

I had forgot the great chair, for your own particular slumbers after a hearty meal.

MARLOW.

Zounds! bring me my bill, I say, and let's hear no more on't.

HARDCASTLE.

Young man, young man, from your father's letter to me I was taught to expect a well-bred, modest man as a visitor here, but now I find him no better than a coxcomb and a bully. But he will be down here presently and shall hear more of it. (*Exit.*)

MARLOW.

How's this! Sure I have not mistaken the house! Everything looks like an inn. The servants cry, "Coming"; the attendance is awkward; the barmaid, too, to attend us. But she's here and will further inform me.—Whither so fast, child?* A word with you.

Enter Miss Hardcastle.

MISS HARDCASTLE.

Let it be short, then. I'm in a hurry. (*Aside.*) I believe he begins to find out his mistake, but it's too soon quite to undeceive him.

MARLOW.

Pray child, answer me one question! What are you, and what may your business in this house be?

MISS HARDCASTLE.

A relation of the family, sir.

MARLOW.

What, a poor relation?

MISS HARDCASTLE.

Yes sir, a poor relation appointed to keep the keys and to see that the guests want* nothing in my power to give them.

MARLOW.

That is, you act as the barmaid of this inn.

MISS HARDCASTLE.

Inn! Oh law, what brought that in your head? One of the best families in the county keep an inn! Ha! ha! ha! Old Mr. Hardcastle's house an inn!

MARLOW.
Mr. Hardcastle's house! Is this house Mr. Hardcastle's house, child?

MISS HARDCASTLE.
Aye, sure. Whose else should it be?

MARLOW.
So then all's out, and I have been damnably imposed on. Oh, confound my stupid head, I shall be laughed at over the whole Town. I shall be stuck up in caricatura in all the print shops: The Dullissimo Macaroni. To mistake this house of all others for an inn and my father's old friend for an innkeeper. What a swaggering puppy must he take me for. What a silly puppy do I find myself. There again, may I be hanged, my dear, but I mistook you for the barmaid.

MISS HARDCASTLE.
Dear me! dear me! I'm sure there's nothing in my *behavour* to put me upon a level with one of that stamp.

MARLOW.
Nothing, my dear, nothing. But I was in for a list of blunders and could not help making you a subscriber. My stupidity saw everything the wrong way. I mistook your assiduity for assurance and your simplicity for allurement. But it's over: this house I no more show *my* face in.

MISS HARDCASTLE.
I hope, sir, I have done nothing to disoblige you. I'm sure I should be sorry to affront any gentleman who has been so polite and said so many civil things to me. I'm sure I should be sorry (*Pretending to cry.*) if he left the family upon my account. I'm sure I should be sorry people said anything amiss, since I have no fortune but my character.[r]

MARLOW. (*Aside.*)
By Heaven, she weeps. This is the first mark of tenderness I ever had from a modest woman, and it touches me. (*To her.*) Excuse me, my lovely girl, you are the only part of the family I leave with reluctance. But to be plain with you, the difference of our birth, fortune, and education make an honorable connection impossible, and I can never harbor a thought of seducing simplicity that trusted in my honor or bringing ruin upon one whose only fault was being too lovely.

MISS HARDCASTLE. (*Aside.*)
Generous man! I now begin to admire him. (*To him.*) But I'm sure my family is as good as Miss Hardcastle's, and though I'm poor, that's no great misfortune to a contented mind, and until this moment, I never thought that it was bad to want* fortune.

MARLOW.
And why now, my pretty simplicity?

MISS HARDCASTLE.
Because it puts me at a distance from one that, if I had a thousand pound, I would give it all to.

MARLOW. (*Aside.*)
This simplicity bewitches me, so that if I stay, I'm undone. I must make one bold effort and leave her. (*To her.*) Your partiality in my favor, my dear, touches me most sensibly, and were I to live for myself alone, I could easily fix my choice. But I owe too much to the opinion of the world, too much to the authority of a father, so that—I can scarcely speak it—it affects me. Farewell. (*Exit.*)

MISS HARDCASTLE.
I never knew half his merit till now. He shall not go, if I have power or art to detain him. I'll still preserve the character in which I stooped to conquer but will undeceive my papa, who, perhaps, may laugh him out of his resolution. (*Exit.*)

Enter Tony, Miss Neville.

TONY.
Aye, you may steal for yourselves the next time. I have done my duty. She has got the jewels again, that's a sure thing, but she believes it was all a mistake of the servants.

MISS NEVILLE.
But my dear cousin, sure you won't forsake us in this distress. If she in the least suspects that I am going off, I shall certainly be locked up or sent to my aunt Pedigree's, which is ten times worse.

TONY.
To be sure, aunts of all kinds are damned bad things. But what can I do? I have got you a pair of horses that will fly like Whistlejacket,[77] and I'm sure you can't say but I have courted you nicely

77 Whistlejacket] a famous racehorse

before her face.—Here she comes. We must court a bit or two more, for fear she should suspect us.

They retire and seem to fondle. Enter Mrs. Hardcastle.

MRS. HARDCASTLE.

Well, I was greatly fluttered, to be sure. But my son tells me it was all a mistake of the servants. I shan't be easy, however, till they are fairly married, and then let her keep her own fortune.—But what do I see! Fondling together, as I'm alive. I never saw Tony so sprightly before. Ah! have I caught you, my pretty doves! What, billing, exchanging stolen glances and broken murmurs. Ah!

TONY.

As for murmurs, mother, we grumble a little now and then, to be sure. But there's no love lost between us.

MRS. HARDCASTLE.

A mere sprinkling, Tony, upon the flame, only to make it burn brighter.

MISS NEVILLE.

Cousin Tony promises to give us more of his company at home. Indeed, he shan't leave us anymore. It won't leave us, Cousin Tony, will it?

TONY.

Oh! it's a pretty creature. No, I'd sooner leave a hare in her form,[78] the dogs in full cry, or[s] my horse in a pound than leave you when you smile upon one so. Your laugh makes you so becoming.

MISS NEVILLE.

Agreeable cousin! Who can help admiring that natural humor,* that pleasant, broad, red, thoughtless—(*Patting his cheek.*) ah! it's a bold face.

MRS. HARDCASTLE.

Pretty innocence.

TONY.

I'm sure I always loved cousin Con's hazel eyes and her pretty long fingers, that she twists this way and that over the haspicholls,[79] like a parcel of bobbins.

MRS. HARDCASTLE.

Ah, he would charm the bird from the tree. I was never so happy before. My boy takes after his father, poor Mr. Lumpkin, exactly.—The jewels, my dear Con, shall be yours incontinently. You shall have them. Isn't he a sweet boy, my dear? You shall be married tomorrow, and we'll put off the rest of his education, like Dr. Drowsy's sermons, to a fitter opportunity.

Enter Diggory.

DIGGORY.

Where's the squire? I have got a letter for your worship.

TONY.

Give it to my mamma. She reads all my letters first.

DIGGORY.

I had orders to deliver it into your own hands.

TONY.

Who does it come from?

DIGGORY.

Your worship mun[80] ask that o'the letter itself. [*Exit.*]

TONY.

I would wish to know, though. (*Turning the letter and gazing on it.*)

MISS NEVILLE. (*Aside.*)

Undone, undone. A letter to him from Hastings. I know the hand. If my aunt sees it, we are ruined forever. I'll keep her employed a little if I can. (*To Mrs. Hardcastle.*) But I have not told you, madam, of my cousin's smart answer just now to Mr. Marlow. We so laughed—you must know, madam—this way a little, for he must not hear us. (*They confer.*)

TONY. (*Still gazing.*)

A damned cramp piece of penmanship, as ever I saw in my life. I can read your print-hand very well. But here there are such handles and shanks and dashes that one can scarce tell the head from the tail. "To Anthony Lumpkin, Esquire." It's very odd, I can read the outside of my letters, where my own name is, well enough. But when I come to open it, it's all—buzz. That's hard, very hard, for the inside of the letter is always the cream of the correspondence.

MRS. HARDCASTLE.

Ha! ha! ha! Very well, very well. And so my son was too hard for the philosopher.

78 form] the nest or lair in which a hare crouches (*OED*)

79 haspicholls] Lumpkin for harpsichord

80 mun] must

MISS NEVILLE.

Yes, madam, but you must hear the rest, madam. A little more this way, or he may hear us. You'll hear how he puzzled him again.

MRS. HARDCASTLE.

He seems strangely puzzled now himself, methinks.

TONY. (*Still gazing.*)

A damned up and down hand, as if it was disguised* in liquor. (*Reading.*) "Dear Sir." Aye, that's that. Then there's an "M" and a "T" and an "S," but whether the next be an "izzard"[81] or an "R," confound me, I cannot tell.

MRS. HARDCASTLE.

What's that, my dear. Can I give you any assistance?

MISS NEVILLE.

Pray, aunt, let me read it. Nobody reads a cramp hand better than I. (*Twitching the letter from her.*) Do you know who it is from?

TONY.

Can't tell, except from Dick Ginger the feeder.[82]

MISS NEVILLE.

Aye, so it is. (*Pretending to read.*) "Dear Squire, Hoping that you're in health, as I am at this present. The gentlemen of the Shake-bag[83] club has cut the gentlemen of Goose-green quite out of feather. The odds"—um—"odd battle"—um—"long fighting"—um—here, here, it's all about cocks and fighting; it's of no consequence, here, put it up, put it up. (*Thrusting the crumpled letter upon him.*)

TONY.

But I tell you, miss, it's of all the consequence in the world. I would not lose the rest of it for a guinea. (*Giving Mrs. Hardcastle the letter.*) Here, mother, do you make it out.—Of no consequence!

MRS. HARDCASTLE.

How's this! (*Reads.*) "Dear Squire, I'm now waiting for Miss Neville with a post chaise and pair at the bottom of the garden, but I find my horses yet unable to perform the journey. I expect you'll assist us with a pair of fresh horses, as you promised. Dispatch is necessary, as the *hag* (aye, the hag) your mother, will otherwise suspect us. Yours, Hastings." Grant me patience. I shall run distracted. My rage chokes me.

MISS NEVILLE.

I hope, madam, you'll suspend your resentment for a few moments and not impute to me any impertinence or sinister design that belongs to another.

MRS. HARDCASTLE. (*Curtseying very low.*)

Fine spoken, madam, you are most miraculously polite and engaging and quite the very pink of courtesy and circumspection, madam. (*Changing her tone.*) And you, you great ill-fashioned oaf, with scarce sense enough to keep your mouth shut. Were you, too, joined against me? But I'll defeat all your plots in a moment.—As for you, madam, since you have got a pair of fresh horses ready, it would be cruel to disappoint them. So, if you please, instead of running away with your spark, prepare, this very moment, to run off with *me.* Your old aunt Pedigree will keep you secure, I'll warrant me.—You too, sir, may mount your horse and guard us upon the way.—Here, Thomas, Roger, Diggory.—I'll show you that I wish you better than you do yourselves. (*Exit.*)

MISS NEVILLE.

So now I'm completely ruined.

TONY.

Aye, that's a sure thing.

MISS NEVILLE.

What better could be expected from being connected with such a stupid fool, and after all the nods and signs I made him.

TONY.

By the laws, miss, it was your own cleverness and not my stupidity that did your business. You were so nice* and so busy with your Shake-bags and Goose-greens that I thought you could never be making believe.

Enter Hastings.

HASTINGS.

So sir, I find by my servant that you have shown my letter and betrayed us. Was this well done, young gentleman.

[81] izzard] an old name for the letter *z*

[82] feeder] trainer of fighting cocks

[83] Shake-bag] large fighting cock

TONY.

Here's another. Ask miss there who betrayed you. Ecod, it was her doing, not mine.

Enter Marlow.

MARLOW.

So I have been finely used here among you: rendered contemptible, driven into ill manners, despised, insulted, laughed at.

TONY.

Here's another. We shall have old Bedlam broke loose presently.

MISS NEVILLE.

And there, sir, is the gentleman to whom we all owe every obligation.

MARLOW.

What can I say to him, a mere boy, an idiot, whose ignorance and age are a protection?

HASTINGS.

A poor contemptible booby, that would but disgrace correction.

MISS NEVILLE.

Yet with cunning and malice enough to make himself merry with all our embarrassments.

HASTINGS.

An insensible cub.

MARLOW.

Replete with tricks and mischief.

TONY.

Baw! damme, but I'll fight you both one after the other—with baskets.[84]

MARLOW.

As for him, he's below resentment. But your conduct, Mr. Hastings, requires an explanation. You knew of my mistakes yet would not undeceive me.

HASTINGS.

Tortured as I am with my own disappointments, is this a time for explanations? It is not friendly, Mr. Marlow.

MARLOW.

But sir—

MISS NEVILLE.

Mr. Marlow, we never kept on your mistake till it was too late to undeceive you. Be pacified.

[84] baskets] basket hilts (q.v.)

Enter servant.

SERVANT.

My mistress desires you'll get ready immediately, madam. The horses are putting to. Your hat and things are in the next room. We are to go thirty miles before morning. (*Exit.*)

MISS NEVILLE.

Well, well, I'll come presently.

MARLOW. (*To Hastings.*)

Was it well done, sir, to assist in rendering me ridiculous? To hang me out for the scorn of all my acquaintance? Depend upon it, sir, I shall expect an explanation.

HASTINGS.

Was it well done, sir, if you're upon that subject, to deliver what I entrusted to yourself to the care of another, sir?

MISS NEVILLE.

Mr. Hastings. Mr. Marlow. Why will you increase my distress by this groundless dispute? I implore, I entreat you—

Enter servant.

SERVANT.

Your cloak, madam. My mistress is impatient. [*Exit.*]

MISS NEVILLE.

I come.—Pray be pacified. If I leave you thus, I shall die with apprehension.

Enter servant.

SERVANT.

Your fan, muff, and gloves, madam. The horses are waiting. [*Exit.*]

MISS NEVILLE.

Oh, Mr. Marlow! if you knew what a scene of constraint and ill nature lies before me, I'm sure it would convert your resentment into pity.

MARLOW.

I'm so distracted with a variety of passions that I don't know what I do. Forgive me, madam.—George, forgive me. You know my hasty temper and should not exasperate it.

HASTINGS.

The torture of my situation is my only excuse.

MISS NEVILLE.

Well my dear Hastings, if you have that esteem for me that I think, that I am sure you have, your constancy for three years will but increase the happiness of our future connection. If—

MRS. HARDCASTLE. (*Within.*)

Miss Neville! Constance, why Constance, I say!

MISS NEVILLE.

I'm coming.—Well, constancy. Remember, constancy is the word. (*Exit.*)

HASTINGS.

My heart! How can I support this? To be so near happiness, and such happiness.

MARLOW. (*To Tony.*)

You see now, young gentleman, the effects of your folly. What might be amusement to you is here disappointment and even distress.

TONY. (*From a reverie.*)

Ecod, I have hit it. It's here. Your hands: yours and yours, my poor Sulky.—My boots there, ho.—Meet me two hours hence at the bottom of the garden, and if you don't find Tony Lumpkin a more good-natured fellow than you thought for, I'll give you leave to take my best horse, and Bet Bouncer into the bargain.[t] Come along. My boots, ho.

Exeunt.

Act V, scene i. Scene continues.

Enter Hastings and servant.

HASTINGS.

You saw the old lady and Miss Neville drive off, you say?

SERVANT.

Yes, your honor. They went off in a post coach, and the young squire went on horseback. They're thirty miles off by this time.

HASTINGS.

Then all my hopes are over.

SERVANT.

Yes, sir. Old Sir Charles is arrived. He and the old gentleman of the house have been laughing at Mr. Marlow's mistake this half hour. They are coming this way.

HASTINGS.

Then I must not be seen. So now to my fruitless appointment at the bottom of the garden. This is about the time.

Exeunt. Enter Sir Charles and Hardcastle.

HARDCASTLE.

Ha! ha! ha! The peremptory tone in which he sent forth his sublime commands.

SIR CHARLES.

And the reserve with which I suppose he treated all your advances.

HARDCASTLE.

And yet he might have seen something in me above a common innkeeper, too.

SIR CHARLES.

Yes Dick, but he mistook you for an uncommon innkeeper, ha! ha! ha!

HARDCASTLE.

Well, I'm in too good spirits to think of anything but joy. Yes my dear friend, this union of our families will make our personal friendships hereditary, and though my daughter's fortune is but small—

SIR CHARLES.

Why Dick, will you talk of fortune to *me*? My son is possessed of more than a competence already and can want* nothing but a good and virtuous girl to share his happiness and increase it. If they like each other, as you say they do—

HARDCASTLE.

If, man? I tell you they *do* like each other. My daughter as good as told me so.

SIR CHARLES.

But girls are apt to flatter themselves, you know.

HARDCASTLE.

I saw him grasp her hand in the warmest manner myself.—And here he comes to put you out of your "ifs," I warrant him.

Enter Marlow.

MARLOW.

I come, sir, once more to ask pardon for my strange conduct. I can scarce reflect on my insolence without confusion.

HARDCASTLE.

Tut boy, a trifle. You take it too gravely. An hour or two's laughing with my daughter will set all to rights again. She'll never like you the worse for it.

MARLOW.

Sir, I shall be always proud of her approbation.

HARDCASTLE.

Approbation is but a cold word, Mr. Marlow; if I am not deceived, you have something more than approbation thereabouts. You take me?

MARLOW.

Really sir, I have not that happiness.

HARDCASTLE.

Come boy, I'm an old fellow and know what's what as well as you that are younger. I know what has passed between you, but mum.

MARLOW.

Sure sir, nothing has passed between us but the most profound respect on my side and the most distant reserve on hers. You don't think, sir, that my impudence has been passed upon all the rest of the family?

HARDCASTLE.

Impudence! No, I don't say that—not quite impudence—though girls like to be played with and rumpled a little, too, sometimes. But she has told no tales, I assure you.

MARLOW.

I never gave her the slightest cause.

HARDCASTLE.

Well, well, I like modesty in its place well enough. But this is overacting, young gentleman. You *may* be open. Your father and I will like you the better for it.

MARLOW.

May I die, sir, if I ever—

HARDCASTLE.

I tell you, she don't dislike you, and as I'm sure you like her—

MARLOW.

Dear sir—I protest, sir—

HARDCASTLE.

I see no reason why you should not be joined as fast as the parson can tie you.

MARLOW.

But hear me, sir—

HARDCASTLE.

Your father approves the match, I admire it, every moment's delay will be doing mischief, so—

MARLOW.

But why won't you hear me? By all that's just and true, I never gave Miss Hardcastle the slightest mark of my attachment or even the most distant hint to suspect me of affection. We had but one interview, and that was formal, modest, and uninteresting.

HARDCASTLE. (*Aside.*)

This fellow's formal, modest impudence is beyond bearing.

SIR CHARLES.

And you never grasped her hand, or made any protestations?

MARLOW.

As Heaven is my witness, I came down in obedience to your commands. I saw the lady without emotion and parted without reluctance. I hope you'll exact no further proofs of my duty nor prevent me from leaving a house in which I suffer so many mortifications. (*Exit.*)

SIR CHARLES.

I'm astonished at the air of sincerity with which he parted.

HARDCASTLE.

And I'm astonished at the deliberate intrepidity of his assurance.

SIR CHARLES.

I dare pledge my life and honor upon his truth.

HARDCASTLE.

Here comes my daughter, and I would stake my happiness upon her veracity.

Enter Miss Hardcastle.

Kate, come hither, child. Answer us sincerely and without reserve: Has Mr. Marlow made you any professions of love and affection?

MISS HARDCASTLE.

The question is very abrupt, sir! But since you require unreserved sincerity, I think he has.

HARDCASTLE. (*To Sir Charles.*)

You see.

SIR CHARLES.

And pray, madam, have you and my son had more than one interview?

MISS HARDCASTLE.

Yes sir, several.

HARDCASTLE. (*To Sir Charles.*)

You see.

SIR CHARLES.

But did he profess any attachment?

MISS HARDCASTLE.
A lasting one.
SIR CHARLES.
Did he talk of love?
MISS HARDCASTLE.
Much, sir.
SIR CHARLES.
Amazing! And all this formally?
MISS HARDCASTLE.
Formally.
HARDCASTLE.
Now my friend, I hope you are satisfied.
SIR CHARLES.
And how did he behave, madam?
MISS HARDCASTLE.
As most professed admirers do: said some civil things of my face, talked much of his want* of merit and the greatness of mine, mentioned his heart, gave a short tragedy speech, and ended with pretended rapture.
SIR CHARLES.
Now I'm perfectly convinced, indeed. I know his conversation among women to be modest and submissive. This forward, canting, ranting manner by no means describes him, and I am confident he never sate for the picture.
MISS HARDCASTLE.
Then what, sir, if I should convince you to your face of my sincerity? If you and my papa in about half an hour will place yourselves behind that screen, you shall hear him declare his passion to me in person.
SIR CHARLES.
Agreed. And if I find him what you describe, all my happiness in him must have an end. (*Exit.*)
MISS HARDCASTLE.
And if you don't find him what I describe—I fear my happiness must never have a beginning.

Exeunt.

Scene ii. The back of the garden.

Enter Hastings.

HASTINGS.
What an idiot am I to wait here for a fellow who probably takes a delight in mortifying me. He never intended to be punctual, and I'll wait no longer.—What do I see? It is he, and perhaps with news of my Constance.

Enter Tony, booted and spattered.

HASTINGS.
My honest squire! I now find you a man of your word. This looks like friendship.
TONY.
Aye, I'm your friend, and the best friend you have in the world, if you knew but all. This riding by night, by the bye, is cursedly tiresome. It has shook me worse than the basket of a stagecoach.
HASTINGS.
But how? Where did you leave your fellow travelers? Are they in safety? Are they housed?
TONY.
Five and twenty miles in two hours and a half is no such bad driving. The poor beasts have smoked[85] for it: rabbit me,[86] but I'd rather ride forty miles after a fox than ten with such varmint.
HASTINGS.
Well, but where have you left the ladies? I die with impatience.
TONY.
Left them? Why, where should I leave them but where I found them?
HASTINGS.
This is a riddle.
TONY.
Riddle me this then: What's that goes round the house and round the house and never touches the house?
HASTINGS.
I'm still astray.
TONY.
Why that's it, mon. I have led them astray. By jingo, there's not a pond or slough within five miles of the place but they can tell the taste of.
HASTINGS.
Ha! ha! ha! I understand; you took them in a round, while they supposed themselves going

85 smoked] The horses have steamed from the sweat of galloping at top speed.

86 rabbit me] an expletive the equivalent of "darn me" or "drat me"

forward. And so you have at last brought them home again.

TONY.

You shall hear: I first took them down Feather-bed Lane, where we stuck fast in the mud; I then rattled them crack over the stones of Up-and-down Hill; I then introduced them to the gibbet on Heavy-tree Heath; and from that, with a circumbendibus,[87] I fairly lodged them in the horse-pond at the bottom of the garden.

HASTINGS.

But no accident, I hope.

TONY.

No, no. Only mother is confoundedly frightened. She thinks herself forty miles off. She's sick of the journey, and the cattle can scarce crawl. So if your own horses be ready, you may whip off with cousin, and I'll be bound that no soul here can budge a foot to follow you.

HASTINGS.

My dear friend, how can I be grateful?

TONY.

Aye, now it's dear friend, noble squire. Just now, it was all idiot, cub, and run me through the guts. Damn *your* way of fighting, I say. After we take a knock in this part of the country, we kiss and be friends. But if you had run me through the guts, then I should be dead, and you might go kiss the hangman.

HASTINGS.

The rebuke is just. But I must hasten to relieve Miss Neville. If you keep the old lady employed, I promise to take care of the young one. (*Exit.*)

TONY.

Never fear me.—Here she comes. Vanish. She's got from the pond and draggled up to the waist like a mermaid.

Enter Mrs. Hardcastle.

MRS. HARDCASTLE.

Oh Tony, I'm killed. Shook. Battered to death. I shall never survive it. That last jolt that laid us against the quickset hedge has done my business.

TONY.

Alack Mama, it was all your own fault. You would be for running away by night without knowing one inch of the way.

MRS. HARDCASTLE.

I wish we were at home again. I never met so many accidents in so short a journey: drenched in the mud, overturned in a ditch, stuck fast in a slough, jolted to a jelly, and at last to lose our way. Whereabouts do you think we are, Tony?

TONY.

By my guess we should be upon Crackskull Common, about forty miles from home.

MRS. HARDCASTLE.

Oh Lud!* Oh Lud! the most notorious spot in all the country. We only want* a robbery to make a complete night on't.

TONY.

Don't be afraid, Mama, don't be afraid. Two of the five that kept here are hanged, and the other three may not find us. Don't be afraid.—Is that a man that's galloping behind us? No, it's only a tree. Don't be afraid.

MRS. HARDCASTLE.

The fright will certainly kill me.

TONY.

Do you see anything like a black hat moving behind the thicket?

MRS. HARDCASTLE.

Oh death!

TONY.

No, it's only a cow. Don't be afraid, Mama, don't be afraid.

MRS. HARDCASTLE.

As I'm alive, Tony, I see a man coming towards us. Ah! I'm sure on't. If he perceives us we are undone.

TONY. (*Aside.*)

Father-in-law, by all that's unlucky, come to take one of his night walks. (*To her.*) Ah, it's a highwayman, with pistols as long as my arm. A damned ill-looking fellow.

MRS. HARDCASTLE.

Good Heaven defend us! He approaches.

TONY.

Do you hide yourself in that thicket, and leave me to manage him. If there be any danger I'll cough and cry "hem." When I cough be sure to keep close.

[87] circumbendibus] a roundabout route (bogus Lat.)

Mrs. Hardcastle hides behind a tree in the back scene. Enter Hardcastle.

HARDCASTLE.
I'm mistaken, or I heard voices of people in want* of help. Oh Tony, is that you? I did not expect you so soon back. Are your mother and her charge in safety?

TONY.
Very safe, sir, at my aunt Pedigree's. Hem!

MRS. HARDCASTLE. (*From behind.*)
Ah death! I find there's danger.

HARDCASTLE.
Forty miles in three hours; sure, that's too much, my youngster.

TONY.
Stout horses and willing minds make short journeys, as they say. Hem!

MRS. HARDCASTLE. (*From behind.*)
Sure he'll do the dear boy no harm.

HARDCASTLE.
But I heard a voice here; I should be glad to know from whence it came.

TONY.
It was I, sir, talking to myself, sir. I was saying that forty miles in four hours was very good going. Hem! As to be sure it was. Hem! I have got a sort of cold by being out in the air. We'll go in, if you please. Hem!

HARDCASTLE.
But if you talked to yourself, you did not answer yourself. I am certain I heard two voices and am resolved (*Raising his voice.*) to find the other out.

MRS. HARDCASTLE. (*From behind.*)
Oh! he's coming to find me out. Oh!

TONY.
What need you go, sir, if I tell you? Hem! I'll lay down my life for the truth—hem!—I'll tell you all, sir. (*Detaining him.*)

HARDCASTLE.
I tell you, I will not be detained. I insist on seeing. It's in vain to expect I'll believe you.

MRS. HARDCASTLE. (*Running forward from behind.*)
Oh Lud, he'll murder my poor boy, my darling. Here, good gentleman, whet your rage upon me. Take my money, my life, but spare that young gentleman, spare my child, if you have any mercy.

HARDCASTLE.
My wife, as I'm a Christian! From whence can she come, or what does she mean?

MRS. HARDCASTLE. (*Kneeling.*)
Take compassion on us, good Mr. Highwayman. Take our money, our watches, all we have, but spare our lives. We will never bring you to justice, indeed we won't, good Mr. Highwayman.

HARDCASTLE.
I believe the woman's out of her senses. What, Dorothy, don't you know *me*?

MRS. HARDCASTLE.
Mr. Hardcastle, as I'm alive! My fears blinded me. But who, my dear, could have expected to meet you here, in this frightful place, so far from home? What has brought you to follow us?

HARDCASTLE.
Sure, Dorothy, you have not lost your wits. So far from home, when you are within forty yards of your own door. (*To Tony.*) This is one of your old tricks, you graceless rogue you. (*To her.*) Don't you know the gate and the mulberry tree? and don't you remember the horsepond, my dear?

MRS. HARDCASTLE.
Yes, I shall remember the horsepond as long as I live, I have caught my death in it. (*To Tony.*) And is it to you, you graceless varlet, I owe all this? I'll teach you to abuse your mother, I will.

TONY.
Ecod, mother, all the parish says you have spoiled me, and so you may take the fruits on't.

MRS. HARDCASTLE.
I'll spoil you, I will.

Follows him off the stage and exeunt.

HARDCASTLE.
There's morality, however, in his reply. (*Exit.*)

Enter Hastings and Miss Neville.

HASTINGS.
My dear Constance, why will you deliberate thus? If we delay a moment, all is lost forever. Pluck up a little resolution, and we shall soon be out of the reach of her malignity.

MISS NEVILLE.

I find it impossible. My spirits are so sunk with the agitations I have suffered that I am unable to face any new danger. Two or three years' patience will at last crown us with happiness.

HASTINGS.

Such a tedious delay is worse than inconstancy. Let us fly, my charmer. Let us date our happiness from this very moment. Perish fortune. Love and content will increase what we possess beyond a monarch's revenue. Let me prevail.

MISS NEVILLE.

No, Mr. Hastings, no. Prudence once more comes to my relief, and I will obey its dictates. In the moment of passion, fortune may be despised, but it ever produces a lasting repentance. I'm resolved to apply to Mr. Hardcastle's compassion and justice for redress.

HASTINGS.

But though he had the will, he has not the power to relieve you.

MISS NEVILLE.

But he has influence, and upon that I am resolved to rely.

HASTINGS.

I have no hopes. But since you persist, I must reluctantly obey you.

Exeunt.

Scene iii.

Enter Sir Charles and Miss Hardcastle.

SIR CHARLES.

What a situation am I in. If what you say appears, I shall then find a guilty son. If what he says be true, I shall then lose one that, of all others, I most wished for a daughter.

MISS HARDCASTLE.

I am proud of your approbation, and to show I merit it, if you place yourselves as I directed, you shall hear his explicit declaration.—But he comes.

SIR CHARLES.

I'll to your father and keep him to the appointment. (*Exit.*)

Enter Marlow.

MARLOW.

Though prepared for setting out, I come once more to take leave, nor did I, till this moment, know the pain I feel in the separation.

MISS HARDCASTLE. (*In her own natural manner.*)

I believe these sufferings cannot be very great, sir, which you can so easily remove. A day or two longer, perhaps, might lessen your uneasiness by showing the little value of what you now think proper to regret.

MARLOW. (*Aside.*)

This girl every moment improves upon me. (*To her.*) It must not be, madam. I have already trifled too long with my heart. My very pride begins to submit to my passion. The disparity of education and fortune, the anger of a parent, and the contempt of my equals begin to lose their weight, and nothing can restore me to myself but this painful effort of resolution.

MISS HARDCASTLE.

Then go, sir. I'll urge nothing more to detain you. Though my family be as good as hers you came down to visit and my education, I hope, not inferior, what are these advantages without equal affluence? I must remain contented with the slight approbation of imputed merit; I must have only the mockery of your addresses, while all your serious aims are fixed on fortune.

Enter Hardcastle and Sir Charles from behind.

SIR CHARLES.

Here, behind this screen.

HARDCASTLE.

Aye, aye, make no noise. I'll engage my Kate covers him with confusion at last.

MARLOW.

By heavens, madam, fortune was ever my smallest consideration. Your beauty at first caught my eye, for who could see that without emotion. But every moment that I converse with you, steals in some new grace, heightens the picture, and gives it stronger expression. What at first seemed rustic plainness now appears refined simplicity. What seemed forward assurance now strikes me as the result of courageous innocence and conscious virtue.

SIR CHARLES.
What can it mean? He amazes me!

HARDCASTLE.
I told you how it would be. Hush!

MARLOW.
I am now determined to stay, madam, and I have too good an opinion of my father's discernment, when he sees you, to doubt his approbation.

MISS HARDCASTLE.
No, Mr. Marlow, I will not, cannot detain you. Do you think I could suffer a connection in which there is the smallest room for repentance? Do you think I would take the mean advantage of a transient passion to load you with confusion? Do you think I could ever relish that happiness which was acquired by lessening yours?

MARLOW.
By all that's good, I can have no happiness but what's in your power to grant me. Nor shall I ever feel repentance but in not having seen your merits before. I will stay, even contrary to your wishes, and though you should persist to shun me, I will make my respectful assiduities atone for the levity of my past conduct.

MISS HARDCASTLE.
Sir, I must entreat you'll desist. As our acquaintance began, so let it end, in indifference. I might have given an hour or two to levity, but seriously, Mr. Marlow, do you think I could ever submit to a connection where *I* must appear mercenary and *you* imprudent? Do you think I could ever catch at the confident addresses of a secure admirer?

MARLOW. (*Kneeling.*)
Does this look like security? Does this look like confidence? No, madam, every moment that shows me your merit only serves to increase my diffidence and confusion. Here let me continue—

SIR CHARLES.
I can hold it no longer. Charles, Charles, how hast thou deceived me! Is this your indifference, your uninteresting conversation?

HARDCASTLE.
Your cold contempt, your formal interview? What have you to say now?

MARLOW.
That I'm all amazement! What can it mean?

HARDCASTLE.
It means that you can say and unsay things at pleasure; that you can address a lady in private and deny it in public; that you have one story for us and another for my daughter.

MARLOW.
Daughter! this lady your daughter!

HARDCASTLE.
Yes sir, my only daughter, my Kate. Whose else should she be?

MARLOW.
Oh, the devil.

MISS HARDCASTLE.
Yes sir, that very* identical tall, squinting lady you were pleased to take me for. (*Curtesying.*) She that you addressed as the mild, modest, sentimental man of gravity, and the bold forward agreeable Rattle of the Ladies Club. Ha! ha! ha!

MARLOW.
Zounds, there's no bearing this; it's worse than death.

MISS HARDCASTLE.
In which of your characters, sir, will you give us leave to address you? As the faltering gentleman, with looks on the ground, that speaks just to be heard and hates hypocrisy, or the loud, confident creature, that keeps it up with Mrs. Mantrap and old Miss Biddy Buckskin till three in the morning; ha! ha! ha!

MARLOW.
Oh, curse on my noisy head. I never attempted to be impudent yet that I was not taken down. I must be gone.

HARDCASTLE.
By the hand of my body, but you shall not. I see it was all a mistake, and I am rejoiced to find it. You shall not stir,[u] I tell you. I know she'll forgive you.—Won't you forgive him, Kate? We'll all forgive you. Take courage, man.

They retire, she tormenting him to the back scene. Enter Mrs. Hardcastle and Tony.

MRS. HARDCASTLE.
So, so, they're gone off. Let them go, I care not.

HARDCASTLE.
Who gone?

MRS. HARDCASTLE.

My dutiful niece and her gentleman, Mr. Hastings, from Town. He who came down with our modest visitor here.

SIR CHARLES.

Who, my honest George Hastings? As worthy a fellow as lives, and the girl could not have made a more prudent choice.

HARDCASTLE.

Then, by the hand of my body, I'm proud of the connection.

MRS. HARDCASTLE.

Well, if he has taken away the lady, he has not taken her fortune; that remains in this family to console us for her loss.

HARDCASTLE.

Sure, Dorothy, you would not be so mercenary?

MRS. HARDCASTLE.

Aye, that's my affair, not yours.

HARDCASTLE.[v]

But you know if your son, when of age, refuses to marry his cousin, her whole fortune is then at her own disposal.

MRS.[w] HARDCASTLE.

Aye, but he's not of age, and she has not thought proper to wait for his refusal.

Enter Hastings and Miss Neville.

(*Aside.*) What, returned so soon? I begin not to like it.

HASTINGS. (*To Hardcastle.*)

For my late attempt to fly off with your niece, let my present confusion be my punishment. We are now come back to appeal from your justice to your humanity. By her father's consent, I first paid her my addresses, and our passions were first founded in duty.

MISS NEVILLE.

Since his death, I have been obliged to stoop to dissimulation to avoid oppression. In an hour of levity, I was ready even to give up my fortune to secure my choice. But I'm now recovered from the delusion and hope from your tenderness what is denied me from a nearer connection.

MRS. HARDCASTLE.

Pshaw, pshaw, this is all but the whining end of a modern novel.

HARDCASTLE.

Be it what it will, I'm glad they're come back to reclaim their due.—Come hither, Tony boy. Do you refuse this lady's hand whom I now offer you?

TONY.

What signifies my refusing? You know I can't refuse her till I'm of age, Father.

HARDCASTLE.

While I thought concealing your age, boy, was likely to conduce to your improvement, I concurred with your mother's desire to keep it secret. But since I find she turns it to a wrong use, I must now declare you have been of age these three months.

TONY.

Of age! Am I of age, Father?

HARDCASTLE.

Above three months.

TONY.

Then you'll see the first use I'll make of my liberty. (*Taking Miss Neville's hand.*) Witness all men by these presents, that I, Anthony Lumpkin, Esquire, of _____* place, refuse you, Constantia Neville, spinster, of no place at all, for my true and lawful wife. So Constance Neville may marry whom she pleases, and Tony Lumpkin is his own man again.

SIR CHARLES.

Oh brave* squire.

HASTINGS.

My worthy friend.

MRS. HARDCASTLE.

My undutiful offspring.

MARLOW.

Joy, my dear George, I give you joy sincerely. And could I prevail upon my little tyrant here to be less arbitrary, I should be the happiest man alive if you would return me the favor.

HASTINGS. (*To Miss Hardcastle.*)

Come madam, you are now driven to the very last scene of all your contrivances. I know you like him, I'm sure he loves you, and you must and shall have him.

HARDCASTLE. (*Joining their hands.*)

And I say so too. And Mr. Marlow, if she makes as good a wife as she has a daughter, I don't believe you'll ever repent your bargain. So now to supper;

tomorrow we shall gather all the poor of the parish about us, and the Mistakes of the Night shall be crowned with a merry morning. So, boy, take her, and as you have been mistaken in the mistress, my wish is, that you may never be mistaken in the wife.

[Exeunt.]

FINIS.

Textual Notes

[a] Copytext is the first edition corrected, a 1773 octavo (Oc). Also consulted: first edition uncorrected, a 1773 octavo (Ou); Larpent ms. in the Huntington Library, the earliest surviving text of the play (not Goldsmith's holograph), prepared before the first performance for the licenser for the theater and used as the basis for some performances up through the 19th century (L); modern editions of 1939, rev. 1969 (Nettleton, Case, Stone—NCS); 1966 (Friedman); 1979 (Davis). If the modern scholarly editions (Friedman and/or Davis) do not incorporate substantive and/or interesting variants from L, they are not noted here.

[b] ackoardingly] L, Friedman; accordingly Oo, NCS, Davis

[c] these] L, NCS, Friedman, Davis; those Oo

[d] (*Noting it down.*)] L, Davis; *om.* Oo, NCS, Friedman

[e] (*Still noting.*)] L, Davis; *om.* Oo, NCS, Friedman

[f] (*Who had been noting.*) L, Davis; *om.* Oo, NCS, Friedman

[g] county] L, Friedman; country Oo, NCS, Davis

[h] this-aways] L, Friedman; this way Oo, NCS, Davis

[i] prepossessing] Oo, NCS, Friedman; professing L, Davis

[j] Charles] L, NCS, Friedman, Davis; George Oo

[k] without ... within] L, Friedman, Davis; within ... without Oo, NCS

[l] *Enter Roger ... fare.*] L, Friedman, Davis; *om.* Oo; *Re-enter Roger* NCS

[m] a pig's face ... pig's face ... pig's face] L, Davis; pig Oo, Friedman, NCS

[n] my boy] L, Davis; boy Oo, NCS, Friedman

[o] I–I–I–as yet have] Oo, NCS, Friedman; I-I-I- MISS HARDCASTLE. Then why take such pains to study and observe them? MARLOW. As yet I have L, Davis

[p] Longhorns,] L, Davis; Langhorns Oo, NCS, Friedman

[q] you] L, NCS, Friedman, Davis; *om.* Oo

[r] fortune but my character.] Oo, NCS, Davis; fortin but my charackter L, Friedman

[s] a hare ... cry, or] L, Davis; *om.* Oo, NCS, Friedman

[t] to take ... the bargain.] Oo, NCS, Friedman; to run me through the guts with a shoulder of mutton L, Davis

[u] not stir,] L, Davis; not, Sir, Oo, NCS, Friedman

[v] HARDCASTLE.] L, NCS, Friedman, Davis; *om.* Oo

[w] MRS.] L, NCS, Friedman, Davis; *om.* Oo

The School for Scandal[a]

by Richard Brinsley Sheridan (1751-1816)
edited by Mita Choudhury

Richard Brinsley Sheridan wrote many plays, including *The Rivals*, *The Critic*, *A Trip to Scarborough*, *The Duenna*, but none was as successful as *The School for Scandal* (premiere at Drury Lane, Thursday, May 8, 1777). On the eighteenth-century London stage, only John Gay's *Beggar's Opera* (1728) came close to this play's performance record. In addition to writing plays, Sheridan was the principal manager of Drury Lane Theater from 1776 on—right after David Garrick withdrew from the theater on grounds of poor health.

The central message of *The School for Scandal* is that appearances are deceptive, so much so that the man of true sentiment and virtue may not necessarily appear to be so. The play deals with the machinations of half a dozen delightfully dubious characters that caricature the late eighteenth-century London society newly invigorated by social mobility, trade, and commerce. Dressing rooms and tea parlors, libraries and picture galleries provide the right blend of settings for gossip and a variety of social schemes. Sir Oliver Surface, the moral arbiter in the play, returns from India with ample means to satisfy the whims of his nephews, only one of whom turns out to have the right values to deserve the uncle's support. While Joseph Surface appears to be a man of sentiment, it is his brother, Charles, who wins the support of their rich uncle and the theater audiences when he reveals his benevolence and compassion, his truly sentimental nature. The two most memorable scenes in the play—the picture and the screen scenes—are also two of the most effective "discovery"* scenes in the history of English drama, designed specifically to reveal the contrasting characters of Oliver Surface's nephews.

Sheridan created most of the characters with specific actors in mind. It is not surprising that William Smith—genteel, debonaire, and charismatic—would be cast, at age forty-seven, as Charles Surface. He looked twenty years younger than his age, and he was able to carry off that role with as much panache much later at age sixty-eight. Likewise, John Palmer, who was cast as Joseph Surface, had a reputation for being hypocritical and unfaithful to his wife. A good friend of Garrick's, Thomas King had become the principal comedian at Drury Lane theater circa mid 1770s. He was the original Sir Peter Teazle, playing opposite Frances Abington as Lady Teazle. Abington was one of the greatest comediennes of her time, and Lady Teazle was her most successful part, following, among many others, Lucy in *The Beggar's Opera* and Mrs. Sullen in *The Beaux' Stratagem.* Richard Yates, the versatile actor and one-time manager of the Birmingham theater, was about seventy when he played the original Sir Oliver Surface.

Good casting alone cannot account for the success of *The School for Scandal*, however. The tone and texture of Sheridan's characters and dialogue add depth to our understanding of a metropolitan public culture at the dawn of London's dynamic role as the imperial capital, the metropolis to which her adventuring colonists, like Sir Oliver, returned with increasing wealth and power.

[I.i]

DRAMATIS PERSONAE

[MEN]

Sir Peter Teazle.
Sir Oliver Surface.
Joseph Surface.
Charles Surface.
Snake.
Rowley.
Moses.
Careless.
Sir Toby Bumper.
Trip.
Sir Benjamin Backbite.
Crabtree.
[Servants.]

[WOMEN]

Lady Teazle.
Lady Sneerwell.
Mrs. Candor.
Maria.

The School for Scandal.

Act I, scene i. [Lady Sneerwell's house.]

Lady Sneerwell at the dressing table; Mr. Snake drinking chocolate.

LADY SNEERWELL.
The paragraphs you say, Mr. Snake, were all inserted?

SNAKE.
They were, madam, and as I copied them myself in a feigned hand, there can be no suspicion whence they came.

LADY SNEERWELL.
Did you circulate the report of Lady Brittle's intrigue with Captain Boastall?

SNAKE.
That is in as fine a train as your ladyship could wish; in the common course of things, I think it must reach Mrs. Clackit's ears within four-and-twenty hours, and then you know the business is as good as done.

LADY SNEERWELL.
Why truly, Mrs. Clackit has a very pretty talent and a great deal of industry.

SNAKE.
True, madam, and has been tolerably successful in her day. To my knowledge she has been the cause of six matches being broken off and three sons being disinherited, of four forced elopements, as many close confinements,[1] nine separate maintenances,* and two divorces. Nay, I have more than once traced her causing a tête-à-tête in the *Town and Country Magazine*[2] when the parties perhaps had never seen each others' faces before in the course of their lives.

LADY SNEERWELL.
She certainly has talents, but her manner is gross.

SNAKE.
'Tis very true: she generally designs well, has a free tongue and a bold invention, but her coloring is too dark and her outline often extravagant. She wants* that delicacy of hint and mellowness of sneer which distinguishes your ladyship's scandal.

LADY SNEERWELL.
Ah! You are partial, Snake.

SNAKE.
Not in the least: everybody allows that Lady Sneerwell can do more with a word or a look than many can with the most labored detail, even when they happen to have a little truth on their side to support it.

LADY SNEERWELL.
Yes, my dear Snake, and I am no hypocrite to deny the satisfaction I reap from the success of my efforts. Wounded myself in the early part of my life by the envenomed tongue of slander, I confess I have since known no pleasure equal to the reducing others to the level of my own reputation.[b]

SNAKE.
Nothing can be more natural. But Lady Sneerwell, there is one affair in which you have lately employed me wherein I confess I am at a loss to guess your motives.

---

[1] close confinements] hushed-up childbirths

[2] *Town and Country Magazine*] a monthly periodical, an early-modern equivalent of today's print tabloid. Celebrities' identities were indicated by pseudonyms or initials; their portraits often accompanied these anecdotes (Price).

LADY SNEERWELL.

I conceive you mean with respect to my neighbor, Sir Peter Teazle, and his family?

SNAKE.

I do. Here are two young men to whom Sir Peter has acted as a kind of guardian since their father's death: the eldest possessing the most amiable character and universally well spoken of; the youngest the most dissipated and extravagant young fellow in the kingdom, without friends or character. The former an avowed admirer of your ladyship's and apparently your favorite; the latter attached to Maria, Sir Peter's ward, and confessedly beloved by her. Now on the face of these circumstances, it is utterly unaccountable to me why you, the widow of a City* knight with a good jointure, should not close with the passion of a man of such character and expectation as Mr. Surface, and more so, why you should be so uncommonly earnest to destroy the mutual attachment between his brother Charles and Maria.

LADY SNEERWELL.

Then at once to unravel this mystery, I must inform you that love has no share whatever in the intercourse between Mr. Surface and me.

SNAKE.

No!

LADY SNEERWELL.

His real attachment is to Maria or her fortune, but finding in his brother a favored rival, he has been obliged to mask his pretensions and profit by my assistance.

SNAKE.

Yet still I am more puzzled why you should interest yourself in his success.

LADY SNEERWELL.

Heavens, how dull you are! Cannot you surmise the weakness which I hitherto through shame have concealed even from you? Must I confess that Charles, that libertine, that extravagant, that bankrupt in fortune and reputation, that he it is for whom I am thus anxious and malicious and to gain whom I would sacrifice everything.

SNAKE.

Now, indeed your conduct appears consistent, but how came you and Mr. Surface so confidential?

LADY SNEERWELL.

For our mutual interest. I have found him out a long time since. I know him to be artful, selfish, and malicious—in short, a sentimental knave—while with Sir Peter, and indeed with all his acquaintance, he passes for a miracle of prudence, good sense, and benevolence.[c]

SNAKE.

Nay, Sir Peter vows he has not his equal in England, and above all he praises him as a Man of Sentiment.

LADY SNEERWELL.

True, and with the assistance of sentiments and hypocrisy, he has brought him entirely into his interest with regard to Maria, while poor Charles has no friend in the house, though I fear he has a powerful one in Maria's heart, against whom we must direct our schemes.

Enter servant.

SERVANT.

Mr. Surface.

LADY SNEERWELL.

Show him up.

Exit servant.

He generally calls about this time; I don't wonder at people's giving him to me for a lover.

Enter Joseph Surface.

JOSEPH SURFACE.

My dear Lady Sneerwell, how do you do to day? Mr. Snake, your most obedient.

LADY SNEERWELL.

Snake has just been arraigning me on our mutual attachment, but I have informed him of our real views. You know how useful he has been to us, and believe me, the confidence is not ill placed.

JOSEPH SURFACE.

Madam, it is impossible for me to suspect a man of Mr. Snake's sensibility and discernment.

LADY SNEERWELL.

Well, well, no compliments now, but tell me when you saw your mistress, Maria, or what is more material to me, your brother.

JOSEPH SURFACE.

I have not seen either since I left you, but I can

inform you that they never meet. Some of your stories have taken a good effect on Maria.

LADY SNEERWELL.
Ah my dear Snake, the merit of this belongs to you.—But do your brother's distresses increase?

JOSEPH SURFACE.
Every hour. I am told he has had another execution[3] in his house yesterday; in short, his dissipation and extravagance exceed everything I ever heard of.

LADY SNEERWELL.
Poor Charles!

JOSEPH SURFACE.
True, madam, notwithstanding his vices, one cannot help feeling for him. Aye, poor Charles indeed. I am sure I wish it was in my power to be of any essential service to him. For the man who does not share in the distresses of a brother, even though merited by his own misconduct, deserves—

LADY SNEERWELL.
Oh Lud!* You are going to be moral and forget that you are among friends.

JOSEPH SURFACE.
Egad that's true. I'll keep that sentiment till I see Sir Peter. However, it is certainly a charity to rescue Maria from such a libertine, who, if he is to be reclaimed, can be so only by one of your ladyship's superior accomplishments and understanding.

SNAKE.
I believe, Lady Sneerwell, here's company coming; I'll go and copy the letter I mentioned to you.—Mr. Surface, your most obedient. (*Exit.*)

JOSEPH SURFACE.
Sir, your very devoted— Lady Sneerwell, I am very sorry you have put any further confidence in that fellow.

LADY SNEERWELL.
Why so?

JOSEPH SURFACE.
I have lately detected him in frequent conference with old Rowley, who was formerly my father's steward and has never, you know, been a friend of mine.

LADY SNEERWELL.
And do you think he would betray us?

JOSEPH SURFACE.
Nothing more likely, take my word for it, Lady Sneerwell, that fellow has not virtue enough to be faithful or constant even to his own villainy.—Hah, Maria!

Enter Maria.

LADY SNEERWELL.
Maria, my dear, how do you do? What's the matter?

MARIA.
Oh, there's that disagreeable lover of mine, Sir Benjamin Backbite, has just called at my guardian's with his odious uncle Crabtree, so I slipped out and ran hither to avoid them.

LADY SNEERWELL.
Is that all?

JOSEPH SURFACE.
If my brother Charles had been of the party, madam, perhaps you would not have been so much alarmed.

LADY SNEERWELL.
Nay now, you are severe, for I dare swear the truth of the matter is, Maria heard you were here.—But my dear, what has Sir Benjamin done that you should avoid him so?

MARIA.
Oh, he has done nothing, but 'tis for what he has said. His conversation is a perpetual libel on all his acquaintance.

JOSEPH SURFACE.
Aye, and the worst of it is, there is no advantage in not knowing him, for he'll abuse a stranger just as soon as his best friend, and his uncle is as bad.

LADY SNEERWELL.
Nay, but we should make allowance: Sir Benjamin is a wit and a poet.

MARIA.
For my part I own, madam, wit loses its respect with me when I see it in company with malice.—What do you think, Mr. Surface?

JOSEPH SURFACE.
Certainly, madam, to smile at the jest which plants a thorn in another's breast is to become a principal in the mischief.

LADY SNEERWELL.
Pshaw! There's no possibility of being witty

[3] execution] deflowering a virgin

without a little ill nature; malice of a good thing is the barb which makes it stick.—What's your opinion, Mr. Surface?

JOSEPH SURFACE.
To be sure, madam, that conversation where the spirit of raillery is suppressed will ever appear tedious and insipid.

MARIA.[d]
Well, I'll not debate how far scandal may be allowable, but in a man I am sure it is always contemptible. We have pride, envy, rivalship, and a thousand little motives to depreciate each other, but the male slanderer must have the cowardice of a woman before he can traduce one.

Enter servant.

SERVANT.
Madam, Mrs. Candor is below and, if your ladyship's at leisure, will leave her carriage.

LADY SNEERWELL.
Beg her to walk in.

[Exit servant.]

Now Maria, however, here is a character to your taste, for though Mrs. Candor is a little talkative, everybody allows her to be the best natured and best sort of woman.

MARIA.
Yet with a very gross affectation of good nature and benevolence, she does more mischief than the direct malice of old Crabtree.

JOSEPH SURFACE.
I'faith, 'tis very true, Lady Sneerwell. Whenever I hear the current running against the characters* of my friends, I never think them in such danger as when Candor undertakes their defence.

LADY SNEERWELL.
Hush! Here she is.

Enter Mrs. Candor.

MRS. CANDOR.
My dear Lady Sneerwell, how have you been this century? Mr. Surface, what news do you hear, though indeed it is no matter, for I think one hears nothing else but scandal.

JOSEPH SURFACE.
Just so indeed, madam.

MRS. CANDOR.
Ah! Maria, child,* is the whole affair off between you and Charles? His extravagance, I presume; the Town* talks of nothing else.

MARIA.
I am very sorry, ma'am, the Town have so little to do.

MRS. CANDOR.
True, true, child, but there is no stopping people's tongues. I own I was hurt to hear it, as indeed I was to learn from the same quarter that your guardian, Sir Peter, and Lady Teazle have not agreed lately so well as could be wished.

MARIA.
'Tis strangely impertinent for people to busy themselves so. I'm sure such reports are—

MRS. CANDOR.
Very true, child, but what's to be done? People will talk, there's no preventing it. Why it was but yesterday I was told that Miss Gadabout had eloped with Sir Filagree Flirt—but Lord, there is no minding what one hears—though to be sure I had this from very good authority.

MARIA.
Such reports are highly scandalous.

MRS. CANDOR.
So they are, child—shameful! shameful! But the world is so censorious no character* escapes. Lord now! Who would have suspected your friend Miss Prim of an indiscretion? Yet such is the ill nature of people that they say her uncle stopped her last week just as she was stepping into the York Diligence with her dancing master.

MARIA.
I'll answer for it, there are no grounds for the report.

MRS. CANDOR.
Oh, no foundation in the world, I dare swear, no more probably than for the story circulated last month of Mrs. Festino's affair with Colonel Cassino, though to be sure that matter was never rightly cleared up.

JOSEPH SURFACE.
The license of invention some people take is monstrous indeed!

MARIA.
'Tis so, but in my opinion those who report such things are equally culpable.

MRS. CANDOR.
To be sure they are: tale bearers are as bad as tale makers; 'tis an old observation and a very true one. But what's to be done, as I said before? How will you prevent people from talking? Today Mrs. Clackit assured me Mr. and Mrs. Honeymoon were at last become mere man and wife like the rest of her acquaintance. She likewise hinted that a certain widow in the next street had got rid of her dropsy and recovered her shape in a most surprising manner, and the same time Miss Tattle, who was by, affirmed that Lord Buffalo had discovered his lady at a house of no extraordinary fame and that Sir Harry Bouquet and Tom Saunter were to measure swords on a similar provocation. But Lord, do you think I would report these things? No, no, tale-bearers, as I said before, are just as bad as tale-makers.

JOSEPH SURFACE.
Oh Mrs. Candor, if everybody had your forbearance and good nature!

MRS. CANDOR.
I confess, Mr. Surface, I cannot bear to hear people attacked behind their backs, and when ugly circumstances come out against one's acquaintances, I own I always love to think the best. By the bye, I hope 'tis not true that your brother is absolutely ruined.

JOSEPH SURFACE.
I am afraid his circumstances are very bad indeed, madam.

MRS. CANDOR.
Ah, I heard so, but you must tell him to keep up his spirits: Sir Thomas Splint,[e] Captain Quinzes, and Mr. Nickit, all up, I hear, within this week, so if Charles is undone, he will find half his acquaintances ruined too, and that, you know, is a consolation.

JOSEPH SURFACE.
Doubtless, ma'am, a very great one.

Enter servant.

SERVANT.
Mr. Crabtree and Sir Benjamin Backbite. [*Exit.*]

LADY SNEERWELL.
So Maria, you see your lover pursues you. Positively you shan't escape.

Enter Crabtree and Sir Benjamin Backbite.

CRABTREE.
Lady Sneerwell, I kiss your hands.—Mrs. Candor, I don't believe you are acquainted with my nephew, Sir Benjamin Backbite. Egad ma'am, he has a pretty wit and is a pretty poet too.—Isn't he, Lady Sneerwell?

SIR BENJAMIN.
Oh fie, Uncle!

CRABTREE.
Nay, egad 'tis true: I'll back him at a rebus or a charade against the best rhymer in the kingdom. Has your ladyship heard the epigram he wrote last week on Lady Frizzle's feather catching fire! Do, Benjamin, repeat it, or the charade you made last night extempore at Mrs. Drowzy's conversazione. Come now, your first is the name of a fish, your second a great naval commander—and—

SIR BENJAMIN.
Uncle—now—prithee!

CRABTREE.
I'faith, madam, 'twould surprise you to hear how ready he is at these things.

LADY SNEERWELL.
I wonder, Sir Benjamin, you never publish anything.

SIR BENJAMIN.
To say truth, ma'am, 'tis very vulgar to print, and as my little productions are mostly satires and lampoons on particular people, I find they circulate more by giving copies in confidence to the friends of the parties; however, I have some love elegies which, when favored with this lady's smiles, I mean to give to the public.

CRABTREE.
Fore Heaven, ma'am, they'll immortalize you; you'll be handed down to posterity like Petrarch's Laura or Waller's Sacharissa.[4]

SIR BENJAMIN.
Yes madam, I think you will like them when you shall see them on a beautiful quarto page, where a neat rivulet of text shall murmur through a meadow of margin. Fore gad, they will be the most elegant things of their kind—

4 Waller's Sacharissa] Edmund Waller (1606-87) wrote verses to Sacharissa, Lady Dorothy Sidney.

CRABTREE.

But ladies, that's true. Have you heard the news?

MRS. CANDOR.

What, sir, do you mean the report of—

CRABTREE.

No ma'am, that's not it. Miss Nicely* is going to be married to her own footman.

MRS. CANDOR.

Impossible!

CRABTREE.

Ask Sir Benjamin.

SIR BENJAMIN.

'Tis very true, ma'am: everything is fixed and the wedding livery bespoke.

CRABTREE.

Yes, and they do say there were pressing reasons for it.

LADY SNEERWELL.

Why, I have heard something of this before.

MRS. CANDOR.

It can't be, and I wonder anyone should believe such a story of so prudent a lady as Miss Nicely.

SIR BENJAMIN.

Oh Lud* ma'am, that's the very reason 'twas believed at once. She has always been so cautious and so reserved that everybody was sure there was some reason for it at bottom.

MRS. CANDOR.

Why, to be sure a tale of scandal is as fatal to the credit of a prudent lady of her stamp as a fever is generally to those of the strongest constitutions. But there is a sort of puny, sickly reputation that is always ailing yet will outlive the robuster character of a hundred prudes.

SIR BENJAMIN.

True madam, there are valetudinarians in reputation as well as constitution, who, being conscious of their weak part, avoid the least breath of air and supply their want* of stamina by care and circumspection.

MRS. CANDOR.

Well, but this may be all a mistake. You know, Sir Benjamin, very trifling circumstances often give rise to the most injurious tales.

CRABTREE.

That they do, I'll be sworn, ma'am. Did you ever hear how Miss Piper came to lose her lover and her character* last summer at Tunbridge? Sir Benjamin, you remember it?

SIR BENJAMIN.

Oh, to be sure! The most whimsical circumstance—

LADY SNEERWELL.

How was it pray?

CRABTREE.

Why, one evening at Mrs. Ponto's assembly the conversation happened to turn on the difficulty of breeding Nova Scotia sheep in this country; says a lady in company, "I have known instances of it, for Miss Laetitia Piper, a first cousin of mine, had a Nova Scotia sheep that produced her twins." "What!" cries the Dowager Lady Dundizzy (who you know is as deaf as a post) "has Miss Laetitia Piper had twins?" This mistake, as you may imagine, threw the whole company into a fit of laughter; however, 'twas the next day reported, and in a few days believed by the whole Town, that Miss Letitia Piper had actually been brought to bed of a fine boy and a girl, and in less than a week there were people who could name the father and the farmhouse where the babies were put out to nurse.

LADY SNEERWELL.

Strange indeed.

CRABTREE.

Matter of fact, I assure you.—Oh Lud, Mr. Surface, pray is it true that your Uncle Sir Oliver is coming home?

JOSEPH SURFACE.

Not that I know of, indeed sir.

CRABTREE.

He has been in the East Indies a long time; you can scarcely remember him, I believe. Sad comfort whenever he returns to hear how your brother has gone on.

JOSEPH SURFACE.

Charles has been imprudent, sir, to be sure, but I hope no busy people have already prejudiced Sir Oliver against him; he may reform.

SIR BENJAMIN.

To be sure he may. For my part I never believed him so utterly void of principle as people say, and though he has lost all his friends, I am told nobody is better spoken of by the Jews.

CRABTREE.
That's true, egad Nephew. If the old Jewry was a ward, I believe Charles would be an alderman. No man more popular there. Fore gad, I hear he pays as many annuities as the Irish tontine[5] and that whenever he's sick they have prayers for the recovery of his health in the synagogue.

SIR BENJAMIN.
Yet no man lives in greater splendor. They tell me when he entertains his friends, he can sit down to dinner with a dozen of his own securities, have a score of tradesman in the anti-chamber and an officer behind every guest's chair.

JOSEPH SURFACE.
This may be entertainment to you, gentlemen, but you pay very little regard to the feelings of a brother.

MARIA. [*Aside.*]
Their malice is intolerable.—Lady Sneerwell, I must wish you a good morning—I'm not very well. (*Exit.*)

MRS. CANDOR.
Oh dear, she changes color very much.

LADY SNEERWELL.
Do Mrs. Candor follow her, she may want* assistance.

MRS. CANDOR.
That I will with all my soul, ma'am. Poor dear creature, who knows what her situation may be? (*Exit.*)

LADY SNEERWELL.
'Twas nothing but that she could not bear to hear Charles reflected on, notwithstanding their difference.

SIR BENJAMIN.
The young lady's penchant is obvious.

CRABTREE.
But Benjamin, you mustn't give up the pursuit for that. Follow her and put her into good humor, repeat her some of your verses. Come, I'll assist you.

SIR BENJAMIN.
Mr. Surface, I did not mean to hurt you, but depend on't, your brother is utterly undone.

CRABTREE.
Oh Lud! Aye! undone as ever man was, can't raise a guinea.

SIR BENJAMIN.
Everything sold, I am told, that was moveable.[6]

CRABTREE.
I have seen one that was at his house: not a thing left but some empty bottles that were overlooked and the family pictures, which I believe are framed in the wainscot.

SIR BENJAMIN.
And I am very sorry to hear also some bad stories against him. (*Going.*)

CRABTREE.
Oh, he has done many mean* things, that's certain.

SIR BENJAMIN.
But however, as he's your brother— (*Going.*)

CRABTREE.
We'll tell you all another opportunity.

Exeunt Sir Benjamin and Crabtree.

LADY SNEERWELL.
Ha, ha, ha! 'tis very hard for them to leave a subject they have not quite run down.

JOSEPH SURFACE.
And I believe their abuse was no more acceptable to your ladyship than Maria.

LADY SNEERWELL.
I doubt* her affections are further engaged than we imagined. But the family are to be here this evening, so you may as well dine where you are, and we shall have an opportunity of observing further; in the meantime, I'll go and plot mischief, and you shall study sentiments.

Exeunt.

Scene ii. Sir Peter Teazle's house.

Enter Sir Peter.

SIR PETER.
When an old bachelor takes a young wife, what is he to expect? 'Tis now six months since Lady Teazle made me the happiest of men, and I have been the

5 Irish tontine] The Anglo-Irish government had set up a tontine to help pay off its debts (Price).

6 moveable] admitting of being removed or displaced; applied to 'personal' as opposed to 'real' property (*OED*)

miserablest dog ever since. We tiffed a little going to church and came to a quarrel before the bells were done ringing. I was more than once nearly choked with gall during the honeymoon and had lost all comfort in life before my friends had done wishing me joy. Yet I chose with caution: a girl bred wholly in the country, who never knew luxury beyond one silk gown nor dissipation above the annual gala of a race ball. Yet now she plays her part in all the extravagant fopperies of the fashion and the Town with as ready a grace as if she had never seen a bush nor a grass plot out of Grosvenor Square.* I am sneered at by my old acquaintance, paragraphed in the newspapers; she dissipates my fortune and contradicts all humors. Yet the worst of it is, I doubt* I love her, or I should never bear all this; however, I'll never be weak enough to own it.

Enter Rowley.

ROWLEY.
Oh Sir Peter, your servant. How is it with you, sir?

SIR PETER.
Very bad, Master Rowley, very bad. I meet with nothing but crosses and vexations.

ROWLEY.
What can have happened to trouble you since yesterday?

SIR PETER.
A good question to a married man.

ROWLEY.
Nay, I'm sure Sir Peter, your lady can't be the cause of your uneasiness.

SIR PETER.
Why, has anyone told you she was dead?

ROWLEY.
Come, come, Sir Peter, you love her, notwithstanding your tempers don't exactly agree.

SIR PETER.
But the fault is entirely hers, Master Rowley. I am myself the sweetest tempered man alive and hate a teazing temper, and so I tell her an hundred times a day.

ROWLEY.
Indeed!

SIR PETER.
Aye, and what is very extraordinary, in all our disputes she is always in the wrong. But Lady Sneerwell and the set she meets at her house encourage the perverseness of her disposition. Then to complete my vexations, Maria, my ward, whom I ought to have the power of a father over, is determined to turn rebel too and absolutely refuses the man whom I have long resolved on for her husband, meaning, I suppose, to bestow herself on his profligate brother.

ROWLEY.
You know, Sir Peter, I have always taken the liberty to differ with you on the subject of these two young gentlemen. I only wish you may not be deceived in your opinion of the elder; for Charles, my life on't, he will retrieve his errors yet. Their worthy father, once my honored master, was at his years nearly as wild a spark, but when he died, he did not leave a more benevolent heart to lament his loss.

SIR PETER.
You are wrong, Master Rowley. On their father's death you know I acted as a kind of guardian to them both 'till their uncle Sir Oliver's eastern liberality gave them an early independence. Of course, no person could have more opportunities of judging of their hearts, and I was never mistaken in my life. Joseph is indeed a model for the young men of the age: he is a man of sentiment and acts up to the sentiments he professes. But for the other, take my word for't, if he had any grains of virtue by descent, he has dissipated them with the rest of his inheritance. Ah, my old friend Sir Oliver will be deeply mortified when he finds how part of his bounty has been misapplied.

ROWLEY.
I am sorry to find you so violent against the young man because this may be the most critical period of his fortune; I came hither with news that will surprise you.

SIR PETER.
What? let me hear.

ROWLEY.
Sir Oliver is arrived and at this moment in Town.

SIR PETER.
How! You astonish me! I thought you did not expect him this month.

ROWLEY.

I did not, but his passage has been remarkably quick.

SIR PETER.

Egad, I shall rejoice to see my old friend; 'tis sixteen years since we met. We have had many a day together. But does he still enjoin us not to inform his nephews of his arrival?

ROWLEY.

Most strictly. He means before it is known to make some trial of their dispositions.

SIR PETER.

Ah, there needs no art to discover their merits; however, he shall have his way. But pray, does he know I am married?

ROWLEY.

Yes, and will soon wish you joy.

SIR PETER.

What, as we drink health to a friend in a consumption? Ah! Oliver will laugh at me. We used to rail at matrimony together, but he has been steady to his text. Well, he must be at my house though. I'll instantly give orders for his reception. But Master Rowley, don't drop a word that Lady Teazle and I disagree.

ROWLEY.

By no means—

SIR PETER.

For I should never be able to stand Noll's jokes, so I'd have him think, Lord forgive me, that we are a very happy couple.

ROWLEY.

I understand you. But then you must be very careful not to differ while he's in the house with you.

SIR PETER.

Egad, and so we must—and that's impossible. Ah Master Rowley, when an old bachelor marries a young wife, he deserves—no, the crime carries the punishment along with it.

Exeunt.

Act II, scene i. Sir Peter Teazle's house.

Enter Sir Peter and Lady Teazle.

SIR PETER.

Lady Teazle, Lady Teazle, I'll not bear it.

LADY TEAZLE.

Sir Peter, Sir Peter, you may bear it or not, as you please, but I ought to have my own way in everything, and what's more, I will too. What, though I was educated in the country, I know very well that women of fashion in London are accountable to nobody after they are married.

SIR PETER.

Very well, ma'am, very well, so a husband is to have no influence, no authority?

LADY TEAZLE.

Authority! No, to be sure. If you wanted authority over me, you should have adopted me and not married me; I am sure you were old enough.

SIR PETER.

Old enough! Aye, there it is, well, well, Lady Teazle, though my life may be made unhappy by your temper, I'll not be ruined by your extravagance.

LADY TEAZLE.

My extravagance? I'm sure I'm not more extravagant than a woman of fashion ought to be.

SIR PETER.

No, no, madam, you shall throw away no more sums on such unmeaning luxury. 'Slife,* to spend as much to furnish your dressing room with flowers in winter, as would suffice to turn the Pantheon* into a greenhouse and give a fête champêtre at Christmas.

LADY TEAZLE.

Lord, Sir Peter, am I to blame because flowers are dear* in cold weather; you should find fault with the climate and not with me. For my part I am sure I wish it were spring all the year round and that roses grew under our feet.

SIR PETER.

'Oons* madam! If you had been born to this, I should not wonder at your talking thus, but you forget what your situation was when I married you.

LADY TEAZLE.

No, no, I don't: 'twas a very disagreeable one, or I should never have married you.

SIR PETER.

Yes, yes, madam, you were then somewhat in an humbler style: the daughter of a plain country squire. Recollect, Lady Teazle, when I first saw you sitting at your tambour in a pretty figured linen gown, with a bunch of keys by your side, your hair combed smoothly over a roll, and your apartment hung round with fruits in worsted of your own working.

LADY TEAZLE.

Oh yes, I remember it very well, and a curious life I led! My daily occupation: to inspect the dairy, superintend the poultry, make extracts from the family receipt* book, and comb my aunt Deborah's lapdog.

SIR PETER.

Yes, yes, madam, 'twas so indeed.

LADY TEAZLE.

And then you know my evening amusements: to draw patterns for ruffles which I had not the materials to make, to play Pope Joan[7] with the curate, read a sermon[f] to my aunt, or be stuck down to an old spinnet to strum my father to sleep after a fox chase.

SIR PETER.

I am glad you have so good a memory. Yes madam, these were the recreations I took you from. But now you must have your coach, vis-à-vis,[8] and three powdered footmen before your chair*—and in summer a pair of white cats[9] to draw you to Kensington Gardens.* No recollection I suppose when you were content to ride double behind the butler on a docked coach horse?

LADY TEAZLE.

No, I swear I never did that, I deny the butler and the coach horse.

SIR PETER.

This, madam, was your situation, and what have I not done for you? I have made you a woman of fashion, of fortune, of rank; in short, I have made you *my wife.*

LADY TEAZLE.

Well then, and there is but one thing more you can make me to add to the obligation—and that is—

SIR PETER.

My widow, I suppose?

LADY TEAZLE.

Hem, hem!

SIR PETER.

Thank you, madam, but don't flatter yourself, for though your ill conduct may disturb my peace, it shall never break my heart, I promise you; however, I am equally obliged to you for the hint.

LADY TEAZLE.

Then why will you endeavor to make yourself so disagreeable to me and thwart me in every little elegant expense?

SIR PETER.

'Slife* madam, I say, had you any of these elegant expenses when you married me?

LADY TEAZLE.

Lord, Sir Peter, would you have me be out of fashion?

SIR PETER.

The fashion indeed! What had you to do with the fashion when you married me?

LADY TEAZLE.

For my part I should think you would like to have your wife thought a woman of taste.

SIR PETER.

Aye, there again—taste—Zounds, Madam! You had no taste when you married me.

LADY TEAZLE.

That's very true indeed, Sir Peter, and after having married you, I should never pretend to taste again, I allow. But now Sir Peter, if we have finished our daily jangle, I presume I may go to my engagement at Lady Sneerwell's?

SIR PETER.

Aye, there's another precious* circumstance, a charming set of acquaintance you have made there.

LADY TEAZLE.

Nay Sir Peter, they are people of rank and fortune, and remarkably tenacious of reputation.

SIR PETER.

Yes, egad, they are tenacious of reputation with a vengeance! For they don't choose anybody should have a character* but themselves. Such a crew! Ah! Many a wretch has rid on a hurdle who has done less mischief than these utterers of forged tales,

7 Pope Joan] a three-handed card game, named after the infamous female pope

8 vis-à-vis] a light carriage for two persons sitting face-to-face (*OED*)

9 cats] ponies (NCS)

coiners of scandal, and clippers* of reputation.

LADY TEAZLE.
What, would you restrain the freedom of speech?

SIR PETER.
Oh, they have made you just as bad as any one of the society.

LADY TEAZLE.
Why I believe I do bear a part with a tolerable grace, but I vow I have no malice against the people I abuse. When I say an ill-natured thing, 'tis out of pure good humor, and I take for granted they'll deal exactly in the same manner with me. But Sir Peter, you know you promised to come to Lady Sneerwell's too.

SIR PETER.
Well, well, I'll call in just to look after my own character.*

LADY TEAZLE.
Then, indeed, you must make haste after me or you'll be too late. So goodbye to you. (*Exit.*)

SIR PETER.
So! I have gained much by my intended expostulations. Yet with what a charming air she contradicts everything I say and how pleasingly she shows her contempt of my authority. Well, though I can't make her love me, there is great satisfaction in quarrelling with her, and I think she never appears to such advantage as when she's doing everything in her power to plague me.

Exit.

Scene ii. Lady Sneerwell's house.

Lady Sneerwell, Mrs. Candor, Crabtree, Sir Benjamin Backbite, and Joseph Surface discovered; servants attending with tea.*

LADY SNEERWELL.
Nay, positively we will have it.

JOSEPH SURFACE.
Yes, yes, the epigram, by all means.

SIR BENJAMIN.
Oh plague on't, Uncle, 'tis mere nonsense.

CRABTREE.
No, no, fore gad, very clever for an extempore.

SIR BENJAMIN.
But ladies, you should be acquainted with the circumstance. You must know that one day last week, as Lady Betty Curricle was taking the dust in Hyde Park* in a sort of duodecimo phaeton, she desired me to write some verses on her ponies, upon which I took out my pocket book and in one moment produced the following:

Sure never were seen two such beautiful ponies,
Other horses are clowns, and these macaronies;
Nay, to give them this title I'm sure is not wrong,
Their legs are so slim, and their tails are so long.

CRABTREE.
There ladies, done in the smack of a whip and on horseback too.

JOSEPH SURFACE.
A very Phoebus mounted indeed, Sir Benjamin.

SIR BENJAMIN.
Oh dear sir, trifles, trifles!

Enter Lady Teazle and Maria.

MRS. CANDOR.
I must have a copy.

LADY SNEERWELL.
Lady Teazle, I hope we shall see Sir Peter.

LADY TEAZLE.
I believe he'll wait on your ladyship presently.

LADY SNEERWELL.
Maria my dear, you look grave. Come, you shall sit down to piquet with Mr. Surface.

MARIA.
I take very little pleasure in cards; however, I'll do as your ladyship pleases.

LADY TEAZLE. [*Aside.*]
I am surprised Mr. Surface should sit down with her. I thought he would have embraced this opportunity of speaking to me before Sir Peter came.

MRS. CANDOR.
Now, I'll die but you are so scandalous, I'll foreswear your society.

LADY TEAZLE.
What's the matter, Mrs. Candor?

MRS. CANDOR.
They'll not allow our friend, Miss Vermillion, to be handsome.

LADY SNEERWELL.
Oh surely, she's a pretty woman.

CRABTREE.
I'm very glad you think so, madam.

MRS. CANDOR.
She has a charming, fresh color.

LADY TEAZLE.
Yes, when it is fresh put on.

MRS. CANDOR.
Oh fie! I'll swear her color is natural. I have seen it come and go.

LADY TEAZLE.
I dare swear you have, ma'am; it goes off at night and comes again in the morning.

MRS. CANDOR.
Ha, ha, ha! How I hate to hear you talk so. But surely now, her sister *is* or *was* very handsome.

CRABTREE.
Who, Mrs. Evergreen? Oh Lord! She's six-and-fifty if she's an hour.

MRS. CANDOR.
Now positively you wrong her, fifty-two or fifty-three is the utmost, and I don't think she looks more.

SIR BENJAMIN.
Oh there's no judging by her looks, unless one could see her face.

LADY SNEERWELL.
Well, well, if Mrs. Evergreen does take some pains to repair the ravages of time, you must allow she effects it with great ingenuity, and surely that's better than the careless manner in which the Widow Ochre caulks her wrinkles.

SIR BENJAMIN.
Nay now Lady Sneerwell, you are severe upon the widow. Come, come, it is not that the widow paints so ill, but when she has finished her face, she joins it on so badly to her neck that she looks like a mended statue in which the connoisseur discovers at once that the head is modern though the trunk's antique.

CRABTREE.
Ha, ha, ha! Well said, Nephew.

MRS. CANDOR.
Well, you make me laugh, but I vow I hate you for't. What do you think of Miss Simper?

SIR BENJAMIN.
Why, she has very pretty teeth.

LADY TEAZLE.
Yes, and on that account when she is neither speaking nor laughing, which very seldom happens, she never absolutely shuts her mouth but leaves it always on ajar as it were.

MRS. CANDOR.
How can you be so ill-natured?

LADY TEAZLE.
I'll allow that's better than the pains Mrs. Prim takes to conceal her losses in front. She draws her mouth till it positively resembles the aperture of a poor box, and all her words appear to slide out edgeways.

LADY SNEERWELL.
Very well, Lady Teazle, I see you can be a little severe.

LADY TEAZLE.
In defense of a friend it is but justice.—But here comes Sir Peter to spoil our pleasantry.

Enter Sir Peter.

SIR PETER.
Ladies, your most obedient— Mercy on me, here is the whole set: a character* dead at every word, I suppose.

MRS. CANDOR.
I am rejoiced you are come, Sir Peter; they have been so censorious, they'll allow good qualities to nobody, not even good nature to our friend, Mrs. Pursey.

LADY TEAZLE.
What, the fat dowager who was at Mrs. Codille's last night?

MRS. CANDOR.
Nay, her bulk is her misfortune, and when she takes such pains to get rid of it, you ought not to reflect on her.

LADY SNEERWELL.
That's very true, indeed.

LADY TEAZLE.
Yes, I know she almost lives upon acids and small whey, laces herself by pullies, and often in the hottest noon in summer you may see her on a little, squat pony with her hair plaited up behind like a drummer and puffing around the Ring* in a full trot.

MRS. CANDOR.
I thank you, Lady Teazle, for defending her.

SIR PETER.
Yes, a good defense, truly.

MRS. CANDOR.
But Sir Benjamin is as censorious as Miss Sallow.

CRABTREE.
Yes, and she is a curious being to pretend to be censorious, an awkward gawky without any one good point under heaven.

MRS. CANDOR.
Positively you shall not be so severe. Miss Sallow is a relation of mine by marriage, and as for her person, great allowance is to be made, for let me tell you, a woman labors under many disadvantages who tries to pass for a girl at six-and-thirty.

LADY SNEERWELL.
Though surely she *is* handsome still, and for the weakness in her eyes, considering how much she reads by candlelight, it is not to be wondered at.

MRS. CANDOR.
True, and then as to her manner, upon my word I think it is particularly graceful, considering she never had the least education, for you know her mother was a Welsh milliner and her father a sugar baker at Bristol.

SIR BENJAMIN.
Ah, you are both of you too good-natured.

SIR PETER.
Yes, damn'd good-natured—this is their own relation, mercy on me!

SIR BENJAMIN.
And Mrs. Candor is of so moral a turn.

MRS. CANDOR.[9]
Well, I will never join in ridiculing a friend. And so I constantly tell my cousin Ogle, and you well know what pretensions she has a to be critical in beauty.

CRABTREE.
Oh, to be sure, she has herself the oddest countenance that ever was seen; 'tis a collection of features from all the different countries of the globe.

SIR BENJAMIN.
She has indeed an Irish front.

CRABTREE.
Caledonian locks.

SIR BENJAMIN.
Dutch nose.

CRABTREE.
Austrian lip.

SIR BENJAMIN.
Complexion of a Spaniard.

CRABTREE.
And teeth *à la chinoise.*[10]

SIR BENJAMIN.
In short, her face resembles a table d'hôte at Spa, where no two guests are of a nation.

CRABTREE.
Or a congress at the close of a general war, where all the members, even to her eyes, appear to have a different interest, and her nose and chin are the only parties likely to join issue.

MRS. CANDOR.
Ha, ha, ha!

SIR PETER.
Mercy on my life! A person they dine with twice a week.

MRS. CANDOR.
Nay, but I vow you shall not carry the laugh off so, for give me leave to say that Mrs. Ogle—

SIR PETER.
Madam, madam, I beg your pardon, there is no stopping these good gentlemen's tongues, but when I tell you, Mrs. Candor, that the lady they are abusing is a particular friend of mine, I hope you'll not take her part.

LADY SNEERWELL.
Well said, Sir Peter, but you are a cruel creature: too phlegmatic yourself for a jest and too peevish to allow it in others.

SIR PETER.
Ah madam, true wit is more nearly allied to good nature than your ladyship is aware of.

LADY TEAZLE.
True, Sir Peter, I believe they are so near of kin they can never be united.

SIR BENJAMIN.
Oh! Rather, ma'am, suppose them man and wife, because one so seldom sees them together.

LADY TEAZLE.
But Sir Peter is such an enemy to scandal, I believe he would have it put down by Parliament.

---

10 *à la chinoise*] of a Chinese woman: stereotypically black

SIR PETER.

Fore Heaven, madam, if they were to consider the sporting with reputation of as much importance as the poaching on manors and pass an Act for the Preservation of Fame, I believe many would thank them for the bill.

LADY SNEERWELL.

Oh Lud!* Sir Peter, would you deprive us of our privileges?

SIR PETER.

Aye madam, and then no person should be permitted to kill characters* or run down reputations but qualified old maids and disappointed widows.

LADY SNEERWELL.

Go, you monster!

MRS. CANDOR.

But sure you would not be quite so severe on those who only report what they hear?

SIR PETER.

Yes madam, I would have law-merchant[11] for them too, and in all cases of slander currency, whenever the drawer of the lie was not to be found, the injured party should have a right to come on any of the endorsers.

CRABTREE.

Well, for my part, I believe there never was a scandalous tale without some foundation.

LADY SNEERWELL.

Come ladies, shall we sit down to cards in the next room?

Enter servant, who whispers to Sir Peter.

SIR PETER.

I'll be with them directly.

[Exit servant.]

[*Aside.*] I'll get away unperceived. (*Going.*)

LADY SNEERWELL.

Sir Peter, you are not leaving us?

SIR PETER.

Your ladyship must excuse me; I'm called away by particular business—but I'll leave my character behind me. (*Exit.*)

SIR BENJAMIN.

Well certainly, Lady Teazle, that lord of yours is a strange being. I would tell you some stories of him that would make you laugh heartily, if he wasn't your husband.

LADY TEAZLE.

Oh pray don't mind that, come, do, let's hear them.

They retire. Joseph Surface and Maria come forward.

JOSEPH SURFACE.

Maria, I see you have no satisfaction in this society.

MARIA.

How is it possible I should? If to raise malicious smiles at the infirmities and misfortunes of those who have never injured us be the province of wit or humor, Heaven grant me a double portion of dullness.

JOSEPH SURFACE.

Yet they appear more ill-natured than they are; they have no malice at heart.

MARIA.

Then is their conduct more inexcusable, for in my opinion, nothing but a depravity of heart could tempt them to such practices.[h]

JOSEPH SURFACE.

But can you, Maria, feel thus for others and be unkind to me alone; is hope to be denied the tenderest passion?

MARIA.

Why will you distress me by renewing the subject?

JOSEPH SURFACE.

Ah Maria! You would not treat me thus and oppose your guardian's, Sir Peter's will but that I see that profligate Charles is still a favored rival.

MARIA.

Ungenerously urged! But whatever my sentiments of that unfortunate young man are, be assured I shall not feel more bound to give him up because his distresses have lost him the regard even of a brother.

Lady Teazle returns.

JOSEPH SURFACE. [*Kneeling.*]

Nay but Maria, do not leave me with a frown. By all that's honest, I swear— (*Aside.*) Gad's life, here is Lady Teazle.—You must not, no, you shall not,

---

11 law-merchant] a special system of rules for the regulation of trade and commerce, differing in some respects from the Common Law (*OED*)

for though I have the greatest regard for Lady Teazle—

MARIA.
Lady Teazle!

JOSEPH SURFACE.
Yet were Sir Peter once to suspect—

LADY TEAZLE. [*Aside.*]
What's this, pray? Does he take her for me?—Child,* you are wanted in the next room.

Exit Maria.

What's all this, pray?

JOSEPH SURFACE.
Oh, the most unlucky circumstance in nature. Maria has somehow suspected the tender concern which I have for your happiness and threatened to acquaint Sir Peter with her suspicions, and I was just endeavoring to reason with her when you came.

LADY TEAZLE.
Indeed! But you seemed to adopt a very tender method of reasoning: Do you usually argue on your knees?

JOSEPH SURFACE.
Oh, she's a child, and I thought a little bombast—But Lady Teazle, when are you to give me your judgment on my library as you promised?

LADY TEAZLE.
No, no, I begin to think it would imprudent, and you know I admit you as a lover no further than fashion requires.

JOSEPH SURFACE.
True, a mere platonic cicisbeo, what every wife[i] is entitled to.

LADY TEAZLE.
Certainly, one must not be out of the fashion; however, I have so many of my country prejudices left that though Sir Peter's ill humor may vex me ever so, it shall never provoke me to—

JOSEPH SURFACE.
The only revenge in you power. Well, I applaud your moderation.

LADY TEAZLE.
Go, you are an insinuating wretch. But we shall be missed; let us join the company.

JOSEPH SURFACE.
But we had best not return together.

LADY TEAZLE.
Well, don't stay, for Maria shan't come to hear any more of your reasoning, I promise you. (*Exit.*)

JOSEPH SURFACE.
A curious dilemma, truly, my politics have run me into: I wanted at first only to ingratiate myself with Lady Teazle that she might not be my enemy with Maria, and I have, I don't know how, become her serious lover! Sincerely, I begin to wish I had never made such a point of gaining so very good a character,* for it has led me into so many rogueries that I doubt* I shall be exposed at last.

Exit.

Scene iii. Sir Peter Teazle's house.

Enter Rowley and Sir Oliver.

SIR OLIVER.
Ha, ha, ha! and so my old friend is married, hey! A young wife out of the country, ha, ha, ha! That he should have stood bluff[12] to old bachelor so long, and sink into husband at last.

ROWLEY.
But you must not rally him on the subject, Sir Oliver; 'tis a tender point I assure you, though he has been married only seven months.

SIR OLIVER.
Then he has been just half a year on the stool of repentance. Poor Peter! But you say he has entirely given up Charles? Never sees him, hey?

ROWLEY.
His prejudice against him is astonishing and, I'm sure, greatly increased by a jealousy of him with Lady Teazle, which he has been industriously led into by a scandalous society in the neighborhood, who have contributed not a little to Charles's ill name, whereas the truth is, I believe, if the lady is partial to either of them, his brother is the favorite.

SIR OLIVER.
Aye, I know there is a set of malicious, prating, prudent gossips, both male and female, who murder characters* to kill time and will rob a young fellow of his good name before he has years to know the value of it. But I am not to be

12 stood bluff] stood firm or stiff (*OED*)

prejudiced against my nephew by such, I promise you; no, no, if Charles has done nothing false or mean,* I shall compound for his extravagance.

ROWLEY.

Then my life on't, you will reclaim him. Ah sir, it gives me new life to find that your heart is not turned against him and that the son of my good old master has one friend, however, left.

SIR OLIVER.

What, shall I forget, Master Rowley, when I was at his years myself? Egad, my brother and I were neither very prudent youths, and yet I believe you have not seen many better men than your old master was.

ROWLEY.

Sir, 'tis this reflection gives me assurance that Charles may yet be a credit to his family.—But here comes Sir Peter.

SIR OLIVER.

Egad, so he does. Mercy on me! he's greatly altered and seems to have a settled, married look! One may read husband in his face at this distance.

Enter Sir Peter.

SIR PETER.

Hah! Sir Oliver, my old friend, welcome to England a thousand times.

SIR OLIVER.

Thank you, thank you, Sir Peter. And i'faith, I'm as glad to find you well, believe me.

SIR PETER.

Ah! 'Tis a long time since we met: sixteen years, I doubt,* Sir Oliver, and many a cross accident in the time.

SIR OLIVER.

Aye, I have had my share. But what, I find you are married, hey, my old boy! Well, well, it can't be helped, and so I wish you joy with all my heart.

SIR PETER.

Thank you, thank you, Sir Oliver. Yes, I have entered into the happy state—but we'll not talk of that now.

SIR OLIVER.

True, true, Sir Peter, old friends should not begin on grievances at first meeting, no, no, no.

ROWLEY. (*To Sir Oliver.*)

Take care, pray sir.

SIR OLIVER.

So, one of my nephews I find is a wild, extravagant young rogue, hey!

SIR PETER.

Wild! Ah my old friend, I grieve for your disappointment there: he's a lost young man indeed. However, his brother will make you amends; Joseph is indeed what a youth should be. Everybody in the world speaks well of him.

SIR OLIVER.

I am sorry to hear it: he has too good a character* to be an honest fellow. Everybody speaks well of him! Pshaw! Then he has bowed as low to knaves and fools as to the honest dignity of genius or virtue.

SIR PETER.

What, Sir Oliver, do you blame him for not making enemies?

SIR OLIVER.

Yes, if he has merit enough to deserve them.

SIR PETER.

Well, well, you'll be convinced when you know him. 'Tis edification to hear him converse. He possesses the noblest sentiments.

SIR OLIVER.

Oh plague of his sentiments! If he salutes* me with a scrap of morality in his mouth, I shall be sick directly. But, however, don't mistake me, Sir Peter, I don't mean to defend Charles's errors, but before I form my judgment of either of them, I intend to make a trial of their hearts, and my friend Rowley and I have planned something for the purpose.

ROWLEY.

And Sir Peter shall own he has been for once mistaken.

SIR PETER.

Oh, my life on Joseph's honor.

SIR OLIVER.

Well, come, give us a bottle of good wine, and we'll drink your lady's good health and tell you all our scheme.

SIR PETER.

Allons[13] then.

SIR OLIVER.

And don't, Sir Peter, be so severe against your old

13 *Allons*] Let's go (Fr.)

friend's son. 'Odd's* my life! I'm not sorry that he has run out of the course a little. For my part, I hate to see prudence clinging to the green suckers of youth. 'Tis like ivy round a sapling and spoils the growth of the tree.

Exeunt.

Act III, scene i. Sir Peter Teazle's house.

Enter Sir Peter, Sir Oliver, and Rowley.

SIR PETER.
Well then, we will see this fellow first and have our wine afterwards. But how is this, Master Rowley? I don't see the gist of your scheme.

ROWLEY.
Why sir, this Mr. Stanley, whom I was speaking of, is nearly related to them by their mother. He was once a merchant in Dublin but has been ruined by a series of undeserved misfortunes. He has applied by letter since his confinement both to Mr. Surface and Charles. From the former he has received nothing but evasive promises of future service, while Charles has done all that his extravagance has left him power to do, and he is at this time endeavoring to raise a sum of money, part of which in the midst of his own distresses, I know, he intends for the service of poor Stanley.

SIR OLIVER.
Ah! He is my brother's son.

SIR PETER.
Well, but how is Sir Oliver personally to—

ROWLEY.
Why sir, I will inform Charles and his brother that Stanley has obtained permission to apply in person to his friends, and as they have neither of them ever seen him, let Sir Oliver assume the character, and he will have a fair opportunity of judging at least of the benevolence of their dispositions. And believe me, sir, you will find in the youngest brother one, who in the midst of folly and dissipation, has still, as our immortal bard expresses it,

A tear for pity and a hand
Open as day for melting charity.[14]

[14] A tear … charity] Shakespeare, *2 Henry IV*, IV.iv.31-32

SIR PETER.
Pshaw! What signifies his having an open hand or a purse either when he has nothing left to give? Well, well, make the trial if you please, but where is the fellow whom you brought for Sir Oliver to examine relative to Charles's affairs?

ROWLEY.
Below, waiting his commands, and no one can give him better intelligence.—This, Sir Oliver, is a friendly Jew, who to do him justice, has done everything in his power to bring your nephew to a proper sense of his extravagance.

SIR PETER.
Pray, let us have him in.

ROWLEY.
Desire Mr. Moses to walk upstairs.

SIR PETER.
But pray, why should you suppose he will speak the truth?

ROWLEY.
Oh, I have convinced him he has no chance of recovering certain sums advanced to Charles but through the bounty of Sir Oliver, who he knows is arrived, so that you may depend on his fidelity to his own interest. I have also another evidence* in my power, one Snake, whom I have detected in a matter little short of forgery, and shall shortly produce him to remove some of *your* prejudices, Sir Peter, relative to Charles and Lady Teazle.

SIR PETER.
I have heard too much on that subject.

ROWLEY.
Here comes the honest Israelite.

Enter Moses.

ROWLEY.
This is Sir Oliver.

SIR OLIVER.
Sir, I understand you have lately had great dealings with my nephew, Charles?

MOSES.
Yes, Sir Oliver. I done all my power for him,[j] but he was ruined before he came to me for assistance.

SIR OLIVER.
That was unlucky, truly, for you have had no opportunity of showing your talents.

MOSES.

None atal. I had not the pleasure of knowing his distresses till he was some thousands worse than nothing.

SIR OLIVER.

Unfortunate indeed! But I suppose you have done all in your power for him, honest Moses?

MOSES.

Yes, he knows that. This very evening I was to have brought him a gentleman from the City,* who does not know him and will, I believe, advance him some money.

SIR PETER.

What, one Charles never had money from before?

MOSES.

Yes, Mr. Premium, of Crutched Friars,[15] formerly a broker.

SIR PETER.

Egad, Sir Oliver, a thought strikes me.—Charles, you say, doesn't know Mr. Premium?

MOSES.

Not atal.

SIR PETER.

Now then, Sir Oliver, you may have an opportunity of satisfying yourself better than by an old romancing tale of a poor relation.—Go with my friend, Moses, and present Mr. Premium.—And then I'll answer for't, you will see your nephew in all his glory.

SIR OLIVER.

Egad, I like this idea better than the other, and I may visit Joseph afterwards as old Stanley.

SIR PETER.

True, so you may.

ROWLEY.

Well, this is taking Charles at a disadvantage to be sure; however, Moses, you understand Sir Peter and will be faithful.

MOSES.

You may depend upon me. This is near the time I was to have gone.

SIR OLIVER.

I'll accompany you as soon as you please, Moses, but hold, I forgot one thing: How the plague shall I be able to pass for a Jew?

MOSES.

There is no need: the principal is Christian.

SIR OLIVER.

Is he? I am sorry to hear it. But then again, an't I too smartly dressed to look like a moneylender?

SIR PETER.

Not atal. 'Twould not be out of character if you went in your own carriage, would it, Moses?

MOSES.

Not in the least.

SIR OLIVER.

Well, but how must I talk? There's certainly some cant of usury and mode of treating that I ought to know.

SIR PETER.

Oh, there's not much to learn. The great point, as I take it, is to be exorbitant enough in your demands, hey Moses?

MOSES.

Yes, that's a very great point.

SIR OLIVER.

I'll answer for't; I'll not be wanting* in that. I'll ask him eight, or ten percent, upon the loan, at least.

MOSES.

If you ask him no more as dat,[k] you'll be discovered immediately.

SIR OLIVER.

Hey, what a plague! How much then?

MOSES.

That depends upon circumstances; if he appears not very anxious for the supply, you should require only forty or fifty percent, but if you find him in great distress and want the monies very bad, you may ask him double.

SIR PETER.

A good, honest trade you are learning, Sir Oliver.

SIR OLIVER.

Truly, I think so, and not unprofitable.

MOSES.

Then, you know, you haven't the monies yourself but are forced to borrow them for him of a friend.

SIR OLIVER.

Oh! I borrow it of a friend, do I?

[15] Crutched Friars] a continuation of Jewry Street, running from Aldgate to Mark Lane (Price)

MOSES.

Yes, and your friend is an unconscionable dog, but you can't help it.

SIR OLIVER.

My friend is an unconscionable dog, is he?

MOSES.

Yes, and he himself has not the monies by him but is forced to sell stock at a great loss.

SIR OLIVER.

He's forced to sell stock at a great loss, is he? Well, that's very kind of him.

SIR PETER.

I'faith, Sir Oliver, Mr. Premium I mean, you'll soon be master of the trade.

SIR OLIVER.

Right, right![1] Well, Moses shall give me further instructions as we go together.

SIR PETER.

You will not have much time, for your nephew lives hard by.

SIR OLIVER.

Oh, never fear, my tutor appears so able that, though Charles lived in the next street, it must be my own fault if I'm not a complete rogue before I turn the corner.

Exeunt Sir Oliver and Moses.

SIR PETER.

So now I think Sir Oliver will be convinced you are partial, Rowley, and would have prepared Charles for the other plot.

ROWLEY.

No, upon my word, Sir Peter.

SIR PETER.

Well, go bring me this Snake, and I'll hear what he has to say presently.—I see Maria and want to speak with her.

Exit Rowley.

I should be glad to be convinced my suspicions of Lady Teazle and Charles were unjust. I have never yet opened my mind on this subject to my friend Joseph; I am determined I will do it: he will give me his opinion sincerely.

Enter Maria.

SIR PETER.

So child,* has Mr. Surface returned with you?

MARIA.

No sir, he was engaged.

SIR PETER.

Well Maria, do you not reflect the more you converse with that amiable young man what return his partiality for you deserves?

MARIA.

Indeed, Sir Peter, your frequent importunity on this subject distresses me extremely; you compel me to declare that I know no man who has ever paid me a particular attention whom I would not prefer to Mr. Surface.

SIR PETER.

So, here's perverseness! No, no, Maria, 'tis Charles only whom you would prefer; 'tis evident his vices and follies have won your heart.

MARIA.

This is unkind, sir. You know I have obeyed you in neither seeing nor corresponding with him. I have heard enough to convince me that he is unworthy my regard, yet I cannot think it culpable if, while my understanding severely condemns his vices, my heart suggests some pity for his distresses.

SIR PETER.

Well, well, pity him as much as you please, but give your heart and hand to a worthier object.

MARIA.

Never to his brother.

SIR PETER.

Go, perverse and obstinate! But take care, madam, you have never yet known what the authority of a guardian is; do not compel me to inform you of it.

MARIA.

I can only say you shall not have just reason. 'Tis true, by my father's will I am for a short period bound to regard you as his substitute but must cease to think you so when you would compel me to be miserable. (*Exit.*)

SIR PETER.

Was there ever man so crossed as I am! Everything conspiring to fret me. I had not been involved in matrimony a fortnight before her father, a hale and hearty man, died, on purpose, I believe, for the pleasure of plaguing me with the care of his daughter. But here comes my helpmate. She appears in great good humor. How happy I should be if I could tease her into loving me, though but a little.

Enter Lady Teazle.

LADY TEAZLE.
Lud!* Sir Peter, I hope you haven't been quarreling with Maria? It isn't using me well to be ill-humored when I'm not by.

SIR PETER.
Ah! Lady Teazle, you might have the power to make me good-humored at all times.

LADY TEAZLE.
I am sure I wish I had, for I want you to be in a charming, sweet temper at this moment. Do be good-humored now and let me have two hundred pounds, will you?

SIR PETER.
Two hundred pounds! What, an't I to be in a good humor without paying for it? But speak to me thus, and i'faith, there's nothing I would refuse you. You shall have it but seal me a bond for the repayment.

LADY TEAZLE.
Oh no! There's my note of hand will do as well.

SIR PETER.
And you shall no longer reproach me with not giving you an independent settlement—I mean shortly to surprise you—but shall we always live thus, hey?

LADY TEAZLE.
If you please. I'm sure I do not care how soon we leave off quarreling, provided you'll own you were tired first.

SIR PETER.
Well then, let our future contest be who shall be most obliging.

LADY TEAZLE.
I assure you, Sir Peter, good nature becomes you; you look now as you did before we were married! When you used to walk with me under the elms and tell me stories of what a gallant you were in your youth, and chuck me under the chin, you would, and ask me if I thought I could love an old fellow who would deny me nothing, didn't you?

SIR PETER.
Yes, yes, and you were as kind and attentive—

LADY TEAZLE.
Aye, so I was and would always take your part when my acquaintance used to abuse you and turn you into ridicule.

SIR PETER.
Indeed!

LADY TEAZLE.
Aye, and when my cousin Sophy called you a stiff, peevish old bachelor and laughed at me for thinking of marrying one who might be my father, I have always defended you and said I didn't think you so ugly by any means.

SIR PETER.
Thank you!

LADY TEAZLE.
And that I dared say you would make a very good sort of a husband.

SIR PETER.
And you prophesied right, and we shall certainly now be the happiest couple—

LADY TEAZLE.
And never differ again.

SIR PETER.
No, never—though at the same time indeed, my dear Lady Teazle, you must watch your temper very narrowly, for in all our little quarrels, my dear,—if you recollect, my love, you always began first.

LADY TEAZLE.
I beg pardon, my dear Sir Peter, indeed you always gave the provocation.

SIR PETER.
Now see my angel, contradicting isn't the way to keep friends.

LADY TEAZLE.
Then don't you begin it, my love.

SIR PETER.
There now—you—you are going on, you don't perceive, my life, that you are just doing the very thing which you know always makes me angry.

LADY TEAZLE.
Nay, you know if you will be angry without any reason—

SIR PETER.
There now, you want to quarrel again.

LADY TEAZLE.
No, I'm sure I don't, but if you will be so peevish—

SIR PETER.
There, *now* who begins first?

LADY TEAZLE.
Why, you, to be sure. I said nothing, but there's no bearing your temper.

SIR PETER.
No, no, madam, the fault is in your own temper.

LADY TEAZLE.
Aye, you are just what my cousin Sophy said you would be—

SIR PETER.
Your cousin Sophy is a forward, impertinent Gypsy.

LADY TEAZLE.
And you a great bear to abuse my relations.

SIR PETER.
Now may all the plagues of marriage be doubled on me if ever I try to be friends with you any more.

LADY TEAZLE.
So much the better.

SIR PETER.
No, no, madam, 'tis evident you never cared a pin for me, and I was a madman to marry you: a pert, rural coquette that had refused half the honest squires in the neighborhood.

LADY TEAZLE.
And I am sure I was a fool to marry you: an old, dangling bachelor, who was single at fifty only because he never could meet with anyone who would have him.

SIR PETER.
Aye, aye, madam, but you were pleased enough to listen to me: you never had such an offer before.

LADY TEAZLE.
No! Didn't I refuse Sir Tivy Terrier, who everybody said would have been a better match? For his estate is just as good as yours, and he has broke his neck since we have been married.

SIR PETER.
Oh, oh, oh! I have done with you, madam. You are unfeeling, ungrateful—but there is an end of everything. I believe you capable of anything that's bad. Yes madam, I now believe the report relative to you and Charles, madam. Madam—yes, madam, you and Charles, not without grounds.

LADY TEAZLE.
Take care, Sir Peter. You had better not insinuate any such thing. I'll not be suspected without a cause, I promise you.

SIR PETER.
Very well, madam, very well, a separate maintenance* as soon as you please—yes madam, or a divorce. I'll make an example of myself for the benefit of all old bachelors. Let us separate, madam.

LADY TEAZLE.
Agreed, agreed. And now my dear Sir Peter, we are of a mind once more; we may be the happiest couple and never differ again, you know, ha, ha! Well, you are going to be in a passion, I see, and I shall only interrupt you, so bye bye. (*Exit.*)

SIR PETER.
Plagues and tortures! Can't I make her angry either? Oh, I am the miserablest fellow! But I'll not bear her presuming to keep her temper. No, she may break my heart, but she shall not keep her temper.

Exit.

Scene ii. A chamber in Charles's house.

Enter Trip, Moses, and Sir Oliver.

TRIP.
Here master, master, if you will stay a moment, I'll try whether—what's the gentleman's name?

SIR OLIVER. [*Aside.*]
Mr. Moses, what is my name?

MOSES.
Mr. Premium.

TRIP.
Premium—very well. (*Exit taking snuff.*)

SIR OLIVER.
To judge by the servants, one would believe the master was ruined. But what! Sure this was my brother's house!

MOSES.
Yes sir, Mr. Charles bought it of Mr. Joseph, with the furniture, pictures, etcetera, just as the old gentleman left it. Sir Peter thought it a great piece of extravagance in him.

SIR OLIVER.
In my mind the other's economy in selling it him was more reprehensible by half.

Enter Trip.

TRIP.
My master says you must wait, gentleman, he has company and can't speak with you yet.

SIR OLIVER.
If he knew who it was wanted to see him, perhaps he wouldn't have sent such a message.

TRIP.
Yes, yes, sir, he knows you are here; I didn't forget little Premium, no, no, no.

SIR OLIVER.
Very well, and I pray sir, what may be your name?

TRIP.
Trip, sir, my name is Trip, at your service.

SIR OLIVER.
Well then Mr. Trip, you have a pleasant sort of place here I guess?

TRIP.
Why yes, here are three or four of us pass our time agreeably enough, but then our wages are sometimes a little in arrear, and not very good either, but fifty pounds a year and find our own bags and bouquets.[16]

SIR OLIVER.
Bags and bouquets! Halters and bastinadoes.

TRIP.
But apropos, Moses! Have you been able to get me that little bill* discounted?

SIR OLIVER. [*Aside.*]
Wants to raise money too—mercy on me—has his distresses, I warrant, like a lord, and affects creditors and duns.

MOSES.
'Twas not to be done indeed, Mr. Trip.

TRIP.
Good lack! You surprise me. My friend Brush has endorsed it, and I thought, when he puts his mark to the back of the bill, 'twas as good as cash.

MOSES.
No, 'twouldn't do.

TRIP.
A small sum—but twenty pounds. Harkee, Moses, do you think you could get it me by way of annuity?

[16] bags and bouquets] extras or perks, including food and clothing

SIR OLIVER. [*Aside.*]
An annuity! Ha, ha, ha! A footman raise money by annuity! Well done, luxury, egad!

MOSES.
But you must insure your place.

TRIP.
Oh, with all my heart I'll insure my place—and my life too if you please.

SIR OLIVER. [*Aside.*]
It's more than I would your neck.[m]

MOSES.
But is there nothing you could deposit?

TRIP.
Why nothing capital of my master's wardrobe has dropped lately, but I could give you a mortgage on some of his winter clothes, with equity and redemption before November, or you shall have the reversion of the French velvet or a post-obit on the blue and silver—these, I should think, Moses, with a few pair of point ruffles, as a collateral security, hey my little fellow?

MOSES.
Well, well—

Bell rings.

TRIP.
Egad, I heard the bell. I believe, gentlemen, I can now introduce you.—Don't forget the annuity, little Moses.—This way, gentlemen.—Insure my place, you know!

SIR OLIVER. [*Aside.*]
If the man be the shadow of the master, this is the temple of dissipation indeed!

Exeunt.

Scene iii.

Charles, Careless, Sir Toby Bumper, etc. discovered at a table drinking wine.*

CHARLES.
Fore Heaven 'tis true, there's the great degeneracy of the age: many of our acquaintance have taste, spirit, and politeness, but plague on't, they won't drink.

CARELESS.
It is so indeed, Charles; they give into all the

substantial luxuries of the table and abstain from nothing but wine and wit.

CHARLES.

Oh certainly, society suffers by it intolerably, for now instead of the social spirit of raillery that used to mantle over a glass of bright burgundy, their conversation is become just like the spa-water they drink, which has all the pertness and flatulence of champagne without its spirit or flavor.

FIRST GENTLEMAN.

But what are they to do, who love play better than wine?

CARELESS.

True, there's Harry diets himself for gaming and is now under a hazard regimen.

CHARLES.

Then he'll have the worst of it. What! You wouldn't train a horse for the course by keeping him from corn?* For my part, egad, I am now never so successful as when I am a little merry; let me throw on a bottle of champagne, and I never lose, at least I never feel my losses, which is exactly the same thing.

SECOND GENTLEMAN.

Aye, that I believe.

CHARLES.

And then, what man can pretend to be a believer in love who is an abjurer of wine? 'Tis the test by which the lover knows his own heart. Fill a dozen bumpers to a dozen beauties, and she that floats at top is the maid that has bewitched you.

CARELESS.

Now then, Charles, be honest and give us your real favorite.

CHARLES.

Why, I have withheld her only in compassion to you; if I toast her, you must give a round of her peers, which is impossible on earth.

CARELESS.

Oh, then we'll find some canonized vestals or heathen goddesses that will do, I warrant.

CHARLES.

Here then, bumpers, you rogues, bumpers. Maria, Maria!

FIRST GENTLEMAN.

Maria who?

CHARLES.

Oh damn the surname, 'tis too formal to be registered in love's calendar.—But now, Sir Toby, beware, we must have beauty's superlative.

CARELESS.

Nay, never study, Sir Toby; we'll stand to the toast though your mistress should want* an eye, and you know you have a song will excuse you.

SIR TOBY.

Egad, so I have, and I'll give him the song instead of the lady.

Song and Chorus.

Here's to the maiden of bashful fifteen;
Here's to the widow of fifty;
Here's to the flaunting, extravagant quean,
And here's to the housewife that's thrifty.

Chorus.

Let the toast pass,
Drink to the lass,
I'll warrant she'll prove an excuse for the glass.

Here's to the charmer whose dimples we prize;
Now to the maid who has none, sir;
Here's to the girl with a pair of blue eyes,
And here's to the nymph with but one, sir.
Let the toast pass, etc.

Here's to the maid with a bosom of snow;
Now to her that's as brown as a berry;
Here's to the wife with her face full of woe,
And now for the damsel that's merry.
Let the toast pass, etc.

For let them be clumsy or let them be slim,
Young or ancient I care not a feather;
So fill a pint bumper quite up to the brim,
And let us e'en toast them together.
Let the toast pass, etc.

ALL.

Bravo, Bravo!

Enter Trip, who whispers Charles.

CHARLES.

Gentlemen, you must excuse me a little.—Careless, take the chair, will you?

CARELESS.
Nay prithee Charles, what now? This is one of your peerless beauties, I suppose, has dropped in by chance.

CHARLES.
No, faith, to tell you the truth, 'tis a Jew and a broker who are come by appointment.

CARELESS.
Oh damn it, let's have the Jew in.

FIRST GENTLEMAN.
Aye, and the broker too, by all means.

SECOND GENTLEMAN.
Yes, yes, the Jew and the broker.

CHARLES.
Egad, with all my heart.—Trip, bid the gentlemen walk in,

Exit Trip

though there's one of them a stranger, I can assure you.

CARELESS.
Charles, let us give them some generous burgundy, and perhaps they'll grow conscientious.

CHARLES.
Oh hang'em, no, wine does but draw forth the natural qualities of a man, and to make them drink would only be to whet their knavery.

Enter Trip, Sir Oliver, and Moses.

CHARLES.
So, honest Moses, walk in, walk in pray, Mr. Premium. That's the gentleman's name, isn't it, Moses?

MOSES.
Yes sir.

CHARLES.
Set chairs, Trip.—Sit down, Mr. Premium.—Glasses, Trip.—Sit down, Moses.—Come, Mr. Premium, I'll give you a sentiment: here's success to usury.—Moses, fill the gentleman a bumper.

MOSES.
Success to usury.

CARELESS.
Right, Moses, usury is prudence and industry and deserves to succeed.

SIR OLIVER.
Then here's all the success it deserves.

CARELESS.
No, no, that won't do, Mr. Premium. You have demurred to the toast and must drink it in a pint-bumper.

FIRST GENTLEMAN.
A pint bumper at least.

MOSES.
Oh pray sir, consider Mr. Premium's a gentleman.

CARELESS.
And therefore loves good wine.

SECOND GENTLEMAN.
Give Moses a quart-glass; this is mutiny and a high contempt of the chair.

CARELESS.
Here now for't. I'll see justice done to the last drop of my bottle.

SIR OLIVER.
Nay, pray gentlemen, I did not expect this usage.

CHARLES.
No, hang it, Careless, you shan't. Mr. Premium's a stranger.

SIR OLIVER. [*Aside.*]
'Odd,* I wish I was well out of their company.

CARELESS.
Plague on them, then. If they won't drink, we'll not sit down with them. Come Harry, the dice are in the next room. Charles, you'll join us when you've finished your business with these gentlemen.

Exeunt Sir Toby and gentlemen.

CHARLES.
I will, I will. Careless!

CARELESS.
Well.

CHARLES.
Perhaps I may want you.

CARELESS.
Oh, you know I am always ready; word, note, or bond, 'tis all the same to me. (*Exit.*)

MOSES.
Sir, this is Mr. Premium, a gentleman of the strictest honor and secresy and always performs what he undertakes. Mr. Premium, this is—

CHARLES.
Pshaw! Have done.—Sir, my friend Moses is a very honest fellow but a little slow at expression; he'll

be an hour giving us our titles. Mr. Premium, the plain state of the matter is this: I am an extravagant young fellow who wants money to borrow; you I take to be a prudent old fellow who has got money to lend. I am blockhead enough to give fifty per cent sooner than not have it, and *you*, I presume, are rogue enough to take an hundred if you can get it. Now sir, you see we are acquainted at once and may proceed to business without any further ceremony.

SIR OLIVER. [*Aside.*]
Exceeding frank, upon my word.—I see, sir, you are not a man of many compliments.

CHARLES.
Oh no, sir, plain dealing in business I always think best.

SIR OLIVER.
Sir, I like you the better for't. However, you are mistaken in one thing: I have no money to lend. But I believe I could procure some of a friend, but then he's an unconscionable dog, isn't he, Moses? and must sell stock to accommodate you, mustn't he, Moses?

MOSES.
Yes indeed. You know I always speak the truth and scorn to tell a lie.

CHARLES.
Right! People that speak the truth generally do.—But these are trifles, Mr. Premium. What, I know money isn't to be bought without paying for't.

SIR OLIVER.
Well, but what security could you give? You have no land, I suppose?

CHARLES.
Not a mole-hill nor a twig but what's in beau-pots[17] out at the window.

SIR OLIVER.
Nor any stock, I presume?

CHARLES.
Nothing but livestock, and that's only a few pointers and ponies. But pray, Mr. Premium, are you acquainted at all with any of my connections?

SIR OLIVER.
Why to say truth, I am.

CHARLES.
Then you must know that I have a devilish rich uncle in the East Indies, Sir Oliver Surface, from whom I have the greatest expectations.

SIR OLIVER.
That you have a wealthy uncle, I have heard, but how your expectations will turn out is more, I believe, than you can tell.

CHARLES.
Oh no! There can be no doubt; they tell me I'm a prodigious favorite and that he talks of leaving me everything.

SIR OLIVER.
Indeed! This is the first I have heard of it.

CHARLES.
Yes, yes, 'tis just so. Moses knows 'tis true, don't you, Moses?

MOSES.
Oh yes, I'll swear to it.

SIR OLIVER. [*Aside.*]
Egad, they'll persuade me presently I'm at Bengal.

CHARLES.
Now I propose, Mr. Premium, if it is agreeable to you, to grant you a post-obit on Sir Oliver's life, though at the same time the old fellow has been so liberal to me that I give you my word I should be very sorry to hear anything had happened to him.

SIR OLIVER.
Not more than I should, I assure you. But the bond you mention happens to be just the worst security you could offer me, for I might live to an hundred and never recover the principal.

CHARLES.
Oh, yes you would, the moment Sir Oliver dies you know you would come on me for the money.

SIR OLIVER.
Then I believe I should be the most unwelcome dun you ever had in your life.

CHARLES.
What, I suppose you are afraid Sir Oliver is too good a life?

SIR OLIVER.
No indeed, I am not though I have heard he is as hale and healthy as any man of his years in Christendom.

CHARLES.
There again you are misinformed; no, no, the

[17] beau-pots] large ornamental vases for cut flowers (*OED*)

climate has hurt him considerably. Poor Uncle Oliver! Yes, he breaks apace, I am told, and so much altered lately that his nearest relations would not know him.

SIR OLIVER.
No? Ha, ha, ha! So much altered lately that his relations would not know him, ha, ha, ha! That's droll, egad, ha, ha, ha!

CHARLES.
Ha, ha, ha! You're glad to hear that, little Premium?

SIR OLIVER.
No, no, I am not.

CHARLES.
Yes, yes, you are, ha, ha, ha! You know that mends your chance.

SIR OLIVER.
But I'm told Sir Oliver is coming over; nay, some say he is actually arrived.

CHARLES.
Pshaw! Sure I must know better than you whether he's coming or not; no, no, rely on't, he is at this moment at Calcutta, isn't he, Moses?

MOSES.
Yes, certainly.

SIR OLIVER.
Very true, as you say, you must know better than I, though I have it from pretty good authority, haven't I, Moses?

MOSES.
Yes, most undoubted.

SIR OLIVER.
But sir, as I understand you want a few hundreds immediately, is there nothing you would dispose of?

CHARLES.
How do you mean?

SIR OLIVER.
For instance, now, I have heard that your father left behind him a great quantity of massy old plate.*

CHARLES.
Oh, Lud!* That's gone long ago; Moses can tell you how better than I.

SIR OLIVER. [*Aside.*]
Good lack! All the family race-cups and corporation bowls!—Then it was also supposed his library was one of the most valuable and complete.

CHARLES.
Yes, yes, so it was, vastly too much so for a private gentleman; for my part I was always of a communicative disposition, so I thought it was a shame to keep so much knowledge to myself.

SIR OLIVER. [*Aside.*]
Mercy on me! Learning that had run in the family like an heirloom.—Pray, what are become of the books?

CHARLES.
You must inquire of the auctioneer, Master Premium, for I don't believe even Moses can direct you there.

MOSES.
I know nothing of books.

SIR OLIVER.
So, so, nothing of the family property left, I suppose?

CHARLES.
Not much indeed, unless you have a mind to the family pictures. I have got a room full of ancestors above, and if you have taste for old paintings, egad, you shall have them a bargain.

SIR OLIVER.
Hey, the devil! Sure you won't sell your forefathers, would you?

CHARLES.
Every man of them to the best bidder.

SIR OLIVER.
What, your great uncles and aunts?

CHARLES.
Yes, and my grandfathers and grandmothers too.

SIR OLIVER. [*Aside.*]
Now I give him up.—What the plague, have you no bowels for your kindred? 'Odd's* life! Do you take me for Shylock in the play, that you would raise money of me on your own flesh and blood?

CHARLES.
Nay, my little broker, don't be angry. What need you care, if you have your money's worth?

SIR OLIVER.
Well, I'll be the purchaser; I think I can dispose of the family canvas. [*Aside.*] Oh! I'll never forgive him this—never.

Enter Careless.

CARELESS.

Come Charles, what keeps you?

CHARLES.

I can't come yet, i'faith; we are going to have a sale above. Here's little Premium will buy all my ancestors.

CARELESS.

Oh, burn your ancestors!

CHARLES.

No, he may do that afterwards, if he pleases. Stay, Careless, we want you; egad, you shall be auctioneer, so come along with us.

CARELESS.

Oh, have with you, if that's the case; I can handle a hammer as well as a dice-box. A-going, a-going, etcetera.

SIR OLIVER. [*Aside.*]

Oh the profligates!

CHARLES.

Come, Moses. You shall be appraiser, if we want one.—Gad's life, little Premium, you don't seem to like the business?

SIR OLIVER.

Oh, yes, I do vastly, ha, ha! Yes, yes, I think it a rare joke to sell one's family by auction, ha, ha! (*Aside.*) Oh the prodigal!

CHARLES.

To be sure! When a man wants* money, where the plague should he get assistance if he can't make free with his own relations?

SIR OLIVER. [*Aside.*]

I'll never forgive him! Never, never!

Exeunt.

Act IV, scene i. Picture room at Charles's house.

Enter Charles, Sir Oliver, Moses, and Careless.

CHARLES.

Walk in, gentlemen, walk in pray. Here they are, the family of the Surfaces up to the Conquest.[18]

SIR OLIVER.

And in my opinion, a goodly collection.

CHARLES.

Aye, aye, they are done in the true spirit of portrait painting, no volunteer grace or expression, not like the works of your* modern Raphael, who gives you the strongest resemblance yet contrives to make your own portrait independent of you, so that you may sink the original and not hurt the pictures. No, no, the merit of these is the inveterate likeness: all stiff and awkward as the originals and like nothing in human nature beside.

SIR OLIVER.

Ah! We shall never see such figures of men again.

CHARLES.

I hope not. Well, you see, Master Premium, what a domestic character I am; here I sit of an evening surrounded by my family. But come, go to your pulpit, Mr. Auctioneer. Here's an old, gouty chair of my grandfather's will answer the purpose.

CARELESS.

Aye, aye, this will do, but Charles, I have ne'er a hammer, and what's an auctioneer without his hammer?

CHARLES.

Egad, that's true. What parchment do we have here? Richard, heir to Thomas[19]— Oh, our genealogy in full.—Here Careless, you shall have no common bit of mahogany; here's the family tree for you, you rogue. This shall be your hammer, and now you may knock down my ancestors with their own pedigree.

SIR OLIVER. [*Aside.*]

What an unnatural rogue! An ex post facto parricide!

CARELESS.

Yes, yes, here's a list of your generation, indeed. 'Faith, Charles, this is the most convenient thing you could have found for the business, for 'twill serve not only as a hammer but a catalog into the bargain. But come, begin, a-going, a-going, a-going—

CHARLES.

Bravo, Careless! Well, here's my great uncle, Sir Richard Raveline, a marvellous good general in his day, I assure you; he served in all the Duke of Marlborough's wars and got that cut over his eye at the Battle of Malplaquet.[20] What say you, Mr.

[18] Conquest] Norman Conquest in 1066

[19] Richard, heir to Thomas] Richard Brinsley Sheridan was the son of Thomas Sheridan.

[20] Battle of Malplaquet] 1709 battle in the War of the Spanish Succession

Premium, look at him, there's a hero: not cut out of his feathers as your modern clipped captains are but enveloped in wig and regimentals as a general should be. What do you bid?

SIR OLIVER. (*Aside to Moses.*)
Bid him speak.

MOSES.
Mr. Premium would have you speak.

CHARLES.
Why, then he shall have him for ten pounds, and I'm sure that's not dear* for a staff officer.

SIR OLIVER. [*Aside.*]
Heaven deliver me! His famous uncle Richard for ten pounds!—Very well, sir, I take him at that.

CHARLES.
Careless, knock down my Uncle Richard. Here now is a maiden sister of his, my great aunt Deborah, done by Kneller in his best manner and esteemed a very formidable likeness; there she is, you see, a shepherdess feeding her flock. You shall have her at five pounds ten; the sheep are worth the money.

SIR OLIVER. [*Aside.*]
Ah, poor Deborah! A woman who set such a value on herself.—Five pounds ten, she is mine.

CHARLES.
Knock down my Aunt Deborah. This[n] now is a grandfather of my mother's, a learned judge, well-known on the western circuit. What do you rate him at, Moses?

MOSES.
Four guineas.

CHARLES.
Four guineas! Gad's life, you don't bid me the price of his wig.—Mr. Premium, you have more respect for the woolsack. Do let us knock his lordship down at fifteen.

SIR OLIVER.
By all means.

CARELESS.
Gone.

CHARLES.
And there are two brothers of his, William and Walter Blunt, Esquires, both members of Parliament and noted speakers, and what's very extraordinary, I believe this is the first time they were ever bought and sold.

SIR OLIVER.
That is very extraordinary indeed! I'll take them at your own price for the honor of Parliament.

CARELESS.
Well said, little Premium; I'll knock them down at forty.

CHARLES.
Here's a jolly fellow. I don't know what relation, but he was Mayor of Norwich. Take him at eight pounds.

SIR OLIVER.
No, no, six will do for the mayor.

CHARLES.
Come, make it guineas, and I'll throw you the two aldermen into the bargain.

SIR OLIVER.
They are mine.

CHARLES.
Careless, knock down the mayor and aldermen. But plague on't, we shall be all day retailing in this manner. Do let us deal wholesale. What say you, Premium, give me three hundred pounds, and take all that remains on each side in the lump.

SIR OLIVER.[o]
Well, well, anything to accommodate you; they are mine. But there is one portrait which you have always passed over.

CARELESS.
What! That little ill-looking fellow over the settee?

SIR OLIVER.
Yes sir, I mean that, though I don't think him so ill-looking a little fellow by any means.

CHARLES.
What, that! Oh, that's my Uncle Oliver; 'twas done before he went to India.

CARELESS.
Your Uncle Oliver! Gad, then you'll never be friends, Charles. That now to me is as stern a looking rogue as ever I saw: an unforgiving eye and a damned disinheriting countenance. An inveterate knave, depend on't. Don't you think so, little Premium?

SIR OLIVER.
Upon my soul, sir, I do not. I think it as honest a looking face as any in the room, dead or alive.—But I suppose your Uncle Oliver goes with the rest of the lumber.*

CHARLES.

No, hang it, I'll not part with poor Noll; the old fellow has been very good to me, and egad, I'll keep his picture while I've a room to put it in.

SIR OLIVER. [*Aside.*]

The rogue's my nephew after all!—But sir, I have somehow taken a fancy to that picture.

CHARLES.

I'm sorry for't, for you certainly will not have it. 'Oons!* Haven't you got enough of 'em.

SIR OLIVER. [*Aside.*]

I forgive him everything!—But sir, when I take a whim in my head, I don't value money. I'll give you as much for that as for all the rest.

CHARLES.

Don't tease me, Master Broker, I tell you I'll not part with it, and there's an end on't.

SIR OLIVER. [*Aside.*]

How like his father the dog is. Well, well, I have done. I did perceive it before, but I never saw such a resemblance.—Well sir, here's a draft for the sum.

CHARLES.

Why, 'tis for eight hundred pounds.

SIR OLIVER.

You will not let Oliver go?

CHARLES.

Zounds! No, I tell you once more.

SIR OLIVER.

Then never mind the difference; we'll balance another time. But give me your hand on the bargain. You are an honest fellow, Charles. I beg pardon for being so free.—Come, Moses.

CHARLES. [*Aside.*]

Egad, this is a whimsical old fellow!—But harkee, Premium, you'll prepare lodgings for these gentlemen?

SIR OLIVER.

Yes, yes, I'll send for them in a day or two.

CHARLES.

But hold, do now send a genteel conveyance for them, for I assure you they were most of them used to ride in their own carriages.

SIR OLIVER.

I will, I will, for all but—Oliver.

CHARLES.

Aye, all but the little nabob.

SIR OLIVER.

You're fixed!

CHARLES.

Peremptorily.

SIR OLIVER. [*Aside.*]

A dear extravagant rogue.—Good day. Come, Moses, let me hear now who dares call him profligate.

Exeunt Sir Oliver and Moses.

CARELESS.

Why this is the oddest genius of the sort I ever saw.

CHARLES.

Egad, he's the prince of brokers, I think. I wonder how the devil Moses got acquainted with so honest a fellow? But hark! Here's Rowley. Do, Careless, say that I'll join the company in a moment.

CARELESS.

I will. But don't now let that old blockhead persuade you to squander any of that money on old musty debts or any such nonsense, for tradesmen, Charles, are the most exorbitant fellows.

CHARLES.

Very true, and paying them is only encouraging them.

CARELESS.

Nothing else.

CHARLES.

Aye, aye, never fear.

Exit Careless.

So, this was an odd fellow indeed—let me see—two thirds of this, five hundred and thirty odd pounds are mine by right. Fore Heaven, I find one's ancestors are more valuable relations than I took them for! Ladies and gentlemen, your most obedient and very grateful humble servant.

Enter Rowley.

Hah! Old Rowley, egad, you are just come in time to take leave of your old acquaintance.

ROWLEY.

Yes, I heard they were going, but I wonder you can have such spirits under so many distresses.

CHARLES.

Why, there's the point: my distresses are so many that I can't afford to part with my spirits. But I shall be rich and splenetic all in good time; however, I suppose that you are surprised that I am not more sorrowful at parting with so many near relations. To be sure, 'tis very affecting, but rot 'em, you see they never move a muscle, so why should I?

ROWLEY.
There's no making you serious a moment.

CHARLES.
Yes, faith I am so now. Here, my honest Rowley, here, get me this changed directly and take a hundred pounds of it immediately to old Stanley.

ROWLEY.
A hundred pounds! Consider only—

CHARLES.
Gad's life, don't talk about. Poor Stanley's wants* are pressing, and if you don't make haste, we shall have someone call that has a better right to the money.

ROWLEY.
Ah! there's the point. I never will cease dunning you with the old proverb—

CHARLES.
"Be just before you're generous." Hey! Why, so I would if I could, but justice is an old, lame, hobbling beldam, and I can't get her to keep pace with generosity for the soul of me.

ROWLEY.
Yet Charles, believe me, one hour's reflection—

CHARLES.
Aye, aye, it is very true, but harkee, Rowley, while I have, by heaven I will give. So damn your economy and now for hazard.

Exeunt.

Scene ii. The parlor.

Enter Sir Oliver and Moses.

MOSES.
Well sir, I think, as Sir Peter said, you have seen Mr. Charles in high glory; 'tis great pity he's so extravagant.

SIR OLIVER.
True, but he wouldn't sell my picture.

MOSES.
And loves wine and women so much.

SIR OLIVER.
But he wouldn't sell my picture.

MOSES.
And game so deep.

SIR OLIVER.
But he wouldn't sell my picture.—Oh, here's Rowley.

Enter Rowley.

ROWLEY.
Oh Sir Oliver, I find you have made a purchase.

SIR OLIVER.
Yes, yes, our young rake has parted with his ancestors like old tapestry.

ROWLEY.
And here has he commissioned me to redeliver you a part of the purchase money, I mean, though, in your necessitous character of Old Stanley.

MOSES.
Ah! There is the pity of all, he's so damned charitable.

ROWLEY.
And I left a hosier and two tailors in the hall, who I'm sure won't be paid, and this hundred would satisfy them.

SIR OLIVER.
Well, well, I'll pay his debts and his benevolence too. But now I'm no more a broker, and you shall introduce me to the brother as Old Stanley.

ROWLEY.
Not yet a while. Sir Peter, I know, means to call there about this time.

Enter Trip.

TRIP.
Oh gentlemen, I beg pardon for not showing you out. This way, gentlemen.—Moses, a word—

Exeunt Trip and Moses.

SIR OLIVER.
There's a fellow for you. Would you believe it, that puppy intercepted the Jew on our coming and wanted to raise money before he got to his master.

ROWLEY.
Indeed!

SIR OLIVER.
Yes, they are now planning an annuity business. Ah Master Rowley, in my days servants were content

with the follies of their masters when they were worn a little threadbare, but now they have their vices like their birthday* clothes, with the gloss on.

Exeunt.

Scene iii. A library.

Enter Joseph Surface and servant.

JOSEPH SURFACE.
No letter from Lady Teazle?

SERVANT.
No sir.

JOSEPH SURFACE.
I am surprised she has not sent if she is prevented from coming. Sir Peter certainly does not suspect me, yet I wish I may not lose the heiress through the scrape I have drawn myself in with the wife. However, Charles's imprudence and bad character* are great points in my favor.

[Knock within.]

SERVANT.
Sir, I believe that must be Lady Teazle.

JOSEPH SURFACE.
Hold! See whether it is or not before you go to the door; I have a particular message for you if it should be my brother.

SERVANT.
'Tis her ladyship, sir, she always leaves her chair* at the milliner's in the next street.

JOSEPH SURFACE.
Stay, stay, draw that screen before the window; that will do. My opposite neighbor is a maiden lady of a curious temper.

Servant draws the screen, and exit.

I have a difficult hand to play in this affair. Lady Teazle has lately suspected my views on Maria, but she must by no means be let into that secret, at least till I have her more in my power.

Enter Lady Teazle.

LADY TEAZLE.
What, sentiment in soliloquy! Have you been very impatient now? O Lud,* don't pretend to look grave. I vow I couldn't come before.

JOSEPH SURFACE.
Oh madam! Punctuality is a species of constancy—very unfashionable quality in a lady.

LADY TEAZLE.
Upon my word, you ought to pity me. Do you know that Sir Peter is grown so ill-natured of late and so jealous of Charles too? That's the best of the story, isn't it?

JOSEPH SURFACE. (*Aside.*)
I am glad my scandalous friends keep that up.

LADY TEAZLE.
I'm sure I wish he would let Maria marry him, and then perhaps he would be convinced. Don't you, Mr. Surface?

JOSEPH SURFACE. (*Aside.*)
Indeed I do not.—Oh, certainly I do, for then my dear Lady Teazle would also be convinced how wrong her suspicions were of my having any design on the silly girl.

LADY TEAZLE.
Well, well, I'm inclined to believe you, but isn't it provoking to have the most ill-natured things said to one. There is my friend Lady Sneerwell has circulated I don't how many scandalous tales of me—and all without any foundation too. That's what vexes me.

JOSEPH SURFACE.
Aye madam, that is the provoking circumstance—without foundation; yes, yes, there's the mortification indeed. For when a scandalous story is believed against one, there certainly is no comfort like the consciousness of having deserved it.

LADY TEAZLE.
No, to be sure. Then I'd forgive their malice. But to attack *me*, who am really so innocent and who never says an ill-natured thing of anybody, that is, of my friends—and then Sir Peter too to have him so peevish and so suspicious—when I know the integrity of my own heart—indeed 'tis monstrous.

JOSEPH SURFACE.
But my dear Lady Teazle, 'tis your own fault if you suffer it. When a husband entertains a groundless suspicion of his wife and withdraws his confidence from her, the original compact is broke, and she owes it to the honor of her sex to endeavor to outwit him.

LADY TEAZLE.

Indeed! So that if he suspects me without cause, it follows that the best way of curing his jealousy is to give him reason for't?

JOSEPH SURFACE.

Undoubtedly, for your husband should never be deceived in you, and in that case it becomes *you* to become frail in compliment to his discernment.

LADY TEAZLE.

To be sure what you say is very reasonable, and when the consciousness of my own innocence—

JOSEPH SURFACE.

Ah, my dear madam, there is the great mistake; 'tis this very conscious innocence that is of the greatest prejudice to you. What is it makes you negligent of forms and careless of the world's opinion? Why, the consciousness of your innocence. What makes you thoughtless in your conduct and apt to run into a thousand little imprudences? Why, the consciousness of your innocence. What makes you impatient of Sir Peter's temper, and outrageous at his suspicions? Why, the consciousness of your own innocence.

LADY TEAZLE.

'Tis very true.

JOSEPH SURFACE.

Now my dear Lady Teazle, if you would but once make a trifling faux-pas, you can't conceive how cautious you would grow and how ready to humor and agree with your husband.

LADY TEAZLE.

Do you think so?

JOSEPH SURFACE.

Oh, I'm sure on't. And then you'd find all scandal would cease at once, for in short, your character at present is like a person in a plethora: absolutely dying of too much health.

LADY TEAZLE.

Why, ifP my understanding were once convinced—

JOSEPH SURFACE.

Oh certainly, madam. Your understanding *should* be convinced—yes, yes. Heaven forbid I should persuade you to do anything you thought wrong—no, no. I have too much honor to desire it.

LADY TEAZLE.

Don't you think we may as well leave honor out of the argument.

JOSEPH SURFACE.

Ah! The ill effects of your country education I see still remain with you.

LADY TEAZLE.

I doubt* they do, indeed, and I will fairly own to you that, if I could be persuaded to do wrong, it would be Sir Peter's ill usage sooner than your honorable logic after all.

JOSEPH SURFACE.

Then by this hand which he is unworthy of—

Enter Servant

'Sdeath,* you blockhead, what do you want?

SERVANT.

I beg pardon, sir, but I thought you wouldn't choose Sir Peter's coming upstairs without announcing him.

JOSEPH SURFACE.

Sir Peter, 'oons,* and the devil!

LADY TEAZLE.

Sir Peter! Oh Lud,* I'm ruined! I'm ruined!

SERVANT.

Sir, 'twasn't I let him in.

LADY TEAZLE.

Oh! I'm undone. What will become of me now, Mr. Logic? Oh mercy, he's on the stairs! I'll get behind here, and if ever I'm so imprudent again! (*Goes behind the screen.*)

JOSEPH SURFACE.

Give me a book.

Enter Sir Peter.

SIR PETER.

Aye, ever improving himself.—Mr. Surface! Mr. Surface!

JOSEPH SURFACE.

Oh my dear Sir Peter, I beg your pardon, (*Gaping and throwing away the book.*) I have been dozing over a stupid* book. Well, I am much obliged to you for this call. You have not been here, I believe, since I fitted up this room. Books, you know, are the only things I am a coxcomb in.

SIR PETER.

'Tis very neat indeed. Well, well, that's proper, and you make even your screen a source of knowledge: hung, I perceive, with maps.

JOSEPH SURFACE.
Oh yes, I find great use in that screen.

SIR PETER.
I dare say you must, certainly, when you want to find anything in a hurry.

JOSEPH SURFACE. (*Aside.*)
Aye, or to hide anything in a hurry either.

SIR PETER.
Well, I have a little private business.

JOSEPH SURFACE.
You needn't stay.

SERVANT.
No sir. (*Exit.*)

JOSEPH SURFACE.
Here's a chair, Sir Peter. I beg—

SIR PETER.
Well now we are alone, there is a subject, my dear friend, on which I wish to unburden my mind to you, a point of greatest moment to my peace—in short, my good friend, Lady Teazle's conduct of late has made me very unhappy.

JOSEPH SURFACE.
Indeed, I am sorry to hear it.

SIR PETER.
Yes, 'tis but too plain she has not the least regard for me, but what's worse, I have pretty good authority to suppose that she must have formed an attachment to another.

JOSEPH SURFACE.
Indeed! You astonish me!

SIR PETER.
Yes, and between ourselves, I think I have discovered the person.

JOSEPH SURFACE.
How! You alarm me exceedingly!

SIR PETER.
Ah my dear friend, I knew you would sympathize with me!

JOSEPH SURFACE.
Yes, believe me, Sir Peter, such a discovery would distress me just as much as it would you.

SIR PETER.
I am convinced of it. Ah, it is a happiness to have a friend whom one can trust even with one's family secrets. But have you no guess who I mean?

JOSEPH SURFACE.
I haven't the most distant idea. It can't be Sir Benjamin Backbite?

SIR PETER.
Oh, no. What say you to Charles?

JOSEPH SURFACE.
My brother! Impossible!

SIR PETER.
It's very true.

JOSEPH SURFACE.
Oh no, Sir Peter, you must not credit the scandalous insinuation you hear. No, no, Charles, to be sure, has been charged many things of this kind, but I can never think he could mediate so gross an injury.

SIR PETER.
Ah, my dear friend! The goodness of your own heart misleads you; you judge of others by yourself.

JOSEPH SURFACE.
Certainly, Sir Peter, the heart that is conscious of its own integrity is ever slow to credit another's baseness.¶

SIR PETER.
True, but your brother has no sentiment; you never hear him talk so.

JOSEPH SURFACE.
Yet I can't but think that Lady Teazle herself has too much principle.

SIR PETER.
Aye, but what's her principle against the flattery of a handsome, lively, young fellow.

JOSEPH SURFACE.
That's very true.

SIR PETER.
And then you know the difference of our ages makes it highly improbable that she should have any violent affection for me, and if she were to be frail, and I were to make it public, why the Town would only laugh at me, the foolish old bachelor who had married a girl.

JOSEPH SURFACE.
That's true. To be sure, they would laugh.

SIR PETER.
Laugh, aye, and make ballads and paragraphs and the devil knows what of me.

JOSEPH SURFACE.
No, you must never make it public.

SIR PETER.

But then again, that the nephew of my old friend, Sir Oliver, should be the person to do such a wrong hurts one more nearly.

JOSEPH SURFACE.

Aye, there's the point: When ingratitude barbs the dart of injury, the wound has double danger in it.

SIR PETER.

Aye, I that was in a manner left his guardian, in whose house he has been so often entertained, who never in my life denied him—my advice.

JOSEPH SURFACE.

Oh 'tis not to be credited. There may be a man capable of such baseness to be sure, but for my part, till you can give me positive proofs, I cannot but doubt it; however, if this should be proved on him, he is no longer a brother of mine. I disclaim kindred with him. For the man who can break through the laws of hospitality and attempt the wife of his friend deserves to branded as the pest of society.

SIR PETER.

What a difference there is between you! What noble sentiments!

JOSEPH SURFACE.

Yet I cannot suspect Lady Teazle's honor.

SIR PETER.

I am sure I wish to think well of her and to remove all ground of quarrel between us. She has lately reproached me more than once with having made no settlement on her, and in our last quarrel she almost hinted that she would not break her heart if I was dead. Now as we seem to differ in our ideas of expense, I have resolved she shall be her own mistress in that respect for the future, and if I were to die, she shall find that I have not been inattentive to her interests while living. Here, my friend, are the drafts of two deeds which I wish to have your opinion on: by one, she will enjoy eight hundred a year, independent, while I live, and by the other, the bulk of my fortune after my death.

JOSEPH SURFACE.

This conduct, Sir Peter, is indeed truly generous! (*Aside.*) I wish it may not corrupt my pupil.

SIR PETER.

Yes, I am determined she shall have no cause to complain, though I would not have her acquainted with the latter instance of my affection yet awhile.

JOSEPH SURFACE. [*Aside.*]

Nor I, if I could help it.

SIR PETER.

And now, my dear friend, if you please, we will talk over the situation of your hopes with Maria.

JOSEPH SURFACE. [*Softly.*]

No, no, Sir Peter, another time if you please.

SIR PETER.

I am sensibly chagrined at the little progress you seem to make in her affections—

JOSEPH SURFACE. (*Softly.*)

I beg you will not mention it, sir. What are my disappointments when your happiness is in debate. [*Aside.*] 'Sdeath,* I shall be ruined every way.

SIR PETER.

And though you are so averse to my acquainting Lady Teazle with your passion, I am sure she is not your enemy in the affair.

JOSEPH SURFACE.

Pray Sir Peter, oblige me—I am really too much affected by the subject we have been talking to bestow a thought on my own concerns. The man who is entrusted with his friend's distresses—can never— Well, sir—

Enter Servant.

SERVANT.

Your brother, sir, is speaking to a gentleman in the street and says he knows you are within.

JOSEPH SURFACE.

'Sdeath! Blockhead, I am not within; I am out for the day.

SIR PETER.

Stay, hold, a thought has struck me: you shall be at home.

JOSEPH SURFACE.

Well, well, let him up.

Exit Servant.

(*Aside.*) He'll interrupt Sir Peter, however.

SIR PETER.

Now my good friend, oblige me, I entreat you: before Charles comes, let me conceal myself somewhere; then do you tax him on the point we have been talking on, and his answers may satisfy me at once.

JOSEPH SURFACE.
Oh fie, Sir Peter! Would you have me join in so mean* a trick—to trepan my brother too—

SIR PETER.
Nay, you tell me you are sure he's innocent; if so, you do him the greatest service in giving him an opportunity to clear himself, and you will set my heart at rest. Come, you shall not refuse me. Here behind this screen will be— Hey! What the devil! There seems to be one listener already. I'll swear I saw a petticoat.

JOSEPH SURFACE.
Ha, ha, ha! Well, this is ridiculous enough. I'll tell you, Sir Peter, though I hold a man of intrigue to be a most despicable character, yet you know it does not follow that one is to be an absolute Joseph either. Harkee, 'tis a little French milliner, a silly* rogue that plagues me, and having some character, on your coming in she ran behind the screen.

SIR PETER.
Ah, you rogue. But egad, she has overheard all I have been saying of my wife.

JOSEPH SURFACE.
Oh, 'twill never go any farther, you may depend on't.

SIR PETER.
No! Then 'ifaith, let her hear it out. Here's a closet will do as well.

JOSEPH SURFACE.
Well, go in then.

SIR PETER.
Sly rogue, sly rogue! (*Goes into the closet.*)

JOSEPH SURFACE.
A narrow escape indeed, and a curious situation I am in, to part man and wife in this manner.

LADY TEAZLE. (*Peeping out.*)
Couldn't I steal off?

JOSEPH SURFACE.
Keep close, my angel.

SIR PETER. (*Peeping out.*)
Joseph, tax him home.

JOSEPH SURFACE.
Back, my dear friend.

LADY TEAZLE.
Couldn't you lock Sir Peter in?

JOSEPH SURFACE.
Lie still, my life.

SIR PETER.
You are sure the little milliner won't blab?

JOSEPH SURFACE.
In, in, my dear Sir Peter. Foregad, I wish I had a key to the door.

Enter Charles.

CHARLES.
Holla, brother! What has been the matter? Your fellow wouldn't let me up at first. What, have you had a Jew or a wench with you?

JOSEPH SURFACE.
Neither brother, I assure you.

CHARLES.
And what has made Sir Peter steal off? I thought he had been with you.

JOSEPH SURFACE.
He was, brother, but hearing you were coming, he did not choose to stay.

CHARLES.
What! Was the old gentleman afraid I wanted to borrow money of him?

JOSEPH SURFACE.
No, sir. But I am sorry to find, Charles, that you have lately given that worthy man grounds for great uneasiness.

CHARLES.
Yes, yes, they tell me I do that to a great many worthy men, but how so pray?

JOSEPH SURFACE.
To be plain with you, brother, he thinks you are endeavoring to gain Lady Teazle's affections from him.

CHARLES.
Who I? Oh Lud!* Not I, upon my word. Ha, ha, ha! So the old fellow has found out that he has got a young wife, has he?[r]

JOSEPH SURFACE.
This is no subject to jest upon, brother. He who can laugh—

CHARLES.
True, true, as you were going to say—then seriously, I never had the least idea of what you charge me with, upon my honor.

JOSEPH SURFACE.
Well, well, it will give Sir Peter great satisfaction to hear it.

CHARLES.
To be sure, I once thought the lady seemed to have taken a fancy to me, but upon my soul, I never gave the least encouragement; besides, you know my attachment to Maria.

JOSEPH SURFACE.
But sure brother, if Lady Teazle had betrayed the fondest partiality for you—

CHARLES.
Why, look ye Joseph, I hope I shall never deliberately do a dishonorable action—but if a pretty woman were purposely to throw herself in my way—and that pretty woman married to a man old enough to be her father—

JOSEPH SURFACE.
Well!

CHARLES.
Why, I believe I should be obliged to borrow a little of your morality, that's all. But brother, do you know now that you surprise me exceedingly by naming me with Lady Teazle, for 'faith, I always understood *you* were her favorite.

JOSEPH SURFACE.
For shame, Charles, this retort is foolish.

CHARLES.
Nay, I swear I have seen you exchange such significant glances.

JOSEPH SURFACE.
Nay, nay sir, this is no jest.

CHARLES.
Egad, I'm serious, don't you remember one day when I called here—

JOSEPH SURFACE.
Nay prithee Charles—

CHARLES.
And found you together—

JOSEPH SURFACE.
Zounds sir! I insist—

CHARLES.
And another time when your servant—

JOSEPH SURFACE.
Brother, brother, a word with you. (*Aside.*) Gad I must stop him.

CHARLES.
Informed me, I say, that—

JOSEPH SURFACE.
Hush! I beg your pardon, but Sir Peter has overheard all we have been saying; I knew you would clear yourself, or I should not have consented.

CHARLES.
How! Sir Peter! Where is he?

JOSEPH SURFACE.
Softly—there. (*Points to the closet.*)

CHARLES.
Oh! Fore Heaven, I'll have him out.—Sir Peter, come forth.

JOSEPH SURFACE.
No, no.

CHARLES.
I say, Sir Peter, come into court. (*Pulls in Sir Peter.*) What, my old guardian! What! Turned inquisitor, and taking evidence incog?

SIR PETER.
Give me your hand, Charles, I believe I have suspected you wrongfully. But you mustn't be angry with Joseph—'twas my plan.

CHARLES.
Indeed!

SIR PETER.
But I acquit you. I promise you, I don't think near so ill of you as I did. What I have heard has given me great satisfaction.

CHARLES.
Egad then! 'twas lucky you didn't hear any more.—Wasn't it, Joseph?

SIR PETER.
Ah! You would have retorted on him.

CHARLES.
Aye, aye, that was a joke.

SIR PETER.
Yes, yes, I know his honor too well.

CHARLES.
But you might as well have suspected *him* as me in this matter for all that.—Mightn't he, Joseph?

SIR PETER.
Well, well, I believe you.

JOSEPH SURFACE. (*Aside.*)
I wish they were both well out of the room.

SIR PETER.
And in future perhaps we may not be such strangers.

Enter servant who speaks to Joseph Surface.

SERVANT.

Sir, Lady Sneerwell is below and says she will come up.

JOSEPH SURFACE. (*To the servant.*)

Lady Sneerwell—Gad's life! She mustn't come here.—Gentlemen, I beg pardon—I must wait on you downstairs—here is a person come on particular business.

CHARLES.

Well, well, you can see him in another room; Sir Peter and I have not met for a long time, and I have something to say to him.

JOSEPH SURFACE. [*Aside.*]

They must not be left together. I'll send Lady Sneerwell away directly.—Sir Peter, not a word of the French milliner.

SIR PETER.

Oh not for the world!

Exit Joseph Surface [and servant].

Ah Charles, if you associated more with your brother, one might indeed hope for your reformation. He is a man of sentiment. Well, there's nothing so noble as a man of sentiment.

CHARLES.

Pshaw, he is too moral by half and so apprehensive of his good name, as he calls it, that I suppose he would as soon let a priest into his house as a wench.

SIR PETER.

No, no, come, come, you wrong him. No, no, Joseph is no rake, but he is no such saint in that respect either. (*Aside.*) I have a great mind to tell him; we should have such a laugh.

CHARLES.

Oh, hang him! He's a very anchorite—a young hermit!

SIR PETER.

Hark ye, you must not abuse him; he may chance to hear of it again, I promise.

CHARLES.

Why, you won't tell him?

SIR PETER.

No—but—this way— [*Aside.*] Egad, I'll tell him.—Hark ye, have you a mind to have a good laugh against Joseph?

CHARLES.

I should like it of all things.

SIR PETER.

Then, faith, we will. [*Aside.*] I'll be quit with him for discovering* me. (*Whispers.*) He had a girl with him when I called.

CHARLES.

What, Joseph! You jest.

SIR PETER.

Hush! A little French milliner—and the best of the jest is—she's in the room now.

CHARLES.

The devil she is! (*Looking at the closet.*)

SIR PETER.

Hush I tell you! (*Points to the screen.*)

CHARLES.

Behind the screen? 'Odd's* life! Let us unveil her.

SIR PETER.

No, no, he's coming, you shan't indeed.

CHARLES.

Oh egad, we'll have a peep at the little milliner!

SIR PETER.

No, not for the world—Joseph will never forgive me.

CHARLES.

I'll stand by you.

SIR PETER.

'Odd's life! Here he is.

Joseph enters as Charles throws down the screen.

CHARLES.

Lady Teazle, by all that's wonderful!

SIR PETER.

Lady Teazle, by all that's damnable![S]

CHARLES.

Sir Peter, this is one of the smartest French milliners I ever saw. Egad, you seem all to have been diverting yourselves at hide and seek. And I don't see who is out of the secret.—Shall I beg your ladyship to inform me? Not a word!—Brother, will you please to explain this matter? What, is morality dumb too?—Sir Peter, though I found you in the dark, perhaps you are not so now. All mute! Well, though I can make nothing of this affair, I suppose you perfectly understand one another, so I shall leave you to yourselves. (*Going.*) Brother, I am sorry to find you have given that worthy man grounds for so much uneasiness.—Sir Peter, there's nothing in the world so noble as a man of sentiment! (*Exit.*)

JOSEPH SURFACE.
Sir Peter, notwithstanding I confess that appearances are against me, if you will afford me your patience, I make no doubt but I shall explain everything to your satisfaction.

SIR PETER.
If you please, sir.

JOSEPH SURFACE.
The fact is, sir—that Lady Teazle, knowing my pretensions to your ward, Maria—I say, sir, Lady Teazle being apprehensive of the jealousy of your temper and knowing my friendship to the family—she, sir, I say, called here, in order that I might explain those pretensions—but on your coming, being apprehensive as I said of your jealousy—she withdrew—and this, you may depend on't, is the whole truth of the matter.

SIR PETER.
A very clear account upon my word, and I dare swear the lady will vouch for every article of it.

LADY TEAZLE.
For not one word of it, Sir Peter.

SIR PETER.
How! Don't you think it worthwhile to agree in the lie?

LADY TEAZLE.
There is not one syllable of truth in what that gentleman has told you.

SIR PETER.
I believe you, upon my soul, madam.

JOSEPH SURFACE.
'Sdeath,* madam, will you betray me?

LADY TEAZLE.
Good Mr. Hypocrite, by your leave, I will speak for myself.

SIR PETER.
Aye, let her alone, sir; you'll find she'll make a better story than you without prompting.

LADY TEAZLE.
Hear me, Sir Peter, I came hither on no matter relating to your ward and even ignorant of this gentleman's pretensions to her. But I came here seduced by his insidious arguments, at least to listen to his pretended passion, if not to sacrifice your honor to his baseness.

SIR PETER.
Now I believe the truth is coming indeed.

JOSEPH SURFACE.
The woman's mad.

LADY TEAZLE.
No sir, she has recovered her senses, and your own arts have furnished her with the means.—Sir Peter, I do not expect you to credit me, but the tenderness you expressed for me, when I'm sure you could not think I was a witness to it, has penetrated so to my heart that, had I left the place without the shame of the discovery, my future life should have spoken the sincerity of my gratitude. As for that smoothed-tongue hypocrite, who would have seduced the wife of his too credulous friend while he affected honorable addresses to his ward, I behold him now in a light so truly despicable that I never again shall respect myself for having listened to him. (*Exit.*)

JOSEPH SURFACE.
Notwithstanding all this, Sir Peter, Heaven knows—

SIR PETER.
That you are a villain, and so I leave you to your conscience.

JOSEPH SURFACE.
You are too rash, Sir Peter—you shall hear me—the man who shuts out conviction by refusing to—

SIR PETER.
Oh, damn your sentiment![t]

Exeunt.

Act V, scene. i. A library.

Enter Joseph Surface and servant.

JOSEPH SURFACE.
Mr. Stanley! and why should you think I would see him? You must know he comes to ask something.

SERVANT.
Sir, I should not have let him in, but that Mr. Rowley came to the door with him.

JOSEPH SURFACE.
Pshaw! Blockhead! To suppose that I should now

be in a temper to receive visits from poor relations! Well, why don't you show the fellow up?

SERVANT.

I will, sir. Why sir, it wasn't my fault that Sir Peter discovered my lady. (*Exit.*)

JOSEPH SURFACE.

Go, fool. Sure, Fortune never played a man of my policy such a trick before. My character* with Sir Peter, my hopes with Maria, destroyed in a moment! I am in a rare humor to listen to other people's distresses! I shan't be able to bestow even a benevolent sentiment on Stanley.—Oh, here he comes, and Rowley with him. I must try to recover myself and put a little charity into my face, however. (*Exit.*)

Enter Sir Oliver and Rowley.

SIR OLIVER.

What, does he avoid us? That was he, was it not?

ROWLEY.

It was, sir, but I doubt* you are come a little[u] too abruptly. His nerves are so weak that the sight of a poor relation may be too much for him. I should have gone first to break you to him.

SIR OLIVER.

A plague of his nerves! Yet this is he whom Sir Peter extols as a man of the most benevolent way of thinking.

ROWLEY.

As to his way of thinking, I cannot pretend to decide, for to do him justice, he appears to have as much speculative benevolence as any private gentleman in the kingdom, though he is seldom so sensual as to indulge himself in the exercise of it.

SIR OLIVER.

Yet has a string of charitable sentiments, I suppose, at his fingers' ends.

ROWLEY.

Or rather at his tongue's end, Sir Oliver, for I believe there is no sentiment he has more faith in than that "Charity begins at home."

SIR OLIVER.

And his, I presume, is of that domestic sort, it never stirs abroad at all.

ROWLEY.

I doubt* you'll find it so. But he's coming. I must not seem to interrupt you, and you know, immediately as you leave him, I come in to announce your arrival in your real character.

SIR OLIVER.

True, and afterwards you'll meet me at Sir Peter's.

ROWLEY.

Without losing a moment. (*Exit.*)

SIR OLIVER.

So! I don't like the complaisance of his features.

Enter Joseph Surface.

JOSEPH SURFACE.

Sir, I beg you ten thousand pardons for keeping you a moment waiting. Mr. Stanley, I presume?

SIR OLIVER.

At your service, sir.

JOSEPH SURFACE.

Sir, I beg you will do me the honor to sit down. I entreat you, sir.

SIR OLIVER.

Dear sir, there's no occasion. (*Aside.*) Too civil by half.

JOSEPH SURFACE.

I have not the pleasure of knowing you, Mr. Stanley, but I am extremely happy to see you look so well. You were nearly related to my mother, Mr. Stanley, I think?

SIR OLIVER.

I was, sir, so nearly that my present poverty, I fear, may do discredit to her wealthy children, else I should not have presumed to trouble you.

JOSEPH SURFACE.

Dear sir, there needs no apology. He that is in distress, though a stranger, has a right to claim kindred with the wealthy. I'm sure I wish I was of that class and had it in my power to offer you even a small relief.

SIR OLIVER.

If your uncle Sir Oliver was here, I should have a friend.

JOSEPH SURFACE.

I wish he was, sir, with all my heart. You should not want* an advocate with him, believe me Sir.

SIR OLIVER.

I should not need one; my distresses would recommend me. But I imagined his bounty had enabled you to become the agent of his charity.

JOSEPH SURFACE.
My dear sir, you are strangely misinformed. Sir Oliver is a worthy man, a very worthy sort of a man, but avarice, Mr. Stanley, is the vice of the age. I will tell you, my good sir, in confidence, what he has done for me has been a mere nothing, though people, I know, have thought otherwise, and for my part, I never chose to contradict the report.

SIR OLIVER.
What! Has he never transmitted you bullion, rupees, pagodas?[21]

JOSEPH SURFACE.
Oh dear sir! Nothing of the kind. No, no, a few presents now and then, china, shawls, congou tea, avadavats,[22] and India crackers, little more, believe me.

SIR OLIVER. [*Aside.*]
Here's gratitude for twelve thousand pounds! Avadavats and India crackers!

JOSEPH SURFACE.
Then, my dear sir, you have heard, I doubt not, of the extravagance of my brother; there are very few would credit what I have done for that unfortunate young man.

SIR OLIVER. (*Aside.*)
Not I, for one.

JOSEPH SURFACE.
The sums I have lent him— Indeed I have been exceedingly to blame. It was an amiable weakness, however. I don't pretend to defend it, and now I feel it doubly culpable since it has deprived me of the power of serving you, Mr. Stanley, as my heart directs.

SIR OLIVER. [*Aside.*]
Dissembler!—Then, sir, you cannot assist me.

JOSEPH SURFACE.
At present it grieves me to say I cannot, but whenever I have the ability, you may depend upon hearing from me.

SIR OLIVER.
I am extremely sorry—

JOSEPH SURFACE.
Not more than I am, believe me; to pity without the power to relieve is still* more painful than to ask and be denied.

SIR OLIVER.
Kind sir, your most obedient humble servant.

JOSEPH SURFACE.
You leave me deeply affected, Mr. Stanley— William, be ready to open the door.

SIR OLIVER.
Oh dear sir, no ceremony!

JOSEPH SURFACE.
Your very obedient.

SIR OLIVER.
Sir, your most obsequious.

JOSEPH SURFACE.
You may depend upon hearing from me, whenever I can be of service.

SIR OLIVER.
Sweet sir, you are too good.

JOSEPH SURFACE.
In the meantime, I wish you health and spirits.

SIR OLIVER.
Your ever grateful and perpetual humble servant.

JOSEPH SURFACE.
Sir, yours as sincerely.

SIR OLIVER.
Now I'm satisfied. (*Exit.*)

JOSEPH SURFACE.
This is one of the bad effects of a good character.* It invites application from the unfortunate, and there needs no small degree of address to gain the reputation of benevolence without incurring the expense. The silver ore of pure charity is an expensive article in the catalog of a man's good qualities, whereas the sentimental French plate I use instead of it makes just as good a show and pays no tax.

Enter Rowley.

ROWLEY.
Mr. Surface, your servant. I was apprehensive of interrupting you, though my business demands immediate action, as this note will inform you.

JOSEPH SURFACE.
Always happy to see Mr. Rowley. (*Aside.*) A rascal![v]—How! Sir Oliver Surface, my uncle, arrived!

---

[21] pagodas] gold (less commonly silver) coins formerly current in Southern India (*OED*)

[22] avadavats] corruption of amadavats, Indian song-birds (*OED*)

ROWLEY.
He is indeed—we have just parted—quite well after a speedy voyage, and impatient to embrace his worthy nephew.

JOSEPH SURFACE.
I am astonished!—William, stop Mr. Stanley if he's not gone.

ROWLEY.
Oh he's out of reach, I believe.

JOSEPH SURFACE.
Why didn't you let me know this when you came in together?

ROWLEY.
I thought you had particular business, but I must be gone to inform your brother and appoint him here to meet his uncle. He will be with you in a quarter of an hour.

JOSEPH SURFACE.
So he says. Well, I'm strangely overjoyed at his coming. (*Aside.*) Never was anything, to be sure, so damned unlucky.

ROWLEY.
You will be delighted to see how well he looks.

JOSEPH SURFACE.
Oh, I am rejoiced to hear it. (*Aside.*) Just at this time.

ROWLEY.
I will tell him how impatient you expect him. (*Exit.*)

JOSEPH SURFACE.
Do, do, pray give my best duty and affection.—Indeed, I cannot express the sensations I feel at the thought of seeing him. Certainly his coming just at this time is the cruellest piece of ill fortune.

Exit.

Scene ii. Sir Peter Teazle's house.

Enter Mrs. Candor and maid.

MAID.
Indeed, ma'am, my lady will see nobody at present.

MRS. CANDOR.
Did you tell her it was her friend, Mrs. Candor?

MAID.
Yes ma'am, but she begs you will excuse her.

MRS. CANDOR.
Do go again. I shall be glad to see her only for a moment, for I'm sure she must be in great distress.

Exit maid.

Dear heart, how provoking! I'm not mistress of half the circumstances. We shall have the whole affair in the newspapers with the names of the parties at full length before I have dropped the story at a dozen houses.

Enter Sir Benjamin Backbite.

Oh dear, Sir Benjamin! You have heard I suppose—

SIR BENJAMIN.
Of Lady Teazle and Mr. Surface.

MRS. CANDOR.
And Sir Peter's discovery.

SIR BENJAMIN.
Oh, the strangest piece of business, to be sure!

MRS. CANDOR.
Well, I never was so surprised in my life. I am sorry for all parties indeed!

SIR BENJAMIN.
Now, I don't pity Sir Peter at all; he was so extravagantly partial to Mr. Surface.

MRS. CANDOR.
Mr. Surface! Why, 'twas with Charles Lady Teazle was detected.

SIR BENJAMIN.
No such thing. Mr. Surface is the gallant.

MRS. CANDOR.
No, no, Charles is the man. 'Twas Mr. Surface brought Sir Peter on purpose to discover them.

SIR BENJAMIN.
I tell you I have it from one—

MRS. CANDOR.
And I have it from one—

SIR BENJAMIN.
Who had it from one—who had it—

MRS. CANDOR.
From one immediately—but here's Lady Sneerwell; perhaps she knows the whole affair.

Enter Lady Sneerwell.

LADY SNEERWELL.
So my dear Mrs. Candor, here's a sad affair of our friend Teazle.

MRS. CANDOR.
Aye, my dear friend, who could have thought it.

LADY SNEERWELL.
Well, there's no trusting to appearances, though indeed she was always too lively for me.

MRS. CANDOR.
To be sure, her manners were a little too free, but she was very young.

LADY SNEERWELL.
And had indeed some good qualities.

MRS. CANDOR.
She had indeed—but have you heard the particulars?

LADY SNEERWELL.
No, but everybody says that Mr. Surface—

SIR BENJAMIN.
Aye, there I told you, Mr. Surface was the man.

MRS. CANDOR.
No, no indeed, the assignation was with Charles.

LADY SNEERWELL.
With Charles! You alarm me, Mrs. Candor.

MRS. CANDOR.
Yes, yes, he was the lover; Mr. Surface, to do him justice, was only the informer.

SIR BENJAMIN.
Well, I'll not dispute with you, Mrs. Candor. Be it which it may, I hope that Sir Peter's wound will not—

MRS. CANDOR.
Sir Peter's wound! Oh mercy, I did not hear a word of their fighting.

LADY SNEERWELL.
Nor I a syllable.

SIR BENJAMIN.
No! What, no mention of the duel!

MRS. CANDOR.
Not a word.

SIR BENJAMIN.
Oh Lord! Yes, yes, they fought before they left the room.

LADY SNEERWELL.
Pray, let us hear.

MRS. CANDOR.
Aye, do oblige us with the duel.

SIR BENJAMIN.
"Sir," says Sir Peter, immediately after the discovery, "you are a most ungrateful fellow"—

MRS. CANDOR.
Aye, to Charles.

SIR BENJAMIN.
No, no, to Mr. Surface—"a most ungrateful fellow, and old as I am, sir," says he, "I insist on immediate satisfaction."

MRS. CANDOR.
Aye, that must have been to Charles, for 'tis very unlikely Mr. Surface should go fight in his own house.

SIR BENJAMIN.
Gad's life, madam, not at all—"giving me immediate satisfaction"—on this, madam, Lady Teazle, seeing Sir Peter in such danger, ran out of the room in strong hysterics and Charles after her, calling for hartshorn and water; then madam, they began to fight with swords—

Enter Crabtree.

CRABTREE.
With pistols, Nephew, I have it from undoubted authority.

MRS. CANDOR.
Oh Mr. Crabtree, then it's all true.

CRABTREE.
Too true indeed, ma'am, and Sir Peter is dangerously wounded.

SIR BENJAMIN.
By a thrust in segoon,[23] quite through his left side.

CRABTREE.
By a bullet lodged in the thorax.

MRS. CANDOR.
Mercy on me, poor Sir Peter!

CRABTREE.
Yes ma'am, though Charles would have avoided the matter if he could.

MRS. CANDOR.
I knew Charles was the person.

SIR BENJAMIN.
My uncle, I see, knows nothing of the matter.

CRABTREE.
But Sir Peter taxed him with the basest ingratitude.

SIR BENJAMIN.
That I told you, you know.

---

23 segoon] seconde, a fencing term for the second of the seven classic thrusts (*OED*)

CRABTREE.
Do, Nephew, let me speak—and insisted on immediate satisfaction.

SIR BENJAMIN.
Just as I said.

CRABTREE.
'Odd's* life! Nephew, allow others to know something too—a pair of pistols lay on the bureau (for Mr. Surface, it seems, had come the night before late from Salt Hill where he had been to see the Montem[24] with a friend who has a son at Eton), so unluckily the pistols were left charged.

SIR BENJAMIN.
I heard nothing of this.

CRABTREE.
Sir Peter forced Charles to take one, and they fired, it seems, pretty nearly together; Charles's shot took place as I tell you, and Sir Peter's missed. But what is very extraordinary, the ball struck against a little bronze Shakespeare[w] that stood over the chimneypiece, grazed out of the window at a right angle, and wounded the postman, who was just coming to the door with a double letter[25] from Northamptonshire.

SIR BENJAMIN.
My uncle's account is more circumstantial, I must confess—but I believe mine is the true one for all that.

LADY SNEERWELL. [*Aside.*]
I am more interested in this affair than they imagine and must have better information. (*Exit.*)

SIR BENJAMIN.
Ah! Lady Sneerwell's alarm is very easily accounted for.

CRABTREE.
Yes, yes, they certainly *do* say— but that's neither here nor there.

MRS. CANDOR.
But pray, where is Sir Peter at present?

CRABTREE.
Oh, they brought him home, and he is now in the house, though the servants are ordered to deny it.

MRS. CANDOR.
I believe so, and Lady Teazle, I suppose, attending him.

CRABTREE.
Yes, yes, I saw one of the Faculty[26] enter just before me.

SIR BENJAMIN.
Hey! Who comes here?

CRABTREE.
Oh this is he! Physician, depend on't.

MRS. CANDOR.
Oh certainly, it must be the physician—and now we shall know.

Enter Sir Oliver.

CRABTREE.
Well, Doctor, what hopes?

MRS. CANDOR.
Aye Doctor, how's your patient?

SIR BENJAMIN.
Now Doctor, isn't it a wound with a small sword?

CRABTREE.
A bullet lodged in the thorax, for a hundred.

SIR OLIVER.
Doctor! A wound with a small sword and a bullet in the thorax! What, are you mad, good people?

SIR BENJAMIN.
Perhaps, sir, you are not a doctor?

SIR OLIVER.
Truly, I am to thank you for my degrees if I am.

CRABTREE.
Only a friend of Sir Peter's then, I presume. But sir, you must have heard of his accident?

SIR OLIVER.
Not a word.

CRABTREE.
Not of his being dangerously wounded?

SIR OLIVER.
The devil he is!

24 Montem] festival wherein the scholars of Eton would go in fancy costumes to "Salt Hill," a mound near Slough, and there collect money from the bystanders (*OED*)

25 double letter] a letter written on two sheets and charged double postage (*OED*)

26 Faculty] of the medical profession (in popular language 'The Faculty') (*OED*)

SIR BENJAMIN.
Run through the body!

CRABTREE.
Shot in the breast.

SIR BENJAMIN.
By one Mr. Surface.

CRABTREE.
Aye, by the younger.

SIR OLIVER.
Hey! What the plague! You seem to differ strangely in your accounts. However, you agree that Sir Peter is dangerously wounded?

SIR BENJAMIN.
Oh yes, we agree in that.

CRABTREE.
Yes, yes, I believe there can be no doubt of that.

SIR OLIVER.
Then upon my word, for a person in that situation, he is the most imprudent man alive, for here he comes walking as if nothing at all was the matter.

Enter Sir Peter.

'Odd's* heart! Sir Peter, you are come in good time, I promise you, for we had just given you over.

SIR BENJAMIN.
Egad Uncle, this is the most sudden recovery—

SIR OLIVER.
Why man, what do you do out of your bed, with a small sword through your body and a bullet lodged in your thorax?

SIR PETER.
A small sword and a bullet?

SIR OLIVER.
Aye, these gentlemen would have killed you without law or physic and wanted to dub me a doctor to make me an accomplice.

SIR PETER.
Why, what is all this?

SIR BENJAMIN.
We rejoice, Sir Peter, that the story of the duel is not true and are sincerely sorry for your other misfortunes.

SIR PETER. [*Aside.*]
So, it's all over the Town already.

CRABTREE.
Though, Sir Peter, you were certainly vastly to blame to marry at all at your years.

SIR PETER.
What business is that of yours, sir?

MRS. CANDOR.
Though indeed, as Sir Peter made so good a husband, he's very much to be pitied.

SIR PETER.
Plague on your pity, ma'am, I desire none of it.

SIR BENJAMIN.
However, Sir Peter, you mustn't mind the laughing and jests you will meet with on the occasion.

SIR PETER.
Sir, I desire to be master of my own house.

CRABTREE.
'Tis no uncommon case—that's one comfort.

SIR PETER.
I insist on being left to myself; without ceremony, I insist on your leaving my house directly.

MRS. CANDOR.
Well, well, we are going—and depend on't, we'll make the best report of you we can.

SIR PETER.
Leave my house.

CRABTREE.
And tell how hard you have been treated.

SIR PETER.
Leave my house.

SIR BENJAMIN.
And how patiently you bear it.

SIR PETER.
Leave my house—

Exeunt Mrs. Candor, Sir Benjamin, and Crabtree.

Fiends! Vipers! Furies! Oh that their own venom would choke them.

SIR OLIVER.
They are very provoking indeed, Sir Peter.

Enter Rowley.

ROWLEY.
I heard high words. What has ruffled you, Sir Peter?

SIR PETER.
Pshaw! What signifies asking? Do I ever pass a day without my vexations?

SIR OLIVER.
Well, I'm not inquisitive. I come only to tell you that I have seen both my nephews in the manner we proposed.

SIR PETER.
A precious* couple they are!

ROWLEY.
Yes, and Sir Oliver is convinced that your judgement was right, Sir Peter.

SIR OLIVER.
Yes, I find Joseph is indeed the man after all.

ROWLEY.
Aye, as Sir Peter says, he's a man of sentiment.

SIR OLIVER.
And acts up to the sentiments he professes.

ROWLEY.
It's certainly edification to hear him talk!

SIR OLIVER.
Oh, he's a model for the young men of the age! But how's this, Sir Peter? You don't join in your friend Joseph's praise, as I expected.

SIR PETER.
Sir Oliver, we live in a damned, wicked world, and the fewer we praise, the better.

ROWLEY.
What, do you say so, Sir Peter, who never were mistaken in your life?

SIR PETER.
Pshaw! Plague on you both. I see by your sneering you have heard the whole affair. I shall go mad among you.

ROWLEY.
Then, to fret you no longer, Sir Peter, we are indeed acquainted with it all. I met Lady Teazle coming from Mr. Surface's so humbled that she deigned to request me to be her advocate with you.

SIR PETER.
And does Sir Oliver know all too?

SIR OLIVER.
Every circumstance.

SIR PETER.
What, of the closet—and the screen, hey?

SIR OLIVER.
Yes, yes, and the little French milliner! Oh, I have been vastly diverted with the story—ha, ha!

SIR PETER.
'Twas very pleasant.

SIR OLIVER.
I never laughed more in my life, I assure you, ha, ha, ha!

SIR PETER.
Oh, vastly diverting, ha, ha, ha!

ROWLEY.
To be sure, Joseph with his sentiments—ha, ha, ha!

SIR PETER.
Yes, yes, his sentiments—ha, ha, ha! A hypocritical villain!

SIR OLIVER.
Aye, and that rogue Charles to pull Sir Peter out of the closet—ha, ha, ha!

SIR PETER.
Ha, ha!—'twas devilish entertaining, to be sure.

SIR OLIVER.
Ha, ha! Egad, Sir Peter, I should like to have seen your face when the screen was thrown down—ha, ha, ha!

SIR PETER.
Yes, yes, my face when the screen was thrown down—ha, ha! Oh, I must never show my head again.

SIR OLIVER.
But come, come, it isn't fair to laugh at you neither, my old friend, though upon my soul I can't help it.

SIR PETER.
Oh pray, don't restrain your mirth on my account; it doesn't hurt me at all. I laugh at the whole affair myself. Yes, yes, I think being a standing jest for all one's acquaintances a very happy situation. Oh yes, and then of a morning to read the paragraphs about Lady T. and Sir P.[x] will be so entertaining. I shall certainly leave town tomorrow and never look mankind in the face again.[y]

ROWLEY.
Without affectation, Sir Peter, you may despise the ridicule of fools. But I see Lady Teazle going towards the next room; I am sure you must desire a reconciliation as much as she does.

SIR OLIVER.
Perhaps my being here prevents her coming to you. Well, I'll leave honest Rowley to mediate between

you—but he must bring you all presently to Mr. Surface's, where I am now returning, if not to reclaim a libertine, at least to expose hypocrisy. (*Exit.*)

SIR PETER.
Ah! I'll be present at your discovering* yourself there with all my heart, though 'tis a vile, unlucky place for discoveries.

ROWLEY.
We'll follow.

SIR PETER.
She's not coming here, you see, Rowley.

ROWLEY.
No. But she has left the door of that room open, you perceive. She's in tears.

SIR PETER.
Certainly a little mortification appears very becoming in a wife. Don't you think 'twill do her good to let her pine a little?

ROWLEY.
Oh! This is ungenerous in you.

SIR PETER.
Well, I know not what to think. You remember, Rowley, the letter I found of hers evidently intended for Charles.

ROWLEY.
Oh mere forgery, Sir Peter, laid in your way on purpose; this is one of the points I intend Snake shall give you conviction on.

SIR PETER.
I wish I was once satisfied of that.—She looks this way. What a remarkably elegant turn of the head she has.—Rowley, I'll go to her.

ROWLEY.
Certainly.

SIR PETER.
Though when 'tis known we are reconciled, people will laugh at me ten times more.

ROWLEY.
Let them laugh, and retort their malice only by showing you are happy in spite of it.

SIR PETER.
I'faith, so I will, and if I am not mistaken we may be the happiest couple in the country.

ROWLEY.
Nay Sir Peter, he who once lays aside suspicion—

SIR PETER.
Hold, Master Rowley! If you have any regard for me, never let me hear you utter anything like a sentiment. I have had enough of *them* to serve me the rest of my life.

Exeunt.

Scene iii. The library.

Enter Joseph Surface and Lady Sneerwell.

LADY SNEERWELL.
Impossible! Will not Sir Peter immediately be reconciled to Charles and of consequence no longer oppose his union with Maria? The thought is distraction to me.

JOSEPH SURFACE.
Can passion furnish a remedy?

LADY SNEERWELL.
No, nor cunning either. Oh, I was a fool! an idiot! to league with such a blunderer.

JOSEPH SURFACE.
Sure Lady Sneerwell, I am the greatest sufferer, yet you see I bear the accident with calmness.

LADY SNEERWELL.
Because the disappointment doesn't reach your heart; your interest only attached you to Maria. Had you felt for her what I have felt for that ungrateful libertine, neither your temper nor hypocrisy could prevent your showing the sharpness of your vexation.

JOSEPH SURFACE.
But why should your reproaches fall on me for this disappointment?

LADY SNEERWELL.
Are you not the cause of it? What had you to do to bate in your pursuit of Maria, to pervert Lady Teazle by the way? Had you not a sufficient field for your roguery in blinding Sir Peter and supplanting your brother? I hate such an avarice of crimes; 'tis an unfair monopoly and never prospers.

JOSEPH SURFACE.
Well, I admit I have been to blame. I confess I have deviated from the direct road of wrong, but I don't think we are so totally defeated either.

LADY SNEERWELL.
No?

JOSEPH SURFACE.
You tell me you have made a trial of Snake since we met and that you still believe him faithful to us?

LADY SNEERWELL.
I do believe so.

JOSEPH SURFACE.
And that he has undertaken, should it be necessary, to swear and prove that Charles is at this time contracted by vows and honor to your ladyship, which some of his former letters to you will serve to support.

LADY SNEERWELL.
This indeed might have assisted.

JOSEPH SURFACE.
Come, come, it is not too late yet.

Knocking.

But hark! This is probably my uncle, Sir Oliver. Retire to that room and we'll consult farther when he's gone.

LADY SNEERWELL.
I have[z] no diffidence of your abilities, only to be constant to one roguery at a time. (*Exit.*)

JOSEPH SURFACE.
I will, I will— So, 'tis confounded hard after such bad fortune to be baited by one's confederate in evil. Well, at all events my character is so much better than Charles's that I certainly— Hey! What! This is not Sir Oliver but old Stanley again. Plague on't that he should return to tease me just now. We shall have Sir Oliver come and find him here and—

Enter Sir Oliver.

Gad's life, Mr. Stanley, you have come back to plague me at this time? You must not stay, upon my word.

SIR OLIVER.
Sir, I hear your uncle Sir Oliver is expected here, and though he has been so penurious to you, I'll try what he will do for me.

JOSEPH SURFACE.
Sir, 'tis impossible for you to stay now. So I must beg you, come any other time, and I promise you, you shall be assisted.

SIR OLIVER.
No. Sir Oliver and I must be acquainted.

JOSEPH SURFACE.
Zounds sir, then I insist on your quitting the room directly.

SIR OLIVER.
Nay sir—

JOSEPH SURFACE.
Sir, I insist on't.—Here William, show this gentleman out.—Since you compel me, sir—not one moment—this is such insolence—

Enter Charles.

CHARLES.
Heyday! What's the matter? What the devil, have you got hold of my little broker here? Zounds, don't hurt little Premium! What's the matter, my little fellow?

JOSEPH SURFACE.
So he has been with you too, has he?

CHARLES.
To be sure he has. Why, 'tis as honest a little— But sure, Joseph, you have not been borrowing money too, have you?

JOSEPH SURFACE.
Borrowing! No. But Brother, you know here we expect Sir Oliver every—

CHARLES.
Oh gad! That's true. Noll musn't find the little broker here, to be sure.

JOSEPH SURFACE.
Yet Mr. Stanley insists—

CHARLES.
Stanley! Why, his name is Premium.

JOSEPH SURFACE.
No, no, Stanley.

CHARLES.
No, no, Premium.

JOSEPH SURFACE.
Well, no matter which—but—

CHARLES.
Aye, aye, Stanley or Premium, 'tis the same thing, as you say, for I suppose he goes by half an hundred names, besides A and B at the coffee house.

Knocking.

JOSEPH SURFACE.
'Sdeath!* Here's Sir Oliver at the door. Now I beg, Mr. Stanley—

CHARLES.
Aye, aye, and I beg, Mr. Premium—

SIR OLIVER.
Gentlemen—

JOSEPH SURFACE.
Sir, by Heaven you shall go.

CHARLES.
Aye, out with him certainly.

SIR OLIVER.
This violence—

JOSEPH SURFACE.
'Tis your own fault.

CHARLES.
Out with him to be sure.

Both forcing Sir Oliver out. Enter Sir Peter, Lady Teazle, Maria and Rowley.

SIR PETER.
My old friend, Sir Oliver, hey! What in the name of wonder! Here are dutiful nephews! assault their uncle at the first visit.

LADY TEAZLE.
Indeed, Sir Oliver, 'twas well we came in to rescue you.

ROWLEY.
Truly it was, for I perceive, Sir Oliver, the character of Old Stanley was not a protection to you.

SIR OLIVER.
No, nor of Premium either: the necessities of the former couldn't extort a shilling from that benevolent gentleman, and with the other I stood a chance of faring worse than my ancestors and being knocked down without being bid for.

JOSEPH SURFACE.
Charles!

CHARLES.
Joseph!

JOSEPH SURFACE.
'Tis now complete.

CHARLES.
Very.

SIR OLIVER.
Sir Peter, my friend, and Rowley too, look on that elder nephew of mine. You know what he has already received from my bounty, and you know also how gladly I would have regarded half my fortune as held in trust for him. Judge then my disappointment in discovering him to be destitute of truth, charity, and gratitude.

SIR PETER.
Sir Oliver, I should be more surprised at this declaration if I had not myself found him to be selfish, treacherous, and hypocritical.

LADY TEAZLE.
And if the gentleman pleads not guilty to these, pray let him call me to his character.*

SIR PETER.
Then I believe we need add no more. If he knows himself, he will consider it as the most perfect punishment that he is known by the world.

CHARLES. [*Aside.*]
If they talk this way to honesty, what will they say to me by and by?

SIR OLIVER.
As for that prodigal his brother there—

CHARLES. [*Aside.*]
Aye, now comes my turn—the damned family pictures will ruin me.

JOSEPH SURFACE.
Sir Oliver! Uncle! If you will honor me with a hearing.

SIR OLIVER. (*Turns from him with contempt.*)
Psha!

CHARLES. (*Aside.*)
Now if Joseph would make one of his long speeches, I might recollect myself a little.

SIR OLIVER.
I suppose you would undertake to justify yourself entirely.

JOSEPH SURFACE.
I trust I could.

SIR OLIVER.
Pshaw. Nay, if you desert your roguery in its distress and try to be justified, you have even less principle than I thought you had.[aa] (*To Charles.*) Well sir, and you could justify yourself yourself too, I suppose.

CHARLES.
Not that I know of, Sir Oliver.

SIR OLIVER.
What, little Premium has been let too much into the secret, I presume.

CHARLES.
True, sir, but they were family secrets and should never be mentioned again, you know.

ROWLEY.
Come, Sir Oliver, I know you cannot speak of Charles's follies with anger.

SIR OLIVER.
'Odd's* heart! No more I can, nor with gravity either.—Sir Peter, do you know the rogue bargained with me for all his ancestors: sold me judges and generals by the foot, and maiden aunts as cheap as broken china.

CHARLES.
To be sure, Sir Oliver, I did make free with the family canvas, that's the truth on't; my ancestors may certainly rise in evidence against me, there's no denying. But believe me sincere when I tell you, and upon my soul I would not say it if it was not, that, if I do not appear mortified at the exposure of my follies, it is because I feel at this moment the warmest satisfaction in seeing *you*, my liberal benefactor.

SIR OLIVER.
Charles, I believe you, give me your hand: the ill-looking little fellow over the settee has made your peace.

CHARLES.
Then sir, my gratitude to the original is still increased.

LADY TEAZLE.
Yet I believe, Sir Oliver, there is one whom Charles is still more anxious to be reconciled to.

SIR OLIVER.
Oh, I have heard of his attachment there, and with the young lady's pardon, if I construe right that blush—

SIR PETER.
Well, child,* speak your sentiments.

MARIA.
Sir, I have little to say but that I shall rejoice to hear that he is happy; for me, whatever claim I had to his attention,[bb] I willingly resign it to one who has a better title.

CHARLES.
How Maria!

SIR PETER.
Heyday! What's the mystery now? While he appeared an incorrigible rake, you would give your hand to no one else, and now that he's likely to reform, I warrant you won't have him.

MARIA.
His own heart and Lady Sneerwell's knows the cause.

CHARLES.
Lady Sneerwell!

JOSEPH SURFACE.
Brother, it is with great concern I am obliged to speak on this point, but my regard to justice obliges me, and Lady Sneerwell's injuries can no longer be concealed. (*Goes to the door.*)

Enter Lady Sneerwell.

ALL.
Lady Sneerwell!!![cc]

SIR PETER.
So! Another French milliner. Egad, he has one in every room in the house, I suppose.

LADY SNEERWELL.
Ungrateful Charles! Well may you be surprised and feel for the indelicate situation which your perfidy has forced me into.

CHARLES.
Pray, Uncle, is this another plot of yours, for as I have life, I don't understand it.

JOSEPH SURFACE.
I believe, sir, there is but the evidence of one person more necessary to make it extremely clear.

SIR PETER.
And that person, I imagine, is Mr. Snake.—Rowley, you were perfectly right to bring him with us, and pray let him appear.

ROWLEY.
Walk in, Mr. Snake.

Enter Snake.

I thought his testimony might be wanted;* however, it happens unluckily that he comes to confront Lady Sneerwell and not to support her.

LADY SNEERWELL.
A villain! treacherous to me at last. Speak fellow, have you conspired against me?

SNAKE.
I beg your ladyship ten thousand pardons: You paid me extremely liberally for the lie in question, but I have unfortunately been offered double the sum to speak the truth.

SIR PETER.
Plot and counterplot.[dd]

LADY SNEERWELL.
The torments of shame and disappointment on you all.

LADY TEAZLE.
Hold, Lady Sneerwell, before you go, let me thank you for the trouble you and that gentleman have taken in writing letters to me from Charles and answering them yourself. And let me also request you to make my respects to the Scandalous College, of which you are president, and inform them that Lady Teazle, licentiate, begs leave to return the diploma they granted her—as she leaves off practice and kills characters* no longer.

LADY SNEERWELL.
You too, madam—provoking—insolent—may your husband live these fifty years. (*Exit.*)[ee]

LADY TEAZLE.
What a malicious creature it is!

SIR PETER.
Hey! What, not for her last wish?

LADY TEAZLE.
Oh, no.

SIR OLIVER.
Well sir, what have you to say now?

JOSEPH SURFACE.
Sir, I am so confounded that Lady Sneerwell could be guilty of suborning Mr. Snake in this manner to impose on us all that I know not what to say; however, lest her revengeful spirit should prompt her to injure my brother, I had certainly better follow her directly. (*Exit.*)

SIR PETER.
Moral to the last drop.

SIR OLIVER.
Aye, and marry her, Joseph, if you can, oil and vinegar, egad you'll do very well together.

ROWLEY.
I believe we have no more occasion for Mr. Snake at present.

SNAKE.
Before I go, I beg pardon once for all for whatever uneasiness I have been the humble instrument of causing to the parties present.

SIR PETER.
Well, well, you have made atonement by a good deed at last.

SNAKE.
But I must request of the company that it shall never be known.

SIR PETER.
Hey! What the plague, are you ashamed of having done a right thing once in your life.

SNAKE.
Ah sir, consider I live by the badness of my character. I have nothing but my infamy to depend on, and if it were once known that I had been betrayed into an honest action, I should lose every friend I have in the world. (*Exit.*)

SIR PETER.
Here's a precious* rogue.[ff]

SIR OLIVER.
Well, well, we'll not traduce you by saying any thing to your praise, never fear.

LADY TEAZLE.
See, Sir Oliver, there needs no persuasion now to reconcile your nephew and Maria.

SIR OLIVER.
Aye, aye, that's as it should be, and egad, we'll have the wedding tomorrow morning.

CHARLES.
Thank you, my dear uncle.

SIR PETER.
What, you rogue! Don't you ask the girl's consent first?

CHARLES.
I have done that a long time—a minute—ago, and she looked—yes.

MARIA.
For shame, Charles.—I protest, Sir Peter, there has not been a word.

SIR OLIVER.
Well then, the fewer the better. May your love for

each other never know abatement.

SIR PETER.

And may you live as happily together as Lady Teazle and I—intend to do.

CHARLES.

Rowley, my old friend, I am sure you congratulate me, and I suspect that I owe you much.

SIR OLIVER.

You do indeed, Charles.

ROWLEY.

If my efforts to serve you had not succeeded, you would have been in my debt for the attempt, but deserve to be happy, and you overpay me.

SIR PETER.

Aye! Honest Rowley always said you would reform.

CHARLES.

Why as to reforming, Sir Peter, I'll make no promises—and that I take to be a proof that I intend to set about it. But here shall be my monitor, my gentle guide. Ah! can I leave the virtuous path those eyes illumine? (*To the audience.*)

For thou, dear maid, shouldst waive thy beauty's sway.
Thou still* must rule because I will obey.
An humbled fugitive from folly view—
No sanctuary near but love and you.
You can indeed each anxious fear remove,
For even scandal dies if you approve.

[Exeunt.]

THE END.

Textual Notes

[a] Because of the complicated publishing history of the play, resulting from Sheridan's refusal to publish it, the copytext chosen is the 1799 Dublin edition (Du), which is generally regarded as being both accurate and complete. Also consulted were modern editions of 1939, revised 1969 (Nettleton, Case, and Stone—NCS) and of 1973 (Price), which is based on the Frampton Court, the Georgetown Crewe, the Second Crewe, the Buckinghamshire, and the Powell mss.

[b] reputation] Du; injured reputation NCS, Price

[c] while with Sir Peter ... benevolence] Du; *om.* NCS, Price

[d] MARIA] Du, NCS; LADY SNEERWELL Price.

[e] his spirits: Sir Thomas Splint] Du; his Spirits—every body almost is in the same way—Lord Spindle, Sir Thomas Splint NCS, Price

[f] sermon] Du; novel NCS, Price

[g] turn. MRS. CANDOR.] Du; turn—she can sit for an hour to hear Lady Stucco talk sentiment. LADY TEAZLE. Nay, I vow Lady Stucco is very well with the dessert after dinner for she's just like the French fruit one cracks for mottoes—made up of paint and proverb. MRS. CANDOR. NCS, Price

[h] opinion ... practices.] Du; opinion—nothing could—excuse the intemperance of their tongues but a natural and ungovernable bitterness of mind. NCS, Price

[i] every wife] Du; every London wife NCS, Price

[j] I ... him] Du; I have done all I could for him NCS, Price

[k] If ... dat] Du; If you ask him no more than that NCS, Price; only the Dublin edition has such speech patterns for Moses.

[l] trade. SIR OLIVER. Right, right!] Du; trade—but Moses—wouldn't you have him run out a little against the annuity Bill? That should be in character, I should think. MOSES. Very much. ROWLEY. And lament that a young man now must be at years of discretion before he is suffered to ruin himself? MOSES. Aye, great pity. SIR PETER. And abuse the public for allowing merit to an act whose only object is to snatch misfortune and imprudence from the rapacious relief of usury, and give the minor a chance of inheriting his estate without being undone by coming into possession. SIR OLIVER. So, so NCS, Price.

[m] neck. MOSES. But] Du; neck. TRIP. But then, Moses, it must be done before this d——d register takes place—one wouldn't like to have one's name made public you know. MOSES. No, certainly, but NCS, Price

[n] Deborah. This] Du; Deborah! Here now are two that were a sort of cousins of theirs.—You see, Moses, these pictures were done some time ago, when beaux wore wigs, and the ladies wore their own hair. SIR OLIVER. Yes, truly, head-dresses appear to have been a little lower in those days. CHARLES. Well, take that couple for the same. MOSES. 'Tis good bargain. CHARLES. Careless!—This NCS, Price

[o] pounds and take ... in the lump. SIR OLIVER.] Du; pounds, for the rest of the family in the lump. CARELESS. Aye—aye—that will be the best way. SIR OLIVER. NCS, Price

[p] health. LADY TEAZLE. Why, if] health. LADY TEAZLE. So, so; then I perceive your prescription is, that I must sin in my own defence and part with my virtue to preserve my reputation? JOSEPH SURFACE. Exactly so, upon my credit, ma'am. LADY TEAZLE. Well, certainly this is the oddest doctrine, and the newest receipt for avoiding calumny? JOSEPH SURFACE. An infallible one, believe me. *Prudence*, like *experience*, must be paid for. LADY TEAZLE. Why, if NCS, Price

[q] baseness] Du; treachery NCS, Price

[r] has he?] Du; has he? Or what's worse has her ladyship discovered that she has an old husband? NCS, Price

[s] damnable] Du; horrible NCS, Price

[t] damn … sentiment!] Du; *om.* NCS, Price

[u] are … little] NCS, Price; Du illegible

[v] (*Aside.*) a rascal!] Du; *om.* NCS, Price

[w] Shakespeare] Du; Pliny NCS, Price

[x] Lady T. and Sir P.] Du; Mr. S—, Lady T—, and Sir P— NCS, Price

[y] I shall … again] Du; *om.* NCS, Price

[z] gone. LADY SNEERWELL. I have] Du; gone. LADY SNEERWELL. Well!—but if *he* should find you out too— JOSEPH SURFACE. Oh I have no fear of that. Sir Peter will hold his tongue for his own credit sake—and you may depend on't I shall soon discover Sir Oliver's weak side! LADY SNEERWELL. I have NCS, Price

[aa] nay … you had.] Du; *om.* NCS, Price

[bb] attention] Du; affection NCS, Price

[cc] ALL… . Sneerwell!!!] Du; *om.* NCS, Price

[dd] counterplot. LADY SNEERWELL.] Du; counterplot. Egad—I wish your ladyship joy of the success of your negotiation. LADY SNEERWELL. NCS, Price

[ee] years. (*Exit.*)] Du; years. Oons what a fury—] NCS, Price

[ff] rogue. SIR OLIVER.] Du; rogue—yet that fellow is a writer and a critic! SIR OLIVER. NCS, Price

The Belle's Stratagem[a]

by Hannah Cowley (1743-1809)

edited by Linda R. Payne

Like a stock character type in the plays of the period, including her own, Hannah Parkhouse Cowley was raised in the rural environs of Tiverton, Devonshire, and was brought to London when she married. Her husband went to India, however, leaving her on her own in London with three children and her writing career, through which she became an acute observer and satirist of English society.

The Belle's Stratagem enjoyed a particularly profitable run of twenty-eight nights beginning February 22, 1780. The role of Letitia Hardy, originated by Elizabeth Younge, drew the best actresses of subsequent generations, most notably Ellen Terry, playing opposite Henry Irving as Doricourt in the late nineteenth century. The original audience enjoyed John Quick, as Mr. Hardy, reprising his role of Isaac Mendoza from *The Duenna* (1779).

The play follows the "laughing comedy" revival popularized by Goldsmith and Sheridan in the 1760s and '70s. Cowley foregrounds a courtship plot involving the witty couple Letitia and Doricourt, backed with a sentimental subplot in which the doting but misguided Touchwoods are educated into a right relationship. The more original features of these plots include Letitia as the blocking figure who subverts her own arranged marriage to a rich, handsome man she adores unrequitedly in order to gamble at re-establishing the relationship on a more equal footing; and the role of Saville, the agent of the subplot who protects the virtue and marriage of a woman he loves without hope of return.

The portrayal of Letitia's unwillingness to settle for a conventionally advantageous marriage, along with the emphasis given her intelligence and courage, can certainly be viewed as a feminist perspective, although complicated by more traditional characteristics. And both of the play's chief strategists triumph from traditionally powerless positions: Letitia as woman and marriage pawn, Saville as second son or descendant of a decayed family who lacks the economic status to marry within the class he deserves.

Both plots build on errors in discerning appearance from reality. There are also strong nationalistic themes inspired by the revolt of the American colonies and tensions with France. Yet the play outlasted its times. Acted 118 times in London by 1800, ranking fourth of full-length plays written between 1776 and 1800, it continued to be frequently produced in both England and America through the nineteenth century.

DRAMATIS PERSONAE

MEN

Doricourt.
Hardy.
Sir George Touchwood.
Flutter.
Saville.
Villers.
Courtall.
Silvertongue.
Crowquill.
First Gentleman.
Second Gentleman.
Mountebank.
French Servant.
Porter.
Dick.
[Mask.]

WOMEN

Letitia Hardy.
Mrs. Racket.
Lady Frances Touchwood.
Miss Ogle.
Kitty Willis.
Lady.
[Mrs. Fagg.]
Masqueraders, tradesmen, servants, etc.

The Belle's Stratagem.

Act I, scene i. Lincoln's Inn.[1]

Enter Saville followed by a servant at the top of the stage, looking round as if at a loss.

SAVILLE.
Lincoln's Inn! Well, but where to find him, now I am in Lincoln's Inn? Where did he say his master was?

SERVANT.
He only said in Lincoln's Inn, sir.

SAVILLE.
That's pretty! And your wisdom never enquired at whose chambers?

SERVANT.
Sir, you spoke to the servant yourself.

SAVILLE.
If I was too impatient to ask questions, you ought to have taken directions, blockhead!

Enter Courtall singing.

Hah, Courtall!—Bid him keep the horses in motion and then enquire at all the chambers round.

Exit servant.

What the devil brings you to this part of the Town?* Have any of the long robes[2] handsome wives, sisters, or chambermaids?

COURTALL.
Perhaps they have, but I came on a different errand, and had thy good fortune brought thee here half an hour sooner, I'd have given thee such a treat, ha, ha, ha!

SAVILLE.
I'm sorry I missed it. What was it?

COURTALL.
I was informed a few days since that my cousins Fallow were come to Town and desired earnestly to see me at their lodgings in Warwick-Court, Holborn.[3] Away drove I, painting them all the way as so many Hebes. They came from the farthest part of Northumberland, had never been in Town, and in course were made up of rusticity, innocence, and beauty.

SAVILLE.
Well!

COURTALL.
After waiting thirty minutes, during which there was a violent bustle, in bounced five sallow damsels, four of them maypoles; the fifth, Nature, by way of variety, had bent in the Aesop style.[4] But they all opened at once like hounds on a fresh scent: "Oh cousin Courtall! How do you do, cousin Courtall! Lord, cousin, I am glad you are come! We want you to go with us to the Park* and

---

1 Lincoln's Inn] one of the Inns of Court*

2 long robes] judges

3 Holborn] a small district of central London sandwiched between the City* and the Town* and dominated by the Inns of Court

4 Aesop style] deformed, as was Aesop, legendarily

the plays and the opera and Almack's[5] and all the fine places!" The devil, thought I, my dears, may attend you, for I am sure I won't. However, I heroically stayed an hour with them and discovered the virgins were all come to Town with the hopes of leaving it—wives: their heads full of knight-baronights,[6] fops, and adventures.

SAVILLE.

Well, how did you get off?

COURTALL.

Oh, pleaded a million engagements. However, conscience twitched me, so I breakfasted with them this morning and afterwards squired them to the gardens here as the most private place in Town and then took a sorrowful leave, complaining of my hard, hard fortune that obliged me to set off immediately for Dorsetshire, ha, ha, ha!

SAVILLE.

I congratulate your escape! Courtall at Almack's with five awkward country cousins! Ha, ha, ha! Why, your existence as a man of gallantry could never have survived it.

COURTALL.

Death and fire! Had they come to Town like the rustics of the last age to see Paul's, the Lions, and the Waxwork[7]—at their service. But the cousins of our days come up ladies, and with the knowledge they glean from magazines and pocket books, fine ladies; laugh at the bashfulness of their grandmothers; and boldly demand their entrées in the first circles.

SAVILLE. [*Aside.*]

Where can this fellow be!—Come, give me some news. I have been at war with woodcocks and partridges these two months and am a stranger to all that has passed out of their region.

COURTALL.

Oh! enough for three gazettes. The ladies are going to petition for a bill that, during the war,[8] every man may be allowed two wives.

SAVILLE.

'Tis impossible they should succeed, for the majority of both Houses know what it is to have one.

COURTALL.

Gallantry was blackballed at the coterie last Thursday, and Prudence and Chastity voted in.

SAVILLE.

Aye, that may hold till the camps break up. But have ye no elopements? no divorces?

COURTALL.

Divorces are absolutely out and the commons-doctors[9] starving, so they are publishing trials of crim. con.[10] with all the separate evidences at large, which they find has always a wonderful effect on their trade, actions tumbling in upon them afterwards like mackerel at Gravesend.

SAVILLE.

What more?

COURTALL.

Nothing—for weddings, deaths, and politics I never talk of but whilst my hair is dressing. But prithee, Saville, how came you in Town, whilst all the qualified gentry are playing at popgun on Coxheath and the country overrun with hares and foxes?[11]

SAVILLE.

I came to meet my friend Doricourt, who, you know, is lately arrived from Rome.

COURTALL.

Arrived! Yes faith, and has cut us all out! His carriage, his liveries, his dress, himself are the rage

---

5 Almack's] popular assembly rooms on King St., St. James, London, exclusive marriage mart for eligible daughters of fashionable London

6 baronights] play off of baronet, whose title of address, like that of knights, was "Sir"

7 Paul's, the Lions, and the Waxwork] typical tourist attractions: St. Paul's Cathedral, the lions of the royal menagerie housed in the Tower of London, exhibits or sales of wax figures, the most famous and popular in the eighteenth century being Mrs. Salmon's Waxwork in Fleet Street, established in 1693.

8 war] the American Revolution and concomitant colonial skirmishes with France and Spain

9 commons-doctors] lawyers at Doctors Commons*

10 crim. con.] criminal conversation

11 playing at popgun ... foxes] Country squires neglected their hunting as they drilled their militia at Coxheath, a village in Kent, its heath the site of encampments where George III reviewed the troops in 1778.

of the day! His first appearance set the whole *ton*[12] in a ferment, and his valet is besieged by levees of tailors, habit-makers, and other ministers of fashion to gratify the impatience of their customers for becoming *à la mode de Doricourt.* Nay, the beautiful Lady Frolic t'other night, with two sister countesses, insisted upon his waistcoat for muffs, and their snowy arms now bear it in triumph about Town, to the heartrending affliction of all our *beaux garçons.*[13]

SAVILLE.

Indeed! Well, those little gallantries will soon be over; he's on the point of marriage.

COURTALL.

Marriage! Doricourt on the point of marriage! 'Tis the happiest tidings you could have given, next to his being hanged. Who is the bride elect?

SAVILLE.

I never saw her, but 'tis Miss Hardy, the rich heiress. The match was made by the parents and the courtship begun on their nurses' knees; Master used to crow at Miss, and Miss used to chuckle at Master.

COURTALL.

Oh! then by this time they care no more for each other than I do for my country cousins.

SAVILLE.

I don't know that; they have never met since thus high and so, probably, have some regard for each other.

COURTALL.

Never met! Odd!

SAVILLE.

A whim of Mr. Hardy's: he thought his daughter's charms would make a more forcible impression if her lover remained in ignorance of them till his return from the continent.

Enter Saville's servant.

SERVANT.

Mr. Doricourt, sir, has been at Counsellor Pleadwell's and gone about five minutes. (*Exit.*)

[12] *ton*] the *bon ton*, beautiful Town, fashionable society (Fr.)

[13] *beaux garçons*] handsome young men; men of fashion (Fr.)

SAVILLE.[b]

Five minutes! Zounds![c] I have been five minutes too late all my lifetime!—Good morrow, Courtall, I must pursue him. (*Going.*)

COURTALL.

Promise to dine with me today. I have some honest fellows. (*Going off on the opposite side.*)

SAVILLE.

Can't promise, perhaps I may.—See there, there's a bevy of female Patagonians coming down upon us.

COURTALL.

By the Lord, then, it must be my strapping cousins. I dare not look behind me. Run, man, run.

Exeunt on the same side.

Scene ii. A hall at Doricourt's.

A gentle knock at the door. Enter the porter.

PORTER.

Tap! What sneaking devil art thou? (*Opens the door.*)

Enter Crowquill.[d]

So! I suppose *you* are one of monsieur's customers, too? He's above stairs, now, overhauling all his honor's things to a parcel of 'em.

CROWQUILL.

No sir, it is with you, if you please, that I want to speak.

PORTER.

Me! Well, what do you want with me?

CROWQUILL.

Sir, you must know that I am—I am the gentleman who writes the tête-à-têtes in the magazines.

PORTER.

Oh, oh! What, you are the fellow that ties folks together in your sixpenny cuts[14] that never meet anywhere else?

CROWQUILL.

Oh dear sir, excuse me! We always go on *foundation*, and if you can help me to a few anecdotes of your master, such as what marchioness he lost money to

[14] sixpenny cuts] cheap tabloids

in Paris, who is his favorite lady in Town, or the name of the girl he first made love* to at college, or any incidents that happened to his grandmother or great aunts—a couple will do, by way of supporters—I'll weave a web of intrigues, losses, and gallantries between them that shall fill four pages, procure me a dozen dinners and you, sir, a bottle of wine for your trouble.

PORTER.

Oh, oh! I heard the butler talk of you when I lived at Lord Tinket's. But what the devil do you mean by bottle of wine! You gave him a crown for a retaining fee.

CROWQUILL.

Oh sir, that was for a lord's amours; a commoner's are never but half. Why, I have had a baronet's for five shillings, though he was a married man and changed his mistress every six weeks.

PORTER.

Don't tell me! What signifies a baronet or a bit of a lord, who maybe was never further than fun and fun round London? *We* have traveled, man! My master has been in Italy and over the whole island of Spain, talked to the Queen of France and danced with her at a masquerade. Aye, and such folks don't go to masquerades for nothing, but mum—not a word more. Unless you'll rank my master with a lord, I'll not be guilty of blabbing his secrets, I assure you.

CROWQUILL.

Well sir, perhaps you'll throw in a hint or two of other families where you've lived that may be worked up into something, and so, sir, here is one, two, three, four, five shillings.

PORTER.

Well, that's honest. (*Pocketing the money.*) To tell you the truth, I don't know much of my master's concerns yet, but here comes Monsieur and his gang, I'll pump them; they have trotted after him all round Europe from the Canaries to the Isle of Wight.

Enter several foreign servants and two tradesmen. The porter takes one of them aside.

TRADESMAN.

Well then, you have showed us all?

FRENCHMAN.

All, *en vérité, messieurs*! you *avez* seen every ting. *Serviteur, serviteur.*

Exeunt tradesmen.

Ah, here comes one *autre* curious Englishman, and dat's one *autre* guinea *pour moi.*

Enter Saville.

Allons,[15] monsieur, dis way; I will shew you tings, such tings you never see, begar,* in England!—velvets by Le Mosse, suits cut by Verdue, trimmings by Grossette, embroidery by Detanville[16]—

SAVILLE.

Puppy!* Where is your master?

PORTER.

Zounds! You chattering, frog-eating, dunderhead, can't you see a gentleman? 'Tis Mr. Saville.

FRENCHMAN. [*Aside.*]

Monsieur Saville! *Je suis mort de peur.*[17]—Ten tousand pardons! *Excuser mon erreur*, and permit me you conduct to Monsieur Doricourt; he be too happy *à vous voir.*[18]

Exeunt Frenchman and Saville.

PORTER.

Step below a bit. We'll make it out somehow! I suppose a slice of sirloin won't make the story go down the worse.

Exeunt Porter and Crowquill.

Scene iii. An apartment at Doricourt's.

Enter Doricourt.

DORICOURT. (*Speaking to a servant behind.*)

I shall be too late for St. James's.* Bid him come immediately.

Enter Frenchman and Saville.

---

15 *Allons*] Let's go (Fr.)

16 LeMosse, Verdue, Grossette, Detanville] popular French merchants

17 *Je suis mort de peur*] I am dead with fear (Fr.)

18 *à vous voir*] to see you (Fr.)

FRENCHMAN.
Monsieur Saville. (*Exit.*)

DORICOURT.
Most fortunate! My dear Saville, let the warmth of this embrace speak the pleasure of my heart.

SAVILLE.
Well, this is some comfort, after the scurvy reception I met with in your hall. I prepared my mind, as I came upstairs, for a bonjour, a grimace, and an adieu.

DORICOURT.
Why so?

SAVILLE.
Judging of the master from the rest of the family.* What the devil is the meaning of that flock of foreigners below, with their parchment faces and snuffy whiskers? What! can't an Englishman stand behind your carriage, buckle your shoe, or brush your coat?

DORICOURT.
Stale, my dear Saville, stale! Englishmen make the best soldiers, citizens, artisans, and philosophers in the world, but the very worst footmen. I keep French fellows and Germans as the Romans kept slaves, because their own countrymen had minds too enlarged and haughty to descend with a grace to the duties of such a station.

SAVILLE.
A good excuse for a bad practice.

DORICOURT.
On my honor, experience will convince you of its truth. A Frenchman neither hears, sees, nor breathes but as his master directs, and his whole system of conduct is comprised in one short word, *obedience*! An Englishman reasons, forms opinions, cogitates, and disputes. He is the mere creature of your will, the other, a being conscious of equal importance in the universal scale with yourself and is therefore your judge, whilst he wears your livery and decides on your actions with the freedom of a censor.

SAVILLE.
And this in defense of a custom I have heard you execrate, together with all the adventitious manners imported by our traveled gentry.

DORICOURT.
Aye, but that was at eighteen; we are always *very* wise at eighteen. But consider this point: we go into Italy where the sole business of the people is to study and improve the powers of music; we yield to the fascination and grow enthusiasts in the charming science. We travel over France and see the whole kingdom composing ornaments and inventing fashions; we condescend to avail ourselves of their industry and adopt their modes. We return to England and find the nation intent on the most important objects: polity, commerce, war, with all the liberal arts, employ her sons. The latent sparks glow afresh within our bosoms; the sweet follies of the continent imperceptibly slide away whilst senators, statesmen, patriots, and heroes emerge from the virtu of Italy and the frippery of France.

SAVILLE.
I may as well give it up! You had always the art of placing your faults in the best light, and I can't help loving you, faults and all. So, to start a subject which must please you, when do you expect Miss Hardy?

DORICOURT.
Oh, the hour of expectation is past. She is arrived, and I this morning had the honor of an interview at Pleadwell's. The writings were ready, and in obedience to the will of Mr. Hardy, we met to sign and seal.

SAVILLE.
Has the event answered? Did your heart leap or sink when you beheld your mistress?

DORICOURT.
Faith, neither one nor t'other. She's a fine girl, as far as mere flesh and blood goes, but—

SAVILLE.
But what?

DORICOURT.
Why, she's *only* a fine girl: complexion, shape, and features—nothing more.

SAVILLE.
Is not that enough?

DORICOURT.
No! she should have spirit! fire! *l'air enjoué*![19] that something, that nothing, which everybody feels

19 *l'air enjoué*] a playful nature (Fr.)

and which nobody can describe in the resistless charmers of Italy and France.

SAVILLE.

Thanks to the parsimony of my father that kept me from travel! I would not have lost my relish for true, unaffected English beauty to have been quarreled for by all the belles of Versailles and Florence.

DORICOURT.

Faugh! thou has no taste. *English* beauty! 'Tis insipidity; it wants* the zest, it wants* poignancy, Frank! Why, I have known a Frenchwoman, indebted to nature for no one thing but a pair of decent eyes, reckon in her suite as many counts, marquises, and *petits maîtres*[20] as would satisfy three dozen of our first-rate toasts. I have known an Italian *marquizina*[21] make ten conquests in stepping from her carriage and carry her slaves from one city to another, whose real intrinsic beauty would have yielded to half the little grisettes that pace your Mall* on a Sunday.

SAVILLE.

And has Miss Hardy nothing of this?

DORICOURT.

If she has, she was pleased to keep it to herself. I was in the room half an hour before I could catch the color of her eyes, and every attempt to draw her into conversation occasioned so cruel an embarrassment that I was reduced to the necessity of news, French fleets, and Spanish captures with her father.

SAVILLE.

So Miss Hardy, with only beauty, modesty, and merit, is doomed to the arms of a husband who will despise her.

DORICOURT.

You are unjust. Though she has not inspired me with violent passion, my honor secures her felicity.

SAVILLE.

Come, come, Doricourt, you know very well that when the honor of a husband is *locum-tenens*[22] for his heart, his wife must be as indifferent as himself, if she is not unhappy.

DORICOURT.

Faugh! never moralize without spectacles. But as we are upon the tender subject, how did you bear Touchwood's carrying Lady Frances?

SAVILLE.

You know I never looked up to her with hope, and Sir George is every way worthy of her.

DORICOURT.

Á la mode Angloise, a philosopher even in love.

SAVILLE.

Come, I detain you, you seem dressed at all points and of course have an engagement.

DORICOURT.

To St. James. I dine at Hardy's and accompany them to the masquerade in the evening. But breakfast with me tomorrow, and we'll talk of our old companions, for I swear to you, Saville, the air of the continent has not effaced one youthful prejudice or attachment.

SAVILLE.

With an exception to the case of ladies and servants.

DORICOURT.

True, there I plead guilty, but I have never yet found any man whom I could cordially take to my heart and call friend who was not born beneath a British sky and whose heart and manners were not truly English.

Exeunt Doricourt and Saville.

Scene iv. An apartment at Mr. Hardy's.

Villers[e] *seated on a sofa, reading. Enter Flutter.*

FLUTTER.

Hah, Villers, have you seen Mrs. Racket? Miss Hardy, I find, is out.

VILLERS.

I have not seen her yet. I have made a voyage to Lapland since I came in. (*Flinging away the book.*) A lady at her toilet* is as difficult to be moved as a Quaker.[23] (*Yawning.*) What events have happened in the world since yesterday? Have you heard?

---

20 *petits maîtres*] lesser gentry (Fr.)

21 *marquizina*] *marchesina*, lesser marchioness (It.)

22 *locum-tenens*] representative or placeholder (Lat.)

23 as difficult … Quaker] Quakers have services without ministers, where members sit silently until an individual feels "moved" to speak.

FLUTTER.

Oh yes, I stopped at Tattersall's[24] as I came by, and there I found Lord James Jessamy, Sir William Wilding, and Mr. _____.* But now I think of it, you shan't know a syllable of the matter, for I have been informed you never believe above one-half of what I say.

VILLERS.

My dear fellow, somebody has imposed upon you most egregiously! Half! Why, I never believe one tenth part of what you say, that is, according to the plain and literal expression. But as I understand you, your intelligence is amusing.

FLUTTER.

That's very hard now, very hard. I never related a falsity in my life, unless I stumbled on it by mistake. And if it were otherwise, your dull matter-of-fact people are infinitely obliged to those warm imaginations which soar into fiction to amuse you. For positively, the common events of this little dirty world are not worth talking about unless you embellish 'em!—Hah! here comes Mrs. Racket: adieu to weeds, I see! All life!

Enter Mrs. Racket.

Enter, madam, in all your charms! Villers has been abusing your toilet* for keeping you so long, but I think we are much obliged to it, and so are you.

MRS. RACKET.

How so, pray? Good morning t'ye both. Here, here's a hand apiece for you. (*They kiss her hands.*)

FLUTTER.

How so! Because it has given you so many beauties.

MRS. RACKET.

Delightful compliment! what do you think of that, Villers?

VILLERS.

That he and his compliments are alike: showy, but won't bear examining. So you brought Miss Hardy to Town last night?

MRS. RACKET.

Yes, I should have brought her before, but I had a fall from my horse that confined me a week. I suppose in her heart she wished me hanged a dozen times an hour.

FLUTTER.

Why?

MRS. RACKET.

Had she not an expecting lover in Town all the time? She meets him this morning at the lawyer's. I hope she'll charm him; she's the sweetest girl in the world.

VILLERS. [*Aside.*]

Vanity, like murder, will out.—You have convinced me you think yourself more charming.

MRS. RACKET.

How can that be?

VILLERS.

No woman ever praises another unless she thinks herself superior in the very perfections she allows.

FLUTTER.

Nor no man ever rails at the sex unless he is conscious he deserves their hatred.

MRS. RACKET.

Thank ye, Flutter, I'll owe ye a bouquet for that. I am going to visit the new-married Lady Frances Touchwood. Who knows her husband?

FLUTTER.

Everybody.

MRS. RACKET.

Is there not something odd in his character?

VILLERS.

Nothing but that he is passionately fond of his wife, and so petulant is his love that he opened the cage of a favorite bullfinch and sent it to catch butterflies because she rewarded its song with her kisses.

MRS. RACKET.

Intolerable monster! Such a brute deserves—

VILLERS.

Nay, nay, nay, nay, this is your sex now. Give a woman but one stroke of character,* off she goes like a ball from a racket, sees the whole man, marks him down for an angel or a devil, and so exhibits him to her acquaintance. This "monster"! this "brute"! is one of the worthiest fellows upon earth—sound sense and a liberal mind—but dotes on his wife to such excess that he quarrels with everything she admires and is jealous of her tippet and nosegay.

24 Tattersall's] an auction establishment specializing in horses

MRS. RACKET.

Oh, less love for me, kind Cupid! I can see no difference between the torment of such an affection and hatred.

FLUTTER.

Oh pardon me, inconceivable difference, inconceivable: I see it as clearly as your bracelet. In the one case the husband would say, as Mr. Snapper said t'other day, "Zounds! madam, do you suppose that *my* table and *my* house and *my* pictures—" *À propos des bottes*,[25] there was the divinest *Plague of Athens* sold yesterday at Langford's![26] The dead figures so natural you would have sworn they had been alive! Lord Primrose bid five hundred. "Six," said Lady Carmine. "A thousand," said Ingot the Nabob. Down went the hammer. "A rouleau for your bargain," said Sir Jeremy Jingle. And what answer do you think Ingot made him?

MRS. RACKET.

Why, took the offer.

FLUTTER.

"Sir, I would oblige you, but I buy this picture to place in the nursery: the children have already got *Whittington and his Cat*;[27] 'tis just this size, and they'll make good companions.

MRS. RACKET.

Ha, ha, ha! Well, I protest that's just the way now. The nabobs and their wives outbid one at every sale, and the creatures have no more taste—

VILLERS.

There again! You forget this story is told by Flutter, who always remembers everything but the circumstances and the person he talks about: 'twas Ingot who offered a rouleau for the bargain, and Sir Jeremy Jingle who made the reply.

FLUTTER.

Egad, I believe you are right. Well, the story is as good one way as t'other, you know. Good morning. I am going to Mrs. Crotchet's concert and in my way back shall make my bow at Sir George's. (*Going.*)

VILLERS.

I'll venture every figure in your tailor's bill you make some blunder there.

FLUTTER. (*Turning back.*)

Done! My tailor's bill has not been paid these two years, and I'll open my mouth with as much care as Mrs. Bridget Button, who wears cork plumpers in each cheek and never hazards more than six words for fear of showing them. (*Exit.*)

MRS. RACKET.

'Tis a good-natured, insignificant creature! let in everywhere and cared for nowhere.—There's Miss Hardy returned from Lincoln's Inn. She seems rather chagrined.

VILLERS.

Then I leave you to your communications.

Enter Letitia followed by her maid.

Adieu!—I am rejoiced to see you so well, madam, but I must tear myself away.

LETITIA.

Don't vanish in a moment.

VILLERS.

Oh inhuman! you are two of the most dangerous women in Town. Staying here to be cannonaded by four such eyes is equal to a rencontre with Paul Jones or a midnight march to Omoa![28] (*Aside.*) They'll swallow the nonsense for the sake of the compliment. (*Exit.*)

LETITIA. (*Gives her cloak to her maid.*)

Order Du Quesne never to come again; he shall positively dress my hair no more.

Exit maid.

And this odious silk, how unbecoming it is! I was bewitched to choose it. (*Throwing herself on a sofa and looking in a pocket glass,* Mrs. Racket staring at her.*) Did you ever see such a fright as I am today?

MRS. RACKET.

Yes, I have seen you look much worse.

[25] *À propos des bottes*] by way of nothing (Fr.)

[26] Langford's] a popular auction house

[27] *Whittington and his Cat*] painting of legendary poor boy whose cat is sold for a fortune and who becomes Lord Mayor of London

[28] Omoa] fortification on the Bay of Honduras, site of a grueling 5-month invasion of Honduras in 1780 with disastrous results to British troops

LETITIA.
How can you be so provoking? If I do not look this morning worse than ever I looked in my life, I am naturally a fright. You shall have it which way you will.

MRS. RACKET.
Just as you please. But pray, what is the meaning of all this?

LETITIA. (*Rising.*)
Men are all dissemblers! flatterers! deceivers! Have I not heard a thousand times of my air, my eyes, my shape—all made for victory! and today, when I bent my whole heart on one poor conquest, I have proved that all those imputed charms amount to nothing—for Doricourt saw them unmoved. A husband of fifteen months could not have examined me with more cutting indifference.

MRS. RACKET.
Then you return it like a wife of fifteen months and be as indifferent as he.

LETITIA.
Aye, there's the sting! The blooming boy who left his image in my young heart is, at four and twenty, improved in every grace that fixed him there. It is the same face that my memory and my dreams constantly painted to me, but its graces are finished and every beauty heightened. How mortifying to feel myself at the same moment his slave and an object of perfect indifference to him![f]

MRS. RACKET.
How are you certain that was the case? Did you expect him to kneel down before the lawyer, his clerks, and your father to make oath of your beauty?

LETITIA.
No, but he should have looked as if a sudden ray had pierced him! He should have been breathless! speechless! For oh, Caroline, all this was I.

MRS. RACKET.
I am sorry you was such a fool. Can you expect a man who has courted and been courted by half the fine women in Europe to feel like a girl from a boarding school? He is the prettiest fellow you have seen and in course bewilders your imagination. But he has seen a million of pretty women, child,* before he saw you, and his first feelings have been over long ago.

LETITIA.
Your raillery distresses me, but I will touch his heart or never be his wife.

MRS. RACKET.
Absurd and romantic! If you have no reason to believe his heart pre-engaged, be satisfied; if he is a man of honor, you'll have nothing to complain of.

LETITIA.
Nothing to complain of! Heavens! shall I marry the man I adore with such an expectation as that?

MRS. RACKET.
And when you have fretted yourself pale, my dear, you'll have mended your expectation greatly.

LETITIA. (*Pausing.*)
Yet I have one hope. If there is any power whose peculiar care is faithful love, that power I invoke to aid me.

Enter Mr. Hardy.

HARDY.
Well now, wasn't I right? Aye, Letty! Aye, cousin Racket! Wasn't I right? I knew 'twould be so. He was all agog to see her before he went abroad and, if he had, he'd have thought no more of her face, maybe, than his own.

MRS. RACKET.
Maybe not half so much.

HARDY.
Aye, maybe so, but I see into things: exactly as I foresaw, today he fell desperately in love with the wench, he! he! he!

LETITIA.
Indeed, sir! how did you perceive it?

HARDY.
That's a pretty question! How do I perceive everything? How did I foresee the fall of corn* and the rise of taxes? How did I know that if we quarreled with America, Norway deals would be dearer? How did I foretell that a war would sink the funds? How did I forewarn Parson Homily that if he didn't some way or other contrive to get more votes than Rubrick, he'd lose the lectureship? How did I—but what the devil makes you so dull, Letitia? I thought to have found you popping about as brisk as the jacks of your harpsichord.

LETITIA.
Surely sir, 'tis a very serious occasion.

HARDY.
Faugh, faugh! girls should never be grave before marriage. How did you feel, cousin, beforehand? Aye!

MRS. RACKET.
Feel! why, exceedingly full of cares.

HARDY.
Did you?

MRS. RACKET.
I could not sleep for thinking of my coach, my liveries, and my chairmen;* the taste of clothes I should be presented in distracted me for a week; and whether I should be married in white or lilac gave me the most cruel anxiety.

LETITIA.
And is it possible that you felt no other care?

HARDY.
And pray, of what sort may your cares be, Mrs.* Letitia? I begin to foresee now that you have taken a dislike to Doricourt.

LETITIA.
Indeed sir, I have not.

HARDY.
Then what's all this melancholy about? Ain't you going to be married? And what's more, to a sensible man? And what's more to a young girl, to a handsome man? And what's all this melancholy for, I say?

MRS. RACKET.
Why, because he *is* handsome and sensible, and because she's over head and ears in love with him; all which, it seems, your foreknowledge had not told you a word of.

LETITIA.
Fie, Caroline!

HARDY.
Well come, do you tell me what's the matter then? If you don't like him, hang the signing and sealing, he shan't have ye—and yet I can't say that, neither, for you know that estate that cost his father and me upwards of fourscore thousand pounds must go all to him if you won't have him; if he won't have you, indeed, 'twill be all yours. All that's clear, engrossed upon parchment, and the poor dear man set his hand to it whilst he was a-dying. "Ah!" said I, "I foresee you'll never live to see 'em come together, but their first son shall be christened Jeremiah after you, that I promise you." But come, I say, what is the matter? Don't you like him?

LETITIA.
I fear, sir—if I must speak—I fear I was less agreeable in Mr. Doricourt's eyes than he appeared in mine.

HARDY.
There you are mistaken, for I asked him, and he told me he liked you vastly.—Don't you think he must have taken a fancy to her?

MRS. RACKET.
Why really I think so, as I was not by.

LETITIA.
My dear sir, I am convinced he has not. But if there is spirit or invention in woman, he shall.

HARDY.
Right, girl, go to your toilet—*

LETITIA.
It is not my toilet* that can serve me. But a plan has struck me, if you will not oppose it, which flatters me with brilliant success.

HARDY.
Oppose it! not I indeed! What is it?

LETITIA.
Why sir, it may seem a little paradoxical, but as he does not like me enough, I want him to like me still less and will at our next interview endeavor to heighten his indifference into dislike.

HARDY.
Who the devil could have foreseen that?

MRS. RACKET.
Heaven and earth! Letitia, are you serious?

LETITIA.
As serious as the most important business of my life demands.

MRS. RACKET.
Why endeavor to make him dislike you?

LETITIA.
Because 'tis much easier to convert a sentiment into its opposite than to transform indifference into tender passion.

MRS. RACKET.
That may be good philosophy, but I am afraid you'll find it a bad maxim.

LETITIA.

I have the strongest confidence in it. I am inspired with unusual spirits and on this hazard willingly stake my chance for happiness. I am impatient to begin my measures. (*Exit.*)

HARDY.

Can you foresee the end of this, cousin?

MRS. RACKET.

No sir, nothing less than your penetration can do that, I am sure, and I can't stay now to consider it. I am going to call on Miss Ogle[g] and then to Lady Frances Touchwood's and then to an auction and then—I don't know where—but I shall be at home time enough to witness this extraordinary interview. Goodbye. (*Exit.*)

HARDY.

Well, 'tis an odd thing—I can't understand it—but I foresee Letty will have her way, and so I shan't give myself the trouble to dispute it.

Exit.

Act II, scene i. Sir George Touchwood's.

Enter Doricourt and Sir George.

DORICOURT.

Married, ha, ha, ha! you, whom I heard in Paris say such things of the sex, are in London a married man.

SIR GEORGE.

The sex is still what it has ever been since *la petite morale*[29] banished substantial virtues, and rather than have given my name to one of your high-bred fashionable dames, I'd have crossed the line[30] in a fire ship and married a Japanese.

DORICOURT.

Yet you have married an English beauty, yea, and a beauty born in high life.

SIR GEORGE.

True, but she has a simplicity of heart and manners that would have become the fair Hebrew damsels toasted by the patriarchs.

DORICOURT.

Ha, ha! Why, thou art a downright matrimonial Quixote. My life on't, she becomes as mere* a Town lady in six months as though she had been bred to the trade.

SIR GEORGE. (*Contemptuously.*)

Common, common. No sir, Lady Frances despises high life so much from the ideas I have given her that she'll live in it like a salamander in fire.

DORICOURT.

Oh, that the circle *dans la Place Victoire*[31] could witness thy extravagance! I'll send thee off to St. Évreux[32] this night, drawn at full length and colored after nature.

SIR GEORGE.

Tell him then, to add to the ridicule, that Touchwood glories in the name of husband, that he has found in one Englishwoman more beauty than Frenchmen ever saw and more goodness than Frenchwomen can conceive.

DORICOURT.

Well, enough of description. Introduce me to this phoenix.[33] I came on purpose.

SIR GEORGE.

Introduce! oh, aye, to be sure—I believe Lady Frances is engaged just now—but another time—(*Aside.*) How handsome the dog looks today!

DORICOURT.

Another time! but I have no other time. 'Sdeath!* this is the only hour I can command this fortnight!

SIR GEORGE. (*Aside.*)

I am glad to hear it, with all my soul.—So then, you can't dine with us today? That's very unlucky.

DORICOURT.

Oh yes, as to dinner, yes I can, I believe, contrive to dine with you today.

SIR GEORGE.

Psha! I didn't think on what I was saying; I meant supper—you can't sup with us?

29 *la petite morale*] small details of politeness and courtesy (Fr.)

30 line] equator

31 *dans la Place Victoire*] in the Place de la Victoire (Victory Square), on the right bank in Paris

32 St. Évreux] The cathedral at Évreux in Normandy was famous for its stained-glass windows from the 12th to the 17th centuries; the "him" in the next line may be a personification or someone from St. Évreux.

33 phoenix] Only one of these mythical birds existed at any given time.

DORICOURT.

Why, supper will be rather more convenient than dinner. But you are fortunate: if you had asked me any other night, I could not have come.

SIR GEORGE.

Tonight—Gad, now I recollect, we are particularly engaged tonight—but tomorrow night—

DORICOURT.

Why look ye, Sir George, 'tis very plain you have no inclination to let me see your wife at all; so here I sit. (*Throws himself on a sofa.*) There's my hat, and here are my legs. Now I shan't stir till I have seen her, and I have no engagements: I'll breakfast, dine, and sup with you every day this week.

SIR GEORGE. [*Aside.*]

Was there ever such a provoking wretch!—But to be plain with you, Doricourt, I and my house are at your service. But you are a damned agreeable fellow and ten years younger than I am, and the women, I observe, always simper when you appear. For these reasons I had rather, when Lady Frances and I are together, that you should forget we are acquainted further than a nod, a smile, or a how-d'ye.

DORICOURT.

Very well.

SIR GEORGE.

It is not merely yourself in propria persona that I object to, but if you are intimate here, you'll make my house still more the fashion than it is, and it is already so much so that my doors are of no use to me. I married Lady Frances to engross her to myself, yet such is the blessed freedom of modern manners that, in spite of me, her eyes, thoughts, and conversation are continually divided amongst all the flirts and coxcombs of fashion.

DORICOURT.

To be sure, I confess that kind of freedom is carried rather too far. 'Tis hard one can't have a jewel in one's cabinet but the whole Town must be gratified with its luster. (*Aside.*) He shan't preach me out of seeing his wife, though.

SIR GEORGE.

Well now, that's reasonable. When you take time to reflect, Doricourt, I always observe you decide right, and therefore I hope—

Enter servant.

SERVANT.

Sir, my lady desires—

SIR GEORGE.

I am particularly engaged.

DORICOURT. (*Leaping from the sofa.*)

Oh Lord, that shall be no excuse in the world. Lead the way, John. I'll attend your lady. (*Exit, following the servant.*)

SIR GEORGE.

What devil possessed me to talk about her!—Here, Doricourt! (*Running after him.*) Doricourt!

Enter Mrs. Racket and Miss Ogle, followed by a servant.

MRS. RACKET.

Acquaint your lady that Mrs. Racket and Miss Ogle are here.

Exit servant.

MISS OGLE.

I shall hardly know Lady Frances, 'tis so long since I was in Shropshire.

MRS. RACKET.

And I'll be sworn you never saw her out of Shropshire. Her father kept her locked up with his caterpillars and shells and loved her beyond anything—but a blue butterfly and a petrified frog!

MISS OGLE.

Ha, ha, ha! Well, 'twas a cheap way of breeding her: you know he was very poor, though a lord, and very high-spirited, though a virtuoso. In Town, her pantheons,* operas, and *robes de cour*,[34] would have swallowed his seaweeds, moths, and monsters in six weeks. Sir George, I find, thinks his wife a most extraordinary creature: he has taught her to despise everything like fashionable life and boasts that example will have no effect on her.

MRS. RACKET.

There's a great degree of impertinence in all that. I'll try to make her a fine lady to humble him.

MISS OGLE.

That's just the thing I wish.

Enter Lady Frances.

---

34 *robes de cour*] fashionable attire to wear at Court (Fr.)

LADY FRANCES.

I beg ten thousand pardons, my dear Mrs. Racket.—Miss Ogle, I rejoice to see you. I should have come to you sooner, but I was detained in conversation by Mr. Doricourt.

MRS. RACKET.

Pray make no apology; I am quite happy that we have your ladyship in Town at last. What stay do you make?

LADY FRANCES.

A short one! Sir George talks with regret of the scenes we have left and, as the ceremony of presentation[35] is over, will, I believe, soon return.

MISS OGLE.

Sure he can't be so cruel! Does your ladyship wish to return so soon?

LADY FRANCES.

I have not the habit of consulting my own wishes, but I think, if they decide, we shall not return immediately. I have yet hardly formed an idea of London.

MRS. RACKET.

I shall quarrel with your lord and master if he dares think of depriving us of you so soon. How do you dispose of yourself today?

LADY FRANCES.

Sir George is going with me this morning to the mercer's to choose a silk, and then—

MRS. RACKET.

Choose a silk for you! Ha, ha, ha! Sir George chooses your laces, too, I hope, your gloves and your pincushions!

LADY FRANCES.

Madam!

MRS. RACKET.

I am glad to see you blush, my dear Lady Frances. These are strange, homespun ways! If you do these things, pray keep them secret. Lord bless us, if the Town should know your husband chooses your gowns!

MISS OGLE.

You are very young, my lady, and have been brought up in solitude. The maxims you learnt among the wood nymphs in Shropshire won't pass current here, I assure you.

MRS. RACKET.

Why my dear creature, you look quite frightened! Come, you shall go with us to an exhibition and an auction. Afterwards, we'll take a turn in the Park* and then drive to Kensington;* so we shall be at home by four to dress, and in the evening I'll attend you to Lady Brilliant's masquerade.

LADY FRANCES.

I shall be very happy to be of your party, if Sir George has no engagements.

MRS. RACKET.

What! Do you stand so low in your own opinion that you dare not trust yourself without Sir George? If you choose to play Darby and Joan,[36] my dear, you should have stayed in the country; 'tis an exhibition not calculated for London, I assure you!

MISS OGLE.

What! I suppose, my lady, you and Sir George will be seen pacing it comfortably round the canal,[37] arm and arm, and then go lovingly into the same carriage, dine tête-à-tête, spend the evening at piquet, and so go soberly to bed at eleven! Such a snug plan may do for an attorney and his wife, but for Lady Frances Touchwood, 'tis as unsuitable as linsey-woolsey or a black bonnet at the festino![38]

LADY FRANCES.

These are rather new doctrines to me! But my dear Mrs. Racket, you and Miss Ogle must judge of these things better than I can. As you observe, I am but young and may have caught absurd opinions. Here is Sir George!

Enter Sir George.

SIR GEORGE. (*Aside.*)

'Sdeath!* another room full!

---

35 ceremony of presentation] formal introduction at Court

36 Darby and Joan] John Darby (d. 1730) and wife Joan, originals for characters of Henry Woodfall's ballad "Darby and Joan; or, The Happy Old Couple"

37 the canal] A system of canals linking London with the rest of the country was begun in the late eighteenth century.

38 festino] a feast and party, sometimes including a masquerade

LADY FRANCES.

My love! Mrs. Racket and Miss Ogle.

MRS. RACKET.

Give you joy, Sir George. We came to rob you of Lady Frances for a few hours.

SIR GEORGE.

A few hours!

LADY FRANCES.

Oh yes! I am going to an exhibition and an auction and the Park* and Kensington and a thousand places! It is quite ridiculous, I find, for married people to be always together. We shall be laughed at!

SIR GEORGE.

I am astonished!—Mrs. Racket, what does the dear creature mean?

MRS. RACKET.

Mean, Sir George! what she says, I imagine.

MISS OGLE.

Why, you know, sir, as Lady Frances had the misfortune to be bred entirely in the country, she cannot be supposed to be versed in fashionable life.

SIR GEORGE.

No, Heaven forbid she should! If she had, madam, she would never have been my wife!

MRS. RACKET.

Are you serious?

SIR GEORGE.

Perfectly so. I should never have had the courage to have married a well-bred, fine lady.

MISS OGLE. (*Sneeringly.*)

Pray sir, what do you take a fine lady to be, that you express such fear of her?

SIR GEORGE.

A being easily described, madam, as she is seen everywhere but in her own house. She sleeps at home, but she lives all over the Town. In her mind, every sentiment gives place to the lust of conquest and the vanity of being particular. The feelings of wife and mother are lost in the whirl of dissipation. If she continues virtuous, 'tis by chance, and if she preserves her husband from ruin, 'tis by her dexterity at the card table! Such a woman I take to be a perfect fine lady!

MRS. RACKET.

And you I take to be a slanderous cynic of two-and-thirty. Twenty years hence, one might have forgiven such a libel! Now sir, hear my definition of a fine lady: she is a creature for whom nature has done much and education more; she has taste, elegance, spirit, understanding. In her manner she is free, in her morals nice.* Her behavior is undistinguishingly polite to her husband and all mankind; her sentiments are for their hours of retirement. In a word, a fine lady is the life of conversation, the spirit of society, the joy of the public! Pleasure follows wherever she appears, and the kindest wishes attend her slumbers.—Make haste, then, my dear Lady Frances, commence fine lady and force your husband to acknowledge the justness of my picture!

LADY FRANCES.

I am sure 'tis a delightful one. How can you dislike it, Sir George? You painted fashionable life in colors so disgusting that I thought I hated it, but on a nearer view, it seems charming. I have hitherto lived in obscurity; 'tis time that I should be a woman of the world. I long to begin; my heart pants with expectation and delight!

MRS. RACKET.

Come then, let us begin directly. I am impatient to introduce you to that society which you were born to ornament and charm.

LADY FRANCES.

Adieu, my love! We shall meet again at dinner. (*Going.*)

SIR GEORGE.

Sure, I am in a dream!—Fanny!

LADY FRANCES. (*Returning.*)

Sir George?

SIR GEORGE.

Will you go without me?

MRS. RACKET.

Will you go without me! Ha, ha, ha! What a pathetic address! Why, sure you would not always be seen side by side, like two beans upon a stalk. Are you afraid to trust Lady Frances with me, sir?

SIR GEORGE.

Heaven and earth! with whom can a man trust his wife in the present state of society? Formerly there were distinctions of character amongst ye: every class of females had its particular description. Grandmothers were pious, aunts discreet, old maids censorious. But now aunts, grandmothers, girls, and maiden gentlewomen are all the same creature; a wrinkle more or less is the sole difference between ye.

MRS. RACKET.

That maiden gentlewomen have lost their censoriousness is surely not in your catalogue of grievances.

SIR GEORGE.

Indeed it is, and ranked amongst the most serious grievances. Things went well, madam, when the tongues of three or four old virgins kept all the wives and daughters of a parish in awe. They were the dragons that guarded the Hesperian fruit,[39] and I wonder they have not been obliged, by act of Parliament, to resume their function.

MRS. RACKET.

Ha, ha, ha! And pensioned, I suppose, for making strict enquiries into the lives and conversations* of their neighbors.

SIR GEORGE.

With all my heart, and empowered to oblige every woman to conform her conduct to her real situation. You, for instance, are a widow: your air should be sedate, your dress grave, your deportment matronly, and in all things an example to the young women growing up about you; instead of which, you are dressed for conquest, think of nothing but ensnaring hearts, are a coquette, a wit, and a fine lady.

MRS. RACKET.

Bear witness to what he says! A coquette! a wit! and a fine lady! Who would have expected a eulogy from such an ill-natured mortal? Valor to a soldier, wisdom to a judge, or glory to a prince is not more than such a character* to a woman.

MISS OGLE.

Sir George, I see, languishes for the charming society of a century and a half ago, when a grave squire and a still graver dame, surrounded by a sober family, formed a stiff group in a moldy old house in the corner of a park.

MRS. RACKET.

Delightful serenity! Undisturbed by any noise but the cawing of rooks and the quarterly rumbling of an old family coach on a state visit, with the happy intervention of a friendly call from the parish apothecary or the curate's wife.

SIR GEORGE.

And what is the society of which you boast? A mere* chaos in which all distinction of rank is lost in a ridiculous affectation of ease and every different order of beings huddled together as they were before the creation. In the same *select party*, you will often find the wife of a bishop and a sharper, of an earl and a fiddler. In short, 'tis one universal masquerade, all disguised in the same habits and manners.

[Enter servant.]

SERVANT.

Mr. Flutter. (*Exit.*)

SIR GEORGE.

Here comes an illustration. Now I defy you to tell from his appearance whether Flutter is a privy counselor or a mercer, a lawyer, or a grocer's prentice.

Enter Flutter.

FLUTTER.

Oh, just which you please, Sir George, so you don't make me a Lord Mayor.—Ah, Mrs. Racket!—Lady Frances, your most obedient, you look—now hang me, if that's not provoking—had your gown been of another color, I should have said the prettiest thing you ever heard in your life.

MISS OGLE.

Pray give it us.

FLUTTER.

I was yesterday at Mrs. Bloomer's. She was dressed all in green; no other color to be seen but that of her face and bosom. So says I, "My dear Mrs. Bloomer! you look like a carnation just bursting from its pod."

SIR GEORGE.

And what said her husband?

FLUTTER.

Her husband! Why, her husband laughed and said a cucumber* would have been a happier simile.

39 dragons … Hesperian fruit] In Greek mythology, Hera had to place a dragon who never slept to protect her tree of golden apples from the Hesperides, the singing daughters of Atlas.

SIR GEORGE.

But there *are* husbands, sir, who would rather have corrected than amended your comparison. I, for instance, should consider a man's complimenting my wife as an impertinence.

FLUTTER.

Why, what harm can there be in compliments? Sure they are not infectious, and, if they were, you, Sir George, of all people breathing, have reason to be satisfied about your lady's attachment. Everybody talks of it: that little bird there that she killed out of jealousy, the most extraordinary instance of affection that ever was given.

LADY FRANCES.

I kill a bird through jealousy! Heavens! Mr. Flutter, how can you impute such a cruelty to me?

SIR GEORGE.

I could have forgiven you, if you had.

FLUTTER.

Oh, what a blundering fool! No, no—now I remember—it was your bird, Lady Frances—that's it, your bullfinch, which Sir George, in one of the refinements of his passion, sent into the wide world to seek its fortune. He took it for a knight in disguise.

LADY FRANCES.

Is it possible! Oh Sir George, could I have imagined it was you who deprived me of a creature I was so fond of?

SIR GEORGE.

Mr. Flutter, you are one of those busy, idle, meddling people who, from mere* vacuity of mind are the most dangerous inmates in a family. You have neither feelings nor opinions of your own but, like a glass in a tavern, bear about those of every blockhead who gives you his. And because you *mean* no harm, think yourselves excused though broken friendships, discords, and murders are the consequences of your indiscretions.

FLUTTER. (*Taking out his tablets.*)

Vacuity of mind!—What was the next? I'll write down this sermon; 'tis the first I have heard since my grandmother's funeral.

MISS OGLE.

Come Lady Frances, you see what a cruel creature your loving husband can be. So let us leave him.

SIR GEORGE.

Madam, Lady Frances shall not go.

LADY FRANCES.

Shall not, Sir George? This is the first time such an expression— (*Weeping.*)

SIR GEORGE.

My love! my life!

LADY FRANCES.

Don't imagine I'll be treated like a child, denied what I wish and then pacified with sweet words.

MISS OGLE. (*Apart.*)

The bullfinch! that's an excellent subject; never let it down.

LADY FRANCES.

I see plainly you would deprive me of every pleasure, as well as of my sweet bird, out of pure love! Barbarous man!

SIR GEORGE.

'Tis well, madam: your resentment of that circumstance proves to me what I did not before suspect, that you are deficient both in tenderness and understanding. Tremble to think the hour approaches in which you would give worlds for such a proof of my love. Go madam, give yourself to the public, abandon your heart to dissipation, and see if, in the scenes of gaiety and folly that await you, you can find a recompense for the lost affection of a doting husband. (*Exit.*)

FLUTTER.

Lord! what a fine thing it is to have the gift of speech! I suppose Sir George practices at Coachmakers-hall[40] or the Black Horse in Bond Street.[41]

LADY FRANCES.

He is really angry. I cannot go.

MRS. RACKET.

Not go! Foolish creature! You are arrived at the moment which some time or other was sure to

---

40 Coachmakers Hall] The hall for the coachmakers guild, in 1780 the site of a fiery speech by Lord George Gordon commencing the Gordon Riots in response to a Parliamentary act granting more tolerance to Roman Catholics

41 Black Horse on Bond Street] The pubs often hosted weekly oratorical events with announced topics, at which all were free to speak.

happen, and everything depends on the use you make of it.

MISS OGLE.

Come, Lady Frances! Don't hesitate: the minutes are precious.

LADY FRANCES.

I could find in my heart—and yet I won't give up neither. If I should in this instance, he'll expect it forever.

Exeunt Lady Frances and Mrs. Racket.

MISS OGLE.

Now you act like a woman of spirit. (*Exit.*)

FLUTTER.

A fair tug, by Jupiter*—between Duty and Pleasure! Pleasure beats and off we go, *Iö triumphe!*[42] (*Exit.*)

Scene [ii].[h] An auction room, with busts, pictures, etc.

Enter Silvertongue with [Mrs. Fagg, Mask, and another] puffer.[43]

SILVERTONGUE.

Very well, very well. This morning will be devoted to curiosity; my sale begins tomorrow at eleven. But Mrs. Fagg, if you do no better than you did in Lord Fillagree's sale, I shall discharge you. You want* a knack terribly. And this dress: why, nobody can mistake you for a gentlewoman.

MRS. FAGG.

Very true, Mr. Silvertongue, but I can't dress like a lady upon half-a-crown a day, as the saying is. If you want me to dress like a lady, you must double my pay. Double or quits, Mr. Silvertongue.

SILVERTONGUE.

Five shillings a day! what a demand! Why woman, there are a thousand parsons in the Town who don't make five shillings a day, though they preach, pray, christen, marry, and bury for the good of the community. Five shillings a day! Why, 'tis the pay of a lieutenant in a marching regiment, who keeps a servant, a mistress, a horse; fights, dresses, ogles, makes love,* and dies upon five shillings a day.

MRS. FAGG.

Oh as to that, all that's very right. A soldier should not be too fond of life, and forcing him to do all these things upon five shillings a day is the readiest way to make him tired on't.

SILVERTONGUE.

Well, Mask, have you been looking into the antiquaries? Have you got all the terms of art in a string, aye?

MASK.

Yes, I have: I know the age of a coin by the taste and can fix the birthday of a medal, anno mundi or anno Domini, though the green rust should have eaten up every character. But you know, the brown suit and the wig I wear when I personate the antiquary are in limbo.

SILVERTONGUE.

Those you have on may do.

MASK.

These! Why, in these I am a young traveled cognoscente. Mr. Glib bought them of Sir Tom Totter's valet, and I am going there directly. You know his picture sale comes on today, and I have got my head full of Parmegiano, Sal Rosa, Metzu, Tarback, and Vandermeer.[44] I talk of the relief of Woovermans, the spirit of Teniers, the coloring of the Venetian School, and the correctness of the Roman.[45] I distinguish Claude by his sheep and

---

42 *Iö triumphe*] hurrah, triumph: the cry of soldiers and spectators greeting a triumphal procession in ancient Rome (Lat.)

43 puffers] bidders hired by auctions to exaggerate the value and pretend interest in items in order to drive up the bidding

44 Parmegiano ... Vandermeer] Parmigianino (real name Francesco Mazzola, 1503-1540), Italian artist; Sal Rosa: Salvatore Rosa (1615-1673), Neopolitan artist; Metzu: Gabriel Metsu (1629-1667), Dutch artist; Tarbaek: Gerard Terborch (1617-1667), Dutch artist; and Vandermeer: Jan Vermeer (1632-75), Dutch genre painter

45 Woovermans ... Roman] Phillips Wouwermans (1619-68), Dutch Baroque painter; Teniers: David Teniers the Younger (1610-90), Flemish Baroque painter; the Venetian School: school of painting in Venice in the later 15th century, exploring color, light, and the sensuous rendering of surface texture; the Roman: Counter-

Ruysdael by his water.[46] The rapidity of Tintoret's pencil strikes me at the first glance, whilst the harmony of Vandyke and the glow of Correggio point out their masters.[47]

Enter company.

FIRST LADY.

Heyday, Mr. Silvertongue! what, nobody here?

SILVERTONGUE.

Oh my lady, we shall have company enough in a trice; if your carriage is seen at my door, no other will pass it, I am sure.

FIRST LADY. (*Aside.*)

Familiar monster!—That's a beautiful Diana, Mr. Silvertongue, but in the name of wonder, how came Actaeon to be placed on the top of a house?

SILVERTONGUE.

That's a David and Bathsheba,[48] ma'am.

FIRST LADY.

Oh, I crave their pardon! I remember the names but know nothing of the story.

More company enters.

FIRST GENTLEMAN.

Was not that Lady Frances Touchwood coming up with Mrs. Racket?

SECOND GENTLEMAN.

I think so—yes, it is, faith. Let us go nearer.

Enter Lady Frances, Mrs. Racket, and Miss Ogle.

Reformation style developed in Rome synthesizing Renaissance, Michelangelesque, Mannerist, and Baroque elements and stressing down-to-earth subjects

[46] Claude ... water] Claude Lorrain (1600-82), French landscape painter, noted for pastorals; Ruysdael: Jacob van Ruisdael (1628-82), Dutch landscape painter, noted for waterfalls and marshes

[47] Tintoret] Jacopo Robusti Tintoretto (1518-94), Italian Mannerist painter; Vandyke: Anthony van Dyck (1599-1641), Flemish religious and narrative painter who spent much of his career in England as artist to Charles I; Correggio: Antonio Allegri Correggio (1489-1534), Italian painter of the high Renaissance

[48] David and Bathsheba] Hebrew King David spied from his roof the beautiful bathing Bathsheba, wife of Uriah the Hittite, lusted after her, had her husband killed in battle, and married her (2 Samuel 11: 2-27).

SILVERTONGUE.

Yes sir, this is to be the first lot: the model of a city in wax.

SECOND GENTLEMAN.

The model of a city! What city?

SILVERTONGUE.

That I have not been able to discover, but call it Rome, Peking, or London, 'tis still a city: you'll find in it the same jarring interests, the same passions, the same virtues and the same vices, whatever the name.

[FIRST] GENTLEMAN.

You may as well present us a map of terra incognita.

SILVERTONGUE.

Oh pardon me, sir! a lively imagination would convert this waxen city into an endless and interesting amusement. For instance, look into this little house on the right hand; there are four old prudes in it taking care of their neighbors' reputations. This elegant mansion on the left, decorated with Corinthian pillars: Who needs to told that it belongs to a Court lord and is the habitation of patriotism, philosophy, and virtue? Here's a City Hall: the rich steams that issue from the windows nourish a neighboring workhouse. Here's a church: we'll pass over that, the doors are shut. The parsonage-house comes next; we'll take a peep here, however. Look at the doctor! He's asleep on a volume of Toland,[49] whilst his lady is putting on rouge for the masquerade. Oh! oh! this can be no English city; our parsons are all orthodox and their wives the daughters of modesty and meekness.

Lady Frances and Miss Ogle come forward, followed by Courtall.

LADY FRANCES.

I wish Sir George was here. This man follows me about and stares at me in such a way that I am quite uneasy.

MISS OGLE.

He has traveled and is heir to an immense estate,

[49] Toland] John Toland (1670-1722), English deistic philosopher, offered a purely rational defense of God's existence.

so he's impertinent by patent.

COURTALL.

You are very cruel, ladies. Miss Ogle, you will not let me speak to you. As to this little scornful beauty, she has frowned me dead fifty times.

LADY FRANCES. (*Confused.*)

Sir—I am a married woman.

COURTALL. (*Aside.*)

A married woman! a good hint.—'Twould be a shame if such a charming woman was not married. But I see you are a Daphne just come from your sheep and your meadows, your crook and your waterfalls. Pray now, who is the happy Damon[50] to whom you have vowed eternal truth and constancy?

MISS OGLE.

'Tis Lady Frances Touchwood, Mr. Courtall, to whom you are speaking.

COURTALL. (*Aside.*)

Lady Frances! By Heaven, that's Saville's old flame.-–I beg your ladyship's pardon. I ought to have believed that such beauty could belong only to your name, a name I have long been enamored of because I knew it to be that of the finest woman in the world.

Mrs. Racket comes forward.

LADY FRANCES. (*Apart.*)

My dear Mrs. Racket, I am so frightened! Here's a man making love* to me, though he knows I am married.

MRS. RACKET.

Oh, the sooner for that, my dear. Don't mind him.—Was you at the Casino last night, Mr. Courtall?

COURTALL.

I looked in. 'Twas impossible to stay. Nobody there but antiques. You'll be at Lady Brilliant's tonight, doubtless?

MRS RACKET.

Yes, I go with Lady Frances.

LADY FRANCES. (*To Miss Ogle.*)

Bless me! I did not know this gentleman was acquainted with Mrs. Racket. I behaved so rude to him!

MRS. RACKET. (*Looking at her watch.*)

Come ma'am, 'tis past one. I protest, if we don't fly to Kensington we shan't find a soul there.

LADY FRANCES.

Won't this gentleman go with us?

COURTALL. (*Looking surprised.*)

To be sure. You make me happy, madam, beyond description.

MRS. RACKET.

Oh, never mind him, he'll follow.

Exeunt Lady Frances, Mrs. Racket, and Miss Ogle.

COURTALL.

Lady *Touchwood*! with a vengeance! But 'tis always so: your reserved ladies are like ice, egad, no sooner begin to soften than they melt.

[Exit following.]

Act III, scene i. Mr. Hardy's.

Enter Letitia and Mrs. Racket.

MRS. RACKET.

Come, prepare, prepare, your lover is coming.

LETITIA.

My lover! Confess now that my absence at dinner was a severe mortification to him.

MRS. RACKET.

I can't absolutely swear it spoilt his appetite; he ate as if he was hungry and drank his wine as though he liked it.

LETITIA.

What was the apology?

MRS. RACKET.

That you were ill. But I gave him a hint that your extreme bashfulness could not support his eye.

LETITIA.

If I comprehend him, awkwardness and bashfulness are the last faults he can pardon in a woman, so expect to see me transformed into the veriest malkin.

MRS. RACKET.

You persevere then?

LETITIA.

Certainly. I know the design is a rash one and the event important. It either makes Doricourt mine by all the tenderest ties of passion or deprives me

---

50 Daphne … Damon] stereotypical pastoral names

of him forever, and never to be his wife will afflict me less than to be his wife and not be beloved.

MRS. RACKET.

So you won't trust to the good old maxim, "Marry first, and love will follow?"

LETITIA.

As readily as I would venture my last guinea that good fortune might follow. The woman that has not touched the heart of a man before he leads her to the altar has scarcely a chance to charm it when possession and security turn their powerful arms against her.—But here he comes. I'll disappear for a moment. Don't spare me. (*Exit.*)

Enter Doricourt (not seeing Mrs. Racket).

DORICOURT. (*Looking at a picture.*)

So, this is my mistress, I presume. Ma foi, the painter has hit her off: the downcast eye, the blushing cheek, timid, apprehensive, bashful. A tear and a prayer book would have made her *La Bella Magdalena.*[51]

Give *me* a woman in whose touching mien
A mind, a soul, a polished art is seen,
Whose motion speaks, whose poignant air can
 move.
Such are the darts to wound with endless love.

MRS. RACKET. (*Touching him on the shoulder with her fan.*)

Is that an impromptu?

DORICOURT. (*Starting.*)

Madam! (*Aside.*) Finely caught!—Not absolutely, it struck me during the dessert as a motto for your picture.

MRS. RACKET.

Gallantly turned! I perceive, however, Miss Hardy's charms have made no violent impression on you. And who can wonder? The poor girl's defects are so obvious.

DORICOURT.

Defects!

MRS. RACKET.

Merely those of education. Her father's indulgence ruined her. *Mauvaise honte,*[52] conceit, and ignorance—all unite in the lady you are to marry.

DORICOURT.

Marry! I marry such a woman? Your picture, I hope, is overcharged. I marry *mauvaise honte,* pertness, and ignorance!

MRS. RACKET.

Thank your stars that ugliness and ill temper are not added to the list. You must think her handsome?

DORICOURT.

Half her personal beauty would content me, but could the Medicean Venus[53] be animated for me and endowed with a vulgar soul, *I* should become the statue and my heart transformed to marble.

MRS. RACKET.

Bless us! We are in a hopeful way then!

DORICOURT. (*Aside.*)

There must be some envy in this! I see she is a coquette.—Ha, ha, ha! And you imagine I am persuaded of the truth of your character?* Ha, ha, ha! Miss Hardy, I have been assured, madam, is elegant and accomplished. But one must allow for a lady's painting.

MRS. RACKET. (*Aside.*)

I'll be even with him for that.—Ha, ha, ha! And so you have found me out! Well, I protest I meant no harm; 'twas only to increase the éclat of her appearance that I threw a veil over her charms.—Here comes the lady; her elegance and accomplishments will announce themselves.

Enter Letitia, running.

LETITIA.

La, cousin, do you know that our John— Oh, dear heart!—I didn't see you, sir. (*Hanging down her head and dropping behind Mrs. Racket.*)

MRS. RACKET.

Fie, Letitia! Mr. Doricourt thinks you a woman of

---

51 *La Bella Magdalena*] The character type-and favorite trope in Renaissance painting—of the penitent Magdalen derives from a confusion of three figures in the Gospels, one of them the sinner who washes Jesus's feet in Luke 7:37-38.

52 *mauvaise honte*] extreme bashfulness (Fr.)

53 Medicean Venus] Venus de Medici, classical statue discovered in many pieces during the 17th century near Tivoli

elegant manners. Stand forward and confirm his opinion.

LETITIA.

No, no, keep before me. He's my sweetheart, and 'tis impudent to look one's sweetheart in the face, you know.

MRS. RACKET.

You'll allow in future for a lady's painting, sir. Ha, ha, ha!

DORICOURT.

I am astonished!

LETITIA.

Well hang it, I'll take heart. Why, he is but a man, you know, cousin, and I'll let him see I wasn't born in a wood to be scared by an owl. (*Half apart, advances, and looks at him through her fingers.*) He, he, he!

Goes up to him and makes a very stiff formal curtsy. He bows.

You have been a great traveler, sir, I hear?

DORICOURT.

Yes madam.

LETITIA.

Then I wish you'd tell us about the fine sights you saw when you went oversea. I have read in a book that there are some countries where the men and women are all horses.[54] Did you see any of them?

MRS. RACKET.

Mr. Doricourt is not prepared, my dear, for these enquiries; he is reflecting on the importance of the question and will answer you—when he can.

LETITIA.

When he can! Why, he's as slow in speech as Aunt Margery when she's reading Thomas Aquinas and stands gaping like mumchance.[55]

MRS. RACKET.

Have a little discretion.

LETITIA.

Hold your tongue! Sure I may say what I please before I am married, if I can't afterwards. Do ye think a body does not know how to talk to a sweetheart? He is not the first I have had.

DORICOURT.

Indeed!

LETITIA.

Oh Lud!* he speaks!—Why, if you must know—there was the curate at home. When Papa was a-hunting, he used to come a-suitoring and make speeches to me out of books. Nobody knows what a *mort* of fine things he used to say to me—and call me Venis, and Jubah, and Dinah![56]

DORICOURT.

And pray, fair lady, how did you answer him?

LETITIA.

Why, I used to say, "Look you, Mr. Curate, don't think to come over me with your flimflams, for a better man than ever trod in your shoes is coming oversea to marry me." But i'fags!* I begin to think I was out. Parson Dobbins was the sprightfuller man of the two.

DORICOURT.

Surely this cannot be Miss Hardy!

LETITIA.

Laws! Why, don't you know me! You saw me today—but I was daunted before my father and the lawyer and all them, and did not care to speak out, so, maybe, you thought I couldn't. But I can talk as fast as anybody when I know folks a little, and now I have shown my parts,* I hope you'll like me better.

Enter Hardy.

HARDY.

I foresee this won't do!—Mr. Doricourt, maybe you take my daughter for a fool, but you are mistaken. She's a sensible girl as any in England.

DORICOURT.

I am convinced she has a very uncommon understanding, sir. (*Aside.*) I did not think he had been such an ass.

LETITIA. [*Aside.*]

My father will undo the whole.—Laws, Papa, how can you think he can take me for a fool, when everybody knows I beat the potecary[57] at conun-

[54] men … horses] allusion to *Gulliver's Travels*, pt. 4

[55] mumchance] a game of dice where silence is indispensable

[56] Venis, Jubah, Dinah] probably corrupted versions of Venus, Jubal, and Diana

[57] potecary] corruption of apothecary

drums last Christmastime? and didn't I make a string of names, all in riddles, for the lady's diary? There was a little river and a great house: that was Newcastle. There was what a lamb says and three letters: that was *Ba*, and *k-e-r*, ker, Baker. There was—

HARDY.
Don't stand ba-a-ing there. You'll make me mad in a moment!—I tell you, sir, that for all that, she's devilish sensible.

DORICOURT.
Sir, I give all possible credit to your assertions.

LETITIA.
Laws, Papa, do come along. If you stand watching, how can my sweetheart break his mind and tell me how he admires me?

DORICOURT.
That would be difficult, indeed, madam.

HARDY.
I tell you, Letty, I'll have no more of this. I see well enough—

LETITIA.
Laws! don't snub me before my husband-that-is-to-be. You'll teach him to snub me, too. And I believe, by his looks, he'd like to begin now. So, let us go.—Cousin, you may tell the gentleman what a genus[58] I have: how I can cut watch papers[59] and work catgut, make quadrille baskets[60] with pins, and take profiles in shade,[61] aye, as well as the lady at No. 62, South Moulton Street, Grosvenor Square.*

Exit Hardy and Letitia.

MRS. RACKET.
What think you of my painting now?

DORICOURT.
Oh, mere watercolors, madam! The lady has caricatured your picture.

MRS. RACKET.
And how does she strike you on the whole?

DORICOURT.
Like a good design, spoilt by the incapacity of the artist. Her faults are evidently the result of her father's weak indulgence. I observed an expression in her eye that seemed to satirize the folly of her lips.

MRS. RACKET.
But at her age, when education is fixed, and manner becomes nature, hopes of improvement—

DORICOURT.
Would be as rational as hopes of gold from a juggler's[62] crucible. Doricourt's wife must be incapable of improvement, but it must be because she's got beyond it.

MRS. RACKET.
I am pleased your misfortune sits no heavier.

DORICOURT.
Your pardon, madam, so mercurial was the hour in which I was born that misfortunes always go plump to the bottom of my heart like a pebble in water and leave the surface unruffled. I shall certainly set off for Bath, or the other world, tonight, but whether I shall use a chaise with four swift coursers, or go off in a tangent from the aperture of a pistol, deserves consideration. So I make my adieus. (*Going.*)

MRS. RACKET.
Oh but I entreat you, postpone your journey till tomorrow. Determine on which you will—you must be this night at the masquerade.

DORICOURT.
Masquerade!

MRS. RACKET.
Why not? If you resolve to visit the other world, you may as well take one night's pleasure first in this, you know.

DORICOURT.
Faith, that's very true; ladies are the best philosophers, after all. Expect me at the masquerade. (*Exit.*)

MRS. RACKET.
He's a charming fellow. I think Letitia shan't have him. (*Going.*)

---

58 genus] corruption of genius

59 watch papers] small circles, cut from pretty paper, silk, or satin, which replaced the ordinary papers that kept the dust out of pocket watches; often intricately ornamented love tokens

60 quadrille baskets] baskets quadrilled, marked with squares

61 take profiles in shade] make silhouettes

62 juggler] trickster, in this case an alchemist

Enter Hardy.

HARDY.

What, 's he gone?

MRS. RACKET.

Yes, and I am glad he is. You would have ruined us! Now I beg, Mr. Hardy, you won't interfere in this business; it is a little out of your way. (*Exit.*)

HARDY.

Hang me, if I don't though. I foresee very clearly what will be the end of it if I leave ye to yourselves. So I'll e'en follow him to the masquerade and tell him all about it. Let me see. What shall my dress be? A great mogul? No. A grenadier? No, no, that, I foresee, would make a laugh. Hang me, if I don't send to my favorite little Quick,[63] and borrow his Jew Isaac's[64] dress. I know the dog likes a glass of good wine, so I'll give him a bottle of my forty-eight[65] and he shall teach me. Aye, that's it: I'll be cunning little Isaac! If they complain of my want* of wit, I'll tell 'em the cursed Duenna wears the breeches[66] and has spoilt my parts.

Exit.

Scene ii. Courtall's.

Enter Courtall, Saville, and three others from an apartment in the back scene. (The last three tipsy.)

COURTALL.

You shan't go yet. Another catch and another bottle!

FIRST GENTLEMAN.

May I be a bottle, and an empty bottle, if you catch me at that! Why, I am going to the masquerade. Jack ____,* you know who I mean, is to meet me, and we are to have a leap at the new lusters.

SECOND GENTLEMAN.

And I am going, too—a Harlequin—(*Hiccups.*) Am not I in a pretty pickle to make Harlequinades? And Tony, here—he is going in the disguise—in the disguise—of a gentleman!

FIRST GENTLEMAN.

We are all very disguised;* so bid them draw up. Do ye hear! (*Exeunt the three gentlemen.*)

SAVILLE.

Thy skull, Courtall, is a lady's thimble. No, an eggshell.

COURTALL.

Nay, then you are gone too; you never aspire to similes but in your cups.

SAVILLE.

No, no, I am steady enough, but the fumes of the wine pass directly through thy eggshell and leave thy brain as cool as— Hey! I am quite sober: my similes fail me.

COURTALL.

Then we'll sit down here and have one sober bottle.—Bring a table and glasses.

SAVILLE.

I'll not swallow another drop, no, though the juice should be the true Falernian.[67]

COURTALL.

By the bright eyes of her you love, you shall drink her health.

SAVILLE.

Ah! (*Sitting down.*) Her I loved is gone. (*Sighing.*) She's married!

COURTALL.

Then bless your stars you are not her husband! I would be husband to no woman in Europe who was not devilish rich and devilish ugly.

SAVILLE.

Wherefore ugly?

COURTALL.

Because she could not have the conscience to exact those attentions that a pretty wife expects. Or if she should, her resentments would be perfectly easy to me; nobody would undertake to revenge her cause.

---

63 Quick] John Quick (d.1831), character actor at Covent Garden Theatre, originated the part of Hardy, and so spoke this line about himself

64 Jew Isaac] the character of Isaac Mendoza in *The Duenna* by Richard Brinsley Sheridan, also played by John Quick

65 forty-eight] vintage of his best wine

66 cursed Duenna wears the breeches] in the play, Mendoza is tricked into marrying Margaret, the old duenna (chaperone), instead of her beautiful young charge

67 Falernian] choice Italian wine celebrated in classical literature

SAVILLE.
Thou art a most licentious fellow!

COURTALL.
I should hate my own wife, that's certain. But I have a warm heart for those of other people, and so here's to the prettiest wife in England—Lady Frances Touchwood.

SAVILLE.
Lady Frances Touchwood! I rise to drink her. (*Drinks.*) How the devil came Lady Frances in your head? I never knew you give[68] a woman of chastity before.

COURTALL.
That's odd, for you have heard me give half the women of fashion in England. But pray now, (*Sneeringly.*) what do you take a woman of chastity to be?

SAVILLE.
Such a woman as Lady Frances Touchwood, sir.

COURTALL.
Oh, you are grave, sir. I remember you was an adorer of hers. Why didn't you marry her?

SAVILLE.
I had not the arrogance to look so high. Had my fortune been worthy of her, she should not have been ignorant of my admiration.

COURTALL.
Precious fellow! What, I suppose you would not dare tell her now that you admire her?

SAVILLE.
No, nor you.

COURTALL.
By the Lord, I have told her so.

SAVILLE.
Have! impossible!

COURTALL.
Ha, ha, ha! Is it so?

SAVILLE.
How did she receive the declaration?

COURTALL.
Why, in the old way: blushed and frowned and said she was married.

SAVILLE.
What amazing things thou art capable of! I could more easily have taken the Pope by the beard than profaned her ears with such a declaration.

COURTALL.
I shall meet her at Lady Brilliant's tonight, where I shall repeat it. And I'll lay my life, under a mask, she'll hear it all without blush or frown.

SAVILLE. (*Rising.*)
'Tis false, sir! She won't.

COURTALL. (*Rising.*)
She will! Nay, I'd venture to lay a round sum that I prevail on her to go out with me—only to taste the fresh air, I mean.

SAVILLE.
Preposterous vanity! From this moment I suspect that half the victories you have boasted are false and slanderous as your pretended influence with Lady Frances.

COURTALL.
Pretended! How should such a fellow as you, now, who never soared beyond a cherry-cheeked daughter of a ploughman in Norfolk, judge of the influence of a man of my figure and habits? I could show thee a list in which there are names to shake thy faith in the whole sex! And to that list I have no doubt of adding the name of Lady—

SAVILLE.
Hold, sir! My ears cannot bear the profanation. You cannot, dare not approach her! For your soul you dare not mention love to her! Her look would freeze the word whilst it hovered on thy licentious lips!

COURTALL.
Hoo hoo! Well, we shall see. This evening, by Jupiter, the trial shall be made. If I fail, I fail.

SAVILLE.
I think thou darest not! But my life, my honor on her purity. (*Exit.*)

COURTALL.
Hotheaded fool! (*Musing.*) But since he has brought it to this point, by Gad I'll try what can be done with her ladyship.[i] (*Rings.*) She's frostwork, and the prejudices of education yet strong; ergo, passionate professions will only inflame her pride and put her on her guard. For other arts then!

Enter Dick.

Dick, do you know any of the servants at Sir George Touchwood's?

[68] give] toast

DICK.

Yes sir, I knows the groom and one of the housemaids; for the matter o'that, she's my own cousin. And it was my mother that holped her to the place.

COURTALL.

Do you know Lady Frances's maid?

DICK.

I can't say as how I know she.

COURTALL.

Do you know Sir George's valet?

DICK.

No sir, but Sally is very thick with Mr. Gibson, Sir George's gentleman.

COURTALL.

Then go there, directly, and employ Sally to discover* whether her master goes to Lady Brilliant's this evening. And if he does, the name of the shop that sold his habit.

DICK.

Yes sir.

COURTALL.

Be exact in your intelligence and come to me at Boodle's.[69]

Exit Dick.

If I cannot otherwise succeed, I'll beguile her as Jove did Alcmene, in the shape of her husband. The possession of so fine a woman, the triumph over Saville, are each a sufficient motive-–and united they shall be resistless.

Exit.

Scene iii. The street.

Enter Saville.

SAVILLE.

The air has recovered me! What have I been doing! Perhaps my petulance may be the cause of her ruin, whose honor I asserted. His vanity is piqued, and where women are concerned, Courtall can be a villain.

Enter Dick. Bows and passes hastily.

Hah! That's his servant!—Dick!

[69] Boodle's] gentlemen's club on St James's Street

DICK. (*Returning.*)

Sir.

SAVILLE.

Where are you going, Dick?

DICK.

Going! I am going, sir, where my master sent me.

SAVILLE.

Well answered. But I have a particular reason for my enquiry, and you must tell me.

DICK.

Why then sir, I am going to call upon a cousin of mine that lives at Sir George Touchwood's.

SAVILLE.

Very well. (*Gives him money.*) There, you must make your cousin drink my health. What are you going about?

DICK.

Why sir, I believe 'tis no harm, or elseways I am sure I would not blab. I am only going to ax if Sir George goes to the masquerade tonight and what dress he wears.

SAVILLE.

Enough! Now Dick, if you will call at my lodgings in your way back and acquaint me with your cousin's intelligence, I'll double the trifle I have given you.

DICK.

Bless your honor, I'll call, never fear. (*Exit.*)

SAVILLE.

Surely the occasion may justify the means; 'tis doubly my duty to be Lady Frances's protector. Courtall, I see, is planning an artful scheme, but Saville shall outplot him.

Exit.

Scene iv. Sir George Touchwood's.

Enter Sir George and Villers.

VILLERS.

For shame, Sir George! You have left Lady Frances in tears. How can you afflict her?

SIR GEORGE.

'Tis I that am afflicted; my dream of happiness is over. Lady Frances and I are disunited.

VILLERS.

The devil! Why, you have been in Town but ten

days. She can have made no acquaintance for a Commons* affair yet.

SIR GEORGE.

Faugh! 'Tis our minds that are disunited. She no longer places her whole delight in me; she has yielded herself up to the world!

VILLERS.

Yielded herself up to the world! Why did you not bring her to Town in a cage? Then she might have taken a peep at the world! But after all, what has the world done? A twelvemonth since you was the gayest fellow in it. If anybody asked, "Who dresses best?" Sir George Touchwood. "Who is the most gallant man?" Sir George Touchwood. "Who is the most wedded to amusement and dissipation?" Sir George Touchwood. And now Sir George is metamorphosed into a sour censor and talks of fashionable life with as much bitterness as the old crabbed fellow in Rome.[70]

SIR GEORGE.

The moment I became possessed of such a jewel as Lady Frances, everything wore a different complexion: that society in which I lived with so much éclat became the object of my terror, and I think of the manners of polite life as I do of the atmosphere of a pesthouse. My wife is already infected; she was set upon this morning by maids, widows, and bachelors who carried her off in triumph, in spite of my displeasure.

VILLERS.

Aye, to be sure, there would have been no triumph in the case if you had not opposed it. But I have heard the whole story from Mrs. Racket, and I assure you, Lady Frances didn't enjoy the morning at all. She wished for you fifty times.

SIR GEORGE.

Indeed! Are you sure of that?

VILLERS.

Perfectly sure.

SIR GEORGE.

I wish I had known it. My uneasiness at dinner was occasioned by very different ideas.

VILLERS.

Here then she comes to receive your apology. But if she is true woman, her displeasure will rise in proportion to your contrition, and till you grow careless about her pardon, she won't grant it. However, I'll leave you. Matrimonial duets are seldom set in the style I like. (*Exit.*)

Enter Lady Frances.

SIR GEORGE. (*Embracing her.*)

The sweet sorrow that glitters in these eyes, I cannot bear. Look cheerfully, you rogue.

LADY FRANCES.

I cannot look otherwise, if you are pleased with me.

SIR GEORGE.

Well Fanny, today you made your entrée in the fashionable world. Tell me honestly the impressions you received.

LADY FRANCES.

Indeed Sir George, I was so hurried from place to place that I had not time to find out what my impressions were.

SIR GEORGE.

That's the very spirit of the life you have chosen.

LADY FRANCES.

Everybody about me seemed happy—but everybody seemed in a hurry to be happy somewhere else.

SIR GEORGE.

And you like this?

LADY FRANCES.

One must like what the rest of the world likes.

SIR GEORGE.

Pernicious maxim!

LADY FRANCES.

But my dear Sir George, you have not promised to go with me to the masquerade.

SIR GEORGE.

'Twould be a shocking indecorum to be seen together, you know.

LADY FRANCES.

Oh no. I asked Mrs. Racket, and she told me that we might be seen together at the masquerade without being laughed at.

---

70 old crabbed fellow in Rome] perhaps Cato the Elder (the Censor), associated with simple life, severe morals, self-denying habits, strict justice, brusque manners, blunt speech

SIR GEORGE.

Really?

LADY FRANCES.

Indeed, to tell you the truth, I could wish it was the fashion for married people to be inseparable, for I have more heartfelt satisfaction in fifteen minutes with you at my side than fifteen days of amusement could give me without you.

SIR GEORGE.

My sweet creature! How that confession charms me! Let us begin the fashion.

LADY FRANCES.

Oh impossible! We should not gain a single proselyte, and you can't conceive what spiteful things would be said of us. At Kensington today a lady met us whom we saw at Court when we were presented. She lifted up her hands in amazement! "Bless me!" said she to her companion, "here's Lady Francis without Sir Hurlo Thrumbo!* —My dear Mrs. Racket, consider what an important charge you have! For Heaven's sake take her home again, or some enchanter on a flying dragon will descend and carry her off." "Oh," said another, "I dare say Lady Frances has a clue at her heel, like the peerless Rosamond:[71] her tender swain would never have trusted her so far without such a precaution."

SIR GEORGE.

Heaven and earth! How shall Innocence preserve its luster amidst manners so corrupt?—My dear Fanny, I feel a sentiment for thee at this moment tenderer than love, more animated than passion. I could weep over that purity exposed to the sullying breath of fashion and the *ton,* in whose latitudinary vortex Chastity herself can scarcely move unspotted.

Enter Gibson.

GIBSON.

Your honor talked, I thought, something about going to the masquerade?

SIR GEORGE.

Well.

[71] peerless Rosamond] Rosamond Clifford, beloved by King Henry II, was hidden away at the end of a maze so intricate that a clue was needed to find the end.

GIBSON.

Isn't it?—hasn't your honor?—I thought your honor had forgot to order a dress.

LADY FRANCES.

Well considered, Gibson.—Come, will you be Jew, Turk, or heretic; a Chinese emperor or a ballad-singer; a rake or a watchman?

SIR GEORGE.

Oh neither, my love, I can't take the trouble to support a character.

LADY FRANCES.

You'll wear a domino then. I saw a pink domino trimmed with blue at the shop where I bought my habit. Would you like it?

SIR GEORGE.

Anything, anything.

LADY FRANCES.

Then go about it directly, Gibson. A pink domino trimmed with blue and a hat of the same.—Come, you have not seen my dress yet. It is most beautiful; I long to have it on.

Exeunt Sir George and Lady Frances.

GIBSON.

A pink domino trimmed with blue and a hat of the same. What the devil can it signify to Sally, now, what his dress is to be? Surely the slut has not made an assignation to meet her master!

Exit.

Act IV, scene i. A masquerade [at Lady Brilliant's].

A party dancing cotillions in front—a variety of characters pass and repass. Enter Folly on a hobbyhorse, with cap and bells.

MASK.[72]

Hey! Tom Fool! what business have you here?

FOLLY.

What sir! Affront a prince in his own dominions! (*Struts off.*)

MOUNTEBANK.

Who'll buy my nostrums? Who'll buy my nostrums?

[72] MASK] a reveler at a masquerade who simply covers the face without being in full costume

MASK.
What are they?

They all come round him.

MOUNTEBANK.
Different sorts and for different customers. Here's a liquor for ladies: it expels the rage of gaming and gallantry. Here's a pill for members of Parliament: good to settle consciences. Here's an eye-water for jealous husbands: it thickens the visual membrane through which they see too clearly. Here's a decoction for the clergy: it never sits easy if the patient has more than one living. Here's a draught for lawyers: a great promoter of modesty. Here's a powder for projectors:* 'twill rectify the fumes of an empty stomach and dissipate their airy castles.

MASK.
Have you a nostrum that can give patience to young heirs whose uncles and fathers are stout and healthy?

MOUNTEBANK.
Yes, and I have an infusion for creditors: it gives resignation and humility when fine gentlemen break their promises or plead their privilege.

MASK.
Come along! I'll find you customers for your whole cargo.

Enter Hardy in the dress of Isaac Mendoza.

HARDY.
Why, isn't it a shame to see so many stout, well-built young fellows masquerading and cutting courantes here at home, instead of making the French cut* capers to the tune of your cannon or sweating the Spaniards with an English fandango? I foresee the end of all this.

MASK.
Why, thou little testy Israelite! back to Duke's Place,[73] and preach your tribe into a subscription for the good of the land on whose milk and honey ye fatten. Where are your Joshuas and your Gideons, aye? What, all dwindled into stock-brokers, peddlers, and ragmen?

[73] Duke's Place] mansion once owned by the Duke of Norfolk, became a center for settling Jews in 1650 and in 1682 became the site for the Great Synagogue

HARDY.
No, not all. Some of us turn Christians and by degrees grow into all the privileges of Englishmen! In the second generation we are patriots, rebels, courtiers, and (*Puts his fingers to his forehead [making horns*].*) husbands.

Two other masks advance.

THIRD MASK.
What, my little Isaac! How the devil came you here? Where's your old Margaret?

HARDY.
Oh, I have got rid of her.

THIRD MASK.
How?

HARDY.
Why, I persuaded a young Irishman that she was a blooming, plump beauty of eighteen, so they made an elopement. Ha, ha, ha! and she is now the toast of Tipperary. [*Aside.*] Hah! there's Cousin Racket and her party; they shan't know me. (*Puts on his mask.*)

Enter Mrs. Racket, Lady Frances, Sir George, and Flutter.

MRS. RACKET.
Look at this dumpling Jew; he must be a Levite by his figure. You have surely practiced the flesh-hook[74] a long time, friend, to have raised that goodly presence.

HARDY.
About as long, my brisk widow, as you have been angling for a second husband, but my hook has been better baited than yours. (*Pointing to Flutter.*) You have only caught gudgeons, I see.

FLUTTER.
Oh! this is one of the geniuses they hire to entertain the company with their *accidental* sallies.—Let me look at your commonplace book, friend. I want* a few good things.

HARDY.
I'd oblige you, with all my heart, but you'll spoil them in repeating. Or if you should not, they'll gain you no reputation, for nobody will believe they are your own.

[74] flesh-hook] a hook for removing meat from the pot

SIR GEORGE.
He knows ye, Flutter; the little gentleman fancies himself a wit, I see.

HARDY.
There's no depending on what *you* see; the eyes of the jealous are not to be trusted. Look to your lady.

FLUTTER.
He knows ye, Sir George.

SIR GEORGE. (*Aside.*)
What, am I the Town talk?

HARDY. [*Aside.*]
I can neither see Doricourt nor Letty. I must find them out. (*Exit.*)

MRS. RACKET.
Well Lady Frances, is not all this charming? Could you have conceived such a brilliant assemblage of objects?

LADY FRANCES.
Delightful! The days of enchantment are restored; the columns glow with sapphires and rubies. Emperors and fairies, beauties and dwarfs, meet me at every step.

SIR GEORGE.
How lively are first impressions on sensible minds! In four hours, vapidity and languor will take place of that exquisite sense of joy which flutters your little heart.

MRS. RACKET.
What an inhuman creature! Fate has not allowed us these sensations above ten times in our lives, and would you have us shorten them by anticipation?

FLUTTER.
Oh Lord! your* wise men are the greatest fools upon earth: they reason about their enjoyments and analyze their pleasures whilst the essence escapes. Look, Lady Frances, do ye see that figure strutting in the dress of an emperor? His father retails oranges in Botolph Lane.[75] That gypsy is a maid of honor, and that ragman a physician.

LADY FRANCES.
Why, you know everybody.

FLUTTER.
Oh, every creature. A mask is nothing at all to me. I can give you the history of half the people here. In the next apartment there's a whole family who, to my knowledge, have lived on watercresses this month to make a figure here tonight. But to make up for that, they'll cram their pockets with cold ducks and chickens for a carnival tomorrow.

LADY FRANCES.
Oh, I should like to see this provident family.

FLUTTER.
Honor me with your arm.

Exeunt Flutter and Lady Frances.

MRS. RACKET.
Come Sir George, you shall be *my* beau. We'll make the tour of the rooms and meet them. Oh! your pardon, you must follow Lady Frances or the wit and fine parts* of Mr. Flutter may drive you out of her head. Ha, ha, ha! (*Exit.*)

SIR GEORGE.
I was going to follow her, and now I dare not. How can I be such a fool as to be governed by the *fear* of that ridicule which I despise! (*Exit.*)

Enter Doricourt, meeting a mask.

DORICOURT.
Hah, my lord! I thought you had been engaged at Westminster[76] on this important night.

MASK.
So I am. I slipped out as soon as Lord Trope got upon his legs; I can *badiner*[77] here an hour or two and be back again before he is down.

Enter Letitia.

There's a fine figure! I'll address her.—Charity, fair lady! Charity for a poor pilgrim.

LETITIA.
Charity! If you mean my prayers, Heaven grant thee wit, pilgrim.

MASK.
That blessing would do from a devotee; from you I ask other charities—such charities as Beauty should bestow: soft looks, sweet words, and kind wishes.

---

[75] Botolph Lane] street and area surrounding and named for St. Botolph Billingsgate Church

[76] Westminster] site of the houses of Parliament

[77] *badiner*] to jest, banter (Fr.)

LETITIA.
Alas! I am bankrupt of these and forced to turn beggar myself. [*Aside.*] There he is! How shall I catch his attention?

MASK.
Will you grant me no favor?

LETITIA.
Yes, one: I'll make you my partner—not for life, but through the soft mazes of a minuet. Dare you dance?

DORICOURT.
Some spirit in that.

MASK.
I dare do anything you command.

DORICOURT.
Do you know her, my lord?

MASK.
No, such a woman as that would formerly have been known in any disguise, but Beauty is now common. Venus seems to have given her cestus[78] to the whole sex.

A minuet.

DORICOURT. (*During the minuet.*)
She dances divinely.

When ended.

Somebody must know her! Let us enquire who she is. (*Exit.*)

Enter Saville and Kitty Willis, habited like Lady Frances.

SAVILLE.
I have seen Courtall in Sir George's habit, though he endeavored to keep himself concealed. Go and seat yourself in the tearoom, and on no account discover* your face. Remember too, Kitty, that the woman you are to personate is a woman of virtue.

KITTY.
I am afraid I shall find that a difficult character; indeed, I believe it is seldom kept up through a whole masquerade.

SAVILLE.
Of that *you* can be no judge. Follow my directions, and you shall be rewarded.

Exit Kitty. Enter Doricourt.

DORICOURT.
Hah! Saville! Did you see a lady dance just now?

SAVILLE.
No.

DORICOURT.
Very odd. Nobody knows her.

SAVILLE.
Where is Miss Hardy?

DORICOURT.
Cutting watch papers and making conundrums, I suppose.

SAVILLE.
What do you mean?

DORICOURT.
Faith, I hardly know. She's not here, however, Mrs. Racket tells me. I asked no further.

SAVILLE.
Your indifference seems increased.

DORICOURT.
Quite the reverse: 'tis advanced thirty-two degrees towards hatred.

SAVILLE.
You are jesting?

DORICOURT.
Then it must be with a very ill grace, my dear Saville, for I never felt so seriously. Do you know the creature's almost an idiot?

SAVILLE.
What?

DORICOURT.
An idiot. What the devil shall I do with her? Egad! I think I'll feign myself mad, and then Hardy will propose to cancel the engagements.

SAVILLE.
An excellent expedient. I must leave you; you are mysterious, and I can't stay to unravel ye. I came here to watch over Innocence and Beauty.

DORICOURT.
The guardian of Innocence and Beauty at three and twenty! Is there not a cloven foot under that black gown, Saville?

SAVILLE.
No, faith. Courtall is here on a most detestable design. I found means to get a knowledge of the

[78] Venus … cestus] Venus's girdle (sash), a metonym for her irresistible sexual attraction

lady's dress and have brought a girl to personate her whose reputation cannot be hurt. You shall know the result tomorrow. Adieu. (*Exit.*)

DORICOURT. (*Musing.*)

Yes, I think that will do. I'll feign myself mad, see the doctor to pronounce me incurable, and when the parchments are destroyed—

As he stands in a musing posture, Letitia enters and sings.

Song.

Wake, thou Son of Dullness, wake!
From thy drowsy senses shake
All the spells that Care employs,
Cheating mortals of their joys.

II.

Light-winged spirits, hither haste,
Who prepare for mortal taste
All the gifts that Pleasure sends,
Every bliss that youth attends.

III.

Touch his feelings, rouse his soul,
Whilst the sparkling moments roll,
Bid them wake to new delight,
Crown the magic of the night.

DORICOURT.

By Heaven, the same sweet creature!

LETITIA.

You have chosen an odd situation for study. Fashion and taste preside in this spot; they throw their spells around you; ten thousand delights spring up at their command—and you, a stoic, a being without senses, are wrapped in reflection.

DORICOURT.

And you, the most charming being in the world, awake me to admiration. Did you come from the stars?

LETITIA.

Yes, and I shall reascend in a moment.

DORICOURT.

Pray show me your face before you go.

LETITIA.

Beware of imprudent curiosity; it lost paradise.

DORICOURT.

Eve's curiosity was raised by the Devil; 'tis an angel tempts mine. So your allusion is not in point.

LETITIA.

But *why* would you see my face?

DORICOURT.

To fall in love with it.

LETITIA.

And what then?

DORICOURT.

Why then— (*Aside.*) Aye, curse it! there's the rub.

LETITIA.

Your mistress will be angry—but perhaps, you have no mistress?

DORICOURT.

Yes, yes, and a sweet one it is!

LETITIA.

What, is she old?

DORICOURT.

No.

LETITIA.

Ugly?

DORICOURT.

No.

LETITIA.

What then?

DORICOURT.

Faugh! don't talk about *her*, but show me your face.

LETITIA.

My vanity forbids it; 'twould frighten you.

DORICOURT.

Impossible! Your shape is graceful, your air bewitching, your bosom transparent, and your chin would tempt me to kiss it, if I did not see a pouting red lip above it that demands—

LETITIA.

You grow too free.

DORICOURT.

Show me your face then, only half a glance.

LETITIA.

Not for worlds.

DORICOURT.

What, you will have a little gentle force? (*Attempts to seize her mask.*)

LETITIA.

I am gone forever! (*Exit.*)

DORICOURT.

'Tis false; I'll follow to the end. (*Exit.*)

Flutter, Lady Frances, and Saville advance.

LADY FRANCES.
How can you be thus interested for a stranger?

SAVILLE.
Goodness will ever interest; its home is heaven. On earth 'tis but a wanderer. Imprudent lady! why have you left the side of your protector? Where is your husband?

FLUTTER.
Why, what's that to him?

LADY FRANCES.
Surely it can't be merely his habit; there's something in him that awes me.

FLUTTER.
Faugh! 'tis only his grey beard.—I know him; he keeps a lottery-office on Cornhill.[79]

SAVILLE.
My province as an enchanter lays open every secret to me. Lady! there are dangers abroad—beware! (*Exit.*)

LADY FRANCES.
'Tis very odd. His manner has made me tremble. Let us seek Sir George.

FLUTTER.
He is coming towards us.

Courtall comes forward habited like Sir George.

COURTALL.
There she is! If I can but disengage her from that fool Flutter, crown me, ye schemers, with immortal wreaths.

LADY FRANCES.
Oh my dear Sir George! I rejoice to meet you. An old conjuror has been frightening me with his prophecies. Where's Mrs. Racket?

COURTALL.
In the dancing room.—I promised to send you to her, Mr. Flutter.

FLUTTER.
Ah! she wants me to dance. With all my heart. (*Exit.*)

LADY FRANCES.
Why do you keep on your mask? 'Tis too warm.

COURTALL.
'Tis very warm—I want* air—let us go.

LADY FRANCES.
You seem quite agitated. Shan't we bid our company adieu?

COURTALL.
No, no, there's no time for forms. I'll just give directions to the carriage and be with you in a moment. (*Going, steps back.*) Put on your mask. I have a particular reason for it. (*Exit.*)

Saville advances with Kitty.

SAVILLE.
Now Kitty, you know your lesson. (*Takes off his mask.*) Lady Frances, let me lead you to your husband.

LADY FRANCES.
Heavens! is Mr. Saville the conjuror? Sir George is just stepped to the door to give directions. We are going home immediately.

SAVILLE.
No madam, you are deceived: Sir George is this way.

LADY FRANCES.
This is astonishing!

SAVILLE.
Be not alarmed: you have escaped a snare and shall be in safety in a moment.

Exit Saville and Lady Frances.

Enter Courtall and seizes Kitty's hand.

COURTALL.
Now!

KITTY.
'Tis pity to go so soon.

COURTALL.
Perhaps I may bring you back, my angel, but go now, you must.

Exeunt [Courtall and Kitty].

Music. Doricourt and Letitia come forward.

DORICOURT.
By heavens! I never was charmed till now. English beauty, French vivacity, wit, elegance. Your name, my angel! tell me your name, though you persist in concealing your face.

LETITIA.
My name has a spell in it.

79 Cornhill] highest hill in London

DORICOURT.
I thought so; it must be *Charming*.

LETITIA.
But if revealed, the charm is broke.

DORICOURT.
I'll answer for its force.

LETITIA.
Suppose it Harriet or Charlotte or Maria or—

DORICOURT.
Hang Harriet and Charlotte and Maria—the name your father gave ye!

LETITIA.
That can't be worth knowing, 'tis so transient a thing.

DORICOURT.
How transient?

LETITIA.
Heaven forbid my name should be *lasting* till I am married.

DORICOURT.
Married! The chains of matrimony are too heavy and vulgar for such a spirit as yours. The flowery wreaths of Cupid are the only bands you should wear.

LETITIA.
They are the lightest, I believe, but 'tis possible to wear those of marriage gracefully: throw 'em loosely round and twist 'em in a true lover's knot for the bosom.

DORICOURT.
An angel! but what will you be when a wife?

LETITIA.
A woman. If my husband should prove a churl, a fool, or a tyrant, I'd break his heart, ruin his fortune, elope with the first pretty fellow that asked me—and return the contempt of the world with scorn, whilst my feelings preyed upon my life.

DORICOURT. (*Aside.*)
Amazing!—What if you loved him and he were worthy of your love?

LETITIA.
Why, then I'd be anything—and all: grave, gay, capricious, the soul of whim, the spirit of variety; live with him in the eye of fashion or in the shade of retirement; change my country, my sex; feast with him in an Eskimo's hut or a Persian pavilion; join him in the victorious war dance on the borders of Lake Ontario or sleep to the soft breathings of the flute in the cinnamon groves of Ceylon; dig with him in the mines of Golconda or enter the dangerous precincts of the Mogul's seraglio, cheat him of his wishes, and overturn his empire to restore the husband of my heart to the blessings of liberty and love.

DORICOURT.
Delightful wildness. Oh, to catch thee and hold thee forever in this little cage! (*Attempting to clasp her.*)

LETITIA.
Hold, sir! Though Cupid must give the bait that tempts me to the snare, 'tis Hymen must spread the net to catch me.

DORICOURT.
'Tis in vain to assume airs of coldness: Fate has ordained you mine.

LETITIA.
How do you know?

DORICOURT.
I feel it *here*. I never met with a woman so perfectly to my taste, and I won't believe it formed you so on purpose to tantalize me.

LETITIA. (*Aside.*)
This moment is worth a whole existence.

DORICOURT.
Come, show me your face and rivet my chains.

LETITIA.
Tomorrow you shall be satisfied.

DORICOURT.
Tomorrow! and not tonight?

LETITIA.
No.

DORICOURT.
Where then shall I wait on you tomorrow? Where see you?

LETITIA.
You shall see me in an hour when you least expect me.

DORICOURT.
Why all this mystery?

LETITIA.
I like to be mysterious. At present be content to know that I am a woman of family and fortune. Adieu!

Enter Hardy.

HARDY. (*Aside.*)
Adieu! Then I am come at the fag end.

DORICOURT.
Let me see you to your carriage.

LETITIA.
As you value knowing me, stir not a step. If I am followed, you never see me more. (*Exit.*)

DORICOURT.
Barbarous creature! She's gone! What, and is this really serious? am I in love? Faugh! it can't be.

Enter Flutter.

Oh, Flutter! do you know that charming creature?

FLUTTER.
What charming creature? I passed a thousand.

DORICOURT.
She went out at that door as you entered.

FLUTTER.
Oh, yes, I know her very well.

DORICOURT.
Do you, my dear fellow? Who?

FLUTTER.
She's kept* by Lord George Jennet.

HARDY. (*Aside.*)
Impudent scoundrel!

DORICOURT.
Kept!!!

FLUTTER.
Yes, Colonel Gorget had her first, then Mr. Loveill—then—I forget exactly how many—and at last she's Lord George's. (*Talks to other masks.*)

DORICOURT.
I'll murder Gorget, poison Lord George, and shoot myself.

HARDY.
Now's the time, I see, to clear up the whole.—Mr. Doricourt! I say—Flutter was mistaken. I know who you are in love with.

DORICOURT.
A strange rencontre! Who?

HARDY.
My Letty.

DORICOURT.
Oh, I understand your rebuke. 'Tis too soon, sir, to assume the father-in-law.

HARDY.
Zounds! what do you mean by that? I tell you that the lady you admire is Letitia Hardy.

DORICOURT.
I am glad *you* are so well satisfied with the state of my heart. I wish *I* was. (*Exit.*)

HARDY.
Stop a moment—stop, I say! What, you won't? Very well, if I don't play you a trick for this, may I never be a grandfather! I'll plot *with* Letty now and not against her, aye, hang me if I don't. There's something in my head that shall tingle in his heart. He shall have a lecture upon impatience that I foresee he'll be the better for as long as he lives. (*Exit.*)

Saville comes forward with other masks.

SAVILLE.
Flutter, come with us. We're going to raise a laugh at Courtall's.

FLUTTER.
With all my heart. "Live to live" was my father's motto; "Live to laugh" is mine.

Exeunt.

Scene [ii]. Courtall's.

Enter Kitty and Courtall.

KITTY.
Where have you brought me, Sir George? This is not our home.

COURTALL. (*Kneels and takes off his mask.*)
'Tis *my* home, beautiful Lady Frances! Oh, forgive the ardency of my passion which has compelled me to deceive you.

KITTY.
Mr. Courtall! what will become of me?

COURTALL.
Oh, say but that you pardon the wretch who adores you. Did you but know the agonizing tortures of my heart since I had the felicity of conversing with you this morning—or the despair that now—

Knock.

KITTY.
Oh! I'm undone!

COURTALL.
Zounds! my dear Lady Frances. [*To servant.*] I am not at home. Rascal! do you hear? Let nobody in; I am not at home.

SERVANT. (*Without.*)
Sir, I told the gentlemen so.

COURTALL.
Eternal curses! they are coming up. Step into this room, adorable creature, *one* moment; I'll throw them out of the window if they stay three.

Exit Kitty through the back scene. Enter Saville, Flutter, and masks.

FLUTTER.
Oh jiminy!* Beg the petticoat's pardon. Just saw a corner of it.

FIRST MASK.
No wonder admittance was so difficult. I thought you took us for bailiffs.

COURTALL.
Upon my soul, I am devilish glad to see you, but you perceive how I am circumstanced. Excuse me at this moment.

SECOND MASK.
Tell us who 'tis then.

COURTALL.
Oh, fie!

FLUTTER.
We won't blab.

COURTALL.
I can't, upon honor. Thus far: she's a woman of the first character and rank. Saville (*Takes him aside.*), have I influence, or have I not?

SAVILLE.
Why sure, you do not insinuate—

COURTALL.
No, not insinuate, but swear that she's now in my bed chamber! By Gad, I don't deceive you. There's generalship, you rogue! Such an humble, distant, sighing fellow as thou art, at the end of a six-month siege would have *boasted* of a kiss from her glove. I only give the signal and—pop—she's in my arms.

SAVILLE.
What, Lady Fran—

COURTALL.
Hush! You shall see her name tomorrow morning in red letters at the end of my list.—Gentlemen, you must excuse me now. Come and drink chocolate at twelve, but—

SAVILLE.
Aye, let us go, out of respect to the lady—'tis a person of rank.

FLUTTER.
Is it? Then I'll have a peep at her. (*Runs to the door in the back scene.*)

COURTALL.
This is too much, sir. (*Trying to prevent him.*)

FIRST MASK.
By Jupiter, we'll all have a peep.

COURTALL.
Gentlemen, consider—for Heaven's sake—a lady of quality.* What will be the consequences?

FLUTTER.
The consequences! Why, you'll have your throat cut, that's all. But I'll write your elegy. So, now for the door!

Part open the door, whilst the rest hold Courtall.

Beg your ladyship's pardon, whoever you are. (*Leads her out.*) Emerge from darkness like the glorious sun and bless the wondering circle with your charms. (*Takes off her mask.*)

SAVILLE.
Kitty Willis! ha, ha, ha!

OMNES.
Kitty Willis! ha, ha, ha! Kitty Willis!

FIRST MASK.
Why, what a fellow you are, Courtall, to attempt imposing on your friends in this manner! A lady of quality—an earl's daughter—your ladyship's most obedient—ha, ha, ha!

SAVILLE.
Courtall, have you influence, or have you not?

FLUTTER.
The man's moonstruck.

COURTALL.
Hell and ten thousand furies seize you all together!

KITTY.
What! me, too, Mr. Courtall? me, whom you have knelt to, prayed to, and adored?

FLUTTER.
That's right, Kitty, give him a little more.

COURTALL.

Disappointed and laughed at!

SAVILLE.

Laughed at and despised. I have fulfilled my design, which was to expose your villainy and laugh at your presumption. Adieu, sir! Remember how you again boast of your influence with women of rank. And when you next want amusement, dare not to look up to the virtuous and to the noble for a companion. (*Exit, leading Kitty.*)

FLUTTER.

And Courtall, before you carry a lady into your bedchamber again, look under her mask, d'ye hear? (*Exit.*)

COURTALL.

There's no bearing this! I'll set off for Paris directly.

Exit.

Act V, scene i. Hardy's.

Enter Hardy and Villers.

VILLERS.

Whimsical enough! Dying for her and hates her; believes her a fool and a woman of brilliant understanding.

HARDY.

As true as you are alive. But when I went up to him last night at the masquerade,j out of downright good nature to explain things, my gentleman whips round upon his heel and snapped me as short as if I had been a beggar woman with six children and he overseer of the parish.

VILLERS.

Here comes the wonder-worker.

Enter Letitia.

Here comes the enchantress who can go to masquerades and sing and dance and talk a man out of his wits! But pray, have we morning masquerades?

LETITIA.

Oh no, but I am so enamored of this all-conquering habit that I could not resist putting it on the moment I had breakfasted. I shall wear it on the day I am married and then lay it by in spices, like the miraculous robes of St. Bridget.[80]

VILLERS.

That's as most brides do. The charms that helped to catch the husband are generally *laid by*, one after another till the lady grows a downright wife and then runs crying to her mother because she has transformed her *lover* into a downright husband.

HARDY.

Listen to me. I han't slept tonight for thinking of plots to plague Doricourt. And they drove one another out of my head so quick that I was as giddy as a goose and could make nothing of 'em. I wish to goodness you could contrive something.

VILLERS.

Contrive to plague him! Nothing so easy. Don't undeceive him, madam, till he is your husband. Marry him whilst he possesses the sentiments you labored to give him of Miss Hardy, and when you are his wife—

LETITIA.

Oh heavens! I see the whole—that's the very thing. My dear Mr. Villers, you are the divinest man.

VILLERS.

Don't make love* to me, hussy.

Enter Mrs. Racket.

MRS. RACKET.

No, pray don't, for I design to have Villers myself in about six years. There's an oddity in him that pleases me. He holds women in contempt, and I should like to have an opportunity of breaking his heart for that.

VILLERS.

And when I am heartily tired of life, I know no woman whom I would with more pleasure make my executioner.

HARDY.

It cannot be. I foresee it will be impossible to bring it about. You know the wedding wasn't to take place this week or more, and Letty will never be able to play the fool so long.

VILLERS.

The knot shall be tied tonight. I have it all here.

---

80 robes of St. Bridget] Healing powers were attributed to St. Bridget's cloak, which became a relic.

(*Pointing to his forehead.*) The license is ready. Feign yourself ill, send for Doricourt, and tell him you can't go out of the world in peace except you see the ceremony performed.

HARDY.

I feign myself ill! I could as soon feign myself a Roman ambassador. I was never ill in my life, but with the toothache. When Letty's mother was a-breeding, I had all the qualms.

VILLERS.

Oh, I have no fears for *you.*—But what says Miss Hardy? Are you willing to make the irrevocable vow before night?

LETITIA.

Oh heavens! I—I— 'Tis so exceeding sudden, that really—

MRS. RACKET.

That really she is frightened out of her wits—lest it should be impossible to bring matters about. But *I* have taken the scheme into my protection, and you shall be Mrs. Doricourt before night. (*To Mr. Hardy.*) Come, to bed directly: your room shall be crammed with phials and all the apparatus of death. Then heigh presto! for Doricourt.

VILLERS. (*To Letty.*)

You go and put off your conquering dress and get all your awkward airs ready. (*To Hardy.*) And you practice a few groans. (*To Mrs. Racket.*) And you—if possible—an air of gravity. I'll answer for the plot.

LETITIA.

Married in jest! 'tis an odd idea! Well, I'll venture it.

Exeunt Letitia and Mrs. Racket.

VILLERS.

Aye, I'll be sworn! (*Looks at his watch.*) 'Tis past three. The budget's to be opened this morning. I'll just step down to the House. Will you go?

HARDY.

What! with a mortal sickness?

VILLERS.

What a blockhead! I believe if half of us were to stay away with mortal sicknesses, it would be for the health of the nation. Good morning. I'll call and feel your pulse as I come back. (*Exit.*)

HARDY.

You won't find 'em over brisk, I fancy. I foresee some ill happening from this making believe to die before one's time. But hang it, ahem! I am a stout man yet, only fifty-six. What's that? In the last yearly bill* there were three lived to above a hundred. Fifty-six! Fiddle-de-dee! I am not afraid, not I.

Exit.

Scene ii. Doricourt's.

Doricourt in his robe de chambre. Enter Saville.

SAVILLE.

Undressed so late?

DORICOURT.

I didn't go to bed till late; 'twas late before I slept, late when I rose. Do you know Lord George Jennet?

SAVILLE.

Yes.

DORICOURT.

Has he a mistress?

SAVILLE.

Yes.

DORICOURT.

What sort of a creature is she?

SAVILLE.

Why, she spends him three thousand a year with the ease of a duchess and entertains his friends with the grace of a Ninon.[81] Ergo, she is handsome, spirited, and clever.

Doricourt walks about disordered.

In the name of caprice, what ails you?

DORICOURT.

You have hit it: *elle est mon caprice.* The mistress of Lord George Jennet is my caprice. Oh, insufferable!

SAVILLE.

What, you saw her at the masquerade?

DORICOURT.

Saw her, *loved* her, *died* for her—without knowing her. And now the curse is, I can't hate her.

---

81 Ninon] nickname for Anne de Lenclos (1620-1705), witty French courtesan noted for her prominent liaisons and salon

SAVILLE.
Ridiculous enough! All this distress about a kept woman whom any man may have, I dare swear, in a fortnight. They've been jarring some time.

DORICOURT.
Have her! The sentiment I have conceived for the witch is so unaccountable that, in that line, I cannot bear her idea. Was she a woman of honor, for a wife I could adore her. But I really believe, if she should send me an assignation, I should hate her.

SAVILLE.
Heyday! This sounds like love. What becomes of poor Miss Hardy?

DORICOURT.
Her name has given me an ague. Dear Saville, how shall I contrive to make old Hardy cancel the engagements? The moiety of the estate which he will forfeit shall be his the next moment by deed of gift.

SAVILLE.
Let me see. Can't you get it insinuated that you are a devilish wild fellow, that you are an infidel and attached to wenching, gaming, and so forth?

DORICOURT.
Aye, such a character* might have done some good two centuries back. But who the devil can it frighten now? I believe it must be the mad scheme, at last. There, will that do for a[k] grin?

SAVILLE.
Ridiculous! But how are you certain that the woman who has so bewildered you belongs to Lord George?

DORICOURT.
Flutter told me so.

SAVILLE.
Then fifty to one against the intelligence.

DORICOURT.
It must be so. There was a mystery in her manner for which nothing else can account.

A violent rap.

Who can this be?

SAVILLE. (*Looking out.*)
The proverb[82] is your answer: 'tis Flutter himself. Tip him a scene of the madman and see how it takes.

DORICOURT.
I will—a good way to send it about Town. Shall it be of the melancholy kind or the raving?

SAVILLE.
Rant! Rant! Here he comes.

DORICOURT.
Talk not to me who can pull comets by the beard and overset an island!

Enter Flutter.

There! this is he! This is he who hath sent my poor soul, without coat or breeches, to be tossed about in ether like a duck feather!—Villain, give me my soul again!

FLUTTER. (*Exceedingly frightened.*)
Upon my soul I haven't got it.

SAVILLE.
Oh Mr. Flutter, what a melancholy sight! I little thought to have seen my poor friend reduced to this.

FLUTTER.
Mercy defend me! What, 's he mad?

SAVILLE.
You see how it is. A cursed Italian lady—Jealousy—gave him a drug, and every full of the moon—

DORICOURT.
Moon! Who dares talk of the moon? The patroness of genius—the rectifier of wits—the—Oh! here she is!—I feel her—she tugs at my brain—she has it—she has it—Oh! (*Exit.*)

FLUTTER.
Well! this is dreadful! exceeding dreadful, I protest. Have you had Monro?[83]

SAVILLE.
Not yet. The worthy Miss Hardy—what a misfortune!

FLUTTER.
Aye, very true. Do they know it?

SAVILLE.
Oh no, the paroxysm seized him but this morning.

FLUTTER.
Adieu! I can't stay. (*Going in great haste.*)

---

82 proverb] "Speak of the devil and he's sure to appear."

83 Monro] John Monro, MD (1715-1791), first physician to Bethlem Hospital, second of five generations of Monros who were eminent mad-doctors

SAVILLE.
But you must. (*Holding him.*) Stay and assist me: perhaps he'll return again in a moment, and when he is in this way, his strength is prodigious.
FLUTTER.
Can't indeed—can't upon my soul. (*Exit[ing].*)
SAVILLE.
Flutter, don't make a mistake now. Remember, 'tis Doricourt that's mad.
FLUTTER.
Yes—you mad.
SAVILLE.
No, no: Doricourt.
FLUTTER.
Egad, I'll say you are both mad, and then I can't mistake.

Exeunt severally.

Scene iii. Sir George Touchwood's.

Enter Sir George and Lady Frances.

SIR GEORGE.
The bird is escaped. Courtall is gone to France!
LADY FRANCES.
Heaven and earth! Have ye been to seek him?
SIR GEORGE.
Seek him! Aye.
LADY FRANCES.
How did you get his name? I should never have told it you.
SIR GEORGE.
I learned it at the first coffeehouse I entered. Everybody is full of the story.
LADY FRANCES.
Thank Heaven, he's gone! But I have a story for you. The Hardy family are forming a plot upon your friend Doricourt, and we are expected in the evening to assist.
SIR GEORGE.
With all my heart, my angel, but I can't stay to hear it unfolded. They told me Mr. Saville would be at home in half an hour, and I am impatient to see him. The adventure of last night—
LADY FRANCES.
Think of it only with gratitude. The danger I was in has overset a new system of conduct that, perhaps, I was too much inclined to adopt. But henceforward, my dear Sir George, you shall be my constant companion and protector. And when they ridicule the unfashionable monsters, the felicity of our hearts shall make their satire pointless.
SIR GEORGE.
Charming angel! You almost reconcile me to Courtall. Hark! here's company. (*Stepping to the door.*) 'Tis your lively widow. I'll step down the back stairs to escape her. (*Exit.*)

Enter Mrs. Racket.

MRS. RACKET.
Oh Lady Frances! I am shocked to death. Have you received a card from us?
LADY FRANCES.
Yes, within these twenty minutes.
MRS. RACKET.
Aye, 'tis of no consequence. 'Tis all over. Doricourt is mad.
LADY FRANCES.
Mad!
MRS. RACKET.
My poor Letitia! Just as we were enjoying ourselves with the prospect of a scheme that was planned for their mutual happiness, in came Flutter, breathless, with the intelligence. I flew here to know if you had heard it.
LADY FRANCES.
No indeed, and I hope it is one of Mr. Flutter's dreams.

Enter Saville.

Apropos, now we shall be informed.—Mr. Saville, I rejoice to see you, though Sir George will be disappointed: he's gone to your lodgings.
SAVILLE.
I should have been happy to have prevented* Sir George. I hope your ladyship's adventure last night did not disturb your dreams?
LADY FRANCES.
Not at all, for I never slept a moment. My escape, and the importance of my obligations to you, employed my thoughts. But we have just had shocking intelligence. Is it true that Doricourt is mad?

SAVILLE. (*Aside.*)
So, the business is done.—Madam, I am sorry to say that I have just been a melancholy witness of his ravings; he was in the height of a paroxysm.

MRS. RACKET.
Oh, there can be no doubt of it. Flutter told us the whole history. Some Italian princess gave him a drug in a box of sweetmeats sent to him by her own page, and it renders him lunatic every month. Poor Miss Hardy! I never felt so much on any occasion in my life.

SAVILLE.
To soften your concern, I will inform you, madam, that Miss Hardy is less to be pitied than you imagine.

MRS. RACKET.
Why so, sir?

SAVILLE.
'Tis rather a delicate subject, but he did not love Miss Hardy.

MRS. RACKET.
He did love Miss Hardy, sir, and would have been the happiest of men.

SAVILLE.
Pardon me, madam, his heart was not only free from that lady's chains but absolutely captivated by another.

MRS. RACKET.
No, sir, no. It was Miss Hardy who captivated him. She met him last night at the masquerade and charmed him in disguise. He professed the most violent passion for her and a plan was laid, this evening to cheat him into happiness.

SAVILLE.
Ha, ha, ha! Upon my soul, I must beg your pardon. I have not eaten of the Italian princess's box of sweetmeats sent by her own page, and yet I am as mad as Doricourt, ha, ha, ha!

MRS. RACKET.
So it appears. What can all this mean?

SAVILLE.
Why madam, he is at present in his perfect senses, but he'll lose 'em in ten minutes through joy. The madness was only a feint to avoid marrying Miss Hardy, ha, ha, ha! I'll carry him the intelligence directly. (*Going.*)

MRS. RACKET.
Not for worlds. I owe him revenge, now, for what he has made us suffer. You must promise not to divulge a syllable I have told you. And when Doricourt is summoned to Mr. Hardy's, prevail on him to come, madness and all.

LADY FRANCES.
Pray do. I should like to see him showing off, now I am in the secret.

SAVILLE.
You must be obeyed, though 'tis inhuman to conceal his happiness.

MRS. RACKET.
I am going home, so I'll set you down at his lodgings and acquaint you, by the way, with our whole scheme. *Allons*!

SAVILLE.
I attend you. (*Leading her out.*)

MRS. RACKET.
You won't fail us?

Exeunt Saville and Mrs. Racket.

LADY FRANCES.
No, depend on us.

Exit.

Scene iv. Doricourt's.

Doricourt seated, reading.

DORICOURT. (*Flings away the book.*)
What effect can the morals of fourscore have on a mind torn with passion? (*Musing.*) Is it possible such a soul as hers can support itself in so humiliating a situation? A kept woman! (*Rising.*) Well, well—I am glad it is so—I am glad it is so!

Enter Saville.

SAVILLE.
What a happy dog you are, Doricourt! I might have been mad or beggared or pistoled myself without its being mentioned. But you, forsooth! the whole female world is concerned for. I reported the state of your brain to five different women: the lip of the first trembled; the white bosom of the second heaved a sigh; the third ejaculated and turned her eye—to the glass;* the fourth blessed

herself; and the fifth said, whilst she pinned a curl, "Well, now, perhaps, he'll be an amusing companion. His native dullness was intolerable."

DORICOURT.
Envy! sheer envy, by the smiles of Hebe! There are not less than forty pair of the brightest eyes in Town will drop crystals when they hear of my misfortune.

SAVILLE.
Well, but I have news for you: poor Hardy is confined to his bed. They say he is going out of the world by the first post, and he wants to give you his blessing.

DORICOURT.
Ill! So ill! I am sorry from my soul. He's a worthy little fellow—if he had not the gift of foreseeing so strongly.

SAVILLE.
Well, you must go and take leave.

DORICOURT.
What! To act the lunatic in the dying man's chamber?

SAVILLE.
Exactly the thing, and will bring your business to a short issue: for his last commands must be that you are not to marry his daughter.

DORICOURT.
That's true, by Jupiter! And yet, hang it, impose upon a poor fellow at so serious a moment! I can't do it.

SAVILLE.
You must, faith. I am answerable for your appearance, though it should be in a strait waistcoat. He knows your situation and seems the more desirous of an interview.

DORICOURT.
I don't like encountering Racket. She's an arch little devil and will discover the cheat.

SAVILLE.
There's a fellow! Cheated ninety-nine women and now afraid of the hundredth.

DORICOURT.
And with reason—for that hundredth is a widow.
Exeunt.

Scene v. Hardy's.

Enter Mrs. Racket and Miss Ogle.

MISS OGLE.
And so Miss Hardy is actually to be married tonight?

MRS. RACKET.
If her fate does not deceive her. You are apprised of the scheme, and we hope it will succeed.

MISS OGLE. (*Aside.*)
Deuce take her! She's six years younger than I am.—Is Mr. Doricourt handsome?

MRS. RACKET.
Handsome, generous, young, and rich. There's a husband for ye! Isn't he worth pulling caps[84] for?

MISS OGLE. (*Aside.*)
I'my conscience, the widow speaks as though she'd give cap, ears, and all for him.—I wonder you didn't try to catch this wonderful man, Mrs. Racket!

MRS. RACKET.
Really Miss Ogle, I had not time. Besides, when I marry, so many stout young fellows will hang themselves that out of regard to society, in these sad times, I shall postpone it for a few years. (*Aside.*) This will cost her a new lace:[85] I heard it crack.

Enter Sir George and Lady Frances.

SIR GEORGE.
Well, here we are. But where's the Knight of the Woeful Countenance?[86]

MRS. RACKET.
Here soon, I hope. For a woeful night it will be without him.

SIR GEORGE.
Oh fie! do you condescend to pun?

MRS. RACKET.
Why not? It requires genius to make a good pun. Some men of bright parts* can't reach it. I know

84 pulling caps] quarreling like two women who pull each other's caps

85 lace] corset lacing

86 Knight of the Woeful Countenance] nickname for Cervantes' Don Quixote

a lawyer who writes them on the back of his briefs and says they are of great use in a dry cause.

Enter Flutter.

FLUTTER.
Here they come! Here they come! Their coach stopped as mine drove off.

LADY FRANCES.
Then Miss Hardy's fate is at a crisis. She plays a hazardous game, and I tremble for her.

SAVILLE.
(*Without.*) Come let me guide you! This way, my poor friend! Why are you so furious?

DORICOURT.
The house of death—to the house of death!

Enter Doricourt and Saville.

Ah! this is the spot!

LADY FRANCES.
How wild and fiery he looks!

MISS OGLE.
Now, I think, he looks terrified.

FLUTTER.
Poor creature, how his eyes work!

MRS. RACKET.
I never saw a madman before. Let me examine him. Will he bite?

SAVILLE.
Pray keep out of his reach, ladies, you don't know your danger. He's like a wildcat if a sudden thought seizes him.

SIR GEORGE.
You talk like a keeper of wildcats. How much do you demand for showing the monster?

DORICOURT. [*Aside.*]
I don't like this. I must rouse their sensibility.—There! there she darts through the air in liquid flames! Down again! Now I have her—oh, she burns, she scorches!—oh! she eats into my very heart!

OMNES.
Ha, ha, ha!

MRS. RACKET.
He sees the apparition of the wicked Italian princess.

FLUTTER.
Keep her highness fast, Doricourt.

MISS OGLE.
Give her a pinch, before you let her go.

DORICOURT.
I am laughed at!

MRS. RACKET.
Laughed at, aye, to be sure. Why, I could play the madman better than you.—There! there she is! Now I have her! Ha, ha, ha!

DORICOURT. (*Aside.*)
I knew that devil would discover me.—I'll leave the house; I'm covered with confusion. (*Going.*)

SIR GEORGE.
Stay, sir. You must not go. 'Twas poorly done, Mr. Doricourt, to affect madness rather than fulfil your engagements.

DORICOURT.
Affect madness!—Saville, what can I do?

SAVILLE.
Since you are discovered, confess the whole.

MISS OGLE.
Aye, turn evidence and save yourself.

DORICOURT.
Yes, since my designs have been so unaccountably discovered, I will avow the whole. I cannot love Miss Hardy—and I will never—

SAVILLE.
Hold, my dear Doricourt! Be not so rash. What will the world say to such—

DORICOURT.
Damn the world! What will the world give me for the loss of happiness? Must I sacrifice my peace to please the world?

SIR GEORGE.
Yes, everything, rather than be branded with dishonor.

LADY FRANCES.
Though *our* arguments should fail, there *is* a pleader whom you surely cannot withstand: the dying Mr. Hardy supplicates you not to forsake his child.

Enter Villers.

VILLERS.
Mr. Hardy requests you to grant him a moment's conversation, Mr. Doricourt, though you should persist to send him miserable to the grave. Let me conduct you to his chamber.

DORICOURT.

Oh, aye, anywhere, to the antipodes, to the moon carry me, do with me what you will.

MRS. RACKET.

Mortification and disappointment, then, are specifics in a case of stubbornness. I'll follow, and let you know what passes.

Exeunt Villers, Doricourt, Mrs. Racket, and Miss Ogle.

FLUTTER.

Ladies, ladies, have the charity to take me with you, that I may make no blunder in repeating the story. (*Exit.*)

LADY FRANCES.

Sir George, you don't know Mr. Saville? (*Exit.*)

SIR GEORGE.

Ten thousand pardons, but I will not pardon myself for not observing you. I have been with the utmost impatience at your door twice today.

SAVILLE.

I am concerned you had so much trouble, Sir George.

SIR GEORGE.

Trouble! what a word!—I hardly know how to address you. I am distressed beyond measure, and it is the highest proof of my opinion of your honor and the delicacy of your mind that I open my heart to you.

SAVILLE.

What has disturbed you, Sir George?

SIR GEORGE.

Your having preserved Lady Frances in so imminent a danger. Start not, Saville. To protect Lady Frances was my right. You have wrested from me my dearest privilege.

SAVILLE.

I hardly know how to answer such a reproach. I cannot apologize for what I have done.

SIR GEORGE.

I do not mean to reproach you; I hardly know what I mean. There is one method by which you may restore peace to me: I cannot endure that my wife should be so infinitely indebted to any man who is less than my brother.

SAVILLE.

Pray explain yourself.

SIR GEORGE.

I have a sister, Saville, who is amiable—and you are worthy of her. I shall give her a commission to steal your heart out of revenge for what you have done.

SAVILLE.

I am infinitely honored, Sir George, but—

SIR GEORGE.

I cannot listen to a sentence which begins with so unpromising a word. You must go with us into Hampshire, and if you see each other with the eyes I do, your felicity will be complete. I know no one to whose heart I would so readily commit the care of my sister's happiness.

SAVILLE.

I will attend you to Hampshire with pleasure, but not on the plan of retirement. Society has claims on Lady Frances that forbid it.

SIR GEORGE.

Claims, Saville!

SAVILLE.

Yes, claims: Lady Frances was born to be the ornament of courts. She is sufficiently alarmed not to wander beyond the reach of her protector. And from the British court, the most tenderly anxious husband could not wish to banish his wife. Bid her keep in her eye the bright example who presides there,[87] the splendor of whose rank yields to the superior luster of her virtue.

SIR GEORGE.

I allow the force of your argument. Now for intelligence!

Enter Mrs. Racket, Lady Frances, [Miss Ogle], and Flutter.

MRS. RACKET.

Oh heavens! do you know—

FLUTTER.

Let me tell the story—as soon as Doricourt—

MRS. RACKET.

I protest you shan't—said Mr. Hardy—

FLUTTER.

No, 'twas Doricourt spoke first. Says he—no, 'twas the parson—says he—

87 bright example who presides there] Queen Charlotte (1744-1818), consort of George III (1738-1820)

MRS. RACKET.
Stop his mouth, Sir George, he'll spoil the tale.
SIR GEORGE.
Never heed circumstances, the result, the result.
MRS. RACKET.
No, no, you shall have it in form. Mr. Hardy performed the sick man like an angel. He sat up in his bed and talked so pathetically that the tears stood in Doricourt's eyes.
FLUTTER.
Aye, stood—they did not drop, but stood. I shall, in future, be very exact. The parson seized the moment; you know, they never miss an opportunity.
MRS. RACKET.
"Make haste," said Doricourt. "If I have time to reflect, poor Hardy will die unhappy."
FLUTTER.
They were got as far as the "day of judgement," when we slipped out of the room.
SIR GEORGE.
Then by this time they must have reached "amazement,"[88] which, everybody knows, is the end of matrimony.
MRS. RACKET.
Aye, the reverend fathers ended the service with that word prophetically, to teach the bride what a capricious monster a husband is.
SIR GEORGE.
I rather think it was sarcastically to prepare the bridegroom for the unreasonable humors and vagaries of his helpmate.
LADY FRANCES.
Here comes the bridegroom of tonight.

Enter Doricourt and Villers. Villers whispers Saville, who goes out.

OMNES.
Joy! joy! joy!
MISS OGLE.
If *he's* a sample of bridegrooms, keep me single! A younger brother from the funeral of his father could not carry a more fretful countenance.
FLUTTER.
Oh! now he's melancholy mad, I suppose.
LADY FRANCES.
You do not consider the importance of the occasion.
VILLERS.
No, nor how shocking a thing it is for a man to be forced to marry one woman whilst his heart is devoted to another.
MRS. RACKET.
Well, now 'tis over, I confess to you, Mr. Doricourt, I think 'twas a most ridiculous piece of quixotism to give up the happiness of a whole life to a man who perhaps has but a few moments to be sensible of the sacrifice.
FLUTTER.
So it appeared to me. But thought I, Mr. Doricourt has traveled; he knows best.
DORICOURT.
Zounds! Confusion! Did ye not all set upon me! Didn't ye talk to me of honor, compassion, justice?
SIR GEORGE.
Very true. You have acted according to their dictates, and I hope the utmost felicity of the married state will reward you.
DORICOURT.
Never, Sir George! To felicity I bid adieu, but I will endeavor to be content. Where is my—I must speak it—where is my *wife*?

Enter Letitia, masked, led by Saville.

SAVILLE.
Mr. Doricourt, this lady was pressing to be introduced to you.
DORICOURT. (*Starting.*)
Oh!
LETITIA.
I told you last night you should see me at a time when you least expected me, and I have kept my promise.
VILLERS.
Whoever you are, madam, you could not have arrived at a happier moment. Mr. Doricourt is just married.
LETITIA.
Married! Impossible! 'Tis but a few hours since he

88 "day of judgment" … "amazement"] phrases near the beginning and the end of the Church of England wedding ceremony

swore to me eternal love. I believed him, gave him up my virgin heart—and now!—ungrateful sex!

DORICOURT.

Your virgin heart! No, lady, my fate, thank Heaven, yet wants* that torture. Nothing but the conviction that you was another's could have made me think one moment of marriage to have saved the lives of half mankind. But this visit, madam, is as barbarous as unexpected. It is now my duty to forget you, which, spite of your situation, I found difficult enough.

LETITIA.

My situation! What situation?

DORICOURT.

I must apologize for explaining it in this company. But madam, I am not ignorant that you are the companion of Lord George Jennet, and this is the only circumstance that can give me peace.

LETITIA.

I—a companion! Ridiculous pretense! No sir, know to your confusion that my heart, my honor, my name is unspotted as hers you have married, my birth equal to your own, my fortune large. That, and my person, might have been yours. But, sir, farewell! (*Going.*)

DORICOURT.

Oh, stay a moment. [*To Flutter.*] Rascal! is she not—

FLUTTER.

Who, she? Oh, Lard no! 'Twas quite a different person that I meant. I never saw that lady before.

DORICOURT.

Then never shalt thou see her more. (*Shakes Flutter.*)

MRS. RACKET.

Have mercy upon the poor man! Heavens! He'll murder him.

DORICOURT.

Murder him! Yes, you, myself, and all mankind. Sir George, Saville, Villers, 'twas you who pushed me on this precipice, 'tis you who have snatched from me joy, felicity, and life.

MRS. RACKET.

There! Now, how well he acts the madman! This is something like! I knew he would do it well enough when the time came.

DORICOURT.

Hard-hearted woman! enjoy my ruin, riot in my wretchedness.

Hardy bursts in.

HARDY.

This is too much. You are now the husband of my daughter, and how dare you show all this passion about another woman?

DORICOURT.

Alive again!

HARDY.

Alive! aye, and merry. Here, wipe off the flour from my face. I was never in better health and spirits in my life. I foresaw 'twould do. Why, my illness was only a fetch, man, to make you marry Letty.

DORICOURT.

It was! Base and ungenerous! Well sir, you shall be gratified. The possession of my heart was no object either with you or your daughter. My fortune and name was all you desired, and these—I leave ye. My native England I shall quit, nor ever behold you more.—But lady, that in my exile I may have one consolation, grant me the favor you denied last night: let me behold all that mask conceals, that your whole image may be impressed on my heart and cheer my distant solitary hours.

LETITIA.

This is the most awful* moment of my life. Oh Doricourt, the slight action of taking off my mask stamps me the most blessed or miserable of women!

DORICOURT.

What can this mean? Reveal your face, I conjure you.

LETITIA.

Behold it.

DORICOURT.

Rapture! Transport! Heaven!

FLUTTER.

Now for a touch of the happy madman.

VILLERS.

This scheme was mine.

LETITIA.

I will not allow that. This little stratagem arose from my disappointment in not having made the impression on you I wished. The timidity of the English character threw a veil over me you could not penetrate. You have forced me to emerge in some measure from my natural reserve and to throw off the veil that hid me.

DORICOURT.

I am yet in a state of intoxication. I cannot answer you. Speak on, sweet angel!

LETITIA.

You see I *can* be anything. Choose then my character. Your taste shall fix it. Shall I be an *English* wife? Or, breaking from the bonds of nature and education, step forth to the world in all the captivating glare of foreign manners?

DORICOURT.

You shall be nothing but yourself; nothing can be captivating that you are not. I will not wrong your penetration by pretending that you won my heart at the first interview. But you have now my whole soul. Your person, your face, your mind I would not exchange for those of any other woman breathing.

HARDY.

A dog! How well he makes up for past slights!—Cousin Racket, I wish you a good husband with all my heart.—Mr. Flutter, I'll believe every word you say this fortnight.—Mr. Villers, you and I have managed this to a "T." I never was so merry in my life. 'Gad, I believe I can dance! (*Footing.*)

DORICOURT.

Charming, charming creature!

LETITIA.

Congratulate me, my dear friends! Can you conceive my happiness?

HARDY.

No, congratulate me, for mine is the greatest.

FLUTTER.

No, congratulate me that I have escaped with life, and give me some sticking plaster. This wildcat has torn the skin from my throat.

SIR GEORGE.

I expect to be among the first who are congratulated, for I have recovered one angel while Doricourt has gained another.

HARDY.

Faugh! Faugh! don't talk of angels, we shall be happier by half as mortals. Come into the next room! I have ordered out every drop of my forty-eight, and I'll invite the whole parish of St. George's[89] but what we'll drink it out—except one dozen which I shall keep under three double locks for a certain christening that I foresee will happen within this twelvemonth.

DORICOURT.

My charming bride! It was a strange perversion of taste that led me to consider the delicate timidity of your deportment as the mark of an uninformed mind or inelegant manners. I feel now it is to that innate modesty *English* husbands owe a felicity the married men of other nations are strangers to. It is a sacred veil to your own charms; it is the surest bulwark to your husband's honor. And cursed be the hour, should it ever arrive, in which *British* ladies shall sacrifice to *foreign graces* the grace of modesty!

[Exeunt.]

FINIS.

---

89 St. George's] another prominent church on Botolph Lane

Textual Notes

[a] Copytext is the first authorized edition, a 1782 quarto (Q1). Also consulted were the 1780 manuscript presented for registration (A), housed in the Larpent collection of the Henry E. Huntington Library and published in *Three Centuries of English Drama*; the second edition, a 1787 quarto (Q2), and the 1813 *Collected Works* (W). I have followed Frederick Link in the 1979 Garland facsimile edition of Q1 in accepting Q1 and Q2 as authoritative over W and have shown only representatives of the many changes made in that posthumously published edition revised by the author in her old age.

[b] SAVILLE] SERV. A, Q1, Q2, W

[c] Zounds] In W, oaths such as zounds, 'sdeath, begar, etc., are eliminated.

[d] Crowquill] In W, I.ii is severely curtailed, with the character of Crowquill excised and the lines about the gossip column eliminated.

[e] Villers] In W the characters of Villers and Saville are collapsed into one character named Saville.

[f] It is the same ... beauty heightened] a typical example of the cosmetic tinkering of W: It is the same face that my memory, or my fancy, constantly painted, its expression more heightened, its graces more finished.

[g] Miss Ogle] the Ogles, A, Q1, Q2, W; one of three references in the published editions to a plurality of Misses Ogle—a holdover from the ms (A); there is only one Miss Ogle in the published play.

[h] Scene ii] A includes nine lines omitted Q1, Q2, and W, in which Silvertongue educates the puffers on their trade.

[i] W gives Courtall a brief moment of contrition: "But softly!—softly—a moment— crise conscience! Wilt thou attempt to blemish her character for virtue—merely to keep up thy own for vice!" But with a "psha" he quickly dismisses his "qualm."

[j] masquerade] Pantheon A, Q1, Q2, W

[k] a] Q2, W; the A, Q1

Glossary

______] blanks for actors to fill in, sometimes with words, sometimes with gestures, such as snapping their fingers, sometimes at their peril

'a] he

admire(ation)] wonder at, wonder; not: esteem

an, an if, an't, and] if, if it; not: the article or the conjunction

angel] angel noble, gold coin stamped with archangel Michael, worth about a half pound

Arratine/Aretino] Pietro Aretino (1492–1556), Italian poet, whose "Lewd Sonnets" (1524) were accompanied by scandalously erotic illustrations.

art] human contrivance, artifice; opposed to nature

awful] awe inspiring; not: terrible

baby] doll; not: infant

basset] card game, resembling faro; not: bandy-legged hound dog

Bear Garden] any of several sites for bear-baiting and other rough sports, also associated with theatrical performances, esp. on the South Bank of the Thames; lower-class folk were often in attendance, like butchers, but fashionable folk frequented them as well

begar] by god, "not a polite use" (*OED*)

bell] A church bell rings the morning of execution, when criminals—including traitors—are carted to the scaffold.

$bill_1$] bill of exchange

$bill_2$] list; bills were published (usually weekly) of all deaths in a parish, along with bills of births and baptisms.

Billingsgate] one of the gates to the city of London and the fish market thereby, known for its abusive language

birthday] referring to the monarch's birthday and its attendant celebration, at which ladies and gentlemen wore fine, new clothes

bite] cheat, flimflam; not: injure with teeth

black] usually dark haired, sometimes dark-skinned; not: racial category

bona roba] compliant woman, courtesan (literally, good gown)

bone] a reference to Eve's creation from Adam's rib; thus he calls her "bone of my bones, and flesh of my flesh" (Gen. 2:21–23)

brave(ly), braw(ly)] excellent(ly); not: courageous(ly)

brutal] animal; not: cruel

bubble] to cheat; victim of a cheat

bug] bogey; not: insect

canonical hours] hours when marriages could be legally performed (before noon)

cast] discarded

Cause (Good Old)] the effort to establish a commonwealth in mid-seventeenth-century England

chair, etc.] sedan, a portable chair borne by chairmen

Change] v. Exchange, New

character] description, as in a character sketch

chariot] light 4-wheel vehicle; not: ancient 2-wheel cart

Chateline's] a fashionable ordinary in Covent Garden*

Cheapside] a business district within the walls of London

Chedreux] fashionable Parisian wig-maker—or one of his products

chemist] alchemist (q.v.); also apothecary

child] term of affection for a young, usually noble, person; not: youngster

China orange] sweet, thin-skinned orange, a delicacy originally from China

cit(s), citizen(s)] inhabitant(s) of the City, usually derogatory

City] the old part of London within the walls, housing the financial district

clip] to shave edges of unmilled coins for the gold or silver

clog] shackles or encumbrance; not: shoe

closet] inner chamber of one's lodgings; not: a wardrobe

clown(ish)] rustic; not: comic pantomime

Commons, Doctors] College of Doctors of Civil Law in London, whose lawyers practiced both canon and civil law; they handled cases of separation and divorce in the ecclesiastical courts; also, where wills were registered

conversation] interchange with company, sometimes sexual intercourse; not limited to talk

corn] grain, e.g. wheat; not: maize

Covent Garden] during the Restoration, a fashionable residential area of the Town*; later, a somewhat disreputable area, haven to prostitutes; also location for a market

coy] shy; not: coquettish

crossbite] outcheat

crowd] fiddle

crown] English coin

cucumber] considered inedible by people in the eighteenth century and discarded

curious] skillfully made, precisely accurate; not: odd

cut (a caper)] to spring from the ground and, while in the air, to twiddle the feet one in front of the other alternately with great rapidity (*OED*)

dear] expensive; not: lovable

decide] figure out; not: come to a decision

Deel] Devil

demean] behave; not: lower (oneself)

despise] to regard as negligible, worthless; not: to loathe

die] to suffer *la petite mort* of sexual orgasm; not: to expire

discover] reveal; not: find

disguised] drunk; not: in masquerade

doubt] suspect or fear; not: call into question

Drawing Room] reception room at the royal palace

ears] Perjury and other offenses were sometimes punished by cutting off one or both of the perpetrator's ears.

en cavalier] in the manner of a fashionable gentleman, gallantly

engine] a tool, mechanical or human, often suspected to be sinister; not: motor

engineer] one who works with engines, often mines planted beneath walls to blow them up, usually with sexual connotations

English wife] proverbially (sexually) liberated

entertain] maintain, receive, or show hospitality to; not: amuse

enthusiasm, etc.] religious frenzy; not: eager interest

evidence] witness; not: material support of a case or testimony

Exchange, New] a meeting place for bankers and merchants, as well as a gallery of fashionable shops located on the Strand in London. The original Exchange burned down in the fire of 1666.

fack(s), fads, fags, fackins] colloquial for "faith"

family] servants or whole household; not: relatives

favor] token gift of remembrance, sometimes sexual; not: help

fit] pay back; not: make appropriate

Flanders] Part of the Spanish Netherlands in the seventeenth century, Flanders was nibbled at by other countries, especially France; noted for elegant lace and expensive coach horses.

fond(ness)] foolish(ness); not: amorous(ness)

fubb(s)] small, chubby person, term of endearment

furniture] livery; not: movables

geese] According to Roman legend, the cackling of the geese in Juno's temple saved the Capitol from invaders by warning the guards.

generous] highborn, demonstrating nobility; not: openhanded

gentle] of birth and its attendant worth; not: soft, kind

genius] attendant spirit, often associated with place (as in *genius loci*); not: inclination, penchant, or creative brilliance

glass] mirror; not: a receptacle for liquid or liquor

go to] a mild oath

gog] eagerness

great man] ironic epithet applied to Robert Walpole by his political opponents

groom-porter's] Until the office was abolished under George III, the groom-porter was a royal officer responsible for regulating gaming.

Grosvenor Square] large square, an eighteenth-century extension of the Town*

grumbletonian] derogatory nickname given to the Country Party by their adversaries at Court

half-seas-over] more than half drunk

heels, lie (lay one) by] manacle or put one in the stocks

hictius doctius] standard part of the magician's (juggler's) repertoire; perhaps from *hicce est doctus*—this is the doctor (Lat.).

his] a spurious spelling out of the meaning of *'s* noting possession

hogoe(s)] piquant, strong-smelling (dishes)—from French *de haut goût*, spicy

honest, -ty] chaste/chastity; not: truthfulness

horns] sign of a cuckold, supposedly sprouting from his forehead

hot-cockles] A game in which a player lay down blindfolded and then guessed who had hit him. Cockle is also a slang term for vagina.

humor, humorous, humorsome] (subject to) a permanent characteristic (from humours theory); not: a temporary state of mind or an ability to laugh

Hurlothumbro] eponymous hero of ridiculous farce by Samuel Johnson of Cheshire in 1729

husband] manager of economic affairs; not: spouse

Hyde Park] large fashionable park and promenade, with a track ("the Ring") for coaches; northwest of the more accessible Park* and Mall*

i'facks, etc.] v. facks

ill] unpropitious; not: sick

influence] specifically astrological influence

Inns of Court] Lincoln's, Middle Temple, Inner Temple, and Gray's: the residences of law students preparing for the bar

jerk] lash or cutting jibe; not: spasmodic motion (or foolish person)

jernie] a mild oath, from the much more profane French oath, *je renie dieu*: I renounce God

Jesuit's Powder] quinine

Jezabel] The shameless wife of King Ahab. In 2 Kings 9: 30–37, eunuchs throw her out of a window, her body eaten by dogs.

jill-flirt(ing)] a familiar, contemptuous term for a young woman or her dismissive behavior

jiminy] a mild oath, perhaps a corruption of *jesu domine*

joy] a term of endearment, often used by the Irish

keep(er)] support(er), especially a mistress; not: take custody of

Kensington] fashionable section west of London during the eighteenth century, noted for large mansions and private schools and Kensington Gardens, a large park that provided a fashionable promenade for wealthy citizens; until the reign of George III (1762) Kensington Palace was the center of court life.

kind, -ness] affection(ate)—often to the point of indulging sexual favors; not: sympathetic or helpful lady] woman of title, not just gentlewoman

lie, give the] to *give the lie direct* was to call someone a liar unambiguously and thus to invite a duel

Lilly] William Lilly, popular astrologer

Locket's, Long's] fashionable ordinaries

lousy or lousey] have lice; not: inferior

Lucrece] virtuous Roman matron, was raped by Sextus Tarquinius and subsequently committed suicide; therefore, the emblem of marital chastity (her story is told in Lee's *Lucius Junius Brutus*)

Lud] euphemism for Lord; mild oath

lumber] surplus or disused articles; not: building material

luxury] lust and free living; not: rich abundance

Machiavel] unscrupulous villain, named after Niccolò Machiavelli for his *Prince*

main (chance)] term from hazard, a contemporary dice game similar to modern craps: used metaphorically to signify playing the odds

make love] pay court; not: copulate

Mall] v. Pall Mall

Marrabone] a corruption of Marylebone, an area northwest of London notorious for gambling and bowling

marry] a mild oath, by St. Mary; not: to wed

mask] woman wearing a visor, often a prostitute

mean] low; not: nasty

mere] no less than; not: no more than

millstone, see into] a proverbial (and ironic) claim to acuteness

month's mind] strong desire or inclination (of considerable duration)

mother, fit of the] hysteric attack

motion] acting or puppetry; not: movement

Mrs.] "Mistress," used for both married and unmarried women

mumping] moving the mouth spasmodically, as in nibbling, gumming

natural] *noun* fool or mistress; *adj.* illegitimate

naught] unworthy, bad, vile, naughty; not: nothing

never] ever

nightgown] robe or dressing gown; not: lingerie

nice, etc.] fastidious, delicate, or picky, sometimes foolish, wanton; not: the generalized term of approval

nose] damage to the nose (both upper and nether) was a common effect of syphilis

nouns] v. 'ouns

nown] contraction of mine own or just baby talk

obnoxious to] exposed to something extremely harmful or distasteful

'Od(d), 'Ud] corruption of God, a mild oath; used often in combination (v. 'sbud)

offer] threaten or gesture or start; not: propose

orange women, wenches] women who sell oranges, especially at plays—and often act as bawds

'oun(d)s ('oons, ou'z)] by Christ's wounds (a mild oath)

owl] proverbially stupid bird; not: wise

pad; padder, footpad] to steal; highway robber

Pall Mall] the Mall, a fashionable promenade in the Town*

Pantheon] In imitation of the temple at Rome, a pantheon was built in London in 1772 for musical entertainments.

Park] St. James's Park, the royal park adjacent to St. James's Palace, a fashionable place to walk

parole] promise; not: criminal surveillance

parts] personal qualities, talents; not: bodily members

patriot] honorific and self-righteous self-identification for Whigs

person] appearance; not: individual

perspective] telescope; not: point of view

pit] area on the "ground" in front of the stage, by this time having benches, notorious for noise, bawdry, assignations

pize] a softened version of "pox"

plantation] entire settlement in a new region (like the New World); not: individual estate

plate] silver (plated); not: dish

play] game, sport, gaming, gambling, or a gambit therein

postures] v. Arratine/Aretino

precious] notorious; not: valuable

prefer] advance; not: choose

present(ly)] instant(ly) or immediate(ly); not: near or soon

pretend] venture, aspire; not: feign

prevent] to come before or to anticipate; not: to keep from

probatum (est)] tried and tested (literally, it is approved [Lat.]), usually written on prescriptions

profession] religious belief; not: occupation

project(or)] scheme(r), generally elaborate and unfeasible

pulvillio(ed)] (treated with) powdered perfume

punk] prostitute; not: hoodlum

pupp(e)y] doll or toy; not: young dog

quality] gentry or nobility; not: value

quarrel] violent fight; not: verbal disagreement

quick] alive, lively, or when referring to a fetus, moving; not: fast

race] family, lineage; not: ethnic identity

receipt] recipe or prescription; not: proof of purchase

resty] restive, stubborn

rib] v. bone

Ring] a circular drive in Hyde Park*

rook] a cheat, con man; not: a chesspiece or a crow

Rosamond's Pond] favorite trysting place, put into St. James's Park and surrounded by trees by Charles II; named after the (in)famous mistress of Henry II

rose, under the] sub rosa, in secret

Rowland...Oliver] tit for tat; Roland and Olivier were two of Charlemagne's Twelve Peers, inseparable heroes of the Medieval chanson de geste, *La Chanson de Roland (The Song of Roland)*.

sack] imported Spanish wine; not: bag

Saint] Puritan (often hypocritical); not: truly holy person

St. James's] St. James's Palace, Park, and Square, at the western end of Pall Mall, near Westminster: a very fashionable district in the Town*

salt] lusty

salute] to greet, often with a kiss or embrace; not: to hold hand to eyebrow or over heart

satyr] satire, incorrectly thought to be derived from the Greek word, rather than from Latin *satura* (mixed dish)

'sbud, 'sdeath, 'slife, 'sheart, 'slid(s)] by God's (Christ's) blood/death/life/heart/(eye)lids

scour] in 17th-18th century slang: to roam about at night uproariously, breaking windows, beating the watch, and molesting wayfarers (*OED*)

separate maintenance] money allotted to a wife separated from her husband

servant] courtly-love term for a professed lover; not: domestic employee

shock] shaggy dog

shore] open sewer

silly] innocent, plain, unsophisticated, usually rustic; not: foolish, frivolous snuff] charred part of a candlewick; not: tobacco product

sophisticate(d)] adulterated, falsified; not: cosmopolitan

sot] fool; not: drunkard

sound] healthy, but especially, free from venereal disease

stairs] steps down the embankment of the Thames; not: steps between stories

steenkirk] lace-trimmed neckcloth, worn tied or twisted through a loop or ring

still] always; not: yet

Strand] major thoroughfare connecting the City* of London with the Town* and the Court, a site of popular, public celebrations like erecting a maypole (for example, the one erected after the Restoration)

stum] wine artificially aged; hence, as a verb, to pass off such bad wine or to impair one with it

stupid(ity)] (of people) torpid, (of things) tiresome, boring; not: unintelligent

sudden(ly)] prompt(ly); not: abrupt(ly)

tale] count, tally; not: story

Teague] A pejorative name for any native Irishman (Tadhg is the Irish for the name Timothy.)

teeth] defiance, opposition; not: dental appurtenances

Temple] one of the Inns of Court*

tickle trout] to seduce a trout into one's hand by rubbing its belly

toilet] dressing table or the act of dressing; not: commode

Toledo] sword made in Toledo, Spain, famous for their fine—and long—steel blades

Tony] a foolish person; a simpleton. (*OED*)

tory rory] boisterous

Tower] main garrison for the City of London, often used as a prison

Town] fashionable area west of the City of London; not: a big village in the country

turtle] dove; not: reptile in a shell

twire] to look at covertly, coyly

Tyburn] Middlesex Gallows, west of the Tyburn River (near the northeast corner of modern Hyde Park)

'ud] v. 'od

unsound] see sound

Vérole] French for syphilis

very] genuine, or legitimate, actual; not: extremely

vile] of little worth or account; not: despicable

villain] lowborn, uncouth; not: deliberate scoundrel

visor, vizard] metonymy for masked prostitute

want] lack or (in) need (of); not: desire

watch waters] to scrutinize conduct closely, often used literally, to examine urine for medical diagnosis, especially pregnancy

Westminster Hall] the law court at Westminster (q.v.)

Whitehall] the English royal palace and the area around it in Westminster

whore of Babylon] in the Christian tradition, second only to Satan in her distance from God (see Revelations 17:1–6); in the Restoration, a figure for the corruption of the Roman Church.

willow] symbol of grief for unrequited love or loss of a mate

woman] waiting-woman, usually of gentry, not peasant, status

your] almost equivalent to "the"; not to be taken personally

'zbud] see 'sbud

Index of Authors and Titles